The Official
SAT

Study Guide™

SECOND EDITION

COLLEGE BOARD, NEW YORK

ABOUT COLLEGE BOARD

College Board reaches more than 7 million students a year, helping them navigate the path from high school to college and career. Our not-for-profit membership organization was founded more than 120 years ago. We pioneered programs like the SAT® and AP® to expand opportunities for students and help them develop the skills they need. Our BigFuture® program helps students plan for college, pay for college, and explore careers. Learn more at **cb.org**.

Copies of this book are available from your bookseller or may be ordered from College Board Publications at **store.collegeboard.org** or by calling 800-323-7155.

Editorial inquiries concerning this book should be submitted to **sat.collegeboard.org/contact**.

This publication was written and edited by College Board. Primary authorship for this edition was by Jim Patterson and Dona Carling, with additional support from Sonia Wilson, Sara Schwindt, Stephanie Wright, and Garrett Ziegler. Special thanks to Carolyn Lieberg, Sergio Frisoli, Jessica Marks, and Andrew Schwartz for contributions to prior editions. Cover and layout design: Joe Gagyi. Project manager: Linda Holbrook. Product owner: Nayoung Joe. Assistant editor: Samantha Herrera. Invaluable contributions and review from the College Board Assessment Design & Development team, notably Kinny Mu, Laurie Moore, and Nancy Burkholder.

ISBN-13: 978-1-4573-1684-5

Printed in the United States of America

1 2 3 4 5 6 7 8 9   26 25

Distributed by Macmillan

Dear Student,

Congratulations on taking an important step toward preparing for the SAT®. *The Official SAT Study Guide*™ is a tool to help you practice for the latest version of the test. By investing in SAT practice, you're making a commitment to your college, career, and life success.

As you start to familiarize yourself with the test, we're excited to share with you some of the many benefits it has to offer. The questions that make up the assessment are modeled on the work you're already doing in school. You'll recognize topics and ideas from your math, English language arts, science, history, and social studies classes. These questions are also aligned with the capabilities that research says matter most for college and career readiness. This means that by practicing for the SAT, you're reinforcing the knowledge and skills that will help you excel both in your coursework and in your future pursuits.

The SAT is clearer than ever. The questions will not be tricky, nor will there be any obscure vocabulary. By being transparent about what's on the test and making preparation materials easily available, we're providing you the foundation for successful practice. The best source of information about the SAT is found right here in the pages of this book, and you've taken an important step by equipping yourself with these key facts.

The SAT is just one component of the College Board commitment to increasing students' access to and success in college and career. We have also partnered with colleges and universities to offer college application fee waivers to every income-eligible senior who takes the SAT (to learn more, visit **sat.org/fee-waivers**). College Board wants you to succeed in your pursuits, and defraying the cost of admission for eligible students is just one way that we can make it easier for you to reach your goals.

Now that you have this great study guide as a tool, we encourage you to begin practicing today.

Keep up the good work.

Priscilla Rodriguez
Senior Vice President, College Readiness Assessments
College Board

Foreword

The Official SAT Study Guide is the latest in a series of SAT preparation books put together by College Board, the makers of the test, to help you, the student, get ready to do your best work on the exam.

In putting this volume together, the various authors and contributors had a single goal in mind: giving students such as you all the information and advice you need to do well on test day. To that end, we've put together detailed overviews of the SAT and its components, provided walkthroughs of the various question formats and types you'll encounter on the test, and created opportunities for you to engage in authentic test practice.

The SAT itself has been crafted to give all students a fair, valid, and reliable way to demonstrate to colleges, career training programs, scholarship organizations, and others what they know and can do in reading and writing and in math. Designed and developed based on careful research and extensive input, including from students, the digital version of the SAT is easier to take, easier to give, more secure, and more relevant than ever before. The ultimate aim of the test is to give you the best possible opportunity to show what you know and can do, to stand out from your peers, and to be seen and recognized by the postsecondary institutions that interest you and that are a good match for your plans and capabilities.

Although the single best preparation for the SAT is engaging actively in a set of challenging high school courses, we've created this book to help you understand and get comfortable with the specific ways in which the SAT assesses your achievement. Equipped with this information and having taken advantage of one or more of the many opportunities this book offers to evaluate and hone your skills and knowledge, you'll be able to test with full confidence.

Jim Patterson, Ph.D.
Co-lead author, *The Official SAT Study Guide*
College Board

Contents

PART 3   The Math Section

PART 4   Practice Tests

CHAPTER 1

Introduction

The Official SAT Study Guide is designed to give you the information and tools you'll need to do your best on the SAT, a college and career readiness assessment. This book has been crafted by College Board, the makers of the SAT, and provides authoritative test-taking advice as well as official sample test questions and practice tests developed by the same College Board staff members who produce the actual tests. By using this book as part of your preparation for test day, you can be confident that you have access to all the resources you need to succeed.

A Word or Two About the SAT

Before we dive into the specifics of preparation, let's make sure that you know a little about the SAT and what testing means for you.

The SAT is one, and the best known, of the tests in College Board's SAT Suite of Assessments. Along with the suite's other tests—the PSAT/NMSQT®, PSAT™ 10, and PSAT™ 8/9—the SAT is designed to measure what research indicates are essential academic requirements for college and career readiness in reading and writing and in math. This means that the SAT is intended to measure the extent to which you've obtained the skills and knowledge needed to be ready to succeed in college and in workforce training. Because the SAT shares the same goal as your high school courses—preparing you for the next stage of your educational career—you should expect that the questions on the SAT will ask you to demonstrate the same sorts of skills and knowledge you use every day in your classes. Moreover, because the SAT provides valuable information about your readiness to succeed in college and career, the results are highly relevant to you. In addition, the SAT serves as an important gateway to additional college and career-planning resources and scholarship opportunities, which can help you make informed decisions supportive of your post–high school aspirations.

The demands of college and workforce training programs are high, and the SAT must be similarly demanding. We've designed the SAT to be an appropriately challenging and equally fair test of what you know and can do. When test questions are challenging, it's because the content you're asked to work with, the questions you're posed, and the problems you're asked to solve require this level of understanding. The difficulty of SAT questions, in other words, comes from the sophistication of the skills and knowledge you're asked to demonstrate; by contrast, the wording of test passages and questions as well as the tasks you're presented with are meant to be as clear and comprehensible as possible. Familiarizing yourself with the test and its content will help you confidently answer questions to the best of your ability.

The Structure of This Book

The Official SAT Study Guide is divided into four parts.

- **Part 1: The SAT** provides an overview of the SAT, what to expect, the test day experience (e.g., what to bring and not bring), and how to understand and use your scores. We also present some general test-taking strategies, which complement those specific to the test sections found in later chapters. Part 1 concludes with a discussion of how to use this book to prepare for PSAT-related tests.

- **Part 2: The Reading and Writing Section** goes into depth on the features and elements of the literacy-focused section of the SAT. Part 2 begins with an overview of the test section. The next two chapters address Reading and Writing test passages and informational graphics in detail so you come away with a strong sense of the kinds of readings and graphics you'll be asked to engage with. After a brief introduction to the Reading and Writing section's four *content domains*—the categories into which we organize test questions by topic—we devote two chapters to each of these domains. The first chapter in each pair is a detailed look at the domain, including its purpose and focus and the kinds of questions you may encounter. The second chapter in each pair consists of drill questions in that domain. These questions are accompanied by answer explanations, so you can check your work. Our intent is for these drills to serve as immediate practice once you've read a given overview chapter. The number of drill questions varies somewhat by domain, and there's no real expectation that you answer these questions under timed conditions. Rather, our goal is just to get you familiar with the full range of questions you may encounter in each domain.

- **Part 3: The Math Section** includes a section overview as well as pairs of chapters devoted to the test section's four content domains. These pairs consist of domain overviews followed by drills with answer explanations. Two additional chapters round out Part 3. The first offers further discussion of the student-produced response (SPR) question format, which requires you to generate and enter your own answers (rather than select from multiple-choice options). The second describes your test day calculator options, including the built-in Desmos graphing calculator.

- **Part 4: Practice Tests** consists of a series of official SAT practice tests accompanied by answer explanations and scoring guidelines. You may choose to use the paper versions of these tests included in this book, or, preferably, you can follow the provided directions to test digitally—just as you will on test day and using the same testing application, Bluebook™. If you do choose to practice on paper, carefully read the introduction to this section of the book so that you're fully aware of the differences between practicing on paper and digitally.

How to Use This Book

If you have **two months or more** to prepare, we recommend proceeding through this whole book.

- Read part 1 to get a clear sense of what the SAT is like, and then read parts 2 and 3 to become fully versed in how the Reading and Writing and Math sections of the test are put together.

- Answer the drill questions spread throughout parts 2 and 3 and use the provided answer explanations to assess your responses and identify areas of weakness to work on. Take a full-length practice test, either in Bluebook or in this book, under timed conditions to better understand how to pace yourself.

- Go through your answers and the provided explanations, figure out what you missed and got right, and identify skills and knowledge you need to brush up on and/or question formats and types you need more practice with. Visit **sat.org/practice** for study ideas and tips on using our free official practice resources effectively.

- Visit Khan Academy® at **khanacademy.org/digital-sat**, the home for free Official SAT Prep, to explore their resources, which include lessons and activities designed to assess and build your skills and knowledge. Take a second practice test to check for improvement and to identify any areas still needing work.

BLUEBOOK PRACTICE TESTS

Most students will take the SAT in **Bluebook**, a digital testing application downloaded onto an appropriate device. Because of this, we recommend that you take the official practice tests in Bluebook, unless you have an accommodation to test on paper. Taking practice tests in Bluebook helps you get familiar with the full testing experience, including the many ways Bluebook makes taking the test easy and efficient. If you take a Bluebook practice test, log in to My Practice with the same credentials you used to log in to Bluebook. Learn more at **satsuite.collegeboard.org/practice/my-practice-101**.

If you have roughly **one month** to prepare, we still recommend doing all the above, though you may need to push a little to get through everything.

- If you must prioritize, pay particular attention to the chapters providing overviews of the SAT (chapter 2), the Reading and Writing section (chapter 7), and the Math section (chapter 19) to ensure that you're familiar with the key features of the test and its two sections.

- Take a full-length practice test under timed conditions and analyze your results. Identify the areas where you need the most improvement and use the resources in this book, on **sat.org/practice**, and/or on Khan Academy to address your most critical shortcomings.

If you have **a week or less** before test day, you'll need to be strategic in your preparation.

- Focus on the overview chapters (chapters 2, 7, and 19) mentioned above so that you have the key test features firmly in mind.

- Take a full-length practice test under timed conditions so that you have a better idea of how the test is put together and how to pace yourself effectively.

- Analyze your results and look for one to two areas in Reading and Writing and in Math that you feel you could improve on quickly.

- Use the drill questions and answer explanations found in various chapters in parts 2 and 3 to gain some quick practice with question formats and types you're not confident on but may be able to master with a bit of effort.

Some Additional Advice

There's a lot of information in this book as well as many options for getting ready for the SAT. We strongly suggest that you begin your preparation for taking the SAT at least a couple of months ahead of your test date so that you can practice at a relatively leisurely pace and have enough time and energy to evaluate and, where needed, improve on your reading and writing and math skills and knowledge.

Although we do recommend devoting effort to preparing for the SAT, we also want to reassure you that the questions you'll be asked are, in many respects, similar to those you'd encounter in challenging high school courses. Thus, **the single best preparation you can undertake for the SAT is what you're already doing: actively engaging in your classes.** The main purposes of specific preparation for the SAT are for you to (1) become comfortable with the kinds of questions we ask and how you're expected to respond and (2) learn to pace yourself during the test so that you have an opportunity to answer each question to the best of your ability.

Most of all, remember: You *can* do this.

BUILD YOUR STUDY PLAN

Visit our website for study activity ideas designed to fit your schedule—whether you have 15 minutes, an hour, or more to dedicate to practice. For more information, visit **satsuite.collegeboard.org/ practice/build-your-study-plan**.

The SAT

CHAPTER 2

Getting to Know the SAT

In this chapter, we provide an overview of the SAT. We begin with a high-level discussion of the key components of the test, including its sections, timing, and number of questions. Following that, we describe some of these features in more detail, with a focus on how you can use this information to better prepare for test day.

The SAT at a Glance

The SAT is composed of two sections:

- A **Reading and Writing section**, which measures your ability to apply reading and writing skills and knowledge you've gained in your classes in English language arts and other subjects.

- A **Math section**, which measures your ability to apply math skills and knowledge you've gained in your classes in math and in other subjects, such as science, in which math is frequently used.

Questions in both sections test the skills and knowledge you've learned in your classes and that our research has found are necessary for you to have to be ready to succeed in college courses.

Table 1 summarizes key features of the SAT, while table 2 summarizes key features of each of the two test sections. These features are discussed in more detail below and throughout this book.

NOTE

Part 1 of this book focuses on the SAT in general terms. In parts 2 and 3, we cover the Reading and Writing section and the Math section, respectively, in depth, including offering you opportunities to immediately practice with questions in each of the test's *content domains*, the categories we use to conceptually organize test questions by topic.

NOTE
The SAT includes a small number of unscored questions in each test section. We include these questions to evaluate them for possible future use on the test, and your answers to them don't affect your section (or total) scores.

Table 1. Key Features of the SAT

Feature	SAT
Administration	Two-stage adaptive testing
Number of questions	98 questions: 54 Reading and Writing 44 Math
Time allotted	134 minutes: 64 Reading and Writing 70 Math
Scores reported	Two **section scores**, each on a scale of 200–800: Reading and Writing Math A **total score**, which is the sum of the two section scores and is on a scale of 400–1600

Table 2. Key Features of the SAT Sections

Feature	Reading and Writing Section	Math Section
Administration	Two-stage adaptive test design; each stage consists of a module of questions	Two-stage adaptive test design; each stage consists of a module of questions
Section composition	Questions divided into two modules, each timed separately	Questions divided into two modules, each timed separately
Number of questions	1st module: 27 questions (including 2 unscored questions) 2nd module: 27 questions (including 2 unscored questions)	1st module: 22 questions (including 2 unscored questions) 2nd module: 22 questions (including 2 unscored questions)
Time per module	1st module: 32 minutes 2nd module: 32 minutes	1st module: 35 minutes 2nd module: 35 minutes
Total number of questions	54 questions	44 questions
Total time allotted	64 minutes	70 minutes
Average time per question	1.19 minutes	1.59 minutes
Score reported	Reading and Writing section score, on a scale of 200–800	Math section score, on a scale of 200–800
Question type(s) used	Multiple-choice Each question is standalone (i.e., there are no question sets)	Multiple-choice (about 75% of the section) Student-produced response (about 25% of the section) Each question is standalone (i.e., there are no question sets)

Feature	Reading and Writing Section	Math Section
Subject areas for passages and contexts	Literature, history/social studies, the humanities, science	Science, social studies, real-world topics
Word count	25–150 words per passage (or pair of passages)	About 30% of questions are set in context; most of these contexts have 50 words or fewer
Informational graphics	Tables, bar graphs, line graphs	A wide range of data displays, geometric figures, and *xy*-plane graphs
Reading and Writing passage text complexity	Passages represent a range of text complexities from grades 6–8 through grades 12–14	—

Key Features of the SAT

In this section, we discuss the key features listed above in detail, with an emphasis on how this information can be used to enhance your preparation for test day.

Two-Stage Adaptive Testing

Large-scale tests such as the SAT have been given in a paper and pencil format, and everyone who took a particular test form was presented with the exact same set of questions. Even when College Board started making the transition to digital testing for the SAT several years ago, these digital forms were essentially paper and pencil tests with some minor adjustments (e.g., answers being selected or entered onscreen rather than marked on a paper answer sheet). For these sorts of test forms, whether printed on paper or displayed on a screen, there's only one "path" through the questions, and the test doesn't change in any way based on how the test taker is performing.

The main alternative to paper and pencil testing is *adaptive* digital testing. Adaptive tests (which are pretty much exclusively delivered on digital devices) are so called because, in one or more ways, they "adapt" during the test based on how the test taker is doing.

One critical way that adaptive tests such as the SAT improve the test-taking experience is by targeting questions to individual test takers' demonstrated achievement level. Put more simply, if a test taker is doing well on an adaptive test, they're given harder questions to determine the upper limits of their skills and knowledge; if a test taker is struggling, they're given easier questions to determine what they *do* know and can do, not just what they don't and can't.

By contrast, paper tests given to lots of test takers at a time must include a large number and broad range of questions of various challenge levels to assess everyone's achievement. Such tests are quite lengthy and nearly all test takers end up being asked at least some questions that are either too easy or too hard for them, because the test doesn't change based on how any one test taker is doing during the exam.

The key benefit that the SAT's adaptive testing model offers you is a shorter exam that nonetheless measures your skills and knowledge as accurately as a longer test. While the last paper version of the SAT clocked in at three hours, the digital format is much closer to two.

There are various models for adaptive testing out there. The method we've chosen for the SAT is called *multistage adaptive testing* (MST). In MST, the testing application adapts after test takers have completed a given *stage* of testing. The SAT uses a simple two-stage model, illustrated in figure 1, below.

Figure 1. The Digital SAT's Multistage Adaptive Testing Model

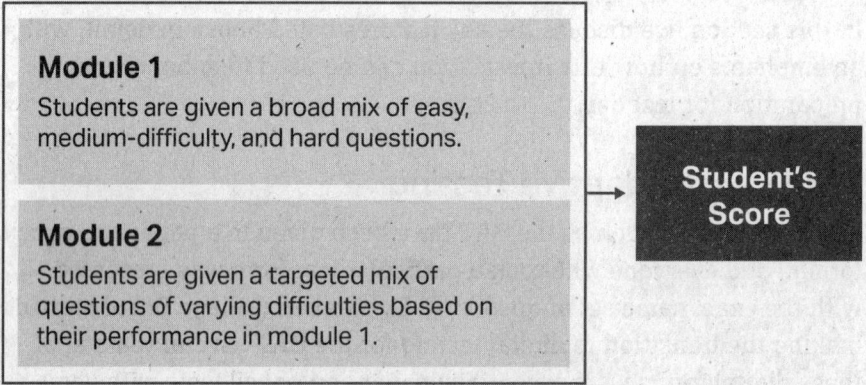

Each section of the digital SAT is divided into two stages, each of which consists of a *module* of questions. Each module contains half the section's test questions (27 Reading and Writing questions or 22 Math questions).

The first module in each test section consists of questions that are, on average, of medium difficulty. (We say "on average" because individual questions may be of high, medium, or low difficulty, but, overall, they average out to moderately challenging.) At the midpoint of each test section, Bluebook, the test application, routes students to one of two possible second-stage modules of questions: one whose questions are, on average, of lower difficulty than those in the first module and the other whose questions are, on average, of higher difficulty than those in the first module. (Again, "on average" means that high-, medium- and low-difficulty questions may appear in either second-stage module.)

Each of the two modules in a test section is separately timed, so you'll be allotted half of the total time for each section for answering questions in the first module and the other half for answering questions in the second module. You'll have 32 minutes for each Reading and Writing module and 35 minutes for each Math module.

It's important to note here that the SAT only "adapts" once per test section and only after you've had a chance to answer half of the section's questions. This means that you'll have a good opportunity to show what you know and can do in each section before the app determines which of the two second-stage modules—higher or lower difficulty—you receive.

Besides reducing any stress you might feel about the adapting the test does, this feature allows you to move around freely among the questions in a given module. You can preview later questions in a module and flag and return to earlier questions if you wish, and even change your answers, as long as time permits.

The Fairness of Adaptive Testing

College Board is deeply committed to ensuring that all its tests, including the SAT, are fair to students from all backgrounds and achievement levels. Put simply, we believe that a test that's not fair is a bad test.

As part of this commitment, we've taken numerous steps to make sure that the adaptive testing model used for the SAT is fair to all students.

- All test takers begin each test section at the same place: with a medium-difficulty module.

- Because this medium-difficulty module contains a large number of questions as well as a mix of low-, medium-, and high-difficulty questions, every student has a fair chance to demonstrate their skills and knowledge.

- Test takers may navigate freely among the questions in a given module as time permits. They may preview later questions and flag, review, and change answers to earlier questions within a particular module.

- The test application only "adapts" once per test section, and only after each student has had a chance to answer many questions and thereby give a strong indication of their achievement. This also means that you won't face a situation in which incorrectly answering the first few questions in a section sends you into a downward spiral of inappropriately easy questions, as could be the case if the test application adapted after each question.

- The specifications ("rules") that control how the SAT is put together ensure that every student, regardless of when or where they take the test, receives a highly comparable experience. In other words, no one receives an SAT test form that's significantly easier or harder than any other student's.

IMPORTANT!
As time permits, you may freely move back and forth among questions in a given module. If you wish, you can change your answers in the current module (the two modules in each section are separate). However, you may **not** return to a previous module after Bluebook moves you to the next module, which happens automatically after time expires. In addition, you may **not** return to the first test section (Reading and Writing) after the test application moves you to the second (and last) test section (Math).

Timing and Pacing

For the Reading and Writing section, you'll have a total of 64 minutes to answer 54 questions. This averages out to 1.19 minutes per question. The questions and total time are evenly split between the two modules of questions in the test section, meaning that you'll have 32 minutes to answer the 27 questions in each module.

For the Math section, you'll have a total of 70 minutes to answer 44 questions. This averages out to 1.59 minutes per question. Like the Reading and Writing section, the Math section is divided evenly into two separately timed modules of questions. You'll have 35 minutes to answer the 22 questions in each module.

Remember that you won't be allowed to return to a given module of questions once time is up, and you won't be able to return to the Reading and Writing section once you've begun the Math section.

Question Types

All questions in the Reading and Writing section and about 75% of questions in the Math section are multiple-choice in format. Each of these multiple-choice questions has four answer choices (also known as *options*), of which one (and only one) is the best answer (*key*). The three other answer choices represent common errors that test takers make or common misconceptions that test takers hold, so they're intended to be plausible to varying degrees without any one of them being a second key.

The other approximately 25% of questions in the Math section are in a format we call *student-produced response* (SPR). These questions have no answer choices; you must solve each problem and enter your own answer into the test application. SPR questions may have more than one possible correct answer, but you'll only ever be asked to enter a single answer. We'll have more to say about SPR questions in chapter 29, and numerous examples of such questions appear throughout this book.

All SAT questions are standalone. (The technical term for this is *discrete*.) This means that each question can be answered independently, without reference to any other question. There are no sets of questions linked to a common passage or set of data. This means that you won't have to worry about answering several questions about a single Reading and Writing passage or Math context that perhaps you feel you don't fully understand. You'll instead be able to give your best effort on each question and then move on to the next.

Context-Based Questions in the Math Section

Roughly a third of the questions in the Math section are set in context. By "in context," we're referring, loosely, to the sorts of questions commonly known as word problems. Although most questions in the section test "pure" math, in-context questions make an important contribution, as they help determine whether you can apply your math skills and knowledge to solving authentic problems in social studies and science as well as those based in real-world scenarios.

Subject Areas

All Reading and Writing questions and some Math questions are set in one of a range of academic subject areas, such as history/social studies and science. We do this for two main (and related) reasons. First, the SAT tests the skills and knowledge you've developed in your classes. It therefore makes sense—and is beneficial to you—to set questions in the subjects you've studied in school. Second, the SAT is a test of your college and career readiness. It therefore follows that your readiness should be tested in relation to the kinds of classes you'll have to take after high school.

It's important to note here that *no* SAT question tests your knowledge of specific topics within the various academic subjects sampled on the test. You won't, for instance, be asked to recall historical facts or scientific theories. All the information needed to answer a given question is provided in the question itself.

That said, we take great pains to ensure that SAT questions set in academic contexts are as authentic as possible. This means that Reading and Writing passages (and informational graphics—more on these below) as well as Math questions set in context present the kinds of topics and ask the kinds of questions that you'd encounter in challenging high school courses as well as in first-year courses at the college level. Your knowledge of and experience with these subjects, therefore, can be beneficial on the SAT, as courses in these subjects teach you how to read, write, and reason in the specific ways required in these fields. We'll have more to say about this later, particularly in chapter 8.

The Reading and Writing section includes passages and informational graphics in the subject areas of literature, history/social studies, the humanities, and science. Some Math section questions set in context address topics in the academic subjects of social studies and science, while others address real-world applications of mathematics. Examples of all of these appear in the chapters later in this book devoted to the Reading and Writing and the Math sections.

IMPORTANT!
We just said it, but it's a critical point worth emphasizing: All the information needed to answer an SAT question is in the question itself.

Passage/Context Word Count

On the SAT, we keep Reading and Writing passages and Math contexts short and focused so that you can concentrate on answering the associated questions. That doesn't mean that you won't encounter some challenging readings—more on that below—but it *does* mean that you'll be presented with only the most important information needed to answer a given question.

Reading and Writing passages are 25 to 150 words in length, while most Math contexts are 50 words or fewer.

Informational Graphics

The SAT includes informational graphics with select Reading and Writing and Math questions. That's because the ability to make skilled use of information from tables and figures is a critical requirement of college and career readiness, not to mention effective participation in civic life.

In the Reading and Writing section, select questions will include a table, bar graph, or line graph. You'll be asked to do various things with the data displayed in these graphics, such as locate specific data points, recognize trends in data, and make connections between the information contained in a graphic with the information and ideas in an accompanying passage. What you *won't* have to do with these questions is perform calculations—and a calculator is neither permitted nor necessary to answer questions in this section. We've limited the types of graphics that appear in the Reading and Writing section to just the three listed above because these are the most common ways in which people in the subject areas sampled by the section organize and display data graphically.

The Math section, by contrast, includes a wider range of informational graphics (e.g., scatterplots, box plots). That's because mathematicians—as well as experts in other fields, such as science, in which math plays a large role—use numerous kinds of data displays, with the choice of which to use depending on what sorts of analyses are being performed. And, unlike in the Reading and Writing section, the Math section *will* require you to perform calculations involving these data. In doing so, you may make use of either the Desmos graphing calculator built into Bluebook or your own approved calculator. (In chapter 30, we'll discuss the features of the built-in graphing calculator as well as where you can find College Board's up-to-date calculator policy that outlines which personal calculators are and aren't acceptable for use on the SAT.) In addition to data displays, select Math section questions may include geometric figures, such as triangles and circles, and *xy*-plane graphs.

Text Complexity (Reading and Writing Section)

The passages you encounter in the Reading and Writing section will vary in terms of how challenging they are to read. Some passages will be relatively straightforward, while others will exhibit a relatively high level of complexity. Technically speaking, passages in the section range in complexity from ones like those you might have encountered in grades 6–8 up to and including ones that are similar in difficulty to those you may be assigned in your first-year college classes. We include some highly challenging passages in the Reading and Writing section because research has shown that the ability to read complex texts is a key indicator of students' college and career readiness. (Text complexity in the Reading and Writing section is a topic we return to in chapter 8.)

Math contexts aren't formally rated for text complexity, in part because the presence of equations and other expressions limits the validity of the kinds of text complexity measures we use, and in part because that test section assesses math skills and knowledge, not reading achievement per se. Each Math context is, however, carefully examined by experts prior to its use to ensure that it's as clear and concise as possible, which helps keep the focus where it belongs: on the math itself.

CHAPTER 3

Understanding and Using Your SAT Scores

In this chapter, we go over how the SAT is scored. We also examine the SAT score report, a critical tool enabling you both to understand your test performance better and to easily take advantage of the many SAT-related services College Board provides.

Your Scores

You'll need to understand your SAT scores to measure your progress toward college and career readiness and determine what your next steps should be. Table 1 shows the score details and score ranges.

Table 1. SAT Scores

SAT Score Reported	Details	Score Range
Section scores (2)	• Reading and Writing	200–800
	• Math	200–800
Total score	Sum of the two section scores	400–1600

Your score on each section is based on your performance on all questions in the section.* Section scores for Reading and Writing and for Math are reported on a scale from 200 to 800. The two section scores are then added together to yield your total score. This total score ranges from 400 to 1600.

The SAT Suite uses adaptive test design with item response theory (IRT) pattern scoring. Adaptive testing allows for fewer questions, in less time, than traditional paper tests. Pattern scoring allows for precise measurement of students' knowledge and skills. Students' scores are determined by whether they answer questions right or wrong, and by considering attributes of the questions, including difficulty level, the questions' ability to differentiate between students with various levels of content knowledge, and the probability that a student is guessing based on their pattern of responses. Every test includes a standardized set of question types and measures the same content domains, so all students have equitable opportunity to demonstrate their strengths. For most students who are trying their best on every question, it is better to guess than leave a question blank, especially if the student can eliminate one or two answer options before guessing.

---

* College Board includes a small number of unscored questions in each test section. We do this to evaluate how these questions perform and to determine whether we can use them in future tests. Your answers to these questions don't affect your section (or total) scores.

Comparing Digital SAT and Paper and Pencil SAT Scores

Scores on the digital SAT are directly linked to scores on the paper and pencil version of the SAT that the digital test has replaced. This means that scores on the paper and pencil SAT can be fairly compared side by side to scores on the digital SAT. However, because the digital and paper and pencil SATs measure slightly different content and do so in somewhat different ways, a paper and pencil SAT score isn't a perfect predictor of how you'd perform on the digital test.

Your Score Report

Your score report gives the meaning behind the numbers by providing a summary of how you did on each section and on the test as a whole. It also serves as a portal connecting you with additional SAT-related services that College Board provides.

You can access your score report online through your College Board account here: **studentscores.collegeboard.org/home**. This account is the same one you use if you register to take the SAT on the weekend. (If you can't access your online score report, your school can print a copy for you.)

We briefly discuss some of the key features of the score report below.

Score Ranges

To better contextualize your actual test scores, we provide score ranges that account for the slight variations in your performance that could occur had you taken the SAT on a different day.

Score Comparisons

Score comparisons let you compare your total and section scores to the average scores of all students who took the SAT in the last three years at your school and in your district, state, and country (as applicable) as well as to all testers worldwide.

Percentiles

Percentiles represent the percentage of students whose score is equal to or lower than your own; the higher your percentile rank, the better. For example, if your score were at the 75th percentile for your state, this would mean that 75% of graduating seniors testing over the past three years in your state achieved scores at or below your score. Percentiles are provided, as applicable, at the state level, country level, and among testers worldwide, contextualizing your scores among those of graduating seniors over the last three years.

College and Career Readiness Benchmarks

Based on extensive, ongoing research, College Board has established college and career readiness benchmark scores for the Reading and Writing and Math sections of the SAT. These benchmarks—480 for the Reading and Writing section and 530 for the Math section—are the minimum scores our research indicates are required for students to have a high chance of succeeding in common entry-level credit-bearing college courses. Students are considered college and career ready when their SAT section scores meet or exceed both the Reading and Writing and the Math benchmarks. If your scores fall below one or both of these benchmarks, we recommend using the Knowledge and Skills section of your report (discussed below) to analyze your results further and to explore options for improving on your weaknesses.

Knowledge and Skills

By themselves, test scores are just numbers. As we illustrated above, test scores can be compared in various ways to give useful information about test performance. But the numbers remain abstractions unless looked at in the context of skills and knowledge they likely demonstrate.

That's why College Board has developed Skills Insight™ for the SAT (and the other tests of the SAT Suite of Assessments). Skills Insight is a set of statements, derived from careful analysis of student performance on hundreds of test questions, describing what test takers earning various scores on the SAT are likely to know and be able to do in reading and writing and in math. Accompanying these statements are sample test questions providing concrete examples of the kinds of skills and knowledge that students scoring in particular ranges on the SAT are typically able to demonstrate. The Skills Insight statements are generalizations, meaning that they don't precisely describe your performance or that of any single student, but they do provide a strong general sense of what students scoring in particular ranges probably know and can do.

The Knowledge and Skills portion of your score report, which is based on Skills Insight, allows you to better understand your performance across the SAT's eight content domains—four for Reading and Writing and four for Math. A link in your score report grants ready access to the Skills Insight Tool, which connects you to the statements and sample test questions associated with your scores.

You can also find Knowledge and Skills results for Bluebook practice tests you've taken on My Practice. There you will see which content domains you may need more work on before test day.

Sharing Your Scores

Your SAT scores can help you better understand your readiness for college and workforce training and how you can further develop your skills and knowledge, but they become more useful still when shared with postsecondary institutions, such as colleges, universities, and scholarship organizations, that are a good match to your achievement and interests.

Sending Scores

You'll have the opportunity when you register for the SAT to choose up to 4 colleges, universities, or scholarship programs to receive your scores for free. You can designate your score recipients (i) at the time you register, (ii) any time until you test, or (iii) within 9 days after you test. For these free score sends, only your scores from the test date on the registration will be sent (or the makeup test for that registration if you take a makeup test), unless you specifically ask to send more existing SAT scores. (Sending scores to additional colleges, universities, or scholarship programs can be requested online for a fee.) We share with your school and district the names of the organizations you select for your 4 free score sends.

If you want to change where your scores are sent, you have until 9 days after the test date to alter your 4 free score reports at no charge. After that, you can't make any changes and you'll need to place a new order. You'll be charged the additional score report request fee. Score Choice™ lets you choose which scores are sent.

The scores you receive and the score reports received by colleges and your high school contain total and section scores. Section scores are converted to a point scale from 200 to 800; these are added together to create a total score between 400 and 1600. Additional score sends include all your available scores unless you choose otherwise, as explained later in this section.

College Board doesn't use your raw score or your reported scaled score by itself or in combination with any other information to predict your individual future academic performance at specific postsecondary institutions. However, College Board does help individual colleges and universities use and interpret SAT scores.

When you request that we send your scores to the colleges, universities, or scholarship programs you choose, we send your scores, certain demographic information about you, and other information you provide when taking the SAT to those organizations, in accordance with **sat. org/scores**. These organizations may use this information to send you information about admissions, educational, financial aid, and scholarship opportunities. Being contacted by these organizations does not mean you have been admitted or are eligible for a scholarship or financial aid program. You must submit an application to be considered for admission at a college or university, and complete any steps required by any scholarship programs to be considered for their opportunities.

In certain college and university systems, once you submit your score to 1 school, other schools within that system will also have access to your score. Please note, however, that if you are applying to more than 1 school within a college or university system, it is still important for you to send your SAT scores to each individual school. If you are not sure whether the specific school you are applying to is part of such a system, contact the school's admissions office.

Score Choice

If you take the SAT more than once, you can have the option of Score Choice, if you choose to send scores online for a fee. With Score Choice, you can choose which scores you send to colleges. Choose by test date for the SAT—but keep in mind that some colleges and scholarship programs require you to send all your scores.

This online service is optional and only applies to scores already received. It is not applicable to any of your 4 free score sends you may select; those scores are automatically included in those score reports. If you don't use Score Choice, we'll send all your SAT scores from your most recent 6 administrations. However, if you want only your highest scores to be seen from already released scores, select Score Choice. Each school or program has its own deadlines and policies for how scores are used. Information is listed on the score-sending site for each participating organization, but check with the individual school or scholarship program to make sure you're following its guidelines. We're not responsible for the accuracy of the information or the consequences of your decisions.

IMPORTANT!

You can only choose which scores to send by test date. You can't send a Reading and Writing section score from one test date and a Math section score from another test date.

Optional Questions to Answer When You Register

When you register for the SAT, you'll have the opportunity to answer questions about yourself, your educational experience, and your plans for after you graduate high school. While you don't have to answer these questions, we strongly recommend that you do. However, if your parent or guardian has told you that you shouldn't provide any optional or voluntary information, you shouldn't do so.

Your responses give your school counselors and college admission officers, as applicable, information they can use to help you plan your future. The more information you provide, the more they can help you.

Your answers will be used by College Board as described in its Privacy Statement at **privacy.collegeboard.org/privacy-statement**, such as for educational research and will be provided to your school, district, and state department of education.

If you choose to participate in Student Search Service™, your answers will be provided to certain participating education organizations, as described under Student Search Service below. Your answers may also be provided to colleges, universities, and scholarship programs to which you choose to send your scores.

Your responses, when combined with those of all other students taking the SAT, contribute to an understanding of the academic preparation, extra- and cocurricular involvement, and post-high-school plans of your graduating class, which can help College Board, colleges, and universities deliver programs and opportunities to serve you and your classmates.

Useful Resources

We offer free resources to help you plan the right next step for you after high school on BigFuture®. Discover future career options based on your interests, explore colleges across the country, and learn about scholarships, financial aid, and more. Visit **bigfuture.org**.

Student Search Service

Student Search Service is a free, voluntary program that connects students with information about opportunities from nearly 1,500 eligible colleges, universities, scholarships and government agencies running education programs. By joining Student Search Service, you can connect with colleges and scholarship programs looking for students like you and discover opportunities you had not previously considered.

Key Facts about Student Search Service

- You can join for free and hear from a diverse group of nonprofit accredited colleges and universities (domestic and international), nonprofit scholarship providers, and government agencies administering educational programs ("Education Organizations"). No other organizations or companies are eligible to participate in Student Search Service.

- When you take a College Board test, you'll be asked to provide certain information about yourself by answering optional questions about yourself during registration.

- You'll have the opportunity to join Student Search Service included as part of the registration. It's entirely up to you whether to opt in. The service is free to you, but Education Organizations may pay us a licensing fee to use the service. We use those fees to support our nonprofit, mission-driven work, including providing fee waivers so that students from lower-income families can take the SAT for free. College Board is a nonprofit organization.

- Being part of Student Search Service is voluntary and you can opt out at any time.

- Being contacted by an Education Organization doesn't mean you've been admitted or received a scholarship. You must submit required information and complete steps requested by the Education Organization for potential admission, enrollment, scholarship and/or financial aid.

How Student Search Service Works

- If you opt in, you may be identified by Education Organizations as a potential match for their programs and opportunities.

- Education Organizations generally look for groups of students based on expected graduation date, where they live, self-reported cumulative grade point average (GPA), test score ranges, intended college major, geography, and other limited parameters. This information may be provided by you to College Board, such as during test registration, testing, and when using the College Board college planning website, BigFuture.

- College Board never shares your actual test scores, grades, disability status, parent information (unless they separately opt in to Student Search Service), or telephone numbers. Please note, we do share test score ranges and GPA. For details on the information shared, please see **bigfuture.collegeboard.org/ student-search-service/what-information-shared**. If you opt in to Student Search Service, we may share information that you provided prior to and after opting in to Student Search Service, but we will not share any information until you opt in.

- If you have opted in and match the Education Organizations search criteria, we will provide them with your contact information so they can reach out to you by postal mail (if you provided your address) and/or email about their programs and opportunities. They have to keep your data secure and may not share your data with any third parties (other than service providers to the Education Organizations).

- Education Organizations send students information about things like:

  - Financial aid, scholarships, or other ways to make college or university more affordable

  - Details on campus life and student services

  - Overviews of majors, courses, and degree options

  - Deadline information

  - Offers of direct admissions to a college

For more information, visit **bigfuture.collegeboard.org/ student-search-service**.

Opting Out of Student Search Service

If at any time you change your mind and want to stop participating, please visit **my.collegeboard.org/profile/ privacy**, complete the Your Privacy Choices webform at **form.collegeboard.org/f/data-subject-rights-request**, or contact us at **SearchCustomerService@collegeboard.org** or 866-825-8051. Please note, Education Organizations that have already received your name and other data may continue to send you information. You may contact such organizations directly to opt out of further communications from them.

CHAPTER 4

What to Expect on Test Day

In this chapter, we review important test day guidelines to help you understand the policies that cover your SAT testing experience. You should expect a similar experience to paper and pencil tests (e.g., prohibited behaviors such as attempting to cheat or communicate with other test takers are the same); however, the digital testing environment will include some unique elements that you should know about in advance.

Get Familiar with the Testing App

To perform at your best on test day, you should be familiar with Bluebook, the digital application delivering the test to you.

Bluebook makes taking the SAT as easy as possible, allowing you to focus on demonstrating your skills and knowledge on test questions. And you don't need to wait till test day to try it out.

To begin your exploration, simply go to **bluebook.app.collegeboard.org** to download Bluebook and get started. This link will specify the hardware requirements your device must meet and then direct you on how to download and install the software. You'll need to sign in to or create a College Board account to use Bluebook for practice or official testing.

Test Day Items

Be prepared for test day by making sure you bring only what you need. Leave all prohibited items at home. You won't be able to use or access your phone during the test.

Here are some SAT regulations:

- For SAT Weekend, you can present your admission ticket on a printed ticket or mobile device. Your phone will be collected and stored away from your desk before testing begins.
- You should bring a pen or pencil for scratch work. (If you choose a pencil, it doesn't have to be a No. 2 pencil, and it may be mechanical.)
- You must have a fully charged, acceptable testing device (see below), with Bluebook already downloaded and exam setup complete.
- A calculator isn't required but is allowed (see below).

IMPORTANT!

Most students taking the SAT will do so using Bluebook. However, for those students who require paper and pencil testing as an accommodation, College Board makes paper versions of the SAT available (these tests are different from the ones included in this guide as they are nonadaptive). These paper tests have the same types of questions as their digital counterparts, but they're somewhat longer. Full-length paper practice tests are available at **satsuite. collegeboard.org/practice/ practice-tests/paper**, and anybody is welcome to use them, but if you expect to take the SAT digitally, you should take your practice tests in Bluebook if you can.

Though not required, consider bringing

- snacks and drinks (which must be under your desk during testing).

- a power cord or portable charger for your eligible testing device.

- an acceptable calculator for use on the Math section of the test (if you prefer using a handheld calculator instead of using the Desmos graphing calculator embedded in Bluebook).*

- extra batteries and backup calculator.

*A battery-operated handheld calculator can be used for testing on the SAT Math section (only). No calculator power cords are allowed. If you have a calculator with characters that are 1 inch or higher, or if your calculator has a raised display that might be visible to other test takers, the testing staff will seat you in a location where other students can't see the display. All scientific calculators, which can perform complex mathematical functions but don't have a graphing feature, are acceptable if they don't have any prohibited features. For a list of acceptable graphing calculators and prohibited calculators, see **sat.org/calculator**. No other calculators are permitted. See also chapter 30 for more information on calculator options.

Testing Devices

You can take the SAT on a wide range of devices, including a personal or school-managed Windows laptop or tablet, a personal or school-managed Mac laptop, a personal or school-managed iPad, or a school-managed Chromebook. You'll need to download Bluebook onto your device before test day. If you're taking the test on a school-managed device, you may need to ask your school's technology department to install the app and adjust device settings for you. Your device must also be able to connect to Wi-Fi and hold a charge for roughly three hours. An internet connection is required to start the test, but Bluebook will keep running even if your connection drops momentarily. We recommend you bring a power cord or portable charger, but we can't guarantee you'll have access to an outlet. You're permitted to bring an external mouse for your device and an external keyboard if your device is a tablet. For Windows tablets, external keyboards are required if you want to use the Highlights & Notes tool. You can't use detachable device privacy screens. All other applications and programs must be closed during the test. You can't simultaneously test on multiple devices.

NOTE
A school-managed device is one owned and/or operated by your school, not a personal device you own.

Testing Guidelines

This section summarizes important guidelines for SAT testing. Make sure you complete all the steps below to successfully prepare to take the test.

- Plan ahead and bring equipment that's in good working order and that has enough battery power to last for three hours. Your testing device must be able to connect to Wi-Fi, and you may need to update your operating system to support the digital test.

- If you're registering for SAT Weekend and think you'll need to borrow a testing device, you'll have a chance to request one. See "Borrowing a Device from College Board," on the next page.

- If you're testing with extended time, bring a power cord; your testing site should provide an outlet for recharging if needed.

- You'll need to download Bluebook from **bluebook.app.collegeboard.org**.

- Between one and five days before the test, you'll need to sign in to the app, agree to the Privacy Policy and Use of This App, and complete exam setup. You'll get access to your admission ticket once you've completed exam setup.

- On test day, you'll follow instructions to complete exam check-in on your testing device and connect to Wi-Fi. Then you'll type a brief statement saying that you agree to follow all test day rules.

- Store any snacks or drinks you bring out of sight in a paper bag under your desk. You may only eat snacks during breaks. If you need to leave the room, the testing staff will tell you where you can go to have your snack.

- Keep your photo ID with you at all times. This is especially important if you leave the testing room. You may be asked to show your ID at any time while at the test site.

- Don't close your device or cover your tablet during testing; leave it open during break time.

- Don't leave the testing room before you're dismissed; if you do, your scores will be canceled.

Borrowing a Device from College Board

For SAT Weekend, students who don't have access to an eligible testing device can request to borrow one from College Board. You may qualify to borrow a testing device if you submit a request at least 30 days before the test date. Submitting a request, however, doesn't guarantee that College Board will grant such a request and provide you with a testing device. If a testing device is provided, additional rules relating to borrowing the device will apply to you. For more information, go to **satsuite.collegeboard.org/digital/device-lending**.

Technical Support on Test Day

The testing staff will provide additional support on test day. They will ensure the Wi-Fi network is working and will assist you if you encounter connectivity issues. Additionally, a help room will be available for you to fix device issues with the testing staff. We'll also have customer service resources ready to troubleshoot issues on test day. Before, during, and after testing, the Help icon in Bluebook enables users to review troubleshooting tips and FAQs.

Makeup Testing

During bad weather, natural disasters, power outages, or other unusual conditions, test sites may close. If a makeup date is confirmed, you'll be notified.

The following policies apply to makeup testing:

- The availability of makeup testing and the conditions that allow test takers to be eligible to take a makeup test are at the sole discretion of College Board.

- Access to scores from makeup administrations may be delayed by several weeks.

CHAPTER 5

SAT Test-Taking Strategies

In this chapter, we offer suggestions for preparing for and taking the SAT. We begin with ways that you can get familiar with the SAT, and then we offer some tips for how you can demonstrate your best work on test day. We wrap up with a brief consideration of whether you should retest.

Getting Familiar with the SAT

As you begin your SAT practice, you should become comfortable with several aspects of the test and how to take it.

Understand the Test's Purpose

The SAT is an assessment of your college and career readiness. It's designed to assess the extent to which you've obtained the necessary prerequisites in reading and writing and in math for success in college and workforce training programs. You should expect that the SAT will call on you to demonstrate academic skills and knowledge that the best available evidence indicates are necessary for you to have to be ready for postsecondary education.

The single best preparation for the SAT is actively participating in a challenging set of academic courses. Such classes and the SAT share the goal of helping ensure that you're ready to succeed in college and career training after you graduate from high school. This means that the skills and knowledge you'll be tested on in the SAT will closely resemble those you're called on to demonstrate in your current classes. While there are specific ways the SAT tests these skills and knowledge (which we'll go over throughout this book), the key point is that what you'll be tested on should be familiar to you from your classes. The test and its results should also be clearly relevant to you since you'll need these same skills and knowledge to succeed in college and workforce training programs.

SECTION PREVIEW

In this section, we cover the following topics:

- Test purpose
- Test basics
- Bluebook
- Digital testing tools in Bluebook
- Adaptive testing
- Test directions
- Question formats
- Question types

Know the Test Basics

Before taking the SAT (or any test), it's important to have a sense of the test's key features. Chapter 2 provides an overview and discussion of all those features. Here, we recap a few of the most relevant points as they pertain to your test preparation.

- **Test components:** A Reading and Writing section and a Math section

- **Number of questions:** 98 (54 Reading and Writing questions, 44 Math questions), with each test section divided into two equal-length, separately timed modules consisting of half the section's questions (27 questions for each Reading and Writing module, 22 questions for each Math module)

- **Time allotted:** 134 minutes (64 minutes for the Reading and Writing section, 70 minutes for the Math section), with each test section divided into two equal-length, separately timed modules of questions (32 minutes for each Reading and Writing module, 35 minutes for each Math module)

- **Scores**
  - Two section scores (Reading and Writing; Math), each on a 200–800 scale
  - A total score (sum of the Reading and Writing and Math section scores) on a 400–1600 scale

STRATEGY

We **strongly recommend** that all students planning to take the SAT spend some time exploring Bluebook using test preview.

Test Preview

One option offered by Bluebook—and one we strongly encourage you to make use of—is test preview. Preview gives you an untimed, stress-free option to explore Bluebook, try out the testing tools, and test out any assistive technology you may be using on test day. Test preview presents you with the directions for each test section and a small selection of sample Reading and Writing and Math questions. These questions aren't primarily to test your skills and knowledge but rather to get you up and running on how to appropriately respond to questions during your practice or on test day itself. You can also gain some experience with the app's tools for annotating text and for flagging questions to return to should time permit, and you can experiment with hiding and revealing the testing app's countdown timer, if you wish. When getting familiar with the Math section, you'll be able to learn how to use the built-in Demos graphing calculator as well as the reference sheet with common math formulas. (Neither of these tools are available—or needed—during the Reading and Writing section.) See chapter 30 for more on your calculator options and chapter 31 for a copy of the reference sheet.

When you finish each mini section in test preview, you'll be reminded of questions you either flagged to return to and/or haven't yet answered. This feature helps ensure that you don't make careless mistakes when responding and will have the best chance to perform up to your achievement level.

Official Full-Length Practice Tests

In addition to hosting test preview, Bluebook is also your hub for official full-length SAT practice tests. Simply sign in to Bluebook to get started. The practice tests have been written by the same developers College Board uses to produce the tests taken on test day, so you can be confident that you'll be measured on the same skills and knowledge, in the same ways, and at the same level of challenge as on test day. These Bluebook practice tests are also adaptive, like those on test day, meaning that you'll gain practical experience with how the adaptive test design used for the SAT works. Finally, because you'll be practicing in the same digital testing application as the one you'll be using on test day, you'll be gaining facility with the testing app while you practice. Log in to My Practice to access answer explanations and information about your practice test scores to make the most of your practice in Bluebook.

Get Familiar with Digital Testing Tools

Bluebook offers several tools that you may choose to use to improve your testing experience. Among the key tools available to all students testing digitally are those that allow test takers to

- cross out answer options in multiple-choice questions.
- highlight any part of a non-math question passage and leave a note.
- display or (until the five-minutes-remaining mark) hide a countdown timer.
- access the test directions and the Math section's reference sheet during testing.
- flag questions within a given test module to return to if time remains.
- access a display informing you of how many questions in each test module you've either flagged or left unanswered and allowing you to jump to any question within a module.
- use the built-in Desmos graphing calculator (Math section only).
- adjust magnification (zoom by using keyboard shortcuts on laptops or by pinching on tablets).
- modify color contrast using system settings before testing.

Remember that you're free to navigate among questions in a given test module as long as testing time remains. This means, for example, that you can preview upcoming questions or return to flagged or unanswered questions should time permit.

LEVEL UP YOUR PRACTICE

Learn helpful strategies to prepare for testing and ideas to get the most out of your practice tests at **satsuite.collegeboard.org/practice/bluebook**.

Build Your Confidence

Taking official practice tests in Bluebook has another benefit too. Research in psychology supports the idea that when we're learning, our brains remember information about the place we're in. When we're in that place again, we feel more confident in our ability to recall that information. In other words, you may not be able to take the SAT from the comfort of your favorite study space, but if you've spent time practicing in Bluebook, we hope you'll feel right at home.

There are other ways to build your confidence as you study as well. If you tend to second-guess yourself, try setting a goal for yourself on how many times you'll "allow" yourself to change your initial answer—maybe once every ten questions, every three minutes, or whatever interval works for you. You can use the Mark for Review tool in Bluebook to flag any questions where you feel the urge to second-guess. When your finish the practice test, go back and look at those flagged questions. If your initial answer was correct, that's a sign you know the material better than you think! If you would have gotten an answer correct if you had gone with your second guess, that's a sign to explore why your initial instinct was off. With a little skill review, you may start to feel more confident in your answers.

For more confidence-boosting exercises like this, visit **satsuite.collegeboard.org/practice/practice-with-confidence**.

Understand the Nature of Adaptive SAT Testing

As discussed in chapter 2, the SAT uses a simple two-stage adaptive model to improve your testing experience, primarily by making it as short as possible while retaining the test's value as a fair, valid, and reliable measure of what you know and can do with respect to college and career readiness requirements.

The key practical implication for you is that each of the two test sections on the SAT is divided into two separately timed, equal-length modules of questions. After you answer the questions in the first module of each test section, Bluebook will automatically route you to either a higher- or lower-difficulty second module of questions, depending on your performance on the first module's questions.

Each of the two possible second modules of questions contains a mix of easy, medium-difficulty, and hard questions, although in different proportions. This means that when you move into the second module, you shouldn't expect to encounter only easy or only hard questions. In fact, the differences between the two possible modules, in terms of average question difficulty, are slight enough that you may not know which of the two possibilities you were routed to.

We suggest not thinking of the two modules in a test section as two separate tests, even though each has its own time limit. Rather, you should think about the two modules as two parts of a single test in either reading and writing or math. Your section scores are based on your performance on *all* test questions in the section (with the exception of the small number of unscored questions College Board includes in each section). If you're routed to the higher-difficulty second module, you don't need to answer every question correctly to get a good score; conversely, if you're routed to the lower-difficulty second module, you'll have a full opportunity to answer questions in the module correctly and show what you know and can do.

The essential point is that, in general terms, you'll get the same section and total scores on the SAT that you would've gotten had the test not been adaptive, except that the test would need to have been significantly longer to reach that conclusion. That's because in typical large-scale nonadaptive testing programs, such as the previous paper-based versions of the SAT, test makers must present each test taker with the same broad range of question difficulties, from very easy to very hard. While this works well enough for test takers in general, this approach isn't particularly efficient because any given individual is likely to encounter questions that are too easy or too hard for them. Such questions don't tell us much about the individual's capabilities. Correctly answering a too-easy question doesn't really help establish the upper limits of what the test taker knows and can do, and incorrectly answering a question that's too hard doesn't reveal much about what the test taker does know and can demonstrate.

The multistage adaptive model used in the SAT improves on this approach by targeting question difficulty more closely to the skills and knowledge of individual students than is possible in a nonadaptive test. This is beneficial to you because it means that the same information about your skills and knowledge can be obtained with fewer questions and less time. It also means you'll more likely be able to give your full effort and attention throughout the test than you would if the test were longer.

Learn the Test Directions Prior to Test Day

We strongly encourage you to become familiar with the directions for the SAT prior to test day. You won't have to memorize them because you'll have access to them throughout the test if you wish, but any time you spend reading directions on test day is time not spent answering questions.

The best way to become familiar with the test directions is through practice activities. Test preview, discussed above, allows you to read the test's directions in advance and to apply your understanding by answering a few sample test questions. Our official full-length practice tests, also discussed previously, contain the directions as well.

A NOTE ON PAPER SAT TESTS

Paper (nonadaptive) versions of SAT tests are available for students who require them as testing accommodations or for other reasons. These tests are longer in terms of number of questions and testing time due to their nonadaptive nature, but otherwise these forms are highly comparable to digital adaptive forms and also yield scores that can be reported to colleges and universities.

The directions for the SAT are straightforward. For most questions, you simply need to select the best (Reading and Writing) or correct (Math) option from among a set of provided answer choices. The exception to this is the SPR question format in Math. These questions lack answer options and require you to generate and enter your own answer. Directions for entering SPR answers in Bluebook can be found in chapter 29 as well as in Bluebook itself.

Know the Two Test Question Formats

Most SAT questions—all Reading and Writing questions and roughly three-quarters of Math questions—are in the multiple-choice format. Each of these questions has four answer choices, and your job is to determine which of these choices is the single best (Reading and Writing) or correct (Math) answer.

About a quarter of Math questions are in the SPR format. As noted above, these questions lack answer options and instead require you to generate and enter your own answers. These questions are essentially tests of whether you can apply your math skills and knowledge in cases where the scaffolding and support of answer choices isn't provided. Examples of questions in the SPR format can be found throughout this book's discussion of the Math section, and chapter 29 is devoted to explaining how to properly enter your answers in Bluebook. Note that some SPR questions may have more than one possible answer, but you're only ever required to enter a single answer to each question in this format.

Get Familiar with the Various Question Types

Chapter 7 (Reading and Writing) and chapter 19 (Math) provide overviews of the types of questions you'll be asked on test day, while subsequent chapters in parts 2 and 3 of this book go into detail about the skills and knowledge these question types require you to demonstrate and provide opportunities for immediate practice.

Becoming aware of and comfortable with the types of questions you'll be asked is a critical element of your preparation for several reasons. First, and most obviously, it's important for you to know what skills and knowledge you'll be required to demonstrate on the SAT. Second, it's important to know how these skills and knowledge are tested (i.e., in what types of questions) so that you're better prepared to answer correctly. Finally, an understanding of question types is helpful for practice, as you can hone your preparation on those topics that you may be struggling with.

The question drills in parts 2 (Reading and Writing) and 3 (Math) of this book are one way for you to gain this familiarity, as these practice sequences include a good representation of question types organized by content domain (e.g., Information and Ideas in Reading and Writing;

NOTE

Some Math multiple-choice questions also have more than one possible real-world answer, but only one correct answer will be provided among the options you're given.

Problem-Solving and Data Analysis in Math). Visiting Khan Academy for free Official SAT Prep at **khanacademy.org/digital-sat** is another excellent option.

Additionally, you can access the Student Question Bank on My Practice to find thousands of official practice questions. Reference your Knowledge and Skill domain results from Bluebook practice tests and filter the question bank by assessment, domain, and different skill levels to get more questions tailored to practice. Learn more at **satsuite.collegeboard.org/practice/student-question-bank**.

Doing Your Best on Test Day

In this section, we focus on specific strategies that you can use on test day to maximize your performance.

Read Every Question Carefully

It's important that you read every question on the SAT carefully to know what you're being asked to demonstrate. Although this takes time and effort, there are compensations.

- You'll know exactly what you're being asked, so you're less likely to make a careless error when answering. This can be particularly important for multiple-choice questions, as the incorrect answers often play into common mistakes that test takers make or misconceptions that they hold.

- You may encounter some important contextual information that changes how you'd otherwise understand the question. This is true in both test sections. Some Reading and Writing questions, especially those associated with the literature subject area, supply important background information to make interpreting a given passage easier. In-context questions in Math, which constitute about 30 percent of questions in the section, require you to read and understand the scenarios presented in order to answer properly.

- You'll notice important qualifiers. A few Math questions, for example, may use "**not**" or "NOT" in the question to signal that you're looking for what's *not* the case. Missing out on that qualifier will leave you adrift in the question.

It's worth noting that College Board takes great pains to ensure the clarity and conciseness of each test question. In other words, we're not trying to trick or overload you with the wording of questions. We want the challenge posed by our test questions to come solely from the ease or difficulty of performing given tasks, not from students struggling to understand what they're being asked to do.

SECTION PREVIEW

In this section, we cover the following topics:

- Reading every question carefully
- Answering every question
- Making use of the question order
- Pacing yourself
- Knowing when to move on

To this end, you may note that we make use of standardized question language whenever it makes sense to do so. For instance, in Rhetorical Synthesis questions in Reading and Writing (see chapter 15 for more details), you'll always be presented with a set of notes taken by a hypothetical student and asked to use relevant information from the notes to meet the student's goal as a writer, such as introducing an artist to an audience unfamiliar with that artist or their work. While the basic framing is the same from one Rhetorical Synthesis question to the next, the hypothetical student's goal varies from question to question, as will, of course, the student's notes and the topic they address. So you'll want to pay close attention to the specified goal in each question, as meeting this goal most effectively is the objective of answering the question.

Answer Every Question to the Best of Your Ability

It is better to make an educated guess than to leave a question blank, so there's no reason not to answer every question in both sections to the best of your ability. But what if you're not sure of the answer? There are a couple of things you can do to improve your odds of responding properly.

- First, you may find it beneficial to flag questions you're having trouble with to return to should time permit. You don't want to flag too many questions, but you don't want to get hung up on one or two questions about which you're uncertain when you could be answering other questions in a module with greater confidence.

- Second, for multiple-choice questions that you're not sure of the answer to, try to eliminate one or more incorrect answer choices. (The Bluebook testing application has an answer elimination option for this very reason.) You're much more likely to answer correctly if you can reduce your possible responses by two or even one than if you randomly guess.

After you've reached the end of a module but before time has expired, the questions you've flagged to return to and the questions you haven't answered at all will appear on your Check Your Work page. Use this information in the remaining moments of your testing to address as many of these questions as possible. Use your timed practice (discussed later) to get a better sense of when you should make this turn toward finalizing your answers to questions in each module.

Make Use of the Question Order

As also discussed in chapter 7 (Reading and Writing) and chapter 19 (Math), SAT questions are ordered in particular ways, and knowing these patterns can help you during testing.

In the Reading and Writing section, each module begins with Craft and Structure questions, followed by Information and Ideas, Standard English Conventions, and Expression of Ideas questions. Within all but the Standard English Conventions content domain, questions are further ordered by type, meaning that similar questions appear together. This is beneficial to you because it allows you to get into a rhythm by answering questions of the same type consecutively, with a minimum of context switching. This can also be an aid to pacing, as we discuss below. Note, however, that Reading and Writing questions aren't strictly ordered by question difficulty, so within each module you can expect to see easy, medium-difficulty, and hard questions mingled.

In Math, questions are ordered by difficulty, from easiest to hardest, within each module. While you're free to navigate through the questions in each module and answer them in any order you choose, you may find more success working from the start of a given module to the end, given that the easier questions appear earlier than the harder ones. Of course, "easy" and "hard" are relative terms, and what's easy for one test taker may be hard for you and vice versa. Nonetheless, you may find that moving sequentially—question by question—through a Math module offers some benefit to you because of the ordering by difficulty.

Pace Yourself

Pacing is critical to success on the SAT. To get your best score, you need to spend the right amount of time on each question—no more, no less.

In Reading and Writing, you'll have about 1.19 minutes to read and answer each question, and you'll have about 1.59 minutes to read and answer each Math question. Since SAT questions are relatively brief, this should give you adequate time to give your best answer in each case as long as you're adequately prepared.

As we've argued, part of that preparation is understanding the purpose of the SAT; the test basics; Bluebook and its tools; the nature of the adaptive testing approach; the test directions; and the question formats and types. Another crucial part is practice under conditions. The question drills throughout part 2 and part 3 of this book are geared toward untimed practice—in other words, the focus is intended to be on getting familiar with the way the SAT presents questions. By contrast, the full-length practice tests available in Bluebook and this book are ideal opportunities to practice under test-like conditions and to get a better handle on how long particular formats and types of questions are going to take you.

In general:

- Reading and Writing questions in the Information and Ideas content domain are usually the lengthiest and require the most time, on average, while questions in the Standard English Conventions domain are typically the briefest and take the least time, on average. Craft and Structure and Expression of Ideas questions usually fall somewhere in between.

- Math questions set in context are likely to take a bit longer to answer than Math questions not in context, as you'll have to spend some time and effort reading and understanding the scenarios being laid out.

Know When to Move On

Finally, it may sometimes be worth it to give up on particular test questions and move on to others for the sake of time. As mentioned above, we still suggest giving your best answer to every question, but there may be some that you really just don't know the answer to or perhaps even how to approach. Grinding away on such questions is probably not worth it, even if you end up getting them right, as there's an opportunity cost in the form of other questions you might have answered more skillfully had you given them adequate time.

This may be obvious, but it's not necessary to get every question on the SAT correct to score well. In that spirit, don't let the perfect be the enemy of the good. Focus on your strengths and avoid getting bogged down in one or more questions that stump you.

Should I Retest?

Let's say you've done everything we suggested, practiced extensively, and taken the SAT. You've gotten your scores back, and while you're not unhappy with them, you feel as though you could've done better. Should you retest?

In general, College Board recommends that students take the SAT at least twice—in the spring of their junior year and the fall of their senior year. The most important reason for this is because research has shown that SAT test takers' scores tend to go up between tests, due to a combination of enhanced learning and greater familiarity with the test itself. What's more, colleges tend to use students' highest SAT scores as the basis for decision-making, and many use a practice known as superscoring in which a student's highest SAT Reading and Writing section score is paired with their highest SAT Math section score.

It's possible that your scores could increase between a first and second testing simply due to you becoming more familiar with the SAT itself. However, you're more likely to improve scores between testing if you spend time identifying and working on academic shortcomings associated with the SAT. This is where additional resources, such as your score report (discussed in more detail in chapter 3), full-length practice tests, My Practice, the Student Question Bank, and Official SAT Prep on Khan Academy, can be hugely beneficial. These various resources can help you pinpoint weaknesses that you need to address and provide information about and suggestions for how to improve on them.

CHAPTER 6

Using This Book to Prepare for the PSAT/NMSQT or PSAT 10

Overview

The SAT is part of a system of tests—the SAT Suite of Assessments—created by College Board to assess students' progress toward college and career readiness. Two other important pieces of this suite are the Preliminary SAT/National Merit Scholarship Qualifying Test (PSAT/NMSQT) and PSAT 10. These two tests are the same in terms of content, differing mainly in when students take them and how they're used. The PSAT/NMSQT is administered in the fall of each year, typically to high school juniors, and serves as the qualifying test for entry to the National Merit® Scholarship Program conducted by National Merit Scholarship Corporation. The PSAT 10 is administered in the spring, typically to high school sophomores, and cannot be used for entry to the National Merit Scholarship Program.

Whether you take the PSAT/NMSQT or PSAT 10, the test and its results are useful to you in several ways. First, as we'll discuss in more detail below, the PSAT/NMSQT and PSAT 10 are highly similar in content to the SAT, meaning that preparation and practice for either of these earlier tests will carry over into getting ready for the SAT and that your PSAT/NMSQT or PSAT 10 scores are good indicators of how well you'd perform on the SAT if you'd taken it instead. Second, the PSAT/NMSQT and PSAT 10 provide important measures of your progress toward attaining college and career readiness. You can use the results to check in on your progress, engage in career exploration, identify areas of strength and weakness in your academic preparation, and plan steps to address any shortcomings. Third, the PSAT/NMSQT is the official qualifying test for the National Merit Scholarship Program.

By design, the PSAT/NMSQT and PSAT 10 tests are very similar to the SAT. Among other things, this means that **you can use the content of this book, including the advice, sample questions, and practice tests, to help you prepare to take either the PSAT/NMSQT or PSAT 10.** There are just a few important differences worth noting.

Table 1 compares the SAT to the PSAT/NMSQT and PSAT 10. The few differences between the SAT and the two PSAT-related assessments are discussed afterward.

Table 1. Comparison of the SAT and PSAT/NMSQT and PSAT 10 Tests

Feature	SAT	PSAT/NMSQT and PSAT 10
Reading and Writing		
Number of questions	54	54
Total time allotted (minutes)	64	64
Average time per question (minutes)	1.19	1.19
Math		
Number of questions	44	44
Total time allotted (minutes)	70	70
Average time per question (minutes)	1.59	1.59
Score scales		
Section	200–800	160–760
Total	400–1600	320–1520
Question distribution—format		
READING AND WRITING:		
Multiple-choice	100%	100%
MATH:		
Multiple-choice	~75%	~75%
Student-produced response	~25%	~25%
Question distribution—content domain		
READING AND WRITING:		
Information and Ideas	~26%	~26%
Craft and Structure	~28%	~28%
Expression of Ideas	~24%	~24%
Standard English Conventions	~22%	~22%
MATH:		
Algebra	~35%	~35%
Advanced Math	~35%	~32.5%
Problem-Solving and Data Analysis	~15%	~20%
Geometry and Trigonometry	~15%	~12.5%
Administration	Two-stage adaptive test design; each stage consists of a module of questions	
Organization	Reading and Writing section, Math section	
	Each section consists of two separately timed modules of questions	
Scores reported	◆ Reading and Writing section score ◆ Math section score ◆ Total score ◆ Selection Index score (PSAT/NMSQT only)	
Skills and knowledge tested	Reading and Writing: ◆ No differences Math: Tested only on the SAT— ◆ Margins of error ◆ Evaluating statistical claims associated with observational studies and experiments ◆ Circles	

Differences between the SAT and the PSAT/NMSQT and PSAT 10

There are only a few differences between the SAT and the PSAT/NMSQT and PSAT 10.

- **Score scales.** The tests of the SAT Suite of Assessments are on the same common scale. This means that your score on any one test in the suite is a good predictor of how well you'd score on a later test in the suite had you taken it instead. One consequence of the common scaling is that the tests' score scales are slightly different to allow for continued growth in subsequent tests. As a result, the PSAT/NMSQT and PSAT 10 have section scores that are on a 160–760 scale and total scores that are on a 320–1520 scale, whereas the SAT's section scores are on a 200–800 scale and its total score is on a 400–1600 scale. Students who take the PSAT/NMSQT will also receive a Selection Index score on a scale from 48–228, which National Merit Scholarship Corporation uses as an initial screen of program entrants.

- **Question distribution—content domains.** The approximate proportion of Reading and Writing questions in each of the section's four content domains is the same on the SAT and the PSAT/NMSQT and PSAT 10. The approximate proportion of Math questions in each of that section's four content domains varies slightly, with the SAT having slightly higher proportions of Advanced Math as well as Geometry and Trigonometry questions and a slightly lower proportion of Problem-Solving and Data Analysis questions.

- **Skills and knowledge tested.** The skills and knowledge tested in the Reading and Writing section are the same in the SAT and the PSAT/NMSQT and PSAT 10. The same is true for Math, with the following exceptions:

  - *Problem-Solving and Data Analysis.* The SAT (only) may have questions about margins of error and about evaluating statistical claims associated with observational studies and experiments.

  - *Geometry and Trigonometry.* The SAT (only) may have questions about circles.

PART 2

The Reading and Writing Section

CHAPTER 7

Reading and Writing: Overview

The Reading and Writing section of the SAT is, along with the Math section, one of the two main portions of the test. In the Reading and Writing section, you'll answer questions that test your ability to read, analyze, and use information and ideas in passages (texts); explain how and why authors make the choices that they do; revise passages to improve how information and ideas are expressed; and edit passages so that they meet expectations of Standard English sentence structure, usage, and punctuation.

In this chapter, we'll cover the whole Reading and Writing section at an overview level so that you'll have a general sense of what you'll be tested on and how. Subsequent chapters will go into more details about the passages, informational graphics, and questions found in the section.

The Section at a Glance

Table 1 provides an overview of the SAT Reading and Writing section. Each feature is discussed in the following subsections.

Number of Questions, Timing, and Pacing

Each Reading and Writing test section is divided into two equal-length *modules* of questions. Each of these modules is separately timed, so you'll have 32 minutes to answer the 27 questions in each module. That averages out to 1.19 minutes per question.

Score

You'll receive a Reading and Writing section score based on your performance. Section scores range from 200 to 800, in 10-point intervals. Your scores on the Reading and Writing and Math sections added together will give you your total score for the SAT, which is on a 400–1600 scale, also in 10-point intervals.

PREVIEW
Chapters 8 and 9 discuss in detail the kinds of passages and informational graphics found in the Reading and Writing section, respectively. Chapters 10–18 cover the kinds of questions you'll encounter and provide drills that you can use for immediate practice.

QUICK TAKE
You'll have **64 minutes** to answer **54 multiple-choice Reading and Writing questions**. This averages out to **1.19 minutes per question**. These questions will be divided into **two separately timed modules** of 32 minutes each.

FOR MORE INFORMATION
For an explanation of why the Reading and Writing (and Math) section is divided into two separately timed modules, see chapter 2.

Table 1. Reading and Writing Section Overview

Feature	SAT Reading and Writing Section
Timing and Pacing	
Number of questions	1st module: 27 questions
	2nd module: 27 questions
	Total: 54 questions
Time per module	1st module: 32 minutes
	2nd module: 32 minutes
	Total: 64 minutes
Average time per question	1.19 minutes
Score	
Score	Reading and Writing section score (200–800 scale); one-half of the SAT total score
Passages	
Words per passage (or passage pair)	25–150
Passage subject areas	Literature
	History/social studies
	Humanities
	Science
Passage text type	Literary
	Informative/explanatory
	Argumentative
Text complexity bands	Grades 6–8
	Grades 9–11
	Grades 12–14
Informational graphics (included with select passages)	Tables
	Bar graphs
	Line graphs
Questions	
Question format	Four-option multiple-choice, each with a single best answer; all questions are independent of each other
Question content domains (categories)	Information and Ideas
	Craft and Structure
	Expression of Ideas
	Standard English Conventions

Passages

Each Reading and Writing question is accompanied by a brief *passage*, which questions in the Reading and Writing section refer to as a *text*. Each passage is short—as few as 25 words to a maximum of 150 words. Some questions will instead include a pair of passages on the same topic or similar topics; together, these passages will be 150 words or fewer in length.

Each passage has a number of important traits, which we'll describe here briefly and focus on in detail in chapter 8.

- Each passage has a **subject area**. This represents the nature of the topic being presented. Passages in the Reading and Writing section represent the subject areas of literature, history/social studies, the humanities, and science. It's helpful to pay attention to the subject area of a given passage because different subjects convey information and ideas in different ways, and knowing something about how each subject shares knowledge can give you an edge in responding to questions. You won't, however, be tested on what you already know about the topic of each passage, as all the information needed to answer each question is contained in the passage itself (and in any accompanying informational graphic).

- Each passage has a **text type**. The three text types represented in the Reading and Writing section are literary, informative/explanatory, and argumentative. It's useful to note the text type of a given passage because, as with subject area, the purpose for which a passage is written (e.g., to entertain, to explain, to convince) influences how its information and ideas are conveyed and organized as well as what kinds of details are included and what roles they serve.

- Each passage has a **text complexity** rating. *Text complexity* is a measure of how easy or difficult a given passage is. When we develop Reading and Writing passages, they get assigned to one of three text complexity bands: grades 6–8, grades 9–11, and grades 12–14. A given passage's text complexity is based on a number of factors, such as how long and sophisticated (or short and straightforward) its sentences are, how challenging (or familiar) its vocabulary is, and how much information it conveys and at what rate. You won't find text complexity ratings listed for passages on the test, and we don't advise paying too much attention to how easy or difficult any passage you encounter on test day is. Still, it's helpful to know that some passages will be relatively straightforward while others will be as challenging as those you'll be assigned in common first-year college courses.

The passages for certain questions will also include an **informational graphic**. Informational graphics in the Reading and Writing section consist of tables, bar graphs, and line graphs, which are among the most common tools authors use to display data visually.

A NOTE ON TERMINOLOGY

Reading and Writing questions refer to the brief readings they include as *texts*. In this guide, we use the term *passages* to refer to these texts in order to avoid possible confusion with other types of real-world texts you may encounter.

QUICK TAKE

Each passage has a **subject area**, **text type**, and **text complexity**, and some passages are accompanied by an **informational graphic**. Understanding these features can help you better prepare to read and understand the passages on test day.

Questions that include a graphic may ask you to locate data, interpret information (e.g., identify a trend), or combine data from the graphic with information in the passage in a meaningful way. You won't, however, have to "do math" with graphics in the Reading and Writing section. No question in the Reading and Writing section will ask you to perform calculations, and the use of a calculator isn't permitted in the section. Instead, you'll apply the numeracy skills you've acquired in various classes, including in history/social studies and science courses, to find and make strategic use of data from tables and graphs to come to a fuller understanding of the topics presented in passages.

Questions

All questions in the Reading and Writing section are multiple-choice. Each question has four answer choices and one (and only one) best answer, known as the *key*. The three incorrect answer choices represent common errors that students may make when answering a given question (which is why, in test-maker lingo, incorrect multiple-choice options are sometimes called *distractors*, because they're meant to be at least somewhat tempting). Your task on test day will be figuring out the best answer for each question using your reading and writing skills and knowledge.

All Reading and Writing questions are independent of each other. (These sorts of questions are sometimes described as *discrete*.) This means that each question is self-contained and can be answered on its own, without reference to any other question. In practical terms, this means that instead of reading a few long passages and answering multiple questions about each one, you'll be reading many short passages and answering a single question about each. This has important implications for preparing for and taking the test: if you struggle with a particular passage, just give your best answer and move on (and possibly flag the question to return to if time permits).

Each Reading and Writing question tests a single skill or knowledge element. The skill/knowledge elements tested by SAT Reading and Writing questions fall into four broad categories, or *content domains*. Each of these domains captures a "big idea" in reading and writing. We'll describe each of these briefly to orient you now and then unpack each content domain in later chapters.

Table 2 offers an overview of the four content domains in the Reading and Writing section, including the "big idea," or main focus, of each domain, the specific skills and knowledge on which you may be tested, and roughly how many questions of each domain appear in the test section.

QUICK TAKE

Each four-option multiple-choice Reading and Writing question has one (and only one) best answer. Your job is to determine which choice that is and to avoid being tempted by incorrect answers. All test questions are independent of each other; there are no question sets.

QUICK TAKE

Each Reading and Writing question falls into one of four categories, or *content domains*: Information and Ideas, Craft and Structure, Expression of Ideas, and Standard English Conventions. **Each question tests one (and only one) skill/knowledge element** (e.g., Central Ideas and Details).

The first two domains—Information and Ideas and Craft and Structure—mainly test reading skills and knowledge, while the second two domains—Expression of Ideas and Standard English Conventions—mainly test writing skills and knowledge.

Questions in each Reading and Writing test module will follow the sequence listed in table 3.

Within the content domains of Information and Ideas, Craft and Structure, and Expression of Ideas, questions testing the same skill/knowledge element (e.g., Central Ideas and Details in the Information and Ideas content domain) appear alongside each other. This is so you can concentrate on one type of question at a time, without having to switch back and forth among the various skills and knowledge tested. Standard English Conventions questions, on the other hand, won't be organized by skill/knowledge element, so you might encounter Boundaries and Form, Structure, and Sense conventions questions in any order on your test form.

Being aware of this sequencing can help you manage your time since some question types can take longer to answer than others. However, it's important to be aware that the exact number of questions per skill/knowledge element within a module can vary.

Questions in each Reading and Writing module aren't strictly ordered by difficulty, so you may come across a hard question followed by an easier one and vice versa. Just do your best to answer each question, and remember that you can flag questions to return to if time permits.

IMPORTANT: UNSCORED QUESTIONS
Four Reading and Writing questions on each test form—two different questions per module—won't count toward your section score. These questions are ones that College Board is studying for potential use on future tests. Your answers to these questions won't impact your section score in any way. You won't be able to tell these questions apart from the ones in the section that do get scored, but there are few enough of them that their presence won't significantly affect your test taking.

Table 2. Reading and Writing Section Content Domains

Reading and Writing Section Content Domain	The Big Idea	Skills and Knowledge Tested	Proportion of Test Section

Information and Ideas	Questions in this domain test your understanding of what you read.	Central Ideas and Details
		Command of Evidence
		  • Textual
		  • Quantitative
		Inferences
			12–14 questions (about 26%)

Craft and Structure	Questions in this domain test your understanding of how and why authors write the way they do.	Words in Context Text Structure and Purpose Cross-Text Connections	13–15 questions (about 28%)
Expression of Ideas	Questions in this domain test your ability to revise passages to meet particular writing goals.	Rhetorical Synthesis Transitions	8–12 questions (about 20%)
Standard English Conventions	Questions in this domain test your ability to edit passages for conventional sentence structure, usage, and punctuation.	Boundaries Form, Structure, and Sense	11–15 questions (about 26%)

Table 3. Reading and Writing Section Question Order

Reading and Writing Modules	Content Domain Sequence
1st module	Craft and Structure questions
	Information and Ideas questions
	Standard English Conventions questions
	Expression of Ideas questions
2nd module	Craft and Structure questions
	Information and Ideas questions
	Standard English Conventions questions
	Expression of Ideas questions

Summary: Reading and Writing Section

Timing and pacing

- 64 minutes to answer 54 questions across two separately timed modules of 32 minutes each

- An average of 1.19 minutes to answer each question

Score

- A Reading and Writing section score on a 200–800 scale, in 10-point intervals (one-half of the total score for the SAT, which is on an 800–1600 scale, also in 10-point intervals)

Passages

- 25–150 words per passage (or passage pair)

- Subject areas of literature, history/social studies, the humanities, and science

- Text types of literary, informative/explanatory, and argumentative

- An informational graphic (table, bar graph, or line graph) included with select passages

- Text complexities of grades 6–8, grades 9–11, and grades 12–14

Questions

- Four-option multiple-choice, each with a single best answer (*key*)

- All questions independent of each other (i.e., no question sets)

- Content domains of Information and Ideas, Craft and Structure, Expression of Ideas, and Standard English Conventions

    - On the test, Craft and Structure questions appear first in each module, followed by Information and Ideas, Standard English Conventions, and Expression of Ideas questions.

    - Except for Standard English Conventions questions, questions within each content domain are grouped together by skill/knowledge element (e.g., Central Ideas and Details) being tested.

- Each question tied to a single skill/knowledge element within one of the four content domains

- Easier and harder questions may appear alongside each other

- 4 unscored questions (2 different questions per module)

CHAPTER 8

Reading and Writing: Passages

This chapter examines the key features of the passages you'll be asked to work with in the Reading and Writing section. This information will help you unpack the passages you read during practice and on test day so that you're better prepared to answer associated test questions correctly. Over the course of this chapter, we'll demonstrate three strategies for unlocking the meaning of Reading and Writing passages: (1) determining a passage's main purpose, (2) identifying its central (main) idea, and (3) analyzing its structure. Using one or more of these strategies can help you obtain a high-level grasp of each passage, which can, in turn, help you answer whatever question you're ultimately presented with.

The Basics

Each Reading and Writing question includes a *passage* (which the test refers to as a *text*) or, in some cases, a pair of passages on the same topic or similar topics. Each passage is tied to one (and only one) question, meaning that you can approach each question separately, without reference to any other question in the section.

As we noted in the previous chapter, all passages have three traits: a **subject area**, a **text type**, and a **text complexity**. Some passages also have a fourth trait: an **informational graphic**, which may be a table, bar graph, or line graph. We'll address the first three traits in this chapter and devote the next chapter to the informational graphics found in the Reading and Writing section.

All the information needed to answer each question is in the passage itself (and in any accompanying informational graphic). This benefits all test takers because it makes the Reading and Writing section a test of literacy skills and knowledge and not a test of what topics students such as you may or may not have had a chance to learn about in school.

This also means that you should **always answer questions based on what's stated or strongly implied in the passage (and any graphic)** rather than on what you know or believe about a topic.

PREVIEW

This chapter discusses traits of Reading and Writing passages and presents several broad strategies to help you better understand the passages.

QUICK TAKE

Each Reading and Writing passage has a **subject area**, **text type**, and **text complexity**. Select passages also have an **informational graphic**. All the information needed to answer each question is contained in its accompanying passage (and any informational graphic). Answer each question based on what's stated or strongly implied in the passage itself (and any graphic).

Subject Area

Each passage belongs to one of **four subject areas: literature, history/social studies, the humanities, and science**. This is important because test passages (as well as real-world texts in these areas) convey information and ideas in differing ways by subject and have differing concerns, or things that authors writing in these subjects care about and are trying to communicate to readers.

Literature passages in the Reading and Writing section are excerpted from previously published works, such as novels, plays, and poems. Passages in all other subject areas are written specifically for the test in ways that simulate real-world texts in these areas.

As we analyze a sample passage from each of the four subject areas, we'll consider how we can determine the **main purpose** and the **central (main) idea** of each passage.

A statement of a passage's **main purpose** focuses on the author's aim in writing the text and is phrased in terms of what the author is trying to accomplish and why. Statements of purpose generally contain two elements:

- a verb signaling intent, such as "[to] persuade," "[to] convince," or "[to] explain," and

- a "that" or "in order to" clause signaling more specifically what the author is trying to do, such as "[to persuade readers] that the proposed policy should be adopted" or "[to explain why the experiment likely failed] in order to prevent similar failures by other scientists."

A statement of a passage's **central idea**, on the other hand, summarizes the informational content of the passage. In simpler terms, it conveys what the primary "message" of the passage is. Statements of central ideas are factual in content and are typically phrased as declarative sentences (e.g., "Researchers found that the new method of crop rotation increased yields by 30 percent on average").

The concepts of main purpose and central idea are closely related. Main purpose is about *why* the author is writing, whereas central idea is about *what* the author is trying to communicate.

With those two concepts in mind, let's examine sample passages from each of the four subject areas represented in the Reading and Writing section. As we look at each sample, we'll work to uncover the main purpose and central idea of each passage using only information and ideas in the passages themselves.

Literature

Authors write literary texts mainly to share ideas and experiences (real or fictional) in vivid, memorable ways that engage readers at many levels—intellectual, emotional, moral, and so on. Works of literature come in many forms, including novels, dramas, and poems. While these forms differ in many specifics, they all exhibit literary techniques such as evocative word choice, telling (revealing, characterizing) details, and figurative language (e.g., symbolism, metaphors). For literature questions in the Reading and Writing section, the reading skills you've developed in your English language arts classes are most applicable.

Literature passages in the Reading and Writing section include excerpts from previously published novels, short stories, plays, and poems as well as works of literary nonfiction (e.g., memoirs, personal essays). The original works from which literature passages are sampled represent a broad range of authors, styles, perspectives, and time periods and include works produced by writers from the United States and around the world; works originally in English as well as in translation; classic and contemporary works; and widely read and less familiar works. You don't need to have read any of the original works beforehand, however, as all the information needed to answer questions based on literature passages is, as always, included in the passages themselves.

Because they're excerpted from previously published works, literature passages in the Reading and Writing section will include some information about the author and the work, such as the author's name, the title of the work, and the year the work was first published. We suggest that you *not* skip over this information, as knowing who the author is and when the author was writing may help you properly set your expectations for what you'll read. For instance, if the work was originally published in the nineteenth century, you can reasonably expect that the vocabulary and style of writing will differ from what we typically find in more modern literature. In addition, this introductory material may include context that will help you understand the passage, such as a description of the setting or a quick summary of prior events to help set the scene.

Because Reading and Writing literature passages are so brief, don't expect to analyze them for complicated plot details or extended character development. Instead, these passages focus on specific moments, relationships, and characterizations that can be analyzed within a few sentences. You may be asked, for instance, to consider what a narrator's description tells us about a character's personality, how two characters feel about each other, or how a character reacts to an important event in their life.

Although the Reading and Writing section includes questions about selections from poems and dramas, you'll be asked to read and analyze these passages in ways similar to how you'd approach works of prose fiction, such as novels and short stories. In other words, you won't be asked to identify the meter or rhyme scheme of a poem, nor will you be asked to explain the conventions of drama, such as how plays are staged. Instead, you may be asked questions about ideas or experiences represented in the work, particular word choices that the author makes, or how one part of the passage relates to another.

QUICK TAKE

Literature passages in the Reading and Writing section convey ideas and experiences in expressive, memorable ways and are notable for their use of **evocative word choice, telling details, and figurative language**. These passages are excerpted from previously published works and include selections from novels, short stories, plays, poems, and works of literary nonfiction.

Don't worry: you don't need to have read these works beforehand. All the information needed to answer questions based on literature passages is in the passages themselves.

STRATEGY

Don't skip the introductory information about the authors and original texts from which literature passages in the Reading and Writing section are excerpted. This information may clue you in to the kind of reading experience you're about to have or provide useful context about the passage itself.

With that out of the way, let's examine a sample Reading and Writing literature passage.

Literature Sample Passage

> The following text is from F. Scott Fitzgerald's 1925 novel *The Great Gatsby*.
>
> [Jay Gatsby] was balancing himself on the dashboard of his car with that resourcefulness of movement that is so peculiarly American—that comes, I suppose, with the absence of lifting work in youth and, even more, with the formless grace of our nervous, sporadic games. This quality was continually breaking through his punctilious manner in the shape of restlessness.

This passage exhibits many of the qualities you'd expect to see in a challenging literary text, including uncommon vocabulary and sophisticated syntax (*syntax* being the arrangement of words, phrases, and clauses into sentences). Before digging into the details, though, let's consider the purpose of this passage in order to get a sense of the passage as a whole, which is useful regardless of the specific question you're being asked.

After reading the passage, we can conclude that its main purpose is to characterize Jay Gatsby. You can tell this (even if you find some of the vocabulary unfamiliar) by noting that all the details in the passage serve to describe Gatsby's manner, or the way in which he generally acts. The narrator indicates, for example, that Gatsby's manner is "peculiarly [i.e., uniquely] American," that he's lived a life of ease marked by participation in sports ("nervous, sporadic games") and freedom from hard labor ("absence of lifting work in youth"), and that he exhibits a kind of bored, infectious energy ("resourcefulness of movement," "formless grace") that fights against his tendency toward being reserved ("continually breaking through his punctilious manner in the shape of restlessness").

If we were asked to determine the central (main) idea of this passage, we could use the understanding we gained from identifying the passage's main purpose to assist us. We've already discovered that the author wants to describe Jay Gatsby's personality. We can now use that understanding to figure out what specifically the author is trying to tell us about that personality—that Gatsby's usual reserve ("his punctilious manner") is routinely disrupted by his restless energy. Going a bit deeper, we might also reasonably conclude that Gatsby is something of a contradictory figure, a person who's both restrained and energetic.

Note that even if you don't know what "punctilious" means, you should still be able to get the basic idea of the word (and the passage) from the more accessible information available to you. In this case, you can examine the language and structure of the passage's second sentence to figure out an approximate meaning for "punctilious."

Here's that last sentence again, with an example of how we might parse it.

> This quality was continually breaking through his punctilious manner in the shape of restlessness.

- "This quality" refers to "resourcefulness of movement," mentioned in the passage's first sentence.

- "Was continually breaking through" suggests a deviation from a pattern.

- "His punctilious manner" indicates Gatsby's usual behavior.

- "In the shape of restlessness" indicates how the pattern is broken.

At a minimum, then, we can discover that the second sentence of the passage describes Gatsby's self-presentation as somewhat contradictory. But we can do a little better than that, even if we don't know what "punctilious" means precisely. Because Gatsby's usual behavior ("his punctilious manner") is disrupted by restlessness, we can reasonably assume that "punctilious" carries a sense of being different from or perhaps the opposite of "restless." While this doesn't get us quite all the way to "reserved," we're much closer to understanding the gist of the passage even after encountering an unfamiliar word. The key point here—which applies generally to the Reading and Writing section—is, don't give up if you come across a word or phrase whose meaning you don't know. There's probably a lot you *can* still figure out, and even getting a general sense of the main purpose or central idea of a passage can go a long way toward helping you eliminate incorrect answer choices.

STRATEGY

If you encounter something in a Reading and Writing passage that you don't know or understand, such as an unfamiliar vocabulary term, focus on what you *do* know and understand. That's often enough to answer the question correctly, or it will at least help you rule out one or more incorrect answer choices. Don't give up.

NOTE

While our focus here is on preparing for the SAT, this advice is true for any reading activity you undertake in or out of school. Use what you *do* know and *can* understand from a text to help you figure out what you don't (yet) know or understand.

AN ALTERNATE FORMAT FOR LITERATURE TEXTS IN THE READING AND WRITING SECTION

Above, we discussed what a typical passage in the literature subject area on the Reading and Writing section looks like. Some questions, however, may vary from that format, though these questions can still be approached in the same basic way we described.

Here's an example of an alternate presentation style you might encounter.

"Ghosts of the Old Year" is an early 1900s poem by James Weldon Johnson. In the poem, the speaker describes experiencing an ongoing cycle of anticipation followed by regretful reflection: _____

Which quotation from "Ghosts of the Old Year" most effectively illustrates the claim?

A) "The snow has ceased its fluttering flight, / The wind sunk to a whisper light, / An ominous stillness fills the night, / A pause—a hush."

B) "And so the years go swiftly by, / Each, coming, brings ambitions high, / And each, departing, leaves a sigh / Linked to the past."

C) "What does this brazen tongue declare, / That falling on the midnight air / Brings to my heart a sense of care / Akin to fright?"

D) "It tells of many a squandered day, / Of slighted gems and treasured clay, / Of precious stores not laid away, / Of fields unreaped."

Instead of being presented as a traditional passage, the literature content in this question is spread across the answer choices. In this case, you're looking for the evidence from the literary work (in the form of a quotation) that best supports the claim that the speaker in the poem experienced "an ongoing cycle of anticipation followed by regretful reflection." The best answer here is B, by the way, because that quotation describes both anticipation ("brings ambitions high") and regret ("and each, departing, leaves a sigh") occurring cyclically ("Each [year]").

QUICK TAKE

History/social studies passages in the Reading and Writing section aim to share information, ideas, and findings from research in history and the social sciences. These passages tend to include several **elements of research reports**:

- **research questions** (what issue researchers are interested in studying).

- **hypotheses** (what researchers think will happen in their study).

- **discussion of previous research** (to put the study in context).

- **methodology** (how researchers performed the study).

- **data** (the information researchers collected in the study).

- **findings** (what researchers discovered in the study).

- **implications** (the impact the study may have on the research field and/or real life).

- **recommendations for future research** (to further address findings from and implications of a study).

History/social studies passages also establish important **sequential, causal, and comparative relationships**, an understanding of which is central to comprehending most of these passages.

All the information needed to answer questions based on history/social studies passages is in the passages themselves.

History/Social Studies

Authors write history/social studies texts mainly to convey information, ideas, and findings from research in the fields of history and social science, the latter including such areas of study as psychology, sociology, geography, and other subfields involving the study of people and societies.

Commonly found in many history/social studies passages are what we might describe collectively as elements of research reports: research questions, hypotheses, discussions of previous research, descriptions of methodology (i.e., how researchers went about conducting their study), data (e.g., statistics, observations), findings (i.e., what the researchers learned from the study), implications (i.e., the potential significance of the findings), and recommendations for further research. Because of their short length, individual Reading and Writing passages may not exhibit all these features, but you can expect to encounter many if not most of these elements across the history/social studies passages found on a test form.

In addition to these elements, you can expect to find a strong emphasis in history/social studies passages on establishing relationships. Passages may stress time or sequence relationships (e.g., what happened *before*, *after*, or *at the same time as* another event), causal relationships (e.g., one event happened *because* another event happened), and comparative relationships (e.g., one quantity was *greater* or *less than* another). Tracing these relationships is critical to success on many of the questions associated with history/social studies passages.

As always, all the information you'll need to answer questions about history/social studies passages is found in the passages themselves.

Reading and analyzing history/social studies passages will call most directly on your skill in and experience with reading texts in history and social studies classes. That's because history/social studies passages in the Reading and Writing section are designed to closely resemble the kinds of texts you'll read in high school and college history/social studies classes and because the associated questions require you to engage in the kinds of thinking typically expected in rich, challenging history/social studies courses.

History/social studies passages in the Reading and Writing section are written specifically for the test. This means that the passages focus only on the most relevant information for answering the associated questions. It also means that we can tailor these passages for maximum clarity and precision while still presenting you with an appropriate challenge.

Let's examine a sample history/social studies passage in terms of structure, one of our three main strategies for analyzing Reading and Writing passages. After noting the research-based elements we find in this passage, we'll consider how the passage establishes and signals relationships between and among the pieces of information presented.

History/Social Studies Sample Passage

> Some studies have suggested that posture can influence cognition, but we should not overstate this phenomenon. A case in point: In a 2014 study, Megan O'Brien and Alaa Ahmed had subjects stand or sit while making risky simulated economic decisions. Standing is more physically unstable and cognitively demanding than sitting; accordingly, O'Brien and Ahmed hypothesized that standing subjects would display more risk aversion during the decision-making tasks than sitting subjects did, since they would want to avoid further feelings of discomfort and complicated risk evaluations. But O'Brien and Ahmed actually found no difference in the groups' performance.

Let's unpack this passage, first, in terms of the elements of research reports that it exhibits.

- **Research question.** Does posture influence cognition (thinking)?

- **Methodology.** The researchers (O'Brien and Ahmed) had study participants stand or sit while making risky simulated economic decisions.

- **Discussion of previous research.** Some earlier studies have suggested that posture can influence cognition. Although not stated explicitly, we can also reasonably infer from the passage that prior studies have found standing to be more unstable and cognitively demanding than sitting.

- **Hypothesis.** The researchers expected that standing participants would be less likely to take risks than sitting participants. (To spell this out more fully: The researchers expected the hypothesized outcome *because* they knew, presumably from prior research, that standing is more difficult than sitting, so standing participants, preoccupied at some level with the challenge of standing, would be less likely to take additional risks.)

- **Finding.** The researchers found no difference in the risk-taking behavior of the standing and sitting participants they studied.

NOTE

While many history/social studies passages describe the results of observational or experimental studies, some passages may instead take other approaches, such as discussing important historical events or sociological concepts.

NOTE

We're going deep into this passage for this exercise, and you may wish to do so yourself with other passages as part of your practice for the SAT, but we wouldn't expect that you'd analyze passages at this level of detail on test day.

The passage doesn't specifically tell us what data the researchers collected, and it doesn't explicitly describe implications of the study's finding.

Now let's take a look at another aspect of text structure: how the passage establishes and signals relationships between and among information and ideas. We'll number the sentences here for ease of reference and use boldface to call out important connectives in the passage, but neither of these features will appear in actual test passages.

(1) Some studies have suggested that posture can influence cognition, **but** we should not overstate this phenomenon. (2) **A case in point:** In a 2014 study, Megan O'Brien and Alaa Ahmed had subjects stand or sit while making risky simulated economic decisions. (3) Standing is more physically unstable and cognitively demanding than sitting; **accordingly,** O'Brien and Ahmed hypothesized that standing subjects would display more risk aversion during the decision-making tasks than sitting subjects did, **since** they would want to avoid further feelings of discomfort and complicated risk evaluations. (4) **But** O'Brien and Ahmed actually found no difference in the groups' performance.

Sentence 1. Sentence 1 first makes a claim about previous investigations to provide context for the research study about to be described in the passage.

> Some studies have suggested that posture can influence cognition

The sentence then uses the coordinating conjunction *but* to introduce the second clause.

> **but** we should not overstate this phenomenon.

Let's consider the two ideas in sentence 1 separately for a moment, omitting the conjunction.

> Some studies have suggested that posture can influence cognition.

> We should not overstate this phenomenon.

If we paraphrase these ideas, or put them into simpler language that still accurately captures the meaning of the original ideas, we might come up with something such as the following:

> *Some research studies have found that a person's posture can affect cognition, or how the person thinks.*

> *It would be a mistake to think that posture always affects cognition.*

Just by examining the content and structure of this sentence, we can learn a lot about the passage.

- The use of a coordinating conjunction indicates that the two ideas presented in the sentence carry equal weight.

- The use of the conjunction *but* signals a contrast between the two ideas in the sentence.

The passage, in other words, is asking us to hold two ideas in our heads and to recognize (*but*) that the second idea should qualify our understanding of the first idea. We might rewrite (or mentally alter) sentence 1 for simplicity so that it reads something like the following:

> *Although some research studies have found that a person's posture can affect cognition, or how they think, it would be a mistake to think that posture always affects cognition.*

Sentence 2. Sentence 2 provides both some information about the specific study discussed in the passage and an important connective link to sentence 1.

> **A case in point:** In a 2014 study, Megan O'Brien and Alaa Ahmed had subjects stand or sit while making risky simulated economic decisions.

The information in the sentence itself is relatively straightforward: two researchers, Megan O'Brien and Alaa Ahmed, conducted a study in which participants either stood or sat while being asked to make economic decisions that carried (simulated) risk.

The phrase *a case in point* is the critical connector here. It acts as a bridge between sentences 1 and 2, letting us know that O'Brien and Ahmed's study is an example (*a case in point*) of the claim made in sentence 1. Recall that the claim, in our paraphrased version, was that although some research studies have found that a person's posture can affect cognition, that's not always true. *A case in point* signals to us, in other words, that sentence 2 (and beyond) provides an example of how it's not always the case that posture affects cognition.

Sentence 3. Due to its length and use of connectives, sentence 3 requires special attention.

> Standing is more physically unstable and cognitively demanding than sitting; **accordingly,** O'Brien and Ahmed hypothesized that standing subjects would display more risk aversion during the decision-making tasks than sitting subjects did, **since** they would want to avoid further feelings of discomfort and complicated risk evaluations.

We have several clauses here. Let's examine each idea separately, so as not to get overwhelmed, while momentarily leaving out the connectives.

> Standing is more physically unstable and cognitively demanding than sitting.

> O'Brien and Ahmed hypothesized that standing subjects would display more risk aversion during the decision-making tasks than sitting subjects did.

> They [standing study participants] would want to avoid further feelings of discomfort and complicated risk evaluations.

Although we need the connectives for a full understanding of the sentence, we can still get a lot of information out of the ideas considered separately. If we paraphrase them, we might come up with something like the following:

> *It's harder, both physically and mentally, to stand than to sit.*

> *The researchers assumed that participants in the study who stood would be less likely to take risks during decision-making tasks than would participants who sat.*

> *The researchers assumed that standing would make study participants feel even more uncomfortable when making complicated economic decisions and therefore encourage them to avoid risks during decision making.*

Now let's consider how we might link these ideas with connectives. The original version of sentence 3 connects the first two ideas with *accordingly*, which here functions like the word "so."

> *It's harder, both physically and mentally, to stand than to sit,* **so** *the researchers assumed that participants in the study who stood would be less likely to take risks during decision-making tasks than would participants who sat.*

This paraphrase now says, in essence, that *because* standing is harder than sitting, the researchers assumed (hypothesized) that standing would make participants less willing to take risks during the decision-making tasks.

Since is used in sentence 3 to link the last two ideas. *Since* is equivalent to "because" in this context, so let's just use that here as we work to tie the two ideas together.

> *The researchers assumed that participants in the study who stood would be less likely to take risks during decision-making tasks than would participants who sat* **because** *standing would make study participants feel even more uncomfortable when making complicated economic decisions.*

Sentence 4. As we observed earlier, sentence 4 states the researchers' finding.

> **But** O'Brien and Ahmed actually found no difference in the groups' performance.

But works here just as it did in sentence 1, signaling a contrast with what came before. Specifically, sentence 4 challenges the researchers' expectation expressed in sentence 3. Put another way, sentence 4 refutes the hypothesis the researchers laid out (sentence 3) by indicating that both sitting and standing participants showed similar degrees of risk tolerance.

As our analysis of this passage shows, paying close attention to text structure enables us to gain a rich understanding of the content of the passage. Even though you may have little or no prior familiarity with the topic of whether posture affects cognition, you can follow what the passage is saying by focusing on how the passage organizes and presents relationships among the ideas and information it discusses.

Humanities

Authors write humanities texts mainly to share ideas and insights about culture, literature, art, language, and philosophy. Texts in the humanities subject area aren't primarily literary themselves, however. Instead, they inform readers about particular works of art or their creators, analyze the arguments of philosophers past and present, or make and support claims about cultural phenomena.

To make this distinction clearer, think about the differences between a movie and a movie review. Most movies are designed to entertain and to immerse viewers in a fictional (or fictionalized) narrative. Movie reviews, on the other hand, inform audiences by telling them what a given movie is about and make evaluative claims about the movie supported with evidence (e.g., discussion of plot details, standout performances, impactful scenes, and appealing filmmaking techniques). Humanities passages in the Reading and Writing section are more like movie reviews than movies themselves. They explain, illuminate, or make and defend claims about the products, expressions, and values of human cultures.

Like literature passages, humanities passages use vivid language and telling details, but because humanities passages seek to inform, explain, or convince, they also have a lot in common with history/social studies and science passages. For example, they present central ideas or claims, flesh out these points with support and evidence, and establish sequential, comparative, and cause-effect relationships.

All humanities passages in the Reading and Writing section are written specifically for the test.

Depending on the classes you've taken in high school, you may or may not have a lot of experience reading and analyzing humanities texts. If these types of texts are new to you, don't worry. As always, all the information you'll need to answer the questions is found in the passages themselves. You're not expected to have previous familiarity with any of the topics discussed in humanities passages.

Let's examine a sample humanities passage now to better understand how you can go about analyzing it productively. In our analysis, we'll focus first on determining the main purpose and the structure of the passage and then on distilling the central idea or claim. We'll again number the sentences in the passage for ease of reference during our discussion, but be aware that sentence numbers don't appear in actual test passages.

QUICK TAKE

Humanities passages in the Reading and Writing section aim to share ideas and insights about culture, literature, art, language, and philosophy.

Humanities passages are something of a hybrid between literature passages and history/social studies and science passages. Like literature passages, humanities passages tend to use **evocative language and telling details**. Like history/social studies and science passages, however, their **aim is to inform, explain, or convince**.

All the information needed to answer questions based on humanities passages is in the passages themselves.

Humanities Sample Passage

> (1) To dye wool, Navajo (Diné) weaver Lillie Taylor uses plants and vegetables from Arizona, where she lives. (2) For example, she achieved the deep reds and browns featured in her 2003 rug *In the Path of the Four Seasons* by using Arizona dock roots, drying and grinding them before mixing the powder with water to create a dye bath. (3) To intensify the appearance of certain colors, Taylor also sometimes mixes in clay obtained from nearby soil.

As we noted in our introduction to humanities passages, these types of texts have as their main purpose either to inform or explain or to convince readers of something. Using that understanding, accompanied by an analysis of the passage's structure, you'll be better prepared to determine the passage's central idea or claim, which will help you regardless of the specific type of question that might be associated with the passage.

Sentence 1. Sentence 1 establishes a straightforward informative purpose for the passage.

> To dye wool, Navajo (Diné) weaver Lillie Taylor uses plants and vegetables from Arizona, where she lives.

While we haven't yet analyzed Reading and Writing passages by text type—that happens in the next section—it's clear here that the author's intent is to explain an artistic process. One clue is the language the author uses. Taylor's approach is described in a neutral and objective way. If the passage were argumentative in type, by contrast, we'd expect to find language that sets out a claim that can be both defended and challenged. There's nothing like that here. Instead, the author provides a statement of fact about how Taylor uses plants and vegetables from the state in which she lives to create dyes for the wool she uses in her art.

Having figured out the main purpose of the passage, we can make some educated guesses about what we're likely to find in the rest of the passage. Because the passage's purpose is to explain, we should expect the rest of the passage to supply additional facts, details, and examples related to Taylor's art and creative process. Furthermore, because sentence 1 signals that the passage will explain a process, we might also reasonably expect that the connectives the author uses will establish sequential or cause-effect relationships, since these are typically key to texts that seek to explain.

Sentences 2 and 3. As we anticipated, sentences 2 and 3 build on and support the point made in sentence 1 with examples. Specifically, we learn how Taylor got the deep reds and browns in her rug *In the Path of the Four Seasons* as well as how Taylor is able to intensify certain other colors.

> For example, she achieved the deep reds and browns featured in her 2003 rug *In the Path of the Four Seasons* by using Arizona dock roots, drying and grinding them before mixing the powder with water to create a dye bath.

To intensify the appearance of certain colors, Taylor also sometimes mixes in clay obtained from nearby soil.

The connective *for example* at the beginning of sentence 2 is important here for two reasons. First, it suggests that what follows in the rest of the passage builds on and supports the point made in sentence 1. Second, in so doing, it lets us know (if we didn't already) that sentence 1 captures the central idea of the passage, because examples (sentences 2 and 3) can't fill that role.

Having now done this analysis, we recognize that the passage uses a simple structure of central idea (sentence 1) followed by supporting examples (sentences 2 and 3). The central idea itself is stated explicitly in sentence 1 and doesn't require much in the way of paraphrasing.

Science

Authors write science texts mainly to convey information, ideas, and findings from research in the natural sciences, such as Earth science, biology, chemistry, and physics. Like history/social studies passages in the Reading and Writing section, science passages typically have elements of research reports: research questions, hypotheses, discussions of previous research, descriptions of methodology, data, findings, implications, and recommendations for future research. Because they're so brief, individual science passages may not have all these features, but you're likely to come across all of them at some point while reading the science passages in the Reading and Writing section.

One thing to note here is that although the general features of research reporting found in history/social studies and science passages are the same, the specific kinds of information and ideas presented often differ between the two subject areas. So instead of encountering data on consumer preferences or political movements, as in history/social studies passages, you may be presented with data on animal behavior or star formation.

You can expect to find relationships between and among information and ideas foregrounded in science passages, just as in history/social studies passages. Science passages, like their history/social studies counterparts, may stress time or sequence, cause-effect, or comparison-contrast relationships—or more than one type of relationship. Understanding these relationships is vital to understanding science passages and to answering many Reading and Writing test questions correctly.

Reading and analyzing science passages will call most directly on your skill in and experience with reading texts in science classes. That's because these classes help students such as you approach science writing with the tools, knowledge, and questions that professional researchers use in their own work. Science passages in the Reading and Writing section mimic the style and substance of real-world

QUICK TAKE

Science passages in the Reading and Writing section aim to share information, ideas, and findings from research in Earth science, biology, chemistry, physics, and other natural science fields. Like history/social studies passages, science passages tend to include several **elements of research reports**:

- **research questions**.

- **hypotheses**.

- **discussion of previous research**.

- **methodology**.

- **data**.

- **findings**.

- **implications**.

- **recommendations for future research**.

Science passages (again like history/social studies passages) also establish important **sequential, causal, and comparative relationships**, an understanding of which is central to comprehending these texts. All the information needed to answer questions based on science passages is in the passages themselves.

scientific texts, meaning that "reading like a scientist" will help you successfully approach associated test questions. This doesn't mean, however, that you need specialized scientific knowledge or prior familiarity with the topics under discussion to answer the questions. As always, all the information you'll need to answer questions about science passages is found in the passages themselves.

Science passages in the Reading and Writing section are written specifically for the test.

Our analysis of a sample science passage will follow the same general approach as the one we used to examine a history/social studies passage. That's because, despite important differences in passage content, history/social studies and science passages in the Reading and Writing section tend to follow the same basic structure. We'll first look at the research reporting elements in the passage and then examine the relationships between and among information and ideas in the passage. We've again numbered the sentences for ease of reference, but these sentence numbers don't appear in actual test passages. Also note that we've modified this passage to include sentence 3, which is the correct answer (key) to the associated test question, in order to make the passage more complete.

Science Sample Passage

(1) Jan Gimsa, Robert Sleigh, and Ulrike Gimsa have hypothesized that the sail-like structure running down the back of the dinosaur *Spinosaurus aegyptiacus* improved the animal's success in underwater pursuits of prey species capable of making quick, evasive movements. (2) To evaluate their hypothesis, a second team of researchers constructed two battery-powered mechanical models of *S. aegyptiacus*, one with a sail and one without, and subjected the models to a series of identical tests in a water-filled tank. (3) The model with a sail took significantly less time to complete a sharp turn while submerged than the model without a sail did.

First, let's identify the research reporting elements found in this passage. When doing so, we'll note where the information can be found in the passage and paraphrase it if doing so seems helpful. This passage is fairly dense, so this will take a bit of time and effort.

Research question. The research question is the main thing the scientists are interested in finding out about. Such questions are usually broad, general statements, without a specific expected result in mind. Sentence 1 of this passage informs us that Gimsa, Sleigh, and Gimsa had previously made a claim (hypothesis) about the movement of a particular kind of dinosaur, *Spinosaurus aegyptiacus*, while sentences 2 and 3 tell us that another team of scientists carried out an experiment based on this hypothesis. Given that, we could reasonably formulate the research question as: How, if at all, was the movement of *S. aegyptiacus* affected by the presence of a sail-like structure running down its back?

Hypothesis. Hypotheses aren't the same as research questions, though they're related. A hypothesis puts the research question into terms that can be tested via observation or experimentation. The goal of the research, then, is to either support or refute (reject) the hypothesis using data collected in the study. This means that a hypothesis will indicate the result the researchers expect, with the rest of the study geared toward evaluating whether the results bolster or challenge that hypothesis.

Sentence 1 tells us that Gimsa, Sleigh, and Gimsa had a hypothesis about the role of *S. aegyptiacus*'s sail-like structure, and sentence 2 tells us that "a second team of researchers" set out to test this hypothesis. The hypothesis being tested is identified explicitly in sentence 1: "the sail-like structure running down the back of the dinosaur *Spinosaurus aegyptiacus* improved the animal's success in underwater pursuits of prey species capable of making quick, evasive movements." This statement passes our "test" for hypotheses because it's capable of being supported or refuted by research: a well-designed study will help determine whether the sail-like structure did or didn't help the dinosaur catch elusive prey underwater.

Discussion of previous research. This passage does mention earlier research, but it does so in a way that's a little subtle. The "earlier research" is actually that of Gimsa, Sleigh, and Gimsa, who came up with the hypothesis (sentence 1) that the "second team of researchers" (sentence 2) designed an experiment to test. This is how science often works, with one study building on another and the conclusion of one study serving to inspire the hypotheses of later studies. We don't know from the passage what the precise nature of Gimsa, Sleigh, and Gimsa's previous work was, only that it led them to the hypothesis stated in sentence 1. Because all the information needed to answer the associated test question is in the passage itself, this tells us that we don't have to worry about how those three scientists came up with their hypothesis, only that they did and that it led another team to test it.

Methodology. Sentence 2 tells us directly what approach the second team of researchers used. They "constructed two battery-powered mechanical models of *S. aegyptiacus*, one with a sail and one without, and subjected the models to a series of identical tests in a water-filled tank." In other words, the second team set up an experiment in which they compared the underwater movements of two dinosaur models, one that had a sail (which, remember, was hypothesized to aid the species' movement) and one that didn't (thereby serving as a control condition for the purpose of comparison).

Data. Sentence 3 says that "the model [dinosaur] with a sail took significantly less time to complete a sharp turn while submerged than the model without a sail did." Put more simply, the model with the sail (the experimental condition) outperformed the model without the sail (the control condition) in the experiment.

It's at this point that we run out of passage. We can, however, draw a reasonable, text-based inference as to what the **finding** was. A *finding* is a conclusion that scientists reach based on their data and hypothesis. We can safely conclude from what we've already read that the finding here was confirmation of the hypothesis. We can reach that conclusion in just a few steps. (You can probably make this leap more quickly than we illustrate below, but we think it's a useful exercise to sometimes slow down during practice to make our thinking and question-answering processes more explicit.)

- The hypothesis was that the sail-like structure on the dinosaur's back would help the dinosaur chase and catch agile prey underwater.

- The second team of researchers designed an experiment to test this hypothesis.

- Data from the study showed that in tests of maneuverability, the dinosaur model with the sail outperformed the model without the sail.

- The finding, therefore, is that the hypothesis is supported.

We can't make any reasonable inferences from the passage about the **implication** of the study, nor are there any stated or implied **recommendations for future research**.

Now that we've studied the passage for elements of research reports, let's examine the relationships in the passage. We'll again highlight key connectives in boldface, though they won't be marked that way on actual test forms.

> Jan Gimsa, Robert Sleigh, and Ulrike Gimsa have hypothesized that the sail-like structure running down the back of the dinosaur *Spinosaurus aegyptiacus* **improved the animal's success** in underwater pursuits of prey species capable of making quick, evasive movements. **To evaluate their hypothesis**, a second team of researchers constructed two battery-powered mechanical models of *S. aegyptiacus*, one with a sail and one without, and subjected the models to a series of identical tests in a water-filled tank. The model with a sail took significantly **less time** to complete a sharp turn while submerged **than the model without a sail did.**

There are three relationship links we want to call attention to. Note that these links aren't in the form of common transition words and phrases, such as *but* and *on the other hand*, like we identified in the history/social studies passage sample earlier, but these phrases establish similar kinds of relationships.

- **"improved the animal's success."** This phrase identifies an important comparative relationship: Gimsa, Sleigh, and Gimsa's hypothesis was that *S. aegyptiacus*'s sail-like structure would have made members of the species better able to catch elusive prey underwater than they otherwise would have been.

- **"To evaluate their hypothesis."** This phrase identifies an important causal relationship: the second team of researchers conducted their experiment because of Gimsa, Sleigh, and Gimsa's earlier hypothesis.

- **"less time . . . than the model without a sail did."** This phrase identifies another important comparative relationship: the experimental model with the sail made sharp turns faster than did the control-condition model lacking a sail.

Summary: Passage Subject Area

Literature passages

- Taken from previously published novels, short stories, dramas, poems, and works of literary nonfiction (e.g., memoirs, personal essays)

- Convey ideas and experiences in expressive, memorable ways to engage readers

- Notable for evocative word choice, telling details, and figurative language

History/social studies and **science** passages

- Written for the test

- Share information, ideas, and findings from research or discuss concepts or events

- Differ from each other in that history/social studies passages focus on people and societies, while science passages focus on natural phenomena

- Tend to include elements of research reports: research questions, hypotheses, discussions of previous research, methodology, data, findings, implications, and recommendations for future research; may also discuss topics other than research (e.g., historical events, emerging theories)

- Signal important sequential, causal, and comparative relationships using common transition words and phrases (e.g., *but*, *on the other hand*) as well as phrases unique to a given passage (e.g., *to evaluate the hypothesis*, *improved the animal's success*)

Humanities passages

- Written for the test

- Share information and insights about culture, literature, art, language, and philosophy

- Similar to literature passages in that they tend to feature evocative language and telling details

- Differ from literature passages in that their main aim is to inform, explain, or convince

In reading and analyzing the sample passages, we used three main strategies, which we'll continue to employ throughout the rest of this chapter:

- Determining the main purpose of the passage

- Determining the central idea of the passage

- Analyzing the passage structurally

Text Type

In addition to having a subject area, each passage on the SAT has a **text type** closely tied to its main purpose.

Table 1 summarizes these text types and their associated main purposes.

Table 1. Passage Text Types and Main Purposes

Text Type	Main Purpose
Literary	To share ideas and insights into the human condition in order to entertain or enlighten
Informative/explanatory	To convey factual information and ideas or to explain a process, procedure, or phenomenon
Argumentative	To convince readers to accept the "rightness" of a claim using logical reasoning and relevant evidence

As we observed when we examined passages by subject area, determining the main purpose of a passage allows us to get a high-level sense of the passage, or its gist. In this section, we'll apply that approach when examining sample passages by text type. We'll also consider the typical style and tone of each text type as well as features you'll commonly encounter in these passages.

Literary Passages

The literary category in the Reading and Writing section is the same as the literature subject area discussed earlier. The literary category includes excerpts from previously published novels, short stories, dramas, and poems as well as works of literary nonfiction, such as memoirs and personal essays.

In the classroom, there are important differences between how we approach, say, a novel and a poem, but in the Reading and Writing section, the focus of questions on literary passages, regardless of what kind of source the passage is taken from, will be similar: reading and understanding what the author says directly or strongly implies, and understanding and explaining how and why the author made the writing choices they did. In other words, you won't have to know what iambic pentameter is or consider how the set for a play might be constructed.

QUICK TAKE

Passages of the **literary text type** consist of passages in the literature subject area (i.e., excerpts from novels, short stories, dramas, poems, and works of literary nonfiction).

The **general main purpose** of literary texts **is to entertain or enlighten**. On the test, literary passages **have specific purposes as well**, such as to describe a character's personality.

The **style and tone** of literary passages **vary widely** from passage to passage.

Common features include **evocative word choice**, **telling details**, and **figurative language**.

Purpose. The **general main purpose** of literary texts—at least in the real world—**is to entertain or enlighten**. In the Reading and Writing section, we focus on the more specific purposes that particular literary passages have, such as describing

- the personality or actions of a character.
- how two characters interact.
- how one character views another character.
- what a particular setting (time, place) is like.
- how a series of events or actions unfolds.

Although this list is only a sampling of some of the more common purposes of literary texts, it should still give you a sense of the kinds of specific purposes found in literary passages in the Reading and Writing section.

Style and tone. Because literary passages in the Reading and Writing section are excerpted from previously published literature texts, their **styles and tones vary widely**. This makes sense because part of authors' goals in writing literary texts is to express ideas and describe experiences in unique ways.

Common features. You can expect that literary passages will use **evocative word choice**, **telling details**, and **figurative language**, among other features, to express ideas and points of view.

Let's consider how these elements play out in a sample literary passage.

Literary Sample Passage

> The following text is from Herman Melville's 1854 short story "The Lightning-Rod Man."
>
> The stranger still stood in the exact middle of the cottage, where he had first planted himself. His singularity impelled a closer scrutiny. A lean, gloomy figure. Hair dark and lank, mattedly streaked over his brow. His sunken pitfalls of eyes were ringed by indigo halos, and played with an innocuous sort of lightning: the gleam without the bolt. The whole man was dripping. He stood in a puddle on the bare oak floor: his strange walking-stick vertically resting at his side.

Before we examine the purpose and features of this passage, note the introductory information provided. Recall that this kind of information is offered only for literature passages because those are the only ones in the Reading and Writing section taken from previously published works. It's tempting to skip over that information and get right to the passage, but this information can provide some important clues about what the passage will contain.

STRATEGY

We recommend that you read the introductory information associated with literary passages, as this information can offer important clues to what you're about to read and/or useful context, such as details about the setting.

In this case, we're told that the passage was excerpted from a Herman Melville short story originally published in 1854. Melville was a famous nineteenth-century U.S. writer probably best known for the novel *Moby-Dick*, so you may know of him or have read some of his writing previously. If so, you might be better prepared for the writing style you encounter in the passage. Even if you don't know who Melville is, though, the fact that the passage is from a short story originally published in 1854 hints that you should expect to find language and literary techniques different from what you might find in a modern short story.

In addition to bibliographical information, the introductory material accompanying literature passages may include important contextual details, such as the setting of a short story or a brief recap of important events that occurred earlier in a novel. So don't skip this information.

Purpose. A close reading of this passage reveals a great many vivid details about "the stranger." We learn, for example, about his build ("lean"), demeanor ("gloomy"), hair ("dark and lank, mattedly streaked over his brow"), and face ("sunken pitfalls of eyes"). We're also told that "the whole man was dripping" and that he "stood in a puddle on the bare oak floor" and possessed an odd walking stick. Considering these details together, we can reasonably conclude that the (specific) main purpose of this passage is to describe the physical appearance of the character.

Common features. In this Melville passage, we find many examples of the three features commonly found in literary passages in the Reading and Writing section.

- **Evocative word choice.** The passage uses language in ways that we often associate with literature. In everyday conversations and in most nonfiction, it's uncommon, for example, to refer to hair being "mattedly streaked" over a brow or to characterize dark circles around the eyes as "indigo halos." The sentence "his singularity impelled a closer scrutiny" is a particularly strong turn of phrase, indicating that the stranger's oddness and uniqueness ("his singularity") inevitably drew ("impelled") careful looks ("a closer scrutiny"). (Even if the meaning of some of the words here is unfamiliar to you, you can still make a good guess about the intent of the sentence by observing that all the details that follow in the passage are related to the stranger's physical appearance.)

- **Telling details.** The passage uses numerous precise details to characterize the stranger. He's "lean" and "gloomy," with dark, lank, matted hair. The description of his eyes—"sunken pitfalls . . . ringed by indigo halos"—suggests that he's exhausted, perhaps due to lack of sleep. He's also described as "dripping," which indicates that he's been in the rain, on the water, or perhaps both.

- **Figurative language.** "Planted," in the passage's first sentence, is one example of figurative language in the passage. The stranger is obviously not "planted" in the literal sense. Instead, Melville uses the word to suggest that the stranger is unmoving, or fixed in place. "Pitfalls," in the passage's fifth sentence, is used in a similarly nonliteral way. According to the dictionary, a *pitfall* is either a trap, such as a pit, or a hidden danger. Based on how the rest of the passage characterizes the stranger, it's more likely that Melville means to indicate that the stranger is exhausted, as sunken eyes with dark rings are common signs of fatigue. The author also employs a metaphor: the stranger's eyes "played with an innocuous sort of lightning: the gleam without the bolt." In this metaphor, the stranger's eyes have a kind of light in them similar to that produced by lightning. However, we're also told that this "gleam" is "innocuous" and lacks the "bolt" associated with lightning. The general idea here is that while the stranger's eyes have a peculiar light to them, they lack the kind of energy, spark, and danger we think of when we think of lightning. Given that other details we've already examined suggest that the stranger is exhausted, it's reasonable to conclude that this detail is intended to add to that picture. (It's also possible that Melville was also or instead suggesting that the stranger is emotionally haunted by some experience that drained him of vitality, but we can't really tell that for sure without more context than the passage provides.)

Informative/Explanatory Passages

History/social studies, humanities, and science passages in the Reading and Writing section may be of the informative/explanatory text type.

Purpose. Informative/explanatory passages, as the name suggests, either **aim to share factual information and ideas or to explain a process, procedure, or phenomenon.** Passages of this type may, for example, describe the cause and consequence of a historical event, reveal how an artist created a particular work, or detail the steps in an experiment.

The chief difference between an informative/explanatory passage and an argumentative passage (which we'll discuss next) lies in their respective purposes. Informative/explanatory passages treat the information and ideas they share as factual, or as describing the real state of things in the world. Arguments, by contrast, deal with matters about which people can reasonably disagree. Whereas informative/explanatory passages assert and support central ideas (main points) that we as readers assume to be true, argumentative passages assert claims that readers must be convinced of the correctness of through logical reasoning and relevant evidence.

The difference is fairly easy to spot in practice. Consider again the following example from the humanities passage we analyzed earlier.

QUICK TAKE

Passages of the **informative/ explanatory text type** may come from the history/social studies, humanities, or science subject areas.

The **main purpose** of informative/ explanatory passages is to **share factual information and ideas or to explain a process, procedure, or phenomenon**.

Informative/explanatory passages tend to have a **formal style** and **objective tone**.

Common features include a **central idea** and **supporting details**.

> To dye wool, Navajo (Diné) weaver Lillie Taylor uses plants and vegetables from Arizona, where she lives.

As a statement of the central idea of an informative/explanatory text, the sentence simply relates a fact: Taylor uses plants and vegetables found in Arizona to make dyes for the wool she weaves. We'd expect—correctly, as we found out beforehand—that the rest of the passage offers factual details to support that central idea.

If, however, the passage had been written as an argument, we'd expect the author to assert a claim that reasonable people could challenge, such as the following hypothetical example.

> Navajo (Diné) weaver Lillie Taylor's use of local plant- and vegetable-based dyes makes her weavings among the most vibrant being made today.

This claim isn't factually true or false. It's an interpretation being made by the author. We can tell this, in part, by the author's use of subjective language. "Among the most vibrant" isn't something that can objectively be proved true (or false). It's an assertion based on the author's assessment. Given that, we'd expect the author to present logical reasoning and relevant evidence to back up that claim. The details found in the informative/explanatory version of the passage could, in fact, be recast in the argumentative mold.

> **Informative/explanatory:** For example, she achieved the deep reds and browns featured in her 2003 rug *In the Path of the Four Seasons* by using Arizona dock roots, drying and grinding them before mixing the powder with water to create a dye bath.
>
> **Argumentative:** For example, the deep browns and reds featured in Taylor's 2003 rug *In the Path of the Four Seasons* stand out far more than do similar colors in other contemporary rugs, thanks to Taylor's use of dried and ground Arizona dock roots.
>
> ....
>
> **Informative/explanatory:** To intensify the appearance of certain colors, Taylor also sometimes mixes in clay obtained from nearby soil.
>
> **Argumentative:** Taylor's occasional use of locally sourced clay in her dyes further adds to the striking appearance of her weavings.

It should be clear by now that claims aren't limited to assertions about controversial topics, such as "pro" or "con" positions in a debate over a hotly contested issue. Claims can be found in any sort of text in which an author is offering their own interpretation or judgment, such as a critic's review of a movie or book, a historian's analysis of why something in the past happened, or a scientist's discussion about why the results of an experiment were different from what had been expected.

Style and tone. Informative/explanatory passages tend to have a **formal style** and **objective tone**. By "formal style," we mean that they tend to use language you'd find more often in academic settings than in everyday conversations, and by "objective tone," we mean that they attempt to describe things as they are in reality.

Common features. As suggested above, informative/explanatory passages contain a **central idea** and **supporting details.** The central idea is the main point the author is trying to make, while the supporting details flesh out that point. Continuing with the Lillie Taylor weaving sample, we can sketch out this structure. In doing so, we'll break down the supporting details into more distinct points than in the original passage to make their individual contributions to the passage clearer.

Central idea: To dye wool, Navajo (Diné) weaver Lillie Taylor uses plants and vegetables from Arizona, where she lives.

Supporting details:

- Taylor created the rug *In the Path of the Four Seasons* in 2003.

- This rug featured deep reds and browns.

- These reds and browns were achieved using Arizona dock roots.

- These dock roots were dried and ground by Taylor, who then mixed the resultant powder with water to create a dye bath.

- Taylor also sometimes mixes clay into her dyes.

- This clay is obtained from nearby soil.

- The use of this clay intensifies the appearance of certain colors.

Before we go on to the argumentative text type, two last points about informative/explanatory passages are worth making here:

- The central idea may be stated explicitly (as in the Lillie Taylor weaving sample), or you may need to infer it using evidence from the passage.

- If stated explicitly, the central idea may appear anywhere in the passage, not just the first sentence. Although authors often begin paragraphs with topic sentences, sometimes the central idea appears at the end or even in the middle of a passage.

Argumentative Passages

History/social studies, humanities, and science passages in the Reading and Writing section may be argumentative in nature instead of informative/explanatory. We've already discussed how arguments differ from informative/explanatory texts, but we'll recap here.

Purpose. Arguments seek to convince readers of the "rightness" of the author's point of view, interpretations, or recommendations.

QUICK TAKE

Passages of the **argumentative text type** may come from the history/social studies, humanities, or science subject areas.

The main purpose of argumentative passages is to **convince readers of the "rightness" of a claim** using logical reasoning and relevant evidence.

Argumentative passages tend to have a **formal style** and **objective tone**.

Common features include a **central claim**, **logical reasoning**, and **relevant evidence**.

We use "convince" here rather than "persuade" because arguments, unlike persuasive pieces, rely chiefly on logical reasoning and relevant evidence to support their claims. Persuasive pieces may use logical reasoning and evidence as well, but they may also draw on other writing techniques, such as appeals to emotion. While we find persuasive writing in many areas of our lives, such as in newspaper opinion columns, in politics, and in advertising, the argumentative mode is more typical of academic writing in the nonliterary subject areas sampled in the Reading and Writing section.

It's worth mentioning here explicitly that when we use the terms *argument* and *argumentative*, we're not using them in the sense of "fight" or "fighting," as in "I had an argument with my friend last night." Rather, we use them in a more technical way to refer to pieces of writing that make logical arguments or that use logical argumentation to assert and support claims. Arguments in this sense sometimes concern issues that people sharply disagree about, but that isn't always the case. As we observed earlier, authors of all sorts, writing texts serving many different purposes, use the argumentative form.

Style and tone. Like informative/explanatory passages, argumentative passages tend to have a formal style and objective tone. The latter is true even though arguments do tend to make greater use of subjective language, or the language of evaluation, than do informative/explanatory texts. Even when authors of arguments offer opinions or judgments, they do so in ways that suggest these assessments describe the way things really are; as part of the "bargain," readers who have weighed the claims and considered the reasoning and evidence supporting them are then free to accept or reject these assessments.

Common features. Argumentative passages contain a **central claim** that is backed up by **logical reasoning** and **relevant evidence**. The central claim is the main point the author is trying to convince readers of. As we noted earlier, this claim doesn't have to be about a controversial issue. It can, in fact, be any sort of assertion about which reasonable people can disagree.

The nature of evidence in arguments varies by subject area, as we've already observed. In other words, what counts as evidence in, for example, the humanities differs from what counts as evidence in science. In humanities passages, such as the Lillie Taylor sample, evidence may come in the form of analyses of specific works of art, such as Taylor's 2003 rug *In the Path of the Four Seasons*, whereas evidence in science passages may consist of data that support a hypothesis. To be meaningful, evidence must be relevant both to the topic and the subject area.

Logical reasoning is, metaphorically speaking, the connective tissue of an argument. It's the analysis—the "thinking"—that the author performs to connect the evidence being presented with the claim being asserted.

Let's consider the following sample argumentative passage in terms of its main purpose, style and tone, and key features.

Argumentative Sample Passage

> (1) Many animals, including humans, must sleep, and sleep is known to have a role in everything from healing injuries to encoding information in long-term memory. (2) But some scientists claim that, from an evolutionary standpoint, deep sleep for hours at a time leaves an animal so vulnerable that the known benefits of sleeping seem insufficient to explain why it became so widespread in the animal kingdom. (3) These scientists therefore imply that prolonged deep sleep is likely advantageous in ways that have yet to be discovered.

Note that we've added the answer to the question associated with this passage into the passage itself so that you can focus on how the text is put together. Also note that we've again numbered the passage's sentences here for ease of reference, but you won't find sentence numbers in the passages you read for practice or on test day.

Purpose. Given that this passage is an argument, we should expect that it would assert a debatable claim. This is, indeed, the case, but just what that central claim is requires some work to uncover.

Sentence 1 states that "many animals, including humans, must sleep" and "sleep is known to have a role in everything from healing injuries to encoding information in long-term memory." Although these statements might broadly be considered claims, neither qualifies as this passage's central claim. Reading through the rest of the passage, we learn that the information in sentence 1 is mostly background. It doesn't, in other words, capture the basic point of the passage.

How about sentence 2? This sentence even uses the word "claim," but it's not actually the passage's claim. It's the hypothesis that "some scientists" believe to be true. In the passage, sentence 2 mainly serves to qualify, or add considerations to, the commonly accepted ideas, cited in sentence 1, that many animals must sleep and that sleep has many known benefits. Sentence 2 doesn't directly challenge earlier findings that sleep is beneficial, but it does qualify these findings. To these scientists, the evolutionary danger to a species of long-lasting deep sleep is so profound that the benefits researchers have already found for sleep ("from healing injuries to encoding information in long-term memory") can't really explain why many species engage in such sleep.

That leaves us with sentence 3, which does, in fact, come closest to capturing the passage's central claim. It asserts that the scientists who found a problem with commonly accepted ideas about deep sleep believe ("imply") that there must be something else beneficial ("advantageous") to deep sleep that science has yet to discover.

If we string the various points made in the three sentences into a single statement of the passage's claim, we might come up with something like the following:

> Some scientists believe that long periods of deep sleep must have evolutionary benefits for animals beyond those already discovered.

This version of the claim leans heavily on sentence 3 but also incorporates ideas from the first two sentences—specifically, that deep sleep has benefits and that deep sleep also has evolutionary drawbacks (i.e., leaves animals vulnerable).

As a side note, it's worth calling out here that the passage doesn't actually explain how the scientists went about trying to prove their hypothesis, as in many passages in the Reading and Writing section. Instead, the focus here is on logical reasoning, and specifically on how these scientists came to believe that conventional explanations for why many animals engage in long periods of deep sleep are inadequate given that deep sleep is a profound evolutionary disadvantage.

Taking a structural approach to analyzing this passage, we might sketch out the following.

Sentence 1	Background: Sleep benefits animals.
Sentence 2	Problem: These benefits aren't sufficient to explain why some animals routinely engage in seemingly dangerous long periods of deep sleep.
Sentence 3	Qualification: While sleep does have known benefits for animals, science hasn't figured out yet why many animals engage in long periods of deep sleep, given how risky it is from an evolutionary standpoint.

Although this passage doesn't strictly follow the research report structure we discussed above, we can still find some research reporting elements.

Sentence 1	Discussion of previous research: Although we're not told directly that the benefits of sleep for animals were discovered by prior scientific research, it's a reasonable, text-supported conclusion.
Sentence 2	Implication: We can consider sentence 2 an implication since it points out a shortcoming of previous research.

REMINDER

Earlier in this chapter, we mentioned that not all science (or history/social studies) passages in the Reading and Writing section strictly follow the research reporting model. This argumentative passage is an example of one that doesn't.

Sentence 3	Recommendation for future research: Again, we're not told directly that "more research is needed," but the idea is strongly implicit, since scientists' understanding of the benefits of sleep for animals has been shown to be inadequate.

Style and tone. The passage clearly adopts a formal style and objective tone. The formality of the style is apparent in the sentence structures used and the vocabulary choices made by the author. Sentence 1 is a good example of an objective tone: the ideas that many animals must sleep and that sleep has many benefits for these animals are presented as facts, and while the passage goes on to point out a limitation of scientific understanding of sleep, it never questions the basic "rightness" of the ideas expressed in sentence 1. Overall, the passage takes on a tone of neutral reporting on a scientific phenomenon.

Common features. We've already discussed the passage's claim. Let's consider how logical reasoning and evidence are used.

The evidence here isn't in the form of data, such as results from an experiment or observational study. Instead, the evidence is in the form of a weakness found in current scientific explanations of the value of sleep to animals. Specifically, the evidence is that current explanations can't account for why some animals engage in long periods of deep sleep, which, from an evolutionary standpoint, is dangerous since it leaves animals defenseless for extended periods of time. We can reasonably infer from the passage that this evidence, as well as the current scientific explanations, are based on research even though the studies leading to those conclusions aren't discussed.

The logical reasoning used here is closely tied to the passage's structure, which we've already analyzed.

Sentence 1	Previous research has found that animals gain many benefits from sleep.
Sentence 2	**However,** some scientists believe that this previous research doesn't adequately explain why some animals engage in long periods of deep sleep.
Sentence 3	**Therefore,** more research is needed to find a better explanation for sleep in animals, one that accounts for why some animals engage in long periods of deep sleep.

We've highlighted the words *however* and *therefore* to call attention to the logical reasoning used in the passage. *However* highlights that sentence 2 challenges or undercuts sentence 1, while *therefore* highlights the conclusion that logically follows from sentence 2 being the case.

Summary: Passage Text Type

Literary passages (same features as for passages in the literature subject area)

- Purpose: In general, to entertain or enlighten; specific purposes vary by passage

- Style and tone: Vary widely from passage to passage

- Common features

  - Evocative word choice

  - Telling details

  - Figurative language

Informative/explanatory passages

- Purpose: To share factual information and ideas or to explain a process, procedure, or phenomenon

- Style and tone: Formal and objective

- Common features

  - A central idea

  - Supporting details

Argumentative passages

- Purpose: To convince readers of the "rightness" of a claim

- Style and tone: Formal and objective

- Common features

  - A central claim

  - Logical reasoning

  - Relevant evidence

Text Complexity

Our last topic specifically related to Reading and Writing passages is text complexity. You should be aware that passages in the Reading and Writing section may vary in terms of how challenging or easy the texts themselves are to read. Some passages may be relatively easy for most test takers, while others may pose a significant challenge. Since the SAT measures your readiness for college and careers, the challenge level of the texts you'll be asked to read on test day has to match the expectations that instructors have for students entering college and workforce training programs.

This may sound daunting, especially if you don't feel you're a strong reader, but don't worry too much about this aspect of the test section. In this chapter, we've given you several ways to examine passages and break them down regardless of their difficulty, and most of the samples we presented were from the middle and the higher end of the text complexity range used in the Reading and Writing section. Remember, too, that all the information needed to answer test questions is found in their associated passages (and sometimes informational graphics, the topic of our next chapter), so even if you run into some unfamiliar words or difficult-to-understand concepts, you likely can use what you *do* know about passages in general and specific passages in particular to get a good handle on what the questions are asking and, at the very least, eliminate some incorrect answer choices, turning your response from a random guess into an educated one (and one with a vastly higher probability of success). Finally, because each Reading and Writing passage has only one question associated with it, you can give your best effort and move on from any one passage that you feel you don't understand well, as there's no penalty for guessing on the SAT.

Summary: Reading and Writing Passages

Each Reading and Writing passage has

- a **subject area** (literature, history/social studies, the humanities, science)

  - **Literature** passages

    - Purpose: To share ideas and experiences in vivid, memorable ways

    - Style and tone: Vary widely from passage to passage

    - Common features

      - Evocative word choice

      - Telling details

      - Figurative language

  - **History/social studies** and **science** passages

    - Purpose: To share ideas and findings from research

    - Common features

      - Elements of research reports

        ○ Research questions

        ○ Hypotheses

        ○ Discussion of previous research

        ○ Methodology

        ○ Data

        ○ Findings

        ○ Implications

        ○ Recommendations for future research

      - Sequential, causal, and comparative relationships

- ◆ **Humanities** passages
  - – Purpose: To share ideas and insights about culture, literature, art, language, and philosophy
  - – Common features
    - • Evocative language
    - • Telling details
- ▪ a **text type** (literary, informative/explanatory, argumentative)
  - ◆ Literary passages
    - – Purpose
      - • In general, to entertain or enlighten
      - • Specific purpose varies by passage (e.g., to describe a character's personality)
    - – Style and tone: Vary widely from passage to passage
    - – Common features
      - • Evocative word choice
      - • Telling details
      - • Figurative language
  - ◆ Informative/explanatory passages
    - – Purpose: To share factual information and ideas or to explain a process, procedure, or phenomenon
    - – Style and tone: Formal and objective
    - – Common features
      - • A central idea
      - • Supporting details
  - ◆ Argumentative passages
    - – Purpose: To convince readers of the "rightness" of a claim
    - – Style and tone: Formal and objective
    - – Common features
      - • A central claim
      - • Logical reasoning
      - • Relevant evidence
- ▪ a **text complexity** (difficulty) ranging from relatively easy to significantly challenging

Some Reading and Writing passages include an informational graphic (the topic of our next chapter).

KEYS TO SUCCESS ON THE READING AND WRITING SECTION

- All the information needed to answer a given question is in the passage itself (or in an associated informational graphic).

- Base your answers to questions on what the passage says explicitly and what the passage strongly implies.

- If you struggle with a passage, give your best answer and move on. (You can always flag questions to return to if time permits.)

- Answer every question to the best of your ability. Make educated rather than random guesses by focusing on what you *do* understand about a passage and eliminating incorrect answer choices. There's no penalty for guessing on the SAT, but random guessing is unlikely to benefit your score.

- Remember that you *can* do this. You have the tools now (if you didn't before) to get the information you need from Reading and Writing passages to answer the associated questions.

CHAPTER 9

Reading and Writing: Informational Graphics

In this chapter, we'll discuss and walk through examples of the three kinds of informational graphics you may encounter in the Reading and Writing section: tables, bar graphs, and line graphs. We'll consider the important features common to all three graphic types so that you'll be better prepared to analyze such figures during practice and on test day. We'll then examine a sample of each type of graphic. We'll also talk about what you'll have to do with the graphics on test day—and what you won't, namely performing calculations (which is why a calculator isn't allowed for the Reading and Writing section).

Why Include Informational Graphics on a Test of Reading and Writing?

Before we get started, though, we should explain why informational graphics are included in the Reading and Writing section in the first place.

The SAT is a test of your college and career readiness. As we found in the previous chapter, Reading and Writing passages simulate the kinds of reading and writing activities you not only engage in now in your high school classes but that you'll also participate in in college or workforce training. An important part of the way that many authors convey information and ideas in several of the subject areas represented in the Reading and Writing section is through the use of informational graphics. These graphics display data in ways that are typically easier to understand and work with than written descriptions are, and they often display more data than the author has an opportunity to discuss in writing (though extraneous data are minimized in graphics in the Reading and Writing section so that you can focus on the data relevant to answering a given question).

You'll also need to be able to read and analyze data from informational graphics in your everyday life. Tables, bar graphs, and line graphs—the three types of informational graphics in the Reading and Writing section—are among the most common ways authors in history/social studies, the humanities, and science as well as in workplace settings and popular media display data visually. You may not need to produce such data displays on your own, but you do need to be an informed consumer of such displays to navigate successfully in our increasingly data-driven world.

In short, the ability to make sense of and critically analyze data displays is important not only in your current and future classes but also in many other areas of your life after high school.

Common Features of Informational Graphics

Regardless of type, each informational graphic in the Reading and Writing section has a **title**, one or more **labels**, and **data**, while some graphics also have a **legend** and/or **additional information**. It's important to recognize and make use of these features, as they provide critical clues to how to read and interpret a given graphic.

To help make this discussion more concrete, we'll refer to the following sample table.

Informational Graphic Sample 1

Participants' Evaluation of the Likelihood That Robots Can Work Effectively in Different Occupations

Occupation	Somewhat or very unlikely (%)	Neutral (%)	Somewhat or very likely (%)
Television news anchor	24	9	67
Teacher	37	16	47
Firefighter	62	9	30
Surgeon	74	9	16
Tour guide	10	8	82

Rows in table may not add up to 100 due to rounding.

Title. Each graphic has a title. This title lets you know what the general topic of the graphic is, but it often provides additional useful information.

Let's consider the title for the sample graphic above.

> Participants' Evaluation of the Likelihood That Robots Can Work Effectively in Different Occupations

Even without the graphic, we can draw some reasonable conclusions about the topic addressed and the kind of data displayed. The graphic focuses on people's perceptions of how likely robots are to successfully take on a range of jobs. Given that, it's likely that the data displayed will be quantitative and drawn from a survey or similar tool.

Labels. Although different kinds of informational graphics label key elements in different ways, all types of graphics use such labels to identify their constituent parts. These labels are vital to understanding what the displayed data represent.

Let's focus on a portion of the sample informational graphic above.

Occupation	Somewhat or very unlikely (%)	Neutral (%)	Somewhat or very likely (%)

This graphic uses the label "Occupation" for the leftmost column. Looking down the column, we see a list of five types of jobs: television news anchor, teacher, firefighter, surgeon, and tour guide. Examining the full graphic, we can reasonably conclude that participants in the study were asked their view of the likelihood that a robot could successfully perform each of those jobs.

The remaining columns are headed by three labels: "Somewhat or very unlikely (%)," "Neutral (%)," and "Somewhat or very likely (%)." Although this table lacks an overarching label for these three columns, we can reasonably infer that each of these columns corresponds to a possible response on the survey (or other tool) participants were given. The "(%)" symbol in each column tells us that the data are percentages, which isn't surprising given that we've already concluded that participants were given a survey (or the like) and asked to rate likelihood.

Data. Data are, of course, the heart of informational graphics. These data can take many forms and can be collected in many different ways. The data you encounter in informational graphics in the Reading and Writing section will typically be quantitative (numeric) in nature, although other types are possible. Quantitative data can consist of counts (e.g., how many times something occurred), percentages (e.g., what proportion of people behave in a given way), measurements (e.g., the body lengths of animals raised under different conditions), monetary values (e.g., the cost, in U.S. dollars, of various items), and so on. There's really no theoretical limit to the kinds of quantitative data that can be displayed.

As we've already determined, our sample table presents percentages— specifically, the percentages of participants who held certain views on the likelihood of robots successfully performing various types of jobs.

Occupation	Somewhat or very unlikely (%)	Neutral (%)	Somewhat or very likely (%)
Television news anchor	24	9	67

These rows from the full table represent the percentages of participants who rated the likelihood of a robot successfully performing the job of television news anchor as somewhat or very unlikely (24 percent) and somewhat or very likely (67 percent), as well as the percentage of participants who had no strong opinion on the matter ("neutral"; 9 percent).

Legend. Graphs used in the Reading and Writing section will also contain a legend. A *legend* is a guide to how to interpret the bars or lines in the figure, as in the sample below.

Informational Graphic Sample 2

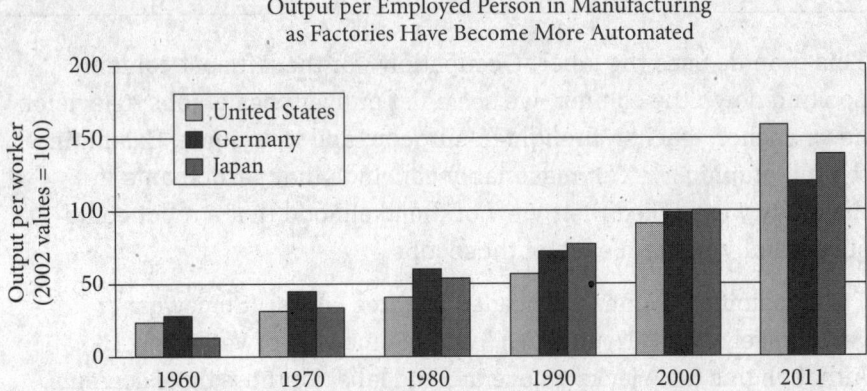

Output per Employed Person in Manufacturing as Factories Have Become More Automated

In this bar graph, which presents data about employee output in factories exhibiting greater levels of automation over time, the legend—the small box in the upper left corner—tells us that the three bars for each year represent three different nations: the United States (light gray), Germany (black), and Japan (dark gray).

Additional information. Creators of informational graphics strive to make the data displayed as clear and understandable as possible. Sometimes, however, they supply additional information to guide how readers interpret the figures.

For example, in the sample table presented earlier in this chapter, we're given this additional information.

Rows in table may not add up to 100 due to rounding.

This note is intended to allay concerns from attentive readers who discover (and may then be distracted by the fact) that the percentages in the table—specifically, the totals for the firefighter and surgeon rows—add up to something other than 100 percent (101 and 99, respectively). Pay attention to these notes, as they can significantly aid your understanding of a graphic and its data.

Informational Graphics in the Reading and Writing Section

Now let's examine each of the three types of informational graphics found in the Reading and Writing section: tables, bar graphs, and line graphs.

Tables

Authors use tables to organize and display a wide variety of data. These authors tend to favor using tables over graphs when the goal is to convey data precisely (e.g., exact percentages of survey participants answering in certain ways) or when they want to display data that don't share a common scale or unit of measurement, such as the length of selected passenger airline routes in miles alongside the average cost in U.S. dollars of tickets to fly those routes.

Let's examine another table, this time about changes to road capacity. Because we already studied a fairly simple table, we've selected a more complex one to discuss here. Bear with us on this because we're going to analyze this table in detail so that you get a better sense of just how much information you can obtain, even though no single question in the Reading and Writing section will require you to go into this much depth on test day.

Informational Graphic Sample 3

Effect of Route Capacity Reductions in Several Regions

Region	Vehicles per day on altered road		Vehicles per day on surrounding roads		Change in regional traffic
	Before alteration	After alteration	Before alteration	After alteration	
Rathausplatz, Nürnberg	24,584	0	67,284	55,824	−146.6%
Southampton city center	5,316	3,081	26,522	24,101	−87.5%
Tower Bridge, London	44,242	0	103,262	111,999	−80.3%
New York highway	110,000	50,000	540,000	560,000	−36.4%
Kinnaird Bridge, Edmonton	1,300	0	2,130	2,885	−41.9%

Title. The title tells us that the data in the table are intended to illustrate a cause-effect relationship ("effect of")—specifically, the impact that reductions in road capacity (i.e., restrictions on the amount of traffic that can use a given road) had on the numbers of vehicles per day on various roads in various regions. We can also reasonably expect, as turns out to be the case, that the data will be quantitative.

Labels. We need to pay attention to several labels here. The label for the leftmost column is "Region," and it heads a list of different locations around the world. Continuing from the left, the second and third columns have two labels. The topmost, "Vehicles per day on altered road," applies to both columns; each column also has its own label: "Before alteration" and "After alteration," respectively. This indicates that these columns display the average number of vehicles

QUICK TAKE

Authors use **tables** when it's important to represent exact values from the data or when the data of interest lack a common scale or unit of measurement (e.g., distances and prices).

per day on an altered road, both before and after the alteration. (The numbers in the third column are all lower than the corresponding numbers in the second column because, as the table's title indicates, the "alteration" referred to involved reducing the traffic capacity of the road(s) in the locations listed in the leftmost column.) The fourth and fifth columns are labeled similarly to the second and third, but this time they describe the effect, in terms of vehicles per day, on roads surrounding those whose capacity was reduced. The rightmost column, "Change in regional traffic," lists negative percentages indicating reductions in traffic.

Data. The data displayed in this table are of two kinds. The first, found in the second through fifth columns (again counting from the left), are counts (or, more likely, estimated averages) of the number of vehicles using a road or roads in a given location (identified in the leftmost column) under various conditions. The second type of data, found in the rightmost column, consists of percentages indicating the extent of change in traffic. As we previously noted, these percentages are all negative because the data pertain to efforts to reduce traffic.

The big question here is, what can we make of these data?

First, let's reconsider the title. From it, we know that the table intends to show a cause-effect relationship between the amount of traffic on roads in several different regions and efforts to reduce the traffic capacity of those roads.

Second, let's consider some of the conclusions we're able to draw from the data. In doing so, we'll identify specific data points as well as patterns.

- Each of the listed regions experienced decreases in traffic on altered roads. For example, traffic on an altered Tower Bridge, London, road decreased from 44,242 vehicles per day before the alteration to 0 after. (Presumably, the road was closed to vehicle traffic.)

- While some of the regions (e.g., Rathausplatz, Nürnberg) experienced a similar drop in traffic (in terms of number of vehicles per day) on surrounding roads after road alteration was complete, other regions (e.g., New York highway) saw increases in such traffic.

- The decrease in traffic across the regions varied from very high (e.g., −146.6% in Rathausplatz) to moderate (−36.4% for New York highway).

Now let's consider whether we can reach a "big picture" understanding of the data in the table, making use of the conclusions we've already drawn.

Let's first remind ourselves of what the table intends to illustrate. As we mentioned when we discussed the title, the table is meant to show a cause-effect relationship. Specifically, it's meant to show the effect of road capacity reduction efforts on the amount of traffic.

When we analyzed the labels and data in the table, we observed that the table not only indicates the effect of road capacity reduction efforts on specific roads but also on surrounding (neighboring) roads. This might lead us to wonder why both capacity-reduced roads and surrounding roads are included in the table. Given what we've already identified as the purpose of the table, the most likely reason is that if traffic is intentionally reduced on specific roads (columns 2 and 3 of the table) but actually goes up on surrounding roads (columns 4 and 5), the *total* amount of vehicle traffic may not be reduced as much as planners may have hoped, and thus road capacity reduction may not always lead to robust reductions in total traffic.

If we go back to our analysis of the data, we find that this was the case. While two regions in the table—Rathausplatz, Nürnberg, and Southampton city center—experienced reductions in both traffic on the altered road and surrounding roads, the other three regions in the table experienced an increase in the amount of traffic on surrounding roads once a given road was altered to reduce traffic. These latter three regions therefore also had smaller percentages in the "change in regional traffic" column.

From all of this, we can reasonably conclude that efforts to reduce vehicle capacity on roads are less likely to be successful in actually reducing vehicle traffic overall if changes to one road just lead drivers to move to surrounding roads. Thus, while all the road alterations presented in the table reduced overall traffic (as indicated by the negative percentages in the rightmost column), the more successful efforts in Rathausplatz and Southampton managed to reduce traffic on specific roads *and* keep displaced traffic from spilling over onto surrounding roads.

Bar Graphs

Authors use bar graphs to display data when they want to highlight comparisons in the data. In doing so, they sacrifice some of the precision of tables to make it easier for readers to grasp these comparisons visually.

Let's start with a straightforward example of a bar graph, which we'll analyze in terms of how the common features of graphics presented above are represented.

QUICK TAKE

Authors use **bar graphs** when they want readers to be able to easily make comparisons with data and when exact figures are less important than overall patterns.

Informational Graphic Sample 4

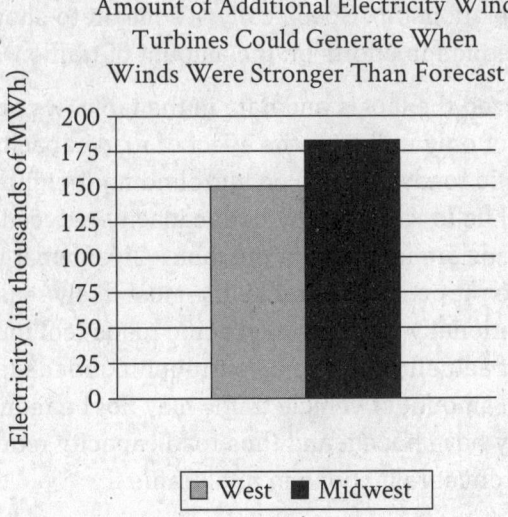

Title. The title for this graphic tells us that the data indicate how much extra electricity wind turbines can generate when the wind is stronger than forecasted. We note from this that the data do *not* represent the total amount of electricity generated by wind turbines but rather the "excess" amount produced when stronger-than-expected winds occur.

Labels. Bar graphs (and line graphs) include labels for one or more axes. In this simple graph, only one axis—the *y*-axis, or vertical axis— is so labeled: "Electricity (in thousands of MWh)." (*MWh* are megawatt hours.) This label is accompanied by a scale, which divides the graph into 25-unit increments from 0 to 200. Note, however, that the label indicates that these numerals represent *thousands* of MWh, so the scale actually ranges from 0 MWh to 200,000 MWh, not 0 to 200. Each increment on the graph represents 25,000 MWh.

Legend. The legend indicates that the light gray bar represents the "West," while the black bar represents the "Midwest." Paying attention to the legend not only allows us to make sense of the bars but also gives us an important hint about what's being compared in the graph— in this case, the additional electricity generated by wind turbines in two regions.

Data. Bringing the above analyses together, we can figure out that the graph is trying to tell us how two different regions (West, Midwest) compare in terms of the amount of "extra" electricity that wind turbines generate during stronger-than-forecasted winds. In this bar graph, we can simply compare the height of the two bars to see that the Midwest generates more such electricity than does the West. Because the bar for the West tops out exactly at the 150 mark, we can precisely determine that output; because the bar for the Midwest, by contrast, tops out at between 175 and 200, we can only really estimate the amount. (This is a key difference between a table and a graph, as we noted before. The graph was doubtlessly built from precise values, but these values have been somewhat obscured here because the exact values are less important than the comparison.)

Now let's take a quick look at another, slightly more complex bar graph.

Informational Graphic Sample 5

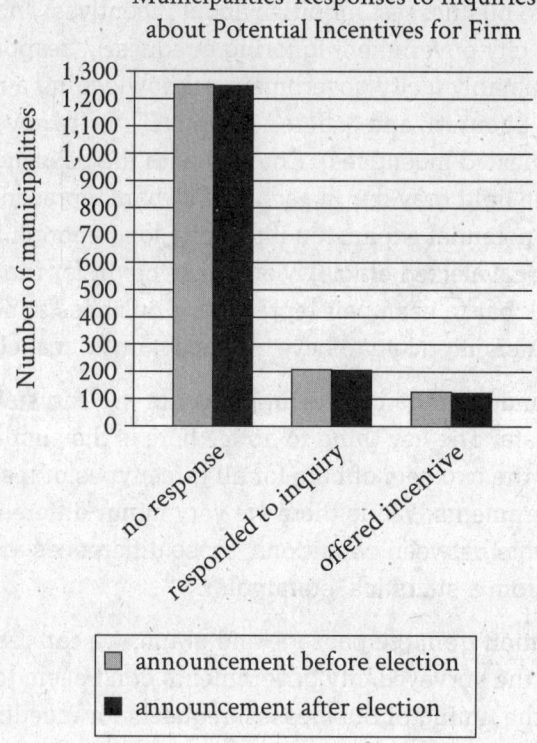

Municipalities' Responses to Inquiries about Potential Incentives for Firm

- announcement before election
- announcement after election

To make sense of this graph, we'll need the context provided in the accompanying passage. This exercise is good practice for test day, as many graphics questions in the Reading and Writing section will not only require you to read and interpret graphics but also make connections between graphics and the passages that accompany them.

Here's the passage for that figure:

> In the United States, firms often seek incentives from municipal governments to expand to those municipalities. A team of political scientists hypothesized that municipalities are much more likely to respond to firms and offer incentives if expansions can be announced in time to benefit local elected officials than if they can't. The team contacted officials in thousands of municipalities, inquiring about incentives for a firm looking to expand and indicating that the firm would announce its expansion on a date either just before or just after the next election.

Pairing the information from the passage and the figure, we can make better sense of the graph's title, "Municipalities' Responses to Inquiries about Potential Incentives for Firm." We can figure out that the graph depicts how various city governments (municipalities) responded to business firms' requests for financial incentives to expand into their cities. By reading the labels, we see that the (vertical) y-axis represents number of city governments, in increments of one hundred, while the (horizontal) x-axis represents three types of responses from city governments to businesses' inquiries about incentives: "no response" (presumably a city government ignoring a request), "responded to inquiry" (presumably a city government acknowledging a request but doing nothing about it), and "offered incentive" (a city government giving out requested incentives). Coupled with the passage, the legend tells us that the light gray bar in each pair of bars represents a business announcing a potential expansion into a city long enough before an election that local elected officials could take credit for the expansion, while the black bar in each pair represents a business announcing a potential expansion too late to have an impact on a local election.

Now that we understand how the graph works, we can start to make sense of the data. The key thing to notice here is the similarity of the heights of the two sets of bars for all three types of responses from city governments. While there are very minor differences in the two bars' heights between conditions, those differences are probably meaningless from a statistical standpoint.

Using information from the passage and graph, we can reasonably conclude that the surveyed city governments don't seem to have been motivated by the timing of businesses' requests for incentives. In the context of the passage, this would further lead us to conclude that the researchers' hypothesis—"municipalities are much more likely to respond to firms and offer incentives if expansions can be announced in time to benefit local elected officials than if they can't"—is incorrect. If the hypothesis *had* been correct, we would expect the light gray bars for at least the "responded to inquiry" and "offered incentive" conditions to be noticeably higher than the corresponding black bars. Instead, they're nearly or exactly equal.

Line Graphs

The third and final informational graphic type you may encounter in the Reading and Writing section is the line graph. Like bar graphs, line graphs prioritize illustrating comparisons, but line graphs also make it easy to spot trends in data.

Let's consider a relatively straightforward line graph.

QUICK TAKE

Authors use **line graphs** when they want to make it easy for readers to draw comparisons and/or identify trends in data, such as change over time.

Informational Graphic Sample 6

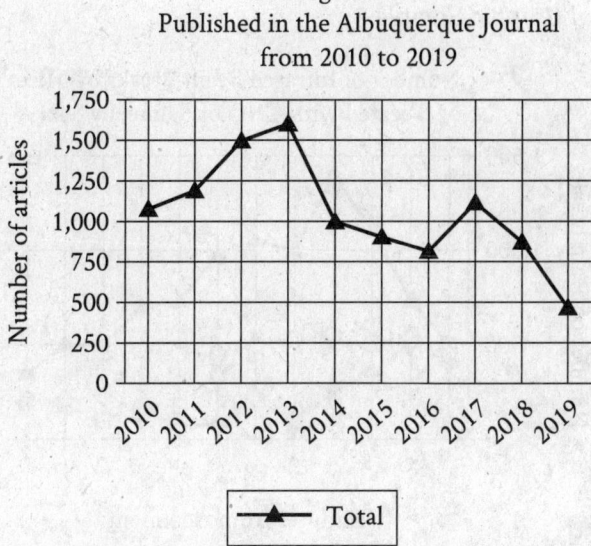

Investigative Articles
Published in the Albuquerque Journal
from 2010 to 2019

As we mentioned above, line graphs excel at illustrating trends. This graph's title informs us that the graph depicts the number of investigative articles published in the *Albuquerque Journal* in the time span from 2010 to 2019. The *y*-axis label tells us that the vertical axis represents the number of articles published, in increments of 250. Although unlabeled, the *x*-axis represents years from 2010 to 2019, inclusive. The legend indicates that each triangle in the graph represents the total number of investigative articles published in a given year. In terms of data, we can (roughly) identify the number of investigative articles published by the *Journal* each year, but the more interesting bit is analyzing how this number has changed over time. The overall trend isn't perfectly consistent, but the general pattern is a decrease in the number of investigative articles published, which reached a low (in the years represented) in 2019 after a peak in 2013.

A more complex line graph in the Reading and Writing section may look like the following:

Informational Graphic Sample 7

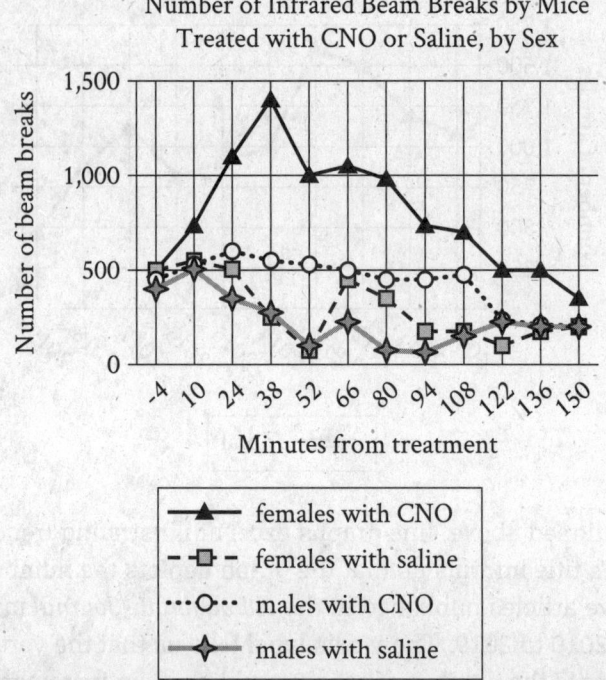

Number of Infrared Beam Breaks by Mice Treated with CNO or Saline, by Sex

Rather than analyze this figure in detail, which would require working through the passage context, we really just want to illustrate here how line graphs can become more complex than the simple example we reviewed previously. But don't worry: more complex line graphs such as this will have the same basic features as simpler ones and can be evaluated in similar ways. The main difference is that in addition to being able to examine a single trend, such as the number of investigative articles a single newspaper published over time, you can compare multiple trends.

In this case, two variables are represented in the graph: (1) sex of the mice (male, female) and (2) treatment condition (treated with CNO, treated with saline). The combination of these two variables—females treated with CNO, females treated with saline, males treated with CNO, males treated with saline—results in the four lines graphed above. As the legend indicates, each of these lines has its own symbol (triangle, square, circle, diamond) and line style (solid black, dash, dot, solid gray), making it easier to tell them apart.

These lines are plotted against a grid in which the *y*-axis represents the number of infrared beam breaks by the mice, in increments of five hundred, and the *x*-axis represents time—specifically, minutes from the time at which the female and male mice were treated with either CNO or saline—in fourteen-minute increments.

Even without knowing more about the scientific study in question, we can both identify some specific data points and recognize some differences in how mice of different sexes responded to the two treatment conditions. For example, thirty-eight minutes after treatment (*x*-axis), female mice treated with CNO (solid black line with triangles) broke infrared beams approximately 1,450 times (*y*-axis). We can also recognize that during the period after the treatment, these mice broke infrared beams more often than did female mice treated with saline or male mice treated with either CNO or saline.

One interesting note about this graph is the inclusion of "−4 minutes" on the *x*-axis. Recall that the *x*-axis represents minutes from treatment. It's reasonable to conclude, then, that "−4 minutes from treatment" represents four minutes *before* the treatment with either CNO or saline was administered. Researchers likely included this information as a baseline—specifically, to indicate, for purposes of comparison, how the mice behaved just before receiving one of the two treatments.

What You Will and Won't Do with Reading and Writing Informational Graphics

Reading and Writing questions associated with informational graphics may ask you to do one or more of the following three things:

- **Locate data**, such as identifying a specific value from a table.

- **Interpret data**, such as recognizing trends in data and making comparisons.

- **Make connections** between data and the information and ideas in the associated passage.

To this point, we've focused primarily on the first two bullets, but you've probably already gotten some idea of how the information and ideas in the passages associated with graphics not only help you figure out what a given graphic means but also provide a context and a purpose for locating and interpreting data. We'll provide a few examples of this third type of task in chapters 11 and 12.

It's important to note here that **you *won't* be asked to perform calculations** with data from graphics in the Reading and Writing section. This means, for example, that you won't have to add, subtract, multiply, or divide using the data from graphics. For this reason, the use of a calculator isn't allowed (and wouldn't be beneficial) in the Reading and Writing section.

QUICK TAKE

When analyzing informational graphics in the Reading and Writing section, you may be asked to **locate data**, **interpret data**, and/or **make connections** between data and the associated passage.

You **won't**, however, have to perform calculations, and the use of a calculator isn't permitted in the Reading and Writing section (nor would it help to have access to one).

Summary: Reading and Writing Informational Graphics

Three types of informational graphics appear in the Reading and Writing section.

- **Tables**

- **Bar graphs**

- **Line graphs**

Regardless of type, informational graphics have certain features in common.

- A **title** indicating the purpose of the graphic

- **Labels** for a graphic's important elements (e.g., x- and y-axes)

- **Data**, typically in quantitative (numerical) form

- In addition, graphics may also have

    - a **legend** that explains the meaning of the bars or lines in a graph.

    - **additional information** that helps you interpret the graphic.

For graphics-related questions in the Reading and Writing section, you may be asked to

- **locate data** (e.g., find a specific value in a table).

- **interpret data** (e.g., identify trends or make comparisons).

- **make connections** between data and the information and ideas in the associated passage.

You *won't* be asked to perform calculations in the Reading and Writing section, and the use of a calculator isn't allowed in that section.

CHAPTER 10

Reading and Writing: Questions—Introduction

The following chapters discuss the kinds of questions you'll encounter in the Reading and Writing section and give you opportunities to immediately practice what you've learned.

Recall that the Reading and Writing section has questions in four broad categories, which we refer to as *content domains*. Each content domain has a "big idea," or common focus, tying all the questions in the domain together at a conceptual level. Table 1 summarizes the section's four content domains and the focus of their respective questions.

Table 1. Reading and Writing Section Content Domains

Reading and Writing Content Domain	The Big Idea
Information and Ideas (chapters 11 and 12)	Testing your understanding of what you read
Craft and Structure (chapters 13 and 14)	Testing your understanding of how and why authors write the way they do
Expression of Ideas (chapters 15 and 16)	Testing your ability to revise passages to meet particular writing goals
Standard English Conventions (chapters 17 and 18)	Testing your ability to edit passages for conventional sentence structure, usage, and punctuation

Each of the following pairs of chapters will

- provide a broad overview of a particular content domain, including the "big idea" (focus) of the domain;

- indicate about how many questions you can expect to encounter from that domain on test day;

- identify the key types of questions included in the domain;

- offer a range of sample questions and answer explanations; and

- give you an opportunity to immediately practice by answering questions from that domain and reading the associated answer explanations.

CHAPTER 11

Reading and Writing: Questions— Information and Ideas

Overview

Reading and Writing questions in the **Information and Ideas** content domain are designed to test your ability to read and demonstrate understanding of passages that represent a range of subject areas, text types, and text complexities as well as of informational graphics. The main goal of these questions is to see whether you can **read carefully to determine what the passages say explicitly and what they strongly imply**.

REMINDER

For a full discussion of the kinds of passages you'll find in the Reading and Writing section as well as analysis of these passages' key features, see chapter 8.

Proportion of the Test Section

About 26 percent of the Reading and Writing section is made up of Information and Ideas questions. This translates to **twelve to fourteen Information and Ideas questions** per test form.

Overview of Information and Ideas Question Types

The Information and Ideas content domain includes three main types of questions:

- **Central Ideas and Details** questions, which test your ability to locate or reasonably infer the main point of a passage and to identify and use supporting details.

- **Command of Evidence** questions, which test your ability to identify and use either textual evidence or quantitative data found in a passage and in any accompanying informational graphic to support or challenge points or claims.

- **Inferences** questions, which test your ability to draw reasonable, text-based conclusions from what you've read in passages.

All questions in this content domain (and in the Reading and Writing section in general) are multiple-choice in format. Each question has a single best answer (*key*) and three incorrect answer choices (*distractors*) that represent common errors students make when answering such questions. All the information needed to answer each question is in the passage (or in any accompanying informational graphic), so you should always base your answers on what a given passage (and/or graphic) says directly and what it strongly implies.

Information and Ideas Question Types in Detail

In this section, we'll discuss each of the three Information and Ideas question types in detail. We'll describe the general purpose of each type so that you understand better how to approach such questions on test day. As part of this discussion, we'll walk through some sample questions so that you get a strong sense of the kinds of skills and knowledge required to successfully answer questions of a given type.

Central Ideas and Details Questions

As the name suggests, **Central Ideas and Details** questions ask you to determine the main point of a given passage and to identify and make use of supporting details.

Questions About Central Ideas

When you're asked to determine the **main point (central idea)** of a passage, the answer you choose should capture all the important information and ideas in the passage. Answer choices that only reflect some of the information and ideas in the passage will be incorrect, as are, of course, choices that mischaracterize the passage or that make assertions about the passage that aren't supported in the text.

Let's begin with a fairly straightforward sample question.

Information and Ideas Sample Question 1

> The following text is from Edith Nesbit's 1902 novel *Five Children and It*. Five young siblings have just moved with their parents from London to a house in the countryside that they call the White House.
>
> > It was not really a pretty house at all; it was quite ordinary, and mother thought it was rather inconvenient, and was quite annoyed at there being no shelves, to speak of, and hardly a cupboard in the place. Father used to say that the ironwork on the roof and coping was like an architect's nightmare. But the house was deep in the country, with no other house in sight, and the children had been in London for two years, without so much as once going to the seaside even for a day by an excursion train, and so the White House seemed to them a sort of Fairy Palace set down in an Earthly Paradise.
>
> Which choice best states the main idea of the text?
>
> A) The house is beautiful and well built, but the children miss their old home in London.
>
> B) The children don't like the house nearly as much as their parents do.
>
> C) Each member of the family admires a different characteristic of the house.
>
> D) Although their parents believe the house has several drawbacks, the children are enchanted by it.

Now let's evaluate each of the answer choices. Recall that we're searching for the answer choice that best captures the main idea of the passage without introducing any misstatements or unsupported assertions.

In this case, choice D is the best answer, as it best reflects the passage's main idea. The passage makes two basic points. First, the parents are well aware of problems with the house. The mother calls the house "inconvenient," and the father describes the ironwork as "like an architect's nightmare." On the other hand, the children view the house as "a sort of Fairy Palace set down in an Earthly Paradise." Choice D clearly reflects both of those ideas.

The other three answer choices mischaracterize what the passage says, making them incorrect options for the main idea. Neither part of choice A is correct, per the passage. Even the narrator refers to the house as "quite ordinary," which undermines the idea that the house is beautiful, and, as we've already seen, both the father and mother recognize that the house has shortcomings. Additionally, nothing in the passage suggests that the children miss their former home in London. Choice B is similarly inaccurate, as the reverse is actually true: the children love the house more than do their parents. Choice C is also incorrect because while the children find things to admire about the house, all we know from the passage about the parents is that the mother finds the house "inconvenient" and that the father complains about the ironwork.

Part of the straightforwardness of this question comes from the fact that choices A, B, and C are simply wrong based on what we know from the passage. More challenging Central Ideas and Details questions focused on main ideas may also require you to distinguish the main idea from statements about the passage that are accurate but still not the best expression of the main idea. In other words, you'll also have to distinguish between a *main* idea and *subordinate* ideas or mere details.

Let's consider another example. This time, we'll have to consider both whether the choices are accurate, given what we know from the passage, and whether they appropriately capture the passage's main idea.

Information and Ideas Sample Question 2

In many of his sculptures, artist Richard Hunt uses broad forms rather than extreme accuracy to hint at specific people or ideas. In his first major work, *Arachne* (1956), Hunt constructed the mythical character Arachne, a weaver who was changed into a spider, by welding bits of steel together into something that, although vaguely human, is strange and machinelike. And his large bronze sculpture *The Light of Truth* (2021) commemorates activist and journalist Ida B. Wells using mainly flowing, curved pieces of metal that create stylized flames.

Which choice best states the text's main idea about Hunt?

A) He often depicts the subjects of his sculptures using an unrealistic style.

B) He uses different kinds of materials depending on what kind of sculpture he plans to create.

C) He tends to base his art on important historical figures rather than on fictional characters.

D) He has altered his approach to sculpture over time, and his works have become increasingly abstract.

When working on this question, it's helpful to remember our discussion in chapter 8 of the structure of passages and how we can use an understanding of structure to help us out. The passage's first sentence makes a general statement about Hunt and his creations, while the second and last sentences provide examples supporting this statement. Because the second and last sentences only offer supporting examples, it's unlikely that we'll find the main point of the passage there.

As it happens, choice A, which is the best answer, is a close paraphrase of the passage's first sentence. The first sentence makes a general statement about Hunt and his work—he often uses "broad forms rather than extreme accuracy" to depict his subjects—while the second and last sentences offer two examples illustrating that general statement. ("Unrealistic style" is a reasonable translation of "broad forms," with *broad* here suggesting a lack of precision or fidelity, in contrast to "extreme accuracy.")

Choice B is an example of a (mostly) accurate statement about the passage that still fails to capture the passage's main point. It's true, or at least highly probable, that Hunt uses different materials depending on the kind of sculpture he plans to create, and we observe from the two examples cited in the second and last sentences of the passage that *Arachne* and *The Light of Truth* do use different materials—steel and bronze, respectively. However, this choice focuses only on the examples and ignores the general statement in the passage's first sentence. Therefore, choice B can't be the best answer.

Choices C and D are more like the incorrect answer options we considered in the previous sample question. Choice C is incorrect because the passage doesn't say that Hunt tends to base his works on important historical figures rather than on fictional characters.

In fact, the passage's first example, *Arachne*, describes a work based on a figure from mythology. (Although you might know that Ida B. Wells is a famous historical figure, this knowledge isn't crucial to answering the question, as the answer choice is still inaccurate based only on what we find directly in the passage.) Choice D is incorrect because the passage gives no indication that Hunt has changed his approach over time.

Let's consider one final Central Ideas and Details example, this time on the more challenging side of things.

Information and Ideas Sample Question 3

> In a study of new technology adoption, Davit Marikyan et al. examined negative disconfirmation (which occurs when experiences fall short of one's expectations) to determine whether it could lead to positive outcomes for users. The team focused on established users of "smart home" technology, which presents inherent utilization challenges but tends to attract users with high expectations, often leading to feelings of dissonance. The researchers found that many users employed cognitive mechanisms to mitigate those feelings, ultimately reversing their initial sense of disappointment.
>
> Which choice best states the main idea of the text?
>
> A) Research suggests that users with high expectations for a new technology can feel content with that technology even after experiencing negative disconfirmation.
>
> B) Research suggests that most users of smart home technology will not achieve a feeling of satisfaction given the utilization challenges of such technology.
>
> C) Although most smart home technology is aimed at meeting or exceeding users' high expectations, those expectations in general remain poorly understood.
>
> D) Although negative disconfirmation has often been studied, little is known about the cognitive mechanisms shaping users' reactions to it in the context of new technology adoption.

NOTE

You may see the phrase "et al." in some passages about scientific (or social scientific) research (e.g., "Davit Marikyan et al." in this sample passage). This just means that the study being discussed was undertaken by several people, not all of whom are named. You may see slight variations on the same idea (e.g., "[researcher's name] and colleagues") in other questions.

Determining the main idea of this passage requires some persistence because of the complexity of the text itself. If you find some of the concepts, vocabulary, and sentence structures challenging, try to focus on the basic points and the connections between them.

In this case, we might say that the first sentence of the passage raises the question of whether "something bad" (negative disconfirmation) can be turned into "something good" (a positive outcome). The second sentence more or less just tells us that the subjects of the study were users of smart-home technology. For the purpose of understanding the passage and answering the associated question, it doesn't really matter what smart-home technology is, only that it's the case that Marikyan and colleagues studied users of this technology because those users are especially likely to experience the bad feeling described in the first sentence. At heart, the last sentence tells us that the researchers found that in many cases, the "something bad" (initial sense of disappointment) could be turned into "something good" (satisfaction).

STRATEGY

Don't get distracted by what a passage doesn't tell you. Focus on what it *does* tell you directly or what it strongly implies. That's all questions will ask you about.

We actually don't know from the passage the specific reason or reasons smart-home technology users' feelings changed, only that "many users employed cognitive mechanisms to mitigate those [negative] feelings." Because Reading and Writing passages are so short, expect that some details will be left out.

Now let's evaluate the answer choices for the question associated with this passage, keeping in mind that we're looking for the passage's main idea. Even from our simple breakdown of the passage above, we can recognize that choice A is the best answer, as it captures all the elements we traced. The first sentence of the passage tells us that the researchers were interested in negative feelings associated with the adoption of new technology. The second sentence informs us that smart-home technology users are prone to disappointment with the technology ("feelings of dissonance") when their high expectations aren't met. The last sentence lets us know that the researchers discovered that many smart-home technology users found a way to feel better about having adopted the technology.

You may have noticed that the key doesn't actually mention smart-home technology, and this might lead you away from choice A (and choice D) and toward choices B and C, which do refer directly to smart-home technology. The best way to avoid this misconception is to recognize that the researchers described in the passage were, first and foremost, interested in a phenomenon—negative disconfirmation—and that smart-home technology users are just one example of a category of people who, in the researchers' view, often experience this phenomenon.

All the other answer choices can be ruled out because they get the passage wrong. Choice B is incorrect because the passage says nearly the opposite: the passage's last sentence tells us that many smart-home technology users do, in fact, get over their initial disappointment. Both parts of choice C lack support in the passage. The passage doesn't tell us that smart-home technology is designed to meet or exceed users' high expectations, nor does it tell us that these expectations remain poorly understood.

Choice D is interesting—and tempting—because it plays into our assumptions, even though the passage doesn't directly support either idea it presents. We might guess that negative disconfirmation has been the subject of a lot of research just from the fact that it has a technical name and was something Marikyan and colleagues analyzed, but the passage never says that the phenomenon has "often" been studied. We might also assume that because the passage doesn't describe the "cognitive mechanisms" that allowed smart-home technology users to cope with their feelings of disappointment, little is known about these mechanisms. But, again, the passage doesn't say that. We therefore shouldn't jump to the conclusion that a lack of detail in the passage about the mechanisms means that scientists themselves don't understand the mechanisms.

Questions About Details

Questions about **details**, as opposed to ones about central ideas, will ask you to locate and use small bits of information from the passage. Sometimes the answer to a details-focused question will be explicitly stated in the passage; other times it will be strongly implicit.

In some cases, the best answer will be straightforward, as in the following example.

Information and Ideas Sample Question 4

Artist Justin Favela explained that he wanted to reclaim the importance of the piñata as a symbol in Latinx culture. To do so, he created numerous sculptures from strips of tissue paper, which is similar to the material used to create piñatas. In 2017, Favela created an impressive life-size, piñata-like sculpture of the Gypsy Rose lowrider car, which was displayed at the Petersen Automotive Museum in Los Angeles, California. The Gypsy Rose lowrider was famously driven by Jesse Valadez, an early president of the Los Angeles Imperials Car Club.

According to the text, which piece of Favela's art was on display in the Petersen Automotive Museum in 2017?

A) A painting of Los Angeles

B) A painting of a piñata

C) A sculpture of Jesse Valadez

D) A sculpture of a lowrider car

Here, we simply need to identify which answer choice is factually accurate per the passage. That option is choice D, as the passage's third sentence informs us that Favela "created an impressive life-size, piñata-like sculpture of the Gypsy Rose lowrider car" and that it was "displayed at the Petersen Automotive Museum." The other choices, by contrast, are inaccurate. The passage's only mentions of Los Angeles are as the location of the Petersen Automotive Museum and the Imperials Car Club, which rules out choice A. Choice B (as well as choice A) can be ruled out because the passage indicates that Favela is a sculptor, not a painter, and because no paintings are mentioned. Choice C is incorrect because the only reference in the passage to Valadez is as a driver of the Gypsy Rose lowrider car.

In other details-focused questions, you'll have to determine what the passage most strongly suggests. By "strongly suggests," we mean that the passage won't directly state the information or idea, but the information or idea will be heavily implied. Think of something "strongly suggested" as being a close paraphrase of what the passage directly says, a synthesis of multiple pieces of information found in the passage, or a statement that can be reasonably regarded as true given the information presented in the passage. The best answer will be put into different words than those found in the passage, but it will be closely connected to evidence in the passage, as in the following example:

Information and Ideas Sample Question 5

In a paper about p-i-n planar perovskite solar cells (one of several perovskite cell architectures designed to collect and store solar power), Lyndsey McMillon-Brown et al. describe a method for fabricating the cell's electronic transport layer (ETL) using a spray coating. Conventional ETL fabrication is accomplished using a solution of nanoparticles. The process can result in a loss of up to 80% of the solution, increasing the cost of manufacturing at scale—an issue that may be obviated by spray coating fabrication, which the researchers describe as "highly reproducible, concise, and practical."

What does the text most strongly suggest about conventional ETL fabrication?

A) It typically entails a greater loss of nanoparticle solution than do other established approaches for ETL fabrication.

B) It is less suitable for manufacturing large volumes of planar p-i-n perovskite solar cells than an alternative fabrication method may be.

C) It is somewhat imprecise and therefore limits the potential effectiveness of p-i-n planar perovskite solar cells at capturing and storing solar power.

D) It is more expensive when manufacturing at scale than are processes for fabricating ETLs used in other perovskite solar cell architectures.

The best answer to this question is choice B. Although this answer choice isn't stated word for word in the passage, it's strongly implied by the combination of information in the second and last sentences. The second sentence lets us know that "conventional ETL fabrication" involves using a solution of nanoparticles. The last sentence tells us that this process is inefficient because it results in "a loss of up to 80% of the solution," which raises the costs of manufacturing. We're also told in that sentence that the new process involving spray coating may represent an improvement. If we flip that around, it's basically the same as saying that the old process is worse ("less suitable") than the new one may be.

Let's digress for a moment to talk about the word *obviated* in the passage's last sentence. You may or may not know that the verb *obviate* means to make something unnecessary. Even if you didn't know that going into the passage, however, you can get a good sense of the meaning of *obviated* from context clues in the passage. If the new spray coating process, as McMillon-Brown and colleagues claim, is "highly reproducible, concise, and practical," while the conventional solution-based process is inefficient, we can make a reasonable guess that *obviated* has something to do with making the problems associated with the solution-based process go away. We'll talk more about how to make use of context clues in chapter 13 when we discuss vocabulary-related questions.

Now let's consider the other answer choices for this question. Choice A is incorrect because the passage only talks about a single conventional (standard) process, not multiple established approaches. Choice C is incorrect because the passage describes the conventional process as inefficient and therefore wastefully expensive, not "imprecise" or ineffective per se. The old process seems to work; it's just costly.

STRATEGY

When you answer questions about Reading and Writing passages, don't fixate on what you don't know or understand. Focus on what you *do* know and understand. This can often be enough to answer a given question correctly, even if some details remain hazy.

Choice D is incorrect because the passage only discusses one type of perovskite solar cell architecture: p-i-n planar perovskite solar cells. Although the passage alludes to other types of architectures, it doesn't tell us anything about them.

Command of Evidence Questions

Command of Evidence questions assess your ability to make use of both textual evidence and quantitative data in passages and informational graphics to answer associated questions. This is an important set of skills because you'll frequently have to recognize and make use of evidence—facts, figures, quotations, data, and the like—as you read, write, participate in discussions, and make presentations in high school and college classes as well as in the workplace and everyday life.

Questions About Textual Evidence

As we noted in chapter 8, the nature of **textual evidence** varies by subject area. In the following example, we'll examine how this bears out in a literature passage.

Information and Ideas Sample Question 6

Sense and Sensibility is an 1811 novel by Jane Austen. In the novel, Austen describes Marianne Dashwood's ability to persuade others of the rightness of her artistic judgments, as is evident when Marianne visits with John Willoughby, a potential suitor: _____

Which quotation from *Sense and Sensibility* most effectively illustrates the claim?

A) "Above all, when she heard him declare, that of music and dancing he was passionately fond, she gave him such a look of approbation as secured the largest share of his discourse to herself for the rest of his stay."

B) "Their taste was strikingly alike. The same books, the same passages were idolized by each—or if any difference appeared, any objection arose, it lasted no longer than till the force of her arguments and the brightness of her eyes could be displayed."

C) "It was only necessary to mention any favourite amusement to engage her to talk. She could not be silent when such points were introduced, and she had neither shyness nor reserve in their discussion."

D) "They speedily discovered that their enjoyment of dancing and music was mutual, and that it arose from a general conformity of judgment in all that related to either. Encouraged by this to a further examination of his opinions, she proceeded to question him on the subject of books."

On first encountering this question, you may wonder where the passage you're supposed to read is and how you're supposed to answer this question if you haven't read *Sense and Sensibility*.

The format of this question is probably different from many you've encountered, but it shouldn't be intimidating. Remember that with all Reading and Writing questions, the information you need to answer correctly is always provided in the passages (and any graphics).

With a question such as this, your task is twofold:

- First, you'll be presented with a **claim** about the work of literature. In this case, the claim is that "Austen describes Marianne Dashwood's ability to persuade others of the rightness of her artistic judgments" and that this is made clear in a scene where Marianne talks with another character, John Willoughby. Recall from chapter 8 that a *claim* is an assertion—in this instance, an interpretation of a literary work—that people can reasonably disagree about.

- Second, you'll have to determine which of the answer choices best **supports** that claim in a way indicated by the question itself. In this case, you're asked to find which choice "most effectively illustrates the claim." The answer choices are carefully selected so that you can understand them on their own, whether or not you've read the literary work in question.

For this question, we're searching for the one quotation among the four offered in the answer choices that best illustrates that Marianne is able to convince others that her views on art are the correct ones.

Choice B does this most effectively. This quotation tells us, first, that Marianne and John have virtually identical opinions on art ("their taste was strikingly alike") and, second, that were John ever to disagree, Marianne's reasoning ("arguments") and physical appeal ("the brightness of her eyes") would quickly convince him to change his mind.

Choice A might seem like it's on the right track, but when we read it closely, we discover that this quotation merely indicates that Marianne approved of ("gave . . . a look of approbation" regarding) John being enthusiastic about ("passionately fond" of) music and dancing. In other words, there's nothing in this quotation about Marianne being persuasive. Choice C is incorrect because this quotation only tells us that Marianne herself was passionate about certain things ("favorite amusement[s]") and would talk boldly and at length about them with others. Again, this choice is in the right neighborhood, so to speak, but it doesn't illustrate Marianne persuading anyone, so it can't be the best answer. Choice D is tempting because, like choice B, it indicates that Marianne and John had a great deal in common, but, again, it doesn't support the point that Marianne was able to persuade John to accept her views on music and dancing.

Let's now shift to looking at a textual Command of Evidence question in a different subject area.

NOTE

It's always safe to assume with questions of this sort that the quotations in the answer choices are accurate excerpts from the literary work in question.

Information and Ideas Sample Question 7

In the 1980s, many musicians and journalists in the English-speaking world began to draw attention to music from around the globe—such as mbaqanga from South Africa and quan họ from Vietnam—that can't be easily categorized according to British or North American popular music genres, typically referring to such music as "world music." While some scholars have welcomed this development for bringing diverse musical forms to prominence in countries where they'd previously been overlooked, musicologist Su Zheng claims that the concept of world music homogenizes highly distinct traditions by reducing them all to a single category.

Which finding about mbaqanga and quan họ, if true, would most directly support Zheng's claim?

A) Mbaqanga is significantly more popular in the English-speaking world than quan họ is.

B) Mbaqanga and quan họ developed independently of each other and have little in common musically.

C) Mbaqanga and quan họ are now performed by a diverse array of musicians with no direct connections to South Africa or Vietnam.

D) Mbaqanga and quan họ are highly distinct from British and North American popular music genres but similar to each other.

NOTE
We use the phrase "if true" in questions such as this because we want to present a range of possibilities in the answer choices for you to consider without making you wonder about what actually happened in the study. At the same time, all the choices will be plausible—things that could reasonably have been discovered during research.

Let's begin by figuring out what the passage is trying to communicate. First, we're told that the category of "world music" was created by English-speaking musicians and journalists to describe types of music that didn't fit conventional British and North American popular music forms. Second, we learn that mbaqanga and quan họ are examples of two musical traditions that have both been categorized as "world music." Third, we're informed that Zheng objects to the concept of "world music" in general terms because, in Zheng's view, it ignores important differences between and among the musical traditions lumped into the category.

The question itself asks which finding about mbaqanga and quan họ, if true, would most directly support Zheng's claim, which is that it's inappropriate to homogenize (blend together) diverse musical traditions into the category of "world music." What we're looking for among the answer choices, in other words, is the best support for Zheng's claim.

Choice B is the best answer here. If mbaqanga and quan họ emerged separately and have little in common musically, this finding would support Zheng's criticism of conceiving of diverse musical traditions as belonging to the single category of "world music."

STRATEGY
When answering textual Command of Evidence questions such as this, read the passage carefully to determine what claim is being made. Then read the question closely to make sure you understand what you're looking for among the answer choices (e.g., support for the claim). And then carefully evaluate each answer choice to determine how it would affect the claim (support or weaken it)—or whether it's even relevant to the claim.

Choice A is incorrect because this finding wouldn't really affect Zheng's claim one way or the other, as the greater popularity of mbaqanga in the English-speaking world relative to quan họ would be irrelevant to what Zheng is arguing. Choice C is incorrect because it also wouldn't directly relate to Zheng's claim, which is about essential differences between and among diverse musical traditions and not about who performs the music. Choice D is incorrect because it would actually weaken Zheng's claim. Zheng asserts that highly distinct musical traditions shouldn't be lumped together, but the finding in choice D would indicate that mbaqanga and quan họ are actually similar to each other, which suggests it might not be such a bad thing to categorize them both as "world music."

Questions About Quantitative Evidence

While some Command of Evidence questions require you to work with textual evidence, others call on you to make use of **quantitative evidence** in the form of data obtained from informational graphics.

Let's examine a pair of examples.

Information and Ideas Sample Question 8

Comfort Range and Temperature-Adjustment Preferences from One Survey

Participant	Comfort rating	Preferred temperature adjustment
20	−2	Cooler
1	+1	Cooler
21	+1	Cooler

Nan Gao and her team conducted multiple surveys to determine participants' levels of comfort in a room where the temperature was regulated by a commercial climate control system. Participants filled out surveys several times a day to indicate their level of comfort on a scale from −3 (very cold) to +3 (very hot), with 0 indicating neutral (neither warm nor cool), and to indicate how they would prefer the temperature to be adjusted. The table shows three participants' responses in one of the surveys. According to the table, all three participants wanted the room to be cooler, _____

Which choice most effectively uses data from the table to complete the statement?

A) and they each reported the same level of comfort.

B) even though each participant's ratings varied throughout the day.

C) but participant 20 reported feeling significantly colder than the other two participants did.

D) but participant 1 reported feeling warmer than the other two participants did.

This question asks you to make some straightforward interpretations of data from the table in order to correctly complete the blank in the passage with the best answer choice.

REMINDER

Chapter 9 covers in detail how to work with informational graphics found in the Reading and Writing section.

NOTE

Some passages in the Reading and Writing section, such as this one, contain a blank. This blank is where the answer choice would go if it were added to the passage.

Choice C is the best answer. According to the table, on the −3 (very cold) to +3 (very hot) scale used in the survey, participant 20 provided a response of −2 (near the "very cold" end of the scale), while the other two participants provided a response of +1 (on the "warm" side of the scale). Given that the scale only includes seven points (−3, −2, −1, 0, +1, +2, +3), a difference of three (−2, +1) can reasonably be considered significant, as choice C describes it.

The same rationale shows why choice A is incorrect. While participants 1 and 21 gave the same comfort rating response (+1), participant 20 gave a response of −2; this establishes clearly that one of the three participants experienced a different level of comfort than did the other two. Choice B is incorrect because the table provides only one rating per participant, so we can't tell whether perceptions changed throughout the day. Choice D is incorrect because participant 21 gave the same response (+1) as participant 1, meaning that participant 1 didn't feel warmer than both of the other participants (though participant 1 did feel warmer than participant 20 [−2]).

Other quantitative Command of Evidence questions, such as our next example, require more—and more complex—interpretation of data on your part.

Information and Ideas Sample Question 9

Distribution of Ecosystem Services Affected by Invasive Species by Service Type			
Region (Overall)	Provisioning (75%)	Regulating (21%)	Cultural (4%)
West	73%	27%	0%
North	88%	12%	0%
South	79%	14%	7%
East	83%	6%	11%
Central	33%	67%	0%

To assess the impact of invasive species on ecosystems in Africa, Benis N. Egoh and colleagues reviewed government reports from those nations about how invasive species are undermining ecosystem services (aspects of the ecosystem on which residents depend). The services were sorted into three categories: provisioning (material resources from the ecosystem), regulating (natural processes such as cleaning the air or water), and cultural (nonmaterial benefits of ecosystems). Egoh and her team assert that countries in each region reported effects on provisioning services and that provisioning services represent the majority of the reported services.

Which choice best describes data from the table that support Egoh and colleagues' assertion?

A) Provisioning services represent 73% of the services reported for the West region and 33% of those for the Central region, but they represent 75% of the services reported overall.

B) None of the percentages shown for provisioning services are lower than 33%, and the overall percentage shown for provisioning services is 75%.

C) Provisioning services are shown for each region, while no cultural services are shown for some regions.

D) The greatest percentage shown for provisioning services is 88% for the North region, and the least shown for provisioning services is 33% for the Central region.

Let's consider first what main points the passage and table are trying to get across. The passage tells us that Egoh and colleagues were trying to determine the effects of invasive species on African ecosystems and that they used government reports to collect data about these effects. From these reports, the researchers calculated what percentage of reports of invasive species, by region, documented effects on three categories of ecosystem services: provisioning, regulating, and cultural. (The passage defines what each of these categories represents.) Let's use the West region as an example. Of the government reports from nations in the West region citing impacts of invasive species on ecosystem services, 73 percent of those reports were about impacts to provisioning services, while the other 27 percent were about impacts to regulating services (and no reports—0 percent—were about impacts to cultural services).

The top row of the table identifies the percentage of all the impact reports across regions that were about each of the three categories of services. According to those data, 75 percent of reports across regions were about impacts to provisioning services, 21 percent were about impacts to regulating services, and 4 percent were about impacts to cultural services. Continuing our previous example of the West region, we see that that the nations in that region reported impacts similar to those reported for Africa as a whole: 73 percent of reports described impacts to provisioning services, 27 percent to regulating services, and 0 percent to cultural services.

The claim the researchers make, as reported in the passage, is that (1) all regions experienced effects on provisioning services and that (2) impacts on provisioning services represent the majority of reports of affected ecosystem services. We're then directed to choose the answer that describes data from the table supporting the researchers' assertion (claim).

Now let's evaluate the answer choices. Choice B is the best answer, as it accurately uses data from the table to support both aspects of the researchers' assertion. We can tell, first, that provisioning services were affected in all regions listed on the table because all regions have a percentage greater than 0 for this category, with (as choice B alludes to) the Central region, at 33 percent, having the lowest percentage of reports of impacts on provisioning services. We can also tell, from the top row of the table, that 75 percent of reports across all regions related to provisioning services.

As we examine the other answer choices, keep in mind that the researchers' assertion (claim) was that each region reported effects on provisioning services and that reports of provisioning services impacts make up the majority of all impact reports.

Choice A is incorrect because it doesn't adequately support the researchers' assertion. Choice A only cites the percentage of impact reports relating to provisioning services for two regions and for the continent as a whole, not for each region. Choice C is incorrect because it also fails to support the assertion adequately. While choice C does mention that each region reported impacts on provisioning services, it doesn't support the part of the assertion that claims that reports of impacts on provisioning services represented the majority of all impact reports. Choice D is incorrect because although it does accurately list the range of percentages of impact reports by region related to provisioning services, it, like choice C, doesn't demonstrate that the majority of all impact reports were related to provisioning services.

Inferences Questions

Finally, let's look at **Inferences** questions. When a Reading and Writing question asks you to draw an inference, it's asking you to come to the most reasonable conclusion (represented by the question's key) based on information and ideas in the passage itself. You won't be asked to make giant leaps in logic or to provide your own subjective interpretation. Instead, you'll read carefully to determine what the passage says directly and what it strongly implies and then use that information to answer the question.

Let's first examine a relatively straightforward example to get a better sense of the kinds of inferences these questions will ask you to make.

Information and Ideas Sample Question 10

Researchers recently found that disruptions to an enjoyable experience, like a short series of advertisements during a television show, often increase viewers' reported enjoyment. Suspecting that disruptions to an unpleasant experience would have the opposite effect, the researchers had participants listen to construction noise for 30 minutes and anticipated that those whose listening experience was frequently interrupted with short breaks of silence would thus _____

Which choice most logically completes the text?

A) rate the listening experience as more negative than those whose listening experience was uninterrupted.

B) rate the experience of listening to construction noise as lasting for less time than it actually lasted.

C) perceive the volume of the construction noise as growing softer over time.

D) find the disruptions more irritating as time went on.

STRATEGY
Higher-complexity quantitative Command of Evidence questions, such as this one, will often present answer choices that accurately represent data from the informational graphic but that are still incorrect because they don't effectively answer the question. Remember that you're not just looking for an accurate statement but rather for one that is accurate *and* best meets the question's requirement (in this case, finding support in the table for a claim made by the researchers).

STRATEGY

You may find it helpful to anticipate what the best answer to a question would be before actually reading the answer choices. Doing so could help you find the right answer more quickly.

In questions with a blank, such as this, we need to select the answer choice that best completes that blank. In the case of Inferences questions, that answer will be the choice that represents the most reasonable inference based on the information and ideas we're supplied with in the passage.

The passage for this question presents a fairly simple scenario. Researchers have found that disruptions in enjoyable experiences often increase participants' perceptions of enjoying the experience. (The passage doesn't tell us why this is so, so we know we won't be asked about the reason.) The passage also tells us that researchers believe disruptions in unenjoyable experiences should have the opposite effect.

Before we consider the answer choices, let's think about what the passage is signaling about the right answer. If (1) interruptions to enjoyable experiences increase participants' positive perceptions of those experiences compared to the perceptions of those who had uninterrupted good experiences and if (2) researchers believe the opposite occurs when unenjoyable experiences are interrupted, we can reasonably conclude, or infer, that interruptions to unenjoyable experiences increase participants' *negative* perceptions of those experiences compared to the perceptions of those who had uninterrupted bad experiences. This is almost, in fact, what we find in choice A, which is the best answer to this question.

We can rule out choices B, C, and D on the same basic grounds. None of the inferences in these choices is supported by the passage, nor do any of the choices describe an effect opposite to the one described in the passage.

This question illustrates nicely two key takeaways about Inferences questions in general:

- The best answer to Inferences questions (as with all Reading and Writing questions) is based on what's explicitly stated and what's strongly implied in the associated passages.

- The best answer to Inferences questions is the choice that most logically completes the passage text (represented by the blank).

Choices B, C, and D might have some appeal because they sound like reasonable statements on their own, but they're neither supported by the passage nor the most logical way to fill in the passage's blank.

Let's now consider a more demanding Inferences question.

Information and Ideas Sample Question 11

As the name suggests, dramaturges originated in theater, where they continue to serve a variety of functions: conducting historical research for directors, compiling character biographies for actors, and perhaps most importantly, helping writers of plays and musicals to hone the works' stories and characters. Performance scholar Susan Manning observes that many choreographers, like playwrights and musical theater writers, are concerned with storytelling and characterization. In fact, some choreographers describe the dances they create as expressions of narrative through movement; it is therefore unsurprising that _____

Which choice most logically completes the text?

A) some directors and actors rely too heavily on dramaturges to complete certain research tasks.

B) choreographers developing dances with narrative elements frequently engage dramaturges to assist in refining those elements.

C) dramaturges can have a profound impact on the artistic direction of plays and musicals.

D) dances by choreographers who incorporate narrative elements are more accessible to audiences than dances by choreographers who do not.

Since this passage is more complex than the last one we analyzed, let's take the text apart to get a better idea of what it's saying.

We might sketch out the passage in these terms:

1. Dramaturges perform a variety of roles, including helping writers of plays and musicals develop stories and characters (first sentence).

2. Many choreographers, like writers of plays and musicals, care about storytelling and character development (second and last sentences).

3. It therefore shouldn't surprise us that _____ (last sentence).

The word *therefore* signals to us that what we place in the blank should be a logical consequence of the preceding information. Put another way, *therefore* tells us that if (1) and (2), above, are true, then (3) logically follows as a result or consequence.

The word *unsurprising* in the passage's last sentence is also useful to note here. The use of this word reinforces the point that what should fill the blank is predictable (unsurprising) based on the information we've been given.

We can figure out this logical consequence, even before considering the answer choices, just from what the passage tells us.

1. Dramaturges help writers of plays and musicals develop stories and characters.

2. Many choreographers also care about developing good stories and characters.

3. It therefore shouldn't surprise us that many choreographers work with dramaturges.

Choice B matches up pretty closely with our own passage-based inference making, and it turns out to be the best answer to the question. We'd expect (i.e., shouldn't be surprised by the fact that) many choreographers would turn to dramaturges for help since many choreographers, like writers of plays and musicals, care about good storytelling and strong characters.

Choice A is incorrect because it's not supported at all by the passage. Nothing in the passage suggests anyone is overly reliant on dramaturges, and the passage adopts a strongly positive tone toward them. Choice C is incorrect because although it's a reasonable assertion on its own, it doesn't make sense in the blank, which is leading us to draw a conclusion about the role of dramaturges in choreography. Choice D, like choice A, isn't supported by the passage, and, like choice C, it doesn't make sense in the blank.

Summary: Information and Ideas Questions

Main purpose: To assess whether you can read carefully to determine what passages (and sometimes informational graphics) say explicitly and what they strongly imply

Proportion of the test section: About 26 percent
(twelve to fourteen questions)

Question types

- Central Ideas and Details: Locate or reasonably infer the main point of a passage; identify and use supporting details

- Command of Evidence: Identify and use textual evidence or quantitative data to support or challenge points or claims

- Inferences: Draw reasonable, text-based conclusions from what you've read in passages

CHAPTER 12

Reading and Writing: Questions—Information and Ideas Drills

1

The ice melted on a Norwegian mountain during a particularly warm summer in 2019, revealing a 1,700-year-old sandal to a mountaineer looking for artifacts. The sandal would normally have degraded quickly, but it was instead well preserved for centuries by the surrounding ice. According to archaeologist Espen Finstad and his team, the sandal, like those worn by imperial Romans, wouldn't have offered any protection from the cold in the mountains, so some kind of insulation, like fabric or animal skin, would have needed to be worn on the feet with the sandal.

What does the text indicate about the discovery of the sandal?

A) The discovery revealed that the Roman Empire had more influence on Norway than archaeologists previously assumed.

B) The sandal would have degraded if it hadn't been removed from the ice.

C) Temperatures contributed to both protecting and revealing the sandal.

D) Archaeologists would have found the sandal eventually without help from the general public.

2

The following text is adapted from María Cristina Mena's 1914 short story "The Vine-Leaf."

It is a saying in the capital of Mexico that Dr. Malsufrido carries more family secrets under his hat than any archbishop.

The doctor's hat is, appropriately enough, uncommonly capacious, rising very high, and sinking so low that it seems to be supported by his ears and eyebrows, and it has a furry look, as if it had been brushed the wrong way, which is perhaps what happens to it if it is ever brushed at all. When the doctor takes it off, the family secrets do not fly out like a flock of parrots, but remain nicely bottled up beneath a dome of old and highly polished ivory.

Based on the text, how do people in the capital of Mexico most likely regard Dr. Malsufrido?

A) Few feel concerned that he will divulge their confidences.

B) Many have come to tolerate him despite his disheveled appearance.

C) Most would be unimpressed by him were it not for his professional expertise.

D) Some dislike how freely he discusses his own family.

3

NASA's *Cassini* probe has detected an unusual wobble in the rotation of Mimas, Saturn's smallest moon. Using a computer model to study Mimas's gravitational interactions with Saturn and tidal forces, geophysicist Alyssa Rhoden and colleagues have proposed that this wobble could be due to a liquid ocean moving beneath the moon's icy surface. The researchers believe other moons should be examined to see if they too might have oceans hidden beneath their surfaces.

Which choice best states the main idea of the text?

A) Rhoden and colleagues were the first to confirm that several of Saturn's moons contain hidden oceans.

B) Research has failed to identify signs that there is an ocean hidden beneath the surface of Mimas.

C) Rhoden and colleagues created a new computer model that identifies moons with hidden oceans without needing to analyze the moons' rotation.

D) Research has revealed that an oddity in the rotation of Mimas could be explained by an ocean hidden beneath its surface.

4

Hip-hop pedagogy is a form of teaching that's gaining popularity across school subjects. It involves incorporating hip-hop and rap music into lessons as well as using hip-hop elements when teaching other subject matters. For example, Quan Neloms's students look for college-level vocabulary and historical events in rap songs. Researchers claim that in addition to developing students' social justice awareness, hip-hop pedagogy encourages student success by raising students' interest and engagement.

Which finding, if true, would most strongly support the underlined claim?

A) Students tend to be more enthusiastic about rap music than they are about hip-hop music.

B) Educators report that they enjoy teaching courses that involve hip-hop and rap music more than teaching courses that don't.

C) Courses that incorporate hip-hop and rap music are among the courses with the highest enrollment and attendance rates.

D) Students who are highly interested in social justice issues typically don't sign up for courses that incorporate hip-hop and rap music.

5

Pulitzer Prize–winning writer Héctor Tobar has built a multifaceted career as both a journalist and an author of short stories and novels. In an essay about Tobar's work, a student claims that Tobar blends his areas of expertise by applying journalism techniques to his creation of works of fiction.

Which quotation from a literary critic best supports the student's claim?

A) "For one novel, an imagined account of a real person's global travels, Tobar approached his subject like a reporter, interviewing people the man had met along the way and researching the man's own writings."

B) "Tobar got his start as a volunteer for *El Tecolote*, a community newspaper in San Francisco, and wrote for newspapers for years before earning a degree in creative writing and starting to publish works of fiction."

C) "Many of Tobar's notable nonfiction articles are marked by the writer's use of techniques usually associated with fiction, such as complex narrative structures and the incorporation of symbolism."

D) "The protagonist of Tobar's third novel is a man who wants to be a novelist and keeps notes about interesting people he encounters so he can use them when developing characters for his stories."

6

Electra is a circa 420–410 BCE play by Sophocles, translated in 1870 by R.C. Jebb. Electra, who is in mourning for her dead father and her long-absent brother, is aware of the intensity of her grief but believes it to be justified: _____

Which quotation from *Electra* most effectively illustrates the claim?

A) "O thou pure sunlight, and thou air, earth's canopy, how often have ye heard the strains of my lament, the wild blows dealt against this bleeding breast, when dark night fails!"

B) "I know my own passion, it escapes me not; but, seeing that the causes are so dire, will never curb these frenzied plaints, while life is in me."

C) "Send to me my brother; for I have no more the strength to bear up alone against the load of grief that weighs me down."

D) "But never will I cease from dirge and sore lament, while I look on the trembling rays of the bright stars, or on this light of day."

7

Tadpole Body Mass and Toxin Production After Three Weeks in Ponds

Population density	Average tadpole body mass (milligrams)	Average number of distinct bufadienolide toxins per tadpole	Average amount of bufadienolide per tadpole (nanograms)	Average bufadienolide concentration (nanograms per milligram of tadpole body mass)
High	193.87	22.69	5,815.51	374.22
Medium	254.56	21.65	5,525.72	230.10
Low	258.97	22.08	4,664.99	171.43

Ecologist Veronika Bókony and colleagues investigated within-species competition among common toads (*Bufo bufo*), a species that secretes various unpleasant-tasting toxins called bufadienolides in response to threats. The researchers tested *B. bufo* tadpoles' responses to different levels of competition by creating ponds with different tadpole population densities but a fixed amount of food. Based on analysis of the tadpoles after three weeks, the researchers concluded that increased competition drove bufadienolide production at the expense of growth.

Which choice uses data from the table to most effectively support the researchers' conclusion?

A) The difference in average tadpole body mass was small between the low and medium population density conditions and substantially larger between the low and high population density conditions.

B) Tadpoles in the low and medium population density conditions had substantially lower average bufadienolide concentrations but had greater average body masses than those in the high population density condition.

C) Tadpoles in the high population density condition displayed a relatively modest increase in the average amount of bufadienolide but roughly double the average bufadienolide concentration compared to those in the low population density condition.

D) Tadpoles produced approximately the same number of different bufadienolide toxins per individual across the population density conditions, but average tadpole body mass decreased as population density increased.

8

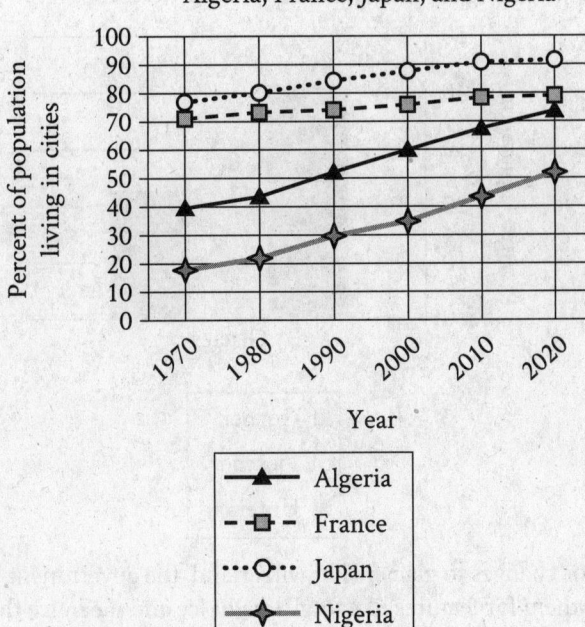

Urban Population of Algeria, France, Japan, and Nigeria

The share of the world's population living in cities has increased dramatically since 1970, but this change has not been uniform. France and Japan, for example, were already heavily urbanized in 1970, with 70% or more of the population living in cities. The main contributors to the world's urbanization since 1970 have been countries like Algeria, whose population went from _____

Which choice most effectively uses data from the graph to complete the assertion?

A) less than 40% urban in 1970 to around 90% urban in 2020.

B) less than 20% urban in 1970 to more than 50% urban in 2020.

C) around 40% urban in 1970 to more than 70% urban in 2020.

D) around 50% urban in 1970 to around 90% urban in 2020.

9

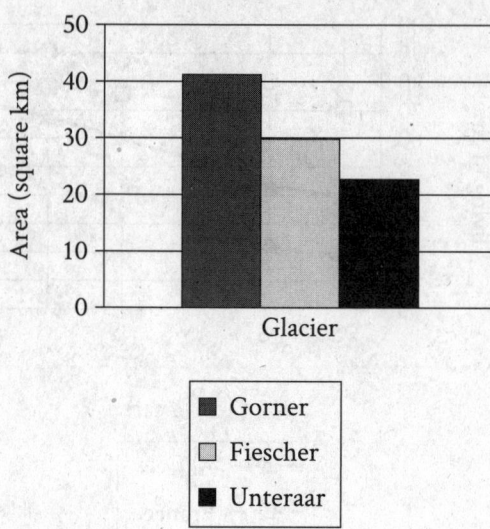

Area of Three Glaciers in the
2016 Swiss Glacier Inventory

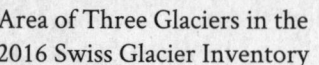

To monitor changes to glaciers in Switzerland, the government periodically measures them for features like total area of ice and mean ice thickness, which are then reported in the Swiss Glacier Inventory. These measurements can be used to compare the glaciers. For example, the Gorner glacier had _____

Which choice most effectively uses data from the graph to complete the example?

A) a larger area than either the Fiescher glacier or the Unteraar glacier.

B) a smaller area than the Fiescher glacier but a larger area than the Unteraar glacier.

C) a smaller area than either the Fiescher glacier or the Unteraar glacier.

D) a larger area than the Fiescher glacier but a smaller area than the Unteraar glacier.

10

Henry Ossawa Tanner's 1893 painting *The Banjo Lesson*, which depicts an elderly man teaching a boy to play the banjo, is regarded as a landmark in the history of works by Black artists in the United States. Scholars should be cautious when ascribing political or ideological values to the painting, however: beliefs and assumptions that are commonly held now may have been unfamiliar to Tanner and his contemporaries, and vice versa. Scholars who forget this fact when discussing *The Banjo Lesson* therefore _____

Which choice most logically completes the text?

A) risk judging Tanner's painting by standards that may not be historically appropriate.

B) tend to conflate Tanner's political views with those of his contemporaries.

C) wrongly assume that Tanner's painting was intended as a critique of his fellow artists.

D) forgo analyzing Tanner's painting in favor of analyzing his political activity.

11

In many cultures, a handshake can create trust between people. Engineer João Avelino and his team are designing a robot to shake hands with a human in order to improve human-robot interactions. The robot hand adjusts its movements and pressure to better imitate the feel of a human hand. The researchers want the robot's handshake to feel realistic because _____

Which choice most logically completes the text?

A) people are less likely to interact with robots that don't look like humans.

B) it's easier to program a robot to perform handshakes than it is to program a robot to perform some other types of greetings.

C) the robot in the researchers' study may have uses other than interacting with humans.

D) lifelike handshakes may make people more comfortable interacting with robots.

12

Tides can deposit large quantities of dead vegetation within a salt marsh, smothering healthy plants and leaving a salt panne—a depression devoid of plants that tends to trap standing water—in the marsh's interior. Ecologist Kathryn Beheshti and colleagues found that burrowing crabs living within these pannes improve drainage by loosening the soil, leading the pannes to shrink as marsh plants move back in. At salt marsh edges, however, crab-induced soil loosening can promote marsh loss by accelerating erosion, suggesting that the burrowing action of crabs _____

Which choice most logically completes the text?

A) can be beneficial to marshes with small pannes but can be harmful to marshes with large pannes.

B) may promote increases in marsh plants or decreases in marsh plants, depending on the crabs' location.

C) tends to be more heavily concentrated in areas of marsh interiors with standing water than at marsh edges.

D) varies in intensity depending on the size of the panne relative to the size of the surrounding marsh.

Answer Explanations

QUESTION 1

Choice C is the best answer because it most clearly identifies what the passage indicates about the discovery of the sandal. A "particularly warm summer" revealed the sandal, and centuries of ice had kept the sandal "well preserved."

Choice A is incorrect because this choice doesn't reflect the information in the passage. The sandal is similar to Roman sandals in its lack of protection from cold, but there's no indication that the sandal itself or its design was a result of Roman influence. *Choice B* is incorrect because the passage says the opposite. The sandal had been preserved by the ice for centuries. *Choice D* is incorrect because there's no information in the passage suggesting that archaeologists would've found the sandal without the help of someone such as the treasure-hunting mountaineer.

QUESTION 2

Choice A is the best answer because it most accurately describes how, according to the passage, the people in the capital of Mexico regard Dr. Malsufrido. The passage cites a saying in the capital that Malsufrido keeps more secrets than any archbishop. It also says that when he takes off his hat, "the family secrets do not fly out . . . but remain nicely bottled up," suggesting that he won't reveal the secrets he's learned.

Choice B is incorrect because it doesn't reflect the passage. While the passage says Malsufrido's hat is large and appears to have been brushed in the wrong direction, it doesn't support a broader characterization of Malsufrido as being regarded as ill-dressed or disheveled. *Choice C* is incorrect because Malsufrido's professional expertise isn't discussed in the passage. *Choice D* is incorrect because the passage indicates that Malsufrido keeps (other) families' secrets "bottled up" in his head, not that he shares details about his own family.

QUESTION 3

Choice D is the best answer because it best states the main idea of the passage. The passage says researchers have proposed that Mimas's wobbly rotation "could be due to a liquid ocean moving beneath the moon's icy surface."

Choice A is incorrect because it doesn't reflect the passage. Rhoden and colleagues proposed, rather than confirmed, that one, and not several, of Saturn's moons may contain a hidden ocean. *Choice B* is incorrect because it conflicts with the passage. Researchers have identified at least one sign—the unusual wobble in Mimas's rotation—that may be due to a hidden ocean beneath the moon's surface. *Choice C* is incorrect because it doesn't reflect the passage. The model Rhoden and colleagues developed was limited to Mimas and was, in fact, the basis for them proposing a hypothesis regarding Mimas's wobbly rotation.

QUESTION 4

Choice C is the best answer because it presents the finding that would most strongly support the underlined claim. Courses incorporating hip-hop and rap music having among the highest enrollment and attendance rates would strongly suggest that these courses encourage student success by raising students' interest and engagement.

Choice A is incorrect because students being more enthusiastic about rap music than about hip-hop music wouldn't support the claim that hip-hop pedagogy, which includes both rap and hip-hop music, encourages student success by raising students' interest and engagement. *Choice B* is incorrect because educators' enthusiasm for hip-hop pedagogy isn't directly relevant to the claim that hip-hop pedagogy encourages student success by raising students' interest and engagement. *Choice D* is incorrect because some students opting out of taking courses influenced by hip-hop pedagogy wouldn't support the claim that hip-hop pedagogy encourages student success by raising the interest and engagement of those students who do take such courses.

QUESTION 5

Choice A is the best answer because it consists of the quotation from a literary critic that best supports the student's claim. The example of Tobar approaching the subject of one of his novels "like a reporter," including conducting interviews and research, shows Tobar applying journalism techniques to his fiction writing.

Choice B is incorrect because although it tells us about Tobar's initial career as a journalist and his transition to creative writing, it doesn't say anything directly about him applying journalism techniques to his fiction. *Choice C* is incorrect because it illustrates Tobar applying fiction techniques to his nonfiction writing, whereas the claim the student makes is that Tobar applied journalism techniques to his fiction writing. *Choice D* is incorrect because while it tells us that a character in one of Tobar's novels applied a journalism technique to his fiction writing, it doesn't tell us that Tobar himself did that.

QUESTION 6

Choice B is the best answer because it consists of the quotation from *Electra* that most effectively illustrates the claim. Electra states that she "know[s] her own passion," which shows that she's aware of the intensity of her grief. But she also claims that the "causes are so dire"—meaning the reasons for her grief are so awful—that she can't let it go, which shows that she believes her grief is justified.

Choice A is incorrect because although "strains of my lament" and "bleeding breast" show that Electra is aware of the intensity of her grief, this choice doesn't suggest that she believes she has a legitimate reason for feeling that way. *Choice C* is incorrect because although "load of grief that weighs me down" shows that Electra is aware of the intensity of her grief, this choice doesn't suggest that she believes she has a legitimate reason for feeling that way. *Choice D* is incorrect because although "dirge" and "sore lament" show that Electra is aware of the intensity of her grief, this choice doesn't suggest that she believes she has a legitimate reason for feeling that way.

QUESTION 7

Choice B is the best answer because it most effectively supports the researchers' conclusion with data from the table. According to the table, tadpoles in the high population density group—that is, the group with the most tadpoles and therefore the highest level of competition among them—had much higher average bufadienolide concentrations (374.22 nanograms per milligram of tadpole body mass) than did the tadpoles in the medium and low population density groups (230.10 and 171.43, respectively). Also according to the table, tadpoles in the high population density group had the lowest average body mass (193.87 mg) relative to the medium and low population density groups (254.56 and 258.97, respectively). These data support the claim that increased competition drove (i.e., increased) bufadienolide production at the expense of growth.

Choice A is incorrect because although this statement is supported by the table, it doesn't mention bufadienolide production, which it would need to do to support the claim. *Choice C* is incorrect because although this statement is supported by the table, it doesn't mention average body mass ("growth"), which it would need to do to support the claim. *Choice D* is incorrect because although this statement is supported by the table, the claim requires support regarding either the average amount of bufadienolide per tadpole or average bufadienolide concentration, not the average number of distinct bufadienolide toxins per tadpole, which is irrelevant to the claim.

QUESTION 8

Choice C is the best answer because it most effectively uses data from the graph to complete the assertion. In the graph, the line representing Algeria's urban population (third line from the top; dark solid line with triangles) indicates that the proportion of the population living in cities was 40 percent in 1970 and slightly above 70 percent in 2020.

Choices A, B, and D are incorrect because they each inaccurately represent data from the graph.

QUESTION 9

Choice A is the best answer because it most effectively uses data from the graph to complete the example. The graph displays area measurements (in square kilometers) for three glaciers. The leftmost (dark gray) bar in the graph, which represents the Gorner glacier, is taller than the two others, with a value of slightly above 40 square kilometers.

Choices B, C, and D are incorrect because the graph establishes that the Gorner glacier (more than 40 square kilometers) is larger than either the Fiescher glacier (middle, light gray bar; 30 square kilometers) or the Unteraar glacier (rightmost, black bar; somewhat more than 20 square kilometers).

QUESTION 10

Choice A is the best answer. The passage warns modern scholars against "ascribing [attributing] political or ideological values" to Tanner's 1893 painting *The Banjo Lesson* that may have been "unfamiliar to Tanner and his contemporaries." The passage's main concern, in other words, is that modern scholars may claim that the painting expresses ideas or values that Tanner may not have intended because he painted the work over a century ago, and thus those scholars may judge the painting by inappropriate standards.

Choice B is incorrect because Tanner's contemporaries are only briefly mentioned in the passage, and there's no suggestion that modern scholars are at risk of conflating (confusing) Tanner's views with those of his contemporaries. *Choice C* is incorrect because the passage offers no support for the idea that Tanner meant to critique his fellow artists with *The Banjo Lesson*, as the passage only briefly mentions Tanner's contemporaries. *Choice D* is incorrect because the passage is mainly concerned with how modern scholars interpret *The Banjo Lesson* and says nothing to suggest that modern scholars are at risk of focusing more on Tanner's political activity than on his painting.

QUESTION 11

Choice D is the best answer because it most logically completes the text. The passage says that handshakes can create trust and that the engineers' goal is to "improve human-robot interactions." This suggests that they want the robot's handshake to feel realistic because they want humans to trust the robot and therefore feel more comfortable interacting with it.

Choice A is incorrect because the passage never discusses the appearance of this robot or any other robots, so there's no basis to make this inference. *Choice B* is incorrect because the passage never discusses any other types of greetings, so there's no basis to make this inference. *Choice C* is incorrect because the passage never discusses any uses for the robot other than interacting with humans, so there's no basis to make this inference.

QUESTION 12

Choice B is the best answer because it most logically completes the text. The passage says that crab burrowing in the pannes enables marsh plants to grow there again. It also says that crab burrowing at the edges of salt marshes speeds up marsh loss. Taken together, these pieces of information suggest that burrowing crabs can either help or hurt marshes, depending on where the crabs are located.

Choice A is incorrect because the passage never discusses pannes of different sizes. *Choice C* is incorrect because the passage never suggests that crabs do more burrowing in the pannes (interior areas prone to standing water) than they do at salt marsh edges. *Choice D* is incorrect because the passage never discusses the intensity of crab burrowing, nor does it discuss the size of pannes relative to the size of surrounding salt marshes.

CHAPTER 13

Reading and Writing: Questions—Craft and Structure

Overview

Reading and Writing questions in the **Craft and Structure** content domain are designed to test your ability to demonstrate understanding of how and why authors write texts the way they do. The passages you'll consider for these questions represent a range of subject areas, text types, and text complexities. There are three main areas of focus in Craft and Structure questions: using and determining the meaning of vocabulary, analyzing the structure and purpose of passages, and making supportable connections between two topically related passages.

Proportion of the Test Section

About 28 percent of the Reading and Writing section is made up of Craft and Structure questions. This translates to **thirteen to fifteen Craft and Structure questions** per test form.

Overview of Craft and Structure Question Types

The Craft and Structure content domain includes three main question types:

- **Words in Context** questions, which test your ability to use and determine the meaning of high-utility academic words and phrases in the contexts in which they appear.

- **Text Structure and Purpose** questions, which test your abilities to analyze and describe how and why passages are put together the way they are and to determine the main purpose of passages.

- **Cross-Text Connections** questions, which test your ability to draw supportable connections between two topically related passages.

All questions in this content domain (and in the Reading and Writing section in general) are multiple-choice in format. Each question has a single best answer (*key*) and three incorrect answer choices (*distractors*) that represent common errors students make when answering such questions. All the information needed to answer each question is in the passage (or passage pair), so you should always base your answers on what a given passage (or pair of passages) says directly and what it strongly implies.

Craft and Structure Question Types in Detail

In this section, we'll discuss each of the three Craft and Structure question types in detail. We'll describe the general purpose of each type so you'll better understand how to approach such questions on test day. As part of this discussion, we'll walk through some sample questions so you get a clear sense of the kinds of skills and knowledge required to answer questions of a given type.

Words in Context Questions

Words in Context questions ask you to either use or determine the meaning of high-utility academic words and phrases in the contexts in which they appear.

WHAT ARE "HIGH-UTILITY ACADEMIC WORDS AND PHRASES"?

We use the term *high-utility academic words and phrases* to describe the vocabulary tested in Words in Context questions in the Reading and Writing section. These words and phrases are ones that you'll encounter fairly often in your readings in class across a range of subject areas. Some examples of high-utility academic vocabulary are *analyze, dissent, simulate,* and *ambiguous.*

The tested words and phrases are ones whose meaning has high value (utility) to you because they're used quite a bit and are often key to unlocking the meaning of texts you'll read, especially the more complex texts you'll encounter in your coursework in high school and in college and workplace settings.

By contrast, Words in Context questions *don't* test the meaning and use of words and phrases that are

- common in casual, everyday speech.
- specific to a given field of study (e.g., *isotope, magma, interest rate, lobbyist*).
- so uncommon that learning their meaning isn't a high college and career readiness priority (e.g., *apricate, ultracrepidarian, lachrymose*).

To answer these questions, you'll need to pay close attention to the *context*, or the language surrounding the tested word or phrase, to get a clear indication of either what word or phrase (among the provided answer choices) should fill a given blank in a passage because it makes the most sense in context or what definition (among those provided in the answer choices) most nearly captures the meaning of the tested word or phrase as it's used in the passage.

It's crucial to note here that you can use clues from this context to help determine the best answer to each question. This is true even if you don't know the precise meaning of a tested word or phrase.

STRATEGY

Passages for Words in Context questions will provide **context clues** that will help you understand the use or meaning of tested words and phrases.

To be clear, strong vocabulary knowledge is beneficial with these sorts of questions, and those students who know the meaning of and how to properly use more high-utility academic words and phrases than other students do will generally be more successful with these questions. However, context clues can help direct you to the answer, or at least help you eliminate incorrect answer choices, even when a tested word or phrase is unfamiliar to you.

PREPARING TO ANSWER WORDS IN CONTEXT QUESTIONS

The single best preparation you can undertake for answering Words in Context questions is reading, especially wide and/or deep reading of challenging texts. That's because the words and phrases tested in Words in Context questions are those you'll commonly find in texts in many different subject areas but not commonly use in casual conversation. Vocabulary lessons in classes can also be beneficial, particularly if they focus on high-utility academic words and phrases (sometimes known as *tier two vocabulary*).

We won't say *not* to use word lists as a vocabulary-building tool, but there are a couple of things you should understand if you do decide to go that route.

First, College Board doesn't publish an official list of words and phrases tested on the SAT, so any list you find out there may or may not match up with the vocabulary you'll encounter in Words in Context questions. Many so-called SAT words, in fact, aren't actually ones we test because they're used so infrequently in the real world that knowing their meaning or how to use them yourself isn't particularly valuable in most circumstances.

Second, learning the isolated (out-of-context) meaning of words and phrases may not be particularly useful when encountering those words and phrases in particular contexts in the Reading and Writing section.

That said, any vocabulary learning is likely to be of at least some benefit to you, whether on the test, in classes, in the workplace, or in your everyday life.

Let's look at some examples of Words in Context questions, starting with those that ask you to fill in a passage's blank with the most logical and precise word or phrase from among the answer choices.

Craft and Structure Sample Question 1

Visual artist Gabriela Alemán states that the bold colors of comics, pop art, and Latinx culture have always fascinated her. This passion for the rich history and colors of her Latinx community translates into the _____ artworks she produces.

Which choice completes the text with the most logical and precise word or phrase?

A) unknown

B) reserved

C) definite

D) vivid

STRATEGY

"Most logical and precise" in this question reminds you that you're looking for the most contextually appropriate word or phrase from among the answer choices.

In questions such as this, you'll have to determine the answer choice that best fills in the blank in the most logical and precise way.

The gist of the passage is that Alemán produces art that reflects her "passion for the rich history and colors of her Latinx community." The position of the blank in the passage as well as the answer choices we're offered indicate that we're looking for an adjective—a descriptive word to modify the noun "artworks."

As we've previously noted, passages associated with Words in Context questions such as these will include context clues pointing to the word or phrase intended to fill the passage's blank. In this case, "bold colors" (first sentence of the passage) and "passion" and "rich history and colors" (last sentence) suggest that we want a word here that conveys the idea that Alemán's artworks are vibrant. This makes choice D the best option, as "vivid" effectively captures the ideas of boldness, vigor, and intensity.

The other choices aren't as logical or precise in this context. "Unknown" (choice A) and "definite" (choice C) make little sense in context, while "reserved" (choice B) suggests the opposite of what's intended by the context.

Here's a more challenging sample question that also asks you to determine the most logical and precise word or phrase in context.

Craft and Structure Sample Question 2

Economist Marco Castillo and colleagues showed that nuisance costs—the time and effort people must spend to make donations—reduce charitable giving. Charities can mitigate this effect by compensating donors for nuisance costs, but those costs, though variable, are largely _____ donation size, so charities that compensate donors will likely favor attracting a few large donors over many small donors.

Which choice completes the text with the most logical and precise word or phrase?

A) predictive of

B) subsumed in

C) independent of

D) supplemental to

Even though this question is more challenging than the first one we considered, you can approach it in the same way.

First, let's make sure we understand the passage. We're told that researchers found that charities can mitigate (reduce) the negative impact of nuisance costs on giving by compensating the donors for these costs. We're also told that because these costs have some kind of relationship to donation size, charities compensating for these costs would likely favor (prefer) working with a few large donors than a lot of small donors.

STRATEGY

Context clues are elements of a text that suggest the meaning of a particular word or phrase found in it. Context clues include, but aren't necessarily limited to, definitions, restatements, and synonyms and antonyms. In this case, the context clues come mainly in the form of the synonym "bold" and the related concept of "passion." Something that's bold and expresses passion is likely to be "vivid" and unlikely to be "unknown," "reserved," or "definite."

The blank in the passage before "donation size" indicates that we're going to need to choose the phrase from the answer options that makes the most sense in context. By doing so, we'll complete the passage logically by describing the relationship that's currently missing between nuisance costs and donation size.

At this point, we should be asking ourselves what kind of relationship between nuisance costs and donation size would lead charities to prefer taking money from a few large donors rather than many small donors. After considering all the choices, we find that choice C makes the most sense in context. "Independent of" indicates that the "amount" of nuisance cost doesn't depend on donation size. In other words, while nuisance costs vary, they're largely not tied to (i.e., are independent of) donation size. In practice, this would mean that charities would have to pay out roughly the same amount of compensation (in whatever form) to small donors as to large ones. Because the charities would be getting a lot of money from each of a few large donors, compensating these donors wouldn't have much impact on how much money the charities ultimately took in. On the other hand, these same charities would have to pay out roughly the same amount to each small donor, of whom there would be many more and each of whom would only be giving a little money. If the compensation were, say, a $5 gift card, the charity would be better off handing out a few $5 gift cards to a small number of big donors than a lot of $5 gift cards to many small donors.

None of the other answer choices makes sense in context. Nothing in the passage indicates that nuisance costs are predictive of (choice A), subsumed in (choice B), or supplemental to (choice D) donation size, and choosing any of those options for the key would leave the passage without a good explanation for why charities compensating donors for nuisance costs would likely prefer to work with fewer large donors than many smaller ones.

Now let's turn to a Words in Context example for which you must determine the context-based meaning of a word or phrase.

Craft and Structure Sample Question 3

> The following text is from Booth Tarkington's 1921 novel *Alice Adams*.
>
> Mrs. Adams had always been fond of vases, she said, and every year her husband's Christmas present to her was a vase of one sort or another—whatever the clerk showed him, underlined{marked} at about twelve or fourteen dollars.
>
> As used in the text, what does the word "marked" most nearly mean?
>
> A) Stained
>
> B) Staged
>
> C) Watched
>
> D) Priced

STRATEGY

The context clues here aren't limited, as in the previous example, to synonyms and closely related concepts. For this question, it's important to use reading and reasoning skills to establish the intended relationship between nuisance costs and donation size. The passage as a whole suggests that nuisance costs have little relation to donation size, so "independent of" (choice C) is the best answer.

For questions such as this, we have to read carefully and consider the context in which the underlined word (in this case, "marked") appears in order to settle on the best definition for this word among the answer choices.

The passage informs us that Mrs. Adams really likes vases and that her husband gave her a vase each year as a present. The passage also informs us that Mrs. Adams's husband let a store clerk pick out each vase and that each vase was marked at around twelve or fourteen dollars.

The main context clue is right in the phrase in which the underlined word appears: "marked at about twelve to fourteen dollars." Choice D, "priced," makes obvious sense here, as what follows the underlined word is a range of costs that Mrs. Adams's husband paid. (Prices being "marked" on items for sale is also a common way in American English to indicate that these items have price tags of some sort on them, but even without that knowledge, you should easily recognize that "marked" in this context is closely related to price.)

By contrast, none of the other answer choices makes much sense in context, as it wouldn't be logical or customary to describe an item for sale as "stained" (choice A), "staged" (choice B), or "watched" (choice C) at about twelve or fourteen dollars. You can mark something by staining it, you can use marks in staging to indicate where actors should stand, and you can "mark" someone or something by observing them or it closely, but none of these options makes sense in relation to a listed price.

STRATEGY

Incorrect answer choices for Words in Context questions that ask you for a definition, such as this question, will often offer real-world meanings for the target word or phrase (in this case, "marked"), but the key will be the most logical and precise in the provided context.

Text Structure and Purpose Questions

Text Structure and Purpose questions ask you to analyze the ways authors put texts together and for what reasons. You may be asked to describe the overall structure or purpose of a passage or to determine the impact on a passage of a particular element (e.g., a detail) in it.

Let's consider an example focusing on a passage-level main purpose.

Craft and Structure Sample Question 4

In 1973, poet Miguel Algarín started inviting other writers who, like him, were Nuyorican—a term for New Yorkers of Puerto Rican heritage—to gather in his apartment to present their work. The gatherings were so well attended that Algarín soon had to rent space in a cafe to accommodate them. Thus, the Nuyorican Poets Cafe was born. Moving to a permanent location in 1981, the Nuyorican Poets Cafe expanded its original scope beyond the written word, hosting art exhibitions and musical performances as well. Half a century since its inception, it continues to foster emerging Nuyorican talent.

Which choice best describes the overall purpose of the text?

A) To explain what motivated Algarín to found the Nuyorican Poets Cafe

B) To situate the Nuyorican Poets Cafe within the cultural life of New York as a whole

C) To discuss why the Nuyorican Poets Cafe expanded its scope to include art and music

D) To provide an overview of the founding and mission of the Nuyorican Poets Cafe

Main purpose questions are essentially central idea questions but with a focus on *why* rather than *what*. Like questions about passages' central ideas, main purpose questions require you to understand the passage as a whole and to provide a summary that incorporates the key ideas without leaving anything critical out or including anything extraneous. The difference is that main purpose questions address authors' intentions, or their aims for writing particular texts. Whereas central ideas questions will have answer choices that are (correct or incorrect) statements about the information and ideas contained in passages, each answer choice in main purpose questions will often begin with a verb (and the particle *to*)—"to explain," "to describe," "to argue," and so on.

This passage narrates the development of the Nuyorican Poets Cafe from its informal founding in 1973 as a workshop for poets to its move in 1981 to a permanent location with an expanded focus on other art forms to its continued support for emerging artists over half a century. Choice D provides the best answer to the question, as the intent of the passage is to provide an overview of the birth and goal of the Nuyorican Poets Cafe.

Choice A is incorrect because Algarín's motivation for founding the cafe isn't specifically discussed in the passage and because the passage continues on from the cafe's founding to talk about its expansion and evolution. Choice B is incorrect because although the passage does mention that the cafe "continues to foster emerging Nuyorican talent," it doesn't do so in enough detail to qualify as situating (contextualizing) the cafe within New York City's cultural life, as the passage's focus is on the cafe itself. Choice C is incorrect because the passage doesn't tell us why the cafe expanded its scope to include art and music, only that it did so. In any case, the passage's overall focus is broader, addressing the cafe itself, its beginnings, and its development over time.

The important thing to note here is that, like central ideas questions, main purpose questions require you to not only determine what's factually correct per the passage but also differentiate the main purpose from subordinate, or minor, purposes. The incorrect answers in this example are primarily wrong on factual grounds (i.e., they aren't supported in the passage), but other main purpose questions—particularly more challenging ones—may ask you to distinguish between main and subordinate purposes. For example, an answer choice such as "To explain why Algarín had to rent space in a cafe for his gatherings of writers" would be true to the facts of the passage—which tells us that Algarín had to rent cafe space because the gatherings were so well attended—but would represent a subordinate purpose of the passage rather than the main purpose, since that explanation is merely one part of the larger account of the Nuyorican Poets Cafe that the passage provides.

REMINDER
Main purpose questions call on the same general skill as central ideas questions. You're looking for the answer choice that best captures the whole passage.

STRATEGY
A key skill required to answer some main purpose questions, especially more challenging ones, is the ability to distinguish the *main* purpose from other, smaller purposes the passage might also be trying to accomplish (i.e., *subordinate* purposes).

While we're thinking about entire passages from a rhetorical standpoint, let's now consider an example about the overall structure of a passage.

Craft and Structure Sample Question 5

Many films from the early 1900s have been lost. These losses include several films by the first wave of Black women filmmakers. We know about these lost movies only from small pieces of evidence. For example, an advertisement for Jennie Louise Toussaint Welcome's documentary *Doing Their Bit* still exists. There's a reference in a magazine to Tressie Souders's film *A Woman's Error*. And Maria P. Williams's *The Flames of Wrath* is mentioned in a letter and a newspaper article, and one image from the movie was discovered in the 1990s.

Which choice best describes the overall structure of the text?

A) The text discusses several notable individuals, then explains commonly overlooked differences between those individuals.

B) The text describes a general situation, then illustrates that situation with specific examples.

C) The text identifies a complex problem, then presents examples of unsuccessful attempts to solve that problem.

D) The text summarizes a debate among researchers, then gives reasons for supporting one side in that debate.

REMINDER

We spent a good deal of time discussing how to analyze the structure of passages in chapter 8.

This question asks us to pick the answer choice that best describes the overall structure of the passage. In chapter 8, we used text structure as one of a few key ways to analyze and make sense of passages. Here, our goal is to describe text structure itself.

The answer choices for this question all follow the same pattern. Each choice presents two ideas linked by the word *then*, which indicates sequence. First the passage does one thing, and then it does another thing.

Before turning to the answer choices, let's break down the passage's structure ourselves. The passage's first three sentences ("Many films . . . evidence") tell us that many early films, including films from "the first wave of Black women filmmakers," have been lost and that we only know those films existed because of "small pieces of evidence." The turning point in the passage is the fourth sentence, which begins with "for example" and introduces a series of cases of early films by Black women of which we have only scant evidence. Our preview of the answer choices led us to anticipate this circumstance, as we saw that each choice consisted of two ideas—two things the passage might do—linked by *then*.

Choice B closely tracks with our analysis of the passage's overall structure. The passage's first three sentences describe a general situation—the loss of many early films and, in particular, the near-total loss of those of many early Black women filmmakers—while the passage's last three sentences provide three examples of early films by Black women of which little trace remains.

Choice A is incorrect because the passage begins with a description of a general situation, not of several notable individuals, and because the passage concludes with examples of the general situation, not a discussion of differences among individuals. Moreover, the individuals mentioned in the passage's last three sentences are more alike than different, as each of their films has all but disappeared. Choice C is incorrect because the first three sentences of the passage present a regrettable set of facts more than a "problem" (complex or otherwise) to be solved and because the last three sentences offer examples illustrating the state of affairs rather than a series of failed solutions. Choice D is incorrect because no debate is presented in the passage.

Now let's examine the third type of Text Structure and Purpose question you may encounter in the Reading and Writing section: questions that ask you to determine the function (role) of part of a passage in relation to the passage as a whole. We'll number the sentences (and the underlined portion) for ease of reference in our discussion, but be aware that sentences in passages aren't numbered in actual test questions.

Craft and Structure Sample Question 6

(1) Horizontal gene transfer occurs when an organism of one species acquires genetic material from an organism of another species through nonreproductive means. (2) The genetic material can then be transferred "vertically" in the second species—that is, through reproductive inheritance. (3) Scientist Atma Ivancevic and her team have hypothesized infection by invertebrate parasites as a mechanism of horizontal gene transfer between vertebrate species: (4) while feeding, a parasite could acquire a gene from one host, then relocate to a host from a different vertebrate species and transfer the gene to it in turn.

Which choice best describes the function of the underlined portion in the text as a whole?

A) It explains why parasites are less susceptible to horizontal gene transfer than their hosts are.

B) It clarifies why some genes are more likely to be transferred horizontally than others are.

C) It contrasts how horizontal gene transfer occurs among vertebrates with how it occurs among invertebrates.

D) It describes a means by which horizontal gene transfer might occur among vertebrates.

Let's first break down the structure of this passage as a whole and then zero in on the role the underlined portion plays in the passage.

As with many opening sentences in Reading and Writing passages (and in real-world texts), sentence 1 here provides background—in this case, a brief explanation of the process of horizontal gene transfer. Sentence 2 continues the explanation by contrasting horizontal gene transfer with vertical transfer. From these sentences, we learn that while vertical gene transfer occurs through reproduction, horizontal gene transfer doesn't. Sentence 3 (before the colon) states the

STRATEGY

To answer questions about the function of parts of passages, you'll want to have a good sense of what the passage as a whole is trying to accomplish. The answer will be the main contribution the tested part of the passage makes to the whole passage.

hypothesis of Ivancevic and colleagues, which involves invertebrate parasites serving as a mechanism (means) for horizontal gene transfer between vertebrate species. In some sense, the parasites, the researchers speculate, act as a genetic "bridge" between other species.

The underlined portion, which we've numbered 4, is the part of the passage for which we need to determine a function in relation to the passage as a whole. In other words, we need to identify what the underlined portion mainly contributes to the passage.

Through careful reading, we can recognize that the underlined portion builds on sentence 3 by further explaining the mechanism posited by the researchers. There are several clues leading us to this interpretation. First, and most obviously, the content of the underlined portion describes a possible method by which parasites could be responsible for horizontal gene transfer: by gaining a gene from one host, moving to another host, and passing on the gene to the second host. Our second clue is the use of the colon in sentence 3. Colons can be used to introduce lists, for example, but their other main use in writing (especially in academic writing, which the Reading and Writing section's passages exemplify) is to introduce an elaboration. *Elaborations* are word(s), phrase(s), or even sentence(s) that build on or clarify the meaning of prior statements—in this case, the statement before the colon marked as sentence 3. This is exactly the role of the underlined portion in this passage. What follows the colon is an extension and clarification of what's said in sentence 3. While sentence 3 describes the way horizontal gene transfer involving parasites may occur, the underlined portion adds specific details about how that mechanism may work. A final clue to the role of sentence 4 is the use of the conditional mood verb "could acquire" in the underlined portion. "Could" here signals that what's being described in the underlined portion is a possible way in which horizontal gene transfer involving parasites may occur. This ties back nicely to sentence 3, which tells us that the researchers had a hypothesis about how parasites may facilitate horizontal gene transfer.

Choice D turns out to match very closely with the reasoning we just detailed and is the best answer to this question. Choice A is incorrect because it's not factually accurate. The passage does describe how parasites could be involved in horizontal gene transfer, but nothing in the passage suggests that parasites are "less susceptible" to such transfers, only that the parasites might facilitate them. Choice B is incorrect because the passage doesn't tell us anything about which genes are capable of or prone to being transferred horizontally. Choice C is incorrect because the passage talks only about horizontal gene transfer among vertebrate species; the only reference to invertebrates is to the parasites themselves, and the only real comparison the passage makes is between horizontal and vertical gene transfer.

Cross-Text Connections Questions

Let's close out this chapter with the third and final main type of Craft and Structure question: questions that require you to make supportable text-based conclusions about how two passages on the same topic or similar topics relate to one another.

In **Cross-Text Connections** questions, you'll be presented with two brief passages that are related by topic. After reading both passages, you'll have to determine which of the question's answer choices is best supported by evidence in each of the passages. Individual questions of this type may focus on similarities or differences between the two passages, and these relationships may be fairly straightforward or quite subtle.

Let's consider some examples.

Craft and Structure Sample Question 7

Text 1
Today the starchy root cassava is found in many dishes across West Africa, but its rise to popularity was slow. Portuguese traders brought cassava from Brazil to the West African coast in the 1500s. But at this time, people living in the capitals further inland had little contact with coastal communities. Thus, cassava remained relatively unknown to most of the region's inhabitants until the 1800s.

Text 2
Cassava's slow adoption into the diet of West Africans is mainly due to the nature of the crop itself. If not cooked properly, cassava can be toxic. Knowledge of how to properly prepare cassava needed to spread before the food could grow in popularity. The arrival of formerly enslaved people from Brazil in the 1800s, who brought their knowledge of cassava and its preparation with them, thus directly fueled the spread of this crop.

Based on the texts, the author of Text 1 and the author of Text 2 would most likely agree with which statement?

A) The climate of the West African coast in the 1500s prevented cassava's spread in the region.

B) Several of the most commonly grown crops in West Africa are originally from Brazil.

C) The most commonly used methods to cook cassava today date to the 1500s.

D) Cassava did not become a significant crop in West Africa until long after it was first introduced.

Our general approach to this question will be similar to how we've tackled questions about single passages. We'll first consider what each passage says separately and then look for one or more supportable connections between the two texts.

The central idea of Text 1 is stated directly in the passage's last sentence: cassava remained relatively unknown in West Africa until the nineteenth century. In terms of purpose, Text 2 mainly serves to explain why cassava remained underutilized in West Africa until

STRATEGY
In many ways, Cross-Text Connections questions can be approached like other questions asking only about a single passage. You'll want to begin by getting a clear sense of the message of each passage separately as well as of the point of view or perspective expressed in each passage.

the 1800s and why the situation changed with the arrival of formerly enslaved people from Brazil who knew how to prepare cassava safely. The two passages together give us a clearer view of the emergence of cassava in West Africa.

Now let's consider the question we're posed. Among the answer choices, we want to find the one that the author of Text 1 and the author of Text 2 would most likely agree on. Before we examine the answer choices closely, let's think about how the information in and the perspectives of the two passages relate. As we already noted, Text 1 focuses on the fact that cassava didn't become well known in West Africa until the 1800s, while Text 2 focuses on why cassava only emerged as an important West African food source in the 1800s. The two texts, in other words, are complementary, as they each present different parts of the story of cassava's introduction into the West African diet. Although the two passages contain different details, they agree on the main points.

Choice D is the best answer because it states a point that both authors would likely agree with. Both passages indicate that a lot of time passed between the introduction of cassava to West Africa and its widespread use as a source of food. Text 1 tells us directly that cassava was introduced to West Africa in the 1500s. Text 2 doesn't dispute that estimate and also characterizes the adoption of cassava as a food source in West Africa as "slow." In addition, Text 1 tells us directly that cassava "remained relatively unknown to most of the region's inhabitants until the 1800s," while Text 2 indicates that cassava didn't take off as a food source in West Africa until the arrival of formerly enslaved people from Brazil in the 1800s. Thus, both passages agree that it took a long time for cassava to become important to West Africans' diets.

Choice A, on the other hand, can be ruled out because neither passage suggests that climate prevented the spread of cassava: Text 1 suggests that the distance from the coasts to the inland capitals impeded the spread of cassava, while Text 2 suggests that cassava's toxicity kept it from being widely adopted as a food source. The passages also tell us only about a single crop, not several crops, coming to West Africa from Brazil, which rules out choice B. Text 2 establishes that successful methods for cooking cassava in West Africa emerged only in the 1800s with the arrival of formerly enslaved people from Brazil, which rules out choice C.

In the preceding example, only one answer choice, the key, was supported by textual evidence from the passages. In more challenging questions of this type, such as the following example, you'll have to consider more plausible choices that require more reasoning to dismiss.

STRATEGY

Once you've grasped the message and point of view of each passage, think about how the two passages intersect. The second passage may, for example, offer details not included in the first passage, offer an example of what's described in the first passage, or support or challenge all or part of the first passage. In each case, the question itself will help guide you, as it will signal the kind of relationship you should be seeking.

Craft and Structure Sample Question 8

Text 1

Although food writing is one of the most widely read genres in the United States, literary scholars have long neglected it. And within this genre, cookbooks attract the least scholarly attention of all, regardless of how well written they may be. This is especially true of works dedicated to regional US cuisines, whose complexity and historical significance are often overlooked.

Text 2

With her 1976 cookbook *The Taste of Country Cooking*, Edna Lewis popularized the refined Southern cooking she had grown up with in Freetown, an all-Black community in Virginia. She also set a new standard for cookbook writing: the recipes and memoir passages interspersing them are written in prose more elegant than that of most novels. Yet despite its inarguable value as a piece of writing, Lewis's masterpiece has received almost no attention from literary scholars.

Based on the two texts, how would the author of Text 1 most likely regard the situation presented in the underlined sentence in Text 2?

A) As typical, because scholars are dismissive of literary works that achieve popularity with the general public

B) As unsurprising, because scholars tend to overlook the literary value of food writing in general and of regional cookbooks in particular

C) As justifiable, because Lewis incorporated memoir into *The Taste of Country Cooking*, thus undermining its status as a cookbook

D) As inevitable, because *The Taste of Country Cooking* was marketed to readers of food writing and not to readers of other genres

Recall that in our first Cross-Text Connections example, the two passages were quite similar in overall focus and perspective, differing only in details. In this example, the relationship between the two passages is more subtle and thus requires more reasoning to infer.

After reading both passages, we can say in broad terms that Text 1 describes a general state of affairs and that Text 2 provides a concrete example of that state. But there's a little bit more going on than that, and the text-based connection we're being asked to draw between the two passages requires a finer-level understanding of both passages.

Let's consider Text 1 first. The author describes a nested set of relationships concerning the esteem (or, rather, lack thereof) in which scholars hold certain forms of writing. Food writing, the broadest category of the three mentioned in Text 1, is "neglected." Within the category of food writing, cookbook writing is particularly devalued. And within the category of cookbook writing, regional cookbook writing is the most devalued. If we wanted to write this out using basic math symbology, we could come up with the following, which uses "greater than" signs to indicate the hierarchy described in Text 1.

(Other, esteemed forms of writing) > food writing > cookbook writing > regional cookbook writing

NOTE

In more challenging Cross-Text Connections questions, both the passages and the relationship between them tend to become more subtle and complex.

Once we've mapped out the relationships described in Text 1 (whether literally or in our heads), it's a fairly straightforward task to understand the intended connection to Text 2. Text 2 tells us that Edna Lewis published *The Art of Country Cooking*, a regional cookbook of "inarguable value," in 1976. Based only on our analysis of Text 1, we would anticipate that Lewis's cookbook wasn't highly valued by scholars, as regional cookbook writing was lowest in the hierarchy described in Text 1. This inference is borne out by evidence in Text 2, which tells us, in the underlined (last) sentence, that "Lewis's masterpiece has received almost no attention from literary scholars."

Let's consider now the answer choices. Each choice consists of two parts, which we might call a *characterization* and a *reason*. From the question itself, we learn that the characterizations—"typical," "unsurprising," "justifiable," and "inevitable"—are posed as possible reactions of the author of Text 1 to the situation described in the underlined sentence of Text 2 (Lewis's cookbook has been ignored by scholars despite its obvious quality). Even before we get to the reasons that follow each characterization, we can easily rule out choice C based on "justifiable." Nothing suggests that the author of Text 1 would regard scholarly neglect of a landmark regional cookbook as justified, as the author is critical of the scholarly neglect of cookbooks in general and regional cookbooks in particular.

To choose the best answer among the remaining choices, we need to consider the reasons—the "because" clauses—provided in each. In doing so, choice B turns out to be the best answer to the question. The underlined portion in Text 2 asserts that Lewis's work has been unfairly overlooked. Based on our analysis of the passages, it's reasonable to conclude that the author of Text 1 would find this neglect unsurprising, and the reason given in choice B—"because scholars tend to overlook the literary value of food writing in general and of regional cookbooks in particular"—tracks with our breakdown of the hierarchy of relationships depicted in Text 1.

Choice A is incorrect because while the characterization "typical" carries about the same meaning as "unsurprising" in choice B, the reason given in choice A is unsupported by Text 1. The author of Text 1 does mention that food writing is "one of the most widely read genres in the United States" but doesn't offer evidence that food writing is dismissed by scholars just because it's popular. It's *possible* that the author of Text 1 believes critics are biased against popular forms of writing, but the text doesn't directly say or strongly imply that, so we can safely rule out this answer option. As we've observed, the characterization "justifiable" in choice C immediately rules out this option, but we can also note that the reason provided— Lewis undermined the status of *The Taste of Country Cooking* by incorporating memoir into it—has no support in either text. Choice D is incorrect because the characterization "inevitable" is a little stronger

STRATEGY

While we strongly recommend that you read and consider the entirety of each answer choice to a given question, it's possible that some choices can be ruled out quickly based on (as here) a single key word or phrase that's clearly incorrect.

STRATEGY

When answering Reading and Writing questions, especially more challenging ones, it's critical to distinguish between what *may* be possible or even plausible in the real world and what's actually supported in the passage(s). The key will be the answer choice with the firmest grounding in the passage(s).

than Text 1 supports and because there's no evidence in either text to support the assertion that *The Taste of Country Cooking* was marketed to readers of food writing and not to readers of other genres.

In our final example for this chapter, we'll examine a Cross-Text Connections question that, unlike the other two discussed, asks you to identify a difference in perspective between two passages.

Craft and Structure Sample Question 9

Text 1
Despite its beautiful prose, *The Guns of August*, Barbara Tuchman's 1962 analysis of the start of World War I, has certain weaknesses as a work of history. It fails to address events in Eastern Europe just before the outbreak of hostilities, thereby giving the impression that Germany was the war's principal instigator. Had Tuchman consulted secondary works available to her by scholars such as Luigi Albertini, she would not have neglected the influence of events in Eastern Europe on Germany's actions.

Text 2
Barbara Tuchman's *The Guns of August* is an engrossing if dated introduction to World War I. Tuchman's analysis of primary documents is laudable, but her main thesis that European powers committed themselves to a catastrophic outcome by refusing to deviate from military plans developed prior to the conflict is implausibly reductive.

Which choice best describes a difference in how the authors of Text 1 and Text 2 view Barbara Tuchman's *The Guns of August*?

A) The author of Text 1 believes that the scope of Tuchman's research led her to an incorrect interpretation, while the author of Text 2 believes that Tuchman's central argument is overly simplistic.

B) The author of Text 1 argues that Tuchman should have relied more on the work of other historians, while the author of Text 2 implies that Tuchman's most interesting claims result from her original research.

C) The author of Text 1 asserts that the writing style of *The Guns of August* makes it worthwhile to read despite any perceived deficiency in Tuchman's research, while the author of Text 2 focuses exclusively on the weakness of Tuchman's interpretation of events.

D) The author of Text 1 claims that Tuchman would agree that World War I was largely due to events in Eastern Europe, while the author of Text 2 maintains that Tuchman would say that Eastern European leaders were not committed to military plans in the same way that other leaders were.

Before we consider differences between the perspectives of the authors of the two passages in this question, let's identify some of the ways in which the two texts are similar in their views. Both authors describe *The Guns of August* as well written, with the author of Text 1 saying it has "beautiful prose" and the author of Text 2 calling it "engrossing." In addition, both authors agree that *The Guns of August* has serious limitations as a work of history. Text 1 argues that Tuchman paid too little attention to prewar events in Eastern Europe, while Text 2 contends that Tuchman gave too much credence to the idea that a refusal to deviate from military plans made before the outbreak of hostilities caused World War I.

STRATEGY

Authors of passages in Cross-Text Connections questions may agree or disagree in whole or in part. More challenging questions of this type will pair passages with subtle or complex relationships that you must use reading, reasoning, and text-based inferencing to determine.

This discussion leads us to an important general point about Cross-Text Connections passages. Even when the authors of such passages disagree, this disagreement may only be partial. You may see pairs of passages in the Reading and Writing section in which two clearly opposing viewpoints are contrasted, but that's not always going to be the case, especially with more challenging questions of this type.

Choice A is the best answer to this question, as it captures an important difference between the two passages. The author of Text 1 objects to Tuchman's lack of attention to prewar events in Eastern Europe and attributes this to her failure to consult appropriate secondary sources. We can fairly conceptualize this, as choice A does, as a narrowness in the scope of Tuchman's work (i.e., not adequately considering secondary sources) leading Tuchman to an incorrect interpretation (i.e., Germany was the war's primary instigator). We find support for the other half of choice A in Text 2, in which the author refers to Tuchman's central argument as "implausibly reductive." Even if the precise meaning of *reductive* (overly simplistic) eludes you, the adverb *implausibly* should clue you in to choice A being the best option.

Choice B is incorrect because although the first half of the answer choice is basically accurate—the author of Text 1 does argue that Tuchman should have consulted more secondary sources—the second half of the answer choice isn't really supported by Text 2. The author of Text 2 clearly respects *The Guns of August* at some level, but Text 2's emphasis is on the book's shortcomings as a work of history. Both halves of choice C are incorrect. The author of Text 1, as we've observed, does praise the prose of *The Guns of August*, but the author never says or implies anything as strongly worded as the proposition that the writing quality of the book transcends (overcomes) its weaknesses as history. Furthermore, although the author of Text 2 does focus primarily on the limitations of *The Guns of August* as a historical account, the author also praises the book, calling it "engrossing" and lauding Tuchman's analysis of primary sources. Choice D is incorrect because, like choice C, it's false on both counts. The author of Text 1 claims that Tuchman ignored prewar events in Eastern Europe, and the author of Text 2 never mentions Eastern Europe specifically, only Europe in general.

As we saw with this question, the most challenging Cross-Text Connections questions will require you to carefully evaluate two (potentially complex) passages while also sorting through answer choices that may be partially but not wholly right. But, as we've also shown, you can use the same basic approach to these questions regardless of the passages' content or the specific question you're asked: read each passage closely, and then establish the nature of the relationship between the two passages. Do they largely agree? Do they largely disagree? Do they simply cover different aspects of the same topic? Getting a strong sense of both passages' content and how the two texts relate will give you a solid basis for answering any question about the pairing.

Summary: Craft and Structure Questions

Main purpose: To test whether you can determine how and why authors write texts the way they do

Proportion of the test section: About 28 percent (thirteen to fifteen questions)

Question types

- Words in Context: Use and determine the meaning of high-utility academic words and phrases in the contexts in which they appear

- Text Structure and Purpose: Analyze and describe how and why passages are put together the way they are; describe the main purpose of passages

- Cross-Text Connections: Draw supportable connections between two topically related passages

CHAPTER 14

Reading and Writing: Questions—Craft and Structure Drills

1

Biologist Jane Edgeloe and colleagues have located what is believed to be the largest individual plant in the world in the Shark Bay area of Australia. The plant is a type of seagrass called *Posidonia australis*, and it _____ approximately 200 square kilometers.

Which choice completes the text with the most logical and precise word or phrase?

A) acknowledges

B) produces

C) spans

D) advances

2

Osage Nation citizen Randy Tinker-Smith produced and directed the ballet *Wahzhazhe*, which vividly chronicles Osage history and culture. Telling Osage stories through ballet is _____ choice because two of the foremost ballet dancers of the twentieth century were Osage: sisters Maria and Marjorie Tallchief.

Which choice completes the text with the most logical and precise word or phrase?

A) an unpredictable

B) an arbitrary

C) a determined

D) a suitable

3

The following text is adapted from Zora Neale Hurston's 1921 short story "John Redding Goes to Sea." John wants to travel far beyond the village where he lives near his mother, Matty.

[John] had on several occasions attempted to <u>reconcile his mother to</u> the notion, but found it a difficult task. Matty always took refuge in self-pity and tears. Her son's desires were incomprehensible to her, that was all.

As used in the text, what does the phrase "reconcile his mother to" most nearly mean?

A) Get his mother to accept

B) Get his mother to apologize for

C) Get his mother to match

D) Get his mother to reunite with

4

Michelene Pesantubbee, a historian and citizen of the Choctaw Nation, has identified a dilemma inherent to research on the status of women in her tribe during the 1600s and 1700s: the primary sources from that era, travel narratives and other accounts by male European colonizers, underestimate the degree of power conferred on Choctaw women by their traditional roles in political, civic, and ceremonial life. Pesantubbee argues that the Choctaw oral tradition and findings from archaeological sites in the tribe's homeland supplement the written record by providing crucial insights into those roles.

Which choice best describes the overall structure of the text?

A) It details the shortcomings of certain historical sources, then argues that research should avoid those sources altogether.

B) It describes a problem that arises in research on a particular topic, then sketches a historian's approach to addressing that problem.

C) It lists the advantages of a particular research method, then acknowledges a historian's criticism of that method.

D) It characterizes a particular topic as especially challenging to research, then suggests a related topic for historians to pursue instead.

5

The following text is from Srimati Svarna Kumari Devi's 1894 novel *The Fatal Garland* (translated by A. Christina Albers in 1910). Shakti is walking near a riverbank that she visited frequently during her childhood.

She crossed the woods she knew so well. <u>The trees seemed to extend their branches like welcoming arms.</u> They greeted her as an old friend. Soon she reached the river-side.

Which choice best describes the function of the underlined portion in the text as a whole?

A) It suggests that Shakti feels uncomfortable near the river.

B) It indicates that Shakti has lost her sense of direction in the woods.

C) It emphasizes Shakti's sense of belonging in the landscape.

D) It conveys Shakti's appreciation for her long-term friendships.

6

The following text is adapted from Oscar Wilde's 1897 nonfiction work *De Profundis*.

> People whose desire is solely for self-realisation never know where they are going. They can't know. In one sense of the word it is of course necessary to know oneself: that is the first achievement of knowledge. But to recognise that the soul of a man is unknowable, is the ultimate achievement of wisdom. The final mystery is oneself. When one has weighed the sun in the balance, and measured the steps of the moon, and mapped out the seven heavens star by star, there still remains oneself. <u>Who can calculate the orbit of his own soul?</u>

Which choice best describes the function of the underlined question in the text as a whole?

A) It cautions readers that the text's directions for how to achieve self-knowledge are hard to follow.

B) It concedes that the definition of self-knowledge advanced in the text is unpopular.

C) It reinforces the text's skepticism about the possibility of truly achieving self-knowledge.

D) It speculates that some readers will share the doubts expressed in the text about the value of self-knowledge.

7

In many agricultural environments, the banks of streams are kept forested to protect water quality, but it's been unclear what effects these forests may have on stream biodiversity. To investigate the issue, biologist Xingli Giam and colleagues studied an Indonesian oil palm plantation, comparing the species richness of forested streams with that of nonforested streams. Giam and colleagues found that species richness was significantly higher in forested streams, a finding the researchers attribute to the role leaf litter plays in sheltering fish from predators and providing food resources.

Which choice best states the main purpose of the text?

A) It presents a study that addresses an unresolved question about the presence of forests along streams in agricultural environments.

B) It explains the differences between stream-protection strategies used in oil palm plantations and stream-protection strategies used in other kinds of agricultural environments.

C) It discusses research intended to settle a debate about how agricultural yields can be increased without negative effects on water quality.

D) It describes findings that challenge a previously held view about how fish that inhabit streams in agricultural environments attempt to avoid predators.

8

Text 1

Dance choreographer Alvin Ailey's deep admiration for jazz music can most clearly be felt in the rhythms and beats his works were set to. Ailey collaborated with some of the greatest jazz legends, like Charles Mingus, Charlie Parker, and perhaps his favorite, Duke Ellington. With his choice of music, Ailey helped bring jazz to life for his audiences.

Text 2

Jazz is present throughout Ailey's work, but it's most visible in Ailey's approach to choreography. Ailey often incorporated improvisation, a signature characteristic of jazz music, in his work. When managing his dance company, Ailey rarely forced his dancers to an exact set of specific moves. Instead, he encouraged his dancers to let their own skills and experiences shape their performances, as jazz musicians do.

Based on the texts, both authors would most likely agree with which statement?

A) Audiences were mostly unfamiliar with the jazz music in Ailey's works.

B) Ailey's work was strongly influenced by jazz.

C) Dancers who worked with Ailey greatly appreciated his supportive approach as a choreographer.

D) Ailey blended multiple genres of music together when choreographing dance pieces.

9

Text 1

The idea that time moves in only one direction is instinctively understood, yet it puzzles physicists. According to the second law of thermodynamics, at a macroscopic level some processes of heat transfer are irreversible due to the production of entropy—after a transfer we cannot rewind time and place molecules back exactly where they were before, just as we cannot unbreak dropped eggs. But laws of physics at a microscopic or quantum level hold that those processes *should* be reversible.

Text 2

In 2015, physicists Tiago Batalhão et al. performed an experiment in which they confirmed the irreversibility of thermodynamic processes at a quantum level, producing entropy by applying a rapidly oscillating magnetic field to a system of carbon-13 atoms in liquid chloroform. But the experiment "does not pinpoint . . . what causes [irreversibility] at the microscopic level," coauthor Mauro Paternostro said.

Based on the texts, what would the author of Text 1 most likely say about the experiment described in Text 2?

A) It is consistent with the current understanding of physics at a microscopic level but not at a macroscopic level.

B) It provides empirical evidence that the current understanding of an aspect of physics at a microscopic level must be incomplete.

C) It supports a claim about an isolated system of atoms in a laboratory, but that claim should not be extrapolated to a general claim about the universe.

D) It would suggest an interesting direction for future research were it not the case that two of the physicists who conducted the experiment disagree on the significance of its findings.

10

Text 1

Because literacy in Nahuatl script, the writing system of the Aztec Empire, was lost after Spain invaded central Mexico in the 1500s, it is unclear exactly how meaning was encoded in the script's symbols. Although many scholars had assumed that the symbols signified entire words, linguist Alfonso Lacadena theorized in 2008 that they signified units of language smaller than words: individual syllables.

Text 2

The growing consensus among scholars of Nahuatl script is that many of its symbols could signify either words or syllables, depending on syntax and content at any given site within a text. For example, the symbol signifying the word *huipil* (blouse) in some contexts could signify the syllable "pil" in others, as in the place name "Chipiltepec." Thus, for the Aztecs, reading required a determination of how such symbols functioned each time they appeared in a text.

Based on the texts, how would the author of Text 2 most likely characterize Lacadena's theory, as described in Text 1?

A) By praising the theory for recognizing that the script's symbols could represent entire words

B) By arguing that the theory is overly influenced by the work of earlier scholars

C) By approving of the theory's emphasis on how the script changed over time

D) By cautioning that the theory overlooks certain important aspects of how the script functioned

Answer Explanations

QUESTION 1

Choice C is the best answer because it completes the text with the most logical and precise word. "Spans" means "extends over a distance of" or "encompasses," which makes sense in describing the area covered by what's believed to be the world's largest individual plant.

Choice A is incorrect because "acknowledges" means "recognizes" or "admits the truth of." Either way, it doesn't make sense here, as a plant can't acknowledge an area. *Choice B* is incorrect because "produces" can mean "makes," "causes," or "presents," but none of those definitions makes sense here, as a plant can't make, cause, or present an area. *Choice D* is incorrect because "advances" means "moves forward" or "progresses," but the plant isn't necessarily moving forward or progressing. Rather, the passage indicates that it already covers an area of 200 square kilometers.

QUESTION 2

Choice D is the best answer because it completes the text with the most logical and precise phrase. "Suitable" means "appropriate for a particular purpose." Since the passage indicates that two of the best ballet dancers of the twentieth century were Osage, we can reasonably infer that the author believes that ballet is a suitable art form for telling Osage stories.

Choice A is incorrect because the passage never suggests that Tinker-Smith's choice was an "unpredictable" one. Rather, the fact that two of the best ballet dancers of the twentieth century were Osage makes ballet especially appropriate for telling Osage stories. *Choice B* is incorrect because the passage implies the opposite. An "arbitrary" choice is a choice based on whim rather than reason, but the passage gives a good reason behind the choice to tell Osage stories through ballet: two of the best ballet dancers of the twentieth century were Osage. *Choice C* is incorrect because the passage never suggests that Tinker-Smith's choice was a "determined" one, which would imply that Tinker-Smith initially faced some kind of obstacle or opposition, or that the choice was made for Tinker-Smith. Nothing like either of those ideas, however, is mentioned in or suggested by the passage.

QUESTION 3

Choice A is the best answer because it most nearly identifies what the underlined phrase means in context. The expression "reconcile . . . to" refers to causing someone to come to accept something difficult or disagreeable. The passage indicates that John wants his mother to accept his desire to travel even though she doesn't like the idea.

Choice B is incorrect because, per the passage, John doesn't want his mother to apologize for his own desire to travel; he just wants her to accept the idea. *Choice C* is incorrect because the passage doesn't suggest that John wants his mother to match, or share, his desire to travel. Rather, he wants her to accept his desire to travel even though she doesn't like the idea. *Choice D* is incorrect because a person can't really "reunite with" a notion, or idea; in any case, "reunite" illogically suggests that John's mother would be once again accepting the notion of John traveling, when the passage gives no indication that she'd previously accepted the idea.

QUESTION 4

Choice B is the best answer because it best describes the overall structure of the text. The passage begins by stating a problem with existing research on the status of Choctaw women during the 1600s and 1700s: because of the nature of their authorship, written primary sources underestimate the power Choctaw women had in their traditional roles. Then it presents one historian's solution: looking to oral tradition and archeological findings for additional insights into these roles.

Choice A is incorrect because the passage never says that research should avoid written primary sources altogether, just that research should also make use of oral tradition and archeological findings as sources. *Choice C* is incorrect because the passage never mentions the advantages of using written primary sources and because it goes beyond critiquing the use of such sources to suggest ways to supplement them. *Choice D* is incorrect because the passage never says that the status of Choctaw women during the 1600s and 1700s is unusually challenging to research compared to other historical topics and because it doesn't mention any other topics for historians to research instead.

QUESTION 5

Choice C is the best answer because it best describes the function of the underlined portion in the text as a whole. The phrase "welcoming arms" reinforces the passage's suggestion that Shakti feels a sense of belonging in the woods "she knew so well," as if the trees are embracing her.

Choice A is incorrect because the phrase "welcoming arms" suggests that Shakti is comfortable, not uncomfortable, in the woods. *Choice B* is incorrect because the phrase "welcoming arms" reinforces the passage's suggestion that the woods are familiar to Shakti, not that she's become lost. *Choice D* is incorrect because the underlined portion doesn't describe actual long-term friendships; it instead uses figurative language to emphasize Shakti's familiarity with the woods.

QUESTION 6

Choice C is the best answer because it best describes the function of the underlined question in the text as a whole. The passage repeatedly claims that true self-knowledge can't be achieved, and the rhetorical question in the underlined portion, which also expresses skepticism, emphasizes that point.

Choice A is incorrect because the passage doesn't provide directions for how to achieve self-knowledge; rather, it claims that true self-knowledge is impossible to achieve. *Choice B* is incorrect because the text doesn't really ever define self-knowledge, much less discuss the popularity of that nonexistent definition. *Choice D* is incorrect because the passage never expresses doubts about the value of self-knowledge; rather, the doubts expressed in the passage are about the possibility of achieving self-knowledge at all. Additionally, there's nothing in the passage to suggest that the author expects some readers to share his views.

QUESTION 7

Choice A is the best answer because it best states the main purpose of the text. The passage first describes an unresolved question: What effect do forests on stream banks have on stream biodiversity? Then the passage presents a study that answers the question: such forests increase stream biodiversity.

Choice B is incorrect because the passage never mentions any specific agricultural environments other than the one Giam and colleagues studied, which was an Indonesian oil palm plantation. *Choice C* is incorrect because the passage never mentions agricultural yields. *Choice D* is incorrect because the passage never mentions any previously held view about how fish in streams in agricultural environments try to avoid predators.

QUESTION 8

Choice B is the best answer because it identifies the statement with which the authors of the two texts would most likely agree. Text 1 states that Ailey had a "deep admiration for jazz music" and that he "helped bring jazz to life for his audiences" with the inclusion of jazz rhythms and beats in his works. Text 2 states that "jazz is present throughout Ailey's work."

Choice A is incorrect because neither passage mentions how familiar or unfamiliar audiences were with any aspect of Ailey's works. *Choice C* is incorrect because neither passage mentions how Ailey's dancers felt about his approach as a choreographer. *Choice D* is incorrect because neither passage mentions Ailey employing any genre of music other than jazz.

QUESTION 9

Choice B is the best answer because it identifies what the author of Text 1 would most likely say about the experiment described in Text 2. Text 1 describes a puzzle that physicists hadn't been able to solve: at a microscopic or quantum level, the laws of physics suggest that we should be able to reverse processes that aren't reversible at a macroscopic level. The researchers discussed in Text 2, however, provided empirical evidence that those processes aren't reversible even at the quantum level, for reasons the researchers themselves don't yet understand. It's reasonable to conclude, then, that the author of Text 1 would say that our understanding of the laws of physics is incomplete since this understanding led to an incorrect assumption.

Choice A is incorrect because the experiment described in Text 2 contradicts, rather than supports, what the physicists mentioned in Text 1 believed to be true at the microscopic or quantum level. Furthermore, per the passage, the experiment described in Text 2 didn't address the macroscopic level at all. *Choice C* is incorrect because neither passage distinguishes between laboratory findings and the way the universe works in general. *Choice D* is incorrect because although Text 2 mentions multiple physicists and that these physicists don't yet know what causes irreversibility at the microscopic level, there's no indication in Text 2 that two of the researchers disagree about the significance of their findings.

QUESTION 10

Choice D is the best answer because it identifies how the author of Text 2 would most likely characterize Lacadena's theory, as described in Text 1. Lacadena's theory is that Nahuatl script symbols signified syllables, but the consensus described in Text 2 is that they could signify either syllables or full words, depending on the context. The author of Text 2 would, therefore, likely consider Lacadena's theory too simplistic: it's missing the importance of context in determining the meaning of the symbols.

Choice A is incorrect because it conflicts with Text 1's description of Lacadena's theory, which is that Nahuatl script symbols signified only syllables. *Choice B* is incorrect because it conflicts with Text 1's description of Lacadena's theory. Text 1 states that Lacadena's theory differed from what earlier scholars had believed. *Choice C* is incorrect because neither passage mentions how or even whether the script changed over time.

CHAPTER 15

Reading and Writing: Questions— Expression of Ideas

Reading and Writing questions in the **Expression of Ideas** content domain are designed to test your ability to revise passages in order to improve how information and ideas are conveyed. There are two main areas of focus in Expression of Ideas questions: selectively using and combining provided information and ideas in order to best meet a specified rhetorical (writerly) goal and using the most logical transition word or phrase to connect information and ideas within a passage.

Proportion of the Test Section

About 20 percent of the Reading and Writing section is made up of Expression of Ideas questions. This translates to **eight to twelve Expression of Ideas questions** per test form.

Overview of Expression of Ideas Question Types

The Expression of Ideas content domain includes two main question types:

- **Rhetorical Synthesis** questions, which test your ability to selectively use and combine provided information and ideas in order to meet specified writerly goals.

- **Transitions** questions, which test your ability to provide the most logical transition in order to link information and ideas in passages.

All questions in this content domain (and in the Reading and Writing section in general) are multiple-choice in format. Each question has a single best answer (*key*) and three incorrect answer choices (*distractors*) that represent common errors students make when answering such questions. All the information needed to answer each question is in the passage, so you should always base your answers on what a given passage says directly and what it strongly implies.

Expression of Ideas Question Types in Detail

In this section, we'll discuss both Expression of Ideas question types in detail. We'll describe the general purpose of each type so that you understand better how to approach such questions on test day. As part of this discussion, we'll walk through some sample questions so that you get a strong indication of the kinds of skills and knowledge required to successfully answer questions of a given type.

Rhetorical Synthesis Questions

Rhetorical Synthesis questions ask you to selectively use and combine provided information and ideas into an effective single sentence that meets the writerly aim specified in the question itself.

A "passage" for a Rhetorical Synthesis question is made up of a bulleted list of statements about a topic. As the question reminds you, these statements are meant to simulate the kinds of notes a student like you might take during a reading assignment or research project. You'll draw on information and ideas in the statements to answer the question, but you'll need to do so selectively because—as is often the case when you take notes—not all the information and ideas may be needed to meet the writerly goal set forth in the question. You'll have to pay close attention to this goal because it will strongly influence how you answer the question. The answer choices in Rhetorical Synthesis questions will consist of single sentences that present differing ways to combine the information and ideas in the passage, but only one of these ways will best meet the specified writerly goal.

Let's begin with a relatively straightforward Rhetorical Synthesis example. Before going through how to answer the question itself, we'll point out the key features of questions of this type.

WHAT IS "RHETORIC"?

Rhetoric is simply the art of effective writing (and speaking). You may sometimes find people referring to empty arguments and insincere flowery language as "mere rhetoric," but the term has a broader and more positive meaning as well.

NOTE

Passages for Rhetorical Synthesis questions don't include the literature subject area.

Expression of Ideas Sample Question 1

While researching a topic, a student has taken the following notes:

- The painter Frida Kahlo is one of the most influential artists of the twentieth century.
- She was born in Coyoacán, Mexico, in 1907.
- She is best known for her vivid and richly symbolic self-portraits.
- *The Two Fridas* (1939) features two versions of Kahlo sitting together.
- One version wears a European-style dress and the other a traditional Tehuana dress.

The student wants to introduce Kahlo to an audience unfamiliar with the artist. Which choice most effectively uses relevant information from the notes to accomplish this goal?

A) The 1939 painting *The Two Fridas* is one example of a self-portrait by Frida Kahlo.

B) One painting by Frida Kahlo features two versions of herself, with one version wearing a European-style dress and the other a traditional Tehuana dress.

C) Known for being vivid and richly symbolic, Frida Kahlo's self-portraits include *The Two Fridas* (1939).

D) One of the most influential artists of the twentieth century, Mexican painter Frida Kahlo is best known for her self-portraits, which are vivid and richly symbolic.

Rhetorical Synthesis questions have several important features.

- *Framing.* The framing of the question, or how it's presented to you, asks you to approach this kind of question as if you were a student taking notes for an assignment. Although this framing isn't really necessary to answering the question, it helps to show you how answering the question is like something you've done many times already (and will continue to do) in your classes.

- *Bulleted list.* The statements in the bulleted list represent the kinds of notes you might take as you read about a topic. Just like real notes, this list includes information and ideas relevant to the specified writing goal and may include additional information and ideas that aren't particularly relevant to that goal. As the question itself reminds you, your job will be, in part, to distinguish between relevant and irrelevant information and ideas when answering. You can safely assume that all the information and ideas in these notes are accurate, and therefore you won't be asked to distinguish what's true from what's not.

- *Rhetorical goal.* The rhetorical (writerly) goal specified in the question is critically important to pay attention to. There are many potential ways that the information and ideas in the question's bulleted list *could* be combined into a single sentence, but only one of the four answer choices will do so in a way that most effectively meets the specified goal.

STRATEGY

Pay close attention to the writerly goal specified in Rhetorical Synthesis questions. There are many possible ways to combine the information and ideas in the bulleted list, but only one answer choice will do so in a way that best meets this goal.

NOTE

Rhetorical Synthesis questions don't test grammar, usage, and punctuation. All answer choices will be grammatical. Your job is to focus on meeting the specified writerly goal most effectively, not correcting sentence-level errors. (You'll do the latter in Standard English Conventions questions, the topic of subsequent chapters.)

STRATEGY

Before or while reading Rhetorical Synthesis answer choices, think about what meeting the writerly goal specified in the question might look like—in this case, how you might go about introducing an artist to an audience unfamiliar with her paintings.

- *Answer choices.* Each answer choice represents one possible way to use and combine information and ideas from the notes in the bulleted list. Each sentence is grammatical, and you won't be tested on conventions of sentence structure, usage, and punctuation in this type of question. Instead, you'll have to carefully consider the answer choices to determine which of them best meets the specified writerly goal.

Let's now turn to the particulars of this question.

The five statements in the bulleted list represent notes that a (hypothetical) student has taken about Frida Kahlo and some of her paintings. Before we set about trying to blend this information together, though, we need to consider the writerly goal specified in the question. In this case, the student wants to "introduce Kahlo to an audience unfamiliar with the artist."

This goal will shape how we evaluate the answer choices. We're not simply searching for the sentence among the answer choices that reads best to us but rather trying to meet the student's goal most effectively. Before (or at least while) reading the actual answer choices carefully, think about what it might mean to meet this goal. In this case, if you were to tell your classmates about an artist you'd researched, and you had good reason to think your fellow students wouldn't know who this artist was, you'd probably want to provide some general information about that artist to orient your listeners. You wouldn't just jump in by, say, describing some of this artist's works but instead would want to give your audience some sense of who the artist was, why they're important (to you or to others), and what they're known for.

Choice D, the best answer to this question, does all these things. It orients and informs readers in general terms about Kahlo and her artistry in a way suitable for an audience unfamiliar with her. This choice tells us that Kahlo was highly influential, worked in the twentieth century, was Mexican, and is best known for her self-portraits, and then characterizes her self-portraits as "vivid and richly symbolic."

Choice A is incorrect because it's simply a factual statement about one of Kahlo's paintings and doesn't provide any background about Kahlo, as the goal requires. Choice B is incorrect for a similar reason, as it jumps right to discussing one of Kahlo's paintings without any effort at an introduction. Choice C is incorrect as well. It gets closer than either choice A or choice B to offering an introductory statement, but it's a general statement about Kahlo's self-portraits, not, as the goal requires, about Kahlo herself, and the more successful choice D includes the same sort of information about Kahlo's self-portraits as choice C highlights.

Before we turn to another example, let's examine, statement by statement, how the information in the bulleted list was used (or not used) in the key to this question.

Bulleted-List Statements	Use In the Key
The painter Frida Kahlo is one of the most influential artists of the twentieth century.	This information is fully incorporated into the key.
She was born in Coyoacán, Mexico, in 1907.	The key uses the information that Kahlo was Mexican, but it leaves out her birthplace and the year she was born.
She is best known for her vivid and richly symbolic self-portraits.	This information is fully incorporated into the key.
The Two Fridas (1939) features two versions of Kahlo sitting together.	This information is left out of the key.
One version wears a European-style dress and the other a traditional Tehuana dress.	This information is left out of the key.

As you'll notice, although some information from the statements is used directly in the key, other pieces of information in the bulleted list are left out entirely, while one piece was only partly incorporated. This is normal: part of the task in Rhetorical Synthesis questions is to distinguish relevant from irrelevant information and ideas in terms of meeting the specified writerly goal.

We already implied this, but it's worth singling out and making more explicit: the best answer to a Rhetorical Synthesis question may, and likely will, selectively incorporate and/or paraphrase the information and ideas in its bulleted list. Although the first and the third bullets in the above example appear in the key nearly word for word, this won't always be the case—particularly for more challenging Rhetorical Synthesis questions, which may make greater use of paraphrasing. In addition, as with the second statement in the bulleted list, the best answer may use only part of the information found in some bulleted points. As we noted, Kahlo's Mexican heritage was relevant to meeting the writerly goal specified in the question, but her birthplace and the year she was born were extraneous details that wouldn't have contributed to the most effective introductory statement (choice D). And the best answer may, as we found in this example, leave out some bulleted statements entirely. In this case, the details about Kahlo's painting *The Two Fridas* were omitted because they were too specific and precise for an introductory statement about Kahlo herself.

Our second Rhetorical Synthesis example also highlights the need when answering this type of question to distinguish relevant from irrelevant information and ideas in order to meet the specified writerly goal.

STRATEGY

The best answer to a Rhetorical Synthesis question does *not* have to—and typically won't—use all the information and ideas found in its bulleted list. It may leave out some statements entirely, paraphrase elements of some statements (putting them into different words while still preserving the original meaning), and/or incorporate only the most relevant portions of some statements while leaving out less relevant portions.

Expression of Ideas Sample Question 2

While researching a topic, a student has taken the following notes:

- A wok is a cooking pan that originated in China during the Han dynasty (206 BCE–220 CE).
- The wok's round, wide base helps to cook food evenly.
- The wok's high, angled sides help to contain oil splatters.
- Grace Young is a cook and culinary historian.
- Her book *The Breath of a Wok* (2004) traces the history of the wok.

The student wants to describe the wok's shape. Which choice most effectively uses relevant information from the notes to accomplish this goal?

A) Grace Young's 2004 book, *The Breath of a Wok*, traces the history of the cooking pan.

B) A wok is a cooking pan with a round, wide base and high, angled sides.

C) The design of a wok, a type of cooking pan that originated in China during the Han dynasty, helps the pan cook food evenly and contain oil splatters.

D) Able to cook food evenly and contain oil splatters, the wok is the subject of Grace Young's 2004 book.

STRATEGY

Don't be afraid to leave out irrelevant information—even one or more whole statements—when answering Rhetorical Synthesis questions. Always keep the specified writerly goal in mind. You may even want to highlight or otherwise annotate the goal before answering to remind you of it.

Two of the five statements in the bulleted list pertain to Grace Young and her history of the wok. Given that forty percent of the information in the list is about Young and her writing, you might reasonably expect that the best answer would include that information somehow. But read the writerly goal closely. The student wants to describe the shape of a wok. Reading the last two sentences in the bulleted list again, we note that knowing that Young is a cook and culinary historian and that she wrote a history of the wok wouldn't add anything to a description of a wok's shape. It's interesting information, certainly, but it's not relevant to answering this particular question.

Choice B is the best answer because it sticks to describing the shape of a wok—it has a "round, wide base" and "high, angled sides." Choice A is incorrect because it focuses on Young's book and doesn't describe the shape of a wok. Choice C is incorrect because although it focuses on woks themselves, it doesn't describe the shape of a wok at all. Choice D is incorrect because it doesn't describe the shape of a wok and because it focuses as much on Young's book as it does on woks themselves.

Let's look at one final example.

Expression of Ideas Sample Question 3

While researching a topic, a student has taken the following notes:

- As engineered structures, many bird nests are uniquely flexible yet cohesive.
- A research team led by Yashraj Bhosale wanted to better understand the mechanics behind these structural properties.
- Bhosale's team used laboratory models that simulated the arrangement of flexible sticks into nest-like structures.
- The researchers analyzed the points where sticks touched one another.
- When pressure was applied to the model nests, the number of contact points between the sticks increased, making the structures stiffer.

The student wants to present the primary aim of the research study. Which choice most effectively uses relevant information from the notes to accomplish this goal?

A) The researchers used laboratory models that simulated the arrangement of flexible sticks and analyzed the points where sticks touched one another.

B) As analyzed by Bhosale's team, bird nests are uniquely flexible yet cohesive engineered structures.

C) Bhosale's team wanted to better understand the mechanics behind bird nests' uniquely flexible yet cohesive structural properties.

D) After analyzing the points where sticks touched, the researchers found that the structures became stiffer when pressure was applied.

This example again requires us to carefully differentiate relevant from irrelevant information in terms of the specified writerly goal. Given that this goal is to present the primary aim of the research study, we should be on the lookout for information about that in the bulleted list. The second statement in the list speaks directly to the researchers' motivation: they "wanted to better understand the mechanics behind" the structural properties of bird nests. We should, therefore, expect to find this statement strongly represented in the best answer.

The best answer to this question, choice C, does, in fact, include the second statement from the list, pairing it with the first statement's characterization of birds' nests as "uniquely flexible but cohesive."

Choice A is incorrect because it describes the researchers' approach during the study (i.e., their methodology), not their motivation for undertaking the study in the first place. Choice B is incorrect because it describes the nature of birds' nests, not the researchers' motivation for studying them. Choice D is incorrect because it describes a finding from the research, not the reason the researchers undertook the study.

STRATEGY

We've noted this before, but we think it's worth repeating: it's a good idea when answering Reading and Writing questions to have a sense of what the best answer ought to be (based on a close reading of the associated passage) before carefully examining the answer choices. Doing so may speed up your test taking and will likely make it easier for you to avoid being distracted by incorrect choices.

Transitions Questions

The other main type of Expression of Ideas question focuses on transitions, or the logical links between information and ideas in passages. In real-world texts, transitions serve to guide and smooth readers' movement between and among sentences, paragraphs, and larger sections of texts (such as chapters). In the Reading and Writing section, however, **Transitions** questions are focused on logical connections between and among sentences in brief passages. Let's study a Transitions example, returning to our strategy of analyzing the underlying structure of a passage to examine the relationship between the information and ideas presented and, more specifically, how the sentences themselves relate to one another.

WHAT ARE TRANSITIONS?

Transitions questions in the Reading and Writing section may offer as answer choices a range of common transition words and phrases. In linguistic terms, these take the form of conjunctions (e.g., *so, but, because*) and conjunctive adverbs (e.g., *however, as such, be that as it may*). Below is a list of some such transitions, though the list is only partial.

Accordingly	For example (for instance)	Moreover
Additionally	For that reason	Nevertheless (nonetheless)
After all	Furthermore	On the contrary
As a result	Hence	On the other hand
As such	In addition	So
Be that as it may	In conclusion (in the end)	Specifically
Because		That is
But	In other words	Therefore
By contrast (in contrast)	In summary (in sum) (to sum up)	Thus
Consequently	In the meantime	To be sure
Conversely	Indeed	Yet
First (second, third, etc.)	Likewise	

Other Transitions questions may in addition or instead present options consisting of words, phrases, or even whole clauses or sentences whose transitional language is specific to the passage. You'll approach these questions the same way: looking for the answer choice that creates the most logical connection and the smoothest movement between information and ideas in the passage.

Expression of Ideas Sample Question 4

(1) Researchers believe that pieces of hull found off Oregon's coast are from a Spanish cargo ship that was lost in 1697. (2) Stories passed down among the area's Confederated Tribes of Siletz Indians support this belief. (3) _____ Siletz stories describe how blocks of beeswax, an item the ship had been carrying, began washing ashore after the ship was lost.

Which choice completes the text with the most logical transition?

A) For this reason,

B) For example,

C) However,

D) Likewise,

In our analysis, we'll omit some details to focus on the role each sentence serves. We've numbered the sentence for ease of reference, but they won't be so marked on test day.

Sentence 1:   Researchers make a claim about a discovered ship hull.

Sentence 2:   Researchers find evidence for the claim in stories.

Sentence 3:   ?

Sentence 2's main function is to provide evidence for the researchers' claim about the ship hull found off Oregon's coast. The passage makes this explicit by noting that stories of the Confederated Tribes of Siletz Indians "support" the researchers' claim.

What, then, is the role of sentence 3? Even with the blank, we can tell that that sentence offers additional detail about how the stories support the researchers' claim. It notes that stories about blocks of beeswax appearing on the shore align with the fact that the wrecked ship was carrying beeswax as cargo. In other words, sentence 3 provides a particular case in which the Siletz Indians' stories (sentence 2) support the researchers' claim (sentence 1).

Returning to our sketch of the passage's structure, we might update it as follows.

Sentence 1:   Researchers make a claim about a discovered ship hull.

Sentence 2:   Researchers find evidence for the claim in stories.

Sentence 3:   _____, these stories' description of beeswax blocks offers evidence for the claim.

We've left the blank where the transition word or phrase is needed. Since sentence 3 is a specific case of the general point made in sentence 2 about Siletz Indians' stories, we should expect to select the answer choice that most clearly signals that relationship.

STRATEGY

When answering Transitions questions, it can be helpful to consider the role of each sentence within the associated passage. In doing so, you can leave out or paraphrase some of the passage's details, as we've done here, in order to focus on the passage's underlying structure.

STRATEGY

While the sentences won't be numbered on test day, remember you can use the Highlights & Notes tool to annotate passages yourself if tips like these are helpful to you.

After we consider the answer choices, choice B emerges as the best option. "For example" makes good sense as a transition phrase here because sentence 3 can be read as a particular instance (example) of how the stories referred to in sentence 2 support the researchers' claim in sentence 1.

Choice A is incorrect. "For this reason" implies that the fact that Siletz Indians' stories support the researchers' claim led to the existence of particular stories describing beeswax blocks washing up on shore, which makes no sense in context. Choice C is incorrect because "however" implies that sentence 3 somehow contradicts or undermines sentence 2, which, as we've observed, isn't the case. Choice D is also incorrect. "Likewise" implies that Siletz Indians' stories in general (sentence 2) and their stories about beeswax blocks (sentence 3) are two separate if similar ("like") things supporting the researchers' claim. As we noted earlier, though, sentence 3 elaborates on sentence 2—we could say that sentence 3 is subordinate to sentence 2—and so it doesn't represent a second distinct example of support for the researchers' claim.

Now let's wrap up this chapter with one more Transitions example. We'll again number elements within the passage for ease of reference in our discussion.

Expression of Ideas Sample Question 5

> (1) Seismologists Kaiqing Yuan and Barbara Romanowicz have proposed that the magma fueling Iceland's more than 30 active volcano systems emerges from deep within Earth. (2) The great depths involved—nearly 3,000 km—mark Iceland's volcanoes as extreme outliers; (3) _____ many of Earth's volcanoes are fed by shallow pockets of magma found less than 15 km below the surface.
>
> Which choice completes the text with the most logical transition?
>
> A) consequently,
>
> B) in addition,
>
> C) indeed,
>
> D) nevertheless,

Let's once again sketch out the relationships among the passage's statements, leaving a blank where the transition word or phrase would appear.

Sentence 1:   Researchers make a claim about Iceland's active volcanoes.

Sentence 2:   The great depth of Iceland's active volcanoes makes them extreme outliers.

Sentence 3:   _____, many active volcanoes are much shallower than Iceland's.

The key task here is to ascertain the role of sentence 3 in relation to sentence 2 and the passage as a whole. Sentence 2 tells us that Iceland's active volcanoes are "extreme outliers" because of their great depth, while sentence 3 informs us that many active volcanoes are much shallower than Iceland's. From this, we realize that sentence 3 amplifies, or strengthens, the point made in sentence 2 by providing more details about shallower active volcanoes.

This might sound like another case in which sentence 3 provides a specific example in support of sentence 2, but that's not quite the case (and "for example" or something similar isn't an answer choice). Rather, sentence 3 essentially restates the point made in sentence 2, only this time with more specifics.

This makes choice C the best answer here. "Indeed" is often used to signal that the statement it introduces builds on what's been written or said previously by reaffirming the underlying truth or accuracy of these previous statements. In this sense, "indeed" is roughly synonymous with a phrase such as "in reality" or "in truth." This makes good sense in the context of this passage. Sentence 2 says that Iceland's active volcanoes are extreme outliers, while sentence 3 says that "in reality" or "in truth," many other active volcanoes are shallower than Iceland's.

Choice A is incorrect. "Consequently" signals a cause-effect relationship, but it's illogical to suggest that many active volcanoes outside of Iceland draw on shallow magma pools *because* Iceland's volcanoes are extreme outliers. Choice B is also incorrect. "In addition" illogically suggests that sentence 3 describes an additional factor related to the point made in sentence 2, but, as we've observed, sentence 3 serves to amplify sentence 2, meaning sentence 3 doesn't function as a separate, distinct point in the way that "in addition" would imply. Choice D is also incorrect. "Nevertheless" suggests that sentence 3 is true despite what's presented in sentence 2, but we've noted already that this isn't the case.

Summary: Expression of Ideas Questions

Main purpose: To test your ability to revise passages in order to improve how information and ideas are conveyed

Proportion of the test section: About 20 percent (eight to twelve questions)

Question types

- Rhetorical Synthesis: Selectively use and combine provided information and ideas in order to meet specified writerly goals

- Transitions: Provide the most logical transition in order to link information and ideas in passages

CHAPTER 16

Reading and Writing: Questions—Expression of Ideas Drills

1

While researching a topic, a student has taken the following notes:

- Annie Wu is a prominent American flutist who graduated from the New England Conservatory.

- She has won multiple national flute competitions.

- She is best known for a 2011 YouTube video that has been viewed over two million times.

- The video shows her performing *Three Beats for Beatbox Flute,* an original work by composer Greg Pattillo.

- Wu combines flute playing and beatboxing in the video.

The student wants to emphasize Wu's most well-known achievement. Which choice most effectively uses relevant information from the notes to accomplish this goal?

A) Among her many achievements, prominent American flutist Annie Wu graduated from the New England Conservatory and has won multiple national flute competitions.

B) Annie Wu is best known for a 2011 YouTube video performance of *Three Beats for Beatbox Flute* that has been viewed over two million times.

C) Composer Greg Pattillo's original work *Three Beats for Beatbox Flute* combines flute playing and beatboxing.

D) Annie Wu, who has won multiple national flute competitions, has also combined flute playing and beatboxing.

2

While researching a topic, a student has taken the following notes:

- A thermal inversion is a phenomenon where a layer of atmosphere is warmer than the layer beneath it.

- In 2022, a team of researchers studied the presence of thermal inversions in twenty-five gas giants.

- Gas giants are planets largely composed of helium and hydrogen.

- The team found that gas giants featuring a thermal inversion were also likely to contain heat-absorbing metals.

- One explanation for this relationship is that these metals may reside in a planet's upper atmosphere, where their absorbed heat causes an increase in temperature.

The student wants to present the study's findings to an audience already familiar with thermal inversions. Which choice most effectively uses relevant information from the notes to accomplish this goal?

A) Gas giants were likely to contain heat-absorbing metals when they featured a layer of atmosphere warmer than the layer beneath it, researchers found; this phenomenon is known as a thermal inversion.

B) The team studied thermal inversions in twenty-five gas giants, which are largely composed of helium and hydrogen.

C) Researchers found that gas giants featuring a thermal inversion were likely to contain heat-absorbing metals, which may reside in the planets' upper atmospheres.

D) Heat-absorbing metals may reside in a planet's upper atmosphere.

3

While researching a topic, a student has taken the following notes:

- Muckrakers were journalists who sought to expose corruption in US institutions during the Progressive Era (1897–1920).

- Ida Tarbell was a muckraker who investigated the Standard Oil Company.

- She interviewed Standard Oil Company executives, oil industry workers, and public officials.

- She examined thousands of pages of the company's internal communications, including letters and financial records.

- Her book *The History of the Standard Oil Company* (1904) exposed the company's unfair business practices.

The student wants to emphasize the thoroughness of Ida Tarbell's investigation of the Standard Oil Company. Which choice most effectively uses relevant information from the notes to accomplish this goal?

A) Ida Tarbell not only interviewed Standard Oil executives, oil industry workers, and public officials but also examined thousands of pages of the company's internal communications.

B) As part of her investigation of the Standard Oil Company, muckraker Ida Tarbell conducted interviews.

C) Published in 1904, muckraker Ida Tarbell's book *The History of the Standard Oil Company* exposed the company's unfair business practices.

D) Ida Tarbell, who investigated the Standard Oil Company, was a muckraker (a journalist who sought to expose corruption in US institutions during the Progressive Era, 1897–1920).

4

While researching a topic, a student has taken the following notes:

- Platinum is a rare and expensive metal.

- It is used as a catalyst for chemical reactions.

- Platinum catalysts typically require a large amount of platinum to be effective.

- Researcher Jianbo Tang and his colleagues created a platinum catalyst that combines platinum with liquid gallium.

- Their catalyst was highly effective and required only trace amounts of platinum (0.0001% of the atoms in the mixture).

The student wants to explain an advantage of the new platinum catalyst developed by Jianbo Tang and his colleagues. Which choice most effectively uses relevant information from the notes to accomplish this goal?

A) Like other platinum catalysts, the new platinum catalyst requires a particular amount of the metal to be effective.

B) While still highly effective, the new platinum catalyst requires far less of the rare and expensive metal than do other platinum catalysts.

C) Platinum is a rare and expensive metal that is used as a catalyst for chemical reactions; however, platinum catalysts typically require a large amount of platinum to be effective.

D) Researcher Jianbo Tang and his colleagues created a platinum catalyst that combines platinum, a rare and expensive metal, with liquid gallium.

5

While researching a topic, a student has taken the following notes:

- *Puntius javanicus* is a species of commercially raised fish.
- Researchers in Indonesia recently found that adding pineapple extract to fish food increased both the feed utilization efficiency and the growth rate of *P. javanicus*.
- Adding the pineapple extract did not affect total food consumption.
- The researchers thus determined that the increased growth rate resulted from the increased feed utilization efficiency.
- The enzyme bromelain in pineapple extract enhances the hydrolysis of ingested proteins.
- This allows the fish to more readily absorb them.

The student wants to explain how pineapple extract increased the growth rate of *P. javanicus*. Which choice most effectively uses relevant information from the notes to accomplish this goal?

A) Researchers in Indonesia recently found that adding pineapple extract to fish food increased the growth rate of *P. javanicus*.

B) An enzyme in pineapple extract, bromelain increased the growth rate of *P. javanicus* by enhancing the hydrolysis of ingested proteins, in turn affecting the fish's total food consumption.

C) According to the researchers, the growth rate of *P. javanicus* was affected not by food consumption but by feed utilization efficiency.

D) The enzyme bromelain enhanced *P. javanicus*'s absorption of ingested proteins, increasing the growth rate of fish fed pineapple extract.

6

A 2017 study of sign language learners tested the role of iconicity—the similarity of a sign to the thing it represents—in language acquisition. The study found that the greater the iconicity of a sign, the more likely it was to have been learned. _____ the correlation between acquisition and iconicity was lower than that between acquisition and another factor studied: sign frequency.

Which choice completes the text with the most logical transition?

A) In fact,

B) In other words,

C) Granted,

D) As a result,

7

Before the 1847 introduction of the US postage stamp, the cost of postage was usually paid by the recipient of a letter rather than the sender, and recipients were not always able or willing to pay promptly. _____ collecting this fee could be slow and arduous, and heaps of unpaid-for, undeliverable mail piled up in post offices.

Which choice completes the text with the most logical transition?

A) Regardless,

B) On the contrary,

C) Consequently,

D) For example,

8

The number of dark spots that appear on the Sun, known as sunspots, can vary greatly. For example, there were about 180 sunspots in November 2001. _____ there were only about 2 sunspots in December 2008.

Which choice completes the text with the most logical transition?

A) In other words,

B) Similarly,

C) Therefore,

D) By comparison,

9

It has long been thought that humans first crossed a land bridge into the Americas approximately 13,000 years ago. _____ based on radiocarbon dating of samples uncovered in Mexico, a research team recently suggested that humans may have arrived more than 30,000 years ago—much earlier than previously thought.

Which choice completes the text with the most logical transition?

A) As a result,

B) Similarly,

C) However,

D) In conclusion,

10

The writer Henry James (1843–1916) was known for revising his novels and stories substantially after their initial publication, often altering dialogue, expanding descriptions of characters, and including prefaces in later editions of his works. _____ in the case of James's novel *A Portrait of a Lady*, some critics regard the 1881 first edition and the 1908 revised edition as essentially two different novels.

A) Indeed, the disparities between editions could be quite stark;

B) However, this wasn't the case for all of James's published works;

C) In particular, James's prefaces introduce each work to new readers;

D) Even so, his novels and stories continue to be lauded by critics;

Answer Explanations

QUESTION 1

Choice B is the best answer because it most effectively emphasizes Wu's most well-known achievement. This choice focuses directly on her 2011 YouTube video performance of *Three Beats for Beatbox Flute*, which the passage identifies as her best-known accomplishment.

Choices A and *D* are incorrect because although each choice mentions some of Wu's accomplishments, neither choice mentions her 2011 YouTube video performance of *Three Beats for Beatbox Flute*, which the passage identifies as what Wu is best known for. *Choice C* is incorrect because it doesn't mention Wu at all.

QUESTION 2

Choice C is the best answer because it most effectively presents the study's findings to an audience already familiar with thermal inversions. This choice presents the findings of the study without unnecessarily explaining what thermal inversions are.

Choice A is incorrect because it focuses on explaining what thermal inversions are, which is unnecessary for an audience already familiar with the concept. *Choice B* is incorrect because it describes the researchers' approach (methodology), not their findings. *Choice D* is incorrect because although it partially identifies the researchers' findings, it doesn't mention the study itself or link the information to the concept of thermal inversion.

QUESTION 3

Choice A is the best answer because it most effectively emphasizes the thoroughness of Ida Tarbell's investigation of the Standard Oil Company. This choice establishes that for *The History of the Standard Oil Company*, Tarbell interviewed many people from various occupations and reviewed a large amount of documentation.

Choice B is incorrect because it's less successful than choice A in establishing the thoroughness of Tarbell's investigation, as it mentions only that Tarbell conducted interviews (without indicating how many or what sorts of people she interviewed) and leaves out that she also analyzed a large number of documents. *Choice C* is incorrect because it merely describes *The History of the Standard Oil Company* without mentioning how much research went into writing it. *Choice D* is incorrect because it merely describes Tarbell and her work in general terms without mentioning how much research went into writing *The History of the Standard Oil Company*.

QUESTION 4

Choice B is the best answer because it most effectively explains an advantage of the new platinum catalyst developed by Jianbo Tang and his colleagues. This choice establishes such an advantage: the new catalyst is highly effective but requires much less of the rare and expensive metal platinum than do typical platinum catalysts.

Choices A and *D* are incorrect because each fails to establish an advantage of the new catalyst; choice A stresses a similarity between the new catalyst and other platinum catalysts, while choice D just describes how the new catalyst was created. *Choice C* is incorrect because it doesn't mention the new catalyst at all.

QUESTION 5

Choice D is the best answer. The sentence effectively explains how pineapple extract increased the fish's growth rate, noting that the enzyme bromelain (which is in pineapple extract) enhanced the absorption of proteins ingested by fish fed pineapple extract.

Choice A is incorrect. The sentence indicates that adding pineapple extract to fish food increased the fish's growth rate; it does not explain how this was accomplished. *Choice B* is incorrect. While the sentence appears to explain how pineapple extract increased the fish's growth rate, it misrepresents the information provided about the effect on the fish's food consumption. As the notes indicate, adding the pineapple extract did not affect total food consumption. *Choice C* is incorrect. The sentence discusses the fish's growth rate but does not indicate how pineapple extract increased that rate.

QUESTION 6

Choice C is the best answer because it completes the text with the most logical transition. The sentence with the blank concedes that sign frequency was found to be more important for sign language acquisition than was iconicity, the factor that the previous two sentences discuss. "Granted" means "admittedly" and would logically signal the kind of concession that the passage makes here.

Choice A is incorrect because "in fact" means "in truth" and would serve to emphasize the correctness of the previous sentences by adding new, amplifying details, which is roughly the opposite of the function the sentence with the blank actually performs in the passage. *Choice B* is incorrect because "in other words" would signal that the sentence with the blank restates in simpler language what's already been said in the passage, whereas the sentence with the blank offers a new piece of information. *Choice D* is incorrect because "as a result" would signal that the sentence with the blank describes the effect of a cause described in the previous sentences, whereas the sentence with a blank offers a concession.

QUESTION 7

Choice C is the best answer because it completes the text with the most logical transition. The sentence with the blank describes two effects—slow fee collection and "heaps" of undeliverable mail—that resulted from the past practice of having the recipient rather than the sender typically pay for postage. "Consequently" means "as a result" and would logically signal this cause-effect relationship.

Choice A is incorrect because "regardless" means "despite everything" and would signal that the sentence with the blank is true in spite of what's described in the previous sentence, whereas the sentence with the blank logically follows from what's already been presented in the passage. *Choice B* is incorrect because "on the contrary" means "just the opposite" and would signal that the sentence with the blank contradicts the previous sentence, whereas the sentence with the blank logically follows from what's already been presented in the passage. *Choice D* is incorrect because "for example" would signal that the sentence with the blank is an example of the situation described in the previous sentence, whereas the sentence with the blank describes a consequence of what's already been presented in the passage.

QUESTION 8

Choice D is the best answer because it completes the text with the most logical transition. The sentence with the blank completes a comparison between the number of sunspots in November 2001 and in December 2008. "By comparison" would logically signal this comparative relationship.

Choice A is incorrect because "in other words" would signal that the sentence with the blank restates in simpler language what's already been said in the passage, whereas the sentence with the blank provides a point of contrast. *Choice B* is incorrect because "similarly" would signal that what's described in the sentence with the blank is comparable to what's described in the previous sentences, whereas the sentence with the blank provides a point of contrast. *Choice C* is incorrect because "therefore" would signal a cause-effect relationship between the sentence with the blank and the previous sentences, whereas the sentence with the blank provides a point of contrast.

QUESTION 9

Choice C is the best answer because it completes the text with the most logical transition. The sentence with the blank offers evidence that contradicts the previous sentence's assertion that humans first crossed a land bridge into the Americas around 13,000 years ago. "However" means "in spite of that" and would logically signal this contrastive relationship.

Choice A is incorrect because "as a result" would signal a cause-effect relationship between the two sentences in the passage, whereas the sentence with the blank contradicts the previous sentence. *Choice B* is incorrect because "similarly" would signal that the sentence with the blank makes an assertion comparable to the one described in the previous sentence, whereas the sentence with the blank contradicts the previous sentence's assertion. *Choice D* is incorrect because "in conclusion" would signal that the sentence with the blank neatly wraps up the discussion begun in the previous sentence, but this makes no sense in context given that the sentence with the blank contradicts the previous sentence.

QUESTION 10

Choice A is the best answer because it completes the text with the most logical transition. The passage's first sentence indicates that Henry James frequently revised his novels and stories extensively after publication, while the passage's last sentence, which contains the blank, provides an example of one such novel that James heavily revised. "Indeed," which here means "in reality," properly signals that the second sentence amplifies, or builds on, the claim made in the first sentence with an example, while "the disparities between editions could be quite stark" closely aligns with the last sentence's example, which contends that the two editions of *A Portrait of a Lady* differ so much that some critics regard them as "essentially two different novels."

Choice B is incorrect because "However, this wasn't the case for all of James's published works" fails to properly set up the last sentence's example, which contends that some critics view the two editions of *A Portrait of a Lady* as "essentially two different novels." *Choice C* is incorrect because "In particular, James's prefaces introduce each work to new readers" is a random assertion that does not serve as an effective transition between the passage's two sentences. *Choice D* is incorrect because "Even so, his novels and stories continued to be lauded by critics" fails to create an adequate transition between the passage's two sentences. Although the passage's last sentence mentions critics, it does so to offer support for the first sentence's claim that James often heavily revised his novels and stories after publication, not to make a general claim that critics continue to be impressed by James's novels and stories.

CHAPTER 17

Reading and Writing: Questions—Standard English Conventions

Reading and Writing questions in the **Standard English Conventions** content domain are designed to test your ability to edit passages so that they conform to core conventions of Standard English sentence structure, usage, and punctuation. There are two main areas of focus in Standard English Conventions questions: ensuring that sentences are conventionally complete and applying a range of usage and punctuation conventions.

Proportion of the Test Section

About 26 percent of the Reading and Writing section is made up of Standard English Conventions questions. This translates to **eleven to fifteen Standard English Conventions questions** per test form.

Overview of Standard English Conventions Question Types

The Standard English Conventions content domain includes two main question types, each with several subtypes:

- **Boundaries** questions, which test your ability to form conventionally complete sentences.

- **Form, Structure, and Sense** questions, which test your ability to edit text to conform to core usage and punctuation conventions.

All questions in this content domain (and in the Reading and Writing section in general) are multiple-choice in format. Each question has a single best answer (*key*) and three incorrect answer choices (*distractors*) that represent common errors students make when answering such questions. All the information needed to answer each question is in the passage, so you won't need prior knowledge of the passages' topics to successfully answer associated questions.

"STANDARD ENGLISH" AND "CONVENTIONS"

Before we start examining test questions in this content domain, we need to be clear on a few key concepts.

Standard English is a specific form of formal English that's typically expected in academic and workplace settings. Because Standard English is widely understood and employed in these settings, it's useful as a tool of communication. Standard English isn't the only variety of English, and other forms of English are equally rich and sophisticated, but questions in the Reading and Writing section will only test your understanding of Standard English because of that variety's connection to college and career readiness expectations.

Conventions in the sense we use the term here describe the "rules" of Standard English. We put the word "rules" in quotation marks because these conventions aren't absolute and unchanging directives but rather agreed-on ways that most users of Standard English adopt to express things. For instance, one expectation of writers using Standard English is that their sentences will express complete thoughts and conform to certain requirements about how sentences are structured and marked with punctuation, such as the inclusion of ending punctuation (periods, question marks, and exclamation points) to denote the conclusion of a sentence. Knowing and applying these conventions makes writing (and, to some extent, speaking) more understandable to others who also know these conventions. In a real sense, the use of conventions is less about conforming to "rules" than it is about enhancing the communicative power of text. To underline that point, all Standard English Conventions questions in the Reading and Writing section appear within realistic contexts, and your task is to edit these contexts to ensure that they exhibit conventional sentence structure, usage, and punctuation.

Because conventions are simply (informal) agreements among writers and speakers about how to express ideas in standard ways, these conventions can—and do—change over time. A commonly cited example of this is the increasing acceptance of the use of the pronouns *they*, *them*, and *theirs* to refer to single individuals. A few language traditionalists still insist that such constructions as "a person . . . they" are incorrect, but the truth is that widely used languages, such as English, grow and evolve over time, and "singular *they*," as this usage is sometimes referred to, has come into much wider acceptance as part of Standard English. (From a linguistic standpoint, singular *they* actually fills a gap that otherwise exists in Standard English: the lack of a set of gender-neutral singular pronouns.)

The important thing to know here is that we won't ask you to try to apply conventions that are contested or rapidly changing. This means, to continue our previous example, that we won't test you on whether "they" is singular or plural in reference to a person whose gender hasn't been identified (and, to the fullest extent possible, we use the pronouns the individuals mentioned in our passages themselves employ).

PREPARING TO ANSWER STANDARD ENGLISH CONVENTIONS QUESTIONS

It's beyond the scope of this chapter to teach you the conventions of Standard English. In working through the sample questions in this chapter, we'll also try to keep grammatical terms to a minimum.

Should you, after reading this chapter, feel the need to brush up on some of the conventions, Khan Academy, which hosts Official SAT Prep (**khanacademy.org/digital-sat**), has a number of resources dedicated to teaching you about these conventions. Your English language arts textbook (if your class uses one) may also have a grammar, usage, and mechanics section. Numerous other resources are also available in print and digital forms.

Standard English Conventions Questions in Detail

In this section, we'll discuss both Standard English Conventions question types in detail. We'll describe the general purpose of each type so that you understand better how to approach such questions on test day. We'll also discuss the various subtypes of questions in each of these categories. As part of this discussion, we'll walk through some sample questions for each type so that you get a clear indication of the kinds of skills and knowledge required to answer questions of a given type.

Boundaries Questions

Boundaries questions test your ability to apply your understanding of Standard English conventions to ensure that sentences in test passages are conventionally complete. By *conventionally complete*, we mean that the sentences express complete thoughts, are structured in standard ways, and are set off from other sentences by appropriate punctuation.

Questions of this type may ask you to edit sentences in a variety of ways, some of which we'll illustrate below.

Standard English Conventions Sample Question 1

In the novel *Things Fall Apart* by Chinua Achebe, Okonkwo is a leader of Umuofia (a fictional Nigerian clan) and takes pride in his culture's traditions. However, when the arrival of European missionaries brings changes to Umuofia, the novel asks a central question: How _____

Which choice completes the text so that it conforms to the conventions of Standard English?

A) will Umuofia's traditions be affected?

B) Umuofia's traditions will be affected?

C) Umuofia's traditions will be affected.

D) will Umuofia's traditions be affected.

This question tests your ability to differentiate between two types of sentences: *declarative* sentences, which convey information and end with periods, and *interrogative* sentences, which pose questions and end with question marks.

The passage tells you, via "central question," that the statement in which the blank appears should be framed as a question (interrogative sentence).

To make this point clearer, consider the statement written in both declarative and interrogative forms.

> *Declarative:* Umuofia's traditions will be affected (in some unspecified way).

> *Interrogative:* How will Umuofia's traditions be affected?

You can observe that not only does the sentence's end punctuation differ between the two versions, but the word order (syntax) also changes.

Since we're told we're looking for a question here, let's consider choices A and B, which are framed as questions. Choice A results in "How will Umuofia's traditions be affected?" This choice matches our analysis and is the best answer because it's the conventionally appropriate choice. Although choice B is similarly presented as a question, it's not in standard interrogative form. "How Umuofia's traditions will be affected?" isn't a conventional way to phrase a question such as this, so choice B can be ruled out as incorrect. Choices C and D are presented as declarative, rather than interrogative, sentences, so we can quickly rule those options out as incorrect.

Standard English Conventions Sample Question 2

> Humans were long thought to have begun occupying the Peruvian settlement of Machu Picchu between 1440 and 1450 CE. However, a team led by anthropologist Dr. Richard Burger used accelerator mass spectrometry to uncover evidence that it was occupied _____ 1420 CE, according to Burger, humans were likely inhabiting the area.
>
> Which choice completes the text so that it conforms to the conventions of Standard English?
>
> A) earlier, which in
>
> B) earlier, in
>
> C) earlier. In
>
> D) earlier in

STRATEGY

Sometimes your "ear" for language may help you recognize obviously incorrect sentence structures. Even if that isn't always the case, it's still a good idea to (silently) read the various answer choices into the sentence by substituting them for the blank.

This question asks you to consider how best to join or separate two statements using words and sometimes punctuation. The passage makes two assertions, one before and one after the blank. To paraphrase:

> Researchers discovered that Machu Picchu was occupied earlier (than 1440–1450 CE).

> In 1420 CE, humans were inhabiting the area.

Choice C is the best answer because turning these two ideas into two separate, complete sentences is one conventional and effective way to structure the information.

The other answer choices violate convention in differing ways. Choice A would result in "it was occupied earlier, which in 1420 CE . . . humans were likely inhabiting the area," which is ungrammatical. *Which* is a relative pronoun, but in this case, it wouldn't precisely refer to anything (i.e., would lack a clear antecedent) in the preceding clause. The relative clause introduced by *which* would also be nonstandard. Choice B is incorrect because it results in a comma splice: two complete sentences joined only by a comma. Choice D is incorrect because it results in a run-on sentence: two complete sentences fused together without an appropriate conjunction and/or punctuation.

Standard English Conventions Sample Question 3

In a 2016 study, Eastern Washington University psychologist Amani El-Alayli found that, among the study participants who experienced frisson (a physiological response akin to goosebumps or getting the chills) while listening to music, there was one personality trait that they scored particularly _____ openness to experience.

Which choice completes the text so that it conforms to the conventions of Standard English?

A) high on;

B) high on

C) high. On

D) high on:

You may find this question more challenging than the previous two examples because it tests, in part, the appropriate use of colons and semicolons to link ideas. Colons and semicolons aren't common in informal writing and even in many published texts, but they make frequent appearance in academic (and, to a lesser extent, formal workplace) writing because they offer powerful ways to establish connections between and among ideas. The colon, for example, can be used to introduce a word, phrase, clause, or sentence (or more than one of these) that directly builds or elaborates on the statement made before the colon. This second word, phrase, clause, or sentence can be an example, a definition, a clarification, a restatement, or the like. A semicolon, on the other hand, can be used to join two (or, less commonly, more) closely related sentences. Its effect is a little different from that of the colon because the semicolon suggests that the two (or more) sentences so connected carry equal weight, whereas the colon implies that what follows that punctuation mark is subordinate to (e.g., exemplifies, defines, clarifies, restates) the statement made before the colon.

Let's turn now to our answer choices for this question. It turns out that choice D, which employs the colon, is the best answer here. The phrase "openness to experience" clarifies what "personality trait" El-Alayli found to be closely associated with study participants who experienced frisson while listening to music.

Choice A is incorrect because a semicolon can't be used in this way to join an independent clause (beginning with "Eastern Washington University") to a phrase ("openness to experience"). As we previously mentioned, conventional use of the semicolon in this manner involves linking two (or more) closely related sentences, not two unequal sentence elements, such as (in this case) an independent clause and a phrase. Choice B is incorrect because some sort of punctuation is required between the independent clause beginning with "Eastern Washington University" and the phrase "openness to experience"; otherwise, the two ideas being expressed run together in a nonstandard and confusing way. Choice C is incorrect because the period after "high" results in two rhetorically unacceptable sentence fragments, one beginning with "in a 2016 study" and the other with "on openness."

Form, Structure, and Sense Questions

The second and final type of Standard English Conventions question consists of those in the **Form, Structure, and Sense** category. Questions of this type ask you to apply your knowledge of Standard English usage and punctuation conventions to a range of tasks. Specifically, these questions test

- subject-verb agreement.

- pronoun-antecedent agreement.

- verb finiteness (i.e., making contextually appropriate uses of verbs and verbals [gerunds, participles, and infinitives]).

- verb tense and aspect (i.e., making contextually proper choice of verb tense and aspect).

- subject-modifier placement (i.e., making contextually appropriate placement of modifying elements in sentences).

- genitives and plurals (i.e., distinguishing between plural and possessive nouns and pronouns as well as among commonly confused possessive determiners, contractions, and adverbs (e.g., *its* vs. *it's*; *their* vs. *they're* vs. *there*).

> **NOTE**
>
> In published writing, especially literature, sentence fragments (incomplete sentences) are sometimes used for dramatic effect.
>
> Like this, for example.
>
> Standard English Conventions questions, however, won't offer a sentence fragment as the best answer.

We provide an example and discussion of each of these question subtypes below.

Standard English Conventions Sample Question 4

Wanda Diaz-Merced, an astrophysicist who is blind, has developed software that can translate astrophysical data into sound. Such tools _____ astrophysicists to detect subtle patterns in data—patterns that may not be evident in graphs and other visual formats.

Which choice completes the text so that it conforms to the conventions of Standard English?

A) has enabled

B) enable

C) is enabling

D) enables

This question primarily tests **subject-verb agreement**. When we talk about subjects and verbs agreeing, we mean that they have the same number: singular subjects take singular verbs, and plural subjects take plural verbs. Sometimes, as in this example, subject and verb are close together in the sentence, so it's fairly easy to find a match. In more challenging questions, however, the subject and verb may be separated by other words, phrases, and clauses, which makes maintaining the link harder. Sometimes this intervening text may seem to suggest a different number for the verb than is required by the subject itself. In a few cases, a verb may even come before its subject. These questions, though, are still answered the same way: by keeping track of the subject and ensuring that it agrees (matches) in number with the verb.

In this question, choice B is the best answer. The subject of the sentence with the blank is "tools," which is plural, and "enable" is a plural verb. Choices A, C, and D are incorrect because "has enabled," "is enabling," and "enables" are singular verbs that don't agree in number with the plural subject.

Standard English Conventions Sample Question 5

Official measurements of the Mississippi River's length vary: according to the US Geologic Survey, the river is 2,300 miles long, whereas the Environmental Protection Agency records its length as 2,320 miles. This disparity can be explained in part by the fact that rivers such as the Mississippi expand and contract as _____ sediment.

Which choice completes the text so that it conforms to the conventions of Standard English?

A) one accumulates

B) they accumulate

C) it accumulates

D) we accumulate

This question primarily tests **pronoun-antecedent agreement**. In Standard English, pronouns are expected to agree in number (singular, plural) and person (first person, second person, third person) with the antecedents they refer to. Note that antecedents typically come before the pronouns that rename them, but this isn't always the case.

Choice B is the best answer here. The antecedent for the pronoun that is to complete the text is "rivers," which is plural, and the plural pronoun "they" is the conventionally correct one to use to refer to a plural noun such as "rivers." Choice A is incorrect because "one" is singular, not plural. ("One" in this sense is typically used to refer to a generic person or thing, such as "One really ought to practice for the SAT.") Choice C is incorrect because "it," too, is singular. Choice D is incorrect because although "we" is plural, it doesn't make any sense in context to refer to "rivers" as "we." (Put slightly more technically, "we" is a first person pronoun, and all nouns referring to things take third person pronouns.)

Standard English Conventions Sample Question 6

In 1990, California native and researcher Ellen Ochoa left her position as chief of the Intelligent Systems Technology Branch at a NASA research center _____ the space agency's astronaut training program.

Which choice completes the text so that it conforms to the conventions of Standard English?

A) to join

B) is joining

C) joined

D) joins

This question primarily tests **verb finiteness**. *Finite verbs* are your average, garden-variety verbs. In a technical sense, verbs are finite when they agree with a subject and take a tense, such as past or present. Finite verbs contrast with a category of words known as *verbals*, which include gerunds (verbs functioning as nouns), participles (verbs functioning as adjectives or that are used as part of compound verbs [e.g., "is walking"]), and infinitives (base forms of verbs, such as "[to] be," that lack the characteristics of agreement or tense and that are used as nouns, adjectives, or adverbs). Conventional sentences require that there be at least one finite verb. Problems with verb finiteness arise when a sentence mistakenly uses a verbal in place of a finite verb, leaving the sentence either incomplete or poorly structured, and when finite verbs are used when verbals are instead called for.

In this case, choice A is the best answer because the context requires the use of the infinitive "to join." This infinitive signals Ochoa's intent in leaving one job for another and results in a conventional expression ("Ochoa left . . . to join"). Choices B, C, and D are incorrect because "is joining," "joined," and "joins" are finite verbs, whereas the context requires the infinitive "to join."

Standard English Conventions Sample Question 7

After winning the 1860 presidential election, Abraham Lincoln appointed Edward Bates, Salmon P. Chase, and William H. Seward to his cabinet. Lincoln's decision was surprising, since each of these men had run against him, but historians have praised it, noting that Lincoln _____ his rivals' diverse talents to strengthen his administration.

Which choice completes the text so that it conforms to the conventions of Standard English?

A) will leverage

B) is leveraging

C) has leveraged

D) leveraged

This question primarily tests **verb tense and aspect**. Verb *tense* identifies whether the verb describes something in the past, present, or future. Verb *aspect* can refine tense by adding a specific indication of whether the action took place once, more than once, or progressively over time. The basic guideline here is that verb tense and aspect have to make sense in context. You don't want a past tense verb to describe present action, for instance, nor do you want to use a verb in, say, the simple past tense (e.g., "ran") when the action took place over an extended time (e.g., "was running").

In this question, the best answer is choice D. The context describes how Lincoln made use of his rivals' talents by appointing several of his former opponents to his cabinet. This event occurred one time in the past (around 1860), so the simple past tense verb "leveraged" makes the most sense.

Choices A, B, and C are incorrect because the simple future tense verb "will leverage," the present progressive verb "is leveraging," and the present perfect verb "has leveraged" are inappropriate in this context, which describes a onetime historical event.

Standard English Conventions Sample Question 8

> In 2015, a team led by materials scientists Anirudha Sumant and Diana Berman succeeded in reducing the coefficient of friction (COF) between two surfaces to the lowest possible level—superlubricity. A nearly frictionless (and, as its name suggests, extremely slippery) state,
>
> _____
>
> Which choice completes the text so that it conforms to the conventions of Standard English?
>
> A) reaching superlubricity occurs when two surfaces' COF drops below 0.01.
>
> B) superlubricity is reached when two surfaces' COF drops below 0.01.
>
> C) when their COF drops below 0.01, two surfaces reach superlubricity.
>
> D) two surfaces, when their COF drops below 0.01, reach superlubricity.

This question primarily tests **subject-modifier placement**. Standard English conventions dictate that modifiers be placed as close as possible to the elements of the sentence they modify. Failure to meet this expectation often results in confusing—and sometimes unintentionally amusing—sentences in which the modifier appears to modify something other than what was intended.

In this question, "a nearly frictionless . . . state" is a phrase intended to modify, or describe, superlubricity. To construct this sentence in a conventional way, the modifying phrase should appear as close as possible to the word it modifies. This is accomplished by choice B, which is the best answer.

Choices A, C, and D are incorrect because they illogically result in "a nearly frictionless . . . state" modifying "reaching superlubricity" (choice A) and "two surfaces" (choices C and D). (In slightly more technical terms, "a nearly frictionless . . . state" becomes a dangling modifier under these circumstances.)

Sample Standard English Conventions Question 9

> When they were first discovered in Australia in 1798, duck-billed, beaver-tailed platypuses so defied categorization that one scientist assigned them the name *Ornithorhynchus paradoxus*: "paradoxical birdsnout." The animal, which lays eggs but also nurses _____ young with milk, has since been classified as belonging to the monotremes group.
>
> Which choice completes the text so that it conforms to the conventions of Standard English?
>
> A) it's
>
> B) their
>
> C) they're
>
> D) its

This question primarily tests appropriate uses of **genitives and plurals**. *Genitives* are a category of (usually) nouns with a range of uses, but for the purposes of answering questions in the Reading and Writing section, genitives are functionally equivalent to possessives— that is, they indicate that something "owns" something else, whether literally ("Alex's jacket") or more loosely, as in a trait ("Sofia's skill"). Essentially, this subtype of Form, Structure, and Sense questions asks you to knowledgeably distinguish among

- possessive nouns.

- plural nouns.

- the possessive determiners (sometimes called *possessive pronouns* and, occasionally, *possessive adjectives*) *my, your, his, her, its, our,* and *their.*

- the contractions *it's,* frequently confused with the possessive determiner *its,* and *they're,* frequently confused with the possessive determiner *their* or the adverb *there.*

The technical distinctions among these categories are fairly easy to grasp, but it's (its?) their (there? they're??) application that messes up many people, including some highly educated people and skilled writers. That's due in part to the fact that *its* and *it's* as well as *their, they're,* and *there* are indistinguishable to the ear and because *its* and *their* break the typical pattern of possessives in English, which generally take an apostrophe.

One common misapplication of genitives is sometimes described as the "grocer's apostrophe," so called because this category of error often appears in signs for the sale of such items as "banana's" and "apple's." The distinctions between *its* (determiner) and *it's* (contraction) as well as among *their* (determiner), *there* (adverb), and *they're* (contraction) are just things one has to learn to apply consistently, although asking yourself what function a given frequently confused word performs in a particular sentence can help you spot or avoid errors.

Back to the sample question. We want to know which of the answer choices should precede the noun "young," as in offspring. This is a possessive (genitive) relationship—in a loose sense, the animal (platypus) "owns" its offspring—so the best answer here is the singular possessive determiner *its,* which is choice D.

Choices A and C are incorrect because "it's" and "they're" are contractions, not possessive determiners. Choice B is incorrect because although "their" is a possessive determiner, it's a plural one and therefore doesn't agree with the singular antecedent "animal."

STRATEGY

If you're one of the many people who struggle making these distinctions consistently in your writing, consider what role the word plays in the sentence. The possessive determiner *its,* for example, identifies "ownership" and typically precedes a noun (e.g., "its color is red"), whereas the contraction *it's* is a shortened form of either "it is" or "it has." One way to double-check whether *it's* rather than *its* is appropriate in context is to "read out" the contraction. "It is color is red" makes no sense, so *its* should be used instead. The same can be done with *they're* and *their.*

Summary: Standard English Conventions

Main purpose: To test your ability to edit passages so that they conform to core conventions of Standard English sentence structure, usage, and punctuation

Proportion of the test section: About 26 percent (eleven to fifteen questions)

Question types

- Boundaries: Form conventionally complete sentences

- Form, Structure, and Sense: Edit text to conform to core usage and punctuation conventions

CHAPTER 18

Reading and Writing: Questions—Standard English Conventions Drills

1

In 1959, marine biologist Dr. Albert Jones founded the Underwater Adventure Seekers, a scuba diving _____ that is the oldest club for Black divers in the United States and that has helped thousands of diving enthusiasts become certified in the field.

Which choice completes the text so that it conforms to the conventions of Standard English?

A) club

B) club, and

C) club—

D) club,

2

Photographer Ansel Adams's landscape portraits are iconic pieces of American art. However, many of the _____ of landscapes were intended not as art but as marketing; a concessions company at Yosemite National Park had hired Adams to take pictures of the park for restaurant menus and brochures.

Which choice completes the text so that it conforms to the conventions of Standard English?

A) photographers early photo's

B) photographers early photos

C) photographer's early photos

D) photographer's early photo's

3

The field of geological oceanography owes much to American _____ Marie Tharp, a pioneering oceanographic cartographer whose detailed topographical maps of the ocean floor and its multiple rift valleys helped garner acceptance for the theories of plate tectonics and continental drift.

Which choice completes the text so that it conforms to the conventions of Standard English?

A) geologist

B) geologist:

C) geologist;

D) geologist,

4

In her book *The Woman Warrior: Memoirs of a Girlhood Among Ghosts*, author Maxine Hong Kingston examines themes _____ childhood, womanhood, and Chinese American identity by intertwining autobiography and mythology.

Which choice completes the text so that it conforms to the conventions of Standard English?

A) of—

B) of

C) of:

D) of,

5

Classical composer Florence Price's 1927 move to Chicago marked a turning point in her career. It was there that Price premiered her First Symphony—a piece that was praised for blending traditional Romantic motifs with aspects of Black folk music—and _____ supportive relationships with other Black artists.

Which choice completes the text so that it conforms to the conventions of Standard English?

A) developing

B) developed

C) having developed

D) to develop

6

A subseasonal weather forecast attempts to predict weather conditions three to four weeks in _____ its predictions are therefore more short-term than those of the seasonal forecast, which attempts to predict the weather more than a month in advance.

Which choice completes the text so that it conforms to the conventions of Standard English?

A) advance and

B) advance

C) advance,

D) advance;

7

In 1881, French chemist Camille Faure redesigned the rechargeable lead-acid battery. Faure's design greatly increased the amount of electricity that the original battery, which the French physicist Gaston Planté _____ fifteen years earlier, could hold.

Which choice completes the text so that it conforms to the conventions of Standard English?

A) is inventing

B) will invent

C) had invented

D) invents

8

The African Games Co-production Market, one of over 180 annual international conferences supporting video game development, _____ the growth of the African gaming industry by helping start-up studios in Africa find partners.

Which choice completes the text so that it conforms to the conventions of Standard English?

A) promotes

B) promote

C) are promoting

D) have promoted

Answer Explanations

QUESTION 1

Choice A is the best answer because it completes the text so that it conforms to the conventions of Standard English. The two declarative content clauses ("that is the oldest club for Black divers in the United States," "that has helped thousands of diving enthusiasts become certified in the field") are essential sentence elements used to describe the Underwater Adventure Seekers and therefore shouldn't be separated from the noun "club" by either punctuation or a conjunction.

Choices B, C, and *D* are incorrect because each separates the noun "club" from the two declarative content clauses with punctuation, a conjunction, or both. *Choice D* is also incorrect because the comma after "club" turns "a scuba diving club" into a nonrestrictive appositive of "Underwater Adventure Seekers," which is inappropriate in this context. The relative clauses that follow ("that is the oldest club for Black divers in the United States," "that has helped thousands of diving enthusiasts become certified in the field") would need to be nonrestrictive themselves and each headed by "which" to make the resultant sentence grammatical.

QUESTION 2

Choice C is the best answer because it completes the text so that it conforms to the conventions of Standard English. The singular possessive noun "photographer's" and the plural noun "photos" are appropriate to indicate that a single photographer (Ansel Adams) took many photographs.

Choices A and *B* are incorrect because the singular possessive noun "photographer's," not the plural noun "photographers," is needed in this context. *Choices A* and *D* are incorrect because the plural noun "photos," not the singular possessive noun "photo's," is needed in this context.

QUESTION 3

Choice A is the best answer because it completes the text so that it conforms to the conventions of Standard English. The essential appositive "Marie Tharp" shouldn't be separated by punctuation from the noun phrase ("American geologist") it renames.

Choices B, C, and *D* are incorrect because each uses punctuation to separate the essential appositive from the noun phrase it renames.

QUESTION 4

Choice B is the best answer because it completes the text so that it conforms to the conventions of Standard English. No punctuation is needed between the preposition "of" and the words "childhood," "womanhood," and "Chinese American identity," each of which functions as an object of the preposition.

Choices A, C, and *D* are incorrect because each uses punctuation to separate the preposition "of" from its objects.

QUESTION 5

Choice B is the best answer because it completes the text so that it conforms to the conventions of Standard English. This choice establishes parallelism between the two verb phrases ("premiered her First Symphony," "developed supportive relationships with other Black artists") that describe what Price did in Chicago after her move there in 1927.

Choices A, C, and *D* are incorrect because the present participle "developing," the present perfect participle "having developed," and the infinitive "to develop" aren't parallel in form to the past tense verb "premiered."

QUESTION 6

Choice D is the best answer because it completes the text so that it conforms to the conventions of Standard English. The semicolon after "advance" is used in a conventional way to join the sentence's two closely related independent clauses, the first of which begins with "a subseasonal weather forecast" and the second of which begins with "its predictions."

Choice A is incorrect because it results in a rambling sentence. It's conventional to place a comma after the conjunction "and" when the conjunction is used to join two lengthy independent clauses. Even if that comma were present, however, the sentence would still be awkward, as the conjunction "and" and the conjunctive adverb "therefore" aren't both needed to establish the logical relationship between the two independent clauses. *Choice B* is incorrect because it results in a run-on sentence. *Choice C* is incorrect because it results in a comma splice.

QUESTION 7

Choice C is the best answer because it completes the text so that it conforms to the conventions of Standard English. The past perfect tense verb "had invented" is appropriate in this context to describe a past event that occurred before another event in the past. In this case, Planté invented the rechargeable lead-acid battery fifteen years before Faure improved on the design.

Choices A, B, and *D* are incorrect because the present progressive tense verb "is inventing," the simple future tense verb "will invent," and the simple present tense verb "invents" are inappropriate to describe a past event that took place before another event in the past.

QUESTION 8

Choice A is the best answer because it completes the text so that it conforms to the conventions of Standard English. The singular verb "promotes" agrees in number with the singular subject "African Games Co-production Market."

Choices B, C, and *D* are incorrect because "promote," "are promoting," and "have promoted" are plural verbs that don't agree in number with the singular subject "African Games Co-production Market."

PART 3

The Math Section

CHAPTER 19

Math: Overview

The Math section of the SAT is, alongside the Reading and Writing section, one of the two main portions of the test. In this test section, you'll answer questions that test your ability to solve problems involving algebra, advanced math, problem-solving and data analysis, and geometry and trigonometry.

In this chapter, we'll provide a high-level overview of the Math section. In the chapters that follow, we'll examine in detail each of the four broad content domains (areas) that compose the section, including the skills and knowledge covered by questions in each of the domains—Algebra, Advanced Math, Problem-Solving and Data Analysis, and Geometry and Trigonometry. Each content domain's overview chapter is followed by a chapter consisting of drill questions (and answer explanations) that you can use for immediate practice.

Three additional chapters round out our discussion of the Math section. The first provides additional details about responding to student-produced response (SPR) questions in the Math section. As the name suggests, these questions require you to generate your own answers instead of selecting one of four multiple-choice answer options. You'll find samples of questions in this format throughout earlier chapters, but we want to make sure that you know how to properly enter your answers on test day. The second chapter provides an overview of the features of the graphing calculator built into the digital test platform, which you may choose to use on test day, as well as guidance about where to obtain up-to-date information on bringing your own approved calculator. The third chapter consists of a copy of the reference sheet with common math formulas that you have access to during testing.

At a Glance

Table 1 provides an overview of the SAT Math section. We then discuss each feature introduced in the table throughout the remainder of the chapter.

PREVIEW

Chapters 20–28 cover the various kinds of questions you'll encounter in the Math section and provide drills that you can use for immediate practice. Chapter 29 offers additional details about the student-produced response (SPR) question format and how to properly enter your answers. Chapter 30 provides an overview of the built-in graphing calculator available to you on the digital test platform as well as guidance about where to obtain up-to-date information on bringing your own approved calculator to test day should you choose to do so. Chapter 31 consists of a copy of the reference sheet available during testing that contains common math formulas.

QUICK TAKE

You'll have a total of **70 minutes** to answer **44 Math questions**, about 75% of which are in the multiple-choice format and the remaining roughly 25% in the SPR format. This averages out to **1.59 minutes per question**. These questions will be divided into **two separately timed modules** of 35 minutes each.

Table 1. Math Section Overview

Feature	SAT Math Section
Timing and Pacing	
Number of questions	1st module: 22 questions
	2nd module: 22 questions
	Total: 44 questions
Time per module	1st module: 35 minutes
	2nd module: 35 minutes
	Total: 70 minutes
Average time per question	1.59 minutes
Score	
Score	Math section score (200–800 scale); one-half of the SAT total score
Contexts	
Proportion of test section	About 30% of questions are in context ("word problems")
Words per context	A majority of in-context questions have 50 words or fewer
Context areas	Science
	Social studies
	Real-world topics
Graphics (included with select questions)	A wide range of types of informational graphics and geometric figures (e.g., xy-plane graphs, bar graphs, scatterplots)
Questions	
Question format	Four-option multiple-choice, each with a single correct answer (about 75% of section)
	SPR (about 25% of section)
Question content domains (categories)	Algebra
	Advanced Math
	Problem-Solving and Data Analysis
	Geometry and Trigonometry
Calculator Use	

A calculator is allowed throughout the Math section. You may use the graphing calculator built into the digital test platform, or you may bring your own approved calculator.

Reference Sheet

You'll have access to a set of common formulas used in math throughout the test section.

Scratch (Scrap) Paper

While you're taking the Math section, you'll have access to notepaper for performing calculations.

Discussion

In this section of the chapter, we'll go over each of the features in table 1.

Number of Questions, Timing, and Pacing

Each Math section is divided into two equal-length *modules* of questions. Each of these modules is separately timed, so you'll have 35 minutes to answer the 22 questions in each module. That averages out to 1.59 minutes per question.

Score

You'll receive a Math section score based on your performance on the section. This section score will range from 200 to 800, depending on how well you did. Your scores on the Math and Reading and Writing sections added together will give you your total score for the SAT, which is on a 400–1600 scale.

Contexts

About 30% of questions in the Math section are set in context. By *context*, we mean that the question presents a brief scenario that you have to read and analyze in order to solve the associated problem. These questions will ask you to consider topics in social studies, science, or real-world settings. Many of these contexts are quite short—a majority of in-context questions are 50 words or fewer—and all contexts are written to be clear and understandable without the need for prior knowledge of the topics being discussed. In other words, all topic-specific information needed to answer an in-context question correctly is in the question itself, and you won't need to have studied a given science, social studies, or real-world topic in school. These sorts of questions are included in the Math section because they help assess your ability to apply your math skills and knowledge in authentic situations. The remaining roughly 70% of questions are "pure" math problems without context.

Graphics

The Math section includes three main varieties of graphics with select questions. One category consists of informational graphics that display data. These include the same sorts of tables, line graphs, and bar graphs that you'll be presented with in the Reading and Writing section as well as other informational graphics types commonly encountered in math classes, such as scatterplots, dot plots, and histograms. The second category consists of graphs of functions in the *xy*-plane, while the third consists of geometric figures, such as triangles. You'll be expected to make skillful use of these graphics and the information they contain and represent to answer associated questions.

QUICK TAKE

About 30% of Math questions are **set in context**. This context may consist of a **science, social studies, or real-world topic**. However, you won't need prior knowledge of these topics to be able to answer the associated questions correctly, as all relevant information about these topics is included in the contexts themselves.

QUICK TAKE

Select Math questions are accompanied by one or more graphics. These may be **informational graphics** (data displays), **graphs of functions in the *xy*-plane**, or **geometric figures**, such as triangles.

201

Questions

Two question formats are used in the Math section. About 75% of the questions are in the multiple-choice format. Each of these questions has four answer choices (options), one (and only one) of which is the correct answer, or *key*. The three incorrect answer choices—which are sometimes called *distractors*—represent common errors that students often make in answering math questions, either in how they approach the question or how they calculate the answer. Your task in these questions is to use your math skills and knowledge to figure out which of the four choices is the correct answer.

The rest of the Math section questions—about 25% of the total—use the SPR format. As the name suggests, these questions don't include answer choices to pick from. Instead, you'll have to find and enter your answers on your own. These questions are intended to find out whether you can successfully apply your math skills and knowledge without the structure of a set of options to choose from. We devote chapter 29 to discussing how to properly enter answers to questions in the SPR format, and examples of SPR questions are found throughout other chapters. For now, you just need to know that about one-quarter of the Math section questions will require you to come up with and enter your own answer. Note that some SPR questions may have more than one possible correct answer, but you'll still enter only one answer per question.

All Math questions are independent of each other, or *discrete*. This means that there are no question sets built around a common source, such as a passage or graphic. This is good news for you because it means you can approach each question separately, give your best answer, and move on to the next question.

Each Math question, whether multiple-choice or SPR, primarily tests a single skill or element of knowledge (e.g., your ability to solve linear equations in one variable). The knowledge and skills tested by Math questions fall into four broad categories, which we call *content domains*. Each of these domains represents a major area of focus in math. Table 2 offers an overview of the four content domains in the Math section, including each domain's "big idea," or main focus; the skills and knowledge each domain covers; and the approximate proportion of the Math section devoted to questions in each domain. Subsequent chapters go into detail about each of the domains in turn and provide opportunities for immediate practice.

Table 2. Math Section Content Domains

Math Section Content Domain	The Big Idea	Skills and Knowledge Tested	Proportion of Test Section
Algebra	Questions in this domain test your understanding of linear relationships.	• Linear equations in one variable • Linear equations in two variables • Linear functions • Systems of two linear equations in two variables • Linear inequalities in one or two variables	13–15 questions (about 35%)
Advanced Math	Questions in this domain test your understanding of nonlinear relationships.	• Equivalent expressions • Nonlinear equations in one variable and systems of equations in two variables • Nonlinear functions	13–15 questions (about 35%)
Problem-Solving and Data Analysis	Questions in this domain test your understanding of proportional relationships, percentages, and probability as well as your ability to use data to analyze and solve problems.	• Ratios, rates, proportional relationships, and units • Percentages • One-variable data: distributions and measures of center and spread • Two-variable data: models and scatterplots • Probability and conditional probability • Inference from sample statistics and margin of error • Evaluating statistical claims: observational studies and experiments	5–7 questions (about 15%)
Geometry and Trigonometry	Questions in this domain test your understanding of concepts central to geometry and trigonometry.	• Area and volume • Lines, angles, and triangles • Right triangles and trigonometry • Circles	5–7 questions (about 15%)

IMPORTANT: UNSCORED QUESTIONS

Four Math questions on each test form—two different questions per module—won't count toward your section score. These questions are ones that College Board is studying for potential use on future tests. Your answers to these questions won't impact your section score in any way. You won't be able to tell these questions apart from the ones in the section that do get scored, but the small number of these unscored questions shouldn't affect your practice or test day performance. Just do your best on each question.

Questions from all four domains appear in each test module (i.e., in each of the two separately timed portions of the Math section). Questions in each module are ordered by difficulty from easiest to hardest, regardless of the content domain the question belongs to, so you may find it advantageous to answer questions in the order in which they appear.

Calculator Use

You're allowed to use a calculator on all questions on the Math section. Bluebook has a built-in graphing calculator that you can use if you wish, or you may instead use your own approved calculator. We recommend basing this choice on which tool you feel more comfortable with. We'll talk more about calculator options in chapter 30. The key thing for the moment is that you may use a calculator with all Math questions if you wish, although, as we'll talk about later, using a calculator won't always be the most efficient way to answer questions.

Reference Sheet

While you're taking the Math section, you'll have access to a reference sheet that includes a set of common math formulas that you can use anytime you want during the test. A copy of this reference sheet appears in chapter 31.

Scratch (Scrap) Paper

Even though you'll take the digital SAT on a laptop, desktop computer, or other device, you'll still have access on test day to notepaper for performing calculations, taking notes, and the like.

Summary: Math Section

Let's quickly recap the basics of the Math section:

Timing and pacing

- 70 minutes to answer 44 questions divided into two separately timed modules

- An average of 1.59 minutes to answer each question

Score

- A Math section score on a 200–800 scale (one-half of the total score for the SAT)

Contexts

- About 30% of Math questions set in context

- Majority of in-context questions have 50 words or fewer

- Contexts drawn from topics in science, social studies, and real-world settings

Graphics

- Informational graphics (data displays), graphs of functions in the *xy*-plane, or geometric figures included with select questions

Questions

- A mix of four-option multiple-choice questions (about 75% of the section total) and SPR questions (about 25% of the section total)

  - Multiple-choice questions: A single correct answer (*key*)

  - SPR questions: May have more than one correct answer, although only a single answer is entered

- All questions independent of each other (i.e., no question sets)

- Content domains of Algebra, Advanced Math, Problem-Solving and Data Analysis, and Geometry and Trigonometry

- Ordered from easiest to hardest within each module

- 4 unscored questions (2 unique questions per module)

Calculators

- Allowed for all Math questions

- May choose between built-in graphing calculator and an approved personal calculator

Reference sheet

- A set of common formulas available anytime while taking the Math section

Scratch (scrap) paper

- Notepaper available during the Math section for making calculations, taking notes, and the like

CHAPTER 20

Math: Questions— Introduction

The following chapters discuss the kinds of questions you'll encounter in the Math section and give you opportunities to immediately practice what you've learned.

Recall that the Math section has questions in four broad categories, which we refer to as *content domains*. Each content domain has a "big idea," or common focus, tying all the questions in the domain together at a conceptual level. Table 1 summarizes the section's four content domains and the focus of their respective questions.

Table 1. Math Section Content Domains

Math Content Domain	The Big Idea
Algebra (chapters 21 and 22)	Testing your understanding of linear relationships
Advanced Math (chapters 23 and 24)	Testing your understanding of nonlinear relationships
Problem-Solving and Data Analysis (chapters 25 and 26)	Testing your understanding of proportional relationships, percentages, and probability as well as your ability to use data to analyze and solve problems
Geometry and Trigonometry (chapters 27 and 28)	Testing your ability to solve problems that focus on area and volume formulas; lines, angles, and triangles; right triangles and trigonometry; and circles

Each of the following pairs of chapters will

- provide a broad overview of a particular content domain, including the "big idea" (focus) of the domain;
- indicate about how many questions you can expect to encounter from that domain on test day;
- identify the key types of questions included in the domain;
- offer a range of sample questions and answer explanations; and
- give you an opportunity to immediately practice by answering questions from that domain and reading the associated answer explanations.

CHAPTER 21

Math: Questions— Algebra

Algebra questions in the Math section focus on the mastery of linear equations and inequalities, linear functions, and systems of linear equations. The ability to interpret, create, use, and solve problems using linear representations and to make connections between different representations of linear relationships is essential for success in college and careers.

Across the Math section, Algebra questions vary significantly in form and appearance. They may be straightforward fluency exercises or pose challenges of strategy or understanding, such as interpreting the relationship between graphical and algebraic representations or solving as a process of reasoning. You'll be required to demonstrate both procedural skill and a deep understanding of concepts.

The questions in the Algebra content domain include both multiple-choice questions and student-produced response (SPR) questions.

Let's explore the content, skills, and knowledge assessed by Algebra questions.

Linear Equations, Linear Inequalities, and Linear Functions in Context

When you use algebra to analyze and solve a problem in real life, a key step is to represent the context of the problem algebraically. To do this, you may need to define one or more variables that represent quantities in the context. Then you may need to write one or more expressions, equations, inequalities, or functions that represent the relationships described in the context. For some algebra questions, you may need to rewrite an equation or interpret a given algebraic representation. For other questions, once you write an equation that represents the context, you then need to solve that equation. Then you may need to interpret the solution to the equation in terms of the context. Questions in the Math section may assess your ability to accomplish any or all of these steps.

QUICK TAKE

Questions in the Math section require you to demonstrate deep understanding of several core algebra topics, namely linear equations and inequalities, linear functions, and systems of linear equations. These topics are fundamental to the learning and work often required in college and careers.

REMINDER

Multiple-choice questions have four answer choices and one (and only one) correct answer, or *key*. Questions in the SPR format require you to generate and enter your own answer.

STRATEGY

Many Algebra questions such as this one will require you to perform the following steps:

1. Define one or more variables that represent quantities in the question.

2. Write one or more equations, expressions, inequalities, or functions that represent the relationships described in the question.

3. Solve the equation.

4. Interpret the solution in terms of what the question is asking.

Ample practice with each of these steps will help you develop the math skills and knowledge needed to successfully answer questions in the Algebra content domain.

REMINDER

There are several different ways you may be tested on the same underlying algebra concepts. Practicing a variety of questions with different contexts is a good way to ensure you'll be ready for the questions you'll come across in the Math section.

Algebra Sample Question 1

In 2014, County X had 783 miles of paved roads. Starting in 2015, the county has been building 8 miles of new paved roads each year. At this rate, how many miles of paved road will County X have in 2030? (Assume that no paved roads go out of service.)

The first step in answering this question is to decide what variable or variables you need to define. Since the number of miles paved depends on the year, we can define a variable to represent the year. The number of years after 2014 can be represented using the variable n. Then, since the question says that County X had 783 miles of paved road in 2014 and has been building 8 miles of new paved roads each year, the expression $783 + 8n$ gives the number of miles of paved roads in County X in the year that is n years after 2014. The year 2030 is $2030 - 2014 = 16$ years after 2014; thus, the year 2030 corresponds to $n = 16$. Hence, to find the number of miles of paved roads in County X in 2030, substitute 16 for n in the expression $783 + 8n$, giving $783 + 8(16)$. This is equivalent to $783 + 128$, or 911. Therefore, at the given rate of building, County X will have 911 miles of paved roads in 2030.

Note that this example provides no answer choices. It's in the student-produced response format mentioned briefly above. To respond to this question, you would enter your answer in Bluebook. Directions for entering your answers to student-produced response questions are presented in chapter 29.

Note that the same context could have generated different sorts of questions, as in samples 2 and 3, below.

Algebra Sample Question 2

In 2014, County X had 783 miles of paved roads. Starting in 2015, the county has been building 8 miles of new paved roads each year. At this rate, which of the following functions f gives the number of miles of paved road there will be in County X n years after 2014? (Assume that no paved roads go out of service.)

A) $f(n) = 8 + 783n$

B) $f(n) = 2{,}014 + 783n$

C) $f(n) = 738 + 8n$

D) $f(n) = 2{,}014 + 8n$

This question already defines the variable and asks you to identify a function that describes the context. The discussion for sample 1 shows that the correct answer is choice C.

Algebra Sample Question 3

> In 2014, County X had 783 miles of paved roads. Starting in 2015, the county has been building 8 miles of new paved roads each year. At this rate, in which year will County X first have at least 1,000 miles of paved roads? (Assume that no paved roads go out of service.)

In this question, you must create and solve an inequality. As in sample 1, let n be the number of years after 2014. Then the expression $783 + 8n$ gives the number of miles of paved roads in County X n years after 2014. The question is asking when there will first be at least 1,000 miles of paved roads in County X. This condition can be represented by the inequality $783 + 8n \geq 1,000$. To find the year in which there will first be at least 1,000 miles of paved roads, you solve this inequality for n. Subtracting 783 from each side of $783 + 8n \geq 1,000$ gives $8n \geq 217$. Then dividing each side of $8n \geq 217$ by 8 gives $n \geq 27.125$. Note that an important part of relating the inequality $783 + 8n \geq 1,000$ back to the context is to notice that n is counting calendar years, and so the value of n must be an integer. The least value of n that satisfies $783 + 8n \geq 1,000$ is 27.125, but the year $2014 + 27.125 = 2041.125$ does not make sense as an answer, and in 2041, there would be only $783 + 8(27) = 999$ miles of paved roads in the county. Therefore, the variable n needs to be rounded up to the next integer, and so the least possible value of n is 28. Therefore, the year that County X will first have at least 1,000 miles of paved roads is 28 years after 2014, which is 2042.

In sample 1, once the variable n was defined, you needed to find an expression that represents the number of miles of paved road in terms of n. In other questions, creating the correct expression, equation, or function may require a more insightful understanding of the context.

Algebra Sample Question 4

> To edit a manuscript, Miguel charges $50 for the first 2 hours and $20 per hour after the first 2 hours. Which of the following expresses the amount, C, in dollars, Miguel charges if it takes him x hours to edit a manuscript, where $x > 2$?
>
> A) $C = 20x$
>
> B) $C = 20x + 10$
>
> C) $C = 20x + 50$
>
> D) $C = 20x + 90$

The question defines the variables C and x and asks you to express C in terms of x. To create the correct equation, you must note that since the $50 that Miguel charges pays for his first 2 hours of editing, he charges $20 per hour only *after* the first 2 hours. Thus, if it takes x hours for Miguel to edit a manuscript, he charges $50 for the first 2 hours and $20 per hour for the remaining time, which is $x - 2$ hours. Thus, his total charge, C, in dollars, can be written as $C = 50 + 20(x - 2)$, where $x > 2$.

STRATEGY

Solving an equation or inequality is often only part of the problem-solving process. You'll also need to interpret the solution in the context of the question, so be sure to remind yourself of the question's context and the meaning of the variables you solved for before selecting your answer.

STRATEGY

When the solution you arrive at doesn't match any of the answer choices provided in a given multiple-choice question, consider whether expanding, simplifying, or rearranging your solution will cause it to match an answer choice. Sometimes this extra step is needed to arrive at the correct answer.

This doesn't match any of the provided answer choices. But when you apply the distributive property to the right-hand side of $C = 50 + 20(x - 2)$, you get $C = 50 + 20x - 40$, or $C = 20x + 10$, which is choice B.

As with samples 1 to 3, different questions could have been asked about this context. For example, you could be asked to find how long it took Miguel to edit a manuscript if he charged $370.

In some questions in the Math section, you'll be given a function that represents a context and be asked to find the value of the output of the function given an input or, as in sample 5, below, the value of the input that corresponds to a given output.

Algebra Sample Question 5

A builder uses the function g defined by $g(x) = 110x + 10,000$ to estimate the cost $g(x)$, in dollars, to build a one-story home of planned floor area of x square feet in Stillwater. If the builder estimates that the cost to build a certain one-story home in Stillwater is $142,000, what is the planned floor area, in square feet, of the home?

This question asks you to find the value of the input of a function when you're given the value of the output and the equation of the function. The estimated cost of the home, in dollars, is the output of the function g for a one-story home of planned floor area of x square feet. That is, the output of the function, $g(x)$, is 142,000, and you need to find the value of the input x that gives an output of 142,000. To do this, substitute 142,000 for $g(x)$ in the equation that defines g: $142,000 = 110x + 10,000$. Now solve for x: First, subtract 10,000 from each side of the equation $142,000 = 110x + 10,000$, which gives $132,000 = 110x$. Then, divide each side of $132,000 = 110x$ by 110, which gives $1,200 = x$. Therefore, a one-story home with an estimated cost of $142,000 to build in Stillwater has a planned floor area of 1,200 square feet.

Systems of Linear Equations and Inequalities in Context

You may need to define more than one variable and create more than one equation or inequality to represent a context and answer a question. Questions on the Math section may require you to create and solve a system of equations or create a system of inequalities.

Algebra Sample Question 6

Maizah bought pants and a briefcase at a department store. The sum of the prices of the pants and the briefcase before sales tax was $130.00. There was no sales tax on the pants and a 9% sales tax on the briefcase. The total Maizah paid, including the sales tax, was $136.75. What was the price, in dollars, of the pants?

To answer the question, you first need to define the variables. The question discusses the prices of pants and a briefcase and asks you to find the price of the pants. So it's appropriate to let P be the price, in dollars, of the pants and to let B be the price, in dollars, of the briefcase. Since the sum of the prices before sales tax was $130.00, the equation $P + B = 130$ represents the sum of the prices. A sales tax of 9% was added to the price of the briefcase. Since 9% is equal to 0.09, the price of the briefcase with tax was $B + 0.09B = 1.09B$. There was no sales tax on the pants, and the total Maizah paid, including tax, was $136.75, so the equation $P + 1.09B = 136.75$ represents the total, in dollars, Maizah paid.

Now you need to solve the system

$$P + B = 130$$
$$P + 1.09B = 136.75$$

Subtracting the left- and right-hand sides of the first equation from the corresponding sides of the second equation gives you $(P + 1.09B) - (P + B) = 136.75 - 130$, which can be rewritten as $0.09B = 6.75$. Now you can divide each side of the equation $0.09B = 6.75$ by 0.09. This gives you $B = \dfrac{6.75}{0.09}$, or $B = 75$. Thus, the price, in dollars, of the briefcase is 75. The question asks for the price, in dollars, of the pants, which is P. You can substitute 75 for B in the equation $P + B = 130$, which gives you $P + 75 = 130$, or $P = 130 - 75$, or $P = 55$, so the price of the pants is $55.

Algebra Sample Question 7

Each morning, John jogs at 6 miles per hour and rides a bike at 12 miles per hour. His goal is to jog and ride his bike a total of at least 9 miles in no more than 1 hour. If John jogs j miles and rides his bike b miles, which of the following systems of inequalities represents John's goal?

A) $\dfrac{j}{6} + \dfrac{b}{12} \le 1$
$j + b \ge 9$

B) $\dfrac{j}{6} + \dfrac{b}{12} \ge 1$
$j + b \le 9$

C) $6j + 12b \ge 9$
$j + b \le 1$

D) $6j + 12b \le 1$
$j + b \ge 9$

It's given that John jogs j miles and rides his bike b miles. It's also given that his goal is to jog and ride his bike a total of at least 9 miles. This goal is represented by the inequality $j + b \ge 9$. This eliminates choices B and C.

STRATEGY

You can use either of two approaches—combination or substitution—when solving a system of linear equations. One may get you to the answer more quickly than the other, depending on the equations you're working with and what you're solving for. Practice using both approaches to give you greater flexibility on test day.

STRATEGY

While this question may seem complex, as it involves numerous steps, solving it calls on the same underlying principles outlined earlier: defining variables, creating equations to represent relationships, solving equations, and interpreting the solution.

STRATEGY

In sample 7, the answer choices each contain two parts. Use this to your advantage by tackling one part at a time and eliminating answers that don't work.

You should be able to quickly rearrange equations such as rate × time = distance by solving for any of the variables. Sample 7 requires you to solve the equation for time.

Since rate × time = distance, it follows that time = $\frac{\text{distance}}{\text{rate}}$. John jogs j miles at 6 miles per hour, so the time he jogs is equal to $\frac{j \text{ miles}}{6 \text{ miles/hour}} = \frac{j}{6}$ hours. Similarly, since John rides his bike b miles at 12 miles per hour, the time he rides his bike is $\frac{b}{12}$ hours. Thus, John's goal to complete his jog and his bike ride in no more than 1 hour can be represented by the inequality $\frac{j}{6} + \frac{b}{12} \leq 1$. The system $j + b \geq 9$ and $\frac{j}{6} + \frac{b}{12} \leq 1$ is choice A.

Fluency in Solving Linear Equations, Linear Inequalities, and Systems of Linear Equations

Creating linear equations, linear inequalities, and systems of linear equations that represent a context are key skills for success in college and careers. It's also essential to be able to fluently solve these linear equations, linear inequalities, and systems of linear equations. Some of the Algebra questions in the Math section may also present equations, inequalities, or systems without a context and directly assess your fluency in solving them.

All such fluency questions in the Math section permit the use of a calculator, and some of them test your ability to solve equations, inequalities, and systems of equations. Even though a calculator is permitted for all Math section questions, you may be able to answer certain questions more quickly without using a calculator, such as in sample 9, below. Part of what the Math section assesses is your ability to decide whether using a calculator to answer a question offers efficiency or whether it's more efficient to solve by hand. Sample 8 is an example of a question that could be solved either by hand or by using a graphing calculator.

Algebra Sample Question 8

$$3\left(\frac{1}{2} - x\right) = \frac{3}{5} + 15x$$

What is the solution to the given equation?

Using the distributive property to rewrite the left-hand side of the equation gives $\frac{3}{2} - 3x = \frac{3}{5} + 15x$. Adding $3x$ to both sides of this equation and then subtracting $\frac{3}{5}$ from both sides of this equation gives $\frac{3}{2} - \frac{3}{5} = 18x$. The equation may be easier to solve if it's transformed into an equation without fractions; to do this, multiply each side of $\frac{3}{2} - \frac{3}{5} = 18x$ by 10, which is the least common multiple of the denominators 2 and 5. This gives $\frac{30}{2} - \frac{30}{5} = 180x$, which can be rewritten as $15 - 6 = 180x$, or $9 = 180x$. Dividing both sides of this equation by 180 gives $x = \frac{1}{20}$.

Alternatively, each side of the given equation can be set equal to y and entered in a graphing calculator. Then the problem can be solved by finding the intersection point of the two lines that each represent one side of the given equation. You would enter $y = 3\left(\frac{1}{2} - x\right)$ and $y = \frac{3}{5} + 15x$ in the graphing interface and draw the graphs. The intersection point is (0.05, 1.35), which means $x = 0.05$, which is equivalent to $x = \frac{1}{20}$. Note that .05 and 1/20 are examples of ways to enter a correct answer.

Algebra Sample Question 9

$$-2(3x + 2.4) = -3(3x + 2.4)$$

What is the solution to the given equation?

You could solve this in the same way as sample 8, by multiplying everything out and simplifying, or by graphing each side of the equation. But the structure of the equation reveals that −2 times a quantity, $3x + 2.4$, is equal to −3 times the same quantity. This is only possible if the quantity $3x + 2.4$ is equal to zero. Thus, $3x + 2.4 = 0$, or $3x = -2.4$. Therefore, the solution is $x = -0.8$.

Algebra Sample Question 10

$$-2x = 4y + 6$$
$$2(2y + 3) = 3x - 5$$

What is the solution (x, y) to the given system of equations?

A) (1, 2)
B) (1, −2)
C) (−1, −1)
D) (−1, 1)

This is an example of a system you can solve more efficiently by substitution than by using the elimination method demonstrated in sample 6. Since $-2x = 4y + 6$, it follows that $-x = 2y + 3$. Now you can substitute $-x$ for $2y + 3$ in the second equation. This gives you $2(-x) = 3x - 5$, which is equivalent to $5x = 5$, or $x = 1$. Substituting 1 for x in the first equation gives you $-2 = 4y + 6$, which is equivalent to $4y = -8$, or $y = -2$. Therefore, the solution to the system is (1, −2).

STRATEGY

While a calculator is permitted on all questions in the Math section, it's important to not rely too much on the tool. Some questions, such as sample 9, can be solved more efficiently without using a calculator. Your ability to choose when to use and when not to use a calculator is one of the things the Math section assesses, so be sure to practice this.

STRATEGY

In sample 6, the elimination method yields an efficient solution to the question. In sample 10, the substitution method turns out to be an efficient approach. These examples illustrate the benefits of knowing both approaches and thinking critically about which approach may be more efficient for a given question.

In the preceding examples, you found a unique solution to linear equations and to systems of two linear equations in two variables. But not all such equations and systems have solutions, and some have infinitely many solutions. Some questions in the Math section assess your ability to determine whether an equation or a system of linear equations has one solution, no solutions, or infinitely many solutions.

The Relationships Among Linear Equations, Lines in the Coordinate Plane, and the Contexts They Describe

A system of two linear equations in two variables can be solved by graphing the lines in the coordinate plane. For example, you can graph the equations of the system in the xy-plane in sample 10, above.

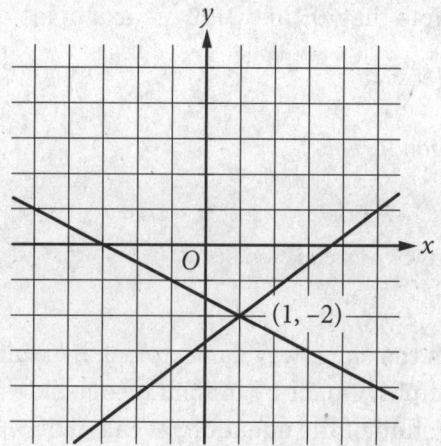

The point of intersection gives the solution to the system.

If the equations in a system of two linear equations in two variables are graphed, each graph will be a line. There are three possibilities:

1. The lines intersect at one point. In this case, the system has a unique solution.

2. The lines are parallel. In this case, the system has no solution.

3. The lines are identical. In this case, every point on the line is a solution, and so the system has infinitely many solutions.

One way that the second and third cases can be identified is by rewriting the equations of the system in slope-intercept form, $y = mx + b$, where m is the slope of the line and b is the y-coordinate of the y-intercept of the line when the system is graphed in the xy-plane. If the lines have the same slope and different y-coordinates of the y-intercepts, the lines are parallel; if both the slope and the y-coordinate of the y-intercept are the same, the lines are identical.

How are the second and third cases represented algebraically? Samples 11 and 12 answer this question.

Algebra Sample Question 11

$$2y + 6x = 3$$
$$y + 3x = 2$$

How many solutions (x, y) does the given system of equations have?

A) Zero

B) Exactly one

C) Exactly two

D) Infinitely many

To rewrite the second equation in slope-intercept form, subtract $3x$ from both sides of the equation, which gives $y = -3x + 2$. To rewrite the first equation in slope-intercept form, subtract $6x$ from both sides of the equation, which gives $2y = -6x + 3$. Next, divide both sides of this equation by 2, which gives $y = -3x + \frac{3}{2}$. Now that the two equations are written in slope-intercept form, you can identify that the slope of each line is -3 and that the y-coordinates of the y-intercepts are $\frac{3}{2}$ and 2.

Since the slopes are the same and the y-coordinates of the y-intercepts are different, the graphs of the lines will show distinct parallel lines. Because parallel lines never intersect, the system of equations has zero solutions.

Alternatively, if you multiply each side of $y + 3x = 2$ by 2, you get $2y + 6x = 4$. Then subtracting each side of $2y + 6x = 3$ from the corresponding side of $2y + 6x = 4$ gives $0 = 1$. This is a false statement. Therefore, the system has zero solutions (x, y).

You could also use graphing technology to graph the two equations. The graphs are parallel lines, so there are no points of intersection, and the system of equations has zero solutions.

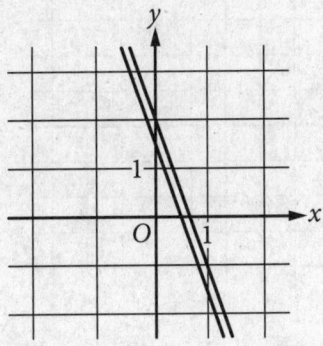

STRATEGY

When the graphs of a system of two linear equations are distinct parallel lines, as in sample 11, the system has zero solutions. If the question states that a system of two linear equations has an infinite number of solutions, as in sample 12, the equations must be equivalent.

STRATEGY

The equations in the system in sample 11 are in a form that allows you to quickly find both the x-intercept and the y-intercept of the graph of the equation. For example, the graph of $y + 3x = 2$ has an x-intercept of $\left(\frac{2}{3}, 0\right)$ because if $y = 0$, then $3x = 2$ and $x = \frac{2}{3}$. Similarly, the graph has a y-intercept of $(0, 2)$ because if $x = 0$, then $y = 2$.

Algebra Sample Question 12

$$3s - 2t = a$$
$$-15s + bt = -7$$

In the given system of equations, a and b are constants. If the system has infinitely many solutions, what is the value of a?

If a system of two linear equations in two variables has infinitely many solutions, the two equations in the system must be equivalent. Since the two equations are presented in the same form, the second equation must be equal to the first equation multiplied by a constant. Since the coefficient of s in the second equation is −5 times the coefficient of s in the first equation, multiply each side of the first equation by −5. This gives you the system

$$-15s + 10t = -5a$$
$$-15s + bt = -7$$

Since these two equations are equivalent and have the same coefficient of s, the coefficients of t and the constants on the right-hand side must also be the same. Thus, $b = 10$ and $-5a = -7$. Therefore, the value of a is $\frac{7}{5}$.

There may also be questions in the Math section that assess your knowledge of the relationship between the algebraic and the geometric representations of a line—that is, between an equation of a line and its graph. The key concepts are

- If the slopes of line ℓ and line k are each defined (that is, if neither line is a vertical line), then

    ◆ Line ℓ and line k are parallel if and only if they have the same slope.

    ◆ Line ℓ and line k are perpendicular if and only if the product of their slopes is −1.

Algebra Sample Question 13

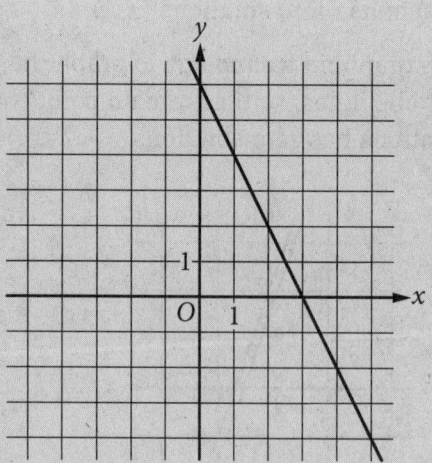

The graph of line k is shown in the xy-plane. Which of the following is an equation of a line that is perpendicular to line k?

A) $y = -2x + 1$

B) $y = -\frac{1}{2}x + 2$

C) $y = \frac{1}{2}x + 3$

D) $y = 2x + 4$

Note that the graph of line k passes through the points (0, 6) and (3, 0). Thus, the slope of line k is $\frac{0-6}{3-0} = -2$. Since the product of the slopes of perpendicular lines is −1, a line that is perpendicular to line k will have slope $\frac{1}{2}$. All the choices are in slope-intercept form, and so the coefficient of x is the slope of the line represented by the equation. Therefore, choice C, $y = \frac{1}{2}x + 3$, is an equation of a line with slope $\frac{1}{2}$, and thus this line is perpendicular to line k.

As we've noted, some contexts can be described with a linear equation. The graph of a linear equation is a line. A nonvertical line has geometric properties such as its slope and its y-intercept. These geometric properties can often be interpreted in terms of the context. The Math section may have questions that assess your ability to make these interpretations. For example, reconsider the contexts in samples 1 to 3. You created a linear function, $f(n) = 783 + 8n$, that describes the number of miles of paved road County X will have n years after 2014. This equation can be graphed in the coordinate plane, with n on the horizontal axis and $f(n)$ on the vertical axis. The points of this graph lie on a line with slope 8 and y-intercept of (0, 783). The slope, 8, gives the number of miles of new paved roads added each year, and the y-intercept gives the number of miles of paved roads in 2014, the year that corresponds to $n = 0$.

Algebra Sample Question 14

A voter registration drive was held in Town Y. The number of voters, V, registered T days after the drive began can be estimated by the equation $V = 3{,}450 + 65T$. What is the best interpretation of the number 65 in this context?

A) The estimated number of registered voters at the beginning of the registration drive

B) The estimated number of registered voters at the end of the registration drive

C) The total estimated number of voters registered during the drive

D) The estimated number of voters registered each day during the drive

The correct answer is choice D. For each day that passes, it's the next day of the registration drive, and so T increases by 1. In the given equation, when T, the number of days after the drive began, increases by 1, V, the estimated number of voters registered, becomes $V = 3{,}450 + 65(T + 1)$, or $V = 3{,}450 + 65T + 65$. That is, the estimated number of voters registered increases by 65 for each day of the drive. Therefore, 65 is the estimated number of voters registered each day during the drive.

You should note that choice A describes the number 3,450, and the numbers described by choices B and C can be found only if you know how many days the registration drive lasted; this information isn't given in the question.

Summary: Algebra Questions

Main purpose: To assess your understanding of linear relationships

Proportion of the test section: About 35 percent (thirteen to fifteen questions)

Question types

- Linear equations in one variable
- Linear equations in two variables
- Linear functions
- Systems of two linear equations in two variables
- Linear inequalities in one or two variables

CHAPTER 22

Math: Questions— Algebra Drills

1

$$3a + 4b = 25$$

A shipping company charged a customer $25 to ship some small boxes and some large boxes. The given equation represents the relationship between a, the number of small boxes, and b, the number of large boxes, the customer had shipped. If the customer had 3 small boxes shipped, how many large boxes were shipped?

A) 3

B) 4

C) 5

D) 6

2

$$ax = 5$$

In the given equation, a is a constant. For which of the following values of a will the equation have no solution?

A) 0

B) 1

C) 5

D) 10

3

Tom scored 85, 78, and 98 on his first three exams in history class. Solving which inequality gives all the possible scores, G, that Tom could get on his fourth exam that will result in a mean score on all four exams of at least 90?

A) $90 - (85 + 78 + 98) \leq 4G$

B) $4G + 85 + 78 + 98 \geq 360$

C) $\dfrac{(G + 85 + 78 + 98)}{4} \geq 90$

D) $\dfrac{(85 + 78 + 98)}{4} \geq 90 - 4G$

4

If $3(3x + 5) = 2x - 8$, what is the value of x?

A) $-\dfrac{23}{7}$

B) $-\dfrac{15}{7}$

C) $-\dfrac{13}{7}$

D) $\dfrac{7}{11}$

5

On Monday, Jao walked a total of 11,400 steps. On Tuesday, Jao has a goal to walk at least 1,500 more steps than he did on Monday. What is the least number of steps Jao could walk on Tuesday to meet his goal?

6

$$x - 3y = 7$$

$$3y = 9$$

If (x, y) is the solution to the given system of equations, what is the value of x?

A) -2

B) 10

C) 16

D) 34

7

$$P = 1.20x + 5.00$$

The given equation gives the total monthly price P, in dollars, for using an online gaming service. The total monthly price for the online service consists of a flat monthly fee and a charge for each game played during a month. Of the following, which is the best interpretation of the value of x in this context?

A) The number of games played during a month

B) The charge, in dollars, for playing x games

C) The flat monthly fee, in dollars, for the gaming service

D) The number of months the gaming service was used

8

$$x + y = 4$$
$$x - y = 2$$

Which of the following is the graph in the *xy*-plane of the given system of equations?

A)

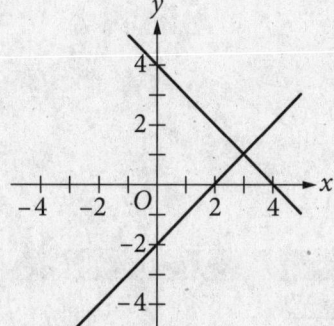

B)

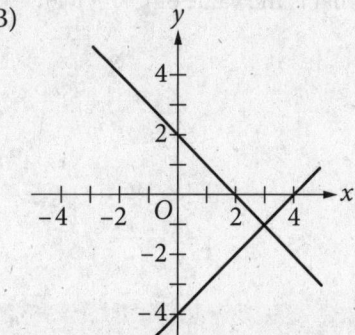

C)

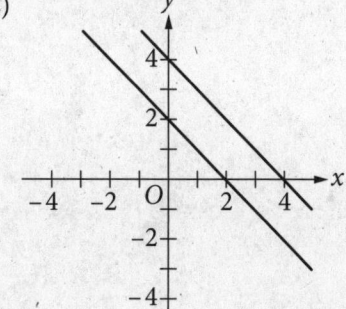

D)

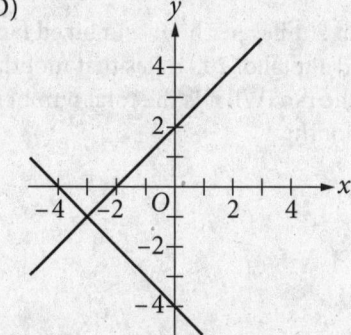

9

Nayya burns 5 kilocalories per minute running on a treadmill and 10 kilocalories per minute pedaling on a stationary bike. Which of the following equations represents the total number of kilocalories, T, Nayya has burned after running on the treadmill for 50 minutes and pedaling on the stationary bike for m minutes?

A) $T = 15m + 50$

B) $T = 50m + 50$

C) $T = 5m + 500$

D) $T = 10m + 250$

10

$$f(x) = \frac{(x+7)}{4}$$

For the function f defined as shown, what is the value of $f(9) - f(1)$?

A) 1

B) 2

C) $\frac{1}{4}$

D) $\frac{9}{4}$

11

In the xy-plane, line l contains the points $(2, 6)$ and $(8, 10)$. Which of the following is an equation of line l?

A) $y = \frac{2}{3}x + \frac{14}{3}$

B) $y = \frac{3}{2}x - 2$

C) $y = 2x + 6$

D) $y = 8x + 10$

12

During a month, Morgan ran r miles at 5 miles per hour and biked b miles at 10 miles per hour. She ran and biked a total of 200 miles that month, and she biked for twice as many hours as she ran. What is the total number of miles that Morgan biked during the month?

A) 80

B) 100

C) 120

D) 160

13

The equation $c = \frac{5}{4}x + 406$ gives the total cost c, in dollars, to produce a quantity of x units. If the quantity of units produced increases by 39 units, what is the corresponding increase in the total cost, in dollars?

14

$$kx - 3y = 4$$
$$4x - 5y = 7$$

In the given system of equations, k is a constant and x and y are variables. For what value of k will the system of equations have no solution?

A) $\frac{12}{5}$

B) $\frac{16}{7}$

C) $-\frac{16}{7}$

D) $-\frac{12}{5}$

15

x	y
−10	66
−5	45
5	3
10	−18

The table shows four values of x and their corresponding values of y. There is a linear relationship between x and y. If an equation representing this relationship is written in the form $Ax + 5y = C$, where A and C are constants, what is the value of C?

16

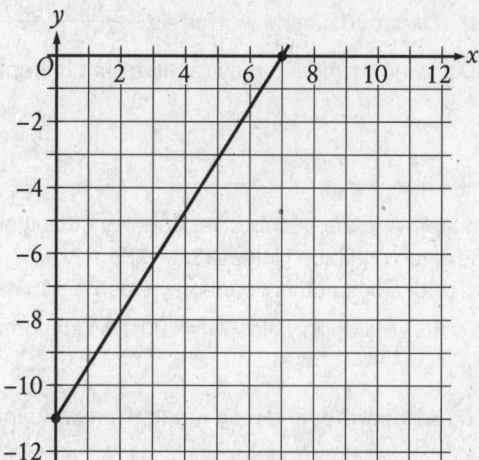

The point $(3, d)$ lies on the line shown. What is the value of d?

Answer Explanations

QUESTION 1

Choice B is correct. It's given that a represents the number of small boxes and b represents the number of large boxes the customer had shipped. If the customer had 3 small boxes shipped, then $a = 3$. Substituting 3 for a in the equation $3a + 4b = 25$ yields $3(3) + 4b = 25$, or $9 + 4b = 25$. Subtracting 9 from both sides of this equation yields $4b = 16$. Dividing both sides of this equation by 4 yields $b = 4$. Therefore, the customer had 4 large boxes shipped.

Choice A is incorrect. If the customer had 3 small boxes and 3 large boxes shipped, then the company would have charged the customer $21, not $25. *Choice C* is incorrect. If the customer had 3 small boxes and 5 large boxes shipped, then the company would have charged the customer $29, not $25. *Choice D* is incorrect. If the customer had 3 small boxes and 6 large boxes shipped, then the company would have charged the customer $33, not $25.

QUESTION 2

Choice A is correct. An equation has no solution when there is no value of x that produces a true statement. To solve the given equation for x, both sides of the equation can be divided by a, yielding $x = \frac{5}{a}$. Since 5 can be divided by any number except 0, it follows that the value of a can't be 0. Therefore, if the value of a is 0, the given equation will have no solution.

Alternate approach: Substituting 0 for a in the given equation yields $0x = 5$, or $0 = 5$, which isn't a true statement. Therefore, when $a = 0$, there is no solution to the given equation.

Choice B is incorrect. If $a=1$, then $x = \frac{5}{1}$, or $x = 5$, which yields exactly one solution rather than no solution. *Choice C* is incorrect. If $a=5$, then $x = \frac{5}{5}$, or $x = 1$, which yields exactly one solution rather than no solution. *Choice D* is incorrect. If $a=10$, then $x = \frac{5}{10}$, or $x = \frac{1}{2}$, which yields exactly one solution rather than no solution.

QUESTION 3

Choice C is correct. The mean of the four scores (G, 85, 78, and 98) can be expressed as $\frac{G + 85 + 78 + 98}{4}$. Thus, an inequality that represents a mean score on all four exams of at least 90 can be written as $\frac{G + 85 + 78 + 98}{4} \geq 90$.

Choices A, B, and *D* are incorrect and may result from conceptual or calculation errors.

QUESTION 4

Choice A is correct. Applying the distributive property of multiplication on the left-hand side of the given equation yields $3(3x) + 3(5) = 2x - 8$, or $9x + 15 = 2x - 8$. Subtracting $2x$ from both sides of this equation yields $7x + 15 = -8$. Subtracting 15 from both sides of this equation yields $7x = -23$. Dividing both sides of this equation by 7 yields $x = -\frac{23}{7}$.

Choices B, C, and *D* are incorrect and may result from conceptual or calculation errors.

QUESTION 5

The correct answer is 12,900. It's given that Jao walked a total of 11,400 steps on Monday. It's also given that Jao has a goal to walk at least 1,500 more steps on Tuesday than he did on Monday. Let x represent the possible number of steps Jao could walk on Tuesday to meet his goal. This situation can be represented by the inequality $x \geq 11,400 + 1,500$, or $x \geq 12,900$. Thus, the least number of steps Jao could walk on Tuesday to meet his goal is 12,900.

QUESTION 6

Choice C is correct. From the given system of equations, adding the second equation, $3y = 9$, to the first equation, $x - 3y = 7$, yields $x - 3y + 3y = 7 + 9$, or $x = 16$.

Choices A, B, and *D* are incorrect and may result from conceptual or calculation errors.

QUESTION 7

Choice A is correct. It's given that the total monthly price P, in dollars, is the sum of a flat monthly fee and a charge for each game played during a month. A charge for each game played implies the multiplication of the rate, in dollars per game, and the number of games played. Therefore, $1.20 must be the charge per game, and x must be the number of games played during a month.

Choice B is incorrect. The charge, in dollars, for playing x games is $1.20x$. *Choice C* is incorrect. The flat monthly fee, in dollars, for the gaming service is $5.00. *Choice D* is incorrect. No information has been provided about the number of months the gaming service was used.

QUESTION 8

Choice A is correct. Each of the equations in the given system can be rewritten in the form $y = mx + b$, where m represents the slope and $(0, b)$ represents the y-intercept of the line. The first equation in the given system can be rewritten as $y = -x + 4$. It follows that this line has a slope of -1 and a y-intercept at $(0, 4)$. The second equation in the given system can be rewritten as $y = x - 2$. It follows that this line has a slope of 1 and a y-intercept at $(0, -2)$. Of the given choices, only the graph in choice A represents these lines.

Choices B and *D* are incorrect. These systems of equations represent lines with y-intercepts at $(0, 2)$ and $(0, -4)$ rather than $(0, 4)$ and $(0, -2)$. *Choice C* is incorrect. This system of equations represents lines with y-intercepts at $(0, 2)$ and $(0, 4)$ rather than $(0, 4)$ and $(0, -2)$.

QUESTION 9

Choice D is correct. It's given that Nayya burns 5 kilocalories per minute running on a treadmill. It follows that Nayya will burn $5(50)$, or 250, kilocalories running on the treadmill for 50 minutes. It's also given that Nayya burns 10 kilocalories per minute pedaling on a stationary bike. It follows that she will burn $10m$ kilocalories pedaling on the stationary bike for m minutes. The sum of the kilocalories burned after running on the treadmill for 50 minutes, 250, and the kilocalories burned after pedaling on the stationary bike for m minutes, $10m$, gives the total number of kilocalories, T, Nayya burned. Therefore, $T = 250 + 10m$, or $T = 10m + 250$.

Choice A is incorrect. This equation represents the total number of kilocalories Nayya has burned if she burns 15, not 10, kilocalories per minute pedaling on a stationary bike and ran on the treadmill for 10, not 50, minutes. *Choice B* is incorrect. This equation represents the total number of kilocalories Nayya has burned if she burns 50, not 10, kilocalories per minute pedaling on a stationary bike and ran on the treadmill for 10, not 50, minutes. *Choice C* is incorrect. This equation represents the total number of kilocalories Nayya has burned if she burns 5, not 10, kilocalories per minute pedaling on a stationary bike and ran on the treadmill for 100, not 50, minutes.

QUESTION 10

Choice B is correct. The value of $f(9)$ represents the value of $f(x)$ when $x = 9$. Substituting 9 for x in the given function yields $f(9) = \frac{(9 + 7)}{4}$, which can be rewritten as $f(9) = \frac{16}{4}$, or $f(9) = 4$. Similarly, the value of $f(1)$ represents the value of $f(x)$ when $x = 1$. Substituting 1 for x in the given function yields $f(1) = \frac{(1 + 7)}{4}$, which can be rewritten as $f(1) = \frac{8}{4}$, or $f(1) = 2$. Therefore, $f(9) - f(1) = 4 - 2$, which is equivalent to 2.

Choices A, C, and *D* are incorrect and may result from conceptual or calculation errors.

QUESTION 11

Choice A is correct. The equation of a line in the xy-plane can be written as $y = mx + b$, where m represents the slope and b represents the y-coordinate of the y-intercept of the line. Given two points on a line, (x_1, y_1) and (x_2, y_2), the slope of the line can be calculated as $m = \frac{y_2 - y_1}{x_2 - x_1}$. Substituting $(2, 6)$ for (x_1, y_1) and $(8, 10)$ for (x_2, y_2) in the equation $m = \frac{y_2 - y_1}{x_2 - x_1}$ yields $m = \frac{10 - 6}{8 - 2}$, which is equivalent to $m = \frac{4}{6}$, or $m = \frac{2}{3}$. Substituting $\frac{2}{3}$ for m in the equation $y = mx + b$ yields $y = \frac{2}{3}x + b$. Since it's given that line *l* contains the point $(2, 6)$, substituting 2 for x and 6 for y in $y = \frac{2}{3}x + b$ yields $6 = \frac{2}{3}(2) + b$, or $6 = \frac{4}{3} + b$. Subtracting $\frac{4}{3}$ from both sides of this equation yields $b = \frac{14}{3}$. Substituting $\frac{14}{3}$ for b in the equation $y = \frac{2}{3}x + b$ gives $y = \frac{2}{3}x + \frac{14}{3}$.

Choice B is incorrect. The line for this equation contains the point $(2, 1)$, not $(2, 6)$. *Choice C* is incorrect. The line for this equation contains the point $(2, 10)$, not $(2, 6)$. *Choice D* is incorrect. The line for this equation contains the point $(2, 26)$, not $(2, 6)$.

QUESTION 12

Choice D is correct. The number of hours Morgan spent running or biking can be calculated by dividing the distance, in miles, she traveled during that activity by her speed, in miles per hour, for that activity. It's given that Morgan ran r miles at 5 miles per hour and biked b miles at 10 miles per hour. It follows that the number of hours she ran can be represented by the expression $\frac{r}{5}$ and the number of hours she biked can be represented by the expression $\frac{b}{10}$. It's given that she biked for twice as many hours as she ran, so this can be represented by the equation $\frac{b}{10} = 2\left(\frac{r}{5}\right)$, which can be rewritten as $5b = 20r$, or $b = 4r$. It's also given that she ran and biked a total of 200 miles. This can be represented by the equation $r + b = 200$. Substituting $4r$ for b in this equation yields $r + 4r = 200$, or $5r = 200$.

Dividing both sides of this equation by 5 yields $r = 40$. Determining the number of miles she biked, b, can be found by substituting 40 for r in the equation $r + b = 200$, which yields $40 + b = 200$. Subtracting 40 from both sides of this equation yields $b = 160$. Therefore, Morgan biked a total of 160 miles during the month.

Choice A is incorrect. If Morgan had biked a total of 80 miles during the month, it follows that Morgan would have run 120 miles, which doesn't satisfy the condition that Morgan biked for twice as many hours as she ran. *Choice B* is incorrect. If Morgan had biked a total of 100 miles during the month, it follows that Morgan would have run 100 miles, which doesn't satisfy the condition that Morgan biked for twice as many hours as she ran. *Choice C* is incorrect. If Morgan had biked a total of 120 miles during the month, it follows that Morgan would have run 80 miles, which doesn't satisfy the condition that Morgan biked for twice as many hours as she ran.

QUESTION 13

The correct answer is 48.75. It's given that the equation $c = \frac{5}{4}x + 406$ gives the total cost c, in dollars, to produce a quantity of x units. Since $c = \frac{5}{4}x + 406$ is a linear equation with a positive rate of change, $\frac{5}{4}$, it follows that the value of c increases by $\frac{5}{4}$ for every increase in x by 1. Therefore, if the value of x increases by 39, the value of c increases by $\frac{5}{4}(39)$, or $\frac{195}{4}$, which is equivalent to 48.75. Thus, if the quantity of units produced increases by 39, the corresponding increase in the total cost, in dollars, is 48.75. Note that 48.75 and 195/4 are examples of ways to enter a correct answer.

QUESTION 14

Choice A is correct. If a system of two linear equations has no solution, then the lines represented by the equations in the coordinate plane are parallel and distinct. The equation $kx - 3y = 4$ can be rewritten as $y = \frac{k}{3}x - \frac{4}{3}$, where $\frac{k}{3}$ is the slope and $\left(0, -\frac{4}{3}\right)$ is the y-intercept of the line. The equation $4x - 5y = 7$ can be rewritten as $y = \frac{4}{5}x - \frac{7}{5}$, where $\frac{4}{5}$ is the slope and $\left(0, -\frac{7}{5}\right)$ is the y-intercept of the line. If the two lines are parallel, then the lines have the same slope and different y-intercepts. Therefore, $\frac{k}{3} = \frac{4}{5}$, or $k = \frac{12}{5}$.

Choice B is incorrect. Substituting $\frac{16}{7}$ for k in the equation $kx - 3y = 4$ yields a line with a slope of $\frac{16}{21}$, not $\frac{4}{5}$. Therefore, for the given system of equations, if $k = \frac{16}{7}$, then the system has exactly one solution. *Choice C* is incorrect. Substituting $-\frac{16}{7}$ for k in the equation $kx - 3y = 4$ yields a line with a slope of $-\frac{16}{21}$, not $\frac{4}{5}$. Therefore, for the given system of equations, if $k = -\frac{16}{7}$, then the system has exactly one solution. *Choice D* is incorrect. Substituting $-\frac{12}{5}$ for k in the equation $kx - 3y = 4$ yields a line with a slope of $-\frac{4}{5}$, not $\frac{4}{5}$. Therefore, for the given system of equations, if $k = -\frac{12}{5}$, then the system has exactly one solution.

QUESTION 15

The correct answer is 120. It's given that there is a linear relationship between x and y and that the table shows four values of x and their corresponding values of y. Based on the given table, when $x = -5$, the corresponding value of y is 45 and when $x = 5$, the corresponding value of y is 3. Substituting -5 for x and 45 for y in the equation $Ax + 5y = C$ yields $A(-5) + 5(45) = C$, or $-5A + 225 = C$. Substituting 5 for x and 3 for y in the equation $Ax + 5y = C$ yields $A(5) + 5(3) = C$, or $5A + 15 = C$. Since $-5A + 225 = C$ and $5A + 15 = C$, it follows that $-5A + 225 = 5A + 15$. Subtracting $5A$ and 225 from both sides of this equation yields $-10A = -210$. Dividing both sides of this equation by -10 yields $A = 21$. Substituting 21 for A in the equation $-5A + 225 = C$ yields $-5(21) + 225 = C$, which is equivalent to $-105 + 225 = C$, or $C = 120$. Therefore, if an equation representing this relationship is written in the form $Ax + 5y = C$, where A and C are constants, the value of C is 120.

QUESTION 16

The correct answer is $-\frac{44}{7}$. It's given from the graph that the points $(7, 0)$ and $(0, -11)$ lie on the line shown in the xy-plane. For two points on a line, (x_1, y_1) and (x_2, y_2), the slope, m, of the line can be calculated using the slope formula $m = \frac{y_2 - y_1}{x_2 - x_1}$. Substituting $(7, 0)$ for (x_1, y_1) and $(0, -11)$ for (x_2, y_2) in this formula, the slope of the line can be calculated as $m = \frac{-11 - 0}{0 - 7}$, or $m = \frac{11}{7}$. It's also given that the point $(3, d)$ lies on the line. Substituting $(7, 0)$ for (x_1, y_1), $(3, d)$ for (x_2, y_2), and $\frac{11}{7}$ for m in the slope formula yields $\frac{11}{7} = \frac{d - 0}{3 - 7}$, or $\frac{11}{7} = \frac{d}{-4}$. Multiplying both sides of this equation by -4 yields $(-4)\left(\frac{11}{7}\right) = d$, or $d = -\frac{44}{7}$. Thus, the value of d is $-\frac{44}{7}$. Note that $-44/7$, -6.285, and -6.286 are examples of ways to enter a correct answer. $\frac{12}{5}$

CHAPTER 23

Math: Questions— Advanced Math

Advanced Math questions in the Math section address topics that are especially important for students to master before studying higher-level math concepts. Chief among these topics is the understanding of the structure of expressions and the ability to analyze, manipulate, and rewrite these expressions. Questions in this content domain also include ones involving reasoning with more complex equations and interpreting and building functions.

Algebra questions focus on the mastery of linear equations and inequalities, systems of linear equations, and linear functions. By contrast, Advanced Math questions focus on the ability to work with and analyze more complex equations. Advanced Math questions may require you to demonstrate procedural skill in adding, subtracting, and multiplying polynomials and in factoring polynomials. You may also be required to work with expressions involving integer and rational exponents, radicals, or fractions with a variable in the denominator. Questions in this domain may ask you to solve quadratic, radical, rational, polynomial, or absolute value equations. They may also ask you to solve a system consisting of a linear equation and a nonlinear equation. You may also be required to manipulate an equation in several variables to isolate a quantity of interest.

Some questions in Advanced Math may ask you to build a quadratic or an exponential function or an equation that describes a context or to interpret the function, the graph of the function, or the solution to an equation in terms of the context.

Advanced Math questions may assess your ability to recognize structure. Expressions and equations that appear complex may use repeated terms or repeated expressions. By noticing these patterns, the complexity of a problem can be reduced. Structure may be used to factor or otherwise rewrite an expression, to solve a quadratic or other equation, or to draw conclusions about the context represented by an expression, equation, or function. You may be asked to identify or derive the form of an expression, equation, or function that reveals information about the expression, equation, or function or the context it represents.

Advanced Math questions may also assess your understanding of functions and their graphs. A question may require you to demonstrate your understanding of function notation, including interpreting an expression in which the argument of a function is an expression rather than a variable. The questions may assess your understanding of how the algebraic properties of a function relate to the geometric characteristics of its graph.

Advanced Math questions include both multiple-choice questions and student-produced response questions. Although you may always use a calculator in the Math section, you must decide whether using it is an effective strategy for a given question.

Let's consider the content, skills, and knowledge assessed by Advanced Math questions.

Operations with Polynomials and Rewriting Expressions

Questions in the Math section may assess your ability to add, subtract, and multiply polynomials.

Advanced Math Sample Question 1

$$x^3 + 6x^2 + 7x - 6 = (x^2 + bx - 2)(x + 3)$$

In the given equation, b is a constant. If the equation is true for all values of x, what is the value of b?

A) 2

B) 3

C) 7

D) 9

The given equation shows two polynomials that are equivalent. To find the value of b, use the distributive property to rewrite the polynomial on the right-hand side of the given equation and then combine like terms so that the polynomial on the right-hand side is in the same form as the polynomial on the left-hand side.

$$x^3 + 6x^2 + 7x - 6 = (x^2 + bx - 2)(x + 3)$$
$$= (x^3 + bx^2 - 2x) + (3x^2 + 3bx - 6)$$
$$= x^3 + (3 + b)x^2 + (3b - 2)x - 6$$

STRATEGY

The skills and knowledge tested in Advanced Math questions build on the knowledge and skills tested by Algebra questions. Develop proficiency with the tested Algebra skills and knowledge before tackling Advanced Math questions.

Since the two polynomials are equal for all values of x, the coefficient of matching powers of x should be the same. Therefore, comparing the coefficients of $x^3 + 6x^2 + 7x - 6$ and $x^3 + (3 + b)x^2 + (3b - 2)x - 6$ reveals that $3 + b = 6$ and $3b - 2 = 7$. Solving either of these equations gives $b = 3$, which is choice B.

Questions may also ask you to use structure to rewrite expressions. For example, the expression may be in the form of a common pattern, such as a difference of squares, where using the difference-of-squares structure allows for efficient rewriting of the expression as the product of two binomials, as shown in sample 2.

Advanced Math Sample Question 2

Which of the following is equivalent to $16s^4 - 4t^2$?

A) $4(s^2 - t)(4s^2 + t)$

B) $4(4s^2 - t)(s^2 + t)$

C) $4(2s^2 - t)(2s^2 + t)$

D) $(8s^2 - 2t)(8s^2 + 2t)$

A close examination reveals that the given expression follows the difference of two perfect squares pattern, $x^2 - y^2$, which factors as the product $(x - y)(x + y)$. The expression $16s^4 - 4t^2$ is also the difference of two squares: $16s^4 - 4t^2 = (4s^2)^2 - (2t)^2$. Therefore, it can be factored as $(4s^2)^2 - (2t)^2 = (4s^2 - 2t)(4s^2 + 2t)$. This expression can be rewritten as $(4s^2 - 2t)(4s^2 + 2t) = 2(2s^2 - t)(2)(2s^2 + t)$, or $4(2s^2 - t)(2s^2 + t)$, which is choice C.

Alternatively, a 4 could be factored out of the given expression: $4(4s^4 - t^2)$. The expression inside the parentheses is a difference of two squares. Therefore, it can be further factored as $4(2s^2 - t)(2s^2 + t)$.

Advanced Math Sample Question 3

Which expression is equivalent to $xy^2 + 2xy^2 + 3xy$?

A) $2xy^2 + 3xy$

B) $3xy^2 + 3xy$

C) $6xy^4$

D) $6xy^5$

There are three terms in the expression, the first two of which are like terms. The like terms can be added together by adding their coefficients: $xy^2 + 2xy^2 + 3xy = (xy^2 + 2xy^2) + 3xy$, which is equivalent to $3xy^2 + 3xy$. Therefore, choice B is correct.

Quadratic Functions and Equations

Advanced Math questions may require you to build a quadratic function or an equation to represent a context.

Advanced Math Sample Question 4

A car is traveling at x feet per second. The driver sees a red light ahead, and after 1.5 seconds reaction time, the driver applies the brake. After the brake is applied, the car takes $\frac{x}{24}$ seconds to stop, during which time the average speed of the car is $\frac{x}{2}$ feet per second. If the car travels 165 feet from the time the driver saw the red light to the time it comes to a complete stop, which of the following equations can be used to find the value of x?

A) $x^2 + 48x - 3{,}960 = 0$

B) $x^2 + 48x - 7{,}920 = 0$

C) $x^2 + 72x - 3{,}960 = 0$

D) $x^2 + 72x - 7{,}920 = 0$

STRATEGY

Sample 4 requires careful translation of an in-context problem into an algebraic equation. It pays to be deliberate and methodical when translating such problems in the Math section into equations.

During the 1.5-second reaction time, the car is still traveling at x feet per second, so it travels a total of $1.5x$ feet. The average speed of the car during the $\frac{x}{24}$-second braking interval is $\frac{x}{2}$ feet per second, so over this interval the car travels $\left(\frac{x}{2}\right)\left(\frac{x}{24}\right) = \frac{x^2}{48}$ feet. Since the total distance the car travels from the time the driver saw the red light to the time the car comes to a complete stop is 165 feet, you have the equation $\frac{x^2}{48} + 1.5x = 165$. This quadratic equation can be rewritten in standard form by subtracting 165 from each side and then multiplying each side by 48, giving $x^2 + 72x - 7{,}920 = 0$, which is choice D.

STRATEGY

Questions in the Advanced Math domain may ask you to solve a quadratic equation. Practice using the various methods (below) until you're comfortable with all of them.

1. Factoring
2. Completing the square
3. Using the quadratic formula
4. Graphing using technology
5. Using structure

Be prepared to identify which strategy may be the most effective for solving a given quadratic equation.

Some questions in the Advanced Math domain may ask you to solve a quadratic equation. You must determine an appropriate procedure: factoring, completing the square, using the quadratic formula, graphing using technology, or using structure. It may be more efficient to solve a quadratic equation if you can make use of one of the following facts:

- The sum of the distinct solutions of $x^2 + bx + c = 0$ is $-b$.

- The product of the distinct solutions of $x^2 + bx + c = 0$ is c.

Each of these facts can be observed from examining the factored form of a quadratic. If r and s are distinct solutions of $x^2 + bx + c = 0$, then $x^2 + bx + c = (x - r)(x - s)$. Thus, $b = -(r + s)$ and $c = (-r)(-s) = rs$. **Note:** To use either of these facts, the coefficient of x^2 must be equal to 1.

Advanced Math Sample Question 5

What are the solutions to the equation $x^2 - 3 = x$?

A) $\dfrac{-1 \pm \sqrt{11}}{2}$

B) $\dfrac{-1 \pm \sqrt{13}}{2}$

C) $\dfrac{1 \pm \sqrt{11}}{2}$

D) $\dfrac{1 \pm \sqrt{13}}{2}$

The equation can be solved by using the quadratic formula or by completing the square. Let's use the quadratic formula. First, subtract x from each side of $x^2 - 3 = x$ to put the equation into standard form: $x^2 - x - 3 = 0$. The quadratic formula states that the solutions, x, of the equation $ax^2 + bx + c = 0$ are $\dfrac{-b \pm \sqrt{b^2 - 4ac}}{2a}$. For the equation $x^2 - x - 3 = 0$, $a = 1$, $b = -1$, and $c = -3$. Substituting these values into the quadratic formula gives $x = \dfrac{-(-1) \pm \sqrt{(-1)^2 - 4(1)(-3)}}{2(1)}$. This equation can be rewritten as $x = \dfrac{1 \pm \sqrt{1-(-12)}}{2}$, or $x = \dfrac{1 \pm \sqrt{13}}{2}$, which is choice D.

Advanced Math Sample Question 6

If $x > 0$ and $2x^2 + 3x - 2 = 0$, what is the value of x?

Note that this example is in the student-produced response (SPR) format and therefore has no answer choices. You have to generate and enter the response yourself.

The left-hand side of the given equation can be factored: $2x^2 + 3x - 2 = (2x - 1)(x + 2)$. Therefore, the given equation can be rewritten as $(2x - 1)(x + 2) = 0$, which implies that either $2x - 1 = 0$, which gives $x = \dfrac{1}{2}$, or $x + 2 = 0$, which gives $x = -2$. Since $x > 0$, the value of x is $\dfrac{1}{2}$.

Advanced Math Sample Question 7

What is the sum of the solutions to $(2x - 1)^2 = (x + 2)^2$?

If a and b are real numbers and $a^2 = b^2$, then either $a = b$ or $a = -b$. It follows then that since $(2x - 1)^2 = (x + 2)^2$, either $2x - 1 = x + 2$ or $2x - 1 = -(x + 2)$. In the first case, subtracting x and adding 1 to both sides of the equation yields $x = 3$. In the second case, applying the distributive property on the right side of the equation gives $2x - 1 = -x - 2$.

Adding x and 1 to both sides of this equation yields $3x = -1$. It follows that $x = -\dfrac{1}{3}$. Therefore, the sum of the solutions of $(2x - 1)^2 = (x + 2)^2$ is $3 + \left(-\dfrac{1}{3}\right)$, or $\dfrac{8}{3}$.

Exponential Functions, Equations, and Expressions and Radicals

Some Advanced Math questions may ask you to build a function that models a given context. Exponential functions model situations in which a quantity is multiplied by a constant factor for each time period. An exponential function can be increasing with time, in which case it models exponential growth, or it can be decreasing with time, in which case it models exponential decay.

Advanced Math Sample Question 8

A researcher estimates that the population of a city is increasing at an annual rate of 0.6%. If the current population of the city is 80,000, which of the following expressions appropriately models the population of the city t years from now according to the researcher's estimate?

A) $80,000(1 + 0.006)^t$

B) $80,000(1 + 0.006^t)$

C) $80,000 + 1.006^t$

D) $80,000(0.006^t)$

REMINDER

A quantity that grows or decays by a fixed percent at regular intervals is said to exhibit exponential growth or decay, respectively.

Exponential growth is represented by the function $y = a(1 + r)^t$, while exponential decay is represented by the function $y = a(1 - r)^t$, where y is the new population, a is the initial population, r is the rate of growth or decay, and t is the number of time intervals that have elapsed.

According to the researcher's estimate, the population is increasing by 0.6% each year. Since 0.6% is equal to 0.006, after the first year the population is $80,000 + 0.006(80,000) = 80,000(1 + 0.006)$. After the second year, the population is $80,000(1 + 0.006) + 0.006(80,000)(1 + 0.006) = 80,000(1 + 0.006)^2$. Similarly, after t years, the population will be $80,000(1 + 0.006)^t$ according to the researcher's estimate. This is choice A.

A well-known example of exponential decay is the decay of a radioactive isotope. One example involves iodine-131, a radioactive isotope used in some medical treatments. The half-life of iodine-131 is 8.02 days; that is, after 8.02 days, half of the iodine-131 in a sample will have decayed. Suppose a sample with a mass of A milligrams of iodine-131 decays for d days. Every 8.02 days, the quantity of iodine-131 is multiplied by $\frac{1}{2}$, or 2^{-1}. In d days, a total of $\frac{d}{8.02}$ different 8.02-day periods will have passed, and so the original quantity will have been multiplied by 2^{-1} a total of $\frac{d}{8.02}$ times. Therefore, the mass, in milligrams, of iodine-131 remaining in the sample will be $A(2^{-1})^{\frac{d}{8.02}} = A\left(2^{-\frac{d}{8.02}}\right)$.

In the preceding discussion, we used the identity $\frac{1}{2} = 2^{-1}$. Advanced Math questions may require you to apply this and other laws of exponents as well as the relationship between powers and radicals.

Some Advanced Math questions may ask you to use properties of exponents to rewrite expressions.

Advanced Math Sample Question 9

Which of the following is equivalent to $\left(\frac{1}{\sqrt{x}}\right)^n$, where $x > 0$?

A) $x^{\frac{n}{2}}$

B) $x^{-\frac{n}{2}}$

C) $x^{n+\frac{1}{2}}$

D) $x^{n-\frac{1}{2}}$

The expression $\sqrt{x}$ is equal to $x^{\frac{1}{2}}$. Thus, $\frac{1}{\sqrt{x}} = x^{-\frac{1}{2}}$, and $\left(\frac{1}{\sqrt{x}}\right)^n = \left(x^{-\frac{1}{2}}\right)^n = x^{-\frac{n}{2}}$. Choice B is the correct answer.

An Advanced Math question may also ask you to solve a radical equation. In solving radical equations, you may square both sides of an equation. Since squaring both sides of an equation may result in an extraneous solution, you may end up with a root to the simplified equation that isn't a root to the original equation. Thus, when solving a radical equation, you must check any solution you get in the original equation.

STRATEGY

Practice your exponent rules. Know, for instance, that $\sqrt{x} = x^{\frac{1}{2}}$ and that $\frac{1}{\sqrt{x}} = x^{-\frac{1}{2}}$.

Advanced Math Sample Question 10

$$x - 12 = \sqrt{x + 44}$$

What are all possible solutions to the given equation?

A) 5

B) 20

C) −5 and 20

D) 5 and 20

Squaring each side of $x - 12 = \sqrt{x + 44}$ gives

$$(x - 12)^2 = (\sqrt{x + 44})^2$$

$$(x - 12)^2 = x + 44$$

$$x^2 - 24x + 144 = x + 44$$

$$x^2 - 25x + 100 = 0$$

$$(x - 5)(x - 20) = 0$$

The solutions to this quadratic equation are $x = 5$ and $x = 20$. However, since the first step was to square each side of the given equation, which may have introduced an extraneous solution, you need to check $x = 5$ and $x = 20$ in the original equation. Substituting 5 for x gives

$$5 - 12 = \sqrt{5 + 44}$$

$$-7 = \sqrt{49}$$

This isn't a true statement (since $\sqrt{49}$ represents the principal square root, or only the positive square root, 7), so $x = 5$ is *not* a solution to $x - 12 = \sqrt{x + 44}$. Substituting 20 for x gives

$$20 - 12 = \sqrt{20 + 44}$$

$$8 = \sqrt{64}$$

STRATEGY

A good strategy to use when solving radical equations is to square both sides of the equation. When doing so, however, be sure to check the solutions in the original equation, as you may end up with a root that isn't a solution to the original equation.

This is a true statement, so $x = 20$ is a solution to $x - 12 = \sqrt{x + 44}$. Therefore, the only solution to the given equation is 20, which is choice B.

Solving Rational Equations

Questions in the Advanced Math domain may assess your ability to work with rational expressions, including fractions with a variable in the denominator. This may include finding the solution to a rational equation.

Advanced Math Sample Question 11

$$\frac{3}{t + 1} = \frac{2}{t + 3} + \frac{1}{4}$$

If t is a solution to the given equation and $t > 0$, what is the value of t?

STRATEGY

When solving for a variable in an equation involving fractions, a good first step is to clear the variable out of the denominators of the fractions. Remember that you can only multiply both sides of an equation by an expression when you know the expression can't be equal to 0.

Since $t > 0$, both sides of the given equation can be multiplied by the lowest common denominator, which is $4(t + 1)(t + 3)$. The resulting equivalent equation won't have any fractions, and the variable will no longer be in the denominator. This gives $12(t + 3) = 8(t + 1) + (t + 1)(t + 3)$. This equation can be rewritten as $12t + 36 = (8t + 8) + (t^2 + 4t + 3)$, or $12t + 36 = t^2 + 12t + 11$. Subtracting $12t$ and 36 from both sides of this equation yields $0 = t^2 - 25$. This equation can be rewritten by factoring the right-hand side as $0 = (t - 5)(t + 5)$. By the zero product property, $t - 5 = 0$ or $t + 5 = 0$. Therefore, the solutions to the equation are $t = 5$ or $t = -5$. Since $t > 0$, the value of t is 5.

Systems of Equations

Questions in the Advanced Math domain may ask you to solve a system of equations in two variables in which one equation is linear and the other equation is quadratic or another nonlinear equation.

Advanced Math Sample Question 12

$$3x + y = -3$$
$$(x + 1)^2 - 4(x + 1) - 6 = y$$

If (x, y) is a solution to the given system of equations and $y > 0$, what is the value of y?

STRATEGY

The first step used to solve this example was substitution, an approach you may use on questions about finding the solution to a system of linear equations as well. The second step used to solve this example was taken after noticing that $(x + 1)$ can be treated as a variable.

One method for solving systems of equations is substitution. If the first equation is solved for y, it can be substituted in the second equation. Subtracting $3x$ from each side of the first equation gives you $y = -3 - 3x$, which can be rewritten as $y = -3(x + 1)$. Substituting $-3(x + 1)$ for y in the second equation gives you $(x + 1)^2 - 4(x + 1) - 6 = -3(x + 1)$. Since the factor $(x + 1)$ appears as a squared term and a linear term, the equation can be thought of as a quadratic equation in the variable $(x + 1)$, so collecting the terms and setting the expression equal to 0 gives you $(x + 1)^2 - (x + 1) - 6 = 0$. Rewriting this equation by factoring gives you $((x + 1) - 3)((x + 1) + 2) = 0$, or $(x - 2)(x + 3) = 0$.

Thus, either $x = 2$, which gives $y = -3 - 3(2) = -9$; or $x = -3$, which gives $y = -3 - 3(-3) = 6$. Therefore, the solutions to the system are $(2, -9)$ and $(-3, 6)$. Since the question states that $y > 0$, the value of y is 6.

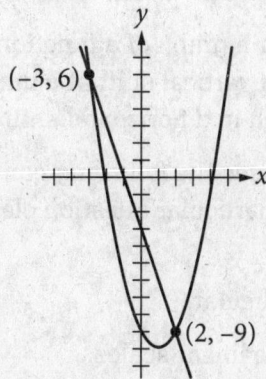

The solutions of the system are given by the intersection points of the two graphs. Questions in the SAT Math section may assess this or other relationships between algebraic and graphical representations of functions.

Relationships Between Algebraic and Graphical Representations of Functions

A function f has a graph in the xy-plane, which is the graph of the equation $y = f(x)$, or, equivalently, consists of all ordered pairs $(x, f(x))$. Some Advanced Math questions may assess your ability to relate properties of the function f to properties of its graph and vice versa. You may be required to apply some of the following relationships:

- **Intercepts.** The x-intercepts of the graph of f correspond to values of x such that $f(x) = 0$, which corresponds to values of x where the graph intersects with the x-axis, also known as the function's zeros; if the function f has no zeros, its graph has no x-intercepts and vice versa. The y-intercept of the graph of f corresponds to the value of $f(0)$, or the value of y where the graph intersects with the y-axis. If $x = 0$ is not in the domain of f, the graph of f has no y-intercept and vice versa.

- **Domain and range.** The domain of f is the set of all x for which $f(x)$ is defined. The range of f is the set of all y such that $y = f(x)$ for some value of x in the domain. The domain and range can be found from the graph of f as the set of all x-coordinates and y-coordinates, respectively, of points on the graph.

- **Maximum and minimum values.** The maximum and minimum values of f can be found by locating the highest and the lowest points on the graph, respectively. For example, suppose P is the highest point on the graph of f. Then the y-coordinate of P is the maximum value of f, and the x-coordinate of P is where f takes on its maximum value.

REMINDER

The domain of a function is the set of all values for which the function is defined. The range of a function is the set of all values that correspond to the values in the domain, given the relationship defined by the function, or the set of all outputs that are associated with all the possible inputs.

- **Increasing and decreasing.** The graph of f shows the intervals over which the function f is increasing and decreasing.

- **End behavior.** The graph of f can indicate if $f(x)$ increases or decreases without limit as x increases or decreases without limit.

- **Transformations.** For a graph of a function f, a change of the form $f(x) + a$ will result in a vertical shift of a units, and a change of the form $f(x - a)$ will result in a horizontal shift of a units.

STRATEGY

Don't assume the size of the units on the two axes are equal unless the question states they're equal or you can conclude they're equal from the information given.

Note: The Math section uses the following conventions about graphs in the xy-plane unless a particular question clearly states or shows a different convention:

- The axes are perpendicular.

- Scales on the axes are linear scales.

- The size of the units on the two axes can't be assumed to be equal unless the question states they're equal or you're given enough information to conclude they're equal.

- The values on the horizontal axis increase as you move to the right.

- The values on the vertical axis increase as you move up.

Advanced Math Sample Question 13

The graph of which of the following functions in the xy-plane has x-intercepts at -4 and 5?

A) $f(x) = (x + 4)(x - 5)$
B) $g(x) = (x - 4)(x + 5)$
C) $h(x) = (x - 4)^2 + 5$
D) $k(x) = (x + 5)^2 - 4$

The x-intercepts of the graph of a function correspond to the zeros of the function. All the functions in the choices are defined by quadratic equations, so the answer must be a quadratic function. If a quadratic function has x-intercepts at -4 and 5, then the values of the function at -4 and 5 are each 0; that is, the zeros of the function occur at $x = -4$ and at $x = 5$. Since the function is defined by a quadratic equation and has zeros at $x = -4$ and $x = 5$, it must have $(x + 4)$ and $(x - 5)$ as factors. Therefore, choice A, $f(x) = (x + 4)(x - 5)$, is correct.

STRATEGY

Another way to think of sample 13 is to ask yourself, "Which answer choice represents a function that has values of 0 when $x = -4$ and $x = 5$?"

The graph in the xy-plane of each of the functions in the previous example is a parabola. Using the defining equations, you can tell that the graph of g has x-intercepts at 4 and -5; the graph of h has its vertex at $(4, 5)$; and the graph of k has its vertex at $(-5, -4)$.

Advanced Math Sample Question 14

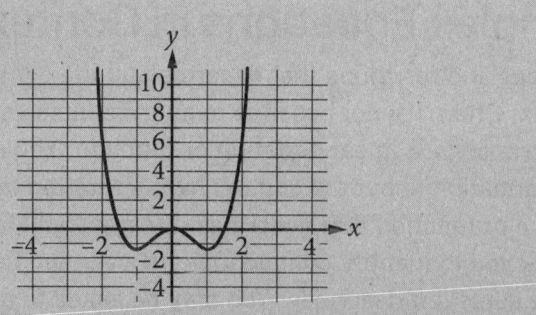

The function $f(x) = x^4 - 2.4x^2$ is graphed in the xy-plane where $y = f(x)$, as shown. If k is a constant such that the equation $f(x) = k$ has 4 solutions, which of the following could be the value of k?

A) 1

B) 0

C) −1

D) −2

Choice C is correct. Since $f(x) = x^4 - 2.4x^2$, the equation $f(x) = k$, or $x^4 - 2.4x^2 = k$, will have four solutions if and only if the graph of the horizontal line with equation $y = k$ intersects the graph of f at four points. The graph shows that of the given choices, only for choice C, −1, does the graph of $y = -1$ intersect the graph of f at four points.

Function Notation

The Math section may assess your understanding of function notation. In such cases, you must be able to evaluate a function given the rule that defines it, and if the function describes a context, you may need to interpret the value of the function in the context. A question may ask you to interpret a function when an expression, such as $2x$ or $x + 1$, is used as the argument instead of the variable x.

Advanced Math Sample Question 15

If $g(x) = 2x + 1$ and $f(x) = g(x) + 4$, what is $f(2)$?

You're given $f(x) = g(x) + 4$; therefore, $f(2) = g(2) + 4$. To determine the value of $g(2)$, use the function $g(x) = 2x + 1$. Thus, $g(2) = 2(2) + 1$, and therefore, $g(2) = 5$. Substituting $g(2)$ gives $f(2) = 5 + 4$, or $f(2) = 9$.

Alternatively, since $f(x) = g(x) + 4$ and $g(x) = 2x + 1$, it follows that $f(x)$ must equal $2x + 1 + 4$, or $2x + 5$. Therefore, $f(2) = 2(2) + 5 = 9$.

STRATEGY

What may seem at first to be a complex question could boil down to straightforward substitution.

Interpreting and Analyzing More Complex Equations in Context

Equations and functions that describe real-life contexts can be complex. Often, it's not possible to analyze them as completely as you can analyze a linear equation or function. You still can acquire key information about the context by interpreting and analyzing the equation or function that describes it. Advanced Math questions may ask you to identify connections between the function, its graph, and the context it describes. You may be asked to use an equation describing a context to determine how a change in one quantity affects another quantity. You may also be asked to manipulate an equation to isolate a quantity of interest on one side of the equation. You may be asked to produce or identify a form of an equation that reveals new information about the context it represents or about the graphical representation of the equation.

Advanced Math Sample Question 16

> For a certain reservoir, the function f gives the water level $f(n)$, to the nearest whole percent of capacity, on the nth day of 2016. Which of the following is the best interpretation of $f(37) = 70$?
>
> A) The water level of the reservoir was at 37% capacity for 70 days in 2016.
> B) The water level of the reservoir was at 70% capacity for 37 days in 2016.
> C) On the 37th day of 2016, the water level of the reservoir was at 70% capacity.
> D) On the 70th day of 2016, the water level of the reservoir was at 37% capacity.

The function f gives the water level, to the nearest whole percent of capacity, on the nth day of 2016. It follows that $f(37) = 70$ means that on the 37th day of 2016, the water level of the reservoir was at 70% capacity. This statement is choice C.

Advanced Math Sample Question 17

> If an object of mass m is moving at speed v, the object's kinetic energy (KE) is given by the equation $KE = \frac{1}{2}mv^2$. If the mass of the object is halved and its speed is doubled, how does the kinetic energy change?
>
> A) The kinetic energy is halved.
> B) The kinetic energy is unchanged.
> C) The kinetic energy is doubled.
> D) The kinetic energy is quadrupled (multiplied by a factor of 4).

STRATEGY

Another way to check your answer in sample 17 is to substitute simple numerical values for the variables m, v, and KE when those values are altered as indicated by the question. If the value 1 is substituted for both m and v, then KE is $\frac{1}{2}$. However, substituting $\frac{1}{2}$ for m and 2 for v yields a value for KE of 1. Since 1 is twice the value of $\frac{1}{2}$, you know that KE is doubled.

Choice C is correct. If the mass of the object is halved, the new mass is $\frac{m}{2}$. If the speed of the object is doubled, its new speed is $2v$. Therefore, the new kinetic energy is $\frac{1}{2}\left(\frac{m}{2}\right)(2v^2) = \frac{1}{2}\left(\frac{m}{2}\right)(4v^2) = mv^2$. This is double the original kinetic energy of the object, which was $\frac{1}{2}mv^2$.

Advanced Math Sample Question 18

A gas in a container will escape through holes of microscopic size, as long as the holes are larger than the gas molecules. This process is called effusion. If a gas of molar mass M_1 effuses at a rate of r_1 and a gas of molar mass M_2 effuses at a rate of r_2, then the following relationship holds.

$$\frac{r_1}{r_2} = \sqrt{\frac{M_2}{M_1}}$$

This is known as Graham's law. Which of the following correctly expresses M_2 in terms of M_1, r_1, and r_2?

A) $M_2 = M_1 \left(\dfrac{r_1^2}{r_2^2} \right)$

B) $M_2 = M_1 \left(\dfrac{r_2^2}{r_1^2} \right)$

C) $M_2 = \sqrt{M_1} \left(\dfrac{r_1}{r_2} \right)$

D) $M_2 = \sqrt{M_1} \left(\dfrac{r_2}{r_1} \right)$

Squaring each side of $\frac{r_1}{r_2} = \sqrt{\frac{M_2}{M_1}}$ gives $\left(\frac{r_1}{r_2} \right)^2 = \left(\sqrt{\frac{M_2}{M_1}} \right)^2$, which can be rewritten as $\frac{M_2}{M_1} = \frac{r_1^2}{r_2^2}$. Multiplying each side of $\frac{M_2}{M_1} = \frac{r_1^2}{r_2^2}$ by M_1 gives $M_2 = M_1 \left(\frac{r_1^2}{r_2^2} \right)$, which is choice A.

Advanced Math Sample Question 19

A store manager estimates that if a video game is sold at a price of p dollars, the store will have weekly revenue, in dollars, of $r(p) = -4p^2 + 200p$ from the sale of the video game. Which of the following equivalent forms of $r(p)$ shows, as constants or coefficients, the maximum possible weekly revenue and the price that results in the maximum revenue?

A) $r(p) = 200p - 4p^2$
B) $r(p) = -2(2p^2 - 100p)$
C) $r(p) = -4(p^2 - 50p)$
D) $r(p) = -4(p - 25)^2 + 2{,}500$

Choice D is correct. The graph of r in the coordinate plane is a parabola that opens downward. The maximum value of revenue corresponds to the vertex of the parabola. Since the square of any real number is always nonnegative, the form $r(p) = -4(p - 25)^2 + 2{,}500$ shows that the vertex of the parabola is (25, 2,500); that is, the maximum must occur where $-4(p - 25)^2$ is 0, which is $p = 25$, and this maximum is $r(25) = 2{,}500$. Thus, the maximum possible weekly revenue and the price that results in the maximum revenue occur as constants in the form $r(p) = -4(p - 25)^2 + 2{,}500$.

STRATEGY

Always start by identifying exactly what the question asks. In sample 18, you're being asked to isolate the variable M_2. Squaring both sides of the equation is a great first step, as it allows you to eliminate the radical sign.

STRATEGY

The fact that the coefficient of the squared term is negative for this function indicates that the graph of r in the coordinate plane is a parabola that opens downward. Thus, the maximum value of revenue corresponds to the vertex of the parabola.

Summary: Advanced Math

Main purpose: To assess your understanding of nonlinear relationships

Proportion of the test section: About 35 percent (thirteen to fifteen questions)

Question types

- Equivalent expressions
- Nonlinear equations in one variable and systems of equations in two variables
- Nonlinear functions

CHAPTER 24

Math: Questions—
Advanced Math Drills

1

Which of the following expressions is equivalent to $2(ab - 3) + 2$?

A) $2ab - 1$

B) $2ab - 4$

C) $2ab - 5$

D) $2ab - 8$

2

$$f(x) = (x + 0.25x)(50 - x)$$

The function f is defined as shown. What is the value of $f(20)$?

A) 250

B) 500

C) 750

D) 2,000

3

$$x^2 + 6x + 9 = 36$$

What is the positive solution to the given equation?

4

The function f is defined by $f(x) = \frac{22}{x+1}$. What is the value of $f(22)$?

5

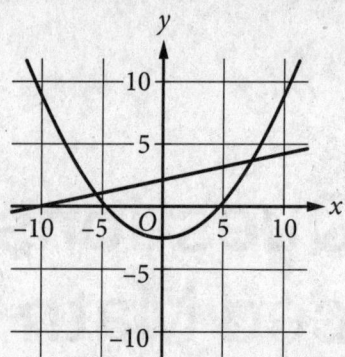

A system of equations consists of a quadratic equation and a linear equation. The equations in this system are graphed in the xy-plane shown. How many solutions does this system have?

A) 0

B) 1

C) 2

D) 3

6

$$S = 4\pi r^2$$

The formula shown gives the surface area, S, of a sphere in terms of the length of its radius, r. Which of the following gives the radius of the sphere in terms of its surface area?

A) $r = \sqrt{\dfrac{S}{4\pi}}$

B) $r = \sqrt{\dfrac{4\pi}{S}}$

C) $r = \dfrac{\sqrt{S}}{4\pi}$

D) $r = \dfrac{\sqrt{4\pi}}{S}$

7

$$\frac{4x}{2(x^2 - 1)} - \frac{3x}{3(x^2 - 1)}$$

Which of the following is equivalent to the given expression for $x \neq -1$ and $x \neq 1$?

A) $\dfrac{1}{6(x - 1)}$

B) $\dfrac{x}{6(x^2 - 1)}$

C) $\dfrac{1}{x - 1}$

D) $\dfrac{x}{x^2 - 1}$

8

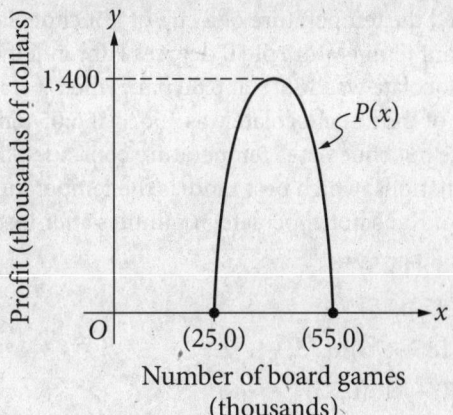

Profit (thousands of dollars)

1,400

P(x)

O   (25,0)   (55,0)

Number of board games
(thousands)

A company produces board games and sells them online and in stores. The quadratic function *P* models the company's monthly profits *P(x)*, in thousands of dollars, when *x* board games, in thousands, are produced and sold. The graph of *y = P(x)*, where $25 \leq x \leq 55$, is shown in the *xy*-plane. How many board games must the company produce and sell in order to earn the maximum profit estimated by the model?

A) 20,000

B) 40,000

C) 60,000

D) 1,400,000

9

$$y - x = 30$$
$$y = x^2 - 28x$$

The graphs of the equations in the given system intersect at the point (x, y) in the *xy*-plane. What is a possible value of *y*?

10

In the equation $9x^2 + 108x + \frac{c}{4} = 0$, *c* is a constant. If the equation has exactly one real solution, what is the value of *c*?

A) 0

B) 324

C) 1,296

D) 11,664

11

Kao measured the temperature of a cup of hot chocolate placed in a room with a constant temperature of 70 degrees Fahrenheit (°F). The temperature of the hot chocolate was 185°F at 6:00 p.m. when it started cooling. The temperature of the hot chocolate was 156°F at 6:05 p.m. and 135°F at 6:10 p.m. The hot chocolate's temperature continued to decrease. Of the following functions, which best models the temperature $T(m)$, in degrees Fahrenheit, of Kao's hot chocolate m minutes after it started cooling?

A) $T(m) = 185(1.25)^m$

B) $T(m) = 185(0.85)^m$

C) $T(m) = (185 - 70)(0.75)^{\frac{m}{5}}$

D) $T(m) = 70 + 115(0.75)^{\frac{m}{5}}$

12

$$\sqrt{5(x - k)} = x - k$$

In the given equation, k is a positive constant. The greatest solution to the equation is 12. What is the value of k?

13

$$g(x) = (5 - 2x)(14 + 2x)$$

The function g is defined by the given equation. For what value of x does $g(x)$ reach its maximum?

14

A rectangular volleyball court has an area of 162 square meters. If the length of the court is twice the width, what is the width of the court, in meters?

A) 9

B) 18

C) 27

D) 54

15

$$x^2 = 6x + y$$

$$y = -6x + 36$$

A solution to the given system of equations is (x, y). Which of the following is a possible value of xy?

A) 0

B) 6

C) 12

D) 36

16

The function f is defined by $f(x) = ax^2 + bx + c$, where a, b, and c are constants and $1 < a < 4$. The graph of $y = f(x)$ in the xy-plane passes through points $(11, 0)$ and $(-2, 0)$. If a is an integer, what could be the value of $a + b$?

Answer Explanations

QUESTION 1

Choice B is correct. Applying the distributive property to the given expression yields $2(ab) + 2(-3) + 2$, or $2ab - 6 + 2$. Adding the like terms -6 and 2 results in the expression $2ab - 4$.

Choice A is incorrect. This expression is equivalent to $2(ab - 3) + 5$. *Choice C* is incorrect. This expression is equivalent to $2(ab - 3) + 1$. *Choice D* is incorrect. This expression is equivalent to $2(ab - 3) - 2$.

QUESTION 2

Choice C is correct. Adding the like terms x and $0.25x$ yields the equation $f(x) = (1.25x)(50 - x)$. Substituting 20 for x yields $f(20) = (1.25(20))(50 - 20)$, or $f(20) = (25)(30)$, which is equivalent to $f(20) = 750$. Therefore, the value of $f(20)$ is 750.

Choices A, B, and *D* are incorrect and may result from conceptual or calculation errors.

QUESTION 3

The correct answer is 3. Subtracting 36 from both sides of the given equation yields $x^2 + 6x - 27 = 0$. Two numbers whose product is -27 and whose sum is 6 are 9 and -3. Therefore, by factoring, the equation $x^2 + 6x - 27 = 0$ can be rewritten as $(x + 9)(x - 3) = 0$. By the zero product property, it follows that $x + 9 = 0$ or $x - 3 = 0$. Subtracting 9 from both sides of the equation $x + 9 = 0$ yields $x = -9$. Adding 3 to both sides of the equation $x - 3 = 0$ yields $x = 3$. Therefore, the two solutions to the given equation are -9 and 3. Thus, the positive solution to the given equation is 3.

Alternate approach: The left-hand side of the given equation is a perfect square trinomial. It follows that the given equation can be rewritten as $(x + 3)^2 = 36$. Taking the square root of both sides of this equation yields two equations: $x + 3 = 6$ and $x + 3 = -6$. Subtracting 3 from both sides of the equation $x + 3 = 6$ yields $x = 3$. Subtracting 3 from both sides of the equation $x + 3 = -6$ yields $x = -9$. Therefore, the two solutions to the given equation are 3 and -9. Thus, the positive solution to the given equation is 3.

QUESTION 4

The correct answer is $\frac{22}{23}$. For the given function f, the value of $f(22)$ is the value of $f(x)$ when $x = 22$. Substituting 22 for x in the equation $f(x) = \frac{22}{x + 1}$ yields $f(22) = \frac{22}{(22) + 1}$, or $f(22) = \frac{22}{23}$. Therefore, the value of $f(22)$ is $\frac{22}{23}$. Note that 22/23, .9565, 0.956, and 0.957 are examples of ways to enter a correct answer.

QUESTION 5

Choice C is correct. The solutions to a system of two equations correspond to points where the graphs of the equations intersect. The given graphs intersect at 2 points; therefore, the system has 2 solutions.

Choice A is incorrect and may result from conceptual or calculation errors. *Choice B* is incorrect and may result from conceptual or calculation errors. *Choice D* is incorrect. It's not possible for the graph of a quadratic equation and the graph of a linear equation to intersect at more than two points.

QUESTION 6

Choice A is correct. Solving the given formula for r yields the radius of the sphere in terms of its surface area. Dividing both sides of the given equation by 4π yields $\frac{S}{4\pi} = r^2$. Taking the square root of both sides of this equation yields $\sqrt{\frac{S}{4\pi}} = r$, which can be rewritten as $r = \sqrt{\frac{S}{4\pi}}$.

Choices B, C, and *D* are incorrect and may result from conceptual or calculation errors.

QUESTION 7

Choice D is correct. Multiplying the first fraction in the given expression by $\frac{3}{3}$ and multiplying the second fraction in the given expression by $\frac{2}{2}$ results in both fractions having a common denominator:

$\frac{4x}{2(x^2 - 1)} - \frac{3x}{3(x^2 - 1)} = \frac{(3)(4x)}{(3)(2)(x^2 - 1)} - \frac{2(3x)}{(2)(3)(x^2 - 1)}$. Rewriting the right-hand side of this equation yields $\frac{12x}{6(x^2 - 1)} - \frac{6x}{6(x^2 - 1)}$, which is equivalent to $\frac{12x - 6x}{6(x^2 - 1)}$, or $\frac{6x}{6(x^2 - 1)}$. Rewriting this fraction yields $\frac{x}{x^2 - 1}$.

Alternate approach: The given expression can be rewritten as $\frac{2x}{x^2 - 1} - \frac{x}{x^2 - 1}$. Since the fractions in this expression have a common denominator of $x^2 - 1$, it follows that this expression is equivalent to $\frac{2x - x}{x^2 - 1}$, or $\frac{x}{x^2 - 1}$.

Choices A, B, and *C* are incorrect and may result from conceptual or calculation errors.

QUESTION 8

Choice B is correct. For each point (x, y) on the graph shown, the x-coordinate gives the number of board games, in thousands, that the company produces and sells, and the y-coordinate gives the monthly profit, in thousands of dollars, from the sale of these board games. The maximum profit is represented by the point on the graph with the greatest y-coordinate. Because P is a quadratic function, the graph of $y = P(x)$ is a parabola and the point with the greatest y-coordinate is the vertex. Because of the symmetry of the parabola, the x-coordinate of its vertex is the mean of the x-coordinates of any two symmetrical points on the graph. For example, the x-intercepts (25, 0) and (55, 0) are symmetrical points on the graph. Therefore, the x-coordinate of the vertex is $\frac{25 + 55}{2}$, or 40. It follows that the vertex of the graph is (40, 1,400). This means that the maximum profit of $1,400,000 is reached when the company produces and sells 40,000 board games.

Choices A and *C* are incorrect and may result from conceptual or calculation errors. *Choice D* is incorrect. This is the maximum profit, in dollars, that corresponds to the production and sale of 40,000 board games.

QUESTION 9

The correct answer is either 29 or 60. It's given that the graphs of the equations in the given system intersect at the point (x, y) in the xy-plane. Therefore, this intersection point represents a solution to the given system. The first equation, $y - x = 30$, can be rewritten as $y = x + 30$. Substituting $x + 30$ for y in the second equation, $y = x^2 - 28x$, yields $x + 30 = x^2 - 28x$. Subtracting x and 30 from both sides of this equation yields $0 = x^2 - 28x - x - 30$, or $0 = x^2 - 29x - 30$, which is equivalent to $0 = (x + 1)(x - 30)$. It follows that $x + 1 = 0$ or $x - 30 = 0$. Therefore, $x = -1$ or $x = 30$. Substituting -1 for x in the equation $y - x = 30$ yields $y - (-1) = 30$, or $y + 1 = 30$, which is equivalent to $y = 29$. Therefore, the graphs of the equations in the given system intersect at the point $(-1, 29)$. Substituting 30 for x in the equation $y - x = 30$ yields $y - 30 = 30$, which is equivalent to $y = 60$. Therefore, the graphs of the equations in the given system intersect at the point $(30, 60)$. Thus, either 29 or 60 is a possible value of y. Note that 29 and 60 are examples of ways to enter a correct answer.

QUESTION 10

Choice C is correct. A quadratic equation of the form $Ax^2 + Bx + C = 0$, where A, B, and C are constants, has exactly one solution if and only if its discriminant, $B^2 - 4AC$, is equal to zero. The given equation is in this form, where $A = 9$, $B = 108$, and $C = \frac{c}{4}$. Substituting 9 for A, 108 for B, and $\frac{c}{4}$ for C into $B^2 - 4AC$ yields $(108)^2 - 4(9)\left(\frac{c}{4}\right)$, or $11{,}664 - 9c$. Therefore, if the given equation has exactly one solution, then $11{,}664 - 9c = 0$. Adding $9c$ to both sides of this equation yields $11{,}664 = 9c$. Dividing both sides of this equation by 9 yields $1{,}296 = c$. Therefore, if the equation has exactly one real solution, the value of c is 1,296.

Choice A is incorrect. This is the value of $9x^2 + 108x + \frac{c}{4}$, not c. *Choice B* is incorrect. This is the value of $\frac{c}{4}$, not c. *Choice D* is incorrect. This is the value of $(108)^2$, not c.

QUESTION 11

Choice D is correct. The temperature, in degrees Fahrenheit (°F), of the cup of hot chocolate, $T(m)$, will decrease as the number of minutes, m, after it starts cooling increases, since the temperature of the room is lower than the starting temperature of the cup of hot chocolate. Each of the answer choices involves the variable m in an exponent. Choices B, C, and D each have a function with the base of the exponent less than 1, so each of them is a decreasing function, where the value of $T(m)$ will decrease over time. It's given that the temperature of the hot chocolate was 185°F at 6:00 p.m. when it started cooling. It follows that $T(0) = 185$. It's also given that at 6:05 p.m., or 5 minutes after it started cooling, the temperature of the hot chocolate was 156°F and that at 6:10 p.m., or 10 minutes after it started cooling, the temperature was 135°F. Therefore, $T(5) = 156$ and $T(10) = 135$. For the function in choice D, substituting 0, 5, and 10 for m in the function yields $T(0) = 70 + 115(0.75)^{\frac{0}{5}}$, or 185; $T(5) = 70 + 115(0.75)^{\frac{5}{5}}$, which is approximately 156; and $T(10) = 70 + 115(0.75)^{\frac{10}{5}}$, which is approximately 135. Therefore, of the given choices, choice D best models the temperature of Kao's hot chocolate m minutes after it started cooling.

Choice A is incorrect because it's a function with the base of the exponent equal to 1.25, which results in the value of $T(m)$ increasing over time, rather than decreasing. *Choice B* is incorrect because substituting 0, 5, and 10 for m in this function yields approximately 185, 82, and 36, respectively, rather than 185, 156, and 135. *Choice C* is incorrect because substituting 0, 5, and 10 for m in this function yields approximately 115, 86, and 65, respectively, rather than 185, 156, and 135.

QUESTION 12

The correct answer is 7. Squaring both sides of the given equation yields $5(x - k) = (x - k)^2$, or $5(x - k) = (x - k)(x - k)$. Subtracting $5(x - k)$ from both sides of this equation yields $0 = (x - k)(x - k) - 5(x - k)$. Factoring out the common factor of $x - k$ from the terms on the right-hand side of this equation yields $0 = (x - k)(x - k - 5)$, or $0 = (x - k)(x - (k + 5))$. By the zero product property, it follows that $x - k = 0$ or $x - (k + 5) = 0$. Adding k to both sides of the equation $x - k = 0$ yields $x = k$. Adding $(k + 5)$ to both sides of the equation $x - (k + 5) = 0$ yields $x = k + 5$. Thus, the two solutions to the given equation are k and $k + 5$. It follows that the greatest solution to the given equation is $k + 5$. It's given that the greatest solution to the given equation is 12. Therefore, $k + 5 = 12$. Subtracting 5 from both sides of this equation yields $k = 7$. Thus, the value of k is 7.

QUESTION 13

The correct answer is $-\frac{9}{4}$. It's given that $g(x) = (5 - 2x)(14 + 2x)$, which can be rewritten as $g(x) = -4x^2 - 18x + 70$. Since the coefficient of the x^2-term is negative, the graph of $y = g(x)$ in the xy-plane opens downward and reaches a maximum value at its vertex. The x-coordinate of the vertex is the value of x such that $g(x)$ reaches its maximum. For the graph of an equation in the form $g(x) = ax^2 + bx + c$, where a, b, and c are constants, the x-coordinate of the vertex is $-\frac{b}{2a}$. For the equation $g(x) = -4x^2 - 18x + 70$, $a = -4$, $b = -18$, and $c = 70$. It follows that the x-coordinate of the vertex is $-\frac{-18}{2(-4)}$, or $-\frac{9}{4}$. Therefore, $g(x)$ reaches its maximum when the value of x is $-\frac{9}{4}$. Note that $-9/4$ and -2.25 are examples of ways to enter a correct answer.

QUESTION 14

Choice A is correct. It's given that the volleyball court is rectangular and has an area of 162 square meters. The formula for the area of a rectangle is $A = l \cdot w$, where A is the area, l is the length, and w is the width of the rectangle. It's also given that the length of the volleyball court is twice the width, thus $l = 2w$. Substituting 162 for A in the formula for the area of a rectangle and using the relationship between length and width for this rectangle yields $162 = (2w)(w)$. This equation can be rewritten as $162 = 2w^2$. Dividing both sides of this equation by 2 yields $81 = w^2$. Taking the square root of both sides of the equation yields $\pm 9 = w$. Since the width of the rectangle is a positive number, the width of the volleyball court is 9 meters.

Choice B is incorrect. This is the length, not the width, of the court. *Choice C* is incorrect. If the width of this volleyball court was 27 meters, the area would be $2(27)^2$ meters, or 1,458 meters, not 162 meters. *Choice D* is incorrect. If the width of this volleyball court was 54 meters, the area would be $2(54)^2$ meters, or 591,872 meters, not 162 meters.

QUESTION 15

Choice A is correct. Solutions to the given systems of equations are ordered pairs (x, y) that satisfy both equations in the system. Adding the left-hand and right-hand sides of the equations in the given system yields $x^2 + y = 6x + -6x + y + 36$, or $x^2 + y = y + 36$. Subtracting y from both sides of this equation yields $x^2 = 36$. Taking the square root of both sides of this equation yields $x = 6$ and $x = -6$. Therefore, there are two solutions to this system of equations, one with an x-coordinate of 6 and the other with an x-coordinate of -6. Substituting 6 for x in the second equation yields $y = -6(6) + 36$, or $y = 0$; therefore, one solution is $(6, 0)$. Similarly, substituting -6 for x in the second equation yields $y = -6(-6) + 36$, or $y = 72$; therefore, the other solution is $(-6, 72)$. Of these possible values of xy, only 0 is given as a choice.

Choice B is incorrect. This is the x-coordinate of one of the solutions, $(6, 0)$. *Choice C* is incorrect and may result from conceptual or calculation errors. *Choice D* is incorrect. This is the square of the x-coordinate of one of the solutions, $(6, 0)$.

QUESTION 16

The correct answer is either -16 or -24. It's given that the function f is defined by the equation $f(x) = ax^2 + bx + c$, where a, b, and c are constants, and $1 < a < 4$. It's also given that the graph of $y = f(x)$ in the xy-plane passes through the points $(11, 0)$ and $(-2, 0)$. Therefore, $f(11) = 0$ and $f(-2) = 0$. It follows that $x - 11$ and $x + 2$ are factors of $f(x)$, and the equation $f(x) = ax^2 + bx + c$ can be rewritten as $f(x) = a(x - 11)(x + 2)$. Applying the distributive property on the right-hand side of this equation yields $f(x) = a(x^2 - 9x - 22)$, or $f(x) = ax^2 - 9ax - 22a$. Since $1 < a < 4$, if a is an integer, it follows that the value of a is either 2 or 3. If $a = 2$, the equation defining f is $f(x) = (2)x^2 - 9(2)x - 22(2)$, or $f(x) = 2x^2 - 18x - 44$. Since it's given that $f(x) = ax^2 + bx + c$, it follows that $ax^2 + bx + c = 2x^2 - 18x - 44$. Therefore, if $a = 2$, then $b = -18$ and the value of $a + b$ is $2 + (-18)$, or -16. If $a = 3$, the equation defining f is $f(x) = (3)x^2 - 9(3)x - 22(3)$, or $f(x) = 3x^2 - 27x - 66$. Since it's given that $f(x) = ax^2 + bx + c$, it follows that $ax^2 + bx + c = 3x^2 - 27x - 66$. Therefore, if $a = 3$, then $b = -27$ and the value of $a + b$ is $3 + (-27)$, or -24. Thus, if a is an integer, then the value of $a + b$ is either -16 or -24. Note that -16 and -24 are examples of ways to enter a correct answer.

CHAPTER 25

Math: Questions— Problem-Solving and Data Analysis

Problem-Solving and Data Analysis questions in the Math section assess your ability to use your math skills and knowledge to solve problems, many of which are set in context. Some of the questions in this content domain may ask you to create a representation of a problem, consider the units involved, pay attention to the meaning of quantities, know and use different properties of mathematical operations and representations, and apply key principles of statistics and probability. Special focus in this domain is given to mathematical models. Models are representations of real-life contexts. They help us to explain or interpret the behavior of certain components of a system and to predict results that are as yet unobserved or unmeasured. You may be asked to create and use a model and to understand the distinction between the predictions of a model and the data that have been collected.

Some of the questions in this content domain may involve quantitative reasoning about ratios, rates, percentages, and proportional relationships and may require understanding and applying unit rates. Some problems may be set in contexts, which may address topics in science, social science, and real-world settings.

Some questions may present information about the relationship between two variables in a graph, scatterplot, table, or another form and ask you to analyze and draw conclusions about the given information. These questions assess your understanding of the key properties of, and the differences between, linear, quadratic, and exponential relationships and how these properties apply to the corresponding contexts.

The Problem-Solving and Data Analysis domain may also include questions that assess your understanding of essential concepts in statistics and probability. You may be asked to analyze univariate data (data involving one variable) presented in dot plots, histograms, box plots, bar graphs, and frequency tables, or bivariate data (data involving two variables) presented in scatterplots, line graphs, and two-way tables. This includes computing, comparing, and interpreting measures of center; interpreting measures of spread; describing overall patterns; and recognizing the effects of outliers on measures of center and spread.

These questions may test your understanding of the conceptual meaning of standard deviation (although you won't be asked to calculate a standard deviation).

Other questions in this domain may ask you to estimate the probability of an event, employing different approaches, rules, or probability models. Special attention is given to the notion of conditional probability, which is tested using two-way tables and in other ways.

Some questions may present you with a description of a study and ask you to decide what conclusion is most appropriate based on the design of the study. Some questions may ask about using data from a sample to draw conclusions about an entire population. These questions may also assess conceptual understanding of the margin of error (although you won't be asked to calculate a margin of error) when a population mean or proportion is estimated from sample data. Other questions may ask about making conclusions about cause-and-effect relationships between two variables.

Problem-Solving and Data Analysis questions include both multiple-choice questions and student-produced response questions.

Let's explore the content, skills, and knowledge assessed by Problem-Solving and Data Analysis questions in the Math section.

Ratio, Proportion, Units, and Percentages

Ratio and proportion is one of the major ideas in math. Introduced well before high school, ratio and proportion is a theme throughout mathematics and has many applications in daily life, career work, and higher-level math courses.

Problem-Solving and Data Analysis Sample Question 1

> On Thursday, 240 adults and children attended a show. The ratio of adults to children was 5 to 1. How many children attended the show?
>
> A) 40
>
> B) 48
>
> C) 192
>
> D) 200

REMINDER

A ratio represents a relationship between quantities, not the actual quantities themselves. Fractions are an especially effective way to represent and work with ratios.

Because the ratio of adults to children was 5 to 1, there were 5 adults for every 1 child. Thus, of every 6 people who attended the show, 5 were adults and 1 was a child. In fractions, $\frac{5}{6}$ of the 240 who attended were adults and $\frac{1}{6}$ were children. Therefore, $\frac{1}{6} \times 240$, or 40 children attended the show, which is choice A.

Ratios in the Math section may be expressed in the forms 3 to 1, 3:1, $\frac{3}{1}$, or simply 3.

Problem-Solving and Data Analysis Sample Question 2

> On an architect's drawing of the floor plan for a house, 1 inch represents 3 feet. If a room is represented on the floor plan by a rectangle that has sides of lengths 3.5 inches and 5 inches, what is the actual floor area of the room, in square feet?
>
> A) 17.5
>
> B) 51.0
>
> C) 52.5
>
> D) 157.5

Because 1 inch represents 3 feet, the actual dimensions of the room are 3 × 3.5, or 10.5 feet, and 3 × 5, or 15 feet. Therefore, the floor area of the room is 10.5 × 15, or 157.5 square feet, which is choice D.

Another classic example of a ratio is the comparison of the length of an object to the length of its shadow. At a given location and time of day, it might be true that a fence post that has a height of 4 feet casts a shadow that is 6 feet long. This ratio of the height of the object to the length of its shadow, 4 to 6, or 2 to 3, remains the same for any object at the same location and time. This could be considered a unit rate: the ratio of the height of the object to the length of its shadow would be equivalent to 1 to $\frac{2}{3}$ or the unit rate $\frac{2}{3}$-foot change in height of the object for every 1-foot change in length of shadow. So, for example, a tree that casts a shadow that's 18 feet long has a height of $18 \times \frac{2}{3}$, or 12 feet. In this situation, in which one variable quantity is always a fixed constant times another variable quantity, the two quantities are said to be directly proportional.

Thus, if variables x and y are said to be directly proportional, then there exists some number k such that $y = kx$, where k is a nonzero constant. The constant k is called the constant of proportionality.

In the preceding example, you'd say that the height of an object is directly proportional to the length of the object's shadow, with constant of proportionality $\frac{2}{3}$. So if you let L be the length of the shadow and H be the height of the object, then $H = \frac{2}{3}L$.

Notice that both L and H are lengths, so the constant of proportionality, $\frac{H}{L} = \frac{2}{3}$, has no units. In contrast, let's consider sample question 2 again. On the scale drawing, 1 inch represents 3 feet. The length of an actual measurement is directly proportional to its length on the scale drawing. But to find the constant of proportionality, you need to keep track of units: $\frac{3 \text{ feet}}{1 \text{ inch}} = \frac{36 \text{ inches}}{1 \text{ inch}} = 36$. Hence, if S is a length on the scale drawing that corresponds to an actual length of R, then $R = 36S$, where R and S have the same units.

Many questions in the Math section require you to pay attention to units. Some questions in the Problem-Solving and Data Analysis content domain require you to convert units either between the U.S. customary system and the metric system or within those systems.

Problem-Solving and Data Analysis Sample Question 3

> Scientists estimate that the Pacific Plate, one of Earth's tectonic plates, has moved about 1,060 kilometers in the past 10.3 million years. About how far, in <u>miles</u>, has the Pacific Plate moved during this same time period? (Use 1 mile = 1.6 kilometers.)
>
> A) 165
> B) 398
> C) 663
> D) 1,696

STRATEGY

Pay close attention to units, and convert units if required by the question. Writing out the unit conversion as a series of multiplication steps, as seen here, will help ensure accuracy. Intermediate units should cancel (as do the kilometers in sample 3), leaving you with the desired unit.

Because 1 mile = 1.6 kilometers, the distance is

$$1,060 \text{ kilometers} \times \frac{1 \text{ mile}}{1.6 \text{ kilometers}} = 662.5 \text{ miles, which is about}$$

663 miles. Therefore, the correct answer is choice C.

Problem-Solving and Data Analysis Sample Question 4

> County Y consists of two districts. One district has an area of 30 square miles and a population density of 370 people per square mile, and the other district has an area of 50 square miles and a population density of 290 people per square mile. What is the population density, in people per square mile, for all of County Y?

Note that this example is in the student-produced response (SPR) format and therefore has no answer choices. You have to generate and enter the response yourself.

The first district has an area of 30 square miles and a population density of 370 people per square mile, so its total population is

$30 \text{ square miles} \times \frac{370 \text{ people}}{\text{square mile}}$, or 11,100 people. The other district has

an area of 50 square miles and a population density of 290 people per

square mile, so its total population is $50 \text{ square miles} \times \frac{290 \text{ people}}{\text{square mile}}$,

or 14,500 people. Thus, County Y has a total population of 11,100 + 14,500 = 25,600 people and a total area of 30 + 50 = 80 square

miles. Therefore, the population density of County Y is $\frac{25,600}{80}$, or

320 people per square mile.

The Problem-Solving and Data Analysis domain also includes questions involving percentages, which are a type of proportion. These questions may involve the concepts of percentage increase and percentage decrease.

Problem-Solving and Data Analysis Sample Question 5

> A furniture store buys its furniture from a wholesaler. For a particular style of table, the usual price of the table is 75% more than the cost of the table from the wholesaler. During a sale, the store sells the table for 15% more than the cost from the wholesaler. If the sale price of the table is $299, what is the usual price for the table?
>
> A) $359
>
> B) $455
>
> C) $479
>
> D) $524

The sale price of the table was $299. This is equal to the cost from the wholesaler plus 15%. Thus, $299 = 1.15 (cost from the wholesaler), and the cost from the wholesaler is $\frac{\$299}{1.15}$ = $260. The usual price is the cost from the wholesaler, $260, plus 75%. Therefore, the usual price the store charges for the table is 1.75 × $260 = $455, which is choice B.

Interpreting Relationships Presented in Scatterplots, Graphs, Tables, and Equations

The behavior of a variable and the relationship between two variables in a context may be explored by considering data presented in scatterplots, tables, and graphs.

The relationship between two quantitative variables may be modeled by a function or an equation. The model may allow very accurate predictions, as, for example, models used in physical sciences, or may only describe a general trend, with considerable variability between the actual and predicted values, as, for example, models used in behavioral and social sciences.

Questions in the Math section may assess your ability to understand and analyze relationships between two variables, the properties of the functions used to model these relationships, and the conditions under which a model is considered to be an appropriate representation of the data. Problem-Solving and Data Analysis questions of these sorts focus on linear, quadratic, and exponential relationships.

Problem-Solving and Data Analysis Sample Question 6

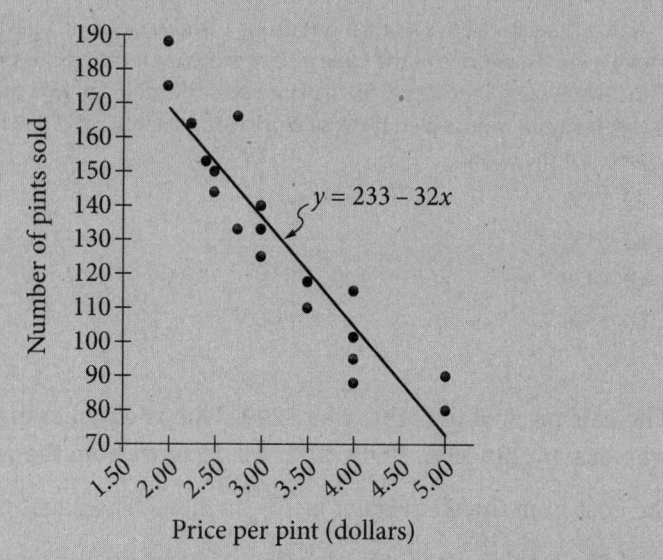

A grocery store sells pints of raspberries and sets the price per pint each week. The scatterplot above shows the price and the number of pints of raspberries sold for 19 weeks, along with a line of best fit for the data and an equation for the line of best fit.

Several different questions could be asked about this context.

REMINDER

A line of best fit is a straight line that best represents the association shown on a scatterplot. It's often written in $y = a + bx$ form.

A. According to the line of best fit, how many pints of raspberries would the grocery store be predicted to sell in a week when the price of raspberries is $4.50 per pint?

Because the line of best fit has equation $y = 233 - 32x$, where x is the price, in dollars, for a pint of raspberries and y is the predicted number of pints of raspberries sold, the number of pints the store would be predicted to sell in a week when the price of raspberries is $4.50 per pint is $233 - 32(4.50) = 89$ pints.

B. For how many of the 19 weeks shown was the number of pints of raspberries sold greater than the number predicted by the line of best fit?

For a given week, the number of pints of raspberries sold is greater than the number predicted by the line of best fit if and only if the point representing that week lies above the line of best fit. For example, at the price of $5 per pint, the number sold in two different weeks was approximately 80 and 90, which is more than the 73 predicted by the line of best fit. Of the 19 points, 8 lie above the line of best fit, so there were 8 weeks in which the number of pints sold was greater than what was predicted by the line of best fit.

C. What is the best interpretation of the slope of the line of best fit in this context?

In the Math section, this question would be followed by multiple-choice answer options. The slope of the line of best fit is −32. This means that the correct answer would state that for each dollar that the price of a pint of raspberries increases, the store is predicted to sell 32 fewer pints of raspberries.

D. What is the best interpretation of the y-intercept of the line of best fit in this context?

In the Math section, this question would be followed by multiple-choice answer options.

In this context, the y-intercept doesn't represent a likely scenario, so it can't be accurately interpreted in this context. According to the model, the y-intercept means that if the store sold raspberries for $0 per pint—that is, if the store gave raspberries away—233 people would be expected to accept the free raspberries. However, it's not realistic that the store would give away raspberries, and if it did, it's likely that far more people would accept the free raspberries. Also notice that in this case, the leftmost line on the graph is not the y-axis. The lower-left corner shows the x- and y-coordinates of (1.5, 70), not (0, 0).

The fact that the y-intercept indicates that 233 people would accept free raspberries is one limitation of the model. Another limitation is that for a price of $7.50 per pint or above, the model predicts that a negative number of people would buy raspberries, which is impossible. In general, you should be cautious about applying a model for values outside of the given data. In this example, you should only be confident in the prediction of sales for prices between $2 and $5 because those are the lowest and highest prices for which data are shown.

Giving a line of best fit, as in this example, assumes that the relationship between the variables is best modeled by a linear function, but that isn't always true. In the Math section, you may see data that are best modeled by a linear, quadratic, or exponential model.

Problem-Solving and Data Analysis Sample Question 7

Time (hours)	Number of bacteria
0	1,000
1	4,000
2	16,000
3	64,000

The table gives the initial number (at time $t = 0$) of bacteria placed in a growth medium and the number of bacteria in the growth medium each hour for 3 hours. Which of the following functions best models the number of bacteria, $N(t)$, after t hours?

A) $N(t) = 4{,}000t$

B) $N(t) = 1{,}000 + 3{,}000t$

C) $N(t) = 1{,}000(4^{-t})$

D) $N(t) = 1{,}000(4^{t})$

STRATEGY

To determine whether a relationship is linear or exponential, examine the change in the quantity between successive time periods. If the difference in the quantity is constant, the relationship is linear. If the ratio in the quantity is constant (for instance, 4 times greater than the preceding time period), the relationship is exponential.

The given choices are linear and exponential models. If a quantity is increasing linearly with time, then the *difference* in the quantity between successive time periods is constant. If a quantity is increasing exponentially with time, then the *ratio* in the quantity between successive time periods is constant. According to the table, after each hour, the number of bacteria in the culture is 4 times as great as it was the preceding hour: $\frac{4,000}{1,000} = \frac{16,000}{4,000} = \frac{64,000}{16,000} = 4$. That is, for each increase of 1 in t, the value of $N(t)$ is multiplied by 4. At $t = 0$, which corresponds to the time when the culture was placed in the medium, there were 1,000 bacteria. This is modeled by the exponential function $N(t) = 1,000(4^t)$, which has the value 1,000 at $t = 0$ and increases by a factor of 4 for each increase of 1 in the value of t. Choice D is the correct answer.

The Math section may include questions that require you to know the difference between linear and exponential growth.

Problem-Solving and Data Analysis Sample Question 8

> Every month, Jamal adds 2 new books to his library. Which of the following types of functions best models the number of books in Jamal's library as a function of time?
>
> A) Increasing linear
>
> B) Decreasing linear
>
> C) Increasing exponential
>
> D) Decreasing exponential

Over equal intervals, linear functions increase or decrease by a constant amount, while exponential functions increase or decrease by a constant factor. Since the number of books is increasing by a constant amount (2 books) over equal intervals (each month), the function is linear. Also, since the number of books is increasing as time increases, the function is increasing, and therefore choice A is correct.

Problem-Solving and Data Analysis Sample Question 9

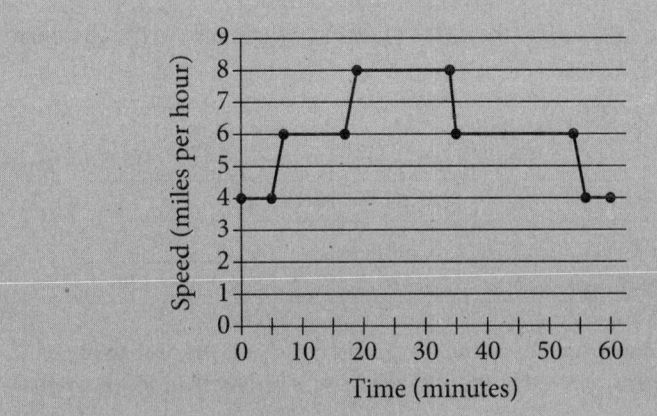

One evening, Maria walks, jogs, and runs for a total of 60 minutes. The graph above shows Maria's speed during the 60 minutes. Which segment of the graph represents the times when Maria's speed is the greatest?

A) The segment from (17, 6) to (19, 8)

B) The segment from (19, 8) to (34, 8)

C) The segment from (34, 8) to (35, 6)

D) The segment from (35, 6) to (54, 6)

The correct answer is choice B. Because the vertical coordinate represents Maria's speed, the part of the graph with the greatest vertical coordinate represents the times when Maria's speed is the greatest. This is the highest part of the graph, the segment from (19, 8) to (34, 8), when Maria runs at 8 miles per hour (mph). Choice A represents the time during which Maria's speed is increasing from 6 to 8 mph; choice C represents the time during which Maria's speed is decreasing from 8 to 6 mph; and choice D represents the longest period of Maria moving at the same speed (6 mph), not the times when Maria's speed is the greatest.

More Data and Statistics

Some questions in the Problem-Solving and Data Analysis domain may assess your ability to understand and analyze data presented in a table, bar graph, histogram, dot plot, box plot, line graph, or other display.

Problem-Solving and Data Analysis Sample Question 10

The given table summarizes the distribution of 200 animals by type of animal and mass, in kilograms.

	Less than 45 kg	45–55 kg	Greater than 55 kg	Total
Cheetah	12	59	4	75
Leopard	24	76	25	125
Total	36	135	29	200

One of these animals will be selected at random. What is the probability of selecting a leopard, given that the animal's mass is greater than 55 kilograms?

A) $\dfrac{25}{29}$

B) $\dfrac{1}{5}$

C) $\dfrac{29}{200}$

D) $\dfrac{1}{8}$

The probability of selecting a leopard given that the animal's mass is greater than 55 kg is the number of leopards with a mass greater than 55 kg divided by the total number of animals with a mass greater than 55 kg. According to the table, there are 29 animals with a mass greater than 55 kg. Of these 29 animals, 25 are leopards. Therefore, if the animal has a mass greater than 55 kg, the probability that the animal is a leopard is $\dfrac{25}{29}$. The correct answer is choice A.

Sample 10 is an example of a conditional probability, the probability of an event given that another event is known to have occurred. The question asks for the probability that an animal chosen at random is a leopard given that the animal has a mass greater than 55 kg.

REMINDER

Mean and median are measures of center for a data set, while range and standard deviation are measures of spread.

You may be asked to answer questions that involve a measure of center for a data set: the mean or the median. A question may ask you to draw conclusions about one or more of these measures of center even if the exact values cannot be calculated. To recall briefly:

- The *mean* of a set of numerical values is the sum of all the values divided by the number of values in the set.

- The *median* of a set of numerical values is the middle value when the values are listed in increasing (or decreasing) order. If the set has an even number of values, then the median is the average of the two middle values. While technically, the median could be any number between the two middle values, it is most often computed as the average of the two middle values and will always be computed this way for questions in the Math section.

Problem-Solving and Data Analysis Sample Question 11

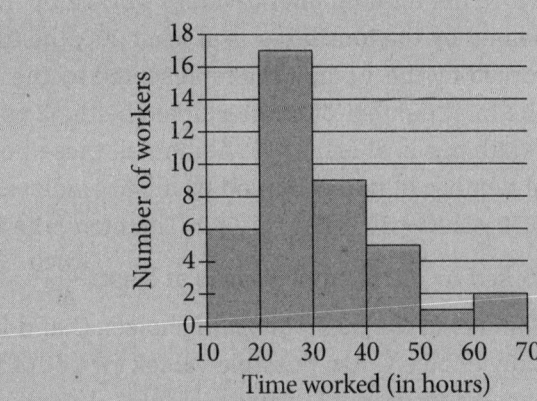

The histogram shown summarizes the distribution of time worked last week, in hours, by the 40 employees of a landscaping company. In the histogram, the first bar represents all workers who worked at least 10 hours but less than 20 hours; the second bar represents all workers who worked at least 20 hours but less than 30 hours; and so on. Which of the following could be the median and mean amount of time worked, in hours, for the 40 employees?

A) Median = 22, mean = 23

B) Median = 24, mean = 22

C) Median = 26, mean = 32

D) Median = 32, mean = 30

Note: In the Math section, all questions that include a histogram will include a description of the boundary condition if interpretation of the boundary is required. That is, the question will include a description of how to interpret the values represented by a bar and whether to include the left endpoint but not the right endpoint or the other way around.

If the number of hours the 40 employees worked is listed in increasing order, the median will be a value between the 20th and the 21st numbers in the list. The first 6 numbers in the list will be workers represented by the first bar; hence, each of the first 6 numbers will be at least 10 but less than 20. The next 17 numbers—that is, the 7th through the 23rd numbers in the list—will be workers represented by the second bar; hence, each of the next 17 numbers will be at least 20 but less than 30. Thus, the 20th and the 21st numbers in the list will be at least 20 but less than 30. Therefore, any of the median values in choices A, B, or C is possible, but the median value in choice D isn't.

Now let's find the possible values of the mean. Each of the 6 employees represented by the first bar worked at least 10 hours but less than 20 hours. Thus, the total number of hours worked by these 6 employees is at least 60. Similarly, the total number of hours worked by the 17 employees represented by the second bar is at least 340; the total

REMINDER

The distribution of a variable provides all possible values of the variable and how often they occur.

number of hours worked by the 9 employees represented by the third bar is at least 270; the total number of hours worked by the 5 employees represented by the fourth bar is at least 200; the total number of hours worked by the 1 employee represented by the fifth bar is at least 50; and the total number of hours worked by the 2 employees represented by the sixth bar is at least 120. Adding all these hours shows that the total number of hours worked by all 40 employees is at least 60 + 340 + 270 + 200 + 50 + 120 = 1,040. Therefore, the mean number of hours worked by all 40 employees is at least $\frac{1,040}{40}$ = 26.

Therefore, only the values of the mean given in choices C and D are possible. Because only choice C has possible values for both the median and the mean, it's the correct answer.

A data set may have a few values that are much larger or smaller than the rest of the values in the set. These values are called *outliers*. An outlier may represent an important piece of data. For example, if a data set consists of rates of a certain illness in various cities, a data point with a very high value could indicate a serious health issue to be investigated.

In general, outliers affect the mean more than the median. Therefore, outliers that are larger than the rest of the points in the data set tend to make the mean greater than the median, and outliers that are smaller than the rest of the points in the data set tend to make the mean less than the median. In sample 11, the mean was larger than the median due to the unusually large amount of time worked by a few employees.

REMINDER

You won't be asked to calculate the standard deviation of a set of data in the Math section, but you will be expected to demonstrate an understanding of what standard deviation measures.

The mean and the median are different ways to describe the center of a data set. Another key characteristic of a data set is the amount of variability, or spread, in the data. One measure of spread is the range, which is equal to the maximum value minus the minimum value. Another measure of spread is the standard deviation, which is a measure of how dispersed, or far away, the points in the data set are from the mean value. A low standard deviation indicates the points in the data set are clustered around the mean value, and a high standard deviation indicates the points in the data set are more spread out from the mean value. In the Math section, you won't be asked to compute the standard deviation of a data set, but you do need to understand that a larger standard deviation corresponds to a data set whose values are more spread out from the mean value.

Problem-Solving and Data Analysis Sample Question 12

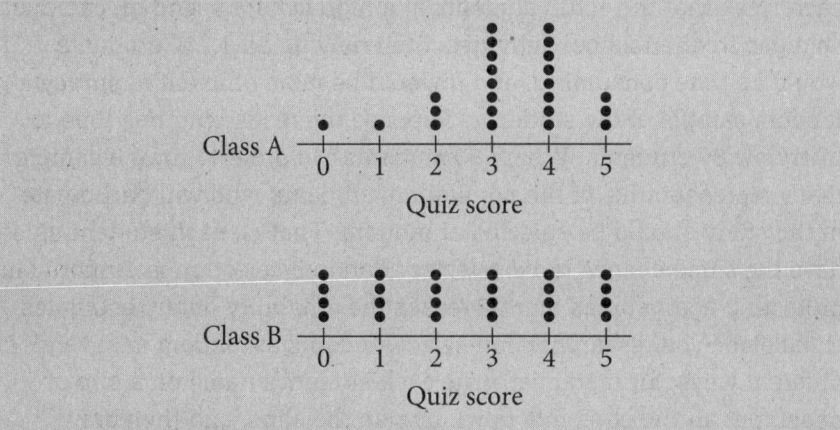

The dot plots show the distributions of scores on a current events quiz for two classes of 24 students each. Which of the following statements about the standard deviations of the two distributions is true?

A) The standard deviation of quiz scores in Class A is less than that of quiz scores in Class B.

B) The standard deviation of quiz scores in Class A is greater than that of quiz scores in Class B.

C) The standard deviation of quiz scores in Class A is equal to that of quiz scores in Class B.

D) There is not enough information to compare the standard deviations.

In Class A, the mean score is between 3 and 4. The large majority of scores are 3 and 4, with only a few scores of 0, 1, 2, and 5. In Class B, the mean score is 2.5, and scores are evenly distributed across all possible scores, with many scores not close to the mean score. Because the scores in Class A are more closely clustered around the mean, the standard deviation of the scores in Class A is smaller. The correct answer is choice A.

A *population parameter* is a numerical value that describes a characteristic of a population. For example, the percentage of registered voters who would vote for a certain candidate is a parameter describing the population of registered voters in an election. In another example, the average income of a household in a city is a parameter describing the population of households in that city. We often don't know the value of the population parameter; thus, an essential purpose of statistics is to estimate a population parameter based on a sample from the population. A common example is election polling, where researchers will interview a random sample of registered voters to estimate the proportion of all registered voters who plan to vote for a certain candidate. The precision of the estimate depends on the variability of the sample data and the sample size. For instance, if household incomes in a city vary widely or the sample is small, the estimate that comes from a sample may differ considerably from the actual value for the population parameter.

STRATEGY

When asked to compare the standard deviations of two data sets, first locate the mean approximately. Then ask yourself which data set has values that are more closely clustered around the mean. That data set will have the smaller standard deviation.

For example, a researcher wants to estimate the mean number of hours each week that the 1,200 students at a high school spend on campus engaged in after-school activities. Interviewing all 1,200 students would be time consuming, and it would be more efficient to survey a random sample of the students. Suppose the researcher has time to interview 80 students. Which 80 students? In order to have a sample that's representative of the population, students who will participate in the study should be selected at random. That is, each student must have the same chance to be selected. Random selection is essential in protecting against bias and increases the reliability of any estimates calculated. The researcher can select students at random in several different ways; for instance, write each student's name on a slip of paper, put all the slips in a bowl, mix up the slips, and then draw 80 names from the bowl. In practice, a computer is often used to select participants at random.

If you don't select a random sample, the sampling method used may introduce bias. For example, if you found 80 students from those attending a game of the school's football team, those people would be more likely to be interested in sports and, in turn, an interest in sports might be related to the average amount of time the students spend on the internet. The result would be that the average time those 80 students spend on the internet might not be an accurate estimate of the average amount of time all students at the school spend on the internet.

Suppose you select 80 students at random from the 1,200 students at the high school. You ask them how much time they spend on campus engaged in after-school activities each week, and you calculate that the mean time is 7.9 hours per week. You also find that 6 of the 80 students spend less than 1 hour each week on campus engaged in after-school activities. Based on these results, what conclusions should be made about the entire population of 1,200 students?

Because the sample was selected at random, the mean of 7.9 hours is a plausible estimate of the mean time spent each week on campus engaged in after-school activities by all 1,200 students. Also, we can use the sample data to estimate how many students spend less than 1 hour on campus engaged in after-school activities each week. In the sample, the percentage is $\frac{6}{80}$, or 7.5%. Applying this percentage to the entire population of 1,200 students, the best estimate is that 90 students at the school spend less than 1 hour per week on campus engaged in after-school activities.

REMINDER

You won't need to calculate margins of error in the Math section, but you should understand what the concept means and be able to interpret margins of error in context.

However, the estimates of the population parameters need to be interpreted carefully. An essential part of statistics is accounting for the variability of the estimate. The estimates above are reasonable, but they're unlikely to be exactly correct. Statistical analysis can also describe how far from the estimates the actual values are expected at most to be. To describe the precision of an estimate, statisticians use the concept of *margin of error*. You won't be expected to compute a margin of error in the Math section, but you should understand how sample size affects margin of error and how to interpret a given margin of error in context.

If the example above had been part of a Math section question, you might have been given survey results indicating that for a random sample of 80 students, the estimated mean was 7.9 hours with an associated margin of error of 0.8 hours. An appropriate interpretation of these results is that it's plausible that the mean number of hours for all 1,200 students in the population is greater than 7.9 − 0.8, or 7.1 hours, but less than 7.9 + 0.8, or 8.7 hours. There are two key points to note.

1. The value of the margin of error is affected by two factors: the variability in the data and the sample size. The larger the standard deviation, the larger the margin of error; the smaller the standard deviation, the smaller the margin of error. Furthermore, increasing the size of the random sample provides more information and typically reduces the margin of error.

2. The margin of error applies to the estimated value of the population parameter only; it doesn't inform the estimated value for an individual. In the example, plausible values for the population mean are in the interval from 7.1 hours to 8.7 hours. The time, in hours, that an individual spends on the internet may or may not fall in this interval.

Problem-Solving and Data Analysis Sample Question 13

A quality control researcher at an electronics company is testing the life of the company's batteries in a certain camera. The researcher selects 100 batteries at random from the daily output of the batteries and finds that the life of the batteries has a mean of 342 pictures with an associated margin of error of 18 pictures. Which of the following is the most appropriate conclusion based on these data?

A) All the batteries produced by the company that day have a life between 324 and 360 pictures.

B) All the batteries ever produced by the company have a life between 324 and 360 pictures.

C) It is plausible that the mean life of batteries produced by the company that day is between 324 and 360 pictures.

D) It is plausible that the mean life of all the batteries ever produced by the company is between 324 and 360 pictures.

The correct answer is choice C. Choices A and B are incorrect because the margin of error gives information about the mean life of all batteries produced by the company that day, not about the life of any individual battery. Choice D is incorrect because the sample of batteries was taken from the population of all the batteries produced by the company on that day. The population of all batteries the company ever produced may have a different mean life because of changes in the formulation of the batteries, wear on machinery, improvements in production processes, and many other factors.

STRATEGY

When a margin of error is provided, determine the value to which the margin of error applies. If the margin of error is associated with a mean, then the margin of error describes the plausible values for individual values in the population.

The statistics examples discussed so far are largely based on investigations intended to estimate some characteristic of a group: the mean amount of time students spend on the internet, the mean life of a battery, and the percentage of registered voters who plan to vote for a candidate. Another primary focus of statistics is to investigate relationships between variables and to draw conclusions about cause and effect. For example, does a new type of physical therapy help people recover from knee surgery faster? For such a study, some people who have had knee surgery will be randomly assigned to the new therapy or to the usual therapy. The medical results of these patients can be compared. The key questions from a statistical viewpoint are

- Is it appropriate to generalize from the sample of patients in the study to the entire population of people who are recovering from knee surgery?

- Is it appropriate to conclude that the new therapy caused any difference in the results for the two groups of patients?

The answers depend on the use of random selection and random assignment.

- If the subjects in the sample of a study were selected at random from the entire population in question, the results can be generalized to the entire population because random sampling ensures that each individual has the same chance to be selected for the sample.

- If the subjects in the sample were randomly assigned to treatments, it may be appropriate to make conclusions about cause and effect because the treatment groups will be roughly equivalent at the beginning of the experiment other than the treatment they receive.

This can be summarized in the following table.

REMINDER

In order for the results of a study to be generalized to an entire population, random sampling is needed. In order for a cause-and-effect relationship to be established, random assignment of individuals to treatments is needed.

	Subjects selected at random	Subjects not selected at random
Subjects randomly assigned to treatments	• Results can be generalized to the entire population. • Conclusions about cause and effect can appropriately be drawn.	• Results *cannot* be generalized to the entire population. • Conclusions about cause and effect can appropriately be drawn.
Subjects not randomly assigned to treatments	• Results can be generalized to the entire population. • Conclusions about cause and effect should *not* be drawn.	• Results *cannot* be generalized to the entire population. • Conclusions about cause and effect should *not* be drawn.

The previous example discussed treatments in a medical experiment. The word *treatment* refers to any factor that is deliberately varied in an experiment.

Problem-Solving and Data Analysis Sample Question 14

A community center offers a Spanish course. This year, all students in the course were offered additional audio lessons they could take at home. The students who took these additional audio lessons did better in the course than students who didn't take the additional audio lessons. Based on these results, which of the following is the most appropriate conclusion?

A) Taking additional audio lessons will cause an improvement for any student who takes any foreign language course.

B) Taking additional audio lessons will cause an improvement for any student who takes a Spanish course.

C) Taking additional audio lessons was the cause of the improvement for the students at the community center who took the Spanish course.

D) No conclusion about cause and effect can be made regarding students at the community center who took the additional audio lessons at home and their performance in the Spanish course.

The correct answer is choice D. The better results of these students may have been a result of being more motivated, as shown in their willingness to do extra work, and not the additional audio lessons. Choice A is incorrect because no conclusion about cause and effect is possible without random assignment to treatments and because the sample was only students taking a Spanish course, so no conclusion can be appropriately made about students taking all foreign language courses. Choice B is incorrect because no conclusion about cause and effect is possible without random assignment to treatments and because the students taking a Spanish course at the community center is not a random sample of all students who take a Spanish course. Choice C is incorrect because the students taking the Spanish course at the community center weren't randomly assigned to use the additional audio lessons or to not use the additional audio lessons.

STRATEGY

Be wary of conclusions that claim a cause-and-effect relationship or that generalize a conclusion to a broader population. Before accepting a conclusion, assess whether the subjects were selected at random from the broader population and whether subjects were randomly assigned to treatments.

Summary: Problem-Solving and Data Analysis Questions

Main purpose: To assess your understanding of proportional relationships, percentages, and probability as well as your ability to use data to analyze and solve problems

Proportion of the test section: About 15 percent (five to seven questions)

Question types

- Ratios, rates, proportional relationships, and units

- Percentages

- One-variable data: distributions and measures of center and spread

- Two-variable data: models and scatterplots

- Probability and conditional probability

- Inference from sample statistics and margin of error

- Evaluating statistical claims: observational studies and experiments

CHAPTER 26

Math: Questions— Problem-Solving and Data Analysis Drills

1

Makayla is planning an event in a 5,400-square-foot room. If there should be at least 8 square feet per person, what is the maximum number of people that could attend this event?

A) 588

B) 675

C) 15,274

D) 43,200

2

Water flows from a pipe at a rate of 6.0 gallons per minute. How many gallons of water will flow from the pipe in 8.4 minutes?

3

The bar graph shows the results from a survey in which a group of students was asked during which month they prefer to have the class picnic.

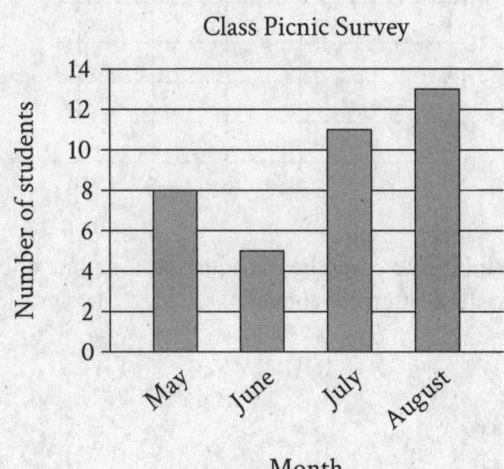

Class Picnic Survey

Based on the graph, how many students did not respond "May"?

4

A fish hatchery has three tanks for holding fish before they are introduced into the wild. Ten fish weighing less than 5 ounces are placed in tank A. Eleven fish weighing at least 5 ounces but no more than 13 ounces are placed in tank B. Twelve fish weighing more than 13 ounces are placed in tank C. Which of the following could be the median of the weights, in ounces, of these 33 fish?

A) 4.5

B) 8

C) 13.5

D) 15

5

A data set of 27 different numbers has a mean of 33 and a median of 33. A new data set is created by adding 7 to each number in the original data set that is greater than the median and subtracting 7 from each number in the original data set that is less than the median. Which of the following measures does NOT have the same value in both the original and new data sets?

A) Median

B) Mean

C) Sum of the numbers

D) Standard deviation

6

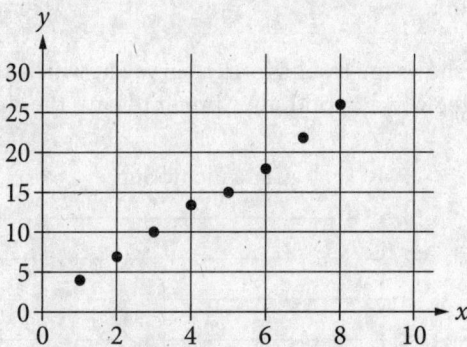

Which of the following could be the equation for a line of best fit for the data shown in the scatterplot above?

A) $y = 0.8 + 3x$

B) $y = 3 + 0.8x$

C) $y = 3 - 0.8x$

D) $y = 0.8 - 3x$

7

A sample of 40 4th-grade students was selected at random from a certain school. The 40 students completed a survey about the morning announcements, and 32 thought the announcements were helpful. Which of the following is the largest population to which the results of the survey can be applied?

A) The 40 students who were surveyed

B) All 4th-grade students at the school

C) All students at the school

D) All 4th-grade students in the county in which the school is located

8

In which of the following tables is the relationship between the values of x and their corresponding y-values nonlinear?

A)

x	1	2	3	4
y	8	11	14	17

B)

x	1	2	3	4
y	4	8	12	16

C)

x	1	2	3	4
y	8	13	18	23

D)

x	1	2	3	4
y	6	12	24	48

9

A bag containing 10,000 beads of assorted colors is purchased from a craft store. To estimate the percent of red beads in the bag, a sample of beads is selected at random. The percent of red beads in the bag was estimated to be 15%, with an associated margin of error of 2%. If r is the actual number of red beads in the bag, which of the following is most plausible?

A) $r > 1,700$

B) $1,300 < r < 1,700$

C) $200 < r < 1,500$

D) $r < 1,300$

10

The table summarizes the distribution of people in a certain city by age group.

Age group	Percent
Less than 18 years old	27%
18–40 years old	22%
41–65 years old	26%
Greater than 65 years old	25%

If a person in this city is selected at random, what is the probability of selecting a person who is greater than 65 years old, given that the person is at least 18 years old? (Express your answer as a decimal or fraction, not as a percent.)

11

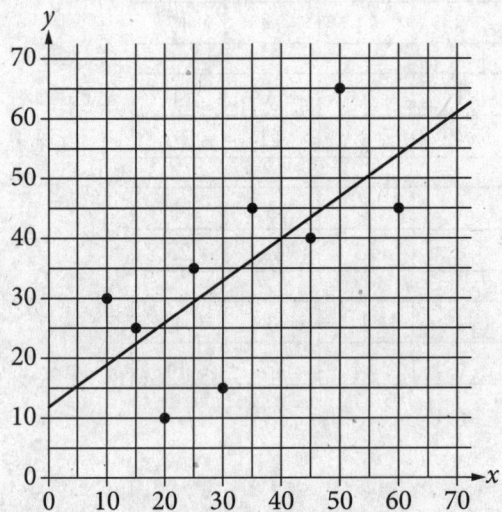

The scatterplot in the xy-plane above shows nine points (x, y) and a line of best fit. Of the following, which best estimates the amount by which the line underestimates the value of y when $x = 50$?

A) 8

B) 10

C) 13

D) 18

12

Sample	Percent in favor	Margin of error
A	52%	4.2%
B	48%	1.6%

The results of two random samples of votes for a proposition are shown. The samples were selected from the same population, and the margins of error were calculated using the same method. Which of the following is the most appropriate reason that the margin of error for sample A is greater than the margin of error for sample B?

A) Sample A had a smaller number of votes that could not be recorded.

B) Sample A had a higher percent of favorable responses.

C) Sample A had a larger sample size.

D) Sample A had a smaller sample size.

13

The number of crane flies in a wildlife sanctuary is 30% less than the number of ladybugs in the sanctuary. The number of honeybees in the sanctuary is 85% greater than the number of crane flies in the sanctuary. The number of honeybees in the sanctuary is how many times the number of ladybugs in the sanctuary?

14

The positive number a is 210% of the number b, and a is 30% of the number c. If c is p% of b, what is the value of p?

Answer Explanations

QUESTION 1

Choice B is correct. It's given that the event will be in a 5,400-square-foot room and that there should be at least 8 square feet per person. The maximum number of people that could attend the event can be found by dividing the total square feet in the room by the minimum number of square feet needed per person, which gives $\frac{5,400}{8}$, or 675.

Choices A, C, and *D* are incorrect and may result from conceptual or calculation errors.

QUESTION 2

The correct answer is 50.4. It's given that water flows from a pipe at a rate of 6.0 gallons per minute. It follows that the number of gallons of water that will flow from the pipe in 8.4 minutes can be determined by multiplying the water flow rate by the number of minutes: $\left(\frac{6.0 \text{ gallons}}{1 \text{ minute}}\right)$(8.4 minutes), or 50.4 gallons.

Therefore, 50.4 gallons of water will flow from the pipe in 8.4 minutes. Note that 50.4 and 252/5 are examples of ways to enter a correct answer.

QUESTION 3

The correct answer is 29. It's given that the bar graph shows the results from a survey in which a group of students was asked during which month they prefer to have the class picnic. Based on the graph, 8 students responded "May," 5 students responded "June," 11 students responded "July," and 13 students responded "August." It follows that the number of students who did not respond "May" is the sum of the number of students who responded "June," "July," or "August," which yields 5 + 11 + 13, or 29. Therefore, 29 students did not respond "May."

QUESTION 4

Choice B is correct. The median of a set of numbers is the middle number when the values in the set are ordered from least to greatest. There are 33 fish, so in an ordered list of the weights, the 17th value would be the median weight. The 10 fish in tank A weigh the least, and these 10 weights would be the first 10 values on the ordered list. The 11 fish in tank B have the next set of greater weights and so would be the 11th through 21st weights in the ordered list, which includes the median weight as the 17th value. The fish in tank B weigh at least 5 ounces but no more than 13 ounces. Of the given choices, only 8 ounces falls within this range of values.

Choice A is incorrect. It's given that tank A has 10 fish weighing less than 5 ounces. Since there are more than 10 fish in tanks B and C combined, the median weight cannot be less than 5 ounces. *Choices C* and *D* are incorrect. It's given that tank C has 12 fish weighing more than 13 ounces. There are more than 12 fish in tanks A and B combined, so the median weight can't be more than 13 ounces.

QUESTION 5

Choice D is correct. When a data set has an odd number of elements, the median can be found by ordering the values from least to greatest and determining the middle value. Out of the 27 different numbers in this data set, 13 numbers are below the median, one number is exactly 33, and 13 numbers are above the median. When 7 is subtracted from each number below the median and added to each number above the median, the distance between these numbers and the median is larger in the new data set compared to the original data set. Since the median of this data set, 33, is equivalent to the mean of the data set, it follows that the distance between these numbers and the mean is larger in the new data set compared to the original data set. Since standard deviation is a measure of how spread out the data are from the mean, a greater spread from the mean indicates an increased standard deviation. Therefore, the standard deviation doesn't have the same value in both the original and new data sets.

Choice A is incorrect. All the numbers less than the median decrease and all the numbers greater than the median increase, but the median itself doesn't change. *Choice B* is incorrect. The mean of a data set is found by dividing the sum of the values by the number of values. The net change from subtracting 7 from 13 numbers and adding 7 to 13 numbers is zero. Therefore, the mean of the numbers doesn't change. *Choice C* is incorrect. The net change from subtracting 7 from 13 numbers and adding 7 to 13 numbers is zero. Therefore, the sum of the numbers doesn't change.

QUESTION 6

Choice A is correct. The data show a strong linear relationship between x and y. The line of best fit for a set of data is a linear equation that minimizes the distances from the data points to the line. An equation for the line of best fit can be written in slope-intercept form, $y = mx + b$, where m is the slope of the graph of the line and b is the y-coordinate of the y-intercept of the graph. Since, for the data shown, the y-values increase as the x-values increase, the slope of a line of best fit must be positive. The data shown lie almost in a line, so the slope can be roughly estimated using the formula for slope, $m = \frac{y_2 - y_1}{x_2 - x_1}$, where (x_1, y_1) and (x_2, y_2) represent two points on the line. The leftmost and rightmost data points have coordinates of about (1, 4) and (8, 26). Substituting (1, 4) for (x_1, y_1) and (8, 26) for (x_2, y_2) in the formula for slope yields $m = \frac{26 - 4}{8 - 1}$, or $m = \frac{22}{7}$. Thus, the slope is approximately $\frac{22}{7}$, which is a little greater than 3. Extension of the line to the left would intersect the y-axis at about (0, 1). Only choice A represents a line with a slope close to 3 and a y-intercept close to (0, 1).

Choice B is incorrect and may result from switching the slope and y-intercept. The line with a y-intercept of (0, 3) and a slope of 0.8 is farther from the data points than the line with a slope of 3 and a y-intercept of (0, 0.8). *Choices C* and *D* are incorrect. These equations represent lines with negative slopes, not positive slopes.

QUESTION 7

Choice B is correct. Selecting a sample of a reasonable size at random to use for a survey allows the results from that survey to be applied to the population from which the sample was selected, but not beyond this population. In this case, the population from which the sample was selected is all 4th-grade students at a certain school. Therefore, the results of the survey can be applied to all 4th-grade students at the school.

Choice A is incorrect. The results of the survey can be applied to the 40 students who were surveyed. However, this isn't the largest group to which the results of the survey can be applied. *Choice C* is incorrect. Since the sample was selected at random from among the 4th-grade students at a certain school, the results of the survey can't be applied to other students at the school. Students in other grades in the school may feel differently about announcements than the 4th-grade students at the school do. *Choice D* is incorrect. Since the sample was selected at random from among the 4th-grade students at a certain school, the results of the survey can't be applied to other 4th-grade students who weren't represented in the survey results. Other 4th-grade students in the county may feel differently about announcements than the 4th-grade students at the school do.

QUESTION 8

Choice D is correct. The relationship between the values of x and their corresponding y-values is nonlinear if the rate of change between these pairs of values isn't constant. The table for choice D gives four pairs of values: (1, 6), (2, 12), (3, 24), and (4, 48). Finding the rate of change, or slope, $\frac{y_2 - y_1}{x_2 - x_1}$, between $(x_1, y_1) = (1, 6)$ and $(x_2, y_2) = (2, 12)$ yields $\frac{12 - 6}{2 - 1}$, or 6. Finding the rate of change between $(x_1, y_1) = (2, 12)$ and $(x_2, y_2) = (3, 24)$ yields $\frac{24 - 12}{3 - 2}$, or 12. Finding the rate of change between $(x_1, y_1) = (3, 24)$ and $(x_2, y_2) = (4, 48)$ yields $\frac{48 - 24}{4 - 3}$, or 24. Since the rate of change isn't constant for these pairs of values, this table shows a nonlinear relationship.

Choices A, B, and *C* are incorrect. The rate of change between the values of x and their corresponding y-values in each of these tables is constant, with slopes of 3, 4, and 5, respectively. Therefore, each of these tables shows a linear relationship.

QUESTION 9

Choice B is correct. It was estimated that 15% of the beads in the bag are red. Since the bag contains 10,000 beads, it follows that there are an estimated 10,000 × 0.15 = 1,500 red beads. It's given that the associated margin of error is 2%, or 10,000 × 0.02 = 200 beads. If the estimate is too high, there could plausibly be 1,500 − 200 = 1,300 red beads. If the estimate is too low, there could plausibly be 1,500 + 200 = 1,700 red beads. Therefore, it is estimated that there are between 1,300 and 1,700 red beads in the bag. Since it's given that r represents the actual number of red beads in the bag, it follows that $1,300 < r < 1,700$.

Choices A and *D* are incorrect and may result from conceptual or calculation errors. *Choice C* is incorrect because 200 is the associated margin of error for the number of red beads, not the lower bound of the range of red beads.

QUESTION 10

The correct answer is $\frac{25}{73}$. It's given that the table summarizes the distribution of people in a certain city by age group. If a person in this city is selected at random and the person is at least 18 years old, the person is either 18–40 years old, 41–65 years old, or greater than 65 years old. Therefore, the percent of the people in the city who are at least 18 years old is the sum of the percentages of the people who are 18–40 years old, 41–65 years old, and greater than 65 years old, which is 22% + 26% + 25%, or 73%. It follows that the proportion of people in the city who are at least 18 years old is $\frac{73}{100}$, or 0.73.

Based on the table, 25% of the people in the city are greater than 65 years old. It follows that the proportion of people in the city who are greater than 65 years old is $\frac{25}{100}$, or 0.25. Therefore, the probability of selecting a person who is greater than 65 years old, given that the person is at least 18 years old, is the proportion of people in the city who are greater than 65 years old divided by the proportion of people in the city who are at least 18 years old, or $\frac{0.25}{0.73}$, which is equivalent to $\frac{25}{73}$. Note that 25/73, .3424, .3425, and 0.342 are examples of ways to enter a correct answer.

QUESTION 11

Choice D is correct. At $x = 50$, the point on the scatterplot is (50, 65) and the point on the line of best fit is approximately (50, 47). Therefore, the amount by which the line of best fit underestimates the value of y at $x = 50$ is approximately $65 - 47$, or 18.

Choices A, B, and *C* are incorrect and may result from conceptual or calculation errors.

QUESTION 12

Choice D is correct. In general, a smaller sample size generally leads to a larger margin of error because the sample may be less representative of the whole population.

Choice A is incorrect. The margin of error will depend on the size of the sample of recorded votes, not the number of votes that could not be recorded. In any case, the smaller number of votes that could not be recorded for sample A would tend to decrease, not increase, the comparative size of the margin of error. *Choice B* is incorrect. Since the percent in favor for sample A is the same distance from 50% as the percent in favor for sample B, the percent of favorable responses doesn't affect the comparative size of the margin of error for the two samples. *Choice C* is incorrect and may result from a conceptual error.

QUESTION 13

The correct answer is 1.295. For this wildlife sanctuary, let x be the number of crane flies, y be the number of ladybugs, and z be the number of honeybees. It's given that the number of crane flies in the sanctuary is 30% less than the number of ladybugs. This means that the number of crane flies is $(100 - 30)\%$, or 70%, of the number of ladybugs. The equation $x = \frac{70}{100}y$, or $x = 0.70y$, represents this situation. It's given that the number of honeybees in the sanctuary is 85% greater than the number of crane flies in the sanctuary. This means that the number of honeybees is $(100 + 85)\%$, or 185%, of the number of crane flies. The equation $z = \frac{185}{100}x$, or $z = 1.85x$, represents this situation. Substituting $0.70y$ for x in the equation $z = 1.85x$ yields $z = 1.85(0.70y)$, or $z = 1.295y$. Therefore, the number of honeybees is 1.295 times the number of ladybugs in the sanctuary.

QUESTION 14

The correct answer is 700. It's given that the positive number a is 210% of the number b. Thus, $a = \frac{210}{100}b$. It's also given that a is 30% of the number c. Thus, $a = \frac{30}{100}c$. Since $a = \frac{210}{100}b$ and $a = \frac{30}{100}c$, it follows that $\frac{210}{100}b = \frac{30}{100}c$. Multiplying both sides of this equation by $\frac{100}{30}$ yields $\left(\frac{100}{30}\right)\left(\frac{210}{100}\right)b = c$, or $c = \frac{210}{30}b$. If c is $p\%$ of b, it follows that $\frac{p}{100} = \frac{210}{30}$. Multiplying both sides of this equation by 100 yields $p = \left(\frac{210}{30}\right)(100)$, or $p = 700$.

CHAPTER 27

Math: Questions— Geometry and Trigonometry

In addition to questions in Algebra, Advanced Math, and Problem-Solving and Data Analysis, the Math section includes several questions that are drawn from geometry and trigonometry. They include both multiple-choice and student-produced response questions.

Let's explore the content and skills assessed by these questions.

Geometry

The Math section includes questions that assess your understanding of the key concepts in the geometry of lines, angles, triangles, circles, and other geometric objects. Other questions may also ask you to find the area, surface area, or volume of an abstract figure or a real-life object. You don't need to memorize a large collection of formulas, but you should be comfortable understanding and using these formulas to solve various types of problems. Many of the geometry formulas are provided in the reference sheet available during testing, and less commonly used formulas required to answer particular questions are given in the questions themselves.

To answer geometry questions in the Math section, you should recall the geometry definitions learned before high school and know the essential concepts extended while learning geometry in high school. You should also be familiar with basic geometric notation.

Here are some of the areas that may be the focus of some geometry questions in the Math section.

- Lines and angles

  - Lengths and midpoints

  - Measures of angles

  - Vertical angles

  - Angle addition

  - Straight angles and the sum of the angles about a point

  - Properties of parallel lines and the angles formed when parallel lines are cut by a transversal

  - Properties of perpendicular lines

REMINDER

You don't need to memorize a large collection of geometry formulas. Many geometry formulas are provided in the reference sheet available throughout testing.

- Triangles and other polygons

  - Right triangles and the Pythagorean theorem

  - Properties of equilateral and isosceles triangles

  - Properties of 30°-60°-90° triangles and 45°-45°-90° triangles

  - Congruent triangles and other congruent figures

  - Similar triangles and other similar figures

  - The triangle inequality theorem

  - Squares, rectangles, parallelograms, trapezoids, and other quadrilaterals

  - Regular polygons

- Circles

  - Radius, diameter, and circumference

  - Measure of central angles and inscribed angles

  - Arc length, arc measure, and area of sectors

  - Tangents and chords

  - Representations in the *xy*-plane

- Area and volume

  - Area of plane figures

  - Volume of solids

  - Surface area of solids

You should be familiar with the geometric notation for points and lines, line segments, angles and their measures, and lengths.

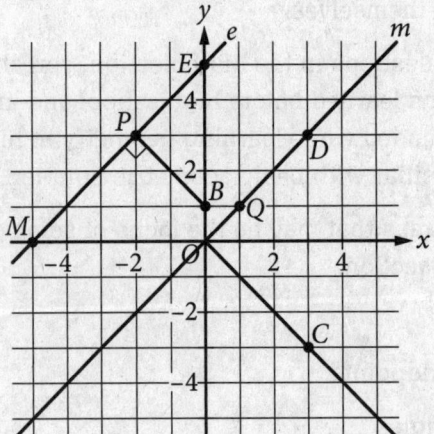

In the figure shown, the *xy*-plane has origin *O*. The values of *x* on the horizontal *x*-axis increase as you move to the right, and the values of *y* on the vertical *y*-axis increase as you move up. Line *e* contains point *P*, which has coordinates (−2, 3); point *E*, which has coordinates (0, 5); and point *M*, which has coordinates (−5, 0). Line *m* passes through the origin *O* (0, 0), the point *Q* (1, 1), and the point *D* (3, 3).

Lines *e* and *m* are parallel—they never meet. This is written *e* ∥ *m*.

You'll also need to know the following notation:

- $\overleftrightarrow{PE}$: The line containing the points *P* and *E* (this is the same as line *e*)

- $\overline{PE}$, or line segment *PE*: The line segment with endpoints *P* and *E*

- *PE*: The length of segment *PE* (you can write $PE = 2\sqrt{2}$)

- $\overrightarrow{PE}$: The ray starting at point *P* and extending indefinitely in the direction of point *E*

- $\overrightarrow{EP}$: The ray starting at point *E* and extending indefinitely in the direction of point *P*

- ∠*DOC*: The angle formed by $\overrightarrow{OD}$ and $\overrightarrow{OC}$

- △*PEB*: The triangle with vertices *P*, *E*, and *B*

- Quadrilateral *BPMO*: The quadrilateral with vertices *B*, *P*, *M*, and *O*

- $\overline{BP} \perp \overline{PM}$: Segment *BP* is perpendicular to segment *PM*. (You should also recognize that the right-angle box within ∠*BPM* means this angle is a right angle.)

Geometry and Trigonometry Sample Question 1

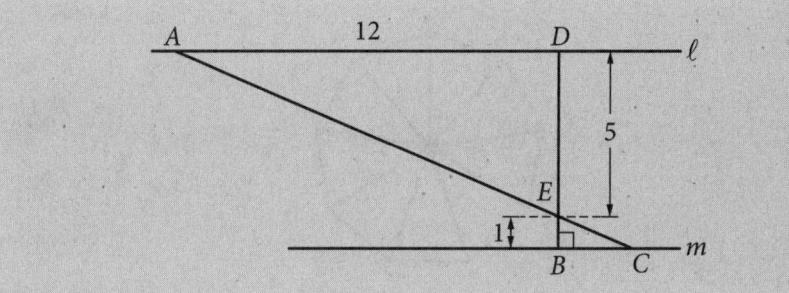

In the figure shown, line ℓ is parallel to line *m*, segment *BD* is perpendicular to line *m*, and segment *AC* and segment *BD* intersect at *E*. What is the length of segment *AC*?

STRATEGY

Familiarize yourself with these notations in order to avoid confusion on test day.

Note that this sample question has no answer choices. It's in the student-produced response (SPR) format. You'll have to come up with your own answer.

Since segment *AC* and segment *BD* intersect at *E*, ∠*AED* and ∠*CEB* are vertical angles, and so the measure of ∠*AED* is equal to the measure of ∠*CEB*. Since line ℓ is parallel to line *m*, ∠*BCE* and ∠*DAE* are alternate interior angles of parallel lines cut by a transversal, and so the measure of ∠*BCE* is equal to the measure of ∠*DAE*. By the angle-angle similarity theorem, △*AED* is similar to △*CEB*, with vertices *A*, *E*, and *D* corresponding to vertices *C*, *E*, and *B*, respectively.

Also, △*AED* is a right triangle, so by the Pythagorean theorem, $AE = \sqrt{AD^2 + DE^2}$. Substituting values for the length of the line segments gives $\sqrt{12^2 + 5^2} = \sqrt{169}$, which means that *AE* = 13.

STRATEGY

A shortcut here is remembering that 5, 12, 13 is a Pythagorean triple (5 and 12 are the lengths of the sides of the right triangle, and 13 is the length of the hypotenuse). Another common Pythagorean triple is 3, 4, 5.

Since $\triangle AED$ is similar to $\triangle CEB$, the ratios of the lengths of corresponding sides of the two triangles are in the same proportion. Since $\frac{ED}{EB} = \frac{AE}{EC}$, then $\frac{5}{1} = \frac{13}{EC}$, and so $EC = \frac{13}{5}$. Therefore, $AC = AE + EC$, or $13 + \frac{13}{5} = \frac{78}{5}$.

Note some of the key concepts that were used in sample 1:

- Vertical angles have the same measure.

- When parallel lines are cut by a transversal, the alternate interior angles have the same measure.

- If two angles of a triangle are congruent to (have the same measure as) two angles of another triangle, the two triangles are similar.

- The Pythagorean theorem: $a^2 + b^2 = c^2$, where a and b are the lengths of the legs of a right triangle and c is the length of the hypotenuse.

- If two triangles are similar, then all ratios of lengths of corresponding sides are equal.

- If point E lies on line segment AC, then $AC = AE + EC$.

Geometry and Trigonometry Sample Question 2

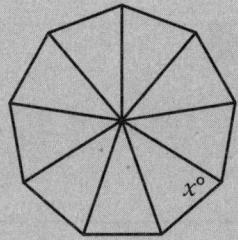

In the figure shown, a regular polygon with 9 sides has been divided into 9 congruent isosceles triangles by line segments drawn from the center of the polygon to its vertices. What is the value of x?

The sum of the measures of the angles around a point is 360°. Since the 9 triangles are congruent, the measures of each of the 9 angles around the center point are equal. Thus, the measure of each of the 9 angles around the center point is $\frac{360°}{9} = 40°$. In any triangle, the sum of the measures of the interior angles is 180°. So in each triangle, the sum of the measures of the remaining two angles is $180° - 40° = 140°$. Since each triangle is isosceles, the measure of each of these two angles is the same. Therefore, the measure of each of these angles is $\frac{140°}{2} = 70°$. Hence, the value of x is 70.

Note some of the key concepts that were used in sample 2:

- The sum of the measures of the angles about a point is 360°.

- Corresponding angles of congruent triangles have the same measure.

- The sum of the measures of the interior angles of any triangle is 180°.

- In an isosceles triangle, the angles opposite the sides of equal length are of equal measure.

Geometry and Trigonometry Sample Question 3

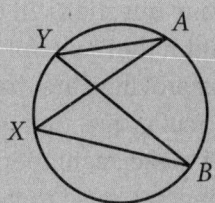

In the figure shown, ∠*AXB* and ∠*AYB* are inscribed in the circle. Which of the following statements is true?

A) The measure of ∠*AXB* is greater than the measure of ∠*AYB*.

B) The measure of ∠*AXB* is less than the measure of ∠*AYB*.

C) The measure of ∠*AXB* is equal to the measure of ∠*AYB*.

D) There is not enough information to determine the relationship between the measure of ∠*AXB* and the measure of ∠*AYB*.

Choice C is correct. Let the measure of arc *AB* be $d°$. Since ∠*AXB* is inscribed in the circle and intercepts arc *AB*, the measure of ∠*AXB* is equal to half the measure of arc *AB*. Thus, the measure of ∠*AXB* is $\frac{d°}{2}$. Similarly, since ∠*AYB* is also inscribed in the circle and intercepts arc *AB*, the measure of ∠*AYB* is also $\frac{d°}{2}$. Therefore, the measure of ∠*AXB* is equal to the measure of ∠*AYB*.

Note the key concept that was used in sample 3:

- The measure of an angle inscribed in a circle is equal to half the measure of its intercepted arc.

You also should know these related concepts:

- The measure of a central angle in a circle is equal to the measure of its intercepted arc.

- An arc is measured in degrees, while arc length is measured in linear units.

You should also be familiar with notation for arcs and circles for questions in the Math section.

- A circle may be identified by the point at its center—for instance, "the circle centered at point *M*" or "the circle with center at point *M*."

- An arc named with only its two endpoints, such as $\overarc{AB}$ or arc *AB*, will always refer to a minor arc. A minor arc has a measure that's less than 180°.

STRATEGY

At first glance, it may appear as though there's not enough information to determine the relationship between the two angle measures. One key to this question is identifying what's the same about the two angle measures. In this case, both angles intercept arc *AB*.

- An arc may also be named with three points: the two endpoints and a third point that the arc passes through. So $\overgroup{ACB}$ or arc *ACB* has endpoints at *A* and *B* and passes through point *C*. Three points may be used to name a minor arc or an arc that has a measure of 180° or more.

In general, figures that accompany questions in the Math section are intended to provide information that's useful in answering the question. Sometimes figures provided are drawn to scale, and sometimes they're not. In a particular question when it's stated that the figure isn't drawn to scale, don't make assumptions about the relative size of angles or segments. In general, even in figures not drawn to scale, the relative positions of points and angles may be assumed to be in the order shown. Also, line segments that extend through points and appear to lie on the same line may be assumed to be on the same line. A point that appears to lie on a line or curve may be assumed to lie on the line or curve.

The text "Note: Figure not drawn to scale" is included with the figure when degree measures may not be accurately shown and specific lengths may not be drawn proportionally. The following example illustrates what information can and can't be assumed from a figure not drawn to scale.

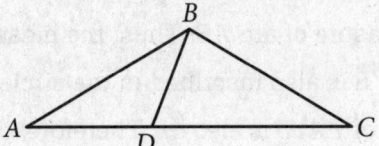

Note: Figure not drawn to scale.

A question may refer to a triangle such as *ABC* above. Although the note indicates that the figure isn't drawn to scale, you may assume the following from the figure:

- *ABC*, *ABD*, and *DBC* are triangles.

- *A*, *D*, and *C* are points on a line.

- *D* is between *A* and *C*.

- The length of $\overline{AD}$ is less than the length of $\overline{AC}$.

- The measure of angle *ABD* is less than the measure of angle *ABC*.

You may *not* assume the following from the figure:

- The length of $\overline{AD}$ is less than the length of $\overline{DC}$.

- The measures of angles *BAD* and *DBA* are equal.

- The measure of angle *DBC* is greater than the measure of angle *ABD*.

- Angle *DBC* is a right angle.

Geometry and Trigonometry Sample Question 4

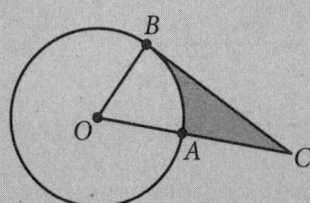

In the given figure, O is the center of the circle, segment BC is tangent to the circle at B, and A lies on segment OC. If the lengths of $\overline{OB}$ and $\overline{AC}$ are each 6, what is the area of the shaded region?

A) $18\sqrt{3} - 3\pi$

B) $18\sqrt{3} - 6\pi$

C) $36\sqrt{3} - 3\pi$

D) $36\sqrt{3} - 6\pi$

Since line segment BC is tangent to the circle at B, it follows that $\overline{BC} \perp \overline{OB}$, and so triangle OBC is a right triangle with its right angle at B. Since $OB = 6$ and $\overline{OB}$ and $\overline{OA}$ are both radii of the circle, $OA = 6$. Since $OC = OA + AC$, $OC = 6 + 6$, or 12. Thus, triangle OBC is a right triangle with the length of the hypotenuse ($OC = 12$) twice the length of one of its legs ($OB = 6$). It follows that triangle OBC is a 30°-60°-90° triangle with its 30° angle at C and its 60° angle at O. The area of the shaded region is the area of triangle OBC minus the area of the sector bounded by radii OA and OB.

In the 30°-60°-90° triangle OBC, the length of side OB, which is opposite the 30° angle, is 6. Thus, the length of side BC, which is opposite the 60° angle, is $6\sqrt{3}$. Hence, the area of triangle OBC is $\frac{1}{2}(6)(6\sqrt{3}) = 18\sqrt{3}$. Since the sector bounded by radii OA and OB has central angle 60°, the area of this sector is $\frac{60}{360} = \frac{1}{6}$ of the area of the circle. Since the circle has radius 6, its area is $\pi(6)^2 = 36\pi$, and so the area of the sector is $\frac{1}{6}(36\pi) = 6\pi$. Therefore, the area of the shaded region is $18\sqrt{3} - 6\pi$, which is choice B.

Note some of the key concepts that were used in sample 4:

- A tangent to a circle is perpendicular to the radius of the circle drawn to the point of tangency.

- Properties of 30°-60°-90° triangles.

- Area of a circle.

- The area of a sector with central angle $x°$ is equal to $\frac{x}{360}$ of the area of the entire circle.

STRATEGY

On complex multistep questions such as sample 4, start by identifying the task (finding the area of the shaded region) and considering the intermediate steps that you'll need to solve for (the area of triangle OBC and the area of sector OBA) in order to get to the final answer. Breaking up this question into a series of smaller questions will make it more manageable.

REMINDER

Arc length, area of a sector, and central angle are all proportional to each other in a circle. This proportionality is written as

$$\frac{\text{arc length}}{\text{circumference}} = \frac{\text{central angle}}{360 \text{ degrees}} = \frac{\text{area of a sector}}{\text{area of a circle}}.$$

Geometry and Trigonometry Sample Question 5

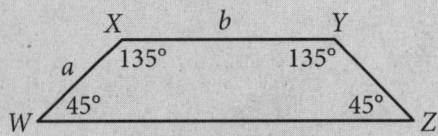

Trapezoid *WXYZ* is shown. How much greater is the area of this trapezoid than the area of a parallelogram with side lengths *a* and *b* and base angles of measures 45° and 135°?

A) $\frac{1}{2}a^2$

B) $\sqrt{2}a^2$

C) $\frac{1}{2}ab$

D) $\sqrt{2}ab$

STRATEGY

Note how drawing the parallelogram within trapezoid *WXYZ* makes it much easier to compare the areas of the two shapes, minimizing the amount of calculation needed to arrive at the solution. Be on the lookout for time-saving shortcuts such as this one.

In the figure, draw a line segment from *Y* to the point *P* on side *WZ* of the trapezoid such that ∠*YPW* has measure 135°, as shown in the figure below.

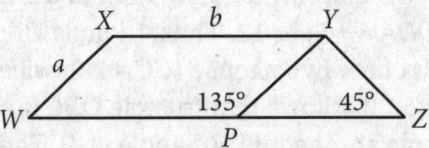

Since in trapezoid *WXYZ* side *XY* is parallel to side *WZ*, it follows that *WXYP* is a parallelogram with side lengths *a* and *b* and base angles of measure 45° and 135°. Thus, the area of the trapezoid is greater than the area of a parallelogram with side lengths *a* and *b* and base angles of measure 45° and 135° by the area of triangle *PYZ*. Since ∠*YPW* has measure 135°, it follows that ∠*YPZ* has measure 45°. Hence, triangle *PYZ* is a 45°-45°-90° triangle with legs of length *a*. Therefore, its area is $\frac{1}{2}a^2$, which is choice A.

Note some of the key concepts that were used in sample 5:

- Properties of trapezoids and parallelograms.

- Area of a 45°-45°-90° triangle.

Some questions in the Math section may ask you to find the area, surface area, or volume of an object, possibly in context.

Geometry and Trigonometry Sample Question 6

A laboratory supply company produces graduated cylinders, each with an internal radius of 2 inches and an internal height between 7.75 inches and 8 inches. What is one possible volume, rounded to the nearest cubic inch, of a graduated cylinder produced by this company?

The volume of a cylinder can be found by using the formula $V = \pi r^2 h$, where r is the radius of the circular base and h is the height of the cylinder. The smallest possible volume, in cubic inches, of a graduated cylinder produced by the laboratory supply company can be found by substituting 2 for r and 7.75 for h, giving $V = \pi(2^2)(7.75)$. This gives a volume of approximately 97.39 cubic inches, which rounds to 97 cubic inches. The largest possible volume, in cubic inches, can be found by substituting 2 for r and 8 for h, giving $V = \pi(2^2)(8)$. This gives a volume of approximately 100.53 cubic inches, which rounds to 101 cubic inches. Therefore, the possible volumes are all the integers greater than or equal to 97 and less than or equal to 101, which are 97, 98, 99, 100, and 101. Any of these numbers may be entered as the correct answer.

Coordinate Geometry

Questions in the Geometry and Trigonometry domain may ask you to use the coordinate plane and equations of lines and circles to describe figures. You may be asked to create the equation of a circle given the figure or use the structure of a given equation to determine a property of a figure in the coordinate plane. You should know that the graph of $(x - a)^2 + (y - b)^2 = r^2$ in the xy-plane is a circle with center (a, b) and radius r.

Geometry and Trigonometry Sample Question 7

$$x^2 + (y + 1)^2 = 4$$

The graph of the given equation in the xy-plane is a circle. A new circle is drawn whose center is 1 unit up from this circle's center and whose radius is 1 more than this circle's radius. Which of the following is an equation of this new circle?

A) $x^2 + y^2 = 5$

B) $x^2 + y^2 = 9$

C) $x^2 + (y + 2)^2 = 5$

D) $x^2 + (y + 2)^2 = 9$

The graph of the given equation $x^2 + (y + 1)^2 = 4$ in the xy-plane is a circle with center $(0, -1)$ and radius $\sqrt{4} = 2$. If the center of the new circle is 1 unit up from the center of the given circle, the center of the new circle will be $(0, 0)$. If the radius of the new circle is 1 more than the given circle, the radius of the new circle will be 3. Therefore, an equation of the new circle in the xy-plane is $x^2 + y^2 = 3^2 = 9$, so choice B is correct.

Geometry and Trigonometry Sample Question 8

$$x^2 + 8x + y^2 - 6y = 24$$

The graph of the given equation in the xy-plane is a circle. What is the radius of the circle?

REMINDER

You should know that the graph of $(x - a)^2 + (y - b)^2 = r^2$ in the xy-plane is a circle with center (a, b) and radius r. You should also be comfortable finding the center or radius of a circle from an equation not written in "standard form" by using the method of completing the square to rewrite the equation in standard form.

The given equation isn't in the standard form $(x - a)^2 + (y - b)^2 = r^2$. You can put it in standard form by completing the square. Since the coefficient of x is 8 and the coefficient of y is −6, you can write the equation in terms of $(x + 4)^2$ and $(y - 3)^2$ as follows:

$$x^2 + 8x + y^2 - 6y = 24$$
$$(x^2 + 8x + 16) - 16 + (y^2 - 6y + 9) - 9 = 24$$
$$(x + 4)^2 - 16 + (y - 3)^2 - 9 = 24$$
$$(x + 4)^2 + (y - 3)^2 = 24 + 16 + 9$$
$$(x + 4)^2 + (y - 3)^2 = 49$$

Since $49 = 7^2$, the radius of the circle is 7. (Also, the center of the circle is (−4, 3).)

Trigonometry and Radians

Questions in the Geometry and Trigonometry domain may ask you to apply the definitions from right triangle trigonometry. You should also know the definition of radian measure; you may also need to convert between angle measure in degrees and radians. You may need to evaluate trigonometric functions at benchmark angle measures such as 0, $\frac{\pi}{6}$, $\frac{\pi}{4}$, $\frac{\pi}{3}$, and $\frac{\pi}{2}$ radians (which are equal to the angle measures $0°$, $30°$, $45°$, $60°$, and $90°$, respectively). You will *not* be asked for values of trigonometric functions that require a calculator.

For an acute angle, the trigonometric functions sine, cosine, and tangent can be defined using right triangles. (Note the functions are often abbreviated as sin, cos, and tan, respectively.)

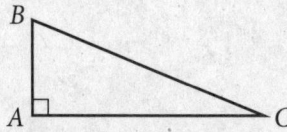

For $\angle C$ in the right triangle shown:

- $\sin \angle C = \dfrac{AB}{BC} = \dfrac{\text{length of leg opposite } \angle C}{\text{length of hypotenuse}}$

- $\cos \angle C = \dfrac{AC}{BC} = \dfrac{\text{length of leg adjacent to } \angle C}{\text{length of hypotenuse}}$

- $\tan \angle C = \dfrac{AB}{AC} = \dfrac{\text{length of leg opposite } \angle C}{\text{length of leg adjacent to } \angle C} = \dfrac{\sin \angle C}{\cos \angle C}$

The functions will often be written as sin C, cos C, and tan C, respectively.

Note that the trigonometric functions are actually functions of the *measures* of an angle, not the angle itself. Thus, if the measure of $\angle C$ is, say, $30°$, you can write sin $30°$, cos $30°$, and tan $30°$, respectively.

REMINDER

The acronym "SOHCAHTOA" may help you remember how to compute sine, cosine, and tangent. SOH stands for Sine equals Opposite over Hypotenuse, CAH stands for Cosine equals Adjacent over Hypotenuse, and TOA stands for Tangent equals Opposite over Adjacent.

Also note that sine and cosine are cofunctions and that

$\sin B = \dfrac{\text{length of leg opposite } \angle B}{\text{length of hypotenuse}} = \dfrac{AC}{BC} = \cos C$. This is the

complementary angle relationship: $\sin x° = \cos (90° - x°)$.

Geometry and Trigonometry Sample Question 9

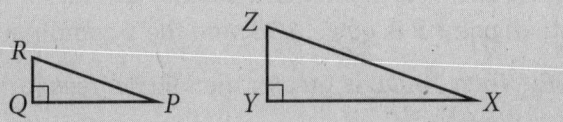

In the figure, right triangle *PQR* is similar to right triangle *XYZ*, with
vertices *P*, *Q*, and *R* corresponding to vertices *X*, *Y*, and *Z*, respectively.
If $\cos R = 0.263$, what is the value of $\cos Z$?

By the definition of cosine, $\cos R = \dfrac{RQ}{RP}$ and $\cos Z = \dfrac{ZY}{ZX}$. Since triangle

PQR is similar to triangle *XYZ*, with vertices *P*, *Q*, and *R* corresponding

to vertices *X*, *Y*, and *Z*, respectively, the ratios $\dfrac{RQ}{RP}$ and $\dfrac{ZY}{ZX}$ are

equal. Therefore, since $\cos R = \dfrac{RQ}{RP}$, or $\cos R = 0.263$, it follows that

$\cos Z = \dfrac{ZY}{ZX}$, or $\cos Z = 0.263$. Note that to find the values of the

trigonometric functions of $d°$, you can use *any* right triangle with an
acute angle of measure $d°$ and then find the appropriate ratio of lengths
of sides.

Note that since an acute angle of a right triangle has a measure
between 0° and 90°, exclusive, right triangles can be used only to find
values of trigonometric functions for angles with measures between
0° and 90°, exclusive. The definitions of sine, cosine, and tangent can
be extended to all values. This is done using radian measure and the
unit circle.

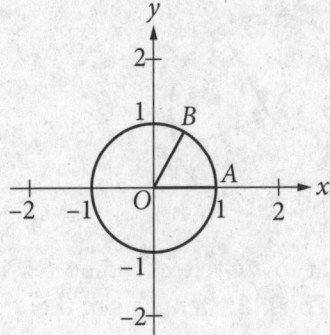

The circle above has radius 1 and is centered on the origin, *O*. An
angle in the coordinate plane is said to be in *standard position* if
it meets these two conditions: (1) its vertex lies at the origin and
(2) one of its sides lies along the positive *x*-axis. Since $\angle AOB$, above,
formed by segments *OA* and *OB*, meets both these conditions, it's in

REMINDER

To convert from degrees to radians, multiply the number of degrees by $\frac{2\pi}{360}$ degrees. To convert from radians to degrees, multiply the number of radians by $\frac{360°}{2\pi \text{ radians}}$.

standard position. As segment *OB*, also called the *terminal side* of ∠*AOB*, rotates counterclockwise about the circle, while *OA* is anchored along the *x*-axis, the *radian* measure of ∠*AOB* is defined to be the length *s* of the arc that ∠*AOB* intercepts on the unit circle. In other words, the measure of ∠*AOB* is *s* radians.

When an acute ∠*AOB* is in standard position within the unit circle, the *x*-coordinate of point *B* is cos ∠*AOB*, and the *y*-coordinate of point *B* is sin ∠*AOB*. When ∠*AOB* is greater than 90 degrees (or $\frac{\pi}{2}$ radians), and point *B* extends beyond the boundaries of the positive *x*-axis and positive *y*-axis, the values of cos ∠*AOB* and sin ∠*AOB* may be negative depending on the coordinates of point *B*. For any ∠*AOB*, place ∠*AOB* in standard position within the circle of radius 1 centered at the origin, with side *OA* along the positive *x*-axis and terminal side *OB* intersecting the circle at point *B*. Then the cosine of ∠*AOB* is the *x*-coordinate of *B*, and the sine of ∠*AOB* is the *y*-coordinate of *B*. The tangent of ∠*AOB* is the sine of ∠*AOB* divided by the cosine of ∠*AOB*.

An angle with a full rotation about point *O* has measure 360°. This angle intercepts the full circumference of the circle, which has length 2π. Thus, $\frac{\text{measure of an angle in radians}}{\text{measure of an angle in degrees}} = \frac{2\pi}{360°}$. It follows that the measure of an angle in radians is $\frac{2\pi}{360°}$ × the measure of the angle in degrees and that the measure of an angle in degrees is $\frac{360°}{2\pi}$ × the measure of the angle in radians.

Also note that since a rotation of 2π about point *O* brings you back to the same point on the unit circle, sin (*s* + 2π) = sin *s*, cos (*s* + 2π) = cos *s*, and tan (*s* + 2π), for any radian measure *s*.

Let angle *DEF* be a central angle in a circle of radius *r*, as shown in the following figure.

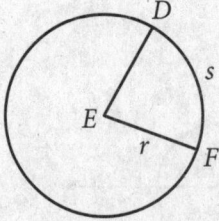

A circle of radius *r* is similar to a circle of radius 1, with constant of proportionality equal to *r*. Thus, the length *s* of the arc intercepted by angle *DEF* is *r* times the length of the arc that would be intercepted by an angle of the same measure in a circle of radius 1. Therefore, in the figure above, *s* = *r* × (radian measure of angle *DEF*), or radian measure of angle *DEF* = $\frac{s}{r}$.

Geometry and Trigonometry Sample Question 10

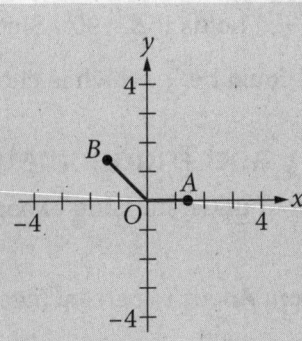

In the figure shown, the coordinates of point B are $(-\sqrt{2}, \sqrt{2})$. What is the measure, in radians, of angle AOB?

A) $\dfrac{\pi}{4}$

B) $\dfrac{\pi}{2}$

C) $\dfrac{3\pi}{4}$

D) $\dfrac{5\pi}{4}$

Let C be the point $(-\sqrt{2}, 0)$. Then triangle BOC, shown in the figure below, is a right triangle with both legs of length $\sqrt{2}$.

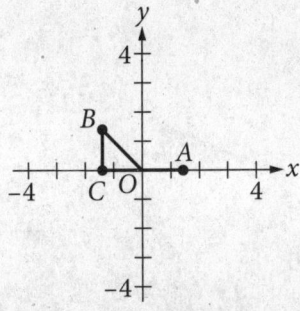

STRATEGY

Always be on the lookout for special right triangles. Here, noticing that segment OB is the hypotenuse of a 45°-45°-90° triangle makes this question easier to solve.

Hence, triangle BOC is a 45°-45°-90° triangle. Thus, angle COB has measure 45°, and angle AOB has measure 180° − 45° = 135°. Therefore, the measure of angle AOB in radians is 135° × $\dfrac{2\pi}{360°}$ = $\dfrac{3\pi}{4}$, which is choice C.

Geometry and Trigonometry Sample Question 11

$$\sin x = \cos (K - x)$$

In the given equation, the angle measures are in radians and K is a constant. Which of the following could be the value of K?

A) 0

B) $\dfrac{\pi}{4}$

C) $\dfrac{\pi}{2}$

D) π

The complementary angle relationship for sine and cosine implies that the equation $\sin x = \cos (K - x)$ holds if $K = 90°$. Since $90° = \frac{2\pi}{360°} \times 90°$, or $\frac{\pi}{2}$ radians, the value of K could be $\frac{\pi}{2}$, which is choice C.

Summary: Geometry and Trigonometry Questions

Main purpose: To assess your understanding of concepts central to geometry and trigonometry

Proportion of the test section: About 15 percent (five to seven questions)

Question types

- Area and volume
- Lines, angles, and triangles
- Right triangles and trigonometry
- Circles

CHAPTER 28

Math: Questions— Geometry and Trigonometry Drills

1

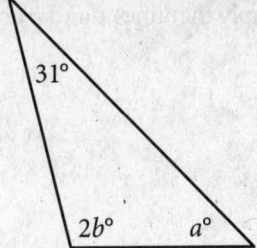

In the triangle shown, $a = 45$. What is the value of b?

A) 52

B) 59

C) 76

D) 104

2

A cube has a surface area of 54 square meters. What is the volume, in cubic meters, of the cube?

A) 18

B) 27

C) 36

D) 81

3

In the xy-plane, a circle with radius 5 has center $(-8, 6)$. Which of the following is an equation of the circle?

A) $(x - 8)^2 + (y + 6)^2 = 25$

B) $(x + 8)^2 + (y - 6)^2 = 25$

C) $(x - 8)^2 + (y + 6)^2 = 5$

D) $(x + 8)^2 + (y - 6)^2 = 5$

4

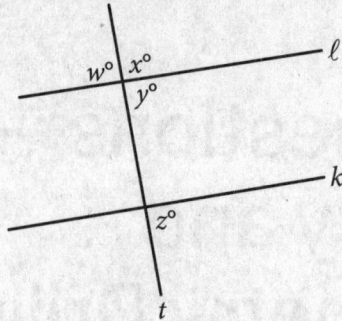

Note: Figure not drawn to scale.

In the figure shown, line t intersects lines ℓ and k. Which of the following statements, if true, would imply that lines ℓ and k are parallel?

A) $w = y$

B) $w = z$

C) $x = z$

D) $x + y = 180$

5

In a right triangle, the tangent of one of the two acute angles is $\frac{\sqrt{3}}{3}$. What is the tangent of the other acute angle?

A) $-\frac{\sqrt{3}}{3}$

B) $-\frac{3}{\sqrt{3}}$

C) $\frac{\sqrt{3}}{3}$

D) $\frac{3}{\sqrt{3}}$

6

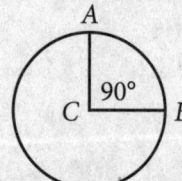

Point C is the center of the circle shown. What is the measure of angle ACB, in radians?

A) 2π

B) π

C) $\frac{\pi}{2}$

D) $\frac{\pi}{4}$

7

The length of one side of square M is 5 times the length of one side of square N. The area of square N is 361 square centimeters. What is the area, in square centimeters, of square M?

8

Triangle *KLM* is similar to triangle *QRS*, where angle *K* corresponds to angle *Q* and where angles *L* and *R* are right angles. If $\sin K = \frac{105}{233}$ and $\sin M = \frac{208}{233}$, what is the value of $\tan S$?

9

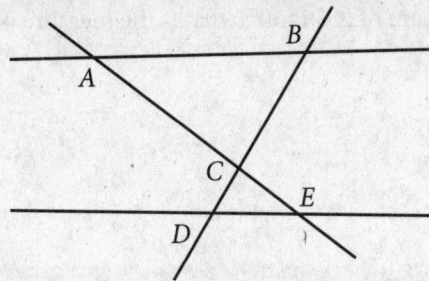

Note: Figure not drawn to scale.

In the figure shown, $\triangle ABC$ is similar to $\triangle EDC$, with $\angle BAC$ corresponding to $\angle CED$ and $\angle ABC$ corresponding to $\angle CDE$. Which of the following must be true?

A) $\overline{AE} \parallel \overline{BD}$

B) $\overline{AE} \perp \overline{BD}$

C) $\overline{AB} \parallel \overline{DE}$

D) $\overline{AB} \perp \overline{DE}$

10

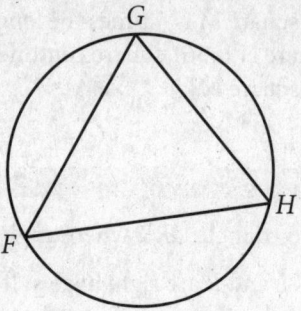

Note: Figure not drawn to scale.

Triangle *FGH* is inscribed in the circle shown. If arc *FG* is congruent to arc *GH* and the measure of ∠*G* is 30°, what is the measure of ∠*H*?

A) 30°

B) 60°

C) 75°

D) 120°

11

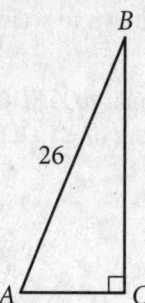

Triangle *ABC* shown is a right triangle, and $\sin B = \frac{5}{13}$. What is the length of side $\overline{BC}$?

12

An architect drew the sketch shown while designing a house roof. The dimensions shown are for the interior of the triangle.

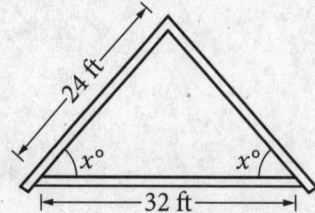

Note: Figure not drawn to scale.

What is the value of cos *x*?

13

Line ℓ is parallel to line m. Points A and B lie on line ℓ, and points P and Q lie on line m. If $\angle ABP$ and $\angle QAB$ each have measure 21° and $\angle AQB$ has measure 76°, what is the measure, in degrees, of $\angle PAQ$?

14

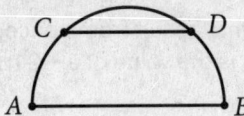

The semicircle shown has a radius of r inches, and chord $\overline{CD}$ is parallel to the diameter $\overline{AB}$. If the length of $\overline{CD}$ is $\frac{2}{3}$ of the length of $\overline{AB}$, what is the distance between the chord and the diameter in terms of r?

A) $\frac{1}{3}\pi r$

B) $\frac{2}{3}\pi r$

C) $\frac{\sqrt{2}}{2}r$

D) $\frac{\sqrt{5}}{3}r$

Answer Explanations

QUESTION 1

Choice A is correct. The sum of the measures of the three interior angles of a triangle is 180°. Therefore, $31 + 2b + a = 180$. Since it's given that $a = 45$, it follows that $31 + 2b + 45 = 180$, or $2b = 104$. Dividing both sides of this equation by 2 yields $b = 52$.

Choice B is incorrect and may result from conceptual or calculation errors. *Choice C* is incorrect. This is the value of $a + 31$. *Choice D* is incorrect. This is the value of $2b$.

QUESTION 2

Choice B is correct. The surface area of a cube with side length s is equal to $6s^2$. Since the surface area is given as 54 square meters, the equation $54 = 6s^2$ can be used to solve for s. Dividing both sides of this equation by 6 yields $9 = s^2$. Taking the square root of both sides of this equation yields $3 = s$ and $-3 = s$. Since the side length of a cube must be a positive value, it follows that $s = 3$. The volume of a cube with side length s is equal to s^3. Therefore, the volume of this cube, in cubic meters, is 3^3, or 27.

Choices A, C, and *D* are incorrect and may result from conceptual or calculation errors.

QUESTION 3

Choice B is correct. An equation of a circle in the xy-plane is $(x - h)^2 + (y - k)^2 = r^2$, where the center of the circle is (h, k) and the radius is r. It's given that the center of this circle is $(-8, 6)$ and the radius is 5. Substituting these values into the equation $(x - h)^2 + (y - k)^2 = r^2$ gives $(x - (-8))^2 + (y - 6)^2 = 5^2$, or $(x + 8)^2 + (y - 6)^2 = 25$.

Choice A is incorrect. This is an equation of a circle that has center $(8, -6)$. *Choice C* is incorrect. This is an equation of a circle that has center $(8, -6)$ and radius $\sqrt{5}$. *Choice D* is incorrect. This is an equation of a circle that has radius $\sqrt{5}$.

QUESTION 4

Choice B is correct. Two lines are parallel if the alternate exterior angles are congruent. The angles with measures of $w°$ and $z°$ are alternate exterior angles. If $w = z$, then these alternate exterior angles would be congruent, which would imply that the lines ℓ and k are parallel.

Choice A is incorrect. Although it's true that $w = y$, since vertical angles are congruent, this doesn't provide enough information to imply that lines ℓ and k are parallel. *Choice C* is incorrect. The angles with measures $x°$ and $z°$ must be supplementary, instead of congruent, to imply that lines ℓ and k are parallel. *Choice D* is incorrect. Although it's true that $x + y = 180$, since the sum of the measures of a linear pair of angles is 180°, this doesn't provide enough information to imply that lines ℓ and k are parallel.

QUESTION 5

Choice D is correct. The tangent of a non-right angle in a right triangle is defined as the ratio of the length of the leg opposite the angle to the length of the leg adjacent to the angle. Using this definition for tangent, in a right triangle with legs that have lengths a and b, the tangent of one acute angle is $\frac{a}{b}$ and the tangent for the other acute angle is $\frac{b}{a}$. It follows that the tangents of the acute angles in a right triangle are reciprocals of each other. Therefore, the tangent of the other acute angle in the given triangle is the reciprocal of $\frac{\sqrt{3}}{3}$, or $\frac{3}{\sqrt{3}}$.

Choices A, B, and C are incorrect and may result from conceptual or calculation errors.

QUESTION 6

Choice C is correct. It's given that the measure of angle *ACB* is 90°. Since 180° is equivalent to π radians and angle *ACB* is the equivalent of $\frac{180°}{2}$, it follows that the measure of angle *ACB*, in radians, is $\frac{\pi}{2}$.

Choices A, B, and D are incorrect and may result from conceptual or calculation errors.

QUESTION 7

The correct answer is 9,025. It's given that the length of one side of square M is 5 times the length of one side of square N. Let *m* and *n* represent the lengths, in centimeters, of each side of square M and square N, respectively. It follows that *m* = 5*n* and the areas, in square centimeters, of squares M and N are m^2 and n^2, respectively. Squaring both sides of the equation *m* = 5*n* yields $m^2 = (5n)^2$, which is equivalent to $m^2 = 25n^2$. It's given that the area of square N is 361 square centimeters. Substituting 361 for n^2 in the equation $m^2 = 25n^2$ yields $m^2 = 25(361)$, or $m^2 = 9{,}025$. Therefore, the area, in square centimeters, of square M is 9,025.

QUESTION 8

The correct answer is 1.981. It's given that triangle *KLM* is similar to triangle *QRS*, where angle *K* corresponds to angle *Q* and where angles *L* and *R* are right angles. Since corresponding angles in similar triangles have equal measures, the sines, cosines, and tangents, respectively, of corresponding angles are equivalent. Therefore, tan *S* = tan *M*. In a right triangle, the sine of an acute angle is the ratio of the length of the leg opposite the angle to the length of the hypotenuse. It follows that in triangle *KLM*, $\sin K = \frac{LM}{MK}$ and $\sin M = \frac{KL}{MK}$. If $\sin K = \frac{105}{233}$ and $\sin M = \frac{208}{233}$, then $\frac{LM}{MK} = \frac{105}{233}$ and $\frac{KL}{MK} = \frac{208}{233}$. It follows from these ratios that for some constant *d*, *LM* = 105*d*, *MK* = 233*d*, and *KL* = 208*d*.

The tangent of an acute angle in a right triangle is the ratio of the length of the leg opposite the angle to the length of the leg adjacent to the angle. It follows that in triangle *KLM*, $\tan M = \frac{KL}{LM}$. Thus, $\tan M = \frac{208d}{105d}$, or $\tan M = \frac{208}{105}$. Since tan *S* = tan *M*, the value of tan *S* is $\frac{208}{105}$, or approximately 1.981. Note that 1.981 and 1.980 are examples of ways to enter a correct answer.

QUESTION 9

Choice C is correct. It's given that $\triangle ABC$ is similar to $\triangle EDC$ and that $\angle BAC$ corresponds to $\angle CED$. Since the two triangles are similar, corresponding angles are congruent. Therefore, $\angle BAC$ is congruent to $\angle CED$. The alternate interior angle theorem states that when two parallel lines are cut by a transversal, alternate interior angles are congruent. The converse of this theorem is also true, which implies that $\overline{AB}$ is parallel to $\overline{DE}$.

Choice A is incorrect. The figure shows that $\overline{AE}$ and $\overline{BD}$ intersect; therefore, they can't be parallel. *Choice B* is incorrect. While $\overline{AE}$ and $\overline{BD}$ appear to form a 90° angle, there isn't sufficient information to prove that $\overline{AE}$ is perpendicular to $\overline{BD}$. *Choice D* is incorrect. $\overline{AB}$ is parallel, not perpendicular, to $\overline{DE}$.

QUESTION 10

Choice C is correct. The measure of an inscribed angle is equal to half the measure of the arc the angle intercepts. Therefore, the measure of $\angle H$ is equal to half the measure of arc FG and the measure of $\angle F$ is equal to half the measure of arc GH. If arcs FG and GH are congruent, it follows that the measures of angles H and F must be equal. Let the measure of $\angle H$ be $x°$. Therefore, the measure of $\angle F$ is also $x°$. It's given that the measure of $\angle G$ is 30°. Since the sum of the three interior angles of a triangle is 180°, it follows that the sum of the measures of angles F, G, and H is 180°. Therefore, $x + x + 30 = 180$. Adding like terms on the left-hand side and subtracting 30 from both sides of this equation gives $2x = 150$. Dividing both sides of this equation by 2 yields $x = 75$. Therefore, the measure of $\angle H$ is 75°.

Choice A is incorrect. This is the measure of $\angle G$, which isn't congruent to $\angle H$. *Choice B* is incorrect. This is twice the measure of $\angle G$, not the measure of $\angle H$. *Choice D* is incorrect and may result from a conceptual or calculation error.

QUESTION 11

The correct answer is 24. The sine of an acute angle in a right triangle is equal to the ratio of the length of the side opposite the angle to the length of the hypotenuse. In the triangle shown, the sine of angle B, or sin B, is equal to the ratio of the length of side AC to the length of side AB. It's given that the length of side AB is 26 and that $\sin (B) = \frac{5}{13}$. Therefore, $\frac{5}{13} = \frac{AC}{26}$. Multiplying both sides of this equation by 26 yields $AC = 10$. Using the Pythagorean theorem, it follows that $AB^2 = AC^2 + BC^2$. Substituting 26 for AB and 10 for AC in this equation gives $26^2 = 10^2 + BC^2$, or $676 = 100 + BC^2$. Subtracting 100 from both sides of this equation yields $576 = BC^2$. Taking the square root of both sides of this equation yields $-24 = BC$ or $24 = BC$. Since the side length of a triangle must be a positive value, the length of side BC is 24.

QUESTION 12

The correct answer is $\frac{2}{3}$. The given sketch of the house roof shows that the two base angles of the triangle are congruent, which means the triangle is isosceles. Constructing a perpendicular line from the vertex of the isosceles triangle to the opposite side will bisect the base of the triangle and create two smaller right triangles. In a right triangle, the cosine of an acute angle is equal to the ratio of the length of the side adjacent to the angle to the length of the hypotenuse. This gives $\cos x = \frac{16}{24}$, which can be rewritten as $\cos x = \frac{2}{3}$. Note that 2/3, .6666, .6667, 0.666, and 0.667 are examples of ways to enter a correct answer.

QUESTION 13

The correct answer is 62. It's given that line ℓ is parallel to line m, where points A and B lie on line ℓ and points P and Q lie on line m. If a line segment is drawn from point B to point P and a line segment is drawn from point A to point Q, then angles ABP and QAB are formed. It's given that each of these angles has a measure of 21°. Let the intersection of $\overline{BP}$ and $\overline{AQ}$ be point T, which lies between lines ℓ and m. Since the sum of the interior angles of a triangle is 180°, it follows that in triangle ABT, the measure of angle ATB is equal to 180° − 2(21°), or 138°. Angles ATB and ATP are adjacent angles that form a straight line segment, $\overline{BP}$. Since a line segment is a straight angle that measures 180°, by the angle addition postulate, it follows that the measure of angle ATP is 180° − 138°, or 42°. Angles ATP and BTQ are vertical angles and are therefore congruent. Therefore, the measure of angle BTQ is also 42°. Angles ABP and BPQ are alternate interior angles. Since lines ℓ and m are parallel, angles ABP and BPQ are congruent. Therefore, the measure of angle BPQ is also 21°. Similarly, angles QAB and AQP are congruent alternate interior angles. Therefore, angle AQP also measures 21°. It follows that triangle ABT is an isosceles triangle, where $AT = BT$, and triangle PQT is an isosceles triangle, where $PT = QT$. If a line segment is drawn from point A to point P and a line segment is drawn from point B to point Q, then triangles ATP and BTQ are formed. Since $AT = BT$, $PT = QT$, and the measure of angle ATP is equal to the measure of angle BTQ, by the side-angle-side theorem, triangle ATP is congruent to triangle BTQ. In triangles ATP and BTQ, angle ATP corresponds to angle BTQ, angle TPA corresponds to angle TQB, and angle PAT corresponds to angle QBT. It's given that the measure of angle AQB is 76°. Since angle AQB and angle TQB are the same angle, the measure of angle TQB is 76°. Therefore, in triangle BTQ, by the triangle angle sum theorem, it follows that the measure of angle QBT is 180° − 42° − 76°, or 62°. In congruent triangles, corresponding angles have equal measure. Therefore, the measure of angle PAT is 62°. Since angle PAT and angle PAQ are the same angle, the measure, in degrees, of angle PAQ is 62.

QUESTION 14

Choice D is correct. Let the semicircle have center O. The diameter $\overline{AB}$ has length $2r$. If chord $\overline{CD}$ is $\frac{2}{3}$ of the length of the diameter, then $CD = \frac{2}{3}(2r)$, or $CD = \frac{4}{3}r$. It follows that $\frac{1}{2}CD = \frac{1}{2}\left(\frac{4}{3}\right)r$, or $\frac{1}{2}CD = \frac{2}{3}r$. The distance between two line segments is the shortest distance between the two segments, or the perpendicular distance between the two segments. The distance, x, between $\overline{AB}$ and $\overline{CD}$ can be found by drawing a right triangle connecting center O, the midpoint of chord $\overline{CD}$, and point C. Using the Pythagorean theorem, it follows that $r^2 = x^2 + \left(\frac{2}{3}r\right)^2$, or $r^2 = x^2 + \frac{4}{9}r^2$. Subtracting $\frac{4}{9}r^2$ from both sides of this equation yields $\frac{5}{9}r^2 = x^2$. Finally, taking the square root of both sides of this equation gives $x = \frac{\sqrt{5}}{3}r$ or $x = -\frac{\sqrt{5}}{3}r$. Since the distance between the chord and the diameter must be positive, this distance in terms of r is $\frac{\sqrt{5}}{3}r$.

Choices A, B, and C are incorrect and may result from conceptual or calculation errors.

CHAPTER 29

Math: Student-Produced Response (SPR) Questions

In earlier chapters, we presented numerous examples of Math section questions in the student-produced response, or SPR, format. In this brief chapter, we go over the directions for entering answers to these sorts of questions.

SPRs IN PRACTICE AND ACTUAL TESTS

The following describes how to enter SPR answers into Bluebook, the digital testing app. This guidance applies to taking a practice test digitally in Bluebook or an actual SAT digitally.

If you're using the paper-based practice test forms at the end of this book to prepare, write your answer to a given SPR question next to or under the question in this book. Once you've written your answer, circle it.

SPR Directions

You'll have ready access to the SPR directions while you take the SAT, so there's no need to memorize them in every detail prior to test day. However, as we discussed in chapter 5, being familiar with the directions in advance of testing is beneficial to you because it will both save you time—you can devote more time to answering questions—and make it less likely that you'll make a careless mistake when entering your answers.

Figure 1 displays the official directions for how to enter responses to SPR questions.

Figure 1. Math Section: Student-Produced Response (SPR) Entry Directions

For student-produced response questions, solve each problem and enter your answer as described below.

- If you find **more than one correct answer,** enter only one answer.

- You can enter up to 5 characters for a **positive** answer and up to 6 characters (including the negative sign) for a **negative** answer.

- If your answer is a **fraction** that doesn't fit in the provided space, enter the decimal equivalent.

- If your answer is a **decimal** that doesn't fit in the provided space, enter it by truncating or rounding at the fourth digit.

- If your answer is a **mixed number** (such as $3\frac{1}{2}$), enter it as an improper fraction (7/2) or its decimal equivalent (3.5).

- Don't enter **symbols** such as a percent sign, comma, or dollar sign.

Examples

Answer	Acceptable ways to enter answer	Unacceptable: will NOT receive credit
3.5	3.5 3.50 7/2	31/2 3 1/2
$\frac{2}{3}$	2/3 .6666 .6667 0.666 0.667	0.66 .66 0.67 .67
$-\frac{1}{3}$	−1/3 −.3333 −0.333	−.33 −0.33

Unacceptable and Acceptable Answers

The directions themselves are clear on what can and can't be entered into an SPR answer field, but let's go over what disqualifies the "unacceptable" answers (as well as a few other examples) to clarify what makes them impermissible and to help you avoid making these (and similar) entry mistakes.

Table 1. Math Section: Examples of Unacceptable and Acceptable SPR Answers

Intended answer	Unacceptable answer(s)	Reason	Acceptable answer(s)
3.5	31/2 3 1/2	Mixed numbers should be entered as improper fractions or as decimal equivalents.	7/2 (improper fraction that fits the space) 3.5 (decimal equivalent)
$\frac{2}{3}$	0.66 .66 0.67 .67	Decimals that don't fit the provided space should be truncated or rounded at the fourth digit.	2/3 (fraction that fits the space) .6666 (decimal truncated at the fourth digit) .6667 (decimal rounded at the fourth digit) 0.666 (decimal truncated at the fourth digit, includes leading zero) 0.667 (decimal rounded at the fourth digit, includes leading zero)
$-\frac{1}{3}$	−0.33	Decimals that don't fit the provided space should be truncated or rounded at the fourth digit.	−1/3 (fraction that fits the space) −.3333 (decimal rounded or truncated at the fourth digit) −0.333 (decimal rounded or truncated at the fourth digit, includes leading zero)
$2.53	$2.53	Answers may not include symbols such as a dollar sign.	2.53
68,132	68,132	Answers may not include symbols such as a comma.	68132
45%	45%	Answers may not include symbols such as a percent sign.	.45 (decimal equivalent of the percent) 0.45 (decimal equivalent of the percent; leading zero allowed but not required)

Confirming Your Answers

The Bluebook test application includes a feature called Answer Preview below each SPR question. Answer Preview shows you how the test interprets the response you entered to a given question so that you can confirm that your intended answer is properly reflected. If it's not, you'll have a chance to change it should time permit.

For example, to continue from the cases presented in the preceding table, let's assume that you had intended your answer to a given SPR question to be $3\frac{1}{2}$ and that, contrary to the guidelines above, you decided to enter this as 31/2, with the goal of representing your answer as a mixed number. Answer Preview would inform you that it interprets this response as the fraction $\frac{31}{2}$, which isn't what you intended. Recognizing your error, you instead enter either 7/2, an improper fraction, or 3.5, the decimal equivalent of $3\frac{1}{2}$.

CHAPTER 30
Calculator Options

The use of a calculator is permitted throughout the Math section (but not the Reading and Writing section) of the SAT. You have two options in terms of tools on test day: (1) you may bring your own approved calculator or (2) you may use the Desmos graphing calculator built into Bluebook, the digital testing app. The choice you make should be based primarily on which tool you're more comfortable with. We recommend that you try out both options during your practice.

Bringing Your Own Calculator

College Board allows SAT test takers to use their own approved calculator on test day. To ensure that you have up-to-date information on which calculators are and aren't permitted, please visit **satsuite.collegeboard.org/digital/what-to-bring-do/calculator-policy**.

REMINDER
If you choose to bring your own calculator, you will be asked to clear all saved formulas on it before you begin testing.

Using the Built-In Desmos Graphing Calculator

The embedded calculator available for test takers in Bluebook is the Desmos graphing calculator, a fully digital, accessible graphing calculator used for computational, graphing, statistical, and other mathematical purposes. You may already be familiar with the Desmos calculator from your classes, as it's an application commonly used in education as well as in other fields. If you aren't familiar with using the Desmos graphing calculator, you may want to consider trying it in Bluebook to see if it works well for you.

The Testing Calculator

The Desmos graphing calculator embedded in Bluebook mimics the experience users see at **desmos.com/calculator**, except that images, folders, and notes (usually available via the Plus Mark button—i.e., the Add Icon button atop the expression list) are removed in the testing calculator.

Figure 1. Desmos Graphing Calculator—Standard View in Bluebook with Keypad Open

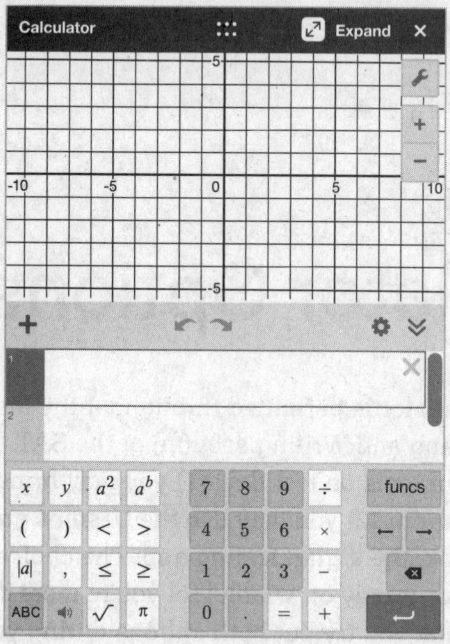

Figure 2. Desmos Graphing Calculator—Expanded View in Bluebook

A PDF document explaining the slight differences between the online Demos graphing calculator and the one embedded in Bluebook, along with a practice calculator that mimics the exact version available in Bluebook, can be found at **desmos.com/testing**. The version of the Desmos graphing calculator for the digital SAT is also available at **desmos.com/practice** and on the Desmos Test Mode app available for Chromebooks (Chrome Web Store) and for iPads and iPhones (Apple's App Store).

Notable Features

For students and users new to the Desmos graphing calculator, please reference the frequently asked questions (FAQ) document (**help.desmos.com/hc/en-us/articles/4406360401677**) available at the Desmos Help Center to get started with basic functionality around plotting points, graphing lines and curves, adjusting display settings, and more.

Accessibility Settings

The Desmos graphing calculator was designed with all learners in mind. Accessibility features available to digital SAT test takers in the Desmos graphing calculator include:

- Text-to-Speech and Audio Trace capabilities: **desmos.com/accessibility#setup**

- Enlarge Display, Reverse Contrast, and additional options: **help.desmos.com/hc/en-us/articles/5685797932813**

- Braille Mode: **desmos.com/braille-examples**

CHAPTER 31
Math: Reference Sheet

You'll have access to the following common formulas at any time as you take the SAT.

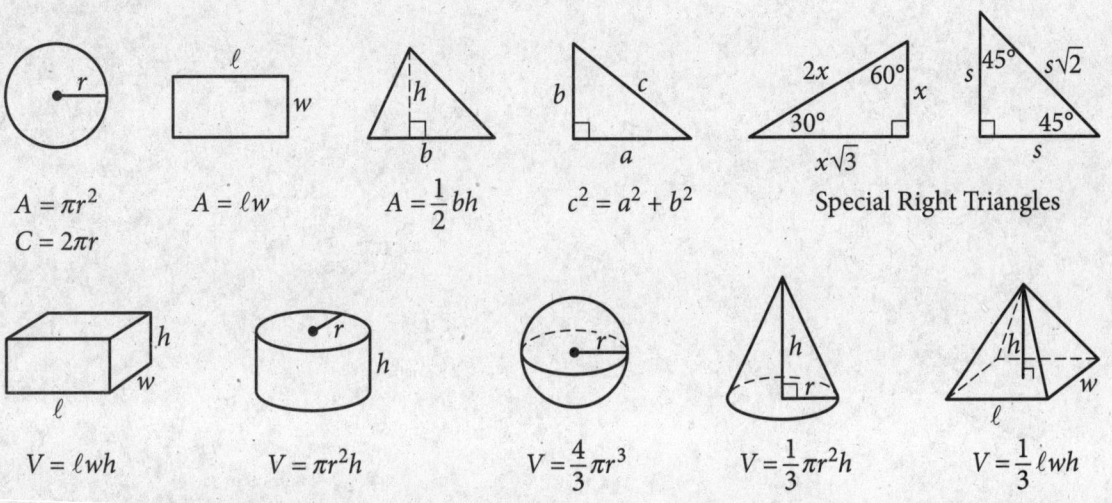

$A = \pi r^2$
$C = 2\pi r$

$A = \ell w$

$A = \dfrac{1}{2} bh$

$c^2 = a^2 + b^2$

Special Right Triangles

$V = \ell wh$

$V = \pi r^2 h$

$V = \dfrac{4}{3} \pi r^3$

$V = \dfrac{1}{3} \pi r^2 h$

$V = \dfrac{1}{3} \ell wh$

The number of degrees of arc in a circle is 360.

The number of radians of arc in a circle is 2π.

The sum of the measures in degrees of the angles of a triangle is 180.

Practice Tests

Introduction to the Practice Tests

Part 4 of this book consists of seven official full-length SAT practice tests accompanied by answer explanations and scoring guidelines. These practice tests were assembled using the same processes and standards College Board employs to construct actual SAT tests, so you can prepare for test day confident in the knowledge that your practice will be as authentic as possible.

We strongly recommend that you take at least one full-length practice test, under timed conditions, prior to test day to get a clear sense of how the test is put together and how to pace yourself.

About These Practice Tests

The seven practice tests included in this book may be used as part of your preparation for test day. For the best and most realistic practice experience, however, **we strongly recommend that you take these tests digitally in the Bluebook testing application** unless you know that you'll be taking the actual test on paper owing to a testing accommodation. Practicing in Bluebook gives you valuable exposure to the app's interface and tools in a low-stakes environment, allows you to experience how adaptive testing works, and yields section and total scores that you don't have to calculate yourself. The practice tests in this book are consistent with those in Bluebook.

Unlike the actual SAT and practice tests in Bluebook, each of the practice tests in this book consists of three modules: (1) a single first-stage (routing) module and (2) two second-stage modules. The two second-stage modules differ by average question difficulty and are marked as either "higher difficulty" or "lower difficulty." **An actual testing experience consists of one routing and one second-stage module per test section.** This means that the best simulation of an actual Reading and Writing or Math test section using the practice tests in this book is to pair a given "module 1" with **one** of the two options for "module 2." If you work through multiple practice tests, you may want to try both options—taking one practice test with the lower-difficulty second-stage module and another practice test with the higher-difficulty second-stage module—to get a clearer sense of the full range of question difficulty you may encounter on test day. For more information on how adaptive testing in the digital SAT works, see chapter 2.

Important

College Board includes a small number of unscored questions in test forms—including these practice test forms—for research purposes. Your answers to these questions don't affect your score in any way.

In the scoring guides that follow each practice test in this book, the rows in the "SAT Practice Test Worksheet: Answer Key" corresponding to unscored questions are grayed out. You should **not** consider these questions when calculating your raw scores for the Reading and Writing and Math sections. (A reminder of this appears in each scoring guide.)

Note also that the placement of unscored questions within SAT test forms isn't fixed. This means that the locations of the unscored questions in the practice tests in this book are only examples and that such questions may appear in different locations in actual SAT test forms. You should give your best effort to answering each and every question on the test.

The SAT®

Practice Test #4

Make time to take the practice test.
It is one of the best ways to get ready for the SAT.

Note: The practice tests in this guide include two second modules so that you can experience both the lower- and higher-difficulty modules. On the actual test, you will be presented with only one second module.

After you have taken the practice test, score it right away using materials provided in *The Official SAT Study Guide*.

This version of the SAT Practice Test is for students using this Study Guide. As a reminder, most students taking the SAT will do so using Bluebook™, the digital testing application. To best prepare for test day, download Bluebook at **bluebook.app.collegeboard.org** to take the practice test in the digital format.

Test begins on the next page.

Reading and Writing

27 QUESTIONS

1

Although critics believed that customers would never agree to pay to pick their own produce on farms, such concerns didn't _____ Booker T. Whatley's efforts to promote the practice. Thanks in part to Whatley's determined advocacy, farms that allow visitors to pick their own apples, pumpkins, and other produce can be found throughout the United States.

Which choice completes the text with the most logical and precise word or phrase?

A) enhance

B) hinder

C) misrepresent

D) aggravate

2

The artisans of the Igun Eronmwon guild in Benin City, Nigeria, typically _____ the bronze- and brass-casting techniques that have been passed down through their families since the thirteenth century, but they don't strictly observe every tradition; for example, guild members now use air-conditioning motors instead of handheld bellows to help heat their forges.

Which choice completes the text with the most logical and precise word or phrase?

A) experiment with

B) adhere to

C) improve on

D) grapple with

Unauthorized copying or reuse of any part of this page is illegal.

324

CONTINUE ➡

3

Set in a world where science fiction tropes exist as everyday realities, Charles Yu's 2010 novel *How to Live Safely in a Science Fictional Universe* traces a time traveler's quest to find his father. Because the journey at the novel's center is so _____, with the protagonist ricocheting chaotically across time, the reader often wonders whether the pair will ever be reunited.

Which choice completes the text with the most logical and precise word or phrase?

A) haphazard

B) premeditated

C) inspirational

D) fruitless

4

In a 2019 study, Jeremy Gunawardena and colleagues found that the single-celled protozoan *Stentor roeseli* not only uses strategies to escape irritating stimuli but also switches strategies when one fails. This evidence of protozoans sophisticatedly "changing their minds" demonstrates that single-celled organisms may not be limited to _____ behaviors.

Which choice completes the text with the most logical and precise word or phrase?

A) aggressive

B) rudimentary

C) evolving

D) advantageous

5

Some economic historians _____ that late nineteenth- and early twentieth-century households in the United States experienced an economy of scale when it came to food purchases—they assumed that large households spent less on food per person than did small households. Economist Trevon Logan showed, however, that a close look at the available data disproves this supposition.

Which choice completes the text with the most logical and precise word or phrase?

A) surmised

B) contrived

C) questioned

D) regretted

6

The following text is adapted from Karel Čapek's 1920 play *R.U.R. (Rossum's Universal Robots)*, translated by Paul Selver and Nigel Playfair in 1923. Fabry and Busman are telling Miss Glory why their company manufactures robots.

FABRY: One Robot can replace two and a half *workmen*. The human machine, Miss Glory, was terribly *imperfect*. It had to be removed sooner or later.

BUSMAN: It was too expensive.

FABRY: It was not *effective*. It no longer <u>answers</u> the requirements of *modern engineering*. Nature has no idea of keeping pace with *modern labor*.

As used in the text, what does the word "answers" most nearly mean?

A) Explains

B) Rebuts

C) Defends

D) Fulfills

CONTINUE

7

In 2014, Amelia Quon and her team at NASA set out to build a helicopter capable of flying on Mars. Because Mars's atmosphere is only one percent as dense as Earth's, the air of Mars would not provide enough resistance to the rotating blades of a standard helicopter for the aircraft to stay aloft. For five years, Quon's team tested designs in a lab that mimicked Mars's atmospheric conditions. The craft the team ultimately designed can fly on Mars because its blades are longer and rotate faster than those of a helicopter of the same size built for Earth.

According to the text, why would a helicopter built for Earth be unable to fly on Mars?

A) Because Mars and Earth have different atmospheric conditions

B) Because the blades of helicopters built for Earth are too large to work on Mars

C) Because the gravity of Mars is much weaker than the gravity of Earth

D) Because helicopters built for Earth are too small to handle the conditions on Mars

8

In West Africa, jalis have traditionally been keepers of information about family histories and records of important events. They have often served as teachers and advisers, too. New technologies may have changed some aspects of the role today, but jalis continue to be valued for knowing and protecting their peoples' stories.

Which choice best states the main idea of the text?

A) Even though there have been some changes in their role, jalis continue to preserve their communities' histories.

B) Although jalis have many roles, many of them like teaching best.

C) Jalis have been entertaining the people within their communities for centuries.

D) Technology can now do some of the things jalis used to be responsible for.

Unauthorized copying or reuse of any part of this page is illegal.

CONTINUE ▶

326

The following text is adapted from Jack London's 1903 novel *The Call of the Wild*. Buck is a sled dog living with John Thornton in Yukon, Canada.

Thornton alone held [Buck]. The rest of mankind was as nothing. Chance travellers might praise or pet him; but he was cold under it all, and from a too demonstrative man he would get up and walk away. When Thornton's partners, Hans and Pete, arrived on the long-expected raft, Buck refused to notice them till he learned they were close to Thornton; after that he tolerated them in a passive sort of way, accepting favors from them as though he favored them by accepting.

Which choice best states the main idea of the text?

A) Buck has become less social since he began living with Thornton.

B) Buck mistrusts humans and does his best to avoid them.

C) Buck has been especially well liked by most of Thornton's friends.

D) Buck holds Thornton in higher regard than any other person.

The Souls of Black Folk is a 1903 book by W.E.B. Du Bois. In the book, Du Bois suggests that upon hearing Black folk songs, he felt an intuitive and sometimes unexpected sense of cultural recognition: _____

Which quotation from *The Souls of Black Folk* most effectively illustrates the claim?

A) "[Black folk music] still remains as the singular spiritual heritage of the nation and the greatest gift of the Negro people."

B) "Ever since I was a child these songs have stirred me strangely. They came out of the South unknown to me, one by one, and yet at once I knew them as of me and of mine."

C) "Caricature has sought again to spoil the quaint beauty of the music, and has filled the air with many debased melodies which vulgar ears scarce know from the real. But the true Negro folk-song still lives in the hearts of those who have heard them truly sung and in the hearts of the Negro people."

D) "The songs are indeed the siftings of centuries; the music is far more ancient than the words, and in it we can trace here and there signs of development."

CONTINUE

11

Percentage of Ondo State Small-Scale Farmers Who Are Female, by Main Crop Grown

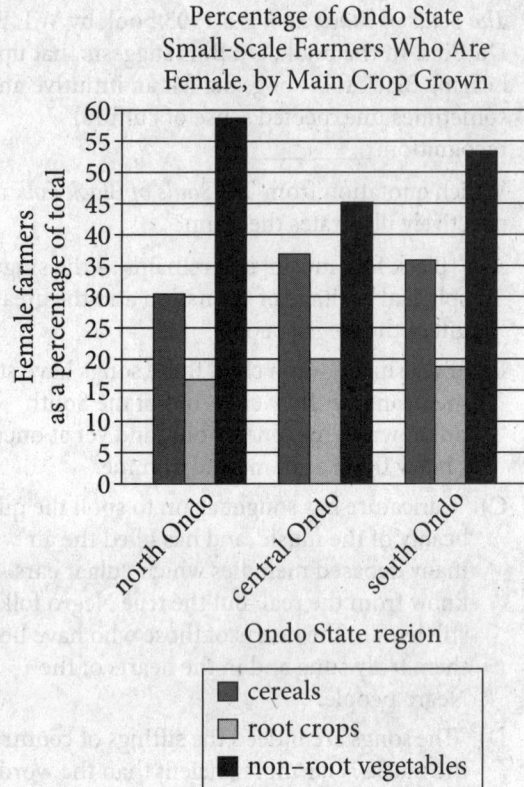

Geographer Adebayo Oluwole Eludoyin and his colleagues surveyed small-scale farmers in three locations in Ondo State, Nigeria—which has mountainous terrain in the north, an urbanized center, and coastal terrain in the south—to learn more about their practices, like the types of crops they mainly cultivated. In some regions, female farmers were found to be especially prominent in the cultivation of specific types of crops and even constituted the majority of farmers who cultivated those crops; for instance, _____.

Which choice most effectively uses data from the graph to complete the example?

A) most of the farmers who mainly cultivated cereals and most of the farmers who mainly cultivated non–root vegetables in south Ondo were women.

B) more women in central Ondo mainly cultivated root crops than mainly cultivated cereals.

C) most of the farmers who mainly cultivated non–root vegetables in north and south Ondo were women.

D) a relatively equal proportion of women across the three regions of Ondo mainly cultivated cereals.

CONTINUE ➡

12

Scholars have noted that F. Scott Fitzgerald's writings were likely influenced in part by his marriage to Zelda Fitzgerald, but many don't recognize Zelda as a writer in her own right. Indeed, Zelda authored several works herself, such as the novel *Save Me the Waltz* and numerous short stories. Thus, those who primarily view Zelda as an inspiration for F. Scott's writings _____

Which choice most logically completes the text?

A) overlook the many other factors that motivated F. Scott to write.

B) risk misrepresenting the full range of Zelda's contributions to literature.

C) may draw inaccurate conclusions about how F. Scott and Zelda viewed each other's works.

D) tend to read the works of F. Scott and Zelda in an overly autobiographical light.

13

Herbivorous sauropod dinosaurs could grow more than 100 feet long and weigh up to 80 tons, and some researchers have attributed the evolution of sauropods to such massive sizes to increased plant production resulting from high levels of atmospheric carbon dioxide during the Mesozoic era. However, there is no evidence of significant spikes in carbon dioxide levels coinciding with relevant periods in sauropod evolution, such as when the first large sauropods appeared, when several sauropod lineages underwent further evolution toward gigantism, or when sauropods reached their maximum known sizes, suggesting that _____

Which choice most logically completes the text?

A) fluctuations in atmospheric carbon dioxide affected different sauropod lineages differently.

B) the evolution of larger body sizes in sauropods did not depend on increased atmospheric carbon dioxide.

C) atmospheric carbon dioxide was higher when the largest known sauropods lived than it was when the first sauropods appeared.

D) sauropods probably would not have evolved to such immense sizes if atmospheric carbon dioxide had been even slightly higher.

14

Known for her massive photorealistic paintings of African American figures floating or swimming in pools, Calida Garcia _____ was the logical choice to design the book cover for Ta-Nehisi Coates's *The Water Dancer*, a novel about an African American man who can travel great distances through water.

Which choice completes the text so that it conforms to the conventions of Standard English?

A) Rawles—

B) Rawles:

C) Rawles,

D) Rawles

15

In 2010, archaeologist Noel Hidalgo Tan was visiting the twelfth-century temple of Angkor Wat in Cambodia when he noticed markings of red paint on the temple _____ the help of digital imaging techniques, he discovered the markings to be part of an elaborate mural containing over 200 paintings.

Which choice completes the text so that it conforms to the conventions of Standard English?

A) walls, with

B) walls with

C) walls so with

D) walls. With

16

Cheng Dang and her colleagues at the University of Washington recently ran simulations to determine the extent to which individual snow _____ affect the amount of light reflecting off a snowy surface.

Which choice completes the text so that it conforms to the conventions of Standard English?

A) grain's physical properties'

B) grains' physical properties

C) grains' physical property's

D) grains physical properties

Unauthorized copying or reuse of any part of this page is illegal.

CONTINUE

329

17

The Mission 66 initiative, which was approved by Congress in 1956, represented a major investment in the infrastructure of overburdened national _____ it prioritized physical improvements to the parks' roads, utilities, employee housing, and visitor facilities while also establishing educational programming for the public.

Which choice completes the text so that it conforms to the conventions of Standard English?

A) parks and

B) parks

C) parks;

D) parks,

18

The Progressive Era in the United States witnessed the rise of numerous Black women's clubs, local organizations that advocated for racial and gender equality. Among the clubs' leaders _____ Josephine St. Pierre Ruffin, founder of the Women's Era Club of Boston.

Which choice completes the text so that it conforms to the conventions of Standard English?

A) was

B) were

C) are

D) have been

19

Eli Eisenberg, a genetics expert at Tel Aviv University in Israel, recently discovered that _____ have a special genetic ability called RNA editing that confers evolutionary advantages.

Which choice completes the text so that it conforms to the conventions of Standard English?

A) cephalopods, ocean dwellers that include the squid, the octopus, and the cuttlefish

B) cephalopods—ocean dwellers—that include the squid, the octopus, and the cuttlefish,

C) cephalopods, ocean dwellers that include: the squid, the octopus, and the cuttlefish,

D) cephalopods—ocean dwellers that include the squid, the octopus, and the cuttlefish—

20

A model created by biologist Luis Valente predicts that the rate of speciation—the rate at which new species form—on an isolated island located approximately 5,000 kilometers from the nearest mainland _____ triple the rate of speciation on an island only 500 kilometers from the mainland.

Which choice completes the text so that it conforms to the conventions of Standard English?

A) being

B) to be

C) to have been

D) will be

CONTINUE

21

Award-winning travel writer Linda Watanabe McFerrin considers the background research she conducts on destinations featured in her travel books to be its own reward. _____ McFerrin admits to finding the research phase of her work just as fascinating and engaging as exploring a location in person.

Which choice completes the text with the most logical transition?

A) By contrast,

B) Likewise,

C) Besides,

D) In fact,

22

While researching a topic, a student has taken the following notes:

- Bharati Mukherjee was an Indian-born author of novels and short stories.
- She published the novel *The Holder of the World* in 1993.
- A central character in the novel is a woman living in twentieth-century United States.
- Another central character is a woman living in seventeenth-century India.

The student wants to introduce the novel *The Holder of the World* to an audience already familiar with Bharati Mukherjee. Which choice most effectively uses relevant information from the notes to accomplish this goal?

A) Bharati Mukherjee's settings include both twentieth-century United States and seventeenth-century India.

B) In addition to her novel *The Holder of the World,* which was published in 1993, Indian-born author Bharati Mukherjee wrote other novels and short stories.

C) Bharati Mukherjee's novel *The Holder of the World* centers around two women, one living in twentieth-century United States and the other in seventeenth-century India.

D) *The Holder of the World* was not the only novel written by Indian-born author Bharati Mukherjee.

23

While researching a topic, a student has taken the following notes:

- Pterosaurs were flying reptiles that existed millions of years ago.
- In a 2021 study, Anusuya Chinsamy-Turan analyzed fragments of pterosaur jawbones located in the Sahara Desert.
- She was initially unsure if the bones belonged to juvenile or adult pterosaurs.
- She used advanced microscope techniques to determine that the bones had few growth lines relative to the bones of fully grown pterosaurs.
- She concluded that the bones belonged to juveniles.

The student wants to present the study and its findings. Which choice most effectively uses relevant information from the notes to accomplish this goal?

A) In 2021, Chinsamy-Turan studied pterosaur jawbones and was initially unsure if the bones belonged to juveniles or adults.

B) Pterosaur jawbones located in the Sahara Desert were the focus of a 2021 study.

C) In a 2021 study, Chinsamy-Turan used advanced microscope techniques to analyze the jawbones of pterosaurs, flying reptiles that existed millions of years ago.

D) In a 2021 study, Chinsamy-Turan determined that pterosaur jawbones located in the Sahara Desert had few growth lines relative to the bones of fully grown pterosaurs and thus belonged to juveniles.

CONTINUE

24

While researching a topic, a student has taken the following notes:

- Samuel Selvon was a Trinidadian author.
- *The Lonely Londoners* is one of his most celebrated novels.
- Selvon published the novel in 1956.
- It is about a group of men who emigrate from the Caribbean to Great Britain after World War II.
- Some of *The Lonely Londoners'* characters also appear in Selvon's later novel *Moses Ascending*.

The student wants to introduce Samuel Selvon and his novel *The Lonely Londoners* to a new audience. Which choice most effectively uses relevant information from the notes to accomplish this goal?

A) In 1956, Trinidadian author Samuel Selvon published one of his most celebrated novels, *The Lonely Londoners*, which is about a group of men who emigrate from the Caribbean to Great Britain after World War II.

B) Samuel Selvon wrote the novel *Moses Ascending* after he wrote *The Lonely Londoners*.

C) *The Lonely Londoners*, a celebrated novel that was published in 1956, depicts post–World War II Caribbean migration from the perspective of a Trinidadian author.

D) Some of the characters who appear in Samuel Selvon's *Moses Ascending* also appear in *The Lonely Londoners*.

25

While researching a topic, a student has taken the following notes:

- Seven species of sea turtle exist today.
- Five sea turtle species can be found in the Atlantic Ocean.
- One of those species is the Kemp's ridley sea turtle.
- Its scientific name is *Lepidochelys kempii*.
- Another of those species is the olive ridley sea turtle.
- Its scientific name is *Lepidochelys olivacea*.

The student wants to emphasize a similarity between the two sea turtle species. Which choice most effectively uses relevant information from the notes to accomplish this goal?

A) Among the seven species of sea turtle is the olive ridley sea turtle, which can be found in the Atlantic Ocean.

B) The Kemp's ridley sea turtle is referred to as *Lepidochelys kempii*, while the olive ridley sea turtle is referred to as *Lepidochelys olivacea*.

C) Both the Kemp's ridley sea turtle and the olive ridley sea turtle can be found in the Atlantic Ocean.

D) The Kemp's ridley sea turtle (*Lepidochelys kempii*) and the olive ridley sea turtle (*Lepidochelys olivacea*) are different species.

CONTINUE ▶

26

While researching a topic, a student has taken the following notes:

- In 2019, Emily Shepard and colleagues in the UK and Germany studied the effect of wind on auks' success in landing at cliffside nesting sites.
- They found as wind conditions intensified, the birds needed more attempts in order to make a successful landing.
- When the wind was still, almost 100% of landing attempts were successful.
- In a strong breeze, approximately 40% of attempts were successful.
- In near-gale conditions, only around 20% of attempts were successful.

The student wants to summarize the study. Which choice most effectively uses relevant information from the notes to accomplish this goal?

A) For a 2019 study, researchers from the UK and Germany collected data on auks' attempts to land at cliffside nesting sites in different wind conditions.

B) Emily Shepard and her colleagues wanted to know the extent to which wind affected auks' success in landing at cliffside nesting sites, so they conducted a study.

C) Knowing that auks often need multiple attempts to land at their cliffside nesting sites, Emily Shepard studied the birds' success rate, which was only around 20% in some conditions.

D) Emily Shepard's 2019 study of auks' success in landing at cliffside nesting sites showed that as wind conditions intensified, the birds' success rate decreased.

27

While researching a topic, a student has taken the following notes:

- Abdulrazak Gurnah was awarded the 2021 Nobel Prize in Literature.
- Gurnah was born in Zanzibar in East Africa and currently lives in the United Kingdom.
- Many readers have singled out Gurnah's 1994 book *Paradise* for praise.
- *Paradise* is a historical novel about events that occurred in colonial East Africa.

The student wants to introduce *Paradise* to an audience unfamiliar with the novel and its author. Which choice most effectively uses relevant information from the notes to accomplish this goal?

A) Abdulrazak Gurnah, who wrote *Paradise* and later was awarded the Nobel Prize in Literature, was born in Zanzibar in East Africa and currently lives in the United Kingdom.

B) Many readers have singled out Abdulrazak Gurnah's 1994 book *Paradise*, a historical novel about colonial East Africa, for praise.

C) A much-praised historical novel about colonial East Africa, *Paradise* (1994) was written by Abdulrazak Gurnah, winner of the 2021 Nobel Prize in Literature.

D) *Paradise* is a historical novel about events that occurred in colonial East Africa, Abdulrazak Gurnah's homeland.

STOP

**If you finish before time is called, you may check your work on this module only.
Do not turn to any other module in the test.**

Reading and Writing

27 QUESTIONS

1

The fashion resale market, in which consumers purchase secondhand clothing from stores and online sellers, generated nearly $30 billion globally in 2019. Expecting to see continued growth, some analysts _____ that revenues will more than double by 2028.

Which choice completes the text with the most logical and precise word or phrase?

A) produced

B) denied

C) worried

D) predicted

2

According to botanists, a viburnum plant experiencing insect damage may develop erineum—a discolored, felty growth—on its leaf blades. A _____ viburnum plant, on the other hand, will have leaves with smooth surfaces and uniformly green coloration.

Which choice completes the text with the most logical and precise word or phrase?

A) struggling

B) beneficial

C) simple

D) healthy

3

When Mexican-American archaeologist Zelia Maria Magdalena Nuttall published her 1886 research paper on sculptures found at the ancient Indigenous city of Teotihuacan in present-day Mexico, other researchers readily _____ her work as groundbreaking; this recognition stemmed from her convincing demonstration that the sculptures were much older than had previously been thought.

Which choice completes the text with the most logical and precise word or phrase?

A) acknowledged

B) ensured

C) denied

D) underestimated

CONTINUE ➤

4

Like other tribal nations, the Muscogee (Creek) Nation is self-governing; its National Council generates laws regulating aspects of community life such as land use and healthcare, while the principal chief and cabinet officials _____ those laws by devising policies and administering services in accordance with them.

Which choice completes the text with the most logical and precise word or phrase?

A) implement

B) presume

C) improvise

D) mimic

5

For a 2020 exhibition, photographer and neurobiologist Okunola Jeyifous _____ a series of new images based on a series of alphabet posters from the 1970s known as the "Black ABCs," which featured Black children from Chicago. Jeyifous photographed the now-adult models and layered the photos over magnified images of the models' cells, resulting in what he called "micro and macro portraiture."

Which choice completes the text with the most logical and precise word or phrase?

A) validated

B) created

C) challenged

D) restored

6

Researcher Haesung Jung led a 2020 study showing that individual acts of kindness can _____ prosocial behavior across a larger group. Jung and her team found that bystanders who witness a helpful act become more likely to offer help to someone else, and in doing so, can inspire still others to act.

Which choice completes the text with the most logical and precise word or phrase?

A) require

B) remember

C) foster

D) discourage

7

Some bird species don't raise their own chicks. Instead, adult females lay their eggs in other nests, next to another bird species' own eggs. Female cuckoos have been seen quickly laying eggs in the nests of other bird species when those birds are out looking for food. After the eggs hatch, the noncuckoo parents will typically raise the cuckoo chicks as if they were their own offspring, even if the cuckoos look very different from the other chicks.

Which choice best describes the function of the underlined sentence in the text as a whole?

A) It introduces a physical feature of female cuckoos that is described later in the text.

B) It describes the appearance of the cuckoo nests mentioned earlier in the text.

C) It offers a detail about how female cuckoos carry out the behavior discussed in the text.

D) It explains how other birds react to the female cuckoo behavior discussed in the text.

Unauthorized copying or reuse of any part of this page is illegal.

CONTINUE

335

8

The following text is adapted from Susan Glaspell's 1912 short story "'Out There.'" An elderly shop owner is looking at a picture that he recently acquired and hopes to sell.

It did seem that the picture failed to fit in with the rest of the shop. A persuasive young fellow who claimed he was closing out his stock let the old man have it for what he called a song. It was only a little out-of-the-way store which subsisted chiefly on the framing of pictures. The old man looked around at his views of the city, his pictures of cats and dogs, his flaming bits of landscape. "Don't belong in here," he fumed.

And yet the old man was secretly proud of his acquisition. There was a hidden dignity in his scowling as he shuffled about pondering the least ridiculous place for the picture.

Which choice best states the main purpose of the text?

A) To reveal the shop owner's conflicted feelings about the new picture

B) To convey the shop owner's resentment of the person he got the new picture from

C) To describe the items that the shop owner most highly prizes

D) To explain differences between the new picture and other pictures in the shop

9

Text 1

Digital art, the use of digital technology to create or display images, isn't really art at all. It doesn't require as much skill as creating physical art. "Painting" with a tablet and stylus is much easier than using paint and a brush: the technology is doing most of the work.

Text 2

The painting programs used to create digital art involve more than just pressing a few buttons. In addition to knowing the fundamentals of art, digital artists need to be familiar with sophisticated software. Many artists will start by drawing an image on paper before transforming the piece to a digital format, where they can apply a variety of colors and techniques that would otherwise require many different traditional tools.

Based on the texts, how would the author of Text 2 most likely respond to the claims of the author of Text 1?

A) By arguing that a piece of art created digitally can still be displayed traditionally

B) By explaining that it's actually much harder to use a tablet and stylus to create art than to use paint and a brush

C) By insisting that digital art requires artistic abilities and skill even if it employs less traditional tools

D) By admitting that most digital artists don't think fundamental drawing skills are important

Unauthorized copying or reuse of any part of this page is illegal.

CONTINUE ▶

336

10

US States with the Greatest Number of
Organic Farms in 2016

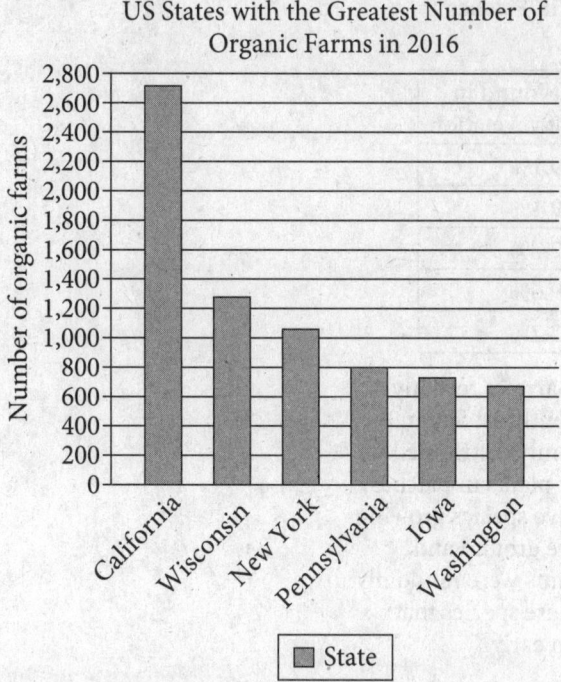

State

Organic farming is a method of growing food that
tries to reduce environmental harm by using natural
forms of pest control and avoiding fertilizers made
with synthetic materials. Organic farms are still a
small fraction of the total farms in the United States,
but they have been becoming more popular.
According to the US Department of Agriculture, in
2016 California had between 2,600 and 2,800
organic farms and _____

Which choice most effectively uses data from the
graph to complete the text?

A) Washington had between 600 and 800 organic
farms.

B) New York had fewer than 800 organic farms.

C) Wisconsin and Iowa each had between 1,200 and
1,400 organic farms.

D) Pennsylvania had more than 1,200 organic farms.

11

"John of God, the Water-Carrier" is a 1913 short
story by María Cristina Mena. In the story, the
narrator presents John as being a hard worker who
is fully dedicated to his job as water carrier, or
aguador: _____

Which quotation from "John of God, the Water-
Carrier" most effectively illustrates the claim?

A) "Very happy, he would jog home, the heavy silver
pieces in his leather pockets making a discreet
and dulcet '*trink-trak*' between his jugs and
his body."

B) "He learned that the city *aguador* may not blow
his whistle to halt the traffic while he gravely
crosses the street, but must wait for the passing
of many vehicles, some with horses and some
outlandishly without."

C) "From early morn to the fall of the afternoon he
would go from fountain to fountain and from
portal to portal, his lean body so accustomed to
bending that he never thought of straightening
it, his head bowed as if in prayer."

D) "When his first jugs had worn out—the sweet-
scented, porous red clay becomes perforated in
time—he had buried them to their necks in the
corner where he slept, and they were now
his treasury."

12

"Loon Point" is a 1912 poem by Amy Lowell.
In the poem, which presents a nighttime scene
on a body of water, Lowell describes an element of
nature as an active participant in the experience,
writing, _____

Which quotation from "Loon Point" most effectively
illustrates the claim?

A) "Through the water the moon writes her legends /
In light, on the smooth, wet sand."

B) "Softly the water ripples / Against the canoe's
curving side."

C) "Or like the snow-white petals / Which drop
from an overblown rose."

D) "But the moon in her wayward beauty / Is ever
and always the same."

CONTINUE ▶

13

Juvenile Plants Found Growing on Bare Ground and in Patches
of Vegetation for Five Species

Species	Bare ground	Patches of vegetation	Total	Percent found in patches of vegetation
T. moroderi	9	13	22	59.1%
T. libanitis	83	120	203	59.1%
H. syriacim	95	106	201	52.7%
H. squamatum	218	321	539	59.6%
H. stoechas	11	12	23	52.2%

Alicia Montesinos-Navarro, Isabelle Storer, and Rocío Perez-Barrales recently examined several plots within a diverse plant community in southeast Spain. The researchers calculated that if individual plants were randomly distributed on this particular landscape, only about 15% would be with other plants in patches of vegetation. They counted the number of juvenile plants of five species growing in patches of vegetation and the number growing alone on bare ground and compared those numbers to what would be expected if the plants were randomly distributed. Based on these results, they claim that plants of these species that grow in close proximity to other plants gain an advantage at an early developmental stage.

Which choice best describes data from the table that support the researchers' claim?

A) For all five species, less than 75% of juvenile plants were growing in patches of vegetation.

B) The species with the greatest number of juvenile plants growing in patches of vegetation was *H. stoechas*.

C) For *T. libanitis* and *T. moroderi*, the percentage of juvenile plants growing in patches of vegetation was less than what would be expected if plants were randomly distributed.

D) For each species, the percentage of juvenile plants growing in patches of vegetation was substantially higher than what would be expected if plants were randomly distributed.

CONTINUE

14

"The Poet Walt Whitman" is an 1887 essay by José Martí, a Cuban author and political activist, originally written in Spanish. In the essay, Martí explores the value of literature, arguing that a society's spiritual well-being depends on the character of its literary culture: _____

Which quotation from a translation of "The Poet Walt Whitman" most effectively illustrates the claim?

A) "Poetry, which brings together or separates, which fortifies or brings anguish, which shores up or demolishes souls, which gives or robs men of faith and vigor, is more necessary to a people than industry itself, for industry provides them with a means of subsistence, while literature gives them the desire and strength for life."

B) "Every society brings to literature its own form of expression, and the history of the nations can be told with greater truth by the stages of literature than by chronicles and decades."

C) "Where will a race of men go when they have lost the habit of thinking with faith about the scope and meaning of their actions? The best among them, those who consecrate Nature with their sacred desire for the future, will lose, in a sordid and painful annihilation, all stimulus to alleviate the ugliness of humanity."

D) "Listen to the song of this hardworking and satisfied nation; listen to Walt Whitman. The exercise of himself exalts him to majesty, tolerance exalts him to justice, and order to joy."

15

The ancient Sumerian civilization formed around 4000 BCE between two large rivers in an area that is now Iraq and Syria. The extremely hot and sunny weather in that area helped crops grow very quickly, but it also made it hard to keep the crops from drying up and dying. So, the Sumerians used water from the rivers in their farming. That method worked so well that they often could harvest even more crops than they needed in a season. As a result, the Sumerians _____

Which choice most logically completes the text?

A) harvested crops only on the hottest days of each season.

B) found ways to shield their crops from the sun.

C) did not begin farming until long after 4000 BCE.

D) were able to store extra crops for later use.

16

In a study of the mechanisms underlying associative memory—or the ability to learn and remember connections between inherently unrelated things—neuroscientists Kei Igarashi, Jasmine Chavez, and others presented mice with memory tests. The team discovered that fan cells, a type of cell found in the medial temporal lobe of the brain, are necessary for the acquisition of new associative memories. They also found that fan cell activity requires dopamine, a chemical the brain produces in response to pleasure and rewards. Consequently, receiving a reward should likely help to _____

Which choice most logically completes the text?

A) decrease an individual's capacity to utilize dopamine.

B) increase an individual's capacity to recognize differences between unrelated things.

C) increase an individual's capacity to form associative memories.

D) decrease an individual's capacity to create fan cells.

CONTINUE ➤

17

In 1637, the price of tulips skyrocketed in Amsterdam, with single bulbs of rare varieties selling for up to the equivalent of $200,000 in today's US dollars. Some historians _____ that this "tulip mania" was the first historical instance of an asset bubble, which occurs when investors drive prices to highs not supported by actual demand.

Which choice completes the text so that it conforms to the conventions of Standard English?

A) claiming

B) claim

C) having claimed

D) to claim

18

In her two major series "Memory Test" and "Autobiography," painter Howardena Pindell explored themes _____ healing, self-discovery, and memory by cutting and sewing back together pieces of canvas and inserting personal artifacts, such as postcards, into some of the paintings.

Which choice completes the text so that it conforms to the conventions of Standard English?

A) of

B) of,

C) of—

D) of:

19

Even though bats prefer very sweet nectar, the plants that attract them have evolved to produce nectar that is only moderately sweet. A recent study _____ why: making sugar is energy-intensive, and it is more advantageous for plants to make a large amount of low-sugar nectar than a small amount of high-sugar nectar.

Which choice completes the text so that it conforms to the conventions of Standard English?

A) explains

B) explaining

C) having explained

D) to explain

20

Bonnie Buratti of NASA's Jet Propulsion Laboratory _____ data about Saturn's rings collected by the *Cassini* spacecraft when she made an interesting discovery: the tiny moons embedded between and within Saturn's rings are shaped by the buildup of ring material on the moons' surfaces.

Which choice completes the text so that it conforms to the conventions of Standard English?

A) studies

B) has been studying

C) will study

D) was studying

CONTINUE ➤

21

In his groundbreaking book *Bengali Harlem and the Lost Histories of South Asian America*, Vivek Bald uses newspaper articles, census records, ships' logs, and memoirs to tell the _____ who made New York City their home in the early twentieth century.

Which choice completes the text so that it conforms to the conventions of Standard English?

A) story's of the South Asian immigrants

B) story's of the South Asian immigrants'

C) stories of the South Asian immigrants

D) stories' of the South Asian immigrant's

22

The life spans of rockfish vary greatly by species. For instance, the colorful calico rockfish (*Sebastes dallii*) can survive for a little over a _____ the rougheye rockfish (*Sebastes aleutianus*) boasts a maximum life span of about two centuries.

Which choice completes the text so that it conforms to the conventions of Standard English?

A) decade: while

B) decade. While

C) decade; while

D) decade, while

23

Scientists believe that, unlike most other species of barnacle, turtle barnacles (*Chelonibia testudinari*) can dissolve the cement-like secretions they use to attach _____ to a sea turtle shell, enabling the barnacles to move short distances across the shell's surface.

Which choice completes the text so that it conforms to the conventions of Standard English?

A) it

B) themselves

C) them

D) itself

24

Small, flat structures called spatulae are found at the tips of the hairs on a spider's leg. These spatulae temporarily bond with the atoms of whatever they touch. _____ spiders are able to cling to and climb almost any surface.

Which choice completes the text with the most logical transition?

A) For instance,

B) However,

C) Similarly,

D) As a result,

CONTINUE ➡

25

Geoscientists have long considered Hawaii's Mauna Loa volcano to be Earth's largest shield volcano by volume, measuring approximately 74,000 cubic kilometers. _____ according to a 2020 study by local geoscientist Michael Garcia, Hawaii's Pūhāhonu shield volcano is significantly larger, boasting a volume of about 148,000 cubic kilometers.

Which choice completes the text with the most logical transition?

A) Secondly,

B) Consequently,

C) Moreover,

D) However,

26

In 2019, researcher Patricia Jurado Gonzalez and food historian Nawal Nasrallah prepared a stew from a 4,000-year-old recipe found on a Mesopotamian clay tablet. When they tasted the dish, known as *pašrūtum* ("unwinding"), they found that it had a mild taste and inspired a sense of calm. _____ the researchers, knowing that dishes were sometimes named after their intended effects, theorized that the dish's name, "unwinding," referred to its function: to help ancient diners relax.

Which choice completes the text with the most logical transition?

A) Therefore,

B) Alternately,

C) Nevertheless,

D) Likewise,

27

While researching a topic, a student has taken the following notes:

- Jon Ching is a Los Angeles-based painter.
- He uses the term "flauna" to describe the plant-animal hybrids that he depicts in his surreal paintings.
- "Flauna" is a combination of the words "flora" and "fauna."
- His painting *Nectar* depicts a parrot with leaves for feathers.
- His painting *Primaveral* depicts a snow leopard whose fur sprouts flowers.

The student wants to provide an explanation and example of "flauna." Which choice most effectively uses relevant information from the notes to accomplish this goal?

A) The term "flauna," used by Los Angeles-based painter Jon Ching, is a combination of the words "flora" and "fauna."

B) Jon Ching uses the term "flauna," a combination of the words "flora" and "fauna," to describe the subjects of his surreal paintings: plant-animal hybrids such as a parrot with leaves for feathers.

C) Jon Ching, who created *Nectar*, refers to the subjects of his paintings as "flauna."

D) The subjects of *Nectar* and *Primaveral* are types of "flauna," a term that the paintings' creator, Jon Ching, uses when describing his surreal artworks.

STOP

**If you finish before time is called, you may check your work on this module only.
Do not turn to any other module in the test.**

Unauthorized copying or reuse of any part of this page is illegal.

342

Test begins on the next page.

Reading and Writing

27 QUESTIONS

1

In studying the use of external stimuli to reduce the itching sensation caused by an allergic histamine response, Louise Ward and colleagues found that while harmless applications of vibration or warming can provide a temporary distraction, such _____ stimuli actually offer less relief than a stimulus that seems less benign, like a mild electric shock.

Which choice completes the text with the most logical and precise word or phrase?

A) deceptive

B) innocuous

C) novel

D) impractical

2

New and interesting research conducted by Suleiman A. Al-Sweedan and Moath Alhaj is inspired by their observation that though there have been many studies of the effect of high altitude on blood chemistry, there is a _____ studies of the effect on blood chemistry of living in locations below sea level, such as the California towns of Salton City and Seeley.

Which choice completes the text with the most logical and precise word or phrase?

A) quarrel about

B) paucity of

C) profusion of

D) verisimilitude in

CONTINUE →

3

Whether the reign of a French monarch such as Hugh Capet or Henry I was historically consequential or relatively uneventful, its trajectory was shaped by questions of legitimacy and therefore cannot be understood without a corollary understanding of the factors that allowed the monarch to _____ his right to hold the throne.

Which choice completes the text with the most logical and precise word or phrase?

A) disengage

B) annotate

C) buttress

D) reciprocate

4

Researcher Haesung Jung led a 2020 study showing that individual acts of kindness can _____ prosocial behavior across a larger group. Jung and her team found that bystanders who witness a helpful act become more likely to offer help to someone else, and in doing so, can inspire still others to act.

Which choice completes the text with the most logical and precise word or phrase?

A) require

B) remember

C) foster

D) discourage

5

The following text is adapted from *Indian Boyhood*, a 1902 memoir by Ohiyesa (Charles A. Eastman), a Santee Dakota writer. In the text, Ohiyesa recalls how the women in his tribe harvested maple syrup during his childhood.

Now the women began to test the trees—moving leisurely among them, axe in hand, and striking a single quick blow, to see if the sap would appear. The trees, like people, have their individual characters; some were ready to yield up their life-blood, while others were more reluctant. Now one of the birchen basins was set under each tree, and a hardwood chip driven deep into the cut which the axe had made. From the corners of this chip—at first drop by drop, then more freely—the sap trickled into the little dishes.

Which choice best describes the function of the underlined sentence in the text as a whole?

A) It portrays the range of personality traits displayed by the women as they work.

B) It foregrounds the beneficial relationship between humans and maple trees.

C) It demonstrates how human behavior can be influenced by the natural environment.

D) It elaborates on an aspect of the maple trees that the women evaluate.

Unauthorized copying or reuse of any part of this page is illegal.

CONTINUE ➤

345

6

The following text is from Charlotte Brontë's 1847 novel *Jane Eyre*. Jane, the narrator, works as a governess at Thornfield Hall.

> I went on with my day's business tranquilly; but ever and anon vague suggestions kept wandering across my brain of reasons why I should quit Thornfield; and I kept involuntarily framing advertisements and pondering conjectures about new situations: these thoughts I did not think to check; they might germinate and bear fruit if they could.

Which choice best states the main purpose of the text?

A) To convey a contrast between Jane's outward calmness and internal restlessness

B) To emphasize Jane's loyalty to the people she works for at Thornfield Hall

C) To demonstrate that Jane finds her situation both challenging and deeply fulfilling

D) To describe Jane's determination to secure employment outside of Thornfield Hall

7

Musician Joni Mitchell, who is also a painter, uses images she creates for her album covers to emphasize ideas expressed in her music. For the cover of her album *Turbulent Indigo* (1994), Mitchell painted a striking self-portrait that closely resembles Vincent van Gogh's *Self-Portrait with Bandaged Ear* (1889). The image calls attention to the album's title song, in which Mitchell sings about the legacy of the postimpressionist painter. In that song, Mitchell also hints that she feels a strong artistic connection to Van Gogh—an idea that is reinforced by her imagery on the cover.

Which choice best describes the overall structure of the text?

A) It presents a claim about Mitchell, then gives an example supporting that claim.

B) It discusses Van Gogh's influence on Mitchell, then considers Mitchell's influence on other artists.

C) It describes a similarity between two artists, then notes a difference between them.

D) It describes the songs on *Turbulent Indigo*, then explains how they relate to the album's cover.

CONTINUE ➤

8

A study by a team including finance professor Madhu Veeraraghavan suggests that exposure to sunshine during the workday can lead to overly optimistic behavior. Using data spanning from 1994 to 2010 for a set of US companies, the team compared over 29,000 annual earnings forecasts to the actual earnings later reported by those companies. The team found that the greater the exposure to sunshine at work in the two weeks before a manager submitted an earnings forecast, the more the manager's forecast exceeded what the company actually earned that year.

Which choice best states the function of the underlined sentence in the overall structure of the text?

A) To summarize the results of the team's analysis

B) To present a specific example that illustrates the study's findings

C) To explain part of the methodology used in the team's study

D) To call out a challenge the team faced in conducting its analysis

9

Text 1

Most animals can regenerate some parts of their bodies, such as skin. But when a three-banded panther worm is cut into three pieces, each piece grows into a new worm. Researchers are investigating this feat partly to learn more about humans' comparatively limited abilities to regenerate, and they're making exciting progress. An especially promising discovery is that both humans and panther worms have a gene for early growth response (EGR) linked to regeneration.

Text 2

When Mansi Srivastava and her team reported that panther worms, like humans, possess a gene for EGR, it caused excitement. However, as the team pointed out, the gene likely functions very differently in humans than it does in panther worms. Srivastava has likened EGR to a switch that activates other genes involved in regeneration in panther worms, but how this switch operates in humans remains unclear.

Based on the texts, what would the author of Text 2 most likely say about Text 1's characterization of the discovery involving EGR?

A) It is reasonable given that Srivastava and her team have identified how EGR functions in both humans and panther worms.

B) It is overly optimistic given additional observations from Srivastava and her team.

C) It is unexpected given that Srivastava and her team's findings were generally met with enthusiasm.

D) It is unfairly dismissive given the progress that Srivastava and her team have reported.

Unauthorized copying or reuse of any part of this page is illegal.

CONTINUE ➜

347

10

Credited Film Output of James Young Deer,
Dark Cloud, Edwin Carewe, and Lillian St. Cyr

Individual	Years active	Number of films known and commonly credited
James Young Deer	1909–1924	33 (actor), 35 (director), 10 (writer)
Dark Cloud	1910–1920	35 (actor), 1 (writer)
Edwin Carewe	1912–1934	47 (actor), 58 (director), 20 (producer), 4 (writer)
Lillian St. Cyr (Red Wing)	1908–1921	66 (actor)

Some researchers studying Indigenous actors and filmmakers in the United States have turned their attention to the early days of cinema, particularly the 1910s and 1920s, when people like James Young Deer, Dark Cloud, Edwin Carewe, and Lillian St. Cyr (known professionally as Red Wing) were involved in one way or another with numerous films. In fact, so many films and associated records for this era have been lost that counts of those four figures' output should be taken as bare minimums rather than totals; it's entirely possible, for example, that _____

Which choice most effectively uses data from the table to complete the example?

A) Dark Cloud acted in significantly fewer films than did Lillian St. Cyr, who is credited with 66 performances.

B) Edwin Carewe's 47 credited acting roles include only films made after 1934.

C) Lillian St. Cyr acted in far more than 66 films and Edwin Carewe directed more than 58.

D) James Young Deer actually directed 33 films and acted in only 10.

Unauthorized copying or reuse of any part of this page is illegal.

CONTINUE ▶

348

11

Mosasaurs were large marine reptiles that lived in the Late Cretaceous period, approximately 100 million to 66 million years ago. Celina Suarez, Alberto Pérez-Huerta, and T. Lynn Harrell Jr. examined oxygen-18 isotopes in mosasaur tooth enamel in order to calculate likely mosasaur body temperatures and determined that mosasaurs were endothermic—that is, they used internal metabolic processes to maintain a stable body temperature in a variety of ambient temperatures. Suarez, Pérez-Huerta, and Harrell claim that endothermy would have enabled mosasaurs to include relatively cold polar waters in their range.

Which finding, if true, would most directly support Suarez, Pérez-Huerta, and Harrell's claim?

A) Mosasaurs' likely body temperatures are easier to determine from tooth enamel oxygen-18 isotope data than the body temperatures of nonendothermic Late Cretaceous marine reptiles are.

B) Fossils of both mosasaurs and nonendothermic marine reptiles have been found in roughly equal numbers in regions known to be near the poles during the Late Cretaceous, though in lower concentrations than elsewhere.

C) Several mosasaur fossils have been found in regions known to be near the poles during the Late Cretaceous, while relatively few fossils of nonendothermic marine reptiles have been found in those locations.

D) During the Late Cretaceous, seawater temperatures were likely higher throughout mosasaurs' range, including near the poles, than seawater temperatures at those same latitudes are today.

12

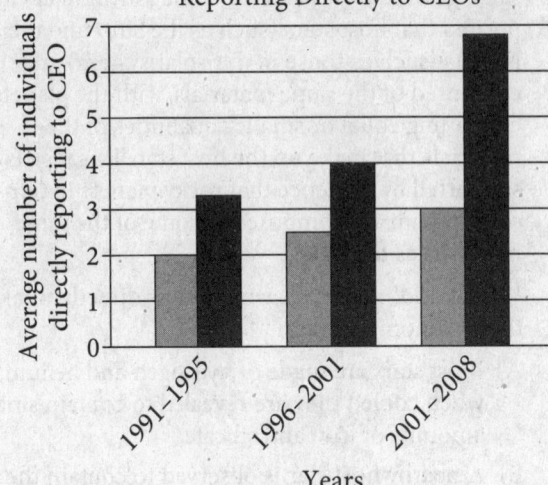

Average Number of Individuals Reporting Directly to CEOs

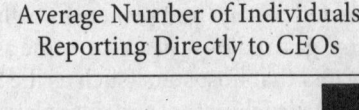

Considering a large sample of companies, economics experts Maria Guadalupe, Julie Wulf, and Raghuram Rajan assessed the number of managers and leaders from different departments who reported directly to a chief executive officer (CEO). According to the researchers, the findings suggest that across the years analyzed, there was a growing interest among CEOs in connecting with more departments in their companies.

Which choice best describes data from the graph that support the researchers' conclusion?

A) The average numbers of managers and department leaders reporting directly to their CEO didn't fluctuate from the 1991–1995 period to the 2001–2008 period.

B) The average number of managers reporting directly to their CEO was highest in the 1996–2001 period.

C) The average number of department leaders reporting directly to their CEO was greater than the average number of managers reporting directly to their CEO in each of the three periods studied.

D) The average number of department leaders reporting directly to their CEO rose over the three periods studied.

CONTINUE ▶

13

Given that stars and planets initially form from the same gas and dust in space, some astronomers have posited that host stars (such as the Sun) and their planets (such as those in our solar system) are composed of the same materials, with the planets containing equal or smaller quantities of the materials that make up the host star. This idea is also supported by evidence that rocky planets in our solar system are composed of some of the same materials as the Sun.

Which finding, if true, would most directly weaken the astronomers' claim?

A) Most stars are made of hydrogen and helium, but when cooled they are revealed to contain small amounts of iron and silicate.

B) A nearby host star is observed to contain the same proportion of hydrogen and helium as that of the Sun.

C) Evidence emerges that the amount of iron in some rocky planets is considerably higher than the amount in their host star.

D) The method for determining the composition of rocky planets is discovered to be less effective when used to analyze other kinds of planets.

14

While attending school in New York City in the 1980s, Okwui Enwezor encountered few works by African artists in exhibitions, despite New York's reputation as one of the best places to view contemporary art from around the world. According to an arts journalist, later in his career as a renowned curator and art historian, Enwezor sought to remedy this deficiency, not by focusing solely on modern African artists, but by showing how their work fits into the larger context of global modern art and art history.

Which finding, if true, would most directly support the journalist's claim?

A) As curator of the Haus der Kunst in Munich, Germany, Enwezor organized a retrospective of Ghanaian sculptor El Anatsui's work entitled *El Anatsui: Triumphant Scale*, one of the largest art exhibitions devoted to a Black artist in Europe's history.

B) In the exhibition *Postwar: Art Between the Pacific and the Atlantic, 1945–1965*, Enwezor and cocurator Katy Siegel brought works by African artists such as Malangatana Ngwenya together with pieces by major figures from other countries, like US artist Andy Warhol and Mexico's David Siqueiros.

C) Enwezor's work as curator of the 2001 exhibition *The Short Century: Independence and Liberation Movements in Africa, 1945–1994* showed how African movements for independence from European colonial powers following the Second World War profoundly influenced work by African artists of the period, such as Kamala Ibrahim Ishaq and Thomas Mukarobgwa.

D) Enwezor organized the exhibition *In/sight: African Photographers, 1940 to the Present* not to emphasize a particular aesthetic trend but to demonstrate the broad range of ways in which African artists have approached the medium of photography.

CONTINUE ➡

15

One challenge when researching whether holding elected office changes a person's behavior is the problem of ensuring that the experiment has an appropriate control group. To reveal the effect of holding office, researchers must compare people who hold elected office with people who do not hold office but who are otherwise similar to the office-holders. Since researchers are unable to control which politicians win elections, they therefore _____

Which choice most logically completes the text?

A) struggle to find valid data about the behavior of politicians who do not currently hold office.

B) can only conduct valid studies with people who have previously held office rather than people who presently hold office.

C) should select a control group of people who differ from office-holders in several significant ways.

D) will find it difficult to identify a group of people who can function as an appropriate control group for their studies.

16

Compiled in the late 1500s largely through the efforts of Indigenous scribes, *Cantares Mexicanos* is the most important collection of poetry in Classical Nahuatl, the principal language of the Aztec Empire. The poems portray Aztec society before the occupation of the empire by the army of Spain, and marginal notes in *Cantares Mexicanos* indicate that much of the collection's content predates the initial invasion. Nonetheless, some of the poems contain inarguable references to beliefs and customs common in Spain during this era. Thus, some scholars have concluded that _____

Which choice most logically completes the text?

A) while its content largely predates the invasion, *Cantares Mexicanos* also contains additions made after the invasion.

B) although those who compiled *Cantares Mexicanos* were fluent in Nahuatl, they had limited knowledge of the Spanish language.

C) before the invasion by Spain, the poets of the Aztec Empire borrowed from the literary traditions of other societies.

D) the references to beliefs and customs in Spain should be attributed to a coincidental resemblance between the societies of Spain and the Aztec Empire.

17

To humans, it does not appear that the golden orb-weaver spider uses camouflage to capture its _____ the brightly colored arachnid seems to wait conspicuously in the center of its large circular web for insects to approach. Researcher Po Peng of the University of Melbourne has explained that the spider's distinctive coloration may in fact be part of its appeal.

Which choice completes the text so that it conforms to the conventions of Standard English?

A) prey, rather,

B) prey rather,

C) prey, rather;

D) prey; rather,

CONTINUE

18

Bonnie Buratti of NASA's Jet Propulsion Laboratory _____ data about Saturn's rings collected by the *Cassini* spacecraft when she made an interesting discovery: the tiny moons embedded between and within Saturn's rings are shaped by the buildup of ring material on the moons' surfaces.

Which choice completes the text so that it conforms to the conventions of Standard English?

A) studies

B) has been studying

C) will study

D) was studying

19

On July 23, 1854, a clipper ship called the *Flying Cloud* entered San Francisco _____ left New York Harbor under the guidance of Captain Josiah Perkins Creesy and his wife, navigator Eleanor Creesy, a mere 89 days and 8 hours earlier, the celebrated ship set a record that would stand for 135 years.

Which choice completes the text so that it conforms to the conventions of Standard English?

A) Bay and having

B) Bay. Having

C) Bay, having

D) Bay having

20

Bengali author Toru Dutt's *A Sheaf Gleaned in French Fields* (1876), a volume of English translations of French poems, _____ scholars' understanding of the transnational and multilingual contexts in which Dutt lived and worked.

Which choice completes the text so that it conforms to the conventions of Standard English?

A) has enhanced

B) are enhancing

C) have enhanced

D) enhance

21

Hegra is an archaeological site in present-day Saudi Arabia and was the second largest city of the Nabataean Kingdom (fourth century BCE to first century CE). Archaeologist Laila Nehmé recently traveled to Hegra to study its ancient _____ into the rocky outcrops of a vast desert, these burial chambers seem to blend seamlessly with nature.

Which choice completes the text so that it conforms to the conventions of Standard English?

A) tombs. Built

B) tombs, built

C) tombs and built

D) tombs built

CONTINUE ➡

22

In 1937, Chinese American screen actor Anna May Wong, who had portrayed numerous villains and secondary characters but never a heroine, finally got a starring role in Paramount Pictures' *Daughter of Shanghai*, a film that _____ "expanded the range of possibilities for Asian images on screen."

Which choice completes the text so that it conforms to the conventions of Standard English?

A) critic, Stina Chyn, claims

B) critic, Stina Chyn, claims,

C) critic Stina Chyn claims

D) critic Stina Chyn, claims,

23

The Arctic-Alpine Botanic Garden in Norway and the Jardim Botânico of Rio de Janeiro in Brazil are two of many botanical gardens around the world dedicated to growing diverse plant _____ fostering scientific research; and educating the public about plant conservation.

Which choice completes the text so that it conforms to the conventions of Standard English?

A) species, both native and nonnative,

B) species, both native and nonnative;

C) species; both native and nonnative,

D) species both native and nonnative,

24

The Babylonian king Hammurabi achieved much during his forty-year reign. He conquered all of Mesopotamia and built Babylon into one of the most powerful cities of the ancient world. Today, _____ he is mainly remembered for a code of laws inscribed on a seven-foot-tall block of stone: the Code of Hammurabi.

Which choice completes the text with the most logical transition?

A) therefore,

B) likewise,

C) however,

D) for instance,

25

In her poetry collection *Thomas and Beulah*, Rita Dove interweaves the titular characters' personal stories with broader historical narratives. She places Thomas's journey from the American South to the Midwest in the early 1900s within the larger context of the Great Migration. _____ Dove sets events from Beulah's personal life against the backdrop of the US Civil Rights Movement.

Which choice completes the text with the most logical transition?

A) Specifically,

B) Thus,

C) Regardless,

D) Similarly,

CONTINUE ➡

26

When designing costumes for film, American artist Suttirat Larlarb typically custom fits the garments to each actor. _____ for the film *Sunshine*, in which astronauts must reignite a dying Sun, she designed a golden spacesuit and had a factory reproduce it in a few standard sizes; lacking a tailor-made quality, the final creations reflected the ungainliness of actual spacesuits.

Which choice completes the text with the most logical transition?

A) Nevertheless,

B) Thus,

C) Likewise,

D) Moreover,

27

While researching a topic, a student has taken the following notes:

- Astronomers estimate that the number of comets orbiting the Sun is in the billions.

- 81P/Wild is one of many comets whose orbit has changed over time.

- 81P/Wild's orbit once lay between the orbits of Uranus and Jupiter.

- The comet's orbit is now positioned between the orbits of Jupiter and Mars.

The student wants to make and support a generalization about the orbits of comets. Which choice most effectively uses relevant information from the notes to accomplish these goals?

A) Astronomers estimate that the number of comets orbiting the Sun is in the billions; the comets' orbits may change over time.

B) Like Uranus, Jupiter, and Mars, billions of comets orbit the Sun.

C) One example of a comet is 81P/Wild, whose orbit around the Sun once lay between Uranus's and Jupiter's orbits but is now positioned between those of Jupiter and Mars.

D) A comet's orbit around the Sun may change over time: the orbit of comet 81P/Wild once lay between the orbits of Uranus and Jupiter but is now positioned between those of Jupiter and Mars.

STOP

**If you finish before time is called, you may check your work on this module only.
Do not turn to any other module in the test.**

Test begins on the next page.

Math

22 QUESTIONS

DIRECTIONS

The questions in this section address a number of important math skills.
Use of a calculator is permitted for all questions.

NOTES

Unless otherwise indicated:

- All variables and expressions represent real numbers.
- Figures provided are drawn to scale.
- All figures lie in a plane.
- The domain of a given function f is the set of all real numbers x for which $f(x)$ is a real number.

REFERENCE

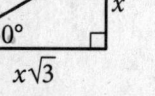 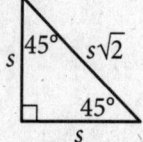

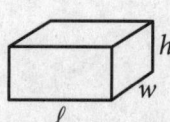  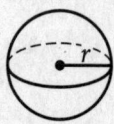  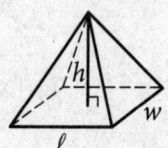

The number of degrees of arc in a circle is 360.

The number of radians of arc in a circle is 2π.

The sum of the measures in degrees of the angles of a triangle is 180.

CONTINUE

For multiple-choice questions, solve each problem, choose the correct answer from the choices provided, and then circle your answer in this book. Circle only one answer for each question. If you change your mind, completely erase the circle. You will not get credit for questions with more than one answer circled, or for questions with no answers circled.

For student-produced response questions, solve each problem and write your answer next to or under the question in the test book as described below.

- Once you've written your answer, circle it clearly. You will not receive credit for anything written outside the circle, or for any questions with more than one circled answer.

- If you find **more than one correct answer**, write and circle only one answer.

- Your answer can be up to 5 characters for a **positive** answer and up to 6 characters (including the negative sign) for a **negative** answer, but no more.

- If your answer is a **fraction** that is too long (over 5 characters for positive, 6 characters for negative), write the decimal equivalent.

- If your answer is a **decimal** that is too long (over 5 characters for positive, 6 characters for negative), truncate it or round at the fourth digit.

- If your answer is a **mixed number** (such as $3\frac{1}{2}$), write it as an improper fraction (7/2) or its decimal equivalent (3.5).

- Don't include **symbols** such as a percent sign, comma, or dollar sign in your circled answer.

Unauthorized copying or reuse of any part of this page is illegal.

CONTINUE →

357

1

If $x = 7$, what is the value of $x + 20$?

A) 13

B) 20

C) 27

D) 34

2

Data set X: 5, 9, 9, 13

Data set Y: 5, 9, 9, 13, 27

The lists give the values in data sets X and Y. Which statement correctly compares the mean of data set X and the mean of data set Y?

A) The mean of data set X is greater than the mean of data set Y.

B) The mean of data set X is less than the mean of data set Y.

C) The means of data set X and data set Y are equal.

D) There is not enough information to compare the means.

3

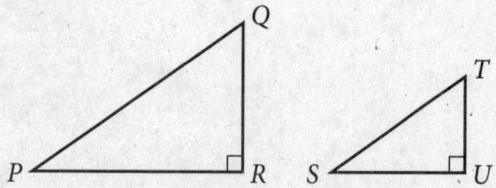

Note: Figures not drawn to scale.

Right triangles PQR and STU are similar, where P corresponds to S. If the measure of angle Q is 18°, what is the measure of angle S?

A) 18°

B) 72°

C) 82°

D) 162°

4

A rocket contained 467,000 kilograms (kg) of propellant before launch. Exactly 21 seconds after launch, 362,105 kg of this propellant remained. On average, approximately how much propellant, in kg, did the rocket burn each second after launch?

A) 4,995

B) 17,243

C) 39,481

D) 104,895

5

$$4x = 20$$

$$-3x + y = -7$$

The solution to the given system of equations is (x, y). What is the value of $x + y$?

A) −27

B) −13

C) 13

D) 27

6

A certain apprentice has enrolled in 85 hours of training courses. The equation $10x + 15y = 85$ represents this situation, where x is the number of on-site training courses and y is the number of online training courses this apprentice has enrolled in. How many more hours does each online training course take than each on-site training course?

7

Square X has a side length of 12 centimeters. The perimeter of square Y is 2 times the perimeter of square X. What is the length, in centimeters, of one side of square Y?

A) 6

B) 10

C) 14

D) 24

CONTINUE

8

$$g(m) = -0.05m + 12.1$$

The given function g models the number of gallons of gasoline that remains from a full gas tank in a car after driving m miles. According to the model, about how many gallons of gasoline are used to drive each mile?

A) 0.05

B) 12.1

C) 20

D) 242.0

9

If $|4x - 4| = 112$, what is the positive value of $x - 1$?

10

$$\frac{1}{7b} = \frac{11x}{y}$$

The given equation relates the positive numbers b, x, and y. Which equation correctly expresses x in terms of b and y?

A) $x = \dfrac{7by}{11}$

B) $x = y - 77b$

C) $x = \dfrac{y}{77b}$

D) $x = 77by$

11

x	10	15	20	25
$f(x)$	82	137	192	247

The table shows four values of x and their corresponding values of $f(x)$. There is a linear relationship between x and $f(x)$ that is defined by the equation $f(x) = mx - 28$, where m is a constant. What is the value of m?

12

$$(5x^3 - 3) - (-4x^3 + 8)$$

The given expression is equivalent to $bx^3 - 11$, where b is a constant. What is the value of b?

13

$$y > 14$$
$$4x + y < 18$$

The point $(x, 53)$ is a solution to the system of inequalities in the xy-plane. Which of the following could be the value of x?

A) -9

B) -5

C) 5

D) 9

14

Bacteria are growing in a liquid growth medium. There were 300,000 cells per milliliter during an initial observation. The number of cells per milliliter doubles every 3 hours. How many cells per milliliter will there be 15 hours after the initial observation?

A) 1,500,000

B) 2,400,000

C) 4,500,000

D) 9,600,000

CONTINUE

15

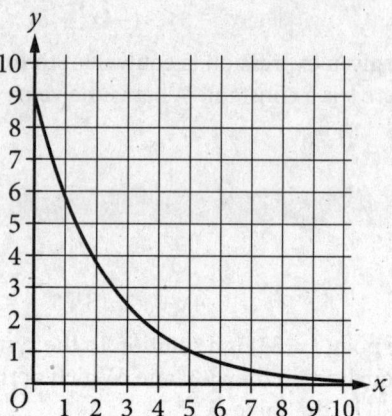

The graph gives the estimated number of catalogs y, in thousands, a company sent to its customers at the end of each year, where x represents the number of years since the end of 1992, where $0 \leq x \leq 10$. Which statement is the best interpretation of the y-intercept in this context?

A) The estimated total number of catalogs the company sent to its customers during the first 10 years was 9,000.

B) The estimated total number of catalogs the company sent to its customers from the end of 1992 to the end of 2002 was 90.

C) The estimated number of catalogs the company sent to its customers at the end of 1992 was 9.

D) The estimated number of catalogs the company sent to its customers at the end of 1992 was 9,000.

16

Which expression is equivalent to $\sqrt[7]{x^9 y^9}$, where x and y are positive?

A) $(xy)^{\frac{7}{9}}$

B) $(xy)^{\frac{9}{7}}$

C) $(xy)^{16}$

D) $(xy)^{63}$

17

The population of City A increased by 7% from 2015 to 2016. If the 2016 population is k times the 2015 population, what is the value of k?

A) 0.07

B) 0.7

C) 1.07

D) 1.7

18

Which of the following systems of linear equations has no solution?

A) $x = 3$
$y = 5$

B) $y = 6x + 6$
$y = 5x + 6$

C) $y = 16x + 3$
$y = 16x + 19$

D) $y = 5$
$y = 5x + 5$

CONTINUE

19

The first term of a sequence is 9. Each term after the first is 4 times the preceding term. If w represents the nth term of the sequence, which equation gives w in terms of n?

A) $w = 4(9^n)$

B) $w = 4(9^{n-1})$

C) $w = 9(4^n)$

D) $w = 9(4^{n-1})$

20

The minimum value of x is 12 less than 6 times another number n. Which inequality shows the possible values of x?

A) $x \leq 6n - 12$

B) $x \geq 6n - 12$

C) $x \leq 12 - 6n$

D) $x \geq 12 - 6n$

21

$RS = 20$

$ST = 48$

$TR = 52$

The side lengths of right triangle RST are given. Triangle RST is similar to triangle UVW, where S corresponds to V and T corresponds to W. What is the value of $\tan W$?

A) $\dfrac{5}{13}$

B) $\dfrac{5}{12}$

C) $\dfrac{12}{13}$

D) $\dfrac{12}{5}$

22

The graph of $9x - 10y = 19$ is translated down 4 units in the xy-plane. What is the x-coordinate of the x-intercept of the resulting graph?

STOP

If you finish before time is called, you may check your work on this module only. Do not turn to any other module in the test.

Math

22 QUESTIONS

DIRECTIONS

The questions in this section address a number of important math skills.
Use of a calculator is permitted for all questions.

NOTES

Unless otherwise indicated:

- All variables and expressions represent real numbers.
- Figures provided are drawn to scale.
- All figures lie in a plane.
- The domain of a given function f is the set of all real numbers x for which $f(x)$ is a real number.

REFERENCE

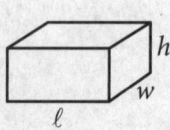

$A = \pi r^2$
$C = 2\pi r$

$A = \ell w$

$A = \frac{1}{2} bh$

$c^2 = a^2 + b^2$

Special Right Triangles

$V = \ell wh$

$V = \pi r^2 h$

$V = \frac{4}{3}\pi r^3$

$V = \frac{1}{3}\pi r^2 h$

$V = \frac{1}{3}\ell wh$

The number of degrees of arc in a circle is 360.

The number of radians of arc in a circle is 2π.

The sum of the measures in degrees of the angles of a triangle is 180.

CONTINUE ➤

For multiple-choice questions, solve each problem, choose the correct answer from the choices provided, and then circle your answer in this book. Circle only one answer for each question. If you change your mind, completely erase the circle. You will not get credit for questions with more than one answer circled, or for questions with no answers circled.

For student-produced response questions, solve each problem and write your answer next to or under the question in the test book as described below.

- Once you've written your answer, circle it clearly. You will not receive credit for anything written outside the circle, or for any questions with more than one circled answer.

- If you find **more than one correct answer**, write and circle only one answer.

- Your answer can be up to 5 characters for a **positive** answer and up to 6 characters (including the negative sign) for a **negative** answer, but no more.

- If your answer is a **fraction** that is too long (over 5 characters for positive, 6 characters for negative), write the decimal equivalent.

- If your answer is a **decimal** that is too long (over 5 characters for positive, 6 characters for negative), truncate it or round at the fourth digit.

- If your answer is a **mixed number** (such as $3\frac{1}{2}$), write it as an improper fraction (7/2) or its decimal equivalent (3.5).

- Don't include **symbols** such as a percent sign, comma, or dollar sign in your circled answer.

CONTINUE ➡

1

If $7x = 28$, what is the value of $8x$?

A) 21

B) 32

C) 168

D) 224

2

Isabel grows potatoes in her garden. This year, she harvested 760 potatoes and saved 10% of them to plant next year. How many of the harvested potatoes did Isabel save to plant next year?

A) 66

B) 76

C) 84

D) 86

3

A printer produces posters at a constant rate of 42 posters per minute. At what rate, in posters per hour, does the printer produce the posters?

4

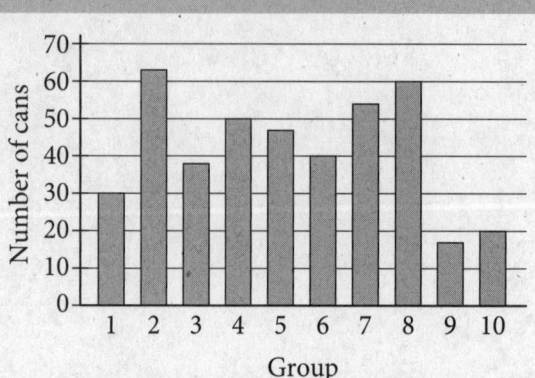

The bar graph shows the distribution of 419 cans collected by 10 different groups for a food drive. How many cans were collected by group 6?

5

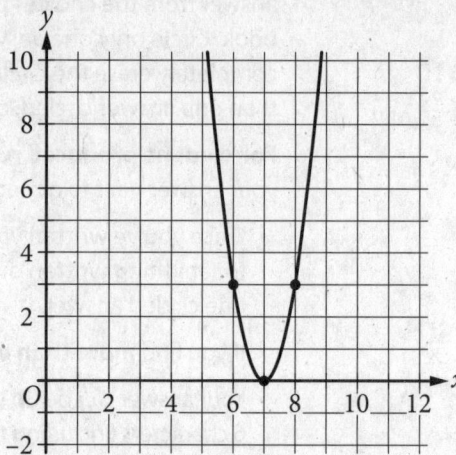

The x-intercept of the graph shown is $(x, 0)$. What is the value of x?

6

The function f is defined by the equation $f(x) = 7x + 2$. What is the value of $f(x)$ when $x = 4$?

7

Each side of a square has a length of 45. What is the perimeter of this square?

CONTINUE

8

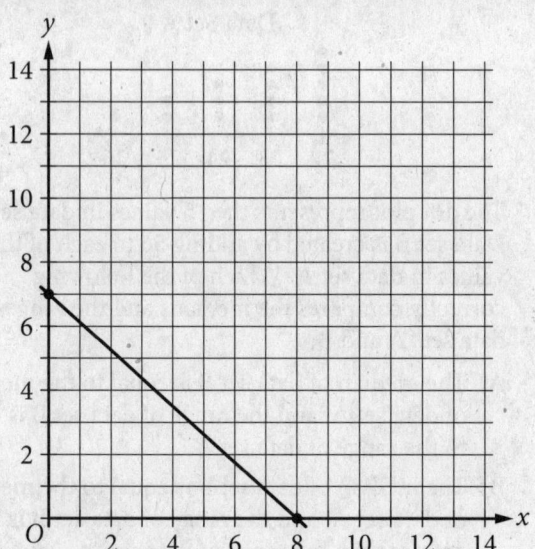

The point with coordinates $(d, 4)$ lies on the line shown. What is the value of d?

A) $\dfrac{7}{2}$

B) $\dfrac{26}{7}$

C) $\dfrac{24}{7}$

D) $\dfrac{27}{8}$

9

Which expression is equivalent to $5x^2 - 50xy^2$?

A) $5x(x - 10y^2)$

B) $5x(x - 50y^2)$

C) $5x^2(10xy^2)$

D) $5x^2(50xy^2)$

10

The function f is defined by $f(x) = 5x^2$. What is the value of $f(8)$?

A) 40

B) 50

C) 80

D) 320

11

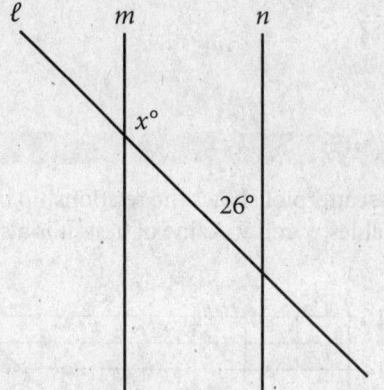

Note: Figure not drawn to scale.

In the figure shown, line m is parallel to line n. What is the value of x?

A) 13

B) 26

C) 52

D) 154

Unauthorized copying or reuse of any part of this page is illegal.

CONTINUE ▶

365

12

Each face of a fair 14-sided die is labeled with a number from 1 through 14, with a different number appearing on each face. If the die is rolled one time, what is the probability of rolling a 2?

A) $\frac{1}{14}$

B) $\frac{2}{14}$

C) $\frac{12}{14}$

D) $\frac{13}{14}$

13

The scatterplot shows the relationship between two variables, x and y. A line of best fit is also shown.

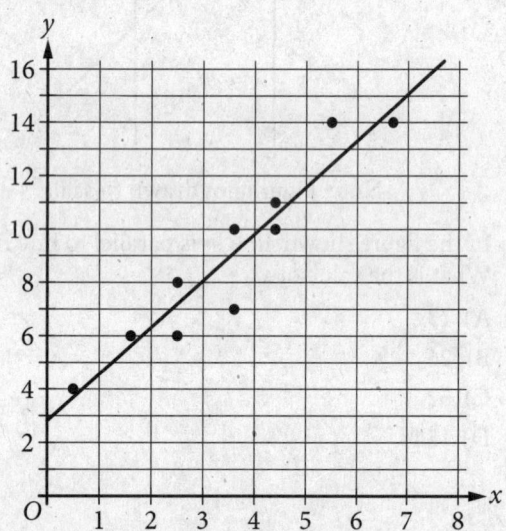

Which of the following equations best represents the line of best fit shown?

A) $y = 2.8 + 1.7x$

B) $y = 2.8 - 1.7x$

C) $y = -2.8 + 1.7x$

D) $y = -2.8 - 1.7x$

14

Data Set A

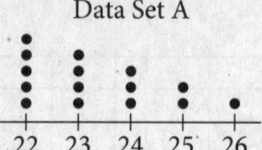

The dot plot represents the 15 values in data set A. Data set B is created by adding 56 to each of the values in data set A. Which of the following correctly compares the medians and the ranges of data sets A and B?

A) The median of data set B is equal to the median of data set A, and the range of data set B is equal to the range of data set A.

B) The median of data set B is equal to the median of data set A, and the range of data set B is greater than the range of data set A.

C) The median of data set B is greater than the median of data set A, and the range of data set B is equal to the range of data set A.

D) The median of data set B is greater than the median of data set A, and the range of data set B is greater than the range of data set A.

15

Last week, an interior designer earned a total of $1,258 from consulting for x hours and drawing up plans for y hours. The equation $68x + 85y = 1,258$ represents this situation. Which of the following is the best interpretation of 68 in this context?

A) The interior designer earned $68 per hour consulting last week.

B) The interior designer worked 68 hours drawing up plans last week.

C) The interior designer earned $68 per hour drawing up plans last week.

D) The interior designer worked 68 hours consulting last week.

Unauthorized copying or reuse of any part of this page is illegal.

CONTINUE ▶

366

16

$$x = 8$$
$$y = x^2 + 8$$

The graphs of the equations in the given system of equations intersect at the point (x, y) in the xy-plane. What is the value of y?

A) 8

B) 24

C) 64

D) 72

17

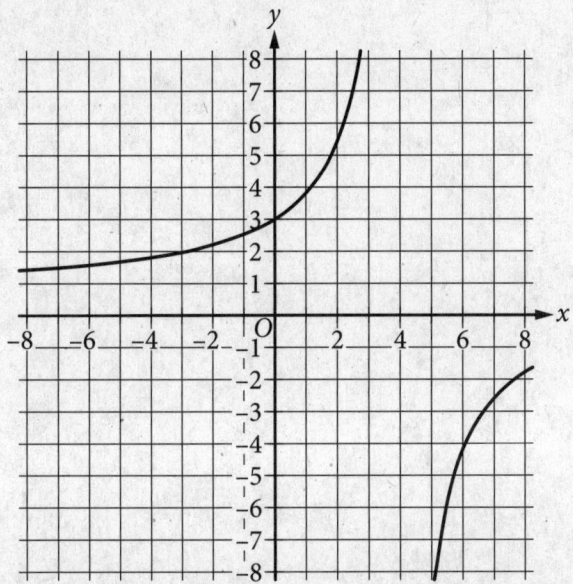

The graph of $y = f(x)$ is shown in the xy-plane. What is the value of $f(0)$?

A) −3

B) 0

C) $\frac{3}{5}$

D) 3

18

The function f is defined by $f(x) = 8\sqrt{x}$. For what value of x does $f(x) = 48$?

A) 6

B) 8

C) 36

D) 64

19

Line t in the xy-plane has a slope of $-\frac{1}{3}$ and passes through the point $(9, 10)$. Which equation defines line t?

A) $y = 13x - \frac{1}{3}$

B) $y = 9x + 10$

C) $y = -\frac{x}{3} + 10$

D) $y = -\frac{x}{3} + 13$

20

A company that provides whale-watching tours takes groups of 21 people at a time. The company's revenue is 80 dollars per adult and 60 dollars per child. If the company's revenue for one group consisting of adults and children was 1,440 dollars, how many people in the group were children?

A) 3

B) 9

C) 12

D) 18

CONTINUE

21

$$5x^2 + 10x + 16 = 0$$

How many distinct real solutions does the given equation have?

A) Exactly one

B) Exactly two

C) Infinitely many

D) Zero

22

The equation $x^2 + (y - 2)^2 = 36$ represents circle A. Circle B is obtained by shifting circle A down 4 units in the xy-plane. Which of the following equations represents circle B?

A) $x^2 + (y + 2)^2 = 36$

B) $x^2 + (y - 6)^2 = 36$

C) $(x - 4)^2 + (y - 2)^2 = 36$

D) $(x + 4)^2 + (y - 2)^2 = 36$

STOP

If you finish before time is called, you may check your work on this module only.
Do not turn to any other module in the test.

Test begins on the next page.

Math

22 QUESTIONS

DIRECTIONS

The questions in this section address a number of important math skills.
Use of a calculator is permitted for all questions.

NOTES

Unless otherwise indicated:

- All variables and expressions represent real numbers.
- Figures provided are drawn to scale.
- All figures lie in a plane.
- The domain of a given function f is the set of all real numbers x for which $f(x)$ is a real number.

REFERENCE

 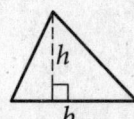 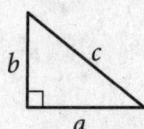 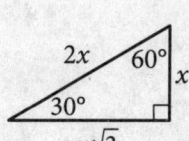

$A = \pi r^2$ $A = \ell w$ $A = \dfrac{1}{2}bh$ $c^2 = a^2 + b^2$ Special Right Triangles
$C = 2\pi r$

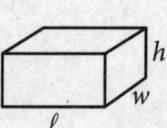 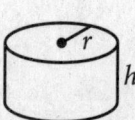  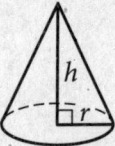 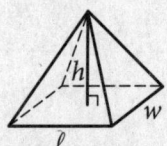

$V = \ell wh$ $V = \pi r^2 h$ $V = \dfrac{4}{3}\pi r^3$ $V = \dfrac{1}{3}\pi r^2 h$ $V = \dfrac{1}{3}\ell wh$

The number of degrees of arc in a circle is 360.

The number of radians of arc in a circle is 2π.

The sum of the measures in degrees of the angles of a triangle is 180.

CONTINUE

For multiple-choice questions, solve each problem, choose the correct answer from the choices provided, and then circle your answer in this book. Circle only one answer for each question. If you change your mind, completely erase the circle. You will not get credit for questions with more than one answer circled, or for questions with no answers circled.

For student-produced response questions, solve each problem and write your answer next to or under the question in the test book as described below.

- Once you've written your answer, circle it clearly. You will not receive credit for anything written outside the circle, or for any questions with more than one circled answer.

- If you find **more than one correct answer**, write and circle only one answer.

- Your answer can be up to 5 characters for a **positive** answer and up to 6 characters (including the negative sign) for a **negative** answer, but no more.

- If your answer is a **fraction** that is too long (over 5 characters for positive, 6 characters for negative), write the decimal equivalent.

- If your answer is a **decimal** that is too long (over 5 characters for positive, 6 characters for negative), truncate it or round at the fourth digit.

- If your answer is a **mixed number** (such as $3\frac{1}{2}$), write it as an improper fraction (7/2) or its decimal equivalent (3.5).

- Don't include **symbols** such as a percent sign, comma, or dollar sign in your circled answer.

CONTINUE

1

There are 55 students in Spanish club. A sample of the Spanish club students was selected at random and asked whether they intend to enroll in a new study program. Of those surveyed, 20% responded that they intend to enroll in the study program. Based on this survey, which of the following is the best estimate of the total number of Spanish club students who intend to enroll in the study program?

A) 11

B) 20

C) 44

D) 55

2

A machine makes large boxes or small boxes, one at a time, for a total of 700 minutes each day. It takes the machine 10 minutes to make a large box or 5 minutes to make a small box. Which equation represents the possible number of large boxes, x, and small boxes, y, the machine can make each day?

A) $5x + 10y = 700$

B) $10x + 5y = 700$

C) $(x + y)(10 + 5) = 700$

D) $(10 + x)(5 + y) = 700$

3

The scatterplot shows the relationship between two variables, x and y. A line of best fit is also shown.

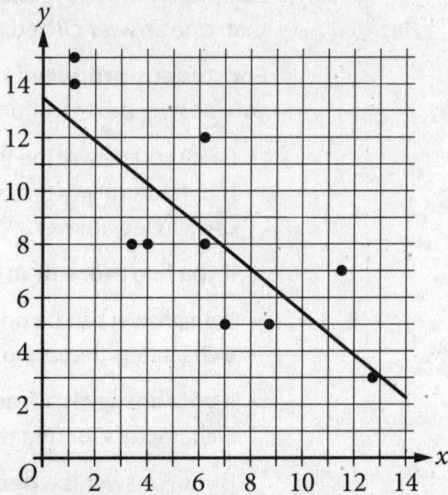

Which of the following equations best represents the line of best fit shown?

A) $y = 13.5 + 0.8x$

B) $y = 13.5 - 0.8x$

C) $y = -13.5 + 0.8x$

D) $y = -13.5 - 0.8x$

CONTINUE ➤

4

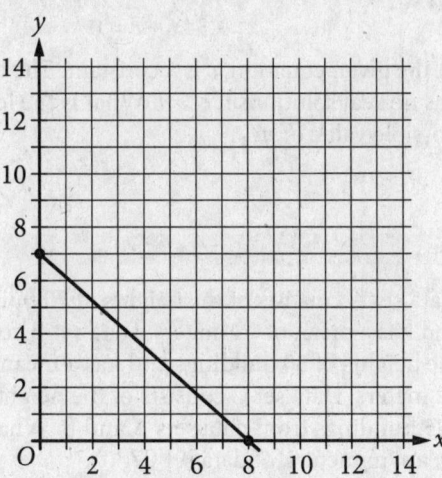

The point with coordinates $(d, 4)$ lies on the line shown. What is the value of d?

A) $\dfrac{7}{2}$

B) $\dfrac{26}{7}$

C) $\dfrac{24}{7}$

D) $\dfrac{27}{8}$

5

x	$f(x)$
-1	10
0	14
1	20

For the quadratic function f, the table shows three values of x and their corresponding values of $f(x)$. Which equation defines f?

A) $f(x) = 3x^2 + 3x + 14$

B) $f(x) = 5x^2 + x + 14$

C) $f(x) = 9x^2 - x + 14$

D) $f(x) = x^2 + 5x + 14$

6

The function f is defined by $f(x) = \dfrac{x + 15}{5}$, and $f(a) = 10$, where a is a constant. What is the value of a?

A) 5

B) 10

C) 35

D) 65

7

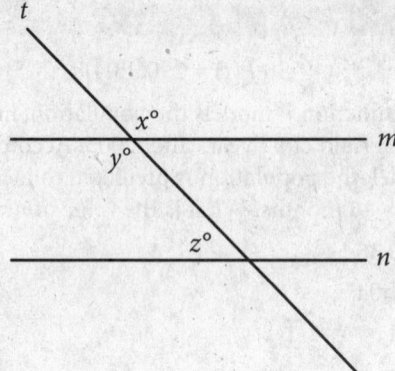

Note: Figure not drawn to scale.

In the figure, lines m and n are parallel. If $x = 6k + 13$ and $y = 8k - 29$, what is the value of z?

A) 3

B) 21

C) 41

D) 139

8

Line p is defined by $2y + 18x = 9$. Line r is perpendicular to line p in the xy-plane. What is the slope of line r?

A) -9

B) $-\dfrac{1}{9}$

C) $\dfrac{1}{9}$

D) 9

CONTINUE

9

A sample of oak has a density of 807 kilograms per cubic meter. The sample is in the shape of a cube, where each edge has a length of 0.90 meters. To the nearest whole number, what is the mass, in kilograms, of this sample?

A) 588

B) 726

C) 897

D) 1,107

10

$$P(t) = 290(1.04)^{\left(\frac{4}{6}\right)t}$$

The function P models the population, in thousands, of a certain city t years after 2005. According to the model, the population is predicted to increase by n% every 18 months. What is the value of n?

A) 0.38

B) 1.04

C) 4

D) 6

11

$$2(kx - n) = -\frac{28}{15}x - \frac{36}{19}$$

In the given equation, k and n are constants and $n > 1$. The equation has no solution. What is the value of k?

12

A gift shop buys souvenirs at a wholesale price of 7.00 dollars each and resells them each at a retail price that is 290% of the wholesale price. At the end of the season, any remaining souvenirs are marked at a discounted price that is 80% off the retail price. What is the discounted price of each remaining souvenir, in dollars?

13

$$x^2 - 34x + c = 0$$

In the given equation, c is a constant. The equation has no real solutions if $c > n$. What is the least possible value of n?

14

Data set A consists of the heights of 75 buildings and has a mean of 32 meters. Data set B consists of the heights of 50 buildings and has a mean of 62 meters. Data set C consists of the heights of the 125 buildings from data sets A and B. What is the mean, in meters, of data set C?

15

The expression $4x^2 + bx - 45$, where b is a constant, can be rewritten as $(hx + k)(x + j)$, where h, k, and j are integer constants. Which of the following must be an integer?

A) $\frac{b}{h}$

B) $\frac{b}{k}$

C) $\frac{45}{h}$

D) $\frac{45}{k}$

16

$$y = -1.5$$
$$y = x^2 + 8x + a$$

In the given system of equations, a is a positive constant. The system has exactly one distinct real solution. What is the value of a?

CONTINUE

17

Data Set A

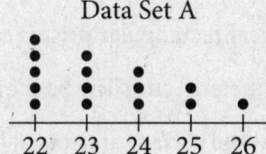

22 23 24 25 26

The dot plot represents the 15 values in data set A. Data set B is created by adding 56 to each of the values in data set A. Which of the following correctly compares the medians and the ranges of data sets A and B?

A) The median of data set B is equal to the median of data set A, and the range of data set B is equal to the range of data set A.

B) The median of data set B is equal to the median of data set A, and the range of data set B is greater than the range of data set A.

C) The median of data set B is greater than the median of data set A, and the range of data set B is equal to the range of data set A.

D) The median of data set B is greater than the median of data set A, and the range of data set B is greater than the range of data set A.

18

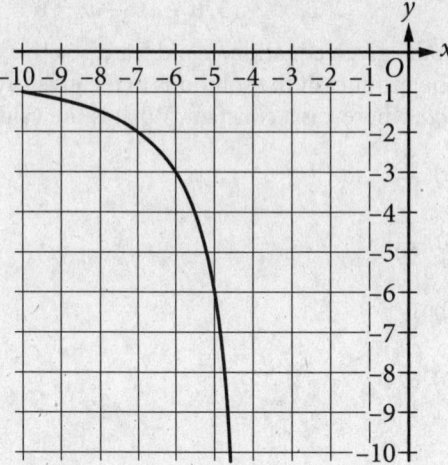

The rational function f is defined by an equation in the form $f(x) = \dfrac{a}{x+b}$, where a and b are constants. The partial graph of $y = f(x)$ is shown. If $g(x) = f(x+4)$, which equation could define function g?

A) $g(x) = \dfrac{6}{x}$

B) $g(x) = \dfrac{6}{x+4}$

C) $g(x) = \dfrac{6}{x+8}$

D) $g(x) = \dfrac{6(x+4)}{x+4}$

CONTINUE

19

$$57x^2 + (57b + a)x + ab = 0$$

In the given equation, a and b are positive constants. The product of the solutions to the given equation is kab, where k is a constant. What is the value of k?

A) $\dfrac{1}{57}$

B) $\dfrac{1}{19}$

C) 1

D) 57

20

The graph of $x^2 + x + y^2 + y = \dfrac{199}{2}$ in the xy-plane is a circle. What is the length of the circle's radius?

21

Two identical rectangular prisms each have a height of 90 centimeters (cm). The base of each prism is a square, and the surface area of each prism is K cm^2. If the prisms are glued together along a square base, the resulting prism has a surface area of $\dfrac{92}{47} K$ cm^2.

What is the side length, in cm, of each square base?

A) 4

B) 8

C) 9

D) 16

22

In the xy-plane, a parabola has vertex $(9, -14)$ and intersects the x-axis at two points. If the equation of the parabola is written in the form $y = ax^2 + bx + c$, where a, b, and c are constants, which of the following could be the value of $a + b + c$?

A) -23

B) -19

C) -14

D) -12

STOP

**If you finish before time is called, you may check your work on this module only.
Do not turn to any other module in the test.**

The SAT®

Practice Test #4

ANSWER EXPLANATIONS

These answer explanations are for students using
The Official SAT Study Guide.

Reading and Writing

Module 1
(27 questions)

QUESTION 1

Choice B is the best answer because it most logically completes the text's discussion of Booker T. Whatley. In this context, "hinder" means hold back or obstruct. The text explains that Whatley encouraged farms to allow customers on site to pick their own produce for a fee. He did so despite critics' concerns that the customers would never pay to do so. This context establishes that the critics' concerns didn't hinder Whatley's efforts to promote the practice.

Choice A is incorrect. The text indicates that critics' skepticism of the idea that customers would pay to pick their own produce didn't have some effect on Whatley's promotion of the practice. The text illustrates this assertion by describing Whatley's "determined advocacy" for the practice. This context suggests that critics' concerns didn't obstruct Whatley's efforts, not that critics' concerns didn't "enhance," or increase or improve, Whatley's efforts. *Choice C* is incorrect because in this context, "misrepresent" would mean portray inaccurately, and the text includes no information relevant to the issue of how Whatley's efforts were portrayed by critics of the practice of charging customers to pick their own produce. *Choice D* is incorrect. The text indicates that critics' skepticism of the idea that customers would pay to pick their own produce didn't have some effect on Whatley's promotion of the practice. The text illustrates this assertion by describing Whatley's "determined advocacy" for the practice. This context suggests that critics' concerns didn't obstruct Whatley's efforts, not that critics' concerns didn't "aggravate," or irritate or make more severe, Whatley's efforts.

QUESTION 2

Choice B is the best answer because it most logically completes the text's discussion of bronze- and brass-casting techniques used by the Igun Eronmwon guild. In this context "adhere to" would mean to act in accordance with. The text states that although members of the Igun Eronmwon guild typically do something with techniques that have been passed down since the thirteenth century, they "don't strictly observe every tradition." By establishing a contrast with not always following traditions, the context suggests that guild members do typically adhere to traditional techniques.

Choice A is incorrect because in this context "experiment with" would mean to do something new with. Although using motors rather than manual bellows is presented as a new approach, the text establishes a contrast between what the guild members typically do with techniques that have been passed down over centuries and the idea that the members "don't strictly observe every tradition." The phrase "experiment with" wouldn't support the contrast because regularly trying new things with the techniques would be an example of not strictly following all traditions. *Choice C* is incorrect because in this context "improve on" would mean to make better. Although using motors rather than manual bellows might be an improved approach, the text establishes a contrast between what the guild members typically do with techniques that have been passed down over centuries and the idea that the members "don't strictly observe every tradition." The phrase "improve on" wouldn't support the contrast because regularly making changes to the techniques would be an example of not strictly following all traditions. *Choice D* is incorrect because in this context "grapple with" would mean to try hard to solve a difficult problem. Although bronze- and brass-casting are likely challenging tasks, nothing in the text suggests that the guild members have any particular difficulties with the techniques passed down since the thirteenth century.

QUESTION 3

Choice A is the best answer because it most logically completes the text's discussion of Yu's novel. In this context, "haphazard" means marked by a lack of plan or order. The text indicates that the quest featured in the novel, which involves the protagonist bouncing across time, is chaotic and causes the reader to often wonder what will happen. This context suggests that the protagonist's journey seems to be marked by a lack of order.

Choice B is incorrect because the text indicates that the journey featured in Yu's novel involves a character "ricocheting chaotically," or bouncing in a disordered way, across time and causes the reader to often wonder what will happen. It wouldn't make sense to say that a chaotic journey seems "premeditated," or characterized by forethought and planning. *Choice C* is incorrect because the text doesn't give any indication that readers regard the journey in Yu's novel as "inspirational," or as causing extraordinarily creative or brilliant thoughts or actions; instead, the text focuses on the idea that the protagonist's journey is chaotic, or disordered, and doesn't give readers a clear sense of what will happen. *Choice D* is incorrect. Rather than suggesting that the journey featured in Yu's novel is "fruitless," or has an unsuccessful outcome, the text focuses on the idea that while reading about the protagonist's chaotic movements across time, readers are often unsure of what will happen—that is, they don't know whether the protagonist will be successful in finding his father.

QUESTION 4

Choice B is the best answer because it most logically completes the text's discussion of single-celled organism behavior. As used in this context, "rudimentary" means basic or unsophisticated. According to the text, a study of the single-celled protozoan *Stentor roeseli* showed that the organisms can switch strategies for escaping certain stimuli, "sophisticatedly 'changing their minds'" and using new strategies should other strategies fail. This context suggests that single-celled organisms may not be limited to behaviors that are basic or rudimentary, since the study showed that single-celled protozoans can respond complexly to irritating stimuli.

Choice A is incorrect because the text doesn't suggest that single-celled organisms may not be limited to behavior that is "aggressive," or threatening. Rather, the text suggests that single-celled organisms may not be limited to behaviors that are basic, since the study of *Stentor roeseli* showed that single-celled protozoans can respond complexly to irritating stimuli.

Choice C is incorrect because the text doesn't suggest that single-celled organisms may not be limited to behavior that is "evolving," or advancing. Rather, the text suggests that single-celled organisms may not be limited to behaviors that are basic, since the study of *Stentor roeseli* showed that single-celled protozoans can respond complexly to irritating stimuli. *Choice D* is incorrect because the text doesn't suggest that single-celled organisms may not be limited to behavior that is "advantageous," or helpful. Rather, the text suggests that single-celled organisms may not be limited to behaviors that are basic, since the study of *Stentor roeseli* showed that single-celled protozoans can respond complexly to irritating stimuli.

QUESTION 5

Choice A is the best answer because it most logically completes the text's discussion of late nineteenth- and early twentieth-century household food purchases. In this context, "surmised" means formed an idea or assumption with little evidence. The text explains that certain economic historians "assumed" that large and small households spent different amounts on food per person, but that another economist found this supposition to be false based on evidence from available data. This context suggests that the economic historians made an incorrect assumption without enough consideration of evidence.

Choice B is incorrect. In this context, "contrived" would mean brought about or created through trickery. Nothing in the text suggests that the economic historians were deliberately trying to trick people with a claim about food purchasing behaviors in late nineteenth- and early twentieth-century households; the text simply suggests that they made an assumption about those behaviors that another historian believes isn't supported by the available data. *Choice C* is incorrect because the text indicates that it's Logan and not the economic historians who "questioned," or doubted, the assumption that large and small households in the late nineteenth and early twentieth centuries spent different amounts on food per person; the economic historians are the ones who made that assumption to begin with. *Choice D* is incorrect because nothing in the text suggests that some economic historians "regretted," or felt sad or remorseful about, the food purchasing behaviors of late nineteenth- and early twentieth-century households. The text focuses on the idea that the economic historians made an assumption about those behaviors that may not be supported by available data, not on the historians' emotional response to what households did in the past.

QUESTION 6

Choice D is the best answer because as used in the text, "answers" most nearly means fulfills. In the text, Fabry and Busman claim that the robots manufactured by their company are more efficient than human workers, which they refer to as "the human machine." Fabry observes that the human machine "no longer answers the requirements of *modern engineering*." That is, human workers are incapable of meeting the rigorous needs of modern, industrialized workplaces.

Choice A is incorrect. Although in some contexts "answers" can mean explains, it doesn't have that meaning in this context because the topic under discussion is human beings' inability to perform labor efficiently, not their inability to engage in discussion or explanation. *Choice B* is incorrect. Although in some contexts "answers" can mean rebuts, or proves a claim or argument to be false, it wouldn't make sense to speak of proving requirements to be false; requirements might or might not be reasonable, but they can't be verified as truthful or untruthful, as claims or accusations can. *Choice C* is incorrect.

Although in some contexts, "answers" can mean defends against criticism, or justifies, it doesn't have that meaning in this context because the opinion that Fabry expresses is that human workers can no longer fulfill the requirements of modern workplaces, not that they have ceased to justify those requirements or to defend them against criticism; indeed, there is no suggestion in the text that workers ever defended those requirements.

QUESTION 7

Choice A is the best answer because it presents an explanation about a helicopter that is directly supported by the text. The text states that Mars's atmosphere is much less dense than Earth's, and as a result, the air on Mars doesn't provide the resistance required to support the blades of a helicopter built for Earth and to keep the helicopter aloft. In other words, a helicopter built for Earth can't fly on Mars because of the differences in the two planets' atmospheres.

Choice B is incorrect because instead of stating that the blades of helicopters built for Earth are too large to work on Mars, the text indicates that the helicopter built to fly on Mars actually has even longer blades than a helicopter built for Earth. *Choice C* is incorrect because the text never addresses the role of gravity on Mars or on Earth; instead, it focuses on atmospheric conditions. *Choice D* is incorrect because the text doesn't indicate that helicopters built for Earth are too small to operate in the conditions on Mars. In fact, the text states that the size of the helicopter built to fly on Mars is the same size as a helicopter built for Earth, even though it has longer blades that rotate faster.

QUESTION 8

Choice A is the best answer because it best states the main idea of the text. According to the text, jalis' traditional role has been to maintain information about families' histories and significant events. The text goes on to say that although technological changes have altered jalis' role somewhat, jalis are still valued for preserving the histories of their communities.

Choice B is incorrect because the text says nothing about jalis' views of the various tasks they perform. There is no information to support the idea that many jalis prefer teaching to other tasks. *Choice C* is incorrect because the text doesn't describe jalis as being sources of entertainment. Rather, jalis are presented as valued sources of knowledge. Additionally, the text gives no indication of how long jalis have been serving their communities. *Choice D* is incorrect because the main focus of the text is on jalis' role and their continued value despite the effects of technology, not on what technology can now do. Although the text indicates that jalis' role has changed as a result of technological changes, the text doesn't present any specific information about technology performing tasks that jalis once performed.

QUESTION 9

Choice D is the best answer because it most accurately states the main idea of the text. After establishing that Buck views most people "as nothing," the text explains that Buck won't acknowledge people other than Thornton unless they appear friendly toward Thornton, and even then he's only reluctantly accepting. Thus, the text focuses on the idea that Thornton has a special status in Buck's mind, with Buck holding him in higher regard than other people.

Choice A is incorrect because the text conveys that Buck isn't social with people other than Thornton but doesn't address Buck's life or temperament before he lived with Thornton. *Choice B* is incorrect because the text conveys that Buck doesn't really care about people other than Thornton and is aloof toward them. However, there's no indication that Buck mistrusts and avoids people generally; indeed, he accepts Thornton, who is a human. *Choice C* is incorrect because the text refers to random travelers praising and petting Buck and Thornton's partners giving Buck favors, but there's no indication that any of these people are Thornton's friends or that they have a particular fondness for Buck.

QUESTION 10

Choice B is the best answer because the quotation from *The Souls of Black Folk* illustrates the claim that Du Bois felt a sense of cultural recognition when he heard Black folk songs. In the quotation, Du Bois explains that for his entire life, Black folk songs "stirred [him] strangely." Even though they originated in the South, a region he wasn't familiar with, he knew the songs "as of me and of mine." That is, he identified strongly with them and associated them with his community. Therefore, Du Bois felt an intuitive sense of cultural recognition when he heard Black folk songs.

Choice A is incorrect. Although the quotation considers the cultural and spiritual value of Black folk music, it doesn't establish that this music inspired in Du Bois a sense of cultural recognition. *Choice C* is incorrect because this quotation addresses the cultural survival of Black folk songs despite attempts to caricature, or parody, them, not Du Bois's sense of cultural connection to them. *Choice D* is incorrect because the quotation indicates that the Black folk songs and music are old, "the siftings of centuries," instead of addressing how Du Bois felt when he heard the songs.

QUESTION 11

Choice C is the best answer because it uses data from the graph to effectively complete the example of Eludoyin and his colleagues' findings concerning female farmers in some regions of Ondo State, Nigeria. The graph presents values for the percentage of Ondo State small-scale farmers who are female, by type of crop and region. The graph shows that of the farmers mainly cultivating non-root vegetables, approximately 57% in north Ondo and approximately 54% in south Ondo are female; in other words, most of those farmers are female, which exemplifies the idea that female farmers make up the majority (more than half) of the farmers cultivating specific types of crops in some regions.

Choice A is incorrect because it inaccurately cites data from the graph: the graph shows that in south Ondo, most of the farmers mainly cultivating non-root vegetables are women (approximately 54%), but that only about 35% (less than half) of the farmers mainly cultivating cereals are women. *Choice B* is incorrect because it inaccurately cites data from the graph: the graph shows that more women in central Ondo mainly cultivate cereals than mainly cultivate root crops (approximately 36% and 20%, respectively). Additionally, it doesn't effectively complete the example because the graph shows that female farmers don't make up the majority (more than half) of the farmers for any type of crop in central Ondo. *Choice D* is incorrect because it doesn't effectively complete the example; it simply states that a relatively equal proportion of women across the three regions mainly cultivate cereals, which doesn't address the value for that proportion and thus doesn't show that a majority (more than half) of the farmers cultivating certain crops are female.

QUESTION 12

Choice B is the best answer because it most logically completes the text's discussion of Zelda Fitzgerald's contributions to literature. The text begins by saying that many scholars view Zelda mainly in terms of her marriage to F. Scott Fitzgerald and "don't recognize Zelda as a writer in her own right." The text then mentions a novel and "numerous short stories" that she wrote and that such scholars tend to ignore. Therefore, those scholars who focus on Zelda only as an inspiration for F. Scott's writings risk misrepresenting the full range of Zelda's contributions to literature.

Choice A is incorrect. Although the text does mention that Zelda Fitzgerald "likely influenced" her husband's literary work, its focus is on Zelda's own writing, not on her husband's writing or factors that might have influenced it. *Choice C* is incorrect because the text does not discuss F. Scott and Zelda Fitzgerald's opinions of each other's works. *Choice D* is incorrect. Although the text does suggest that F. Scott Fitzgerald's works were "likely influenced in part" by his marriage to Zelda, it does not discuss autobiographical interpretations of the works of either F. Scott or Zelda.

QUESTION 13

Choice B is the best answer because it presents the conclusion that most logically follows from the text's discussion of the relationship between atmospheric carbon dioxide and sauropod body size. The text establishes that sauropods evolved to reach enormous sizes, and it notes that some scientists have asserted that the cause of this phenomenon was increased plant production that resulted from increased atmospheric carbon dioxide. The text goes on to state, however, that atmospheric carbon dioxide levels didn't increase around the time of important periods in sauropods' evolution of larger body sizes. If significant periods of sauropod evolution toward larger sizes occurred without increased atmospheric carbon dioxide levels, that suggests that the evolution of larger sizes didn't depend on increased carbon dioxide in the atmosphere.

Choice A is incorrect because the text doesn't describe any fluctuations in atmospheric carbon dioxide, so there's no evidence in the text to support the conclusion that such fluctuations had different effects on different sauropod lineages. All that the text says about atmospheric carbon dioxide levels is that there weren't increases at particular points that correspond with key moments in sauropod evolution. *Choice C* is incorrect because the text indicates that there weren't significant increases in atmospheric carbon dioxide around the time of important periods in sauropods' evolution toward larger body sizes, not that atmospheric carbon dioxide was higher when the largest sauropods lived than when sauropods first appeared. *Choice D* is incorrect because the text indicates that atmospheric carbon dioxide levels didn't increase at important periods in sauropod evolution, not that higher levels would have affected that evolution. The text provides no information about how higher levels of atmospheric carbon dioxide might have affected sauropods.

QUESTION 14

Choice D is the best answer. The convention being tested is punctuation between a subject and a verb. When, as in this case, a subject ("Calida Garcia Rawles") is immediately followed by a verb ("was"), no punctuation is needed.

Choice A is incorrect because no punctuation is needed between the subject and the verb. *Choice B* is incorrect because no punctuation is needed between the subject and the verb. *Choice C* is incorrect because no punctuation is needed between the subject and the verb.

QUESTION 15

Choice D is the best answer. The convention being tested is punctuation use between sentences. In this choice, the period after "walls" is used correctly to mark the boundary between the first sentence ("In...walls") and the second sentence ("With...techniques"), which starts with a supplementary phrase.

Choice A is incorrect because it results in a comma splice. A comma can't be used in this way to mark the boundary between sentences. *Choice B* is incorrect because it results in a run-on sentence. The sentences ("In...walls" and "with...paintings") are fused without punctuation and/or a conjunction. *Choice C* is incorrect. Without a comma preceding it, the conjunction "so" can't be used in this way to join sentences.

QUESTION 16

Choice B is the best answer. The convention being tested is the use of plural and possessive nouns. The plural possessive noun "grains" and the plural noun "properties" correctly indicate that the simulations involved multiple snow grains and that those snow grains had several properties.

Choice A is incorrect because the context requires the plural possessive noun "grains" and the plural noun "properties," not the singular possessive noun "grain's" and the plural possessive noun "properties'." *Choice C* is incorrect because the context requires the plural noun "properties," not the singular possessive noun "property's." *Choice D* is incorrect because the context requires the plural possessive noun "grains'," not the plural noun "grains."

QUESTION 17

Choice C is the best answer. The convention being tested is the coordination of main clauses within a sentence. This choice uses a semicolon to correctly join the first main clause ("The Mission...parks") and the second main clause that begins with "it."

Choice A is incorrect. When coordinating two longer main clauses such as these, it's conventional to use a comma before the coordinating conjunction. *Choice B* is incorrect because it results in a run-on sentence. The two main clauses are fused without punctuation and/or a conjunction. *Choice D* is incorrect because it results in a comma splice. Without a conjunction following it, a comma can't be used in this way to join two main clauses.

QUESTION 18

Choice A is the best answer. The convention being tested here is subject-verb agreement. The singular verb "was" agrees in number with the singular subject "Josephine St. Pierre Ruffin."

Choice B is incorrect because the plural verb "were" doesn't agree in number with the singular subject "Josephine St. Pierre Ruffin." *Choice C* is incorrect because the plural verb "are" doesn't agree in number with the singular subject "Josephine St. Pierre Ruffin." *Choice D* is incorrect because the plural verb "have been" doesn't agree in number with the singular subject "Josephine St. Pierre Ruffin."

QUESTION 19

Choice D is the best answer. The convention being tested is the punctuation of a supplementary element within a sentence. In this choice, the dash after "cephalopods" pairs with the dash after "cuttlefish" to clearly separate the supplementary element "ocean dwellers that include the squid, the octopus, and the cuttlefish" from the rest of the sentence. This supplementary element functions to explain what cephalopods are, and the pair of dashes indicates that this element could be removed without affecting the grammatical coherence of the sentence.

Choice A is incorrect because it fails to use appropriate punctuation to separate the supplementary element that explains what cephalopods are from the rest of the sentence. *Choice B* is incorrect because it fails to use appropriate punctuation to separate the supplementary element that explains what cephalopods are from the rest of the sentence. *Choice C* is incorrect because it fails to use appropriate punctuation to separate the supplementary element that explains what cephalopods are from the rest of the sentence.

QUESTION 20

Choice D is the best answer. The convention being tested is finite and nonfinite verb forms within a sentence. Relative clauses, such as the one beginning with "that," require a finite verb, a verb that can function as the main verb of a clause. This choice correctly supplies the clause with the finite future tense verb "will be."

Choice A is incorrect because the nonfinite participle "being" doesn't supply the clause with a finite verb. *Choice B* is incorrect because the nonfinite to-infinitive "to be" doesn't supply the clause with a finite verb. *Choice C* is incorrect because the nonfinite to-infinitive "to have been" doesn't supply the clause with a finite verb.

QUESTION 21

Choice D is the best answer. "In fact" logically signals that the information in this sentence—that McFerrin finds the research phase of her work to be just as fascinating as travel—emphasizes and elaborates on the previous sentence's point that McFerrin regards background research as a rewarding activity.

Choice A is incorrect because "by contrast" illogically signals that the information in this sentence contrasts with the previous sentence's point about McFerrin's attitude toward background research. Instead, it emphasizes and elaborates on that point. *Choice B* is incorrect because "likewise" illogically signals that this sentence merely adds a second, similar point to the previous sentence's point about McFerrin's attitude toward background research. Instead, it emphasizes and elaborates on that point. *Choice C* is incorrect because "besides" illogically signals that this sentence provides a separate point in addition to, or apart from, the previous sentence's point about McFerrin's attitude toward background research. Instead, it emphasizes and elaborates on that point.

QUESTION 22

Choice C is the best answer. The sentence effectively introduces *The Holder of the World* to an audience already familiar with Mukherjee, explaining that the novel centers around two women and mentioning the author without providing any other identifying information.

Choice A is incorrect. The sentence provides a detail about Mukherjee's settings; it doesn't introduce, or even mention, the novel. *Choice B* is incorrect. The sentence provides introductory information about Mukherjee; it doesn't effectively introduce her novel to an audience already familiar with the author. *Choice D* is incorrect. The sentence provides introductory information about Mukherjee; it doesn't effectively introduce her novel to an audience already familiar with the author.

QUESTION 23

Choice D is the best answer. The sentence presents both the study and its findings, noting the study's date and the researcher's name as well as describing what the researcher determined about the jawbones and how she determined it.

Choice A is incorrect. While the sentence describes the study and the researcher's initial assessment, it doesn't present the study's findings. *Choice B* is incorrect. While the sentence describes the study and its focus, it doesn't present the study's findings or the name of the researcher who conducted it. *Choice C* is incorrect. While the sentence mentions the study's methodology and provides information about pterosaurs, it doesn't present the study's findings.

QUESTION 24

Choice A is the best answer. By noting that Selvon is a Trinidadian author and indicating that *The Lonely Londoners*, published in 1956, is about a group of men who emigrate from the Caribbean to Great Britain after World War II, the sentence effectively introduces Samuel Selvon and his novel to a new audience.

Choice B is incorrect. The sentence indicates the order in which two of Selvon's novels were written; it doesn't introduce Samuel Selvon and *The Lonely Londoners* to a new audience. *Choice C* is incorrect. While the sentence describes the novel *The Lonely Londoners*, it doesn't mention its author, Samuel Selvon, by name and thus doesn't effectively introduce him to a new audience. *Choice D* is incorrect. The sentence indicates that two of Selvon's novels include the same characters; it doesn't introduce Samuel Selvon and *The Lonely Londoners* to a new audience.

QUESTION 25

Choice C is the best answer. The sentence emphasizes a similarity between the two sea turtle species: both can be found in the Atlantic Ocean.

Choice A is incorrect. The sentence indicates that the olive ridley sea turtle is one of seven species of sea turtle; it fails to mention the Kemp's ridley sea turtle. *Choice B* is incorrect. The sentence emphasizes a difference between the two sea turtle species rather than a similarity. *Choice D* is incorrect. The sentence emphasizes a difference between the two sea turtle species rather than a similarity.

QUESTION 26

Choice D is the best answer. The sentence effectively summarizes the study, noting who conducted it, when it was conducted, and what its results showed: that auks' landing success rate decreased as wind conditions intensified.

Choice A is incorrect. While the sentence presents the methodology of the study—that is, the approach taken by the researchers—it fails to summarize the study as a whole. *Choice B* is incorrect. While the sentence presents the aim, or goal, of the study, it fails to summarize the study as a whole. *Choice C* is incorrect. While the sentence indicates what Shepard studied, it fails to mention a key factor: the effect of wind. It thus fails to summarize the study as a whole.

QUESTION 27

Choice C is the best answer. The sentence effectively introduces *Paradise* to an audience unfamiliar with the novel and its author, describing *Paradise* as a historical novel about colonial East Africa and its author as the winner of the 2021 Nobel Prize in Literature.

Choice A is incorrect. While the sentence introduces Abdulrazak Gurnah to an audience unfamiliar with the author, it doesn't effectively introduce *Paradise*. *Choice B* is incorrect. While the sentence provides background information about *Paradise*, it doesn't effectively introduce the novel to an audience unfamiliar with its author. *Choice D* is incorrect. While the sentence provides background information about *Paradise*, it doesn't effectively introduce the novel to an audience unfamiliar with its author.

Reading and Writing

Module 2 — Lower Difficulty
(27 questions)

QUESTION 1

Choice D is the best answer because it most logically completes the text's discussion of the fashion resale market's continued growth. As used in this context, "predicted" means forecast, or indicated that something would happen in the future. The text indicates that the fashion resale market made a lot of money in 2019 and that some analysts expected the market to continue to grow. This context suggests that the analysts believed that the fashion resale market was going to make more money than it had already made, with the analysts indicating that revenues would more than double by 2028.

Choice A is incorrect because it wouldn't make sense in context to say that some analysts "produced," or manufactured or brought about, the increase in future revenues of the fashion resale market. The analysts themselves couldn't have brought about the future revenue growth, since, as the text suggests, they were merely in the position of drawing conclusions about future fashion resale market revenue based on 2019 revenue. *Choice B* is incorrect because the text indicates that some analysts expected the fashion resale market to continue to grow in the future, not that they "denied," or rejected, this notion. Nothing in the text supports the idea that these analysts thought the revenues wouldn't grow. *Choice C* is incorrect because the text indicates that some analysts expected the fashion resale market to continue to grow in the future, not that they "worried," or felt concerned, that revenue would significantly increase by 2028. Nothing in the text suggests that the analysts felt concerned about the increase; rather, the text suggests that the increase would represent a favorable outcome, since it would mean that the fashion resale market grew to generate even more revenue.

QUESTION 2

Choice D is the best answer because it most logically completes the text's discussion of damage to viburnum plants. In this context, "healthy" would mean not distressed or diseased. The text states that insect damage may cause viburnum plants to be discolored and have abnormal growths. In the next sentence, the phrase "on the other hand" indicates a contrast with the description of plants suffering from damage. Thus, the context contrasts the appearance of healthy, undamaged plants with the appearance of damaged plants.

Choice A is incorrect because in this context, "struggling" would mean working against difficulties. The text first describes viburnum plants experiencing damage by insects, and the phrase "on the other hand" then establishes a contrast with that description. It wouldn't make sense to contrast struggling viburnum plants with those being damaged by insects, because in both cases the plants would be experiencing difficulties. *Choice B* is incorrect because in this context, "beneficial" would mean producing good or helpful effects. The text doesn't discuss how viburnum plants affect other things or suggest that the plants are helpful in some way; rather, it focuses on how viburnum plants are affected by certain conditions. *Choice C* is incorrect because in this context "simple" would mean plain or uncomplicated. The text doesn't discuss whether certain viburnum plants are complicated or uncomplicated; rather, it focuses on how viburnum plants are affected by certain conditions.

QUESTION 3

Choice A is the best answer because it most logically completes the text's discussion of Nuttall's 1886 research paper. In this context, "acknowledged" means recognized as having a certain status. The text indicates that other researchers recognized Nuttall's work as groundbreaking because of its "convincing demonstration" related to the age of the ancient sculptures. In other words, the researchers recognized the groundbreaking status of Nuttall's work.

Choice B is incorrect because in this context, "ensured" would mean to have guaranteed or made sure something was the case. The text states that other researchers gave Nuttall's work recognition after it was published, but there's no indication that they contributed to the work or had any involvement that would have allowed them to make sure the work would be groundbreaking. *Choice C* is incorrect because the text doesn't suggest that other researchers "denied," or refused to admit or accept, that Nuttall's work was groundbreaking; on the contrary, it indicates that researchers praised the work, recognizing it as groundbreaking due to its "convincing demonstration" related to the age of the ancient sculptures. *Choice D* is incorrect because the text doesn't suggest that other researchers "underestimated," or undervalued, Nuttall's work; on the contrary, it indicates that researchers praised the work, recognizing it as groundbreaking due to its "convincing demonstration" related to the age of the ancient sculptures.

QUESTION 4

Choice A is the best answer because it most logically completes the text's discussion of self-government among the Muscogee (Creek) Nation. In this context, "implement" means to carry out or put into effect. The text states that the National Council generates laws, while the principal chief and cabinet officials are responsible for "devising policies and administering services in accordance with" those laws. This context suggests that the principal chief and cabinet officials implement the laws: they put the laws into effect by creating policies and administering services that accord with those laws.

Choice B is incorrect because "presume" in this context would mean to assume based on incomplete information, and the text does not suggest that the principal chief and cabinet officials either made assumptions about the content of the laws or had incomplete information about them. *Choice C* is incorrect because in this context "improvise" would mean to create something without preparation, and the text does not suggest that the principal chief and cabinet officials create policies and administer services without advance preparation. *Choice D* is incorrect because nothing in the text suggests that the principal chief and cabinet officials "mimic," or imitate, the laws generated by the National Council. To mimic laws would mean to generate new laws that are imitations of existing laws, but the text indicates that the National Council, not the principal chief and cabinet officials, is responsible for generating laws. Instead of generating laws, the principal chief and cabinet officials put laws into effect by "devising policies and administering services in accordance with" the laws.

QUESTION 5

Choice B is the best answer because it most logically and precisely completes the text's discussion of Jeyifous's series of images for the 2020 exhibition. In this context, "created" means produced. The text explains that Jeyifous, a photographer and neurobiologist, photographed adults who had appeared as children in posters from the 1970s, then combined those photographs with magnified images of the adults' cells—a process that resulted in what he called "micro and macro portraiture." This context suggests that Jeyifous drew on his dual interests in photography and neurobiology to produce the images for display in the exhibition.

Choice A is incorrect because there's nothing in the text to suggest that Jeyifous "validated," or corroborated, the series of images. The text describes Jeyifous's process for composing the images but doesn't describe Jeyifous making an effort to evaluate the images for their artistic or scientific legitimacy. *Choice C* is incorrect because there's nothing in the text to suggest that Jeyifous "challenged," or disputed, an aspect of the images; rather, the focus of the text is on the inspiration behind the images and the method Jeyifous used to achieve them. *Choice D* is incorrect because the text indicates that Jeyifous made the images himself using a combination of photography and magnified pictures of cells, not that he "restored," or reconditioned, the images from a deteriorated state.

QUESTION 6

Choice C is the best answer because it most logically completes the text's discussion of Jung and her team's study of acts of kindness. In this context, "foster" means encourage or promote the development of. The text indicates that Jung and her team found that seeing a helpful (or prosocial) act makes a bystander more likely to help someone else, which can in turn inspire additional people to help others. That is, the team showed that single acts of kindness can foster additional prosocial acts across a group.

Choice A is incorrect because nothing in the text suggests that Jung and her team found that single acts of kindness "require," or depend on or make obligatory, broader prosocial (or helpful) behavior across a group. There's no suggestion in the text that individual acts of kindness can only occur if other prosocial acts have already occurred, and the text indicates only that an act of kindness can inspire additional helpful acts, not that it necessarily will do so. *Choice B* is incorrect because the text focuses on a possible direct effect of individual acts of kindness, or single helpful actions, and it wouldn't make sense to suggest that actions can "remember," or hold a memory of, something. *Choice D* is incorrect because the text doesn't indicate that Jung and her team found that single acts of kindness can "discourage," or hinder, prosocial (or helpful) behavior across a group. On the contrary, the text states that Jung and her team found that seeing a helpful act makes a bystander more likely to help someone else, which can in turn inspire even more people to help others.

QUESTION 7

Choice C is the best answer because it best describes how the underlined sentence functions in the text as a whole. The first two sentences establish that birds of some species don't raise their own young; instead, they lay their eggs in the nests of birds of other species. The underlined sentence then states that female cuckoo birds engage in this behavior, having been observed specifically laying their eggs in other nests while the other birds are out finding food. According to the text, the cuckoo chicks are then raised by the other birds. Thus, the underlined sentence provides a particular detail about how female cuckoos carry out the behavior of laying eggs for other birds to raise.

Choice A is incorrect. Rather than mentioning a physical feature of female cuckoos, the underlined sentence introduces a specific behavior of female cuckoos: laying eggs in the nests of birds of other species when the other birds are away. The only reference to physical features is the last sentence's general mention of cuckoo chicks looking different from chicks of other species. *Choice B* is incorrect because the underlined sentence refers to the nests of birds other than cuckoos and doesn't describe how any nests look, cuckoo or otherwise. Instead, the sentence addresses how female cuckoos use other birds' nests. *Choice D* is incorrect because the underlined sentence describes only female cuckoo behavior (laying eggs in the nests of birds of other species when the other birds are away); it's the last sentence of the text that addresses the other birds' reaction, indicating that those birds usually raise the cuckoo chicks once they've hatched.

QUESTION 8

Choice A is the best answer because it most accurately describes the main purpose of the text. The text begins by stating that the new picture "failed to fit in" with the other items that the shop owner has. The text goes on to illustrate that point by describing the other pictures the shop owner has, indicating that the shop owner is fuming because he doesn't think the new picture belongs in the store. In the second paragraph, however, the text indicates that the shop owner is "secretly proud of his acquisition." The main purpose of the text is thus to reveal the shop owner's conflicted feelings about the new picture.

Choice B is incorrect because the text doesn't suggest that the shop owner resents the young man who sold him the new picture; in fact, the text gives no indication of the owner's feelings about the young man at all. *Choice C* is incorrect. Although the text indicates that the new picture is different from the other items in the shop, there's no suggestion that the shop owner prizes either the new picture or the pictures of the city, pets, and landscapes more than he prizes any other items. *Choice D* is incorrect because the text doesn't describe what the new picture looks like; rather, the text identifies some of the other kinds of images that the shop owner has and states that they're different from the new picture without explaining how they're different.

QUESTION 9

Choice C is the best answer because it reflects how the author of Text 2 would respond to the claims in Text 1. Both texts address skills needed to produce digital art. Text 1 claims that digital art doesn't require the same amount of skill as creating physical art and that "the technology is doing most of the work." Text 2 states that digital art requires "knowing the fundamentals of art" and that many digital artists begin their work on paper and then transfer it to a digital format using "sophisticated software" and "a variety of colors and techniques." Therefore, the author of Text 2 would most likely insist that digital art requires artistic abilities even if it employs less traditional tools.

Choice A is incorrect because neither text discusses nondigital means of displaying art. *Choice B* is incorrect because the author of Text 2 doesn't address whether it's harder to use a tablet and stylus than it is to use paint and a brush. Text 2 does argue that digital art requires skills that aren't part of the traditional methods for producing art, but the text doesn't address relative difficulty. *Choice D* is incorrect because the author of Text 2 states that digital artists still need to know "the fundamentals of art" and that many digital artists begin their work by drafting on paper before transferring the work to a digital format.

QUESTION 10

Choice A is the best answer because it uses data from the graph to accurately complete the text. The graph shows the number of organic farms located in each of six US states in 2016: between 2,600 and 2,800 in California; between 1,200 and 1,400 in Wisconsin; between 1,000 and 1,200 in New York; approximately 800 in Pennsylvania; and between 600 and 800 in both Iowa and Washington. The last sentence of the text provides information about the number of organic farms in 2016, first describing the number in California. The best completion of the sentence is the choice that accurately describes the number of organic farms in 2016 in another state, which the assertion that Washington had between 600 and 800 organic farms provides.

Choice B is incorrect because it doesn't accurately reflect the data from the graph. The graph indicates that there were between 1,000 and 1,200 organic farms in New York, not fewer than 800 organic farms. *Choice C* is incorrect because it doesn't accurately reflect the data from the graph. While the graph indicates that there were between 1,200 and 1,400 organic farms in Wisconsin in 2016, there were only between 600 and 800 in Iowa. *Choice D* is incorrect because it doesn't accurately reflect the data from the graph. The graph indicates that in 2016 there were approximately 800 organic farms in Pennsylvania, not more than 1,200.

QUESTION 11

Choice C is the best answer because it most effectively illustrates the claim in the text that John is hard-working and dedicated to his job. In the quotation, John is portrayed as spending "early morn to the fall of the afternoon" working hard as a water carrier. John is also described as "so accustomed to bending" while doing his work "that he never thought of straightening" his body, instead remaining deeply focused on his work. These details portray John as a dedicated worker.

Choice A is incorrect because this quotation portrays John as happy about heading home after being paid. It doesn't showcase John being hard at work. *Choice B* is incorrect because this quotation doesn't pertain to John's commitment to his work; it describes difficulties the traffic in the city causes John in the performance of his work. *Choice D* is incorrect because this quotation doesn't pertain to John's commitment to his work; it discusses what John does with his worn-out water jugs.

QUESTION 12

Choice A is the best answer because it most effectively illustrates the claim that Lowell describes an element of nature as an active participant in the experience of a nighttime scene on a body of water. The quotation presents the image of the moon shining on a body of water. However, instead of describing the moon in passive terms or simply stating that it reflects through the water and onto the sandy shore, the quotation portrays the moon as being engaged in the humanlike action of writing a legend. In other words, the moon is participating actively in the nighttime scene.

Choice B is incorrect. Although the quotation describes a nighttime scene on a body of water, the element of nature in these lines—the waves—isn't portrayed as an active participant in an experience; instead, the waves merely ripple softly against a canoe, as waves would normally do. *Choice C* is incorrect because the quotation doesn't present a nighttime scene on a body of water; instead, it describes petals falling from a rose. *Choice D* is incorrect. Although the quotation presents an image of an element of nature—the moon—it doesn't mention a body of water; moreover, it portrays the moon not as an active participant in a scene but instead as static or unchanging ("ever and always the same").

QUESTION 13

Choice D is the best answer because it provides the most direct support from the table for the claim that the plants growing in close proximity to other plants gained an advantage at an early developmental stage. The table shows the total number of juvenile plants from five species that were found growing on bare ground and in patches of vegetation as well as the percentage of the total number of each species that were growing in patches of vegetation. For each of the five species, more than 50% of the juvenile plants were growing in patches of vegetation. The text notes, however, that a random distribution of plants across the landscape should result in only about 15% of the plants being found in patches of vegetation. In other words, for each of the five species, the percentage of juvenile plants found growing in patches of vegetation was substantially higher than could be explained by chance alone. This finding supports the claim in the text: if plants growing in patches are overrepresented among plants that have survived to the juvenile stage, as the data show they are, then it suggests that it's advantageous for plants at an early stage of development to grow in patches of vegetation.

Choice A is incorrect because the statement that less than 75% of juvenile plants were found growing in patches of vegetation, while true, doesn't clearly support the claim that the plants growing in close proximity to other plants gained an advantage at an early developmental stage. Saying that less than 75% of plants were found in patches doesn't indicate how the percentage growing in patches compares with the percentage that would be expected to grow in patches on the basis of chance alone, which is the information necessary to evaluate whether the claim in the text has support in the table. Put another way, if the percentage of plants found growing in patches was 15% or less, it would be true that less than 75% were found in patches, but the data would in fact weaken the claim in the text, not strengthen it, since the data would show that growing in patches wasn't advantageous. *Choice B* is incorrect because only 12 plants of this species were found growing in patches, which was the lowest number of any species, not the greatest number. Additionally, even if it were true that this species had the greatest number of plants growing in patches, the finding would be irrelevant to the claim that plants of all five species gained an advantage by growing in close proximity to other plants. *Choice C* is incorrect because 59.1% of the plants of these species were found growing in patches, which is a far greater percentage, not a lower percentage, than what would be expected if plants were randomly distributed (around 15%). Additionally, if it were true that the percentage of plants growing in patches was lower for these species than what would be expected from chance alone, that finding would weaken, not strengthen, the claim that growing in patches is advantageous.

QUESTION 14

Choice A is the best answer because it most effectively illustrates the claim that Martí argues that a society's spiritual well-being depends on the character of its literary culture. In the quotation, Martí asserts that poetry is "more necessary to a people than industry itself" and that it has the power to provide people with "faith and vigor." He also adds that literature gives people "the desire and strength for life." Therefore, this quotation shows that Martí believes that literature is a societal necessity because it uplifts people and nourishes their spiritual well-being.

Choice B is incorrect. Although this quotation emphasizes the importance of literature, it focuses on how the nature of a society is reflected in that society's literature rather than on literature's value for people's spiritual well-being. *Choice C* is incorrect. Although this quotation involves an element of spirituality, it doesn't discuss literature. The quotation instead focuses on humanity's actions. *Choice D* is incorrect because this quotation mainly focuses on the importance of Walt Whitman rather than on the value of literature in general.

QUESTION 15

Choice D is the best answer because it presents the conclusion that most logically completes the text's discussion of Sumerian civilization and crop growth. The text mentions the hot, sunny weather in the area where the Sumerians lived, which made crops grow quickly but also made it difficult to keep them alive. The Sumerians solved this problem by using river water for their farming—as a result, they often harvested more crops than were needed in a season. It follows that the Sumerians must have needed to find something to do with the surplus crops—that is, they stored the extra crops for later use.

Choice A is incorrect because it doesn't logically follow that a surplus in crops would lead the Sumerians to choose only certain days of the season to harvest. Nor is there any indication in the text that the Sumerians improved their farming methods with the goal of reducing the time spent farming. *Choice B* is incorrect because the text doesn't suggest that the Sumerians tried to shield their crops from the sun: in fact, the text indicates that the sunny weather helped crops grow very quickly and that the Sumerians used river water to allow crops to be exposed to the sun without dying. *Choice C* is incorrect. Having a surplus of crops wouldn't have caused the Sumerians to begin farming until long after 4000 BCE: in fact, since the text indicates that the Sumerian civilization formed around 4000 BCE and farming was a part of that civilization, the statement that Sumerians only began farming long after 4000 BCE isn't supported by the text.

QUESTION 16

Choice C is the best answer because it most logically completes the text's discussion of the mechanisms underlying associative memory. The text explains that fan cells—a type of brain cell—are necessary for the acquisition of new associative memories, and that activity among these cells requires a chemical known as dopamine, which the brain produces in response to rewards. Since the brain cells that enable the formation of associative memories require dopamine in order to function, and since the brain produces dopamine in response to rewards, it can be inferred that receiving a reward should likely help to increase an individual's capacity to form associative memories.

Choice A is incorrect because the relationship between rewards and dopamine sketched by the text is that rewards result in the production of dopamine, not that they cause an individual's capacity to utilize dopamine to decrease.

Choice B is incorrect. The text suggests that receiving a reward would produce dopamine and thereby assist with associate memory formation. However, the text never suggests that associative memory involves the capacity to recognize differences between unrelated things, indicating only that associative memory involves remembering what connects those things. *Choice D* is incorrect because the text never discusses how fan cells are initially created and therefore provides no evidence for a conclusion about how receiving a reward would affect their creation.

QUESTION 17

Choice B is the best answer. The convention being tested is the use of finite and nonfinite verb forms within a sentence. A main clause requires a finite verb to perform the action of the subject (in this case, "some historians"), and this choice supplies the finite present tense verb "claim" to indicate what some historians do.

Choice A is incorrect because the nonfinite participle "claiming" doesn't supply the main clause with a finite verb. *Choice C* is incorrect because the nonfinite participle "having claimed" doesn't supply the main clause with a finite verb. *Choice D* is incorrect because the nonfinite to-infinitive "to claim" doesn't supply the main clause with a finite verb.

QUESTION 18

Choice A is the best answer. The convention being tested is punctuation between a preposition and its complement. No punctuation is needed between the preposition "of" and its complement, the noun phrase "healing, self-discovery, and memory."

Choice B is incorrect because no punctuation is needed between a preposition and its complement. *Choice C* is incorrect because no punctuation is needed between a preposition and its complement. *Choice D* is incorrect because no punctuation is needed between a preposition and its complement.

QUESTION 19

Choice A is the best answer. The convention being tested is the use of finite and nonfinite verb forms within a sentence. A main clause requires a finite verb to perform the action of the subject (in this case, "a recent study"), and this choice supplies the finite present tense verb "explains" to indicate that the study explains why plants that attract bats have evolved to produce moderately sweet nectar.

Choice B is incorrect because the nonfinite participle "explaining" doesn't supply the main clause with a finite verb. *Choice C* is incorrect because the nonfinite participle "having explained" doesn't supply the main clause with a finite verb. *Choice D* is incorrect because the nonfinite to-infinitive "to explain" doesn't supply the main clause with a finite verb.

QUESTION 20

Choice D is the best answer. The convention being tested is the use of verbs to express tense in a sentence. In this choice, the past progressive tense verb "was studying" is consistent with the other past tense verbs (e.g., "made" and "collected") used to describe Buratti's discovery. Further, the past progressive tense correctly indicates that an ongoing action in the past was occurring (she was studying) at the same time that another event occurred in the past (she made an interesting discovery).

Choice A is incorrect because the present tense verb "studies" isn't consistent with the past tense verbs used to describe Buratti's discovery. *Choice B* is incorrect because the present perfect progressive tense verb "has been studying" isn't consistent with the past tense verbs used to describe Buratti's discovery. *Choice C* is incorrect because the future tense verb "will study" isn't consistent with the past tense verbs used to describe Buratti's discovery.

QUESTION 21

Choice C is the best answer. The convention being tested is the use of plural and possessive nouns. The plural nouns "stories" and "immigrants" correctly indicate that the memoir tells multiple stories of multiple immigrants.

Choice A is incorrect because the context requires the plural noun "stories," not the singular possessive noun "story's." *Choice B* is incorrect because the context requires the plural nouns "stories" and "immigrants," not the singular possessive noun "story's" and the plural possessive noun "immigrants'." *Choice D* is incorrect because the context requires the plural nouns "stories" and "immigrants," not the plural possessive noun "stories'" and the singular possessive noun "immigrant's."

QUESTION 22

Choice D is the best answer. The convention being tested is punctuation between a main clause and a subordinate clause. This choice correctly uses a comma to mark the boundary between the main clause ("the colorful...decade") and the subordinate clause ("while...centuries") that provides contrasting information about the life span of rougheye rockfish.

Choice A is incorrect because a colon can't be used in this way to join a main clause and a subordinate clause. *Choice B* is incorrect because it results in a rhetorically unacceptable sentence fragment beginning with "while." *Choice C* is incorrect because a semicolon can't be used in this way to join a main clause and a subordinate clause.

QUESTION 23

Choice B is the best answer. The convention being tested is pronoun-antecedent agreement. The plural reflexive pronoun "themselves" agrees in number with the plural antecedent "turtle barnacles," correctly indicating what is attached to a sea turtle shell.

Choice A is incorrect because the singular pronoun "it" doesn't agree in number with the plural antecedent "turtle barnacles." *Choice C* is incorrect because it results in an unclear and confusing sentence. In this context, it's unclear what the plural pronoun "them" refers to. *Choice D* is incorrect because the singular reflexive pronoun "itself" doesn't agree in number with the plural antecedent "turtle barnacles."

QUESTION 24

Choice D is the best answer. "As a result" logically signals that the claim in this sentence—that spiders can cling to and climb almost any surface—is because of the previous information about the bonding properties of spiders' spatulae.

Choice A is incorrect because "for instance" illogically signals that the claim in this sentence exemplifies the information in the previous sentences. Instead, the claim is because of the previous information about the bonding properties of spiders' spatulae. *Choice B* is incorrect because "however" illogically signals that the claim in this sentence contrasts with the information in the previous sentences. Instead, the claim is because of the previous information about the bonding properties of spiders' spatulae. *Choice C* is incorrect because "similarly" illogically signals that the claim in this sentence is similar to, but separate from, the information in the previous sentences. Instead, the claim is because of the previous information about the bonding properties of spiders' spatulae.

QUESTION 25

Choice D is the best answer. "However" logically signals that this sentence, which indicates that the Pūhāhonu volcano may be larger than the Mauna Loa volcano, offers a contrast to or refutation of the previous assumption that Mauna Loa is the largest shield volcano.

Choice A is incorrect because "secondly" illogically signals that this sentence merely offers an additional or secondary point concerning the previous assumption that Mauna Loa is the largest shield volcano. Instead, the sentence offers a contrast to or refutation of that assumption. *Choice B* is incorrect because "consequently" illogically signals that this sentence offers a result or consequence of the previous assumption that Mauna Loa is the largest shield volcano. Instead, the sentence offers a contrast to or refutation of that assumption. *Choice C* is incorrect because "moreover" illogically signals that this sentence merely adds to the previous assumption that Mauna Loa is the largest shield volcano. Instead, the sentence offers a contrast to or refutation of that assumption.

QUESTION 26

Choice A is the best answer. "Therefore" logically signals that the action described in this sentence—the researchers theorizing that the dish was named for its effect on diners—is a result or consequence of the previous observation that the dish had a calming effect.

Choice B is incorrect because "alternately" illogically signals that the action described in this sentence offers an alternative or contrast to the previous observation that the dish had a calming effect. Instead, the action is a result or consequence of that observation. *Choice C* is incorrect because "nevertheless" illogically signals that the action described in this sentence occurs despite the previous observation that the dish had a calming effect. Instead, the action is a result or consequence of that observation. *Choice D* is incorrect because "likewise" illogically signals that this sentence merely adds a second, similar detail to the previous observation that the dish had a calming effect. Instead, this sentence describes an action that is a result or consequence of that observation.

QUESTION 27

Choice B is the best answer because it provides both an explanation and an example of "flauna." The sentence explains that flauna, a combination of the words "flora" and "fauna," is a term used by Jon Ching to describe the plant-animal hybrids in his paintings. The sentence also mentions an example of Ching's flauna: a parrot with leaves for feathers.

Choice A is incorrect. While the sentence partially explains what "flauna" is, it doesn't provide a full explanation or specific example of Ching's flauna. *Choice C* is incorrect. While the sentence partially explains what "flauna" is and includes a title of a Ching painting, it doesn't provide a full explanation or specific example of Ching's flauna. *Choice D* is incorrect. While the sentence partially explains what "flauna" is and includes the titles of two Ching paintings, it doesn't provide a full explanation of Ching's flauna.

Reading and Writing

Module 2 — Higher Difficulty
(27 questions)

QUESTION 1

Choice B is the best answer because it most logically completes the text's discussion of Ward and colleagues' findings. As used in this context, "innocuous" means mild or unharmful. The text describes the vibration and warming that Ward and colleagues used to alleviate itching as "harmless applications" and goes on to contrast these applications with another stimulus that actually offers more relief even though it seems to be stronger and "less benign." This context conveys the idea that vibration and warming were innocuous stimuli.

Choice A is incorrect because the text focuses on a distinction between harmless stimuli and those that seem to be less benign. Nothing in the text suggests that any of the treatments are "deceptive," or misleading; indeed, even the less effective ones are described as offering some relief. *Choice C* is incorrect because the text focuses on the amount of relief from itching offered by harmless stimuli and those that seem to be less benign. The text doesn't suggest that any of these stimuli are "novel," or original and new; heat, vibration, and electricity aren't new inventions. *Choice D* is incorrect because it wouldn't make sense to describe an application of vibration or warming as "impractical," or not suitable for use. The text indicates that these harmless applications are useful in that they offer at least some temporary relief.

QUESTION 2

Choice B is the best answer because it most logically and precisely completes the text's discussion of studies of altitude's effect on blood chemistry. In this context, "paucity of" means lack of. In describing the inspiration behind Al-Sweedan and Alhaj's research, the text uses the word "though" to suggest a contrasting relationship between two types of studies: those examining the effect on blood chemistry of living at a high altitude and those examining the effect on blood chemistry of living in locations below sea level. This contrasting relationship and the text's use of the word "many" provide context suggesting that there are few, if any, examples of the second type of study, whereas there are numerous examples of the first type.

Choice A is incorrect because it wouldn't make sense in context for there to be a "quarrel about," or open disagreement about, studies of the effect on blood chemistry of living in locations below sea level. The text's use of the words "though" and "many" suggests a contrasting relationship in terms of amount between two types of studies: those examining the effect on blood chemistry of living at a high altitude and those examining the effect on blood chemistry of living in locations below sea level. There's nothing in the text to suggest that the contrast between the two types of studies involves the extent to which researchers broadly agree or disagree about the contents of either type. *Choice C* is incorrect because it wouldn't make sense in context for there to be a "profusion of," or great abundance of, studies of the effect on blood chemistry of living in locations below sea level. The text's use of the words "though" and "many" suggests a contrasting relationship in terms of amount between two types of studies: those examining the effect on blood chemistry of living at a high altitude and those examining the effect on blood chemistry of living in locations below sea level. Rather than logically completing this contrast, "profusion of" would indicate that the two types of studies are similar in terms of amount, with many examples existing of both types. *Choice D* is incorrect because it wouldn't make sense in context for there to be a "verisimilitude in," or appearance of truth in, studies of the effect on blood chemistry of living in locations below sea level. The text's use of the words "though" and "many" suggests a contrasting relationship in terms of amount between two types of studies: those examining the effect on blood chemistry of living at a high altitude and those examining the effect on blood chemistry of living in locations below sea level. There's nothing in the text to suggest that the contrast between the two types of studies involves the extent to which either type of study presents an appearance of truth.

QUESTION 3

Choice C is the best answer because it most logically completes the text's discussion of the legitimacy of the reigns of French monarchs such as Hugh Capet and Henry I. As used in this context, "buttress" means to strengthen or defend. The text indicates that regardless of whether a French monarch's reign was significant or uneventful, each monarch faced questions about his right to the throne. The text goes on to say that in order to understand the path of a French monarch's reign, it's important to understand what contributed to the monarch's ability to "hold the throne." This context suggests that French monarchs such as Hugh Capet and Henry I had to buttress, or defend, their right to be monarch.

Choice A is incorrect because it wouldn't make sense in context to discuss factors that enabled a monarch to "disengage," or withdraw his right to the French throne. The text focuses on an examination of people who reigned as French monarchs, not on people who didn't choose to rule. *Choice B* is incorrect because it wouldn't make sense in context to discuss factors that enabled a monarch to "annotate," or add notes to or explain, his right to the French throne. Nothing in the text suggests that the monarchs were writing notes about their right to the throne; instead, faced with questions about the legitimacy of their reign, the monarchs defended their right. *Choice D* is incorrect. Saying that a monarch who is faced with questions about the legitimacy of his reign was able to "reciprocate" his right to the French throne would mean that he either returned his right to the throne or that he responded in kind to the challenge. Neither of these meanings would make sense in context because the text focuses on people who did reign as French monarchs and defended their right to do so.

QUESTION 4

Choice C is the best answer because it most logically completes the text's discussion of Jung and her team's study of acts of kindness. In this context, "foster" means encourage or promote the development of. The text indicates that Jung and her team found that seeing a helpful (or prosocial) act makes a bystander more likely to help someone else, which can in turn inspire additional people to help others. That is, the team showed that single acts of kindness can foster additional prosocial acts across a group.

Choice A is incorrect because nothing in the text suggests that Jung and her team found that single acts of kindness "require," or depend on or make obligatory, broader prosocial (or helpful) behavior across a group. There's no suggestion in the text that individual acts of kindness can only occur if other prosocial acts have already occurred, and the text indicates only that an act of kindness can inspire additional helpful acts, not that it necessarily will do so. *Choice B* is incorrect because the text focuses on a possible direct effect of individual acts of kindness, or single helpful actions, and it wouldn't make sense to suggest that actions can "remember," or hold a memory of, something. *Choice D* is incorrect because the text doesn't indicate that Jung and her team found that single acts of kindness can "discourage," or hinder, prosocial (or helpful) behavior across a group. On the contrary, the text states that Jung and her team found that seeing a helpful act makes a bystander more likely to help someone else, which can in turn inspire even more people to help others.

QUESTION 5

Choice D is the best answer because it best describes the function of the underlined sentence in the text's overall portrayal of how the women in Ohiyesa's tribe harvested maple syrup. The text states that the women used an axe to strike the maple trees in order to find out which ones would produce sap. The underlined sentence compares the trees to people, with the sap described as the trees' "life-blood." Some of the trees are ready to give out their sap, while others are unwilling to do so. Using personification, the sentence provides greater detail about the aspect of the maple trees—their potential to give sap—that the women are evaluating.

Choice A is incorrect because the personalities of the women are not discussed in the text. Although the underlined sentence does mention "individual characters," this reference is not to the women in the text but rather to the maple trees, which the sentence compares to people with individual character traits. *Choice B* is incorrect because the underlined sentence focuses on the trees' willingness or refusal to yield sap, not on the beneficial relationship between the women and the trees. Additionally, although the text does suggest that the women and their tribe benefit from the maple trees since the trees allow the women to harvest syrup, there is nothing in the text to suggest that the trees benefit from this relationship in turn. *Choice C* is incorrect because the underlined sentence is comparing maple trees to humans, not addressing the influence of the natural environment on how the actual humans in the text, the women, behave.

QUESTION 6

Choice A is the best answer because it most accurately describes the main purpose of the text, which is to show that while Jane calmly goes about her daily tasks, she is experiencing internal agitation about possibly seeking a new job. At the start of the text, Jane says, "I went on with my day's business tranquilly," indicating that she is outwardly calm. This outward calmness is then contrasted with her intense internal restlessness, as Jane says that thoughts of leaving her job keep running through her mind, that she is "involuntarily framing advertisements" (meaning that she can't stop herself from thinking up potential listings for jobs), and that she often wonders what new "situations" (or jobs) would be like.

Choice B is incorrect because the text gives no indication of Jane's feelings, either positive or negative, about the people she works for at Thornfield Hall. And rather than emphasizing that Jane feels particularly loyal to her employers, the text focuses on her constant consideration of leaving her job. *Choice C* is incorrect because the text gives no indication that Jane finds her current situation fulfilling, or satisfying. Given that much of the text is focused on Jane's thoughts about possibly leaving her job for a new one, it might be the case that she finds her situation challenging, but there is no evidence in the text that Jane also finds that situation satisfying—she says nothing positive about her current job at all, in fact. *Choice D* is incorrect because the text describes Jane as wondering about getting a new job, not as determined to definitely do so. Jane keeps thinking about reasons why she "should" quit her current job (indicating that she hasn't yet decided to) and imagining possible new situations she could find, but she says at the end of the text that these thoughts "might germinate and bear fruit if they could," meaning that the thoughts haven't yet led to a decision—that Jane isn't yet determined to get a new job somewhere else.

QUESTION 7

Choice A is the best answer because it accurately describes the organization of the elements within the text. The text begins with the claim that Joni Mitchell's album covers use images she creates in order to emphasize ideas embedded in her albums. It then goes on to provide an example of how Mitchell's self-portrait on the cover of *Turbulent Indigo* resembles a painting by Van Gogh, which the text indicates helps emphasize the strong connection Mitchell feels toward Van Gogh, a connection that is also expressed in the album's title song.

Choice B is incorrect because there are no references in the text to artists other than Joni Mitchell and Van Gogh. *Choice C* is incorrect because there is nothing in the text that calls attention to any similarities or differences between Joni Mitchell and Van Gogh. Instead, it mentions that Mitchell feels a strong "artistic connection" to Van Gogh. *Choice D* is incorrect because the text discusses the cover before referring to any songs, and it only references one song from the album not all the songs.

QUESTION 8

Choice C is the best answer because it best describes how the underlined sentence functions in the text as a whole. The first sentence presents the implications of Veeraraghavan's team's study: sunshine exposure during work hours can cause overly optimistic behavior. The underlined sentence then describes the data the team consulted and how they were used (comparing predictions about earnings to what the companies actually earned), and the final sentence presents what the team found in their examination of the data. Thus, the underlined sentence mainly functions to explain part of the methodology used in the team's study.

Choice A is incorrect because the underlined sentence explains in part how the team conducted their analysis of the effect of sunshine but doesn't address what the team found; a broad summary is instead given in the other two sentences. *Choice B* is incorrect because the underlined sentence doesn't present any specific examples from the team's comparisons of 29,000 earnings predictions to actual earnings; it simply explains in part how the team conducted their analysis. *Choice D* is incorrect because the underlined sentence simply explains in part how the team conducted their analysis; the text never mentions any challenges that the team encountered in their study.

QUESTION 9

Choice B is the best answer because it reflects how the author of Text 2 would most likely respond to Text 1 based on the information provided. Text 1 discusses the discovery of a regeneration-linked gene, EGR, in both three-banded panther worms (which are capable of full regeneration) and humans (who have relatively limited regeneration abilities). Text 1 characterizes this discovery as "especially promising" and a sign of "exciting progress" in understanding human regeneration. The author of Text 2, on the other hand, focuses on the fact that the team that reported the EGR finding pointed out that while EGR's function in humans isn't yet known, it's likely very different from its function in panther worms. Therefore, the author of Text 2 would most likely say that Text 1's enthusiasm about the EGR discovery is overly optimistic given Srivastava's team's observations about EGR in humans.

Choice A is incorrect because the author of Text 2 explains that Srivastava and her team explicitly reported that they haven't yet identified how EGR functions in humans; therefore, the author of Text 2 wouldn't say that Text 1's excitement is reasonable for the stated reason. Instead, the author of Text 2 would likely characterize Text 1's excitement as premature and overly optimistic. *Choice C* is incorrect because Text 1 does treat Srivastava's team's findings with enthusiasm; it describes the discovery of EGR in both three-banded panther worms and humans as promising and exciting. It would be illogical for the author of Text 2 to say that because most others treat the discovery with enthusiasm, Text 1's enthusiastic characterization of the discovery is unexpected. *Choice D* is incorrect because Text 1 isn't at all dismissive of Srivastava's team's findings; instead, Text 1 is optimistic about the EGR discovery, characterizing it as promising and exciting. There's nothing in Text 2 to suggest that the author of Text 2 would say that Text 1's praise for the discovery is dismissive, or disdainful.

QUESTION 10

Choice C is the best answer because it uses data from the table to effectively exemplify the idea that the film outputs of the four individuals included in the table should be considered bare minimums—that is, that we should assume that the individuals actually had higher outputs than those recorded. The table presents the years during which the individuals were active and the number of known films the individuals are credited in. The table indicates that Lillian St. Cyr has 66 film credits as an actor and that Edwin Carewe has 58 film credits as a director; it follows that if some films and records for the era were lost, it's possible that Lillian St. Cyr acted in far more than 66 films and that Edwin Carewe directed more than 58 films.

Choice A is incorrect because it doesn't effectively exemplify the idea that the film outputs of the four individuals included in the table should be considered bare minimums. Rather than addressing the idea that the individuals likely had higher outputs than those presented in the table, this choice simply compares data from the table to make the point that Dark Cloud has fewer credited acting roles than Lillian St. Cyr (35 and 66, respectively). *Choice B* is incorrect because it misrepresents data from the table, even though it may exemplify the idea that the film outputs of the four individuals included in the table should be considered bare minimums by implying that Edwin Carewe acted in more than 47 films. The table indicates that Edwin Carewe was active from 1912 to 1934, meaning that his 47 credited acting roles were in films made before or during 1934, not after that time. *Choice D* is incorrect because it doesn't effectively exemplify the idea that the film outputs of the four individuals included in the table should be considered bare minimums. Instead of addressing the idea that the individuals likely had higher outputs than those recorded, this choice suggests that James Young Deer actually acted in and directed fewer films than presented in the table (only 33 known films as a director instead of 35, and only 10 known films as an actor instead of 33).

QUESTION 11

Choice C is the best answer because it presents the finding that, if true, would best support Suarez, Pérez-Huerta, and Harrell's claim about mosasaurs. The text states that Suarez, Pérez-Huerta, and Harrell's research on mosasaur tooth enamel led them to conclude that mosasaurs were endothermic, which means that they could live in waters at many different temperatures and still maintain a stable body temperature. The researchers claim that endothermy enabled mosasaurs to live in relatively cold waters near the poles. If several mosasaur fossils have been found in areas that were near the poles during the period when mosasaurs were alive and fossils of nonendothermic marine reptiles are rare in such locations, that would support the researchers' claim: it would show that mosasaurs inhabited polar waters but nonendothermic marine mammals tended not to, suggesting that endothermy may have been the characteristic that enabled mosasaurs to include polar waters in their range.

Choice A is incorrect because finding that it's easier to determine mosasaur body temperatures from tooth enamel data than it is to determine nonendothermic reptile body temperatures wouldn't support the researchers' claim. Whether one research process is more difficult than another indicates nothing about the results of those processes and therefore is irrelevant to the issue of where mosasaurs lived and what enabled them to live in those locations. *Choice B* is incorrect because finding roughly equal numbers of mosasaur and nonendothermic marine reptile fossils in areas that were near the poles in the Late Cretaceous would suggest that endothermy didn't give mosasaurs any particular advantage when it came to expanding their range to include relatively cold polar waters, thereby weakening the researchers' claim rather than supporting it. *Choice D* is incorrect because finding that the temperature of seawater in the Late Cretaceous was warmer than seawater today wouldn't weaken the researchers' claim. Seawater in the Late Cretaceous could have been warmer than seawater today but still cold enough for endothermy to be advantageous to mosasaurs, so this finding wouldn't provide enough information to either support or weaken the researchers' claim.

QUESTION 12

Choice D is the best answer because it describes data from the graph that support the researchers' conclusion that there is a growing interest among CEOs in connecting with more departments in their companies. The graph shows the average number of individuals reporting directly to CEOs during three different time periods: the individuals are divided into managers and department leaders. The average number of department leaders directly reporting to their CEO during the 1991–1995 period was slightly more than three, during the 1996–2001 period it was four, and during the 2001–2008 period it was almost seven. Thus, the average number of department leaders reporting directly to their CEO rose over the three periods studied, which suggests that CEOs were connecting with more departments.

Choice A is incorrect because the average number of managers and department leaders reporting directly to their CEO rose for both categories between the 1991–1995 and 2001–2008 periods; thus, it isn't true that the average numbers didn't fluctuate. *Choice B* is incorrect because the average number of managers reporting directly to their CEO was highest in the 2001–2008 period, not in the 1996–2001 period. *Choice C* is incorrect.

Although it correctly describes a feature of the graph, the observation that more department leaders than managers are reporting to CEOs does not by itself address the question of whether CEOs are connecting with more departments over time—to address that question, one needs to know whether the number of department leaders reporting to CEOs is increasing over time.

QUESTION 13

Choice C is the best answer because it presents a finding that, if true, would weaken the astronomers' claim about the makeup of host stars and their planets. The text explains that because stars and planets begin forming from the same gas and dust, astronomers believe planets should be composed of the same materials as their host stars, but in equal or smaller quantities. The finding that the amount of iron in some rocky planets is much higher than the amount in their host star would weaken the astronomers' claim because it would show that some planets contain the same material as their host star, but in higher quantities.

Choice A is incorrect because a finding only about the makeup of stars, whether they've cooled or not, would provide no information about the makeup of planets. Thus, it wouldn't have any bearing on the claim that planets and their host stars are composed of the same materials in differing quantities. *Choice B* is incorrect because a finding about two host stars having similar proportions of certain materials wouldn't provide any information about the makeup of planets. Thus, it wouldn't be relevant to the claim that planets and their host stars are composed of the same materials in differing quantities. *Choice D* is incorrect because the text indicates that the astronomers' claim is based on a fact—that stars and planets begin forming from the same gas and dust in space—which would remain true regardless of the effectiveness of a method for analysis of compositions. The text does cite analysis of rocky planets in our solar system and the Sun, but only as a single piece of evidence that is consistent with the claim and not as the source of the claim; the finding that the method used for that analysis is less effective in other scenarios wouldn't weaken a claim that's based on knowledge of how stars and planets initially form.

QUESTION 14

Choice B is the best answer because it presents a finding that, if true, would most directly support the arts journalist's claim about Enwezor's work as a curator and art historian. In the text, the arts journalist asserts that Enwezor wished not just to focus on modern African artists but also to show "how their work fits into the larger context of global modern art and art history," or how their work relates to artistic developments and work by other artists elsewhere in the world. The description of *Postwar: Art Between the Pacific and the Atlantic, 1945–1965* indicates that Enwezor and Siegel's exhibition brought works by African artists together with works by artists from other countries, thus supporting the arts journalist's claim that Enwezor sought to show works by African artists in a context of global modern art and art history.

Choice A is incorrect because it describes a retrospective that wouldn't support the arts journalist's claim that Enwezor wanted to show how works by modern African artists fit into the larger context of global modern art and art history. The description of *El Anatsui: Triumphant Scale* indicates that the retrospective focused only on the work of a single African artist, El Anatsui. The description doesn't suggest that the exhibition showed how El Anatsui's works fit into a global artistic context. *Choice C* is incorrect because it describes an exhibition that wouldn't support the arts journalist's claim that Enwezor wanted to show how works by modern African artists relate to the larger context of global modern art and art history. The description of *The Short Century: Independence and Liberation Movements in Africa, 1945–1994* indicates that the exhibition showed how African artists were influenced by movements for independence from European colonial powers following the Second World War. Although this suggests that Enwezor intended the exhibition to place works by African artists in a political context, it doesn't indicate that the works were placed in a global artistic context. *Choice D* is incorrect because it describes an exhibition that wouldn't support the arts journalist's claim that Enwezor wanted to show how works by modern African artists relate to the larger context of global modern art and art history. The description of *In/sight: African Photographers, 1940 to the Present* indicates that the exhibition was intended to reveal the broad range of approaches taken by African photographers, not that the exhibition showed how photography by African artists fits into a global artistic context.

QUESTION 15

Choice D is the best answer because it presents the conclusion that most logically follows from the text's discussion of the challenge researchers face when studying the effects of holding elected office on a person's behavior. The text explains that it's hard for researchers to test for the effects that elected office has on people because finding people to serve as a control group is difficult. The text indicates that a control group needs to be made up of people who share characteristics of the group being tested but don't have the variable being tested (in this case, holding elected office). Because researchers aren't able to influence who wins elections, they're also unable to determine who would serve as an appropriately similar member of a control group. Thus, it logically follows that researchers will find it difficult to identify a group of people who can function as an appropriate control group for their studies.

Choice A is incorrect because the text focuses on the struggle to put together a control group for experiments; it doesn't suggest that finding information about politicians' behavior is difficult. *Choice B* is incorrect because the experiments mentioned in the text are testing the effects of holding elected office on a person's behavior. Studying people who have already held elected office wouldn't provide an opportunity to note any behavioral changes that the position might cause. *Choice C* is incorrect because the text defines people in a control group as those "who are otherwise similar to the office-holders"; selecting people who differ from the office-holders wouldn't fit the criteria for an appropriate control group.

QUESTION 16

Choice A is the best answer because it most logically completes the text. The text explains that the *Cantares Mexicanos* contains poems about the Aztec Empire from before the Spanish invasion. Furthermore, it indicates that notes in the collection attest that some of these poems predate the Spanish invasion, while some customs depicted are likely Spanish in origin. The implication is that some poems were composed before the invasion but the references to Spanish customs could have come about only after the invasion, and thus that the collection includes content that predates the invasion and also content from after the invasion.

Choice B is incorrect because the text clearly indicates that the collection is in Nahuatl, not Spanish, so the compilers' unfamiliarity with Spanish is irrelevant to whether the collection contains material composed after the Spanish invasion. *Choice C* is incorrect because the text mentions only the Aztec Empire and

Spain: there is no information about the relationship of Aztec literature to any traditions other than its own or Spain's. *Choice D* is incorrect because the text states that some of the poems make "inarguable references" to common Spanish customs, which conflicts with the idea that these references can reasonably be attributed to mere coincidence.

QUESTION 17

Choice D is the best answer. The convention being tested is the coordination of main clauses within a sentence. The semicolon is correctly used to join the first main clause ("To humans...prey") and the second main clause ("rather... approach"). Further, the comma after the adverb "rather" is correctly used to separate the adverb from the main clause ("the brightly...approach") it modifies, logically indicating that the information in this clause (how the spider's behavior appears to humans) is contrary to the information in the previous clause (how the spider's behavior does not appear to humans.)

Choice A is incorrect because it results in a comma splice. Without a conjunction following it, a comma can't be used in this way to join two main clauses. *Choice B* is incorrect because it results in a run-on sentence. The two main clauses are fused without appropriate punctuation and/or a conjunction. *Choice C* is incorrect. Placing the comma between the first main clause "To humans...prey" and the adverb "rather" illogically indicates that the information in the first main clause is contrary to what came before, which doesn't make sense in this context.

QUESTION 18

Choice D is the best answer. The convention being tested is the use of verbs to express tense in a sentence. In this choice, the past progressive tense verb "was studying" is consistent with the other past tense verbs (e.g., "made" and "collected") used to describe Buratti's discovery. Further, the past progressive tense correctly indicates that an ongoing action in the past was occurring (she was studying) at the same time that another event occurred in the past (she made an interesting discovery).

Choice A is incorrect because the present tense verb "studies" isn't consistent with the past tense verbs used to describe Buratti's discovery. *Choice B* is incorrect because the present perfect progressive tense verb "has been studying" isn't consistent with the past tense verbs used to describe Buratti's discovery. *Choice C* is incorrect because the future tense verb "will study" isn't consistent with the past tense verbs used to describe Buratti's discovery.

QUESTION 19

Choice B is the best answer. The convention being tested is punctuation use between sentences. In this choice, the period after "Bay" is used correctly to mark the boundary between one sentence ("On...Bay") and another sentence that begins with a supplementary phrase ("Having...years"). Here, the supplementary phrase beginning with "having" modifies the subject of the second sentence, "the celebrated ship."

Choice A is incorrect. Without a comma preceding it, the conjunction "and" can't be used in this way to join sentences. *Choice C* is incorrect because it results in a comma splice. A comma can't be used in this way to join two sentences. *Choice D* is incorrect because it results in a run-on sentence. The sentences ("On...Bay" and "having...years") are fused without punctuation and/or a conjunction.

QUESTION 20

Choice A is the best answer. The convention being tested is subject-verb agreement. The singular verb "has enhanced" agrees in number with the singular subject "*A Sheaf Gleaned in French Fields*," which is the title of a book of poems.

Choice B is incorrect because the plural verb "are enhancing" doesn't agree in number with the singular subject "*A Sheaf Gleaned in French Fields*." *Choice C* is incorrect because the plural verb "have enhanced" doesn't agree in number with the singular subject "*A Sheaf Gleaned in French Fields*." *Choice D* is incorrect because the plural verb "enhance" doesn't agree in number with the singular subject "*A Sheaf Gleaned in French Fields*."

QUESTION 21

Choice A is the best answer. The convention being tested is punctuation use between sentences. In this choice, the period after "tombs" is used correctly to mark the boundary between one sentence ("Archaeologist...tombs") and another ("Built...nature").

Choice B is incorrect because it results in a comma splice. A comma can't be used in this way to mark the boundary between sentences. *Choice C* is incorrect. Without a comma preceding it, the conjunction "and" can't be used in this way to join the two sentences. *Choice D* is incorrect because it results in a run-on sentence. The sentences ("Archaeologist...tombs" and "Built...nature") are fused without punctuation and/or a conjunction.

QUESTION 22

Choice C is the best answer. The conventions being tested are punctuation use between titles and proper nouns and between verbs and integrated quotations. No punctuation is needed to set off the proper noun "Stina Chyn" from the title that describes Chyn, "critic." Because "Stina Chyn" is essential information identifying the "critic," no punctuation is necessary. Further, no punctuation is needed between the verb "claims" and the following quotation because the quotation is integrated into the structure of the sentence.

Choice A is incorrect because no punctuation is needed before or after the proper noun "Stina Chyn." Setting the critic's name off with commas suggests that it could be removed without affecting the coherence of the sentence, which isn't the case. *Choice B* is incorrect because no punctuation is needed before or after the proper noun "Stina Chyn." Setting the critic's name off with commas suggests that it could be removed without affecting the coherence of the sentence, which isn't the case. Additionally, no punctuation is needed between "claims" and the integrated quotation. *Choice D* is incorrect because no punctuation is needed between the verb "claims" and its subject, "critic Stina Chyn." Additionally, no punctuation is needed between the verb "claims" and the integrated quotation.

QUESTION 23

Choice B is the best answer. The convention being tested is the punctuation of items in a complex series (a series including internal punctuation). The semicolon after "nonnative" is correctly used to separate the first item ("growing diverse plant species, both native and nonnative") and the second item ("fostering scientific research") in the series of things that botanical gardens are dedicated to. Further, the comma after "species" is correctly used to separate the noun phrase "diverse plant species" and the supplementary phrase "both native and nonnative" that modifies it.

Choice A is incorrect because a comma (specifically, the comma after "nonnative") can't be used in this way to separate items in a complex series. *Choice C* is incorrect because a semicolon can't be used in this way to separate the noun phrase "diverse plant species" and the supplementary phrase "both native and nonnative" that modifies it. Further, a comma can't be used in this way to separate items in a complex series. *Choice D* is incorrect because it fails to use appropriate punctuation to separate the noun phrase "diverse plant species" and the supplementary phrase "both native and nonnative" that modifies it. Further, a comma can't be used in this way to separate items in a complex series.

QUESTION 24

Choice C is the best answer. "However" logically signals that the information in this sentence—that Hammurabi is mainly remembered for just a single achievement, the Code of Hammurabi—is contrary to what might be assumed from the previous information about Hammurabi's many achievements.

Choice A is incorrect because "therefore" illogically signals that the information in this sentence is a result of the previous information about Hammurabi's many achievements. Instead, this sentence makes a point that is contrary to what might be assumed from the previous information. *Choice B* is incorrect because "likewise" illogically signals that the information in this sentence is similar to the previous information about Hammurabi's many achievements. Instead, this sentence makes a point that is contrary to what might be assumed from the previous information. *Choice D* is incorrect because "for instance" illogically signals that this sentence exemplifies the previous information about Hammurabi's many achievements. Instead, this sentence makes a point that is contrary to what might be assumed from the previous information.

QUESTION 25

Choice D is the best answer. "Similarly" logically signals that the information in the sentence—that Dove situates Beulah's life in the context of the US Civil Rights Movement—is similar to the previous information about Thomas and the Great Migration. Both sentences support the first sentence's claim that Dove portrays her characters in the context of broader historical narratives.

Choice A is incorrect because "specifically" illogically signals that the information about Beulah in this sentence provides specific details elaborating on the previous information about Thomas. Instead, it's similar to the previous information about Thomas. *Choice B* is incorrect because "thus" illogically signals that the information about Beulah in this sentence is a result or consequence of the previous information about Thomas. Instead, it's similar to the previous information about Thomas. *Choice C* is incorrect because "regardless" illogically signals that the information about Beulah in this sentence is true despite the previous information about Thomas. Instead, it's similar to the previous information about Thomas.

QUESTION 26

Choice A is the best answer. "Nevertheless" logically signals that the information in this sentence—that the spacesuits Suttirat Larlarb designed for the film *Sunshine* were made in standard sizes in a factory—presents a notable exception to Larlarb's typical approach of custom-fitting garments to actors, which is described in the previous sentence.

Choice B is incorrect because "thus" illogically signals that the information in this sentence is a result or consequence of the previous information about Larlarb's typical approach of custom-fitting garments to actors. Instead, it presents a notable exception to Larlarb's typical approach. *Choice C* is incorrect because "likewise" illogically signals that the information in this sentence is similar to the previous information about Larlarb's typical approach of custom-fitting garments to actors. Instead, it presents a notable exception to Larlarb's typical approach. *Choice D* is incorrect because "moreover" illogically signals that the information in this sentence merely adds to the previous information about Larlarb's typical approach of custom-fitting garments to actors. Instead, it presents a notable exception to Larlarb's typical approach.

QUESTION 27

Choice D is the best answer. The sentence makes a generalization—that a comet's orbit around the Sun may change over time—and supports the generalization with the example of the orbit of comet 81P/Wild, which once lay between the orbits of Uranus and Jupiter but is now positioned between the orbits of Jupiter and Mars.

Choice A is incorrect. The sentence emphasizes the number of comets orbiting the Sun and makes a generalization about their orbits, but it doesn't support the generalization with an example. *Choice B* is incorrect. The sentence makes a generalization about comets and compares them to the planets Uranus, Jupiter, and Mars; it doesn't make and support a generalization about comets' orbits. *Choice C* is incorrect. While the sentence provides an example of a comet whose orbit has changed, it doesn't make a generalization about the orbits of comets.

Math

Module 1
(22 questions)

QUESTION 1

Choice C is correct. It's given that $x = 7$. Substituting 7 for x into the given expression $x + 20$ yields $7 + 20$, which is equivalent to 27.

Choice A is incorrect. This is the value of $x + 6$. *Choice B* is incorrect. This is the value of $x + 13$. *Choice D* is incorrect. This is the value of $x + 27$.

QUESTION 2

Choice B is correct. The mean of a data set is the sum of the values in the data set divided by the number of values in the data set. It follows that the mean of data set X is $\frac{5 + 9 + 9 + 13}{4}$, or 9, and the mean of data set Y is $\frac{5 + 9 + 9 + 13 + 27}{5}$, or 12.6. Since 9 is less than 12.6, the mean of data set X is less than the mean of data set Y.

Alternate approach: Data set Y consists of the 4 values in data set X and one additional value, 27. Since the additional value, 27, is larger than any value in data set X, the mean of data set X is less than the mean of data set Y.

Choice A is incorrect and may result from conceptual or calculation errors. *Choice C* is incorrect and may result from conceptual or calculation errors. *Choice D* is incorrect and may result from conceptual or calculation errors.

QUESTION 3

Choice B is correct. In similar triangles, corresponding angles are congruent. It's given that right triangles *PQR* and *STU* are similar, where angle *P* corresponds to angle *S*. It follows that angle *P* is congruent to angle *S*. In the triangles shown, angle *R* and angle *U* are both marked as right angles, so angle *R* and angle *U* are corresponding angles. It follows that angle *Q* and angle *T* are corresponding angles, and thus, angle *Q* is congruent to angle *T*. It's given that the measure of angle *Q* is 18°, so the measure of angle *T* is also 18°. Angle *U* is a right angle, so the measure of angle *U* is 90°. The sum of the measures of the interior angles of a triangle is 180°. Thus, the sum of the measures of the interior angles of triangle *STU* is 180 degrees. Let *s* represent the measure, in degrees, of angle *S*. It follows that $s + 18 + 90 = 180$, or $s + 108 = 180$. Subtracting 108 from both sides of this equation yields $s = 72$. Therefore, if the measure of angle *Q* is 18 degrees, then the measure of angle *S* is 72 degrees.

Choice A is incorrect. This is the measure of angle *T*. *Choice C* is incorrect and may result from conceptual or calculation errors. *Choice D* is incorrect. This is the sum of the measures of angle *S* and angle *U*.

QUESTION 4

Choice A is correct. It's given that the rocket contained 467,000 kilograms (kg) of propellant before launch and had 362,105 kg remaining exactly 21 seconds after launch. Finding the difference between the amount, in kg, of propellant before launch and the remaining amount, in kg, of propellant after launch gives the amount, in kg, of propellant burned during the 21 seconds: 467,000 − 362,105 = 104,895. Dividing the amount of propellant burned by the number of seconds yields $\frac{104,895}{21}$ = 4,995. Thus, an average of 4,995 kg of propellant burned each second after launch.

Choice B is incorrect and may result from conceptual or calculation errors. *Choice C* is incorrect and may result from conceptual or calculation errors. *Choice D* is incorrect and may result from finding the amount of propellant burned, rather than the amount of propellant burned each second.

QUESTION 5

Choice C is correct. It's given that $4x = 20$ and $-3x + y = -7$ is a system of equations with a solution (x, y). Adding the second equation in the given system to the first equation yields $4x + (-3x + y) = 20 + (-7)$, which is equivalent to $x + y = 13$. Thus, the value of $x + y$ is 13.

Choice A is incorrect. This represents the value of $-2(x + y) - 1$. *Choice B* is incorrect. This represents the value of $-(x + y)$. *Choice D* is incorrect. This represents the value of $2(x + y) + 1$.

QUESTION 6

The correct answer is 5. It's given that the equation $10x + 15y = 85$ represents the situation, where x is the number of on-site training courses, y is the number of online training courses, and 85 is the total number of hours of training courses the apprentice has enrolled in. Therefore, $10x$ represents the number of hours the apprentice has enrolled in on-site training courses, and $15y$ represents the number of hours the apprentice has enrolled in online training courses. Since x is the number of on-site training courses and y is the number of online training courses the apprentice has enrolled in, 10 is the number of hours each on-site course takes and 15 is the number of hours each online course takes. Subtracting these numbers gives 15 − 10, or 5 more hours each online training course takes than each on-site training course.

QUESTION 7

Choice D is correct. The perimeter, P, of a square can be found using the formula $P = 4s$, where s is the length of each side of the square. It's given that square X has a side length of 12 centimeters. Substituting 12 for s in the formula for the perimeter of a square yields $P = 4(12)$, or $P = 48$. Therefore, the perimeter of square X is 48 centimeters. It's also given that the perimeter of square Y is 2 times the perimeter of square X. Therefore, the perimeter of square Y is 2(48), or 96, centimeters. Substituting 96 for P in the formula $P = 4s$ gives $96 = 4s$. Dividing both sides of this equation by 4 gives $24 = s$. Therefore, the length of one side of square Y is 24 centimeters.

Choice A is incorrect and may result from conceptual or calculation errors.
Choice B is incorrect and may result from conceptual or calculation errors.
Choice C is incorrect and may result from conceptual or calculation errors.

QUESTION 8

Choice A is correct. It's given that the function g models the number of gallons that remain from a full gas tank in a car after driving m miles. In the given function $g(m) = -0.05m + 12.1$, the coefficient of m is -0.05. This means that for every increase in the value of m by 1, the value of $g(m)$ decreases by 0.05. It follows that for each mile driven, there is a decrease of 0.05 gallons of gasoline. Therefore, 0.05 gallons of gasoline are used to drive each mile.

Choice B is incorrect and represents the number of gallons of gasoline in a full gas tank. *Choice C* is incorrect and may result from conceptual errors. *Choice D* is incorrect and may result from conceptual errors.

QUESTION 9

The correct answer is 28. The given absolute value equation can be rewritten as two linear equations: $4x - 4 = 112$ and $-(4x - 4) = 112$, or $4x - 4 = -112$. Adding 4 to both sides of the equation $4x - 4 = 112$ results in $4x = 116$. Dividing both sides of this equation by 4 results in $x = 29$. Adding 4 to both sides of the equation $4x - 4 = -112$ results in $4x = -108$. Dividing both sides of this equation by 4 results in $x = -27$. Therefore, the two values of $x - 1$ are $29 - 1$, or 28, and $-27 - 1$, or -28. Thus, the positive value of $x - 1$ is 28.

Alternate approach: The given equation can be rewritten as $|4(x - 1)| = 112$, which is equivalent to $4|x - 1| = 112$. Dividing both sides of this equation by 4 yields $|x - 1| = 28$. This equation can be rewritten as two linear equations: $x - 1 = 28$ and $-(x - 1) = 28$, or $x - 1 = -28$. Therefore, the positive value of $x - 1$ is 28.

QUESTION 10

Choice C is correct. Multiplying each side of the given equation by y yields the equivalent equation $\frac{y}{7b} = 11x$. Dividing each side of this equation by 11 yields $\frac{y}{77b} = x$, or $x = \frac{y}{77b}$.

Choice A is incorrect. This equation is not equivalent to the given equation. *Choice B* is incorrect. This equation is not equivalent to the given equation. *Choice D* is incorrect. This equation is not equivalent to the given equation.

QUESTION 11

The correct answer is 11. It's given that $f(x)$ is defined by the equation $f(x) = mx - 28$, where m is a constant. It's also given in the table that when $x = 10$, $f(x) = 82$. Substituting 10 for x and 82 for $f(x)$ in the equation $f(x) = mx - 28$ yields $82 = m(10) - 28$. Adding 28 to both sides of this equation yields $110 = 10m$. Dividing both sides of this equation by 10 yields $11 = m$. Therefore, the value of m is 11.

QUESTION 12

The correct answer is 9. The given expression can be rewritten as $(5x^3 - 3) + (-1)(-4x^3 + 8)$. By applying the distributive property, this expression can be rewritten as $5x^3 - 3 + 4x^3 + (-8)$, which is equivalent to $(5x^3 + 4x^3) + (-3 + (-8))$. Adding like terms in this expression yields $9x^3 - 11$.

Since it's given that $(5x^3 - 3) - (-4x^3 + 8)$ is equivalent to $bx^3 - 11$, it follows that $9x^3 - 11$ is equivalent to $bx^3 - 11$. Therefore, the coefficients of x^3 in these two expressions must be equivalent, and the value of b must be 9.

QUESTION 13

Choice A is correct. It's given that the point $(x, 53)$ is a solution to the given system of inequalities in the xy-plane. This means that the coordinates of the point, when substituted for the variables x and y, make both of the inequalities in the system true. Substituting 53 for y in the inequality $y > 14$ yields $53 > 14$, which is true. Substituting 53 for y in the inequality $4x + y < 18$ yields $4x + 53 < 18$. Subtracting 53 from both sides of this inequality yields $4x < -35$. Dividing both sides of this inequality by 4 yields $x < -8.75$. Therefore, x must be a value less than -8.75. Of the given choices, only -9 is less than -8.75.

Choice B is incorrect. Substituting -5 for x and 53 for y in the inequality $4x + y < 18$ yields $4(-5) + 53 < 18$, or $33 < 18$, which is not true. *Choice C* is incorrect. Substituting 5 for x and 53 for y in the inequality $4x + y < 18$ yields $4(5) + 53 < 18$, or $73 < 18$, which is not true. *Choice D* is incorrect. Substituting 9 for x and 53 for y in the inequality $4x + y < 18$ yields $4(9) + 53 < 18$, or $89 < 18$, which is not true.

QUESTION 14

Choice D is correct. Let y represent the number of cells per milliliter x hours after the initial observation. Since the number of cells per milliliter doubles every 3 hours, the relationship between x and y can be represented by an exponential equation of the form $y = a(b)^{\frac{x}{k}}$, where a is the number of cells per milliliter during the initial observation and the number of cells per milliliter increases by a factor of b every k hours. It's given that there were 300,000 cells per milliliter during the initial observation. Therefore, $a = 300{,}000$. It's also given that the number of cells per milliliter doubles, or increases by a factor of 2, every 3 hours. Therefore, $b = 2$ and $k = 3$. Substituting 300,000 for a, 2 for b, and 3 for k in the equation $y = a(b)^{\frac{x}{k}}$ yields $y = 300{,}000(2)^{\frac{x}{3}}$. The number of cells per milliliter there will be 15 hours after the initial observation is the value of y in this equation when $x = 15$. Substituting 15 for x in the equation $y = 300{,}000(2)^{\frac{x}{3}}$ yields $y = 300{,}000(2)^{\frac{15}{3}}$, or $y = 300{,}000(2)^5$. This is equivalent to $y = 300{,}000(32)$, or $y = 9{,}600{,}000$. Therefore, 15 hours after the initial observation, there will be 9,600,000 cells per milliliter.

Choice A is incorrect and may result from conceptual or calculation errors. *Choice B* is incorrect and may result from conceptual or calculation errors. *Choice C* is incorrect and may result from conceptual or calculation errors.

QUESTION 15

Choice D is correct. The y-intercept of the graph is the point at which the graph crosses the y-axis, or the point for which the value of x is 0. Therefore, the y-intercept of the given graph is the point $(0, 9)$. It's given that x represents the number of years since the end of 1992. Therefore, $x = 0$ represents 0 years since the end of 1992, which is the same as the end of 1992. It's also given that y represents the estimated number of catalogs, in thousands, that the company sent to its customers at the end of the year. Therefore, $y = 9$ represents 9,000 catalogs. It follows that the y-intercept $(0, 9)$ means that the estimated number of catalogs the company sent to its customers at the end of 1992 was 9,000.

Choice A is incorrect and may result from conceptual or calculation errors.
Choice B is incorrect and may result from conceptual or calculation errors.
Choice C is incorrect and may result from conceptual or calculation errors.

QUESTION 16

Choice B is correct. For positive values of a and b, $a^m b^m = (ab)^m$, $\sqrt[n]{a} = (a)^{\frac{1}{n}}$, and $(a^j)^k = a^{jk}$. Therefore, the given expression, $\sqrt[7]{x^9 y^9}$, can be rewritten as $\sqrt[7]{(xy)^9}$. This expression is equivalent to $\left((xy)^9\right)^{\frac{1}{7}}$, which can be rewritten as $(xy)^{9 \cdot \frac{1}{7}}$, or $(xy)^{\frac{9}{7}}$.

Choice A is incorrect and may result from conceptual or calculation errors.
Choice C is incorrect and may result from conceptual or calculation errors.
Choice D is incorrect and may result from conceptual or calculation errors.

QUESTION 17

Choice C is correct. It's given that the population of City A increased by 7% from 2015 to 2016. Therefore, the population of City A in 2016 includes 100% of the population of City A in 2015 plus an additional 7% of the population of City A in 2015. This means that the population of City A in 2016 is 107% of the population in 2015. Thus, the population of City A in 2016 is $\frac{107}{100}$, or 1.07, times the 2015 population. Therefore, the value of k is 1.07.

Choice A is incorrect. This would be the value of k if the population in 2016 was 7% of the population in 2015. *Choice B* is incorrect. This would be the value of k if the population in 2016 was 70% of the population in 2015. *Choice D* is incorrect. This would be the value of k if the population increased by 70%, not 7%, from 2015 to 2016.

QUESTION 18

Choice C is correct. A system of two linear equations in two variables, x and y, has no solution if the graphs of the lines represented by the equations in the xy-plane are distinct and parallel. The graphs of two lines in the xy-plane represented by equations in slope-intercept form, $y = mx + b$, where m and b are constants, are parallel if their slopes, m, are the same and are distinct if their y-coordinates of the y-intercepts, b, are different. In the equations $y = 16x + 3$ and $y = 16x + 19$, the values of m are each 16, and the values of b are 3 and 19, respectively. Since the slopes of these lines are the same, and the y-coordinates of the y-intercepts are different, it follows that the system of linear equations in choice C has no solution.

Choice A is incorrect. The lines represented by the equations in this system are a vertical line and a horizontal line. Therefore, this system has a solution, (3, 5), rather than no solution. *Choice B* is incorrect. The two lines represented by these equations have different slopes and the same y-coordinate of the y-intercept. Therefore, this system has a solution, (0, 6), rather than no solution. *Choice D* is incorrect. The two lines represented by these equations are a horizontal line and a line with a slope of 5 that have the same y-coordinate of the y-intercept. Therefore, this system has a solution, (0, 5), rather than no solution.

QUESTION 19

Choice D is correct. Since w represents the nth term of the sequence and 9 is the first term of the sequence, the value of w is 9 when the value of n is 1. Since each term after the first is 4 times the preceding term, the value of w is 9(4) when the value of n is 2. Therefore, the value of w is 9(4)(4), or $9(4)^2$, when the value of n is 3. More generally, the value of w is $9(4^{n-1})$ for a given value of n. Therefore, the equation $w = 9(4^{n-1})$ gives w in terms of n.

Choice A is incorrect. This equation describes a sequence for which the first term is 36, rather than 9, and each term after the first is 9, rather than 4, times the preceding term. *Choice B* is incorrect. This equation describes a sequence for which the first term is 4, rather than 9, and each term after the first is 9, rather than 4, times the preceding term. *Choice C* is incorrect. This equation describes a sequence for which the first term is 36, rather than 9.

QUESTION 20

Choice B is correct. It's given that the minimum value of x is 12 less than 6 times another number n. Therefore, the possible values of x are all greater than or equal to the value of 12 less than 6 times n. The value of 6 times n is given by the expression $6n$. The value of 12 less than $6n$ is given by the expression $6n - 12$. Therefore, the possible values of x are all greater than or equal to $6n - 12$. This can be shown by the inequality $x \geq 6n - 12$.

Choice A is incorrect. This inequality shows the possible values of x if the maximum, not the minimum, value of x is 12 less than 6 times n. *Choice C* is incorrect. This inequality shows the possible values of x if the maximum, not the minimum, value of x is 6 times n less than 12, not 12 less than 6 times n. *Choice D* is incorrect. This inequality shows the possible values of x if the minimum value of x is 6 times n less than 12, not 12 less than 6 times n.

QUESTION 21

Choice B is correct. It's given that right triangle RST is similar to triangle UVW, where S corresponds to V and T corresponds to W. It's given that the side lengths of the right triangle RST are $RS = 20$, $ST = 48$, and $TR = 52$. Corresponding angles in similar triangles are equal. It follows that the measure of angle T is equal to the measure of angle W. The hypotenuse of a right triangle is the longest side. It follows that the hypotenuse of triangle RST is side TR. The hypotenuse of a right triangle is the side opposite the right angle. Therefore, angle S is a right angle. The adjacent side of an acute angle in a right triangle is the side closest to the angle that is not the hypotenuse. It follows that the adjacent side of angle T is side ST. The opposite side of an acute angle in a right triangle is the side across from the acute angle. It follows that the opposite side of angle T is side RS. The tangent of an acute angle in a right triangle is the ratio of the length of the opposite side to the length of the adjacent side. Therefore, $\tan T = \frac{RS}{ST}$. Substituting 20 for RS and 48 for ST in this equation yields $\tan T = \frac{20}{48}$, or $\tan T = \frac{5}{12}$. The tangents of two acute angles with equal measures are equal. Since the measure of angle T is equal to the measure of angle W, it follows that $\tan T = \tan W$. Substituting $\frac{5}{12}$ for $\tan T$ in this equation yields $\frac{5}{12} = \tan W$. Therefore, the value of $\tan W$ is $\frac{5}{12}$.

Choice A is incorrect. This is the value of $\sin W$. *Choice C* is incorrect. This is the value of $\cos W$. *Choice D* is incorrect. This is the value of $\frac{1}{\tan W}$.

QUESTION 22

The correct answer is $\frac{59}{9}$. When the graph of an equation in the form

$Ax + By = C$, where A, B, and C are constants, is translated down k units in the xy-plane, the resulting graph can be represented by the equation $Ax + B(y + k) = C$. It's given that the graph of $9x - 10y = 19$ is translated down 4 units in the xy-plane. Therefore, the resulting graph can be represented by the equation $9x - 10(y + 4) = 19$, or $9x - 10y - 40 = 19$. Adding 40 to both sides of this equation yields $9x - 10y = 59$. The x-coordinate of the x-intercept of the graph of an equation in the xy-plane is the value of x in the equation when $y = 0$. Substituting 0 for y in the equation $9x - 10y = 59$ yields $9x - 10(0) = 59$,

or $9x = 59$. Dividing both sides of this equation by 9 yields $x = \frac{59}{9}$. Therefore,

the x-coordinate of the x-intercept of the resulting graph is $\frac{59}{9}$. Note that 59/9,

6.555, and 6.556 are examples of ways to enter a correct answer.

Math

Module 2 — Lower Difficulty
(22 questions)

QUESTION 1

Choice B is correct. Dividing both sides of the given equation 7x = 28 by 7 yields x = 4. Substituting 4 for x in the expression 8x yields 8(4), which is equivalent to 32.

Choice A is incorrect. This is the value of $\frac{21}{4}x$. *Choice C* is incorrect. This is the value of 42x. *Choice D* is incorrect. This is the value of 56x.

QUESTION 2

Choice B is correct. The number of harvested potatoes Isabel saved to plant next year can be calculated by multiplying the total number of potatoes Isabel harvested, 760, by the proportion of potatoes she saved. Since she saved 10% of the potatoes she harvested, the proportion of potatoes she saved is $\frac{10}{100}$, or 0.1. Multiplying 760 by this proportion gives 760(0.1), or 76, potatoes that she saved to plant next year.

Choice A is incorrect and may result from conceptual or calculation errors. *Choice C* is incorrect and may result from conceptual or calculation errors. *Choice D* is incorrect and may result from conceptual or calculation errors.

QUESTION 3

The correct answer is 2,520. There are 60 minutes in one hour. At a rate of 42 posters per minute, the number of posters produced in one hour can be determined by $\left(\frac{42 \text{ posters}}{1 \text{ minute}}\right)\left(\frac{60 \text{ minutes}}{1 \text{ hour}}\right)$, which is 2,520 posters per hour.

QUESTION 4

The correct answer is 40. The height of each bar in the bar graph shown represents the number of cans collected by the group specified at the bottom of the bar. The bar for group 6 reaches a height of 40. Therefore, group 6 collected 40 cans.

QUESTION 5

The correct answer is 7. It's given that the x-intercept of the graph shown is $(x, 0)$. The graph passes through the point $(7, 0)$. Therefore, the value of x is 7.

QUESTION 6

The correct answer is 30. The value of $f(x)$ when $x = 4$ can be found by substituting 4 for x in the given equation $f(x) = 7x + 2$. This yields $f(4) = 7(4) + 2$, or $f(4) = 30$. Therefore, when $x = 4$, the value of $f(x)$ is 30.

QUESTION 7

The correct answer is 180. The perimeter of a polygon is equal to the sum of the lengths of the sides of the polygon. It's given that each side of the square has a length of 45. Since a square is a polygon with 4 sides, the perimeter of this square is $45 + 45 + 45 + 45$, or 180.

QUESTION 8

Choice C is correct. It's given from the graph that the points $(0, 7)$ and $(8, 0)$ lie on the line. For two points on a line, (x_1, y_1) and (x_2, y_2), the slope of the line can be calculated using the slope formula $m = \dfrac{y_2 - y_1}{x_2 - x_1}$. Substituting $(0, 7)$ for (x_1, y_1) and $(8, 0)$ for (x_2, y_2) in this formula, the slope of the line can be calculated as $m = \dfrac{0 - 7}{8 - 0}$, or $m = -\dfrac{7}{8}$. It's also given that the point $(d, 4)$ lies on the line. Substituting $(d, 4)$ for (x_1, y_1), $(8, 0)$ for (x_2, y_2), and $-\dfrac{7}{8}$ for m in the slope formula yields $-\dfrac{7}{8} = \dfrac{0 - 4}{8 - d}$, or $-\dfrac{7}{8} = \dfrac{-4}{8 - d}$. Multiplying both sides of this equation by $8 - d$ yields $-\dfrac{7}{8}(8 - d) = -4$. Expanding the left-hand side of this equation yields $-7 + \dfrac{7}{8}d = -4$. Adding 7 to both sides of this equation yields $\dfrac{7}{8}d = 3$. Multiplying both sides of this equation by $\dfrac{8}{7}$ yields $d = \dfrac{24}{7}$. Thus, the value of d is $\dfrac{24}{7}$.

Choice A is incorrect. This is the value of y when $x = 4$. *Choice B is incorrect and may result from conceptual or calculation errors. Choice D is incorrect and may result from conceptual or calculation errors.*

QUESTION 9

Choice A is correct. Since each term of the given expression has a factor of $5x$, it can be rewritten as $5x(x) - 5x(10y^2)$, or $5x(x - 10y^2)$.

Choice B is incorrect and may result from conceptual or calculation errors. Choice C is incorrect and may result from conceptual or calculation errors. Choice D is incorrect and may result from conceptual or calculation errors.

QUESTION 10

Choice D is correct. It's given that the function f is defined by $f(x) = 5x^2$. Substituting 8 for x in $f(x) = 5x^2$ yields $f(8) = 5(8)^2$, which is equivalent to $f(8) = 5(64)$, or $f(8) = 320$. Therefore, the value of $f(8)$ is 320.

Choice A is incorrect. This is the value of $f(8)$ if $f(x) = 5x$. *Choice B is incorrect.* This is the value of $f(8)$ if $f(x) = 5(x + 2)$. *Choice C is incorrect.* This is the value of $f(8)$ if $f(x) = (5x)(2)$.

QUESTION 11

Choice D is correct. The sum of consecutive interior angles between two parallel lines and on the same side of the transversal is 180 degrees. Since it's given that line *m* is parallel to line *n*, it follows that $x + 26 = 180$. Subtracting 26 from both sides of this equation yields 154. Therefore, the value of *x* is 154.

Choice A is incorrect. This is half of the given angle measure. *Choice B* is incorrect. This is the value of the given angle measure. *Choice C* is incorrect. This is twice the value of the given angle measure.

QUESTION 12

Choice A is correct. The total number of possible outcomes for rolling a fair 14-sided die is 14. The number of possible outcomes for rolling a 2 is 1. The probability of rolling a 2 is the number of possible outcomes for rolling a 2 divided by the total number of possible outcomes, or $\frac{1}{14}$.

Choice B is incorrect. This is the probability of rolling a number no greater than 2. *Choice C* is incorrect. This is the probability of rolling a number greater than 2. *Choice D* is incorrect. This is the probability of rolling a number other than 2.

QUESTION 13

Choice A is correct. The line of best fit shown intersects the *y*-axis at a positive *y*-value and has a positive slope. The graph of an equation of the form $y = a + bx$, where *a* and *b* are constants, intersects the *y*-axis at a *y*-value of *a* and has a slope of *b*. Of the given choices, only choice A represents a line that intersects the *y*-axis at a positive *y*-value, 2.8, and has a positive slope, 1.7.

Choice B is incorrect. This equation represents a line that has a negative slope, not a positive slope. *Choice C* is incorrect. This equation represents a line that intersects the *y*-axis at a negative *y*-value, not a positive *y*-value. *Choice D* is incorrect. This equation represents a line that intersects the *y*-axis at a negative *y*-value, not a positive *y*-value, and has a negative slope, not a positive slope.

QUESTION 14

Choice C is correct. The median of a data set with an odd number of values, in ascending or descending order, is the middle value of the data set, and the range of a data set is the positive difference between the maximum and minimum values in the data set. Since the dot plot shown gives the values in data set A in ascending order and there are 15 values in the data set, the eighth value in data set A, 23, is the median. The maximum value in data set A is 26 and the minimum value is 22, so the range of data set A is 26 − 22, or 4. It's given that data set B is created by adding 56 to each of the values in data set A. Increasing each of the 15 values in data set A by 56 will also increase its median value by 56, making the median of data set B 79. Increasing each value of data set A by 56 does not change the range, since the maximum value of data set B is 26 + 56, or 82, and the minimum value is 22 + 56, or 78, making the range of data set B 82 − 78, or 4. Therefore, the median of data set B is greater than the median of data set A, and the range of data set B is equal to the range of data set A.

Choice A is incorrect and may result from conceptual or calculation errors. *Choice B* is incorrect and may result from conceptual or calculation errors. *Choice D* is incorrect and may result from conceptual or calculation errors.

QUESTION 15

Choice A is correct. It's given that $68x + 85y = 1,258$ represents the situation where an interior designer earned a total of \$1,258 last week from consulting for x hours and drawing up plans for y hours. Thus, $68x$ represents the amount earned, in dollars, from consulting for x hours, and $85y$ represents the amount earned, in dollars, from drawing up plans for y hours. Since $68x$ represents the amount earned, in dollars, from consulting for x hours, it follows that the interior designer earned \$68 per hour consulting last week.

Choice B is incorrect. The interior designer worked y hours, not 68 hours, drawing up plans last week. *Choice C* is incorrect. The interior designer earned \$85 per hour, not \$68 per hour, drawing up plans last week. *Choice D* is incorrect. The interior designer worked x hours, not 68 hours, consulting last week.

QUESTION 16

Choice D is correct. Since the graphs of the equations in the given system intersect at the point (x, y), the point (x, y) represents a solution to the given system of equations. The first equation of the given system of equations states that $x = 8$. Substituting 8 for x in the second equation of the given system of equations yields $y = 8^2 + 8$, or $y = 72$. Therefore, the value of y is 72.

Choice A is incorrect. This is the value of x, not y. *Choice B* is incorrect and may result from conceptual or calculation errors. *Choice C* is incorrect and may result from conceptual or calculation errors.

QUESTION 17

Choice D is correct. Because the graph of $y = f(x)$ is shown, the value of $f(0)$ is the value of y on the graph that corresponds with $x = 0$. When $x = 0$, the corresponding value of y is 3. Therefore, the value of $f(0)$ is 3.

Choice A is incorrect and may result from conceptual errors. *Choice B* is incorrect and may result from conceptual errors. *Choice C* is incorrect and may result from conceptual errors.

QUESTION 18

Choice C is correct. It's given that $f(x) = 8\sqrt{x}$. Substituting 48 for $f(x)$ in this equation yields $48 = 8\sqrt{x}$. Dividing both sides of this equation by 8 yields $6 = \sqrt{x}$. This can be rewritten as $\sqrt{x} = 6$. Squaring both sides of this equation yields $x = 36$. Therefore, the value of x for which $f(x) = 48$ is 36.

Choice A is incorrect. If $x = 6$, $f(x) = 8\sqrt{6}$, not 48. *Choice B* is incorrect. If $x = 8$, $f(x) = 8\sqrt{8}$, not 48. *Choice D* is incorrect. If $x = 64$, $f(x) = 8\sqrt{64}$, which is equivalent to 64, not 48.

QUESTION 19

Choice D is correct. The equation that defines line t in the xy-plane can be written in slope-intercept form $y = mx + b$, where m is the slope of line t and $(0, b)$ is its y-intercept. It's given that line t has a slope of $-\frac{1}{3}$. Therefore, $m = -\frac{1}{3}$. Substituting $-\frac{1}{3}$ for m in the equation $y = mx + b$ yields $y = -\frac{1}{3}x + b$, or $y = -\frac{x}{3} + b$. It's also given that line t passes through the point $(9, 10)$.

Substituting 9 for x and 10 for y in the equation $y = -\frac{x}{3} + b$ yields $10 = -\frac{9}{3} + b$,

or $10 = -3 + b$. Adding 3 to both sides of this equation yields $13 = b$.

Substituting 13 for b in the equation $y = -\frac{x}{3} + b$ yields $y = -\frac{x}{3} + 13$.

Choice A is incorrect and may result from conceptual or calculation errors. *Choice B* is incorrect. This equation defines a line that has a slope of 9, not $-\frac{1}{3}$, and passes through the point (0, 10), not (9, 10). *Choice C* is incorrect. This equation defines a line that passes through the point (0, 10), not (9, 10).

QUESTION 20

Choice C is correct. Let x represent the number of children in a whale-watching tour group. Let y represent the number of adults in this group. Because it's given that 21 people are in a group and the group consists of adults and children, it must be true that $x + y = 21$. Since the company's revenue is 60 dollars per child, the total revenue from x children in this group was $60x$ dollars. Since the company's revenue is 80 dollars per adult, the total revenue from y adults in this group was $80y$ dollars. Because it's given that the total revenue for this group was 1,440 dollars, it must be true that $60x + 80y = 1,440$. The equations $x + y = 21$ and $60x + 80y = 1,440$ form a linear system of equations that can be solved to find the value of x, which represents the number of children in the group, using the elimination method. Multiplying both sides of the equation $x + y = 21$ by 80 yields $80x + 80y = 1,680$. Subtracting $60x + 80y = 1,440$ from $80x + 80y = 1,680$ yields $(80x + 80y) - (60x + 80y) = 1,680 - 1,440$, which is equivalent to $80x - 60x + 80y - 80y = 240$, or $20x = 240$. Dividing both sides of this equation by 20 yields $x = 12$. Therefore, 12 people in the group were children.

Choice A is incorrect and may result from conceptual or calculation errors. *Choice B* is incorrect. This is the number of adults in the group, not the number of children in the group. *Choice D* is incorrect and may result from conceptual or calculation errors.

QUESTION 21

Choice D is correct. The number of solutions of a quadratic equation of the form $ax^2 + bx + c = 0$, where a, b, and c are constants, can be determined by the value of the discriminant, $b^2 - 4ac$. If the value of the discriminant is positive, then the quadratic equation has exactly two distinct real solutions. If the value of the discriminant is equal to zero, then the quadratic equation has exactly one real solution. If the value of the discriminant is negative, then the quadratic equation has zero real solutions. In the given equation, $5x^2 + 10x + 16 = 0$, $a = 5$, $b = 10$, and $c = 16$. Substituting these values for a, b, and c in $b^2 - 4ac$ yields $(10)^2 - 4(5)(16)$, or -220. Since the value of its discriminant is negative, the given equation has zero real solutions. Therefore, the number of distinct real solutions the given equation has is zero.

Choice A is incorrect and may result from conceptual or calculation errors. *Choice B* is incorrect and may result from conceptual or calculation errors. *Choice C* is incorrect and may result from conceptual or calculation errors.

QUESTION 22

Choice A is correct. The standard form of an equation of a circle in the xy-plane is $(x - h)^2 + (y - k)^2 = r^2$, where the coordinates of the center of the circle are (h, k) and the length of the radius of the circle is r. The equation of circle A, $x^2 + (y - 2)^2 = 36$, can be rewritten as $(x - 0)^2 + (y - 2)^2 = 6^2$. Therefore, the center of circle A is at $(0, 2)$ and the length of the radius of circle A is 6. If circle A is shifted down 4 units, the y-coordinate of its center will decrease by 4; the radius of the circle and the x-coordinate of its center will not change. Therefore, the center of circle B is at $(0, 2 - 4)$, or $(0, -2)$, and its radius is 6. Substituting 0 for h, -2 for k, and 6 for r in the equation $(x - h)^2 + (y - k)^2 = r^2$ yields $(x - 0)^2 + (y - (-2))^2 = (6)^2$, or $x^2 + (y + 2)^2 = 36$. Therefore, the equation $x^2 + (y + 2)^2 = 36$ represents circle B.

Choice B is incorrect. This equation represents a circle obtained by shifting circle A up, rather than down, 4 units. *Choice C* is incorrect. This equation represents a circle obtained by shifting circle A right, rather than down, 4 units. *Choice D* is incorrect. This equation represents a circle obtained by shifting circle A left, rather than down, 4 units.

Math

Module 2 — Higher Difficulty
(22 questions)

QUESTION 1

Choice A is correct. It's given that 20% of the students surveyed responded that they intend to enroll in the study program. Therefore, the proportion of students in Spanish club who intend to enroll in the study program, based on the survey, is 0.20. Since there are 55 total students in Spanish club, the best estimate for the total number of these students who intend to enroll in the study program is 55(0.20), or 11.

Choice B is incorrect. This is the best estimate for the percentage, rather than the total number, of students in Spanish club who intend to enroll in the study program. *Choice C* is incorrect. This is the best estimate for the total number of Spanish club students who do not intend to enroll in the study program. *Choice D* is incorrect. This is the total number of students in Spanish club.

QUESTION 2

Choice B is correct. It's given that it takes the machine 10 minutes to make a large box. It's also given that x represents the possible number of large boxes the machine can make each day. Multiplying 10 by x gives $10x$, which represents the amount of time spent making large boxes. It's given that it takes the machine 5 minutes to make a small box. It's also given that y represents the possible number of small boxes the machine can make each day. Multiplying 5 by y gives $5y$, which represents the amount of time spent making small boxes. Combining the amount of time spent making x large boxes and y small boxes yields $10x + 5y$. It's given that the machine makes boxes for a total of 700 minutes each day. Therefore $10x + 5y = 700$ represents the possible number of large boxes, x, and small boxes, y, the machine can make each day.

Choice A is incorrect and may result from associating the time of 10 minutes with small, rather than large, boxes and the time of 5 minutes with large, rather than small, boxes. *Choice C* is incorrect and may result from conceptual errors. *Choice D* is incorrect and may result from conceptual errors.

QUESTION 3

Choice B is correct. The line of best fit shown intersects the y-axis at a positive y-value and has a negative slope. The graph of an equation of the form $y = a + bx$, where a and b are constants, intersects the y-axis at a y-value of a and has a slope of b. Of the given choices, only choice B represents a line that intersects the y-axis at a positive y-value, 13.5, and has a negative slope, −0.8.

Choice A is incorrect. This equation represents a line that has a positive slope, not a negative slope. *Choice C* is incorrect. This equation represents a line that intersects the *y*-axis at a negative *y*-value, not a positive *y*-value, and has a positive slope, not a negative slope. *Choice D* is incorrect. This equation represents a line that intersects the *y*-axis at a negative *y*-value, not a positive *y*-value.

QUESTION 4

Choice C is correct. It's given from the graph that the points $(0, 7)$ and $(8, 0)$ lie on the line. For two points on a line, (x_1, y_1) and (x_2, y_2), the slope of the line can be calculated using the slope formula $m = \frac{y_2 - y_1}{x_2 - x_1}$. Substituting $(0, 7)$ for (x_1, y_1) and $(8, 0)$ for (x_2, y_2) in this formula, the slope of the line can be calculated as $m = \frac{0 - 7}{8 - 0}$, or $m = -\frac{7}{8}$. It's also given that the point $(d, 4)$ lies on the line. Substituting $(d, 4)$ for (x_1, y_1), $(8, 0)$ for (x_2, y_2), and $-\frac{7}{8}$ for m in the slope formula yields $-\frac{7}{8} = \frac{0 - 4}{8 - d}$, or $-\frac{7}{8} = \frac{-4}{8 - d}$. Multiplying both sides of this equation by $8 - d$ yields $-\frac{7}{8}(8-d) = -4$. Expanding the left-hand side of this equation yields $-7 + \frac{7}{8}d = -4$. Adding 7 to both sides of this equation yields $\frac{7}{8}d = 3$. Multiplying both sides of this equation by $\frac{8}{7}$ yields $d = \frac{24}{7}$. Thus, the value of *d* is $\frac{24}{7}$.

Choice A is incorrect. This is the value of *y* when *x* = 4. *Choice B* is incorrect and may result from conceptual or calculation errors. *Choice D* is incorrect and may result from conceptual or calculation errors.

QUESTION 5

Choice D is correct. The equation of a quadratic function can be written in the form $f(x) = a(x - h)^2 + k$, where *a*, *h*, and *k* are constants. It's given in the table that when *x* = −1, the corresponding value of *f(x)* is 10. Substituting −1 for *x* and 10 for *f(x)* in the equation $f(x) = a(x - h)^2 + k$ gives $10 = a(-1 - h)^2 + k$, which is equivalent to $10 = a(1 + 2h + h^2) + k$, or $10 = a + 2ah + ah^2 + k$. It's given in the table that when *x* = 0, the corresponding value of *f(x)* is 14. Substituting 0 for *x* and 14 for *f(x)* in the equation $f(x) = a(x - h)^2 + k$ gives $14 = a(0 - h)^2 + k$, or $14 = ah^2 + k$. It's given in the table that when *x* = 1, the corresponding value of *f(x)* is 20. Substituting 1 for *x* and 20 for *f(x)* in the equation $f(x) = a(x - h)^2 + k$ gives $20 = a(1 - h)^2 + k$, which is equivalent to $20 = a(1 - 2h + h^2) + k$, or $20 = a - 2ah + ah^2 + k$. Adding $20 = a - 2ah + ah^2 + k$ to the equation $10 = a + 2ah + ah^2 + k$ gives $30 = 2a + 2ah^2 + 2k$. Dividing both sides of this equation by 2 gives $15 = a + ah^2 + k$. Since $14 = ah^2 + k$, substituting 14 for $ah^2 + k$ into the equation $15 = a + ah^2 + k$ gives $15 = a + 14$. Subtracting 14 from both sides of this equation gives $a = 1$. Substituting 1 for *a* in the equations $14 = ah^2 + k$ and $20 = ah^2 - 2ah + a + k$ gives $14 = h^2 + k$ and $20 = 1 - 2h + h^2 + k$, respectively. Since $14 = h^2 + k$, substituting 14 for $h^2 + k$ in the equation $20 = 1 - 2h + h^2 + k$ gives $20 = 1 - 2h + 14$, or $20 = 15 - 2h$. Subtracting 15 from both sides of this equation gives $5 = -2h$. Dividing both sides of this equation by −2 gives $-\frac{5}{2} = h$. Substituting $-\frac{5}{2}$ for *h* into the equation $14 = h^2 + k$ gives $14 = \left(-\frac{5}{2}\right)^2 + k$, or $14 = \frac{25}{4} + k$. Subtracting $\frac{25}{4}$ from both sides of this equation gives $\frac{31}{4} = k$. Substituting 1 for *a*, $-\frac{5}{2}$ for *h*, and $\frac{31}{4}$ for *k* in the equation

$f(x) = a(x - h)^2 + k$ gives $f(x) = \left(x + \frac{5}{2}\right)^2 + \frac{31}{4}$, which is equivalent to

$f(x) = x^2 + 5x + \frac{25}{4} + \frac{31}{4}$, or $f(x) = x^2 + 5x + 14$. Therefore, $f(x) = x^2 + 5x + 14$

defines f.

Choice A is incorrect. If $f(x) = 3x^2 + 3x + 14$, then when $x = -1$, the corresponding value of $f(x)$ is 14, not 10. *Choice B* is incorrect. If $f(x) = 5x^2 + x + 14$, then when $x = -1$, the corresponding value of $f(x)$ is 18, not 10. *Choice C* is incorrect. If $f(x) = 9x^2 - x + 14$, then when $x = -1$, the corresponding value of $f(x)$ is 24, not 10, and when $x = 1$, the corresponding value of $f(x)$ is 22, not 20.

QUESTION 6

Choice C is correct. It's given that $f(x) = \frac{x + 15}{5}$ and $f(a) = 10$, where a is a

constant. Therefore, for the given function f, when $x = a$, $f(x) = 10$. Substituting

a for x and 10 for $f(x)$ in the given function f yields $10 = \frac{a + 15}{5}$. Multiplying both

sides of this equation by 5 yields $50 = a + 15$. Subtracting 15 from both sides of this equation yields $35 = a$. Therefore, the value of a is 35.

Choice A is incorrect. This is the value of a if $f(a) = 4$. *Choice B* is incorrect. This is the value of a if $f(a) = 5$. *Choice D* is incorrect. This is the value of a if $f(a) = 16$.

QUESTION 7

Choice C is correct. Vertical angles, which are angles that are opposite each other when two lines intersect, are congruent. The figure shows that lines t and m intersect. It follows that the angle with measure $x°$ and the angle with measure $y°$ are vertical angles, so $x = y$. It's given that $x = 6k + 13$ and $y = 8k - 29$. Substituting $6k + 13$ for x and $8k - 29$ for y in the equation $x = y$ yields $6k + 13 = 8k - 29$. Subtracting $6k$ from both sides of this equation yields $13 = 2k - 29$. Adding 29 to both sides of this equation yields $42 = 2k$, or $2k = 42$. Dividing both sides of this equation by 2 yields $k = 21$. It's given that lines m and n are parallel, and the figure shows that lines m and n are intersected by a transversal, line t. If two parallel lines are intersected by a transversal, then the same-side interior angles are supplementary. It follows that the same-side interior angles with measures $y°$ and $z°$ are supplementary, so $y + z = 180$. Substituting $8k - 29$ for y in this equation yields $8k - 29 + z = 180$. Substituting 21 for k in this equation yields $8(21) - 29 + z = 180$, or $139 + z = 180$. Subtracting 139 from both sides of this equation yields $z = 41$. Therefore, the value of z is 41.

Choice A is incorrect and may result from conceptual or calculation errors. *Choice B* is incorrect. This is the value of k, not z. *Choice D* is incorrect. This is the value of x or y, not z.

QUESTION 8

Choice C is correct. It's given that line r is perpendicular to line p in the xy-plane. This means that the slope of line r is the negative reciprocal of the slope of line p. If the equation for line p is rewritten in slope-intercept form $y = mx + b$, where m and b are constants, then m is the slope of the line and $(0, b)$ is its y-intercept. Subtracting $18x$ from both sides of the equation $2y + 18x = 9$ yields $2y = -18x + 9$. Dividing both sides of this equation by

2 yields $y = -9x + \frac{9}{2}$. It follows that the slope of line p is -9. The negative reciprocal of a number is -1 divided by the number. Therefore, the negative reciprocal of -9 is $\frac{-1}{-9}$, or $\frac{1}{9}$. Thus, the slope of line r is $\frac{1}{9}$.

Choice A is incorrect. This is the slope of line p, not line r. Choice B is incorrect. This is the reciprocal, not the negative reciprocal, of the slope of line p. Choice D is incorrect. This is the negative, not the negative reciprocal, of the slope of line p.

QUESTION 9

Choice A is correct. It's given that the sample is in the shape of a cube with edge lengths of 0.9 meters. Therefore, the volume of the sample is 0.90^3, or 0.729, cubic meters. It's also given that the sample has a density of 807 kilograms per 1 cubic meter. Therefore, the mass of this sample is 0.729 cubic meters $\left(\frac{807 \text{ kilograms}}{1 \text{ cubic meter}} \right)$, or 588.303 kilograms. Rounding this mass to the nearest whole number gives 588 kilograms. Therefore, to the nearest whole number, the mass, in kilograms, of this sample is 588.

Choice B is incorrect and may result from conceptual or calculation errors. Choice C is incorrect and may result from conceptual or calculation errors. Choice D is incorrect and may result from conceptual or calculation errors.

QUESTION 10

Choice C is correct. It's given that the function P models the population of the city t years after 2005. Since there are 12 months in a year, 18 months is equivalent to $\frac{18}{12}$ years. Therefore, the expression $\frac{18}{12}x$ can represent the number of years in x 18-month periods. Substituting $\frac{18}{12}x$ for t in the given equation yields $P\left(\frac{18}{12}x\right) = 290(1.04)^{\left(\frac{4}{6}\right)\left(\frac{18}{12}x\right)}$, which is equivalent to $P\left(\frac{18}{12}x\right) = 290(1.04)^x$. Therefore, for each 18-month period, the predicted population of the city is 1.04 times, or 104% of, the previous population. This means that the population is predicted to increase by 4% every 18 months.

Choice A is incorrect and may result from conceptual or calculation errors. Choice B is incorrect. Each year, the predicted population of the city is 1.04 times the previous year's predicted population, which is not the same as an increase of 1.04%. Choice D is incorrect and may result from conceptual or calculation errors.

QUESTION 11

The correct answer is $-\frac{14}{15}$. A linear equation in the form $ax + b = cx + d$ has no solution only when the coefficients of x on each side of the equation are equal and the constant terms are not equal. Dividing both sides of the given equation by 2 yields $kx - n = -\frac{28}{30}x - \frac{36}{38}$, or $kx - n = -\frac{14}{15}x - \frac{18}{19}$. Since it's given that the equation has no solution, the coefficient of x on both sides of this equation must be equal, and the constant terms on both sides of this equation must not be equal. Since $\frac{18}{19} < 1$, and it's given that $n > 1$, the second condition is true. Thus, k must be equal to $-\frac{14}{15}$. Note that $-14/15$, $-.9333$, and -0.933 are examples of ways to enter a correct answer.

QUESTION 12

The correct answer is 4.06. It's given that the retail price is 290% of the wholesale price of \$7.00. Thus, the retail price is $\$7.00\left(\frac{290}{100}\right)$, which is equivalent to \$7.00(2.9), or \$20.30. It's also given that the discounted price is 80% off the retail price. Thus, the discounted price is $\$20.30\left(1 - \frac{80}{100}\right)$, which is equivalent to \$20.30(0.20), or \$4.06.

QUESTION 13

The correct answer is 289. A quadratic equation of the form $ax^2 + bx + c = 0$, where a, b, and c are constants, has no real solutions when the value of the discriminant, $b^2 - 4ac$, is less than 0. In the given equation, $x^2 - 34x + c = 0$, $a = 1$ and $b = -34$. Therefore, the discriminant of the given equation can be expressed as $(-34)^2 - 4(1)(c)$, or $1,156 - 4c$. It follows that the given equation has no real solutions when $1,156 - 4c < 0$. Adding $4c$ to both sides of this inequality yields $1,156 < 4c$. Dividing both sides of this inequality by 4 yields $289 < c$, or $c > 289$. It's given that the equation $x^2 - 34x + c = 0$ has no real solutions when $c > n$. Therefore, the least possible value of n is 289.

QUESTION 14

The correct answer is 44. The mean of a data set is computed by dividing the sum of the values in the data set by the number of values in the data set. It's given that data set A consists of the heights of 75 buildings and has a mean of 32 meters. This can be represented by the equation $\frac{x}{75} = 32$, where x represents the sum of the heights of the buildings, in meters, in data set A. Multiplying both sides of this equation by 75 yields $x = 75(32)$, or $x = 2,400$ meters. Therefore, the sum of the heights of the buildings in data set A is 2,400 meters. It's also given that data set B consists of the heights of 50 buildings and has a mean of 62 meters. This can be represented by the equation $\frac{y}{50} = 62$, where y represents the sum of the heights of the buildings, in meters, in data set B. Multiplying both sides of this equation by 50 yields $y = 50(62)$, or $y = 3,100$ meters. Therefore, the sum of the heights of the buildings in data set B is 3,100 meters. Since it's given that data set C consists of the heights of the 125 buildings from data sets A and B, it follows that the mean of data set C is the sum of the heights of the buildings, in meters, in data sets A and B divided by the number of buildings represented in data sets A and B, or $\frac{2,400 + 3,100}{125}$, which is equivalent to 44 meters. Therefore, the mean, in meters, of data set C is 44.

QUESTION 15

Choice D is correct. It's given that $4x^2 + bx - 45$ can be rewritten as $(hx + k)(x + j)$. The expression $(hx + k)(x + j)$ can be rewritten as $hx^2 + jhx + kx + kj$, or $hx^2 + (jh + k)x + kj$. Therefore, $hx^2 + (jh + k)x + kj$ is equivalent to $4x^2 + bx - 45$.

It follows that $kj = -45$. Dividing each side of this equation by k yields $j = \frac{-45}{k}$.

Since j is an integer, $-\frac{45}{k}$ must be an integer. Therefore, $\frac{45}{k}$ must also be

an integer.

Choice A is incorrect and may result from conceptual or calculation errors.
Choice B is incorrect and may result from conceptual or calculation errors.
Choice C is incorrect and may result from conceptual or calculation errors.

QUESTION 16

The correct answer is $\frac{29}{2}$. According to the first equation in the given system,

the value of y is -1.5. Substituting -1.5 for y in the second equation in the given system yields $-1.5 = x^2 + 8x + a$. Adding 1.5 to both sides of this equation yields $0 = x^2 + 8x + a + 1.5$. If the given system has exactly one distinct real solution, it follows that $0 = x^2 + 8x + a + 1.5$ has exactly one distinct real solution. A quadratic equation in the form $0 = px^2 + qx + r$, where p, q, and r are constants, has exactly one distinct real solution if and only if the discriminant, $q^2 - 4pr$, is equal to 0. The equation $0 = x^2 + 8x + a + 1.5$ is in this form, where $p = 1$, $q = 8$, and $r = a + 1.5$. Therefore, the discriminant of the equation $0 = x^2 + 8x + a + 1.5$ is $(8)^2 - 4(1)(a + 1.5)$, or $58 - 4a$. Setting the discriminant equal to 0 to solve for a yields $58 - 4a = 0$. Adding $4a$ to both sides of this equation yields $58 = 4a$.

Dividing both sides of this equation by 4 yields $\frac{58}{4} = a$, or $\frac{29}{2} = a$. Therefore,

if the given system of equations has exactly one distinct real solution,

the value of a is $\frac{29}{2}$. Note that 29/2 and 14.5 are examples of ways to enter a

correct answer.

QUESTION 17

Choice C is correct. The median of a data set with an odd number of values, in ascending or descending order, is the middle value of the data set, and the range of a data set is the positive difference between the maximum and minimum values in the data set. Since the dot plot shown gives the values in data set A in ascending order and there are 15 values in the data set, the eighth value in data set A, 23, is the median. The maximum value in data set A is 26 and the minimum value is 22, so the range of data set A is 26 − 22, or 4. It's given that data set B is created by adding 56 to each of the values in data set A. Increasing each of the 15 values in data set A by 56 will also increase its median value by 56, making the median of data set B 79. Increasing each value of data set A by 56 does not change the range, since the maximum value of data set B is 26 + 56, or 82, and the minimum value is 22 + 56, or 78, making the range of data set B 82 − 78, or 4. Therefore, the median of data set B is greater than the median of data set A, and the range of data set B is equal to the range of data set A.

Choice A is incorrect and may result from conceptual or calculation errors.
Choice B is incorrect and may result from conceptual or calculation errors.
Choice D is incorrect and may result from conceptual or calculation errors.

QUESTION 18

Choice C is correct. It's given that $f(x) = \frac{a}{x + b}$ and that the graph shown is a partial graph of $y = f(x)$. Substituting y for $f(x)$ in the equation $f(x) = \frac{a}{x + b}$ yields $y = \frac{a}{x + b}$. The graph passes through the point $(-7, -2)$. Substituting -7 for x and -2 for y in the equation $y = \frac{a}{x + b}$ yields $-2 = \frac{a}{-7 + b}$. Multiplying each side of this equation by $-7 + b$ yields $-2(-7 + b) = a$, or $14 - 2b = a$. The graph also passes through the point $(-5, -6)$. Substituting -5 for x and -6 for y in the equation $y = \frac{a}{x + b}$ yields $-6 = \frac{a}{-5 + b}$. Multiplying each side of this equation by $-5 + b$ yields $-6(-5 + b) = a$, or $30 - 6b = a$. Substituting $14 - 2b$ for a in this equation yields $30 - 6b = 14 - 2b$. Adding $6b$ to each side of this equation yields $30 = 14 + 4b$. Subtracting 14 from each side of this equation yields $16 = 4b$. Dividing each side of this equation by 4 yields $4 = b$. Substituting 4 for b in the equation $14 - 2b = a$ yields $14 - 2(4) = a$, or $6 = a$. Substituting 6 for a and 4 for b in the equation $f(x) = \frac{a}{x + b}$ yields $f(x) = \frac{6}{x + 4}$. It's given that $g(x) = f(x + 4)$. Substituting $x + 4$ for x in the equation $f(x) = \frac{6}{x + 4}$ yields $f(x + 4) = \frac{6}{x + 4 + 4}$, which is equivalent to $f(x + 4) = \frac{6}{x + 8}$. It follows that $g(x) = \frac{6}{x + 8}$.

Choice A is incorrect. This could define function g if $g(x) = f(x - 4)$. *Choice B is incorrect.* This could define function g if $g(x) = f(x)$. *Choice D is incorrect.* This could define function g if $g(x) = f(x) \cdot (x + 4)$.

QUESTION 19

Choice A is correct. The left-hand side of the given equation is the expression $57x^2 + (57b + a)x + ab$. Applying the distributive property to this expression yields $57x^2 + 57bx + ax + ab$. Since the first two terms of this expression have a common factor of $57x$ and the last two terms of this expression have a common factor of a, this expression can be rewritten as $57x(x + b) + a(x + b)$. Since the two terms of this expression have a common factor of $(x + b)$, it can be rewritten as $(x + b)(57x + a)$. Therefore, the given equation can be rewritten as $(x + b)(57x + a) = 0$. By the zero product property, it follows that $x + b = 0$ or $57x + a = 0$. Subtracting b from both sides of the equation $x + b = 0$ yields $x = -b$. Subtracting a from both sides of the equation $57x + a = 0$ yields $57x = -a$.

Dividing both sides of this equation by 57 yields $x = \frac{-a}{57}$. Therefore, the solutions to the given equation are $-b$ and $\frac{-a}{57}$. It follows that the product of the solutions of the given equation is $(-b)\left(\frac{-a}{57}\right)$, or $\frac{ab}{57}$. It's given that the product of the solutions of the given equation is kab. It follows that $\frac{ab}{57} = kab$, which can also be written as $ab\left(\frac{1}{57}\right) = ab(k)$. It's given that a and b are positive constants. Therefore, dividing both sides of the equation $ab\left(\frac{1}{57}\right) = ab(k)$ by ab yields $\frac{1}{57} = k$. Thus, the value of k is $\frac{1}{57}$.

Choice B is incorrect and may result from conceptual or calculation errors. *Choice C is incorrect and may result from conceptual or calculation errors.* *Choice D is incorrect and may result from conceptual or calculation errors.*

QUESTION 20

The correct answer is 10. It's given that the graph of $x^2 + x + y^2 + y = \frac{199}{2}$ in the

xy-plane is a circle. The equation of a circle in the xy-plane can be written in the form $(x - h)^2 + (y - k)^2 = r^2$, where the coordinates of the center of the circle are (h, k) and the length of the radius of the circle is r. The term $(x - h)^2$ in this equation can be obtained by adding the square of half the coefficient of x to both sides of the given equation to complete the square. The coefficient of x is 1. Half the

coefficient of x is $\frac{1}{2}$. The square of half the coefficient of x is $\frac{1}{4}$. Adding $\frac{1}{4}$ to

each side of $(x^2 + x) + (y^2 + y) = \frac{199}{2}$ yields $\left(x^2 + x + \frac{1}{4}\right) + (y^2 + y) = \frac{199}{2} + \frac{1}{4}$,

or $\left(x + \frac{1}{2}\right)^2 + (y^2 + y) = \frac{199}{2} + \frac{1}{4}$. Similarly, the term $(y - k)^2$ can be obtained by

adding the square of half the coefficient of y to both sides of this equation, which

yields $\left(x + \frac{1}{2}\right)^2 + \left(y^2 + y + \frac{1}{4}\right) = \frac{199}{2} + \frac{1}{4} + \frac{1}{4}$, or $\left(x + \frac{1}{2}\right)^2 + \left(y + \frac{1}{2}\right)^2 = \frac{199}{2} + \frac{1}{4} + \frac{1}{4}$.

This equation is equivalent to $\left(x + \frac{1}{2}\right)^2 + \left(y + \frac{1}{2}\right)^2 = 100$, or $\left(x + \frac{1}{2}\right)^2 + \left(y + \frac{1}{2}\right)^2 = 10^2$.

Therefore, the length of the circle's radius is 10.

QUESTION 21

Choice B is correct. Let x represent the side length, in cm, of each square base. If the two prisms are glued together along a square base, the resulting prism has a surface area equal to twice the surface area of one of the prisms, minus the area of the two square bases that are being glued together, which yields

$2K - 2x^2$ cm^2. It's given that this resulting surface area is equal to $\frac{92}{47}K$ cm^2,

so $2K - 2x^2 = \frac{92}{47}K$. Subtracting $\frac{92}{47}K$ from both sides of this equation yields

$2K - \frac{92}{47}K - 2x^2 = 0$. This equation can be rewritten by multiplying $2K$ on the

left-hand side by $\frac{47}{47}$, which yields $\frac{94}{47}K - \frac{92}{47}K - 2x^2 = 0$, or $\frac{2}{47}K - 2x^2 = 0$.

Adding $2x^2$ to both sides of this equation yields $\frac{2}{47}K = 2x^2$. Multiplying both

sides of this equation by $\frac{47}{2}$ yields $K = 47x^2$. The surface area K, in cm^2, of each

rectangular prism is equivalent to the sum of the areas of the two square bases and the areas of the four lateral faces. Since the height of each rectangular prism is 90 cm and the side length of each square base is x cm, it follows that the area of each square base is x^2 cm^2 and the area of each lateral face is $90x$ cm^2. Therefore, the surface area of each rectangular prism can be represented by the expression $2x^2 + 4(90x)$, or $2x^2 + 360x$. Substituting this expression for K in the equation $K = 47x^2$ yields $2x^2 + 360x = 47x^2$. Subtracting $2x^2$ and $360x$ from both sides of this equation yields $0 = 45x^2 - 360x$. Factoring x from the right-hand side of this equation yields $0 = x(45x - 360)$. Applying the zero product property, it follows that $x = 0$ and $45x - 360 = 0$. Adding 360 to both sides of the equation $45x - 360 = 0$ yields $45x = 360$. Dividing both sides of this equation by 45 yields $x = 8$. Since a side length of a rectangular prism can't be 0, the length of each square base is 8 cm.

Choice A is incorrect and may result from conceptual or calculation errors.
Choice C is incorrect and may result from conceptual or calculation errors.
Choice D is incorrect and may result from conceptual or calculation errors.

QUESTION 22

Choice D is correct. The equation of a parabola in the xy-plane can be written in the form $y = a(x - h)^2 + k$, where a is a constant and (h, k) is the vertex of the parabola. If a is positive, the parabola will open upward, and if a is negative, the parabola will open downward. It's given that the parabola has vertex $(9, -14)$. Substituting 9 for h and -14 for k in the equation $y = a(x - h)^2 + k$ gives $y = a(x - 9)^2 - 14$, which can be rewritten as $y = a(x - 9)(x - 9) - 14$, or $y = a(x^2 - 18x + 81) - 14$. Distributing the factor of a on the right-hand side of this equation yields $y = ax^2 - 18ax + 81a - 14$. Therefore, the equation of the parabola, $y = ax^2 - 18ax + 81a - 14$, can be written in the form $y = ax^2 + bx + c$, where $a = a$, $b = -18a$, and $c = 81a - 14$. Substituting $-18a$ for b and $81a - 14$ for c in the expression $a + b + c$ yields $(a) + (-18a) + (81a - 14)$, or $64a - 14$. Since the vertex of the parabola, $(9, -14)$, is below the x-axis, and it's given that the parabola intersects the x-axis at two points, the parabola must open upward. Therefore, the constant a must have a positive value. Setting the expression $64a - 14$ equal to the value in choice D yields $64a - 14 = -12$. Adding 14 to both sides of this equation yields $64a = 2$. Dividing both sides of this equation by 64 yields $a = \frac{2}{64}$, which is a positive value. Therefore, if the equation of the parabola is written in the form $y = ax^2 + bx + c$, where a, b, and c are constants, the value of $a + b + c$ could be -12.

Choice A is incorrect. If the equation of a parabola with a vertex at $(9, -14)$ is written in the form $y = ax^2 + bx + c$, where a, b, and c are constants and $a + b + c = -23$, then the value of a will be negative, which means the parabola will open downward, not upward, and will intersect the x-axis at zero points, not two points. *Choice B* is incorrect. If the equation of a parabola with a vertex at $(9, -14)$ is written in the form $y = ax^2 + bx + c$, where a, b, and c are constants and $a + b + c = -19$, then the value of a will be negative, which means the parabola will open downward, not upward, and will intersect the x-axis at zero points, not two points. *Choice C* is incorrect. If the equation of a parabola with a vertex at $(9, -14)$ is written in the form $y = ax^2 + bx + c$, where a, b, and c are constants and $a + b + c = -14$, then the value of a will be 0, which is inconsistent with the equation of a parabola.

Scoring Your Paper SAT Practice Test #4

Congratulations on completing an SAT® practice test. To score your test, follow the instructions in this scoring guide.

IMPORTANT: *This scoring guide is for students who completed SAT Practice Test #4 in The Official SAT Study Guide™. We recommend reading through these instructions and explanations before scoring so that you understand the specifics and limitations of scoring this practice test.*

The total score on your practice test reflects the sum of the (1) Reading and Writing and (2) Math section scores, as indicated below. If you decided to take both the lower- and higher-difficulty modules, choose which one you will use to score.

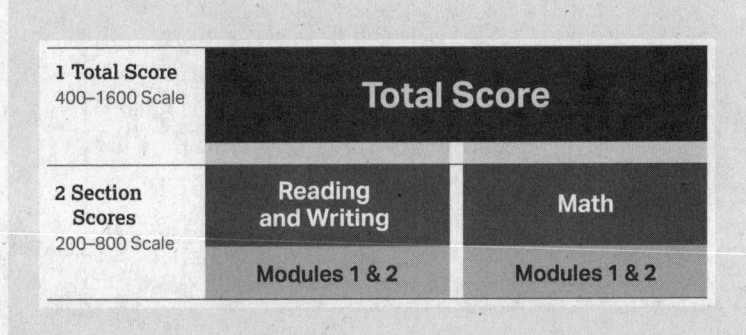

1 Total Score 400–1600 Scale	Total Score	
2 Section Scores 200–800 Scale	Reading and Writing	Math
	Modules 1 & 2	Modules 1 & 2

Scores Overview

Each assessment in the SAT Suite (SAT, PSAT/NMSQT®, PSAT™ 10, and PSAT™ 8/9) reports test scores on a common scale.

For more details about scores, visit **sat.org/scores**.

How to Calculate Your Practice Test Scores

The worksheets on the pages that follow help you calculate your test scores.

GET SET UP

1 In addition to your practice test, you'll need the answer keys and conversion tables at the end of this scoring guide.

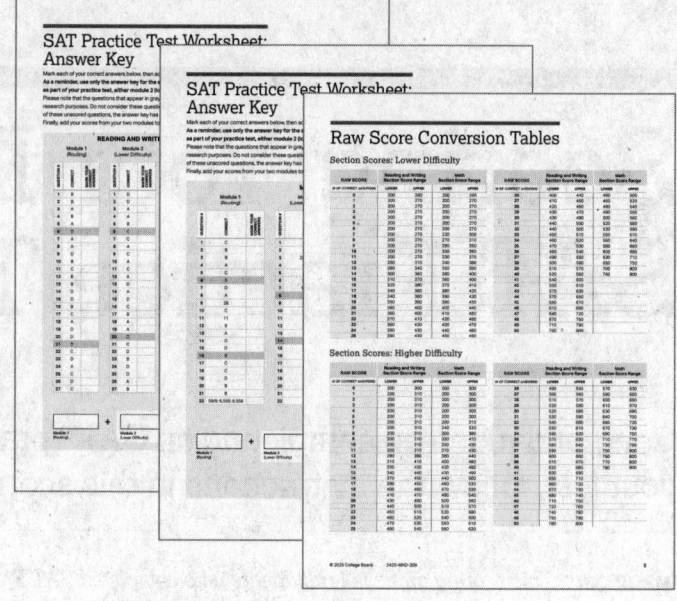

SCORE YOUR PRACTICE TEST

2 Compare your answers to the answer keys later in this scoring guide and count up the total number of correct answers for each section. Write the number of correct answers for each section in the boxes at the bottom of the pages.

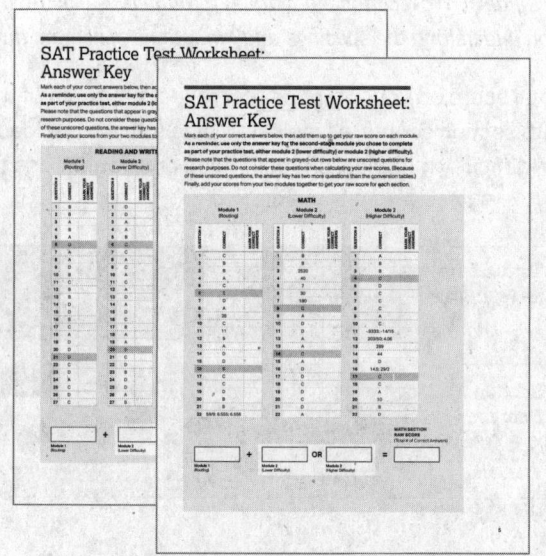

CALCULATE YOUR SCORES

3 Using your marked-up answer keys and the conversion tables, follow the directions on the SAT Practice Test Worksheet: Section and Total Scores page to get your section and total scores.

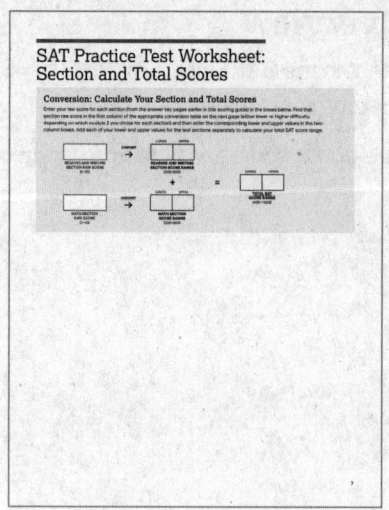

Get Section and Total Scores

Section and total scores for this paper version of SAT Practice Test #4 are expressed as ranges. That's because the scoring method described in this guide is a different (and therefore less precise) version of the one used in the actual adaptive test.

This practice test contains three modules for each test section: (1) a single first-stage (routing) module and (2) two second-stage modules. The two second-stage modules differ by average question difficulty and are marked as either "module 2 (lower difficulty)" or "module 2 (higher difficulty)." You get to choose which module 2 you would like to take for this practice test. **An actual testing experience consists of one routing and one second-stage module per test section.** To obtain your Reading and Writing and Math section scores, you will refer to the answer key and conversion table for the second-stage module you chose (either lower or higher difficulty).

GET YOUR READING AND WRITING SECTION SCORE

Calculate your SAT Reading and Writing section score (it's on a scale of 200–800).

1 Use the answer key for Reading and Writing to find the number of questions in module 1 and the module 2 you chose (either lower or higher difficulty) that you answered correctly.

2 To determine your Reading and Writing raw score, add the number of correct answers you got in module 1 and the module 2 you chose (either lower or higher difficulty). **Exclude the questions in grayed-out rows in your calculation.**

3 Use the appropriate Raw Score Conversion Table to turn your raw score into your Reading and Writing section score.

4 The lower and upper values associated with your raw score establish the range of scores you might expect to receive had this been an actual adaptive test.

GET YOUR MATH SECTION SCORE

Calculate your SAT Math section score (it's on a scale of 200–800).

1 Use the answer key for Math to find the number of questions in module 1 and the module 2 you chose (either lower or higher difficulty) that you answered correctly.

2 To determine your Math raw score, add the number of correct answers you got in module 1 and the module 2 you chose (either lower or higher difficulty). **Exclude the questions in grayed-out rows in your calculation.**

3 Use the appropriate Raw Score Conversion Table to turn your raw score into your Math section score.

4 The lower and upper values associated with your raw score establish the range of scores you might expect to receive had this been an actual adaptive test.

GET YOUR TOTAL SCORE

Add together the lower values for the Reading and Writing and Math sections, and then add together the upper values for the two sections. The result is your total score, expressed as a range, for this SAT practice test. The total score is on a scale of 400–1600.

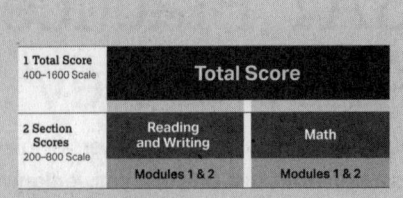

1 Total Score 400–1600 Scale	Total Score	
2 Section Scores 200–800 Scale	Reading and Writing	Math
	Modules 1 & 2	Modules 1 & 2

Your total score on this SAT practice test is the sum of your Reading and Writing section score and your Math section score. For this practice test, you'll receive a lower and upper score for each test section and the total score. This is the range of scores that you might expect to receive.

Use the worksheets on the pages that follow to calculate your section and total scores.

SAT Practice Test Worksheet: Answer Key

Mark each of your correct answers below, then add them up to get your raw score on each module.
As a reminder, use only the answer key for the second-stage module you chose to complete as part of your practice test, either module 2 (lower difficulty) or module 2 (higher difficulty).
Please note that the questions that appear in grayed-out rows below are unscored questions for research purposes. Do not consider these questions when calculating your raw scores. (Because of these unscored questions, the answer key has two more questions than the conversion tables.)
Finally, add your scores from your two modules together to get your raw score for each section.

READING AND WRITING

Module 1 (Routing)			Module 2 (Lower Difficulty)			Module 2 (Higher Difficulty)		
QUESTION #	CORRECT	MARK YOUR CORRECT ANSWERS	QUESTION #	CORRECT	MARK YOUR CORRECT ANSWERS	QUESTION #	CORRECT	MARK YOUR CORRECT ANSWERS
1	B		1	D		1	B	
2	B		2	D		2	B	
3	A		3	A		3	C	
4	B		4	A		4	C	
5	A		5	B		5	D	
6	D		6	C		6	A	
7	A		7	C		7	A	
8	A		8	A		8	C	
9	D		9	C		9	B	
10	B		10	A		10	C	
11	C		11	C		11	C	
12	B		12	A		12	D	
13	B		13	D		13	C	
14	D		14	A		14	B	
15	D		15	D		15	D	
16	B		16	C		16	A	
17	C		17	B		17	D	
18	A		18	A		18	D	
19	D		19	A		19	B	
20	D		20	D		20	A	
21	D		21	C		21	A	
22	C		22	D		22	C	
23	D		23	B		23	B	
24	A		24	D		24	C	
25	C		25	D		25	D	
26	D		26	A		26	A	
27	C		27	B		27	D	

READING AND WRITING SECTION RAW SCORE
(Total # of Correct Answers)

[ ] + [ ] OR [ ] = [ ]

Module 1 (Routing) Module 2 (Lower Difficulty) Module 2 (Higher Difficulty)

SAT Practice Test Worksheet: Answer Key

Mark each of your correct answers below, then add them up to get your raw score on each module. **As a reminder, use only the answer key for the second-stage module you chose to complete as part of your practice test, either module 2 (lower difficulty) or module 2 (higher difficulty).** Please note that the questions that appear in grayed-out rows below are unscored questions for research purposes. Do not consider these questions when calculating your raw scores. (Because of these unscored questions, the answer key has two more questions than the conversion tables.) Finally, add your scores from your two modules together to get your raw score for each section.

MATH

Module 1 (Routing)				Module 2 (Lower Difficulty)				Module 2 (Higher Difficulty)		
QUESTION #	CORRECT	MARK YOUR CORRECT ANSWERS		QUESTION #	CORRECT	MARK YOUR CORRECT ANSWERS		QUESTION #	CORRECT	MARK YOUR CORRECT ANSWERS
1	C			1	B			1	A	
2	B			2	B			2	B	
3	B			3	2520			3	B	
4	A			4	40			4	C	
5	C			5	7			5	D	
6	5			6	30			6	C	
7	D			7	180			7	C	
8	A			8	C			8	C	
9	28			9	A			9	A	
10	C			10	D			10	C	
11	11			11	D			11	-.9333; -14/15	
12	9			12	A			12	203/50; 4.06	
13	A			13	A			13	289	
14	D			14	C			14	44	
15	D			15	A			15	D	
16	B			16	D			16	14.5; 29/2	
17	C			17	D			17	C	
18	C			18	C			18	C	
19	D			19	D			19	A	
20	B			20	C			20	10	
21	B			21	D			21	B	
22	59/9; 6.555; 6.556			22	A			22	D	

MATH SECTION RAW SCORE (Total # of Correct Answers)

[ ] **+** [ ] **OR** [ ] **=** [ ]

Module 1 (Routing) Module 2 (Lower Difficulty) Module 2 (Higher Difficulty)

Understanding the SAT Practice Test Conversion Tables and Total Score Ranges

As mentioned earlier in this scoring guide, the scoring method for the practice tests that appear in *The Official SAT Study Guide* is different (and therefore less precise) than the method used in the actual adaptive test. Your practice test may result in a larger score range than what you hoped to see, but it's not feasible to estimate your performance on the practice tests in the study guide as precisely as we could for an actual test. As the test developers, College Board is committed to providing the most accurate conversion possible to help you understand your scores and guide your practice most effectively.

There are two conversion tables in this scoring guide. Use the conversion table labelled lower difficulty if you took module 2 (lower difficulty). Use the conversion table labelled higher difficulty if you took module 2 (higher difficulty). You might need both conversion tables if you took the lower-difficulty option for one section (e.g., Reading and Writing) and the higher-difficulty option for the other section (e.g., Math).

Because the lower- and higher-difficulty conversion tables share the same questions for module 1 (routing), you may encounter different score ranges based on the conversion table you use. For example, if you got all the module 1 (routing) questions correct, the lower-difficulty conversion table and the higher-difficulty conversion table will give you different score ranges. This is to be expected because the conversion tables account for all items within the two modules that make up the test. Answering only items on the first half of the test assumes you answered the other questions (module 2) incorrectly. Recall that when taking the actual SAT on test day, the test will adapt to your ability based on how you perform on the first half. Because of the differences between the actual test and providing a paper approximation of that (the practice test you're currently scoring), you should select the second-stage module that feels most appropriate for you. For example, if you were to answer all items on the first module correctly on the actual test, you would not be routed to the easier second-stage module. The converse would also be true. For many users of moderate ability either second-stage would be acceptable, but very high or low performers should be cautioned about taking the second-stage module that doesn't align well with their ability.

SAT Practice Test Worksheet: Section and Total Scores

Conversion: Calculate Your Section and Total Scores

Enter your raw score for each section (from the answer key pages earlier in this scoring guide) in the boxes below. Find that section raw score in the first column of the appropriate conversion table on the next page (either lower or higher difficulty, depending on which module 2 you chose for each section) and then enter the corresponding lower and upper values in the two-column boxes. Add each of your lower and upper values for the test sections separately to calculate your total SAT score range.

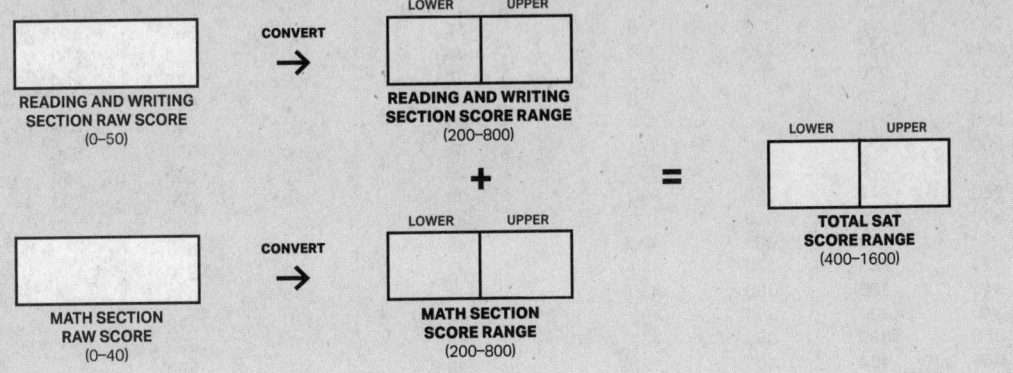

READING AND WRITING
SECTION RAW SCORE
(0–50)

CONVERT →

LOWER   UPPER

READING AND WRITING
SECTION SCORE RANGE
(200–800)

+

MATH SECTION
RAW SCORE
(0–40)

CONVERT →

LOWER   UPPER

MATH SECTION
SCORE RANGE
(200–800)

=

LOWER   UPPER

TOTAL SAT
SCORE RANGE
(400–1600)

Raw Score Conversion Tables

Section Scores: Lower Difficulty

RAW SCORE (# OF CORRECT ANSWERS)	Reading and Writing Section Score Range		Math Section Score Range	
	LOWER	UPPER	LOWER	UPPER
0	200	260	200	260
1	200	270	200	270
2	200	270	200	270
3	200	270	200	270
4	200	270	200	270
5	200	270	200	270
6	200	270	200	270
7	200	270	220	300
8	200	270	270	310
9	200	270	290	350
10	200	270	300	360
11	200	270	330	370
12	250	310	340	380
13	280	340	350	390
14	300	360	360	400
15	310	370	360	400
16	320	380	370	410
17	340	380	380	420
18	340	380	390	430
19	350	390	390	430
20	360	400	400	440
21	360	400	410	450
22	370	410	420	460
23	380	420	430	470
24	390	430	440	480
25	390	430	450	490
26	400	440	460	500
27	410	450	460	520
28	420	460	480	540
29	430	470	490	550
30	430	490	500	560
31	440	500	520	580
32	440	500	530	590
33	450	510	550	610
34	460	520	560	640
35	470	530	580	660
36	480	540	600	680
37	490	550	630	710
38	500	560	650	750
39	510	570	700	800
40	520	580	760	800
41	540	600		
42	550	610		
43	570	630		
44	570	650		
45	590	670		
46	610	690		
47	640	720		
48	670	750		
49	710	790		
50	760	800		

Section Scores: Higher Difficulty

RAW SCORE (# OF CORRECT ANSWERS)	Reading and Writing Section Score Range		Math Section Score Range	
	LOWER	UPPER	LOWER	UPPER
0	200	300	200	300
1	200	310	200	300
2	200	310	200	300
3	200	310	200	300
4	200	310	200	300
5	200	310	200	300
6	200	310	200	310
7	200	310	240	320
8	200	310	300	380
9	200	310	330	410
10	200	310	350	430
11	200	310	370	430
12	280	380	380	440
13	310	410	400	460
14	330	430	420	480
15	340	440	430	490
16	370	450	440	500
17	390	450	460	520
18	400	460	470	530
19	410	470	480	540
20	430	490	500	560
21	440	500	510	570
22	450	510	520	580
23	460	520	540	600
24	470	530	550	610
25	480	540	560	620
26	490	550	570	630
27	500	560	590	650
28	510	570	600	660
29	520	580	610	670
30	520	580	630	690
31	530	590	640	700
32	540	600	660	720
33	550	610	670	730
34	560	620	690	750
35	570	630	710	770
36	580	640	730	790
37	590	650	750	800
38	600	660	760	800
39	610	670	770	800
40	620	680	780	800
41	630	690		
42	650	710		
43	660	720		
44	670	730		
45	680	740		
46	710	750		
47	720	760		
48	740	780		
49	750	790		
50	780	800		

The SAT®

Practice Test #5

Make time to take the practice test. It is one of the best ways to get ready for the SAT.

Note: The practice tests in this guide include two second modules so that you can experience both the lower- and higher-difficulty modules. On the actual test, you will be presented with only one second module.

After you have taken the practice test, score it right away using materials provided in *The Official SAT Study Guide*.

This version of the SAT Practice Test is for students using this Study Guide. As a reminder, most students taking the SAT will do so using Bluebook™, the digital testing application. To best prepare for test day, download Bluebook at **bluebook.app.collegeboard.org** to take the practice test in the digital format.

Test begins on the next page.

Reading and Writing

27 QUESTIONS

DIRECTIONS

The questions in this section address a number of important reading and writing skills. Each question includes one or more passages, which may include a table or graph. Read each passage and question carefully, and then choose the best answer to the question based on the passage(s).

All questions in this section are multiple-choice with four answer choices. Each question has a single best answer.

1

According to a team of neuroeconomists from the University of Zurich, ease of decision making may be linked to communication between two brain regions, the prefrontal cortex and the parietal cortex. Individuals tend to be more decisive if the information flow between the regions is intensified, whereas they make choices more slowly when information flow is _____.

Which choice completes the text with the most logical and precise word or phrase?

A) reduced

B) evaluated

C) determined

D) acquired

2

Ecologist Exequiel Ezcurra and colleagues found that the inhabitants of the Mexica empire used natural landmarks to track time with a high degree of _____. By observing the sun's position in relation to various points on the mountains surrounding the Basin of Mexico, the Mexica were able to precisely identify the dates when significant events such as solstices occurred.

Which choice completes the text with the most logical and precise word or phrase?

A) precariousness

B) exactitude

C) resilience

D) inconspicuousness

CONTINUE ➤

3

In editor Lisa Yaszek's introduction to her anthology *The Future Is Female! More Classic Science Fiction Stories by Women*, Yaszek identifies an increasing sense of _____ feminist mode of writing in the 1970s, in contrast to many woman-authored science fiction stories of the 1920s to 1960s whose politics were less deliberately signaled.

Which choice completes the text with the most logical and precise word or phrase?

A) a prudently

B) an overtly

C) a cordially

D) an inadvertently

4

K.D. Leka and colleagues found that the Sun's corona provides an advance indication of solar flares—intense eruptions of electromagnetic radiation that emanate from active regions in the Sun's photosphere and can interfere with telecommunications on Earth. Preceding a flare, the corona temporarily exhibits increased brightness above the region where the flare is _____.

Which choice completes the text with the most logical and precise word or phrase?

A) antecedent

B) impending

C) innocuous

D) perpetual

5

The following text is adapted from Jean Webster's 1912 novel *Daddy-Long-Legs*. The narrator is a young college student writing letters detailing her weekly experiences.

[The college is] organizing the Freshman basket-ball team and there's just a chance that I shall make it. I'm little of course, but terribly quick and wiry and tough. While the others are hopping about in the air, I can dodge under their feet and grab the ball.

Which choice best states the main purpose of the text?

A) To compare basketball with other sports

B) To provide details of how to play basketball

C) To state how players will be chosen for the basketball team

D) To explain why the narrator thinks she might make the basketball team

6

Researchers have long hypothesized that woolly mammoths were hunted to extinction in North America by humans using spears with grooved tips known as Clovis points. One anthropologist set out to test this hypothesis. Using a mechanical spear-thrower, he launched spears with Clovis points into mounds of clay—substitutes for the animals' large bodies. The projectiles generally penetrated only a few inches into the clay, an amount insufficient to have harmed most woolly mammoths. This led the anthropologist to conclude that hunters using spears with Clovis points likely weren't the principal drivers of the extinction.

Which choice best states the main purpose of the text?

A) To argue for the significance of new findings amid an ongoing debate among researchers

B) To discuss the advantages and disadvantages of the method used in an experiment

C) To summarize two competing hypotheses and a major finding associated with each one

D) To describe an experiment whose results cast doubt on an established hypothesis

CONTINUE

7

The ancient writing system used in the Maya kingdoms of southern Mexico and Central America had a symbol for the number zero. The earliest known example of the symbol dates to more than 2,000 years ago. At that time, almost none of the writing systems elsewhere in the world possessed a zero symbol. And the use of zero in Mexico and Central America may be even more ancient. Some historians suggest that Maya mathematicians inherited it from the Olmec civilization, which flourished in the region 2,400–3,600 years ago.

According to the text, what do some historians suggest about Maya civilization?

A) Maya civilization acquired the use of zero from the Olmec civilization.

B) Maya civilization respected its historians more than it respected its mathematicians.

C) Maya civilization was highly secretive about its intellectual achievements.

D) Maya civilization tried to introduce its writing system to other civilizations.

8

A subject of much speculation, distinctive sets of parallel ridges mark the icy crust of Europa, Jupiter's smallest moon. Researchers now claim that the ridges' formation mechanism mirrors that of a strikingly similar pair on Greenland's ice sheet. There, surface water seeped through fissures in the sheet and formed a water pocket that subsequently disrupted the overlying ice, forcing fragments of it upward and outward into peaks, as the pocket froze and expanded. Although Europa lacks liquid surface water, the same process could be driven by the moon's subsurface ocean.

Which choice best states the main idea of the text?

A) Researchers think that the ridges on Europa and the ridges in Greenland may have been formed by the same process even though Europa, unlike Greenland, doesn't have liquid water on its surface.

B) The primary difference between the ridges on Europa and the ridges in Greenland is that unlike the Europa ridges, the Greenland ridges are parallel.

C) The pair of ridges found on Greenland's ice sheet appear to have formed long before the recently discovered sets of ridges on Europa formed.

D) Researchers don't understand why Europa is marked by so many sets of ridges when the moon doesn't have any liquid water on its surface that could have collected and expanded under the icy crust.

CONTINUE

9

To understand how Paleolithic artists navigated dark caves, archaeologist Mª Ángeles Medina-Alcaide and her team tested different lighting methods in a cave in Spain using replicas of artifacts found in European caves with art. They used three different Paleolithic light sources—torches, animal-fat lamps, and fireplaces—determining that each likely had a specific purpose. For instance, the team learned that the animal-fat lamps were less useful than torches while walking because the lamps didn't illuminate the cave floor.

Which choice best states the main idea of the text?

A) Medina-Alcaide and her team's study demonstrated that fireplaces were essential to the creators of Paleolithic cave art.

B) Medina-Alcaide and her team discovered that Paleolithic cave artists in Spain used animal-fat lamps more often than they used torches.

C) Medina-Alcaide and her team were reluctant to draw many conclusions from their study because of the difficulty they had replicating light sources based on known artifacts.

D) Medina-Alcaide and her team tested Paleolithic light sources and learned some details about how Paleolithic artists traveled within dark caves.

10

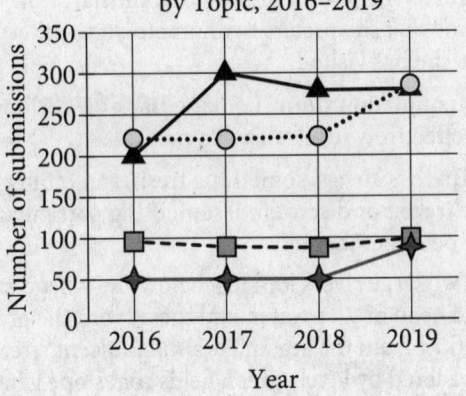

Total Science Research Submissions by Topic, 2016–2019

Legend:
— cellular and molecular biology
- - ■ - - physics and space science
··· ○ ··· medicine and health
✦ animal science

A student is researching the trends in the topics submitted to a national science fair for high school students. The graph shows the number of submissions by topic that were made each year. Based on the data in the graph, the student claims that there were more medicine and health research topics submitted in 2019 than in any other year.

Which choice most effectively uses data from the graph to support the underlined claim?

A) In 2016, the number of cellular and molecular biology topic submissions was the same as the number of animal science topic submissions.

B) In 2019, there were more physics and space science topic submissions than there were medicine and health topic submissions.

C) The lowest number of animal science topic submissions in a year was approximately 95 in 2016.

D) The highest number of medicine and health topic submissions during the period shown is approximately 285 in 2019.

CONTINUE

447

11

"Looking Back on Girlhood" is an 1892 short story by Sarah Orne Jewett. In the story, the narrator explains that she prefers her hometown to other places she has visited: _____

Which quotation from "Looking Back on Girlhood" most effectively illustrates this claim?

A) "There is always something fresh, something to be traced or discovered, something particularly to be remembered."

B) "Two large rivers join just below the village at the head of tide-water, and these, with the great inflow from the sea, make a magnificent stream, bordered by lovely green fields that slope gently to long lines of willows at the water's edge."

C) "I have had a good deal of journeying in my life, and taken great delight in it, but I have never taken greater delight than in my rides and drives and tramps and voyages within the borders of my native town."

D) "There is never-ending pleasure in making one's self familiar with such a region."

12

External shopping cues are a type of marketing that uses obvious messaging—a display featuring a new product, for example, or a "buy one, get one free" offer—to entice consumers to make spontaneous purchases. In a study, data scientist Sam K. Hui and colleagues found that this effect can also be achieved with a less obvious cue: rearranging a store's layout. The researchers explain that trying to find items in new locations causes shoppers to move through more of the store, exposing them to more products and increasing the likelihood that they'll buy an item they hadn't planned on purchasing.

Which response from a survey given to shoppers who made a purchase at a retail store best supports the researchers' explanation?

A) "I needed to buy some cleaning supplies, but they weren't in their regular place. While I was looking for them, I saw this interesting notebook and decided to buy it, too."

B) "I didn't buy everything on my shopping list today. I couldn't find a couple of the items in the store, even though I looked all over for them."

C) "The store sent me a coupon for a new brand of soup, so I came here to find out what kinds of soup that brand offers. I decided to buy a few cans because I had the coupon."

D) "This store is larger than one that's closer to where I live, and it carries more products. I came here to buy some things that the other store doesn't always have."

CONTINUE ➡

13

Even with the widespread adoption of personal computers, many authors still choose to write and revise their novels by hand and only then transcribe the final version on a computer. It may be tempting to speculate about how a novel written this way would be affected if it had been exclusively typed instead, but each novel is a unique entity resulting from a specific set of circumstances. Therefore, _____

Which choice most logically completes the text?

A) in order to increase their efficiency, authors who currently write their novels largely by hand should instead work only on a computer.

B) authors who do most of their drafting and revising by hand likely have more success than those who work entirely on a computer.

C) novels written by hand take less time to produce, on average, than novels written on a computer do.

D) there is no way to reasonably evaluate how a work would be different if it had been written by other means.

14

Behavioral ecologists Will Wiggins, Sarah Bounds, and Shawn Wilder recently examined the behavior of field-collected and laboratory-reared bold jumping spiders (*Phidippus audax*). They found a positive association between experimental high-protein diets and aggressive behavior in field-collected males and a similar association between experimental high-lipid diets and aggressive behavior in lab-reared males; additionally, field-collected spiders showed a preference for flowers manipulated to display ultraviolet fluorescence, whereas lab-reared spiders showed a preference for flowers dyed with red food coloring that was not fluorescent. Wiggins, Bounds, and Wilder therefore concluded that _____

Which choice most logically completes the text?

A) rearing conditions likely affect the responses of bold jumping spiders to experimental stimuli.

B) being raised in a laboratory setting reduces aggression among male bold jumping spiders.

C) laboratory settings are more suitable for studying bold jumping spiders' diets than their flower preferences.

D) experiments involving bold jumping spiders should make use of lab-reared individuals.

CONTINUE ➤

15

In forecasting weather events, meteorologists sometimes discuss the role of atmospheric rivers. What are atmospheric rivers, and how _____ Part of the water cycle, atmospheric rivers are narrow channels of moisture moving through the atmosphere. In certain conditions, these "rivers" can release some of their moisture as precipitation.

Which choice completes the text so that it conforms to the conventions of Standard English?

A) do they affect our weather.

B) they do affect our weather.

C) do they affect our weather?

D) they do affect our weather?

16

The soundtrack to Mira Nair's 1991 film *Mississippi Masala* expressively captures the clashing of cultures that happens when _____ (a young Indian woman from Uganda and a young African American man from Mississippi) meet. Featured throughout the film are songs from Uganda's Afrigo Band, the Indian composer L. Subramaniam, and the Mississippi blues musician Sam Chatmon.

Which choice completes the text so that it conforms to the conventions of Standard English?

A) it's two protagonists

B) its two protagonist's

C) it's two protagonist's

D) its two protagonists

17

Julia Alvarez's 1994 novel *In the Time of the Butterflies,* a fictionalized account of the lives of the Mirabal _____ can serve as a starting point for those wanting to explore how the rule of dictator Rafael Trujillo has been represented in Dominican American literature.

Which choice completes the text so that it conforms to the conventions of Standard English?

A) sisters, and

B) sisters and

C) sisters,

D) sisters

18

On March 23, 2021, a gust of wind wreaked havoc on global trade. *Ever Given,* an international shipping container vessel, became lodged in Egypt's Suez Canal, a major shipping route between Europe and Asia. The vessel took six days to _____ it's as heavy as two thousand blue whales when fully loaded.

Which choice completes the text so that it conforms to the conventions of Standard English?

A) dislodge in part due to its sheer size,

B) dislodge, in part due to its sheer size:

C) dislodge, in part due to its sheer size,

D) dislodge, in part, due to its sheer size

CONTINUE ➔

19

Woven from recycled yarn and hand tufted using a carpet weaving technique passed down by the artist's Turkish grandmother, _____ so lush and tactilely inviting that you are tempted to reach out and touch them.

Which choice completes the text so that it conforms to the conventions of Standard English?

A) the topological tapestries of Argentine textile artist Alexandra Kehayoglou are

B) the Argentine textile artist Alexandra Kehayoglou creates topological tapestries that are

C) when she creates her topological tapestries, Argentine textile artist Alexandra Kehayoglou makes them

D) Alexandra Kehayoglou is an Argentine textile artist whose topological tapestries are

20

Jamaican British artist Willard Wigan is known for his remarkable _____ so small that they are best viewed through a microscope, Wigan's sculptures are made from tiny natural materials, such as spiderweb strands.

Which choice completes the text so that it conforms to the conventions of Standard English?

A) microsculptures creations

B) microsculptures, creations

C) microsculptures. Creations

D) microsculptures and creations

21

After appropriate permissions are granted, a typical archaeological dig begins with a surveyor making a detailed grid of the excavation site. Then, the site is carefully dug, and any artifacts found are recorded and mapped onto the site grid. _____ the artifacts are removed, cataloged, and analyzed in a laboratory.

Which choice completes the text with the most logical transition?

A) For instance,

B) On the contrary,

C) Earlier,

D) Finally,

22

In 1949, Frank Zamboni developed an ice rink resurfacing machine. As Zamboni's machine moved along the rink's surface, it first scraped off the top layer of ice. _____ it sprayed water into the deep grooves left behind by customers' skates. Lastly, it smoothed over the newly formed ice.

Which choice completes the text with the most logical transition?

A) For example,

B) Next,

C) Similarly,

D) In contrast,

CONTINUE

23

In the 1880s, inventor Lewis Latimer improved upon Thomas Edison's design for the electric light bulb. _____ Latimer made the light bulb more durable by placing cardboard around its carbon filament. With this innovation, Latimer became the first Black inventor to contribute to the electrification of the world.

Which choice completes the text with the most logical transition?

A) Soon,

B) Regardless,

C) However,

D) Specifically,

24

Jeffrey Gibson's sculptural object *KNOW YOUR MAGIC, BABY*, an Everlast-brand exercise bag embroidered with multicolored beads and a fringe associated with the dances of the Ojibwe people, stitches together—literally and figuratively—recognizable symbols from both Native and non-Native cultures. _____ Gibson's piece also blurs the distinction between contemporary art and traditional crafts.

Which choice completes the text with the most logical transition?

A) Conversely,

B) In so doing,

C) For instance,

D) In particular,

25

While researching a topic, a student has taken the following notes:

- In World War I, US soldiers who were members of the Choctaw Nation in Oklahoma participated in the Choctaw Code Talkers program.

- The Choctaw Code Talkers were trained to relay coded military information in their native language.

- In World War II, the US Army recruited Navajo (Diné) soldiers to transmit coded messages in their native language.

- These soldiers were known as the Navajo Code Talkers.

The student wants to emphasize a similarity between the Choctaw Code Talkers and the Navajo Code Talkers. Which choice most effectively uses relevant information from the notes to accomplish this goal?

A) US soldiers who were members of the Choctaw Nation in Oklahoma used their native language to relay coded information.

B) In World War II, one group of Navajo (Diné) soldiers was known as the Navajo Code Talkers.

C) Both the Choctaw Code Talkers and the Navajo Code Talkers transmitted coded military messages in the soldiers' native languages.

D) The Choctaw Code Talkers, not the Navajo Code Talkers, served in World War I.

CONTINUE

26

While researching a topic, a student has taken the following notes:

- The International Center for the Arts of the Americas (ICAA) is directed by Mari Carmen Ramírez.
- Ramírez oversaw an initiative to create an online archive of historical documents related to the history of Latin American and Latino visual art.
- The ICAA digitized over 10,000 documents, including the writings of Latin American and Latino artists and critics.
- The creation of the archive didn't require historical documents to be removed from their countries of origin.
- Scholars now have more access to these documents.

The student wants to explain an advantage of the ICAA's archive being digital. Which choice most effectively uses relevant information from the notes to accomplish this goal?

A) Over 10,000 documents related to the history of Latin American and Latino visual art are part of the ICAA archive.

B) By offering online versions of historical documents, the ICAA's archive provides more access to these materials without removing them from their countries of origin.

C) Among the historical documents in the ICAA's archive are the writings of Latin American and Latino artists and critics.

D) The ICAA's director, Mari Carmen Ramírez, oversaw the creation of an online archive of historical documents related to Latin American and Latino visual art.

27

While researching a topic, a student has taken the following notes:

- Sister Rosetta Tharpe (1915–1973) was a gospel musician.
- She was known for her passionate vocals and electric guitar performances.
- In 2018, Tharpe was inducted into the Rock and Roll Hall of Fame for her major impact on the genre.
- According to songwriter Roxie Moore, "[Tharpe] would sing until you cried and then she would sing until you danced for joy."
- According to guitarist Celisse Henderson, "Tharpe is the unquestioned founding mother of rock 'n' roll."

The student wants to use a quotation to support a claim about Tharpe's contribution to rock 'n' roll. Which choice most effectively uses relevant information from the notes to accomplish this goal?

A) Gospel musician Sister Rosetta Tharpe had a major impact on rock 'n' roll, and she was known for her passionate electric guitar performances.

B) Celisse Henderson believes that Sister Rosetta Tharpe had a major impact on the development of rock 'n' roll.

C) Sister Rosetta Tharpe had such a major impact on rock 'n' roll that Celisse Henderson called her "the unquestioned founding mother" of the genre.

D) A gospel musician, Sister Rosetta Tharpe had the ability to "sing until you cried" and also "until you danced for joy," according to Roxie Moore.

STOP

If you finish before time is called, you may check your work on this module only. Do not turn to any other module in the test.

Reading and Writing

27 QUESTIONS

DIRECTIONS

The questions in this section address a number of important reading and writing skills. Each question includes one or more passages, which may include a table or graph. Read each passage and question carefully, and then choose the best answer to the question based on the passage(s).

All questions in this section are multiple-choice with four answer choices. Each question has a single best answer.

1

The following text is adapted from Elizabeth von Arnim's 1922 novel *The Enchanted April*. Mrs. Wilkins and her friend Rose are traveling in Italy.

"I'm going to have one of these gorgeous oranges," said Mrs. Wilkins, staying where she was and <u>reaching across to</u> a black bowl piled with them. "Rose, how can you resist them. Look—have this one. Do have this beauty—" And she held out a big one.

As used in the text, what does the phrase "reaching across to" most nearly mean?

A) Joining with

B) Gaining on

C) Stretching toward

D) Arriving at

2

Many ancient sculptures of people's heads are missing their noses. This is because the nose is the most _____ part of a sculpture of a person's head. It is delicate and sticks out from the rest of the sculpture, making it especially easy to break.

Which choice completes the text with the most logical and precise word or phrase?

A) recognizable

B) fragile

C) common

D) sophisticated

CONTINUE ➤

3

A team of paleontologists has found a rich fossil deposit near Gulgong, Australia. The fossils are so well preserved that the team has been able to _____ detailed information about the life forms that left them behind, such as color patterns and how they interacted with other species.

Which choice completes the text with the most logical and precise word or phrase?

A) occupy

B) hoard

C) reserve

D) obtain

4

Urban planning expert Francisco Lara-Valencia and colleagues have argued that managing environmental matters along the US-Mexico border _____ coordination between the two countries' governments. Since ecosystems extend across the border, actions taken on one side can have environmental effects on the other side, making international cooperation essential.

Which choice completes the text with the most logical and precise word or phrase?

A) requires

B) praises

C) reports

D) advises

5

Though not closely related, the hedgehog tenrecs of Madagascar share basic _____ true hedgehogs, including protective spines, pointed snouts, and small body size—traits the two groups of mammals independently developed in response to equivalent roles in their respective habitats.

Which choice completes the text with the most logical and precise word or phrase?

A) examples of

B) concerns about

C) indications of

D) similarities with

6

The following text is from Paul Laurence Dunbar's 1913 poem "The Poet and His Song."

> A song is but a little thing,
> And yet what joy it is to sing!
> In hours of toil it gives me zest,
> And when at eve I long for rest;
> When cows come home along the bars,
> And in the fold I hear the bell,
> As Night, the shepherd, herds his stars,
> I sing my song, and all is well.

Which choice best states the main purpose of the text?

A) To convey how engaging in song makes the speaker feel

B) To compare the speaker to a singing shepherd

C) To portray the speaker's excitement about farming

D) To describe the pieces of music the speaker enjoys hearing

CONTINUE ➤

7

In the late 1800s, Spanish-language newspapers flourished in cities across Texas. San Antonio alone produced eleven newspapers in Spanish between 1890 and 1900. But El Paso surpassed all other cities in the state. This city produced twenty-two newspapers in Spanish during that period. El Paso is located on the border with Mexico and has always had a large population of Spanish speakers. Thus, it is unsurprising that this city became such a rich site for Spanish-language journalism.

Which choice best states the main purpose of the text?

A) To compare Spanish-language newspapers published in Texas today with ones published there during the late 1800s

B) To explain that Spanish-language newspapers thrived in Texas and especially in El Paso during the late 1800s

C) To argue that Spanish-language newspapers published in El Paso influenced the ones published in San Antonio during the late 1800s

D) To explain why Spanish-language newspapers published in Texas were so popular in Mexico during the late 1800s

8

Text 1
In 1954 George Balanchine choreographed a production of *The Nutcracker,* a ballet by Pyotr Ilyich Tchaikovsky. It has since become a tradition for hundreds of dance companies in North America to stage *The Nutcracker* each year. But the show is stuck in the past, with an old-fashioned story and references, so it should no longer be produced. Ballet needs to create new traditions if it wants to stay relevant to contemporary audiences.

Text 2
The Nutcracker is outdated, but it should be kept because it's a holiday favorite and provides substantial income for some dance companies. Although it can be behind the times, there are creative ways to update the show. For example, Debbie Allen successfully modernized the story. Her show *Hot Chocolate Nutcracker* combines ballet, tap, hip-hop, and other styles, and it has been gaining in popularity since it opened in 2009.

Based on the texts, how would the author of Text 2 most likely respond to the underlined claim in Text 1?

A) By questioning the idea that the story of *The Nutcracker* is stuck in the past and by rejecting the suggestion that contemporary audiences would enjoy an updated version

B) By agreeing that contemporary audiences have largely stopped going to see performances of *The Nutcracker* because it's so old-fashioned

C) By pointing out that most dance companies could increase their incomes by offering modernized versions of *The Nutcracker*

D) By suggesting that dance companies should consider offering revised versions of *The Nutcracker* instead of completely rejecting the show

CONTINUE

9

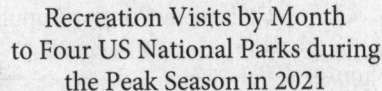

Recreation Visits by Month
to Four US National Parks during
the Peak Season in 2021

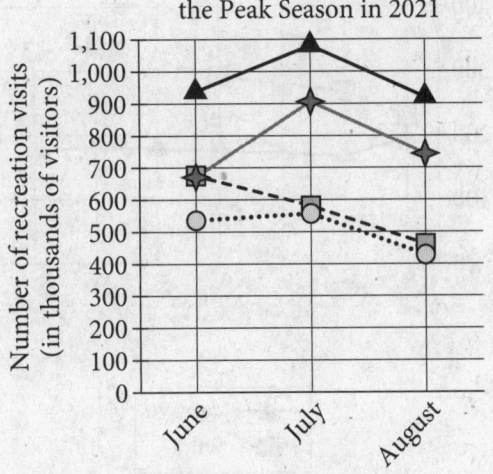

Month

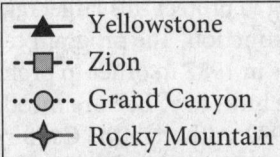

In 2021, four of the United States national parks that were among the most visited were Grand Canyon National Park, Rocky Mountain National Park, Yellowstone National Park, and Zion National Park. The graph shows the number of visits for recreation to each of these parks during the three-month period with the highest number of visitors.

A student notes that among the parks shown in the graph, the park with the highest monthly recreation visits in all three months was _____

Which choice most effectively uses data from the graph to complete the text?

A) Zion National Park.

B) Rocky Mountain National Park.

C) Yellowstone National Park.

D) Grand Canyon National Park.

10

Average Clothing Prices, 2019–2022

Clothing type	2019	2020	2021	2022
button-down shirts	$44.05	$40.54	$45.73	$47.75
sweaters	$66.40	$58.30	$64.64	$55.28
dresses	$128.17	$95.96	$106.98	$101.29
jackets	$131.20	$89.79	$133.87	$99.20

An employee at a clothing retailer is writing a report and needs to determine whether there are any clothing types for which the average sales price of an article of clothing was lower in 2019 than in 2022. Consulting the table, she finds that this was the case for _____

Which choice most effectively uses data from the table to complete the assertion?

A) dresses.

B) jackets.

C) button-down shirts.

D) sweaters.

CONTINUE

11

Male túngara frogs make complex calls to attract mates, but their calls also attract frog-biting midges, insects that feed on the frogs' blood. Researchers Ximena Bernal and Priyanka de Silva wondered if the calls alone are sufficient for midges to locate the frogs or if midges use carbon dioxide emitted by frogs as an additional cue to their prey's whereabouts, like mosquitoes do. In an experiment, the researchers placed two midge traps in a túngara frog breeding area. One trap played recordings of túngara frog calls and the other released carbon dioxide along with playing the calls. Bernal and de Silva concluded that carbon dioxide does not serve as an additional cue to frog-biting midges.

Which finding from the experiment, if true, would most directly support Bernal and de Silva's conclusion?

A) Only a small number of midges were found in the traps, though the majority were found in the trap that played calls and released carbon dioxide.

B) Midges entered the trap that released carbon dioxide and played calls only during or immediately after periods of carbon dioxide release.

C) More midges were found in the trap that only played calls than in the trap that played calls and released carbon dioxide.

D) The trap that released carbon dioxide and played calls attracted few midges when carbon dioxide concentrations were low but attracted many midges when carbon dioxide concentrations were high.

12

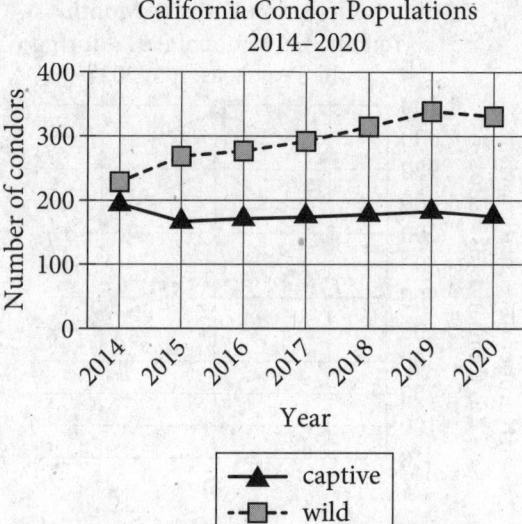

The California Condor Recovery Program is working to protect this large, rare American vulture from extinction. The program captured 27 wild condors in 1987 in order to protect and breed them. Captive birds have been reintroduced into the wild since 1992. Although the California condor is still a rare species, many biologists claim that the program has been reasonably successful.

Which choice best describes data from the graph that support the biologists' claim?

A) The number of captive California condors steadily decreased between 2014 and 2020.

B) The numbers of California condors living both in captivity and in the wild decreased only slightly from 2019 to 2020.

C) The difference between the number of captive and wild California condors remained relatively steady between 2014 and 2017.

D) The number of wild California condors increased overall from 2014 to 2020 and exceeded the number of those living in captivity.

Unauthorized copying or reuse of any part of this page is illegal.

CONTINUE

458

13

Annual Spending by
International Tourists in Four Countries
(in billions of US dollars)

Country	2016	2017	2018
South Korea	$21.0	$17.2	$23.1
Japan	$33.5	$37.0	$45.3
Thailand	$48.5	$57.1	$61.4
Malaysia	$19.7	$20.3	$21.8

One measure of international tourism is how much money visitors from abroad spend in a country. A student writing a report about tourism in several Asian countries notes that among the countries in the table, most had annual increases in international tourism revenue in 2017 and 2018, but that trend wasn't universal. For example, _____

Which choice most effectively uses data from the table to complete the example?

A) in each year shown, the revenue from tourism by residents of those countries was greater than the revenue from international tourism.

B) Japan's international tourism revenue was higher in 2016 than it was in 2018.

C) South Korea's annual international tourism revenue decreased from 2016 to 2017.

D) in each year shown, Thailand had higher international tourism income than any of the other countries.

14

Fish whose DNA has been modified to include genetic material from other species are known as transgenic. Some transgenic fish have genes from jellyfish that result in fluorescence (that is, they glow in the dark). Although these fish were initially engineered for research purposes in the 1990s, they were sold as pets in the 2000s and can now be found in the wild in creeks in Brazil. A student in a biology seminar who is writing a paper on these fish asserts that their escape from Brazilian fish farms into the wild may have significant negative long-term ecological effects.

Which quotation from a researcher would best support the student's assertion?

A) "In one site in the wild where transgenic fish were observed, females outnumbered males, while in another the numbers of females and males were equivalent."

B) "Though some presence of transgenic fish in the wild has been recorded, there are insufficient studies of the impact of those fish on the ecosystems into which they are introduced."

C) "The ecosystems into which transgenic fish are known to have been introduced may represent a subset of the ecosystems into which the fish have actually been introduced."

D) "Through interbreeding, transgenic fish might introduce the trait of fluorescence into wild fish populations, making those populations more vulnerable to predators."

Unauthorized copying or reuse of any part of this page is illegal.

CONTINUE →

459

15

The practice of logging (cutting down trees for commercial and other uses) is often thought to be at odds with forest conservation (the work of preserving forests). However, a massive study in forest management and preservation spanning 700,000 hectares in Oregon's Malheur National Forest calls that view into question. So far, results of the study suggest that forest plots that have undergone limited logging (the careful removal of a controlled number of trees) may be more robust than plots that haven't been logged at all. These results, in turn, suggest that _____

Which choice most logically completes the text?

A) logging may be useful for maintaining healthy forests, provided it is limited.

B) other forest management strategies are more effective than limited logging.

C) as time passes, it will be difficult to know whether limited logging has any benefits.

D) the best way to support forest health may be to leave large forests entirely untouched.

16

The Boston Saloon was one of the most popular African American–owned establishments in nineteenth-century Nevada. _____ by businessman William A.G. Brown, the saloon was known to offer elegant accommodations and an inclusive environment.

Which choice completes the text so that it conforms to the conventions of Standard English?

A) Created

B) Creates

C) Creating

D) Create

17

Lê Lương Minh became the thirteenth secretary-general of the Association of Southeast Asian Nations (ASEAN) in January 2013, making _____ the first time the organization would appoint a Vietnamese leader.

Which choice completes the text so that it conforms to the conventions of Standard English?

A) these

B) those

C) this

D) some

Unauthorized copying or reuse of any part of this page is illegal.

CONTINUE ▶

460

18

Louise Bennett (1919–2006), also known as "Miss Lou," was an influential Jamaican poet and folklorist. Her innovative poems _____ the use of Jamaican Creole (a spoken language) in literature.

Which choice completes the text so that it conforms to the conventions of Standard English?

A) popularized;

B) popularized,

C) popularized

D) popularized:

19

Researchers Amit Kumar and Nicholas Epley investigated how _____ In a series of experiments conducted in 2022, they found that people performing small acts of kindness underestimated the positive effect their actions had on others.

Which choice completes the text so that it conforms to the conventions of Standard English?

A) do people perceive acts of kindness.

B) do people perceive acts of kindness?

C) people perceive acts of kindness?

D) people perceive acts of kindness.

20

One of the few African American global explorers during the turn of the 20th century, _____

Which choice completes the text so that it conforms to the conventions of Standard English?

A) Matthew Henson made several treks across Greenland between 1891 and 1909.

B) 1891 and 1909 were the years between which Matthew Henson made several treks across Greenland.

C) Greenland was where Matthew Henson made several treks between 1891 and 1909.

D) several treks across Greenland were made by Matthew Henson between 1891 and 1909.

21

Oyster mushrooms typically get their nutrients from the damp logs on which they grow, but the fungi are also carnivorous, with the ability to kill and consume microscopic worms known as nematodes. As researcher Yen-Ping Hsueh has shown, the mushrooms release a toxin that is deadly to nematodes that _____ in contact with it.

Which choice completes the text so that it conforms to the conventions of Standard English?

A) has come

B) comes

C) is coming

D) come

Unauthorized copying or reuse of any part of this page is illegal.

CONTINUE

461

22

In the search for extraterrestrial life, astrobiologists Stuart Bartlett and Michael L. Wong propose that scientists avoid using the term "life." _____ researchers should use another word: "lyfe." This new term, they argue, could be used to draw distinctions between the known characteristics of life on Earth and the potentially differing characteristics of lyfe on other planets.

Which choice completes the text with the most logical transition?

A) Previously,

B) Regardless,

C) There,

D) Instead,

23

To guarantee the validity of experimental results, scientists rely on precise, unchanging standards of measurement. _____ metrologists (scientists who study measurement) developed the SI, or International System of Units. The SI's units of measurement are based on unchanging values in nature, such as the mass of an electron or the speed of light.

Which choice completes the text with the most logical transition?

A) In contrast,

B) Regardless,

C) In addition,

D) For this reason,

24

My interest in old public libraries has led me to seek them out whenever I visit a new part of the United States. _____ I could visit every state in the US and still not find the oldest public library in the Western Hemisphere. That library, the Biblioteca Palafoxiana, is located in Puebla, Mexico.

Which choice completes the text with the most logical transition?

A) As a result,

B) Nevertheless,

C) Earlier,

D) In other words,

25

While researching a topic, a student has taken the following notes:

- In astronomy, the mass of stars can be described in units called solar masses.
- One solar mass is roughly equal to the mass of the Sun.
- The mass of the star Proxima Centauri is 0.122 solar masses.
- The mass of the star Sirius A is 2.063 solar masses.

The student wants to emphasize the mass of Sirius A. Which choice most effectively uses relevant information from the notes to accomplish this goal?

A) The mass of stars, like Proxima Centauri, can be described in units called solar masses.

B) In astronomy, the mass of stars can be described in units called solar masses, and one solar mass is roughly equal to the mass of the Sun.

C) The Sun is more massive than Proxima Centauri, which has a mass of 0.122 solar masses.

D) With a mass of 2.063 solar masses, Sirius A is more massive than the Sun.

Unauthorized copying or reuse of any part of this page is illegal.

CONTINUE

462

26

While researching a topic, a student has taken the following notes:

- A lever is a simple machine consisting of a rigid beam and a fulcrum.
- The fulcrum is the point about which the beam pivots.
- The input force (effort) is the force applied to the lever.
- The output force (load) is the force that the lever exerts on another object.
- In first-class levers, the fulcrum is located between the effort and the load.
- In second-class levers, the load is located between the effort and the fulcrum.

The student wants to contrast first-class levers and second-class levers. Which choice most effectively uses relevant information from the notes to accomplish this goal?

A) In levers, the effort is the force applied to the lever; the load, in contrast, is the force that the lever exerts on another object.

B) In first-class and second-class levers, the fulcrum and the load are in different locations.

C) First-class levers are simple machines consisting of a rigid beam and a fulcrum, but then again, the same is true of second-class levers.

D) In first-class levers, the fulcrum is located between the effort and the load, but in second-class levers, the load is located between the effort and the fulcrum.

27

While researching a topic, a student has taken the following notes:

- The melting rate of glaciers varies based on air temperature.
- In the warm summer months, massive glaciers on the coast of Greenland melt into the surrounding water.
- The melting glaciers contribute to rising sea levels each summer.
- Huge icebergs also break off Greenland's glaciers into the water and melt.
- In 2017, geoscientist Twila Moon found that the iceberg melting rate depends not on air temperature but on water temperature.
- Because water temperature is consistent, melting icebergs contribute to rising sea levels all year.

The student wants to emphasize a similarity between glaciers and icebergs in Greenland. Which choice most effectively uses relevant information from the notes to accomplish this goal?

A) Because icebergs break off Greenland's glaciers into the water, their melting rate depends on water temperature.

B) Greenland's glaciers and icebergs both melt during the year, contributing to rising sea levels.

C) Geoscientist Twila Moon found that the melting rate of Greenland's icebergs, unlike that of glaciers, does not depend on air temperature.

D) Glaciers on the coast of Greenland melt during the warm summer months into the surrounding water, the temperature of which remains consistent throughout the year.

STOP

If you finish before time is called, you may check your work on this module only.
Do not turn to any other module in the test.

Reading and Writing

27 QUESTIONS

1

Mary Engle Pennington, a chemist who helped advance home refrigeration, undoubtedly made a substantial impact on society, but her place in our historical memory is perhaps more _____ than that of Stephanie Kwolek, who invented the incredibly strong material known as Kevlar, an accomplishment for which she will long be remembered.

Which choice completes the text with the most logical and precise word or phrase?

A) permanent

B) tentative

C) warranted

D) prominent

2

To demonstrate that the integrity of underground metal pipes can be assessed without unearthing the pipes, engineer Aroba Saleem and colleagues _____ the tendency of some metals' internal magnetic fields to alter under stress: the team showed that such alterations can be measured from a distance and can reveal concentrations of stress in the pipes.

Which choice completes the text with the most logical and precise word or phrase?

A) hypothesized

B) discounted

C) redefined

D) exploited

CONTINUE ➡

3

Despite the generalizations about human behavior they have produced, many studies of behavioral psychology have used highly unrepresentative subject pools: students at the colleges and universities where the researchers are employed. To _____ this situation, it is necessary to actively recruit subjects from diverse backgrounds and locations.

Which choice completes the text with the most logical and precise word or phrase?

A) sanction

B) ameliorate

C) rationalize

D) postulate

4

Though not closely related, the hedgehog tenrecs of Madagascar share basic _____ true hedgehogs, including protective spines, pointed snouts, and small body size—traits the two groups of mammals independently developed in response to equivalent roles in their respective habitats.

Which choice completes the text with the most logical and precise word or phrase?

A) examples of

B) concerns about

C) indications of

D) similarities with

5

While recent scholarship has undermined claims that the works of twelfth-century Islamic philosopher Ibn Rushd were _____ other Muslim philosophers of his time, it is indisputable that his location in the Muslim-ruled area of what is now Spain meant that his works were primarily available thousands of miles west of the era's center of Islamic thought.

Which choice completes the text with the most logical and precise word or phrase?

A) controversial among

B) antagonistic toward

C) imitated by

D) inconsequential to

6

The following text is adapted from Herman Melville's 1855 novel *Israel Potter*. Israel is a young man wandering through New England during the late eighteenth century.

He hired himself out for three months; at the end of that time to receive for his wages two hundred acres of land lying in New Hampshire. […] His employer proving false to the contract in the matter of the land, and there being no law in the country to force him to fulfil it, Israel—who, however brave-hearted, and even much of a dare-devil upon a pinch, seems nevertheless to have evinced, throughout many parts of his career, a singular patience and mildness—was obliged to look round for other means of livelihood than clearing out a farm for himself in the wilderness.

Which choice best describes the function of the underlined portion in the text as a whole?

A) It implies that Israel treasures a particular characteristic of his personality when that characteristic should usually be regarded as a flaw.

B) It suggests that if not for a certain aspect of his character, Israel might not have been as easily thwarted in his ambition to establish a farm.

C) It shows why Israel would not have been able to undertake the enormous amount of labor necessary to run a farm even if he had owned the necessary property.

D) It explains why, when the situation requires it, Israel is able to undertake courageous acts that others would generally avoid.

CONTINUE ▶

7

Changes to vegetation cover and other human activities influence carbon and nitrogen levels in soil, though how deep these effects extend is unclear. Hypothesizing that differences in land use lead to differences in carbon and nitrogen levels that are not restricted to the topsoil layer (0–30 cm deep), Chukwuebuka Okolo and colleagues sampled soils across multiple land-use types (e.g., grazing land, cropland, forest) within each of several Ethiopian locations. They found, though, that across land-use types, carbon and nitrogen decreased to comparably low levels beyond depths of 30 cm.

Which choice best describes the overall structure of the text?

A) It describes a phenomenon that scientists do not fully understand, explains a research team's hypothesis about that phenomenon, and then describes a finding that led the team to refine the hypothesis.

B) It introduces an unresolved scientific question, presents a research team's hypothesis pertaining to that question, and then describes an observation made by the team that conflicts with that hypothesis.

C) It discusses a process that scientists are somewhat unclear about, introduces competing hypotheses about that process, and then explains how a research team concluded that one of those hypotheses is likely correct.

D) It explains a hypothesis that has been the subject of scientific debate, discusses how a research team tested that hypothesis, and then presents data the team collected that validate the hypothesis.

8

Text 1
Efforts to automate classification of paintings into different artistic styles have had little success, and we have probably reached the technological limit of this work. Furthermore, it's not obvious that this is even a useful endeavor—as several critics have argued, differences between artistic styles are inherently subjective and often not the best way to understand relationships between works.

Text 2
Baroque painting utilized a very similar color palette as Renaissance painting did to depict largely the same subjects that Renaissance painting depicted. Automated artistic style classifiers often struggle to draw distinctions between these two styles, but Ravneet Singh Arora and Ahmed Elgammal were able to achieve a high degree of accuracy in Baroque/Renaissance comparisons by running one classification model atop another, an approach that demonstrates how much innovation is possible in this realm.

Based on the texts, how would the author of Text 2 most likely respond to the claim in the underlined sentence of Text 1?

A) By emphasizing that there are still advances being made in automated artistic style classification

B) By criticizing previous research into automated artistic style classification systems for focusing on a narrow group of styles

C) By arguing that most people are not able to correctly identify the style of paintings that they are shown

D) By suggesting that people may eventually develop more uniform and accepted ideas about artistic styles and their boundaries

CONTINUE

9

To understand how temperature change affects microorganism-mediated cycling of soil nutrients in alpine ecosystems, Eva Kaštovská et al. collected plant-soil cores in the Tatra Mountains at elevations around 2,100 meters and transplanted them to elevations of 1,700–1,800 meters, where the mean air temperature was warmer by 2°C. Microorganism-mediated nutrient cycling was accelerated in the transplanted cores; crucially, microorganism community composition was unchanged, allowing Kaštovská et al. to attribute the acceleration to temperature-induced increases in microorganism activity.

It can most reasonably be inferred from the text that the finding about the microorganism community composition was important for which reason?

A) It provided preliminary evidence that microorganism-mediated nutrient cycling was accelerated in the transplanted cores.

B) It suggested that temperature-induced changes in microorganism activity may be occurring at increasingly high elevations.

C) It ruled out a potential alternative explanation for the acceleration in microorganism-mediated nutrient cycling.

D) It clarified that microorganism activity levels in the plant-soil cores varied depending on which microorganisms comprised the community.

10

Mean Ratings for Patients after 21 Days

Measure	Mean rating for participants aware of taking a placebo	Mean rating for participants in the control group
Global improvement	5.0	3.9
Symptom severity reduction	92.00	46.00
Quality of life improvement	11.4	5.4

To test whether a medication is effective, scientists compare outcomes for patients taking it and patients taking a placebo (a medically inactive substance). Patients normally aren't told they're receiving a placebo, but a research team conducted a study to see if there might be a medical benefit to telling them. The team used various measures to evaluate participants, with higher ratings indicating greater well-being in each measure. Compared to the mean ratings after 21 days for participants in the control group, the mean ratings for participants who were aware of taking a placebo _____

Which choice most effectively uses data from the table to complete the statement?

A) ranged from 5.0 to 92.00, indicating that well-being varied widely from participant to participant.

B) were lower for two measures, with the rating for only one measure indicating greater well-being for these participants.

C) ranged from 3.9 to 46.00, with no rating indicating greater well-being in any measure for these participants.

D) were higher for all three measures, indicating greater overall well-being for these participants.

Unauthorized copying or reuse of any part of this page is illegal.

CONTINUE ▶

467

11

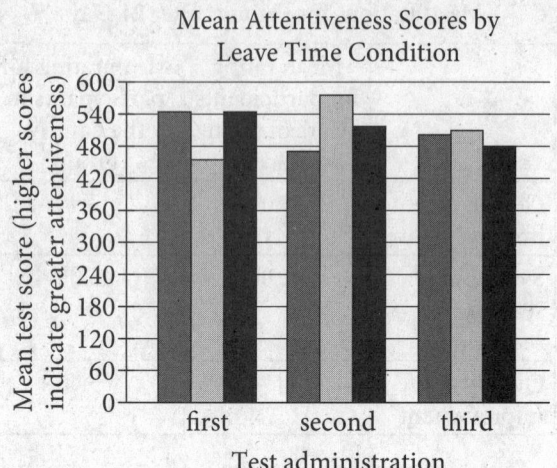

Mean Attentiveness Scores by Leave Time Condition

Mean test score (higher scores indicate greater attentiveness)

Test administration

- ■ no leave
- ■ 2–4 days leave
- ■ 1–5 weeks leave

To investigate potential cognitive benefits of taking leave from work, psychologist Jan Packer and colleagues conducted a six-month study of Australian university staff members who took no leave from work during the study, took 2–4 days of leave, or took 1–5 weeks of leave. Tests of attentiveness were administered to participants three times during the study: at random for the no-leave staff, and for the rest, one week before their leave, one week following their return to work, and one week after the second test administration. After analyzing the results, the researchers concluded that longer leave times might not confer a greater cognitive benefit than shorter leave times do.

Which choice best describes data from the graph that support the researchers' conclusion?

A) In the second test administration, participants who took 2–4 days of leave had higher average attentiveness scores than did those who took no leave, but in the third test administration, those who took no leave had higher average scores than those who took 1–5 weeks of leave.

B) In the first test administration, participants who took 2–4 days of leave had lower average attentiveness scores than did those who took 1–5 weeks of leave and those who took no leave.

C) In both the second and third test administrations, participants who took 2–4 days of leave had higher average attentiveness scores than did participants who took 1–5 weeks of leave.

D) In the second and third test administrations, participants who took 2–4 days of leave had higher average attentiveness scores than did those who took no leave.

CONTINUE ➡

12

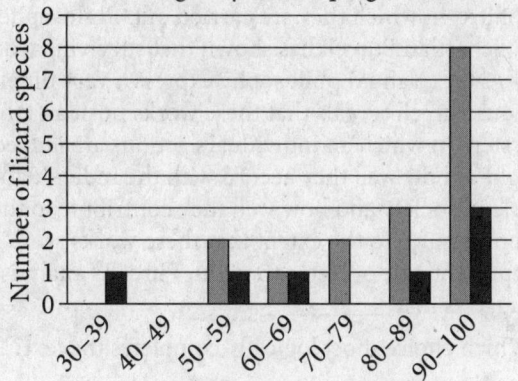

Number of Lizard Species by Average
Percent of Maximal Speed Used When
Pursuing Prey or Escaping Predators

escaping   ■ pursuing

It may seem that the optimal strategy for an animal
pursuing prey or escaping predators is to move at
maximal speed, but the energy expense of exploiting
full speed capacity can disfavor such a strategy
even in escape contexts, as evidenced by the fact
that _____

Which choice most effectively uses data from the
graph to complete the text?

A) most lizard species use about the same percentage
of their maximal speed when escaping predation
as they do when pursuing prey.

B) multiple lizard species move at an average of
less than 90% of their maximal speed while
escaping predation.

C) more lizard species use, on average, 90%–100%
of their maximal speed while escaping
predation than use any other percentage of
their maximal speed.

D) at least 4 lizard species use, on average,
less than 100% of their maximal speed while
pursuing prey.

13

"Poetry" is a 1919 poem by Marianne Moore.
The poem highlights an ambivalence toward
poetry as the speaker acknowledges its merits
while also expressing a sense of displeasure,
writing _____

Which quotation from "Poetry" most effectively
illustrates the claim?

A) "nor is it valid / to discriminate against 'business
documents and / school-books'; all these
phenomena are important."

B) "One must make a distinction / however: when
dragged into prominence by half poets, the result
is not / poetry"

C) "when [poems] become so derivative as to
become unintelligible, the / same thing may be
said for all of us—that we / do not admire what /
we cannot understand."

D) "Reading [poetry], however, with a perfect
contempt for it, one discovers that there is in /
it after all, a place for the genuine."

CONTINUE ➡

14

The Cretaceous pterosaur *Tupandactylus navigans* is known for having an anomalously oversized head crest. Until an almost complete fossil skeleton was found in Brazil, paleontologists had been able to study only skull specimens from *T. navigans*, though it was presumed that, like other pterosaurs, the species's primary form of locomotion was powered flight. Examining the fuller skeleton in 2016, Victor Beccari and his team determined that *T. navigans* had long hind legs, short wings, and an unusually long neck—characteristics that, combined with the creature's large-crested head, would have made sustained flight difficult and walking upright relatively comfortable. Based on these findings the team suggests that *T. navigans* likely _____

Which choice most logically completes the text?

A) flew for longer distances than did other pterosaur species that had oversized head crests.

B) had longer wings than other pterosaur species considered to have been comfortable walking.

C) had a smaller head than researchers expected based on the earlier *T. navigans* skull specimens.

D) flew for shorter distances and spent more time walking than researchers previously thought.

15

Some ethicists hold that the moral goodness of an individual's actions depends solely on whether the actions themselves are good, irrespective of the context in which they are carried out. Philosopher L. Sebastian Purcell has shown that surviving works of Aztec (Nahua) philosophy express a very different view. Purcell reveals that these works posit an ethical system in which an individual's actions are judged in light of how well they accord with the individual's role in society and how well they contribute to the community. To the extent that these works are representative of Aztec thought, Purcell's analysis suggests that _____

Which choice most logically completes the text?

A) the Aztecs would have disputed the idea that the morality of an individual's actions can be assessed by appealing to standards of behavior that are independent of the individual's social circumstances.

B) the Aztecs would not have accepted the notion that the morality of an individual's actions can be fairly evaluated by people who do not live in the same society as that individual.

C) actions by members of Aztec society who contributed a great deal to their community could be judged as morally good even if those actions were inconsistent with behaviors the Aztecs regarded as good in all contexts.

D) similar actions performed by people in different social roles in Aztec society would have been regarded as morally equivalent unless those actions led to different outcomes for the community.

CONTINUE

16

The Boston Saloon was one of the most popular African American-owned establishments in nineteenth-century Nevada. _____ by businessman William A.G. Brown, the saloon was known to offer elegant accommodations and an inclusive environment.

Which choice completes the text so that it conforms to the conventions of Standard English?

A) Created

B) Creates

C) Creating

D) Create

17

In a painting titled "The Milkmaid" by Johannes Vermeer, the artist prominently features a bread basket, milk pitcher, and bowl. Such quotidian objects, depicted in exquisite detail by Vermeer, a painter celebrated for his naturalism, _____ the daily minutiae of a seventeenth-century Dutch household.

Which choice completes the text so that it conforms to the conventions of Standard English?

A) was revealing

B) has revealed

C) reveals

D) reveal

18

Physical materials can be classified by how much light passes through them. Clear glass, which is classified as transparent, allows all (or almost all) light to pass _____ wax paper, which is classified as translucent, allows only some light to pass through.

Which choice completes the text so that it conforms to the conventions of Standard English?

A) through,

B) through

C) through;

D) through and

19

In her 1983 book *The Managed Heart: Commercialization of Human Feeling*, sociologist Arlie Russell Hochschild first explored at length her conception of a "sociology of emotions"—the idea that the various cultural and ideological frameworks a person has internalized (class, gender, political affiliation, etc.) _____ each emotional reaction that person has within a situation.

Which choice completes the text so that it conforms to the conventions of Standard English?

A) underlies

B) is underlying

C) underlie

D) has been underlying

20

Latin America is known to have dozens, if not hundreds, of popular dance forms. Only five of these dances are included in international ballroom dance _____ rumba, samba, cha-cha-cha, paso doble, and jive—the last of which is grouped with the other Latin dances despite not having Latin roots.

Which choice completes the text so that it conforms to the conventions of Standard English?

A) competitions, however:

B) competitions, however,

C) competitions, however;

D) competitions; however,

21

For thousands of years, humans have used domesticated goats (*Capra hircus*) to clear land of unwanted vegetation. When it comes to their diets, goats are notoriously _____ they will devour all kinds of shrubs and weeds, leaving virtually no part of any plant unconsumed.

Which choice completes the text so that it conforms to the conventions of Standard English?

A) indiscriminate and

B) indiscriminate,

C) indiscriminate

D) indiscriminate:

Unauthorized copying or reuse of any part of this page is illegal.

CONTINUE ▶

471

22

Working together with the Navajo Nation Department of Water Resources, Dr. Lani Tsinnajinnie analyzed data about snowpack levels in the Chuska Mountains. She found that the snowpack (the amount of snow on the ground) was deepest in early March at lower elevations. At higher elevations, _____ the snowpack was deepest in mid-March.

Which choice completes the text with the most logical transition?

A) in other words,

B) for instance,

C) on the other hand,

D) in summary,

23

According to Duverger's law, countries with single-ballot majoritarian elections for single-member districts tend to polarize into two-party systems, wherein dueling political parties consistently dominate the political system. _____ countries with proportional-representation electoral systems tend to support multi-partyism, under which power gets distributed among many political parties.

Which choice completes the text with the most logical transition?

A) Subsequently,

B) Conversely,

C) For instance,

D) In other words,

24

A turtle shell appears external to the animal, protecting its body like armor. _____ the shell is often incorrectly assumed to be an exoskeleton, a rigid outer casing like that of a crustacean or an insect, when in fact it is an endoskeleton, a part of the turtle's internal bone structure, more akin to a spine or a pair of ribs.

Which choice completes the text with the most logical transition?

A) That being said,

B) However,

C) For instance,

D) Hence,

25

In retrospect, one of the lessons of the 2003 Human Genome Project is that a gene is affected by many factors, not the least of which is its interactions with the protein products of other genes. _____ rather than just focusing on the human genome, efforts to better understand gene mutations related to disease have begun to consider the human proteome; the complete set of proteins expressed by human genes.

Which choice completes the text with the most logical transition?

A) In other words,

B) That said,

C) For example,

D) Accordingly,

CONTINUE ➤

26

While researching a topic, a student has taken the following notes:

- Elizabeth Catlett's sculpture *Recognition* (1970) shows two African American figures with rounded, indistinct features.
- The figures reach out to each other in a pose that symbolizes a close, supportive relationship.
- Her sculpture *Students Aspire* (1978) shows two African American figures with sharply defined features.
- The figures hold an equal sign above their heads with one hand and embrace each other with the other hand.
- This pose symbolizes their support for each other in the pursuit of equality.

The student wants to emphasize a similarity between the two sculptures. Which choice most effectively uses relevant information from the notes to accomplish this goal?

A) Catlett's *Students Aspire* depicts two figures supporting each other in the pursuit of equality.

B) *Recognition* and *Students Aspire* both show African American figures in poses that symbolize supportive relationships.

C) Catlett completed *Recognition* in 1970 and *Students Aspire* in 1978.

D) The figures in *Recognition* have features that are rounded and indistinct, while the figures in *Students Aspire* have sharply defined features.

27

While researching a topic, a student has taken the following notes:

- The US government classifies sensitive information according to the degree to which disclosure could affect the nation's security.
- Information that could cause "damage" to national security is classified as Confidential.
- Information that could cause "serious damage" to national security is classified as Secret.
- Most routine diplomatic correspondence, if disclosed, could cause damage but not serious damage to national security.
- Diplomatic correspondence includes communication with both allies and adversaries.

The student wants to indicate which category most routine diplomatic correspondence belongs in, based on how sensitive information is classified. Which choice most effectively uses relevant information from the notes to accomplish this goal?

A) According to the US government, which classifies such sensitive information as routine diplomatic correspondence, Confidential information could damage national security if disclosed.

B) Most routine diplomatic correspondence is classified according to the degree to which disclosure could affect the nation's security.

C) Having the potential to damage national security if disclosed, most routine diplomatic correspondence is classified as Confidential.

D) If disclosed, communication with both allies and adversaries could affect the nation's security.

STOP

**If you finish before time is called, you may check your work on this module only.
Do not turn to any other module in the test.**

Math

22 QUESTIONS

The questions in this section address a number of important math skills.
Use of a calculator is permitted for all questions.

NOTES

Unless otherwise indicated:

- All variables and expressions represent real numbers.

- Figures provided are drawn to scale.

- All figures lie in a plane.

- The domain of a given function f is the set of all real numbers x for which $f(x)$ is a real number.

REFERENCE

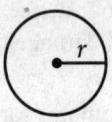 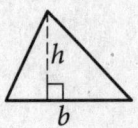 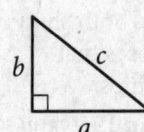 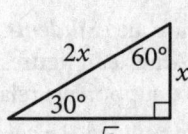 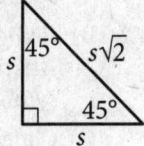

$A = \pi r^2$ $\quad$ $A = \ell w$ $\quad$ $A = \frac{1}{2}bh$ $\quad$ $c^2 = a^2 + b^2$ $\quad$ Special Right Triangles

$C = 2\pi r$

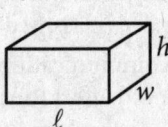 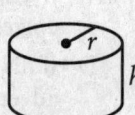   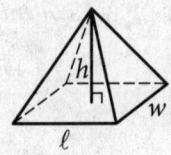

$V = \ell wh$ $\quad$ $V = \pi r^2 h$ $\quad$ $V = \frac{4}{3}\pi r^3$ $\quad$ $V = \frac{1}{3}\pi r^2 h$ $\quad$ $V = \frac{1}{3}\ell wh$

The number of degrees of arc in a circle is 360.

The number of radians of arc in a circle is 2π.

The sum of the measures in degrees of the angles of a triangle is 180.

CONTINUE

For multiple-choice questions, solve each problem, choose the correct answer from the choices provided, and then circle your answer in this book. Circle only one answer for each question. If you change your mind, completely erase the circle. You will not get credit for questions with more than one answer circled, or for questions with no answers circled.

For student-produced response questions, solve each problem and write your answer next to or under the question in the test book as described below.

- Once you've written your answer, circle it clearly. You will not receive credit for anything written outside the circle, or for any questions with more than one circled answer.

- If you find **more than one correct answer**, write and circle only one answer.

- Your answer can be up to 5 characters for a **positive** answer and up to 6 characters (including the negative sign) for a **negative** answer, but no more.

- If your answer is a **fraction** that is too long (over 5 characters for positive, 6 characters for negative), write the decimal equivalent.

- If your answer is a **decimal** that is too long (over 5 characters for positive, 6 characters for negative), truncate it or round at the fourth digit.

- If your answer is a **mixed number** (such as $3\frac{1}{2}$), write it as an improper fraction (7/2) or its decimal equivalent (3.5).

- Don't include **symbols** such as a percent sign, comma, or dollar sign in your circled answer.

Unauthorized copying or reuse of any part of this page is illegal.

CONTINUE

475

1

A veterinarian recommends that each day a certain rabbit should eat 25 calories per pound of the rabbit's weight, plus an additional 11 calories. Which equation represents this situation, where c is the total number of calories the veterinarian recommends the rabbit should eat each day if the rabbit's weight is x pounds?

A) $c = 25x$

B) $c = 36x$

C) $c = 11x + 25$

D) $c = 25x + 11$

2

A special camera is used for underwater ocean research. The camera is at a depth of 39 fathoms. What is the camera's depth in <u>feet</u>? (1 fathom = 6 feet)

A) 234

B) 117

C) 45

D) 7

3

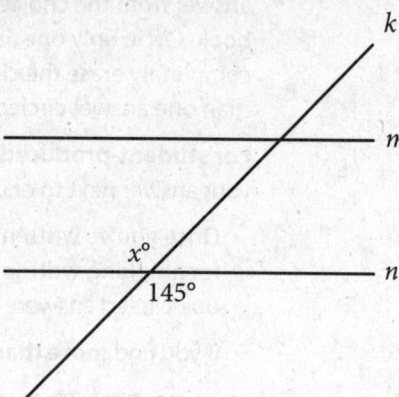

Note: Figure not drawn to scale.

In the figure, line m is parallel to line n, and line k intersects both lines. Which of the following statements is true?

A) The value of x is less than 145.

B) The value of x is greater than 145.

C) The value of x is equal to 145.

D) The value of x cannot be determined.

CONTINUE ▶

4

$$f(x) = 14 + 4x$$

The function f represents the total cost, in dollars, of attending an arcade when x games are played. How many games can be played for a total cost of $58?

5

If $4x - 28 = -24$, what is the value of $x - 7$?

A) -24

B) -22

C) -6

D) -1

6

The amount of Hanna's bill for a food order was $50. Hanna gave a tip of 20% of the amount of the bill. What is the amount, in dollars, of the tip Hanna gave?

7

Five *Eretmochelys imbricata*, a type of sea turtle, each have a nest. The table shows an original data set of the number of eggs that each turtle laid in its nest.

Nest	Number of eggs
A	149
B	144
C	148
D	136
E	139

A sixth nest with 121 eggs is added to create a new data set. Which of the following correctly compares the means of the two data sets?

A) The mean of the original data set is greater than the mean of the new data set.

B) The mean of the original data set is less than the mean of the new data set.

C) The means of both data sets are equal.

D) There is not enough information to compare the means.

Unauthorized copying or reuse of any part of this page is illegal.

CONTINUE

477

8

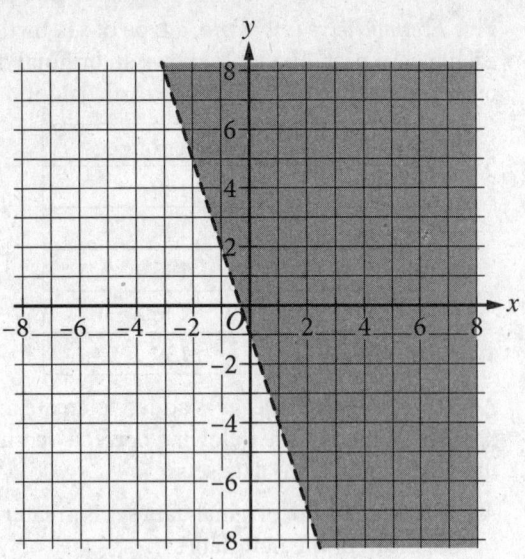

The shaded region shown represents the solutions to which inequality?

A) $y < -1 + 3x$

B) $y < -1 - 3x$

C) $y > -1 + 3x$

D) $y > -1 - 3x$

9

Which expression is equivalent to $(8x^3 + 8) - (x^3 - 2)$?

A) $8x^3 + 6$

B) $7x^3 + 10$

C) $8x^3 + 10$

D) $7x^3 + 6$

10

In the xy-plane, line t passes through the points $(0, 9)$ and $(1, 17)$. Which equation defines line t?

A) $y = \frac{1}{8}x + 9$

B) $y = x + \frac{1}{8}$

C) $y = x + 8$

D) $y = 8x + 9$

11

$$(d - 30)(d + 30) - 7 = -7$$

What is a solution to the given equation?

12

A store sells two different-sized containers of blueberries. The store's sales of these blueberries totaled 896.86 dollars last month. The equation $4.51x + 6.07y = 896.86$ represents this situation, where x is the number of smaller containers sold and y is the number of larger containers sold. According to the equation, what is the price, in dollars, of each smaller container?

13

$$f(t) = 500(0.5)^{\frac{t}{12}}$$

The function f models the intensity of an X-ray beam, in number of particles in the X-ray beam, t millimeters below the surface of a sample of iron. According to the model, what is the estimated number of particles in the X-ray beam when it is at the surface of the sample of iron?

A) 500

B) 12

C) 5

D) 2

CONTINUE ➡

14

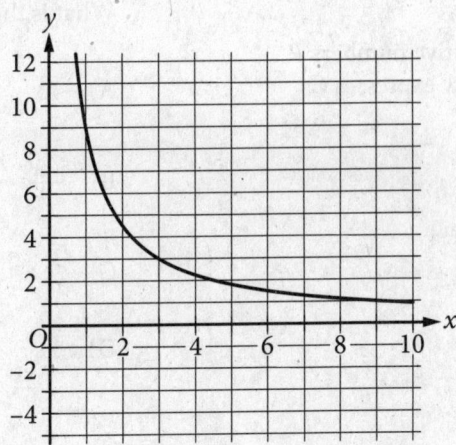

The graph of the rational function f is shown, where $y = f(x)$ and $x \geq 0$. Which of the following is the graph of $y = f(x) + 5$, where $x \geq 0$?

A)

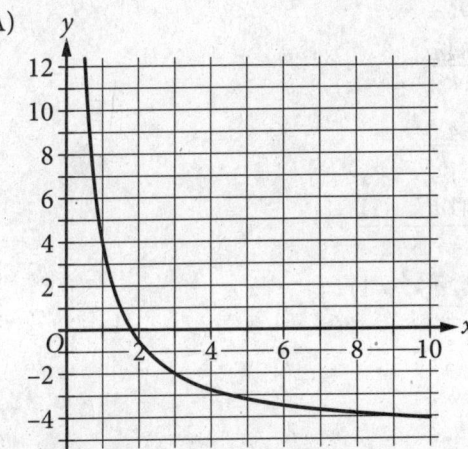

B)

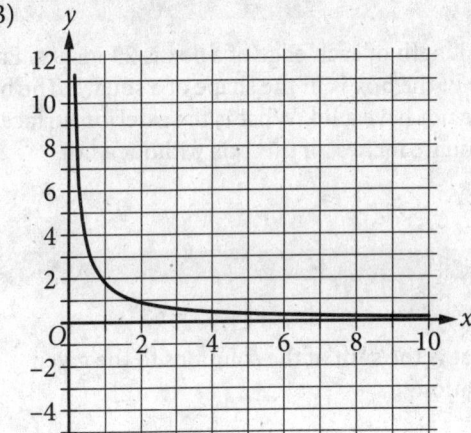

C)

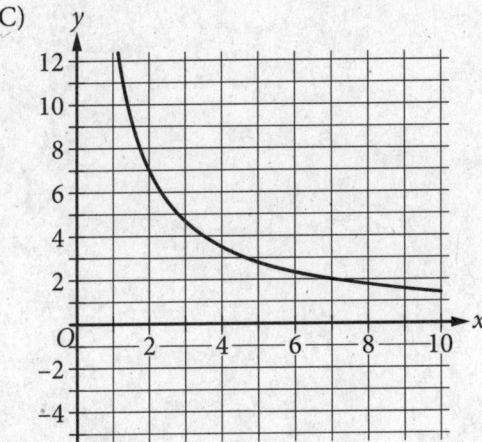

D)

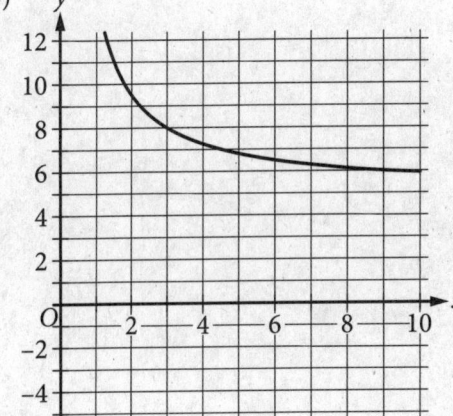

CONTINUE

15

$$P = N(19 - C)$$

The given equation relates the positive numbers P, N, and C. Which equation correctly expresses C in terms of P and N?

A) $C = \dfrac{19 + P}{N}$

B) $C = \dfrac{19 - P}{N}$

C) $C = 19 + \dfrac{P}{N}$

D) $C = 19 - \dfrac{P}{N}$

16

The length of each edge of a box is 29 inches. Each side of the box is in the shape of a square. The box does not have a lid. What is the exterior surface area, in square inches, of this box without a lid?

17

$$|x - 9| + 45 = 63$$

What is the sum of the solutions to the given equation?

18

What is the value of $\tan \dfrac{92\pi}{3}$?

A) $-\sqrt{3}$

B) $-\dfrac{\sqrt{3}}{3}$

C) $\dfrac{\sqrt{3}}{3}$

D) $\sqrt{3}$

19

Which expression is equivalent to $\dfrac{42a}{k} + 42ak$, where $k > 0$?

A) $\dfrac{84a}{k}$

B) $\dfrac{84ak^2}{k}$

C) $\dfrac{42a(k + 1)}{k}$

D) $\dfrac{42a(k^2 + 1)}{k}$

CONTINUE

20

$$(x + 4)^2 + (y - 19)^2 = 121$$

The graph of the given equation is a circle in the xy-plane. The point (a, b) lies on the circle. Which of the following is a possible value for a?

A) −16

B) −14

C) 11

D) 19

21

A right rectangular prism has a height of 9 inches. The length of the prism's base is x inches, which is 7 inches more than the width of the prism's base. Which function V gives the volume of the prism, in cubic inches, in terms of the length of the prism's base?

A) $V(x) = x(x + 9)(x + 7)$

B) $V(x) = x(x + 9)(x - 7)$

C) $V(x) = 9x(x + 7)$

D) $V(x) = 9x(x - 7)$

22

The function f is defined by $f(x) = a\sqrt{x + b}$, where a and b are constants. In the xy-plane, the graph of $y = f(x)$ passes through the point $(-24, 0)$, and $f(24) < 0$. Which of the following must be true?

A) $f(0) = 24$

B) $f(0) = -24$

C) $a > b$

D) $a < b$

STOP

**If you finish before time is called, you may check your work on this module only.
Do not turn to any other module in the test.**

Math

22 QUESTIONS

DIRECTIONS

The questions in this section address a number of important math skills.
Use of a calculator is permitted for all questions.

NOTES

Unless otherwise indicated:

- All variables and expressions represent real numbers.
- Figures provided are drawn to scale.
- All figures lie in a plane.
- The domain of a given function f is the set of all real numbers x for which $f(x)$ is a real number.

REFERENCE

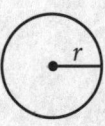
$A = \pi r^2$
$C = 2\pi r$

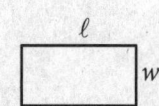
$A = \ell w$

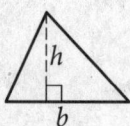
$A = \frac{1}{2}bh$

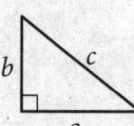
$c^2 = a^2 + b^2$

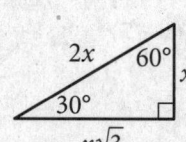
Special Right Triangles

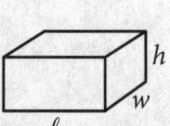
$V = \ell wh$

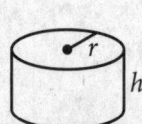
$V = \pi r^2 h$

$V = \frac{4}{3}\pi r^3$

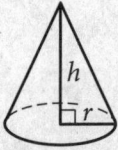
$V = \frac{1}{3}\pi r^2 h$

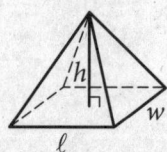
$V = \frac{1}{3}\ell wh$

The number of degrees of arc in a circle is 360.

The number of radians of arc in a circle is 2π.

The sum of the measures in degrees of the angles of a triangle is 180.

CONTINUE

For multiple-choice questions, solve each problem, choose the correct answer from the choices provided, and then circle your answer in this book. Circle only one answer for each question. If you change your mind, completely erase the circle. You will not get credit for questions with more than one answer circled, or for questions with no answers circled.

For student-produced response questions, solve each problem and write your answer next to or under the question in the test book as described below.

- Once you've written your answer, circle it clearly. You will not receive credit for anything written outside the circle, or for any questions with more than one circled answer.

- If you find **more than one correct answer**, write and circle only one answer.

- Your answer can be up to 5 characters for a **positive** answer and up to 6 characters (including the negative sign) for a **negative** answer, but no more.

- If your answer is a **fraction** that is too long (over 5 characters for positive, 6 characters for negative), write the decimal equivalent.

- If your answer is a **decimal** that is too long (over 5 characters for positive, 6 characters for negative), truncate it or round at the fourth digit.

- If your answer is a **mixed number** (such as $3\frac{1}{2}$), write it as an improper fraction (7/2) or its decimal equivalent (3.5).

- Don't include **symbols** such as a percent sign, comma, or dollar sign in your circled answer.

Unauthorized copying or reuse of any part of this page is illegal.

CONTINUE

483

1

The graph shows the predicted value y, in dollars, of a certain sport utility vehicle x years after it is first purchased.

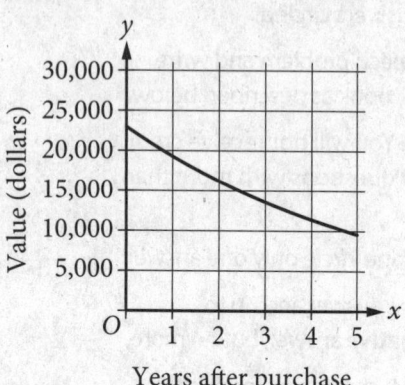

Years after purchase

Which of the following is closest to the predicted value of the sport utility vehicle 3 years after it is first purchased?

A) $9,619

B) $13,632

C) $19,320

D) $23,000

2

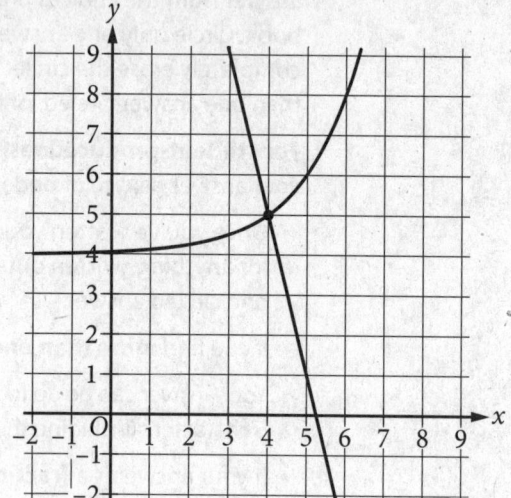

The graph of a system of a linear equation and a nonlinear equation is shown. What is the solution (x, y) to this system?

A) (0, 0)

B) (0, 4)

C) (4, 5)

D) (5, 0)

CONTINUE

3

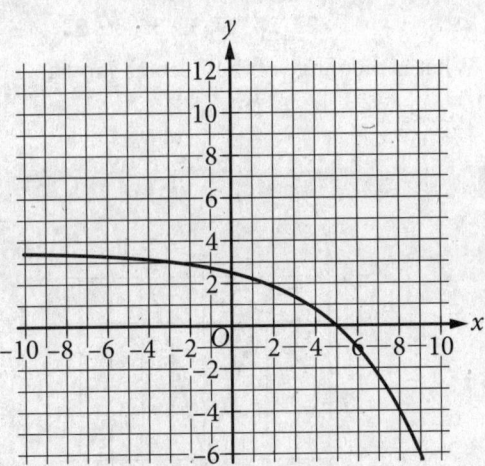

What is the x-intercept of the graph shown?

A) $(-5, 0)$

B) $(5, 0)$

C) $(-2, 0)$

D) $(2, 0)$

4

On a street with 7 houses, 2 houses are blue. If a house from this street is selected at random, what is the probability of selecting a house that is blue?

A) $\frac{1}{7}$

B) $\frac{2}{7}$

C) $\frac{5}{7}$

D) $\frac{7}{7}$

5

The graph of function f is shown, where $y = f(x)$.

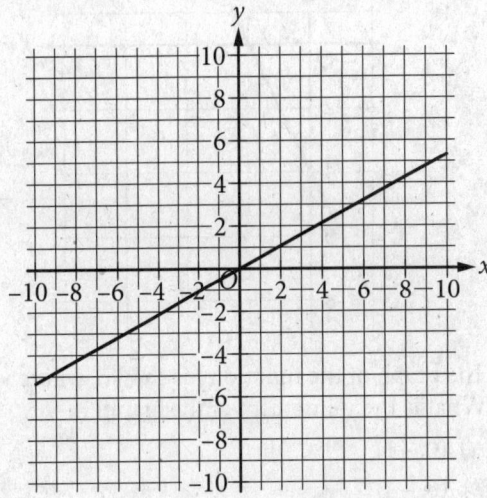

Which of the following describes function f?

A) Increasing linear

B) Decreasing linear

C) Increasing exponential

D) Decreasing exponential

6

If $6n = 12$, what is the value of $n + 4$?

7

The function f is defined by $f(x) = 4x - 3$. What is the value of $f(10)$?

A) -30

B) 37

C) 40

D) 43

CONTINUE ➤

8

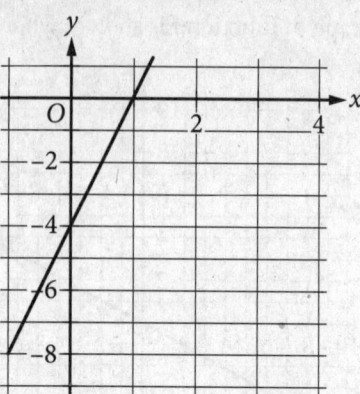

The graph of the function *f* is shown, where $y = f(x)$. What is the *y*-intercept of the graph?

A) $(0, -1)$

B) $(0, -4)$

C) $(0, 1)$

D) $(0, 4)$

9

$$y = 12x - 20$$
$$y = 28$$

What is the solution (x, y) to the given system of equations?

A) $(4, 28)$

B) $(20, 28)$

C) $(28, 4)$

D) $(28, 20)$

10

23, 27, 27, 32, 35, 36, 52

What is the range of the 7 scores shown?

11

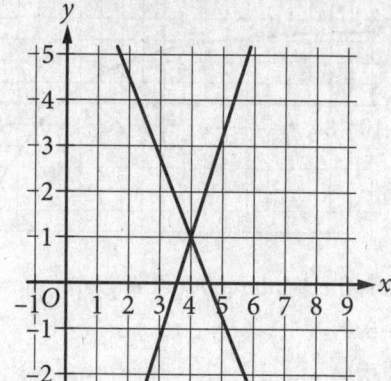

The graph of a system of linear equations is shown. The solution to the system is (x, y). What is the value of *x*?

12

The function *h* is defined by $h(x) = \dfrac{8}{5x + 6}$. What is the value of $h(2)$?

CONTINUE ▶

13

For the linear function f, the graph of $y = f(x)$ in the xy-plane has a slope of 39 and passes through the point $(0, 0)$. Which equation defines f?

A) $f(x) = -39x$

B) $f(x) = \dfrac{1}{39}x$

C) $f(x) = x - 39$

D) $f(x) = 39x$

14

For a snowstorm in a certain town, the minimum rate of snowfall recorded was 0.6 inches per hour, and the maximum rate of snowfall recorded was 1.8 inches per hour. Which inequality is true for all values of s, where s represents a rate of snowfall, in inches per hour, recorded for this snowstorm?

A) $s \geq 2.4$

B) $s \geq 1.8$

C) $0 \leq s \leq 0.6$

D) $0.6 \leq s \leq 1.8$

15

The function f defined by $f(t) = 14t + 9$ gives the estimated length, in inches, of a vine plant t months after Tavon purchased it. Which of the following is the best interpretation of 9 in this context?

A) Tavon will keep the vine plant for 9 months.

B) The vine plant is expected to grow 9 inches each month.

C) The vine plant is expected to grow to a maximum length of 9 inches.

D) The estimated length of the vine plant was 9 inches when Tavon purchased it.

16

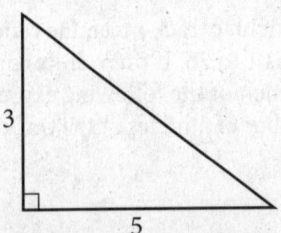

Note: Figure not drawn to scale.

The figure shows the lengths, in inches, of two sides of a right triangle. What is the area of the triangle, in square inches?

17

x	1	2	3
y	11	16	21

The table shows three values of x and their corresponding values of y. Which equation represents the linear relationship between x and y?

A) $y = 5x + 6$

B) $y = 5x + 11$

C) $y = 6x + 5$

D) $y = 6x + 11$

18

$$y = 4x$$
$$y = x^2 - 12$$

A solution to the given system of equations is (x, y), where $x > 0$. What is the value of x?

Unauthorized copying or reuse of any part of this page is illegal.

CONTINUE

487

19

At a particular track meet, the ratio of coaches to athletes is 1 to 26. If there are x coaches at the track meet, which of the following expressions represents the number of athletes at the track meet?

A) $\frac{x}{26}$

B) $26x$

C) $x + 26$

D) $\frac{26}{x}$

20

$$f(x) = (1.84)^{\frac{x}{4}}$$

The function f is defined by the given equation. The equation can be rewritten as $f(x) = \left(1 + \frac{p}{100}\right)^x$, where p is a constant. Which of the following is closest to the value of p?

A) 16

B) 21

C) 46

D) 96

21

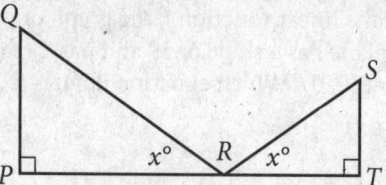

Note: Figure not drawn to scale.

$\triangle QPR$ is similar to $\triangle STR$. The lengths represented by $\overline{ST}$, $\overline{QP}$, $\overline{PR}$, and $\overline{QR}$ in the figure are 14, 15, 20, and 25, respectively. What is the length of $\overline{SR}$?

A) $\frac{350}{15}$

B) $\frac{350}{20}$

C) $\frac{210}{20}$

D) $\frac{210}{25}$

22

In triangle ABC, angle B is a right angle. The length of side AB is $10\sqrt{37}$ and the length of side BC is $24\sqrt{37}$. What is the length of side AC?

A) $14\sqrt{37}$

B) $26\sqrt{37}$

C) $34\sqrt{37}$

D) $\sqrt{34 \cdot 37}$

STOP

If you finish before time is called, you may check your work on this module only. Do not turn to any other module in the test.

Test begins on the next page.

Math

22 QUESTIONS

The questions in this section address a number of important math skills.
Use of a calculator is permitted for all questions.

NOTES

Unless otherwise indicated:

- All variables and expressions represent real numbers.

- Figures provided are drawn to scale.

- All figures lie in a plane.

- The domain of a given function f is the set of all real numbers x for which $f(x)$ is a real number.

REFERENCE

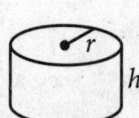
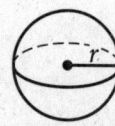
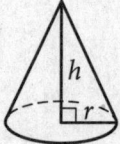
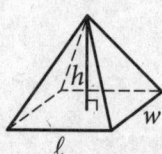

$A = \pi r^2$ $A = \ell w$ $A = \frac{1}{2} bh$ $c^2 = a^2 + b^2$ Special Right Triangles
$C = 2\pi r$

$V = \ell wh$ $V = \pi r^2 h$ $V = \frac{4}{3}\pi r^3$ $V = \frac{1}{3}\pi r^2 h$ $V = \frac{1}{3}\ell wh$

The number of degrees of arc in a circle is 360.

The number of radians of arc in a circle is 2π.

The sum of the measures in degrees of the angles of a triangle is 180.

CONTINUE

For multiple-choice questions, solve each problem, choose the correct answer from the choices provided, and then circle your answer in this book. Circle only one answer for each question. If you change your mind, completely erase the circle. You will not get credit for questions with more than one answer circled, or for questions with no answers circled.

For student-produced response questions, solve each problem and write your answer next to or under the question in the test book as described below.

- Once you've written your answer, circle it clearly. You will not receive credit for anything written outside the circle, or for any questions with more than one circled answer.

- If you find **more than one correct answer**, write and circle only one answer.

- Your answer can be up to 5 characters for a **positive** answer and up to 6 characters (including the negative sign) for a **negative** answer, but no more.

- If your answer is a **fraction** that is too long (over 5 characters for positive, 6 characters for negative), write the decimal equivalent.

- If your answer is a **decimal** that is too long (over 5 characters for positive, 6 characters for negative), truncate it or round at the fourth digit.

- If your answer is a **mixed number** (such as $3\frac{1}{2}$), write it as an improper fraction (7/2) or its decimal equivalent (3.5).

- Don't include **symbols** such as a percent sign, comma, or dollar sign in your circled answer.

CONTINUE ➡

1

A right triangle has legs with lengths of 11 centimeters and 9 centimeters. What is the length of this triangle's hypotenuse, in centimeters?

A) $\sqrt{40}$

B) $\sqrt{202}$

C) 20

D) 202

2

For the linear function h, the graph of $y = h(x)$ in the xy-plane passes through the points $(7, 21)$ and $(9, 25)$. Which equation defines h?

A) $h(x) = \frac{1}{2}x - \frac{7}{2}$

B) $h(x) = 2x + 7$

C) $h(x) = 7x + 21$

D) $h(x) = 9x + 25$

3

A company that produces socks wants to estimate the percent of the socks produced in a typical week that are defective. A random sample of 310 socks produced in a certain week were inspected. Based on the sample, it is estimated that 12% of all socks produced by the company in this week are defective, with an associated margin of error of 3.62%. Based on the estimate and associated margin of error, which of the following is the most appropriate conclusion about all socks produced by the company during this week?

A) 3.62% of the socks are defective.

B) It is plausible that between 8.38% and 15.62% of the socks are defective.

C) 12% of the socks are defective.

D) It is plausible that more than 15.62% of the socks are defective.

4

A truck can haul a maximum weight of 5,630 pounds. During one trip, the truck will be used to haul a 190-pound piece of equipment as well as several crates. Some of these crates weigh 25 pounds each and the others weigh 62 pounds each. Which inequality represents the possible combinations of the number of 25-pound crates, x, and the number of 62-pound crates, y, the truck can haul during one trip if only the piece of equipment and the crates are being hauled?

A) $25x + 62y \le 5,440$

B) $25x + 62y \ge 5,440$

C) $62x + 25y \le 5,630$

D) $62x + 25y \ge 5,630$

5

$$y - 9x = 13$$
$$5x = 2y$$

What is the solution (x, y) to the given system of equations?

A) $\left(\frac{5}{2}, 1\right)$

B) $\left(1, \frac{2}{5}\right)$

C) $(-2, -5)$

D) $(-5, -2)$

6

$$23, 27, 27, 32, 35, 36, 52$$

What is the range of the 7 scores shown?

CONTINUE ▶

7

Two customers purchased the same kind of bread and eggs at a store. The first customer paid 12.45 dollars for 1 loaf of bread and 2 dozen eggs. The second customer paid 19.42 dollars for 4 loaves of bread and 1 dozen eggs. What is the cost, in dollars, of 1 dozen eggs?

A) 3.77

B) 3.88

C) 4.15

D) 4.34

8

$$y = 18$$
$$y = -3(x - 18)^2 + 15$$

If the given equations are graphed in the xy-plane, at how many points do the graphs of the equations intersect?

A) Exactly one

B) Exactly two

C) Infinitely many

D) Zero

9

$$y = x + 9$$
$$y = x^2 + 16x + 63$$

A solution to the given system of equations is (x, y). What is the greatest possible value of x?

A) −6

B) 7

C) 9

D) 63

10

In the xy-plane, line p has a slope of $-\frac{5}{3}$ and an x-intercept of $(-6, 0)$. What is the y-coordinate of the y-intercept of line p?

11

How many solutions does the equation $12(x - 3) = -3(x + 12)$ have?

A) Exactly one

B) Exactly two

C) Infinitely many

D) Zero

12

Kaylani used fabric measuring 5 yards in length to make each suit for a men's choir. The relationship between the number of suits that Kaylani made, x, and the total length of fabric that she purchased y, in yards, is represented by the equation $y - 5x = 6$. What is the best interpretation of 6 in this context?

A) Kaylani made 6 suits.

B) Kaylani purchased a total of 6 yards of fabric.

C) Kaylani used a total of 6 yards of fabric to make the suits.

D) Kaylani purchased 6 yards more fabric than she used to make the suits.

13

Which quadratic equation has no real solutions?

A) $x^2 + 14x - 49 = 0$

B) $x^2 - 14x + 49 = 0$

C) $5x^2 - 14x - 49 = 0$

D) $5x^2 - 14x + 49 = 0$

CONTINUE

14

$$f(x) = (1.84)^{\frac{x}{4}}$$

The function f is defined by the given equation. The equation can be rewritten as $f(x) = \left(1 + \frac{p}{100}\right)^x$, where p is a constant. Which of the following is closest to the value of p?

A) 16

B) 21

C) 46

D) 96

15

$$6 + 7r = pw$$

$$7r - 5w = 5w + 11$$

In the given system of equations, p is a constant. If the system has no solution, what is the value of p?

16

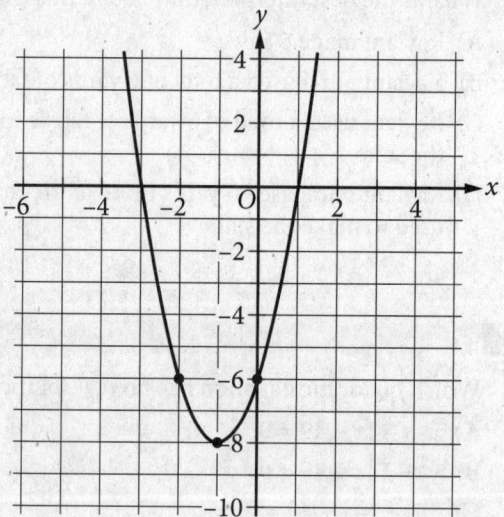

The graph of $y = 2x^2 + bx + c$ is shown, where b and c are constants. What is the value of bc?

17

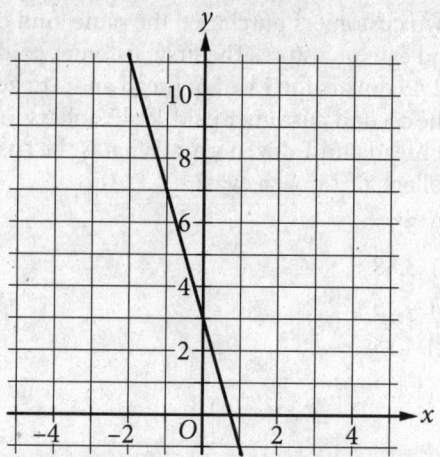

The graph of the linear function $y = f(x) + 19$ is shown. If c and d are positive constants, which equation could define f?

A) $f(x) = -d - cx$

B) $f(x) = d - cx$

C) $f(x) = -d + cx$

D) $f(x) = d + cx$

18

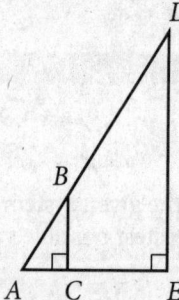

Note: Figure not drawn to scale.

In the figure shown, $AB = \sqrt{34}$ units, $AC = 3$ units, and $CE = 21$ units. What is the area, in square units, of triangle ADE?

CONTINUE ➡

19

The result of increasing the quantity x by 400% is 60. What is the value of x?

A) 12

B) 15

C) 240

D) 340

20

In the xy-plane, a circle has center C with coordinates (h, k). Points A and B lie on the circle. Point A has coordinates $(h + 1, k + \sqrt{102})$, and $\angle ACB$ is a right angle. What is the length of $\overline{AB}$?

A) $\sqrt{206}$

B) $2\sqrt{102}$

C) $103\sqrt{2}$

D) $103\sqrt{3}$

21

For an electric field passing through a flat surface perpendicular to it, the electric flux of the electric field through the surface is the product of the electric field's strength and the area of the surface. A certain flat surface consists of two adjacent squares, where the side length, in meters, of the larger square is 3 times the side length, in meters, of the smaller square. An electric field with strength 29.00 volts per meter passes uniformly through this surface, which is perpendicular to the electric field. If the total electric flux of the electric field through this surface is 4,640 volts · meters, what is the electric flux, in volts · meters, of the electric field through the larger square?

22

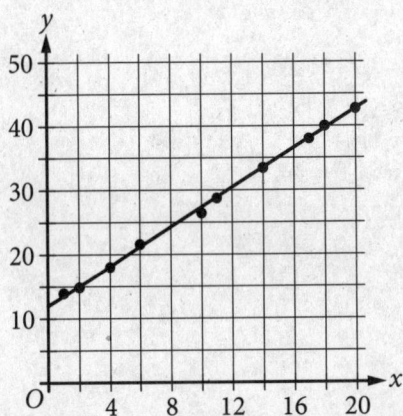

The scatterplot shows the relationship between two variables, x and y, for data set E. A line of best fit is shown. Data set F is created by multiplying the y-coordinate of each data point from data set E by 3.9. Which of the following could be an equation of a line of best fit for data set F?

A) $y = 46.8 + 5.9x$

B) $y = 46.8 + 1.5x$

C) $y = 12 + 5.9x$

D) $y = 12 + 1.5x$

STOP

**If you finish before time is called, you may check your work on this module only.
Do not turn to any other module in the test.**

The SAT®

Practice Test #5

ANSWER EXPLANATIONS

These answer explanations are for students using
The Official SAT Study Guide.

Reading and Writing

Module 1
(27 questions)

QUESTION 1

Choice A is the best answer because it most logically completes the text's discussion of how the flow of information between two regions of the brain may affect the ease of people's decision making. In this context, "reduced" means decreased. The text presents the finding from a team of neuroeconomists that decision making may be connected to communication between the prefrontal cortex and the parietal cortex. In presenting this finding, the text suggests a contrast between people who tend to be more decisive and people who make decisions more slowly. According to the text, people tend to be more decisive when the flow of information between the two brain regions is intensified, or strengthened. On the other hand, this context suggests that people make choices more slowly when the flow of information between the two brain regions is decreased.

Choice B is incorrect because "evaluated" means assessed, which wouldn't make sense in context. According to the text, people tend to be more decisive when the flow of information between two brain regions is intensified, or strengthened. This suggests that people's ease of decision making varies based on the rate of information traveling between the regions, not based on an effort to assess the information. *Choice C* is incorrect because "determined" means judged or influenced, neither of which would make sense in context. According to the text, people tend to be more decisive when the flow of information between two brain regions is intensified, or strengthened. This suggests that people's ease of decision making varies based on the rate of information traveling between the regions, not based on an effort to judge or influence the information. *Choice D* is incorrect because "acquired" means developed or attained, neither of which would make sense in context. According to the text, people tend to be more decisive when the flow of information between two brain regions is intensified, or strengthened. This suggests that people's ease of decision making varies based on the rate of information traveling between the regions, not based on the development or attainment of the information.

QUESTION 2

Choice B is the best answer because it most logically completes the text's discussion of the method the inhabitants of the Mexica empire used to track time. In this context, "exactitude" means precision. The text indicates that the

Mexica used the sun's position relative to various natural landmarks to track the passage of time, explaining that such methods allowed the Mexica to accurately determine the dates of important events such as solstices. This context supports the idea that the Mexica people were able to track time with a high degree of precision, or exactitude.

Choice A is incorrect because in this context "precariousness" would mean instability, and there's nothing in the text to suggest that the method used by the Mexica people to track time was unstable or produced unstable results. Rather, the text indicates that the method yielded precise results, allowing the Mexica to accurately determine the dates of significant events. *Choice C* is incorrect because in this context "resilience" would mean persistence, and there's nothing in the text to suggest that the Mexica worked stubbornly in spite of obstacles in order to track time. *Choice D* is incorrect because in this context "inconspicuousness" would mean discreetness, and there's nothing in the text to suggest that the Mexica wanted to track time without being noticed.

QUESTION 3

Choice B is the best answer because it most logically completes the text's discussion of Yaszek's introduction to her science fiction anthology. In this context "overtly" means openly or without concealment. The text draws a contrast between the lack of "deliberately signaled" political themes in woman-authored science fiction from the 1920s to the 1960s and what Yaszek notes about woman-authored science fiction from the 1970s. This contrast implies that the work from the 1970s did clearly reflect feminist political themes. In other words, the text indicates that unlike women who wrote science fiction in the 1920s to the 1960s, the women who wrote science fiction in the 1970s expressed overtly feminist themes.

Choice A is incorrect. In this context "prudently" would mean cautiously, which might plausibly describe the women who wrote science fiction from the 1920s to the 1960s, in that they tended to avoid revealing their political views; however, the text contrasts these authors with the women writing science fiction in the 1970s, thereby suggesting that the authors writing in the 1970s were not restrained in that way. *Choice C* is incorrect because in this context "cordially" would mean politely, and nothing in the text indicates that politeness was a significant factor for women writing science fiction either from the 1920s to the 1960s or in the 1970s. The text draws a contrast between the lack of "deliberately signaled" political themes in woman-authored science fiction from the 1920s to the 1960s and what Yaszek notes about woman-authored science fiction from the 1970s. It's unclear how "less deliberately signaled" politics and an increasing sense of politeness toward feminism would constitute a meaningful contrast. *Choice D* is incorrect because in this context, "inadvertently" would mean unintentionally, and nothing in the text suggests that Yaszek thought the feminist elements of the woman-authored science fiction from the 1970s arose without deliberate effort.

QUESTION 4

Choice B is the best answer because it most logically completes the text's discussion of advance indications of solar flares. In this context the word "impending" means imminent or approaching. The text mentions a study by Leka and colleagues that found that the Sun's corona provides an advance indication of solar flares. The text then points out why such an advance indication would be useful—solar flares can interfere with communications on Earth—and concludes by describing the characteristic of the corona that gives warning of a solar flare. The text indicates that this characteristic—increased brightness in a particular region of the corona—comes before the appearance of the flare. Therefore, in context, the best answer would indicate that the flare is approaching, or impending.

Choice A is incorrect. The best answer would be one that indicates that the increased brightness of the Sun's corona precedes the appearance of the flare. But if the flare were "antecedent," or previous, then the flare would instead precede the appearance of the increased brightness of the corona, a statement that is logically inconsistent. *Choice C* is incorrect. The word "innocuous," or harmless, does not logically complete the text; since solar flares can interfere with communications on Earth, they cannot reasonably be described as innocuous. *Choice D* is incorrect. If the solar flares have an advance indication of their appearance, then there must therefore be a time before the appearance of the flares when they do not exist. But the word "perpetual," or never-ending, would in context indicate that the flare exists at the same time as the advance indication provided by the Sun's corona, which would not make logical sense.

QUESTION 5

Choice D is the best answer because it most accurately describes the main purpose of the text. In the first sentence of the text, the narrator states that she thinks there's a chance she will become part of the basketball team at her college. She goes on to explain that she is "quick" and "tough." Based on these characteristics, she thinks she has a chance to join the team. Thus, the main purpose of the text is to explain why the narrator thinks she might make the basketball team.

Choice A is incorrect because the text focuses solely on basketball and doesn't mention any other kinds of sports. *Choice B* is incorrect because the text doesn't describe aspects of the game of basketball. Instead, it provides the narrator's reasoning for thinking that she might make her school basketball team. *Choice C* is incorrect. Although the narrator explains why she thinks she will be chosen for the basketball team at her school, the text doesn't go into the general decision-making process or the requirements for being picked for the team.

QUESTION 6

Choice D is the best answer because it most accurately states the main purpose of the text, which is to describe an experiment whose results cast doubt on an established hypothesis. The text begins by noting that researchers have long believed that woolly mammoths were hunted to extinction in North America by humans using spears with Clovis points. The text then describes an experiment conducted by an anthropologist to test this hypothesis. According to the text, the results of the experiment led the anthropologist to conclude that hunters using spears with Clovis points likely weren't the primary cause of the extinction. The anthropologist's results cast doubt on the long-held hypothesis presented at the beginning of the text and suggest that woolly mammoths may have become extinct in North America due to some other cause.

Choice A is incorrect because there's nothing in the text to suggest that researchers have been involved in an ongoing debate. On the contrary, the text suggests that most researchers agree on the cause of the woolly mammoth's extinction in North America. *Choice B* is incorrect because the text never mentions any advantages or disadvantages of the method used in the experiment, focusing instead on the results achieved using that method. *Choice C* is incorrect because the text addresses only one hypothesis, that mammoths were hunted to extinction in North America by humans using spears with Clovis points. Rather than present a competing hypothesis, the text explains how one anthropologist designed an experiment to test this long-held hypothesis.

QUESTION 7

Choice A is the best answer because it presents information about Maya civilization that is supported by the text. The text states that the writing system used in the Maya kingdoms had a symbol for the number zero. It goes on to say that at the time of the zero symbol's earliest example, more than 2,000 years ago, almost no other writing systems in the world featured such a symbol. The text also points out that some historians suggest that Maya mathematicians inherited the use of zero from the Olmec civilization, which existed in the same area as the Maya civilization at an earlier date. Thus, according to the text, some historians suggest that the Maya civilization acquired the use of zero from the Olmec civilization.

Choice B is incorrect because although the text mentions present-day historians and Maya mathematicians, it does not say anything about how much the Maya civilization respected its historians and mathematicians. *Choice C* is incorrect because the text does not indicate that the Maya civilization treated its use of the zero symbol, or any other intellectual achievements, as secrets to be kept from other civilizations. *Choice D* is incorrect because although the text mentions historians who suggest that the writing system of the Maya civilization inherited some features from the earlier Olmec civilization, the text does not describe any attempts of Maya civilization to introduce its writing system to other civilizations.

QUESTION 8

Choice A is the best answer because it accurately states the main idea of the text. The text focuses on formations of parallel ice ridges on Jupiter's moon Europa that are said to be formed by the same mechanism that formed a parallel set of ridges on Greenland's ice sheet. The text indicates that in Greenland, water on the surface seeps to the lower portion of the ice sheet, resulting in uplift that creates the ridges, and it states that although Europa lacks liquid water on its surface, the same process could be driven by an ocean below Europa's surface. In other words, the main idea of the text is that parallel ridges in the ice on Europa and Greenland are likely caused by similar processes even though in Greenland the process begins with liquid water on the surface while Europa lacks liquid water on the surface.

Choice B is incorrect because the text states outright that the ridges on Europa are parallel and furthermore refers to Greenland's ridges as "strikingly similar" to those on Europa. *Choice C* is incorrect because the text makes no mention of when any of the ice ridges formed, either separately or relative to one another. *Choice D* is incorrect because the text does not indicate any uncertainty about the reason for the ice ridges on Europa and, in fact, clearly states that researchers now claim to know the mechanism that created the ridges.

QUESTION 9

Choice D is the best answer because it most accurately states the main idea of the text. The text indicates that archaeologist Mª Ángeles Medina-Alcaide and her team used replicas of Paleolithic light sources to understand how Paleolithic artists moved through dark caves. The researchers learned, for example, that torches were more helpful for moving through caves than animal-fat lamps were. Thus, the main idea of the text is that Medina-Alcaide and her team tested Paleolithic light sources and learned some details about how Paleolithic artists traveled within dark caves.

Choice A is incorrect because the text doesn't address the usefulness of fireplaces for Paleolithic cave artists; it only mentions fireplaces briefly as one of the three lighting methods the researchers tested. *Choice B* is incorrect because the text doesn't discuss how often Paleolithic cave artists used each kind of light source tested. Although the text does compare animal-fat lamps with another lighting method, the point of that comparison is that animal-fat lamps were less useful than torches when walking, not that one method was used more often than another. *Choice C* is incorrect because the text doesn't discuss either how difficult it was for Medina-Alcaide and her team to replicate light sources or how the team felt about drawing conclusions from their study. Instead, the text reveals that the team was able to conclude that each light source likely had a distinct purpose.

QUESTION 10

Choice D is the best answer because it effectively uses data from the graph to support the underlined claim that more medicine and health topics were submitted to a national science fair in 2019 than in any of the other years shown. This choice indicates that the approximately 285 medicine and health topics submitted in 2019 are more than the number of medicine and health submissions in any other year shown—a description that is supported by information in the graph, which shows that medicine and health topic submissions were below 250 in 2016, 2017, and 2018, but above 250 (approximately 285 submissions) in 2019.

Choice A is incorrect because it doesn't support the underlined claim or accurately reflect the information in the graph. This choice refers to 2016 and discusses cellular and molecular biology and animal science, whereas the underlined claim refers to 2019 and discusses medicine and health. Moreover, the claim that in 2016 there were equal numbers of submissions in the cellular and molecular biology category and in the animal science category is contradicted by the graph, which shows approximately 200 submissions and 50 submissions, respectively, for those categories in 2016. *Choice B* is incorrect because it doesn't accurately reflect the information in the graph. This choice claims that in 2019 there were more physics and space submissions than there were medicine and health submissions, but the graph shows that there were approximately 100 space and science submissions that year and approximately 285 medicine and health submissions. *Choice C* is incorrect because it doesn't accurately reflect the information in the graph or support the underlined claim about medicine and health research topics. This choice claims that there were approximately 95 submissions for the animal science category in 2016, but the graph shows that the number was closer to 50 in 2016.

QUESTION 11

Choice C is the best answer because it most effectively illustrates the claim that the narrator prefers her hometown to other places she has visited. In the quotation, the narrator compares how she feels about places she has traveled to how she feels about the town she's from. The narrator states that although the many journeys she has made in her lifetime have brought her much pleasure, she has gained the most enjoyment from her experiences inside the borders of her hometown.

Choice A is incorrect because it doesn't express that the narrator likes her hometown better than other places she has visited; instead, the quotation describes something unspecified in positive terms, saying it continues to offer new things to explore and remember. *Choice B* is incorrect. Although the quotation praises a landscape surrounding a village, it doesn't specify that this village is the narrator's hometown, nor does it express a preference for this village over other places the narrator has visited. *Choice D* is incorrect. Although the quotation describes enjoyment from getting to know a region, it doesn't compare the narrator's feelings for this region with her feelings for her hometown.

QUESTION 12

Choice A is the best answer because it best supports the researchers' explanation of the results of rearranging a store's layout. According to the text, Sam K. Hui and colleagues found that rearranging a store's layout can encourage customers to make spontaneous purchases. The text states that the researchers explain that a change in layout causes shoppers to hunt for items' new locations, which exposes the shoppers to more products and increases the likelihood that they'll make an unplanned purchase. This quotation from a surveyed shopper indicates that the shopper spontaneously purchased a notebook while looking for cleaning supplies that weren't in their usual place. The quotation therefore supports the researchers' explanation that rearranging a store's layout can lead shoppers to make unanticipated purchases.

Choice B is incorrect because it doesn't support the researchers' explanation that rearranging a store's layout can lead shoppers to make unanticipated purchases. Instead of attributing an unplanned purchase to a change in layout, the quotation notes that the shopper searched for but couldn't find some items, and as a result the shopper purchased less, not more, than what was anticipated. *Choice C* is incorrect because the quotation attributes what was purchased to coupons that the shopper received, not to a new store layout. Thus, the quotation doesn't support the researchers' explanation that rearranging a store's layout can lead shoppers to make unanticipated purchases. *Choice D* is incorrect because the quotation attributes what was purchased to the size and stock of the store, not to a new store layout. The shopper simply purchased products that the shopper wanted in a particular store because other stores didn't carry those products, so the quotation doesn't support the researchers' explanation that rearranging a store's layout can lead shoppers to make spontaneous purchases.

QUESTION 13

Choice D is the best answer because it presents the conclusion that most logically follows from the text's discussion of the means authors use to write and revise their novels. After stating that many authors still choose to draft novels by hand even though computers are now widely used, the text acknowledges the speculation that the opposite choice—using only a computer—would have had an effect on such novels. However, the text then points out that every novel is the singular result of a combination of the particular conditions surrounding its creation. This suggests that it isn't possible to determine the effect of any single condition (such as the means of writing) on its own; thus, there would be no way to reasonably evaluate how a novel would have turned out differently if it had been written by other means.

Choice A is incorrect because the text doesn't suggest that it's more efficient to write a novel on a computer than to write it by hand; it doesn't address efficiency at all. Therefore, it isn't logical to conclude that authors who currently choose to write novels largely by hand should instead work only on a computer to increase their efficiency. *Choice B* is incorrect because the text doesn't suggest anything about how successful authors are, regardless of the means by which they choose to write; therefore, it isn't logical to conclude that authors who write largely by hand are likely to be more successful than those who work only on a computer. *Choice C* is incorrect because the text makes no mention of the time it takes to produce a novel, regardless of the means by which it's written; therefore, it isn't logical to conclude that novels written by hand take less time on average to produce than those written on a computer do.

QUESTION 14

Choice A is the best answer because it most logically completes the text's discussion of the behavior observed in field-collected and laboratory-reared bold jumping spiders when the spiders are exposed to certain experimental stimuli. The text indicates that researchers were exposing two groups of male bold jumping spiders (field-collected and laboratory-reared) to different stimuli and observing their subsequent behaviors. The text goes on to detail the observations made by the research team: field-collected spiders displayed aggressive behaviors when fed a high-protein diet and preferred flowers manipulated to display ultraviolet fluorescence, while laboratory-reared spiders displayed aggressive behaviors when fed a high-lipid diet and preferred nonfluorescent flowers that were dyed red. It can be inferred from the text that the rearing conditions (field versus laboratory) of the spiders was the independent variable for the experiment. Thus, it follows that the conditions in which the spiders were reared likely affect their response to the different experimental stimuli presented.

Choice B is incorrect because the text indicates that both groups of male bold jumping spiders (field-collected and lab-reared) displayed aggressive behaviors depending on the experimental diet they were exposed to. Additionally, the researchers observed the response of the spiders to different experimental stimuli, not the effect of rearing location on male spider aggression. *Choice C* is incorrect. The experiment detailed in the text compared two groups of bold jumping spiders reared in different settings—a lab setting, in which spiders were fed a high-lipid diet, and a field setting, in which spiders were fed a high-protein diet. The text does not speculate about whether the laboratory setting was more suitable to studying some aspects of the spiders' behavior than to studying other aspects of it. *Choice D* is incorrect. Although the experiment discussed in the text involved both lab-reared and field-collected specimens of the bold jumping spider, the text never suggests that lab-reared specimens were somehow superior to field-collected specimens or necessarily recommends the use of lab-reared specimens in experiments.

QUESTION 15

Choice C is the best answer. The convention being tested is end-of-sentence punctuation. This choice correctly uses a question mark to punctuate the coordinated interrogative clauses "What are atmospheric rivers" and "how do they affect our weather," both of which ask direct questions.

Choice A is incorrect because a period can't be used in this way to punctuate an interrogative clause, such as "how do they affect our weather," at the end of a sentence. *Choice B* is incorrect because the structure requires an interrogative clause and a question mark at the end of the sentence. *Choice D* is incorrect because the structure requires an interrogative clause at the end of the sentence.

QUESTION 16

Choice D is the best answer. The conventions being tested are the use of possessive determiners and the use of plural nouns. The singular possessive determiner "its"—which agrees in number with the singular noun phrase "Mira Nair's 1991 film *Mississippi Masala*"—and the plural noun "protagonists" correctly indicate that Nair's film has multiple protagonists.

Choice A is incorrect because "it's" is the contraction for "it is," not a possessive determiner. *Choice B* is incorrect because the context requires the plural noun "protagonists," not the singular possessive noun "protagonist's."

Choice C is incorrect because the context requires the possessive determiner "its" and the plural noun "protagonists," not the contraction "it's" or the singular possessive noun "protagonist's."

QUESTION 17

Choice C is the best answer. The convention being tested is the punctuation of a supplementary element within a sentence. The comma after "sisters" pairs with the comma after "Butterflies" to separate the supplementary element "a fictionalized account of the lives of the Mirabal sisters" from the rest of the sentence. This supplementary element functions to describe the novel *In the Time of the Butterflies*, and the pair of commas indicates that this element could be removed without affecting the grammatical coherence of the sentence.

Choice A is incorrect because a comma and conjunction can't be used in this way to separate the supplementary element from the rest of the sentence. *Choice B* is incorrect because it fails to use appropriate punctuation to separate the supplementary element from the rest of the sentence. *Choice D* is incorrect because it fails to use appropriate punctuation to separate the supplementary element from the rest of the sentence.

QUESTION 18

Choice B is the best answer. The convention being tested is punctuation between main clauses and a supplementary element. This choice correctly uses a comma to mark the boundary between the main clause ("The vessel took six days to dislodge") and the supplementary element ("in part due to its sheer size") that provides additional information on why the vessel was difficult to dislodge. Additionally, this choice correctly uses a colon to introduce another main clause that describes the vessel's size ("it's as heavy as two thousand blue whales when fully loaded").

Choice A is incorrect because it results in a comma splice. A comma can't be used in this way to mark the boundary between two main clauses ("The vessel…size" and "it's…loaded"). Additionally, it fails to mark the boundary between the main clause ("The vessel took six days to dislodge") and the supplementary element ("in part due to its sheer size"). *Choice C* is incorrect because it results in a comma splice. A comma can't be used in this way to mark the boundary between two main clauses ("The vessel…size" and "it's…loaded"). *Choice D* is incorrect because it results in a run-on sentence. The two main clauses ("The vessel…size" and "it's… loaded") are fused without punctuation and/or a conjunction.

QUESTION 19

Choice A is the best answer. The convention being tested is subject-modifier placement. This choice makes the noun phrase "topological tapestries" the subject of the sentence and places it immediately after the modifying phrase "woven…grandmother." In doing so, this choice clearly establishes that the topological tapestries—and not another noun in the sentence—are being described as woven from recycled yarn and hand tufted.

Choice B is incorrect because it results in a dangling modifier. The placement of the noun phrase "Argentine textile artist Alexandra Kehayoglou" immediately after the modifying phrase illogically suggests that Kehayoglou is woven from recycled yarn and hand tufted. *Choice C* is incorrect because it results in a dangling modifier. The placement of the pronoun "she" and the noun phrase "Argentine textile artist Alexandra Kehayoglou" after the modifying phrase illogically suggests that Kehayoglou is woven from recycled yarn and hand tufted. *Choice D* is incorrect because it results in a dangling modifier.

The placement of the noun "Alexandra Kehayoglou" immediately after the modifying phrase illogically suggests that Kehayoglou is woven from recycled yarn and hand tufted.

QUESTION 20

Choice C is the best answer. The convention being tested is punctuation between sentences. In this choice, the period is used to correctly mark the boundary between one sentence ("Jamaican...microsculptures") and another ("Creations...strands"). The noun phrase beginning with "creations" modifies the subject of the next sentence, "Wigan's sculptures."

Choice A is incorrect because it results in a run-on sentence. The sentences ("Jamaican...microsculptures" and "Creations...strands") are fused without punctuation and/or a conjunction. *Choice B* is incorrect because it results in a comma splice. A comma can't be used in this way to mark the boundary between sentences. *Choice D* is incorrect. Without a comma preceding it, the conjunction "and" can't be used in this way to join sentences.

QUESTION 21

Choice D is the best answer. "Finally" logically signals that the actions in this sentence—the removal, cataloging, and analysis of artifacts—are the next and final steps in a process, following the previous actions of surveying, digging, recording, and mapping.

Choice A is incorrect because "for instance" illogically signals that the actions in this sentence are an example of the actions in the previous sentence. Instead, the removal, cataloging, and analysis of artifacts are the next and final steps in a process. *Choice B* is incorrect because "on the contrary" illogically signals that the actions in this sentence are directly opposed to the actions in the previous sentence. Instead, the removal, cataloging, and analysis of artifacts are the next and final steps in a process. *Choice C* is incorrect because "earlier" illogically signals that the actions in this sentence occur before the actions in the previous sentence. Instead, the removal, cataloging, and analysis of artifacts are the next and final steps in a process.

QUESTION 22

Choice B is the best answer. "Next" logically signals that the action in this sentence—the water spraying—is the next step in the resurfacing process, following the ice scraping mentioned in the previous sentence.

Choice A is incorrect because "for example" illogically signals that the action in this sentence is an example of the action in the previous sentence. Instead, the water spraying is the next step in a process that begins with the ice scraping. *Choice C* is incorrect because "similarly" illogically signals that the action in this sentence is similar to the action in the previous sentence. Instead, the water spraying is the next step in a process that begins with the ice scraping. *Choice D* is incorrect because "in contrast" illogically signals that the action in this sentence contrasts with the action in the previous sentence. Instead, the water spraying is the next step in a process that begins with the ice scraping.

QUESTION 23

Choice D is the best answer. "Specifically" logically signals that the information in this sentence—Latimer making the light bulb more durable—provides a specific detail elaborating on the more general claim in the previous sentence that Latimer improved the light bulb.

Choice A is incorrect because "soon" illogically signals that the information in this sentence occurred shortly after Latimer improved the light bulb. Instead, Latimer making the bulb more durable was the specific improvement. *Choice B* is incorrect because "regardless" illogically signals that the information in this sentence is true despite the previous claim about Latimer. Instead, the information about Latimer making the bulb more durable provides a specific detail elaborating on that claim. *Choice C* is incorrect because "however" illogically signals that the information in this sentence contrasts with the previous claim about Latimer. Instead, the information about Latimer making the bulb more durable provides a specific detail elaborating on that claim.

QUESTION 24

Choice B is the best answer. "In so doing" logically signals that the information in this sentence about Gibson's piece—that it blurs the distinction between contemporary art and traditional crafts—is a result or consequence of the piece's blending of particular Native and non-Native cultural symbols.

Choice A is incorrect. "Conversely" illogically signals that the information in this sentence contrasts with the previous information about the blending of particular cultural symbols in Gibson's piece. Instead, it presents a result or consequence of that information. *Choice C* is incorrect. "For instance" illogically signals that this sentence provides an example supporting the previous information about the blending of particular cultural symbols in Gibson's piece. Instead, it presents a result or consequence of that information. *Choice D* is incorrect. "In particular" illogically signals that this sentence provides specific details elaborating on the previous information about the blending of particular cultural symbols in Gibson's piece. Instead, it presents a result or consequence of that information.

QUESTION 25

Choice C is the best answer. The sentence emphasizes a similarity between the Choctaw Code Talkers and the Navajo Code Talkers by explaining that both groups used their native languages to transmit coded messages for the military.

Choice A is incorrect. The sentence describes the Choctaw Code Talkers; it doesn't emphasize a similarity between the Choctaw Code Talkers and the Navajo Code Talkers. *Choice B* is incorrect. The sentence introduces the Navajo Code Talkers; it doesn't emphasize a similarity between the Choctaw Code Talkers and the Navajo Code Talkers. *Choice D* is incorrect. The sentence emphasizes a difference between the Choctaw Code Talkers and the Navajo Code Talkers; it doesn't emphasize a similarity.

QUESTION 26

Choice B is the best answer. The sentence explains an advantage of the ICAA's archive being digital, noting that the archive provides more access to historical documents since they don't have to be removed from their countries of origin.

Choice A is incorrect. The sentence emphasizes the number of documents in the ICAA archive; it doesn't explain an advantage of the archive being digital. *Choice C* is incorrect. The sentence notes the types of historical documents the ICAA's archive contains; it doesn't explain an advantage of the archive being digital. *Choice D* is incorrect. The sentence identifies who oversaw the creation of the ICAA's online archive; it doesn't explain an advantage of the archive being digital.

QUESTION 27

Choice C is the best answer. The sentence uses the quotation from Henderson to support a claim about Tharpe's contribution to rock 'n' roll, noting that the impact Tharpe had on the genre led Henderson to call her "the unquestioned founding mother of rock 'n' roll."

Choice A is incorrect. While the sentence makes the claim that Tharpe had a major impact on rock 'n' roll, it doesn't use a quotation to support this claim. *Choice B* is incorrect. The sentence presents Henderson's opinion that Tharpe had a major impact on rock 'n' roll, but it doesn't use a quotation to support this claim. *Choice D* is incorrect. While the sentence includes a quotation about audience reactions to Tharpe's music, the sentence describes Tharpe as a gospel musician; it doesn't support a claim about her contribution to rock 'n' roll.

Reading and Writing

Module 2 — Lower Difficulty
(27 questions)

QUESTION 1

Choice C is the best answer because as used in the text "reaching across to" most nearly means stretching toward. The text begins with Mrs. Wilkins stating that she wants to have one of the oranges that she's admiring. The text then indicates that Mrs. Wilkins, staying where she is, holds out a big orange to her friend. This context suggests that when the text describes Mrs. Wilkins as reaching across to the bowl of oranges, it means that she is stretching toward the bowl.

Choice A is incorrect because the text never suggests that Mrs. Wilkins is joining with, or becoming attached to, the bowl of oranges. Rather, the text indicates that she is stretching toward the bowl so she can pick out oranges for herself and her friend Rose to eat. *Choice B* is incorrect because the text never suggests that Mrs. Wilkins is gaining on, or overtaking in a competition or race, the bowl of oranges. The text suggests instead that the bowl is sitting still on a surface and that Mrs. Wilkins is extending her arm toward the bowl so she can pick out oranges for herself and her friend Rose to eat. *Choice D* is incorrect because the text doesn't indicate that Mrs. Wilkins is arriving at the bowl of oranges. In fact, the text states that Mrs. Wilkins stays where she is when reaching across to the bowl, meaning that she remains at a distance from it.

QUESTION 2

Choice B is the best answer because it most logically completes the text's discussion of noses on ancient sculptures. In this context, "fragile" means weak or delicate. This matches the text's description of noses on ancient sculptures, which are often missing from sculptures' heads because they are "especially easy to break." Therefore, this context indicates that noses on ancient sculptures are the most fragile part of the sculptures' heads.

Choice A is incorrect. In this context, "recognizable" would mean identifiable, and since the text indicates that noses are often missing from ancient statues, they therefore cannot be the most recognizable part of the statue. *Choice C* is incorrect because the text indicates that many ancient statues are missing noses, so noses wouldn't be "common," or frequent, aspects of ancient statues; they would conversely be uncommon. *Choice D* is incorrect because the text only indicates that noses on ancient statues often stick out and end up missing from the heads, which doesn't relate to the noses being "sophisticated," or knowledgeable or refined.

QUESTION 3

Choice D is the best answer because it most logically completes the text's discussion of the fossil deposit. In this context, "obtain" means gain or acquire. According to the text, a team of paleontologists has found fossils that are very well preserved. For this reason, the text suggests, the paleontologists have been able to gain detailed information from the fossils, such as the color patterns of the life forms that left them behind.

Choice A is incorrect because "occupy" means engage or inhabit, neither of which would make sense in context. It's unclear what it would mean for detailed information revealed by fossils to be engaged or inhabited. *Choice B* is incorrect because the text gives no indication that the paleontologists wanted to "hoard," or collect and hide, the detailed information revealed by the well-preserved fossils. *Choice C* is incorrect because the text gives no indication that the paleontologists wanted to "reserve," or withhold, the detailed information revealed by the well-preserved fossils.

QUESTION 4

Choice A is the best answer because it most logically completes the text's discussion of environmental management along the US and Mexican border. In this context, "requires" means needs in order to perform a task. The text indicates that because ecosystems span the border, actions taken by the government on one side of the border can affect the environment in the nation on the other side of the border, which makes international cooperation crucial. In other words, because actions on one side of the US and Mexican border can affect the other side of the border, managing environmental matters along the border requires coordination between the two governments.

Choice B is incorrect because "praises" in this context would mean to express a favorable judgment, but the text doesn't describe approval expressed by anyone, and it wouldn't make sense to say that environmental management itself praises intergovernmental coordination. *Choice C* is incorrect. In this context, "reports" would mean gives an account. Although coordination between the US and Mexican governments likely would involve some sort of reporting, the text doesn't describe any such practice. *Choice D* is incorrect. In this context, "advises" would mean recommends a course of action, and although governments can advise one another, it wouldn't make sense to say that environmental management itself makes recommendations.

QUESTION 5

Choice D is the best answer because in context, sharing "similarities with" means having some resemblance to. The text establishes a comparison between two groups of mammals, stating that although they aren't closely related, hedgehog tenrecs and true hedgehogs play similar roles in their habitats, a circumstance that has resulted in the independent development of some of the same physical traits. This context supports the idea that hedgehog tenrecs resemble, or share basic similarities with, true hedgehogs in some respects.

Choice A is incorrect because the text doesn't suggest that hedgehog tenrecs are "examples of," or representative of, true hedgehogs. The text states that despite some shared physical traits, the two groups of mammals aren't closely related; therefore, hedgehog tenrecs can't be examples of true hedgehogs. *Choice B* is incorrect because in this context, "concerns about" would mean worries about or interests in. The text focuses on the various physical traits that hedgehog tenrecs and true hedgehogs share. There's nothing in the text to suggest why hedgehog tenrecs would be worried about true hedgehogs, or why they would be interested in them. *Choice C* is incorrect because in this context, "indications of" would mean evidence of. By listing a set of traits that hedgehog tenrecs share with true hedgehogs, the text establishes a comparison between the two groups of mammals, and saying that the traits shared within one group of mammals provide evidence of another group of mammals wouldn't be an effective way to establish the similarities between the two groups.

QUESTION 6

Choice A is the best answer because is accurately states the main purpose of the text. The text begins by declaring that although a song is "but a little thing," or seemingly insignificant, singing it brings joy and gives the speaker of the text "zest," or excitement, in "hours of toil." The remainder of the text explores the idea that as night is falling, singing allows the speaker to feel that "all is well." Thus, the main purpose of the text is to convey how engaging in song makes the speaker feel.

Choice B is incorrect. Although the text mentions a shepherd, it neither indicates that the shepherd is singing nor does it compare the shepherd to the speaker. *Choice C* is incorrect. The text indicates that the speaker works hard, engaging in "hours of toil," and it can be inferred that the speaker likely lives in a rural area, since cows and a cowbell can be heard nearby. However, the text does not suggest that the speaker is a farmer or feels excited about farming. Moreover, the shepherd in the text is not a literal reference to someone who herds sheep but instead a figurative description of the moon as the shepherd of the stars. *Choice D* is incorrect because in the text, the speaker is singing a song, not listening to others sing one. Moreover, the text describes the feelings that the speaker has when singing a song, not the song itself.

QUESTION 7

Choice B is the best answer because it most accurately describes the main purpose of the text. The text begins by stating that there were many Spanish-language newspapers in cities across Texas in the late 1800s, citing San Antonio as a city that produced eleven such newspapers. The text then goes on to note that in El Paso, there were twenty-two newspapers published in Spanish in the late 1800s, more than any other Texas city. The text then concludes by explaining that the reason for this large number of Spanish-language newspapers was likely El Paso's location near Mexico and its large population of Spanish speakers. Therefore, the main purpose of the text is to explain that Spanish-language newspapers thrived in Texas cities, especially in El Paso, in the late 1800s.

Choice A is incorrect because the text doesn't discuss Spanish-language newspapers published in Texas today, let alone compare them with newspapers that were published in the 1800s. *Choice C* is incorrect. Although the text characterizes El Paso as a particularly rich site for Spanish-language journalism in the late 1800s, the text doesn't discuss whether newspapers published in El Paso influenced the newspapers published in other cities across Texas, including San Antonio. *Choice D* is incorrect because the text doesn't mention whether Spanish-language newspapers published in Texas were also widely read in Mexico. The text only focuses on the popularity of Spanish-language newspapers within Texas, and especially in El Paso.

QUESTION 8

Choice D is the best answer because it reflects how the author of Text 2 would most likely respond to the underlined claim in Text 1. Text 1 begins by noting the success of *The Nutcracker* but then claims that the ballet is "stuck in the past" and should "no longer be produced." Text 2 begins by conceding that *The Nutcracker* is indeed outdated but argues that it should continue to be performed, states that the show can be updated to include more contemporary dance styles, and provides an example of one such modernized version, *Hot Chocolate Nutcracker.* Hence, the author of Text 2 would most likely respond to the underlined claim in Text 1 by suggesting that dance companies should consider offering revised versions of *The Nutcracker* instead of completely rejecting the show.

Choice A is incorrect because the author of Text 2 advocates for using creative ways to update *The Nutcracker* and therefore wouldn't respond to the underlined claim by rejecting the suggestion that contemporary audiences would enjoy an updated version. *Choice B* is incorrect because although the authors of both texts claim that *The Nutcracker* is outdated, neither text suggests that contemporary audiences have largely stopped attending productions of the show. On the contrary, Text 2 states that *The Nutcracker* is a holiday favorite and generates substantial income for some dance companies. *Choice C* is incorrect because although Text 2 provides an example of a contemporized version of *The Nutcracker*, the text doesn't suggest that offering modernized versions is a way to increase income for most dance companies. Rather, the author of Text 2 suggests that offering modernized versions is a way to make the ballet discussed in Text 1 feel less outdated.

QUESTION 9

Choice C is the best answer because it most effectively uses data from the graph to complete the statement about the US national park with the highest number of recreation visits during a three-month period. The line graph shows the number of recreation visits to four US national parks for the months of June, July, and August 2021. According to the graph, the number of recreation visits to Yellowstone National Park in June was approximately 940,000; in July, the number of visits was approximately 1,080,000; and in August, the number of visits was approximately 920,000. In all three months, the number of visits to Yellowstone was higher than the number of visits to any other park in each month.

Choice A is incorrect. According to the graph, the number of recreation visits to Zion National Park was approximately 680,000 in June, about 580,000 in July, and about 470,000 in August, each of which is lower than the number of visits to Yellowstone in the same months. *Choice B* is incorrect. According to the graph, the number of recreation visits to Rocky Mountain National Park was approximately 670,000 in June, about 900,000 in July, and about 750,000 in August, each of which is lower than the number of visits to Yellowstone in the same months. *Choice D* is incorrect. According to the graph, the number of recreation visits to Grand Canyon National Park was approximately 540,000 in June, about 560,000 in July, and about 430,000 in August, each of which is lower than the total visits to Yellowstone in the same months.

QUESTION 10

Choice C is the best answer because it most effectively uses data from the table to complete the assertion about average sale prices at a clothing retailer. The table displays the average clothing prices for button-down shirts, sweaters, dresses, and jackets at a particular retailer for the years 2019–2022. According to the table, the average sales price for button-down shirts in 2019 was $44.05, while the average sales price for them in 2022 was higher at $47.75. The average sales prices for all other articles of clothing shown in the table were lower in 2022 than they were in 2019. Therefore, the average sales price was lower in 2019 than in 2022 for only button-down shirts.

Choice A is incorrect because according to the table the average sales price of dresses was higher in 2019 ($128.17) than in 2022 ($101.29), not lower. *Choice B* is incorrect because according to the table the average sales price of jackets was higher in 2019 ($131.20) than in 2022 ($99.20), not lower. *Choice D* is incorrect because according to the table the average sales price of sweaters was higher in 2019 ($66.40) than in 2022 ($55.28), not lower.

QUESTION 11

Choice C is the best answer because it presents a finding that, if true, would most directly support the researchers' conclusion that carbon dioxide does not serve as an additional cue to frog-biting midges regarding the location of male túngara frogs. The text begins by stating that the mating call of the male túngara frogs also attracts frog-biting midges, which prey on the frogs' blood. Researchers Bernal and de Silva were curious if the mating calls were sufficient signals for the midges to locate the frogs or if midges also used carbon dioxide emitted by the frogs to locate their prey. The text then details the procedure the researchers used to investigate their question and summarizes their conclusion—that carbon dioxide does not serve as an additional cue to the midges. Thus, if more midges were found in the researchers' trap that only played calls than in the trap that played calls and released carbon dioxide, it follows that the frog calls seem sufficient without the carbon dioxide cue. This finding supports the researchers' conclusion that carbon dioxide does not serve as an additional cue to frog-biting midges.

Choice A is incorrect because finding that the majority of frog-biting midges were found in the traps that both played the mating call and released carbon dioxide would present evidence that directly refutes the researchers' conclusion—that carbon dioxide does not serve as an additional cue to the frog-biting midges regarding the location of túngara frogs. *Choice B* is incorrect because if the midges entered the trap that played calls and released carbon dioxide only during or immediately after carbon dioxide was released, that would suggest that the midges used the carbon dioxide as a way to locate their prey, a finding that would contradict the researchers' conclusion that carbon dioxide was not an additional cue to the midges. *Choice D* is incorrect because a trap attracting larger numbers of midges with high carbon dioxide concentrations than a trap with low carbon dioxide concentrations suggests that carbon dioxide might serve as an additional cue to the midges as to the location on the frogs, a finding contrary to the researchers' conclusion.

QUESTION 12

Choice D is the best answer because it best describes data from the graph that support the biologists' claim. The text accompanying the graph describes the efforts of the California Condor Recovery Program, which is working to protect the condor from extinction. The program captured some condors in 1987 in order to breed them and has been reintroducing captive birds into the wild since 1992. Many biologists claim the program has been a success, as the text explains, and it is reasonable to infer that an indication of the program's success would be an increase in the wild condor population compared to the captive condor population. The graph shows the wild and captive condor populations in California between 2014 and 2020. In 2014 there were slightly more than 200 wild condors in California, but by 2020 there were more than 300. Meanwhile, over the same period the captive condor population remained under 200. Thus, the biologists' claim about the program's success is supported by data from the graph showing that the number of wild California condors increased overall from 2014 to 2020 and exceeded the number of those living in captivity.

Choice A is incorrect because it does not accurately describe data from the graph. The number of captive California condors did not steadily decrease between 2014 and 2020: rather, it increased slightly during some years and decreased slightly during others, generally remaining at slightly less than 200. *Choice B* is incorrect. Even though the graph does show a slight decrease in both the captive and wild condor populations from 2019 to 2020, such a decrease during a particular year would not demonstrate the program's success. *Choice C* is incorrect because it does not accurately describe data from the graph. The difference between the number of captive and wild California condors did not remain relatively steady between 2014 and 2017. While the number of captive condors remained roughly the same during that period, the number of wild condors increased, so the difference between the number of captive and wild condors increased as well.

QUESTION 13

Choice C is the best answer because it most effectively uses data from the table to complete the text, providing an example that illustrates that the annual increases in international tourism revenue in 2017 and 2018 weren't universal. The table shows the annual spending by international tourists (which indicates annual international tourism revenue) in 2016–2018 in four Asian countries. According to the table, annual spending by international tourists in South Korea was $21.0 billion in 2016 and then decreased to $17.2 billion in 2017. This decrease shows that not all of the countries included in the table saw increases in annual international tourism revenue in 2017.

Choice A is incorrect because the table doesn't provide any data regarding revenue from tourism by residents of those countries. Even if that data were provided, it wouldn't be relevant to the claim that the trend of annual increases in international tourism revenue in 2017 and 2018 was not universal. *Choice B* is incorrect because the data in the table do not support the statement that Japan's international tourism revenue was higher in 2016 than it was in 2018: the table indicates that Japan's annual international tourism revenue was $33.5 billion in 2016, which is less than Japan's annual international tourism revenue of $45.3 billion in 2018. *Choice D* is incorrect. Although the table does indicate that Thailand's revenue from international tourism was higher than that of the other three Asian countries in 2016, 2017, and 2018, this information has no direct bearing on the text's claim that not all the Asian countries represented in the table saw an increase in revenue from international tourism.

QUESTION 14

Choice D is the best answer because this quotation would best support the student's assertion that the escape of transgenic fish from Brazilian fish farms into the wild may have significant negative long-term ecological effects. The text explains that transgenic fish have DNA that includes genetic material from other species, that some transgenic fish have genes from jellyfish that make them glow in the dark, and that glow-in-the-dark transgenic fish can now be found in the wild in Brazilian creeks. The quotation indicates why the escape of these fish may have negative long-term ecological effects: glow-in-the-dark transgenic fish might introduce fluorescence into wild fish populations by breeding with wild fish, causing wild fish to glow in the dark and thereby allowing predators to prey on them much more easily.

Choice A is incorrect because this quotation doesn't mention any negative effects of the introduction of fluorescent transgenic fish into the wild. The quotation merely compares the ratio of females to males at two sites in the wild where transgenic fish have been observed. *Choice B* is incorrect because this quotation doesn't support the idea that the escape of fluorescent transgenic fish from Brazilian fish farms may have significant negative long-term ecological effects. Rather, the quotation suggests that more research is needed to understand the effects. *Choice C* is incorrect because this quotation supports the idea that transgenic fish may be present in more ecosystems than has been observed; it doesn't address whether the presence of fluorescent transgenic fish affects these ecosystems.

QUESTION 15

Choice A is the best answer because it most logically completes the text's discussion of the potential effects of logging on forest conservation. The text begins by stating that logging practices are often thought of as being contrary to forest conservation efforts. Then, the text presents the results of a research study examining the effect of limited logging practices on specific forest plots, finding that the plots with limited logging may be "more robust" (healthier) than the plots that hadn't been logged at all. Given these results, it follows that logging may be a useful practice for maintaining healthy forests if it is practiced in a limited way.

Choice B is incorrect because the study referenced in the text only provides information on limited logging as a potential forest management strategy. There is no information in the text about how other forest management strategies support forest conservation efforts. Therefore, the text does not support the assertion that other forest management strategies are more successful than limited logging. *Choice C* is incorrect because the text presents a research study with findings that specific plots of forest with limited logging may be more robust than the forest plots that were not logged. Rather than suggesting that it is hard to know whether limited logging might be beneficial, the text suggests that the practice could be useful in forest conservation efforts. *Choice D* is incorrect. The text discusses the results of a research study that compares the health of forest plots with limited logging to forest plots that were not logged. It does not take a position on the best way to support forest health but rather presents a research study with findings that question conventionally held thoughts regarding the practice of logging.

QUESTION 16

Choice A is the best answer. The convention being tested is the use of verb forms within a sentence. The nonfinite past participle "created" is correctly used to form a supplementary element that modifies the noun phrase "the saloon," identifying who established the Boston Saloon.

Choice B is incorrect because it results in an ungrammatical sentence. The finite present tense verb "creates" can't be used in this way to form a supplementary element to modify the noun phrase "the saloon." *Choice C* is incorrect because it results in an ungrammatical sentence. The nonfinite present participle "creating" can't be used in this way to form a supplementary element to modify the noun phrase "the saloon." *Choice D* is incorrect because it results in an ungrammatical sentence. The finite present tense verb "create" can't be used in this way to form a supplementary element to modify the noun phrase "the saloon."

QUESTION 17

Choice C is the best answer. The convention being tested is pronoun-antecedent agreement. The singular pronoun "this" agrees in number with the singular antecedent "Lê Lương Minh became the thirteenth secretary-general of the Association of Southeast Asian Nations (ASEAN) in January 2013." The pronoun "this" is referring back to the singular event described earlier in the sentence in which Minh became secretary-general of ASEAN.

Choice A is incorrect because the plural pronoun "these" doesn't agree in number with the singular antecedent "Lê Lương Minh became the thirteenth secretary-general of the Association of Southeast Asian Nations (ASEAN) in January 2013." *Choice B* is incorrect because the plural pronoun "those" doesn't agree in number with the singular antecedent "Lê Lương Minh became the thirteenth secretary-general of the Association of Southeast Asian Nations (ASEAN) in January 2013." *Choice D* is incorrect because the indefinite pronoun "some" is ambiguous in this context; the resulting sentence leaves unclear what marks the first time the organization appointed a Vietnamese leader.

QUESTION 18

Choice C is the best answer. The convention being tested is punctuation use between a verb and an object. No punctuation is needed between the verb "popularized" and its object "the use of Jamaican Creole." The object helps complete the idea of the verb—in this case, it explains what Louise Bennett popularized—and any punctuation between the two results in an ungrammatical sentence.

Choice A is incorrect because no punctuation is needed between the verb and its object. *Choice B* is incorrect because no punctuation is needed between the verb and its object. *Choice D* is incorrect because no punctuation is needed between the verb and its object.

QUESTION 19

Choice D is the best answer. The convention being tested is end-of-sentence punctuation. This choice correctly uses a period to punctuate a declarative sentence that asks an indirect question ("Researchers Amit Kumar and Nicholas Epley investigated how people perceive acts of kindness").

Choice A is incorrect. The structure of the sentence requires a declarative clause at the end of the sentence that states what Kumar and Epley did, not an interrogative clause that asks a direct question, such as "how do people perceive acts of kindness." *Choice B* is incorrect. The structure of the sentence requires a declarative clause at the end of the sentence that states what Kumar and Epley did, not an interrogative clause that asks a direct question, such as "how do people perceive acts of kindness?" *Choice C* is incorrect. It's unconventional to use a question mark in this way to punctuate a declarative sentence that asks an indirect question, such as "Researchers...kindness."

QUESTION 20

Choice A is the best answer. The convention being tested is subject-modifier placement. This choice makes the proper noun "Matthew Henson" the subject of the sentence and places it immediately after the modifying phrase "one…century." In doing so, this choice clearly establishes that Matthew Henson—and not another noun in the sentence—is being described as one of the few African American global explorers during the turn of the 20th century.

Choice B is incorrect because it results in a dangling modifier. The placement of the noun phrase "1891 and 1909" immediately after the modifying phrase illogically suggests that those years were one of the few African American global explorers during the turn of the 20th century. *Choice C* is incorrect because it results in a dangling modifier. The placement of the proper noun "Greenland" immediately after the modifying phrase illogically suggests that Greenland was one of the few African American global explorers during the turn of the 20th century. *Choice D* is incorrect because it results in a dangling modifier. The placement of the noun phrase "several treks across Greenland" immediately after the modifying phrase illogically suggests that the treks were one of the few African American global explorers during the turn of the 20th century.

QUESTION 21

Choice D is the best answer. The convention being tested is subject-verb agreement. The plural verb "come" agrees in number with the plural subject "nematodes."

Choice A is incorrect because the singular verb "has come" doesn't agree in number with the plural subject "nematodes." *Choice B* is incorrect because the singular verb "comes" doesn't agree in number with the plural subject "nematodes." *Choice C* is incorrect because the singular verb "is coming" doesn't agree in number with the plural subject "nematodes."

QUESTION 22

Choice D is the best answer. "Instead" logically signals that the idea in this sentence—that researchers should use the word "lyfe"—is an alternative to the idea mentioned in the previous sentence (scientists' use of the word "life").

Choice A is incorrect because "previously" illogically signals that the idea in this sentence occurs before the action in the first sentence. Instead, the use of "lyfe" is an alternative to the previously mentioned use of "life." *Choice B* is incorrect because "regardless" illogically signals that the idea in this sentence is true despite the information in the first sentence. Instead, the use of "lyfe" is an alternative to the previously mentioned use of "life." *Choice C* is incorrect because "there" illogically signals that the idea in this sentence occurs in a place mentioned in the previous sentence. Instead, the use of "lyfe" is an alternative to the previously mentioned use of "life."

QUESTION 23

Choice D is the best answer. "For this reason" logically signals that the information that follows—that metrologists developed the SI based on unchanging values in nature—is a result of the previous claim that scientists rely on precise, unchanging standards of measurement to guarantee the validity of experimental results.

Choice A is incorrect because "in contrast" illogically signals that the information that follows contrasts with the previous claim that scientists rely on precise, unchanging standards of measurement. Instead, the information that metrologists developed the SI based on unchanging values in nature is a result of that claim. *Choice B* is incorrect because "regardless" illogically signals that the information that follows is true despite the previous claim that scientists rely on precise, unchanging standards of measure. Instead, the information that metrologists developed the SI based on unchanging values in nature is a result of that claim. *Choice C* is incorrect because "in addition" illogically signals that the information that follows is merely an additional fact related to the previous claim that scientists rely on precise, unchanging standards of measurement. Instead, the information that metrologists developed the SI based on unchanging values in nature is a result of that claim.

QUESTION 24

Choice B is the best answer. "Nevertheless" logically signals that the claim in the sentence—that the speaker could visit every state in the US and not find the oldest public library in the Western Hemisphere—is true despite the previous claim about the speaker seeking out old public libraries.

Choice A is incorrect because "as a result" illogically signals that the claim in the sentence is a consequence of the previous claim about the speaker seeking out old public libraries. Instead, the claim is true despite the previous claim. *Choice C* is incorrect because "earlier" illogically signals that the claim in the sentence occurs earlier in a chronological sequence of events than the previous claim about the speaker seeking out old public libraries. Instead, the claim is true despite the previous claim. *Choice D* is incorrect because "in other words" illogically signals that the claim in the sentence is merely a paraphrase or restatement of the previous claim about the speaker seeking out old public libraries. Instead, the claim is true despite the previous claim.

QUESTION 25

Choice D is the best answer. The sentence emphasizes the mass of Sirius A, noting that it has a mass of 2.063 solar masses and that it is larger than the Sun.

Choice A is incorrect. The sentence makes a generalization about how the mass of stars can be measured; it doesn't emphasize the mass of Sirius A. *Choice B* is incorrect. The sentence introduces solar masses as a unit of measurement; it doesn't emphasize the mass of Sirius A. *Choice C* is incorrect. The sentence emphasizes the mass of Proxima Centauri, not the mass of Sirius A.

QUESTION 26

Choice D is the best answer. The sentence contrasts first-class levers and second-class levers, explaining that the fulcrum in a first-class lever is between the effort and the load, whereas in a second-class lever the load is between the effort and the fulcrum.

Choice A is incorrect. The sentence defines two terms associated with levers; it doesn't contrast first-class levers and second-class levers. *Choice B* is incorrect. While the sentence seems to acknowledge a general difference in fulcrum and load locations between first-class and second-class levers, it does not specify what this difference is. Moreover, the sentence could be read as emphasizing a similarity—that in both types of levers, the fulcrum and load are in different locations. The sentence thus fails to effectively contrast the two types of levers. *Choice C* is incorrect. The sentence describes a similarity between first-class and second-class levers; it doesn't contrast them.

QUESTION 27

Choice B is the best answer. The sentence emphasizes a similarity between glaciers and icebergs in Greenland, noting that both melt and thereby contribute to rising sea levels.

Choice A is incorrect. The sentence provides information about the melting rate of icebergs in Greenland; it doesn't emphasize a similarity between glaciers and icebergs in Greenland. *Choice C* is incorrect. The sentence emphasizes a difference between glaciers and icebergs in Greenland, noting that their melting rates depend on different factors; it doesn't emphasize a similarity. *Choice D* is incorrect. The sentence explains the conditions under which glaciers in Greenland melt; it doesn't emphasize a similarity between glaciers and icebergs in Greenland.

Reading and Writing

Module 2 — Higher Difficulty
(27 questions)

QUESTION 1

Choice B is the best answer because it most logically completes the text's discussion of Mary Engle Pennington and Stephanie Kwolek. In this context, "tentative" means unsettled or not definite. The text indicates a contrast between Pennington and Kwolek in terms of their memorability ("place in our historical memory") and states that Kwolek "will long be remembered" for her invention of Kevlar material. This context suggests that although Pennington had an impact on society, she may be less likely than Kwolek to be remembered for a very long time—in other words, that her memorability may be more tentative, or less definite, than Kwolek's.

Choice A is incorrect because the text establishes a contrast between Pennington and Kwolek in terms of their "place in our historical memory" for their achievements, and the statement that Kwolek "will be long remembered" while Pennington's memorability may be more "permanent," or enduring, wouldn't supply a contrast; it would instead suggest that both people will remain memorable. *Choice C* is incorrect because the text establishes a contrast between Pennington and Kwolek in terms of their memorability, suggesting that Pennington is less likely than Kwolek to be "long remembered," but doesn't address how "warranted," or based on good reason, each person's "place in our historical memory" is. In fact, the text suggests that both Pennington and Kwolek had significant achievements, even if one may be more memorable. *Choice D* is incorrect because the text establishes a contrast between Pennington and Kwolek in terms of their "place in our historical memory" for their achievements, and the statement that Kwolek "will be long remembered" while Pennington's memorability may be more "prominent," or widely known, wouldn't supply a contrast; it would instead suggest that both people are very memorable.

QUESTION 2

Choice D is the best answer because it most logically completes the text's discussion of using magnetism to detect stress in buried metal pipes. In this context, "exploited" means made productive use of. The text indicates that the magnetic fields of some metals change under stress and that Saleem and colleagues showed that it is possible to measure those changes from a distance, thereby demonstrating that the integrity of underground metal pipes can be evaluated without having to unearth them. This context thus indicates that Saleem and colleagues made productive use of, or exploited, this tendency of the metals' magnetic fields.

Choice A is incorrect because in this context, "hypothesized" would mean made a tentative assumption to be evaluated in a study or experiment. Although Saleem and colleagues may have had one or more hypotheses for these experiments, the text presents the information about the tendency of some metals' magnetic fields to change under stress as a known fact that the researchers made productive use of, not as a hypothesis to be evaluated. The text after the colon indicates that the researchers were not evaluating whether such changes occur but whether those changes can be measured at a distance. *Choice B* is incorrect because in this context, "discounted" would mean downplayed or ignored, but the text does not suggest that Saleem and colleagues minimized or ignored the tendency of the magnetic fields of some metals to change under stress. Rather, the text indicates that this tendency is the basis for Saleem and colleagues' method of assessing the pipes' integrity. *Choice C* is incorrect because nothing in the text indicates that Saleem and colleagues "redefined," or reevaluated or reformulated, the tendency of some metals' magnetic fields to change under stress. Instead, the text indicates that the researchers made use of that tendency to demonstrate that it is possible to evaluate the integrity of underground pipes without unearthing them.

QUESTION 3

Choice B is the best answer because it most logically completes the text's discussion of behavioral psychology studies. In this context, "ameliorate" means to help remedy or improve. The text states that many behavioral psychology studies are flawed because the subjects used are "highly unrepresentative." It is then suggested that researchers should recruit subjects from "diverse backgrounds and locations" in order to help address the issue of unrepresentative subject pools. Thus, this context conveys that recruitment efforts focused on diversity would help ameliorate the problems outlined in the text.

Choice A is incorrect. In this context, "sanction" could have two meanings: to give official approval for something or to enact a penalty, neither of which makes sense in this context. The text describes a situation known to be problematic in behavioral psychology studies and then presents a potential remedy to that situation; the text does not suggest that the situation is officially approved or results in any type of penalty. *Choice C* is incorrect because rather than "rationalize," or explain or justify, a situation, the text presents a situation and its potential remedy. *Choice D* is incorrect because the text is not attempting to "postulate," or suggest a claim or theory, related to the situation described in the text but is rather presenting a potential remedy for the situation.

QUESTION 4

Choice D is the best answer because in context, sharing "similarities with" means having some resemblance to. The text establishes a comparison between two groups of mammals, stating that although they aren't closely related, hedgehog tenrecs and true hedgehogs play similar roles in their habitats, a circumstance that has resulted in the independent development of some of the same physical traits. This context supports the idea that hedgehog tenrecs resemble, or share basic similarities with, true hedgehogs in some respects.

Choice A is incorrect because the text doesn't suggest that hedgehog tenrecs are "examples of," or representative of, true hedgehogs. The text states that despite some shared physical traits, the two groups of mammals aren't closely related; therefore, hedgehog tenrecs can't be examples of true hedgehogs. *Choice B* is incorrect because in this context, "concerns about" would mean worries about or interests in. The text focuses on the various physical traits that hedgehog tenrecs and true hedgehogs share. There's nothing in the text to suggest why hedgehog tenrecs would be worried about true hedgehogs, or why they would be interested in them. *Choice C* is incorrect because in this context, "indications of" would mean evidence of. By listing a set of traits that hedgehog tenrecs share with true hedgehogs, the text establishes a comparison between the two groups of mammals, and saying that the traits shared within one group of mammals provide evidence of another group of mammals wouldn't be an effective way to establish the similarities between the two groups.

QUESTION 5

Choice D is the best answer because it most logically completes the text's discussion of the twelfth-century Islamic philosopher Ibn Rushd. As used in this context, "inconsequential to" means not significant to. According to the text, Ibn Rushd's works were primarily available in Spain, where he lived, far from central areas of the Muslim world, a fact that could support the conclusion that his influence on Muslim contemporaries was limited. The text implies, however, that recent scholarship has shown that his works still had an impact on other Muslim philosophers of his time. This context supports the idea that his works weren't inconsequential to Islamic thought in this period.

Choice A is incorrect because the issue under consideration in the text is whether other Muslim philosophers of Ibn Rushd's time had access to his works, not whether his works were "controversial among," or causing dispute among, other philosophers. *Choice B* is incorrect. The text implies that other Muslim philosophers of Ibn Rushd's era were aware of his works, not that they were "antagonistic toward," or hostile toward, them. There is no suggestion that Ibn Rushd's writings elicited hostility from his contemporaries. *Choice C* is incorrect because in this context, "imitated by" would mean followed as a model by. Although the text implies that Ibn Rushd's works were at least somewhat available in regions that were at the center of Islamic thought during the period, it doesn't specifically address in what ways his works influenced contemporary Muslim philosophers. Thus, the text doesn't support the idea that other philosophers modeled their own works after Ibn Rushd's works.

QUESTION 6

Choice B is the best answer because it best describes the function of the underlined portion in the text as a whole. The text describes the failed attempt of Israel Potter to establish a farm in New England during the late eighteenth century: according to his contract, he was to receive two hundred acres in exchange for three months' work, but his employer then refused to fulfill the bargain and Israel had no recourse to law to obtain the land he was owed. Israel was therefore forced to find another means of supporting himself. To explain why Israel was particularly susceptible to his employer's dishonesty, the underlined portion states that though Israel was "brave-hearted, and even much of a dare-devil upon a pinch," he also possessed "a singular patience and mildness." In other words, Israel could be courageous in certain circumstances, but he was usually meek and disinclined to argument, from which it is reasonable to infer that Israel was often taken advantage of.

Thus, the underlined portion suggests that if not for a certain aspect of his character, Israel might not have been as easily thwarted in his ambition to establish a farm.

Choice A is incorrect because although the underlined portion describes aspects of Israel's personality, it does not address how he feels about his own personality. *Choice C* is incorrect because the underlined portion addresses Israel's occasional courage and frequent meekness but does not address whether he would have the skills and resolve necessary to operate a farm if he owned sufficient property. *Choice D* is incorrect. Though the underlined portion does indicate that Israel could be courageous in certain circumstances, it does not say that he undertook acts of courage that others avoided, but rather that he was habitually meek. Even if the underlined portion did say that Israel was more courageous than most, this would not explain why he found himself under the circumstances described in the text—that is, as a consequence of his meek nature, cheated of the property to which he had a right.

QUESTION 7

Choice B is the best answer because it most accurately describes the overall structure of the text. The text begins by explaining that human activities influence carbon and nitrogen levels in soil, but how deeply these effects are seen in the soil remains an unresolved question. Next, the text summarizes Okolo and colleagues' hypothesis regarding this question—which is that the different effects on carbon and nitrogen levels associated with different types of land use would also be observed below the topsoil layer—and then briefly explains the methods they used to test this hypothesis. Finally, the text states that the researchers found that at depths below the topsoil layer, carbon and nitrogen decreased to similarly low levels across all land-use types, a finding that conflicts with the team's hypothesis presented earlier in the text. Thus, the text introduces an unresolved scientific question, presents a research team's hypothesis pertaining to that question, and then describes an observation that the team made that conflicted with their hypothesis.

Choice A is incorrect. Although the text introduces a phenomenon (the fact that human activities influence carbon and nitrogen levels in the soil) that isn't fully understood by scientists and explains a research team's hypothesis about the phenomenon, the text doesn't describe how the team refined their hypothesis when a research finding contradicted it. *Choice C* is incorrect because the text doesn't discuss a process at all; rather, it poses an unsolved scientific question and presents a hypothesis that Okolo and colleagues tested to answer that question. Moreover, the text only describes one hypothesis; it doesn't mention any competing hypotheses, nor does it suggest that Okolo's team was able to determine which hypothesis was correct. *Choice D* is incorrect because the text doesn't begin by presenting a hypothesis that is under scientific debate; rather, it presents a question that scientists have been unable to answer and then introduces a hypothesis formulated by Okolo and colleagues. While the text does explain how Okolo's team tested their hypothesis, the text goes on to say that their data conflicted with their hypothesis, not that the data validated, or supported, their hypothesis.

QUESTION 8

Choice A is the best answer because it reflects how the author of Text 2 would most likely respond to the claim in the underlined sentence of Text 1. Text 1 begins by asserting that efforts to automate classification of paintings into different styles have been largely unsuccessful and that technological limits are likely to prevent significant success. Text 2 concedes that automated artistic style classifiers have found it difficult to distinguish between Baroque paintings and Renaissance paintings, but the text goes on to describe the work of Ravneet Singh Arora and Ahmed Elgammal, who have achieved a greater accuracy in classification by running one model on top of another. Text 2 concludes by describing Arora and Elgammal's approach as one that demonstrates that innovation is still possible in the field. Thus, the author of Text 2 would not agree with the underlined claim in Text 1 that the technological limits of automated painting classification models have been reached; instead, the author of Text 2 would emphasize that there are still advances being made in automated artistic style classification.

Choice B is incorrect because there's nothing in Text 2 to suggest that its author would criticize previous research into automated artistic style classification systems for focusing on a narrow group of styles. Additionally, such a criticism, if it were present in Text 2, would not address the claim in the underlined sentence of Text 1, since Text 1's claim is concerned with the lack of success of automated classifiers and their technological limits, not with the focus of previous research into automated artistic style classification systems. *Choice C* is incorrect. While Text 1 does argue that differences between artistic styles are subjective, implying that two reasonable people might disagree about whether a painting is an example of one style or another, neither Text 1 nor Text 2 addresses whether most people can accurately identify the styles of paintings they are shown. Rather, both texts are concerned mainly with the potential accuracy of automated artistic style classifiers. *Choice D* is incorrect. Text 2 provides no support for the assertion that its author would suggest that people may develop more uniform and accepted ideas regarding artistic classifications. Additionally, such a suggestion, if it were present in Text 2, would not address the claim in the underlined sentence of Text 1, since Text 1's claim is concerned with the lack of success of automated classifiers and their technological limits, not with the uniformity or acceptability of people's ideas about artistic styles and their boundaries.

QUESTION 9

Choice C is the best answer because it accurately describes why the finding about the microorganism community composition was important. The text describes an experiment by Eva Kaštovská and her team in which they collected plant-soil cores at one elevation and transplanted them to sites at a lower elevation, where the mean air temperature was warmer. Kaštovská and her team observed that microorganism-mediated nutrient cycling was accelerated in the transplanted cores and that "crucially, microorganism community composition was unchanged," which allowed the team to attribute the acceleration to changes in microorganism activity brought about by the difference in temperature. This strongly implies that the team wouldn't have been able to make that attribution otherwise, meaning that a change in microorganism composition represented another possible explanation for the acceleration that had to be ruled out.

Choice A is incorrect. Although the text says microorganism-mediated cycling of soil nutrients increased in the transplanted cores, this is unrelated to what's important about the finding that the microorganism composition didn't change—that it allowed the team to attribute the change in activity solely to the change in temperature. *Choice B* is incorrect. Although the text compares activity in one core at two different elevations, the text doesn't address changes in activity at various elevations over time. *Choice D* is incorrect. Although different microorganisms likely exhibit different levels of activity, the text indicates that there was no change in microorganism composition, and there is nothing in the text about different microorganisms having different activity levels.

QUESTION 10

Choice D is the best answer because it most effectively uses data from the table to complete the statement comparing the mean ratings for two different groups of participants in a study. The text explains that a research team evaluated the study's participants using various measures in order to learn whether there might be a medical benefit to telling patients they're receiving a placebo. The table shows the team's mean ratings for participants after 21 days for three of the measures: global improvement, symptom severity reduction, and quality of life improvement. According to the table, the mean ratings were higher for all three measures for participants aware of taking a placebo than for participants in the control group. Given that higher ratings indicate greater well-being, as the text states, the mean ratings in the table indicate greater overall well-being for participants aware of taking a placebo than for participants in the control group.

Choice A is incorrect because the table doesn't include data about individual participants; rather, it presents means, or mathematical averages, of ratings. For this reason, no conclusions can be drawn from data in the table about the extent to which well-being may have varied from participant to participant. *Choice B* is incorrect because according to the table, the mean ratings for participants aware of taking a placebo were higher for all three measures than for participants in the control group, not lower for two of the measures. *Choice C* is incorrect because it cites data from the table related to participants in the control group, not to participants aware of taking a placebo. Additionally, the mean ratings in the table for participants aware of taking a placebo are higher for all three measures than for participants in the control group. Given that higher ratings indicate greater well-being, as the text states, the ratings in the table for participants aware of taking a placebo indicate greater well-being for these participants in all three measures.

QUESTION 11

Choice C is the best answer because it describes data from the graph that support Jan Packer and colleagues' conclusion about the effect of leave time on the attentiveness of university employees. According to the text, the researchers' study design included a group of employees who took no leave, a group who took 2–4 days of leave, and a group who took 1–5 weeks of leave. The participants who took leave were tested for attentiveness one week before their leave (the first test administration), one week after their return to work (the second test administration), and two weeks after their return (the third test administration). The participants who took no leave were tested three times at random. The graph shows that at one week after their return to work, participants who took only 2–4 days of leave had an average attentiveness score of between 540 and 600, while participants who took 1–5 weeks of leave had an average score of between 480 and 540. At two weeks after their return to work, those who took only 2–4 days of leave had an average score of between 480 and 540, while those who took 1–5 weeks of leave had an average score of approximately 480. In other words, the graph shows that on both post-leave testing dates, participants with longer leave times had lower average attentiveness scores than those with shorter leave times. Since attentiveness is an indicator of cognitive functioning, these data confirm Packer and colleagues' conclusion that longer leave times might not confer a greater cognitive benefit than shorter leave times do.

Choice A is incorrect. The graph does show that in the second test administration, participants who took 2–4 days of leave had higher average attentiveness scores than did those who took no leave and also shows that in the third test administration, those who took no leave had higher average scores than those who took 1–5 weeks of leave. But neither of these findings has a direct bearing on the researchers' conclusion, which concerns a comparison of participants who took 2–4 days of leave with those who took 1–5 weeks, rather than a comparison of either group with participants who took no leave. *Choice B* is incorrect. Although the graph does show that in the first test administration, participants who took 2–4 days of leave had lower average attentiveness scores than did those who took 1–5 weeks of leave and those who took no leave, this test administration occurred before any participants went on leave; therefore, these results have no bearing on the researchers' conclusion about how the amount of leave taken by participants affected their cognitive functioning. *Choice D* is incorrect. Although the graph does show that in the second and third test administrations, participants who took 2–4 days of leave had higher average attentiveness scores than did those who took no leave, the researchers' conclusion is about the effects of short leave compared with the effects of long leave, not the effects of short leave compared with the effects of no leave. These results are therefore irrelevant to the conclusion.

QUESTION 12

Choice B is the best answer because it describes data from the graph that complete the text's discussion of lizard species' use of maximal speed when escaping predators. According to the text, moving at maximal speed (the highest speed possible) requires so much energy that it is not always an effective strategy for animals, even when they are escaping predators. The graph displays data on the average percent of maximal speed used by lizard species while either escaping predators or pursuing prey. The graph categorizes the data for both pursuing and escaping by the number of species using 30%–39% of maximal speed, 40%–49% of maximal speed, 50%–59% of maximal speed, 60%–69% of maximal speed, 70%–79% of maximal speed, 80%–89% of maximal speed, and 90%–100% of maximal speed, respectively. In the graph, there is at least one species in each of the following percent categories for maximal speed while escaping predators: 50%–59%, 60%–69%, 70%–79%, and 80%–89%. Thus, the data in the graph show that multiple lizard species move at an average of less than 90% of their maximal speed while escaping predation.

Choice A is incorrect because the data in the graph isn't organized in such a way that a comparison of the percentage of maximal speed used when escaping predation with the percentage used when pursuing prey is possible at the level of individual species. *Choice C* is incorrect. It is true that in the graph, the percent category with the largest number of species using maximal speed while escaping predators is 90%–100% (8 species total). However, these data don't complete the text, which is concerned instead with how animals are discouraged from using maximal speed even when escaping predators because of the amount of energy required to use it. *Choice D* is incorrect because these data from the graph pertain to maximal speed while pursuing prey and therefore don't complete the text's discussion of lizard species' use of maximal speed when escaping predators.

QUESTION 13

Choice D is the best answer because it most effectively uses a quotation from "Poetry" to illustrate the claim that the poem highlights an ambivalence, or a conflicted attitude, toward poetry. In the quotation, the speaker suggests that one might read poetry with "contempt," or disdain, for it, but even with this negative attitude one will find "a place for the genuine." Because the quotation expresses conflicting attitudes toward poetry, it effectively illustrates the speaker's ambivalence in discussing the merits and displeasure of reading poetry.

Choice A is incorrect because it doesn't mention poetry or show ambivalence. *Choice B* is incorrect. Although the idea of "half poets" may seem to relate to ambivalence, the speaker mentions only negative attitudes toward certain works and the quotation therefore lacks a contrasting positive or neutral attitude that would be needed to indicate ambivalence. *Choice C* is incorrect because the speaker mentions only negative attitudes toward certain works and the quotation therefore lacks a contrasting positive or neutral attitude that would be needed to indicate ambivalence.

QUESTION 14

Choice D is the best answer because it most logically completes the text's discussion of the Cretaceous pterosaur *Tupandactylus navigans.* The text first describes what paleontologists initially speculated to be true of *T. navigans* based on observing only fossilized skulls of the pterosaur rather than complete skeletons—namely, that *T. navigans* had an oversized head crest and that, like other pterosaurs, its main mode of movement must have been flight. The text goes on to describe what researcher Victor Beccari and his team concluded based on studying a nearly complete fossilized skeleton of *T. navigans*, which provided additional information that fossilized skulls alone could not. Beccari and colleagues determined that *T. navigans* had long hind legs, short wings, and an unusually long neck, in addition to the oversized head crest previously observed by paleontologists. Taken together, these characteristics would have made sustained flight difficult and upright walking comfortable, which would make *T. navigans* different from other pterosaurs that moved mainly through flight. Thus, Beccari and colleagues suggest that previously held speculations of paleontologists are inaccurate: that instead of moving mainly through powered flight, *T. navigans* likely flew for shorter distances and spent more time walking than researchers previously thought.

Choice A is incorrect because Beccari and his team determined, based on their examination of a nearly complete skeleton, that *T. navigans* would have found "sustained flight difficult," which would differentiate it from most other pterosaurs that moved mainly through flight. Therefore, Beccari's team would not suggest that *T. navigans* flew for longer distances than did other pterosaur species with large head crests. *Choice B* is incorrect because the fossilized skeleton studied by Beccari and colleagues was notable for its short wings, and because no indication in the text is made that other pterosaurs were thought by paleontologists to be comfortable walking. Therefore, Beccari's team would not suggest that *T. navigans* had longer wings than other pterosaur species considered to have been comfortable walking. *Choice C* is incorrect because the text indicates that Beccari and his team agree with the paleontologists mentioned earlier in the text that *T. navigans* had a large-crested head. Therefore, Beccari's team would not suggest that *T. navigans* had a smaller head than researchers previously expected.

QUESTION 15

Choice A is the best answer because it most logically completes the text's discussion about Aztec (Nahua) ethics. The text indicates that, according to Purcell's interpretation of available Aztec philosophical works, the Aztec ethical system views an individual's actions in relation to that individual's societal role and how the actions affect the community. The text contrasts this view with another held by some ethicists, namely that actions are morally good or bad regardless of the context in which they occur. Thus, Purcell's analysis suggests that the Aztecs would have asserted that the morality of an individual's actions are rooted in that person's position in the community and the actions' effects and therefore cannot be determined in the absence of that context.

Choice B is incorrect. Although the text indicates that morally judging an action according to Aztec ethics requires an understanding of the action's effects and the individual's social circumstances, it does not specify that only members of that society can acquire this information. *Choice C* is incorrect because it implies that the Aztecs considered some actions good or bad regardless of the surrounding context, which contradicts the text's claim that the Aztecs believed that the morality of an individual's action is dependent on the action's effects on the community and the person's specific circumstances. *Choice D* is incorrect. Although the text indicates that in Aztec ethics the morality of an action depends in part on how it affects the community, this is only one of the two factors—the other being the person's societal role—that need to be considered. Therefore, it is possible that two actions with the same effect on the community could be considered morally distinct if they are performed by individuals in different social roles.

QUESTION 16

Choice A is the best answer. The convention being tested is the use of verb forms within a sentence. The nonfinite past participle "created" is correctly used to form a supplementary element that modifies the noun phrase "the saloon," identifying who established the Boston Saloon.

Choice B is incorrect because it results in an ungrammatical sentence. The finite present tense verb "creates" can't be used in this way to form a supplementary element to modify the noun phrase "the saloon." *Choice C* is incorrect because it results in an ungrammatical sentence. The nonfinite present participle "creating" can't be used in this way to form a supplementary element to modify the noun phrase "the saloon." *Choice D* is incorrect because it results in an ungrammatical sentence. The finite present tense verb "create" can't be used in this way to form a supplementary element to modify the noun phrase "the saloon."

QUESTION 17

Choice D is the best answer. The convention being tested is subject-verb agreement. The plural verb "reveal" agrees in number with the plural subject "objects."

Choice A is incorrect because the singular verb "was revealing" doesn't agree in number with the plural subject "objects." *Choice B* is incorrect because the singular verb "has revealed" doesn't agree in number with the plural subject "objects." *Choice C* is incorrect because the singular verb "reveals" doesn't agree in number with the plural subject "objects."

QUESTION 18

Choice C is the best answer. The convention being tested is the coordination of main clauses within a sentence. This choice uses a semicolon in a conventional way to join the first main clause ("Clear...through") and the second main clause ("wax...through").

Choice A is incorrect because it results in a comma splice. Without a conjunction following it, a comma can't be used in this way to join two main clauses. *Choice B* is incorrect because it results in a run-on sentence. The two main clauses ("Clear...through" and "wax...through") are fused without punctuation and/or a conjunction. Furthermore, it results in a confusing and illogical sentence that suggests clear glass allows light to pass through wax paper, which doesn't make sense in this context. *Choice D* is incorrect because when coordinating two longer main clauses such as these, it's conventional to use a comma before the coordinating conjunction.

QUESTION 19

Choice C is the best answer. The convention being tested is subject-verb agreement. The plural verb "underlie" agrees in number with the plural subject "frameworks."

Choice A is incorrect because the singular verb "underlies" doesn't agree in number with the plural subject "frameworks." *Choice B* is incorrect because the singular verb "is underlying" doesn't agree in number with the plural subject "frameworks." *Choice D* is incorrect because the singular verb "has been underlying" doesn't agree in number with the plural subject "frameworks."

QUESTION 20

Choice A is the best answer. The convention being tested is the punctuation of supplementary elements within a sentence. This choice correctly uses a comma to separate the supplementary adverb "however" from the preceding main clause ("only...competitions"), and it uses a colon to introduce the list of dances that follows ("rumba...jive"). Further, placing the colon after "however" rather than before indicates that the information in the preceding main clause (only...competitions) is contrary to what might be assumed from the information in the previous sentence (Latin America has many more dance forms).

Choice B is incorrect. The comma after "however" can't be used in this way to introduce a series ("rumba...jive"). *Choice C* is incorrect because it isn't conventional to use a semicolon in this way to introduce a series of items, such as the list of dances. *Choice D* is incorrect because placing the semicolon after "competitions" illogically indicates that the following list of five Latin American dances ("rumba...jive") is contrary to the information in the previous clause (only five Latin American dances are included in international ballroom dance competitions).

QUESTION 21

Choice D is the best answer. The convention being tested is punctuation use between two main clauses. In this choice, a colon is correctly used to mark the boundary between one main clause ("goats are notoriously indiscriminate") and another main clause ("they will devour all kinds of shrubs and weeds") and to introduce the following explanation of goats' nondiscriminatory behavior when it comes to what they eat.

Choice A is incorrect because when coordinating two longer main clauses such as these, it's conventional to use a comma before the coordinating conjunction. Furthermore, the conjunction "and" fails to indicate that what follows is an explanation of goats' nondiscriminatory behavior when it comes to their diets. *Choice B* is incorrect because it results in a comma splice. A comma can't be used in this way to join two main clauses ("goats...indiscriminate" and "they...weeds"). *Choice C* is incorrect because it results in a run-on sentence. The two main clauses ("goats...indiscriminate" and "they...weeds") are fused without punctuation and/or a conjunction.

QUESTION 22

Choice C is the best answer. "On the other hand" logically signals that the information in the sentence—that the snowpack at higher elevations in the Chuska Mountains was deepest in mid-March—contrasts with the previous information about the snowpack at lower elevations being deepest in early March.

Choice A is incorrect because "in other words" illogically signals that information in the sentence is merely a paraphrase or restatement of the previous information about the snowpack at lower elevations. Instead, the information about the snowpack at higher elevations contrasts with that information. *Choice B* is incorrect because "for instance" illogically signals that the information in the sentence exemplifies the previous information about the snowpack at lower elevations. Instead, the information about the snowpack at higher elevations contrasts with that information. *Choice D* is incorrect because "in summary" illogically signals that the information in the sentence summarizes the previous information about the snowpack at lower elevations. Instead, the information about the snowpack at higher elevations contrasts with that information.

QUESTION 23

Choice B is the best answer. "Conversely" logically signals that the information in this sentence—that countries with proportional-representation electoral systems tend toward multi-partyism—contrasts with the previous information about countries with single-ballot majoritarian elections, which tend to have two-party systems.

Choice A is incorrect because "subsequently" illogically signals that the information in this sentence about countries with proportional-representation electoral systems occurs later in a chronological sequence of events than the information in the previous sentence. Instead, it contrasts with the previous information. *Choice C* is incorrect because "for instance" illogically signals that the information in this sentence about countries with proportional-representation electoral systems is an example supporting the previous statement about countries with single-ballot majoritarian elections. Instead, it contrasts with the previous statement. *Choice D* is incorrect because "in other words" illogically signals that the information in this sentence about countries with proportional-representation electoral systems is a paraphrase or restatement of the previous information about countries with single-ballot majoritarian elections. Instead, it contrasts with the previous information.

QUESTION 24

Choice D is the best answer. "Hence" logically signals that the information in this sentence about turtle shells—that people incorrectly assume they are exoskeletons—is a consequence of the shells appearing external to the animal.

Choice A is incorrect because "that being said" illogically signals that this sentence qualifies or contrasts with the previous information about turtle shells appearing external to the animal. Instead, it presents a consequence of that information. *Choice B* is incorrect because "however" illogically signals that this sentence contrasts with the previous information about turtle shells appearing external to the animal. Instead, it presents a consequence of that information. *Choice C* is incorrect because "for instance" illogically signals that this sentence provides an example supporting the previous information about turtle shells appearing external to the animal. Instead, it presents a consequence of that information.

QUESTION 25

Choice D is the best answer. "Accordingly" logically signals that this sentence states a result or consequence of the previous information about the 2003 Human Genome Project. Taking into account an important lesson of the 2003 project (that a gene is affected by interactions with the protein products of other genes), research has begun to consider the human proteome instead of just the genome.

Choice A is incorrect because "in other words" illogically signals that the information in this sentence is a paraphrase or restatement of the previous information about the 2003 Human Genome Project. Instead, this sentence states a result or consequence of that information. *Choice B* is incorrect because "that said" illogically signals that the information in this sentence qualifies or contrasts with the previous information about the 2003 Human Genome Project. Instead, this sentence states a result or consequence of that information. *Choice C* is incorrect because "for example" illogically signals that this sentence provides an example supporting the previous information about the 2003 Human Genome Project. Instead, this sentence states a result or consequence of that information.

QUESTION 26

Choice B is the best answer. The sentence emphasizes a similarity between the sculptures *Recognition* and *Students Aspire*, noting that both sculptures show African American figures in poses that symbolize supportive relationships.

Choice A is incorrect. The sentence describes one of the sculptures; it doesn't emphasize a similarity between the two sculptures. *Choice C* is incorrect. The sentence specifies the different years the sculptures were completed in; it doesn't emphasize a similarity between the two sculptures. *Choice D* is incorrect. The sentence emphasizes a difference between the two sculptures, noting that the figures in the sculptures have different feature definition; it doesn't emphasize a similarity between the two sculptures.

QUESTION 27

Choice C is the best answer. The sentence indicates which classification category most routine diplomatic correspondence belongs in, explaining that it is classified as Confidential because it has the potential to damage national security if disclosed.

Choice A is incorrect. While the sentence makes a claim about information classified as Confidential, it doesn't indicate which category routine diplomatic correspondence belongs in. *Choice B* is incorrect. The sentence makes a generalization about how routine diplomatic correspondence is classified; it doesn't indicate which classification category the correspondence belongs in. *Choice D* is incorrect. This sentence explains that routine diplomatic correspondence could affect national security if disclosed; it doesn't indicate which category of sensitive information this correspondence belongs in.

Math

Module 1
(22 questions)

QUESTION 1

Choice D is correct. It's given that a veterinarian recommends that each day the rabbit should eat 25 calories per pound of the rabbit's weight, plus an additional 11 calories. If the rabbit's weight is x pounds, then multiplying 25 calories per pound by the rabbit's weight, x pounds, yields $25x$ calories. Adding the additional 11 calories that the rabbit should eat each day yields $25x + 11$ calories. It's given that c is the total number of calories the veterinarian recommends the rabbit should eat each day if the rabbit's weight is x pounds. Therefore, this situation can be represented by the equation $c = 25x + 11$.

Choice A is incorrect. This equation represents a situation where a veterinarian recommends that each day the rabbit should eat 25 calories per pound of the rabbit's weight. *Choice B* is incorrect. This equation represents a situation where a veterinarian recommends that each day the rabbit should eat 25 + 11, or 36, calories per pound of the rabbit's weight. *Choice C* is incorrect. This equation represents a situation where a veterinarian recommends that each day the rabbit should eat 11 calories per pound of the rabbit's weight, plus an additional 25 calories.

QUESTION 2

Choice A is correct. It's given that a special camera is used for underwater ocean research, and this camera is at a depth of 39 fathoms. It's also given that 1 fathom is equal to 6 feet. Thus, 39 fathoms is equivalent to $(39 \text{ fathoms})\left(\frac{6 \text{ feet}}{1 \text{ fathom}}\right)$, or 234 feet. Therefore, the camera's depth, in feet, is 234.

Choice B is incorrect. This is the camera's depth, in feet, if the camera is at a depth of 19.5 fathoms. *Choice C* is incorrect. This is the camera's depth, in feet, if the camera is at a depth of 7.5 fathoms. *Choice D* is incorrect and may result from conceptual or calculation errors.

QUESTION 3

Choice C is correct. Vertical angles, or angles that are opposite each other when two lines intersect, are congruent. It's given that line k intersects line n. Based on the figure, the angle with measure $x°$ and the angle with measure 145° are vertical angles. Therefore, the value of x is equal to 145.

Choice A is incorrect and may result from conceptual or calculation errors.
Choice B is incorrect and may result from conceptual or calculation errors.
Choice D is incorrect and may result from conceptual or calculation errors.

QUESTION 4

The correct answer is 11. It's given that the function $f(x) = 14 + 4x$ represents the total cost, in dollars, of attending an arcade when x games are played. Substituting 58 for $f(x)$ in the given equation yields $58 = 14 + 4x$. Subtracting 14 from each side of this equation yields $44 = 4x$. Dividing each side of this equation by 4 yields $11 = x$. Therefore, 11 games can be played for a total cost of $58.

QUESTION 5

Choice C is correct. Dividing all terms in the given equation by 4 yields

$\frac{4x}{4} - \frac{28}{4} = -\frac{24}{4}$, or $x - 7 = -6$. Therefore, the value of $x - 7$ is -6.

Choice A is incorrect. This is the value of $4x - 28$, not $x - 7$. *Choice B* is incorrect and may result from conceptual or calculation errors. *Choice D* is incorrect and may result from conceptual or calculation errors.

QUESTION 6

The correct answer is 10. It's given that the amount of Hanna's food order was $50 and that Hanna gave a tip of 20% of the amount of the bill. 20% of 50 can be calculated as $\left(\frac{20}{100}\right)(50)$, which yields $\frac{1000}{100}$, or 10. Therefore, the amount, in dollars, of the tip Hanna gave is 10.

QUESTION 7

Choice A is correct. It's given that the table shows an original data set of 5 values. It's also given that a sixth value is added to create a new data set. The new data set consists of the 5 values in the original data set and one additional value, 121. Since the additional value, 121, is less than any value in the original data set, the mean of the original data set is greater than the mean of the new data set.

Choice B is incorrect and may result from conceptual or calculation errors.
Choice C is incorrect and may result from conceptual or calculation errors.
Choice D is incorrect and may result from conceptual or calculation errors.

QUESTION 8

Choice D is correct. The equation for the line representing the boundary of the shaded region can be written in slope-intercept form $y = b + mx$, where m is the slope and $(0, b)$ is the y-intercept of the line. For the graph shown, the boundary line passes through the points $(0, -1)$ and $(1, -4)$. Given two points on a line, (x_1, y_1) and (x_2, y_2), the slope of the line can be calculated using the equation

$m = \frac{y_2 - y_1}{x_2 - x_1}$. Substituting the points $(0, -1)$ and $(1, -4)$ for (x_1, y_1) and (x_2, y_2) in

this equation yields $m = \frac{-4 - (-1)}{1 - 0}$, which is equivalent to $m = \frac{-3}{1}$, or $m = -3$.

Since the point $(0, -1)$ represents the y-intercept, it follows that $b = -1$. Substituting -3 for m and -1 for b in the equation $y = b + mx$ yields $y = -1 - 3x$ as the equation of the boundary line. Since the shaded region represents all the points above this boundary line, it follows that the shaded region shown represents the solutions to the inequality $y > -1 - 3x$.

Choice A is incorrect. This inequality represents a region below, not above, a boundary line with a slope of 3, not −3. *Choice B* is incorrect. This inequality represents a region below, not above, the boundary line shown. *Choice C* is incorrect. This inequality represents a region whose boundary line has a slope of 3, not −3.

QUESTION 9

Choice B is correct. The given expression is equivalent to $8x^3 + 8 − x^3 − (−2)$, or $8x^3 + 8 − x^3 + 2$. Combining like terms in this expression yields $7x^3 + 10$.

Choice A is incorrect. This expression is equivalent to $(8x^3 + 8) − 2$, not $(8x^3 + 8) − (x^3 − 2)$. *Choice C* is incorrect. This expression is equivalent to $(8x^3 + 8) − (−2)$, not $(8x^3 + 8) − (x^3 − 2)$. *Choice D* is incorrect. This expression is equivalent to $(8x^3 + 8) − (x^3 + 2)$, not $(8x^3 + 8) − (x^3 − 2)$.

QUESTION 10

Choice D is correct. An equation defining a line in the xy-plane can be written in the form $y = mx + b$, where m represents the slope and $(0, b)$ represents the y-intercept of the line. It's given that line t passes through the point $(0, 9)$; therefore, $b = 9$. The slope, m, of a line can be found using any two points on the line, (x_1, y_1) and (x_2, y_2), and the slope formula $m = \frac{y_2 − y_1}{x_2 − x_1}$. Substituting $(0, 9)$ and $(1, 17)$ for (x_1, y_1) and (x_2, y_2), respectively, in the slope formula yields $m = \frac{17 − 9}{1 − 0}$, or $m = 8$. Substituting 8 for m and 9 for b in the equation $y = mx + b$ yields $y = 8x + 9$.

Choice A is incorrect and may result from conceptual or calculation errors.
Choice B is incorrect and may result from conceptual or calculation errors.
Choice C is incorrect and may result from conceptual or calculation errors.

QUESTION 11

The correct answer is either −30 or 30. Adding 7 to each side of the given equation yields $(d − 30)(d + 30) = 0$. Since a product of two factors is equal to 0 if and only if at least one of the factors is 0, either $d − 30 = 0$ or $d + 30 = 0$. Adding 30 to each side of the equation $d − 30 = 0$ yields $d = 30$. Subtracting 30 from each side of the equation $d + 30 = 0$ yields $d = −30$. Therefore, the solutions to the given equation are −30 and 30. Note that −30 and 30 are examples of ways to enter a correct answer.

QUESTION 12

The correct answer is 4.51. It's given that the equation $4.51x + 6.07y = 896.86$ represents this situation, where x is the number of smaller containers sold, y is the number of larger containers sold, and 896.86 is the store's total sales, in dollars, of blueberries last month. Therefore, $4.51x$ represents the store's sales, in dollars, of smaller containers, and $6.07y$ represents the store's sales, in dollars, of larger containers. Since x is the number of smaller containers sold, the price, in dollars, of each smaller container is 4.51.

QUESTION 13

Choice A is correct. It's given that the function f models the intensity of an X-ray beam, in number of particles in the X-ray beam, t millimeters below the surface of a sample of iron. When the X-ray beam is at the surface of the sample of iron, it is 0 millimeters below the surface, so the value of t is 0.

Substituting 0 for t in the function $f(t) = 500(0.5)^{\frac{t}{12}}$ yields $f(0) = 500(0.5)^{\frac{0}{12}}$. Since any positive number raised to the power of 0 is equal to 1, it follows that $f(0) = 500(1)$, or $f(0) = 500$. Therefore, the estimated number of particles in the X-ray beam at the surface of the sample of iron is 500.

Choice B is incorrect and may result from conceptual or calculation errors.
Choice C is incorrect and may result from conceptual or calculation errors.
Choice D is incorrect and may result from conceptual or calculation errors.

QUESTION 14

Choice D is correct. It's given that the graph of the rational function f is shown, where $y = f(x)$ and $x \geq 0$. The graph shown passes through the point $(3, 3)$. It follows that when the value of x is 3, the value of $f(x)$ is 3. When the value of $f(x)$ is 3, the value of $f(x) + 5$ is $3 + 5$, or 8. Therefore, the graph of $y = f(x) + 5$ passes through the point $(3, 8)$. Of the given choices, choice D is the only graph that passes through the point $(3, 8)$ and is therefore the graph of $y = f(x) + 5$.

Choice A is incorrect. This is the graph of $y = f(x) - 5$, rather than $y = f(x) + 5$.

Choice B is incorrect. This is the graph of $y = \frac{f(x)}{5}$, rather than $y = f(x) + 5$.

Choice C is incorrect and may result from conceptual or calculation errors.

QUESTION 15

Choice D is correct. It's given that the values of P, N, and C are positive. Therefore, dividing each side of the given equation by N yields $\frac{P}{N} = 19 - C$. Subtracting 19 from each side of this equation yields $\frac{P}{N} - 19 = -C$. Dividing each side of this equation by -1 yields $19 - \frac{P}{N} = C$, or $C = 19 - \frac{P}{N}$.

Choice A is incorrect. This equation is equivalent to $P = NC - 19$, not $P = N(19 - C)$.
Choice B is incorrect. This equation is equivalent to $P = 19 - NC$, not $P = N(19 - C)$.
Choice C is incorrect. This equation is equivalent to $P = N(C - 19)$, not $P = N(19 - C)$.

QUESTION 16

The correct answer is 4,205. The exterior surface area of a figure is the sum of the areas of all its faces. It's given that the box does not have a lid and that each side of the box is in the shape of a square. Therefore, the box consists of 5 congruent square faces. It's also given that the length of each edge is 29 inches. Let s represent the length of an edge of a square. It follows that the area of a square is equal to s^2. Therefore, the area of each of the 5 square faces is equal to 29^2, or 841, square inches. Since the box consists of 5 congruent square faces, it follows that the sum of the areas of all its faces, or the exterior surface area of this box without a lid, is $5(841)$, or 4,205, square inches.

QUESTION 17

The correct answer is 18. Subtracting 45 from each side of the given equation yields $|x - 9| = 18$. By the definition of absolute value, if $|x - 9| = 18$, then $x - 9 = 18$ or $x - 9 = -18$. Adding 9 to each side of the equation $x - 9 = 18$ yields $x = 27$. Adding 9 to each side of the equation $x - 9 = -18$ yields $x = -9$. Therefore, the solutions to the given equation are 27 and -9, and it follows that the sum of the solutions to the given equation is $27 + (-9)$, or 18.

QUESTION 18

Choice A is correct. A trigonometric ratio can be found using the unit circle, that is, a circle with radius 1 unit. If a central angle of a unit circle in the *xy*-plane centered at the origin has its starting side on the positive *x*-axis and its terminal side intersects the circle at a point (*x*, *y*), then the value of the tangent of the central angle is equal to the *y*-coordinate divided by the *x*-coordinate. There are 2π radians in a circle. Dividing $\frac{92\pi}{3}$ by 2π yields $\frac{92}{6}$, which is equivalent to $15 + \frac{2}{3}$. It follows that on the unit circle centered at the origin in the *xy*-plane, the angle $\frac{92\pi}{3}$ is the result of 15 revolutions from its starting side on the positive *x*-axis followed by a rotation through $\frac{2\pi}{3}$ radians. Therefore, the angles $\frac{92\pi}{3}$ and $\frac{2\pi}{3}$ are coterminal angles and $\tan\left(\frac{92\pi}{3}\right)$ is equal to $\tan\left(\frac{2\pi}{3}\right)$. Since $\frac{2\pi}{3}$ is greater than $\frac{\pi}{2}$ and less than π, it follows that the terminal side of the angle is in quadrant II and forms an angle of $\frac{\pi}{3}$, or 60°, with the negative *x*-axis. Therefore, the terminal side of the angle intersects the unit circle at the point $\left(-\frac{1}{2}, \frac{\sqrt{3}}{2}\right)$. It follows that the value of $\tan\left(\frac{2\pi}{3}\right)$ is $\frac{\frac{\sqrt{3}}{2}}{-\frac{1}{2}}$, which is equivalent to $-\sqrt{3}$. Therefore, the value of $\tan\left(\frac{92\pi}{3}\right)$ is $-\sqrt{3}$.

Choice B is incorrect. This is the value of $\dfrac{1}{\tan\left(\frac{92\pi}{3}\right)}$, not $\tan\left(\frac{92\pi}{3}\right)$. *Choice C* is incorrect. This is the value of $\dfrac{1}{\tan\left(\frac{\pi}{3}\right)}$, not $\tan\left(\frac{92\pi}{3}\right)$. *Choice D* is incorrect. This is the value of $\tan\left(\frac{\pi}{3}\right)$, not $\tan\left(\frac{92\pi}{3}\right)$.

QUESTION 19

Choice D is correct. Two fractions can be added together when they have a common denominator. Since $k > 0$, multiplying the second term in the given expression by $\frac{k}{k}$ yields $\frac{(42ak)k}{k}$, which is equivalent to $\frac{42ak^2}{k}$. Therefore, the expression $\frac{42a}{k} + 42ak$ can be written as $\frac{42a}{k} + \frac{42ak^2}{k}$ which is equivalent to $\frac{42a + 42ak^2}{k}$. Since each term in the numerator of this expression has a factor of $42a$, the expression $\frac{42a + 42ak^2}{k}$ can be rewritten as $\frac{42a(1) + 42a(k^2)}{k}$, or $\frac{42a(1 + k^2)}{k}$, which is equivalent to $\frac{42a(k^2 + 1)}{k}$.

Choice A is incorrect. This expression is equivalent to $\frac{42a}{k} + \frac{42a}{k}$. *Choice B* is incorrect and may result from conceptual or calculation errors. *Choice C* is incorrect. This expression is equivalent to $\frac{42a}{k} + 42a$.

QUESTION 20

Choice B is correct. An equation of the form $(x - h)^2 + (y - k)^2 = r^2$, where h, k, and r are constants, represents a circle in the xy-plane with center (h, k) and radius r. Therefore, the circle represented by the given equation has center $(-4, 19)$ and radius 11. Since the center of the circle has an x-coordinate of -4 and the radius of the circle is 11, the least possible x-coordinate for any point on the circle is $-4 - 11$, or -15. Similarly, the greatest possible x-coordinate for any point on the circle is $-4 + 11$, or 7. Therefore, if the point (a, b) lies on the circle, it must be true that $-15 \le a \le 7$. Of the given choices, only -14 satisfies this inequality.

Choice A is incorrect and may result from conceptual or calculation errors. *Choice C* is incorrect and may result from conceptual or calculation errors. *Choice D* is incorrect and may result from conceptual or calculation errors.

QUESTION 21

Choice D is correct. The volume of a right rectangular prism can be represented by a function V that gives the volume of the prism, in cubic inches, in terms of the length of the prism's base. The volume of a right rectangular prism is equal to the area of its base times its height. It's given that the length of the prism's base is x inches, which is 7 inches more than the width of the prism's base. This means that the width of the prism's base is $x - 7$ inches. It follows that the area of the prism's base, in square inches, is $x(x - 7)$ and the volume, in cubic inches, of the prism is $x(x - 7)(9)$. Thus, the function V that gives the volume of this right rectangular prism, in cubic inches, in terms of the length of the prism's base, x, is $V(x) = 9x(x - 7)$.

Choice A is incorrect. This function would give the volume of the prism if the height were 9 inches more than the length of its base and the width of the base were 7 inches more than its length. *Choice B* is incorrect. This function would give the volume of the prism if the height were 9 inches more than the length of its base. *Choice C* is incorrect. This function would give the volume of the prism if the width of the base were 7 inches more than its length, rather than the length of the base being 7 inches more than its width.

QUESTION 22

Choice D is correct. It's given that $f(24) < 0$. Substituting 24 for $f(x)$ in the equation $f(x) = a\sqrt{x + b}$ yields $f(24) = a\sqrt{24 + b}$. Therefore, $a\sqrt{24 + b} < 0$. Since $\sqrt{24 + b}$ can't be negative, it follows that $a < 0$. It's also given that the graph of $y = f(x)$ passes through the point $(-24, 0)$. It follows that when $x = -24$, $f(x) = 0$. Substituting -24 for x and 0 for $f(x)$ in the equation $f(x) = a\sqrt{x + b}$ yields $0 = a\sqrt{-24 + b}$. By the zero product property, either $a = 0$ or $\sqrt{-24 + b} = 0$. Since $a < 0$, it follows that $\sqrt{24 + b} = 0$. Squaring both sides of this equation yields $-24 + b = 0$. Adding 24 to both sides of this equation yields $b = 24$. Since $a < 0$ and b is 24, it follows that $a < b$ must be true.

Choice A is incorrect. The value of $f(0)$ is $a\sqrt{b}$, which must be negative. *Choice B* is incorrect. The value of $f(0)$ is $a\sqrt{b}$, which could be -24, but doesn't have to be. *Choice C* is incorrect and may result from conceptual or calculation errors.

Math

Module 2 — Lower Difficulty
(22 questions)

QUESTION 1

Choice B is correct. For the graph shown, the horizontal axis represents the number of years after a certain sport utility vehicle is first purchased, and the vertical axis represents the predicted value, in dollars, of the sport utility vehicle. According to the graph, 3 years after the sport utility vehicle is purchased, the predicted value of the sport utility vehicle is between $10,000 and $15,000. Of the given choices, only $13,632 is between $10,000 and $15,000. Therefore, $13,632 is closest to the predicted value of the sport utility vehicle 3 years after it is first purchased.

Choice A is incorrect. This is closest to the predicted value of the sport utility vehicle 5 years after it is first purchased. *Choice C* is incorrect. This is closest to the predicted value of the sport utility vehicle 1 year after it is first purchased. *Choice D* is incorrect. This is closest to the predicted value of the sport utility vehicle when it is first purchased.

QUESTION 2

Choice C is correct. The solution to the system of two equations corresponds to the point where the graphs of the equations intersect. The graphs of the linear equation and the nonlinear equation shown intersect at the point (4, 5). Thus, the solution to the system is (4, 5).

Choice A is incorrect and may result from conceptual or calculation errors. *Choice B* is incorrect and may result from conceptual or calculation errors. *Choice D* is incorrect and may result from conceptual or calculation errors.

QUESTION 3

Choice B is correct. An x-intercept of a graph in the xy-plane is a point at which the graph crosses the x-axis. The graph shown crosses the x-axis at the point (5, 0). Therefore, the x-intercept of the graph shown is (5, 0).

Choice A is incorrect and may result from conceptual or calculation errors. *Choice C* is incorrect and may result from conceptual or calculation errors. *Choice D* is incorrect and may result from conceptual or calculation errors.

QUESTION 4

Choice B is correct. If a house from the street is selected at random, the probability of selecting a house that is blue is equal to the number of houses on the street that are blue divided by the total number of houses on the street. Since there are 2 blue houses on a street with 7 total houses, the probability of selecting a house that is blue from this street is $\frac{2}{7}$.

Choice A is incorrect. This is the probability of selecting a house that is blue from a street on which 1 of the 7 houses is blue. *Choice C* is incorrect. This is the probability of selecting a house that is not blue from this street. *Choice D* is incorrect. This is the probability of selecting a house that is blue from a street on which all the houses are blue.

QUESTION 5

Choice A is correct. The graph of function f shows that as x increases, $f(x)$ also increases, which means $f(x)$ is an increasing function. The graph of f is a line, which indicates a constant rate of change. A function that has a constant rate of change is a linear function. Therefore, function f can be described as increasing linear.

Choice B is incorrect. For a decreasing function, as x increases, $f(x)$ decreases, rather than increases. *Choice C* is incorrect. For a decreasing function, as x increases, $f(x)$ decreases, rather than increases, and the graph of an exponential function isn't a line. *Choice D* is incorrect. The graph of an exponential function isn't a line.

QUESTION 6

The correct answer is 6. Dividing both sides of the equation $6n = 12$ by 6 yields $n = 2$. Substituting 2 for n in the expression $n + 4$ yields $2 + 4$, or 6.

QUESTION 7

Choice B is correct. It's given that the function f is defined by $f(x) = 4x - 3$. Substituting 10 for x in the given function yields $f(10) = 4(10) - 3$, which is equivalent to $f(10) = 40 - 3$, or $f(10) = 37$. Therefore, the value of $f(10)$ is 37.

Choice A is incorrect and may result from conceptual or calculation errors. *Choice C* is incorrect. This is the value of $f(10)$ for the function $f(x) = 4x$, not $f(x) = 4x - 3$. *Choice D* is incorrect. This is the value of $f(10)$ for the function $f(x) = 4x + 3$, not $f(x) = 4x - 3$.

QUESTION 8

Choice B is correct. The y-intercept of a graph is the point where the graph intersects the y-axis. The graph of function f shown intersects the y-axis at the point $(0, -4)$. Therefore, the y-intercept of the graph is $(0, -4)$.

Choice A is incorrect and may result from conceptual or calculation errors. *Choice C* is incorrect and may result from conceptual or calculation errors. *Choice D* is incorrect and may result from conceptual or calculation errors.

QUESTION 9

Choice A is correct. The second equation in the given system is $y = 28$. Substituting 28 for y in the first equation in the given system yields $28 = 12x - 20$. Adding 20 to both sides of this equation yields $48 = 12x$. Dividing both sides of this equation by 12 yields $4 = x$. Therefore, the solution (x, y) to the given system of equations is $(4, 28)$.

Choice B is incorrect and may result from conceptual or calculation errors. *Choice C* is incorrect. This is the solution (*y*, *x*), not (*x*, *y*), to the given system of equations. *Choice D* is incorrect and may result from conceptual or calculation errors.

QUESTION 10

The correct answer is 29. The range of a data set is the difference between its maximum value and its minimum value. For the data set shown, the maximum score is 52 and the minimum score is 23. The difference between those scores is 52 − 23, or 29. Therefore, the range of the 7 scores shown is 29.

QUESTION 11

The correct answer is 4. A solution to a system of equations must satisfy each equation in the system. It follows that if (*x*, *y*) is a solution to the system, the point (*x*, *y*) lies on the graph in the *xy*-plane of each equation in the system. According to the graph, the point (*x*, *y*) that lies on the graph of each equation in the system is (4, 1). Therefore, the solution to the system is (4, 1). It follows that the value of *x* is 4.

QUESTION 12

The correct answer is $\frac{1}{2}$. The value of *h*(2) is the value of *h*(*x*) when *x* = 2.

Substituting 2 for *x* in the given equation yields $h(2) = \frac{8}{5(2) + 6}$, which is

equivalent to $h(2) = \frac{8}{16}$, or $h(2) = \frac{1}{2}$. Therefore, the value of *h*(2) is $\frac{1}{2}$. Note that

1/2 and .5 are examples of ways to enter a correct answer.

QUESTION 13

Choice D is correct. An equation defining a linear function can be written in the form *f*(*x*) = *mx* + *b*, where *m* is the slope and (0, *b*) is the *y*-intercept of the graph of *y* = *f*(*x*) in the *xy*-plane. It's given that the graph of *y* = *f*(*x*) has a slope of 39, so *m* = 39. It's also given that the graph of *y* = *f*(*x*) passes through the point (0, 0), so *b* = 0. Substituting 39 for *m* and 0 for *b* in *f*(*x*) = *mx* + *b* yields *f*(*x*) = 39*x* + 0, or *f*(*x*) = 39*x*. Thus, the equation that defines *f* is *f*(*x*) = 39*x*.

Choice A is incorrect. This equation defines a function whose graph has a slope of −39, not 39. *Choice B* is incorrect. This equation defines a function whose

graph has a slope of $\frac{1}{39}$, not 39. *Choice C* is incorrect. This equation defines a

function whose graph has a slope of 1, not 39, and passes through the point (0, −39), not (0, 0).

QUESTION 14

Choice D is correct. It's given that for a snowstorm in a certain town, the minimum rate of snowfall recorded was 0.6 inches per hour, the maximum rate of snowfall recorded was 1.8 inches per hour, and *s* represents a rate of snowfall, in inches per hour, recorded for this snowstorm. It follows that the inequality 0.6 ≤ *s* ≤ 1.8 is true for all values of *s*.

Choice A is incorrect and may result from conceptual or calculation errors. *Choice B* is incorrect and may result from conceptual or calculation errors. *Choice C* is incorrect and may result from conceptual or calculation errors.

QUESTION 15

Choice D is correct. It's given that the function *f* defined by $f(t) = 14t + 9$ gives the estimated length, in inches, of a vine plant *t* months after Tavon purchased it. For a function defined by an equation of the form $f(t) = mt + b$, where *m* and *b* are constants, *b* represents the value of $f(0)$, or the value of $f(t)$ when the value of *t* is 0. Therefore, for the function defined by $f(t) = 14t + 9$, 9 represents the value of $f(t)$ when the value of *t* is 0. This means that 0 months after the vine plant was purchased, the estimated length of the vine plant was 9 inches. Therefore, the best interpretation of 9 in this context is the estimated length of the vine plant was 9 inches when Tavon purchased it.

Choice A is incorrect and may result from conceptual or calculation errors. *Choice B* is incorrect. The vine plant is expected to grow 14 inches, not 9 inches, each month. *Choice C* is incorrect and may result from conceptual or calculation errors.

QUESTION 16

The correct answer is $\frac{15}{2}$. The area, *A*, of a triangle is given by the formula $A = \frac{1}{2}bh$, where *b* is the length of the base of the triangle and *h* is the height of the triangle. In the right triangle shown, the length of the base of the triangle is 5 inches, and the height is 3 inches. It follows that $b = 5$ and $h = 3$. Substituting 5 for *b* and 3 for *h* in the formula $A = \frac{1}{2}bh$ yields $A = \frac{1}{2}(5)(3)$, which is equivalent to $A = \frac{1}{2}(15)$, or $A = \frac{15}{2}$. Therefore, the area of the triangle, in square inches, is $\frac{15}{2}$. Note that 15/2 and 7.5 are examples of ways to enter a correct answer.

QUESTION 17

Choice A is correct. The linear relationship between *x* and *y* can be represented by the equation $y = mx + b$, where *m* is the slope of the line in the *xy*-plane that represents the relationship, and *b* is the *y*-coordinate of the *y*-intercept. The slope can be computed using any two points on the line. The slope of a line between any two points, (x_1, y_1) and (x_2, y_2), on the line can be calculated using the slope formula, $m = \frac{y_2 - y_1}{x_2 - x_1}$. In the given table, each value of *x* and its corresponding value of *y* can be represented by a point (x, y). In the given table, when the value of *x* is 1, the corresponding value of *y* is 11 and when the value of *x* is 2, the corresponding value of *y* is 16. Therefore, the points (1, 11) and (2, 16) are on the line. Substituting (1, 11) and (2, 16) for (x_1, y_1) and (x_2, y_2), respectively, in the slope formula yields $m = \frac{16 - 11}{2 - 1}$, or $m = 5$. Substituting 5 for *m* in the equation $y = mx + b$ yields $y = 5x + b$. Substituting the first value of *x* in the table, 1, and its corresponding value of *y*, 11, for *x* and *y*, respectively, in this equation yields $11 = 5(1) + b$, or $11 = b + 5$. Subtracting 5 from both sides of this equation yields $6 = b$. Substituting 6 for *b* in the equation $y = 5x + b$ yields $y = 5x + 6$. Therefore, the equation $y = 5x + 6$ represents the linear relationship between *x* and *y*.

Choice B is incorrect. For this relationship, when the value of *x* is 1, the corresponding value of *y* is 16, not 11. *Choice C* is incorrect. For this relationship, when the value of *x* is 2, the corresponding value of *y* is 17, not 16. *Choice D* is incorrect. For this relationship, when the value of *x* is 1, the corresponding value of *y* is 17, not 11.

QUESTION 18

The correct answer is 6. It's given that $y = 4x$ and $y = x^2 - 12$. Since $y = 4x$, substituting $4x$ for y in the second equation of the given system yields $4x = x^2 - 12$. Subtracting $4x$ from both sides of this equation yields $0 = x^2 - 4x - 12$. This equation can be rewritten as $0 = (x - 6)(x + 2)$. By the zero product property, $x - 6 = 0$ or $x + 2 = 0$. Adding 6 to both sides of the equation $x - 6 = 0$ yields $x = 6$. Subtracting 2 from both sides of the equation $x + 2 = 0$ yields $x = -2$. Therefore, solutions to the given system of equations occur when $x = 6$ and when $x = -2$. It's given that a solution to the given system of equations is (x, y), where $x > 0$. Since 6 is greater than 0, it follows that the value of x is 6.

QUESTION 19

Choice B is correct. It's given that at a particular track meet, the ratio of coaches to athletes is 1 to 26. If one number in a ratio is multiplied by a value, the other number must be multiplied by the same value in order to maintain the same ratio. If there are x coaches at the track meet, multiplying both numbers in the ratio by x yields $1(x)$ to $26(x)$, or x to $26x$. Therefore, the expression $26x$ represents the number of athletes at the track meet.

Choice A is incorrect and may result from conceptual or calculation errors.
Choice C is incorrect and may result from conceptual or calculation errors.
Choice D is incorrect and may result from conceptual or calculation errors.

QUESTION 20

Choice A is correct. The equation $f(x) = (1.84)^{\frac{x}{4}}$ can be rewritten as $f(x) = (1.84)^{\left(\frac{1}{4}\right)(x)}$, which is equivalent to $f(x) = \left(1.84^{\frac{1}{4}}\right)^x$, or approximately $f(x) = (1.16467)^x$. Since it's given that $f(x) = (1.84)^{\frac{x}{4}}$ can be rewritten as $f(x) = \left(1 + \frac{p}{100}\right)^x$, where p is a constant, it follows that $1 + \frac{p}{100}$ is approximately equal to 1.16467. Therefore, $\frac{p}{100}$ is approximately equal to 0.16467. It follows that the value of p is approximately equal to 16.467. Of the given choices, 16 is closest to the value of p.

Choice B is incorrect and may result from conceptual or calculation errors.
Choice C is incorrect and may result from conceptual or calculation errors.
Choice D is incorrect and may result from conceptual or calculation errors.

QUESTION 21

Choice A is correct. The figure shows that angle P in $\triangle QPR$ and angle T in $\triangle STR$ are right angles. It follows that angle P is congruent to angle T. The figure also shows that the measures of angle QRP and angle SRT are both $x°$. Therefore, angle QRP is congruent to angle SRT. It's given that $\triangle QPR$ is similar to $\triangle STR$. Since angle P is congruent to angle T, and angle QRP is congruent to angle SRT, it follows that $\overline{QR}$ corresponds to $\overline{SR}$, and $\overline{QP}$ corresponds to $\overline{ST}$. Since corresponding sides of similar triangles are proportional, it follows that $\frac{SR}{QR} = \frac{ST}{QP}$. It's also given that the lengths of $\overline{ST}$, $\overline{QP}$, and $\overline{QR}$ are 14, 15, and 25, respectively. Substituting 14 for ST, 15 for QP, and 25 for QR in the equation $\frac{SR}{QR} = \frac{ST}{QP}$ yields $\frac{SR}{25} = \frac{14}{15}$. Multiplying each side of this equation by 25 yields $SR = \left(\frac{14}{15}\right)(25)$, or $SR = \frac{350}{15}$. Thus, the length of $\overline{SR}$ is $\frac{350}{15}$.

Choice B is incorrect. This is the result of solving the equation $\frac{SR}{25} = \frac{14}{20}$, not $\frac{SR}{25} = \frac{14}{15}$. *Choice C* is incorrect. This is the result of solving the equation $\frac{SR}{14} = \frac{15}{25}$, not $\frac{SR}{25} = \frac{14}{15}$. *Choice D* is incorrect. This is the result of solving the equation $\frac{SR}{14} = \frac{15}{25}$, not $\frac{SR}{25} = \frac{14}{15}$.

QUESTION 22

Choice B is correct. The Pythagorean theorem states that for a right triangle, $c^2 = a^2 + b^2$, where c represents the length of the hypotenuse and a and b represent the lengths of the legs. It's given that in triangle ABC, angle B is a right angle. Therefore, triangle ABC is a right triangle, where the hypotenuse is side AC and the legs are sides AB and BC. It's given that the lengths of sides AB and BC are $10\sqrt{37}$ and $24\sqrt{37}$, respectively. Substituting these values for a and b in the formula $c^2 = a^2 + b^2$ yields $c^2 = (10\sqrt{37})^2 + (24\sqrt{37})^2$, which is equivalent to $c^2 = 100(37) + 576(37)$, or $c^2 = 676(37)$. Taking the square root of both sides of this equation yields $c = \pm 26\sqrt{37}$. Since c represents the length of the hypotenuse, side AC, c must be positive. Therefore, the length of side AC is $26\sqrt{37}$.

Choice A is incorrect. This is the result of solving the equation $c = 24\sqrt{37} - 10\sqrt{37}$, not $c^2 = (10\sqrt{37})^2 + (24\sqrt{37})^2$. *Choice C* is incorrect. This is the result of solving the equation $c = 10\sqrt{37} + 24\sqrt{37}$, not $c^2 = (10\sqrt{37})^2 + (24\sqrt{37})^2$. *Choice D* is incorrect and may result from conceptual or calculation errors.

Math

Module 2—Higher Difficulty
(22 questions)

QUESTION 1

Choice B is correct. The Pythagorean theorem states that for a right triangle, $c^2 = a^2 + b^2$, where c represents the length of the hypotenuse and a and b represent the lengths of the legs. It's given that a right triangle has legs with lengths of 11 centimeters and 9 centimeters. Substituting 11 for a and 9 for b in the formula $c^2 = a^2 + b^2$ yields $c^2 = 11^2 + 9^2$, which is equivalent to $c^2 = 121 + 81$, or $c^2 = 202$. Taking the square root of each side of this equation yields $c = \pm\sqrt{202}$. Since c represents a length, c must be positive. Therefore, the length of the triangle's hypotenuse, in centimeters, is $\sqrt{202}$.

Choice A is incorrect. This is the result of solving the equation $c^2 = 11(2) + 9(2)$, not $c^2 = 11^2 + 9^2$. *Choice C is incorrect.* This is the result of solving the equation $c(2) = 11(2) + 9(2)$, not $c^2 = 11^2 + 9^2$. *Choice D is incorrect.* This is the result of solving the equation $c = 11^2 + 9^2$, not $c^2 = 11^2 + 9^2$.

QUESTION 2

Choice B is correct. It's given that the graph of the linear function h, where $y = h(x)$, passes through the points $(7, 21)$ and $(9, 25)$ in the xy-plane. An equation defining h can be written in the form $y = mx + b$, where $y = h(x)$, m represents the slope of the graph in the xy-plane, and b represents the y-coordinate of the y-intercept of the graph. The slope can be found using any two points, (x_1, y_1) and (x_2, y_2), and the formula $m = \frac{(y_2 - y_1)}{(x_2 - x_1)}$. Substituting $(7, 21)$ and $(9, 25)$ for (x_1, y_1) and (x_2, y_2), respectively, in the slope formula yields $m = \frac{25 - 21}{9 - 7}$, which is equivalent to $m = \frac{4}{2}$, or $m = 2$. Substituting 2 for m and $(7, 21)$ for (x, y) in the equation $y = mx + b$ yields $21 = (2)(7) + b$, or $21 = 14 + b$. Subtracting 14 from each side of this equation yields $7 = b$. Substituting 2 for m and 7 for b in the equation $y = mx + b$ yields $y = 2x + 7$. Since $y = h(x)$, it follows that the equation that defines h is $h(x) = 2x + 7$.

Choice A is incorrect. For this function, the graph of $y = h(x)$ in the xy-plane would pass through $(7, 0)$, not $(7, 21)$, and $(9, 1)$, not $(9, 25)$. *Choice C is incorrect.* For this function, the graph of $y = h(x)$ in the xy-plane would pass through $(7, 70)$, not $(7, 21)$, and $(9, 84)$, not $(9, 25)$. *Choice D is incorrect.* For this function, the graph of $y = h(x)$ in the xy-plane would pass through $(7, 88)$, not $(7, 21)$, and $(9, 106)$, not $(9, 25)$.

QUESTION 3

Choice B is correct. It's given that, based on the sample, an estimate of 12% of all socks produced by the company in a certain week are defective, with an associated margin of error of 3.62%. This estimate, plus or minus the margin of error, gives an interval of plausible values for the actual percent of all socks produced by the company that week that are defective. Subtracting 3.62% from 12% yields 8.38%. Adding 3.62% to 12% yields 15.62%. Therefore, it is plausible that between 8.38% and 15.62% of all socks produced by the company are defective.

Choice A is incorrect and may result from conceptual errors. *Choice C* is incorrect. 12% is the estimated percent of defective socks based on the sample. However, since the margin of error for this estimate is known, the most appropriate conclusion is not that the percent of defective socks is exactly 12% but instead that it lies in an interval of plausible percents. *Choice D* is incorrect and may result from conceptual errors.

QUESTION 4

Choice A is correct. It's given that a truck can haul a maximum of 5,630 pounds. It's also given that during one trip, the truck will be used to haul a 190-pound piece of equipment as well as several crates. It follows that the truck can haul at most $5{,}630 - 190$, or 5,440, pounds of crates. Since x represents the number of 25-pound crates, the expression $25x$ represents the weight of the 25-pound crates. Since y represents the number of 62-pound crates, $62y$ represents the weight of the 62-pound crates. Therefore, $25x + 62y$ represents the total weight of the crates the truck can haul. Since the truck can haul at most 5,440 pounds of crates, the total weight of the crates must be less than or equal to 5,440 pounds, or $25x + 62y \leq 5{,}440$.

Choice B is incorrect. This represents the possible combinations of the number of 25-pound crates, x, and the number of 62-pound crates, y, the truck can haul during one trip if it can haul a minimum, not a maximum, of 5,630 pounds. *Choice C* is incorrect. This represents the possible combinations of the number of 62-pound crates, x, and the number of 25-pound crates, y, the truck can haul during one trip if only crates are being hauled. *Choice D* is incorrect. This represents the possible combinations of the number of 62-pound crates, x, and the number of 25-pound crates, y, the truck can haul during one trip if it can haul a minimum, not a maximum, weight of 5,630 pounds and only crates are being hauled.

QUESTION 5

Choice C is correct. Adding $9x$ to both sides of the first equation in the given system yields $y = 9x + 13$. Substituting the expression $9x + 13$ for y in the second equation in the given system yields $5x = 2(9x + 13)$. Distributing the 2 on the right-hand side of this equation yields $5x = 18x + 26$. Subtracting $18x$ from both sides of this equation yields $-13x = 26$. Dividing both sides of this equation by -13 yields $x = -2$. Substituting -2 for x in the equation $y = 9x + 13$ yields $y = 9(-2) + 13$, or $y = -5$. Therefore, the solution (x, y) to the given system of equations is $(-2, -5)$.

Choice A is incorrect and may result from conceptual or calculation errors. *Choice B* is incorrect and may result from conceptual or calculation errors. *Choice D* is incorrect. This is the solution (y, x), not (x, y), to the given system of equations.

QUESTION 6

The correct answer is 29. The range of a data set is the difference between its maximum value and its minimum value. For the data set shown, the maximum score is 52 and the minimum score is 23. The difference between those scores is 52 − 23, or 29. Therefore, the range of the 7 scores shown is 29.

QUESTION 7

Choice D is correct. Let ℓ represent the cost, in dollars, of 1 loaf of bread, and let d represent the cost, in dollars, of 1 dozen eggs. It's given that the first customer paid 12.45 dollars for 1 loaf of bread and 2 dozen eggs. Therefore, the first customer's purchase can be represented by the equation $\ell + 2d = 12.45$. It's also given that the second customer paid 19.42 dollars for 4 loaves of bread and 1 dozen eggs. Therefore, the second customer's purchase can be represented by the equation $4\ell + d = 19.42$. The equations $\ell + 2d = 12.45$ and $4\ell + d = 19.42$ form a system of linear equations, which can be solved by elimination to find the value of d. Multiplying the first equation in the system by −4 yields $-4\ell - 8d = -49.8$. Adding $-4\ell - 8d = -49.8$ to the second equation, $4\ell + d = 19.42$, yields $(-4\ell + 4\ell) + (-8d + d) = (-49.8 + 19.42)$, which is equivalent to $-7d = -30.38$. Dividing both sides of this equation by −7 yields $d = 4.34$. Therefore, the cost, in dollars, of 1 dozen eggs is 4.34.

Choice A is incorrect. This is the cost, in dollars, of 1 loaf of bread. *Choice B* is incorrect and may result from conceptual or calculation errors. *Choice C* is incorrect and may result from conceptual or calculation errors.

QUESTION 8

Choice D is correct. A point (x, y) is a solution to a system of equations if it lies on the graphs of both equations in the xy-plane. In other words, a solution to a system of equations is a point (x, y) at which the graphs intersect. It's given that the first equation is $y = 18$. Substituting 18 for y in the second equation yields $18 = -3(x - 18)^2 + 15$. Subtracting 15 from each side of this equation yields $3 = -3(x - 18)^2$. Dividing each side of this equation by −3 yields $-1 = (x - 18)^2$. Since the square of a real number is at least 0, this equation can't have any real solutions. Therefore, the graphs of the equations intersect at zero points.

Alternate approach: The graph of the second equation is a parabola that opens downward and has a vertex at (18, 15). Therefore, the maximum value of this parabola occurs when $y = 15$. The graph of the first equation is a horizontal line at 18 on the y-axis, or $y = 18$. Since 18 is greater than 15, or the horizontal line is above the vertex of the parabola, the graphs of these equations intersect at zero points.

Choice A is incorrect. The graph of $y = 15$, not $y = 18$, and the graph of the second equation intersect at exactly one point. *Choice B* is incorrect. The graph of any horizontal line such that the value of y is less than 15, not greater than 15, and the graph of the second equation intersect at exactly two points. *Choice C* is incorrect and may result from conceptual or calculation errors.

QUESTION 9

Choice A is correct. It's given that $y = x + 9$ and $y = x^2 + 16x + 63$; therefore, it follows that $x + 9 = x^2 + 16x + 63$. This equation can be rewritten as $x + 9 = (x + 9)(x + 7)$. Subtracting $(x + 9)$ from both sides of this equation yields $0 = (x + 9)(x + 7) - (x + 9)$. This equation can be rewritten as $0 = (x + 9)((x + 7) - 1)$, or $0 = (x + 9)(x + 6)$. By the zero product property, $x + 9 = 0$ or $x + 6 = 0$. Subtracting 9 from both sides of the equation $x + 9 = 0$ yields $x = -9$. Subtracting 6 from both sides of the equation $x + 6 = 0$ yields

$x = -6$. Therefore, the given system of equations has solutions, (x, y), that occur when $x = -9$ and $x = -6$. Since -6 is greater than -9, the greatest possible value of x is -6.

Choice B is incorrect. This is the negative of the greatest possible value of x when $y = 0$ for the second equation in the given system of equations. *Choice C* is incorrect. This is the value of y when $x = 0$ for the first equation in the given system of equations. *Choice D* is incorrect. This is the value of y when $x = 0$ for the second equation in the given system of equations.

QUESTION 10

The correct answer is -10. A line in the xy-plane can be represented by the equation $y = mx + b$, where m is the slope of the line and b is the y-coordinate of the y-intercept. It's given that line p has a slope of $-\frac{5}{3}$. Therefore, $m = -\frac{5}{3}$. It's also given that line p has an x-intercept of $(-6, 0)$. Therefore, when $x = -6$, $y = 0$. Substituting $-\frac{5}{3}$ for m, -6 for x, and 0 for y in the equation $y = mx + b$ yields $0 = \left(-\frac{5}{3}\right)(-6) + b$, which is equivalent to $0 = 10 + b$. Subtracting 10 from both sides of this equation yields $-10 = b$. Therefore, the y-coordinate of the y-intercept of line p is -10.

QUESTION 11

Choice A is correct. Distributing 12 on the left-hand side and -3 on the right-hand side of the given equation yields $12x - 36 = -3x - 36$. Adding $3x$ to each side of this equation yields $15x - 36 = -36$. Adding 36 to each side of this equation yields $15x = 0$. Dividing each side of this equation by 15 yields $x = 0$. This means that 0 is the only solution to the given equation. Therefore, the given equation has exactly one solution.

Choice B is incorrect and may result from conceptual or calculation errors. *Choice C* is incorrect and may result from conceptual or calculation errors. *Choice D* is incorrect and may result from conceptual or calculation errors.

QUESTION 12

Choice D is correct. It's given that the equation $y - 5x = 6$ represents the relationship between the number of suits that Kaylani made, x, and the total length of fabric she purchased, y, in yards. Adding $5x$ to both sides of the given equation yields $y = 5x + 6$. Since Kaylani made x suits and used 5 yards of fabric to make each suit, the expression $5x$ represents the total amount of fabric she used to make the suits. Since y represents the total length of fabric Kaylani purchased, in yards, it follows from the equation $y = 5x + 6$ that Kaylani purchased $5x$ yards of fabric to make the suits, plus an additional 6 yards of fabric. Therefore, the best interpretation of 6 in this context is that Kaylani purchased 6 yards more fabric than she used to make the suits.

Choice A is incorrect. Kaylani made a total of x suits, not 6 suits. *Choice B* is incorrect. Kaylani purchased a total of y yards of fabric, not a total of 6 yards of fabric. *Choice C* is incorrect. Kaylani used a total of $5x$ yards of fabric to make the suits, not a total of 6 yards of fabric.

QUESTION 13

Choice D is correct. The number of solutions to a quadratic equation in the form $ax^2 + bx + c = 0$, where a, b, and c are constants, can be determined by the value of the discriminant, $b^2 - 4ac$. If the value of the discriminant is greater than zero, then the quadratic equation has two distinct real solutions. If the value of the discriminant is equal to zero, then the quadratic equation has exactly one real solution. If the value of the discriminant is less than zero, then the quadratic equation has no real solutions. For the quadratic equation in choice D, $5x^2 - 14x + 49 = 0$, $a = 5$, $b = -14$, and $c = 49$. Substituting 5 for a, -14 for b, and 49 for c in $b^2 - 4ac$ yields $(-14)^2 - 4(5)(49)$, or -784. Since -784 is less than zero, it follows that the quadratic equation $5x^2 - 14x + 49 = 0$ has no real solutions.

Choice A is incorrect. The value of the discriminant for this quadratic equation is 392. Since 392 is greater than zero, it follows that this quadratic equation has two real solutions. *Choice B* is incorrect. The value of the discriminant for this quadratic equation is 0. Since zero is equal to zero, it follows that this quadratic equation has exactly one real solution. *Choice C* is incorrect. The value of the discriminant for this quadratic equation is 1,176. Since 1,176 is greater than zero, it follows that this quadratic equation has two real solutions.

QUESTION 14

Choice A is correct. The equation $f(x) = (1.84)^{\frac{x}{4}}$ can be rewritten as $f(x) = (1.84)^{\left(\frac{1}{4}\right)(x)}$, which is equivalent to $f(x) = \left(1.84^{\frac{1}{4}}\right)^x$, or approximately $f(x) = (1.16467)^x$. Since it's given that $f(x) = (1.84)^{\frac{x}{4}}$ can be rewritten as $f(x) = \left(1 + \frac{p}{100}\right)^x$, where p is a constant, it follows that $1 + \frac{p}{100}$ is approximately equal to 1.16467. Therefore, $\frac{p}{100}$ is approximately equal to 0.16467. It follows that the value of p is approximately equal to 16.467. Of the given choices, 16 is closest to the value of p.

Choice B is incorrect and may result from conceptual or calculation errors. *Choice C* is incorrect and may result from conceptual or calculation errors. *Choice D* is incorrect and may result from conceptual or calculation errors.

QUESTION 15

The correct answer is 10. Solving by substitution, the given system of equations, where p is a constant, can be written so that the left-hand side of each equation is equal to $7r$. Subtracting 6 from each side of the first equation in the given system, $6 + 7r = pw$, yields $7r = pw - 6$. Adding $5w$ to each side of the second equation in the given system, $7r - 5w = 5w + 11$, yields $7r = 10w + 11$. Since the left-hand side of each equation is equal to $7r$, setting the right-hand side of the equations equal to each other yields $pw - 6 = 10w + 11$. A linear equation in one variable, w, has no solution if and only if the equation is false; that is, when there's no value of w that produces a true statement. For the equation $pw - 6 = 10w + 11$, there's no value of w that produces a true statement when $pw = 10w$. Therefore, for the equation $pw - 6 = 10w + 11$, there's no value of w that produces a true statement when the value of p is 10. It follows that in the given system of equations, the system has no solution when the value of p is 10.

QUESTION 16

The correct answer is −24. Since the graph passes through the point (0, −6), it follows that when the value of x is 0, the value of y is −6. Substituting 0 for x and −6 for y in the given equation yields $-6 = 2(0)^2 + b(0) + c$, or $-6 = c$. Therefore, the value of c is −6. Substituting −6 for c in the given equation yields $y = 2x^2 + bx - 6$. Since the graph passes through the point (−1, −8), it follows that when the value of x is −1, the value of y is −8. Substituting −1 for x and −8 for y in the equation $y = 2x^2 + bx - 6$ yields $-8 = 2(-1)^2 + b(-1) - 6$, or $-8 = 2 - b - 6$, which is equivalent to $-8 = -4 - b$. Adding 4 to each side of this equation yields $-4 = -b$. Dividing each side of this equation by −1 yields $4 = b$. Since the value of b is 4 and the value of c is −6, it follows that the value of bc is $(4)(-6)$, or −24.

Alternate approach: The given equation represents a parabola in the xy-plane with a vertex at (−1, −8). Therefore, the given equation, $y = 2x^2 + bx + c$, which is written in standard form, can be written in vertex form, $y = a(x - h)^2 + k$, where (h, k) is the vertex of the parabola and a is the value of the coefficient on the x^2 term when the equation is written in standard form. It follows that $a = 2$. Substituting 2 for a, −1 for h, and −8 for k in this equation yields $y = 2(x - (-1))^2 + (-8)$, or $y = 2(x + 1)^2 - 8$. Squaring the binomial on the right-hand side of this equation yields $y = 2(x^2 + 2x + 1) - 8$. Multiplying each term inside the parentheses on the right-hand side of this equation by 2 yields $y = 2x^2 + 4x + 2 - 8$, which is equivalent to $y = 2x^2 + 4x - 6$. From the given equation $y = 2x^2 + bx + c$, it follows that the value of b is 4 and the value of c is −6. Therefore, the value of bc is $(4)(-6)$, or −24.

QUESTION 17

Choice A is correct. It's given that the graph of the linear function $y = f(x) + 19$ is shown. This means that the graph of $y = f(x) + 19$ can be translated down 19 units to create the graph of $y = f(x)$ and the y-coordinate of every point on the graph of $y = f(x) + 19$ can be decreased by 19 to find the resulting point on the graph of $y = f(x)$. The y-intercept of the graph of $y = f(x) + 19$ is (0, 3). Translating the graph of $y = f(x) + 19$ down 19 units results in a y-intercept of the graph of $y = f(x)$ at the point (0, 3 − 19), or (0, −16). The graph of $y = f(x) + 19$ slants down from left to right, so the slope of the graph is negative. The translation of a linear graph changes its position, but does not change its slope. It follows that the slope of the graph of $y = f(x)$ is also negative. The equation of a linear function f can be written in the form $f(x) = b + mx$, where b is the y-coordinate of the y-intercept and m is the slope of the graph of $y = f(x)$. It's given that c and d are positive constants. Since the y-coordinate of the y-intercept and the slope of the graph of $y = f(x)$ are both negative, it follows that $f(x) = -d - cx$ could define f.

Choice B is incorrect. This could define a linear function where its graph has a positive, not negative, y-intercept. *Choice C* is incorrect. This could define a linear function where its graph has a positive, not negative, slope. *Choice D* is incorrect. This could define a linear function where its graph has a positive, not negative, y-intercept and a positive, not negative, slope.

QUESTION 18

The correct answer is 480. It's given in the figure that angle ACB and angle AED are right angles. It follows that angle ACB is congruent to angle AED. It's also given that angle BAC and angle DAE are the same angle. It follows that angle BAC is congruent to angle DAE. Since triangles ABC and ADE have two pairs of congruent angles, the triangles are similar. Sides AB and AC in triangle ABC correspond to sides AD and AE, respectively, in triangle ADE. Corresponding sides in similar triangles are proportional. Therefore, $\frac{AD}{AB} = \frac{AE}{AC}$. It's given that

AC = 3 units and CE = 21 units. Therefore, AE = 24 units. It's also given that $AB = \sqrt{34}$ units. Substituting 3 for AC, 24 for AE, and $\sqrt{34}$ for AB in the

equation $\frac{AD}{AB} = \frac{AE}{AC}$ yields $\frac{AD}{\sqrt{34}} = \frac{24}{3}$, or $\frac{AD}{\sqrt{34}}$ = 8. Multiplying each side of this

equation by $\sqrt{34}$ yields $AD = 8\sqrt{34}$. By the Pythagorean theorem, if a right triangle has a hypotenuse with length c and legs with lengths a and b, then $a^2 + b^2 = c^2$. Since triangle ADE is a right triangle, it follows that AD represents the length of the hypotenuse, c, and DE and AE represent the lengths of the legs, a and b. Substituting 24 for b and $8\sqrt{34}$ for c in the equation $a^2 + b^2 = c^2$ yields $a^2 + (24)^2 = (8\sqrt{34})^2$, which is equivalent to $a^2 + 576 = 64(34)$, or $a^2 + 576 = 2{,}176$. Subtracting 576 from both sides of this equation yields $a^2 = 1{,}600$. Taking the square root of both sides of this equation yields $a = \pm40$. Since a represents a length, which must be positive, the value of a is 40. Therefore, DE = 40. Since DE and AE represent the lengths of the legs of triangle ADE, it follows that DE and AE can be used to calculate the area,

in square units, of the triangle as $\frac{1}{2}(40)(24)$, or 480. Therefore, the area,

in square units, of triangle ADE is 480.

QUESTION 19

Choice A is correct. It's given that the result of increasing the quantity x

by 400% is 60. This can be written as $x + \left(\frac{400}{100}\right)x = 60$, which is equivalent to

$x + 4x = 60$, or $5x = 60$. Dividing each side of this equation by 5 yields $x = 12$. Therefore, the value of x is 12.

Choice B is incorrect. The result of increasing the quantity 15 by 400% is 75, not 60. *Choice C* is incorrect. The result of increasing the quantity 240 by 400% is 1,200, not 60. *Choice D* is incorrect. The result of increasing the quantity 340 by 400% is 1,700, not 60.

QUESTION 20

Choice A is correct. It's given that points A and B lie on the circle with center C. Therefore, $\overline{AC}$ and $\overline{BC}$ are both radii of the circle. Since all radii of a circle are congruent, $\overline{AC}$ is congruent to $\overline{BC}$. The length of $\overline{AC}$, or the distance from point A to point C, can be found using the distance formula, which gives the distance

between two points, (x_1, y_1) and (x_2, y_2), as $\sqrt{(x_1 - x_2)^2 + (y_1 - y_2)^2}$.

Substituting the given coordinates of point A, $(h + 1, k + \sqrt{102})$, for (x_1, y_1) and the given coordinates of point C, (h, k), for (x_2, y_2) in the distance formula yields

$\sqrt{(h + 1 - h)^2 + (k + \sqrt{102} - k)^2}$, or $\sqrt{1^2 + (\sqrt{102})^2}$, which is equivalent to $\sqrt{1 + 102}$, or $\sqrt{103}$. Therefore, the length of $\overline{AC}$ is $\sqrt{103}$ and the length of $\overline{BC}$ is $\sqrt{103}$. It's given that angle ACB is a right angle. Therefore, triangle ACB is a right triangle with legs $\overline{AC}$ and $\overline{BC}$ and hypotenuse $\overline{AB}$. By the Pythagorean theorem, if a right triangle has a hypotenuse with length c and legs with lengths a and b, then $a^2 + b^2 = c^2$. Substituting $\sqrt{103}$ for a and b in this equation yields $(\sqrt{103})^2 + (\sqrt{103})^2 = c^2$, or $103 + 103 = c^2$, which is equivalent to $206 = c^2$. Taking the positive square root of both sides of this equation yields $\sqrt{206} = c$. Therefore, the length of $\overline{AB}$ is $\sqrt{206}$.

Choice B is incorrect and may result from conceptual or calculation errors. *Choice C* is incorrect. This would be the length of $\overline{AB}$ if the length of $\overline{AC}$ were 103, not $\sqrt{103}$. *Choice D* is incorrect and may result from conceptual or calculation errors.

QUESTION 21

The correct answer is 4,176. It's given that the side length of the larger square is 3 times the side length of the smaller square. This means that the area of the larger square is 3^2, or 9, times the area of the smaller square. If the area of the smaller square is represented by x, then the area of the larger square can be represented by $9x$. Therefore, the flat surface of the two adjacent squares has a total area of $x + 9x$, or $10x$. It's given that an electric field with strength 29.00 volts per meter passes uniformly through this surface and the total electric flux of the electric field through this surface is 4,640 volts · meters. Since it's given that the electric flux is the product of the electric field's strength and the area of the surface, the equation $29.00(10x) = 4,640$, or $290x = 4,640$, can be used to represent this situation. Dividing each side of this equation by 290 yields $x = 16$. Substituting 16 for x in the expression for the area of the larger square, $9x$, yields $9(16)$, or 144, square meters. Since the area of the larger square is 144 square meters, the electric flux, in volts · meters, of the electric field through the larger square can be determined by multiplying the area of the larger square by the strength of the electric field. Thus, the electric flux is $(144 \text{ square meters})\left(\dfrac{29.00 \text{ volts}}{\text{meter}}\right)$, or 4,176 volts · meters.

QUESTION 22

Choice A is correct. An equation of a line of best fit for data set F can be written in the form $y = a + bx$, where a is the y-coordinate of the y-intercept of the line of best fit and b is the slope. The line of best fit shown for data set E has a y-intercept at approximately (0, 12). It's given that data set F is created by multiplying the y-coordinate of each data point from data set E by 3.9. It follows that a line of best fit for data set F has a y-intercept at approximately (0, 12(3.9)), or (0, 46.8). Therefore, the value of a is approximately 46.8. The slope of a line that passes through points (x_1, y_1) and (x_2, y_2) can be calculated as $\dfrac{(y_2 - y_1)}{(x_2 - x_1)}$.

Since the line of best fit shown for data set E passes approximately through the point (12, 30), it follows that a line of best fit for data set F passes approximately through the point (12, 30(3.9)), or (12, 117). Substituting (0, 46.8) and (12, 117) for (x_1, y_1) and (x_2, y_2), respectively, in $\dfrac{(y_2 - y_1)}{(x_2 - x_1)}$ yields $\dfrac{117 - 46.8}{12 - 0}$, which is equivalent to $\dfrac{70.2}{12}$, or 5.85. Therefore, the value of b is approximately 5.85, or approximately 5.9. Thus, $y = 46.8 + 5.9x$ could be an equation of a line of best fit for data set F.

Choice B is incorrect and may result from conceptual or calculation errors. *Choice C* is incorrect and may result from conceptual or calculation errors. *Choice D* is incorrect. This could be an equation of a line of best fit for data set E, not data set F.

Scoring Your Paper SAT Practice Test #5

Congratulations on completing an SAT® practice test. To score your test, follow the instructions in this scoring guide.

IMPORTANT: *This scoring guide is for students who completed SAT Practice Test #5 in The Official SAT Study Guide™. We recommend reading through these instructions and explanations before scoring so that you understand the specifics and limitations of scoring this practice test.*

The total score on your practice test reflects the sum of the (1) Reading and Writing and (2) Math section scores, as indicated below. If you decided to take both the lower- and higher-difficulty modules, choose which one you will use to score.

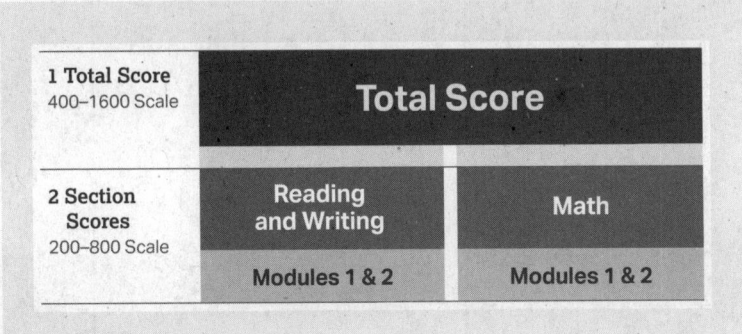

1 Total Score 400–1600 Scale	Total Score	
2 Section Scores 200–800 Scale	Reading and Writing	Math
	Modules 1 & 2	Modules 1 & 2

Scores Overview

Each assessment in the SAT Suite (SAT, PSAT/NMSQT®, PSAT™ 10, and PSAT™ 8/9) reports test scores on a common scale.

For more details about scores, visit **sat.org/scores**.

How to Calculate Your Practice Test Scores

The worksheets on the pages that follow help you calculate your test scores.

GET SET UP

1 In addition to your practice test, you'll need the answer keys and conversion tables at the end of this scoring guide.

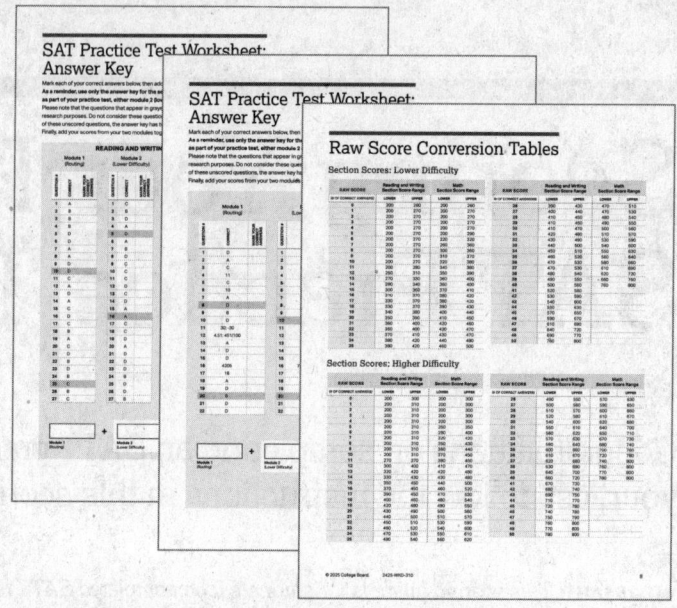

SCORE YOUR PRACTICE TEST

2 Compare your answers to the answer keys later in this scoring guide, and count up the total number of correct answers for each section. Write the number of correct answers for each section in the boxes at the bottom of the pages.

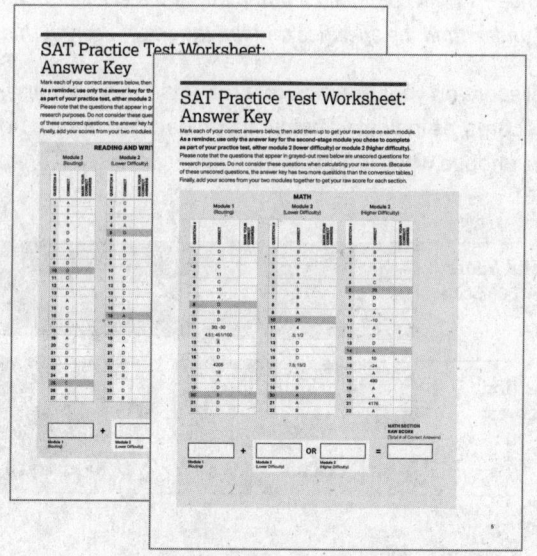

CALCULATE YOUR SCORES

3 Using your marked-up answer keys and the conversion tables, follow the directions on the SAT Practice Test Worksheet: Section and Total Scores page to get your section and total scores.

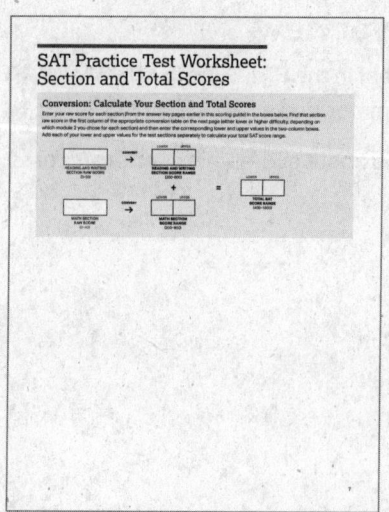

Get Section and Total Scores

Section and total scores for this paper version of SAT Practice Test #5 are expressed as ranges. That's because the scoring method described in this guide is a different (and therefore less precise) version of the one used in the actual adaptive test.

This practice test contains three modules for each test section: (1) a single first-stage (routing) module and (2) two second-stage modules. The two second-stage modules differ by average question difficulty and are marked as either "module 2 (lower difficulty)" or "module 2 (higher difficulty)." You get to choose which module 2 you would like to take for this practice test. **An actual testing experience consists of one routing and one second-stage module per test section.** To obtain your Reading and Writing and Math section scores, you will refer to the answer key and conversion table for the second-stage module you chose (either lower or higher difficulty).

GET YOUR READING AND WRITING SECTION SCORE

Calculate your SAT Reading and Writing section score (it's on a scale of 200–800).

1 Use the answer key for Reading and Writing to find the number of questions in module 1 and the module 2 you chose (either lower or higher difficulty) that you answered correctly.

2 To determine your Reading and Writing raw score, add the number of correct answers you got in module 1 and the module 2 you chose (either lower or higher difficulty). **Exclude the questions in grayed-out rows in your calculation.**

3 Use the appropriate Raw Score Conversion Table to turn your raw score into your Reading and Writing section score.

4 The lower and upper values associated with your raw score establish the range of scores you might expect to receive had this been an actual adaptive test.

GET YOUR MATH SECTION SCORE

Calculate your SAT Math section score (it's on a scale of 200–800).

1 Use the answer key for Math to find the number of questions in module 1 and the module 2 you chose (either lower or higher difficulty) that you answered correctly.

2 To determine your Math raw score, add the number of correct answers you got in module 1 and the module 2 you chose (either lower or higher difficulty). **Exclude the questions in grayed-out rows in your calculation.**

3 Use the appropriate Raw Score Conversion Table to turn your raw score into your Math section score.

4 The lower and upper values associated with your raw score establish the range of scores you might expect to receive had this been an actual adaptive test.

GET YOUR TOTAL SCORE

Add together the lower values for the Reading and Writing and Math sections, and then add together the upper values for the two sections. The result is your total score, expressed as a range, for this SAT practice test. The total score is on a scale of 400–1600.

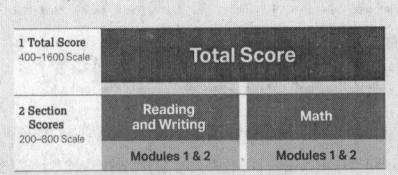

1 Total Score 400–1600 Scale	Total Score	
2 Section Scores 200–800 Scale	Reading and Writing	Math
	Modules 1 & 2	Modules 1 & 2

Your total score on this SAT practice test is the sum of your Reading and Writing section score and your Math section score. For this practice test, you'll receive a lower and upper score for each test section and the total score. This is the range of scores that you might expect to receive.

Use the worksheets on the pages that follow to calculate your section and total scores.

SAT Practice Test Worksheet: Answer Key

Mark each of your correct answers below, then add them up to get your raw score on each module.

As a reminder, use only the answer key for the second-stage module you chose to complete as part of your practice test, either module 2 (lower difficulty) or module 2 (higher difficulty).

Please note that the questions that appear in grayed-out rows below are unscored questions for research purposes. Do not consider these questions when calculating your raw scores. (Because of these unscored questions, the answer key has two more questions than the conversion tables.)

Finally, add your scores from your two modules together to get your raw score for each section.

READING AND WRITING

Module 1 (Routing)			Module 2 (Lower Difficulty)			Module 2 (Higher Difficulty)		
QUESTION #	CORRECT	MARK YOUR CORRECT ANSWERS	QUESTION #	CORRECT	MARK YOUR CORRECT ANSWERS	QUESTION #	CORRECT	MARK YOUR CORRECT ANSWERS
1	A		1	C		1	B	
2	B		2	B		2	D	
3	B		3	D		3	B	
4	B		4	A		4	D	
5	D		5	D		5	D	
6	D		6	A		6	B	
7	A		7	B		7	B	
8	A		8	D		8	A	
9	D		9	C		9	C	
10	D		10	C		10	D	
11	C		11	C		11	C	
12	A		12	D		12	B	
13	D		13	C		13	D	
14	A		14	D		14	D	
15	C		15	A		15	A	
16	D		16	A		16	A	
17	C		17	C		17	D	
18	B		18	C		18	C	
19	A		19	D		19	C	
20	C		20	A		20	A	
21	D		21	D		21	D	
22	B		22	D		22	C	
23	D		23	D		23	B	
24	B		24	B		24	D	
25	C		25	D		25	D	
26	B		26	D		26	B	
27	C		27	B		27	C	

READING AND WRITING SECTION RAW SCORE
(Total # of Correct Answers)

[ ]	**+**	[ ]	**OR**	[ ]	**=**	[ ]

Module 1 (Routing)   Module 2 (Lower Difficulty)   Module 2 (Higher Difficulty)

SAT Practice Test Worksheet: Answer Key

Mark each of your correct answers below, then add them up to get your raw score on each module.
As a reminder, use only the answer key for the second-stage module you chose to complete as part of your practice test, either module 2 (lower difficulty) or module 2 (higher difficulty).
Please note that the questions that appear in grayed-out rows below are unscored questions for research purposes. Do not consider these questions when calculating your raw scores. (Because of these unscored questions, the answer key has two more questions than the conversion tables.)
Finally, add your scores from your two modules together to get your raw score for each section.

MATH

Module 1 (Routing)			Module 2 (Lower Difficulty)			Module 2 (Higher Difficulty)		
QUESTION #	CORRECT	MARK YOUR CORRECT ANSWERS	QUESTION #	CORRECT	MARK YOUR CORRECT ANSWERS	QUESTION #	CORRECT	MARK YOUR CORRECT ANSWERS
1	D		1	B		1	B	
2	A		2	C		2	B	
3	C		3	B		3	B	
4	11		4	B		4	A	
5	C		5	A		5	C	
6	10		6	6		6	29	
7	A		7	B		7	D	
8	D		8	B		8	D	
9	B		9	A		9	A	
10	D		10	29		10	-10	
11	30; -30		11	4		11	A	
12	4.51; 451/100		12	.5; 1/2		12	D	
13	A		13	D		13	D	
14	D		14	D		14	A	
15	D		15	D		15	10	
16	4205		16	7.5; 15/2		16	-24	
17	18		17	A		17	A	
18	A		18	6		18	480	
19	D		19	B		19	A	
20	B		20	A		20	A	
21	D		21	A		21	4176	
22	D		22	B		22	A	

MATH SECTION RAW SCORE
(Total # of Correct Answers)

[ ]	+	[ ]	OR	[ ]	= [ ]
Module 1 (Routing)		Module 2 (Lower Difficulty)		Module 2 (Higher Difficulty)	

Understanding the SAT Practice Test Conversion Tables and Total Score Ranges

As mentioned earlier in this scoring guide, the scoring method for the practice tests that appear in *The Official SAT Study Guide* is different (and therefore less precise) than the method used in the actual adaptive test. Your practice test may result in a larger score range than what you hoped to see, but it's not feasible to estimate your performance on the practice tests in the study guide as precisely as we could for an actual test. As the test developers, College Board is committed to providing the most accurate conversion possible to help you understand your scores and guide your practice most effectively.

There are two conversion tables in this scoring guide. Use the conversion table labelled lower difficulty if you took module 2 (lower difficulty). Use the conversion table labelled higher difficulty if you took module 2 (higher difficulty). You might need both conversion tables if you took the lower-difficulty option for one section (e.g., Reading and Writing) and the higher-difficulty option for the other section (e.g., Math).

Because the lower- and higher-difficulty conversion tables share the same questions for module 1 (routing), you may encounter different score ranges based on the conversion table you use. For example, if you got all the module 1 (routing) questions correct, the lower-difficulty conversion table and the higher-difficulty conversion table will give you different score ranges. This is to be expected because the conversion tables account for all items within the two modules that make up the test. Answering only items on the first half of the test assumes you answered the other questions (module 2) incorrectly. Recall that when taking the actual SAT on test day, the test will adapt to your ability based on how you perform on the first half. Because of the differences between the actual test and providing a paper approximation of that (the practice test you're currently scoring), you should select the second-stage module that feels most appropriate for you. For example, if you were to answer all items on the first module correctly on the actual test, you would not be routed to the easier second-stage module. The converse would also be true. For many users of moderate ability either second-stage would be acceptable, but very high or low performers should be cautioned about taking the second-stage module that doesn't align well with their ability.

SAT Practice Test Worksheet: Section and Total Scores

Conversion: Calculate Your Section and Total Scores

Enter your raw score for each section (from the answer key pages earlier in this scoring guide) in the boxes below. Find that section raw score in the first column of the appropriate conversion table on the next page (either lower or higher difficulty, depending on which module 2 you chose for each section) and then enter the corresponding lower and upper values in the two-column boxes. Add each of your lower and upper values for the test sections separately to calculate your total SAT score range.

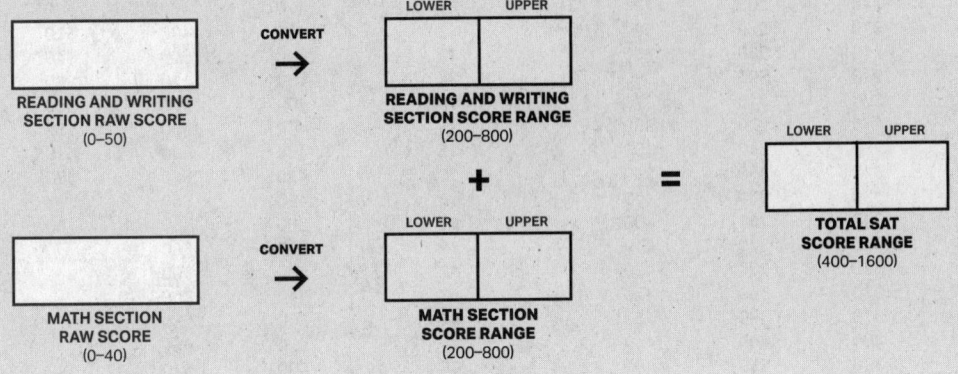

READING AND WRITING SECTION RAW SCORE (0–50)

CONVERT →

LOWER | UPPER

READING AND WRITING SECTION SCORE RANGE (200–800)

+

MATH SECTION RAW SCORE (0–40)

CONVERT →

LOWER | UPPER

MATH SECTION SCORE RANGE (200–800)

=

LOWER | UPPER

TOTAL SAT SCORE RANGE (400–1600)

Raw Score Conversion Tables

Section Scores: Lower Difficulty

RAW SCORE (# OF CORRECT ANSWERS)	Reading and Writing Section Score Range		Math Section Score Range		RAW SCORE (# OF CORRECT ANSWERS)	Reading and Writing Section Score Range		Math Section Score Range	
	LOWER	UPPER	LOWER	UPPER		LOWER	UPPER	LOWER	UPPER
0	200	260	200	260	26	390	430	470	510
1	200	270	200	270	27	400	440	470	530
2	200	270	200	270	28	410	450	480	540
3	200	270	200	270	29	410	450	490	550
4	200	270	200	270	30	410	470	500	560
5	200	270	200	290	31	420	480	510	570
6	200	270	220	320	32	430	490	530	590
7	200	270	260	360	33	440	500	540	600
8	200	270	300	360	34	450	510	550	630
9	200	270	310	370	35	460	520	560	640
10	200	270	320	380	36	470	530	580	660
11	200	280	340	380	37	470	530	610	690
12	250	310	350	390	38	480	540	620	720
13	270	330	360	400	39	490	550	660	760
14	280	340	360	400	40	500	560	760	800
15	300	360	370	410	41	520	580		
16	310	370	380	420	42	530	590		
17	330	370	380	420	43	540	600		
18	330	370	390	430	44	550	630		
19	340	380	400	440	45	570	650		
20	350	390	410	450	46	590	670		
21	360	400	420	460	47	610	690		
22	360	400	430	470	48	640	720		
23	370	410	430	470	49	690	770		
24	380	420	440	480	50	760	800		
25	380	420	460	500					

Section Scores: Higher Difficulty

RAW SCORE (# OF CORRECT ANSWERS)	Reading and Writing Section Score Range		Math Section Score Range		RAW SCORE (# OF CORRECT ANSWERS)	Reading and Writing Section Score Range		Math Section Score Range	
	LOWER	UPPER	LOWER	UPPER		LOWER	UPPER	LOWER	UPPER
0	200	300	200	300	26	490	550	570	630
1	200	310	200	300	27	500	560	590	650
2	200	310	200	300	28	510	570	600	660
3	200	310	200	300	29	520	580	610	670
4	200	310	200	300	30	540	600	620	680
5	200	310	250	350	31	550	610	640	700
6	200	310	280	400	32	560	620	650	710
7	200	310	320	420	33	570	630	670	730
8	200	310	350	430	34	580	640	680	740
9	200	310	360	440	35	600	660	700	760
10	200	310	370	450	36	610	670	720	780
11	270	370	390	450	37	620	680	740	800
12	300	400	410	470	38	630	690	760	800
13	320	420	420	480	39	640	700	770	800
14	330	430	430	490	40	660	720	780	800
15	350	450	440	500	41	670	730		
16	370	450	460	520	42	680	740		
17	390	450	470	530	43	690	750		
18	400	460	480	540	44	710	770		
19	420	480	490	550	45	720	780		
20	430	490	500	560	46	740	780		
21	440	500	510	570	47	750	790		
22	450	510	530	590	48	760	800		
23	460	520	540	600	49	770	800		
24	470	530	550	610	50	780	800		
25	480	540	560	620					

The SAT®

Practice Test #6

Make time to take the practice test. It is one of the best ways to get ready for the SAT.

Note: The practice tests in this guide include two second modules so that you can experience both the lower- and higher-difficulty modules. On the actual test, you will be presented with only one second module.

After you have taken the practice test, score it right away using materials provided in *The Official SAT Study Guide*.

This version of the SAT Practice Test is for students using this Study Guide. As a reminder, most students taking the SAT will do so using Bluebook™, the digital testing application. To best prepare for test day, download Bluebook at **bluebook.app.collegeboard.org** to take the practice test in the digital format.

Test begins on the next page.

Reading and Writing

27 QUESTIONS

DIRECTIONS

The questions in this section address a number of important reading and writing skills. Each question includes one or more passages, which may include a table or graph. Read each passage and question carefully, and then choose the best answer to the question based on the passage(s).

All questions in this section are multiple-choice with four answer choices. Each question has a single best answer.

1

Whether Carmen Lomas Garza is creating small paintings and illustrations or large public artworks—such as *Baile*, a copper cutout of traditional Mexican dance in the San Francisco International Airport—she is _____ direct experience, drawing from memories of her childhood in Texas or details of her current surroundings in California.

Which choice completes the text with the most logical and precise word or phrase?

A) complimented by

B) uncertain about

C) unbothered by

D) inspired by

2

Disproving the common misconception of Native art as _____, the painters whose work appears in the collection at the National Museum of the American Indian employ a range of styles. There are artists working in the traditional arts of their specific tribal communities, artists working in European modernist or American abstract expressionist art traditions, and artists blending various traditions into something wholly new.

Which choice completes the text with the most logical and precise word or phrase?

A) uncontroversial

B) individualistic

C) theoretical

D) homogeneous

CONTINUE ➤

3

Recent measurements of the mass of the *W* boson (a subatomic particle) were notable not only for the mere fact that the particle's mass differed from expectations but for the _____ of that difference: the measured mass of the *W* boson was seven standard deviations higher than predicted by the standard model of particle physics.

Which choice completes the text with the most logical and precise word or phrase?

A) cause

B) existence

C) implication

D) scale

4

Birds sing to communicate over potentially great distances. For this reason, many researchers believe that birds in densely vegetated habitats generally sing at lower frequencies than birds living in comparatively sparse habitats, since dense vegetation tends to _____ the distance that high-frequency sounds can travel.

Which choice completes the text with the most logical and precise word or phrase?

A) exceed

B) diminish

C) encompass

D) conceal

5

The following text is from Betty Smith's 1943 novel *A Tree Grows in Brooklyn*. Francie, a young girl, visits the library often.

Francie thought that all the books in the world were in that library and she had a plan about reading all the books in the world. She was reading a book a day in alphabetical order and not skipping the dry ones. She remembered that the first author had been Abbott. She had been reading a book a day for a long time now and she was still in the B's. Already she had read about bees and buffaloes, Bermuda vacations and Byzantine architecture. For all her enthusiasm, she had to admit that some of the B's had been hard going. But Francie was a reader.

©1947 by Betty Smith

Which choice best states the main purpose of the text?

A) To illustrate Francie's enjoyment of an unusual topic

B) To explain why Francie prefers reading over other activities

C) To portray Francie's determination to meet a goal

D) To describe a book that Francie greatly admires

CONTINUE

6

The people of medieval Europe have traditionally been seen as uninterested in cleanliness and hygiene, but modern research has shown that this is largely a myth. According to historian Eleanor Janega, most medieval towns in Europe had at least one public bathhouse, which often offered both full-immersion baths and—more affordably—steam baths. <u>While such amenities were available mainly to town dwellers</u>, regular bathing in rivers and streams or daily sponge baths at home were common practices throughout medieval Europe.

Which choice best describes the function of the underlined portion?

A) It asserts that in medieval Europe steam baths were more popular in rural areas than in urban ones.

B) It describes a limitation of earlier historians' studies of medieval European bathing habits.

C) It concedes that not all people in medieval Europe had access to public bathhouses.

D) It explains why Janega decided to study the popularity of public bathhouses in medieval Europe.

7

When classical pianist Martha Argerich performs, it appears as if the music is coming to her spontaneously. She's highly skilled technically, but because of how freely she plays and her willingness to take risks, she seems relaxed and natural. Her apparent ease, however, is due to a tremendous amount of preparation. Despite Argerich's experience and virtuosity, she never takes for granted that she knows a piece of music. Instead, she approaches the music as if encountering it for the first time and tries to understand it anew.

Which choice best states the main purpose of the text?

A) To provide details about how Argerich identifies which pieces of music she will perform

B) To assert that Argerich's performances look effortless because of how she prepares for them

C) To discuss the kinds of music Argerich feels most comfortable encountering for the first time

D) To describe the unique way that Argerich approaches music she hasn't performed before

CONTINUE ➤

8

Text 1

An excavation in Chiquihuite Cave in central Mexico has upended the belief that approximately 13,000 years ago, a group known as the Clovis people were the first human inhabitants of North America. More than 200 crude stone tools were found embedded in a layer of earth that is up to 33,150 years old, <u>revealing that humans occupied the cave thousands of years before the Clovis people reached the continent.</u>

Text 2

The objects uncovered in Chiquihuite Cave are intriguing, but it is premature to characterize them as tools. The stone pieces are so roughly shaped that they may have simply fractured from rocks during natural geological activity in the cave. Moreover, their unearthing has thus far not been accompanied by discoveries of other signs of human activity or even traces of human DNA from surfaces.

Based on the texts, how would the author of Text 2 most likely respond to the underlined claim in Text 1?

A) By suggesting that it draws a plausible connection between two groups of people but will need to be confirmed with further study

B) By asserting that it rests on an assumption about the stone pieces that is not sufficiently supported by available evidence

C) By acknowledging that it will most likely be proved correct when the stone pieces undergo more detailed analysis

D) By pointing out that it fails to account for evidence that the Clovis people were active on the continent as early as is commonly thought

9

Many literary theorists distinguish between *fabula*, a narrative's content, and *syuzhet*, a narrative's arrangement and presentation of events. In the film *The Godfather Part II*, the *fabula* is the story of the Corleone family, and the *syuzhet* is the presentation of the story as it alternates between two timelines in 1901 and 1958. But literary theorist Mikhail Bakhtin maintained that *fabula* and *syuzhet* are insufficient to completely describe a narrative—he held that systematic categorizations of artistic phenomena discount the subtle way in which meaning is created by interactions between the artist, the work, and the audience.

Which choice best states the main idea of the text?

A) Literary theorist Mikhail Bakhtin argued that there are important characteristics of narratives that are not fully encompassed by two concepts that other theorists have used to analyze narratives.

B) Literary theorist Mikhail Bakhtin claimed that meaning is not inherent in a narrative but is created when an audience encounters a narrative so that narratives are interpreted differently by different people.

C) The storytelling methods used in *The Godfather Part II* may seem unusually complicated, but they can be easily understood when two concepts from literary theory are utilized.

D) Narratives that are told out of chronological order are more difficult for audiences to understand than are narratives presented chronologically.

Unauthorized copying or reuse of any part of this page is illegal.

CONTINUE ➡

567

10

Partial List of Candidate Species for De-extinction

Common name	Scientific name	Became extinct
Huia	*Heteralocha acutirostris*	1907
Caribbean monk seal	*Monachus tropicalis*	1952
Passenger pigeon	*Ectopistes migratorius*	1914
Saber-toothed cat	*Smilodon*	11,000 years before present
Woolly mammoth	*Mammuthus primigenius*	6,400 years before present

The passage of time is among the many obstacles faced by scientists who are pursuing de-extinction efforts—that is, efforts to use breeding or a mixture of cloning and genetic engineering to bring back extinct species. Specifically, researchers are concerned that the longer a species has been extinct, the less likely it is that a suitable habitat still exists for that species. Among candidate species for de-extinction, this problem would be especially concerning for the _____.

Which choice most effectively uses data from the table to complete the statement?

A) passenger pigeon (*Ectopistes migratorius*), which became extinct only a few years after the huia (*Heteralocha acutirostris*).

B) saber-toothed cat (*Smilodon*), which became extinct 11,000 years ago.

C) woolly mammoth (*Mammuthus primigenius*), which became extinct several thousand years before the saber-toothed cat (*Smilodon*).

D) Caribbean monk seal (*Monachus tropicalis*), which became extinct in 1952.

11

"The Yellow Wallpaper" is an 1892 short story by Charlotte Perkins Gilman. In the story, the narrator expresses mixed feelings about her surroundings: _____.

Which quotation from "The Yellow Wallpaper" most effectively illustrates the claim?

A) "This wallpaper has a kind of sub-pattern in a different shade, a particularly irritating one, for you can only see it in certain lights, and not clearly then."

B) "By moonlight—the moon shines in all night when there is a moon—I wouldn't know it was the same paper."

C) "I'm really getting quite fond of the big room, all but that horrid [wall]paper."

D) "The color is repellant, almost revolting; a smouldering, unclean yellow, strangely faded by the slow-turning sunlight."

CONTINUE

12

Land Area Covered by Native Flowering Plants
at a Site in Antarctica

Species	Area covered in 2009 (in square meters)	Area covered in 2018 (in square meters)	Percent increase in area covered from 2009 to 2018
Deschampsia antarctica	1,230	1,576	28%
Colobanthus quitensis	6.9	10.7	55%

The only flowering plant species native to Antarctica, *Colobanthus quitensis* and *Deschampsia antarctica* grow in places where the earth remains free of ice for much of the year. Botanist Niccoletta Cannone wondered how the warming of Antarctica's climate in recent years had affected these species, so she visited a site in Antarctica, first in 2009 and later in 2018, to count the number of plants growing there. Cannone found that the area of land covered by the two species had significantly expanded during the nine-year period. While both species likely benefited from warming temperatures, *Colobanthus quitensis* _____

Which choice most effectively uses data from the table to complete the comparison?

A) suppressed the growth of *Deschampsia antarctica*, which covered a smaller area of land in 2018 than it had in 2009.

B) saw a greater expansion than *Deschampsia antarctica* did, increasing the area of land it covered by more than half.

C) showed a greater increase in the average size of individual plants than *Deschampsia antarctica* did.

D) covered land newly freed from ice at a rate 55% faster than that of *Deschampsia antarctica*.

13

As media consumption has become increasingly multiplatform and socially mediated, active news acquisition has diminished in favor of an attitude known as "news finds me" (NFM), in which people passively rely on their social networks and ambient media environments for information about current events. Homero Gil de Zúñiga and Trevor Diehl examined data on a representative group of adults in the United States to determine participants' strength of NFM attitude, political knowledge, and political interest. Although no major election took place sufficiently near the study for Gil de Zúñiga and Diehl to identify causality between NFM and voting behavior, they did posit that NFM may reduce voting probability through an indirect effect.

Which finding, if true, would most directly support the idea advanced by Gil de Zúñiga and Diehl?

A) NFM attitude tends to increase in strength as major elections approach, and people are significantly more likely to vote in major elections than in minor elections.

B) NFM attitude has a strong negative effect on political knowledge and interest, and there is known to be a strong positive correlation between political knowledge and interest and the likelihood of voting.

C) Political interest is known to have a strong positive effect on likelihood of voting but shows only a weak positive effect on political knowledge, and NFM attitude shows little correlation with either political knowledge or political interest.

D) The likelihood of voting increases as political knowledge increases, and the relationship between NFM attitude and political knowledge tends to strengthen as the size of people's social networks increases.

Unauthorized copying or reuse of any part of this page is illegal.

CONTINUE

569

14

In dialects of English spoken in Scotland, the "r" sound is strongly emphasized when it appears at the end of syllables (as in "car") or before other consonant sounds (as in "bird"). English dialects of the Upland South, a region stretching from Oklahoma to western Virginia, place similar emphasis on "r" at the ends of syllables and before other consonant sounds. Historical records show that the Upland South was colonized largely by people whose ancestors came from Scotland. Thus, linguists have concluded that _____

Which choice most logically completes the text?

A) the English dialects spoken in the Upland South acquired their emphasis on the "r" sound from dialects spoken in Scotland.

B) emphasis on the "r" sound will eventually spread from English dialects spoken in the Upland South to dialects spoken elsewhere.

C) the English dialects spoken in Scotland were influenced by dialects spoken in the Upland South.

D) people from Scotland abandoned their emphasis on the "r" sound after relocating to the Upland South.

15

In 2016 biological anthropologist Heather F. Smith and her team investigated the evolution of the appendix, an intestinal organ that is present in some mammals, including humans, but is generally thought to have no function. Studying 533 mammal species, the team found that the appendix has emerged independently across multiple lineages in separate instances and, significantly, hasn't disappeared after emerging in specific lineages. Moreover, the team determined that species with the organ tend to have higher concentrations of lymphoid tissue, which supports immune responses, in the cecum, the organ the appendix is attached to. Therefore, the team hypothesized that the appendix likely _____

Which choice most logically completes the text?

A) was once present in many nonmammal species but has since disappeared from those lineages.

B) has been preserved in certain mammal species because it benefits their immune systems.

C) will emerge in a greater number of mammal species because it may serve a necessary function in the immune system.

D) produced higher concentrations of lymphoid tissue in mammals in the past than it does currently.

16

A harpsichord may look just like a piano, but the difference between the two instruments is easy to hear. When a harpsichord's keys are pressed, the strings inside the _____ are plucked, not struck.

Which choice completes the text so that it conforms to the conventions of Standard English?

A) instrument:

B) instrument

C) instrument—

D) instrument,

Unauthorized copying or reuse of any part of this page is illegal.

CONTINUE

570

17

"He was just the man for such a place, and it was just the place for such a man." This line is from Frederick Douglass's autobiography *Narrative of the Life of Frederick Douglass* (1845). It's an example of antimetabole, a writing technique that _____ emphasis by repeating a statement in a reversed order.

Which choice completes the text so that it conforms to the conventions of Standard English?

A) create

B) are creating

C) have created

D) creates

18

Technologies such as microphones and inkjet printers are made using piezoelectric materials, which generate an internal electric field when pressure is applied to them. The toxic nature of some of these materials recently led a team from the University of Sheffield to investigate how _____

Which choice completes the text so that it conforms to the conventions of Standard English?

A) could their use be better regulated?

B) their use could be better regulated.

C) their use could be better regulated?

D) could their use be better regulated.

19

Each night in Gijón, Spain, a section of the city's marina is bathed in a soft green glow. The source of the glow is the Árbol de la Sidra, a large sculpture made up of 3,200 recycled glass bottles. A lamp inside the tree-shaped structure _____ the green glass.

Which choice completes the text so that it conforms to the conventions of Standard English?

A) will be illuminating

B) illuminates

C) would illuminate

D) illuminated

20

French philosopher René Descartes doubted whether he could prove his own existence. Eventually, he found proof in his famous phrase "I think, therefore I am." The _____ complexity: only those who exist would be able to ponder their existence.

Which choice completes the text so that it conforms to the conventions of Standard English?

A) phrases' simplicity masks its

B) phrases simplicity masks their

C) phrase's simplicity masks their

D) phrase's simplicity masks its

21

Fans of the film *Moana* (2016) may not know that the deep and humorous voice behind the _____ belongs to comedian, actor, and musician Jemaine Clement. The versatile performer has appeared in everything from television commercials to action movies, but voice acting, specifically, has become a notable part of his career.

Which choice completes the text so that it conforms to the conventions of Standard English?

A) character Tamatoa the crab

B) character Tamatoa the crab,

C) character: Tamatoa the crab,

D) character, Tamatoa the crab

22

Celebrated Tewa potter Maria Martinez (1887–1980) made her signature all-black ceramic vessels using a heating technique called reduction firing. This technique involves smothering the flame surrounding the clay vessel. _____ the vessel takes on a shiny, black hue.

Which choice completes the text with the most logical transition?

A) On the contrary,

B) For example,

C) Previously,

D) As a result,

Unauthorized copying or reuse of any part of this page is illegal.

CONTINUE

571

23

In the early 1970s, Albert Popa took up graffiti art, spraying his work onto what was at the time an unconventional surface: concrete. _____ Albert's son David has chosen an unusual canvas for his new art project, *Fractured*. In this remarkable work, the artist draws charcoal faces onto fragmented ice floes in Finland, creating the visual effect of a face slowly fracturing.

Which choice completes the text with the most logical transition?

A) However,

B) Indeed,

C) Second,

D) Likewise,

24

Mary Ellen Pleasant, a successful entrepreneur during the gold rush era, earned the moniker "Mother of Human Rights in California" after successfully challenging discrimination in the state. _____ in 1866, she sued a streetcar company for denying her and other Black riders service, a suit she eventually won when the California Supreme Court declared it illegal for carriers to exclude passengers based on race.

Which choice completes the text with the most logical transition?

A) For this reason,

B) Then,

C) In addition,

D) Specifically,

25

The Inca of South America used intricately knotted string devices called quipus to record countable information, like population data and payments. _____ they may have used quipus to record more complex information, like stories and myths, according to researchers.

Which choice completes the text with the most logical transition?

A) As a result,

B) In other words,

C) In addition,

D) For example,

Unauthorized copying or reuse of any part of this page is illegal.

572

CONTINUE

26

While researching a topic, a student has taken the following notes:

- In the 1930s, the Imperial Sugar Cane Institute in India sought to limit the country's dependence on imported sugarcane.
- The institute enlisted botanist Janaki Ammal to breed a local variety of sugarcane.
- She crossbred the imported sugarcane species *Saccharum officinarum* with grasses native to India.
- She succeeded in creating sugarcane hybrids well suited to India's climate.

The student wants to emphasize Janaki Ammal's achievement. Which choice most effectively uses relevant information from the notes to accomplish this goal?

A) By crossbreeding the imported sugarcane species *Saccharum officinarum* with grasses native to India, Ammal succeeded in creating sugarcane hybrids well suited to India's climate.

B) In the 1930s, the Imperial Sugar Cane Institute, which enlisted Ammal, sought to limit dependence on imported sugarcane.

C) Ammal was enlisted by the Imperial Sugar Cane Institute at a time when a local variety of sugarcane needed to be produced.

D) As part of efforts to breed a local variety of sugarcane, an imported sugarcane species called *Saccharum officinarum* was crossbred with grasses native to India.

27

While researching a topic, a student has taken the following notes:

- Scientists have developed a "freeze-thaw" battery that can retain 92% of its charge after twelve weeks.
- The battery contains molten salt (a type of salt that liquifies when heated and solidifies at room temperature).
- When the salt is in a liquid state, energy flows through the battery.
- When the salt is in a solid state, energy stops flowing and is stored in the battery.
- The stored (frozen) energy can be used by reheating (thawing) the battery.

The student wants to specify how the salt enables energy storage. Which choice most effectively uses relevant information from the notes to accomplish this goal?

A) Scientists have developed a freeze-thaw battery that contains molten salt, which liquifies when heated and solidifies at room temperature.

B) The stored energy in a freeze-thaw battery, which contains molten salt, can be used by reheating the battery.

C) When the molten salt in a freeze-thaw battery solidifies at room temperature, energy stops flowing and can be stored in the battery.

D) Molten salt allows a freeze-thaw battery to retain 92% of its charge after twelve weeks.

STOP

If you finish before time is called, you may check your work on this module only. Do not turn to any other module in the test.

Reading and Writing

27 QUESTIONS

1

The following text is from the 1913 story "The King's Coin" by Emily Pauline Johnson, a Kanienkahagen (Mohawk) writer also known as Tekahionwake. Fox-Foot, a young Ojibwe man, is guiding a group of fur traders who are traveling by canoe and suspects that they are being followed.

At supper time, Fox-Foot would allow no fire to be built, no landing to be made, no <u>trace</u> of their passing to be left. They ate canned meat and marmalade, drank again of the stream and pushed on, until just at dusk they reached the edge of a long, still lake, with shores of granite and dense fir forest.

As used in the text, what does the word "trace" most nearly mean?

A) Evidence

B) Blemish

C) Amount

D) Sketch

2

The works of Chicana artist Ester Hernandez are now _____ in museums both in the United States and abroad, but the murals she contributed to as a member of Las Mujeres Muralistas early in her artistic career were displayed in outdoor public spaces across San Francisco.

Which choice completes the text with the most logical and precise word or phrase?

A) invented

B) adjusted

C) featured

D) recommended

3

Animal researcher Amalia P.M. Bastos led a 2021 study about a wild kea parrot that used small stones as tools to preen its feathers. Skeptical colleagues had initially suggested to Bastos that the kea's interactions with the stones might simply be _____, but Bastos and her team showed that the kea was using the stones deliberately.

Which choice completes the text with the most logical and precise word or phrase?

A) intriguing

B) obvious

C) accidental

D) observable

Unauthorized copying or reuse of any part of this page is illegal.

574

CONTINUE →

4

Eighteenth-century historian Edward Gibbon thought the only character defect of the Roman emperor Marcus Aurelius was his mild temperament—though the emperor was widely considered virtuous, his overly permissive nature led him to _____ the vices of those who surrounded him.

Which choice completes the text with the most logical and precise word or phrase?

A) indulge

B) despise

C) moderate

D) criticize

5

Chile's Atacama Desert is one of the driest places on Earth. Mary Beth Wilhelm and other astrobiologists search for life, or its remains, in this harsh place because the desert closely mirrors the extreme environment on Mars. The algae and bacteria found in Atacama's driest regions may offer clues about Martian life. By studying how these and other microorganisms survive such extreme conditions on Earth, Wilhelm's team hopes to determine whether similar life might have existed on Mars and to develop the best tools to look for evidence of it.

Which choice best describes the function of the underlined sentence in the text as a whole?

A) To contrast the conditions in the Atacama Desert with those on Mars

B) To explain why many life-forms cannot survive in the Atacama Desert

C) To indicate why astrobiologists choose to conduct research in the Atacama Desert

D) To describe certain limitations to conducting scientific study in the Atacama Desert

6

In Koasati, an Indigenous language from what is now the southeastern United States, *misip-lin* is the singular form of "to wink," whereas *mis-lin* is the plural form of "to wink"; similarly, *lataf-kan* is the singular form of "to kick something," whereas the plural form is *lat-kan*. These are instances of subtractive morphology, in which a base word is truncated—removing the *ip* and *af*, in these cases—to form a new, related word. This kind of subtractive morphology is pervasive in Koasati.

Which choice best describes the overall structure of the text?

A) It describes the relationship between Koasati and several other languages, raises a question about the nature of that relationship, and then answers that question.

B) It identifies the most frequently occurring words in Koasati, explains why it is difficult to translate those words into English, then provides examples of languages other than English into which those words can be translated.

C) It presents some specific words in Koasati, describes the general linguistic phenomenon exemplified by those words, then states that this phenomenon occurs frequently in Koasati.

D) It explains the phenomenon of subtractive morphology, discusses why subtractive morphology has been controversial among scholars, then argues that an analysis of Koasati could help resolve that controversy.

Unauthorized copying or reuse of any part of this page is illegal.

CONTINUE ➤

575

7

The following text is adapted from Ann Petry's 1946 novel *The Street*. Lutie lives in an apartment in Harlem, New York.

> The glow from the sunset was making the street radiant. The street is nice in this light, [Lutie] thought. It was swarming with children who were playing ball and darting back and forth across the sidewalk in complicated games of tag. Girls were skipping double dutch rope, going tirelessly through the exact center of a pair of ropes, jumping first on one foot and then the other.

> ©1946 by Ann Petry

Which choice best describes what is happening in the text?

A) Lutie is observing the appearance of the street at a particular time of day and the events occurring on it.

B) Lutie is annoyed by the noise of children playing games on her street.

C) Lutie is puzzled by the rules of certain children's games.

D) Lutie is spending time alone in her apartment because she doesn't want to interact with her neighbors.

8

In 1935 Hallie Flanagan was chosen to lead the Federal Theatre Project (FTP). This project was part of the new Works Progress Administration (WPA), a program created by President Franklin D. Roosevelt to provide jobs for unemployed people during the Great Depression. As the director of the FTP, Flanagan created jobs for over 12,500 performers, designers, and other theater professionals across the country. She also kept ticket prices low for the shows they staged, which meant that many people could afford to experience theater for the first time.

Which choice best states the main idea of the text?

A) Jobs provided by the FTP were intended mainly for performers, designers, and other theater professionals.

B) President Roosevelt created the WPA to provide jobs for unemployed people.

C) During the Great Depression, many people couldn't afford to buy theater tickets.

D) As the director of the FTP, Flanagan succeeded in creating many jobs and introducing people to theater.

CONTINUE

9

Recently, scientists looked at data collected by NASA's InSight lander to learn more about seismic activity on Mars, known as marsquakes. The data show that the marsquakes all started from the same location on the planet. This discovery was surprising to scientists, as they expected that the marsquakes would originate from all over the planet because of the cooling of the planet's surface. Now, scientists believe that there could be areas of active magma flows deep beneath the planet's surface that trigger the marsquakes.

According to the text, what was surprising to scientists studying the seismic activity data from NASA's InSight lander?

A) The surface temperature of Mars has been rising.

B) There were different types of seismic waves causing marsquakes.

C) NASA's InSight lander collected less data than scientists had expected.

D) All the marsquakes started from the same location on the planet.

10

Annual Car Production in the United States, 1910–1925

Year	Number of cars produced	Number of companies producing cars
1910	123,990	320
1915	548,139	224
1920	1,651,625	197
1925	3,185,881	80

A student is using the table as part of a social studies class presentation on the US auto industry in the early twentieth century. The student notes that, according to the table, from 1910 to 1925 _____

Which choice most effectively uses data from the table to complete the statement?

A) the number of cars produced increased but the number of companies producing cars decreased.

B) both the number of cars produced and the number of companies producing cars remained unchanged.

C) the number of cars produced decreased but the number of companies producing cars remained unchanged.

D) both the number of cars produced and the number of companies producing cars increased.

CONTINUE

11

"The Bet" is an 1889 short story by Anton Chekhov. In the story, a banker is described as being very upset about something: _____

Which quotation from "The Bet" most effectively illustrates the claim?

A) "Then the banker cautiously broke the seals off the door and put the key in the keyhole."

B) "It struck three o'clock, the banker listened; everyone was asleep in the house and nothing could be heard outside but the rustling of the chilled trees."

C) "The banker, spoilt and frivolous, with millions beyond his reckoning, was delighted at the bet."

D) "When [the banker] got home he lay on his bed, but his tears and emotion kept him for hours from sleeping."

12

Dated Ages of Lunar Samples from Select Missions

Mission name	Year	Landing site	Approximate age of lunar samples (billions of years)
Apollo 11	1969	Mare Tranquillitatis	3.6
Apollo 15	1971	Mare Imbrium	3.3
Apollo 17	1972	Mare Serenitatis	3.8
Chang'e 5	2020	Oceanus Procellarum	2.0

The Apollo program missions were spaceflights to the moon led by the United States during the 1960s and 1970s during which astronauts collected some samples of the moon's surface. More recently, China launched the Chang'e 5 mission, which returned additional lunar surface samples. Researchers have analyzed and dated each of the samples, concluding that the lunar samples collected during the Chang'e 5 mission are significant because _____

Which choice most effectively uses data from the table to complete the claim?

A) they are much younger than the samples brought back from any of the Apollo missions.

B) they were collected from the same landing site as the Apollo 11 mission.

C) they are closest in age to the samples brought back by the Apollo 17 mission.

D) they helped confirm the predicted ages of the lunar samples from the Apollo missions.

CONTINUE ▶

13

Under normal atmospheric pressure at Earth's surface, water molecules form a tetrahedral network stabilized by hydrogen bonds between adjacent molecules. Extreme high pressure, such as can be found in deep ocean waters, destabilizes these bonds and compresses water's structure, allowing water molecules within organisms to permeate proteins and impede crucial biological functions; yet deep-sea organisms known as piezophiles have adapted to extreme pressure. Studies have found a positive correlation between the depths that various piezophiles inhabit and concentrations of a compound called trimethylamine N-oxide (TMAO) in their muscle tissues, which has led a team of researchers to hypothesize that TMAO reduces water's compressibility.

Which finding, if true, would most directly support the researchers' hypothesis?

A) Water molecules are found to be impervious to TMAO even when the water molecules' tetrahedral configuration has been distorted by high pressure.

B) Examination of TMAO's molecular structure shows that TMAO molecules retain their shape even as pressure increases.

C) A positive correlation is found between concentrations of TMAO and the rate at which water's molecular structure compresses as pressure increases.

D) Analysis of water's molecular structure under high pressure reveals that hydrogen bonds are more stable when TMAO is present than when it is not.

14

The Younger Dryas was a period of extreme cooling from 11,700 to 12,900 years ago in the Northern Hemisphere. Some scientists argue that a comet fragment hitting Earth brought about the cooling. Others disagree, partly because there is no known crater from such an impact that dates to the beginning of the period. In 2015, a team led by Kurt Kjær detected a 19-mile-wide crater beneath a glacier in Greenland. The scientists who believe an impact caused the Younger Dryas claim that this discovery supports their view. However, Kjær's team hasn't yet been able to determine the age of the crater. Therefore, the team suggests that _____

Which choice most logically completes the text?

A) it can't be concluded that the impact that made the crater was connected to the beginning of the Younger Dryas.

B) it can't be determined whether a comet fragment could make a crater as large as 19 miles wide.

C) scientists have ignored the possibility that something other than a comet fragment could have made the crater.

D) the scientists who believe an impact caused the Younger Dryas have made incorrect assumptions about when the period began.

15

How did whales, once no bigger than seals, evolve to become the largest animals on Earth? Brazilian biologist Mariana Nery believes the answer might be found in whales' DNA. In January 2023, Nery and her colleagues _____ a study showing changes over time in four whale genes associated with body size.

Which choice completes the text so that it conforms to the conventions of Standard English?

A) published

B) publishing

C) having published

D) to publish

CONTINUE ➤

16

In 1929, Edwin Herbert Land invented a polarizing filter that was featured in a number of products, from sunglasses to 3D movies. A decade later, Land _____ his technology to invent the world's first instant camera, the Polaroid Land camera.

Which choice completes the text so that it conforms to the conventions of Standard English?

A) used
B) to have used
C) to use
D) using

17

When they were first introduced to western Europe from Byzantium in the eleventh century, table forks were met with much resistance. The Bishop of Ostia, St. Peter Damian, condemned the eating utensils because he considered _____ dangerous and unnecessary luxury items.

Which choice completes the text so that it conforms to the conventions of Standard English?

A) them
B) this
C) that
D) it

18

An online content creator who uses copyrighted songs without permission risks being demonetized (prohibited from including paid advertisements in content). The best way to avoid demonetization is to choose music from the public domain. Using one of these noncopyrighted songs _____ a creator won't lose advertising revenue.

Which choice completes the text so that it conforms to the conventions of Standard English?

A) are ensuring
B) have ensured
C) ensure
D) ensures

19

What makes the theremin a unique musical instrument? You play it without touching it. When you place your _____ the pitch will shift as your hands move through the air.

Which choice completes the text so that it conforms to the conventions of Standard English?

A) hand's between the two antenna's,
B) hands between the two antennas,
C) hands' between the two antennas',
D) hands' between the two antennas,

20

While light is known as one of the fastest-moving substances, it slows down when passing through some types of matter. One such type of matter is a form of cooled, condensed gas called a Bose-Einstein condensate _____ Dutch physicist Lene Hau famously used a BEC to slow a beam of light to a complete halt.

Which choice completes the text so that it conforms to the conventions of Standard English?

A) (BEC),
B) (BEC) and
C) (BEC);
D) (BEC)

21

The French directors Colas Koola and Vivien Mermet-Guyenet (known as Koola and Viv) founded the video game studio Blue Twelve. They also love cats. _____ they created an award-winning cat video game, *Stray* (2021), that lets the player explore a dystopian city from the perspective of a clever orange house cat.

Which choice completes the text with the most logical transition?

A) Intermittently,
B) On the other hand,
C) In fact,
D) Nevertheless,

Unauthorized copying or reuse of any part of this page is illegal.

CONTINUE

580

22

In most deer species, males grow antlers, and females don't. _____ reindeer are different. They are the only deer species in which the females grow antlers, too.

Which choice completes the text with the most logical transition?

A) Similarly,

B) Next,

C) However,

D) Thus,

23

In 2014, Nestor Gomez won his first-ever storytelling competition, relating a tale about his life as a Guatemalan immigrant living in Chicago. _____ in 2017, Gomez created the show *80 Minutes Around the World* as a platform for others to share stories about their immigration experiences.

Which choice completes the text with the most logical transition?

A) Instead,

B) For example,

C) Later,

D) In other words,

24

Historians agree that the jazz pianist Jelly Roll Morton was exaggerating when he claimed to have invented jazz music. No one can deny, _____ that Morton's innovative compositions and remarkable improvisational skills helped shape jazz as a genre during its early years.

Which choice completes the text with the most logical transition?

A) therefore,

B) in the second place,

C) in other words,

D) though,

25

While researching a topic, a student has taken the following notes:

- In 1965, Yale University historians claimed that a world map called the Vinland Map was drawn in the fifteenth century.

- Since that time, the map's age has been the subject of debate.

- In 2021, researchers conducted a study to analyze the elemental composition of the map's ink.

- Their analysis revealed that the ink contains a titanium compound not used in inks until the 1920s.

- The researchers concluded that the map was drawn in the twentieth century.

The student wants to present the study and its findings. Which choice most effectively uses relevant information from the notes to accomplish this goal?

A) Given the debate about the Vinland Map's age, researchers in 2021 conducted a study to analyze the elemental composition of the map's ink.

B) A 2021 study of the Vinland Map's ink revealed that it contains a titanium compound not used in inks until the 1920s, indicating that the map was drawn in the twentieth century.

C) The Vinland Map, believed by some to have been drawn in the fifteenth century, was the focus of a 2021 study.

D) Aware that a certain titanium compound was not used in inks until the 1920s, researchers in 2021 studied the elemental composition of the Vinland Map's ink.

CONTINUE ➡

26

While researching a topic, a student has taken the following notes:

- Traditionally, manufacturers have dyed denim jeans blue by dipping them in a solution containing indigo powder.
- Indigo doesn't dissolve in just water, so manufacturers must mix hazardous chemicals with water to dissolve the powder.
- Textile researcher Smriti Rai discovered a process for dyeing blue jeans without chemicals.
- Rai added indigo powder to a hydrogel containing nanocellulose and produced a dye that could be spread directly onto the denim.
- Nanocellulose is a natural, plant-based substance that separates the molecules of indigo powder.

The student wants to emphasize a difference between the two approaches to dyeing blue jeans. Which choice most effectively uses relevant information from the notes to accomplish this goal?

A) Though created using a different process, Rai's dye contains the same ingredient as the dye produced by blue jean manufacturers.

B) Nanocellulose is a natural, plant-based substance that separates the molecules of indigo powder, which doesn't dissolve in water.

C) The traditional approach to dyeing blue jeans is to dip them in a solution containing hazardous chemicals.

D) Rai's approach substitutes a natural, plant-based substance for the hazardous chemicals that manufacturers have traditionally used.

27

While researching a topic, a student has taken the following notes:

- Leigh Torres is a marine ecologist.
- She conducted a study of blue whales in New Zealand's South Taranaki Bight region.
- She wanted to know how ocean temperature affects where the whales forage for krill in that region.
- She found that during a marine heat wave, the whales foraged farther offshore than they had during cooler periods.
- The offshore waters, which were colder than areas closer to shore, had a higher relative abundance of krill.

The student wants to emphasize the aim of the research study. Which choice most effectively uses relevant information from the notes to accomplish this goal?

A) Analyzing ocean temperature data, Torres found that during a marine heat wave, blue whales foraged farther offshore than they had during cooler periods.

B) In her study, Torres sought to determine how ocean temperature affects where blue whales forage for krill in the South Taranaki Bight region.

C) Torres's study revealed that blue whales were attracted to offshore waters with a relatively high abundance of krill.

D) Torres, a marine ecologist, studied blue whales in the South Taranaki Bight region, where the whales forage.

STOP

If you finish before time is called, you may check your work on this module only.
Do not turn to any other module in the test.

Test begins on the next page.

Reading and Writing

27 QUESTIONS

1

The War of 1812 has _____ place in historical memory in Britain, partly because it is overshadowed by the much larger concurrent conflict against Napoleonic France and partly because it essentially maintained the geopolitical status quo for Britain: the country neither gained nor lost significant territory or position as a result of its participation in the war.

Which choice completes the text with the most logical and precise word or phrase?

A) a tenuous

B) an enduring

C) a contentious

D) a conspicuous

2

In 1891, design artist William Morris cofounded the Kelmscott Press, which printed editions of books using preindustrial methods. Historians argue that Morris's repudiation of industrialization is _____ the Kelmscott editions' use of handmade materials and intricate ornamentation reminiscent of medieval manuscripts: these meticulously handcrafted elements exemplify the artistry involved.

Which choice completes the text with the most logical and precise word or phrase?

A) insensible to

B) manifest in

C) scrutinized by

D) complicated by

CONTINUE ➔

3

_____ the long-standing trend of overemphasizing teenagers and young adults in research on social media use, scholars have recently begun to expand their focus to include the fastest-growing cohort of social media users: senior citizens.

Which choice completes the text with the most logical and precise word or phrase?

A) Exacerbating

B) Redressing

C) Epitomizing

D) Precluding

4

The following text is adapted from James Baldwin's 1956 novel *Giovanni's Room*. The narrator is riding in a taxi down a street lined with food vendors and shoppers in Paris, France.

The multitude of Paris seems to be dressed in blue every day but Sunday, when, for the most part, they put on an unbelievably festive black. Here they were now, in blue, <u>disputing</u>, every inch, our passage, with their wagons, handtrucks, their bursting baskets carried at an angle steeply self-confident on the back.

©1956 by James Baldwin

As used in the text, what does the word "disputing" most nearly mean?

A) Arguing about

B) Disapproving of

C) Asserting possession of

D) Providing resistance to

CONTINUE ➡

5

On painter William H. Johnson's return to the United States in 1938 after a decade in Europe, his style underwent an abrupt transformation. <u>Turning away from landscapes painted in an expressionist style—a style that often involves using fluid, distorted shapes and thick, textured brushstrokes to express the artist's subjective experience of reality—Johnson began painting portraits of Black Americans in a bold new way.</u> Evocative of African sculpture and American and Scandinavian folk art, these portraits feature flat, deliberately oversimplified figures in a vibrant but limited color palette.

Which choice best describes the function of the underlined sentence in the text as a whole?

A) It elaborates on the previous sentence's statement about a transitional moment in Johnson's artistic career.

B) It provides information about Johnson's travels in support of a claim about his artistic influences, which is advanced in the following sentence.

C) It recounts a moment in Johnson's personal life that enabled the success of his subsequent career, which is summarized in the following sentence.

D) It presents evidence that calls into question the previous sentence's characterization of Johnson's artistic development.

6

Scholarly accounts of the Chicano movement— a movement that advocated for the social, political, and cultural empowerment of Mexican Americans and reached its zenith in the 1960s and 1970s— <u>tend to focus on the most militant, outspoken figures in the movement</u>, making it seem uniformly radical. Geographer Juan Herrera has shown, however, that if we shift our focus toward the way the movement manifested in comparatively low-profile neighborhood institutions and projects, we see participants espousing an array of political orientations and approaches to community activism.

Which choice best describes the function of the underlined portion in the text as a whole?

A) It presents a trend in scholarship on the Chicano movement that the text claims has been reevaluated by researchers in light of Herrera's work on the movement's participants.

B) It identifies an aspect of the Chicano movement that the text implies was overemphasized by scholars due to their own political orientations.

C) It describes a common approach to studying the Chicano movement that, according to the text, obscures the ideological diversity of the movement's participants.

D) It summarizes the conventional method for analyzing the Chicano movement, which the text suggests creates a misleading impression of the effectiveness of neighborhood institutions and projects.

Unauthorized copying or reuse of any part of this page is illegal.

CONTINUE

586

7

Since its completion in 2014, Bosco Verticale (Vertical Forest)—a pair of residential towers in Milan, Italy, covered by vegetation—has become a striking symbol of environmental sustainability in architecture. Stefano Boeri intended his design, which features balconies that are home to hundreds of trees, to serve as a model for promoting urban biodiversity. However, the concept has faced skepticism: critics note that although the trees used in Bosco Verticale were specifically cultivated for the project, it's too early to tell if they can thrive in this unusual setting.

According to the text, why are some critics skeptical of the concept behind Bosco Verticale?

A) Some essential aspects of Bosco Verticale's design are difficult to adapt to locations other than Milan.

B) The plant life on Bosco Verticale ended up being less varied than Boeri had envisioned it would be.

C) The construction of Bosco Verticale was no less environmentally damaging than the construction of more conventional buildings is.

D) It is unclear whether Bosco Verticale can support the plant life included in its design.

8

Elizabeth Asiedu has identified a negative correlation between the share of developing countries' economies derived from natural-resource extraction and those countries' receipts of foreign investment. This may appear counterintuitive—resource extraction requires initial investments (in extractive technology, for instance) at scales best met by multinational corporations—but Asiedu notes that natural-resource industries' boom-bust cycle can destabilize local currencies and increase developing countries' vulnerability to external shocks, creating levels of uncertainty to which foreign investors are typically averse.

Which choice best states the main idea of the text?

A) Although it may seem surprising that foreign investment declines in developing countries as natural-resource extraction makes up a larger share of those countries' economies, that decline happens because resource extraction requires initial investments too large for foreign investors to supply.

B) Although developing countries tend to become less dependent on foreign investment as natural-resource industries make up a larger share of their economies, this change may not occur if the boom-bust cycle of those industries destabilizes local currencies or increases countries' vulnerability to external shocks.

C) Although one might expect that foreign investment would increase as natural-resource extraction makes up a larger share of developing countries' economies, the opposite happens because heavy reliance on natural resources can lead to unattractive conditions for investors.

D) Although foreign investors tend to avoid initial investments in natural-resource industries in developing countries, foreign investment may increase significantly as those industries stabilize and the risks associated with them decline.

Unauthorized copying or reuse of any part of this page is illegal.

CONTINUE

587

9

Some astronomers searching for extraterrestrial life have proposed that atmospheric NH_3 (ammonia) can serve as a biosignature gas—an indication that a planet harbors life. Jingcheng Huang, Sara Seager, and colleagues evaluated this possibility, finding that on rocky planets, atmospheric NH_3 likely couldn't reach detectably high levels in the absence of biological activity. But the team also found that on so-called mini-Neptunes—gas planets smaller than Neptune but with atmospheres similar to Neptune's—atmospheric pressure and temperature can be high enough to produce atmospheric NH_3.

Based on the text, Huang, Seager, and colleagues would most likely agree with which statement about atmospheric NH_3?

A) Its presence is more likely to indicate that a planet is a mini-Neptune than that the planet is a rocky planet that could support life.

B) Its absence from a planet that's not a mini-Neptune indicates that the planet probably doesn't have life.

C) It should be treated as a biosignature gas if detected in the atmosphere of a rocky planet but not if detected in the atmosphere of a mini-Neptune.

D) It doesn't reliably reach high enough concentrations in the atmospheres of rocky planets or mini-Neptunes to be treated as a biosignature gas.

10

"Lines Written in Early Spring" is a 1798 poem by William Wordsworth. In the poem, the speaker describes having contradictory feelings while experiencing the sights and sounds of a spring day: _____

Which quotation from "Lines Written in Early Spring" most effectively illustrates the claim?

A) "Through primrose-tufts, in that sweet bower, / The periwinkle trail'd its wreathes; / And 'tis my faith that every flower / Enjoys the air it breathes."

B) "The budding twigs spread out their fan, / To catch the breezy air; / And I must think, do all I can, / That there was pleasure there."

C) "The birds around me hopp'd and play'd: / Their thoughts I cannot measure, / But the least motion which they made, / It seem'd a thrill of pleasure."

D) "I heard a thousand blended notes, / While in a grove I [sat] reclined, / In that sweet mood when pleasant thoughts / Bring sad thoughts to the mind."

Unauthorized copying or reuse of any part of this page is illegal.

CONTINUE

588

11

Modeled Radial Growth of Sugar Maple Trees

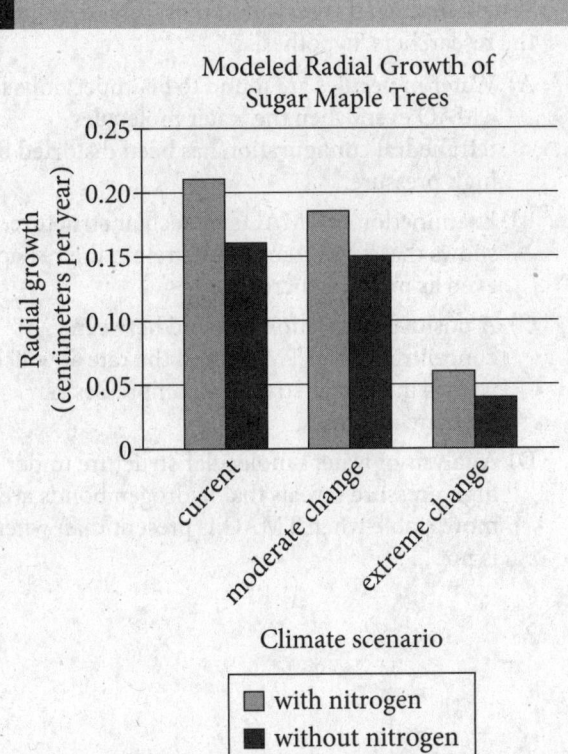

Climate scenario

- ■ with nitrogen
- ■ without nitrogen

Inés Ibáñez and colleagues studied a forest site in which some sugar maple trees receive periodic fertilization with nitrogen to mimic the broader trend of increasing anthropogenic nitrogen deposition in soil. Ibáñez and colleagues modeled the radial growth of the trees with and without nitrogen fertilization under three different climate scenarios (the current climate, moderate change, and extreme change). Although they found that climate change would negatively affect growth, they concluded that anthropogenic nitrogen deposition could more than offset that effect provided that change is moderate rather than extreme.

Which choice best describes data from the graph that support Ibáñez and colleagues' conclusion?

A) Growth with nitrogen under the current climate exceeded growth with nitrogen under moderate change, but the latter exceeded growth without nitrogen under extreme change.

B) Growth without nitrogen under the current climate exceeded growth without nitrogen under moderate change, but the latter exceeded growth with nitrogen under extreme change.

C) Growth with nitrogen under moderate change exceeded growth without nitrogen under moderate change, but the latter exceeded growth without nitrogen under extreme change.

D) Growth with nitrogen under moderate change exceeded growth without nitrogen under the current climate, but the latter exceeded growth with nitrogen under extreme change.

Unauthorized copying or reuse of any part of this page is illegal.

CONTINUE ▶

589

12

Under normal atmospheric pressure at Earth's surface, water molecules form a tetrahedral network stabilized by hydrogen bonds between adjacent molecules. Extreme high pressure, such as can be found in deep ocean waters, destabilizes these bonds and compresses water's structure, allowing water molecules within organisms to permeate proteins and impede crucial biological functions; yet deep-sea organisms known as piezophiles have adapted to extreme pressure. Studies have found a positive correlation between the depths that various piezophiles inhabit and concentrations of a compound called trimethylamine N-oxide (TMAO) in their muscle tissues, which has led a team of researchers to hypothesize that TMAO reduces water's compressibility.

Which finding, if true, would most directly support the researchers' hypothesis?

A) Water molecules are found to be impervious to TMAO even when the water molecules' tetrahedral configuration has been distorted by high pressure.

B) Examination of TMAO's molecular structure shows that TMAO molecules retain their shape even as pressure increases.

C) A positive correlation is found between concentrations of TMAO and the rate at which water's molecular structure compresses as pressure increases.

D) Analysis of water's molecular structure under high pressure reveals that hydrogen bonds are more stable when TMAO is present than when it is not.

CONTINUE

13

Simulated Change in Annual Aquifer Input and Irrigation Output if
Precipitation Concentration Increases as Climate Models Predict

Baseline concentration of annual precipitation	% change in water entering aquifers	% change in surface water used for irrigation	% change in groundwater used for irrigation
Precipitation is currently somewhat concentrated	4.9	0.4	0.9
Precipitation is currently evenly distributed	11.0	9.0	7.9

Some climate models for the western United States predict that while total annual precipitation may remain unchanged from the present level, precipitation will become concentrated into fewer but more intense rain and snow events. University of Texas climate scientist Geeta Persad and her colleagues simulated how the amount of water entering aquifers and the amount being used for irrigation purposes would change if this were to occur. Persad and her colleagues concluded that concentration of precipitation into fewer events would result in a higher number of dry days, triggering more irrigation, but that this change in irrigation output is highly sensitive to the baseline concentration of precipitation that currently exists in an area.

Which choice best describes data from the table that support Persad and her colleagues' conclusion?

A) If baseline precipitation is somewhat concentrated, the amount of water being used for irrigation will increase 0.4% for surface water and 0.9% for groundwater, whereas the amount of water entering aquifers will increase 11.0% if baseline precipitation is evenly distributed.

B) If baseline precipitation is somewhat concentrated, water use for irrigation will increase only slightly, whereas it will increase 9.0% for surface water and 7.9% for groundwater if baseline precipitation is evenly distributed.

C) If baseline precipitation is somewhat concentrated, the amount of water entering aquifers will increase 4.9%, while the amount being used for irrigation will increase 0.4% for surface water and 0.9% for groundwater.

D) If baseline precipitation is somewhat concentrated, water use for irrigation will decline by a small amount, whereas it will increase 11.0% for surface water and 9.0% for groundwater if baseline precipitation is evenly distributed.

CONTINUE

14

In a 2013 study, Agness Gidna, José Yravedra, and Manuel Domínguez-Rodrigo compared the feeding behaviors of wild lions in Tanzania's Tarangire National Park with those of captive lions in Spain's Cabárceno Reserve. The researchers noted that previous studies focused on other carnivores have shown that providing animals with food at regular intervals, as is common in captive settings, may inadvertently facilitate the development of novel stereotypic (i.e., purposelessly repetitive) behaviors by reducing the need for a high degree of cognitive engagement with the environment; the researchers were therefore not altogether surprised to find that _____

Which choice most logically completes the text?

A) bones from carcasses provided to captive lions showed signs of extensive gnawing beyond the point of nutrient extraction, whereas bones from prey hunted by wild lions did not.

B) during feeding episodes, captive male lions showed much more aggression than did wild male lions, whereas female captive and wild lions showed similar levels of aggression.

C) when caretakers placed food in boxes that were cognitively demanding to open, captive lions showed repeated behaviors similar to those that wild lions show when stalking prey.

D) captive lions showed a stereotypic behavior of pacing in their enclosures as feeding times approached, whereas wild lions showed a stereotypic behavior of pacing before embarking on a hunt.

15

In Auguste Escoffier's 1903 cookbook titled *Le Guide Culinaire*, the chef included over 5,000 dishes, including Oeufs Aurore (baked eggs), Gambas (jumbo shrimp) in garlic sauce, and Tarte aux Pignons (pine nut tart). Such iconic French recipes, described in surprisingly brief detail in *Le Guide Culinaire*, _____ the Victorian French cuisine Escoffier sought to preserve in his encyclopedic book.

Which choice completes the text so that it conforms to the conventions of Standard English?

A) epitomize

B) has epitomized

C) epitomizes

D) was epitomizing

16

Consider the mechanics of the pinhole camera: light passes through a small hole, resulting in a focused projected image. A ray diagram reveals how this _____ the hole's small size restricts light to a single ray, all light passing through the hole can only arrive at a single destination, eliminating diffraction and ensuring a clear image.

Which choice completes the text so that it conforms to the conventions of Standard English?

A) works because

B) works. Because

C) works, it's because

D) works: it's because

CONTINUE →

17

Long attributed to Jacques-Louis David, the preeminent Neoclassical painter of his day, the 1801 painting *Marie Joséphine Charlotte du Val d'Ognes* gained fresh attention in the 1990s when art historians discovered that the painting—which depicts a solitary young woman sketching—was actually the work of little-known French portrait _____ Marie-Denise Villers (1774–1821).

Which choice completes the text so that it conforms to the conventions of Standard English?

A) artist—

B) artist

C) artist:

D) artist,

18

In 1986, conceptual artist Sophie Calle asked twenty-three people, all of whom had been born without sight, to describe "their image of beauty" in rich detail. Calle paired excerpts of these conversations with photographs—both of interviewees and the items they _____ to powerful effect in her exhibition *The Blind.*

Which choice completes the text so that it conforms to the conventions of Standard English?

A) described, from hair to grass to sculptures

B) described, from hair to grass to sculptures—

C) described—from hair to grass to sculptures,

D) described: from hair to grass to sculptures

19

American abstract artist Richard _____ his installations to make passersby keenly aware of how one's movements are affected by the physical features of one's environment, assembles large-scale steel plates into sculptures that dominate the outdoor spaces they occupy.

Which choice completes the text so that it conforms to the conventions of Standard English?

A) Serra is intending

B) Serra, intends

C) Serra, intending

D) Serra intends

20

A species of *Byropsis* algae produces toxins to avoid being eaten by predators. However, in some cases, the toxins the organism uses to protect itself from predation actually _____ its attractiveness to predators. The Hawaiian sea slug, for example, not only tolerates *Byropsis* toxins but actually uses them for protection in the same way the algae does.

Which choice completes the text so that it conforms to the conventions of Standard English?

A) is increasing

B) increase

C) increases

D) has increased

21

Historians agree that the jazz pianist Jelly Roll Morton was exaggerating when he claimed to have invented jazz music. No one can deny, _____ that Morton's innovative compositions and remarkable improvisational skills helped shape jazz as a genre during its early years.

Which choice completes the text with the most logical transition?

A) therefore,

B) in the second place,

C) in other words,

D) though,

Unauthorized copying or reuse of any part of this page is illegal.

CONTINUE

593

22

Biographer Michael Gorra notes that the novelist Henry James "lived in a world of second thoughts," frequently tinkering with his novels and stories after their initial publication. However, the differences between the 1881 first edition and the 1908 edition of his novel *A Portrait of a Lady* are extreme, even by James's standards; _____ some critics regard the two editions as two different novels altogether.

Which choice completes the text with the most logical transition?

A) by contrast,

B) in fact,

C) nevertheless,

D) in other words,

23

In hindsight, given the ideas about the natural world circulating among British scientists in the 1800s, the theory of natural selection was an obvious next step. It may not have been a coincidence, _____ that Charles Darwin and Alfred Wallace arrived at the concept independently. Indeed, contrary to the popular myth of the lone genius, theirs is not the first paradigm-shifting theory to have emerged from multiple scholars working in parallel.

Which choice completes the text with the most logical transition?

A) however,

B) then,

C) moreover,

D) for example,

24

In a recent study, researchers examined the sleeping and waking habits of a group of dairy cows to determine if the cows' patterns of activity suggested that the animals were diurnal, nocturnal, or crepuscular. _____ the researchers studied whether the cows were most active in the daytime (diurnal), nighttime (nocturnal), or at dawn and dusk (crepuscular).

Which choice completes the text with the most logical transition?

A) Afterward,

B) In other words,

C) Additionally,

D) However,

25

While researching a topic, a student has taken the following notes:

- Earthquakes start at a point called a "focus" and spread out from there as seismic waves.
- The two types of seismic waves that travel beneath Earth's surface are primary waves (P waves) and secondary waves (S waves).
- P waves travel more quickly beneath Earth's surface than do S waves.
- P waves compress and expand the ground, causing it to move backward and forward.
- S waves cause the ground to move from side to side.

The student wants to emphasize a similarity between P waves and S waves. Which choice most effectively uses relevant information from the notes to accomplish this goal?

A) P waves and S waves both travel beneath Earth's surface, causing the ground to move.

B) P waves travel away from an earthquake's starting point at a higher rate of speed than do S waves.

C) Spreading out from the focus of an earthquake, P waves move the ground backward and forward.

D) Although P waves and S waves start at the same point, they behave very differently.

Unauthorized copying or reuse of any part of this page is illegal.

594

CONTINUE

26

While researching a topic, a student has taken the following notes:

- The US Fish and Wildlife Service (FWS) keeps a list of all at-risk species.
- Species on the list are classified as either endangered or threatened.
- A species that is in danger of extinction throughout most or all of its range is classified as endangered.
- A species that is likely to soon become endangered is classified as threatened.
- The California red-legged frog (*Rana draytonii*) is likely to soon become endangered, according to the FWS.

The student wants to indicate the California red-legged frog's FWS classification category. Which choice most effectively uses relevant information from the notes to accomplish this goal?

A) Species on the FWS list, which includes the California red-legged frog (*Rana draytonii*), are classified as either endangered or threatened.

B) The California red-legged frog (*Rana draytonii*) appears on the FWS list of at-risk species.

C) According to the FWS, the California red-legged frog is in the endangered category, in danger of extinction throughout most or all of its range.

D) Likely to soon become endangered, the California red-legged frog is classified as threatened by the FWS.

27

While researching a topic, a student has taken the following notes:

- The ancient Arab dhow was a sailing vessel distinguishable by its triangular sails and stitched hull construction.
- Dhows were used primarily for trade along the coasts of Arab, South Asian, and East African countries.
- Contemporary shipbuilders in Oman use a mix of modern and traditional materials to build replicas of ancient dhows.
- Most of the materials used are traditional.
- Replica hulls are stitched together using the same traditional coconut palm fiber rope used on the hulls of ancient dhows.

The student wants to make a generalization about the materials used in dhow replicas. Which choice most effectively uses relevant information from the notes to accomplish this goal?

A) A traditional material that was used to stitch together the hulls of ancient dhows, coconut palm fiber rope is still used by shipbuilders.

B) The ancient Arab dhow was a sailing vessel used primarily for trade and distinguishable by its triangular sails.

C) Although most materials used in dhow replicas are traditional, some modern materials are used.

D) Contemporary shipbuilders in Oman build replicas of the dhow, which was an ancient sailing vessel with a stitched hull construction.

STOP

If you finish before time is called, you may check your work on this module only. Do not turn to any other module in the test.

Math

22 QUESTIONS

DIRECTIONS

The questions in this section address a number of important math skills.
Use of a calculator is permitted for all questions.

NOTES

Unless otherwise indicated:

- All variables and expressions represent real numbers.
- Figures provided are drawn to scale.
- All figures lie in a plane.
- The domain of a given function f is the set of all real numbers x for which $f(x)$ is a real number.

REFERENCE

$A = \pi r^2$
$C = 2\pi r$

$A = \ell w$

$A = \frac{1}{2}bh$

$c^2 = a^2 + b^2$

Special Right Triangles

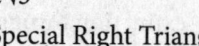

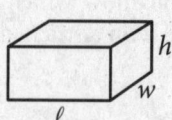

$V = \ell wh$

$V = \pi r^2 h$

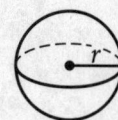

$V = \frac{4}{3}\pi r^3$

$V = \frac{1}{3}\pi r^2 h$

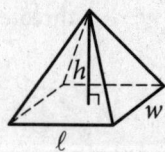

$V = \frac{1}{3}\ell wh$

The number of degrees of arc in a circle is 360.

The number of radians of arc in a circle is 2π.

The sum of the measures in degrees of the angles of a triangle is 180.

CONTINUE ➜

For multiple-choice questions, solve each problem, choose the correct answer from the choices provided, and then circle your answer in this book. Circle only one answer for each question. If you change your mind, completely erase the circle. You will not get credit for questions with more than one answer circled, or for questions with no answers circled.

For student-produced response questions, solve each problem and write your answer next to or under the question in the test book as described below.

- Once you've written your answer, circle it clearly. You will not receive credit for anything written outside the circle, or for any questions with more than one circled answer.

- If you find **more than one correct answer**, write and circle only one answer.

- Your answer can be up to 5 characters for a **positive** answer and up to 6 characters (including the negative sign) for a **negative** answer, but no more.

- If your answer is a **fraction** that is too long (over 5 characters for positive, 6 characters for negative), write the decimal equivalent.

- If your answer is a **decimal** that is too long (over 5 characters for positive, 6 characters for negative), truncate it or round at the fourth digit.

- If your answer is a **mixed number** (such as $3\frac{1}{2}$), write it as an improper fraction (7/2) or its decimal equivalent (3.5).

- Don't include **symbols** such as a percent sign, comma, or dollar sign in your circled answer.

CONTINUE

1

A certain bird species can fly at an average speed of 16 meters per second when in continuous flight. At this rate, how many meters would this bird species fly in 4 seconds?

A) 64

B) 20

C) 16

D) 12

2

Line r in the xy-plane has a slope of 4 and passes through the point $(0, 6)$. Which equation defines line r?

A) $y = -6x + 4$

B) $y = 6x + 4$

C) $y = 4x - 6$

D) $y = 4x + 6$

3

Which expression is equivalent to $5x^5 - 6x^4 + 8x^3$?

A) $x^4(5x - 6)$

B) $x^3(5x^2 - 6x + 8)$

C) $8x^3(5x^2 - 6x + 1)$

D) $6x^5(-6x^4 + 8x^3 + 1)$

4

The equation $x + y = 1,440$ represents the number of minutes of daylight (between sunrise and sunset), x, and the number of minutes of non-daylight, y, on a particular day in Oak Park, Illinois. If this day has 670 minutes of daylight, how many minutes of non-daylight does it have?

A) 670

B) 770

C) 1,373

D) 1,440

5

Scott selected 20 employees at random from all 400 employees at a company. He found that 16 of the employees in this sample are enrolled in exactly three professional development courses this year. Based on Scott's findings, which of the following is the best estimate of the number of employees at the company who are enrolled in exactly three professional development courses this year?

A) 4

B) 320

C) 380

D) 384

CONTINUE

6

$$7(2x - 3) = 63$$

Which equation has the same solution as the given equation?

A) $2x - 3 = 9$

B) $2x - 3 = 56$

C) $2x - 21 = 63$

D) $2x - 21 = 70$

7

$$c - 7 = 25p + k$$

The given equation relates the positive numbers c, p, and k. Which equation correctly expresses c in terms of p and k?

A) $c = 25p + k + 7$

B) $c = 25p + k - 7$

C) $c = 7(25p + k)$

D) $c = \dfrac{25p + k}{7}$

8

A function p estimates that there were 2,000 animals in a population in 1998. Each year from 1998 to 2010, the function estimates that the number of animals in this population increased by 3% of the number of animals in the population the previous year. Which equation defines this function, where $p(x)$ is the estimated number of animals in the population x years after 1998?

A) $p(x) = 2,000(3)^x$

B) $p(x) = 2,000(1.97)^x$

C) $p(x) = 2,000(1.03)^x$

D) $p(x) = 2,000(0.97)^x$

9

Which expression is equivalent to $(x^2 + 11)^2 + (x - 5)(x + 5)$?

A) $x^4 + 23x^2 - 14$

B) $x^4 + 23x^2 + 96$

C) $x^4 + 12x^2 + 121$

D) $x^4 + x^2 + 146$

10

An egg is thrown from a rooftop. The equation $h = -4.9t^2 + 9t + 18$ represents this situation, where h is the height of the egg above the ground, in meters, t seconds after it is thrown. According to the equation, what is the height, in meters, from which the egg was thrown?

11

If $4\sqrt{2x} = 16$, what is the value of $6x$?

A) 24

B) 48

C) 72

D) 96

12

The relationship between two variables, x and y, is linear. For every increase in the value of x by 1, the value of y increases by 8. When the value of x is 2, the value of y is 18. Which equation represents this relationship?

A) $y = 2x + 18$

B) $y = 2x + 8$

C) $y = 8x + 2$

D) $y = 3x + 26$

CONTINUE

13

$$x^2 = -841$$

How many distinct real solutions does the given equation have?

A) Exactly one

B) Exactly two

C) Infinitely many

D) Zero

14

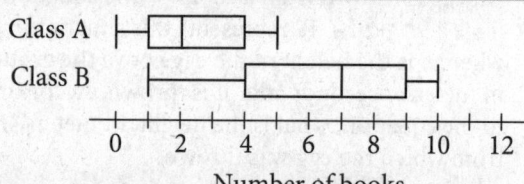

The two box plots show the distribution of number of books read over the summer by the students in two different English classes. What is the positive difference between the ranges of number of books read over the summer for the two classes?

15

The length of the edge of the base of a right square prism is 6 units. The volume of the prism is 2,880 cubic units. What is the height, in units, of the prism?

A) $4\sqrt{30}$

B) 36

C) $24\sqrt{5}$

D) 80

16

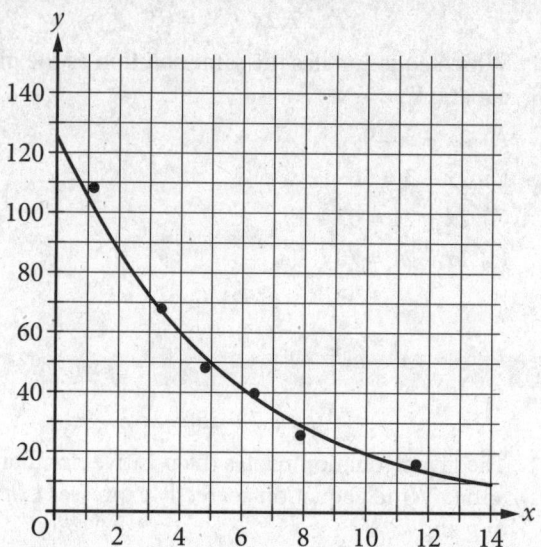

The scatterplot shows the relationship between two variables, x and y. An equation for the exponential model shown can be written as $y = a(b)^x$, where a and b are positive constants. Which of the following is closest to the value of b?

A) 0.83

B) 1.83

C) 18.36

D) 126.35

17

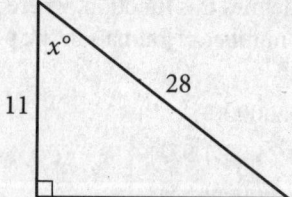

Note: Figure not drawn to scale.

In the triangle shown, what is the value of $\cos x°$?

CONTINUE

$$(x + 2)(x - 5)(x + 9) = 0$$

What is a positive solution to the given equation?

A) 3

B) 4

C) 5

D) 18

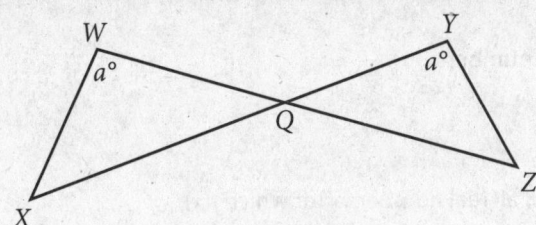

Note: Figure not drawn to scale.

In the figure shown, $\overline{WZ}$ and $\overline{XY}$ intersect at point Q. $YQ = 63$, $WQ = 70$, $WX = 60$, and $XQ = 120$. What is the length of $\overline{YZ}$?

The function g is defined by $g(x) = (x + 14)(t - x)$, where t is a constant. In the xy-plane, the graph of $y = g(x)$ passes through the point $(24, 0)$. What is the value of $g(0)$?

21

The number of zebras in a population in 2018 was 1.27 times the number of zebras in this population in 2014. If the number of zebras in this population in 2014 is p% of the number of zebras in this population in 2018, what is the value of p, to the nearest whole number?

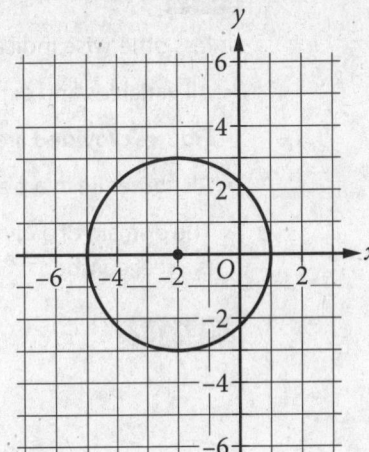

22

Circle A (shown) is defined by the equation $(x + 2)^2 + y^2 = 9$. Circle B (not shown) is the result of shifting circle A down 6 units and increasing the radius so that the radius of circle B is 2 times the radius of circle A. Which equation defines circle B?

A) $(x + 2)^2 + (y + 6)^2 = (4)(9)$

B) $2(x + 2)^2 + 2(y + 6)^2 = 9$

C) $(x + 2)^2 + (y - 6)^2 = (4)(9)$

D) $2(x + 2)^2 + 2(y - 6)^2 = 9$

STOP

If you finish before time is called, you may check your work on this module only.
Do not turn to any other module in the test.

Math

22 QUESTIONS

The questions in this section address a number of important math skills.
Use of a calculator is permitted for all questions.

NOTES

Unless otherwise indicated:

- All variables and expressions represent real numbers.

- Figures provided are drawn to scale.

- All figures lie in a plane.

- The domain of a given function f is the set of all real numbers x for which $f(x)$ is a real number.

REFERENCE

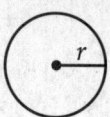 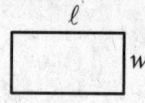 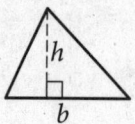 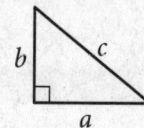 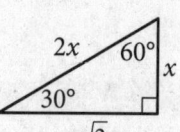

$A = \pi r^2$ $A = \ell w$ $A = \frac{1}{2}bh$ $c^2 = a^2 + b^2$ Special Right Triangles
$C = 2\pi r$

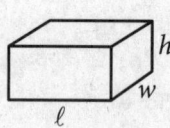 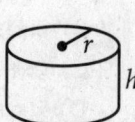  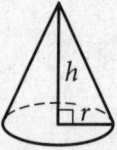 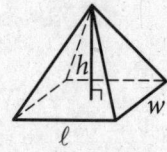

$V = \ell wh$ $V = \pi r^2 h$ $V = \frac{4}{3}\pi r^3$ $V = \frac{1}{3}\pi r^2 h$ $V = \frac{1}{3}\ell wh$

The number of degrees of arc in a circle is 360.

The number of radians of arc in a circle is 2π.

The sum of the measures in degrees of the angles of a triangle is 180.

Unauthorized copying or reuse of any part of this page is illegal.

CONTINUE ➡

602

For multiple-choice questions, solve each problem, choose the correct answer from the choices provided, and then circle your answer in this book. Circle only one answer for each question. If you change your mind, completely erase the circle. You will not get credit for questions with more than one answer circled, or for questions with no answers circled.

For student-produced response questions, solve each problem and write your answer next to or under the question in the test book as described below.

- Once you've written your answer, circle it clearly. You will not receive credit for anything written outside the circle, or for any questions with more than one circled answer.

- If you find **more than one correct answer**, write and circle only one answer.

- Your answer can be up to 5 characters for a **positive** answer and up to 6 characters (including the negative sign) for a **negative** answer, but no more.

- If your answer is a **fraction** that is too long (over 5 characters for positive, 6 characters for negative), write the decimal equivalent.

- If your answer is a **decimal** that is too long (over 5 characters for positive, 6 characters for negative), truncate it or round at the fourth digit.

- If your answer is a **mixed number** (such as $3\frac{1}{2}$), write it as an improper fraction (7/2) or its decimal equivalent (3.5).

- Don't include **symbols** such as a percent sign, comma, or dollar sign in your circled answer.

Unauthorized copying or reuse of any part of this page is illegal.

CONTINUE ➡

603

1

How many <u>meters</u> are equivalent to 2,300 centimeters? (100 centimeters = 1 meter)

A) 0.043

B) 23

C) 2,400

D) 230,000

2

The function f is defined by $f(x) = 8x$. For what value of x does $f(x) = 72$?

A) 8

B) 9

C) 64

D) 80

3

What is 20% of 440?

A) 44

B) 88

C) 880

D) 1,760

4

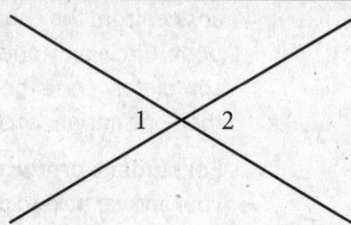

Note: Figure not drawn to scale.

In the figure, two lines intersect at a point. Angle 1 and angle 2 are vertical angles. The measure of angle 1 is 72°. What is the measure of angle 2?

A) 72°

B) 108°

C) 144°

D) 288°

5

$$(p + 3) + 8 = 10$$

What value of p is the solution to the given equation?

A) −1

B) 5

C) 15

D) 21

CONTINUE ➡

6

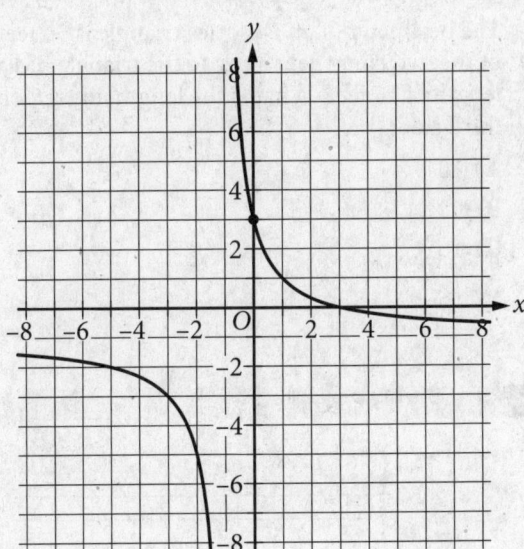

What is the y-coordinate of the y-intercept of the graph shown?

7

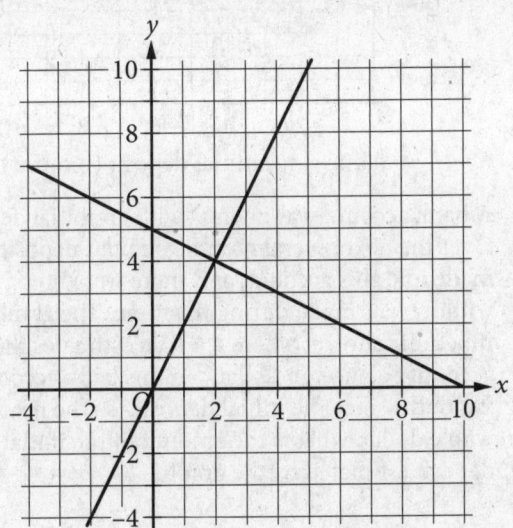

The graph of a system of linear equations is shown. What is the solution (x, y) to the system?

A) $(0, 5)$

B) $(2, 4)$

C) $(5, 10)$

D) $(10, 0)$

8

$$k^2 - 53 = 91$$

What is the positive solution to the given equation?

A) 144

B) 72

C) 38

D) 12

9

$$x = 8$$
$$x + 3y = 26$$

The solution to the given system of equations is (x, y). What is the value of y?

10

During a portion of a flight, a small airplane's cruising speed varied between 150 miles per hour and 170 miles per hour. Which inequality best represents this situation, where s is the cruising speed, in miles per hour, during this portion of the flight?

A) $s \leq 20$

B) $s \leq 150$

C) $s \leq 170$

D) $150 \leq s \leq 170$

CONTINUE

11

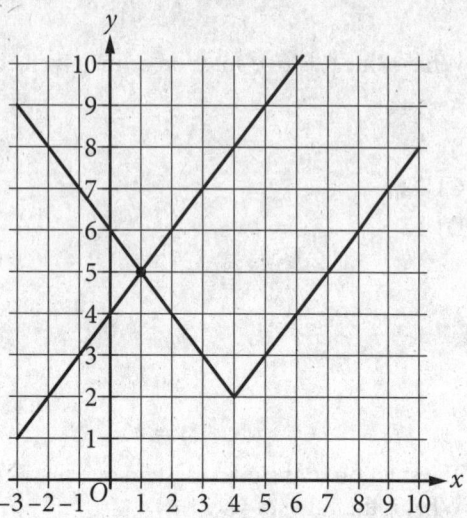

The graph of a system of an absolute value function and a linear function is shown. What is the solution (x, y) to this system of two equations?

A) $(-1, 5)$

B) $(0, 4)$

C) $(1, 5)$

D) $(4, 2)$

12

The function g is defined by $g(x) = |x + 18|$. What is the value of $g(4)$?

A) -18

B) -4

C) 14

D) 22

13

The perimeter of an isosceles triangle is 36 feet. Each of the two congruent sides of the triangle has a length of 10 feet. What is the length, in feet, of the third side?

A) 10

B) 12

C) 16

D) 18

14

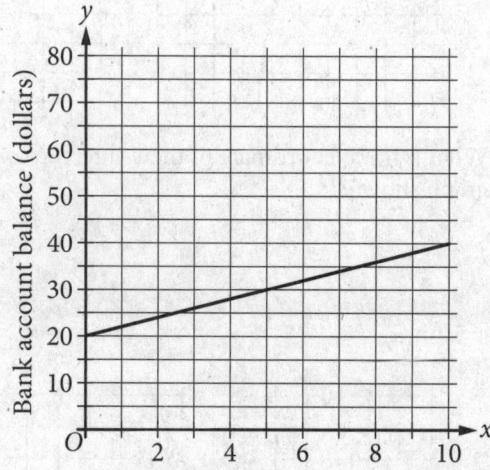

Time since initial deposit (months)

A bank account was opened with an initial deposit. Over the next several months, regular deposits were made into this account, and there were no withdrawals made during this time. The graph of the function f shown, where $y = f(x)$, estimates the account balance, in dollars, in this bank account x months since the initial deposit. To the nearest whole dollar, what is the amount of the initial deposit estimated by the graph?

CONTINUE

15

At a movie theater, there are a total of 350 customers. Each customer is located in either theater A, theater B, or theater C. If one of these customers is selected at random, the probability of selecting a customer who is located in theater A is 0.48, and the probability of selecting a customer who is located in theater B is 0.24. How many customers are located in theater C?

A) 28

B) 40

C) 84

D) 98

16

Brian saves $\frac{2}{5}$ of the \$215 he earns each week from his job. If Brian continues to save at this rate, how much money, in dollars, will Brian save in 9 weeks?

$$q(x) = 32(2^x)$$

Which table gives three values of x and their corresponding values of $q(x)$ for function q?

A)

x	−1	0	1
$q(x)$	−64	0	64

B)

x	−1	0	1
$q(x)$	$\frac{1}{16}$	2	64

C)

x	−1	0	1
$q(x)$	$\frac{1}{16}$	32	64

D)

x	−1	0	1
$q(x)$	16	32	64

A right circular cylinder has a base diameter of 22 centimeters and a height of 6 centimeters. What is the volume, in cubic centimeters, of the cylinder?

A) 132π

B) 264π

C) 726π

D) $2,904\pi$

What is the slope of the graph of $y = \frac{1}{3}(29x + 10) + 5x$

in the xy-plane?

A rectangle is inscribed in a circle, such that each vertex of the rectangle lies on the circumference of the circle. The diagonal of the rectangle is twice the length of the shortest side of the rectangle. The area of the rectangle is $1,089\sqrt{3}$ square units. What is the length, in units, of the diameter of the circle?

CONTINUE

21

$$2x - y > 883$$

For which of the following tables are all the values of x and their corresponding values of y solutions to the given inequality?

A)

x	y
440	0
441	−2
442	−4

B)

x	y
440	0
442	−2
441	−4

C)

x	y
442	0
440	−2
441	−4

D)

x	y
442	0
441	−2
440	−4

22

The combined original price for a mirror and a vase is $60. After a 25% discount to the mirror and a 45% discount to the vase are applied, the combined sale price for the two items is $39. Which system of equations gives the original price m, in dollars, of the mirror and the original price v, in dollars, of the vase?

A) $m + v = 60$
$0.55m + 0.75v = 39$

B) $m + v = 60$
$0.45m + 0.25v = 39$

C) $m + v = 60$
$0.75m + 0.55v = 39$

D) $m + v = 60$
$0.25m + 0.45v = 39$

STOP

If you finish before time is called, you may check your work on this module only.
Do not turn to any other module in the test.

Test begins on the next page.

Math

22 QUESTIONS

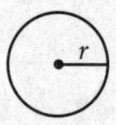 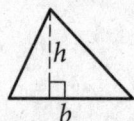 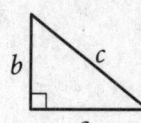 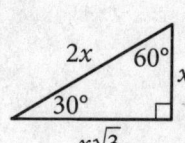

$A = \pi r^2$
$C = 2\pi r$ $\qquad A = \ell w \qquad A = \frac{1}{2}bh \qquad c^2 = a^2 + b^2 \qquad$ Special Right Triangles

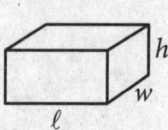 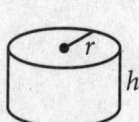  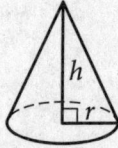 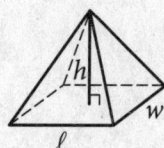

$V = \ell wh \qquad V = \pi r^2 h \qquad V = \frac{4}{3}\pi r^3 \qquad V = \frac{1}{3}\pi r^2 h \qquad V = \frac{1}{3}\ell wh$

The number of degrees of arc in a circle is 360.

The number of radians of arc in a circle is 2π.

The sum of the measures in degrees of the angles of a triangle is 180.

Unauthorized copying or reuse of any part of this page is illegal.

CONTINUE ➤

610

For multiple-choice questions, solve each problem, choose the correct answer from the choices provided, and then circle your answer in this book. Circle only one answer for each question. If you change your mind, completely erase the circle. You will not get credit for questions with more than one answer circled, or for questions with no answers circled.

For student-produced response questions, solve each problem and write your answer next to or under the question in the test book as described below.

- Once you've written your answer, circle it clearly. You will not receive credit for anything written outside the circle, or for any questions with more than one circled answer.

- If you find **more than one correct answer**, write and circle only one answer.

- Your answer can be up to 5 characters for a **positive** answer and up to 6 characters (including the negative sign) for a **negative** answer, but no more.

- If your answer is a **fraction** that is too long (over 5 characters for positive, 6 characters for negative), write the decimal equivalent.

- If your answer is a **decimal** that is too long (over 5 characters for positive, 6 characters for negative), truncate it or round at the fourth digit.

- If your answer is a **mixed number** (such as $3\frac{1}{2}$), write it as an improper fraction (7/2) or its decimal equivalent (3.5).

- Don't include **symbols** such as a percent sign, comma, or dollar sign in your circled answer.

Unauthorized copying or reuse of any part of this page is illegal.

CONTINUE ▶

611

1

A manager is responsible for ordering supplies for a shaved ice shop. The shop's inventory starts with 4,500 paper cups, and the manager estimates that 70 of these paper cups are used each day. Based on this estimate, in how many days will the supply of paper cups reach 1,700?

A) 20

B) 40

C) 60

D) 80

2

In $\triangle RST$, the measure of $\angle R$ is 63°. Which of the following could be the measure, in degrees, of $\angle S$?

A) 116

B) 118

C) 126

D) 180

3

$$y > 4x + 8$$

For which of the following tables are all the values of x and their corresponding values of y solutions to the given inequality?

A)

x	y
2	19
4	30
6	41

B)

x	y
2	8
4	16
6	24

C)

x	y
2	13
4	18
6	23

D)

x	y
2	13
4	21
6	29

4

The function f is defined by $f(x) = \frac{9}{7}x + \frac{8}{7}$. For what value of x does $f(x) = 5$?

CONTINUE

5

During a portion of a flight, a small airplane's cruising speed varied between 150 miles per hour and 170 miles per hour. Which inequality best represents this situation, where s is the cruising speed, in miles per hour, during this portion of the flight?

A) $s \leq 20$

B) $s \leq 150$

C) $s \leq 170$

D) $150 \leq s \leq 170$

6

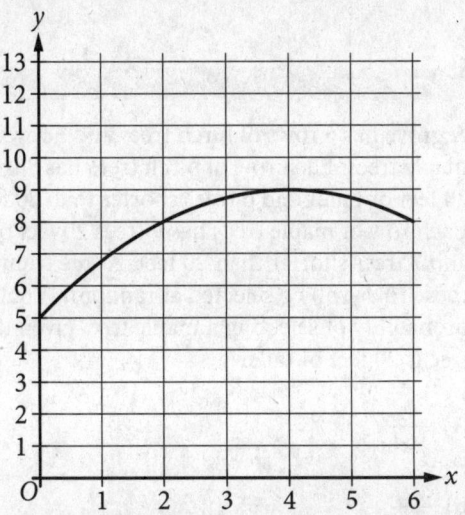

The graph models the number of active projects a company was working on x months after the end of November 2012, where $0 \leq x \leq 6$. According to the model, what is the predicted number of active projects the company was working on at the end of November 2012?

A) 0

B) 5

C) 8

D) 9

7

In the linear function h, $h(28) = 15$ and $h(26) = 22$. Which equation defines h?

A) $h(x) = -\frac{2}{7}x + 23$

B) $h(x) = -\frac{2}{7}x + 113$

C) $h(x) = -\frac{7}{2}x + 23$

D) $h(x) = -\frac{7}{2}x + 113$

8

Number of cars	Maximum number of passengers and crew
3	174
5	284
10	559

The table shows the linear relationship between the number of cars, c, on a commuter train and the maximum number of passengers and crew, p, that the train can carry. Which equation represents the linear relationship between c and p?

A) $55c - p = -9$

B) $55c - p = 9$

C) $55p - c = -9$

D) $55p - c = 9$

9

$$w^2 + 12w - 40 = 0$$

Which of the following is a solution to the given equation?

A) $6 - 2\sqrt{19}$

B) $2\sqrt{19}$

C) $\sqrt{19}$

D) $-6 + 2\sqrt{19}$

CONTINUE

10

What is the y-coordinate of the y-intercept of the graph of $\frac{3x}{7} = -\frac{5y}{9} + 21$ in the xy-plane?

11

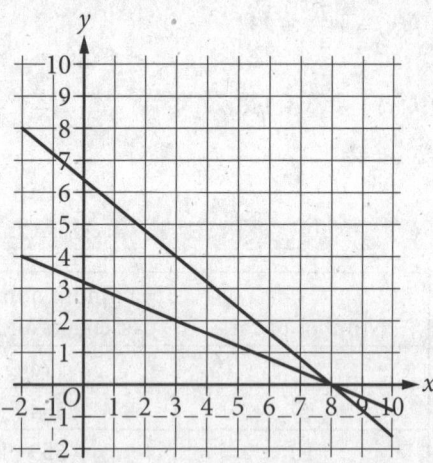

What system of linear equations is represented by the lines shown?

A) $8x + 4y = 32$
   $-10x - 4y = -64$

B) $8x - 4y = 32$
   $-10x + 4y = -64$

C) $4x - 10y = 32$
   $-8x + 10y = -64$

D) $4x + 10y = 32$
   $-8x - 10y = -64$

12

$$(x - 2) - 4(y + 7) = 117$$
$$(x - 2) + 4(y + 7) = 442$$

The solution to the given system of equations is (x, y). What is the value of $6(x - 2)$?

13

$$f(x) = x^2 - 48x + 2{,}304$$

What is the minimum value of the given function?

14

$$-49x = -98x$$

How many solutions does the given equation have?

A) Zero

B) Exactly one

C) Exactly two

D) Infinitely many

15

The function g is defined by $g(x) = x(x - 2)(x + 6)^2$. The value of $g(7 - w)$ is 0, where w is a constant. What is the sum of all possible values of w?

16

A grove has 6 rows of birch trees and 5 rows of maple trees. Each row of birch trees has 8 trees 20 feet or taller and 6 trees shorter than 20 feet. Each row of maple trees has 9 trees 20 feet or taller and 7 trees shorter than 20 feet. A tree from one of these rows will be selected at random. What is the probability of selecting a maple tree, given that the tree is 20 feet or taller?

A) $\frac{9}{164}$

B) $\frac{3}{10}$

C) $\frac{15}{31}$

D) $\frac{9}{17}$

17

A rectangle is inscribed in a circle, such that each vertex of the rectangle lies on the circumference of the circle. The diagonal of the rectangle is twice the length of the shortest side of the rectangle. The area of the rectangle is $1{,}089\sqrt{3}$ square units. What is the length, in units, of the diameter of the circle?

CONTINUE

18

The positive number a is 2,241% of the sum of the positive numbers b and c, and b is 83% of c. What percent of b is a?

A) 23.24%

B) 49.41%

C) 2,324%

D) 4,941%

19

$$\frac{7}{8}y - \frac{5}{8}x = \frac{4}{7} - \frac{7}{8}y$$

$$\frac{5}{4}x + \frac{7}{4} = py + \frac{15}{4}$$

In the given system of equations, p is a constant. If the system has no solution, what is the value of p?

20

x	$g(x)$
−27	3
−9	0
21	5

The table shows three values of x and their corresponding values of $g(x)$, where $g(x) = \dfrac{f(x)}{x+3}$ and f is a linear function. What is the y-intercept of the graph of $y = f(x)$ in the xy-plane?

A) $(0, 36)$

B) $(0, 12)$

C) $(0, 4)$

D) $(0, -9)$

21

A circle has center G, and points M and N lie on the circle. Line segments MH and NH are tangent to the circle at points M and N, respectively. If the radius of the circle is 168 millimeters and the perimeter of quadrilateral $GMHN$ is 3,856 millimeters, what is the distance, in millimeters, between points G and H?

A) 168

B) 1,752

C) 1,760

D) 1,768

22

The function f is defined by $f(x) = ax^2 + bx + c$, where a, b, and c are constants. The graph of $y = f(x)$ in the xy-plane passes through the points $(7, 0)$ and $(-3, 0)$. If a is an integer greater than 1, which of the following could be the value of $a + b$?

A) −6

B) −3

C) 4

D) 5

STOP

**If you finish before time is called, you may check your work on this module only.
Do not turn to any other module in the test.**

The SAT®

Practice Test #6

ANSWER EXPLANATIONS

These answer explanations are for students using
The Official SAT Study Guide.

Reading and Writing

Module 1
(27 questions)

QUESTION 1

Choice D is the best answer because it most logically completes the text's discussion of Carmen Lomas Garza's artistic process. In this context, "inspired by" means influenced by or motivated by. The text refers to how, regardless of the scale of the work, Garza uses her memories of Texas and details from California to create her art. If Garza is basing her work on her direct experiences, then they play a part in her artistic process. This context thus suggests that Garza's art is inspired by the experiences of her childhood in Texas and her current life in California.

Choice A is incorrect because it wouldn't make logical sense to indicate that Garza is "complimented by"—or praised by—something inanimate such as direct experience. *Choice B* is incorrect because describing Garza as "uncertain about"—or unsure or doubtful of—direct experience would suggest that she had misgivings about it. If Garza were unsure of her experiences, that would suggest that she couldn't recall them, and Garza wouldn't be able to represent direct experience in her art if she were uncertain of the memories or details. *Choice C* is incorrect because describing Garza as "unbothered by"—or uninterested in—her experience would imply the opposite of what the text suggests about Garza's artistic process. The text indicates that Garza's art comes from memories of her childhood in Texas and details of her surroundings in California.

QUESTION 2

Choice D is the best answer because it most logically completes the text's discussion of the art at the National Museum of the American Indian. In this context, "homogenous" means uniform or highly similar. The text explains that the painters whose works are included in this museum's collection employ an array of artistic styles, both Native and non-Native, traditional and new. Given this high degree of stylistic diversity, it is a misconception that Native art is uniform, or homogenous.

Choice A is incorrect because the text doesn't consider whether Native art is controversial, or causes disagreement or discussion; instead, the text discusses the stylistic diversity of the collection of the National Museum of the American Indian. *Choice B* is incorrect. Although the text indicates that some of the artists whose work is represented in the collection of the National Museum of the American Indian blend various artistic traditions into highly individual styles of their own, this is not the primary focus of the text. Instead, the text is concerned with how Native art is often mistakenly perceived as uniform, when in fact it is stylistically diverse. *Choice C* is incorrect because the text never implies that people mistakenly conceive of Native art as theoretical, or concerned with philosophical or abstract issues; instead, the text's discussion of Native art is framed around this art's stylistic diversity versus the misconception of it as homogenous.

QUESTION 3

Choice D is the best answer because it most logically completes the text's discussion of the *W* boson. In this context, "scale" means size or extent. The text indicates that recent measurements of the *W* boson were remarkable because they revealed the subatomic particle's mass to be much greater ("seven standard deviations higher") than had been expected based on a standard model. This context conveys not only that the measurements differed from predictions but also that the extent of the difference was very large.

Choice A is incorrect. Although the text indicates that there was a very large difference between the predicted mass and the actual measured mass of the subatomic particle, it doesn't explain the cause of, or reason behind, that difference. *Choice B* is incorrect because it wouldn't make sense to say that the measurements of the subatomic particle were notable because they differed from expectations and also because a difference existed between the measurements and what had been predicted; the text would be repeating the idea that there was a difference instead of adding to that idea. *Choice C* is incorrect because the text doesn't convey any implications of, or consequences of or conclusions drawn from, the fact that the mass of the subatomic particle differed from expectations; the context indicates only that the actual measured mass was much higher than the predicted mass.

QUESTION 4

Choice B is the best answer because it most logically completes the text's discussion of birdsong. In this context, "diminish" means reduce or lessen. The text establishes that birds sing to communicate over potentially large distances and that researchers believe that birds that live in densely vegetated habitats sing at lower frequencies than birds that live in comparatively sparsely vegetated habitats. The text then explains that researchers hold this belief due to some effect of dense vegetation on the distance that high-frequency sounds can travel. If birds sing to communicate over long distances, it would be logical to conclude that researchers believe that birds in densely vegetated habitats sing at lower frequencies than birds in relatively sparse habitats do because dense vegetation diminishes the distance that high-frequency sounds can travel.

Choice A is incorrect because nothing in the text suggests that dense vegetation can "exceed," or surpass or go beyond, the distance that high-frequency sounds can travel. The text suggests that dense vegetation reduces the distance that high-frequency sounds can travel, not that dense vegetation goes farther than that distance. *Choice C* is incorrect because it would not be sensible to say that dense vegetation can "encompass," or enclose or encircle, the distance that high-frequency sounds can travel. The distance that sounds can travel is not an object that can be enclosed or encircled by vegetation. *Choice D* is incorrect because there is no information in the text indicating that dense vegetation can "conceal," or hide or keep from being observed, the distance that high-frequency sounds travel. Instead, the text suggests that dense vegetation reduces the distance that high-frequency sounds can travel.

QUESTION 5

Choice C is the best answer because it most accurately describes the main purpose of the text, which is to portray Francie's determination to reach her goal of reading all the books in the world. The text indicates that to achieve this aim, Francie works systematically and persistently: she reads all the books in the library in alphabetical order and devotes much time and effort to the project, finishing one book per day over a long period of time. The text then suggests that even though she progresses slowly ("she was still in the B's") and that she struggled with some books ("some of the B's had been hard going"), she doesn't give up because she thinks of herself as "a reader." These details show Francie's resolve.

Choice A is incorrect. Although the text mentions several topics (bees and buffaloes, Bermuda vacations, and Byzantine architecture) that Francie has read about, it doesn't indicate that any of these topics are unusual or that she especially enjoyed reading about one of these topics in particular. If anything, the text suggests that she may have found some of these topics to be dull, saying that she even read the "dry ones"—that is, the boring books—and that some of the books were "hard going," meaning they were difficult to get through. *Choice B* is incorrect because the text doesn't discuss Francie's involvement in other activities, only her dedication to reading. Although it's possible that Francie dedicates herself to reading because she prefers it to other activities, the text doesn't indicate whether this is the case. *Choice D* is incorrect. Although the text mentions one author (Abbott) whose book Francie has read as well as several topics (bees and buffaloes, Bermuda vacations, and Byzantine architecture) she has encountered, the text doesn't say whether Francie admires any of the books she's read so far. Instead, the text focuses on the time and effort she devotes to reaching her goal of reading all the books in the world—even ones she doesn't enjoy.

QUESTION 6

Choice C is the best answer because it most effectively describes the function of the underlined portion. The text discusses the long-standing misconception that people in medieval Europe were uninterested in cleanliness and hygiene. As evidence that this idea is false, the text cites historian Eleanor Janega's assertion that in medieval Europe, towns usually had at least one bathhouse, where people could take immersion baths or steam baths for a fee. The underlined portion then notes that mainly town dwellers had access to these bathhouses. The remainder of the text explains that those who lacked such access were nonetheless able to bathe in outdoor waterways or take sponge baths at home. Therefore, the underlined portion concedes that some people in medieval Europe lacked access to public bathhouses.

Choice A is incorrect. The underlined portion establishes that amenities such as steam baths were mainly available to town dwellers, which suggests in turn that steam baths were largely unavailable to people in rural areas. Thus, the distinction made by the underlined portion is not between the popularity of steam baths in towns versus their lack of popularity in rural areas but instead between their presence in towns and absence in rural areas. *Choice B* is incorrect. Although the text does explain that recent historians have disproved the idea that medieval Europeans rarely bathed, it doesn't attribute that misconception to earlier historians of medieval Europe or suggest that their research was subject to limitations. Moreover, the underlined portion addresses a limitation of life in medieval Europe, not of historical research. *Choice D* is incorrect because the underlined portion doesn't address why historian Eleanor Janega decided to study the popularity of public bathhouses in medieval

Europe—nor does any portion of the text. The text mentions Janega in passing, but it doesn't go into detail about why she decided to study the popularity of public bathhouses in medieval Europe.

QUESTION 7

Choice B is the best answer because it most accurately describes the main purpose of the text, which is to establish that pianist Martha Argerich's performances appear easy because of her work to prepare for them. The text begins by stating that Argerich plays in such a way that it looks like the music is coming to her naturally in the moment, without planning. It goes on to point out that despite her skill and experience, Argerich works tirelessly and treats each piece of music as if it is new each time she performs it, and that it is this preparation that causes her playing to appear relaxed and natural. These details establish that the purpose of the text is to assert that Argerich's performances look effortless because of how she prepares for them.

Choice A is incorrect because the text doesn't address how Argerich selects the music she'll perform; instead, it describes how she approaches a piece of music in preparation for a performance. *Choice C* is incorrect because the text doesn't discuss kinds of music beyond stating that Argerich is a classical pianist, and it doesn't mention Argerich actually encountering any music for the first time; it indicates only that she approaches a piece of music she is going to perform as if she has never played it before. *Choice D* is incorrect because the text doesn't mention music that Argerich is actually performing for the first time, only that Argerich approaches the pieces she performs as if they are new each time; further, the text doesn't characterize this approach as unique, or something only Argerich does.

QUESTION 8

Choice B is the best answer because it reflects how the author of Text 2 would most likely respond to the underlined claim about the Clovis people in Text 1. Text 1 explains that the idea that the Clovis people were the first human inhabitants of North America has been overturned by the unearthing of stone tools in Chiquihuite Cave in Mexico. The tools were found in a layer of earth that is over 33,000 years old—much older than the Clovis people's arrival 13,000 years ago. The text ends with the claim that the tools reveal that humans lived in the cave long before the Clovis people reached the continent. Text 2, on the other hand, disputes the idea that the stone pieces are definitely tools. Text 2 states that the pieces are so roughly shaped that they may have simply naturally broken off from rocks and, moreover, that no other signs of human activity have been found in the cave. In other words, Text 2 argues that there is no proof yet that humans made the pieces as tools or were even present in the cave. Therefore, the author of Text 2 would most likely say that the claim that humans occupied Chiquihuite Cave long before the Clovis people reached North America rests on an assumption about the stone pieces—that they are human-made tools—that is not sufficiently supported by available evidence.

Choice A is incorrect because Text 1 doesn't claim that human inhabitants of Chiquihuite Cave and the Clovis people had any connection; the author of Text 1 focuses only on the timing of each group's presence in North America. Further, the author of Text 2 makes no mention of the Clovis people and indicates that it isn't clear yet that any human group did inhabit Chiquihuite Cave. *Choice C* is incorrect because nothing in Text 2 suggests that the author believes the stone pieces probably are human-made tools and will be confirmed as such by further analysis; instead, the author of Text 2 emphasizes the current lack of evidence of human activity in the cave. *Choice D* is incorrect because Text 2 focuses on the issue of characterizing the stone pieces as tools made by humans, not on the timing of any particular group's activity in North America; further, Text 1 seems to support the common belief that the Clovis people reached North America 13,000 years ago and challenges only the idea that they were the continent's first inhabitants. Therefore, there's no reason to think the author of Text 2 would say that the author of Text 1 overlooks evidence that the Clovis people were active as early as is commonly thought.

QUESTION 9

Choice A is the best answer because it most accurately states the main idea of the text. The text begins by explaining that many literary theorists rely on the concepts of *fabula* (a narrative's content) and *syuzhet* (a narrative's arrangement and presentation of events) and illustrates these concepts by explaining how they can be applied to the film *The Godfather Part II*. The text then discusses how Mikhail Bakhtin, a literary theorist, argued that *fabula* and *syuzhet* can't fully describe a narrative, since systematic categorizations such as these fail to account for all the ways in which interactions between the artist, the work, and the audience produce meaning. Thus, the main idea is that Bakhtin argued that there are important characteristics of narratives that are not fully encompassed by two concepts that other theorists have used to analyze narratives.

Choice B is incorrect because according to the text, Mikhail Bakhtin believed that meaning was created through the interactions of the artist, narrative, and audience, not simply through the interaction between the audience and narrative; moreover, the text doesn't address whether Bakhtin focused on the ways in which different people interpret narratives differently. *Choice C* is incorrect. Although the text implies that the storytelling methods used in *The Godfather Part II* are complicated, it discusses the film only to illustrate how the concepts of *fabula* and *syuzhet* may be applied to a narrative. The film's storytelling methods aren't the primary focus of the text. *Choice D* is incorrect. The text discusses *The Godfather Part II*, whose narrative doesn't adhere to a single chronological order, only to illustrate the concepts of *fabula* (a narrative's content) and *syuzhet* (a narrative's arrangement and presentation of events). The primary focus of this text isn't the structure of this film or of other narratives that are told out of chronological order; moreover, the text doesn't consider whether such structures make it harder for audiences to understand narratives.

QUESTION 10

Choice B is the best answer because it uses data from the table to complete the statement regarding a species for which the problem of finding a suitable habitat would be especially concerning. For each candidate species, the table lists its common name, scientific name, and when the species became extinct. The text explains that scientists pursuing de-extinction for the candidate species also consider the length of time that has passed since the species' extinction, noting that the longer the animal has been extinct, the less likely it is that a suitable habitat would exist for the species today. The possibility of not having a suitable habitat would be especially concerning for the candidate species for which the most time has passed since its extinction. According to the table this species would be the saber-toothed cat, which became extinct 11,000 years before present.

Choice A is incorrect because it compares the time since the extinction of the passenger pigeon to the time since the extinction of the huia instead of citing the species listed in the table that has been extinct the longest (the saber-toothed cat). The text indicates that the longer a species has been extinct, the lower the chances are that a suitable habitat exists for it today. Neither the table nor the text supports the claim that the passenger pigeon is especially vulnerable to this problem. *Choice C* is incorrect because the text states that the longer a species has been extinct, the less likely it is that there would be a suitable habitat available for the species today. So, the problem would be especially concerning for the saber-toothed cat, which became extinct several thousand years before the woolly mammoth did—not the other way around. *Choice D* is incorrect because the text states that the longer a species has been extinct, the lower the chances are that a suitable habitat would be available for that species today. According to the table, the Caribbean monk seal became extinct in 1952, which is the most recent extinction listed for a candidate species in the table.

QUESTION 11

Choice C is the best answer because it most effectively illustrates the claim that the narrator of "The Yellow Wallpaper" has mixed feelings about her surroundings. She says she is "really getting quite fond of the big room," a positive sentiment, but also describes the room's wallpaper as "horrid," a negative sentiment. Since some of her feelings about her surroundings are positive and others are negative, they are best described as mixed.

Choice A is incorrect because though the narrator describes the room's wallpaper as "irritating," a negative sentiment, she does not mention a positive sentiment. Thus, the quotation does not effectively illustrate the claim that the narrator has mixed feelings about her surroundings. *Choice B* is incorrect because it describes how the appearance of the room's wallpaper changes at night but does not mention the narrator's feelings about her surroundings. *Choice D* is incorrect because though the narrator describes the room's wallpaper as "repellant," a negative sentiment, she does not mention a positive sentiment. Thus, the quotation does not effectively illustrate the claim that the narrator has mixed feelings about her surroundings.

QUESTION 12

Choice B is the best answer because it most effectively uses data from the table to complete the comparison of how *Colobanthus quitensis* benefited from warming temperatures with how *Deschampsia antarctica* benefited from them. The table shows the land area covered by these two plant species at a site in Antarctica. According to the table, *Colobanthus quitensis* increased the area it covered by 55% from 2009 to 2018, whereas *Deschampsia antarctica* increased the area it covered by 28% during the same period. It therefore follows that *Colobanthus quitensis* saw a greater expansion than *Deschampsia antarctica* did and that *Colobanthus quitensis* increased the area of land it covered by more than half.

Choice A is incorrect because according to the table, *Deschampsia antarctica* covered 1,230 square meters of land in 2009 and 1,576 square meters of land in 2018. *Deschampsia antarctica* therefore covered a larger, not a smaller, area of land in 2018 than in 2009. Moreover, there's no information in the text or the table that suggests that one species of the plant suppressed the other. *Choice C* is incorrect because it inaccurately describes the data in the table. The table shows the land area covered by *Colobanthus quitensis* and *Deschampsia antarctica* and the percent increase in area covered by the two species from 2009 to 2018, not the average size of individual plants belonging to the two species. The data in the table therefore can't be used to make a comparison of the increase in individual plants' average size. *Choice D* is incorrect because the table shows the land area covered by *Colobanthus quitensis* and *Deschampsia antarctica* and the percent increase in area covered by the two species from

2009 to 2018, not the rate at which the species increased the area they covered. Moreover, there's nothing in the table or the text that suggests that the areas covered by the two species were newly freed from ice.

QUESTION 13

Choice B is the best answer because it presents a finding that, if true, would most directly support the idea advanced by Homero Gil de Zúñiga and Trevor Diehl that NFM ("news finds me") attitude may reduce voting probability through an indirect effect. The text describes NFM as an attitude that has lowered people's interest in actively acquiring news and introduces Gil de Zúñiga and Diehl's study on the effects of NFM on people in the United States' political knowledge and interest. The text goes on to say that despite the fact that the study didn't occur near a major election, Gil de Zúñiga and Diehl still conclude that NFM may reduce voting probability. If the likelihood, or probability, that a person will vote is linked to that person's level of political knowledge and interest, that would suggest that negatively affecting a person's level of political knowledge and interest would also negatively affect how likely that person is to vote. Thus, if NFM attitude has a negative effect on political knowledge and interest, then it would also likely reduce voting probability.

Choice A is incorrect because the finding that NFM attitude increases as major elections approach wouldn't address the effect of NFM on the likelihood of voting, which is the idea advanced by Gil de Zúñiga and Diehl. Moreover, although the text mentions that there were no major elections that occurred near the time of the study, it doesn't discern between major and minor elections when discussing voting probability. *Choice C* is incorrect because finding that NFM attitude shows little correlation with either political knowledge or political interest would undermine, not support, Gil de Zúñiga and Diehl's idea that NFM may reduce voting probability because it suggests that NFM has no effect on political knowledge or political interest. *Choice D* is incorrect. Although Gil de Zúñiga and Diehl's idea would be supported by the finding that the likelihood of voting increases as political knowledge increases, nothing in the text suggests that the researchers' idea hinges on the size of people's social networks.

QUESTION 14

Choice A is the best answer because it most logically completes the text's discussion of English dialects spoken in Scotland and the Upland South. The text indicates that these dialects share a feature: putting emphasis on the "r" sound when it appears in certain positions in words. The text goes on to state that records indicate the Upland South was colonized largely by people of Scottish ancestry. It is reasonable to assume that the English dialects spoken by these colonizers were influenced by the English dialects spoken by their ancestors in Scotland. It follows, then, that the emphasis on the "r" sound in the dialects in Scotland carried over into the Upland South dialects as they developed—that is, that the Upland South dialects likely acquired it from dialects spoken in Scotland.

Choice B is incorrect because the text suggests that Scottish ancestry explains the origin of the emphasis on the "r" sound in English dialects spoken in the Upland South, since that linguistic feature is also found in dialects spoken in Scotland; the text doesn't address any other dialects or suggest that the feature will spread elsewhere. *Choice C* is incorrect because the text indicates that many Upland South colonizers were the descendants of Scottish people, suggesting that the English dialects spoken by these colonizers had been influenced by the English dialects spoken by the colonizers' ancestors in Scotland and had acquired their emphasis on the "r" sound from those ancestors' dialects—not the other way around. *Choice D* is incorrect because the text indicates that the emphasis on the "r" sound is part of English dialects spoken in the Upland South today, which almost certainly wouldn't be the case if people from Scotland, who were the main colonizers of the Upland South, had eliminated that linguistic feature from their dialects.

QUESTION 15

Choice B is the best answer because it most logically completes the text's discussion of Smith and colleagues' investigation of the evolution and biological role of the appendix. The text indicates that the team found several instances of the appendix emerging and not disappearing in the lineages of various mammal species the team examined. Furthermore, the text states that species that possess an appendix also tend to have relatively high amounts of lymphoid tissue—a type of tissue that supports immune system function. Taken together, these details strongly support the hypothesis that the appendix has persisted in some species because it has a function that contributes to effective immune responses in those species.

Choice A is incorrect because the text doesn't address any nonmammalian species. *Choice C* is incorrect because the text doesn't make predictions about the evolutionary future of the species Smith and colleagues examined, and although the implication of the text is that the appendix likely does serve a function for the immune system, nothing in the text indicates that the appendix will become more widespread in the future. *Choice D* is incorrect. Although the text does suggest an association between having an appendix and relatively high concentrations of lymphoid tissue, it doesn't claim that the appendix causes the tissue to grow, nor does it address the relative production of the tissue at different periods of time.

QUESTION 16

Choice B is the best answer. The convention being tested is punctuation use between a subject and a verb. When, as in this case, a subject ("the strings inside the instrument") is immediately followed by a main verb ("are plucked"), no punctuation is needed.

Choice A is incorrect because no punctuation is needed between the subject and the verb. *Choice C* is incorrect because no punctuation is needed between the subject and the verb. *Choice D* is incorrect because no punctuation is needed between the subject and the verb.

QUESTION 17

Choice D is the best answer. The convention being tested is subject-verb agreement. The singular verb "creates" agrees in number with the singular subject "technique."

Choice A is incorrect because the plural verb "create" doesn't agree in number with the singular subject "technique." *Choice B* is incorrect because the plural verb "are creating" doesn't agree in number with the singular subject "technique." *Choice C* is incorrect because the plural verb "have created" doesn't agree in number with the singular subject "technique."

QUESTION 18

Choice B is the best answer. The convention being tested is end-of-sentence punctuation. This choice correctly uses a period to punctuate a declarative sentence that asks an indirect question ("The toxic nature of some of these materials recently led a team from the University of Sheffield to investigate how their use could be better regulated").

Choice A is incorrect because the structure requires a period and a declarative clause at the end of the sentence that states what the team investigated, not an interrogative clause that asks a direct question, such as "how could their use be better regulated?" *Choice C* is incorrect because it's unconventional to use a question mark in this way to punctuate a declarative sentence. *Choice D* is incorrect because the structure requires a declarative clause at the end of the sentence that states what the team investigated, not an interrogative clause that asks a direct question, such as "how could their use be better regulated?"

QUESTION 19

Choice B is the best answer. The convention being tested is the use of verbs to express tense. In this choice, the present tense verb "illuminates" is consistent with the other present tense verb ("is") used to describe the sculpture, correctly indicating that the sculpture habitually glows ("each night") and that the lamp inside is the source of its illumination.

Choice A is incorrect because the future progressive tense verb "will be illuminating" isn't consistent with the other present tense verb used to describe the sculpture and the source of its glow. *Choice C* is incorrect because the modal "would," which is used to indicate a typical behavior in the past, isn't consistent with the other present tense verb used to describe the sculpture and the source of its glow. *Choice D* is incorrect because the past tense verb "illuminated" isn't consistent with the other present tense verb used to describe the sculpture and the source of its glow.

QUESTION 20

Choice D is the best answer. The conventions being tested are the use of possessive nouns and the use of possessive determiners. The singular possessive noun "phrase's" correctly indicates that there is only one simple phrase. The singular possessive determiner "its" agrees in number with the singular possessive noun "phrase's," reinforcing the idea that there is only one simple yet complex phrase.

Choice A is incorrect because the context requires the singular possessive noun "phrase's," not the plural possessive noun "phrases'." *Choice B* is incorrect because the context requires the singular possessive noun "phrase's" and the corresponding singular possessive determiner "its," not the plural noun "phrases" and the corresponding plural possessive determiner "their." *Choice C* is incorrect because the context requires the singular possessive determiner "its," not the plural possessive determiner "their."

QUESTION 21

Choice A is the best answer. The convention being tested is the use of punctuation around noun phrases. No punctuation is needed because the noun phrase "Tamatoa the crab" is a restrictive appositive, meaning that it provides essential identifying information about the noun phrase before it, "the character." Additionally, no punctuation is needed between the noun phrase "the deep and humorous voice...crab" and the verb "belongs" that indicates whom the voice belongs to.

Choice B is incorrect because no punctuation is needed. *Choice C* is incorrect because no punctuation is needed. *Choice D* is incorrect because no punctuation is needed.

QUESTION 22

Choice D is the best answer. "As a result" logically signals that the information in this sentence—the vessel turning black—is a result of the heating technique discussed in the previous sentence.

Choice A is incorrect because "on the contrary" illogically signals that the information in this sentence directly opposes the heating technique in the previous sentence. Instead, the vessel turns black as a result of that technique. *Choice B* is incorrect because "for example" illogically signals that the information in this sentence is an example of the heating technique in the previous sentence. Instead, the vessel turns black as a result of that technique. *Choice C* is incorrect because "previously" illogically signals that the information in this sentence occurs earlier in a chronological series of events than does the heating technique discussed in the first two sentences. Instead, the vessel turns black as a result of that technique.

QUESTION 23

Choice D is the best answer. "Likewise" logically signals that the information about Albert's son David is similar to the previous information about Albert Popa. Both artists have used unconventional surfaces for their work: Albert used concrete, and David is using ice floes.

Choice A is incorrect because "however" illogically signals that the information about David contrasts with the previous information about Albert Popa. Instead, it is similar to the previous information about Albert Popa. *Choice B* is incorrect because "indeed" illogically signals that the information about David emphasizes or strengthens the previous point about Albert Popa. Instead, it is similar to the previous information; it highlights a similarity between father and son. *Choice C* is incorrect because "second" illogically signals that the information about David is a second point or reason separate from the previous information about Albert Popa. Instead, it is similar to the previous information; it highlights a similarity between father and son.

QUESTION 24

Choice D is the best answer. "Specifically" logically signals that the information about Pleasant's 1866 lawsuit provides specific, precise details elaborating on the previous point that Pleasant successfully challenged discrimination in California.

Choice A is incorrect because "for this reason" illogically signals that Pleasant's 1866 lawsuit was a result of her successful challenge to discrimination in California. Instead, this sentence provides specific details elaborating on her challenge to discrimination in the state. *Choice B* is incorrect because "then" illogically signals that Pleasant's 1866 lawsuit was subsequent to or resulted from her successful challenge to discrimination in California. Instead, this sentence provides specific, precise details elaborating on how she challenged discrimination in the state. *Choice C* is incorrect because "in addition" illogically signals that the information about Pleasant's 1866 lawsuit is merely additional to the previous point that Pleasant successfully challenged discrimination in California. Instead, this sentence provides specific details elaborating on how she did so.

QUESTION 25

Choice C is the best answer. "In addition" logically signals that the claim in this sentence—that the Inca of South America may have used quipus to record more complex information—is an additional point related to the previous statement about the Inca using quipus to record countable information.

Choice A is incorrect because "as a result" illogically signals that the claim in the sentence is a consequence or result of the previous statement about the Inca using quipus to record countable information. Instead, the possibility that the Inca used quipus to record more complex information is an additional point about how the quipus were used. *Choice B* is incorrect because "in other words" illogically signals that the claim in the sentence is merely a paraphrase or restatement of the previous statement about the Inca using quipus to record countable information. Instead, the possibility that the Inca used quipus to record more complex information is an additional point about how the quipus were used. *Choice D* is incorrect because "for example" illogically signals that the claim in the sentence exemplifies the previous statement about the Inca using quipus to record countable information. Instead, the possibility that the Inca used quipus to record more complex information is an additional point about how the quipus were used.

QUESTION 26

Choice A is the best answer. The sentence emphasizes Janaki Ammal's achievement, explaining that she successfully created sugarcane hybrids that are well suited to India's climate by crossbreeding an imported sugarcane species with grasses native to India.

Choice B is incorrect. The sentence emphasizes the goal of the Imperial Sugar Cane Institute in the 1930s; it doesn't emphasize Janaki Ammal's achievement. *Choice C* is incorrect. While the sentence mentions Ammal, it doesn't emphasize her achievement of successfully creating sugarcane hybrids. *Choice D* is incorrect. While the sentence mentions the achievement of crossbreeding imported sugarcane species with grasses native to India, it doesn't emphasize the achievement as belonging to Janaki Ammal.

QUESTION 27

Choice C is the best answer. The sentence specifies how the salt in a freeze-thaw battery enables energy storage, explaining that energy stops flowing and can be stored when the salt solidifies at room temperature.

Choice A is incorrect. The sentence explains some properties of molten salt; it doesn't specify how that salt enables energy storage. *Choice B* is incorrect. The sentence indicates how the energy in a freeze-thaw battery can be released; it doesn't specify how the salt in the battery enables energy storage. *Choice D* is incorrect. The sentence specifies how much charge the freeze-thaw battery retains when storing energy; it doesn't specify how the salt in the battery enables energy storage.

Reading and Writing

Module 2 — Lower Difficulty
(27 questions)

QUESTION 1

Choice A is the best answer because the text indicates that Fox-Foot doesn't let the group build a fire or create a canoe landing when it's time for supper. This context suggests that he doesn't want anyone who might be following the group to see any sign of them or their activities. In other words, Fox-Foot doesn't want there to be any trace, or evidence, of the group's movements ("their passing") through the area.

Choice B is incorrect because the text conveys that Fox-Foot doesn't want the group to be detected, not that he doesn't want their presence to create a blemish, or a spoiling flaw, in the area; human activity could disturb a natural environment, but the context emphasizes that Fox-Foot is instead focused on avoiding giving any sign of the group's movements through a place ("their passing") to anyone who might be following them. *Choice C* is incorrect because the text focuses on Fox-Foot's desire to avoid detection by those who might be following the group. This context conveys that Fox-Foot doesn't want to create any signs or evidence of the group moving through a place ("their passing"), not that he doesn't want to leave behind some quantity of their presence; indeed, it isn't clear what an amount of a group's movement would be. *Choice D* is incorrect because nothing in the text suggests that the group has a sketch, or rough drawing, of their movements through that area ("their passing") that might be left behind. Rather, the context emphasizes that Fox-Foot is focused on ensuring that the group doesn't give any kind of indication of their presence, as he wants to avoid detection by anyone who might be following the group.

QUESTION 2

Choice C is the best answer because it most logically completes the text's discussion of Ester Hernandez's art. In this context, "featured" means shown prominently. The text focuses on where Hernandez's works have been and continue to be displayed, explaining that her early works, which consisted of murals, could be viewed in outdoor spaces in San Francisco. The central contrast developed in the text is between where her early works could be viewed and where her works can be viewed now, which is in museums across the United States and around the world. The context therefore supports the idea that Hernandez's works are now shown, or featured, in museums globally.

Choice A is incorrect because in this context "invented" would mean created something for the first time, which isn't supported since the text doesn't discuss where Hernandez creates her works or whether they're original or innovative. *Choice B* is incorrect because "adjusted" in this context would mean adapted. Although the text mentions that many of Hernandez's early works were outdoor murals and thus it may be reasonable to infer that Hernandez altered her approach to creating art so that her works could be displayed in indoor venues instead, the text makes no mention of how Hernandez's works might have been adapted for such venues. The text focuses on where Hernandez's works have been and continue to be displayed, not on how she or anyone else may have adapted, or adjusted, her works. *Choice D* is incorrect because "recommended" in this context would mean endorsed or put forth as a suggestion for something that is worth seeing. Although it may be reasonable to say that in choosing to display certain works, museum curators believe such works are worth seeing, the text doesn't discuss the reasons why museums display Hernandez's works. Instead, the text mainly develops a contrast between where Hernandez's early works could once be viewed and where her work can be viewed now.

QUESTION 3

Choice C is the best answer because it most logically completes the text's discussion of Bastos's study of a wild kea parrot. In this context, "accidental" means unplanned or unintentional. The text first describes Bastos's study, which concerns a kea that is observed using small stones to preen its feathers. The text then mentions colleagues who are skeptical (that is, they have doubt) about Bastos's findings, and finally describes how Bastos and her team responded to the skepticism of those colleagues. Given that the colleagues mentioned in the text expressed skepticism regarding Bastos's findings, the best answer choice must be one that completes the text in a manner such that the skeptics' opinion regarding the kea's use of stones disagrees with that held by Bastos and her team. Since Bastos and her team showed that the kea's use of stones was deliberate (that is, intentional), the skeptics' opinion in this context must be that the kea's use of stones was unintentional, or accidental.

Choice A is incorrect because the best answer choice is one that portrays skepticism, or doubt, of Bastos's claim that the kea's usage of stones was deliberate, or intentional. If the skeptics found the kea's usage of stones "intriguing," or fascinating, this would not be at odds with the position of Bastos and her team; in fact, it is reasonable to believe that someone who agreed that the kea's stone usage was deliberate would also find it intriguing. *Choice B* is incorrect because if the skeptics believed that the kea's usage of small stones was "obvious," or evident, this would not be contrary to the observation of Bastos and her team that the kea's usage of stones was deliberate: in fact, these opinions would be consistent with each other. *Choice D* is incorrect because if the skeptics believed that the kea's usage of small stones was "observable," or visible, this would not conflict with the claim of Bastos and her team that the kea's usage of stones was deliberate: instead, these positions would agree.

QUESTION 4

Choice A is the best answer because it most logically completes the text's discussion of the Roman emperor Marcus Aurelius. In this context, "indulge" means treat with excessive leniency. The text states that according to historian Edward Gibbon, Marcus Aurelius, who was widely considered virtuous, had only a single character flaw: his mild temperament. The text suggests that because of this flaw, Marcus Aurelius had an overly permissive nature.

This context, in turn, supports the idea that Marcus Aurelius treated the vices, or evils, of those around him with excessive leniency, indulging rather than punishing those vices.

Choice B is incorrect. While the text does state that Marcus Aurelius was widely considered virtuous, it gives no indication that he was inclined to "despise," or hate, others' vices. Rather, the text suggests that he showed undue tolerance for these vices because of his overly permissive nature—that is, his inclination to allow others to do as they wished. *Choice C* is incorrect because the text's description of Marcus Aurelius as overly permissive suggests that he showed undue tolerance for others' vices, not that he tried to "moderate" those vices, or lessen their intensity. *Choice D* is incorrect because the text's description of Marcus Aurelius as overly permissive suggests that he showed undue tolerance for others' vices, not that he attempted to "criticize," or speak disapprovingly of, those vices.

QUESTION 5

Choice C is the best answer because it most accurately describes how the underlined sentence functions in the text as a whole. The first sentence describes a unique location on Earth, the Atacama Desert. The next sentence, which is the underlined sentence, states that the reason why astrobiologists study life, or its remains, in this unique location is that Atacama is a harsh environment that closely resembles the extreme environment of Mars. The remainder of the text explains that the researchers hope their work in Atacama will support inquiry into life on Mars. Thus, the underlined portion functions mainly to indicate why astrobiologists choose to conduct research in the Atacama Desert.

Choice A is incorrect because to contrast two things means to show the differences between them, and the phrase "closely mirrors" in the underlined sentence indicates that the extreme environment in the Atacama Desert is similar to, not different from, that on Mars. This similarity is why, according to the underlined sentence, astrobiologists conduct research in Atacama. *Choice B* is incorrect because the underlined sentence doesn't address forms of life that are unable to survive the harsh environment of the Atacama Desert. Instead, the underlined sentence explains why astrobiologists study life, or its remains, in this environment. *Choice D* is incorrect because the underlined sentence doesn't suggest that the scientific research in the Atacama Desert is limited in any way; instead, the sentence explains that the similarity between the environments of Atacama and Mars is the reason why astrobiologists search for life, or its remains, in Atacama.

QUESTION 6

Choice C is the best answer because it most accurately describes the overall structure of the text. The text begins by providing some examples of words in Koasati (*misip-lin, mis-lin, lataf-kan, lat-kan*) and their English translations. Then, the text explains that these words are examples of a linguistic phenomenon called subtractive morphology. The text concludes by asserting that the kind of subtractive morphology exemplified in the text is "pervasive," or common, in Koasati. Thus, the text presents some specific words in Koasati, describes the general linguistic phenomenon exemplified by those words, and then states that this phenomenon occurs frequently in Koasati.

Choice A is incorrect. Although the text mentions English translations of some Koasati words, it doesn't describe the relationship between Koasati and several additional languages, nor does it raise or answer any particular question about how Koasati relates to other languages. *Choice B* is incorrect because the

Koasati words named in the text are presented as examples of subtractive morphology, not as examples of the most frequently occurring words in the language. Furthermore, the text doesn't suggest that these words are difficult to translate into English, nor does it mention any other languages besides English. *Choice D* is incorrect. Although the text does explain the phenomenon of subtractive morphology, it doesn't describe any kind of scholarly controversy surrounding the phenomenon, nor does it advocate for additional analysis to resolve the controversy.

QUESTION 7

Choice A is the best answer because it most accurately states what is happening in the text. The narrator notes that Lutie thinks the street looks nice in the light of the sunset. The narrator goes on to describe what Lutie can see in the street: children playing ball or tag and girls skipping rope. Thus, what is happening in the text is that Lutie is observing the appearance of the street at a particular time of day and the events occurring on it.

Choice B is incorrect. Although Lutie is observing children playing games on her street, the text doesn't suggest that she is annoyed by the noise of the games. Instead, the text says that Lutie thinks the street looks nice in the light of the sunset. *Choice C* is incorrect. Although Lutie is observing children playing games on her street, the text doesn't suggest that she is puzzled by the rules of the games. *Choice D* is incorrect because there is no evidence in the text that Lutie doesn't want to interact with her neighbors or that she is in her apartment alone. All the text indicates about Lutie is that she is watching the events on the street and thinks the street looks nice in the light of the sunset.

QUESTION 8

Choice D is the best answer because it most accurately states the main idea of the text. The text begins by stating that Flanagan was chosen in 1935 to lead the Federal Theatre Project (FTP), which was part of a program created by President Franklin D. Roosevelt. The text then explains that as the director of the FTP, Flanagan created jobs for more than 12,500 theater professionals and ensured that ticket prices stayed low so that many people could afford to experience theater for the first time. Thus, the main idea of the text is that as the FTP's director, Flanagan succeeded in creating many jobs and introducing people to theater.

Choice A is incorrect. The text does suggest that jobs provided by the FTP were intended mainly for theater professionals, but this isn't the text's main idea. The focus of the text is Hallie Flanagan's work as the director of the FTP, with the text's main point being that Flanagan succeeded in creating many jobs and introducing people to theater. *Choice B* is incorrect. The text does state that President Roosevelt created the WPA to provide jobs for unemployed people, but this is supporting information, not the text's main idea. The focus of the text is Hallie Flanagan's work as the director of the FTP, which was part of the WPA, and the text's main point is that Flanagan succeeded in creating many jobs and introducing people to theater. *Choice C* is incorrect. It's true that many people couldn't afford to buy theater tickets during the Great Depression, but this isn't the text's main idea. The focus of the text is Hallie Flanagan's work as the director of the FTP, with the text's main point being that Flanagan succeeded in creating many jobs and introducing people to theater.

QUESTION 9

Choice D is the best answer because it presents a statement about what surprised the scientists that is supported by the text. The text states that the marsquakes described in the data from NASA's InSight lander originated from the same location on Mars. The text goes on to say that because they had expected the opposite (that marsquakes would originate from all over the planet) this discovery surprised the scientists.

Choice A is incorrect because the text doesn't say that the data from NASA's InSight lander revealed any surprising information about the planet's surface surface temperature. Instead, the text mentions the cooling of Mars's surface as a reason the scientists expected that marsquakes had multiple origins. In addition, cooling would indicate that the temperature has been falling rather than rising. *Choice B* is incorrect. Although the text indicates that by studying seismic activity scientists found a possible explanation for what causes marsquakes, the text doesn't say that they discovered that marsquakes are caused by different types of seismic waves. Rather, the text states that based on the data from NASA's InSight lander, scientists now believe that this seismic activity happens because of areas of active magma that flow below the planet's surface. *Choice C* is incorrect because the text doesn't discuss the amount of data NASA's InSight lander collected or whether scientists who studied the data found the amount to be as expected. Instead, the text focuses on what the data revealed about where on Mars the marsquakes originated.

QUESTION 10

Choice A is the best answer because it most effectively uses data from the table to complete the statement about the US auto industry in the early twentieth century. The table shows the number of cars produced annually and number of companies producing cars in the United States between 1910 and 1925 in increments of five years. According to the table, the number of cars produced consistently increased from one increment to the next, going from 123,990 cars in 1910 to 3,185,881 cars in 1925. At the same time, the table shows that the number of companies producing cars consistently decreased, going from 320 companies in 1910 to only 80 companies in 1925. Thus, the table shows that the number of cars produced increased from 1910 to 1925, even as the number of companies producing cars decreased.

Choice B is incorrect. The table shows that the number of cars produced in the US increased, going from 123,990 in 1910 to 3,185,881 in 1925, instead of remaining unchanged, and the table also shows that the number of companies producing cars decreased from 320 to 80 instead of remaining unchanged. *Choice C* is incorrect because the table indicates that the number of cars produced consistently increased from 1910 to 1925, going from 123,990 cars to 3,185,881 cars, instead of decreasing; moreover, the table shows that the number of companies producing cars from 1910 to 1925 declined from 320 to 80 instead of remaining unchanged. *Choice D* is incorrect because the table indicates that the number of companies producing cars consistently decreased from 1910 to 1925, going from 320 companies to only 80 companies.

QUESTION 11

Choice D is the best answer because it most effectively uses a quotation from "The Bet" to illustrate the claim that the banker was very upset about something. The quotation indicates that the banker shed tears, which suggests that he was likely unhappy about something, and that his emotions were so strong that they kept him from sleeping for hours. These details suggest that the banker was very upset.

Choice A is incorrect because this quotation mainly describes the banker cautiously unlocking a door; it doesn't suggest that he was particularly upset about anything. *Choice B* is incorrect because this quotation doesn't mention whether the banker was experiencing any particularly strong negative feelings; instead, the quotation focuses on the quietness of the setting. *Choice C* is incorrect because this quotation states that the banker was feeling "delighted," not that he was upset.

QUESTION 12

Choice A is the best answer because it effectively uses data from the table to complete the claim about the significance of the Chang'e 5 lunar samples. The table shows the approximate ages of lunar samples from four different missions: three Apollo missions and the Chang'e 5 mission. The Chang'e 5 samples are said to be approximately 2 billion years old, while the Apollo samples are each said to be more than 3 billion years old. In other words, based on the data in the table, the Chang'e 5 samples are much younger than those from the Apollo missions.

Choice B is incorrect because the table shows that the Chang'e 5 samples were taken from a landing site at Oceanus Procellarum, which none of the Apollo missions are shown to have visited. *Choice C* is incorrect because the table shows the Apollo 17 samples as approximately 3.8 billion years old, the Apollo 15 samples as approximately 3.3 billion years old, and the Chang'e 5 samples as approximately 2 billion years old, and therefore, the Chang'e samples are closer in age to the Apollo 15 samples than they are to the Apollo 17 samples. *Choice D* is incorrect because nothing in the text or table suggests that the Chang'e 5 samples were used to confirm the ages of the Apollo samples.

QUESTION 13

Choice D is the best answer because it presents a finding that, if true, would support the researchers' hypothesis that TMAO reduces water's compressibility. The text explains that at great depths in the ocean, extreme pressure compresses the molecular structure of water by destabilizing the hydrogen bonds between adjacent molecules, thereby allowing water to penetrate proteins and harm the associated organisms. However, deep-sea organisms called piezophiles have adapted to live at these depths and previous studies show a positive correlation between the depth at which a piezophile species lives and the species' level of the compound TMAO. Because this hypothesis links TMAO levels with reduced compressibility of water's tetrahedral molecular structure, a finding that TMAO helps maintain the hydrogen bonds between water molecules under high pressure would strongly support that hypothesis.

Choice A is incorrect. Although the researchers' hypothesis suggests a relationship between TMAO and water molecules' tetrahedral molecular structure, that relationship involves TMAO helping maintain water's tetrahedral molecular structure under high pressure; as presented in the text, the hypothesis doesn't contend that water molecules are impervious to, or incapable of being penetrated by, TMAO. *Choice B* is incorrect because the text discusses how the molecular structure of water, not TMAO, is compressed under extreme pressure and never addresses how TMAO might be affected by such pressure. *Choice C* is incorrect because the researchers' hypothesis holds that water under extreme pressure is more resistant, not less, to being compressed when TMAO concentrations are higher. Moreover, the positive correlation mentioned in the text is between TMAO concentrations and the depths at which piezophiles live, not between concentrations of TMAO and the rate at which water's molecular structure compresses as pressure increases.

QUESTION 14

Choice A is the best answer because it most logically completes the text's discussion of a crater's connection to the start of the Younger Dryas. According to the text, some scientists believe that a comet fragment hitting Earth caused the cooling of the Younger Dryas period to come about. The text then indicates that a team of scientists found a crater in Greenland, which some believe supports the theory of a comet fragment hitting Earth to initiate the Younger Dryas. However, the text also notes that the team was unable to determine the age of the crater. If the age of the crater can't be determined, then its connection to the Younger Dryas period of time can't be confirmed either. Thus, it can't be concluded that the impact that made the crater was connected to the beginning of the Younger Dryas.

Choice B is incorrect because though the text suggests that the age of the comet crater found by a team of scientists is uncertain, it doesn't address whether a comet fragment can make a crater as large as 19 miles wide. The text doesn't consider the size of comet fragments and how they relate to the size of craters they might make. *Choice C* is incorrect because the debate in the text centers on the age of the crater found, not the cause of the crater. The text doesn't indicate uncertainty about what caused the discovered crater. *Choice D* is incorrect because the text suggests that the age of the crater found by the team of scientists is uncertain, not that the dates of the Younger Dryas are uncertain or incorrect. The text states that "the Younger Dryas was a period of extreme cooling from 11,700 to 12,900 years ago" but doesn't indicate any debate about the timing of the period.

QUESTION 15

Choice A is the best answer. The convention being tested is the use of verb forms within a sentence. A main clause requires a finite (tensed) verb to perform the action of the subject (in this case, Nery and her colleagues), and this choice supplies the finite past tense verb "published" to indicate that these biologists shared their findings about changes in whale genes associated with body size.

Choice B is incorrect because it results in an ungrammatical sentence. The nonfinite participle "publishing" doesn't supply the main clause with a finite verb. *Choice C* is incorrect because it results in an ungrammatical sentence. The nonfinite participle "having published" doesn't supply the main clause with a finite verb. *Choice D* is incorrect because it results in an ungrammatical sentence. The nonfinite to-infinitive "to publish" doesn't supply the main clause with a finite verb.

QUESTION 16

Choice A is the best answer. The convention being tested is the use of verb forms within a sentence. A main clause requires a finite (tensed) verb to perform the action of the subject (in this case, Land), and this choice supplies the finite past tense verb "used" to indicate what Land did with the technology he had invented.

Choice B is incorrect because it results in an ungrammatical sentence. The nonfinite perfect infinitive "to have used" doesn't supply the main clause with a finite verb. *Choice C* is incorrect because it results in an ungrammatical sentence. The nonfinite to-infinitive "to use" doesn't supply the main clause with a finite verb. *Choice D* is incorrect because it results in an ungrammatical sentence. The nonfinite participle "using" doesn't supply the main clause with a finite verb.

QUESTION 17

Choice A is the best answer. The convention being tested is pronoun-antecedent agreement. The plural pronoun "them" agrees in number with the plural antecedent "utensils."

Choice B is incorrect because the singular pronoun "this" doesn't agree in number with the plural antecedent "utensils." *Choice C* is incorrect because the singular pronoun "that" doesn't agree in number with the plural antecedent "utensils." *Choice D* is incorrect because the singular pronoun "it" doesn't agree in number with the plural antecedent "utensils."

QUESTION 18

Choice D is the best answer. The convention being tested is subject-verb agreement. The singular verb "ensures" agrees in number with the singular subject "using."

Choice A is incorrect because the plural verb "are ensuring" doesn't agree in number with the singular subject "using." *Choice B* is incorrect because the plural verb "have ensured" doesn't agree in number with the singular subject "using." *Choice C* is incorrect because the plural verb "ensure" doesn't agree in number with the singular subject "using."

QUESTION 19

Choice B is the best answer. The convention being tested is the use of plural nouns in a sentence. The plural noun "hands" and the plural noun "antennas" correctly indicate that two hands are placed between two antennas when playing the theremin.

Choice A is incorrect because the context requires the plural nouns "hands" and "antennas," not the singular possessive nouns "hand's" and "antenna's." *Choice C* is incorrect because the context requires the plural nouns "hands" and "antennas," not the plural possessive nouns "hands'" and "antennas'." *Choice D* is incorrect because the context requires the plural noun "hands," not the plural possessive noun "hands'."

QUESTION 20

Choice C is the best answer. The convention being tested is the coordination of main clauses within a sentence. This choice correctly uses a semicolon to join the first main clause ("One…(BEC)") and the second main clause ("Dutch…halt").

Choice A is incorrect because it results in a comma splice. Without a conjunction following it, a comma can't be used in this way to join two main clauses. *Choice B* is incorrect because it results in a run-on sentence. Without a comma preceding it, a conjunction can't be used in this way to join two main clauses. *Choice D* is incorrect because it results in a run-on sentence. The two main clauses are fused without punctuation and/or a conjunction.

QUESTION 21

Choice C is the best answer. "In fact" logically signals that the information in this sentence about the creation of the video game offers additional emphasis in support of the previous claim that video game studio founders Koola and Viv love cats.

Choice A is incorrect because "intermittently" illogically signals that the information in this sentence occurs sporadically or in intervals. Instead, the creation of the video game offers additional emphasis in support of the previous claim about Koola and Viv. *Choice B* is incorrect because "on the other hand" illogically signals that the information in this sentence contrasts with the previous claim about Koola and Viv. Instead, the creation of the video game offers additional emphasis in support of that claim. *Choice D* is incorrect because "nevertheless" illogically signals that the information in this sentence is true despite the previous claim that Koola and Viv love cats. Instead, the creation of the video game offers additional emphasis in support of that claim.

QUESTION 22

Choice C is the best answer. "However" logically signals that the claim about reindeer in this sentence contrasts with the information about most deer species in the previous sentence.

Choice A is incorrect because "similarly" illogically signals that the claim in this sentence is similar to the previous information about most deer species. Instead, it contrasts with that information. *Choice B* is incorrect because "next" illogically signals that the claim about reindeer in this sentence is the next step in a process. Instead, it contrasts with the previous information about most deer species. *Choice D* is incorrect because "thus" illogically signals that the claim in this sentence results from the previous information about most deer species. Instead, it contrasts with that information.

QUESTION 23

Choice C is the best answer. "Later" logically signals that the information in the sentence—that in 2017 Gomez created a platform for others to share stories about their immigration experiences—occurs later in a chronological series of events than the previous information about Gomez winning his first storytelling competition in 2014.

Choice A is incorrect because "instead" illogically signals that Gomez created a platform for others to share stories about their immigration experiences as an alternative to winning his first storytelling competition. Rather, Gomez created the platform later—in a chronological series of events—than when he won the competition. *Choice B* is incorrect because "for example" illogically signals that the information about Gomez creating a platform for others to share stories exemplifies his winning his first storytelling competition. Rather, Gomez created the platform later—in a chronological series of events—than when he won the competition. *Choice D* is incorrect because "in other words" illogically signals that the information about Gomez creating a platform for others to share stories is merely a paraphrase or restatement of the previous information about Gomez winning his first storytelling competition. Rather, Gomez created the platform later—in a chronological series of events—than when he won the competition.

QUESTION 24

Choice D is the best answer. "Though" logically signals that the claim in the sentence—that Morton's improvisational skills helped shape jazz as a genre during its early years ("No one can deny" it)—is true despite the previous information about Morton's exaggerated claim to have invented jazz.

Choice A is incorrect because "therefore" illogically signals that the claim in the sentence is a result of the previous information about Morton's claim to have invented jazz. Instead, the sentence states that Morton helped to shape jazz—even if his claim was an exaggeration. *Choice B* is incorrect because "in the second place" illogically signals that the claim in the sentence is a second, separate point in addition to Morton's claim to have invented jazz. Instead, the sentence states that

Morton helped to shape jazz—even if his claim was an exaggeration. *Choice C* is incorrect because "in other words" illogically signals that the claim in the sentence is merely a paraphrase or restatement of the previous information about Morton's claim to have invented jazz. Instead, the sentence states that Morton helped to shape jazz—even if his claim was an exaggeration.

QUESTION 25

Choice B is the best answer. The sentence effectively presents the study and its findings, providing relevant information: a 2021 study of the Vinland Map found that the map's ink contains a compound not used in inks until the twentieth century.

Choice A is incorrect. While the sentence introduces the study, it does not present the study's findings. *Choice C* is incorrect. While the sentence mentions the study, it does not effectively present the study or its findings. *Choice D* is incorrect. While the sentence introduces the study, it does not present the study's findings.

QUESTION 26

Choice D is the best answer. The sentence emphasizes a difference between the two approaches to dyeing blue jeans, noting that Rai's approach uses a natural, plant-based substance in place of hazardous chemicals.

Choice A is incorrect. The sentence emphasizes a similarity between the dyes used in the two approaches, noting that the dyes contain the same ingredient; it doesn't emphasize a difference between the two approaches to dyeing blue jeans. *Choice B* is incorrect. The sentence explains what nanocellulose is; it doesn't emphasize a difference between the two approaches to dyeing blue jeans. *Choice C* is incorrect. The sentence explains the traditional approach to dyeing blue jeans; it doesn't emphasize a difference between the traditional approach and Rai's approach.

QUESTION 27

Choice B is the best answer. The sentence emphasizes the aim, or goal, of the research study, noting that Torres sought to determine how ocean temperature affects where blue whales forage for krill.

Choice A is incorrect. The sentence emphasizes the results of the study, noting what Torres found at the end; it doesn't emphasize the aim, or goal, of the study, which is what Torres sought at the beginning. *Choice C* is incorrect. The sentence makes a claim about the study's results; it doesn't emphasize the aim, or goal, of the study. *Choice D* is incorrect. The sentence indicates the location of Torres's study; it doesn't emphasize the aim, or goal, of the study.

Reading and Writing

Module 2 — Higher Difficulty
(27 questions)

QUESTION 1

Choice A is the best answer because it most logically completes the text's discussion of the significance of the War of 1812 in British historical memory. In this context, "tenuous" means vulnerable or uncertain. The text indicates that the War of 1812 was both smaller, and less prominent, than the conflict with France, and resulted in no significant geopolitical changes. These details imply that the War of 1812 is less likely than other British historical events to be remembered, giving the War of 1812 a tenuous place in British historical memory.

Choice B is incorrect because in this context "enduring" would mean lasting or durable, but the text describes the War of 1812 as being overshadowed by, and smaller than, the simultaneous conflict with France. This seems to conflict with the notion that the War of 1812 has an enduring place in British historical memory. *Choice C* is incorrect because in this context "contentious" would mean likely to cause disagreement, and while there likely are contentious issues related to the War of 1812, nothing in the text discusses or implies any such disagreement. *Choice D* is incorrect because in this context "conspicuous" would mean obvious, but the text describes the War of 1812 as being overshadowed by, and smaller than, the simultaneous conflict with France. Rather than suggesting that the War of 1812 has a conspicuous place in British historical memory, these descriptions suggest that its place is not particularly obvious.

QUESTION 2

Choice B is the best answer because it most logically completes the text's discussion of the Kelmscott Press's books. In this context, "manifest in" means evident or apparent from. The text states that the Kelmscott Press, which was cofounded by William Morris, produced its books using preindustrial methods. The text notes the similarity between those methods, which include the use of handmade materials and intricate ornamentation, and methods used in the creation of medieval manuscripts. This context suggests that Morris's repudiation of industrialization is apparent from, or manifest in, the methods and materials his company employed.

Choice A is incorrect because there is nothing in the text to suggest that Morris's repudiation of industrialization is "insensible to," or unaware of or lacking perception of, the use of handmade materials and intricate ornamentation in the production of the Kelmscott editions. Instead, the text suggests that the methods and materials used to produce the Kelmscott editions are evidence of Morris's repudiation of industrialization. *Choice C* is incorrect because it would not make sense to say that Morris's repudiation of industrialization was "scrutinized by," or examined closely by, the Kelmscott editions' use of handmade materials and intricate ornamentation. Although creating the Kelmscott editions may have involved examining the books closely, the text does not mention this aspect of Morris's work, and in any case, the action of using certain materials to create those editions cannot scrutinize Morris's attitude toward industrialization. *Choice D* is incorrect because the text gives no indication that Morris's repudiation of industrialization is "complicated by," or made more complex or difficult by, the Kelmscott Press's use of preindustrial methods and handcrafted elements to produce books. Instead, the text presents those methods as exemplifying Morris's repudiation of industrialization.

QUESTION 3

Choice B is the best answer because it most logically completes the text's discussion about research into social media use. In context, "redressing" means remedying or compensating for. The text indicates that there is a long-standing trend of overemphasizing teenagers and young adults in studies of social media use. It goes on to say that scholars have recently broadened the kinds of social media users they study by including senior citizens. This suggests that scholars are redressing the long-standing trend of overemphasis on younger users by studying older users as well.

Choice A is incorrect because "exacerbating" means making worse or aggravating, which would not make logical sense in context. Expanding the focus of studies of social media use to include senior citizens would not make the long-standing trend of overemphasizing teenagers and young adults in studies of social media use worse; instead, it would help to remedy this trend. *Choice C* is incorrect because "epitomizing" means illustrating or providing an example, which would not make logical sense in context. Expanding the groups of social media users that scholars study to include senior citizens would not provide an example of the long-standing trend of overemphasizing teenagers and young people in research on social media use. *Choice D* is incorrect because "precluding" means making impossible in advance or preventing, which would not make logical sense in context. The text indicates that there is a long-standing trend of overemphasizing teenagers and young adults in social media research. Expanding the focus of social media research to include senior citizens, as the text indicates scholars have begun to do, could help to rectify the trend, but it could not prevent the trend or make the trend impossible in advance, since the trend started long before scholars started expanding their focus.

QUESTION 4

Choice D is the best answer because as used in the text, "disputing" most nearly means providing resistance to. The narrator is in a taxi as it drives down a street lined with so many food vendors and shoppers that the narrator describes them as "the multitude of Paris," meaning an immense group of people. The street is essentially a large open-air market, and there are so many people pushing small wagons of goods and carrying shopping baskets that "every inch" of the taxi's progress is impeded. In other words, the people are providing resistance to the taxi's attempt to drive down the street.

Choice A is incorrect. Although in some contexts, "disputing" can mean arguing, the narrator doesn't portray the shoppers and vendors as arguing with the driver of the taxi or, indeed, arguing at all. *Choice B* is incorrect. Although in some contexts, "disputing" can mean expressing disapproval, the narrator doesn't suggest that the shoppers and vendors necessarily disapprove of the taxi's attempt to drive down the street. Instead, their combined presence along the street has the effect of impeding the taxi's progress. *Choice C* is incorrect because, as the narrator explains, both the multitude of people and the taxi are using a public space (a street) at the same time. The narrator doesn't go so far as to suggest that the people feel that they, and not the taxi, possess exclusive access to the street.

QUESTION 5

Choice A is the best answer because it most accurately describes the function of the underlined sentence in the text as a whole. The first sentence of the text indicates that Johnson returned to the US in 1938 at which time his painting style suddenly changed. The second sentence is underlined and gives more detail about this stylistic change, noting that his earlier work consisted largely of landscapes in an expressionist style and his new works were highly stylized portraits of Black Americans. In other words, the function of the underlined sentence is to elaborate on a transitional moment in Johnson's painting career.

Choice B is incorrect. Although the text does mention that Johnson spent a decade in Europe, it does not discuss what other travel Johnson might have done. Furthermore, although the text mentions African, American, and Scandinavian artistic elements in Johnson's work, it does not indicate that he traveled to different locations to learn about these practices. *Choice C* is incorrect because the text does not focus on Johnson's personal life nor does it address how successful his career was in general. *Choice D* is incorrect because, rather than call it into question, the underlined sentence continues the discussion of Johnson's career by adding further relevant detail of Johnson's artistic transformation.

QUESTION 6

Choice C is the best answer because it most accurately describes how the underlined portion functions in the text as a whole. The text begins by mentioning scholarly accounts of the Chicano movement, which the underlined portion describes as tending "to focus on the most militant, outspoken figures in the movement," making the movement as a whole seem uniformly radical. The text then indicates that the work of geographer Juan Herrera shows that focusing less on such militant figures and instead paying more attention to manifestations of the Chicano movement in less widely known neighborhood institutions and projects would reveal that the movement's participants embraced a range of political orientations and approaches. Thus, the underlined portion describes a common approach to studying the Chicano movement that, according to the text, obscures the ideological diversity of the movement's participants.

Choice A is incorrect. Though the underlined portion does present a trend in scholarship on the Chicano movement, the text does not indicate that other scholars have reevaluated their methods in light of Herrera's work. It only indicates that Herrera's work suggests that the work of those other scholars does not provide a complete picture of the Chicano movement. *Choice B* is incorrect. Though the underlined portion does identify an aspect of the Chicano movement that the text indicates has been overemphasized, the text does not discuss the political orientations of the scholars whose work is mentioned in the text. *Choice D* is incorrect. Though the underlined portion does summarize the conventional method for analyzing the Chicano movement, the rest of the text does not address the effectiveness of "comparatively low-profile neighborhood institutions and projects." Instead, the text suggests that those projects were led by people with a variety of approaches to community activism.

QUESTION 7

Choice D is the best answer because it presents a statement about critics' skepticism of Bosco Verticale that is supported by the text. The text states that Boeri's design for Bosco Verticale features hundreds of trees on balconies and is intended to serve as a model for promoting urban biodiversity. But the text goes on to state that some critics believe that it is too early to determine if the trees planted on Bosco Verticale can thrive there. Therefore, according to the text, critics are skeptical of the concept behind Bosco Verticale because it is unclear whether Bosco Verticale can support the plant life included in its design.

Choice A is incorrect. Although the text states that one of Boeri's goals was for Bosco Verticale to serve as a model for promoting biodiversity in architecture, which suggests that Boeri would likely support the idea of reproducing the same concept in other locations, the text does not discuss whether it is feasible to adapt the design to locations other than Milan. Instead, the text describes critics' concerns that the plant life that currently exists on Bosco Verticale might not thrive in its current setting. *Choice B* is incorrect. Although the text states that one of Boeri's goals in creating Bosco Verticale was to promote biodiversity, which implies a goal of including varied plant life in the design, it does not mention whether the hundreds of trees that were planted on its balconies failed to meet this goal. Rather, the text states that some critics are concerned that the trees on Bosco Verticale's balconies may not thrive in this setting. *Choice C* is incorrect because the text does not mention how Bosco Verticale was constructed, let alone how environmentally destructive its construction may have been relative to the construction of more conventional buildings.

QUESTION 8

Choice C is the best answer because it accurately states the main idea of the text. According to the text, contrary to what some might expect, foreign investment is typically lower in developing countries whose economies are more dependent on natural-resource extraction. The text explains that high reliance on natural-resource extraction can subject a developing country to economic shocks that can destabilize the local currency and introduce economic uncertainty that tends to keep investors away. In other words, although we may think otherwise, foreign investors are less willing to invest in projects in developing countries whose economies are heavily dependent on natural-resource extraction because those economies tend to exhibit instability that investors want to avoid.

Choice A is incorrect. The text does indicate that foreign investment is typically lower in developing countries whose economies are more dependent on natural-resource extraction; the text further indicates that natural-resource extraction requires substantial initial investments (to acquire things like required technologies) for which there are fewer investors willing to participate at this stage than one might think. But the text does not implicate the cost of these initial investments as a reason why foreign investment is less widely available than some might think. *Choice B* is incorrect. The text indicates that greater dependence on natural-resource extraction makes a developing country less appealing to foreign investors because of associated economic instability. Rather than arguing that the goal of developing countries is to become less dependent on foreign investment, as the phrasing of choice B suggests, the text focuses only on why foreign investors become less involved with such countries, which suggests that more investment would be preferable. *Choice D* is incorrect. Although the text indicates that natural-resource extraction requires substantial initial investments (to acquire things like required technologies) and that there are fewer likely investors willing to participate at this stage than one might think, the text does not address what investors are likely to do over time as the industry stabilizes itself.

QUESTION 9

Choice C is the best answer because it states a conclusion the researchers likely agree with, given the details in the text. The text explains that a biosignature gas is a gas that can be used as an indicator that a planet harbors some form of life and some astronomers have proposed that NH_3 could serve as a biosignature gas. The researchers evaluating this claim found that the atmosphere of rocky planets would be unlikely to reach "detectably high levels" of NH_3 without biological activity, which would support the proposal of NH_3 serving as a biosignature gas. However, the text also states that mini-Neptune planets can produce NH_3 in the absence of biological activity. Thus, the text is structured to lead to the conclusion that detectable levels of NH_3 in the atmospheres of rocky planets could constitute a biosignature, but that is not the case for detectable levels of the gas in the atmospheres of mini-Neptune planets.

Choice A is incorrect because the text indicates that biological activity likely accounts for detectable levels of NH_3 in the atmospheres of rocky planets but mini-Neptune planets can have detectable levels of NH_3 in their atmospheres in the absence of biological activity. Therefore, both rocky planets and mini-Neptune planets can have detectable levels of atmospheric NH_3. *Choice B* is incorrect because the text states that for NH_3 to reach detectable levels in the atmospheres of rocky planets likely means they harbor biological activity, meaning that rocky planets with detectable NH_3 usually harbor biological activity. However, that does not entail that every rocky planet with biological activity will have detectable levels of NH_3 in their atmospheres. *Choice D* is incorrect because the text claims only that some astronomers have proposed using NH_3 as a biosignature gas without mentioning a minimum concentration of atmospheric NH_3 that must be met for it to function as a biosignature gas.

QUESTION 10

Choice D is the best answer because it most effectively illustrates the claim that the speaker has contradictory feelings while experiencing the sights and sounds of spring. This quotation indicates that the speaker is reclined in a grove listening to a thousand sounds. Even though the speaker is in a "sweet mood" and thinking "pleasant thoughts," those pleasant thoughts also bring to mind "sad thoughts." In other words, these lines illustrate the claim that the speaker is having contradictory thoughts while immersed in the sights and sounds of spring.

Choice A is incorrect. Although this quotation refers to several flowers (primroses and periwinkles) and indicates that the speaker is in a "bower," or shady spot among the trees—details which suggest that the speaker is experiencing the sights of spring—it doesn't suggest that the speaker is having contradictory feelings, only that the speaker believes that the flowers are experiencing enjoyment. *Choice B* is incorrect. Although this quotation focuses on the sights of spring—namely, new leaves on nearby trees appear to be opening up ("The budding twigs spread out their fan") to feel the breeze—the quotation doesn't suggest that the speaker feels conflicted about this: the statement "And I must think, do all I can" suggests the speaker's determination to attribute feelings of pleasure to the trees, not that the speaker is experiencing contradictory feelings. *Choice C* is incorrect. Although this quotation indicates that the speaker isn't certain what the birds are thinking ("Their thoughts I cannot measure"), there's nothing to suggest that the speaker is experiencing contradictory feelings. Rather, the quotation suggests that although the speaker is uncertain about the birds' feelings, the speaker believes that the birds' movements likely suggest their pleasure.

QUESTION 11

Choice D is the best answer because it describes data from the graph that support Ibáñez and colleagues' conclusion that increasing anthropogenic nitrogen deposition can compensate for the negative effect of climate change on tree growth if that change is moderate but not if it's extreme. The bar graph shows the growth of sugar maple trees with and without nitrogen fertilization under three different climate-change scenarios: current conditions, a moderate change, and an extreme change. According to the graph, radial growth without nitrogen fertilization is projected to be about 0.16 centimeters (cm) under current conditions, 0.15 cm under a moderate change, and 0.04 cm under an extreme change. The graph also shows that with nitrogen fertilization, growth is projected to be about 0.18 centimeters under a moderate change but only about 0.06 centimeters under an extreme change. Thus, the data in the graph support the researchers' conclusion by showing greater growth for a moderate change using nitrogen fertilization than they do either under current conditions without nitrogen fertilization or under an extreme change with nitrogen fertilization.

Choice A is incorrect. Although it accurately represents the data in the graph, this fact pattern doesn't support Ibáñez and colleagues' conclusion that the decline in radial growth due to climate change will be partly offset by higher levels of anthropogenic nitrogen, but only if change to the climate is moderate and not if it's extreme. To support this would require comparing radial growth without nitrogen fertilization under current climate conditions to the growth with nitrogen fertilization under both moderate and extreme changes. This choice mentions only growth with nitrogen fertilization under current climate conditions and moderate change and growth without nitrogen fertilization under an extreme change, which don't provide a basis to determine whether higher nitrogen in the future will be able to offset reduced growth due to climate change. *Choice B* is incorrect. Although it accurately represents the data in the graph, this fact pattern doesn't support Ibáñez and colleagues' conclusion that the decline in radial growth due to climate change will be partly offset by higher levels of atmospheric nitrogen, but only if change to the climate is moderate and not if it's extreme. The support needed would compare radial growth under current climate conditions without nitrogen fertilization to the growth with nitrogen fertilization under moderate and extreme changes. This choice mentions only growth without nitrogen fertilization under current conditions and moderate change and growth with nitrogen fertilization under extreme change, which don't provide a basis to determine whether higher nitrogen in the future will be able to offset reduced growth due to climate change. *Choice C* is incorrect. Although it accurately represents the data in the graph, this fact pattern doesn't support Ibáñez and colleagues' conclusion that the decline in radial growth due to climate change will be partly offset by higher levels of atmospheric nitrogen, but only if change to the climate is moderate and not if it's extreme. The support needed would compare radial growth without adding nitrogen under current climate conditions to the growth with nitrogen fertilization under moderate and extreme changes. This choice mentions only the growth with and without nitrogen fertilization under moderate climate change and growth without nitrogen fertilization under extreme change, which don't provide a basis to determine whether higher nitrogen in the future will be able to offset reduced growth due to climate change.

QUESTION 12

Choice D is the best answer because it presents a finding that, if true, would support the researchers' hypothesis that TMAO reduces water's compressibility. The text explains that at great depths in the ocean, extreme pressure compresses the molecular structure of water by destabilizing the hydrogen bonds between adjacent molecules, thereby allowing water to penetrate proteins and harm the associated organisms. However, deep-sea organisms called piezophiles have adapted to live at these depths and previous studies show a positive correlation between the depth at which a piezophile species lives and the species' level of the compound TMAO. Because this hypothesis links TMAO levels with reduced compressibility of water's tetrahedral molecular structure, a finding that TMAO helps maintain the hydrogen bonds between water molecules under high pressure would strongly support that hypothesis.

Choice A is incorrect. Although the researchers' hypothesis suggests a relationship between TMAO and water molecules' tetrahedral molecular structure, that relationship involves TMAO helping maintain water's tetrahedral molecular structure under high pressure; as presented in the text, the hypothesis doesn't contend that water molecules are impervious to, or incapable of being penetrated by, TMAO. *Choice B* is incorrect because the text discusses how the molecular structure of water, not TMAO, is compressed under extreme pressure and never addresses how TMAO might be affected by such pressure. *Choice C* is incorrect because the researchers' hypothesis holds that water under extreme pressure is more resistant, not less, to being compressed when TMAO concentrations are higher. Moreover, the positive correlation mentioned in the text is between TMAO concentrations and the depths at which piezophiles live, not between concentrations of TMAO and the rate at which water's molecular structure compresses as pressure increases.

QUESTION 13

Choice B is the best answer because it describes data from the table that support Persad and her colleagues' conclusion. The text explains that, according to some climate models, precipitation in the western United States will become concentrated into fewer, more intense rain and snow events. According to the text, Persad and her colleagues concluded that more irrigation will consequently be needed but that the change in irrigation output will be highly sensitive to, or greatly affected by, the baseline concentration of precipitation in an area. This conclusion is supported by data from the researchers' simulations of changes in annual irrigation output in two different scenarios—one in which an area's annual precipitation is already somewhat concentrated and one in which its annual precipitation is evenly distributed. The table shows that if baseline precipitation is somewhat concentrated, water use for irrigation will increase only slightly, whereas if baseline precipitation is evenly distributed, water use for irrigation will increase much more—9.0% for surface water and 7.9% for groundwater. This difference illustrates the researchers' conclusion that the amount of additional water needed for irrigation will vary greatly depending on how concentrated or spread out the annual precipitation in an area already is.

Choice A is incorrect because it compares changes in the amount of water being used for irrigation to changes in the amount of water entering aquifers. Persad and her colleagues' conclusion doesn't focus on changes to the amount of water entering aquifers; rather, the researchers' conclusion focuses on changes to irrigation output relative to how concentrated or spread out the annual precipitation in an area is. *Choice C* is incorrect because it supports only part of Persad and her colleagues' conclusion. According to the text, the researchers concluded that the concentration of precipitation into fewer events will trigger more irrigation but that this change in irrigation output will be highly sensitive to an area's baseline concentration of annual precipitation. The data in this choice support the idea that more irrigation will be needed, but to support the rest of the researchers' conclusion, additional data from the table are required to show that the increases in water use for irrigation will vary depending on how concentrated or spread out the annual precipitation in an area already is. *Choice D* is incorrect because data in the table indicate no declines in water use for irrigation, showing only increases in the form of positive values.

QUESTION 14

Choice A is the best answer because it most logically completes the text's discussion of the research on feeding behaviors of wild and captive lions. The text indicates that Gidna, Yravedra, and Domínguez-Rodrigo compared the behaviors of wild lions in a national park with those of captive lions in a reserve. The text also establishes that the researchers were familiar with earlier studies showing that regularly offering food to captive animals reduces the need for cognitive engagement with the environment and can lead the animals to develop novel stereotypic behaviors, or new behaviors that are repetitive without a clear purpose. It follows, then, that the researchers weren't surprised to find that unlike the wild lions, the captive lions continued gnawing on the bones of provided carcasses even when the bones no longer provided nutrients, because this would be an example of captive animals developing a new and purposelessly repetitive behavior.

Choice B is incorrect because the text suggests that the researchers' findings were consistent with earlier findings that animals may develop novel stereotypic behaviors in captivity, and there's no reason to think that displaying aggression during feeding is a purposelessly repetitive behavior or that it was newly developed by lions in captivity, especially if the researchers found that wild lions also showed aggression during feeding. *Choice C* is incorrect because the text suggests that the researchers' findings were consistent with previous findings that novel stereotypic behaviors can develop when captive animals lack cognitive engagement with their environments. It therefore isn't logical to conclude that the researchers weren't surprised to find that captive lions engaged in repetitive behaviors in an environment with a cognitively demanding feeding system, especially if those behaviors were similar to those seen in wild lions, because that finding wouldn't be an example of a new behavior developing in captivity as a result of low cognitive engagement. *Choice D* is incorrect because the text suggests that the researchers' findings were consistent with earlier findings that animals may develop new purposelessly repetitive behaviors in captivity. It isn't logical to conclude that the researchers weren't surprised to find that both captive and wild lions engage in stereotypic pacing before a feeding activity, since that finding would be an example of a repetitive behavior shared by wild and captive animals rather than one that newly developed in captivity.

QUESTION 15

Choice A is the best answer. The convention being tested is subject-verb agreement. The plural verb "epitomize" agrees in number with the plural subject "recipes."

Choice B is incorrect because the singular verb "has epitomized" doesn't agree in number with the plural subject "recipes." *Choice C* is incorrect because the singular verb "epitomizes" doesn't agree in number with the plural subject "recipes." *Choice D* is incorrect because the singular verb "was epitomizing" doesn't agree in number with the plural subject "recipes."

QUESTION 16

Choice B is the best answer. The convention being tested is punctuation use between sentences. In this choice, the period is used to correctly mark the boundary between one sentence ("A ray...works") and another ("Because...image").

Choice A is incorrect because it results in a run-on sentence. The two sentences ("A ray...works" and "Because...image") are fused without punctuation and/or a conjunction. *Choice C* is incorrect because it results in a comma splice. A comma can't be used in this way to mark the boundary between sentences. *Choice D* is incorrect because it results in a comma splice. Since the contraction "it's" creates a main clause, the comma after "single ray" can't be used in this way to mark the boundary between two main clauses ("it's...ray" and "all light...image").

QUESTION 17

Choice B is the best answer. The convention being tested is the use of punctuation between titles and proper nouns. No punctuation is needed to set off the proper noun "Marie-Denise Villers" from the title that describes Villers, "little-known French portrait artist."

Choice A is incorrect because no punctuation is needed. *Choice C* is incorrect because no punctuation is needed. *Choice D* is incorrect because no punctuation is needed.

QUESTION 18

Choice B is the best answer. The convention being tested is the punctuation of supplementary elements within a sentence. The comma after "described" separates the first supplementary element ("both of interviewees and the items they described") from the second supplementary element ("from hair to grass to sculptures"). Furthermore, the dash after "sculptures" pairs with the dash after "photographs" to separate these two supplementary elements from the rest of the sentence. The pair of dashes, which operate at a higher organizing level than the comma, indicates that the elements between the dashes function together—in this case, the second supplement ("from...sculptures") describes the range of items mentioned in the first supplement—and could be removed without affecting the grammatical coherence of the sentence.

Choice A is incorrect because it fails to appropriately punctuate the supplementary elements in the sentence. A dash is needed after "sculptures" to separate the supplementary elements ("both...sculptures") from the rest of the sentence. *Choice C* is incorrect because it fails to appropriately punctuate the supplementary elements in the sentence. The two supplementary elements "both...described" and "from...sculptures" function together to describe the photographs, and placing a dash between them would make this relationship less clear, suggesting that the supplement "both...described" is a standalone element that could be removed without affecting the grammatical coherence of the sentence, which isn't the case. *Choice D* is incorrect because it fails to appropriately punctuate the supplementary elements in the sentence. A colon isn't conventionally used in this way to separate a supplementary element ("from hair to grass to sculptures") from the noun phrase it is modifying ("items they described"). Additionally, a dash is needed after "sculptures" to separate the supplementary elements ("both...sculptures") from the rest of the sentence.

QUESTION 19

Choice C is the best answer. The convention being tested is the use of verb forms within a sentence. This choice pairs the comma after "Serra" with the comma after "environment" and uses the nonfinite present participle "intending" to correctly form a supplementary phrase describing the reaction Serra intends his sculptures to provoke. This supplementary phrase appears between the noun phrase that it modifies ("American abstract artist Richard Serra") and the finite present tense verb ("assembles"), which functions as the sentence's main verb and describes what Serra does.

Choice A is incorrect because it results in an ungrammatical sentence. The finite present continuous tense verb "is intending" can't be used in this way in conjunction with the finite present tense verb "assembles," which already functions as the main verb in the sentence. *Choice B* is incorrect because it results in an ungrammatical sentence. The finite present tense verb "intends" can't be used in this way to supplement the noun phrase "American abstract artist Richard Serra." *Choice D* is incorrect because it results in an ungrammatical sentence. The finite present tense verb "intends" can't be used in this way in conjunction with the finite present tense verb "assembles," which already functions as the main verb in the sentence.

QUESTION 20

Choice B is the best answer. The convention being tested is subject-verb agreement. The plural verb "increase" agrees in number with the plural subject "toxins."

Choice A is incorrect because the singular verb "is increasing" doesn't agree in number with the plural subject "toxins." *Choice C* is incorrect because the singular verb "increases" doesn't agree in number with the plural subject "toxins." *Choice D* is incorrect because the singular verb "has increased" doesn't agree in number with the plural subject "toxins."

QUESTION 21

Choice D is the best answer. "Though" logically signals that the claim in the sentence—that Morton's improvisational skills helped shape jazz as a genre during its early years ("No one can deny" it)—is true despite the previous information about Morton's exaggerated claim to have invented jazz.

Choice A is incorrect because "therefore" illogically signals that the claim in the sentence is a result of the previous information about Morton's claim to have invented jazz. Instead, the sentence states that Morton helped to shape jazz—even if his claim was an exaggeration. *Choice B* is incorrect because "in the second place" illogically signals that the claim in the sentence is a second, separate point in addition to Morton's claim to have invented jazz. Instead, the sentence states that Morton helped to shape jazz—even if his claim was an exaggeration. *Choice C* is incorrect because "in other words" illogically signals that the claim in the sentence is merely a paraphrase or restatement of the previous information about Morton's claim to have invented jazz. Instead, the sentence states that Morton helped to shape jazz—even if his claim was an exaggeration.

QUESTION 22

Choice B is the best answer. "In fact" logically signals that the critics' claim at the end of this sentence—that the two editions are essentially two different novels altogether—offers additional emphasis in support of the previous claim that the differences between the editions are extreme.

Choice A is incorrect because "by contrast" illogically signals that the claim at the end of this sentence contrasts with the previous claim about the differences between the editions. Instead, the critics' opinion offers additional emphasis in support of that claim. *Choice C* is incorrect because "nevertheless" illogically signals that the claim at the end of this sentence is true despite the previous claim about the differences between the two editions. Instead, the critics' opinion offers additional emphasis in support of that claim. *Choice D* is incorrect because "in other words" illogically signals that the claim at the end of this sentence is merely paraphrasing the previous claim about the differences between the two editions. The critics' opinion adds new information to the previous claim rather than simply paraphrasing it.

QUESTION 23

Choice B is the best answer. "Then" signals that this sentence's claim about Darwin and Wallace follows logically from the previous information. In other words, both scientists independently arriving at the theory of natural selection was, arguably, an expected outcome of the circumstances mentioned in the previous sentence.

Choice A is incorrect because "however" illogically signals that the claim in this sentence contrasts with the previous information about the ideas circulating among British scientists in the 1800s. Instead, this claim follows logically from that information. *Choice C* is incorrect because "moreover" illogically signals that the claim in this sentence merely adds to the previous information about the ideas circulating among British scientists in the 1800s. Instead, this claim follows logically from that information. *Choice D* is incorrect because "for example" illogically signals that this sentence provides an example supporting the previous information about the ideas circulating among British scientists in the 1800s. Instead, it presents a claim that follows logically from that information.

QUESTION 24

Choice B is the best answer. "In other words" logically signals that this sentence is a paraphrase of the previous description of the researchers' study. It summarizes what the researchers examined and clarifies several terms used in the previous sentence (diurnal, nocturnal, and crepuscular).

Choice A is incorrect because "afterward" illogically signals that the information in this sentence occurs later in a chronological sequence of events than the previous information about the researchers' study. Instead, this sentence is a paraphrase of that information. *Choice C* is incorrect because "additionally" illogically signals that this sentence provides a separate point in addition to the previous information about the researchers' study. Instead, this sentence is a paraphrase of that information. *Choice D* is incorrect because "however" illogically signals that the information in this sentence contrasts with the previous information about the researchers' study. Instead, this sentence is a paraphrase of that information.

QUESTION 25

Choice A is the best answer. The sentence emphasizes a similarity between P waves and S waves, noting that they both travel beneath Earth's surface, thereby causing the ground to move.

Choice B is incorrect. The sentence emphasizes a difference between P waves and S waves, noting that P waves travel faster than S waves; it doesn't emphasize a similarity between the two types of waves. *Choice C* is incorrect. The sentence emphasizes how P waves move; it doesn't emphasize a similarity between

P waves and S waves. *Choice D* is incorrect. While the sentence acknowledges that P waves and S waves start at the same point, it doesn't emphasize a similarity; instead, the sentence emphasizes a difference between the two types of waves, noting that they behave very differently.

QUESTION 26

Choice D is the best answer. The sentence effectively indicates the California red-legged frog's FWS classification category, noting that the FWS classifies the frog as threatened, a classification given to species that are likely to soon become endangered.

Choice A is incorrect. The sentence specifies the classification categories of the FWS list; it doesn't indicate the classification category of the California red-legged frog. *Choice B* is incorrect. While the sentence does note that the California red-legged frog is among the species classified by the FWS, it doesn't indicate what classification category the California red-legged frog occupies. *Choice C* is incorrect. While the sentence does appear to indicate the California red-legged frog's FWS classification category, the sentence is factually incorrect and therefore ineffective; the frog's classification category is threatened, not endangered.

QUESTION 27

Choice C is the best answer. The sentence makes a generalization about the materials used in dhow replicas, noting that while some modern materials are used, most of the materials are traditional.

Choice A is incorrect. The sentence provides an example of a traditional material used in ancient dhows; it doesn't indicate that the material is used in dhow replicas or make any other generalization about materials used in those replicas. *Choice B* is incorrect. The sentence explains what an ancient dhow was; it doesn't make a generalization about materials used to make dhow replicas. *Choice D* is incorrect. The sentence introduces the construction of dhow replicas to an audience unfamiliar with the vessel; it doesn't make a generalization about the materials used in those replicas.

Math

Module 1
(22 questions)

QUESTION 1

Choice A is correct. It's given that a certain bird species can fly at an average speed of 16 meters per second when in continuous flight. At this rate, in 4 seconds this bird species would fly $\left(\dfrac{16 \text{ meters}}{\text{second}}\right)$ (4 seconds), or 64 meters.

Choice B is incorrect. This is the value of 16 + 4, not 16(4). *Choice C* is incorrect. This is the distance the bird would fly in 1 second, not 4 seconds. *Choice D* is incorrect. This is the value of 16 − 4, not 16(4).

QUESTION 2

Choice D is correct. A line in the *xy*-plane with a slope of *m* and a *y*-intercept of (0, *b*) can be defined by an equation in the form $y = mx + b$. It's given that line *r* has a slope of 4 and passes through the point (0, 6). It follows that *m* = 4 and *b* = 6. Substituting 4 for *m* and 6 for *b* in the equation $y = mx + b$ yields $y = 4x + 6$. Therefore, the equation $y = 4x + 6$ defines line *r*.

Choice A is incorrect. This equation defines a line that has a slope of −6, not 4, and passes through the point (0, 4), not (0, 6). *Choice B* is incorrect. This equation defines a line that has a slope of 6, not 4, and passes through the point (0, 4), not (0, 6). *Choice C* is incorrect. This equation defines a line that passes through the point (0, −6), not (0, 6).

QUESTION 3

Choice B is correct. Since x^3 is a common factor of each term in the given expression, the expression can be rewritten as $x^3(5x^2 - 6x + 8)$.

Choice A is incorrect. This expression is equivalent to $5x^5 - 6x^4$. *Choice C* is incorrect. This expression is equivalent to $40x^5 - 48x^4 + 8x^3$. *Choice D* is incorrect. This expression is equivalent to $-36x^9 + 48x^8 + 6x^5$.

QUESTION 4

Choice B is correct. It's given that the equation $x + y = 1{,}440$ represents the number of minutes of daylight, *x*, and the number of minutes of non-daylight, *y*, on a particular day in Oak Park, Illinois. It's also given that this day has 670 minutes of daylight. Substituting 670 for *x* in the equation $x + y = 1{,}440$ yields $670 + y = 1{,}440$. Subtracting 670 from both sides of this equation yields $y = 770$. Therefore, this day has 770 minutes of non-daylight.

Choice A is incorrect. This is the number of minutes of daylight, not non-daylight, on this day. *Choice C* is incorrect and may result from conceptual or calculation errors. *Choice D* is incorrect. This is the total number of minutes of daylight and non-daylight.

QUESTION 5

Choice B is correct. It's given that from the sample of 20 employees at the company, 16 of the employees are enrolled in exactly three professional development courses this year. Since $\left(\frac{16}{20}\right)$ is equal to 0.80, or $\frac{80}{100}$, it follows that 80% of the employees in the sample are enrolled in exactly three professional development courses this year. Therefore, the best estimate for the percentage of employees at the company who are enrolled in exactly three professional development courses this year is 80%. It's given that there are a total of 400 employees at the company. Therefore, the best estimate of the number of employees at the company who are enrolled in exactly three professional development courses this year is $\left(\frac{80}{100}\right)(400)$, or 320.

Choice A is incorrect. This is the number of employees from the sample who aren't enrolled in exactly three professional development courses this year. *Choice C* is incorrect. This is the number of employees who weren't selected for the sample. *Choice D* is incorrect and may result from conceptual or calculation errors.

QUESTION 6

Choice A is correct. Dividing each side of the given equation by 7 yields $\frac{7(2x - 3)}{7} = \frac{63}{7}$, or $2x - 3 = 9$. Therefore, the equation $2x - 3 = 9$ is equivalent to the given equation and has the same solution.

Choice B is incorrect. This equation is equivalent to $7(2x - 3) = 392$, not $7(2x - 3) = 63$. *Choice C* is incorrect. Distributing 7 on the left-hand side of the given equation yields $14x - 21 = 63$, not $2x - 21 = 63$. *Choice D* is incorrect. Distributing 7 on the left-hand side of the given equation yields $14x - 21 = 63$, not $2x - 21 = 70$.

QUESTION 7

Choice A is correct. Adding 7 to each side of the given equation yields $c = 25p + k + 7$.

Choice B is incorrect. This equation is equivalent to $c + 7 = 25p + k$, not $c - 7 = 25p + k$. *Choice C* is incorrect. This equation is equivalent to $\frac{c}{7} = 25p + k$, not $c - 7 = 25p + k$. *Choice D* is incorrect. This equation is equivalent to $7c = 25p + k$, not $c - 7 = 25p + k$.

QUESTION 8

Choice C is correct. It's given that a function p estimates that there were 2,000 animals in a population in 1998 and that each year from 1998 to 2010, the number of animals in this population increased by 3% of the number of animals in the population the previous year. It follows that this situation can be represented by the function $p(x) = a\left(1 + \frac{r}{100}\right)^x$, where $p(x)$ is the estimated number of animals in the population x years after 1998, a is the estimated number of animals in the population in 1998, and each year the estimated number of animals increased by $r\%$. Substituting 2,000 for a and 3 for r in this function yields $p(x) = 2,000\left(1 + \frac{3}{100}\right)^x$, or $p(x) = 2,000(1.03)^x$.

Choice A is incorrect. This function represents a population in which each year the number of animals increased by 200%, not 3%, of the number of animals in the population the previous year. *Choice B* is incorrect. This function represents a population in which each year the number of animals increased by 97%, not 3%, of the number of animals in the population the previous year. *Choice D* is incorrect. This function represents a population in which each year the number of animals decreased, rather than increased, by 3% of the number of animals in the population the previous year.

QUESTION 9

Choice B is correct. The expression $(x^2 + 11)^2$ can be written as $(x^2 + 11)(x^2 + 11)$, which is equivalent to $x^2(x^2 + 11) + 11(x^2 + 11)$. Distributing x^2 and 11 to $(x^2 + 11)$ yields $x^4 + 11x^2 + 11x^2 + 121$, or $x^4 + 22x^2 + 121$. The expression $(x - 5)(x + 5)$ is equivalent to $(x - 5)x + (x - 5)5$. Distributing x and 5 to $(x - 5)$ yields $x^2 - 5x + 5x - 25$, or $x^2 - 25$. Therefore, the expression $(x^2 + 11)^2 + (x - 5)(x + 5)$ is equivalent to $(x^4 + 22x^2 + 121) + (x^2 - 25)$, or $x^4 + 22x^2 + 121 + x^2 - 25$. Combining like terms in this expression yields $x^4 + 23x^2 + 96$.

Choice A is incorrect. Equivalent expressions must be equivalent for any value of x. Substituting 0 for x in this expression yields -14, whereas substituting 0 for x in the given expression yields 96. *Choice C* is incorrect. Equivalent expressions must be equivalent for any value of x. Substituting 0 for x in this expression yields 121, whereas substituting 0 for x in the given expression yields 96. *Choice D* is incorrect. Equivalent expressions must be equivalent for any value of x. Substituting 0 for x in this expression yields 146, whereas substituting 0 for x in the given expression yields 96.

QUESTION 10

The correct answer is 18. It's given that an egg is thrown from a rooftop and that the equation $h = -4.9t^2 + 9t + 18$ represents this situation, where h is the height of the egg above the ground, in meters, t seconds after it is thrown. If follows that the height, in meters, from which the egg was thrown is the value of h when $t = 0$. Substituting 0 for t in the equation $h = -4.9t^2 + 9t + 18$ yields $h(0) = -4.9(0)^2 + 9(0) + 18$, or $h = 18$. Therefore, according to the equation, the height, in meters, from which the egg was thrown is 18.

QUESTION 11

Choice B is correct. Dividing each side of the given equation by 4 yields $\sqrt{2x} = 4$. Squaring both sides of this equation yields $2x = 16$. Multiplying each side of this equation by 3 yields $6x = 48$. Therefore, the value of $6x$ is 48.

Choice A is incorrect. This is the value of $3x$, not $6x$. *Choice C* is incorrect. This is the value of $9x$, not $6x$. *Choice D* is incorrect. This is the value of $12x$, not $6x$.

QUESTION 12

Choice C is correct. It's given that the relationship between x and y is linear. An equation representing a linear relationship can be written in the form $y = mx + b$, where m is the slope and b is the y-coordinate of the y-intercept of the graph of the relationship in the xy-plane. It's given that for every increase in the value of x by 1, the value of y increases by 8. The slope of a line can be expressed as the change in y over the change in x. Thus, the slope, m, of the line representing this relationship can be expressed as $\frac{8}{1}$, or 8. Substituting 8 for m in the equation $y = mx + b$ yields $y = 8x + b$. It's also given that when the value of x is 2, the value of y is 18. Substituting 2 for x and 18 for y in the equation $y = 8x + b$ yields $18 = 8(2) + b$, or $18 = 16 + b$. Subtracting 16 from each side of this equation yields $2 = b$. Substituting 2 for b in the equation $y = 8x + b$ yields $y = 8x + 2$. Therefore, the equation $y = 8x + 2$ represents this relationship.

Choice A is incorrect. This equation represents a relationship where for every increase in the value of x by 1, the value of y increases by 2, not 8, and when the value of x is 2, the value of y is 22, not 18. *Choice B* is incorrect. This equation represents a relationship where for every increase in the value of x by 1, the value of y increases by 2, not 8, and when the value of x is 2, the value of y is 12, not 18. *Choice D* is incorrect. This equation represents a relationship where for every increase in the value of x by 1, the value of y increases by 3, not 8, and when the value of x is 2, the value of y is 32, not 18.

QUESTION 13

Choice D is correct. Since the square of a real number is never negative, the given equation isn't true for any real value of x. Therefore, the given equation has zero distinct real solutions.

Choice A is incorrect and may result from conceptual or calculation errors.
Choice B is incorrect and may result from conceptual or calculation errors.
Choice C is incorrect and may result from conceptual or calculation errors.

QUESTION 14

The correct answer is 4. It's given that the two box plots show the distribution of number of books read over the summer by the students in two different English classes. In a box plot, the first vertical line represents the minimum value of the data set and the last vertical line represents the maximum value of the data set. The range of a data set is the difference between its maximum value and its minimum value. In class A, the maximum number of books read is 5 and the minimum number of books read is 0. The difference between those values is 5 − 0, or 5. Therefore, the range of the number of books read in class A is 5. In class B, the maximum number of books read is 10 and the minimum number of books read is 1. The difference between those values is 10 − 1, or 9. Therefore, the range of the number of books read in class B is 9. To find the positive difference between the ranges of the number of books read for the two classes, the smaller range must be subtracted from the larger range. Therefore, the positive difference between the ranges of number of books read over the summer for the two classes is 9 − 5, or 4.

QUESTION 15

Choice D is correct. The volume, V, of a right square prism is given by the formula $V = s^2 h$, where s represents the length of the edge of the base and h represents the height of the prism. It's given that the volume of a right square prism is 2,880 cubic units and the length of the edge of the base is 6 units.

Substituting 2,880 for V and 6 for s in the formula $V = s^2h$ yields $2,880 = (6^2)h$, or $2,880 = 36h$. Dividing both sides of this equation by 36 yields $80 = h$. Therefore, the height, in units, of the prism is 80.

Choice A is incorrect. This is the height, in units, of a right square prism where the length of the edge of the base is 6 units and the volume of the prism is $144\sqrt{30}$, not 2,880, units. *Choice B* is incorrect. This is the area, in square units, of the base, not the height, in units, of the prism. *Choice C* is incorrect. This is the height, in units, of a right square prism where the length of the edge of the base is 6 units and the volume of the prism is $864\sqrt{5}$, not 2,880, units.

QUESTION 16

Choice A is correct. It's given that an equation for the exponential model shown can be written as $y = a(b)^x$, where a and b are positive constants. For an exponential model written in this form, if the value of b is greater than 0 but less than 1, the model is decreasing. If the value of b is greater than 1, the model is increasing. The exponential model shown is decreasing. Therefore, the value of b is greater than 0 but less than 1. Of the given choices, only 0.83 is a value greater than 0 but less than 1. Thus, 0.83 is closest to the value of b.

Choice B is incorrect and may result from conceptual or calculation errors.
Choice C is incorrect and may result from conceptual or calculation errors.
Choice D is incorrect and may result from conceptual or calculation errors.

QUESTION 17

The correct answer is $\frac{11}{28}$. The cosine of an acute angle in a right triangle is defined as the ratio of the length of the leg adjacent to the angle to the length of the hypotenuse. In the triangle shown, the length of the leg adjacent to the angle with measure $x°$ is 11 units and the length of the hypotenuse is 28 units. Therefore, the value of $\cos x°$ is $\frac{11}{28}$. Note that 11/28, .3928, .3929, 0.392, and 0.393 are examples of ways to enter a correct answer.

QUESTION 18

Choice C is correct. Applying the zero product property to the given equation yields three equations: $x + 2 = 0$, $x - 5 = 0$, and $x + 9 = 0$. Subtracting 2 from both sides of the equation $x + 2 = 0$ yields $x = -2$. Adding 5 to both sides of the equation $x - 5 = 0$ yields $x = 5$. Subtracting 9 from both sides of the equation $x + 9 = 0$ yields $x = -9$. Therefore, the solutions to the given equation are -2, 5, and -9. It follows that a positive solution to the given equation is 5.

Choice A is incorrect and may result from conceptual or calculation errors.
Choice B is incorrect and may result from conceptual or calculation errors.
Choice D is incorrect and may result from conceptual or calculation errors.

QUESTION 19

The correct answer is 54. The figure shown includes two triangles, triangle WQX and triangle YQZ, such that angle WQX and angle YQZ are vertical angles. It follows that angle WQX is congruent to angle YQZ. It's also given in the figure that the measures of angle W and angle Y are $a°$. Therefore angle W is congruent to angle Y. Since triangle WQX and triangle YQZ have two pairs of congruent angles, triangle WQX is similar to triangle YQZ by the angle-angle similarity postulate, where $\overline{YZ}$ corresponds to $\overline{WX}$, and $\overline{YQ}$ corresponds to $\overline{WQ}$.

Since the lengths of corresponding sides in similar triangles are proportional, it follows that $\frac{YZ}{WX} = \frac{YQ}{WQ}$. It's given that $YQ = 63$, $WQ = 70$, and $WX = 60$. Substituting 63 for YQ, 70 for WQ, and 60 for WX in the equation $\frac{YZ}{WX} = \frac{YQ}{WQ}$ yields $\frac{YZ}{60} = \frac{63}{70}$. Multiplying each side of this equation by 60 yields $YZ = \left(\frac{63}{70}\right)(60)$, or $YZ = 54$. Therefore, the length of $\overline{YZ}$ is 54.

QUESTION 20

The correct answer is 336. By the zero product property, if $(x + 14)(t - x) = 0$, then $x + 14 = 0$, which gives $x = -14$, or $(t - x) = 0$, which gives $x = t$. Therefore, $g(x) = 0$ when $x = -14$ and when $x = t$. Since the graph of $y = g(x)$ passes through the point $(24, 0)$, it follows that $g(24) = 0$, so $t = 24$. Substituting 24 for t in the equation $g(x) = (x + 14)(t - x)$ yields $g(x) = (x + 14)(24 - x)$. The value of $g(0)$ can be calculated by substituting 0 for x in this equation, which yields $g(0) = (0 + 14)(24 - 0)$, or $g(0) = 336$.

QUESTION 21

The correct answer is 79. Let x represent the number of zebras in the population in 2014 and let y represent the number of zebras in the population in 2018. It's given that the number of zebras in this population in 2018 was 1.27 times the number of zebras in this population in 2014. It follows that the equation $y = 1.27x$ represents this situation. Dividing both sides of this equation by 1.27 yields $\frac{y}{1.27} = x$, or $\left(\frac{1}{1.27}\right)y = x$. Therefore, the number of zebras in this population in 2014 is $\frac{1}{1.27}$ times the number of zebras in this population in 2018. If the number of zebras in this population in 2014 is p% of the number of zebras in this population in 2018, then $x = \frac{p}{100}y$. It follows that $\frac{1}{1.27} = \frac{p}{100}$, or $\frac{100}{1.27} = p$, which means p is approximately equal to 78.74. Therefore, the value of p, to the nearest whole number, is 79.

QUESTION 22

Choice A is correct. According to the graph, the center of circle A has coordinates $(-2, 0)$, and the radius of circle A is 3. It's given that circle B is the result of shifting circle A down 6 units and increasing the radius so that the radius of circle B is 2 times the radius of circle A. It follows that the center of circle B is 6 units below the center of circle A. The point that's 6 units below $(-2, 0)$ has the same x-coordinate as $(-2, 0)$ and has a y-coordinate that is 6 less than the y-coordinate of $(-2, 0)$. Therefore, the coordinates of the center of circle B are $(-2, 0 - 6)$, or $(-2, -6)$. Since the radius of circle B is 2 times the radius of circle A, the radius of circle B is $(2)(3)$. A circle in the xy-plane can be defined by an equation of the form $(x - h)^2 + (y - k)^2 = r^2$, where the coordinates of the center of the circle are (h, k) and the radius of the circle is r. Substituting -2 for h, -6 for k, and $(2)(3)$ for r in this equation yields $(x - (-2))^2 + (y - (-6))^2 = ((2)(3))^2$, which is equivalent to $(x + 2)^2 + (y + 6)^2 = (2)^2(3)^2$, or $(x + 2)^2 + (y + 6)^2 = (4)(9)$. Therefore, the equation $(x + 2)^2 + (y + 6)^2 = (4)(9)$ defines circle B.

Choice B is incorrect and may result from conceptual or calculation errors. *Choice C* is incorrect. This equation defines a circle that's the result of shifting circle A up, not down, by 6 units and increasing the radius. *Choice D* is incorrect and may result from conceptual or calculation errors.

Math

Module 2 — Lower Difficulty
(22 questions)

QUESTION 1

Choice B is correct. It's given that 100 centimeters is equal to 1 meter. Therefore, 2,300 centimeters is equivalent to $(2{,}300 \text{ centimeters})\left(\dfrac{1 \text{ meter}}{100 \text{ centimeters}}\right)$, or 23 meters.

Choice A is incorrect. 0.043 meters is equivalent to 4.3, not 2,300, centimeters. *Choice C* is incorrect. 2,400 meters is equivalent to 240,000, not 2,300, centimeters. *Choice D* is incorrect. 230,000 meters is equivalent to 23,000,000, not 2,300, centimeters.

QUESTION 2

Choice B is correct. Substituting 72 for $f(x)$ in the given function yields $72 = 8x$. Dividing each side of this equation by 8 yields $9 = x$. Therefore, $f(x) = 72$ when the value of x is 9.

Choice A is incorrect. This is the value of x for which $f(x) = 64$, not $f(x) = 72$. *Choice C* is incorrect. This is the value of x for which $f(x) = 512$, not $f(x) = 72$. *Choice D* is incorrect. This is the value of x for which $f(x) = 640$, not $f(x) = 72$.

QUESTION 3

Choice B is correct. 20% of 440 can be calculated as $\left(\dfrac{20}{100}\right)(440)$, which is equivalent to $\dfrac{8{,}800}{100}$, or 88.

Choice A is incorrect. This is 10%, not 20%, of 440. *Choice C* is incorrect. This is 200%, not 20%, of 440. *Choice D* is incorrect. This is 400%, not 20%, of 440.

QUESTION 4

Choice A is correct. It's given that angle 1 and angle 2 are vertical angles, and the measure of angle 1 is 72°. Vertical angles have equal measures. Therefore, the measure of angle 2 is 72°.

Choice B is incorrect. This is the measure of an angle that is supplementary, not congruent, to angle 1. *Choice C* is incorrect. This is the sum of the measures of angle 1 and angle 2. *Choice D* is incorrect and may result from conceptual or calculation errors.

QUESTION 5

Choice A is correct. Subtracting 8 from both sides of the given equation yields $p + 3 = 2$. Subtracting 3 from both sides of this equation yields $p = -1$.

Choice B is incorrect and may result from conceptual or calculation errors.
Choice C is incorrect and may result from conceptual or calculation errors.
Choice D is incorrect and may result from conceptual or calculation errors.

QUESTION 6

The correct answer is 3. A y-intercept of a graph in the xy-plane is a point (x, y) on the graph where $x = 0$. For the graph shown, at $x = 0$, the corresponding value of y is 3. Therefore, the y-coordinate of the y-intercept of the graph shown is 3.

QUESTION 7

Choice B is correct. A solution to a system of equations must be the solution to each equation in the system. It follows that if (x, y) is a solution to the system, the point (x, y) lies on the graph in the xy-plane of each equation in the system. The point that lies on each graph of the system of linear equations shown is their intersection point $(2, 4)$. Therefore, the solution to the system is $(2, 4)$.

Choice A is incorrect. The point $(0, 5)$ lies on one, but not both, of the graphs of the linear equations shown. *Choice C* is incorrect. The point $(5, 10)$ lies on one, but not both, of the graphs of the linear equations shown. *Choice D* is incorrect. The point $(10, 0)$ lies on one, but not both, of the graphs of the linear equations shown.

QUESTION 8

Choice D is correct. Adding 53 to each side of the given equation yields $k^2 = 144$. Taking the square root of each side of this equation yields $k = \pm12$. Therefore, the positive solution to the given equation is 12.

Choice A is incorrect. This is the positive solution to the equation $k^2 - 53 = 20{,}683$, not $k^2 - 53 = 91$. *Choice B* is incorrect. This is the positive solution to the equation $k^2 - 53 = 5{,}131$, not $k^2 - 53 = 91$. *Choice C* is incorrect. This is the positive solution to the equation $k^2 - 53 = 1{,}391$, not $k^2 - 53 = 91$.

QUESTION 9

The correct answer is 6. The first equation in the given system is $x = 8$. Substituting 8 for x in the second equation in the given system yields $8 + 3y = 26$. Subtracting 8 from both sides of this equation yields $3y = 18$. Dividing both sides of this equation by 3 yields $y = 6$. Therefore, the value of y is 6.

QUESTION 10

Choice D is correct. It's given that during a portion of a flight, a small airplane's cruising speed varied between 150 miles per hour and 170 miles per hour. It's also given that s represents the cruising speed, in miles per hour, during this portion of the flight. It follows that the airplane's cruising speed, in miles per hour, was at least 150, which means $s \geq 150$, and was at most 170, which means $s \leq 170$. Therefore, the inequality that best represents this situation is $150 \leq s \leq 170$.

Choice A is incorrect and may result from conceptual or calculation errors.
Choice B is incorrect and may result from conceptual or calculation errors.
Choice C is incorrect and may result from conceptual or calculation errors.

QUESTION 11

Choice C is correct. The solution to the system of two equations corresponds to the point where the graphs of the equations intersect. The graphs of the linear function and the absolute value function shown intersect at the point (1, 5). Thus, the solution to the system is (1, 5).

Choice A is incorrect and may result from conceptual or calculation errors. *Choice B* is incorrect. This is the *y*-intercept of the graph of the linear function. *Choice D* is incorrect. This is the vertex of the graph of the absolute value function.

QUESTION 12

Choice D is correct. The value of $g(4)$ is the value of $g(x)$ when $x = 4$. Substituting 4 for x in the given equation yields $g(4) = |4 + 18|$, which is equivalent to $g(4) = |22|$, or $g(4) = 22$. Therefore, the value of $g(4)$ is 22.

Choice A is incorrect. This would be the value of $g(4)$ if function g was defined by $g(x) = -|18|$, not $g(x) = |x + 18|$. *Choice B* is incorrect. This would be the value of $g(4)$ if function g was defined by $g(x) = -|x|$, not $g(x) = |x + 18|$. *Choice C* is incorrect. This would be the value of $g(4)$ if function g was defined by $g(x) = |-x + 18|$, not $g(x) = |x + 18|$.

QUESTION 13

Choice C is correct. It's given that the perimeter of an isosceles triangle is 36 feet and that each of the two congruent sides has a length of 10 feet. The perimeter of a triangle is the sum of the lengths of its three sides. The equation $10 + 10 + x = 36$ can be used to represent this situation, where x is the length, in feet, of the third side. Combining like terms on the left-hand side of this equation yields $20 + x = 36$. Subtracting 20 from each side of this equation yields $x = 16$. Therefore, the length, in feet, of the third side is 16.

Choice A is incorrect. This would be the length, in feet, of the third side if the perimeter was 30 feet, not 36 feet. *Choice B* is incorrect. This would be the length, in feet, of the third side if the perimeter was 32 feet, not 36 feet. *Choice D* is incorrect. This would be the length, in feet, of the third side if the perimeter was 38 feet, not 36 feet.

QUESTION 14

The correct answer is 20. For the graph shown, the *x*-axis represents the time since the initial deposit, in months, and the *y*-axis represents the bank account balance, in dollars. The amount of the initial deposit is estimated by the *y*-coordinate of the point on the graph that represents 0 months since the initial deposit. Therefore, the amount of the initial deposit is estimated by the corresponding *y*-value for the point when $x = 0$. When $x = 0$, it is estimated that $y = 20$. Thus, the amount of the initial deposit estimated by the graph, to the nearest whole dollar, is 20.

QUESTION 15

Choice D is correct. It's given that at a movie theater, there are a total of 350 customers and that each customer is located in either theater A, theater B, or theater C. If the probability of selecting a customer in theater A is 0.48, then (0.48)(350), or 168, customers are located in theater A. If the probability of selecting a customer in theater B is 0.24, then (0.24)(350), or 84, customers are located in theater B. It follows that there are 168 + 84, or 252, customers in theater A and theater B. Therefore, there are 350 − 252, or 98, customers in theater C.

Choice A is incorrect. This is the percent, not the number, of the customers that are located in theater C. *Choice B* is incorrect and may result from conceptual or calculation errors. *Choice C* is incorrect. This is the number of customers that are located in theater B, not theater C.

QUESTION 16

The correct answer is 774. It's given that Brian saves $\frac{2}{5}$ of the $215 he earns each week from his job. Therefore, Brian saves $\left(\frac{2}{5}\right)$($215), or $86, per week.

If Brian continues to save at this rate of $86 per week for 9 weeks, then he will save a total of (9)(86), or 774, dollars.

QUESTION 17

Choice D is correct. Substituting −1 for x in the given function yields

$q(-1) = 32(2)^{-1}$, which is equivalent to $q(-1) = 32\left(\frac{1}{2}\right)$, or $q(-1) = 16$. Therefore,

when $x = -1$, the corresponding value of $q(x)$ for function q is 16. Substituting 0 for x in the given function yields $q(0) = 32(2)^{0}$, which is equivalent to $q(0) = 32(1)$, or $q(0) = 32$. Therefore, when $x = 0$, the corresponding value of $q(x)$ for function q is 32. Substituting 1 for x in the given function yields $q(1) = 32(2)^{1}$, which is equivalent to $q(1) = 32(2)$, or $q(1) = 64$. Therefore, when $x = 1$, the corresponding value of $q(x)$ for function q is 64. Of the choices given, only the table in choice D gives these three values of x and their corresponding values of $q(x)$ for function q.

Choice A is incorrect. This table gives three values of x and their corresponding values of $q(x)$ for the function $q(x) = 32(2x)$. *Choice B* is incorrect. This table gives three values of x and their corresponding values of $q(x)$ for the function $q(x) = 2(32)^{x}$. *Choice C* is incorrect and may result from conceptual or calculation errors.

QUESTION 18

Choice C is correct. The volume, V, of a right circular cylinder is given by the formula $V = \pi r^2 h$, where r is the radius of the base of the cylinder and h is the height of the cylinder. It's given that a right circular cylinder has a height of 6 centimeters. Therefore, $h = 6$. It's also given that the cylinder has a base diameter of 22 centimeters. The radius of a circle is half the diameter of the circle. Since the base of a right circular cylinder is a circle, it follows that

the radius of the base of the right circular cylinder is $\frac{22}{2}$, or 11, centimeters.

Therefore, $r = 11$. Substituting 11 for r and 6 for h in the formula $V = \pi r^2 h$ yields $V = \pi(11)^2(6)$, which is equivalent to $V = \pi(121)(6)$, or $V = 726\pi$. Therefore, the volume, in cubic centimeters, of the cylinder is 726π.

Choice A is incorrect. This is the volume of a right circular cylinder that has a base diameter of $2\sqrt{22}$, not 22, centimeters and a height of 6 centimeters. *Choice B* is incorrect. This is the volume of a right circular cylinder that has a base diameter of $4\sqrt{11}$, not 22, centimeters and a height of 6 centimeters. *Choice D* is incorrect. This is the volume of a right circular cylinder that has a base diameter of 44, not 22, centimeters and a height of 6 centimeters.

QUESTION 19

The correct answer is $\frac{44}{3}$. A linear equation can be written in the form $y = mx + b$, where m is the slope of the graph of the equation in the xy-plane and $(0, b)$ is the y-intercept. Distributing the $\frac{1}{3}$ in the equation $y = \frac{1}{3}(29x + 10) + 5x$ yields $y = \frac{29}{3}x + \frac{10}{3} + 5x$. Combining like terms on the right-hand side of this equation yields $y = \frac{44}{3}x + \frac{10}{3}$. This equation is in the form $y = mx + b$, where $m = \frac{44}{3}$ and $b = \frac{10}{3}$. Therefore, the slope of the graph of the given equation in the xy-plane is $\frac{44}{3}$. Note that 44/3, 14.66, and 14.67 are examples of ways to enter a correct answer.

QUESTION 20

The correct answer is 66. It's given that each vertex of the rectangle lies on the circumference of the circle. Therefore, the length of the diameter of the circle is equal to the length of the diagonal of the rectangle. The diagonal of a rectangle forms a right triangle with the shortest and longest sides of the rectangle, where the shortest side and the longest side of the rectangle are the legs of the triangle and the diagonal of the rectangle is the hypotenuse of the triangle. Let s represent the length, in units, of the shortest side of the rectangle. Since it's given that the diagonal is twice the length of the shortest side, $2s$ represents the length, in units, of the diagonal of the rectangle. By the Pythagorean theorem, if a right triangle has a hypotenuse with length c and legs with lengths a and b, then $a^2 + b^2 = c^2$. Substituting s for a and $2s$ for c in this equation yields $s^2 + b^2 = (2s)^2$, or $s^2 + b^2 = 4s^2$. Subtracting s^2 from both sides of this equation yields $b^2 = 3s^2$. Taking the positive square root of both sides of this equation yields $b = s\sqrt{3}$. Therefore, the length, in units, of the rectangle's longest side is $s\sqrt{3}$. The area of a rectangle is the product of the length of the shortest side and the length of the longest side. The lengths, in units, of the shortest and longest sides of the rectangle are represented by s and $s\sqrt{3}$, and it's given that the area of the rectangle is $1{,}089\sqrt{3}$ square units. It follows that $1{,}089\sqrt{3} = s(s\sqrt{3})$, or $1{,}089\sqrt{3} = s^2\sqrt{3}$. Dividing both sides of this equation by $\sqrt{3}$ yields $1{,}089 = s^2$. Taking the positive square root of both sides of this equation yields $33 = s$. Since the length, in units, of the diagonal is represented by $2s$, it follows that the length, in units, of the diagonal is $2(33)$, or 66. Since the length of the diameter of the circle is equal to the length of the diagonal of the rectangle, the length, in units, of the diameter of the circle is 66.

QUESTION 21

Choice D is correct. All the tables in the choices have the same three values of x, 440, 441, and 442, so each of the three values of x can be substituted in the given inequality to compare the corresponding values of y in each of the tables. Substituting 440 for x in the given inequality yields $2(440) - y > 883$, or $880 - y > 883$. Subtracting 880 from both sides of this inequality yields $-y > 3$. Dividing both sides of this inequality by -1 yields $y < -3$. Therefore, when $x = 440$, the corresponding value of y must be less than -3. Substituting 441 for x in the given inequality yields $2(441) - y > 883$, or $882 - y > 883$. Subtracting 882 from both sides of this inequality yields $-y > 1$. Dividing both sides of this inequality by -1 yields $y < -1$. Therefore, when $x = 441$, the corresponding value of y must be less than -1. Substituting 442 for x in the given inequality yields $2(442) - y > 883$, or $884 - y > 883$. Subtracting 884 from both sides of this inequality yields $-y > -1$. Dividing both sides of this inequality by -1 yields $y < 1$. Therefore, when $x = 442$, the corresponding value of y must be less than 1. For the table in choice D, when $x = 440$, the corresponding value of y is -4, which is less than -3; when $x = 441$, the corresponding value of y is -2, which is less than -1; when $x = 442$, the corresponding value of y is 0, which is less than 1. Therefore, the table in choice D gives values of x and their corresponding values of y that are all solutions to the given inequality.

Choice A is incorrect. When $x = 440$, the corresponding value of y in this table is 0, which isn't less than -3. *Choice B* is incorrect. When $x = 440$, the corresponding value of y in this table is 0, which isn't less than -3. *Choice C* is incorrect. When $x = 440$, the corresponding value of y in this table is -2, which isn't less than -3.

QUESTION 22

Choice C is correct. It's given that m represents the original price, in dollars, of the mirror, and v represents the original price, in dollars, of the vase. It's also given that the combined original price for the mirror and the vase is $60. This can be represented by the equation $m + v = 60$. After a 25% discount to the mirror is applied, the sale price of the mirror is 75% of its original price. This can be represented by the expression $0.75m$. After a 45% discount to the vase is applied, the sale price of the vase is 55% of its original price. This can be represented by the expression $0.55v$. It's given that the combined sale price for the two items is $39. This can be represented by the equation $0.75m + 0.55v = 39$. Therefore, the system of equations consisting of the equations $m + v = 60$ and $0.75m + 0.55v = 39$ gives the original price m, in dollars, of the mirror and the original price v, in dollars, of the vase.

Choice A is incorrect. The second equation in this system of equations represents a 45% discount to the mirror and a 25% discount to the vase. *Choice B* is incorrect. The second equation in this system of equations represents a 55% discount to the mirror and a 75% discount to the vase. *Choice D* is incorrect. The second equation in this system of equations represents a 75% discount to the mirror and a 55% discount to the vase.

Math

Module 2 — Higher Difficulty
(22 questions)

QUESTION 1

Choice B is correct. It's given that the shop's inventory starts with 4,500 paper cups and that the manager estimates that 70 of these paper cups are used each day. Let x represent the number of days in which the estimated supply of paper cups will reach 1,700. The equation $4{,}500 - 70x = 1{,}700$ represents this situation. Subtracting 4,500 from both sides of this equation yields $-70x = -2{,}800$. Dividing both sides of this equation by -70 yields $x = 40$. Therefore, based on this estimate, the supply of paper cups will reach 1,700 in 40 days.

Choice A is incorrect. After 20 days, the estimated supply of paper cups would be $4{,}500 - 70(20)$, or 3,100 cups, not 1,700 cups. *Choice C* is incorrect. After 60 days, the estimated supply of paper cups would be $4{,}500 - 70(60)$, or 300 cups, not 1,700 cups. *Choice D* is incorrect. After 80 days, the estimated supply of paper cups would be $4{,}500 - 70(80)$, or $-1{,}100$ cups, which isn't possible.

QUESTION 2

Choice A is correct. The sum of the measures of the angles of a triangle is 180°. Therefore, the sum of the measures of $\angle R$, $\angle S$, and $\angle T$ is 180°. It's given that the measure of $\angle R$ is 63°. It follows that the sum of the measures of $\angle S$ and $\angle T$ is $(180 - 63)°$, or 117°. Therefore, the measure of $\angle S$, in degrees, must be less than 117. Of the given choices, only 116 is less than 117. Thus, the measure, in degrees, of $\angle S$ could be 116.

Choice B is incorrect. If the measure of $\angle S$ is 118°, then the sum of the measures of the angles of the triangle is greater than, not equal to, 180°. *Choice C* is incorrect. If the measure of $\angle S$ is 126°, then the sum of the measures of the angles of the triangle is greater than, not equal to, 180°. *Choice D* is incorrect. This is the sum of the measures of the angles of a triangle, in degrees.

QUESTION 3

Choice A is correct. In each choice, the values of x are 2, 4, and 6. Substituting the first value of x, 2, for x in the given inequality yields $y > 4(2) + 8$, or $y > 16$. Therefore, when $x = 2$, the corresponding value of y must be greater than 16. Of the given choices, only choice A is a table where the value of y corresponding to $x = 2$ is greater than 16. To confirm that the other values of x in this table and their corresponding values of y are also solutions to the given inequality, the values of *x* and *y* in the table can be substituted for *x* and *y* in the given inequality. Substituting 4 for *x* and 30 for *y* in the given inequality yields 30 > 4(4) + 8, or 30 > 24, which is true. Substituting 6 for *x* and 41 for *y* in the given inequality yields 41 > 4(6) + 8, or 41 > 32, which is true. It follows that for choice A, all the values of *x* and their corresponding values of *y* are solutions to the given inequality.

Choice B is incorrect. Substituting 2 for *x* and 8 for *y* in the given inequality yields 8 > 4(2) + 8, or 8 > 16, which is false. *Choice C* is incorrect. Substituting 2 for *x* and 13 for *y* in the given inequality yields 13 > 4(2) + 8, or 13 > 16, which is false. *Choice D* is incorrect. Substituting 2 for *x* and 13 for *y* in the given inequality yields 13 > 4(2) + 8, or 13 > 16, which is false.

QUESTION 4

The correct answer is 3. Substituting 5 for *f*(*x*) in the given function yields $5 = \frac{9}{7}x + \frac{8}{7}$. Multiplying each side of this equation by 7 yields $7(5) = 7\left(\frac{9}{7}x + \frac{8}{7}\right)$, or 35 = 9*x* + 8. Subtracting 8 from each side of this equation yields 27 = 9*x*. Dividing each side of this equation by 9 yields 3 = *x*. Therefore, *f*(*x*) = 5 when the value of *x* is 3.

QUESTION 5

Choice D is correct. It's given that during a portion of a flight, a small airplane's cruising speed varied between 150 miles per hour and 170 miles per hour. It's also given that *s* represents the cruising speed, in miles per hour, during this portion of the flight. It follows that the airplane's cruising speed, in miles per hour, was at least 150, which means *s* ≥ 150, and was at most 170, which means *s* ≤ 170. Therefore, the inequality that best represents this situation is 150 ≤ *s* ≤ 170.

Choice A is incorrect and may result from conceptual or calculation errors. *Choice B* is incorrect and may result from conceptual or calculation errors. *Choice C* is incorrect and may result from conceptual or calculation errors.

QUESTION 6

Choice B is correct. It's given that the graph models the number of active projects a company was working on *x* months after the end of November 2012. Therefore, the value of *x* that corresponds to the end of November 2012 is 0. The point at which *x* = 0 is the *y*-intercept of the graph. It follows that the *y*-intercept of the graph shown is the point (0, 5). Therefore, according to the model, the predicted number of active projects the company was working on at the end of November 2012 is 5.

Choice A is incorrect. This is the value of *x* that corresponds to the end of November 2012, not the predicted number of active projects the company was working on at the end of November 2012. *Choice C* is incorrect. This is the predicted number of active projects the company was working on 2 months after the end of November 2012. *Choice D* is incorrect. This is the predicted number of active projects the company was working on 4 months after the end of November 2012.

QUESTION 7

Choice D is correct. An equation defining *h* can be written in the form *y* = *mx* + *b*, where *y* = *h*(*x*), *m* represents the slope of the graph of *y* = *h*(*x*) in the *xy*-plane, and *b* represents the *y*-coordinate of the *y*-intercept of the graph. It's given that *h*(28) = 15 and *h*(26) = 22. It follows that the points (28, 15) and (26, 22) are on the graph of $y = h(x)$ in the *xy*-plane. The slope can be found by using any two points, (x_1, y_1) and (x_2, y_2), and the formula $m = \frac{y_2 - y_1}{x_2 - x_1}$. Substituting (28, 15) and (26, 22) for (x_1, y_1) and (x_2, y_2), respectively, in the slope formula yields $m = \frac{22 - 15}{26 - 28}$, or $m = -\frac{7}{2}$. Substituting $-\frac{7}{2}$ for m and (28, 15) for (x, y) in the equation $y = mx + b$ yields $15 = \left(-\frac{7}{2}\right)(28) + b$, or $15 = -98 + b$. Adding 98 to both sides of this equation yields $113 = b$. Substituting $-\frac{7}{2}$ for m and 113 for b in the equation $y = mx + b$ yields $y = -\frac{7}{2}x + 113$. Since $y = h(x)$, it follows that the equation that defines h is $h(x) = -\frac{7}{2}x + 113$.

Choice A is incorrect. For this function, $h(26) = \frac{109}{7}$, not $h(26) = 22$. *Choice B is incorrect.* For this function, $h(28) = 105$, not $h(28) = 15$, and $h(26) = \frac{739}{7}$, not $h(26) = 22$. *Choice C is incorrect.* For this function, $h(28) = -75$, not $h(28) = 15$, and $h(26) = -68$, not $h(26) = 22$.

QUESTION 8

Choice A is correct. It's given that there is a linear relationship between the number of cars, *c*, on a commuter train and the maximum number of passengers and crew, *p*, that the train can carry. It follows that this relationship can be represented by an equation of the form $p = mc + b$, where *m* is the rate of change of *p* in this relationship and *b* is a constant. The rate of change of *p* in this relationship can be calculated by dividing the difference in any two values of *p* by the difference in the corresponding values of *c*. Using two pairs of values given in the table, the rate of change of *p* in this relationship is $\frac{284 - 174}{5 - 3}$, or 55.

Substituting 55 for *m* in the equation $p = mc + b$ yields $p = 55c + b$. The value of *b* can be found by substituting any value of *c* and its corresponding value of *p* for *c* and *p*, respectively, in this equation. Substituting 10 for *c* and 559 for *p* yields $559 = 55(10) + b$, or $559 = 550 + b$. Subtracting 550 from both sides of this equation yields $9 = b$. Substituting 9 for *b* in the equation $p = 55c + b$ yields $p = 55c + 9$. Subtracting 9 from both sides of this equation yields $p - 9 = 55c$. Subtracting *p* from both sides of this equation yields $-9 = 55c - p$, or $55c - p = -9$.

Choice B is incorrect and may result from conceptual or calculation errors.
Choice C is incorrect and may result from conceptual or calculation errors.
Choice D is incorrect and may result from conceptual or calculation errors.

QUESTION 9

Choice D is correct. Adding 40 to both sides of the given equation yields $w^2 + 12w = 40$. To complete the square, adding $\left(\frac{12}{2}\right)^2$, or 6^2, to both sides of this equation yields $w^2 + 12w + 6^2 = 40 + 6^2$, or $(w + 6)^2 = 76$. Taking the square root of both sides of this equation yields $w + 6 = \pm\sqrt{76}$, or $w + 6 = \pm 2\sqrt{19}$. Subtracting 6 from both sides of this equation yields $w = -6 \pm 2\sqrt{19}$. Therefore, the solutions to the given equation are $-6 + 2\sqrt{19}$ and $-6 - 2\sqrt{19}$. Of these two solutions, only $-6 + 2\sqrt{19}$ is given as a choice.

Choice A is incorrect and may result from conceptual or calculation errors.
Choice B is incorrect and may result from conceptual or calculation errors.
Choice C is incorrect and may result from conceptual or calculation errors.

QUESTION 10

The correct answer is $\frac{189}{5}$. A y-intercept of a graph in the xy-plane is a point where the graph intersects the y-axis, which is a point with an x-coordinate of 0. Substituting 0 for x in the given equation yields $\frac{3(0)}{7} = -\frac{5y}{9} + 21$, or $0 = -\frac{5y}{9} + 21$. Subtracting 21 from both sides of this equation yields $-21 = -\frac{5y}{9}$. Multiplying both sides of this equation by -9 yields $189 = 5y$. Dividing both sides of this equation by 5 yields $\frac{189}{5} = y$. Therefore, the y-coordinate of the y-intercept of the graph of the given equation in the xy-plane is $\frac{189}{5}$. Note that 189/5 and 37.8 are examples of ways to enter a correct answer.

QUESTION 11

Choice D is correct. A line in the xy-plane that passes through the points (x_1, y_1) and (x_2, y_2) has slope m, where $m = \frac{y_2 - y_1}{x_2 - x_1}$, and can be defined by an equation of the form $y - y_1 = m(x - x_1)$. One of the lines shown in the graph passes through the points $(8, 0)$ and $(3, 4)$. Substituting 8 for x_1, 0 for y_1, 3 for x_2, and 4 for y_2 in the equation $m = \frac{y_2 - y_1}{x_2 - x_1}$ yields $m = \frac{4 - 0}{3 - 8}$, or $m = -\frac{4}{5}$. Substituting $-\frac{4}{5}$ for m, 8 for x_1, and 0 for y_1 in the equation $y - y_1 = m(x - x_1)$ yields $y - 0 = -\frac{4}{5}(x - 8)$, which is equivalent to $y = -\frac{4}{5}x + \frac{32}{5}$. Adding $\frac{4}{5}x$ to both sides of this equation yields $\frac{4}{5}x + y = \frac{32}{5}$. Multiplying both sides of this equation by -10 yields $-8x - 10y = -64$. Therefore, an equation of this line is $-8x - 10y = -64$. Similarly, the other line shown in the graph passes through the points $(8, 0)$ and $(3, 2)$. Substituting 8 for x_1, 0 for y_1, 3 for x_2, and 2 for y_2 in the equation $m = \frac{y_2 - y_1}{x_2 - x_1}$ yields $m = \frac{2 - 0}{3 - 8}$, or $m = -\frac{2}{5}$. Substituting $-\frac{2}{5}$ for m, 8 for x_1, and 0 for y_1 in the equation $y - y_1 = m(x - x_1)$ yields $y - 0 = -\frac{2}{5}(x - 8)$, which is equivalent to $y = -\frac{2}{5}x + \frac{16}{5}$. Adding $\frac{2}{5}x$ to both sides of this equation yields $\frac{2}{5}x + y = \frac{16}{5}$. Multiplying both sides of this equation by 10 yields $4x + 10y = 32$.

Therefore, an equation of this line is $4x + 10y = 32$. So, the system of linear equations represented by the lines shown is $4x + 10y = 32$ and $-8x - 10y = -64$.

Choice A is incorrect and may result from conceptual or calculation errors.
Choice B is incorrect and may result from conceptual or calculation errors.
Choice C is incorrect and may result from conceptual or calculation errors.

QUESTION 12

The correct answer is 1,677. Adding the first equation to the second equation in the given system yields $(x - 2) + (x - 2) + (-4)(y + 7) + 4(y + 7) = 117 + 442$, or $2(x - 2) = 559$. Multiplying both sides of this equation by 3 yields $6(x - 2) = 1,677$. Therefore, the value of $6(x - 2)$ is 1,677.

QUESTION 13

The correct answer is 1,728. The given function can be rewritten in the form $f(x) = a(x - h)^2 + k$, where a is a positive constant and the minimum value, k, of the function occurs when the value of x is h. By completing the square,

$f(x) = x^2 - 48x + 2,304$ can be written as $f(x) = x^2 - 48x + \left(\frac{48}{2}\right)^2 + 2,304 - \left(\frac{48}{2}\right)^2$,

or $f(x) = (x - 24)^2 + 1,728$. This equation is in the form $f(x) = a(x - h)^2 + k$, where $a = 1$, $h = 24$, and $k = 1,728$. Therefore, the minimum value of the given function is 1,728.

QUESTION 14

Choice B is correct. Adding $98x$ to each side of the given equation yields $49x = 0$. Dividing each side of this equation by 49 yields $x = 0$. This means that 0 is the only solution to the given equation. Therefore, the given equation has exactly one solution.

Choice A is incorrect and may result from conceptual or calculation errors. *Choice C* is incorrect and may result from conceptual or calculation errors. *Choice D* is incorrect and may result from conceptual or calculation errors.

QUESTION 15

The correct answer is 25. The value of $g(7 - w)$ is the value of $g(x)$ when $x = 7 - w$, where w is a constant. Substituting $7 - w$ for x in the given equation yields $g(7 - w) = (7 - w)(7 - w - 2)(7 - w + 6)^2$, which is equivalent to $g(7 - w) = (7 - w)(5 - w)(13 - w)^2$. It's given that the value of $g(7 - w)$ is 0. Substituting 0 for $g(7 - w)$ in the equation $g(7 - w) = (7 - w)(5 - w)(13 - w)^2$ yields $0 = (7 - w)(5 - w)(13 - w)^2$. Since the product of the three factors on the right-hand side of this equation is equal to 0, at least one of these three factors must be equal to 0. Therefore, the possible values of w can be found by setting each factor equal to 0. Setting the first factor equal to 0 yields $7 - w = 0$. Adding w to both sides of this equation yields $7 = w$. Therefore, 7 is one possible value of w. Setting the second factor equal to 0 yields $5 - w = 0$. Adding w to both sides of this equation yields $5 = w$. Therefore, 5 is a second possible value of w. Setting the third factor equal to 0 yields $(13 - w)^2 = 0$. Taking the square root of both sides of this equation yields $13 - w = 0$. Adding w to both sides of this equation yields $13 = w$. Therefore, 13 is a third possible value of w. Adding the three possible values of w yields $7 + 5 + 13$, or 25. Therefore, the sum of all possible values of w is 25.

QUESTION 16

Choice C is correct. If a tree from one of these rows is selected at random, the probability of selecting a maple tree, given that the tree is 20 feet or taller, is equal to the number of maple trees that are 20 feet or taller divided by the total number of trees that are 20 feet or taller. It's given that there are 6 rows of birch trees, and each row of birch trees has 8 trees that are 20 feet or taller. This means that there are a total of 6(8), or 48, birch trees that are 20 feet or taller. It's given that there are 5 rows of maple trees, and each row of maple trees has 9 trees that are 20 feet or taller. This means that there are a total of 5(9), or 45, maple trees that are 20 feet or taller. It follows that there are a total of 48 + 45, or 93, trees that are 20 feet or taller. Therefore, the probability of selecting a

maple tree, given that the tree is 20 feet or taller, is $\frac{45}{93}$, or $\frac{15}{31}$.

Choice A is incorrect and may result from conceptual or calculation errors. *Choice B* is incorrect and may result from conceptual or calculation errors. *Choice D* is incorrect and may result from conceptual or calculation errors.

QUESTION 17

The correct answer is 66. It's given that each vertex of the rectangle lies on the circumference of the circle. Therefore, the length of the diameter of the circle is equal to the length of the diagonal of the rectangle. The diagonal of a rectangle forms a right triangle with the shortest and longest sides of the rectangle, where the shortest side and the longest side of the rectangle are the legs of the triangle and the diagonal of the rectangle is the hypotenuse of the triangle. Let s represent the length, in units, of the shortest side of the rectangle. Since it's given that the diagonal is twice the length of the shortest side, $2s$ represents the length, in units, of the diagonal of the rectangle. By the Pythagorean theorem, if a right triangle has a hypotenuse with length c and legs with lengths a and b, then $a^2 + b^2 = c^2$. Substituting s for a and $2s$ for c in this equation yields $s^2 + b^2 = (2s)^2$, or $s^2 + b^2 = 4s^2$. Subtracting s^2 from both sides of this equation yields $b^2 = 3s^2$. Taking the positive square root of both sides of this equation yields $b = s\sqrt{3}$. Therefore, the length, in units, of the rectangle's longest side is $s\sqrt{3}$. The area of a rectangle is the product of the length of the shortest side and the length of the longest side. The lengths, in units, of the shortest and longest sides of the rectangle are represented by s and $s\sqrt{3}$, and it's given that the area of the rectangle is $1{,}089\sqrt{3}$ square units. It follows that $1{,}089\sqrt{3} = s(s\sqrt{3})$, or $1{,}089\sqrt{3} = s^2\sqrt{3}$. Dividing both sides of this equation by $\sqrt{3}$ yields $1{,}089 = s^2$. Taking the positive square root of both sides of this equation yields $33 = s$. Since the length, in units, of the diagonal is represented by $2s$, it follows that the length, in units, of the diagonal is $2(33)$, or 66. Since the length of the diameter of the circle is equal to the length of the diagonal of the rectangle, the length, in units, of the diameter of the circle is 66.

QUESTION 18

Choice D is correct. It's given that a is 2,241% of the sum of b and c. This can be represented by the equation $a = \left(\frac{2{,}241}{100}\right)(b + c)$, or $a = 22.41(b + c)$. It's also given that that b is 83% of c. This can be represented by the equation $b = \left(\frac{83}{100}\right)c$, or $b = 0.83c$. Dividing both sides of this equation by 0.83 yields $\frac{b}{0.83} = c$. Substituting $\frac{b}{0.83}$ for c in the equation $a = 22.41(b + c)$ yields $a = 22.41\left(b + \frac{b}{0.83}\right)$, or $a = 22.41\left(\frac{1.83b}{0.83}\right)$, which is equivalent to $a = \frac{41.0103b}{0.83}$, or $a = 49.41b$. This equation is equivalent to $a = \left(\frac{4{,}941}{100}\right)b$; therefore, a is 4,941% of b.

Choice A is incorrect and may result from conceptual or calculation errors.
Choice B is incorrect and may result from conceptual or calculation errors.
Choice C is incorrect and may result from conceptual or calculation errors.

QUESTION 19

The correct answer is $\frac{7}{2}$. A system of two linear equations in two variables, x and y, has no solution if the lines represented by the equations in the xy-plane are distinct and parallel. Two lines represented by equations in standard form $Ax + By = C$, where A, B, and C are constants, are parallel if the coefficients for x and y in one equation are proportional to the corresponding coefficients in the other equation. The first equation in the given system, $\frac{7}{8}y - \frac{5}{8}x = \frac{4}{7} - \frac{7}{8}y$, can be written in standard form by adding $\frac{7}{8}y$ to both sides of the equation, which yields $\frac{14}{8}y - \frac{5}{8}x = \frac{4}{7}$, or $-\frac{5}{8}x + \frac{14}{8}y = \frac{4}{7}$. Multiplying each term in this equation by -8 yields $5x - 14y = -\frac{32}{7}$. The second equation in the given system, $\frac{5}{4}x + \frac{7}{4} = py + \frac{15}{4}$, can be written in standard form by subtracting $\frac{7}{4}$ and py from both sides of the equation, which yields $\frac{5}{4}x - py = \frac{8}{4}$. Multiplying each term in this equation by 4 yields $5x - 4py = 8$. The coefficient of x in the first equation, $5x - 14y = -\frac{32}{7}$, is equal to the coefficient of x in the second equation, $5x - 4py = 8$. For the lines to be parallel, and for the coefficients for x and y in one equation to be proportional to the corresponding coefficients in the other equation, the coefficient of y in the second equation must also be equal to the coefficient of y in the first equation. Therefore, $-14 = -4p$. Dividing both sides of this equation by -4 yields $\frac{-14}{-4} = p$, or $p = \frac{7}{2}$. Therefore, if the given system of equations has no solution, the value of p is $\frac{7}{2}$. Note that 7/2 and 3.5 are examples of ways to enter a correct answer.

QUESTION 20

Choice A is correct. It's given that the table shows values of x and their corresponding values of $g(x)$, where $g(x) = \frac{f(x)}{x+3}$. It's also given that f is a linear function. It follows that an equation that defines f can be written in the form $f(x) = mx + b$, where m represents the slope and b represents the y-coordinate of the y-intercept $(0, b)$ of the graph of $y = f(x)$ in the xy-plane. The slope of the graph of $y = f(x)$ can be found using two points, (x_1, y_1) and (x_2, y_2), that are on the graph of $y = f(x)$, and the formula $m = \frac{y_2 - y_1}{x_2 - x_1}$. Since the table shows values of x and their corresponding values of $g(x)$, substituting values of x and $g(x)$ in the equation $g(x) = \frac{f(x)}{x+3}$ can be used to define function f. Using the first pair of values from the table, $x = -27$ and $g(x) = 3$, yields $3 = \frac{f(-27)}{-27+3}$, or $3 = \frac{f(-27)}{-24}$. Multiplying each side of this equation by -24 yields $-72 = f(-27)$, so the point $(-27, -72)$ is on the graph of $y = f(x)$. Using the second pair of values from the table, $x = -9$ and $g(x) = 0$, yields $0 = \frac{f(-9)}{-9+3}$, or $0 = \frac{f(-9)}{-6}$. Multiplying each side of this equation by -6 yields $0 = f(-9)$, so the point $(-9, 0)$ is on the graph of $y = f(x)$. Substituting $(-27, -72)$ and $(-9, 0)$ for (x_1, y_1) and (x_2, y_2), respectively, in the formula $m = \frac{y_2 - y_1}{x_2 - x_1}$ yields $m = \frac{0 - (-72)}{-9 - (-27)}$, or $m = 4$. Substituting 4 for m in the equation $f(x) = mx + b$ yields $f(x) = 4x + b$. Since $0 = f(-9)$, substituting -9 for x and 0 for $f(x)$ in the equation $f(x) = 4x + b$ yields $0 = 4(-9) + b$, or $0 = -36 + b$. Adding 36 to both sides of this equation yields $36 = b$. It follows that 36 is the y-coordinate of the y-intercept $(0, b)$ of the graph of $y = f(x)$. Therefore, the y-intercept of the graph of $y = f(x)$ is $(0, 36)$.

Choice B is incorrect. 12 is the y-coordinate of the y-intercept of the graph of $y = g(x)$. *Choice C* is incorrect. 4 is the slope of the graph of $y = f(x)$. *Choice D* is incorrect. -9 is the x-coordinate of the x-intercept of the graph of $y = f(x)$.

QUESTION 21

Choice D is correct. It's given that the radius of the circle is 168 millimeters. Since points *M* and *N* both lie on the circle, segments *GM* and *GN* are both radii. Therefore, segments *GM* and *GN* each have length 168 millimeters. Two segments that are tangent to a circle and have a common exterior endpoint have equal length. Therefore, segment *MH* and segment *NH* have equal length. Let *x* represent the length of segment *MH*. Then *x* also represents the length of segment *NH*. It's given that the perimeter of quadrilateral *GMHN* is 3,856 millimeters. Since the perimeter of a quadrilateral is equal to the sum of the lengths of the sides of the quadrilateral, $3,856 = 168 + 168 + x + x$, or $3,856 = 336 + 2x$. Subtracting 336 from both sides of this equation yields $3,520 = 2x$, and dividing both sides of this equation by 2 yields $1,760 = x$. Therefore, the length of segment *MH* is 1,760 millimeters. A line segment that's tangent to a circle is perpendicular to the radius of the circle at the point of tangency. Therefore, segment *GM* is perpendicular to segment *MH*. Since perpendicular segments form right angles, angle *GMH* is a right angle. Therefore, triangle *GMH* is a right triangle with legs of length 1,760 millimeters and 168 millimeters, and hypotenuse *GH*. By the Pythagorean theorem, if a right triangle has a hypotenuse with length *c* and legs with lengths *a* and *b*, then $a^2 + b^2 = c^2$. Substituting 1,760 for *a* and 168 for *b* in this equation yields $1,760^2 + 168^2 = c^2$, or $3,125,824 = c^2$. Taking the square root of both sides of this equation yields $\pm 1,768 = c$. Since *c* represents a length, which must be positive, the value of *c* is 1,768. Therefore, the length of segment *GH* is 1,768 millimeters, so the distance between points *G* and *H* is 1,768 millimeters.

Choice A is incorrect. This is the distance between points *G* and *M* and between points *G* and *N*, not the distance between points *G* and *H*. *Choice B* is incorrect and may result from conceptual or calculation errors. *Choice C* is incorrect. This is the distance between points *M* and *H* and between points *N* and *H*, not the distance between points *G* and *H*.

QUESTION 22

Choice A is correct. It's given that the graph of $y = f(x)$ in the *xy*-plane passes through the points (7, 0) and (−3, 0). It follows that when the value of *x* is either 7 or −3, the value of *f(x)* is 0. It's also given that the function *f* is defined by $f(x) = ax^2 + bx + c$, where *a*, *b*, and *c* are constants. It follows that the function *f* is a quadratic function and, therefore, may be written in factored form as $f(x) = a(x − u)(x − v)$, where the value of *f(x)* is 0 when *x* is either *u* or *v*. Since the value of *f(x)* is 0 when the value of *x* is either 7 or −3, and the value of *f(x)* is 0 when the value of *x* is either *u* or *v*, it follows that *u* and *v* are equal to 7 and −3. Substituting 7 for *u* and −3 for *v* in the equation $f(x) = a(x − u)(x − v)$ yields $f(x) = a(x − 7)(x − (−3))$, or $f(x) = a(x − 7)(x + 3)$. Distributing the right-hand side of this equation yields $f(x) = a(x^2 − 7x + 3x − 21)$, or $f(x) = ax^2 − 4ax − 21a$. Since it's given that $f(x) = ax^2 + bx + c$, it follows that $b = −4a$. Adding *a* to each side of this equation yields $a + b = −3a$. Since $a + b = −3a$, if *a* is an integer, the value of $a + b$ must be a multiple of 3. If *a* is an integer greater than 1, it follows that $a \geq 2$. Therefore, $−3a \leq −3(2)$. It follows that the value of $a + b$ is less than or equal to −3(2), or −6. Of the given choices, only −6 is a multiple of 3 that's less than or equal to −6.

Choice B is incorrect. This is the value of $a + b$ if *a* is equal to, not greater than, 1. *Choice C* is incorrect and may result from conceptual or calculation errors. *Choice D* is incorrect and may result from conceptual or calculation errors.

Scoring Your Paper SAT Practice Test #6

Congratulations on completing an SAT® practice test. To score your test, follow the instructions in this scoring guide.

IMPORTANT: *This scoring guide is for students who completed SAT Practice Test #6 in The Official SAT Study Guide™. We recommend reading through these instructions and explanations before scoring so that you understand the specifics and limitations of scoring this practice test.*

The total score on your practice test reflects the sum of the (1) Reading and Writing and (2) Math section scores, as indicated below. If you decided to take both the lower- and higher-difficulty modules, choose which one you will use to score.

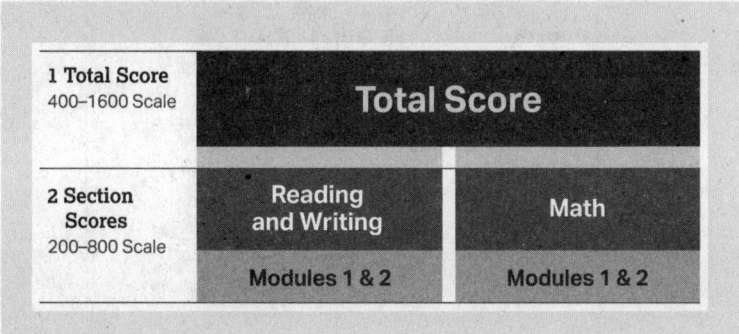

Scores Overview

Each assessment in the SAT Suite (SAT, PSAT/NMSQT®, PSAT™ 10, and PSAT™ 8/9) reports test scores on a common scale.

For more details about scores, visit **sat.org/scores**.

How to Calculate Your Practice Test Scores

The worksheets on the pages that follow help you calculate your test scores.

GET SET UP

1 In addition to your practice test, you'll need the answer keys and conversion tables at the end of this scoring guide.

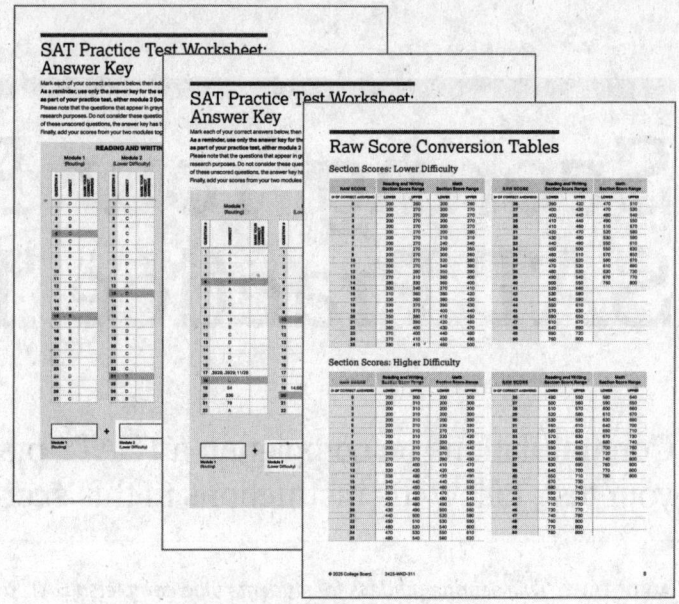

SCORE YOUR PRACTICE TEST

2 Compare your answers to the answer keys later in this scoring guide, and count up the total number of correct answers for each section. Write the number of correct answers for each section in the boxes at the bottom of the pages.

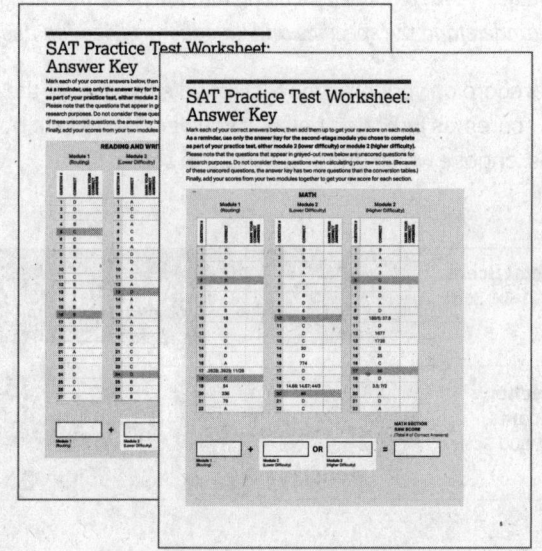

CALCULATE YOUR SCORES

3 Using your marked-up answer keys and the conversion tables, follow the directions on the SAT Practice Test Worksheet: Section and Total Scores page to get your section and total scores.

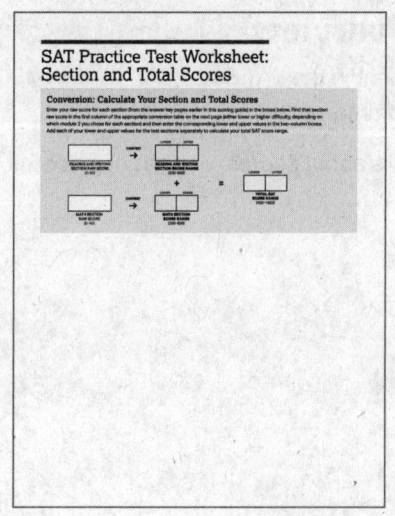

Get Section and Total Scores

Section and total scores for this paper version of SAT Practice Test #6 are expressed as ranges. That's because the scoring method described in this guide is a different (and therefore less precise) version of the one used in the actual adaptive test.

This practice test contains three modules for each test section: (1) a single first-stage (routing) module and (2) two second-stage modules. The two second-stage modules differ by average question difficulty and are marked as either "module 2 (lower difficulty)" or "module 2 (higher difficulty)." You get to choose which module 2 you would like to take for this practice test. **An actual testing experience consists of one routing and one second-stage module per test section.** To obtain your Reading and Writing and Math section scores, you will refer to the answer key and conversion table for the second-stage module you chose (either lower or higher difficulty).

GET YOUR READING AND WRITING SECTION SCORE

Calculate your SAT Reading and Writing section score (it's on a scale of 200–800).

1. Use the answer key for Reading and Writing to find the number of questions in module 1 and the module 2 you chose (either lower or higher difficulty) that you answered correctly.

2. To determine your Reading and Writing raw score, add the number of correct answers you got in module 1 and the module 2 you chose (either lower or higher difficulty). **Exclude the questions in grayed-out rows in your calculation.**

3. Use the appropriate Raw Score Conversion Table to turn your raw score into your Reading and Writing section score.

4. The lower and upper values associated with your raw score establish the range of scores you might expect to receive had this been an actual adaptive test.

GET YOUR MATH SECTION SCORE

Calculate your SAT Math section score (it's on a scale of 200–800).

1. Use the answer key for Math to find the number of questions in module 1 and the module 2 you chose (either lower or higher difficulty) that you answered correctly.

2. To determine your Math raw score, add the number of correct answers you got in module 1 and the module 2 you chose (either lower or higher difficulty). **Exclude the questions in grayed-out rows in your calculation.**

3. Use the appropriate Raw Score Conversion Table to turn your raw score into your Math section score.

4. The lower and upper values associated with your raw score establish the range of scores you might expect to receive had this been an actual adaptive test.

GET YOUR TOTAL SCORE

Add together the lower values for the Reading and Writing and Math sections, and then add together the upper values for the two sections. The result is your total score, expressed as a range, for this SAT practice test. The total score is on a scale of 400–1600.

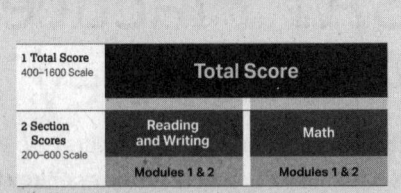

1 Total Score 400–1600 Scale	Total Score	
2 Section Scores 200–800 Scale	Reading and Writing	Math
	Modules 1 & 2	Modules 1 & 2

Your total score on this SAT practice test is the sum of your Reading and Writing section score and your Math section score. For this practice test, you'll receive a lower and upper score for each test section and the total score. This is the range of scores that you might expect to receive.

Use the worksheets on the pages that follow to calculate your section and total scores.

SAT Practice Test Worksheet: Answer Key

Mark each of your correct answers below, then add them up to get your raw score on each module.

As a reminder, use only the answer key for the second-stage module you chose to complete as part of your practice test, either module 2 (lower difficulty) or module 2 (higher difficulty).

Please note that the questions that appear in grayed-out rows below are unscored questions for research purposes. Do not consider these questions when calculating your raw scores. (Because of these unscored questions, the answer key has two more questions than the conversion tables.)

Finally, add your scores from your two modules together to get your raw score for each section,

READING AND WRITING

Module 1 (Routing)			Module 2 (Lower Difficulty)			Module 2 (Higher Difficulty)		
QUESTION #	CORRECT	MARK YOUR CORRECT ANSWERS	QUESTION #	CORRECT	MARK YOUR CORRECT ANSWERS	QUESTION #	CORRECT	MARK YOUR CORRECT ANSWERS
1	D		1	A		1	A	
2	D		2	C		2	B	
3	D		3	C		3	B	
4	B		4	A		4	D	
5	C		5	C		5	A	
6	C		6	C		6	C	
7	B		7	A		7	D	
8	B		8	D		8	C	
9	A		9	D		9	C	
10	B		10	A		10	D	
11	C		11	D		11	D	
12	B		12	A		12	D	
13	B		13	D		13	B	
14	A		14	A		14	A	
15	B		15	A		15	A	
16	B		16	A		16	B	
17	D		17	A		17	B	
18	B		18	D		18	B	
19	B		19	B		19	C	
20	D		20	C		20	B	
21	A		21	C		21	D	
22	D		22	C		22	B	
23	D		23	C		23	B	
24	D		24	D		24	B	
25	C		25	B		25	A	
26	A		26	D		26	D	
27	C		27	B		27	C	

READING AND WRITING SECTION RAW SCORE
(Total # of Correct Answers)

[ ] Module 1 (Routing)	**+**	[ ] Module 2 (Lower Difficulty) **OR** [ ] Module 2 (Higher Difficulty)	**=** [ ]

SAT Practice Test Worksheet: Answer Key

Mark each of your correct answers below, then add them up to get your raw score on each module.
As a reminder, use only the answer key for the second-stage module you chose to complete as part of your practice test, either module 2 (lower difficulty) or module 2 (higher difficulty).
Please note that the questions that appear in grayed-out rows below are unscored questions for research purposes. Do not consider these questions when calculating your raw scores. (Because of these unscored questions, the answer key has two more questions than the conversion tables.)
Finally, add your scores from your two modules together to get your raw score for each section.

MATH

Module 1 (Routing)			Module 2 (Lower Difficulty)			Module 2 (Higher Difficulty)		
QUESTION #	CORRECT	MARK YOUR CORRECT ANSWERS	QUESTION #	CORRECT	MARK YOUR CORRECT ANSWERS	QUESTION #	CORRECT	MARK YOUR CORRECT ANSWERS
1	A		1	B		1	B	
2	D		2	B		2	A	
3	B		3	B		3	A	
4	B		4	A		4	3	
5	B		5	A		5	D	
6	A		6	3		6	B	
7	A		7	B		7	D	
8	C		8	D		8	A	
9	B		9	6		9	D	
10	18		10	D		10	189/5; 37.8	
11	B		11	C		11	D	
12	C		12	D		12	1677	
13	D		13	C		13	1728	
14	4		14	20		14	B	
15	D		15	D		15	25	
16	A		16	774		16	C	
17	.3928; .3929; 11/28		17	D		17	66	
18	C		18	C		18	D	
19	54		19	14.66; 14.67; 44/3		19	3.5; 7/2	
20	336		20	66		20	A	
21	79		21	D		21	D	
22	A		22	C		22	A	

**MATH SECTION
RAW SCORE**
(Total # of Correct Answers)

[ ] **+** [ ] **OR** [ ] **=** [ ]

Module 1
(Routing)

Module 2
(Lower Difficulty)

Module 2
(Higher Difficulty)

Understanding the SAT Practice Test Conversion Tables and Total Score Ranges

As mentioned earlier in this scoring guide, the scoring method for the practice tests that appear in *The Official SAT Study Guide* is different (and therefore less precise) than the method used in the actual adaptive test. Your practice test may result in a larger score range than what you hoped to see, but it's not feasible to estimate your performance on the practice tests in the study guide as precisely as we could for an actual test. As the test developers, College Board is committed to providing the most accurate conversion possible to help you understand your scores and guide your practice most effectively.

There are two conversion tables in this scoring guide. Use the conversion table labelled lower difficulty if you took module 2 (lower difficulty). Use the conversion table labelled higher difficulty if you took module 2 (higher difficulty). You might need both conversion tables if you took the lower-difficulty option for one section (e.g., Reading and Writing) and the higher-difficulty option for the other section (e.g., Math).

Because the lower- and higher-difficulty conversion tables share the same questions for module 1 (routing), you may encounter different score ranges based on the conversion table you use. For example, if you got all the module 1 (routing) questions correct, the lower-difficulty conversion table and the higher-difficulty conversion table will give you different score ranges. This is to be expected because the conversion tables account for all items within the two modules that make up the test. Answering only items on the first half of the test assumes you answered the other questions (module 2) incorrectly. Recall that when taking the actual SAT on test day, the test will adapt to your ability based on how you perform on the first half. Because of the differences between the actual test and providing a paper approximation of that (the practice test you're currently scoring), you should select the second-stage module that feels most appropriate for you. For example, if you were to answer all items on the first module correctly on the actual test, you would not be routed to the easier second-stage module. The converse would also be true. For many users of moderate ability either second-stage would be acceptable, but very high or low performers should be cautioned about taking the second-stage module that doesn't align well with their ability.

SAT Practice Test Worksheet: Section and Total Scores

Conversion: Calculate Your Section and Total Scores

Enter your raw score for each section (from the answer key pages earlier in this scoring guide) in the boxes below. Find that section raw score in the first column of the appropriate conversion table on the next page (either lower or higher difficulty, depending on which module 2 you chose for each section) and then enter the corresponding lower and upper values in the two-column boxes. Add each of your lower and upper values for the test sections separately to calculate your total SAT score range.

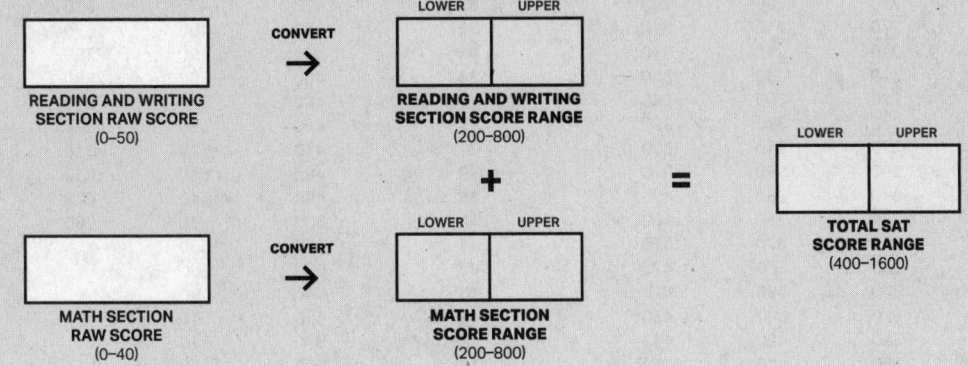

READING AND WRITING
SECTION RAW SCORE
(0–50)

CONVERT →

LOWER   UPPER

READING AND WRITING
SECTION SCORE RANGE
(200–800)

+

=

LOWER   UPPER

TOTAL SAT
SCORE RANGE
(400–1600)

MATH SECTION
RAW SCORE
(0–40)

CONVERT →

LOWER   UPPER

MATH SECTION
SCORE RANGE
(200–800)

Raw Score Conversion Tables

Section Scores: Lower Difficulty

RAW SCORE (# OF CORRECT ANSWERS)	Reading and Writing Section Score Range		Math Section Score Range	
	LOWER	UPPER	LOWER	UPPER
0	200	260	200	260
1	200	270	200	270
2	200	270	200	270
3	200	270	200	270
4	200	270	200	270
5	200	270	200	280
6	200	270	210	310
7	200	270	240	340
8	200	270	290	350
9	200	270	300	360
10	200	270	320	380
11	200	270	340	380
12	250	280	350	390
13	270	310	360	400
14	280	330	360	400
15	300	340	370	410
16	310	360	380	420
17	330	360	380	420
18	330	370	390	430
19	340	370	400	440
20	350	380	410	450
21	360	390	420	460
22	360	400	430	470
23	370	400	440	480
24	370	410	450	490
25	380	410	460	500

RAW SCORE (# OF CORRECT ANSWERS)	Reading and Writing Section Score Range		Math Section Score Range	
	LOWER	UPPER	LOWER	UPPER
26	390	420	470	510
27	400	430	470	530
28	400	440	480	540
29	410	440	490	550
30	410	460	510	570
31	420	470	520	580
32	430	480	530	590
33	440	490	550	610
34	450	500	550	630
35	460	510	570	650
36	460	520	590	670
37	470	520	610	690
38	480	530	630	730
39	490	540	670	770
40	500	550	760	800
41	520	560		
42	530	580		
43	540	590		
44	550	610		
45	570	630		
46	590	650		
47	610	670		
48	640	690		
49	690	720		
50	760	800		

Section Scores: Higher Difficulty

RAW SCORE (# OF CORRECT ANSWERS)	Reading and Writing Section Score Range		Math Section Score Range	
	LOWER	UPPER	LOWER	UPPER
0	200	300	200	300
1	200	310	200	300
2	200	310	200	300
3	200	310	200	300
4	200	310	200	300
5	200	310	230	330
6	200	310	270	370
7	200	310	320	420
8	200	310	350	430
9	200	310	360	440
10	200	310	370	450
11	270	370	390	450
12	300	400	410	470
13	320	420	420	480
14	330	430	430	490
15	340	440	440	500
16	370	450	460	520
17	390	450	470	530
18	400	460	480	540
19	420	480	490	550
20	430	490	500	560
21	440	500	520	580
22	450	510	530	590
23	460	520	540	600
24	470	530	550	610
25	480	540	560	620

RAW SCORE (# OF CORRECT ANSWERS)	Reading and Writing Section Score Range		Math Section Score Range	
	LOWER	UPPER	LOWER	UPPER
26	490	550	580	640
27	500	560	590	650
28	510	570	600	660
29	520	580	610	670
30	530	590	630	690
31	550	610	640	700
32	560	620	650	710
33	570	630	670	730
34	580	640	680	740
35	590	650	700	760
36	600	660	720	780
37	620	680	740	800
38	630	690	760	800
39	640	700	770	800
40	650	710	780	800
41	670	730		
42	680	740		
43	690	750		
44	700	760		
45	710	770		
46	730	770		
47	740	780		
48	760	800		
49	770	800		
50	780	800		

The SAT®

Practice Test #7

Make time to take the practice test.
It is one of the best ways to get ready for the SAT.

Note: The practice tests in this guide include two second modules so that you can experience both the lower- and higher-difficulty modules. On the actual test, you will be presented with only one second module.

After you have taken the practice test, score it right away using materials provided in *The Official SAT Study Guide.*

This version of the SAT Practice Test is for students using this Study Guide. As a reminder, most students taking the SAT will do so using Bluebook™, the digital testing application. To best prepare for test day, download Bluebook at **bluebook.app.collegeboard.org** to take the practice test in the digital format.

Test begins on the next page.

Reading and Writing

27 QUESTIONS

1

Botanist Al Kovaleski has pointed out that maple trees already thrive in a wide variety of climates and thus may _____ changes in climate better than some other tree species do. The alterations maples may undergo in response to a changing climate are likely to be relatively small and easily achieved.

Which choice completes the text with the most logical and precise word or phrase?

A) relocate from

B) refer to

C) originate from

D) adapt to

2

The following text is from John Muir's 1913 autobiography *The Story of My Boyhood and Youth*. Muir describes being on a boat.

The water was so <u>clear</u> that it was almost invisible, and when we floated slowly out over the plants and fishes, we seemed to be miraculously sustained in the air while exploring a veritable fairyland.

As used in the text, what does the word "clear" most nearly mean?

A) Simple

B) Understandable

C) Obvious

D) Transparent

Unauthorized copying or reuse of any part of this page is illegal.

CONTINUE ▶

682

3

The recently observed gamma ray burst GRB 230307A lasted for 200 seconds, _____ for a burst generated by the merger of neutron stars. Bursts caused by neutron mergers typically last fewer than 2 seconds.

Which choice completes the text with the most logical and precise word or phrase?

A) a coincidence

B) a reprieve

C) an incident

D) an oddity

4

In 1776, the United States sent Benjamin Franklin to France to try to win the country's support in the United States' fight for independence from Great Britain. Franklin was very popular in France. This _____ surely helped him to convince France to assist the United States.

Which choice completes the text with the most logical and precise word or phrase?

A) thoughtfulness

B) esteem

C) controversy

D) sincerity

5

In the 1950s, scientists didn't know much about the ocean floor. Many scientists at the time believed that the ocean floor was mostly flat. But geologist Marie Tharp and her research partner, Bruce Heezen, proved that this idea was wrong. Using sonar data collected from the Atlantic Ocean, Tharp and Heezen showed that the floor was filled with canyons, mountains, and valleys.

Which choice best describes the function of the underlined sentence in the text as a whole?

A) It identifies a scientific belief that Tharp and Heezen showed to be wrong.

B) It describes the design of Tharp and Heezen's experiment.

C) It emphasizes a disagreement between Tharp and Heezen.

D) It presents data to support a claim that Tharp and Heezen made.

6

In the early days of television in the 1940s, many people thought that US television programs would rely on the financial support of ad agencies and commercial sponsors, much like radio did. But advertisers hesitated to jump into a new space, particularly at a time when the manufacturing of new television sets was stalled due to the US's involvement in World War II. Broadcasters, like the National Broadcasting Company (NBC), needed to persuade advertisers to support their programming despite not knowing whether there would be a robust television audience to begin with.

Which choice best describes the function of the underlined phrase in the text as a whole?

A) It compares the beginning of radio programming with the beginnings of television programming in the United States.

B) It identifies a specific reason behind some advertisers' hesitance to support television.

C) It describes how broadcasters attempted to convince advertisers to support television.

D) It explains why a type of television programming was popular at the time.

CONTINUE ▶

7

Pteropods are small swimming snails with thin, delicate calcium carbonate shells. These animals are thought to be especially vulnerable to ocean acidification due to calcium carbonate's susceptibility to dissolution at lower pH values. Victoria L. Peck and colleagues recently found that the periostracum (a protective coating on pteropods' outer shells) prevents this dissolution when intact. Moreover, the team was surprised to discover that even when the periostracum is breached, pteropods can still mitigate damage by rebuilding the inner shell wall.

Which choice best describes the main purpose of the text?

A) To call for additional research on biological mechanisms that improve pteropod survival rates

B) To discuss a conclusion drawn in a study of calcium carbonate's role in protecting the periostracum of pteropods

C) To address some of the ways ocean acidification has altered pteropod behavior over time

D) To present findings that suggest that a concern about the effects of ocean acidification on pteropod shells may be unwarranted

8

Text 1
Little is known about how plate tectonics—wherein slabs of Earth's crust move over, under, away from, and against one another—began. Some researchers contend that tectonic movements began around 3 billion years ago, often noting that computer models of Earth's mantle temperature at the time indicate that the mantle would have been sufficiently molten to enable the plates to move.

Text 2
Ultimately, any plausible claim about the inception of tectonic movement must rest on empirical evidence from the geological record. Researcher Wriju Chowdhury and his team analyzed the geochemistry of zircon crystals to gain insight into the chemical composition of the magma from which the crystals formed and, based on the data, compellingly argue that plate tectonics may have been occurring as early as 4.2 billion years ago.

Based on the texts, how would the author of Text 2 most likely respond to what "some researchers contend" as described in Text 1?

A) By suggesting that the temperature of Earth's mantle 3 billion years ago was likely insufficient to allow for the level of tectonic movement predicted by computer models

B) By distinguishing between computer models of Earth's mantle temperature that reliably predict the onset of plate tectonics and those that do not

C) By indicating that computer models of Earth's mantle temperature are still being improved such that new models tend to be much more reliable than their predecessors

D) By asserting that a more definitive form of evidence than the computer models suggests a different timeline for the onset of plate tectonics on Earth

CONTINUE

In 2018, scientists discovered an immense aggregation of *Muusoctopus robustus* (pearl octopuses) along a hydrothermal vent 3,200 meters beneath the ocean's surface. Water temperatures at this site—named the Octopus Garden—climb as high as 11°C, much warmer than the ambient 1.6°C typical at this depth. Based on observations made over three years, scientists concluded that temperatures at the site likely confer reproductive benefits and that the site is used exclusively for reproduction—6,000 *M. robustus* adults, hatchlings, and eggs were observed at the garden, but no juveniles were present.

Which statement about *M. robustus* and the Octopus Garden is best supported by the text?

A) *M. robustus* leave the Octopus Garden upon reaching an intermediary stage of development.

B) The *M. robustus* population at the Octopus Garden remains stable despite variations in water temperature.

C) *M. robustus* nests in the Octopus Garden contain on average fewer but larger eggs than nests at similar ocean depths.

D) The Octopus Garden provides an ideal feeding ground for *M. robustus* hatchlings.

Conservationists worldwide are working to protect ecosystems from habitat destruction and biodiversity loss, and in many cases, initiatives that rely on natural features or processes can help address such challenges. In response to a rapidly dwindling population of blueback salmon, the Quinault Indian Nation (a tribe in Washington State) partnered with the conservation organization Wild Salmon Center to restore naturally occurring logjams in the Quinault River. The logjams create shady pools where the blueback salmon can rest and spawn, thus promoting blueback population recovery.

Which choice best states the main idea of the text?

A) A partnership between the Quinault Indian Nation and Wild Salmon Center shows the importance of collaborative approaches to preserving biodiversity.

B) Nature-based approaches can be effective ways to achieve conservation goals.

C) As indicated by a recent project, logjams help the blueback salmon thrive and reproduce.

D) Scientists now realize that nature-based conservation methods offer better long-term solutions to environmental issues than methods that are not nature-based do.

CONTINUE →

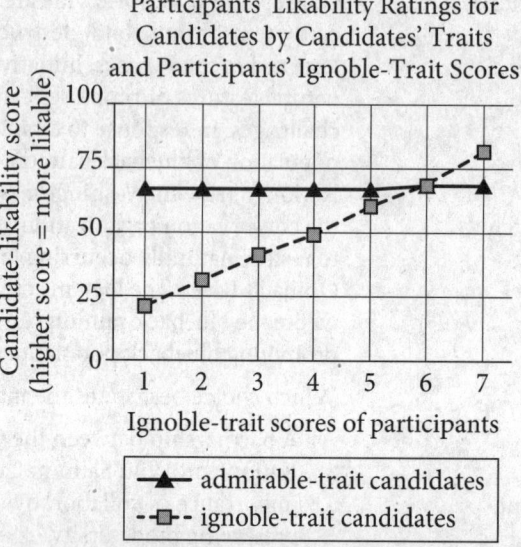

Participants' Likability Ratings for
Candidates by Candidates' Traits
and Participants' Ignoble-Trait Scores

Candidate-likability score (higher score = more likable)

Ignoble-trait scores of participants

▲ admirable-trait candidates

- -■- ignoble-trait candidates

Alessandro Nai et al. presented study participants with vignettes about fictive
political candidates, portraying them as embodying a personality trait widely
considered admirable (e.g., agreeableness) or one considered ignoble
(e.g., cynicism). A survey recorded participants' ratings of the candidates'
likability and showed that across participants, ignoble-trait candidates were less
likable than admirable-trait candidates. However, when the researchers factored
in the participants' own personality-trait scores, on a scale of 1 (least ignoble) to
7 (most ignoble), they concluded that this relative ranking of candidates persisted
except among the participants with high ignobility scores.

Which choice best describes data from the graph that support the researchers'
conclusion?

A) There was a strong positive correlation between participants' ignobility scores
and admirable-trait candidates' likability ratings, but there was no correlation
between ignobility scores and ignoble-trait candidates' likability ratings.

B) Participants with an ignobility score of 5 or less rated admirable-trait
candidates as more likable than ignoble-trait candidates, whereas participants
with an ignobility score of 6 or more rated ignoble-trait candidates as equally
likable as or even more likable than admirable-trait candidates.

C) Overall, participants rated admirable-trait candidates as quite likable, and that
rating was not significantly affected by the participants' ignobility scores.

D) Unlike participants with an ignobility score of 6, participants with an
ignobility score either greater or less than 6 gave admirable-trait candidates
and ignoble-trait candidates different likability ratings.

CONTINUE ➡

12

Puerto Rico is an island in the Caribbean Sea. Indigenous people there started raising guinea pigs about 1,700 years ago. Guinea pigs had originally been domesticated much earlier in both Colombia and Peru. So were guinea pigs brought to Puerto Rico from Colombia or from Peru? Ancient Caribbean trade routes connected Puerto Rico with Colombia but not with Peru. Therefore, guinea pigs in Puerto Rico probably came from Colombia and descended from Colombian guinea pigs.

Which finding, if true, would most directly weaken the underlined claim?

A) Ancient guinea pigs in Puerto Rico were genetically less similar to ancient guinea pigs in Colombia than to ancient guinea pigs in Peru.

B) Guinea pigs are common in ancient Puerto Rican art, especially in pottery.

C) Modern breeds of guinea pigs don't look like images of guinea pigs in ancient art from Puerto Rico, Colombia, and Peru.

D) The guinea pig population of ancient Colombia was much larger than the guinea pig population of ancient Peru.

13

"Ad recall" measures how memorable an advertising campaign is. To provide advertisers with information about their ads' memorability, a social media site regularly surveys users about whether they remember ads they had recently interacted with on the site. In a study that drew on this survey data, advertising researcher Kristen Sussman and colleagues noted that different kinds of social media interactions involve different levels of cognitive engagement: commenting on or sharing a post is more cognitively demanding than is clicking on embedded links or on a "like" button. The researchers hypothesized that interactions indicating high levels of cognitive engagement with ad content would result in relatively high levels of ad recall.

Which finding, if true, would most directly support the researchers' hypothesis?

A) Users who interacted with an ad were much more likely to do so by clicking on the ad's "like" button than they were to interact with the ad in any other way.

B) Users who interacted with an ad were significantly more likely to purchase the advertised product at the time they saw the ad than were users who saw the ad but did not interact with it.

C) Compared with users who clicked on links in an ad, users who commented on that same ad were significantly more likely to remember seeing the ad when surveyed two days later.

D) Although users who shared an ad were highly likely to remember details from the ad when surveyed two days later, those same users tended to forget those details when surveyed again a week later.

CONTINUE

14

Properties of Select Rotating Radio Transients

Name	Right ascension (hours)	Period (seconds)	Frequency (hertz)
J0545-03	5:45	1.074	0.931
J1654-2335	16:54:03	0.545	1.834
J0103+54	1:03:37	0.354	2.822
J0121+53	1:21	2.725	0.367
J0614-03	6:15	0.136	7.353

A student is researching rotating radio transients (RRATs), a subclass of pulsar stars characterized by short pulses of radio waves. The time between consecutive pulses of an RRAT is referred to as a period. Looking at the table, the student determines that _____

Which choice most effectively uses data from the table to complete the statement?

A) J0614-03 has the shortest amount of time between consecutive pulses of all the RRATs in the table.

B) J0545-03 and J0121+53 have the same amount of time between consecutive pulses.

C) J1654-2335 has the longest amount of time between consecutive pulses of all the RRATs in the table.

D) J0103+54 and J0121+53 both have more than one second of time between consecutive pulses.

15

Narwhals are shy whales that live in the remote Arctic Ocean. Some of them have a long tusk, like a unicorn horn, with sensitive nerves. Narwhals are known for this tusk, but many actually don't have one and its purpose is unknown. One group of scientists came up with a possible purpose in 2014. The scientists suggested that the tusk may help narwhals determine when water around them is likely to start freezing and become dangerous for them. Marine biologist Kristin Laidre disagrees with that idea, though. She reasons that if the narwhal's tusk serves such an important purpose, then it's most likely that _____

Which choice most logically completes the text?

A) some narwhals would seek a new habitat.

B) fewer marine animals would also have tusks.

C) more narwhals would have a tusk.

D) narwhals would become less shy over time.

16

Zydeco music originated in the French Creole community of southwest Louisiana. One instrument that gives zydeco its unique sound is the vest frottoir. The vest frottoir _____ a wearable washboard that is played by rubbing spoons or bottle openers against it.

Which choice completes the text so that it conforms to the conventions of Standard English?

A) have been

B) is

C) were

D) are

CONTINUE →

17

Featuring jagged peaks of black ink surrounded by hazy swirls of blue and green paint, Zhang Daqian's 1983 painting *Panorama of Mount Lu* is inspired by the tradition of *qinglü shanshui*, a type of Chinese landscape painting _____ by the use of blue and green hues to depict ethereal, otherworldly landscapes.

Which choice completes the text so that it conforms to the conventions of Standard English?

A) has been characterized

B) will be characterized

C) characterized

D) is characterized

18

In his *Naturalis historia*, Pliny the Elder praised Hipparchus's star catalog, a second-century BCE list of roughly 850 different stars' celestial positions. For centuries, scholars dreamed about locating a copy of this legendary lost _____ fantasy (partially) became reality in 2022, when researchers uncovered traces of the star catalog on a palimpsest, a reused parchment.

Which choice completes the text so that it conforms to the conventions of Standard English?

A) work, that

B) work that

C) work. That

D) work and that

19

With a blend of traditional design elements, such as arched Gothic ceilings, and modern ones, such as floor-to-ceiling _____ design splits the difference between old and new, a mixture that is increasingly seen in home interior in the US.

Which choice completes the text so that it conforms to the conventions of Standard English?

A) windows; transitional

B) windows—transitional

C) windows. Transitional

D) windows, transitional

20

When a given industry—water and electricity are two well-known examples—carries high infrastructural start-up costs and other barriers that discourage competition, _____ of just one or two suppliers per municipality. Such industries are known as natural monopolies.

Which choice completes the text so that it conforms to the conventions of Standard English?

A) these often consist

B) they often consist

C) it often consists

D) this often consists

21

Famous for its four-degree tilt, the leaning Garisenda Tower is a popular attraction in Bologna's city center. However, measurements taken in 2023 showed that the tower was rotating in a concerning way. _____ city officials closed the area around the tower so experts could explore solutions to stabilize the historical twelfth-century structure.

Which choice completes the text with the most logical transition?

A) Similarly,

B) As a result,

C) For example,

D) In comparison,

22

Guard cells are specialized cells that are part of a plant's pores. These cells help regulate the amount of carbon dioxide a plant takes in. _____ they help regulate a plant's water loss.

Which choice completes the text with the most logical transition?

A) Additionally,

B) Previously,

C) In conclusion,

D) Instead,

CONTINUE ➡

23

Marcel Duchamp intended his 1917 so-called ready-made sculpture *Fountain* to challenge then-prevailing conceptions about the nature of art. _____ Duchamp's *Fountain* did just that, raising the question of whether displaying any object in an art gallery could be said to transform the object—even, as Duchamp's sculpture was, a urinal—into a legitimate work of art.

Which choice completes the text with the most logical transition?

A) Similarly,

B) Indeed,

C) Instead,

D) In addition,

24

In 2021, a model developed by astrophysicist Catherine Zucker and her research team revealed that the same supernovas responsible for the creation and ongoing expansion of the Local Bubble—a 14-million-year-old cavity in the Milky Way—are likely responsible for the formation of new stars. _____ this model detailed how the bubble's expansion trapped interstellar clouds of gas and dust that became stars upon their eventual collapse.

Which choice completes the text with the most logical transition?

A) Hence,

B) However,

C) Admittedly,

D) Specifically,

25

While researching a topic, a student has taken the following notes:

- Musicians around the world have used protest songs to raise awareness about human rights violations.

- US folk singer Aunt Molly Jackson released the protest song "Poor Miner's Farewell" in 1932.

- It exposed the unlivable wages and dangerous working conditions coal miners faced in Kentucky during the 1920s and 1930s.

- South African singer-songwriter Hugh Masekela released the protest song "Bring Him Back Home" in 1987.

- It called on the South African government to free Nelson Mandela, an anti-apartheid leader who'd been unjustly imprisoned.

The student wants to contrast the song "Poor Miner's Farewell" with the song "Bring Him Back Home." Which choice most effectively uses relevant information from the notes to accomplish this goal?

A) The songs "Poor Miner's Farewell" and "Bring Him Back Home" both raised awareness about human rights violations.

B) While both are protest songs, "Poor Miner's Farewell" is about coal miners in Kentucky, whereas "Bring Him Back Home" is about the anti-apartheid leader Nelson Mandela.

C) Hugh Masekela's song "Bring Him Back Home," released in 1987, called on the South African government to free Nelson Mandela.

D) Released in 1932 by Aunt Molly Jackson, the song "Poor Miner's Farewell" was a protest against the unlivable wages and dangerous working conditions faced by Kentucky coal miners.

CONTINUE →

While researching a topic, a student has taken the following notes:

- Tibetan mastiffs are large dogs native to the Himalayas.
- A mutation in their EPAS1 gene prevents excess hemoglobin production.
- A mutation in their HBB gene boosts hemoglobin's oxygen-carrying ability.
- These mutations enable the dogs to withstand hypoxic (low-oxygen) conditions at high altitudes.
- In a 2016 study, Zhen Wang and colleagues noted that Tibetan wolves' DNA has the same EPAS1 and HBB mutations.
- Wang and colleagues determined that the dogs first acquired these mutations by interbreeding with Tibetan wolves around 24,000 years ago.

The student wants to present the conclusion of Zhen Wang and colleagues' 2016 study. Which choice most effectively uses relevant information from the notes to accomplish this goal?

A) Like Tibetan mastiffs, Tibetan wolves can withstand hypoxic conditions at high altitudes.

B) Both Tibetan mastiffs and Tibetan wolves have mutations in their EPAS1 and HBB genes, which prevent excess hemoglobin production and boost hemoglobin's oxygen-carrying ability, respectively.

C) In addition to preventing excess hemoglobin production, a mutation in Tibetan mastiffs' HBB gene boosts hemoglobin's oxygen-carrying ability.

D) By interbreeding with Tibetan wolves around 24,000 years ago, Tibetan mastiffs acquired the genetic mutations that enable them to withstand hypoxic conditions.

While researching a topic, a student has taken the following notes:

- Bike-share programs provide bicycles for shared use.
- In docked bike sharing, riders rent a bike and return it to designated docking stations.
- Docked programs are orderly and offer consistency to riders but require significant space and money to implement.
- In dockless bike sharing, riders locate a bike and leave it wherever they choose.
- Dockless programs are relatively simple and inexpensive to implement and offer flexibility to riders.
- Dockless programs can be disorganized.

The student wants to compare some disadvantages of docked and dockless bike-share programs. Which choice most effectively uses relevant information from the notes to accomplish this goal?

A) Dockless programs can be disorganized; docked programs, on the other hand, offer order and consistency.

B) Worth noting is that while dockless programs are relatively easy and inexpensive to implement, they are less flexible than docked programs.

C) Docked programs are more resource-intensive than dockless programs, but they avoid some of the latter's organizational challenges.

D) Though dockless programs offer flexibility, docked bike-share programs provide bicycles for shared use.

STOP

If you finish before time is called, you may check your work on this module only.
Do not turn to any other module in the test.

Reading and Writing

27 QUESTIONS

1

On the basis of extensive calculations and models, astronomers in the 1990s predicted that the collision of two neutron stars or a neutron star and a black hole could release a massive burst of gamma rays in an event called a kilonova. This _____ was confirmed with observations in 2017.

Which choice completes the text with the most logical and precise word or phrase?

A) theory

B) evidence

C) constant

D) experiment

2

Taking photographs in the mid-1800s was complicated and expensive, but this changed with the 1854 invention of the *carte de visite*, a small photo that cost little to make. *Carte de visite* photos helped to _____ photography: they made it easy and enjoyable for everyday people to have their pictures taken, and people at the time loved exchanging these small photos with friends and family.

Which choice completes the text with the most logical and precise word or phrase?

A) weaken

B) praise

C) popularize

D) isolate

3

Painter Alma W. Thomas was fascinated by the colors and shapes found in nature. The flowers and trees in the garden at her home in Washington, DC, _____ her work. For example, Thomas's use of broken brushstrokes was inspired by the way that light would shine through the leaves of a tree in front of her house.

Which choice completes the text with the most logical and precise word or phrase?

A) restricted

B) announced

C) distracted

D) influenced

CONTINUE

4

In the 1990s, conservationists began planting more than 500,000 native trees in the habitat of the Azores bullfinch to boost the bird's numbers. This approach was apparently _____: the Azores bullfinch's population size increased from as few as 100 birds at the end of the 1980s to around 1,300 in 2023.

Which choice completes the text with the most logical and precise word or phrase?

A) amusing

B) costly

C) successful

D) disastrous

5

The majority of plastics today wind up in landfills or are, at best, recycled into materials that have a very limited range of applications. To address this problem, chemist Guoliang Liu and colleagues designed a reactor that melts polyethylene and polypropylene—two widely used plastics—into a wax. The wax can then be transformed into a surfactant (a chemical compound usable as a detergent). With this promising new method, plastic waste could be turned into a range of useful cleaning products.

Which choice best states the function of the underlined portion of the text?

A) It clarifies the meaning of a scientific term.

B) It describes an environmental concern.

C) It explains the significance of a scientific discovery.

D) It identifies a result that confused the team.

6

Archaeologists studying the ancient city of Pompeii in Italy recently discovered a well-preserved food shop known as a *thermopolium*. The site contains food remains, artworks, and decorations. These items give researchers a better understanding of what daily life in Pompeii may have been like. For example, the archaeologists found a ceramic jar that they believe likely contained a meat and seafood stew.

Which choice best states the main purpose of the text?

A) To compare ancient artworks with modern ones

B) To discuss the political system of Italy

C) To present a recent archaeological discovery

D) To describe a region's climate

Unauthorized copying or reuse of any part of this page is illegal.

CONTINUE

693

7

In 2023 literary scholar Jeremy Douglass cautioned technology investors and enthusiasts who predict conventional books' ultimate displacement by newer forms of media. Douglass observed that <u>the concept of an "interactive" text is much older than technologists assume, extending back to the first time readers scratched notes into a text's margins.</u> In addition, newer media, such as video games, haven't replaced older forms of entertainment, such as comic books, but rather exist alongside them. Douglass believes that rather than supplanting books, technology is simply making new forms of expression possible.

Which choice best describes the function of the underlined portion in the text as a whole?

A) It challenges the stance of the investors and enthusiasts who are mentioned earlier in the text.

B) It explains the basis for the claim made by the technologists mentioned in the text.

C) It suggests that academics are better suited than investors to see the potential uses of contemporary interactive texts.

D) It provides a historical anecdote about the technological challenges involved in reading the earliest interactive texts.

8

Hevea brasiliensis, a tree in the Amazon rainforest, is the world's main source of natural rubber. The tree produces a milky substance called latex that is used to make rubber. The bark of *Hevea brasiliensis* is helpful for the process of making rubber because it has a unique structure that makes it easy to collect latex. A network of tubes in the tree's inner bark helps the latex to flow out easily when people make small cuts into the bark.

What feature of *Hevea brasiliensis* does the text say is helpful for the process of making rubber?

A) Its latex produces rubber of an especially high quality.

B) Its bark has a unique structure that makes it easy to collect latex.

C) It is able to grow in a wide variety of climates around the world.

D) It is one of only two trees in the Amazon that produce latex.

9

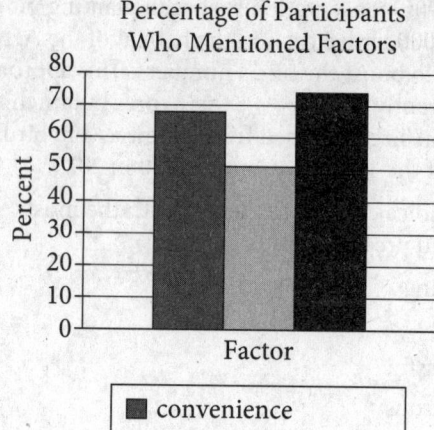

Percentage of Participants Who Mentioned Factors

- ■ convenience
- ▢ costs
- ■ established behaviors

Researcher Judith Hilton and her team interviewed 55 people about which factors would make them switch from using single-use plastic containers to reusable containers. The graph shows three of the factors mentioned in the interviews and the percentage of participants who mentioned them.

According to the graph, about what percentage of participants mentioned costs in the interview?

A) 10%

B) 95%

C) 25%

D) 50%

CONTINUE →

10

Total Areas and 2022 Populations of
Smallest Arabian Peninsula Countries

Country	Total area (square miles)	Population
Kuwait	6,880	4,268,873
Bahrain	304	1,472,233
Qatar	4,471	2,695,122

In terms of area and population, the three smallest Arabian Peninsula countries are Bahrain, Qatar, and Kuwait.

According to the table, what is the total area of Bahrain?

A) 4,268,873 square miles

B) 4,471 square miles

C) 304 square miles

D) 6,880 square miles

11

"The Mountain" is a 1914 poem by Robert Frost. In the poem, the speaker visits a town next to a mountain. The speaker claims to feel protected by the mountain, saying _____

Which quotation from "The Mountain" most effectively illustrates the claim?

A) "A dry ravine emerged under boughs / Into the pasture."

B) "The mountain stood there to be pointed at."

C) "I felt it like a wall / Behind which I was sheltered from a wind."

D) "I crossed the river and swung round the mountain."

12

Treasure Island is an 1883 novel by Robert Louis Stevenson. When the narrator was a child, his father ran a hotel. A mysterious sailor came to stay at the hotel. The narrator was frightened of the sailor, as can be seen when the narrator says, _____

Which quotation from *Treasure Island* most effectively illustrates the claim?

A) "I remember [the sailor] as if it were yesterday, as he came plodding to the inn door, his sea-chest following behind him in a hand-barrow."

B) "[The sailor] was a very silent man by custom. All day he hung round the cove or upon the cliffs with a brass telescope."

C) "All the time he lived with us [the sailor] made no change whatever in his dress but to buy some stockings from a hawker. One of the [corners] of his hat having fallen down, he let it hang from that day forth, though it was a great annoyance when it blew."

D) "How [the sailor] haunted my dreams, I need scarcely tell you. On stormy nights, when the wind shook the four corners of the house and the surf roared along the cove and up the cliffs, I would see him in a thousand forms, and with a thousand diabolical expressions."

Unauthorized copying or reuse of any part of this page is illegal.

CONTINUE

695

13

The Nacional tree is a rare variety of cacao. Nacionals were thought to have gone extinct by the twentieth century due to a fungus. This fungus can spread from tree to nearby tree through the air and causes disease. But around 2013, cacao expert Servio Pachard located some of these Nacional trees. The trees were in the Piedra de Plata coastal forest, within a hard-to-reach valley in Ecuador. Conservationists inferred that the Nacional trees in Piedra de Plata might have avoided the diseases that wiped out the other Nacionals because _____

Which choice most logically completes the text?

A) early twentieth-century scientists did not know why so many Nacionals were becoming infected.

B) the ability of the fungus to travel through the air was only recently discovered.

C) they were too far from the other Nacional trees infected by the fungus to become infected themselves.

D) the chocolate made from their pods was highly valued.

14

Pigments give paints and dyes their color. Ocher is a mineral-based pigment used to make several colors, including red. Red ocher gets its color from iron oxide. Pigments can also be plant-based; plant-based pigments contain a high level of carbon. In a 2023 study, archaeologists tested the red pigment on decorated beads made by members of the Natufian culture approximately 15,000 years ago. The test showed that the pigment found on several beads contained no iron but had a high level of carbon. This finding led the researchers to conclude that _____

Which choice most logically completes the text?

A) the Natufian beads examined in the study are the oldest surviving examples of the use of plant-based pigments for decorating beads.

B) the Natufian beadmakers used plant-based pigments rather than ocher to decorate some of the beads examined in the study.

C) the Natufian beadmakers preferred to use plant-based pigments because they are much brighter than mineral-based pigments are.

D) the pigments used by the Natufian beadmakers likely came from plants because ocher was difficult to find.

15

One of the earliest known maps is a Babylonian clay tablet thought to be almost 4,500 years old. The map _____ the area of a plot of land, shows a river valley, and includes the cardinal directions.

Which choice completes the text so that it conforms to the conventions of Standard English?

A) describes

B) describe

C) have described

D) are describing

Unauthorized copying or reuse of any part of this page is illegal.

CONTINUE

696

16

Eighteen letters written by Louisa May Alcott, author of the popular novel *Little Women* (1868), can be found at the New York Historical Society. _____ letters demonstrate Alcott's keen business sense in her interactions with publishers.

Which choice completes the text so that it conforms to the conventions of Standard English?

A) One

B) That

C) This

D) These

17

The Dust Bowl was a period of severe drought that plagued the Great Plains of the US during the 1930s. During this time, dust storms _____ over 100 million acres of land. They even reached as far east as New York City.

Which choice completes the text so that it conforms to the conventions of Standard English?

A) are affecting

B) will have affected

C) will affect

D) affected

18

Increasing the heat on an uncovered boiling pot of water does not increase the temperature of the water. What increases is the rate at which the water turns to _____ a pressure cooker pot, though, an airtight seal traps the vapor in the pot, creating pressure that allows the temperature of the water to increase past its boiling point.

Which choice completes the text so that it conforms to the conventions of Standard English?

A) vapor. With

B) vapor with

C) vapor, with

D) vapor and with

19

Between 322 and 184 BCE, the Maurya Empire established a complex economic system that, through trade and centralized _____ funded major infrastructure projects throughout the Indian subcontinent. This included the building of many roads, canals, and hospitals.

Which choice completes the text so that it conforms to the conventions of Standard English?

A) taxation:

B) taxation,

C) taxation—

D) taxation

20

Wanting to celebrate the 100th anniversary of the Alaska Purchase, _____ up with a motto that best captured the state's unique character. The commission selected "North to the Future," submitted by Juneau journalist Richard Peter, as its winning entry.

Which choice completes the text so that it conforms to the conventions of Standard English?

A) a contest sponsored by the Alaska Centennial Commission would award $300 to an individual who came

B) an award of $300 would go to an individual in a contest sponsored by the Alaska Centennial Commission for coming

C) $300 would be awarded to an individual by the Alaska Centennial Commission in a contest for coming

D) the Alaska Centennial Commission sponsored a contest that would award $300 to an individual who came

Unauthorized copying or reuse of any part of this page is illegal.

CONTINUE →

697

21

Many mechanical calculators were powered by a notched cylinder mechanism called the Leibniz wheel. Leibniz wheel calculators were popular in the first half of the twentieth _____ these ingenious devices were eventually replaced by electronic calculators.

Which choice completes the text so that it conforms to the conventions of Standard English?

A) century

B) century,

C) century, but

D) century that

22

In his painting *At the Cycle-Race Track*, Jean Metzinger aims to depict a bike race in four-dimensional space. Of course, Metzinger's painting doesn't technically represent a fourth dimension; humans can only see in three dimensions. _____ by depicting the race through multiple, simultaneous perspectives, Metzinger offers a fascinating glimpse at what this other universe might look like.

Which choice completes the text with the most logical transition?

A) Moreover,

B) That said,

C) In other words,

D) For example,

23

While researching a topic, a student has taken the following notes:

- "Raymond's Run" is a short story.

- It was written by African American author Toni Cade Bambara.

- It was first published in her book *Gorilla, My Love* in 1972.

- It is told from a first person perspective.

- It takes place in Harlem.

The student wants to indicate where the short story takes place. Which choice most effectively uses relevant information from the notes to accomplish this goal?

A) "Raymond's Run" takes place in Harlem.

B) "Raymond's Run" was published in *Gorilla, My Love*.

C) "Raymond's Run" is told from a first person perspective.

D) "Raymond's Run" was written by Toni Cade Bambara.

CONTINUE ➤

While researching a topic, a student has taken the following notes:

- Georeferencing is the process of assigning geographic coordinates to an image.
- This process enables mapping software to place the image in its real-world location.
- A 2017 project by Tania López Marrero and colleagues georeferenced a set of aerial photographs of Puerto Rico's coastline taken in 1930.
- These photographs are the earliest known aerial photographs of Puerto Rico.
- López Marrero's project provided data that can help researchers analyze changes in Puerto Rico's coastline.

The student wants to define the term "georeferencing." Which choice most effectively uses relevant information from the notes to accomplish this goal?

A) A 2017 project by Tania López Marrero and colleagues assigned geographic coordinates to photographs of Puerto Rico's coastline and also used georeferencing.

B) Tania López Marrero and colleagues used georeferencing in their analysis of the earliest known aerial photographs of Puerto Rico.

C) Georeferenced aerial photographs from 1930 can help researchers analyze changes in Puerto Rico's coastline.

D) Georeferencing is the process of assigning geographic coordinates to an image so that mapping software can place it in its real-world location.

While researching a topic, a student has taken the following notes:

- The engineer Robert Fulton designed the *Clermont* steamboat in 1807.
- He designed it in New York City.
- *Clermont* was the world's first commercially successful steamboat.
- The city of Fulton, Missouri, is named after Robert Fulton.
- New York City's Fulton Street is named after him.

The student wants to indicate how Fulton, Missouri, got its name. Which choice most effectively uses relevant information from the notes to accomplish this goal?

A) Fulton, Missouri, shares its name with Fulton Street in New York City.

B) Fulton Street is in New York City, where the steamboat *Clermont* was designed in 1807.

C) Designed in 1807 in New York City, *Clermont* was the first commercially successful steamboat.

D) Fulton, Missouri, is named after Robert Fulton, designer of the first commercially successful steamboat.

Unauthorized copying or reuse of any part of this page is illegal.

CONTINUE

699

26

While researching a topic, a student has taken the following notes:

- The Royal Alcázar of Seville is a historic royal palace in Andalucía, Spain.
- The palace is famous for its intricate tilework.
- The palace features majolica and arista tiles.
- In the majolica style, designs are painted directly on the ceramic tiles.
- In the arista style, designs are stamped into the ceramic tiles.

The student wants to contrast the two styles of tiles. Which choice most effectively uses relevant information from the notes to accomplish this goal?

A) Tiles in the majolica and arista styles can be found in the Royal Alcázar of Seville in Andalucía, Spain.

B) Featuring tiles in the majolica and arista styles, the Royal Alcázar of Seville in Spain is famous for its intricate tilework.

C) In the arista style, designs are stamped into the ceramic tiles, whereas in the majolica style, the designs are painted directly on them.

D) Among the famous tilework of the Royal Alcázar of Seville are majolica style tiles, made by painting designs directly on the ceramic tiles.

27

While researching a topic, a student has taken the following notes:

- Political scientist Graham Allison is known for this Thucydides trap theory.
- Allison's theory states that whenever "a rising power is threatening to displace a ruling power," conflict is likely.
- The theory is based on Thucydides's explanation of the conflict between Athens and Sparta.
- Thucydides wrote that "the rise of Athens and the fear this instilled in Sparta" made conflict "inevitable."
- History professor Edmund Stewart recently challenged the historical basis of the theory.
- Stewart claimed that Athens was not a rising power and that the rivals experienced a "clash of cultures" instead.

The student wants to use a quotation to challenge Thucydides's explanation of the conflict between Athens and Sparta. Which choice most effectively uses relevant information from the notes to accomplish this goal?

A) According to Allison's Thucydides trap theory, whenever "a rising power is threatening to displace a ruling power," conflict is likely.

B) Thucydides wrote that conflict between the two powers was "inevitable," although Stewart later challenged the historical basis of this claim.

C) According to Stewart, a "clash of cultures" between Athens and Sparta caused the conflict, not Athens's rise.

D) Thucydides explained that conflict was caused by "the rise of Athens and the fear this instilled in Sparta," but Allison disagreed, seeing the conflict as an example of the Thucydides trap.

STOP

**If you finish before time is called, you may check your work on this module only.
Do not turn to any other module in the test.**

Test begins on the next page.

Reading and Writing

27 QUESTIONS

1

At the turn of the twentieth century, Black residents of Richmond, Virginia, had few formal options for banking and other financial services. To _____ this situation, Maggie Lena Walker chartered the St. Luke Penny Savings Bank in 1903. The bank went on to provide home loans and savings opportunities to thousands of Black families over the following decades.

Which choice completes the text with the most logical and precise word or phrase?

A) prolong

B) rectify

C) retain

D) highlight

2

The creation of Lotte Reiniger's 1926 animated film *The Adventures of Prince Achmed* was _____ process. Over the course of three years, Reiniger and her collaborators painstakingly made more than 250,000 individual images of hand-cut paper silhouettes and repeatedly had to invent entirely new methods and tools to create the special effects Reiniger envisioned.

Which choice completes the text with the most logical and precise word or phrase?

A) a haphazard

B) a contentious

C) an ineffectual

D) an arduous

Unauthorized copying or reuse of any part of this page is illegal.

702

CONTINUE ▶

3

Diadromous fish migrate between freshwater and marine biomes during their life cycle. The migration's obligate nature is why diadromous fish can be _____ those that are merely euryhaline (able to tolerate high salinity): the euryhaline blackchin tilapia can survive high salinity, but its life cycle does not involve relocation to a different biome, as does that of the diadromous wild salmon.

Which choice completes the text with the most logical and precise word or phrase?

A) demarcated from

B) reconstituted as

C) conflated with

D) derived from

4

One popular theory of the origin of the Moon, the "big whack," posits that a protoplanet called Theia collided with Earth, flinging debris into orbit that eventually coalesced into the Moon. Until recently, Theia was _____, but researcher Qian Yuan and colleagues now claim to have identified pieces of the protoplanet in the lowermost section of Earth's mantle.

Which choice completes the text with the most logical and precise word or phrase?

A) desultory

B) spurious

C) veritable

D) notional

5

The following text is from H.D.'s 1916 poem "Mid-Day." In the poem, the speaker is on a path in an outdoor setting.

> A slight wind shakes the seed-pods—
> my thoughts are spent
> as the black seeds.
> My thoughts tear me,
> I dread their fever.
> I am scattered in its whirl.
> I am scattered like
> the hot shrivelled seeds.

Which choice best describes the function of the underlined portion in the text as a whole?

A) It illustrates a change in the natural environment that the speaker implies is responsible for the growing misgivings described in the text.

B) It establishes an example of consistency in the natural landscape that the speaker then contrasts with the unpredictability of human emotions.

C) It presents an observation of an occurrence in the natural world that the speaker then expands on to convey a sense of a turbulent interior state.

D) It evokes the ordinariness of an event in nature to suggest that the critical self-evaluation the speaker engages in is a common pursuit.

Unauthorized copying or reuse of any part of this page is illegal.

CONTINUE

703

6

The Bayeux Tapestry, from eleventh-century France, depicts 75 scenes over 250 feet of fabric. It was likely produced by workers embroidering in sections and then joining the resulting panels together. It's plausible that the workshop that produced the tapestry had never produced one so large, and some researchers claim that a close examination of the joins—the places where the panels are stitched together—suggests that the workers developed and refined their joining process over the course of production. <u>For example, the first join the workers completed exhibits a clear misalignment of the borders of the two panels, whereas the later joins are virtually invisible.</u>

Which choice best describes the function of the underlined sentence in the text as a whole?

A) It identifies the people and events depicted in the Bayeux Tapestry.

B) It supports an argument about the workers who produced the Bayeux Tapestry.

C) It compares the Bayeux Tapestry with other tapestries from eleventh-century France.

D) It describes how researchers determined where the Bayeux Tapestry was produced.

7

The following text is from Thomas Mann's 1924 novel *The Magic Mountain*, translated by John E. Woods in 1995.

> The story of Hans Castorp that we intend to tell here—not for his sake (for the reader will come to know him as a perfectly ordinary, if engaging young man), but for the sake of the story itself, which seems to us to be very much worth telling (although in Hans Castorp's favor it should be noted that it is *his* story, and that not every story happens to everybody)—is a story that took place long ago, and is, so to speak, covered with the patina of history and must necessarily be told with verbs whose tense is that of the deepest past.

©1995 by Alfred A. Knopf, Inc.

What does the text most strongly suggest about the story of Hans Castorp?

A) Though it is true that stories of even the most uninteresting people are themselves interesting because all people are unique, the reason this story is interesting is nonetheless difficult to understand because of the passage of time.

B) Even though it is a story of a person of no particular importance, its age and the manner in which it therefore must be told are both indicators that the story itself is important.

C) Like all stories about the lives of inconsequential people, this story must necessarily be related in a particular way if the reason the story is consequential is to be made evident to the audience.

D) It is a remarkable story that happened to an unremarkable person, though one could plausibly argue that because the story is valuable, some of its value accrues to the person at its center.

Unauthorized copying or reuse of any part of this page is illegal.

CONTINUE ▶

704

8

Early Earth is thought to have been characterized by a stagnant lid tectonic regime, in which the upper lithosphere (the outer rocky layer) was essentially immobile and there was no interaction between the lithosphere and the underlying mantle. Researchers investigated the timing of the transition from a stagnant lid regime to a tectonic plate regime, in which the lithosphere is fractured into dynamic plates that in turn allow lithospheric and mantle material to mix. Examining chemical data from lithospheric and mantle-derived rocks ranging from 285 million to 3.8 billion years old, the researchers dated the transition to 3.2 billion years ago.

Which finding, if true, would most directly support the researchers' conclusion?

A) Among rocks known to be older than 3.2 billion years, significantly more are mantle derived than lithospheric, but the opposite is true for the rocks younger than 3.2 billion years.

B) Mantle-derived rocks older than 3.2 billion years show significantly more compositional diversity than lithospheric rocks older than 3.2 billion years do.

C) There is a positive correlation between the age of lithospheric rocks and their chemical similarity to mantle-derived rocks, and that correlation increases significantly in strength at around 3.2 billion years old.

D) Mantle-derived rocks younger than 3.2 billion years contain some material that is not found in older mantle-derived rocks but is found in older and contemporaneous lithospheric rocks.

9

Almost all works of fiction contain references to the progression of time, including the time of day when events in a story take place. In a 2020 study, Allen Kim, Charuta Pethe, and Steven Skiena claim that an observable pattern in such references reflects a shift in human behavior prompted by the spread of electric lighting in the late nineteenth century. The researchers drew this conclusion from an analysis of more than 50,000 novels spanning many centuries and cultures, using software to recognize and tally both specific time references—that is, clock phrases, such as 7 a.m. or 2:30 p.m.—and implied ones, such as mentions of meals typically associated with a particular time of day.

Which finding from the study, if true, would most directly support the researchers' conclusion?

A) Novels published after the year 1800 include the clock phrase 10 a.m. less often than novels published before the year 1800 do.

B) Novels published after 1880 contain significantly more references to activities occurring after 10 p.m. than do novels from earlier periods.

C) Among novels published in the nineteenth century, implied time references become steadily more common than clock phrases as publication dates approach 1900.

D) The time references of noon (12 p.m.) and midnight (12 a.m.) are used with roughly the same frequency in the novels.

CONTINUE

10

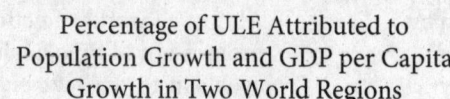

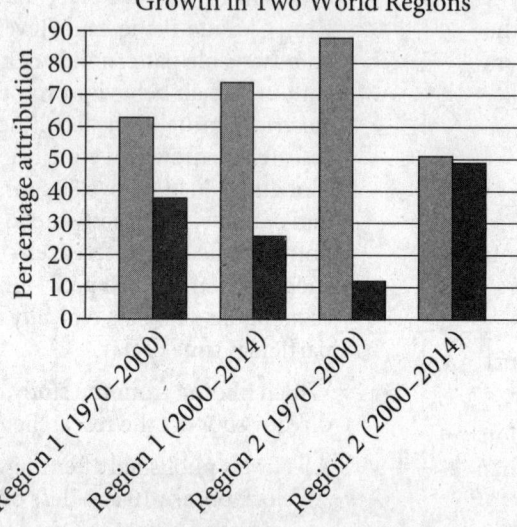

Percentage of ULE Attributed to
Population Growth and GDP per Capita
Growth in Two World Regions

Region, by time period

- urban population growth
- GDP per capita growth

In a study of urban physical expansion, Richa Mahtta et al. conducted a meta-analysis of more than 300 cities worldwide to determine whether urban land expansion (ULE) was more strongly influenced by urban population growth or by growth in gross domestic product (GDP) per capita, a measure of economic activity. Because efficient national government is necessary to provide urban services and infrastructure that attract economic investment, Mahtta et al. propose that absent other factors, the importance of GDP per capita growth to ULE would likely increase relative to the importance of population growth as governments become more efficient. If true, this suggests the possibility that _____

Which choice most effectively uses data from the graph to complete the statement?

A) national governments of countries in Region 1 experienced declines in efficiency in the period from 2000 to 2014, relative to the period from 1970 to 2000.

B) countries in Region 1 experienced a slower rate of economic growth in the period from 2000 to 2014 than countries in Region 2 did, despite increasing national government efficiency in Region 1.

C) national governments of most countries in Region 2 became more efficient in the period from 2000 to 2014 than they had been in the period from 1970 to 2000, but those of several countries in this region did not.

D) national governments of countries in Region 1 and in Region 2 generally became more efficient in the period from 2000 to 2014 than they had been in the period from 1970 to 2000, but at different rates.

Unauthorized copying or reuse of any part of this page is illegal.

CONTINUE

706

11

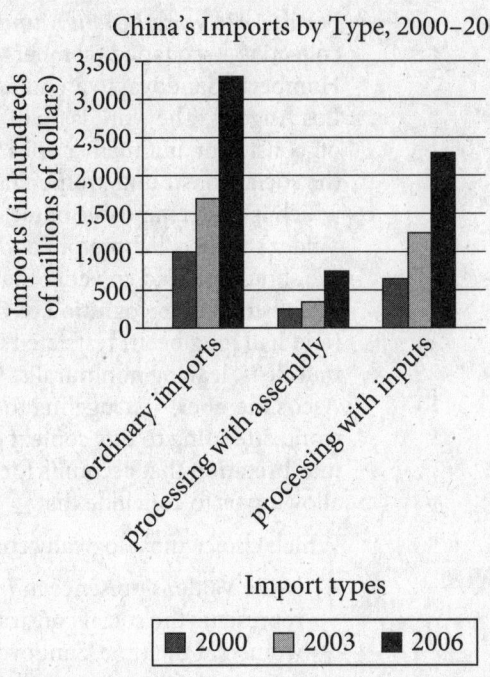

China's Imports by Type, 2000–2006

Imports (in hundreds of millions of dollars)

Import types

■ 2000   ■ 2003   ■ 2006

A student is researching the Chinese government's 1992 shift to a market economy that emphasizes trade liberalization. One means of trade liberalization involves expanding from ordinary imports into an emphasis on processing imports, which have two types: processing with assembly (in which a firm obtains raw materials from a foreign trading partner without payment and sells the final goods to that partner, charging for assembly) and processing with inputs (in which a firm expends capital to buy raw materials from a trading partner, processes them into final goods, and sells those goods to whichever trading partner it chooses). The student asserts that while initial efforts at trade liberalization were shaped by Chinese firms' limited capital, this situation resolved during the 2000s.

Which choice best describes data from the graph that support the student's assertion?

A) Processing imports with inputs were greater than both ordinary imports and processing imports with assembly in 2006.

B) From 2000 to 2006, processing imports with inputs rose much more sharply than processing imports with assembly did.

C) From 2000 to 2006, neither processing imports with inputs nor processing imports with assembly were greater than ordinary imports.

D) Processing imports with assembly were greater in 2006 than processing imports with inputs in 2000.

CONTINUE

12

The Uto-Aztecan language family is divided into a northern branch, which includes the Shoshone language of present-day Idaho and Utah, and a southern one, whose best-known representative is Nahuatl, the language of the Aztec Empire in Mexico. Lexical similarities across the family, including of botanical terms, confirm descent from a single language spoken millennia ago, and the family's geographical distribution suggests an origin in what is now the US Southwest. However, vocabulary pertaining to maize isn't shared between northern and southern branches, despite the crop's universal cultivation among Uto-Aztecan tribes. Given archaeological evidence that maize originated in Mexico and diffused northward into what became the US Southwest, some linguists reason that _____

Which choice most logically completes the text?

A) northern Uto-Aztecan tribes likely obtained the crop directly from a southern Uto-Aztecan tribe rather than from a non-Uto-Aztecan tribe.

B) variation in maize-related vocabulary within each branch of the Uto-Aztecan family likely reflects regionally specific methods for cultivating the crop.

C) southern Uto-Aztecan tribes likely acquired maize at roughly the same time as northern Uto-Aztecan tribes did, though from different sources.

D) the family's division into northern and southern branches likely preceded the acquisition of the crop by the Uto-Aztecan tribes.

13

For its 1974 work *Instant Mural*, the Chicano art collective Asco taped members Patssi Valdez and Humberto Sandoval to an outdoor wall in East Los Angeles. The work is manifestly a commentary on constraint, but many critics focus on Valdez and the social constraints women faced at the time, which is understandable but leaves the presence of Valdez's male collaborator Sandoval unexplained. We should instead consider that in 1974, the art establishment's recognition of Chicano artists was (and had long been) restricted to sociohistorical muralists, leaving nonmuralist Chicano artists—like Asco's members—struggling to even exhibit their work; attending to this context opens an interpretation that accounts for all the evidence, allowing us to conclude that _____

Which choice most logically completes the text?

A) while Valdez's presence in *Instant Mural* represents the social constraints placed on women at the time, Sandoval's presence represents Chicano muralists' frustration at their lack of recognition by the art establishment.

B) the main subject of *Instant Mural* is female Chicano artists' experience of being doubly constrained by gender-role expectations and the marginalization of certain types of art.

C) *Instant Mural* is a reflection on the constraining aesthetic expectations placed on Chicano artists in general rather than on the social constraints placed on women specifically.

D) *Instant Mural* is best understood not as a critique of the social constraints placed on women but rather as a critique of sociohistorical muralists' depictions of Chicano culture.

Unauthorized copying or reuse of any part of this page is illegal.

CONTINUE ➡

708

14

An analysis by Alain Elayi and colleagues of coins minted in Sidon in the fifth and fourth centuries BCE reveals a change in their composition over time: while a coin from circa 450 BCE contains about 98% silver and 1% copper, a coin from 367 BCE (the end of Ba'alšillem II's reign) contains 74.2% silver and 24.7% copper, giving it a relatively yellowish appearance that traders would have noticed. Because coins with a silver content below 80% were widely considered unsuitable for trade, Elayi et al. speculate that a crisis in confidence in the currency occurred in Sidon around 367 BCE, which was likely relieved—despite Sidon's persistent oppressive financial obligations—as a result of Ba'alšillem II's successor Abd'aštart I's decision to _____

Which choice most logically completes the text?

A) proclaim that the percentage of silver in coins suitable for trade would be raised to a threshold higher than 80%.

B) keep the amount of silver in Sidonian coins consistent with that in coins minted in 367 BCE but decrease their weight.

C) begin minting heavier coins with a proportion of silver to copper similar to that in coins minted in 367 BCE.

D) fund the mining of some copper deposits that were not available to Ba'alšillem II.

15

Nigerian American artist Toyin Ojih Odutola uses black-ink pens to create highly detailed drawings of human figures. Her portrait of novelist Zadie _____ is displayed in the National Portrait Gallery in London.

Which choice completes the text so that it conforms to the conventions of Standard English?

A) Smith:

B) Smith—

C) Smith

D) Smith,

16

A government body officially known as the Althing, _____

Which choice completes the text so that it conforms to the conventions of Standard English?

A) the world's oldest parliaments include one which first met in 930 CE, Iceland's.

B) Iceland's parliament is one of the oldest in the world, first meeting in 930 CE.

C) the first meeting of one of the oldest parliaments in the world, Iceland's, was in 930 CE.

D) 930 CE was the year when Iceland's parliament, one of the oldest parliaments in the world, first met.

17

As the fourteenth US librarian of Congress, Carla Hayden has many responsibilities. These include overseeing the Library of Congress's collections, which boast more than 162 million _____ the US Copyright Office, which registers copyright claims and advises Congress on copyright law; and appointing the US poet laureate.

Which choice completes the text so that it conforms to the conventions of Standard English?

A) items managing

B) items, managing

C) items; managing

D) items. Managing

Unauthorized copying or reuse of any part of this page is illegal.

CONTINUE ▶

709

18

Recently unearthed Neronian tools in France dating to 54,000 years ago and attributed to *Homo sapiens* may provide evidence that interactions between Neanderthals and modern humans occurred 10,000 years earlier than was previously _____ finding that, if true, would overturn current theories about *H. sapiens* migration during the Upper Paleolithic.

Which choice completes the text so that it conforms to the conventions of Standard English?

A) supposed; a

B) supposed. A

C) supposed a

D) supposed, a

19

Digital artist Jung (Lulu) Chen primarily uses a suite of software tools to create illustrations for children's books. To manifest the warm and welcoming atmospheres that are a signature of her _____ she occasionally relies on more traditional art techniques, such as painting with watercolors.

Which choice completes the text so that it conforms to the conventions of Standard English?

A) work, though,

B) work, though

C) work; though,

D) work, though;

20

Chondrites are stony meteorites that are undifferentiated—that is, their contents have not melted and separated into distinct layers. They are hardly _____ many chondrites experience aqueous alteration as a result of exposure to fluids, as well as fracturing, veining, and localized melting due to collisions with other objects.

Which choice completes the text so that it conforms to the conventions of Standard English?

A) pristine, though

B) pristine, though;

C) pristine; though

D) pristine, though,

21

That the geographic center of North America lay in the state of North Dakota was conceded by all _____ establishing its precise coordinates proved more divisive.

Which choice completes the text so that it conforms to the conventions of Standard English?

A) involved:

B) involved,

C) involved

D) involved;

22

Following the American Revolutionary War, North American foodways underwent a radical transformation, fueled in large part by spiking consumer demand for certain grains. The cultivation, trade, and transportation of maize and wheat, _____ reconfigured the continent's existing regional foodways into a globally oriented food system.

Which choice completes the text with the most logical transition?

A) in particular,

B) alternatively,

C) by comparison,

D) second of all,

Unauthorized copying or reuse of any part of this page is illegal.

CONTINUE

710

23

When printing paper money for the colony of Pennsylvania in the 1730s, Benjamin Franklin—then a Philadelphia shop owner—took steps to combat the circulation of counterfeit notes, such as weaving blue threads and muscovite (a reflective mineral) into the paper he used. _____ he stamped the notes with detailed imprints of sage leaves that proved difficult for forgers to replicate.

Which choice completes the text with the most logical transition?

A) Specifically,

B) That said,

C) For example,

D) Moreover,

24

While researching a topic, a student has taken the following notes:

- Angana Chaudhuri is a scientist.

- Chaudhuri studies sedimentary rocks.

- A scientist who studies sedimentary rocks is called a sedimentologist.

- Shale, chalk, and sandstone are examples of sedimentary rocks.

The student wants to identify what type of scientist Chaudhuri is. Which choice most effectively uses relevant information from the notes to accomplish this goal?

A) Chalk is a type of sedimentary rock.

B) Some scientists study shale, chalk, and sandstone.

C) There are scientists who study sedimentary rocks.

D) Chaudhuri is a sedimentologist.

25

While researching a topic, a student has taken the following notes:

- Chiura Obata was a Japanese American artist who lived in California.

- *Yosemite Falls* is a notable painting by Obata.

- It uses a Japanese method of black ink painting called sumi-e.

- This painting was completed in 1930.

The student wants to indicate the year *Yosemite Falls* was completed. Which choice most effectively uses relevant information from the notes to accomplish this goal?

A) While living in California, Obata created black ink paintings.

B) Obata, a Japanese American artist, created a notable painting.

C) *Yosemite Falls* was completed in 1930.

D) Obata used a Japanese painting method called sumi-e.

Unauthorized copying or reuse of any part of this page is illegal.

CONTINUE

711

26

While researching a topic, a student has taken the following notes:

- Researchers in a 2021 study wanted to determine the rate at which 17 languages conveyed both information and syllables.
- They calculated the bits of information conveyed per second (the IR, or information rate).
- The IR was found to be approximately consistent across the 17 languages (an average of 39 bits per second).
- They calculated the number of syllables spoken per second (the SR, or syllable rate).
- Spanish had the second-fastest SR (7.7 syllables per second).
- Vietnamese had the sixteenth-fastest SR (5.3 syllables per second).

The student wants to present an overview of the study's findings. Which choice most effectively uses relevant information from the notes to accomplish this goal?

A) The 2021 study determined the information rate (IR) of 17 languages in bits of information conveyed per second.

B) Researchers found that information was conveyed more quickly in Spanish, at 7.7 syllables per second, than in Vietnamese, at 5.3 syllables per second.

C) Vietnamese had the sixteenth-fastest syllable rate, lower than that of Spanish, which had the second-fastest; however, Spanish had the lower information rate of the two.

D) Though some of the languages differed in number of syllables spoken per second, all 17 conveyed information at roughly the same rate.

27

While researching a topic, a student has taken the following notes:

- The fifth Solvay Conference on Physics was held in 1927.
- It brought together twenty-nine of the era's preeminent scientists to discuss the emerging field of quantum theory.
- The conference famously featured a debate between physicists Albert Einstein and Niels Bohr.
- Bohr proposed that subatomic entities like electrons had only probable realities until they were observed.
- Einstein argued that subatomic entities like electrons had a reality independent of observation.
- Bohr's position, later called the Copenhagen interpretation, remains the most widely accepted theory of quantum mechanics.

The student wants to place Einstein's argument within its historical context. Which choice most effectively uses relevant information from the notes to accomplish this goal?

A) During the dawn of quantum theory, Einstein maintained the independent reality of some subatomic entities, although Bohr's opposing interpretation would become the widely accepted view.

B) At the 1927 Solvay Conference on Physics, Einstein disagreed with Bohr's argument that subatomic entities like electrons had a reality independent of observation.

C) The attendees of the 1927 Solvay Conference were among the preeminent scientists of their era, including Einstein, who opposed Bohr's proposal.

D) In 1927, Einstein and Bohr engaged in a famous debate; Bohr's argument, later called the Copenhagen interpretation, would remain popular decades after.

STOP

If you finish before time is called, you may check your work on this module only. Do not turn to any other module in the test.

Test begins on the next page.

Math

22 QUESTIONS

$A = \pi r^2$
$C = 2\pi r$

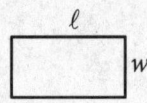

$A = \ell w$

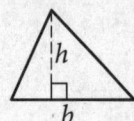

$A = \frac{1}{2}bh$

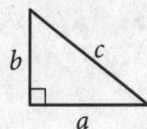

$c^2 = a^2 + b^2$

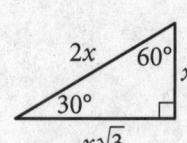

Special Right Triangles

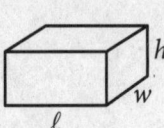

$V = \ell w h$

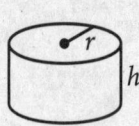

$V = \pi r^2 h$

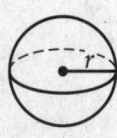

$V = \frac{4}{3}\pi r^3$

$V = \frac{1}{3}\pi r^2 h$

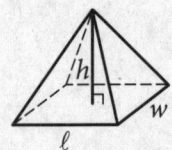

$V = \frac{1}{3}\ell w h$

The number of degrees of arc in a circle is 360.

The number of radians of arc in a circle is 2π.

The sum of the measures in degrees of the angles of a triangle is 180.

Unauthorized copying or reuse of any part of this page is illegal.

714

CONTINUE ➤

For multiple-choice questions, solve each problem, choose the correct answer from the choices provided, and then circle your answer in this book. Circle only one answer for each question. If you change your mind, completely erase the circle. You will not get credit for questions with more than one answer circled, or for questions with no answers circled.

For student-produced response questions, solve each problem and write your answer next to or under the question in the test book as described below.

- Once you've written your answer, circle it clearly. You will not receive credit for anything written outside the circle, or for any questions with more than one circled answer.

- If you find **more than one correct answer**, write and circle only one answer.

- Your answer can be up to 5 characters for a **positive** answer and up to 6 characters (including the negative sign) for a **negative** answer, but no more.

- If your answer is a **fraction** that is too long (over 5 characters for positive, 6 characters for negative), write the decimal equivalent.

- If your answer is a **decimal** that is too long (over 5 characters for positive, 6 characters for negative), truncate it or round at the fourth digit.

- If your answer is a **mixed number** (such as $3\frac{1}{2}$), write it as an improper fraction (7/2) or its decimal equivalent (3.5).

- Don't include **symbols** such as a percent sign, comma, or dollar sign in your circled answer.

CONTINUE ▶

1

Lorenzo purchased a box of cereal and some strawberries at the grocery store. Lorenzo paid $2 for the box of cereal and $1.90 per pound for the strawberries. If Lorenzo paid a total of $9.60 for the box of cereal and the strawberries, which of the following equations can be used to find p, the number of pounds of strawberries Lorenzo purchased? (Assume there is no sales tax.)

A) $1.90p + 2 = 9.60$

B) $1.90p - 2 = 9.60$

C) $1.90 + 2p = 9.60$

D) $1.90 - 2p = 9.60$

2

The function f is defined by $f(x) = 25x + 30$. What is the value of $f(x)$ when $x = 2$?

A) 50

B) 57

C) 80

D) 110

3

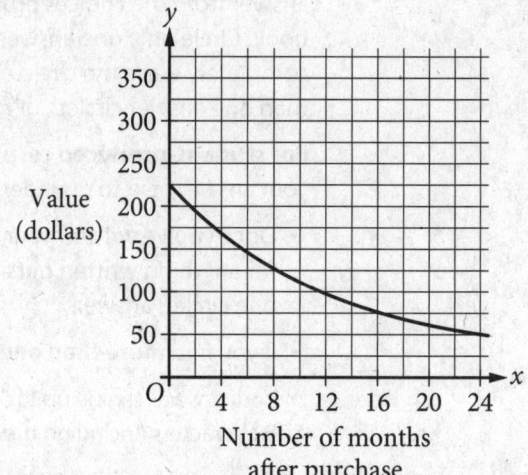

Number of months
after purchase

The graph shown gives the estimated value, in dollars, of a tablet as a function of the number of months since it was purchased. What is the best interpretation of the y-intercept of the graph in this context?

A) The estimated value of the tablet was $225 when it was purchased.

B) The estimated value of the tablet 24 months after it was purchased was $225.

C) The estimated value of the tablet had decreased by $225 in the 24 months after it was purchased.

D) The estimated value of the tablet decreased by approximately 2.25% each year after it was purchased.

CONTINUE

4

$$|p| + 61 = 65$$

Which value is a solution to the given equation?

A) $\frac{65}{61}$

B) 4

C) 126

D) 130

5

Triangles *EFG* and *JKL* are congruent, where *E*, *F*, and *G* correspond to *J*, *K*, and *L*, respectively. The measure of angle *E* is 45° and the measure of angle *F* is 20°. What is the measure of angle *J*?

A) 20°

B) 45°

C) 135°

D) 160°

CONTINUE

6

During the first part of an experiment, a ball was launched from a 7-foot-tall platform. The graph shows the height y, in feet, of the ball x seconds after it was launched during the first part of the experiment.

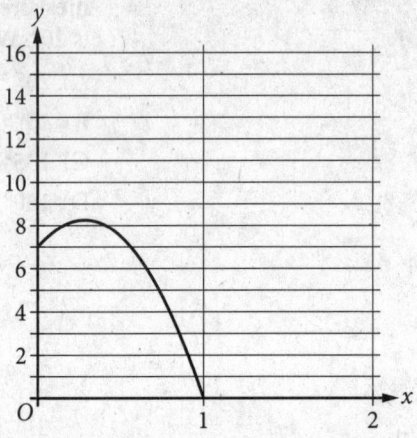

During the second part of the experiment, the ball was launched the same way, but from a platform that is 2 feet shorter than the first platform. Which of the following graphs could represent the height y, in feet, of the ball x seconds after it was launched during the second part of the experiment?

A)

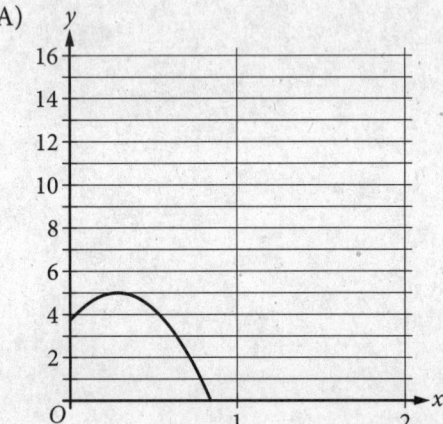

B)

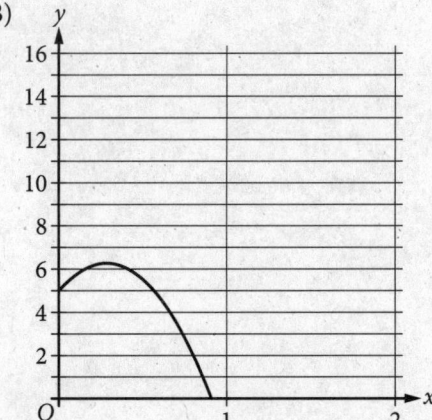

C)

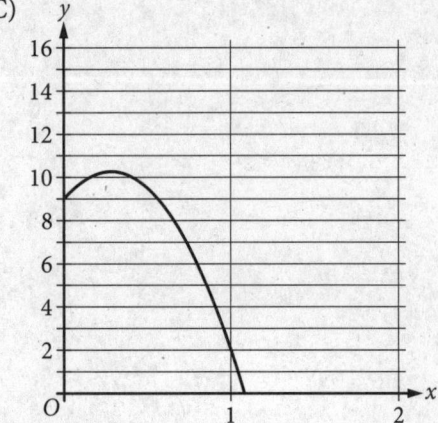

D)

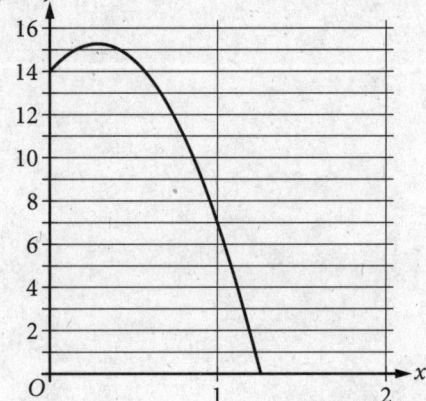

CONTINUE

7

The ratio x to y is equivalent to the ratio 9 to 5. If the value of x is 162, what is the value of y?

8

At a state fair, attendees can win tokens that are worth a different number of points depending on the shape. One attendee won S square tokens and C circle tokens worth a total of 1,120 points. The equation $80S + 90C = 1,120$ represents this situation. How many more points is a circle token worth than a square token?

A) 950

B) 90

C) 80

D) 10

9

$$\frac{(x+9)(x-9)}{x+9} = 7$$

What is the solution to the given equation?

A) 7

B) 9

C) 16

D) 63

10

The equation $12t + b = c$ relates the variables t, b, and c. Which of the following correctly expresses the value of $c - b$ in terms of t?

A) $\frac{t}{12}$

B) t

C) $t + \frac{1}{12}$

D) $12t$

11

What is an x-coordinate of an x-intercept of the graph of $y = 3(x - 14)(x + 5)(x + 4)$ in the xy-plane?

12

The function f is defined by $f(x) = 5\left(\frac{1}{4} - x\right)^2 + \frac{11}{4}$. What is the value of $f\left(\frac{1}{4}\right)$?

13

A circle in the xy-plane has the equation $(x - 13)^2 + (y - k)^2 = 64$. Which of the following gives the center of the circle and its radius?

A) The center is at $(13, k)$ and the radius is 8.

B) The center is at $(k, 13)$ and the radius is 8.

C) The center is at $(k, 13)$ and the radius is 64.

D) The center is at $(13, k)$ and the radius is 64.

14

A circle has a radius of 2.1 inches. The area of the circle is $b\pi$ square inches, where b is a constant. What is the value of b?

CONTINUE

15

During a study, the temperature, in degrees Celsius (°C), of the air in a chamber was recorded to the nearest integer at certain times. The scatterplot shows the recorded temperature y, in °C, of the air in the chamber x minutes after the start of the study.

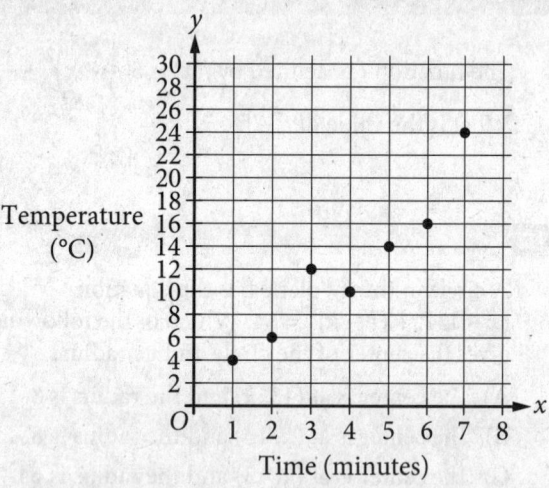

What was the average rate of change, in °C per minute, of the recorded temperature of the air in the chamber from $x = 5$ to $x = 7$?

16

$$3y = 4x + 17$$
$$-3y = 9x - 23$$

The solution to the given system of equations is (x, y). What is the value of $39x$?

A) −18

B) −6

C) 6

D) 18

17

The function $f(t) = 40,000(2)^{\frac{t}{790}}$ gives the number of bacteria in a population t minutes after an initial observation. How much time, in minutes, does it take for the number of bacteria in the population to double?

A) 2

B) 790

C) 1,580

D) 40,000

18

If $5 - 7(2 - 4x) = 16 - 8(2 - 4x)$, what is the value of $2 - 4x$?

19

A scientist studying the life cycle of dragonflies counted the number of dragonflies in a certain habitat each day for 46 days. On February 15, there were 99 dragonflies in the habitat. The percent increase in the number of dragonflies in the habitat from January 1 to February 15 was 12.50%. How many dragonflies were in the habitat on January 1?

A) 88

B) 87

C) 12

D) 8

CONTINUE ➤

20

$$2x^2 - 8x - 7 = 0$$

One solution to the given equation can be written as $\frac{8 - \sqrt{k}}{4}$, where k is a constant. What is the value of k?

21

The function $f(x)$ is defined as 19 more than 4 times a number x. If $y = f(x)$ is graphed in the xy-plane, what is the best interpretation of the x-intercept?

A) When $f(x) = 0$, the number is $-\frac{19}{4}$.

B) When the number is 0, $f(x) = 19$.

C) The value of $f(x)$ increases by 1 for each increase of 4 in the value of the number.

D) For each increase of 1 in the value of the number, $f(x)$ increases by 4.

22

Which of the following expressions is equivalent to $(\sin 24°)(\cos 66°) + (\cos 24°)(\sin 66°)$?

A) $2(\cos 66°)(\sin 24°)$

B) $2(\cos 66°) + 2(\cos 24°)$

C) $(\cos 66°)^2 + (\cos 24°)^2$

D) $(\cos 66°)^2 + (\sin 24°)^2$

STOP

If you finish before time is called, you may check your work on this module only.
Do not turn to any other module in the test.

Math

22 QUESTIONS

DIRECTIONS

The questions in this section address a number of important math skills.
Use of a calculator is permitted for all questions.

NOTES

Unless otherwise indicated:

- All variables and expressions represent real numbers.
- Figures provided are drawn to scale.
- All figures lie in a plane.
- The domain of a given function f is the set of all real numbers x for which $f(x)$ is a real number.

REFERENCE

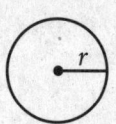 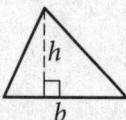 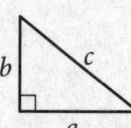 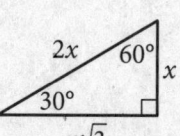

$A = \pi r^2$
$C = 2\pi r$

$A = \ell w$

$A = \frac{1}{2}bh$

$c^2 = a^2 + b^2$

Special Right Triangles

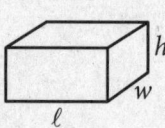    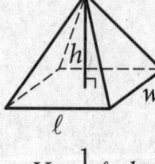

$V = \ell w h$

$V = \pi r^2 h$

$V = \frac{4}{3}\pi r^3$

$V = \frac{1}{3}\pi r^2 h$

$V = \frac{1}{3}\ell w h$

The number of degrees of arc in a circle is 360.

The number of radians of arc in a circle is 2π.

The sum of the measures in degrees of the angles of a triangle is 180.

CONTINUE ➤

For multiple-choice questions, solve each problem, choose the correct answer from the choices provided, and then circle your answer in this book. Circle only one answer for each question. If you change your mind, completely erase the circle. You will not get credit for questions with more than one answer circled, or for questions with no answers circled.

For student-produced response questions, solve each problem and write your answer next to or under the question in the test book as described below.

- Once you've written your answer, circle it clearly. You will not receive credit for anything written outside the circle, or for any questions with more than one circled answer.

- If you find **more than one correct answer**, write and circle only one answer.

- Your answer can be up to 5 characters for a **positive** answer and up to 6 characters (including the negative sign) for a **negative** answer, but no more.

- If your answer is a **fraction** that is too long (over 5 characters for positive, 6 characters for negative), write the decimal equivalent.

- If your answer is a **decimal** that is too long (over 5 characters for positive, 6 characters for negative), truncate it or round at the fourth digit.

- If your answer is a **mixed number** (such as $3\frac{1}{2}$), write it as an improper fraction (7/2) or its decimal equivalent (3.5).

- Don't include **symbols** such as a percent sign, comma, or dollar sign in your circled answer.

CONTINUE ➤

1

A total of 165 people contributed to a charity event as either a donor or a volunteer. 130 people contributed as a donor. How many people contributed as a volunteer?

A) 35

B) 130

C) 165

D) 330

2

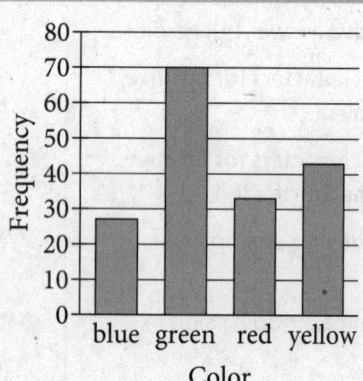

A data set consists of 173 colors. The bar graph shows the number of times each color appears in the data set. Which color appears 70 times?

A) Blue

B) Green

C) Red

D) Yellow

3

What value of p satisfies the equation $2p + 275 = 325$?

A) 5

B) 25

C) 48

D) 300

4

The scatterplot shows the temperature, in degrees Fahrenheit (°F), and the distance above sea level, in feet, measured at 6 locations on Mount Jefferson. A line of best fit is also shown.

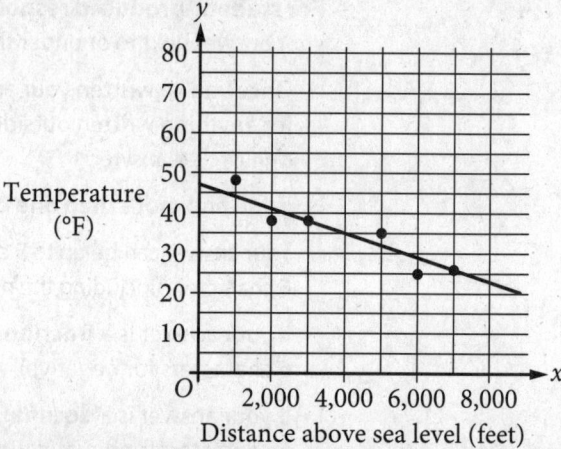

At a distance of 4,000 feet above sea level, what is the temperature, in °F, predicted by the line of best fit?

A) 47

B) 35

C) 25

D) 0

5

Rectangle P has an area of 72 square inches. If a rectangle with an area of 20 square inches is removed from rectangle P, what is the area, in square inches, of the resulting figure?

A) 92

B) 84

C) 80

D) 52

CONTINUE

6

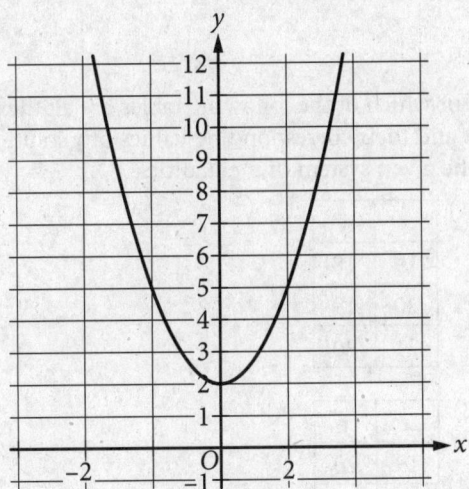

The graph of the quadratic function $y = f(x)$ is shown. What is the vertex of the graph?

A) $(0, -2)$

B) $(0, -3)$

C) $(0, 2)$

D) $(0, 3)$

7

The number of raccoons in a 131-square-mile area is estimated to be 2,358. What is the estimated population density, in raccoons per square mile, of this area?

A) 18

B) 131

C) 149

D) 2,376

8

If $8x = 6$, what is the value of $72x$?

A) 3

B) 15

C) 54

D) 57

9

$$-11, -9, 26$$

A data set of three numbers is shown. If a number from this data set is selected at random, what is the probability of selecting a positive number?

A) 0

B) $\frac{1}{3}$

C) $\frac{2}{3}$

D) 1

10

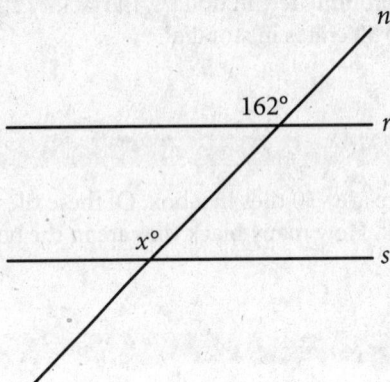

Note: Figure not drawn to scale.

In the figure, line n intersects lines r and s. Line r is parallel to line s. What is the value of x?

11

Which expression is equivalent to $23x^3 + 2x^2 + 9x$?

A) $23x(x^2 + 2x + 9)$

B) $9x(23x^3 + 2x^2 + 1)$

C) $x(23x^2 + 2x + 9)$

D) $34(x^3 + x^2 + x)$

CONTINUE →

12

Which expression is equivalent to
$(9x^3 + 5x + 7) + (6x^3 + 5x^2 - 5)$?

A) $15x^6 + 5x^2 - 5x - 35$

B) $15x^3 + 10x^2 + 2$

C) $15x^6 + 5x^2 + 5x + 2$

D) $15x^3 + 5x^2 + 5x + 2$

13

$$f(x) = 45x + 600$$

The function f gives the monthly fee $f(x)$, in dollars, a facility charges to keep x crates in storage. What is the monthly fee, in dollars, the facility charges to keep 50 crates in storage?

14

There are 450 tiles in a box. Of these tiles, 6% are black. How many black tiles are in the box?

15

An investment account was opened with an initial value of $890. The value of the account doubled every 10 years. Which equation represents the value of the account $M(t)$, in dollars, t years after the account was opened?

A) $M(t) = 890\left(\frac{1}{2}\right)^{\frac{t}{10}}$

B) $M(t) = 890\left(\frac{1}{10}\right)^{\frac{t}{2}}$

C) $M(t) = 890(2)^{\frac{t}{10}}$

D) $M(t) = 890(10)^{\frac{t}{2}}$

16

$$y < x$$
$$x < 22$$

For which of the following tables are all the values of x and their corresponding values of y solutions to the given system of inequalities?

A)

x	y
19	18
20	19
21	20

B)

x	y
19	20
20	21
21	22

C)

x	y
23	22
24	23
25	24

D)

x	y
23	24
24	25
25	26

17

A line in the xy-plane has a slope of 9 and passes through the point $(0, -5)$. The equation $y = px + r$ defines the line, where p and r are constants. What is the value of p?

CONTINUE

18

The function f is defined by $f(x) = \frac{1}{2}(x + 6)$. What is the value of $f(4)$?

A) 20

B) 12

C) 10

D) 5

19

What is the slope of the graph of $10x - 5y = -12$ in the xy-plane?

A) -2

B) $-\frac{5}{6}$

C) $\frac{5}{6}$

D) 2

20

$$y = 6x + 3$$

One of the two equations in a system of linear equations is given. The system has infinitely many solutions. Which equation could be the second equation in this system?

A) $y = 2(6x) + 3$

B) $y = 2(6x + 3)$

C) $2(y) = 2(6x) + 3$

D) $2(y) = 2(6x + 3)$

21

The function f is defined by $f(x) = |x - 4x|$. What value of a satisfies $f(5) - f(a) = -15$?

A) -20

B) 5

C) 10

D) 45

22

In August, a car dealer completed 15 more than 3 times the number of sales the car dealer completed in September. In August and September, the car dealer completed 363 sales. How many sales did the car dealer complete in September?

STOP

**If you finish before time is called, you may check your work on this module only.
Do not turn to any other module in the test.**

Math

22 QUESTIONS

DIRECTIONS

The questions in this section address a number of important math skills.
Use of a calculator is permitted for all questions.

NOTES

Unless otherwise indicated:

- All variables and expressions represent real numbers.
- Figures provided are drawn to scale.
- All figures lie in a plane.
- The domain of a given function f is the set of all real numbers x for which $f(x)$ is a real number.

REFERENCE

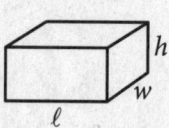

$A = \pi r^2$
$C = 2\pi r$

$A = \ell w$

$A = \frac{1}{2}bh$

$c^2 = a^2 + b^2$

Special Right Triangles

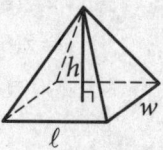

$V = \ell wh$ $V = \pi r^2 h$ $V = \frac{4}{3}\pi r^3$ $V = \frac{1}{3}\pi r^2 h$ $V = \frac{1}{3}\ell wh$

The number of degrees of arc in a circle is 360.

The number of radians of arc in a circle is 2π.

The sum of the measures in degrees of the angles of a triangle is 180.

CONTINUE ➤

For multiple-choice questions, solve each problem, choose the correct answer from the choices provided, and then circle your answer in this book. Circle only one answer for each question. If you change your mind, completely erase the circle. You will not get credit for questions with more than one answer circled, or for questions with no answers circled.

For student-produced response questions, solve each problem and write your answer next to or under the question in the test book as described below.

- Once you've written your answer, circle it clearly. You will not receive credit for anything written outside the circle, or for any questions with more than one circled answer.

- If you find **more than one correct answer**, write and circle only one answer.

- Your answer can be up to 5 characters for a **positive** answer and up to 6 characters (including the negative sign) for a **negative** answer, but no more.

- If your answer is a **fraction** that is too long (over 5 characters for positive, 6 characters for negative), write the decimal equivalent.

- If your answer is a **decimal** that is too long (over 5 characters for positive, 6 characters for negative), truncate it or round at the fourth digit.

- If your answer is a **mixed number** (such as $3\frac{1}{2}$), write it as an improper fraction (7/2) or its decimal equivalent (3.5).

- Don't include **symbols** such as a percent sign, comma, or dollar sign in your circled answer.

CONTINUE

1

The bar graph summarizes the charge, in kilowatt-hours (kWh), a battery received each day for 15 days.

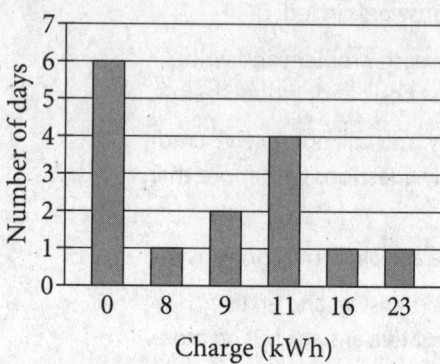

For how many of these 15 days did the battery receive a charge of 0 kWh?

A) 0

B) 1

C) 4

D) 6

2

In the given scatterplot, a line of best fit for the data is shown.

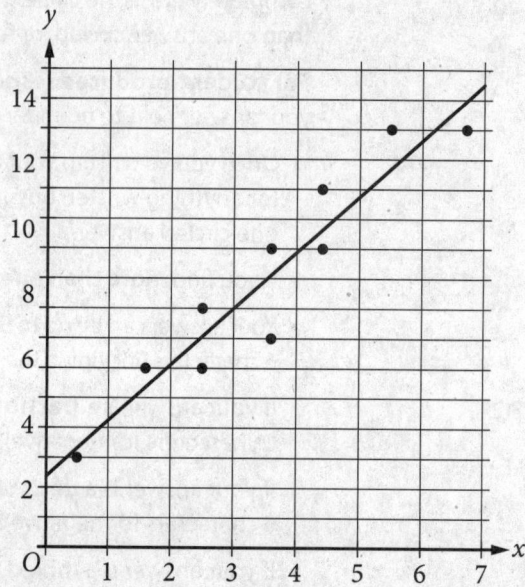

Which of the following is closest to the slope of the line of best fit shown?

A) 0

B) $\frac{1}{2}$

C) 1

D) 2

3

In a sample, 80% of the items are faulty. There are 88 faulty items in the sample. How many total items are in the sample?

CONTINUE

4

x	$g(x)$
-1	25
0	1
1	$\dfrac{1}{25}$
2	$\dfrac{1}{625}$

For the exponential function g, the table shows four values of x and their corresponding values of $g(x)$. Which equation defines g?

A) $g(x) = -25^x$

B) $g(x) = -\left(\dfrac{1}{25}\right)^x$

C) $g(x) = 25^x$

D) $g(x) = \left(\dfrac{1}{25}\right)^x$

5

If $8x = 6$, what is the value of $72x$?

A) 3

B) 15

C) 54

D) 57

6

Which expression is equivalent to $\dfrac{h^{15}q^7}{h^5 q^{21}}$, where $h > 0$ and $q > 0$?

A) $\dfrac{h^{10}}{q^{14}}$

B) $\dfrac{h^3}{q^3}$

C) $h^{10}q^{14}$

D) $h^3 q^3$

7

A company fills boxes with approximately 23 pounds of oranges. To test the accuracy of the filling process, 344 boxes of oranges were selected at random and weighed. Based on the sample, it is estimated that the average weight of all boxes of oranges filled by the company in an 8-hour period is 23.1 pounds, with an associated margin of error of 0.19 pounds. Which of the following is the best interpretation of this estimate?

A) Plausible values for the average weight of all boxes of oranges filled by the company are between 22.91 pounds and 23.29 pounds.

B) Plausible values for the average weight of all boxes of oranges filled by the company are less than 22.91 pounds or greater than 23.29 pounds.

C) The average weight of all boxes of oranges filled by the company is less than 23.01 pounds.

D) The average weight of all boxes of oranges filled by the company is greater than 23.01 pounds.

8

$$\frac{1}{3}(x + 6) - \frac{1}{2}(x + 6) = -8$$

What value of x is the solution to the given equation?

9

$$f(x) = x^2 + bx$$
$$g(x) = 9x^2 - 27x$$

Functions f and g are given, and in function f, b is a constant. If $f(x) \cdot g(x) = 9x^4 - 26x^3 - 3x^2$, what is the value of b?

A) -26

B) $-\dfrac{26}{9}$

C) $\dfrac{1}{9}$

D) 9

Unauthorized copying or reuse of any part of this page is illegal.

CONTINUE

731

10

In the xy-plane, line s passes through the point $(0, 0)$ and is parallel to the line represented by the equation $y = 18x + 2$. If line s also passes through the point $(4, d)$, what is the value of d?

A) 2

B) 18

C) 72

D) 74

11

$$f(x) = (x - 44)(x - 46)$$

The function f is defined by the given equation. For what value of x does $f(x)$ reach its minimum?

A) 46

B) 45

C) 44

D) −1

12

In triangle XYZ, angle Y is a right angle, point P lies on $\overline{XZ}$, and point Q lies on $\overline{YZ}$ such that $\overline{PQ}$ is parallel to $\overline{XY}$. If the measure of angle XZY is 63°, what is the measure, in degrees, of angle XPQ?

13

In a set of four consecutive odd integers, where the integers are ordered from least to greatest, the first integer is represented by x. The product of 12 and the fourth odd integer is at most 26 less than the sum of the first and third odd integers. Which inequality represents this situation?

A) $12(x + 6) \le x + (x + 4) - 26$

B) $12(x + 6) \ge 26 - (x + (x + 4))$

C) $12(x + 4) \le x + (x + 3) - 26$

D) $12(x + 4) \ge 26 - (x + (x + 3))$

14

$$\frac{2}{5}x + \frac{7}{5}y = \frac{2}{7}$$

$$gx + ky = \frac{5}{2}$$

In the given system of equations, g and k are constants. The system has infinitely many solutions. What is the value of $\frac{g}{k}$?

15

x	y
$-2s$	24
$-s$	21
s	15

The table shows three values of x and their corresponding values of y, where s is a constant. There is a linear relationship between x and y. Which of the following equations represents this relationship?

A) $sx + 3y = 18s$

B) $3x + sy = 18s$

C) $3x + sy = 18$

D) $sx + 3y = 18$

16

$$y + k = x + 26$$

$$y - k = x^2 - 5x$$

In the given system of equations, k is a constant. The system has exactly one distinct real solution. What is the value of k?

CONTINUE

17

The function f is defined by $f(x) = \frac{1}{2}(x + 6)$. What is the value of $f(4)$?

A) 20

B) 12

C) 10

D) 5

18

The area of a rectangular banner is 2,661 square inches. The banner's length x, in inches, is 24 inches longer than its width, in inches. Which equation represents this situation?

A) $0 = x^2 - 24x - 2{,}661$

B) $0 = x^2 - 24x + 2{,}661$

C) $0 = x^2 + 24x - 2{,}661$

D) $0 = x^2 + 24x + 2{,}661$

19

A right circular cone has a volume of $71{,}148\pi$ cubic centimeters and the area of its base is $5{,}929\pi$ square centimeters. What is the slant height, in centimeters, of this cone?

A) 12

B) 36

C) 77

D) 85

20

$$7x + 6y = 5$$
$$28x + 24y = 20$$

For each real number r, which of the following points lies on the graph of each equation in the xy-plane for the given system?

A) $\left(r, -\frac{6r}{7} + \frac{5}{7}\right)$

B) $\left(r, \frac{7r}{6} + \frac{5}{6}\right)$

C) $\left(\frac{r}{4} + 5, -\frac{r}{4} + 20\right)$

D) $\left(-\frac{6r}{7} + \frac{5}{7}, r\right)$

21

The cost of renting a carpet cleaner is $52 for the first day and $26 for each additional day. Which of the following functions gives the cost $C(d)$, in dollars, of renting the carpet cleaner for d days, where d is a positive integer?

A) $C(d) = 26d + 26$

B) $C(d) = 26d + 52$

C) $C(d) = 52d - 26$

D) $C(d) = 52d + 78$

22

The speed of a vehicle is increasing at a rate of 7.3 meters per second squared. What is this rate, in **miles per minute squared**, rounded to the nearest tenth? (Use 1 mile = 1,609 meters.)

A) 0.3

B) 16.3

C) 195.8

D) 220.4

STOP

**If you finish before time is called, you may check your work on this module only.
Do not turn to any other module in the test.**

The SAT®

Practice Test #7

ANSWER EXPLANATIONS

These answer explanations are for students using
The Official SAT Study Guide.

Reading and Writing

Module 1
(27 questions)

QUESTION 1

Choice D is the best answer because it most logically completes the text's discussion of how maple trees may respond to changes in climate. As used in this context, "adapt to" means to adjust to new conditions. The text first notes that maple trees already thrive in a wide variety of climates and then goes on to say that alterations maples may undergo are likely to be relatively small and easily achieved. This context supports the idea that maple trees will more easily adjust or adapt to a changing climate.

Choice A is incorrect. Although the text discusses how maple trees adjust to change, the trees do not "relocate from," or physically move from one place to another. *Choice B* is incorrect because "refer to" means to mention or allude to something, and the trees are not doing either of these actions. *Choice C* is incorrect because the text is discussing how maple trees may respond to changes in climate, not where they "originate from," or came from originally.

QUESTION 2

Choice D is the best answer because as used in the text, "clear" most nearly means transparent, or see-through. Muir states that the water beneath the boat "was so clear that it was almost invisible," suggesting that those on the boat were able to see through the water and easily observe plants and fish below the surface.

Choice A is incorrect. In some contexts "clear" can mean "simple," or uncomplicated, but Muir is describing the water, and water isn't typically described as either simple or complicated. Muir emphasizes the water's transparency, not its simplicity. *Choice B* is incorrect. In some contexts "clear" can mean "understandable," or reasonable or easily comprehended, but Muir is describing the water, and it doesn't make much sense to describe water as understandable. Muir emphasizes the water's transparency, not how easily the water can be understood. *Choice C* is incorrect. Although "clear" can mean "obvious," or easily seen or understood, in some contexts, Muir's description emphasizes that the water "was almost invisible" and that the boat seemed to be "sustained in the air," suggesting that the water was almost impossible to see, not that it was obvious.

QUESTION 3

Choice D is the best answer because it most logically completes the text's discussion of the duration of gamma ray burst GRB 230307A. In this context, "an oddity" is something that is odd or unusual. The text explains that the burst lasted for 200 seconds and that other bursts generated by neutron mergers have usually lasted fewer than 2 seconds. In other words, the duration of gamma ray burst GRB 230307A was unusual.

Choice A is incorrect because the text focuses on a difference between the duration of gamma ray burst GRB 230307A and the typical duration of bursts caused by neutron mergers, not "a coincidence," or a point of correspondence, between them; the text indicates that GRB 230307A lasted much longer than what is typical of other bursts. *Choice B* is incorrect. In this context, "a reprieve" would be either a temporary relief from something or a delay of a punishment, neither of which would make sense as something that the duration of a gamma ray burst could provide to the burst itself. *Choice C* is incorrect. Although it would make sense to refer to gamma ray burst GRB 230307A itself as "an incident," or a thing that occurred, the missing word describes the duration of the burst, and it doesn't make much sense to describe a length of time as an incident. Further, the sentence emphasizes that the burst's duration was very unusual, not simply that the burst occurred.

QUESTION 4

Choice B is the best answer because it most logically completes the text's discussion of Benjamin Franklin's popularity in France. In this context, "esteem" means high regard. The text indicates that Franklin was very popular, or highly regarded, in France, where he sought the country's support for the United States in its fight for independence, and indicates that his status helped him achieve his goal. The context therefore suggests that being held in high regard by the people likely helped Franklin convince France to help the United States.

Choice A is incorrect because the text directly indicates that it was Franklin's popularity that likely helped him convince France to help the United States, not his "thoughtfulness" (which in this context would mean either his careful reasoning and attention or his kind consideration of others' needs). *Choice C* is incorrect because the text doesn't suggest that there was any "controversy," or dispute, about Franklin's presence in France; instead, the text states that Franklin was very popular in France and directly indicates that this status likely helped him convince France to help the United States. *Choice D* is incorrect because the text directly indicates that it was Franklin's popularity that likely helped him convince France to help the United States, not his "sincerity," or his honesty.

QUESTION 5

Choice A is the best answer because it most accurately describes how the underlined sentence functions in the text as a whole. The first sentence of the text establishes that scientists didn't know much about the ocean floor in the 1950s. The second sentence, which is underlined, describes what many scientists thought at the time—that the ocean floor was mostly flat. The remainder of the text establishes that the ocean floor is far from flat, citing research conducted by Marie Tharp and Bruce Heezen. Thus, the purpose of the underlined sentence is to identify a scientific belief that Tharp and Heezen showed to be wrong.

Choice B is incorrect. Although Tharp and Heezen's work with sonar data in the Atlantic Ocean is mentioned later in the text, the underlined sentence doesn't describe the design of their experiment. Instead, it identifies a belief held by scientists that Tharp and Heezen demonstrated to be wrong. *Choice C* is incorrect because the underlined sentence presents a belief held by many scientists in the 1950s; nowhere does the text mention a disagreement between Tharp and Heezen, whom the text describes as research partners working together to map the ocean floor. *Choice D* is incorrect because the underlined sentence doesn't present data in support of a claim; instead, it presents a scientific belief that Tharp and Heezen's work showed to be wrong.

QUESTION 6

Choice B is the best answer because it accurately describes the function of the underlined phrase in the text as a whole. According to the text, advertisers were reluctant to support television in its early days. The underlined phrase then indicates that this reluctance was partly due to the US's involvement in World War II, which hindered television production. Thus, the underlined phrase identifies a specific reason behind some advertisers' hesitance to support television.

Choice A is incorrect. The text merely mentions that television was expected to be financed through advertising, as radio was at the time. Nothing in the text compares the origins of radio and television. *Choice C* is incorrect. The underlined phrase focuses on a reason advertisers were reluctant to support television, not measures taken to convince advertisers to support television. *Choice D* is incorrect. The underlined phrase focuses on a reason advertisers were reluctant to support television, not what types of television programming were popular.

QUESTION 7

Choice D is the best answer because it most accurately describes the main purpose of the text, which is to present findings that suggest a previously held concern about the effects of ocean acidification on pteropod shells may be unwarranted. The text introduces the concern that pteropods are thought to be particularly vulnerable to ocean acidification, or lower pH levels, due to the susceptibility of their calcium carbonate shells to dissolution at lower pH levels. However, the text then describes findings from a recent study that suggest this concern may be unjustified, insofar as the protective periostracum coating on a pteropod's shell prevents dissolution, and even when the coating is breached, a pteropod can rebuild the inner shell wall, reducing the damage.

Choice A is incorrect because the text doesn't call for additional research or suggest that more research is needed on biological mechanisms that improve pteropod survival rates. Instead, the text discusses a recent study showing that pteropods may not be as vulnerable to ocean acidification as is feared. *Choice B* is incorrect because the study discussed in the text doesn't address calcium carbonate's role in protecting the periostracum of pteropods. According to the text, the study addresses the periostracum's role in protecting pteropods' calcium carbonate shells from dissolution due to ocean acidification. *Choice C* is incorrect because the text doesn't address how ocean acidification has altered pteropod behavior over time. Instead, the text focuses on the potential effects of ocean acidification on pteropods' shells and the mechanisms protecting against those effects.

QUESTION 8

Choice D is the best answer because it reflects how the author of Text 2 would most likely respond to what the researchers mentioned in Text 1 contend. Text 1 discusses the lack of knowledge of how plate tectonics on Earth began. Text 1 also mentions researchers who contend that movements of tectonic plates began around 3 billion years ago. As support for this assertion, these researchers cite computer models (which are simulations, not empirical evidence) of the temperature in Earth's mantle that show that at that time, the mantle would have been sufficiently molten for plates to move. However, the author of Text 2 asserts that empirical evidence from the geological record is necessary to make plausible claims about when tectonic movement began. Text 2 mentions an analysis performed by Wriju Chowdhury and his team of the geochemistry of zircon crystals (which would constitute empirical evidence). Chowdhury and his team argue, based on this analysis, that tectonic plates may have begun to move as early as 4.2 billion years ago. Therefore, since the author of Text 2 would consider Chowdhury et al.'s empirical evidence to be more conclusive than the computer models cited in Text 1, the author of Text 2 would most likely assert that a more definitive form of evidence than the computer models suggests a different timeline for the onset of plate tectonics on Earth.

Choice A is incorrect because the author of Text 2 makes no claims about the temperature of Earth's mantle and therefore wouldn't argue that the temperature of Earth's mantle 3 billion years ago was insufficient to allow tectonic movement. *Choice B* is incorrect because the author of Text 2 claims that empirical evidence is needed to fix the earliest date of tectonic movement. Computer models are simulations, not empirical evidence, so the author of Text 2 wouldn't distinguish between different kinds of computer models but would instead argue that no computer models can reliably predict the onset of plate tectonics. *Choice C* is incorrect because the author of Text 2 wouldn't consider any computer model to be able to provide evidence to support a plausible claim about tectonic movement, no matter how much such models were improved. The author of Text 2 would only accept empirical evidence.

QUESTION 9

Choice A is the best answer because it most logically completes the text's discussion of the *M. robustus* population at the Octopus Garden. The text states that the scientists concluded that the site is likely used only for reproduction because over three years they saw many adults, freshly hatched octopuses, and eggs but didn't see any juveniles. This suggests that the *M. robustus* octopuses that hatch at the Octopus Garden leave the site when they reach an intermediary state of development, returning only as adults for reproductive purposes.

Choice B is incorrect because the text never discusses the stability of the *M. robustus* population at the site, only that the scientists observed 6,000 adults, hatchlings, and eggs there. Further, the text presents the site's temperatures as likely beneficial. *Choice C* is incorrect because the text doesn't provide any details about the eggs at the site and makes no mention of nests; it indicates only that eggs are present along with hatchlings and adults. *Choice D* is incorrect because the text makes no mention of the hatchlings feeding at the Octopus Garden, indicating only that the temperatures at the site are probably beneficial and that the site is likely used for reproduction.

QUESTION 10

Choice B is the best answer because it best states the main idea of the text: that nature-based approaches can be effective for achieving conservation goals. The text indicates that in many cases where conservationists are trying to protect ecosystems, their methods depend on natural processes or features. The text then gives an example of this phenomenon, a project with the Quinault Indian Nation that allowed logjams to form naturally in a river, creating spawning habitats for blueback salmon.

Choice A is incorrect. Although the text does suggest that the partnership with the Quinault Indian Nation was beneficial, this is not the central aim of the text; the text primarily argues that nature-based approaches to conservation can be effective. *Choice C* is incorrect. Although the text indicates that logjams are helpful to blueback salmon, the example of the blueback salmon project is included to illustrate the larger point made earlier in the text: that nature-based approaches to conservation are often effective. *Choice D* is incorrect. There is no evidence in the text to support a direct comparison of the efficacy of nature-based conservation approaches to other types of approaches. The text merely indicates that nature-based approaches can often be effective.

QUESTION 11

Choice B is the best answer because it describes data from the graph that support the researchers' conclusion that the trend of admirable-trait candidates being rated as more likable than ignoble-trait candidates held true when participants' own personality-trait scores were factored in, except among participants with high ignobility scores. The values on the *x*-axis represent survey participants grouped by their own ignobility scores, from low ignobility (1) to high ignobility (7), while the values on the *y*-axis represent the likability scores given to the political candidates. The graph shows that the full range of participants (from least to most ignoble) gave the admirable-trait candidates (represented by the line with triangles) a likability rating of approximately 70 out of 100; that is, regardless of their own level of ignobility, participants generally found admirable-trait candidates quite likable. However, the graph shows that participants varied in their views of ignoble-trait candidates (represented by the line with squares); likability ratings increased as the participants' own ignobility scores increased. Participants with low to medium-high ignobility scores (1 to 5) still rated the ignoble-trait candidates as less likable than the admirable-trait candidates, with all ratings falling below approximately 70, but participants with high ignobility scores (6 and 7) gave ratings equal to or higher than approximately 70. In other words, the previously observed trend of ranking admirable-trait candidates as more likable than ignoble-trait candidates persisted for participants with low to medium-high ignobility but not for participants with high ignobility.

Choice A is incorrect because it describes the opposite of what the graph shows. The graph shows a positive correlation between participants' ignobility scores and ignoble-trait candidates' likability ratings (as participants' ignobility scores increased, so did their ratings for ignoble-trait candidates' likability) and no correlation between ignobility scores and admirable-trait candidates' likability ratings (all participants gave admirable-trait candidates a rating of approximately 70 out of 100). *Choice C* is incorrect. The graph does show that regardless of their own ignobility scores, participants rated admirable-trait candidates as quite likable (a rating of approximately 70 out of 100). However, this doesn't support the researchers' conclusion because the conclusion has to do with how participants rated both types of candidates, not just the admirable-trait ones; moreover, the conclusion is that relative ratings were actually affected by the participants' ignobility scores. *Choice D* is incorrect.

The graph does show that only participants with an ignobility score of 6 gave the same likability score to both admirable- and ignoble-trait candidates while participants with other ignobility scores gave a different rating for each candidate, but this doesn't support the researchers' conclusion. The conclusion isn't just that participants gave different ratings to the two types of candidates—it's that participants with low to medium-high ignobility scores specifically gave higher likability ratings to admirable-trait candidates than to ignoble-trait candidates and that participants with high ignobility scores didn't.

QUESTION 12

Choice A is the best answer because it presents a finding that, if true, would most directly weaken the underlined claim that guinea pigs in Puerto Rico probably came from Colombia and descended from Colombian guinea pigs. The text makes this claim based on the fact that ancient trade routes connected Puerto Rico with Colombia but not with Peru. However, if it's true that ancient guinea pigs in Puerto Rico were genetically less similar to ancient guinea pigs in Colombia than to ancient guinea pigs in Peru, this would suggest that the Puerto Rican guinea pigs didn't descend from Colombian guinea pigs. Instead, Puerto Rican guinea pigs' greater genetic similarity to Peruvian guinea pigs implies that ancient guinea pigs in Puerto Rico were likely brought to the island from Peru, despite the lack of direct ancient trade routes between the two regions.

Choice B is incorrect. While a finding about how common guinea pig imagery is in ancient Puerto Rican art would indicate the cultural significance of guinea pigs, it wouldn't be relevant to a claim about the geographical origin or descent of the guinea pig population on the island. The guinea pigs depicted in the artwork could have descended from guinea pigs in either Colombia or Peru; therefore, the finding would neither weaken nor strengthen the claim that guinea pigs in Puerto Rico probably came from Colombia and descended from Colombian guinea pigs. *Choice C* is incorrect because the finding that modern breeds of guinea pigs don't look like images of guinea pigs in ancient art from Puerto Rico, Colombia, and Peru wouldn't address the ancestral relationships between ancient guinea pig populations in these three regions. Therefore, the finding would neither weaken nor strengthen the claim that guinea pigs in Puerto Rico probably came from Colombia and descended from Colombian guinea pigs. *Choice D* is incorrect because a finding about the population sizes of guinea pigs in ancient Colombia and ancient Peru wouldn't be relevant to a claim about which population the Puerto Rican guinea pigs likely descended from. The smaller guinea pig population of Peru could still have been the source for the Puerto Rican guinea pig population.

QUESTION 13

Choice C is the best answer because it details a finding that, if true, would most directly support the researchers' hypothesis about ad recall. According to the text, the researchers found that commenting on an ad that appears as a social media post is more cognitively demanding for users than simply clicking on embedded links in such an ad. The researchers then hypothesized that a high level of cognitive engagement with ad content would result in a high level of ad recall, or memory of ad content. This hypothesis would be supported by the finding that users who had commented on an ad were more likely to recall its content when surveyed two days later than users who had simply clicked on links in the same ad.

Choice A is incorrect. Although the text compares one form of social media user interaction with ads—clicking on the ad's "like" button—with other forms of interaction—commenting on the ad and sharing it through social media—

it does so in order to determine which form of interaction is associated with a higher level of ad recall. The text doesn't note whether users were more likely to click on the "like" button than they were to interact with the ad in other ways. *Choice B* is incorrect because the text doesn't indicate that the study attempted to track whether social media users purchased the advertised product or to determine which form of interaction with ad content was more strongly associated with making a purchase. *Choice D* is incorrect. Finding that social media users who shared an ad forgot the content one week later would weaken, not support, the researchers' hypothesis that cognitive engagement is associated with a high level of recall.

QUESTION 14

Choice A is the best answer because it most accurately uses data from the table to complete the statement about certain rotating radio transients (RRATs). The table contains information about the right ascensions, periods, and frequencies of various pulsar stars called RRATs. According to the text, the period of an RRAT is defined as the time between consecutive pulses. The table shows that the period of RRAT J0614-03 is 0.136 seconds, which is the lowest number of all the periods of the RRATs listed in the table. If the period is the time between consecutive pulses, and J0614-03 has the shortest period, then J0614-03 has the shortest amount of time between consecutive pulses of all the RRATs in the table.

Choice B is incorrect because according to the table, J0545-03 has a period of 1.074 seconds and J0121+53 has a period of 2.725 seconds. According to the text, the period of an RRAT is the time between consecutive pulses. Therefore, since J0545-03 and J0121+53 have different periods, they do not have the same amount of time between consecutive pulses. *Choice C* is incorrect because according to the table, J1654-2335 has a period of 0.545 seconds, which is not the longest period of all the RRATs listed in the table. According to the text, the period of an RRAT is the time between consecutive pulses, and both J0545-03 and J0121+53 have longer periods than J1654-2335, so J1654-2335 does not have the longest time between consecutive pulses of all the RRATs in the table. *Choice D* is incorrect because according to the table, J0103+54 has a period of 0.354 seconds, and J0121+53 has a period of 2.725 seconds. According to the text, the period of an RRAT is the time between consecutive pulses, and only J0121+53 has more than one second of time between consecutive pulses, not J0103+54.

QUESTION 15

Choice C is the best answer because it most logically completes the text's discussion of Kristin Laidre's reasoning about the purpose of the tusk that many, but not all, narwhals have. The text explains that one group of scientists thinks the tusk may help narwhals detect the threat of freezing water and that Laidre disagrees with that idea, given the importance of avoiding a dangerous situation. It's logical to suggest that if the tusk serves such an important purpose for narwhals, the trait would be more common among them—specifically, that more narwhals would have a tusk.

Choice A is incorrect because there's no reason to think Laidre would say that if the tusk has the important function of helping narwhals detect when the water around them is about to freeze (meaning that it isn't always freezing), some narwhals would choose a different habitat altogether. Indeed, if it's true that the tusk helps narwhals avoid areas with dangerous conditions when they occur in their Arctic Ocean habitat, the tusk would likely enable the narwhals to continue living in that habitat rather than drive them elsewhere entirely. *Choice B* is incorrect because the text focuses only on narwhals and makes no mention of other marine animals or how having a tusk might affect them. And if anything, it would be more logical to expect a very important trait to be more widespread, not less common, among other similar types of animals. *Choice D is incorrect.* Although the text describes narwhals as shy, it doesn't indicate that the scientists' conclusion has anything to do with shyness. And because shyness and detection of the threat of freezing water aren't logically connected, there's no reason to think that Laidre would expect narwhals to become less shy over time if the tusk serves that important purpose.

QUESTION 16

Choice B is the best answer. The convention being tested is subject-verb agreement. The singular verb "is" agrees in number with the singular subject "vest frottoir."

Choice A is incorrect because the plural verb "have been" doesn't agree in number with the singular subject "vest frottoir." *Choice C* is incorrect because the plural verb "were" doesn't agree in number with the singular subject "vest frottoir." *Choice D* is incorrect because the plural verb "are" doesn't agree in number with the singular subject "vest frottoir."

QUESTION 17

Choice C is the best answer. The convention being tested is the use of verb forms within a sentence. The nonfinite past participle "characterized" is correctly used within a supplementary element that modifies the main clause "Zhang...*shanshui*," defining *qinglü shanshui* and explaining some of its identifying traits.

Choice A is incorrect because it results in a comma splice. Using the finite present perfect tense verb "has been characterized" creates a second main clause in the sentence, and the two main clauses can't be joined in this way by only the comma before "a type." *Choice B* is incorrect because it results in a comma splice. Using the finite future tense verb "will be characterized" creates a second main clause in the sentence, and the two main clauses can't be joined in this way by only the comma before "a type." *Choice D* is incorrect because it results in a comma splice. Using the finite present tense verb "is characterized" creates a second main clause in the sentence, and the two main clauses can't be joined in this way by only the comma before "a type."

QUESTION 18

Choice C is the best answer. The convention being tested is punctuation use between sentences. In this choice, the period is used correctly to mark the boundary between one sentence ("For...work") and another ("That...parchment").

Choice A is incorrect because it results in a comma splice. A comma can't be used in this way to mark the boundary between sentences. *Choice B* is incorrect because it results in a run-on sentence. The sentences ("For...work" and "that...parchment") are fused without punctuation and/or a conjunction. *Choice D* is incorrect. Without a comma preceding it, the conjunction "and" can't be used in this way to join sentences.

QUESTION 19

Choice D is the best answer. The convention being tested is the use of punctuation within a sentence. This choice correctly uses a comma to mark the boundary between the introductory subordinate clause ("With...windows") and the main clause ("transitional design splits the difference between old and new").

Choice A is incorrect because a semicolon can't be used in this way to separate the subordinate clause ("With...windows") from the main clause ("transitional... new"). *Choice B* is incorrect because a dash can't be used in this way to separate the subordinate clause ("With...windows") from the main clause ("transitional...new"). *Choice C* is incorrect because it results in a rhetorically unacceptable sentence fragment beginning with "with."

QUESTION 20

Choice C is the best answer. The convention being tested is pronoun-antecedent agreement. The singular pronoun "it" agrees in number with the singular antecedent "industry" and clearly indicates that the industry consists of just one or two suppliers per municipality.

Choice A is incorrect. The plural pronoun "these" neither agrees in number with the singular antecedent "industry" nor clearly indicates that the industry—not another plural noun in the sentence, such as "start-up costs" or "barriers"—consists of just one or two suppliers per municipality. *Choice B* is incorrect because the plural pronoun "they" doesn't agree in number with the singular antecedent "industry." *Choice D* is incorrect because the singular pronoun "this" is ambiguous in this context; the resulting sentence leaves unclear what consists of just one or two suppliers per municipality.

QUESTION 21

Choice B is the best answer. "As a result" logically signals that the action described in this sentence—closing the area around Garisenda Tower to explore stabilization solutions—occurred as a consequence or result of measurements revealing the tower's concerning rotation.

Choice A is incorrect because "similarly" illogically signals that the action of closing the tower area is similar to the discovery of concerning rotation described in the previous sentence. Instead, closing the area around the tower to explore solutions occurred as a result of the measurements revealing the rotation. *Choice C* is incorrect because "for example" illogically signals that the action of closing the tower area serves as an example of the tower's concerning rotation described in the previous sentence. Instead, closing the area around the tower to explore solutions occurred as a result of the measurements revealing the rotation. *Choice D* is incorrect because "in comparison" illogically signals that the action of closing the tower area is being compared to the discovery of concerning rotation described in the previous sentence. Instead, closing the area around the tower to explore solutions occurred as a result of the measurements revealing the rotation.

QUESTION 22

Choice A is the best answer. "Additionally" logically signals that guard cells' role in regulating water loss is an additional function of these specialized plant cells that is separate from the function of regulating carbon dioxide intake.

Choice B is incorrect because "previously" illogically signals that the activity described in this sentence occurs earlier in a chronological sequence of events than the regulation of carbon dioxide intake described in the previous sentence. Instead, regulating water loss is an additional function of guard cells that is separate from the function of regulating carbon dioxide intake. *Choice C* is incorrect because "in conclusion" illogically signals that the description of guard cells' role in regulating water loss concludes or summarizes the information about guard cells provided in the previous sentences. Instead, regulating water loss is one of the two distinct functions of guard cells described in the text. *Choice D* is incorrect because "instead" illogically signals that the activity described in this sentence happens in place of the activity of regulating carbon dioxide intake described in the previous sentence. Rather, regulating water loss is an additional function of guard cells.

QUESTION 23

Choice B is the best answer. "Indeed" logically signals that the information in this sentence—that the sculpture raised the question of whether displaying any object in an art gallery transforms the object into a work of art—offers emphasis in support of the claim in the previous sentence that the sculpture was intended to challenge conceptions about the nature of art.

Choice A is incorrect because "similarly" illogically signals that information in this sentence is similar to the claim about the sculptor's intention in the previous sentence. Instead, the information about the question raised by the sculpture offers emphasis in support of that claim. *Choice C* is incorrect because "instead" illogically signals that the information in this sentence is an alternative to the claim about the sculptor's intention in the previous sentence. Rather, the information about the question raised by the sculpture offers emphasis in support of that claim. *Choice D* is incorrect because "in addition" illogically signals that the information in this sentence is merely an additional fact related to the claim about the sculptor's intention in the previous sentence. Instead, the information about the question raised by the sculpture offers emphasis in support of that claim.

QUESTION 24

Choice D is the best answer. "Specifically" logically signals that the information in this sentence—that the Local Bubble's expansion trapped clouds of gas and dust that formed new stars—provides specific, precise details elaborating on the more general information in the previous sentence about the relationship between the Local Bubble's expansion and the formation of new stars.

Choice A is incorrect because "hence" illogically signals that the information in this sentence is a result of the information in the previous sentence about the relationship between the Local Bubble's expansion and the formation of new stars. Instead, this sentence provides specific, precise details elaborating on that information. *Choice B* is incorrect because "however" illogically signals that the information in this sentence contrasts with the information in the previous sentence about the relationship between the Local Bubble's expansion and the formation of new stars. Instead, this sentence provides specific, precise details elaborating on that information. *Choice C* is incorrect because "admittedly" illogically signals that the information in this sentence provides an exception or caveat to the previous information about the relationship between the Local Bubble's expansion and the formation of new stars. Instead, this sentence provides specific, precise details elaborating on that information.

QUESTION 25

Choice B is the best answer. The sentence contrasts the two songs, noting that "Poor Miner's Farewell" is about coal miners in Kentucky, whereas "Bring Him Back Home" is about Nelson Mandela.

Choice A is incorrect. The sentence emphasizes a similarity between "Poor Miner's Farewell" and "Bring Him Back Home"; it doesn't contrast the two songs. *Choice C* is incorrect. While the sentence provides a description of the song "Bring Him Back Home," it doesn't mention "Poor Miner's Farewell" or contrast the two songs.

Choice D is incorrect. While the sentence provides a description of the song "Poor Miner's Farewell," it doesn't mention "Bring Him Back Home" or contrast the two songs.

QUESTION 26

Choice D is the best answer. The sentence presents the conclusion of Zhen Wang and colleagues' 2016 study: Tibetan mastiffs are able to withstand hypoxic conditions due to their interbreeding with Tibetan wolves 24,000 years ago (which allowed the mastiffs to acquire the necessary genetic mutations).

Choice A is incorrect. The sentence emphasizes a similarity between Tibetan mastiffs and Tibetan wolves; it doesn't present the conclusions of the 2016 study. *Choice B* is incorrect. The sentence emphasizes a similarity between the genes of Tibetan mastiffs and Tibetan wolves; it doesn't present the conclusions of the 2016 study. *Choice C* is incorrect. The sentence misrepresents information from the notes by indicating that a mutation in mastiffs' HBB gene prevents excess hemoglobin production; moreover, it doesn't present the conclusions of the 2016 study.

QUESTION 27

Choice C is the best answer. The sentence compares some disadvantages of docked and dockless bike-share programs, explaining that while docked programs are more resource-intensive (requiring significant space and money), dockless programs have greater organizational challenges.

Choice A is incorrect. The sentence compares dockless programs to docked programs, noting an advantage of docked programs: they offer order and consistency. It doesn't compare disadvantages of the two types of programs. *Choice B* is incorrect. The sentence compares dockless programs to docked programs, noting an advantage of dockless programs: they are easy and inexpensive to implement. However, it misrepresents information from the notes, stating that dockless programs are less flexible than docked programs. In addition, it doesn't compare disadvantages of the two types of programs. *Choice D* is incorrect. The sentence emphasizes an advantage of dockless programs, then makes a general statement that applies to both types of programs; it doesn't compare disadvantages of the two types of programs.

Reading and Writing

Module 2 — Lower Difficulty
(27 questions)

QUESTION 1

Choice A is the best answer because it most logically completes the text's discussion of a prediction about a kilonova. In this context, a "theory" is an explanation that is considered scientifically acceptable. The text states that astronomers predicted in the 1990s that a collision between a black hole and a neutron star or between two neutron stars could release a massive gamma ray burst called a kilonova, explaining that they determined this possibility based on their extensive work with existing data and simulations ("calculations and models"). In other words, the prediction was a theory—a well-supported explanation—that, as the text indicates, was later confirmed with observations in 2017.

Choice B is incorrect because the text indicates that it is the prediction made by astronomers in the 1990s that was confirmed in 2017, and a prediction of an event isn't "evidence," or proof, of that event's existence, even when the prediction is based on extensive study. Further, there would be no need for later confirmation of something that was already recognized as evidence. *Choice C* is incorrect because in this context, a "constant" is a situation or factor that doesn't change. The text indicates that it is the prediction made by astronomers in the 1990s that was confirmed in 2017, and there is no reason to describe the prediction as a constant because the text doesn't suggest that the prediction was completely unchanged over time— it addresses only the making of the prediction and its later confirmation. *Choice D* is incorrect because the text indicates that it is the prediction made by astronomers in the 1990s that was confirmed in 2017; although a prediction might be informed by an "experiment," or a controlled test, a prediction is an idea rather than a test.

QUESTION 2

Choice C is the best answer because it most logically completes the text's discussion of *carte de visite* photos. To "popularize" a technology is to allow it to be used and appreciated widely. The text explains that unlike the photos produced by earlier forms of photographic technology, *carte de visite* photos were inexpensive and could easily be obtained by "everyday people," who enjoyed exchanging the images. Therefore, *carte de visite* photos helped popularize photography.

Choice A is incorrect because the text indicates that instead of weakening the emerging technology of photography, *carte de visite* photos allowed it to be more widely accessed and enjoyed by people. *Choice B* is incorrect. The text establishes that large numbers of people enjoyed using *carte de visite* photos, so it can be inferred that these photos caused photography to be praised, or celebrated. However, it wouldn't make sense to say that inanimate objects—in this case, photos—had praised photography; instead, *carte de visite* consumers themselves would have praised it. *Choice D* is incorrect because the text explains that rather than isolating photography, or limiting its availability, *carte de visite* technology made photography more widely accessible to people.

QUESTION 3

Choice D is the best answer because it most logically completes the text's discussion of painter Alma W. Thomas's work. In this context, "influenced" means to have had an effect on something's development. The text indicates that there is a connection between Thomas's work and the flowers and trees in her home's garden, giving the example of Thomas's brushstrokes being inspired by light shining through the leaves of a tree in front of her house. This context conveys that Thomas's work was influenced by the flowers and trees in the garden.

Choice A is incorrect because the text conveys that Thomas drew inspiration for her work from the plants in her garden, which suggests that the flowers and trees contributed positively to her work, not that they "restricted," or limited, her work. *Choice B* is incorrect because it wouldn't make sense to suggest that flowers and trees in a garden could have "announced," or made known, a painter's work. *Choice C* is incorrect because the text conveys that Thomas drew inspiration for her work from the plants in her garden, which suggests that the flowers and trees contributed positively to her work, not that they were a distraction. Further, it's not clear how an artist's work could itself be "distracted."

QUESTION 4

Choice C is the best answer because it most logically completes the text's discussion of the conservationists' efforts to increase Azores bullfinch's numbers. In this context, "successful" means accomplishing a goal or purpose. According to the text, conservationists planted more than 500,000 native trees in an Azores bullfinch habitat in order to boost the bird's population size. The text then indicates that the population size did indeed grow as a result of the planted trees. Thus, in this context, the conservationists' approach of planting native trees was successful because it achieved the goal of increasing the bird's population size.

Choice A is incorrect because the text gives no indication that the conservationists' approach of planting native trees to increase Azores bullfinch's numbers was "amusing," or comical or entertaining. Instead, the approach was seriously undertaken and ultimately accomplished. *Choice B* is incorrect because the text doesn't address how much it cost to achieve the goal of planting native trees to increase Azores bullfinch's numbers. The text indicates that the approach was beneficial and successful rather than "costly," or expensive or harmful. *Choice D* is incorrect. According to the text, the conservationists' approach of planting native trees to increase Azores bullfinch's numbers was beneficial and successful rather than "disastrous," or damaging or unsuccessful.

QUESTION 5

Choice A is the best answer because it most accurately describes how the underlined phrase functions in the text as a whole. The text states that the wax produced by Liu and colleagues' reactor can be turned into a surfactant. The underlined phrase, which is set off with parentheses, then provides a definition for the term "surfactant," explaining that it's a chemical compound that can be used as a detergent. Thus, the underlined portion of the text functions to clarify the meaning of a scientific term.

Choice B is incorrect. Though the text as a whole focuses broadly on an environmental concern, the underlined phrase does not; it simply indicates what a surfactant is. *Choice C* is incorrect. Though the text as a whole focuses on a scientific discovery (Liu and colleagues' solution to the problem of plastic recycling), the underlined phrase does not explain its significance; it simply defines a scientific term used in the discussion. *Choice D* is incorrect. Though the text as a whole includes discussion of the result found by Liu and colleagues, the underlined phrase does not discuss it; it simply defines a scientific term used in the discussion. Additionally, at no point in the text is it mentioned that the team was confused.

QUESTION 6

Choice C is the best answer because it most accurately describes the main purpose of the text. The text states that archaeologists recently discovered a well-preserved food shop, or *thermopolium*, in Pompeii, Italy. The text then further describes the contents of the discovery and provides an example of what was found. Thus, the overall purpose of the text is to present a recent archaeological discovery.

Choice A is incorrect. Although the text states that archaeologists found ancient artworks, it doesn't compare these artworks to modern ones or to any other artworks. Choice B is incorrect. Although the archaeological discovery discussed in the text was made in Italy, the text doesn't provide any information about politics or government in Italy. Choice D is incorrect because the text doesn't discuss the climate where the archaeological discovery was made or in any other region.

QUESTION 7

Choice A is the best answer because it most accurately describes how the underlined portion functions in the text as a whole. The first sentence of the text introduces literary scholar Jeremy Douglass's warning to technology investors and enthusiasts against predicting the displacement of conventional books by newer media forms. The next sentence, which is underlined in part, presents Douglass's observation that interactive texts are hardly new; they have been available for longer than technologists assume, beginning with the first time readers wrote notes in texts' margins. Thus, the function of the underlined portion is to challenge the stance of the technology investors and enthusiasts mentioned earlier in the text. As the remainder of the text points out, newer media doesn't necessarily replace older media, but rather, as Douglass believes, leads to new forms of expression.

Choice B is incorrect because the underlined portion challenges the position taken by investors and enthusiasts; it doesn't provide context for their claims. *Choice C* is incorrect because the underlined portion doesn't mention academics or compare them to investors regarding their ability to see potential in using contemporary interactive texts; instead, the underlined portion challenges the position of investors and enthusiasts who predict that conventional books will be replaced by newer forms of media. *Choice D* is incorrect because the underlined portion doesn't address technological challenges; instead, it disputes the stance taken by investors and enthusiasts, suggesting that conventional books haven't been displaced by traditional interactions with texts, such as writing in the margins, and won't be supplanted by newer forms of media either.

QUESTION 8

Choice B is the best answer because it most accurately states what feature of *Hevea brasiliensis* is helpful for the process of making rubber. According to the text, this tree species produces latex, which is used to make rubber, and its inner bark contains a "network of tubes" that, when cut, enables the latex to flow out. The text explicitly states that this feature of *Hevea brasiliensis* is "helpful for the process of making rubber."

Choice A is incorrect because the text doesn't mention the quality of the rubber produced from the latex of *Hevea brasiliensis* or compare its quality to that of rubber produced from other sources. *Choice C* is incorrect because the text never discusses the climates in which *Hevea brasiliensis* grows. Moreover, the text mentions only one region where this tree is found: the Amazon rainforest. *Choice D* is incorrect. Because the text states that *Hevea brasiliensis* is the world's "main source of natural rubber," it can be inferred that there is at least one other source. However, the text doesn't specify whether that other source is also a tree species and, if so, whether that species grows in the Amazon rainforest.

QUESTION 9

Choice D is the best answer because it states the percentage of participants who mentioned costs in the interviews conducted by Judith Hilton and her team. The text states that Hilton and her team interviewed participants about factors that would encourage them to switch from single-use plastic containers to reusable containers. The graph presents three factors mentioned in the interviews (convenience, costs, and established behaviors) and the percentage of participants who mentioned each one. The graph shows that about 50% of participants mentioned costs as a factor.

Choice A is incorrect because the graph shows that about 50% of participants, not 10%, mentioned costs as a factor. *Choice B* is incorrect because the graph shows that about 50% of participants, not 95%, mentioned costs as a factor. *Choice C* is incorrect because the graph shows that about 50% of participants, not 25%, mentioned costs as a factor.

QUESTION 10

Choice C is the best answer because it states the total area of Bahrain that is indicated in the table. The table presents the total area (in square miles) and population for Bahrain, Qatar, and Kuwait, and it indicates that the total area of Bahrain is 304 square miles.

Choice A is incorrect because the table indicates that 4,268,873 is the population of Kuwait, not the total area of Bahrain. *Choice B* is incorrect because the table indicates that 4,471 square miles is the total area of Qatar, not of Bahrain. *Choice D* is incorrect because the table indicates that 6,880 square miles is the total area of Kuwait, not of Bahrain.

QUESTION 11

Choice C is the best answer because it most effectively uses a quotation from "The Mountain" to illustrate the claim that the speaker feels protected by the mountain. In the quotation, the speaker recounts that the mountain felt like a wall that offers shelter from the wind. That the speaker felt sheltered by the mountain suggests that it offered the speaker a sense of being protected.

Choice A is incorrect because this quotation doesn't express the speaker's feeling of being protected by the mountain. Instead, it notes that the speaker has seen a dry ravine and a pasture. *Choice B* is incorrect because this quotation doesn't express the speaker's feeling of being protected by the mountain. Instead, it simply states that there is a mountain, which is meant to be viewed. *Choice D* is incorrect because this quotation doesn't express the speaker's feeling of being protected by the mountain. Instead, it indicates that the speaker has gone around the mountain.

QUESTION 12

Choice D is the best answer because it most effectively illustrates the claim that the narrator was frightened of the sailor. The quotation describes the sailor haunting the narrator's dreams, appearing in "a thousand forms" with "a thousand diabolical expressions." This vivid imagery conveys the intense psychological fear the narrator experienced when thinking about the sailor. Furthermore, the quotation evokes the narrator's terror and dread by describing a stormy night setting with wind shaking the house and a roaring surf.

Choice A is incorrect because this quotation does not provide any details to suggest that the narrator was afraid of the sailor. It simply describes the narrator's memory of the sailor arriving at the inn with his sea chest. *Choice B* is incorrect because this quotation does not effectively illustrate the claim that the narrator was frightened of the sailor. The quotation provides several details about the sailor, including that it was his custom to remain silent. However, the quotation does not relate these details to the narrator's experience of being frightened of the sailor. *Choice C* is incorrect because this quotation focuses on aspects of the sailor's appearance and dress. There is no connection made in the quotation between these physical details and the narrator's sense of being frightened of the sailor.

QUESTION 13

Choice C is the best answer because it most logically completes the text's discussion of the Nacional trees' survival in Piedra de Plata. The text states that the fungus that caused Nacional trees elsewhere to become diseased spreads from tree to nearby tree through the air. The text also mentions that the surviving Nacional trees were found in a hard-to-reach valley in Ecuador. Given this information, it's logical to conclude that these trees might have avoided infection because they were geographically isolated from infected Nacional trees, which prevented the airborne fungus from reaching them.

Choice A is incorrect because early twentieth-century scientists' lack of knowledge about the infection that affected many Nacionals doesn't explain how the trees in the Piedra de Plata coastal forest survived. The text is concerned with the physical factors that allowed certain trees to avoid infection, not with scientists' understanding of the disease. *Choice B* is incorrect. Although the text mentions that the fungus spreads through the air, it doesn't indicate when this ability was discovered. Moreover, even if the ability to move through the air was recently discovered, that wouldn't explain how the trees in Piedra de Plata avoided infection in the past. *Choice D* is incorrect because the value of the chocolate made from Nacional pods doesn't explain how the trees in the Piedra de Plata coastal forest avoided disease. The text focuses on the physical spread of the fungus that caused most Nacionals to become diseased, not on economic factors related to the trees' products.

QUESTION 14

Choice B is the best answer because it presents the conclusion that most logically follows from the text's discussion of the chemical content of pigments. The text begins by differentiating between two kinds of pigments: mineral-based pigments such as red ocher, which get their color from iron oxide, and plant-based pigments, which have a high level of carbon. The text then goes on to describe an analysis by archaeologists of the pigment of decorated beads made by members of the Natufian culture around 15,000 years ago. The archaeologists found that the red pigment on some of the beads contained no iron but had a high level of carbon. Since red ocher gets its color from iron oxide, while plant-based pigments have a high level of carbon, the researchers concluded that the Natufian beadmakers used plant-based pigments to decorate some of the beads examined in the study.

Choice A is incorrect because the text does not indicate that the Natufians were the first to use plant-based pigments, so it cannot be concluded that the beads in the study were the oldest surviving examples of the use of plant-based pigments for decorating beads. *Choice C* is incorrect because the text does not compare the brightness of plant-based and mineral-based pigments. *Choice D* is incorrect. While it can be concluded that the Natufian beadmakers used plant-based pigments because the pigment found on several beads had a high level of carbon, the text offers no evidence that ocher was difficult to find.

QUESTION 15

Choice A is the best answer. The convention being tested is the use of verb forms within a sentence. The singular verb "describes" agrees in number with the singular subject "map."

Choice B is incorrect because the plural verb "describe" doesn't agree in number with the singular subject "map." *Choice C* is incorrect because the plural verb "have described" doesn't agree in number with the singular subject "map." *Choice D* is incorrect because the plural verb "are describing" doesn't agree in number with the singular subject "map."

QUESTION 16

Choice D is the best answer. The convention being tested is the use of determiners in a sentence. The plural determiner "these" agrees in number with the plural noun "letters" that it modifies. This choice clearly indicates that the letters demonstrate Alcott's business sense.

Choice A is incorrect because the singular determiner "one" doesn't agree in number with the plural noun "letters." *Choice B* is incorrect because the singular determiner "that" doesn't agree in number with the plural noun "letters." *Choice C* is incorrect because the singular determiner "this" doesn't agree in number with the plural noun "letters."

QUESTION 17

Choice D is the best answer. The convention being tested is the use of verbs to express tense in a sentence. In this choice, the past tense verb "affected," used in conjunction with the phrase "during this time," correctly indicates that the dust storms occurred in the 1930s.

Choice A is incorrect because the present progressive tense verb "are affecting" doesn't indicate that the dust storms occurred in the 1930s. *Choice B* is incorrect because the future perfect tense verb "will have affected" doesn't indicate that the dust storms occurred in the 1930s. *Choice C* is incorrect because the future tense verb "will affect" doesn't indicate that the dust storms occurred in the 1930s.

QUESTION 18

Choice A is the best answer. The convention being tested is punctuation use between sentences. In this choice, the period is used correctly to mark the boundary between one sentence ("What...vapor") and another ("With...point").

Choice B is incorrect because it results in a run-on sentence. The sentences ("What...vapor" and "with...point") are fused without punctuation and/or a conjunction. *Choice C* is incorrect because it results in a comma splice. A comma can't be used in this way to mark the boundary between sentences. *Choice D* is incorrect. Without a comma preceding it, the conjunction "and" can't be used in this way to join sentences.

QUESTION 19

Choice B is the best answer. The convention being tested is the use of punctuation within a sentence. The comma after "taxation" pairs with the comma after "that" to separate the supplementary element "through trade and centralized taxation" from the rest of the sentence. This supplementary element functions to identify the funding source of the Mauryan economy, and the pair of commas indicates that this element could be removed without affecting the grammatical coherence of the sentence.

Choice A is incorrect because a colon can't be paired with a comma in this way to separate the supplementary element from the rest of the sentence. *Choice C* is incorrect because a dash can't be paired with a comma in this way to separate the supplementary element from the rest of the sentence. *Choice D* is incorrect because it fails to use appropriate punctuation to separate the supplementary element from the rest of the sentence.

QUESTION 20

Choice D is the best answer. The convention being tested is subject-modifier placement. This choice makes the noun phrase "the Alaska Centennial Commission" the subject of the sentence and places it immediately after the modifying phrase "wanting...Purchase." In doing so, this choice clearly establishes that the Alaska Centennial Commission—and not another noun in the sentence—wanted to celebrate the 100th anniversary of the Alaska Purchase.

Choice A is incorrect because it results in a dangling modifier. The placement of the noun phrase "a contest" immediately after the modifying phrase illogically suggests that the contest wanted to celebrate the 100th anniversary of the Alaska Purchase. *Choice B* is incorrect because it results in a dangling modifier. The placement of the noun phrase "an award of $300" immediately after the modifying phrase illogically suggests that the award of $300 wanted to celebrate the 100th anniversary of the Alaska Purchase. *Choice C* is incorrect because it results in a dangling modifier. The placement of the noun phrase "$300" immediately after the modifying phrase illogically suggests that the $300 wanted to celebrate the 100th anniversary of the Alaska Purchase.

QUESTION 21

Choice C is the best answer. The convention being tested is the coordination of main clauses within a sentence. This choice correctly uses a comma and a coordinating conjunction ("but") to join the first main clause ("Leibniz...century") and the second main clause ("these ingenious...calculators").

Choice A is incorrect because it results in a run-on sentence. The two main clauses are fused without punctuation and/or a conjunction. *Choice B* is incorrect because it results in a comma splice. Without a conjunction following it, a comma can't be used in this way to join two main clauses. *Choice D* is incorrect because joining the two main clauses in this way with the subordinating conjunction "that" results in an ungrammatical and illogical sentence.

QUESTION 22

Choice B is the best answer. "That said" logically signals that the statement in this sentence—that Metzinger offers a glimpse of four-dimensional space by depicting multiple, simultaneous perspectives—is true despite the point in the previous sentence (that Metzinger's painting doesn't technically represent a fourth dimension because humans can only see in three dimensions).

Choice A is incorrect because "moreover" illogically signals that the information in this sentence merely adds to the previous point about Metzinger's painting. Instead, it provides information that is true despite that previous point. *Choice C* is incorrect because "in other words" illogically signals that the information in this sentence is a paraphrase or restatement of the previous point about Metzinger's painting. Instead, it provides information that is true despite that previous point. *Choice D* is incorrect because "for example" illogically signals that the information in this sentence provides an example that supports the previous point about Metzinger's painting. Instead, it provides information that is true despite that previous point.

QUESTION 23

Choice A is the best answer. The sentence indicates where "Raymond's Run" takes place, stating that it takes place in Harlem.

Choice B is incorrect. The sentence identifies the book in which the story "Raymond's Run" was published; it doesn't indicate where the story takes place. *Choice C* is incorrect. The sentence indicates the point of view used in "Raymond's Run"; it doesn't indicate where the story takes place. *Choice D* is incorrect. The sentence identifies the author of "Raymond's Run"; it doesn't indicate where the story takes place.

QUESTION 24

Choice D is the best answer. The sentence defines the term "georeferencing," stating that it is the process of assigning geographic coordinates to an image so that mapping software can place the image in its real-world location.

Choice A is incorrect. The sentence describes López Marrero's team's 2017 project; it doesn't provide a definition of the term "georeferencing." Moreover, it misrepresents the information in the notes by characterizing the team's assignment of geographic coordinates to photographs as a process distinct from georeferencing. *Choice B* is incorrect. The sentence states that López Marrero's team used georeferencing, but it doesn't provide a definition of the term. *Choice C* is incorrect. The sentence explains why a particular group of georeferenced aerial photographs is potentially useful for researchers; it doesn't provide a definition of the term "georeferencing."

QUESTION 25

Choice D is the best answer. The sentence indicates how Fulton, Missouri, got its name, noting that the city was named after the designer of the first commercially successful steamboat, Robert Fulton.

Choice A is incorrect. The sentence indicates that Fulton, Missouri, has the same name as a street in New York City; it doesn't indicate how the city of Fulton got its name. *Choice B* is incorrect. The sentence indicates that Fulton Street is in New York City; it doesn't indicate how Fulton, Missouri, got its name. *Choice C* is incorrect. The sentence provides details about Fulton's steamboat; it doesn't indicate how Fulton, Missouri, got its name.

QUESTION 26

Choice C is the best answer. The sentence contrasts the two styles of tiles, noting that tiles in the arista style have designs stamped into them, whereas tiles in the majolica style have designs painted directly on them.

Choice A is incorrect because the sentence indicates that the two styles of tile can be found in the same location; it doesn't contrast the two styles of tile. *Choice B* is incorrect because the sentence indicates that the Royal Alcázar of Seville features tiles in both the majolica and arista styles; it doesn't contrast the two styles of tile. *Choice D* is incorrect because the sentence indicates that the tilework of the Royal Alcázar of Seville includes tiles in the majolica style; it doesn't contrast tiles in the majolica style with tiles in the arista style.

QUESTION 27

Choice C is the best answer. Using a quotation from Stewart, the sentence challenges Thucydides's explanation that the rise of Athens caused the conflict, suggesting that it was instead caused by a "clash of cultures."

Choice A is incorrect. While the sentence uses a quotation, the quotation doesn't challenge Thucydides's explanation of the conflict. *Choice B* is incorrect. While the sentence mentions that Stewart challenged Thucydides's explanation of the conflict, it doesn't use a quotation to challenge Thucydides's explanation: the quoted word "inevitable" is from Thucydides. *Choice D* is incorrect. While the sentence appears to refute Thucydides's explanation, it does so in a way that misrepresents the information in the notes; Allison's Thucydides trap theory is based on Thucydides's explanation of the conflict. Thus, Allison's theory affirms, rather than challenges, Thucydides's explanation.

Reading and Writing

Module 2 — Higher Difficulty
(27 questions)

QUESTION 1

Choice B is the best answer because it most logically completes the text's discussion of how Maggie Lena Walker addressed the lack of financial services available to Black residents in Richmond, Virginia, at the turn of the twentieth century. In this context, "rectify" means to correct or remedy something undesirable. The text indicates that by chartering the St. Luke Penny Savings Bank in 1903, Walker took action to provide local Black residents with greater access to financial services like home loans and savings opportunities. This context supports the idea that she aimed to rectify the undesirable situation affecting these residents.

Choice A is incorrect because in this context, "prolong" would mean to lengthen something in time. The text indicates that at the turn of the twentieth century, Black residents in Richmond, Virginia, were faced with a lack of formal banking options. The text then states that Walker founded a new bank that provided these residents with financial services. Therefore, instead of prolonging the situation, she took steps to rectify, or correct it. *Choice C* is incorrect because in this context, "retain" would mean to continue to have or to keep something. According to the text, at the turn of the twentieth century, Black residents in Richmond, Virginia, had few formal banking options, and Walker chartered a new institution to provide these residents with expanded financial services; therefore, she took steps to rectify, not retain, the situation. *Choice D* is incorrect because in this context, "highlight" would mean to emphasize or call attention to something, but the text indicates that Walker took concrete steps beyond merely drawing attention to the situation Black residents were facing in Richmond, Virginia, at the turn of the twentieth century. According to the text, Walker worked to rectify, or correct, the lack of formal banking options that were available to these residents by establishing a bank that provided them with home loans and savings opportunities.

QUESTION 2

Choice D is the best answer because it most logically completes the text's discussion of the creation of *The Adventures of Prince Achmed*. In this context, "arduous" means that the process is marked by great labor or effort. According to the text, the creation of the 1926 animated film *The Adventures of Prince Achmed* took three years and was a painstaking process. Since the process was so long and required great efforts by Lotte Reiniger and her team, the creation of the film was therefore an arduous process.

Choice A is incorrect because the text doesn't indicate that the creation of Reiniger's film was "a haphazard," or disorganized, process. In fact, the text suggests that the creation process was quite meticulous and the team worked hard together to produce the envisioned effects. *Choice B* is incorrect. While the text does suggest that the creation of Reiniger's film was a long and difficult process, it doesn't suggest that the process was "a contentious" one, or one causing controversy or argument. The text suggests that the team worked together to produce the envisioned effects. *Choice C* is incorrect because rather than describing the process of creating the film as "ineffectual," or not having the effect it was intended to have, the text describes the process as ultimately successful despite the difficulty it involved.

QUESTION 3

Choice A is the best answer because it most logically completes the text's discussion of diadromous fish. In this context, "demarcated from" means separate or set apart from. The text indicates that diadromous fish differ from euryhaline fish in that diadromous fish "migrate between freshwater and marine biomes during their life," whereas euryhaline fish do not relocate to a different biome because they can tolerate higher salinity environments. Therefore, this context suggests that because of differences between their migration patterns, diadromous fish are distinct and can be demarcated from euryhaline fish.

Choice B is incorrect. Although the text states that diadromous fish migrate and relocate, the text does not suggest that diadromous fish would be "reconstituted as," or formed again as, anything new. Only their environments change and not the fish themselves. *Choice C* is incorrect because the text does not suggest that diadromous fish can be "conflated with," or combined with, euryhaline fish. Instead, the text distinguishes the two types of fish by pointing out their differences with regard to migration and tolerance for salinity. *Choice D* is incorrect because the text indicates that based on migration habits and tolerance for salinity, diadromous fish are different from euryhaline fish; so it would not make logical sense to say that diadromous fish would be "derived from," or be an extension of or result from, euryhaline fish.

QUESTION 4

Choice D is the best answer because it most logically completes the text's discussion of Theia and the origin of the Moon. In this context, "notional" means theoretical or only an idea. The text indicates that although something was once true of Theia, the protoplanet one theory holds collided with Earth and created debris that became the Moon, researchers now claim to have identified pieces of it deep in Earth's mantle. In other words, having direct evidence of Theia is a new development. This context suggests that before evidence was found, Theia was only theoretical—that is, that it was notional.

Choice A is incorrect because the text doesn't suggest that Theia, a protoplanet, was "desultory," which in this context would mean moving away from the matter at hand; indeed, the text focuses on the "big whack" theory of the origin of the Moon and indicates that Theia is a central part of that theory. *Choice B* is incorrect because the text makes the point that something was true of Theia until recently and suggests that this has changed now that researchers believe they have found pieces of the protoplanet deep in Earth's mantle. It wouldn't make sense to say that Theia was actually "spurious," or false, until researchers found direct evidence of the protoplanet. (Although Theia's existence might not have been certain, it would not have been false simply because there was no evidence of it.) *Choice C* is incorrect because the text makes the point that something was true of Theia until recently and suggests that this has changed now that researchers believe they have found pieces of the protoplanet deep in Earth's mantle. It wouldn't make sense to say that Theia was "veritable," or real, before researchers found direct evidence of its existence: the evidence would instead confirm that Theia was real.

QUESTION 5

Choice C is the best answer because it best describes the function of the underlined portion in the text as a whole. In the text, the speaker mentions the occurrence in nature of seedpods being shaken by a slight wind. The speaker then goes on to compare the black seeds to thoughts, using language that indicates that the speaker's state of mind is unsettled (e.g., "my thoughts are spent"; "My thoughts tear me, I dread their fever"). The text concludes with a comparison between the speaker's "scattered" state of mind and the "hot shrivelled seeds." Thus, the underlined portion of the text presents an observation of an occurrence in the natural world that the speaker then expands on to convey a sense of a turbulent interior state.

Choice A is incorrect because the text does not indicate that the seedpods are the cause of the speaker's state of mind; thus, they could not be responsible for any misgivings the speaker has. *Choice B* is incorrect because the text does not contrast the natural landscape with the speaker's state of mind or describe the wind shaking the seedpods as consistent; rather, the text suggests that the state of the natural world and the speaker's state of mind are similar in that both are unsettled. *Choice D* is incorrect because there is no indication in the text that the speaker regularly engages in critical self-evaluation, only that in this particular instance the speaker's state of mind is turbulent.

QUESTION 6

Choice B is the best answer because it most accurately describes the function of the underlined sentence in the text as a whole. The text discusses the Bayeux Tapestry, making the point that the workers who produced the huge tapestry in the eleventh century might not have ever produced a tapestry so large before. The text goes on to suggest that because of this lack of previous experience, the workers developed and refined the process of joining the tapestry's panels over time as they worked. The last sentence of the text then provides an example of an observation that suggests the workers' process changed: clear misalignment of the borders of the two panels the workers joined first and virtually invisible joins completed later. Thus, the underlined sentence serves to support an argument about the workers who produced the tapestry.

Choice A is incorrect because the example given in the last sentence of the text has to do with how the panels of the Bayeux Tapestry were joined by the workers, not with what is depicted in those panels; the text never identifies any people or places depicted in the tapestry. *Choice C* is incorrect because the last sentence compares how early panels in the Bayeux Tapestry were joined with how later panels in the same tapestry were joined; it doesn't make any comparison between the Bayeux Tapestry and other tapestries from the same time in France. *Choice D* is incorrect because the last sentence doesn't address the location where the Bayeux Tapestry was created; the first sentence of the text presents it as a given that the tapestry was created in France, but nothing in the text indicates how that origin was determined.

QUESTION 7

Choice D is the best answer because it presents a statement about Hans Castorp's story that is suggested by the text. The narrator of the text indicates that the story about Hans Castorp will be told not because there is something particularly notable about him, since he is pleasant but "perfectly ordinary," but because the story itself is remarkable ("very much worth telling"). The narrator then notes that there is a benefit in being at the heart of the story— that it is "in Hans Castorp's favor" that the story is his, and maybe uniquely so ("not every story happens to everybody"). Thus, the text suggests both that the story that will be told is a remarkable one that happened to an unremarkable person and that it is reasonable to argue that the person at the center of a valuable story takes on some of the story's value.

Choice A is incorrect. Although the narrator of the text makes the point that "not every story happens to everybody," the narrator doesn't state that stories are interesting simply because the people they are about are unique. Rather, the narrator suggests that one particular story is "very much worth telling" on its own and that Hans Castorp benefits from the fact that the story is remarkable and may be unique to him. Further, the narrator never suggests that the story will be hard to understand even though it is old. *Choice B* is incorrect. Although the narrator of the text suggests that Hans Castorp is of no particular importance, since he is a "perfectly ordinary" person, the narrator never reveals what makes the story of Castorp important, just that "the story itself" is "very much worth telling." The narrator states that the story "took place long ago," is "covered with the patina of history," and can be told only "with verbs whose tense is that of the deepest past," but the story's age and the way it must be told aren't presented as reasons the story is important; the narrator is simply providing details about how the story will be told. *Choice C* is incorrect because the narrator of the text doesn't suggest that all stories about people who are "perfectly ordinary" (like Hans Castorp) must be told in particular ways to make it clear why those stories are consequential. Further, the narrator suggests that Hans Castorp's story must be told "with verbs whose tense is that of the deepest past" because it took place so long ago, not because telling it that way will convey the story's importance.

QUESTION 8

Choice D is the best answer because it presents a finding that, if true, would most directly support the researchers' conclusion that the transition from a stagnant lid regime to a tectonic plate regime occurred around 3.2 billion years ago. The text explains that early in Earth's history, Earth exhibited a stagnant lid regime in which there's no interaction between the lithosphere and the underlying mantle. The text further explains that, by contrast, once Earth began to exhibit a tectonic plate regime, its lithospheric and mantle material began to mix. If mantle-derived rocks younger than 3.2 billion years contain material not found in older mantle-derived rocks, that material must have originated somewhere other than the mantle. And if this material is found in both older and contemporaneous lithospheric rocks, that would imply that the lithosphere was able to mix with mantle material beginning around 3.2 billion years ago, as the researchers concluded.

Choice A is incorrect. The text gives no basis for comparing the quantities of lithospheric and mantle-derived rocks. *Choice B* is incorrect. The text gives no basis for comparing the material makeup of lithospheric rocks to that of mantle-derived rocks. *Choice C* is incorrect. A positive correlation between the age of lithospheric rocks and these rocks' chemical similarity to mantle-derived rocks would mean that the oldest rocks would be the most similar, which contradicts the text's claim that lithospheric and mantle-derived rocks were completely separate until 3.2 billion years ago. If the researchers' conclusion about the onset of tectonics on Earth is correct, then younger lithospheric rocks would show greater chemical similarity to mantle-derived rocks than older lithospheric rocks do.

QUESTION 9

Choice B is the best answer because it presents a finding that, if true, would most directly support the researchers' conclusion that an observable pattern in time references in novels reflects a shift in human behavior prompted by the spread of electric lighting in the late nineteenth century. If novels published after 1880 contain significantly more references to activities occurring after 10 p.m. than novels from earlier periods do, this would suggest a change in human behavior and daily routines enabled by the availability of electric lighting. Before electric lighting—which provided illumination more easily than other available forms of light—many activities ceased after nightfall, so references to late-night activities would be less common in earlier novels. An increase in such references after 1880 would align with the researchers' conclusion, reflecting an increase in late-night activities made possible by electric lighting.

Choice A is incorrect because a decrease in references to 10 a.m. after the year 1800 would not support the researchers' conclusion involving a shift in human behavior prompted by the spread of electric lighting toward the end of the 1800s. The time of 10 a.m. is in the morning and, in most places, characterized by daylight, so a change in references to that time would not be clearly linked to the impact of electric lighting. *Choice C* is incorrect because while an increase in implied time references relative to clock phrases in nineteenth-century novels could suggest a change in writing style or conventions, it does not directly support the conclusion involving a shift in human behavior prompted by the spread of electric lighting. The text indicates that the researchers' conclusion is based on the content of the time references themselves, not the phrasing used. *Choice D* is incorrect. If references to noon and midnight are used with roughly the same frequency in all the novels analyzed by the researchers, this would reflect a lack of change in human behavior with regard to time and therefore would not support the researchers' conclusion involving a shift in human behavior that occurred in response to the spread of electric lighting.

QUESTION 10

Choice A is the best answer because it most effectively uses data from the graph to complete the statement about Mahtta et al.'s proposal regarding factors that affect urban land expansion (ULE). According to the text, ULE is influenced by urban population growth and by gross domestic product (GDP) growth per capita. Reasoning that efficient national governments provide urban services and infrastructure needed to attract economic investment, Mahtta et al. suggest that, as governments become more efficient at providing urban services and infrastructure, GDP growth per capita will account for more ULE and urban population growth will account for less. But according to the graph, Region 1 saw an increase in the percentage attributed to urban population growth from 1970–2000 (between 60 and 65%) to 2000–2014 (between 70 and 75%) and a decrease in the percentage attributed to GDP growth per capita from 1970–2000 (between 35 and 40%) to 2000–2014 (about 25%). Because the percentage attributed to GDP growth per capita decreased (the opposite of what Mahtta et al. claimed would happen if the governments had become more efficient), the data suggest that the governments of Region 1 became less efficient at providing urban services and infrastructure over that period.

Choice B is incorrect. Neither the graph nor the text gives the regions' relative levels of economic growth or what effect Mahtta et al. would expect such growth to have. Furthermore, Mahtta et al.'s proposal suggests that Region 1's decline in the percentage of ULE attributed to GDP growth per capita from 1970–2000 (between 35 and 40%) to 2000–2014 (about 25%) would suggest decreasing, not increasing, government efficiency over this time.

Choice C is incorrect. Neither the text nor the graph provides information about the relative efficiencies of different governments in Region 2. *Choice D* is incorrect. Mahtta et al.'s proposal suggests that more efficient governments will have a higher percentage of their ULE driven by GDP growth per capita and a lower percentage driven by urban population growth. For Region 2, the percentage of ULE attributed to GDP growth per capita increased from 1970–2000 (between 10 and 15%) to 2000–2014 (between 45 and 50%), but the opposite is true for Region 1, which saw the percentage of ULE attributed to GDP growth per capita decline over the same period. Thus, whereas the data suggest governments in Region 2 became more efficient, the data for Region 1 suggest that those governments became less efficient, not more.

QUESTION 11

Choice B is the best answer because it describes data from the graph that best support the student's assertion that initial efforts at trade liberalization in China were shaped by firms having limited capital (assets available for use) and that this situation resolved during the 2000s. The text explains that an approach to trade liberalization involves engaging in processing imports, one type of which doesn't require payment to a trade partner (processing with assembly) and one type of which requires upfront payment to a trade partner for raw materials (processing with inputs). The graph, which presents China's imports for ordinary imports and both types of processing imports in the years 2000, 2003, and 2006, shows that while processing imports with assembly rose from about 250 hundred million dollars in 2000 to about 750 hundred million dollars in 2006, processing imports with inputs rose much more sharply, increasing from approximately 650 hundred million dollars in 2000 to about 2,300 hundred million dollars in 2006. Because processing with inputs requires firms to pay for materials (expending capital) and processing with assembly doesn't, the sharper rise in processing imports with inputs suggests that Chinese firms' assets—and thus their ability to engage in that type of processing imports— were relatively limited in (and before) 2000 and then substantially increased from 2000 to 2006. In other words, the data suggest that the situation of having limited capital resolved during the 2000s.

Choice A is incorrect because the graph indicates that ordinary imports were greater than both types of processing imports in 2006, not that processing imports with inputs were greater than ordinary imports and processing imports with assembly that year. *Choice C* is incorrect because the observation that ordinary imports were greater than both types of processing imports in 2000, 2003, and 2006 doesn't address a change within any type of imports from 2000 to 2006, and an indication of a change in that period that might be related to the availability of assets is needed to support the assertion that the situation of having limited capital resolved during the 2000s. *Choice D* is incorrect because the fact that processing imports with assembly were greater at the end of the period from 2000 to 2006 than processing imports with inputs were at the start of the same period doesn't address a change within either type of imports during the period, and an indication of such a change that might be related to the availability of assets is needed to support the assertion that the situation of having limited capital resolved during the 2000s.

QUESTION 12

Choice D is the best answer because it most logically completes the discussion of Uto-Aztecan languages. The text explains that the northern and southern branches of the Uto-Aztecan language family descended from a single language (believed to have originated in what is now the US Southwest), resulting in similarities across the family's languages; however, the branches don't have similar vocabulary for maize, even though maize has been cultivated by all Uto-Aztecan tribes. The text also indicates that maize originated in Mexico and spread northward into what is now the US Southwest—the area where the Uto-Aztecan language family originated. It follows, then, that the language family had already divided into northern and southern branches before maize reached that area; if maize had been present before the division occurred, the family's origin language would have had terminology for it that likely would have been reflected in the branches, meaning they would have had similar vocabulary for maize. If maize arrived after the division occurred, however, the tribes in the two regions likely would have developed vocabulary pertaining to maize separately, at the times when they acquired the crop.

Choice A is incorrect because the text focuses on vocabulary pertaining to maize in the branches of the Uto-Aztecan language family, and referring only to how some Uto-Aztecan tribes obtained maize wouldn't directly address the role of language. Moreover, if northern Uto-Aztecan tribes had acquired maize from a southern Uto-Aztecan tribe, it's reasonable to assume that the northern tribes might have also picked up southern Uto-Aztecan terminology for maize in that exchange. *Choice B* is incorrect because the text discusses the fact that the northern and southern branches of the Uto-Aztecan language family don't have shared vocabulary pertaining to maize, not the idea that there are variations in such vocabulary within each branch—that is, the text focuses on differences between the two branches, not on differences between languages within a branch. *Choice C* is incorrect because the text focuses on vocabulary pertaining to maize in the branches of the Uto-Aztecan language family, and referring only to the timing and source of maize acquisition wouldn't directly address the role of language. Furthermore, the text implies that southern Uto-Aztecan tribes probably acquired maize before the northern tribes did, given the evidence that maize originated in Mexico—the location of the best-known representative of the southern branch of the Uto-Aztecan language family—before spreading to the north.

QUESTION 13

Choice C is the best answer because it most logically completes the text's discussion of *Instant Mural*. According to the text, the 1974 work *Instant Mural* involved taping two Asco members (Patssi Valdez and Humberto Sandoval) to an outdoor wall as a direct commentary on constraint (limitation or restriction). The text suggests that instead of focusing on Valdez's role in the work and on social limitations women faced at the time—an approach that fails to explain the role of Sandoval, a man—people should consider that in 1974 (and long before) the art establishment limited recognition of Chicano artists to those who created murals with social and historical subjects, making it challenging for nonmuralist Chicano artists (such as Asco's members) to show their work. The text suggests that considering the situation with the art establishment leads to a conclusion that accounts for the fact that *Instant Mural* is explicitly about constraint and features both a woman and a man taped to the wall: *Instant Mural* isn't a reflection of the social constraints placed on women specifically but instead is a reflection on the constraining aesthetic expectations placed on Chicano artists in general (that is, the limits resulting from the lack of recognition of Chicano artists of any gender who did not create sociohistorical murals).

Choice A is incorrect. The text indicates that the art establishment in 1974 (and earlier) did recognize Chicano muralists to the exclusion of other Chicano artists, so there's no reason to assume Asco's work *Instant Mural* was intended to represent Chicano muralists' frustration; it's far more likely that Asco's members—described as Chicano nonmuralists—were representing their own frustration at being unrecognized by the art establishment. *Choice B* is incorrect. The text emphasizes that while a common approach to *Instant Mural* focuses on Valdez and the social limitations women faced in 1974 but fails to account for the presence of a man in the work, there is a conclusion that explains Sandoval's role. But concluding that *Instant Mural* represents a double constraint experienced specifically by female Chicano artists would still fail to account for the inclusion of a man in the work. *Choice D* is incorrect. Although the text suggests that *Instant Mural* can be understood as something other than a commentary on social constraints women faced in 1974, it doesn't suggest that the work is best understood as a critique of the content of any other artworks. The text doesn't address how Chicano culture is depicted in sociohistorical murals; it discusses such murals only to make the point that in 1974 (and earlier) the art establishment recognized Chicano artists who produced them to the exclusion of Chicano nonmuralists, indicating a constraint all of Asco's members faced, regardless of gender.

QUESTION 14

Choice B is the best answer because it most logically completes the text's discussion of Sidonian coins. As the text explains, researchers determined that Sidonian coins were made of silver and copper and that from 450 BCE to 367 BCE, the percentage of silver in each coin decreased from 98% to 74.2% while the percentage of copper increased from 1% to 24.7%. The text indicates that because the coins containing less than 80% silver weren't considered suitable for trade (suggesting that copper was less valuable than silver) and looked different from coins containing more silver, the researchers suspect there was a serious loss in confidence in the currency in Sidon in 367 BCE when the copper content was high. It's reasonable to assume that it wasn't possible to boost confidence simply by devoting a greater amount of valuable silver to the currency, since Sidon was under significant and ongoing financial pressure; however, keeping the total amount of silver the same and reducing the amount of copper in the coins would have resulted in smaller coins with a higher percentage of silver. Therefore, it makes sense to suggest that Abd'aštart I (the ruler after 367 BCE) likely restored confidence in the currency by deciding to keep the amount of silver in Sidonian coins consistent with that in coins minted in 367 BCE but to decrease the coins' weight.

Choice A is incorrect because the text conveys that a crisis in confidence in the currency of Sidon likely occurred around 367 BCE because the percentage of silver in coins had fallen below 80% (presumably because Sidon's financial pressures meant that less silver was available for currency), making the coins unsuitable for trade. Thus, announcing that the threshold for the percentage of silver in coins would be raised—that is, that coins would need to contain even more than 80% silver to be suitable for trade—likely would have worsened the crisis rather than relieved it. *Choice C* is incorrect because the text strongly suggests that a crisis in confidence in the currency of Sidon was caused by the proportion of silver to copper in the coins in 367 BCE, with 74.2% being too little silver for the coins to be considered suitable for trade; therefore, it's unlikely that minting coins with a similar proportion of silver to copper (that is, still around 74.2% silver) would have restored confidence, even if the coins were heavier. *Choice D* is incorrect because the text gives no indication that funding the mining of more copper would have relieved a crisis in confidence in the currency of Sidon. The text establishes that Sidonian coins that visibly contained copper weren't considered suitable for trade, so Abd'aštart I wouldn't have wanted to add even more copper to them, and it's unclear how else copper mining would affect views of the currency.

QUESTION 15

Choice C is the best answer. The convention being tested is punctuation use between a subject and a verb. No punctuation is needed when, as in this case, a subject ("Her portrait of novelist Zadie Smith") is immediately followed by a main verb ("is displayed").

Choice A is incorrect because no punctuation is needed between the subject and the verb. *Choice B* is incorrect because no punctuation is needed between the subject and the verb. *Choice D* is incorrect because no punctuation is needed between the subject and the verb.

QUESTION 16

Choice B is the best answer. The convention being tested is subject-modifier placement. This choice makes the noun phrase "Iceland's parliament" the subject of the sentence and places it immediately after the modifying phrase "a government body officially known as the Althing." In doing so, this choice clearly establishes that Iceland's parliament—and not another noun in the sentence—is the government body known as the Althing.

Choice A is incorrect because it results in a dangling modifier. The placement of the noun phrase "the world's oldest parliaments" immediately after the modifying phrase illogically suggests that the world's oldest parliaments are a government body known as the Althing. *Choice C* is incorrect because it results in a dangling modifier. The placement of the noun phrase "the first meeting" immediately after the modifying phrase illogically suggests that the first meeting of Iceland's parliament was a government body known as the Althing. *Choice D* is incorrect because it results in a dangling modifier. The placement of the noun phrase "930 CE" immediately after the modifying phrase illogically suggests that the year 930 CE is a government body known as the Althing.

QUESTION 17

Choice C is the best answer. The convention being tested is the punctuation of elements in a complex series. It's conventional to use a semicolon to separate items in a complex series with internal punctuation, and in this choice, the semicolon after "items" is conventionally used to separate the first item ("overseeing...items") and the second item ("managing...law") in a list of Hayden's responsibilities.

Choice A is incorrect because it fails to use appropriate punctuation to separate the first item and the second item in the complex series. *Choice B* is incorrect because a comma after "items" doesn't match the semicolon used later to separate the second and third items in the series ("managing...law" and "and appointing the US poet laureate"). *Choice D* is incorrect because it results in a rhetorically unacceptable sentence fragment beginning with "Managing."

QUESTION 18

Choice D is the best answer. The convention being tested is the use of punctuation within a sentence. This choice correctly uses a comma to mark the boundary between the main clause ("Recently...supposed") and the supplementary element ("a finding...Paleolithic") that provides additional information about the implications of the Neronian tool discovery.

Choice A is incorrect because a semicolon can't be used in this way to join the main clause ("Recently...supposed") and the supplementary element ("a finding...Paleolithic"). *Choice B* is incorrect because it results in a rhetorically unacceptable sentence fragment beginning with "a finding." *Choice C* is incorrect because it results in a run-on sentence. The main clause ("Recently...supposed") and the supplementary element ("a finding...Paleolithic") are fused without punctuation and/or a conjunction.

QUESTION 19

Choice A is the best answer. The convention being tested is the use of punctuation within a sentence. The comma after "work" pairs with the comma after "though" to separate the supplementary element "though" from the rest of the sentence. This supplementary element signals that what follows is an exception to Chen using software tools to create illustrations, and the pair of commas indicates that this element could be removed without affecting the grammatical coherence of the sentence.

Choice B is incorrect because the comma after "work" must be paired with a comma after "though" to separate the supplementary element from the rest of the sentence. *Choice C* is incorrect because a semicolon can't be paired with a comma in this way to separate the supplementary element from the rest of the sentence. *Choice D* is incorrect because a semicolon can't be paired with a comma in this way to separate the supplementary element from the rest of the sentence.

QUESTION 20

Choice B is the best answer. The convention being tested is the use of punctuation within a sentence. This choice correctly uses a comma to separate the supplementary adverb "though" from the preceding main clause ("They are hardly pristine") and uses a semicolon to join the two main clauses ("They...though" and "many...objects"). Further, placing the semicolon after "though" indicates that the information in the preceding main clause (chondrites are far from pristine) is contrary to what might be assumed from the information in the previous sentence (chondrites have been generally unaltered by their environment).

Choice A is incorrect because placing the comma after "pristine" and using "though" as a subordinating conjunction illogically indicates that the information in the next main clause (many chondrites have experienced damage) is contrary to the information in the previous clause (chondrites are far from pristine). *Choice C* is incorrect because placing the semicolon after "pristine" illogically indicates that the information in the next main clause (many chondrites have experienced damage) is contrary to the information in the previous clause (chondrites are far from pristine). *Choice D* is incorrect because it results in a comma splice. Without a conjunction following it, the comma after "though" can't be used in this way to join two main clauses.

QUESTION 21

Choice D is the best answer. The convention being tested is the use of punctuation within a sentence. This choice uses a semicolon in a conventional way to join the first main clause ("That the...involved") and the second main clause ("establishing...divisive"). Further, the semicolon is the most appropriate choice when joining two separate, parallel statements, such as here, where the information following the semicolon contrasts with the information before.

Choice A is incorrect because placing a colon after "involved" illogically indicates that the information in the second main clause (the precise location was the subject of disagreement) explains or amplifies the information in the previous main clause (the general location was agreed upon by all). Instead, the information in the second clause contrasts with the previous information.

Choice B is incorrect because it results in a comma splice. Without a conjunction following it, a comma can't be used in this way to join two main clauses. *Choice C* is incorrect because it results in a run-on sentence. The two main clauses are fused without punctuation and/or a conjunction.

QUESTION 22

Choice A is the best answer. "In particular" logically signals that the information in this sentence—that maize and wheat supply chains transformed North American foodways into a global food system—provides specific, precise details elaborating on the more general information in the previous sentence about the transformation of North American foodways (with maize and wheat the "certain grains" at the center of it).

Choice B is incorrect because "alternatively" illogically signals that the information in this sentence is an alternative option to the previous information about the transformation of North American foodways. Instead, the roles of maize and wheat in creating a global food system are specific, precise details elaborating on that information. *Choice C* is incorrect because "by comparison" illogically signals that the information in this sentence is being compared to the previous information about the transformation of North American foodways. Instead, the roles of maize and wheat in creating a global food system are specific, precise details elaborating on that information. *Choice D* is incorrect because "second of all" illogically signals that the information in this sentence is a second, separate claim from the previous claim that North American foodways were transformed. Instead, the roles of maize and wheat in creating a global food system are specific, precise details elaborating on that information, rather than a separate claim.

QUESTION 23

Choice D is the best answer. "Moreover" logically signals that the information in this sentence—that Franklin stamped imprints on paper money to make forgery more difficult—adds to the previous information by describing Franklin's other strategy for combatting forgers: weaving materials into the paper used for printing money.

Choice A is incorrect because "specifically" illogically signals that the information in this sentence provides specific, precise details elaborating on the previous information about Franklin's other strategy for combatting forgers (weaving materials into paper). Instead, this information about stamping imprints on money adds new information. *Choice B* is incorrect because "that said" illogically signals that the information in this sentence is an exception to the previous information about Franklin's other strategy for combatting forgers (weaving materials into paper). Instead, this information about stamping imprints on money adds new information. *Choice C* is incorrect because "for example" illogically signals that the information in this sentence serves as an example of the previous information about Franklin's other strategy for combatting forgers (weaving materials into paper). Instead, this information about stamping imprints on money adds new information.

QUESTION 24

Choice D is the best answer. The sentence identifies the type of scientist Chaudhuri is, noting that she is a sedimentologist.

Choice A is incorrect. The sentence provides an example of a type of sedimentary rock; it doesn't identify what type of scientist Chaudhuri is. *Choice B* is incorrect. The sentence indicates types of rock that some scientists study; it doesn't identify what type of scientist Chaudhuri is. *Choice C* is incorrect. While the sentence states that some scientists study sedimentary rocks, it doesn't identify Chaudhuri as this type of scientist.

QUESTION 25

Choice C is the best answer. The sentence indicates the year *Yosemite Falls* was completed, stating that it was completed in 1930.

Choice A is incorrect. The sentence indicates where Obata created black ink paintings; it doesn't indicate when the painting was completed. *Choice B* is incorrect. While the sentence identifies Obata as an artist who created a notable painting, it doesn't indicate when that painting was completed. *Choice D* is incorrect. The sentence identifies the method Obata used; it doesn't indicate when the painting was completed.

QUESTION 26

Choice D is the best answer. The sentence presents an overview of the study's findings, noting that, for some of the languages (the examples of Spanish and Vietnamese are given in the notes), the number of syllables spoken per second varied, while the amount of information conveyed per second remained roughly constant across all 17 languages.

Choice A is incorrect. While the sentence describes one of the metrics the study assessed, it doesn't present any of the study's findings. *Choice B* is incorrect. While the sentence compares specific findings about two of the languages studied, it doesn't provide an overview of the study's findings across all 17 languages. *Choice C* is incorrect. The sentence compares specific findings about two of the languages studied; it doesn't provide an overview of the study's findings across all 17 languages. It also misrepresents the information from the notes about Spanish's information rate.

QUESTION 27

Choice A is the best answer. The sentence places Einstein's argument within the historical context of the development of quantum theory, noting that his argument—made during the dawn of the field—conflicted with Bohr's argument, which became the widely accepted view.

Choice B is incorrect. The sentence misrepresents information from the notes, attributing the argument that electrons had a reality independent of observation to Bohr, not Einstein. In addition, while the sentence provides the date of the conference, it doesn't place Einstein's argument in the context of the development of quantum theory. *Choice C* is incorrect. The sentence indicates that Einstein attended the 1927 Solvay Conference; it doesn't identify Einstein's argument or place it in the historical context of the development of quantum theory. *Choice D* is incorrect. The sentence explains that Einstein and Bohr had a famous debate in 1927 and that Bohr's argument remained popular decades afterward; it doesn't identify Einstein's argument or place it in the context of the development of quantum theory.

Math

Module 1
(22 questions)

QUESTION 1

Choice A is correct. It's given that p represents the number of pounds of strawberries Lorenzo purchased and Lorenzo paid $1.90 per pound for the strawberries. It follows that the total amount, in dollars, Lorenzo paid for strawberries can be represented by $1.90p$. It's given that Lorenzo paid $2 for the box of cereal. If Lorenzo paid a total of $9.60 for the box of cereal and strawberries, it follows that the equation $1.90p + 2 = 9.60$ can be used to find p.

Choice B is incorrect and may result from conceptual errors. *Choice C* is incorrect and may result from conceptual errors. *Choice D* is incorrect and may result from conceptual errors.

QUESTION 2

Choice C is correct. It's given that the function f is defined by $f(x) = 25x + 30$. Substituting 2 for x in this equation yields $f(2) = 25(2) + 30$, which is equivalent to $f(2) = 50 + 30$, or $f(2) = 80$. Therefore, the value of $f(x)$ is 80 when $x = 2$.

Choice A is incorrect. This is the value of $25(2)$, not $25(2) + 30$. *Choice B* is incorrect. This is the value of $25 + 2 + 30$, not $25(2) + 30$. *Choice D* is incorrect. This is the value of $(25 + 30(2)$, not $25(2) + 30$.

QUESTION 3

Choice A is correct. It's given that the graph shown gives the estimated value y, in dollars, of a tablet as a function of the number of months since it was purchased, x. The y-intercept of a graph is the point at which the graph intersects the y-axis, or when x is 0. The graph shown intersects the y-axis at the point $(0, 225)$. It follows that 0 months after the tablet was purchased, or when the tablet was purchased, the estimated value of the tablet was 225 dollars. Therefore, the best interpretation of the y-intercept is that the estimated value of the tablet was $225 when it was purchased.

Choice B is incorrect. The estimated value of the tablet 24 months after it was purchased was $50, not $225. *Choice C* is incorrect. The estimated value of the tablet had decreased by $225 − $50, or $175, not $225, in the 24 months after it was purchased. *Choice D* is incorrect and may result from conceptual errors.

QUESTION 4

Choice B is correct. Subtracting 61 from each side of the given equation yields $|p| = 4$. By the definition of absolute value, if $|p| = 4$, then $p = 4$ or $p = -4$. Of the given choices, 4 is a solution to the given equation.

Choice A is incorrect. This is the quotient, not the difference, of 65 and 61. *Choice C* is incorrect. This is the sum, not the difference, of 65 and 61. *Choice D* is incorrect and may result from conceptual or calculation errors.

QUESTION 5

Choice B is correct. It's given that triangles *EFG* and *JKL* are congruent such that angle *E* corresponds to angle *J*. Corresponding angles of congruent triangles are congruent, so angle *E* and angle *J* must be congruent. Therefore, if the measure of angle *E* is 45°, then the measure of angle *J* is also 45°.

Choice A is incorrect. This is the measure of angle *K*, not angle *J*. *Choice C* is incorrect and may result from conceptual or calculation errors. *Choice D* is incorrect and may result from conceptual or calculation errors.

QUESTION 6

Choice B is correct. It's given that *y* represents the height, in feet, of the ball *x* seconds after it was launched. It's also given that during the first part of an experiment, a ball was launched from a 7-foot-tall platform. Therefore, the *y*-coordinate of the *y*-intercept of the given graph, 7, represents the platform height, in feet. During the second part of the experiment, the platform the ball was launched from was 2 feet shorter than the platform in the first part of the experiment. It follows that the height of the platform in the second part of the experiment was 7 − 2 feet, or 5 feet. Therefore, the *y*-coordinate of the *y*-intercept of the graph representing the second part of the experiment must be 5. Only choice B satisfies this condition.

Choice A is incorrect. This could represent the graph if the ball were launched from a platform that was about 3 feet shorter rather than 2 feet shorter. *Choice C* is incorrect. This could represent the graph if the ball were launched from a platform that was 2 feet taller rather than 2 feet shorter. *Choice D* is incorrect. This could represent the graph if the ball were launched from a platform that was twice as tall rather than 2 feet shorter.

QUESTION 7

The correct answer is 90. It's given that the ratio of *x* to *y* is equivalent to the ratio 9 to 5. It follows that $\frac{x}{y} = \frac{9}{5}$. Multiplying each side of this equation by 5*y* yields $\frac{(5y)x}{y} = \frac{9(5y)}{5}$, or $5x = 9y$. Dividing each side of this equation by 9 yields $\frac{5x}{9} = y$. Substituting 162 for *x* in this equation yields $\frac{5(162)}{9} = y$, which is equivalent to $\frac{810}{9} = y$, or $90 = y$. Therefore, if the value of *x* is 162, the value of *y* is 90.

QUESTION 8

Choice D is correct. It's given that the equation $80S + 90C = 1,120$ represents this situation, where *S* is the number of square tokens won, *C* is the number of circle tokens won, and 1,120 is the total number of points the tokens are worth. It follows that $80S$ represents the total number of points the square tokens are worth. Therefore, each square token is worth 80 points. It also follows that 90*C* represents the total number of points the circle tokens are worth. Therefore, each circle token is worth 90 points. Since a circle token is worth 90 points and a square token is worth 80 points, then a circle token is worth 90 – 80, or 10, more points than a square token.

Choice A is incorrect and may result from conceptual or calculation errors. *Choice B* is incorrect. This is the number of points a circle token is worth. *Choice C* is incorrect. This is the number of points a square token is worth.

QUESTION 9

Choice C is correct. Since the left-hand side of the given equation has a factor of $x + 9$ in both the numerator and the denominator, the solution to the given equation can be found by solving the equation $x - 9 = 7$. Adding 9 to both sides of this equation yields $x = 16$. Substituting 16 for x in the given equation yields $\frac{(16 + 9)(16 - 9)}{16 + 9} = 7$, or $7 = 7$. Therefore, the solution to the given equation is 16.

Choice A is incorrect. Substituting 7 for x in the given equation yields $\frac{(7 + 9)(7 - 9)}{7 + 9} = 7$, or $-2 = 7$, which is false. *Choice B* is incorrect. Substituting 9 for x in the given equation yields $\frac{(9 + 9)(9 - 9)}{9 + 9} = 7$, or $0 = 7$, which is false. *Choice D* is incorrect. Substituting 63 for x in the given equation yields $\frac{(63 + 9)(63 - 9)}{63 + 9} = 7$, or $54 = 7$, which is false.

QUESTION 10

Choice D is correct. Subtracting b from each side of the given equation yields $12t = c - b$. Therefore, the expression $12t$ correctly expresses the value of $c - b$ in terms of t.

Choice A is incorrect and may result from conceptual or calculation errors. *Choice B* is incorrect and may result from conceptual or calculation errors. *Choice C* is incorrect and may result from conceptual or calculation errors.

QUESTION 11

The correct answer is either 14, –5, or –4. The x-intercepts of a graph in the xy-plane are the points at which the graph intersects the x-axis, or when the value of y is 0. Substituting 0 for y in the given equation yields $0 = 3(x - 14)(x + 5)(x + 4)$. Dividing both sides of this equation by 3 yields $0 = (x - 14)(x + 5)(x + 4)$. Applying the zero product property to this equation yields three equations: $x - 14 = 0$, $x + 5 = 0$, and $x + 4 = 0$. Adding 14 to both sides of the equation $x - 14 = 0$ yields $x = 14$, subtracting 5 from both sides of the equation $x + 5 = 0$ yields $x = -5$, and subtracting 4 from both sides of the equation $x + 4 = 0$ yields $x = -4$. Therefore, the x-coordinates of the x-intercepts of the graph of the given equation are 14, –5, and –4. Note that 14, –5, and –4 are examples of ways to enter a correct answer.

QUESTION 12

The correct answer is $\frac{11}{4}$. It's given that the function f is defined by

$f(x) = 5\left(\frac{1}{4} - x\right)^2 + \frac{11}{4}$. Substituting $\frac{1}{4}$ for x in this equation yields

$f\left(\frac{1}{4}\right) = 5\left(\frac{1}{4} - \frac{1}{4}\right)^2 + \frac{11}{4}$, which is equivalent $f\left(\frac{1}{4}\right) = 5(0)^2 + \frac{11}{4}$, or $f\left(\frac{1}{4}\right) = \frac{11}{4}$.

Therefore, the value of $f\left(\frac{1}{4}\right)$ is $\frac{11}{4}$. Note that 11/4 or 2.75 are examples of ways

to enter a correct answer.

QUESTION 13

Choice A is correct. For a circle in the xy-plane that has the equation $(x - h)^2 + (y - k)^2 = r^2$, where h, k, and r are constants, (h, k) is the center of the circle and the positive value of r is the radius of the circle. In the given equation, $h = 13$ and $r^2 = 64$. Taking the square root of each side of $r^2 = 64$ yields $r = \pm 8$. Therefore, the center of the circle is at $(13, k)$ and the radius is 8.

Choice B is incorrect. This gives the center and radius of a circle with equation $(x - k)^2 + (y - 13)^2 = 64$, not $(x - 13)^2 + (y - k)^2 = 64$. *Choice C* is incorrect. This gives the center and radius of a circle with equation $(x - k)^2 + (y - 13)^2 = 4,096$, not $(x - 13)^2 + (y - k)^2 = 64$. *Choice D* is incorrect. This gives the center and radius of a circle with equation $(x - 13)^2 + (y - k)^2 = 4,096$, not $(x - 13)^2 + (y - k)^2 = 64$.

QUESTION 14

The correct answer is 4.41. The area, A, of a circle is given by the formula $A = \pi r^2$, where r is the radius of the circle. It's given that the area of the circle is $b\pi$ square inches, where b is a constant, and the radius of the circle is 2.1 inches. Substituting $b\pi$ for A and 2.1 for r in the formula $A = \pi r^2$ yields $b\pi = \pi(2.1^2)$. Dividing both sides of this equation by π yields $b = 4.41$. Therefore, the value of b is 4.41.

QUESTION 15

The correct answer is 5. For the graph shown, x represents time, in minutes, and y represents temperature, in degrees Celsius (°C). Therefore, the average rate of change, in °C per minute, of the recorded temperature of the air in the chamber between two x-values is the difference in the corresponding y-values divided by the difference in the x-values. The graph shows that at $x = 5$, the corresponding y-value is 14. The graph also shows that at $x = 7$, the corresponding y-value is 24. It follows that the average rate of change, in °C per minute, from $x = 5$ to $x = 7$

is $\frac{24 - 14}{7 - 5}$, which is equivalent to $\frac{10}{2}$, or 5.

QUESTION 16

Choice D is correct. Adding the second equation to the first equation in the given system of equations yields $3y - 3y = 4x + 9x + 17 - 23$, or $0 = 13x - 6$. Adding 6 to each side of this equation yields $6 = 13x$. Multiplying each side of this equation by 3 yields $18 = 39x$. Therefore, the value of $39x$ is 18.

Choice A is incorrect. This is the value of $-39x$, not $39x$. *Choice B* is incorrect. This is the value of $-13x$, not $39x$. *Choice C* is incorrect. This is the value of $13x$, not $39x$.

QUESTION 17

Choice B is correct. It's given that t minutes after an initial observation, the number of bacteria in a population is $40{,}000(2)^{\frac{t}{790}}$. This expression consists of the initial number of bacteria, 40,000, multiplied by the expression $2^{\frac{t}{790}}$. The time, in minutes, it takes for the number of bacteria to double is the increase in the value of t that causes the expression $2^{\frac{t}{790}}$ to double. Since the base is 2, the expression $2^{\frac{t}{790}}$ will double when the exponent increases by 1. Since the exponent of this expression is $\frac{t}{790}$, the exponent will increase by 1 when t increases by 790. Therefore, the time, in minutes, it takes for the number of bacteria in the population to double is 790.

Alternate approach: The initial number of bacteria in the population can be found by substituting 0 for t in the given function. This yields $f(0) = 40{,}000(2)^{\frac{0}{790}}$, or $f(0) = 40{,}000$. Therefore, the initial number of bacteria present in the population is 40,000, so the bacteria population will have doubled when $f(t) = 80{,}000$.

Substituting 80,000 for $f(t)$ in the given function yields $80{,}000 = 40{,}000(2)^{\frac{t}{790}}$. Dividing both sides of this equation by 40,000 yields $2 = 2^{\frac{t}{790}}$, or $2^1 = 2^{\frac{t}{790}}$. It follows that $1 = \frac{t}{790}$. Multiplying both sides of this equation by 790 yields $790 = t$. Therefore, the time, in minutes, it takes for the number of bacteria in the population to double is 790.

Choice A is incorrect. This is the base of the exponent, not the time it takes for the number of bacteria in the population to double. *Choice C* is incorrect. This is the number of minutes it takes for the population to double twice. *Choice D* is incorrect. This is the number of bacteria that are initially observed, not the time it takes for the number of bacteria in the population to double.

QUESTION 18

The correct answer is 11. Subtracting 5 from each side of the given equation yields $-7(2 - 4x) = 11 - 8(2 - 4x)$. Adding $8(2 - 4x)$ to each side of this equation yields $2 - 4x = 11$. Therefore, the value of $2 - 4x$ is 11.

QUESTION 19

Choice A is correct. It's given that a scientist studying the life cycle of dragonflies counted the number of dragonflies in a certain habitat each day for 46 days. It's also given that on February 15, there were 99 dragonflies in the habitat and that the percent increase in the number of dragonflies in the habitat from January 1 to February 15 was 12.50%. This can be represented by the equation $99 = \left(1 + \frac{12.50}{100}\right)x$, where x represents the number of dragonflies in the habitat on January 1. This equation can be rewritten as $99 = 1.125x$. Dividing both sides of this equation by 1.125 yields $88 = x$. Therefore, there were 88 dragonflies in the habitat on January 1.

Choice B is incorrect and may result from conceptual or calculation errors. *Choice C* is incorrect and may result from conceptual or calculation errors. *Choice D* is incorrect and may result from conceptual or calculation errors.

QUESTION 20

The correct answer is 120. The solutions to a quadratic equation of the form $ax^2 + bx + c = 0$ can be calculated using the quadratic formula and are given by

$x = \dfrac{-b \pm \sqrt{b^2 - 4ac}}{2a}$. The given equation is in the form $ax^2 + bx + c = 0$, where

$a = 2$, $b = -8$, and $c = -7$. It follows that the solutions to the given equation are

$x = \dfrac{8 \pm \sqrt{(-8)^2 - 4(2)(-7)}}{2(2)}$, which is equivalent to $x = \dfrac{8 \pm \sqrt{64 + 56}}{4}$, or

$x = \dfrac{8 \pm \sqrt{120}}{4}$. It's given that one solution to the equation $2x^2 - 8x - 7 = 0$ can be

written as $\dfrac{8 - \sqrt{k}}{4}$. The solution $\dfrac{8 - \sqrt{120}}{4}$ is in this form. Therefore, the value of k

is 120.

QUESTION 21

Choice A is correct. It's given that the function $f(x)$ is defined as 19 more than 4 times a number x. This can be represented by the equation $f(x) = 4x + 19$. The x-intercept of the graph of $y = f(x)$ in the xy-plane is the point where the graph intersects the x-axis, or the point on the graph where the value of $f(x)$ is equal to 0. Substituting 0 for $f(x)$ in the equation $f(x) = 4x + 19$ yields $0 = 4x + 19$. Subtracting 19 from each side of this equation yields $-19 = 4x$. Dividing each

side of this equation by 4 yields $x = -\dfrac{19}{4}$. Therefore, when $f(x) = 0$, the number

is $-\dfrac{19}{4}$.

Choice B is incorrect. This is the best interpretation of the y-intercept, not the x-intercept, of the graph of the function. *Choice C* is incorrect and may result from conceptual or calculation errors. *Choice D* is incorrect. This is the best interpretation of the slope, not the x-intercept, of the graph of the function.

QUESTION 22

Choice C is correct. The sine of an angle is equal to the cosine of its complementary angle. Since angles with measures 24° and 66° are complementary to each other, sin 24° is equal to cos 66° and sin 66° is equal to cos 24°. Substituting cos 66° for sin 24° and cos 24° for sin 66° in the given expression yields (cos 66°)(cos 66°) + (cos 24°)(cos 24°), or (cos 66°)^2 + (cos 24°)^2.

Choice A is incorrect and may result from conceptual or calculation errors. *Choice B* is incorrect and may result from conceptual or calculation errors. *Choice D* is incorrect and may result from conceptual or calculation errors.

Math

Module 2 — Lower Difficulty
(22 questions)

QUESTION 1

Choice A is correct. It's given that a total of 165 people contributed to a charity event as either a donor or a volunteer. It's also given that 130 people contributed as a donor. It follows that 165 – 130, or 35, people contributed as a volunteer.

Choice B is incorrect. This is the number of people who contributed as a donor, not a volunteer. *Choice C* is incorrect. This is the total number of people who contributed as either a donor or a volunteer, not the number of people who contributed as a volunteer. *Choice D* is incorrect and may result from conceptual or calculation errors.

QUESTION 2

Choice B is correct. It's given that a data set consists of 173 colors and the bar graph shows the number of times each color appears in the data set. Therefore, for each color specified at the bottom of the bar, the frequency corresponds to the number of times that color appears in the data set. The color that appears 70 times in the data set has a frequency of 70 on the bar graph. Since the bar with a frequency of 70 corresponds to green, green is the color that appears 70 times.

Choice A is incorrect. The color blue appears about 27 times, not 70 times. *Choice C* is incorrect. The color red appears about 33 times, not 70 times. *Choice D* is incorrect. The color yellow appears about 43 times, not 70 times.

QUESTION 3

Choice B is correct. Subtracting 275 from both sides of the given equation yields $2p = 50$. Dividing both sides of this equation by 2 yields $p = 25$. Therefore, the value of p that satisfies the given equation is 25.

Choice A is incorrect and may result from conceptual or calculation errors. *Choice C* is incorrect. This is the value of p that satisfies the equation $(2 + p) + 275 = 325$, not $2p + 275 = 325$. *Choice D* is incorrect. This is the value of p that satisfies the equation $2p - 275 = 325$, not $2p + 275 = 325$.

QUESTION 4

Choice B is correct. In the given scatterplot, the *x*-values represent the distance above sea level, in feet, and the *y*-values represent the temperature, in °F. The point on the line of best fit with an *x*-value of 4,000 has a corresponding *y*-value of 35. Therefore, at a distance of 4,000 feet above sea level, the temperature predicted by the line of best fit is 35°F.

Choice A is incorrect. This is the temperature, in °F, predicted by the line of best fit at a distance of 0 feet above sea level. *Choice C* is incorrect. This is the measured temperature, in °F, at a distance of 6,000 feet above sea level. *Choice D* is incorrect and may result from conceptual or calculation errors.

QUESTION 5

Choice D is correct. It's given that rectangle P has an area of 72 square inches. If a rectangle with an area of 20 square inches is removed from rectangle P, the area, in square inches, of the resulting figure is 72 − 20, or 52.

Choice A is incorrect and may result from conceptual or calculation errors. *Choice B* is incorrect and may result from conceptual or calculation errors. *Choice C* is incorrect and may result from conceptual or calculation errors.

QUESTION 6

Choice C is correct. The vertex of the graph of a quadratic function in the *xy*-plane is the point at which the graph is either at its minimum or maximum *y*-value. In the graph shown, the minimum *y*-value occurs at the point (0, 2).

Choice A is incorrect. The graph shown doesn't pass through the point (0, −2). *Choice B* is incorrect. The graph shown doesn't pass through the point (0, −3). *Choice D* is incorrect. The graph shown doesn't pass through the point (0, 3).

QUESTION 7

Choice A is correct. It's given that there are 2,358 raccoons in a 131-square-mile area. The estimated population density, in raccoons per square mile, is the estimated number of raccoons divided by the number of square miles. Therefore, the estimated population density of this area is $\frac{2,358 \text{ raccoons}}{131 \text{ square miles}}$, or 18 raccoons per square mile.

Choice B is incorrect. This is the number of square miles in the area, not the estimated number of raccoons per square mile in this area. *Choice C* is incorrect and may result from conceptual or calculation errors. *Choice D* is incorrect and may result from conceptual or calculation errors.

QUESTION 8

Choice C is correct. It's given that 8*x* = 6. Multiplying each side of this equation by 9 yields 72*x* = 54. Therefore, the value of 72*x* is 54.

Choice A is incorrect. This is the value of 4*x*, not 72*x*. *Choice B* is incorrect and may result from conceptual or calculation errors. *Choice D* is incorrect and may result from conceptual or calculation errors.

QUESTION 9

Choice B is correct. The probability of selecting a positive number is the number of positive numbers in the data set divided by the total number of numbers in the data set. There is 1 positive number in this data set. There are 3 total numbers in this data set. Thus, if a number from this data set is selected at random, the probability of selecting a positive number is $\frac{1}{3}$.

Choice A is incorrect and may result from conceptual or calculation errors. *Choice C* is incorrect. This is the probability of selecting a negative number from this data set. *Choice D* is incorrect and may result from conceptual or calculation errors.

QUESTION 10

The correct answer is 162. It's given that line *r* is parallel to line *s*. Since line *n* intersects both lines *r* and *s*, it's a transversal. The angles in the figure marked as 162° and *x*° are on the same side of the transversal, where one is an interior angle with line *s* as a side, and the other is an exterior angle with line *r* as a side. Thus, the marked angles are corresponding angles. When two parallel lines are intersected by a transversal, corresponding angles are congruent and, therefore, have equal measure. It follows that the value of *x* is 162.

QUESTION 11

Choice C is correct. Since *x* is a common factor of each term in the given expression, the given expression can be rewritten as $x(23x^2 + 2x + 9)$.

Choice A is incorrect. This expression is equivalent to $23x^3 + 46x^2 + 207x$. *Choice B* is incorrect. This expression is equivalent to $207x^4 + 18x^3 + 9x$. *Choice D* is incorrect. This expression is equivalent to $34x^3 + 34x^2 + 34x$.

QUESTION 12

Choice D is correct. The given expression can be rewritten as $(9x^3 + 6x^3) + 5x^2 + 5x + (7 - 5)$. Combining like terms in this expression yields $15x^3 + 5x^2 + 5x + 2$.

Choice A is incorrect and may result from conceptual or calculation errors. *Choice B* is incorrect and may result from conceptual or calculation errors. *Choice C* is incorrect and may result from conceptual or calculation errors.

QUESTION 13

The correct answer is 2,850. It's given that the function $f(x) = 45x + 600$ gives the monthly fee, in dollars, a facility charges to keep *x* crates in storage. Substituting 50 for *x* in this function yields $f(50) = 45(50) + 600$, or $f(50) = 2,850$. Therefore, the monthly fee, in dollars, the facility charges to keep 50 crates in storage is 2,850.

QUESTION 14

The correct answer is 27. It's given that 6% of the 450 tiles in a box are black. Therefore, the number of black tiles in the box can be calculated by multiplying the number of tiles in the box by $\frac{6}{100}$, which is equivalent to $450\left(\frac{6}{100}\right)$, or 27.

QUESTION 15

Choice C is correct. It's given that t represents the number of years since the account was opened. Therefore, $\frac{t}{10}$ represents the number of 10-year periods since the account was opened. Since the value of the account doubles during each of these 10-year periods, the value of the account can be found by multiplying the initial value by $\frac{t}{10}$ factors of 2. This is equivalent to $2^{\frac{t}{10}}$. It's given that the initial value of the account is $890. Therefore, the value of the account $M(t)$, in dollars, t years after the account was opened can be represented by $M(t) = 890(2)^{\frac{t}{10}}$.

Choice A is incorrect. This equation represents the value of an account if the value of the account halves, not doubles, every 10 years. *Choice B* is incorrect. This equation represents the value of an account if the value of the account decreases by 90%, not doubles, every 2, not 10, years. *Choice D* is incorrect. This equation represents the value of an account if the value of the account increases by a factor of 10, not doubles, every 2, not 10, years.

QUESTION 16

Choice A is correct. The inequality $y < x$ indicates that for any solution to the given system of inequalities, the value of x must be greater than the corresponding value of y. The inequality $x < 22$ indicates that for any solution to the given system of inequalities, the value of x must be less than 22. Of the given choices, only choice A contains values of x that are each greater than the corresponding value of y and less than 22. Therefore, for choice A, all the values of x and their corresponding values of y are solutions to the given system of inequalities.

Choice B is incorrect. The values in this table aren't solutions to the inequality $y < x$. *Choice C* is incorrect. The values in this table aren't solutions to the inequality $x < 22$. *Choice D* is incorrect. The values in this table aren't solutions to the inequality $y < x$ or the inequality $x < 22$.

QUESTION 17

The correct answer is 9. It's given that the equation $y = px + r$ defines the line. In this equation, p represents the slope of the line and r represents the y-coordinate of the y-intercept of the line. It's given that the line has a slope of 9. Therefore, the value of p is 9.

QUESTION 18

Choice D is correct. It's given that the function f is defined by $f(x) = \frac{1}{2}(x + 6)$. Substituting 4 for x in the given function yields $f(4) = \frac{1}{2}(4 + 6)$, or $f(4) = 5$. Therefore, the value of $f(4)$ is 5.

Choice A is incorrect. This is the value of $2(4 + 6)$, not $\frac{1}{2}(4 + 6)$. *Choice B* is incorrect. This is the value of $2 + (4 + 6)$, not $\frac{1}{2}(4 + 6)$. *Choice C* is incorrect. This is the value of $4 + 6$, not $\frac{1}{2}(4 + 6)$.

QUESTION 19

Choice D is correct. A linear equation can be written in the form $y = mx + b$, where m is the slope of the graph of the equation in the xy-plane and $(0, b)$ is the y-intercept. Subtracting $10x$ from each side of the given equation, $10x - 5y = -12$, yields $-5y = -10x - 12$. Dividing each side of this equation by -5 yields $y = 2x + \frac{12}{5}$. This equation is in the form $y = mx + b$, where $m = 2$. Therefore, the slope of the graph of the given equation in the xy-plane is 2.

Choice A is incorrect and may result from conceptual or calculation errors. *Choice B* is incorrect and may result from conceptual or calculation errors. *Choice C* is incorrect and may result from conceptual or calculation errors.

QUESTION 20

Choice D is correct. It's given that the system has infinitely many solutions. A system of two linear equations has infinitely many solutions when the two linear equations are equivalent. When one equation is a multiple of another equation, the two equations are equivalent. Multiplying each side of the given equation by 2 yields $2(y) = 2(6x + 3)$. Thus, $2(y) = 2(6x + 3)$ is equivalent to the given equation and could be the second equation in the system.

Choice A is incorrect. The system consisting of this equation and the given equation has one solution rather than infinitely many solutions. *Choice B* is incorrect. The system consisting of this equation and the given equation has one solution rather than infinitely many solutions. *Choice C* is incorrect. The system consisting of this equation and the given equation has no solutions rather than infinitely many solutions.

QUESTION 21

Choice C is correct. It's given that the function f is defined by $f(x) = |x - 4x|$. It's also given that $f(5) - f(a) = -15$. Substituting 5 for x in the function $f(x) = |x - 4x|$ yields $f(5) = |5 - 4(5)|$ and substituting a for x in the function $f(x) = |x - 4x|$ yields $f(a) = |a - 4a|$. Therefore, $f(5) = 15$ and $f(a) = |-3a|$. Substituting 15 for $f(5)$ and $|-3a|$ for $f(a)$ in the equation $f(a) - f(a) = -15$ yields $15 - |-3a| = -15$. Subtracting 15 from both sides of this equation yields $-|-3a| = -30$. Dividing both sides of this equation by -1 yields $|-3a| = 30$. By the definition of absolute value, if $|-3a| = 30$, then $-3a = 30$ or $-3a = -30$. Dividing both sides of each of these equations by -3 yields $a = -10$ or $a = 10$, respectively. Thus, of the given choices, a value of a that satisfies $f(5) - f(a) = -15$ is 10.

Choice A is incorrect and may result from conceptual or calculation errors. *Choice B* is incorrect and may result from conceptual or calculation errors. *Choice D* is incorrect and may result from conceptual or calculation errors.

QUESTION 22

The correct answer is 87. It's given that in August, the car dealer completed 15 more than 3 times the number of sales the car dealer completed in September. Let x represent the number of sales the car dealer completed in September. It follows that $3x + 15$ represents the number of sales the car dealer completed in August. It's also given that in August and September, the car dealer completed 363 sales. It follows that $x + (3x + 15) = 363$, or $4x + 15 = 363$. Subtracting 15 from each side of this equation yields $4x = 348$. Dividing each side of this equation by 4 yields $x = 87$. Therefore, the car dealer completed 87 sales in September.

Math

Module 2 — Higher Difficulty
(22 questions)

QUESTION 1

Choice D is correct. It's given that the bar graph summarizes the charge, in kilowatt-hours (kWh), a battery received each day for 15 days. The height of each bar in the bar graph shown represents the number of days the battery received the charge, in kWh, specified at the bottom of the bar. The bar for a charge of 0 kWh reaches a height of 6. Therefore, the battery received a charge of 0 kWh for 6 of these days.

Choice A is incorrect. This is the charge, in kWh, that the battery received, not the number of days the battery received this charge. *Choice B* is incorrect. This is the number of days the battery received a charge of either 8, 16, or 23 kWh. *Choice C* is incorrect. This is the number of days the battery received a charge of 11 kWh.

QUESTION 2

Choice D is correct. A line in the *xy*-plane that passes through the points (x_1, y_1) and (x_2, y_2) has a slope of $\frac{y_2 - y_1}{x_2 - x_1}$. The line of best fit shown passes approximately through the points (1, 3.3) and (7, 14.5). It follows that the slope of this best fit line is approximately $\frac{14.5 - 3.3}{7 - 1}$, which is equivalent to $\frac{11.2}{6}$, or approximately 1.87. Therefore, of the given choices, 2 is closest to the slope of the line of best fit shown.

Choice A is incorrect and may result from conceptual or calculation errors. *Choice B* is incorrect and may result from conceptual or calculation errors. *Choice C* is incorrect and may result from conceptual or calculation errors.

QUESTION 3

The correct answer is 110. Let *x* represent the total number of items in the sample. It's given that 80% of the items are faulty and that there are 88 faulty items in the sample. Therefore, 80% of *x* is 88. Since 80% can be rewritten as $\frac{80}{100}$, it follows that $\frac{80}{100}x = 88$. Multiplying both sides of this equation by 100 yields $80x = 8{,}800$. Dividing both sides of this equation by 80 yields $x = 110$. Therefore, there are 110 total items in the sample.

QUESTION 4

Choice D is correct. It's given that function g is exponential. Therefore, an equation defining g can be written in the form $g(x) = a(b)^x$, where a and b are constants. The table shows that when $x = 0$, $g(x) = 1$. Substituting 0 for x and 1 for $g(x)$ in the equation $g(x) = a(b)^x$ yields $1 = a(b)^0$, which is equivalent to $1 = a$. Substituting 1 for a in the equation $g(x) = a(b)^x$ yields $g(x) = (b)^x$. The table also shows that when $x = 1$, $g(x) = \frac{1}{25}$. Substituting 1 for x and $\frac{1}{25}$ for $g(x)$ in the equation $g(x) = (b)^x$ yields $\frac{1}{25} = (b)^1$, which is equivalent to $\frac{1}{25} = b$. Substituting $\frac{1}{25}$ for b in the equation $g(x) = (b)^x$ yields $g(x) = \left(\frac{1}{25}\right)^x$.

Choice A is incorrect. For this function, $g(1)$ is equal to -25, not $\frac{1}{25}$. *Choice B* is incorrect. For this function, $g(1)$ is equal to $-\frac{1}{25}$, not $\frac{1}{25}$. *Choice C* is incorrect. For this function, $g(1)$ is equal to 25, not $\frac{1}{25}$.

QUESTION 5

Choice C is correct. It's given that $8x = 6$. Multiplying each side of this equation by 9 yields $72x = 54$. Therefore, the value of $72x$ is 54.

Choice A is incorrect. This is the value of $4x$, not $72x$. *Choice B* is incorrect and may result from conceptual or calculation errors. *Choice D* is incorrect and may result from conceptual or calculation errors.

QUESTION 6

Choice A is correct. For positive values of a, $\frac{a^m}{a^n} = a^{(m-n)}$, where m and n are integers. Since it's given that $h > 0$ and $q > 0$, this property can be applied to rewrite the given expression as $(h^{(15-5)})(q^{(7-21)})$, which is equivalent to $h^{10}q^{-14}$. For positive values of a, $a^{-n} = \frac{1}{a^n}$. This property can be applied to rewrite the expression $h^{10}q^{-14}$ as $(h^{10})\left(\frac{1}{q^{14}}\right)$, which is equivalent to $\frac{h^{10}}{q^{14}}$.

Choice B is incorrect and may result from conceptual or calculation errors. *Choice C* is incorrect and may result from conceptual or calculation errors. *Choice D* is incorrect and may result from conceptual or calculation errors.

QUESTION 7

Choice A is correct. It's given that the estimate for the average weight of all boxes of oranges filled by the company in an 8-hour period is 23.1 pounds, with an associated margin of error of 0.19 pounds. It follows that plausible values for this average weight are between $23.1 - 0.19$ pounds and $23.1 + 0.19$ pounds. Therefore, plausible values for the average weight of all boxes of oranges filled by the company are between 22.91 pounds and 23.29 pounds.

Choice B is incorrect and may result from conceptual or calculation errors. *Choice C* is incorrect and may result from conceptual or calculation errors. *Choice D* is incorrect and may result from conceptual or calculation errors.

QUESTION 8

The correct answer is 42. The expression $(x + 6)$ is a factor of both terms on the left-hand side of the given equation. Therefore, the given equation can be written as $(x + 6)\left(\frac{1}{3} - \frac{1}{2}\right) = -8$, or $(x + 6)\left(-\frac{1}{6}\right) = -8$. Multiplying each side of this equation by -6 yields $x + 6 = 48$. Subtracting 6 from each side of this equation yields $x = 42$. Therefore, the value of x that is the solution to the given equation is 42.

QUESTION 9

Choice C is correct. Multiplying the given functions f and g yields $f(x) \cdot g(x) = (x^2 + bx)(9x^2 - 27x)$. Applying the distributive property to the right-hand side of this equation yields $f(x) \cdot g(x) = (x^2)(9x^2 - 27x) + (bx)(9x^2 - 27x)$. Applying the distributive property once again to the right-hand side of this equation yields $f(x) \cdot g(x) = (x^2)(9x^2) - (x^2)(27x) + (bx)(9x^2) - (bx)(27x)$, which is equivalent to $f(x) \cdot g(x) = 9x^4 - 27x^3 + 9bx^3 - 27bx^2$. Factoring out x^3 from the second and third terms yields $f(x) \cdot g(x) = 9x^4 + (-27 + 9b)x^3 - 27bx^2$. Since the left-hand sides of $f(x) \cdot g(x) = 9x^4 + (-27 + 9b)x^3 - 27bx^2$ and $f(x) \cdot g(x) = 9x^4 - 26x^3 - 3x^2$ are equal, it follows that $(-27 + 9b)x^3 = -26x^3$, or $-27 + 9b = -26$, and $-27bx^2 = -3x^2$, or $-27b = -3$. Adding 27 to each side of $-27 + 9b = -26$ yields $9b = 1$. Dividing each side of this equation by 9 yields $b = \frac{1}{9}$. Similarly, dividing each side of $-27b = -3$ by -27 yields $b = \frac{1}{9}$. Therefore, the value of b is $\frac{1}{9}$.

Choice A is incorrect and may result from conceptual or calculation errors.
Choice B is incorrect and may result from conceptual or calculation errors.
Choice D is incorrect and may result from conceptual or calculation errors.

QUESTION 10

Choice C is correct. A line in the xy-plane can be represented by an equation of the form $y = mx + b$, where m is the slope and b is the y-coordinate of the y-intercept of the line. It's given that line s passes through the point $(0, 0)$. Therefore, the y-coordinate of the y-intercept of line s is 0. It's also given that line s is parallel to the line represented by the equation $y = 18x + 2$. Since parallel lines have the same slope, it follows that the slope of line s is 18. Therefore, line s can be represented by the equation $y = mx + b$, where $m = 18$ and $b = 0$. Substituting 18 for m and 0 for b in $y = mx + b$ yields the equation $y = 18x + 0$, or $y = 18x$. If line s passes through the point $(4, d)$, then when $x = 4$, $y = d$ for the equation $y = 18x$. Substituting 4 for x and d for y in this equation yields $d = 18(4)$, or $d = 72$.

Choice A is incorrect. This is the y-coordinate of the y-intercept of the line represented by the equation $y = 18x + 2$. *Choice B* is incorrect. This is the slope of the line represented by the equation $y = 18x + 2$. *Choice D* is incorrect. The line represented by the equation $y = 18x + 2$, not line s, passes through the point $(4, 74)$.

QUESTION 11

Choice B is correct. It's given that $f(x) = (x - 44)(x - 46)$, which can be rewritten as $f(x) = x^2 - 90x + 2,024$. Since the coefficient of the x^2-term is positive, the graph of $y = f(x)$ in the xy-plane opens upward and reaches its minimum value at its vertex. For an equation in the form $f(x) = ax^2 + bx + c$, where a, b, and c

are constants, the *x*-coordinate of the vertex is $-\frac{b}{2a}$. For the equation

$f(x) = x^2 - 90x + 2{,}024$, $a = 1$, $b = -90$, and $c = 2{,}024$. It follows that the

x-coordinate of the vertex is $-\frac{(-90)}{2(1)}$, or 45. Therefore, $f(x)$ reaches its minimum when the value of *x* is 45.

Alternate approach: The graph of $y = f(x)$ in the *xy*-plane is a parabola. The value of *x* for the vertex of a parabola is the *x*-value of the midpoint between the two *x*-intercepts of the parabola. Since it's given that $f(x) = (x - 44)(x - 46)$, it follows that the two *x*-intercepts of the graph of $y = f(x)$ in the *xy*-plane occur when $x = 44$ and $x = 46$, or at the points (44, 0) and (46, 0). The midpoint between

two points, (x_1, y_1) and (x_2, y_2), is $\left(\frac{x_1 + x_2}{2}, \frac{y_1 + y_2}{2}\right)$. Therefore, the midpoint

between (44, 0) and (46, 0) is $\left(\frac{44 + 46}{2}, \frac{0 + 0}{2}\right)$, or (45, 0). It follows that $f(x)$

reaches its minimum when the value of *x* is 45.

Choice A is incorrect. This is one of the *x*-coordinates of the *x*-intercepts of the graph of $y = f(x)$ in the *xy*-plane. *Choice C* is incorrect. This is one of the *x*-coordinates of the *x*-intercepts of the graph of $y = f(x)$ in the *xy*-plane. *Choice D* is incorrect. This is the *y*-coordinate of the vertex of the graph of $y = f(x)$ in the *xy*-plane.

QUESTION 12

The correct answer is 153. Since it's given that $\overline{PQ}$ is parallel to $\overline{XY}$ and angle *Y* is a right angle, angle *ZQP* is also a right angle. Angle *ZPQ* is complementary to angle *XZY*, which means its measure, in degrees, is 90 – 63, or 27. Since angle *XPQ* is supplementary to angle *ZPQ*, its measure, in degrees, is 180 – 27, or 153.

QUESTION 13

Choice A is correct. It's given that the four odd integers are consecutive, ordered from least to greatest, and that the first odd integer is represented by *x*. It follows that the second odd integer is represented by $x + 2$, the third odd integer is represented by $x + 4$, and the fourth odd integer is represented by $x + 6$. Therefore, the product of 12 and the fourth odd integer is represented by $12(x + 6)$, and 26 less than the sum of the first and third odd integers is represented by $x + (x + 4) - 26$. Since the product of 12 and the fourth odd integer is at most 26 less than the sum of the first and third odd integers, it follows that $12(x + 6) \le x + (x + 4) - 26$.

Choice B is incorrect and may result from conceptual or calculation errors. *Choice C* is incorrect and may result from conceptual or calculation errors. *Choice D* is incorrect and may result from conceptual or calculation errors.

QUESTION 14

The correct answer is $\frac{2}{7}$. It's given that the system has infinitely many solutions.

A system of two linear equations has infinitely many solutions if and only if the two linear equations are equivalent. Multiplying each side of the first equation

in the system by $\frac{35}{4}$ yields $\frac{35}{4}\left(\frac{2}{5}x + \frac{7}{5}y\right) = \frac{35}{4}\left(\frac{2}{7}\right)$, or $\frac{7}{2}x + \frac{49}{4}y = \frac{5}{2}$. Since this

equation is equivalent to the second equation and has the same right side as the second equation, the coefficients of x and y, respectively, should also

be the same. It follows that $g = \frac{7}{2}$ and $k = \frac{49}{4}$. Therefore, the value of $\frac{g}{k}$ is $\frac{\frac{7}{2}}{\frac{49}{4}}$,

or $\frac{2}{7}$. Note that 2/7, .2857, 0.285, and 0.286 are examples of ways to enter a

correct answer.

QUESTION 15

Choice B is correct. The linear relationship between x and y can be represented by an equation of the form $y - y_1 = m(x - x_1)$, where m is the slope of the graph of the equation in the xy-plane and (x_1, y_1) is a point on the graph. The slope of a line can be found using two points on the line and the slope formula

$m = \frac{y_2 - y_1}{x_2 - x_1}$. Each value of x and its corresponding value of y in the table can

be represented by a point (x, y). Substituting the points (−s, 21) and (s, 15) for

(x_1, y_1) and (x_2, y_2), respectively, in the slope formula yields $m = \frac{15 - 21}{s - (-s)}$, which

gives $m = \frac{-6}{2s}$, or $m = -\frac{3}{s}$. Substituting $-\frac{3}{s}$ for m and the point (s, 15) for (x_1, y_1)

in the equation $y - y_1 = m(x - x_1)$ yields $y - 15 = -\frac{3}{s}(x - s)$. Distributing $-\frac{3}{s}$ on the

right-hand side of this equation yields $y - 15 = -\frac{3x}{s} + 3$. Adding 15 to each side

of this equation yields $y = -\frac{3x}{s} + 18$. Multiplying each side of this equation

by s yields $sy = -3x + 18s$. Adding 3x to each side of this equation yields $3x + sy = 18s$. Therefore, the equation $3x + sy = 18s$ represents this relationship.

Choice A is incorrect and may result from conceptual or calculation errors.
Choice C is incorrect and may result from conceptual or calculation errors.
Choice D is incorrect and may result from conceptual or calculation errors.

QUESTION 16

The correct answer is $\frac{35}{2}$. Subtracting the second equation from the first

equation yields $(y + k) - (y - k) = x + 26 - (x^2 - 5x)$, or $2k = -x^2 + 6x + 26$. This is equivalent to $x^2 - 6x + (2k - 26) = 0$. It's given that the system has exactly one distinct real solution; therefore, this equation has exactly one distinct real solution. An equation of the form $ax^2 + bx + c = 0$, where a, b, and c are constants, has exactly one distinct real solution when the discriminant, $b^2 - 4ac$, is equal to 0. The equation $x^2 - 6x + (2k - 26) = 0$ is of this form, where a = 1, b = −6, and c = 2k − 26. Substituting these values into the discriminant, $b^2 - 4ac$, yields $(-6)^2 - 4(1)(2k - 26)$. Setting the discriminant equal to 0 yields $(-6)^2 - 4(1)(2k - 26) = 0$, or $-8k + 140 = 0$. Subtracting 140 from both sides of this equation yields $-8k = -140$. Dividing both sides of this equation by −8 yields

$k = \frac{35}{2}$. Note that 35/2 and 17.5 are examples of ways to enter a correct answer.

QUESTION 17

Choice D is correct. It's given that the function f is defined by $f(x) = \frac{1}{2}(x + 6)$.

Substituting 4 for x in the given function yields $f(4) = \frac{1}{2}(4 + 6)$, or f(4) = 5.

Therefore, the value of f(4) is 5.

Choice A is incorrect. This is the value of $2(4 + 6)$, not $\frac{1}{2}(4 + 6)$. *Choice B* is incorrect. This is the value of $2 + (4 + 6)$, not $\frac{1}{2}(4 + 6)$. *Choice C* is incorrect. This is the value of $4 + 6$, not $\frac{1}{2}(4 + 6)$.

QUESTION 18

Choice A is correct. It's given that the banner's length x, in inches, is 24 inches longer than its width, in inches. It follows that the banner's width, in inches, can be represented by the expression $x - 24$. The area of a rectangle is the product of its length and its width. It's given that the area of the banner is 2,661 square inches, so it follows that $2,661 = x(x - 24)$, or $2,661 = x^2 - 24x$. Subtracting 2,661 from each side of this equation yields $0 = x^2 - 24x - 2,661$. Therefore, the equation that represents this situation is $0 = x^2 - 24x - 2661$.

Choice B is incorrect and may result from representing the width, in inches, of the banner as $24 - x$, rather than $x - 24$. *Choice C* is incorrect and may result from representing the width, in inches, of the banner as $x + 24$, rather than $x - 24$. *Choice D* is incorrect and may result from conceptual or calculation errors.

QUESTION 19

Choice D is correct. The volume, V, of a right circular cone is given by the formula $V = \frac{1}{3}\pi r^2 h$, where πr^2 is the area of the circular base of the cone and h is the height. It's given that this right circular cone has a volume of $71,148\pi$ cubic centimeters and the area of its base is $5,929\pi$ square centimeters. Substituting $71,148\pi$ for V and $5,929\pi$ for πr^2 in the formula $V = \frac{1}{3}\pi r^2 h$ yields $71,148\pi = \left(\frac{1}{3}\right)(5,929\pi)(h)$. Dividing each side of this equation by $5,929\pi$ yields $12 = \frac{h}{3}$. Multiplying each side of this equation by 3 yields $36 = h$. Let s represent the slant height, in centimeters, of this cone. A right triangle is formed by the radius, r, height, h, and slant height, s, of this cone, where r and h are the legs of the triangle and s is the hypotenuse. Using the Pythagorean theorem, the equation $r^2 + h^2 = s^2$ represents this relationship. Because $5,929\pi$ is the area of the base and the area of the base is πr^2, it follows that $5,929\pi = \pi r^2$. Dividing both sides of this equation by π yields $5,929 = r^2$. Substituting 5,929 for r^2 and 36 for h in the equation $r^2 + h^2 = s^2$ yields $5,929 + 36^2 = s^2$, which is equivalent to $5,929 + 1,296 = s^2$, or $7,225 = s^2$. Taking the positive square root of both sides of this equation yields $85 = s$. Therefore, the slant height of the cone is 85 centimeters.

Choice A is incorrect. This is one-third of the height, in centimeters, not the slant height, in centimeters, of this cone. *Choice B* is incorrect. This is the height, in centimeters, not the slant height, in centimeters, of this cone. *Choice C* is incorrect. This is the radius, in centimeters, of the base, not the slant height, in centimeters, of this cone.

QUESTION 20

Choice D is correct. Dividing each side of the second equation in the given system by 4 yields $7x + 6y = 5$. It follows that the two equations in the given system are equivalent and any point that lies on the graph of one equation will also lie on the graph of the other equation. Substituting r for y in the equation $7x + 6y = 5$ yields $7x + 6r = 5$. Subtracting $6r$ from each side of this equation yields $7x = -6r + 5$. Dividing each side of this equation by 7 yields $x = -\frac{6r}{7} + \frac{5}{7}$.

Therefore, the point $\left(-\frac{6r}{7} + \frac{5}{7}, r\right)$ lies on the graph of each equation in the

xy-plane for each real number *r*.

Choice A is incorrect. Substituting *r* for *x* in the equation $7x + 6y = 5$ yields
$7r + 6y = 5$. Subtracting $7r$ from each side of this equation yields $6y = -7r + 5$.

Dividing each side of this equation by 6 yields $y = -\frac{7r}{6} + \frac{5}{6}$. Therefore, the

point $\left(r, -\frac{7r}{6} + \frac{5}{6}\right)$, not the point $\left(r, -\frac{6r}{7} + \frac{5}{7}\right)$, lies on the graph of each equation.

Choice B is incorrect. Substituting *r* for *x* in the equation $7x + 6y = 5$ yields
$7r + 6y = 5$. Subtracting $7r$ from each side of this equation yields $6y = -7r + 5$.

Dividing each side of this equation by 6 yields $y = -\frac{7r}{6} + \frac{5}{6}$. Therefore, the

point $\left(r, -\frac{7r}{6} + \frac{5}{6}\right)$, not the point $\left(r, -\frac{7r}{6} + \frac{5}{6}\right)$, lies on the graph of each equation.

Choice C is incorrect. Substituting $\frac{r}{4} + 5$ for *x* in the equation $7x + 6y = 5$ yields

$7\left(\frac{r}{4} + 5\right) + 6y = 5$, or $\left(\frac{7r}{4} + 35\right) + 6y = 5$. Subtracting $\left(\frac{7r}{4} + 35\right)$ from each side of

this equation yields $6y = -\frac{7r}{4} - 35 + 5$, or $6y = -\frac{7r}{4} - 30$. Dividing each side of

this equation by 6 yields $y = -\frac{7r}{24} - 5$. Therefore, the point $\left(\frac{r}{4} + 5, -\frac{7r}{24} - 5\right)$, not

the point $\left(\frac{r}{4} + 5, -\frac{r}{4} + 20\right)$, lies on the graph of each equation.

QUESTION 21

Choice A is correct. It's given that the cost of renting a carpet cleaner is $52 for
the first day and $26 for each additional day. Therefore, the cost $C(d)$, in dollars,
of renting the carpet cleaner for *d* days is the sum of the cost for the first day,
$52, and the cost for the additional $d - 1$ days, $26($d - 1$)$. It follows that
$C(d) = 52 + 26(d - 1)$, which is equivalent to $C(d) = 52 + 26d - 26$, or
$C(d) = 26d + 26$.

Choice B is incorrect. This function gives the cost of renting a carpet cleaner
for *d* days if the cost is $78, not $52, for the first day and $26 for each
additional day. *Choice C* is incorrect. This function gives the cost of renting a
carpet cleaner for *d* days if the cost is $26, not $52, for the first day and $52,
not $26, for each additional day. *Choice D* is incorrect. This function gives the
cost of renting a carpet cleaner for *d* days if the cost is $130, not $52, for the
first day and $52, not $26, for each additional day.

QUESTION 22

Choice B is correct. It's given that the speed of a vehicle is increasing at a rate
of 7.3 meters per second squared. It's given to use 1 mile = 1,609 meters. There
are 60 seconds in 1 minute; therefore, 60^2 or 3,600 seconds squared is equal to
1 minute squared. It follows that the rate of 7.3 meters per second squared is

equivalent to $\left(\frac{7.3 \text{ meters}}{1 \text{ second squared}}\right)\left(\frac{1 \text{ mile}}{1,609 \text{ meters}}\right)\left(\frac{3,600 \text{ seconds squared}}{1 \text{ minute squared}}\right)$,

or approximately 16.33 miles per minute squared. The rate, in miles per minute
squared, rounded to the nearest tenth is 16.3.

Choice A is incorrect and may result from conceptual or calculation errors.
Choice C is incorrect and may result from conceptual or calculation errors.
Choice D is incorrect and may result from conceptual or calculation errors.

Scoring Your Paper SAT Practice Test #7

Congratulations on completing an SAT® practice test. To score your test, follow the instructions in this scoring guide.

IMPORTANT: *This scoring guide is for students who completed SAT Practice Test #7 in The Official SAT Study Guide™. We recommend reading through these instructions and explanations before scoring so that you understand the specifics and limitations of scoring this practice test.*

The total score on your practice test reflects the sum of the (1) Reading and Writing and (2) Math section scores, as indicated below. If you decided to take both the lower- and higher-difficulty modules, choose which one you will use to score.

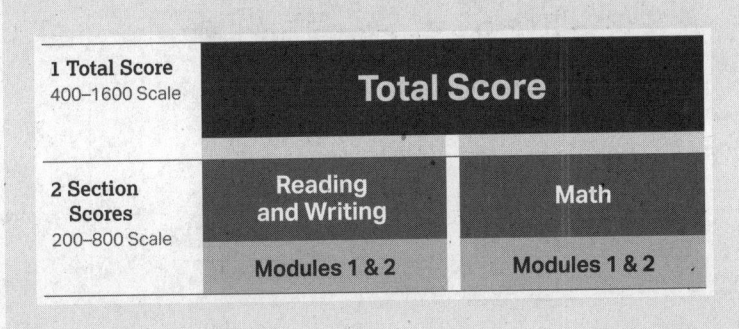

1 Total Score 400–1600 Scale	Total Score	
2 Section Scores 200–800 Scale	Reading and Writing	Math
	Modules 1 & 2	Modules 1 & 2

Scores Overview

Each assessment in the SAT Suite (SAT, PSAT/NMSQT®, PSAT™ 10, and PSAT™ 8/9) reports test scores on a common scale.

For more details about scores, visit **sat.org/scores**.

How to Calculate Your Practice Test Scores

The worksheets on the pages that follow help you calculate your test scores.

GET SET UP

1 In addition to your practice test, you'll need the answer keys and conversion tables at the end of this scoring guide.

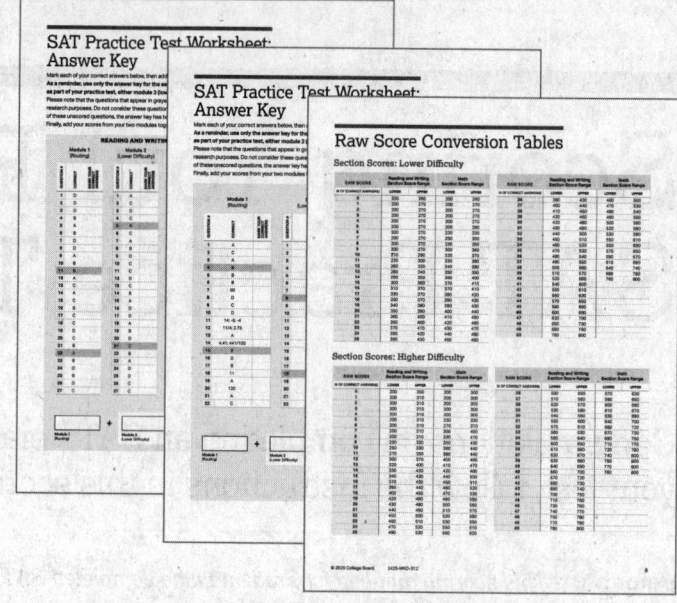

SCORE YOUR PRACTICE TEST

2 Compare your answers to the answer keys later in this scoring guide and count up the total number of correct answers for each section. Write the number of correct answers for each section in the boxes at the bottom of the pages.

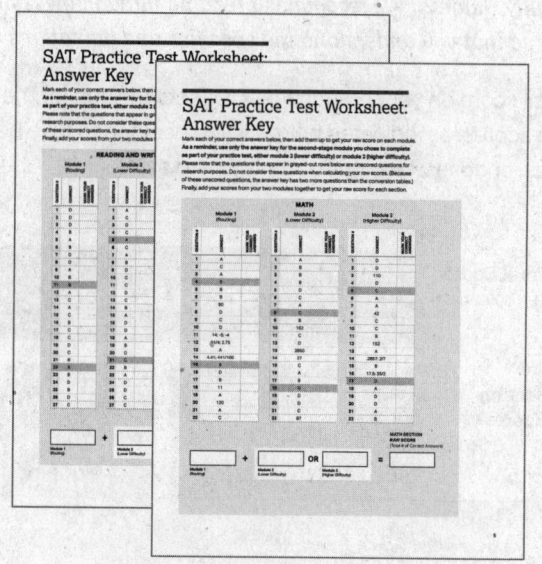

CALCULATE YOUR SCORES

3 Using your marked-up answer keys and the conversion tables, follow the directions on the SAT Practice Test Worksheet: Section and Total Scores page to get your section and total scores.

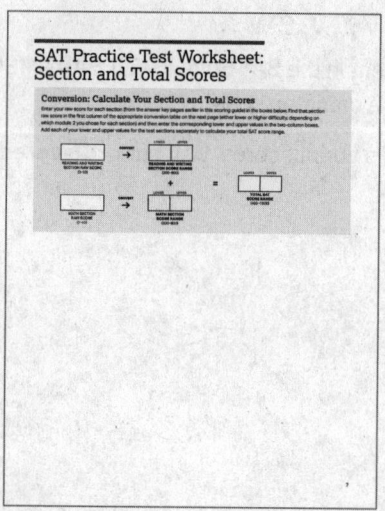

Get Section and Total Scores

Section and total scores for this paper version of SAT Practice Test #7 are expressed as ranges. That's because the scoring method described in this guide is a different (and therefore less precise) version of the one used in the actual adaptive test.

This practice test contains three modules for each test section: (1) a single first-stage (routing) module and (2) two second-stage modules. The two second-stage modules differ by average question difficulty and are marked as either "module 2 (lower difficulty)" or "module 2 (higher difficulty)." You get to choose which module 2 you would like to take for this practice test. **An actual testing experience consists of one routing and one second-stage module per test section.** To obtain your Reading and Writing and Math section scores, you will refer to the answer key and conversion table for the second-stage module you chose (either lower or higher difficulty).

GET YOUR READING AND WRITING SECTION SCORE

Calculate your SAT Reading and Writing section score (it's on a scale of 200–800).

1 Use the answer key for Reading and Writing to find the number of questions in module 1 and the module 2 you chose (either lower or higher difficulty) that you answered correctly.

2 To determine your Reading and Writing raw score, add the number of correct answers you got in module 1 and the module 2 you chose (either lower or higher difficulty). **Exclude the questions in grayed-out rows in your calculation.**

3 Use the appropriate Raw Score Conversion Table to turn your raw score into your Reading and Writing section score.

4 The lower and upper values associated with your raw score establish the range of scores you might expect to receive had this been an actual adaptive test.

GET YOUR MATH SECTION SCORE

Calculate your SAT Math section score (it's on a scale of 200–800).

1 Use the answer key for Math to find the number of questions in module 1 and the module 2 you chose (either lower or higher difficulty) that you answered correctly.

2 To determine your Math raw score, add the number of correct answers you got in module 1 and the module 2 you chose (either lower or higher difficulty). **Exclude the questions in grayed-out rows in your calculation.**

3 Use the appropriate Raw Score Conversion Table to turn your raw score into your Math section score.

4 The lower and upper values associated with your raw score establish the range of scores you might expect to receive had this been an actual adaptive test.

GET YOUR TOTAL SCORE

Add together the lower values for the Reading and Writing and Math sections, and then add together the upper values for the two sections. The result is your total score, expressed as a range, for this SAT practice test. The total score is on a scale of 400–1600.

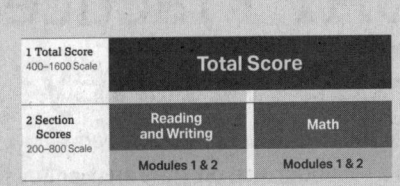

1 Total Score 400–1600 Scale	Total Score	
2 Section Scores 200–800 Scale	Reading and Writing	Math
	Modules 1 & 2	Modules 1 & 2

Your total score on this SAT practice test is the sum of your Reading and Writing section score and your Math section score. For this practice test, you'll receive a lower and upper score for each test section and the total score. This is the range of scores that you might expect to receive.

Use the worksheets on the pages that follow to calculate your section and total scores.

SAT Practice Test Worksheet: Answer Key

Mark each of your correct answers below, then add them up to get your raw score on each module. **As a reminder, use only the answer key for the second-stage module you chose to complete as part of your practice test, either module 2 (lower difficulty) or module 2 (higher difficulty).** Please note that the questions that appear in grayed-out rows below are unscored questions for research purposes. Do not consider these questions when calculating your raw scores. (Because of these unscored questions, the answer key has two more questions than the conversion tables.) Finally, add your scores from your two modules together to get your raw score for each section.

READING AND WRITING

Module 1 (Routing)			Module 2 (Lower Difficulty)			Module 2 (Higher Difficulty)		
QUESTION #	CORRECT	MARK YOUR CORRECT ANSWERS	QUESTION #	CORRECT	MARK YOUR CORRECT ANSWERS	QUESTION #	CORRECT	MARK YOUR CORRECT ANSWERS
1	D		1	A		1	B	
2	D		2	C		2	D	
3	D		3	D		3	A	
4	B		4	C		4	D	
5	A		5	A		5	C	
6	B		6	C		6	B	
7	D		7	A		7	D	
8	D		8	B		8	D	
9	A		9	D		9	B	
10	B		10	C		10	A	
11	B		11	C		11	B	
12	A		12	D		12	D	
13	C		13	C		13	C	
14	A		14	B		14	B	
15	C		15	A		15	C	
16	B		16	D		16	B	
17	C		17	D		17	C	
18	C		18	A		18	D	
19	C		19	B		19	A	
20	C		20	D		20	B	
21	B		21	C		21	D	
22	A		22	B		22	A	
23	B		23	A		23	D	
24	D		24	D		24	D	
25	B		25	D		25	C	
26	D		26	C		26	D	
27	C		27	C		27	A	

READING AND WRITING SECTION RAW SCORE
(Total # of Correct Answers)

[ ] Module 1 (Routing) **+** [ ] Module 2 (Lower Difficulty) **OR** [ ] Module 2 (Higher Difficulty) **=** [ ]

SAT Practice Test Worksheet: Answer Key

Mark each of your correct answers below, then add them up to get your raw score on each module. **As a reminder, use only the answer key for the second-stage module you chose to complete as part of your practice test, either module 2 (lower difficulty) or module 2 (higher difficulty).** Please note that the questions that appear in grayed-out rows below are unscored questions for research purposes. Do not consider these questions when calculating your raw scores. (Because of these unscored questions, the answer key has two more questions than the conversion tables.) Finally, add your scores from your two modules together to get your raw score for each section.

MATH

Module 1 (Routing)			Module 2 (Lower Difficulty)			Module 2 (Higher Difficulty)		
QUESTION #	CORRECT	MARK YOUR CORRECT ANSWERS	QUESTION #	CORRECT	MARK YOUR CORRECT ANSWERS	QUESTION #	CORRECT	MARK YOUR CORRECT ANSWERS
1	A		1	A		1	D	
2	C		2	B		2	D	
3	A		3	B		3	110	
4	B		4	B		4	D	
5	B		5	D		5	C	
6	B		6	C		6	A	
7	90		7	A		7	A	
8	D		8	C		8	42	
9	C		9	B		9	C	
10	D		10	162		10	C	
11	14; -5; -4		11	C		11	B	
12	11/4; 2.75		12	D		12	153	
13	A		13	2850		13	A	
14	4.41; 441/100		14	27		14	.2857; 2/7	
15	5		15	C		15	B	
16	D		16	A		16	17.5; 35/2	
17	B		17	9		17	D	
18	11		18	D		18	A	
19	A		19	D		19	D	
20	120		20	D		20	D	
21	A		21	C		21	A	
22	C		22	87		22	B	

MATH SECTION RAW SCORE
(Total # of Correct Answers)

[ ] **+** [ ] **OR** [ ] **=** [ ]

Module 1 (Routing) | Module 2 (Lower Difficulty) | Module 2 (Higher Difficulty)

Understanding the SAT Practice Test Conversion Tables and Total Score Ranges

As mentioned earlier in this scoring guide, the scoring method for the practice tests that appear in *The Official SAT Study Guide* is different (and therefore less precise) than the method used in the actual adaptive test. Your practice test may result in a larger score range than what you hoped to see, but it's not feasible to estimate your performance on the practice tests in the study guide as precisely as we could for an actual test. As the test developers, College Board is committed to providing the most accurate conversion possible to help you understand your scores and guide your practice most effectively.

There are two conversion tables in this scoring guide. Use the conversion table labelled lower difficulty if you took module 2 (lower difficulty). Use the conversion table labelled higher difficulty if you took module 2 (higher difficulty). You might need both conversion tables if you took the lower-difficulty option for one section (e.g., Reading and Writing) and the higher-difficulty option for the other section (e.g., Math).

Because the lower- and higher-difficulty conversion tables share the same questions for module 1 (routing), you may encounter different score ranges based on the conversion table you use. For example, if you got all the module 1 (routing) questions correct, the lower-difficulty conversion table and the higher-difficulty conversion table will give you different score ranges. This is to be expected because the conversion tables account for all items within the two modules that make up the test. Answering only items on the first half of the test assumes you answered the other questions (module 2) incorrectly. Recall that when taking the actual SAT on test day, the test will adapt to your ability based on how you perform on the first half. Because of the differences between the actual test and providing a paper approximation of that (the practice test you're currently scoring), you should select the second-stage module that feels most appropriate for you. For example, if you were to answer all items on the first module correctly on the actual test, you would not be routed to the easier second-stage module. The converse would also be true. For many users of moderate ability either second-stage would be acceptable, but very high or low performers should be cautioned about taking the second-stage module that doesn't align well with their ability.

SAT Practice Test Worksheet: Section and Total Scores

Conversion: Calculate Your Section and Total Scores

Enter your raw score for each section (from the answer key pages earlier in this scoring guide) in the boxes below. Find that section raw score in the first column of the appropriate conversion table on the next page (either lower or higher difficulty, depending on which module 2 you chose for each section) and then enter the corresponding lower and upper values in the two-column boxes. Add each of your lower and upper values for the test sections separately to calculate your total SAT score range.

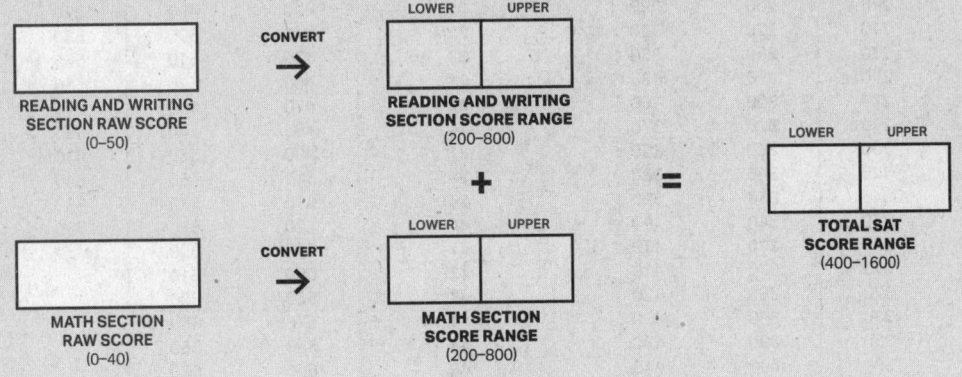

Raw Score Conversion Tables

Section Scores: Lower Difficulty

RAW SCORE (# OF CORRECT ANSWERS)	Reading and Writing Section Score Range		Math Section Score Range	
	LOWER	UPPER	LOWER	UPPER
0	200	260	200	260
1	200	270	200	270
2	200	270	200	270
3	200	270	200	270
4	200	270	200	270
5	200	270	200	290
6	200	270	220	320
7	200	270	250	350
8	200	270	290	350
9	200	270	300	360
10	210	290	320	370
11	220	300	330	380
12	260	320	340	380
13	280	340	350	390
14	290	350	360	400
15	300	360	370	410
16	310	370	370	410
17	330	370	380	420
18	330	370	390	430
19	340	380	390	430
20	350	390	400	440
21	360	400	410	450
22	360	400	420	460
23	370	410	430	470
24	380	420	440	480
25	390	430	450	490

RAW SCORE (# OF CORRECT ANSWERS)	Reading and Writing Section Score Range		Math Section Score Range	
	LOWER	UPPER	LOWER	UPPER
26	390	430	460	500
27	400	440	470	530
28	410	450	480	540
29	420	460	490	550
30	420	480	500	560
31	430	490	520	580
32	440	500	530	590
33	450	510	550	610
34	460	520	550	630
35	470	530	570	650
36	480	540	590	670
37	490	550	610	690
38	500	560	640	740
39	510	570	680	780
40	520	580	760	800
41	540	600		
42	550	610		
43	560	620		
44	570	650		
45	580	660		
46	600	680		
47	620	700		
48	650	730		
49	680	760		
50	760	800		

Section Scores: Higher Difficulty

RAW SCORE (# OF CORRECT ANSWERS)	Reading and Writing Section Score Range		Math Section Score Range	
	LOWER	UPPER	LOWER	UPPER
0	200	300	200	300
1	200	310	200	300
2	200	310	200	300
3	200	310	200	300
4	200	310	200	300
5	200	310	230	330
6	200	310	270	370
7	200	310	300	400
8	200	310	330	410
9	230	320	350	430
10	250	330	360	440
11	270	350	380	440
12	300	370	400	460
13	320	400	410	470
14	330	420	420	480
15	340	430	440	500
16	370	430	450	510
17	390	440	460	520
18	400	450	470	530
19	420	460	490	550
20	430	480	500	560
21	440	490	510	570
22	450	500	520	580
23	460	510	530	590
24	470	520	550	610
25	490	530	560	620

RAW SCORE (# OF CORRECT ANSWERS)	Reading and Writing Section Score Range		Math Section Score Range	
	LOWER	UPPER	LOWER	UPPER
26	500	550	570	630
27	510	560	590	650
28	520	570	600	660
29	530	580	610	670
30	540	590	630	690
31	550	600	640	700
32	570	610	660	720
33	580	630	670	730
34	590	640	690	750
35	600	650	710	770
36	610	660	720	780
37	620	670	740	800
38	630	680	760	800
39	640	690	770	800
40	660	700	780	800
41	670	720		
42	680	730		
43	690	740		
44	700	750		
45	710	760		
46	730	760		
47	740	770		
48	750	780		
49	770	790		
50	780	800		

2425-WKD-312

The SAT®

Practice Test #8

Make time to take the practice test. It is one of the best ways to get ready for the SAT.

Note: The practice tests in this guide include two second modules so that you can experience both the lower- and higher-difficulty modules. On the actual test, you will be presented with only one second module.

After you have taken the practice test, score it right away using materials provided in *The Official SAT Study Guide*.

This version of the SAT Practice Test is for students using this Study Guide. As a reminder, most students taking the SAT will do so using Bluebook™, the digital testing application. To best prepare for test day, download Bluebook at **bluebook.app.collegeboard.org** to take the practice test in the digital format.

Test begins on the next page.

Reading and Writing

27 QUESTIONS

1

As Mexico's first president from an Indigenous community, Benito Juarez became one of the most _____ figures in his country's history: among the many significant accomplishments of his long tenure in office (1858–1872), Juarez consolidated the authority of the national government and advanced the rights of Indigenous peoples.

Which choice completes the text with the most logical and precise word or phrase?

A) unpredictable

B) important

C) secretive

D) ordinary

2

Artist Marilyn Dingle's intricate, coiled baskets are _____ sweetgrass and palmetto palm. Following a Gullah technique that originated in West Africa, Dingle skillfully winds a thin palm frond around a bunch of sweetgrass with the help of a "sewing bone" to create the basket's signature look that no factory can reproduce.

Which choice completes the text with the most logical and precise word or phrase?

A) indicated by

B) handmade from

C) represented by

D) collected with

Unauthorized copying or reuse of any part of this page is illegal.

798

CONTINUE →

3

The Mule Bone, a 1930 play written by Zora Neale Hurston and Langston Hughes, is perhaps the best-known of the few examples of _____ in literature. Most writers prefer working alone, and given that working together cost Hurston and Hughes their friendship, it is not hard to see why.

Which choice completes the text with the most logical and precise word or phrase?

A) characterization

B) interpretation

C) collaboration

D) commercialization

4

Diego Velázquez was the leading artist in the court of King Philip IV of Spain during the seventeenth century, but his influence was hardly _____ Spain: realist and impressionist painters around the world employed his techniques and echoed elements of his style.

Which choice completes the text with the most logical and precise word or phrase?

A) derived from

B) recognized in

C) confined to

D) repressed by

5

Researchers and conservationists stress that biodiversity loss due to invasive species is _____. For example, people can take simple steps such as washing their footwear after travel to avoid introducing potentially invasive organisms into new environments.

Which choice completes the text with the most logical and precise word or phrase?

A) preventable

B) undeniable

C) common

D) concerning

6

Companies are providing consumers with more opportunities to purchase customized products than ever before. Whether buying customized sneakers, jewelry, or clothing, consumers can participate in the design of products to meet their specific needs and tastes. In turn, companies profit too: studies have shown that consumers are willing to pay more and wait longer for a customized product. Still, it can be difficult for companies to offer customization while keeping costs low, as the standard methods of mass production may not be able to accommodate making a unique product each time.

Which choice best describes the overall structure of the text?

A) It discusses several recent innovations in product manufacturing and then suggests some potential applications of those innovations.

B) It describes a company's recent success with new products and then explains multiple factors that may have contributed to that success.

C) It introduces a trend in consumer products and then explains how the trend both benefits and poses a challenge to companies.

D) It presents two contrasting product-marketing techniques and then provides examples of one of those techniques.

CONTINUE

7

The following text is from the 1924 poem "Cycle" by D'Arcy McNickle, who was a citizen of the Confederated Salish and Kootenai Tribes.

> There shall be new roads wending,
> A new beating of the drum—
> Men's eyes shall have fresh seeing,
> Grey lives reprise their span—
> But under the new sun's being,
> Completing what night began,
> There'll be the same backs bending,
> The same sad feet shall drum—
> When this night finds its ending
> And day shall have come....

Which choice best states the main purpose of the text?

A) To consider how the repetitiveness inherent in human life can be both rewarding and challenging

B) To question whether activities completed at one time of day are more memorable than those completed at another time of day

C) To refute the idea that joy is a more commonly experienced emotion than sadness is

D) To demonstrate how the experiences of individuals relate to the experiences of their communities

8

The north celestial pole (NCP)—the fixed point around which stars in the Northern Hemisphere (including the Sun) appear to rotate—is discernible only at night. Inspired by the navigational strategies of some insects and birds, researchers devised a method for locating the NCP in daytime using skylight polarization, which occurs as atmospheric particles scatter sunlight. A polarimetric camera captures images of polarization patterns, which rotate as the Sun's position in the sky changes; temporal variances across images can then be used to determine an observer's latitude and bearing relative to the NCP.

Which choice best describes the overall structure of the text?

A) It illustrates how most navigational tools utilize the NCP, recounts how researchers discovered that certain animals are able to navigate without using the NCP, and then proposes that this discovery could be used to avoid problems in navigation associated with reliance on the NCP.

B) It presents a celestial-based method of navigation, enumerates the comparative benefits of an alternative method used by certain animals that is based on an unrelated natural occurrence, and then indicates how researchers assessed the relative accuracy of the two methods.

C) It explains how the NCP is typically located, emphasizes a key difference between how humans and certain animals use the NCP for navigation, and then suggests an alternative way of using the NCP to improve existing navigational instruments.

D) It notes an obstacle to observing an astronomical phenomenon, mentions a navigational ability of certain animals that inspired a solution to that obstacle, and then explains how researchers used an optical device to mimic that ability.

CONTINUE

9

Culinary anthropologist Vertamae Smart-Grosvenor may be known for her decades of work in national public television and radio, but her book *Vibration Cooking: or, the Travel Notes of a Geechee Girl* is likely her most influential project. The 1970 book, whose title refers to Smart-Grosvenor's roots in the Low Country of South Carolina, was unusual for its time. It combined memoir, recipes, travel writing, and social commentary and challenged notions about conventions of food and cooking. Long admired by many, the book and its author have shaped contemporary approaches to writing about cuisine.

Which choice best describes the main idea of the text?

A) Smart-Grosvenor's unconventional book *Vibration Cooking: or, the Travel Notes of a Geechee Girl* is an important contribution to food writing.

B) Smart-Grosvenor held many different positions over her life, including reporter and food writer.

C) Smart-Grosvenor's groundbreaking book *Vibration Cooking: or, the Travel Notes of a Geechee Girl* didn't receive the praise it deserved when it was first published in 1970.

D) Smart-Grosvenor was a talented chef whose work inspired many people to start cooking for themselves.

10

The following text is from William Shakespeare's play *The Tempest*, first performed in 1611. Miranda has lived on an island with her father, Prospero, since she was three years old. Prospero has stated that Miranda likely does not remember anything other than her life on the island.

MIRANDA: 'Tis far off,
And rather like a dream than an assurance
That my remembrance warrants. Had I not
Four or five women once that tended me?

PROSPERO: Thou hadst, and more, Miranda.
But how is it
That this lives in thy mind? What seest thou else
In the dark backward and abysm of time?
If thou remember'st ought ere thou camest here,
How thou camest here thou mayst.

In the text, which point does Prospero most directly make about Miranda and her memories?

A) Miranda's reminiscences about her early childhood have a melancholy quality that betrays her discontented view of her current circumstances.

B) Miranda's doubts about the accuracy of one recollection of a place other than the island are clouding her judgment and seem to be making her reluctant to explore her recollection of traveling to the island.

C) Miranda's ability to summon details of an experience she had before arriving on the island suggests that she may also be able to summon details of her arrival on the island.

D) Miranda's impression of a scene is vague because she is remembering a scenario she had daydreamed about as a child rather than a scenario that had occurred in reality.

Unauthorized copying or reuse of any part of this page is illegal.

CONTINUE ➡

801

11

In a research paper, a student criticizes some historians of modern African politics, claiming that they have evaluated Patrice Lumumba, the first prime minister of what is now the Democratic Republic of the Congo, primarily as a symbol rather than in terms of his actions.

Which quotation from a work by a historian would best illustrate the student's claim?

A) "Lumumba is a difficult figure to evaluate due to the starkly conflicting opinions he inspired during his life and continues to inspire today."

B) "The available information makes it clear that Lumumba's political beliefs and values were largely consistent throughout his career."

C) "Lumumba's practical accomplishments can be passed over quickly; it is mainly as the personification of Congolese independence that he warrants scholarly attention."

D) "Many questions remain about Lumumba's ultimate vision for an independent Congo; without new evidence coming to light, these questions are likely to remain unanswered."

12

Researchers hypothesized that a decline in the population of dusky sharks near the mid-Atlantic coast of North America led to a decline in the population of eastern oysters in the region. Dusky sharks do not typically consume eastern oysters but do consume cownose rays, which are the main predators of the oysters.

Which finding, if true, would most directly support the researchers' hypothesis?

A) Declines in the regional abundance of dusky sharks' prey other than cownose rays are associated with regional declines in dusky shark abundance.

B) Eastern oyster abundance tends to be greater in areas with both dusky sharks and cownose rays than in areas with only dusky sharks.

C) Consumption of eastern oysters by cownose rays in the region substantially increased before the regional decline in dusky shark abundance began.

D) Cownose rays have increased in regional abundance as dusky sharks have decreased in regional abundance.

CONTINUE

13

The musical *Hadestown* was produced off-Broadway in New York in 2016. A revised version of the musical premiered on Broadway in 2019, in a larger production. In a review of the Broadway production, theater critic Jesse Green enthusiastically praised the musical's storytelling. However, Green also explained that he had seen the earlier version of *Hadestown* in 2016 and had found the storytelling to be very confusing. This suggests that in Green's view, _____

Which choice most logically completes the text?

A) the 2016 version of *Hadestown* had fewer storytelling problems than the 2019 version did.

B) *Hadestown* should have had a larger production in 2019 than it actually did.

C) the 2019 version of *Hadestown* was less enjoyable than the 2016 version.

D) *Hadestown* improved greatly between 2016 and its premiere on Broadway.

14

If some artifacts recovered from excavations of the settlement of Kuulo Kataa, in modern Ghana, date from the thirteenth century CE, that may lend credence to claims that the settlement was founded before or around that time. There is other evidence, however, strongly supporting a fourteenth century CE founding date for Kuulo Kataa. If both the artifact dates and the fourteenth century CE founding date are correct, that would imply that _____

Which choice most logically completes the text?

A) artifacts from the fourteenth century CE are more commonly recovered than are artifacts from the thirteenth century CE.

B) the artifacts originated elsewhere and eventually reached Kuulo Kataa through trade or migration.

C) Kuulo Kataa was founded by people from a different region than had previously been assumed.

D) excavations at Kuulo Kataa may have inadvertently damaged some artifacts dating to the fourteenth century CE.

15

Birds of many species ingest foods containing carotenoids, pigmented molecules that are converted into feather coloration. Coloration tends to be especially saturated in male birds' feathers, and because carotenoids also confer health benefits, the deeply saturated colors generally serve to communicate what is known as an honest signal of a bird's overall fitness to potential mates. However, ornithologist Allison J. Shultz and others have found that males in several species of the tanager genus *Ramphocelus* use microstructures in their feathers to manipulate light, creating the appearance of deeper saturation without the birds necessarily having to maintain a carotenoid-rich diet. These findings suggest that _____

Which choice most logically completes the text?

A) individual male tanagers can engage in honest signaling without relying on carotenoid consumption.

B) feather microstructures may be less effective than deeply saturated feathers for signaling overall fitness.

C) scientists have yet to determine why tanagers have a preference for mates with colorful appearances.

D) a male tanager's appearance may function as a dishonest signal of the individual's overall fitness.

Unauthorized copying or reuse of any part of this page is illegal.

CONTINUE

803

16

Formed in 1967 to foster political and economic stability within the Asia-Pacific region, the Association of Southeast Asian Nations was originally made up of five members: Thailand, the Philippines, Singapore, Malaysia, and Indonesia. By the end of the 1990s, the organization _____ its initial membership.

Which choice completes the text so that it conforms to the conventions of Standard English?

A) has doubled

B) had doubled

C) doubles

D) will double

17

In 1930, Japanese American artist Chiura Obata depicted the natural beauty of Yosemite National Park in two memorable woodcuts: *Evening at Carl Inn* and *Lake Basin in the High Sierra*. In 2019, _____ exhibited alongside 150 of Obata's other works in a single-artist show at the Smithsonian American Art Museum.

Which choice completes the text so that it conforms to the conventions of Standard English?

A) it was

B) they were

C) this was

D) some were

18

The city of Pompeii, which was buried in ash following the eruption of Mount Vesuvius in 79 CE, continues to be studied by archaeologists. Unfortunately, as _____ attest, archaeological excavations have disrupted ash deposits at the site, causing valuable information about the eruption to be lost.

Which choice completes the text so that it conforms to the conventions of Standard English?

A) researchers, Roberto Scandone and Christopher Kilburn,

B) researchers, Roberto Scandone and Christopher Kilburn

C) researchers Roberto Scandone and Christopher Kilburn

D) researchers Roberto Scandone, and Christopher Kilburn

19

Journalists have dubbed Gil Scott-Heron the "godfather of rap," a title that has appeared in hundreds of articles about him since the 1990s. Scott-Heron himself resisted the godfather _____ feeling that it didn't encapsulate his devotion to the broader African American blues music tradition as well as "bluesologist," the moniker he preferred.

Which choice completes the text so that it conforms to the conventions of Standard English?

A) nickname, however

B) nickname, however;

C) nickname, however,

D) nickname; however,

CONTINUE

20

Over twenty years ago, in a landmark experiment in the psychology of choice, professor Sheena Iyengar set up a jam-tasting booth at a grocery store. The number of jams available for tasting _____ some shoppers had twenty-four different options, others only six. Interestingly, the shoppers with fewer jams to choose from purchased more jam.

Which choice completes the text so that it conforms to the conventions of Standard English?

A) varied:

B) varied,

C) varied, while

D) varied while

21

Sociologist Todd Gitlin co-opted the term "recombinant," normally used in reference to genetic engineering, to describe serialized television shows of the 1980s. Gitlin's use of the term referenced TV studios' practice of repackaging successful narrative formulas as new _____ even shows that varied only slightly from other shows still attracted sizeable audiences.

Which choice completes the text so that it conforms to the conventions of Standard English?

A) content, in that era

B) content; in that era,

C) content in that era,

D) content, in that era,

22

Although those who migrated to California in 1849 dreamed of finding gold nuggets in streambeds, the state's richest deposits were buried deeply in rock, beyond the reach of individual prospectors. _____ by 1852, many had given up their fortune-hunting dreams and gone to work for one of the large companies capable of managing California's complex mining operations.

Which choice completes the text with the most logical transition?

A) Furthermore,

B) Still,

C) Consequently,

D) Next,

23

In 1974, Mexican chemist Mario Molina and US chemist F. Sherwood Rowland discovered that chemicals called CFCs were harmful to the ozone layer. Their research was extremely influential in the fight against CFCs. _____ it laid the foundation for a 1987 treaty that phased out the use of CFCs across the globe.

Which choice completes the text with the most logical transition?

A) Regardless,

B) Specifically,

C) However,

D) Earlier,

CONTINUE

24

While researching a topic, a student has taken the following notes:

- On January 3, 1959, Alaska became the 49th state to join the US.
- On August 21, 1959, Hawaii became the 50th state to join the US.
- A new 50-star US flag was unveiled the same day.

The student wants to emphasize the order in which Alaska and Hawaii became US states. Which choice most effectively uses relevant information from the notes to accomplish this goal?

A) Alaska, the 49th US state, became a state several months before Hawaii, the 50th state, did.

B) On August 21, 1959, a new 50-star US flag was unveiled.

C) The 49th and 50th states to join the US did so in the same year.

D) The same day that Hawaii became a US state— August 21, 1959—a new US flag was unveiled.

25

While researching a topic, a student has taken the following notes:

- Physicist Muluneh Abebe was working on a garment suited for both warm and cold conditions.
- He analyzed the emissivity, or ability to emit heat, of the materials he planned to use.
- Abebe found that reflective metal fibers emitted almost no heat and had an emissivity of 0.02.
- He found that silicon carbide fibers absorbed large amounts of heat and had an emissivity of 0.74.
- The amount of heat a material absorbs is equal to the amount of heat it emits.

The student wants to contrast the emissivity of reflective metal fibers with that of silicon carbide fibers. Which choice most effectively uses relevant information from the notes to accomplish this goal?

A) The ability of reflective metal fibers and silicon carbide fibers to emit heat was determined by an analysis of each material's emissivity.

B) The amount of heat a material absorbs is equal to the amount it emits, as evidenced in Abebe's analyses.

C) Though the reflective metal fibers and silicon carbide fibers had different rates of emissivity, Abebe planned to use both in a garment.

D) Whereas the reflective metal fibers had an emissivity of just 0.02, the silicon carbide fibers absorbed large amounts of heat, resulting in an emissivity of 0.74.

CONTINUE

26

While researching a topic, a student has taken the following notes:

- *Las sergas de Esplandián* was a novel popular in sixteenth-century Spain.

- The novel featured a fictional island inhabited solely by Black women and known as California.

- That same century, Spanish explorers learned of an "island" off the west coast of Mexico.

- They called it California after the island in the novel.

- The "island" was actually the peninsula now known as Baja California ("Lower California"), which lies to the south of the US state of California.

The student wants to emphasize the role a misconception played in the naming of a place. Which choice most effectively uses relevant information from the notes to accomplish this goal?

A) The novel *Las sergas de Esplandián* featured a fictional island known as California.

B) To the south of the US state of California lies Baja California ("Lower California"), originally called California after a fictional place.

C) In the sixteenth century, Spanish explorers learned of a peninsula off the west coast of Mexico and called it California.

D) Thinking it was an island, Spanish explorers called a peninsula California after an island in a popular novel.

27

While researching a topic, a student has taken the following notes:

- Most, but not all, of the Moon's oxygen comes from the Sun, via solar wind.

- Cosmochemist Kentaro Terada from Osaka University wondered if some of the unaccounted-for oxygen could be coming from Earth.

- In 2008, he analyzed data from the Japanese satellite Kaguya.

- Kaguya gathered data about gases and particles it encountered while orbiting the Moon.

- Based on the Kaguya data, Terada confirmed his suspicion that Earth is sending oxygen to the Moon.

The student wants to emphasize the aim of the research study. Which choice most effectively uses relevant information from the notes to accomplish this goal?

A) As it orbited the Moon, the Kaguya satellite collected data that was later analyzed by cosmochemist Kentaro Terada.

B) Before 2008, Kentaro Terada wondered if the Moon was receiving some of its oxygen from Earth.

C) Cosmochemist Kentaro Terada set out to determine whether some of the Moon's oxygen was coming from Earth.

D) Kentaro Terada's study determined that Earth is sending a small amount of oxygen to the Moon.

STOP

If you finish before time is called, you may check your work on this module only.
Do not turn to any other module in the test.

Reading and Writing

27 QUESTIONS

DIRECTIONS

The questions in this section address a number of important reading and writing skills. Each question includes one or more passages, which may include a table or graph. Read each passage and question carefully, and then choose the best answer to the question based on the passage(s).

All questions in this section are multiple-choice with four answer choices. Each question has a single best answer.

1

Predatory animals differ widely in how they _____ food for their young. Some leave dead prey nearby for their young to consume, some bring live prey to their young, and some feed their young directly from their own mouths.

Which choice completes the text with the most logical and precise word or phrase?

A) avoid

B) guess

C) provide

D) describe

2

One challenge of generating electricity from ocean waves is that wave power isn't _____: it varies in unpredictable ways that pose technological and planning problems for electricity generation.

Which choice completes the text with the most logical and precise word or phrase?

A) accidental

B) confident

C) expensive

D) consistent

3

For painter Jacob Lawrence, being _____ was an important part of the artistic process. Because he paid close attention to all the details of his Harlem neighborhood, Lawrence's artwork captured nuances in the beauty and vitality of the Black experience during the Harlem Renaissance and the Great Migration.

Which choice completes the text with the most logical and precise word or phrase?

A) skeptical

B) observant

C) critical

D) confident

4

In 1929 the *Atlantic Monthly* published several articles based on newly discovered letters allegedly exchanged between President Abraham Lincoln and a woman named Ann Rutledge. Historians were unable to _____ the authenticity of the letters, however, and quickly dismissed them as a hoax.

Which choice completes the text with the most logical and precise word or phrase?

A) validate

B) interpret

C) relate

D) accommodate

Unauthorized copying or reuse of any part of this page is illegal.

808

CONTINUE ▶

5

In 2007, computer scientist Luis von Ahn was working on converting printed books into a digital format. He found that some words were distorted enough that digital scanners couldn't recognize them, but most humans could easily read them. Based on that finding, von Ahn invented a simple security test to keep automated "bots" out of websites. The first version of the reCAPTCHA test asked users to type one known word and one of the many words scanners couldn't recognize. Correct answers proved the users were humans and added data to the book-digitizing project.

Which choice best states the main purpose of the text?

A) To discuss von Ahn's invention of reCAPTCHA

B) To explain how digital scanners work

C) To call attention to von Ahn's book-digitizing project

D) To indicate how popular reCAPTCHA is

6

The following text is adapted from Cynthia Kadohata's 2004 novel *Kira-Kira*.

[Uncle Katsuhisa] was as loud as my father was quiet. Even when he wasn't talking, he made a lot of noise, clearing his throat and sniffing and tapping his fingers.

©2004 by Cynthia Kadohata

Which choice best describes the function of the underlined sentence?

A) It lists the kinds of topics Uncle Katsuhisa enjoys discussing.

B) It suggests that Uncle Katsuhisa dislikes meeting new people.

C) It contrasts Uncle Katsuhisa with the narrator's father.

D) It describes a conversation between the narrator and the narrator's father.

7

Text 1
A tiny, unusual fossil in a piece of 99-million-year-old amber is of the extinct species *Oculudentavis khaungraae*. The *O. khaungraae* fossil consists of a rounded skull with a thin snout and a large eye socket. Because these features look like they are avian, or related to birds, researchers initially thought that the fossil might be the smallest avian dinosaur ever found.

Text 2
Paleontologists were excited to discover a second small fossil that is similar to the strange *O. khaungraae* fossil but has part of the lower body along with a birdlike skull. Detailed studies of both fossils revealed several traits that are found in lizards but not in dinosaurs or birds. Therefore, paleontologists think the two creatures were probably unusual lizards, even though the skulls looked avian at first.

Based on the texts, what would the paleontologists in Text 2 most likely say about the researchers' initial thought in Text 1?

A) It is understandable because the fossil does look like it could be related to birds, even though *O. khaungraae* is probably a lizard.

B) It is confusing because it isn't clear what caused the researchers to think that *O. khaungraae* might be related to birds.

C) It is flawed because the researchers mistakenly assumed that *O. khaungraae* must be a lizard.

D) It is reasonable because the *O. khaungraae* skull is about the same size as the skull of the second fossil but is shaped differently.

Unauthorized copying or reuse of any part of this page is illegal.

CONTINUE ▶

809

8

The following text is adapted from Oscar Wilde's 1891 novel *The Picture of Dorian Gray*. Dorian Gray is taking his first look at a portrait that Hallward has painted of him.

> Dorian passed listlessly in front of his picture and turned towards it. When he saw it he drew back, and his cheeks flushed for a moment with pleasure. A look of joy came into his eyes, as if he had recognized himself for the first time. He stood there motionless and in wonder, dimly conscious that Hallward was speaking to him, but not catching the meaning of his words. The sense of his own beauty came on him like a revelation. He had never felt it before.

According to the text, what is true about Dorian?

A) He wants to know Hallward's opinion of the portrait.

B) He is delighted by what he sees in the portrait.

C) He prefers portraits to other types of paintings.

D) He is uncertain of Hallward's talent as an artist.

9

The following text is from Jane Austen's 1811 novel *Sense and Sensibility*. Elinor lives with her younger sisters and her mother, Mrs. Dashwood.

> Elinor, this eldest daughter, whose advice was so effectual, possessed a strength of understanding, and coolness of judgment, which qualified her, though only nineteen, to be the counsellor of her mother, and enabled her frequently to counteract, to the advantage of them all, that eagerness of mind in Mrs. Dashwood which must generally have led to imprudence. She had an excellent heart;—her disposition was affectionate, and her feelings were strong; but she knew how to govern them: it was a knowledge which her mother had yet to learn; and which one of her sisters had resolved never to be taught.

According to the text, what is true about Elinor?

A) Elinor often argues with her mother but fails to change her mind.

B) Elinor can be overly sensitive with regard to family matters.

C) Elinor thinks her mother is a bad role model.

D) Elinor is remarkably mature for her age.

CONTINUE ➡

10

Utah is home to Pando, a colony of about 47,000 quaking aspen trees that all share a single root system. Pando is one of the largest single organisms by mass on Earth, but ecologists are worried that its growth is declining in part because of grazing by animals. The ecologists say that strong fences could prevent deer from eating young trees and help Pando start thriving again.

According to the text, why are ecologists worried about Pando?

A) It isn't growing at the same rate it used to.

B) It isn't producing young trees anymore.

C) It can't grow into new areas because it is blocked by fences.

D) Its root system can't support many more new trees.

11

Video Game Availability by Initial Release Years

Initial release years	Percentage of games still available
1975–1979	0.89
1980–1984	3.65
1985–1989	15.38
1990–1994	19.33
1995–1999	14.22

In a recent study, researchers found that relatively few video games released over the decades remain available today. For example, only 14.22 percent of games are still available that were initially released in _____

Which choice most effectively uses data from the table to complete the statement?

A) 2000–2004.

B) 1995–1999.

C) 1970–1974.

D) 1985–1989.

CONTINUE

12

Depths at Which Four Deep-Sea Fish Species Live

Species	Depth below the ocean surface
Footballfish	200–1,000 meters
Southern stoplight loosejaw	500–2,000 meters
Black seadevil	250–2,000 meters
Bollons' rattail	300–800 meters

Some oceanic fish species live very deep underwater. Researchers collected data about the depths at which various species live.

Based on the information in the table, at what depth does the southern stoplight loosejaw live?

A) More than 2,000 meters below the surface

B) 150 to 400 meters below the surface

C) 500 to 2,000 meters below the surface

D) 250 to 500 meters below the surface

13

O Pioneers! is a 1913 novel by Willa Cather. In the novel, Cather portrays Alexandra Bergson as having a deep emotional connection to her natural surroundings: _____

Which quotation from *O Pioneers!* most effectively illustrates the claim?

A) "She had never known before how much the country meant to her. The chirping of the insects down in the long grass had been like the sweetest music. She had felt as if her heart were hiding down there, somewhere, with the quail and the plover and all the little wild things that crooned or buzzed in the sun. Under the long shaggy ridges, she felt the future stirring."

B) "Alexandra talked to the men about their crops and to the women about their poultry. She spent a whole day with one young farmer who had been away at school, and who was experimenting with a new kind of clover hay. She learned a great deal."

C) "Alexandra drove off alone. The rattle of her wagon was lost in the howling of the wind, but her lantern, held firmly between her feet, made a moving point of light along the highway, going deeper and deeper into the dark country."

D) "It was Alexandra who read the papers and followed the markets, and who learned by the mistakes of their neighbors. It was Alexandra who could always tell about what it had cost to fatten each steer, and who could guess the weight of a hog before it went on the scales closer than John Bergson [her father] himself."

CONTINUE ➡

14

Maximum Height of Maple Trees When Fully Grown

Tree type	Maximum height (feet)	Native to North America
Sugar maple	75	yes
Silver maple	70	yes
Red maple	60	yes
Japanese maple	25	no
Norway maple	50	no

For a school project, a forestry student needs to recommend a maple tree that is native to North America and won't grow more than 60 feet in height. Based on the characteristics of five common maple trees, she has decided to select a _____

Which choice most effectively uses data from the table to complete the text?

A) silver maple.

B) sugar maple.

C) red maple.

D) Norway maple.

15

In his 1963 exhibition *Exposition of Music—Electronic Television*, Korean American artist Nam June Paik showed how television images could be manipulated to express an artist's perspective. Today, Paik _____ considered the first video artist.

Which choice completes the text so that it conforms to the conventions of Standard English?

A) will be

B) had been

C) was

D) is

16

In the historical novel *The Surrender Tree*, Cuban American author Margarita Engle uses poetry rather than prose _____ the true story of Cuban folk hero Rosa La Bayamesa.

Which choice completes the text so that it conforms to the conventions of Standard English?

A) tells

B) told

C) is telling

D) to tell

17

The classic children's board game Chutes and Ladders is a version of an ancient Nepalese game, Paramapada Sopanapata. In both games, players encounter "good" or "bad" spaces while traveling along a path; landing on one of the good spaces _____ a player to skip ahead and arrive closer to the end goal.

Which choice completes the text so that it conforms to the conventions of Standard English?

A) allows

B) are allowing

C) have allowed

D) allow

CONTINUE ▶

18

In winter, the diets of Japanese macaques, also known as snow monkeys, are influenced more by food availability than by food preference. Although the monkeys prefer to eat vegetation and land-dwelling invertebrates, those food sources may become unavailable because of extensive snow and ice cover, _____ the monkeys to hunt for marine animals in any streams that have not frozen over.

Which choice completes the text so that it conforms to the conventions of Standard English?

A) forces

B) to force

C) forcing

D) forced

19

The Alvarez theory, developed in 1980 by physicist Luis Walter Alvarez and his geologist son Walter Alvarez, maintained that the secondary effects of an asteroid impact caused many dinosaurs and other animals to die _____ it left unexplored the question of whether unrelated volcanic activity might have also contributed to the mass extinctions.

Which choice completes the text so that it conforms to the conventions of Standard English?

A) out but

B) out, but

C) out

D) out,

20

In the 1950s, a man named Joseph McVicker was struggling to keep his business afloat when his sister-in-law Kay Zufall advised him to repurpose the company's product, a nontoxic, clay-like substance for removing soot from wallpaper, as a modeling putty for kids. In addition, Zufall _____ selling the product under a child-friendly name: Play-Doh.

Which choice completes the text so that it conforms to the conventions of Standard English?

A) suggested

B) suggests

C) had suggested

D) was suggesting

21

The term "retroflex" derives from Latin and means "bent back," an apt descriptor for the branch of consonants—retroflex consonants—pronounced with the tongue curling up and back in the mouth. In many languages, including English, these consonants are _____ in some dialects of Mandarin, however, four such consonants ("ch," "sh," "zh," and "r") are relatively common.

Which choice completes the text so that it conforms to the conventions of Standard English?

A) rare and

B) rare,

C) rare

D) rare;

Unauthorized copying or reuse of any part of this page is illegal.

CONTINUE ➡

814

22

There are three basic steps you should follow when planning a scientific inquiry. First, thoroughly research the question you wish to answer. _____ come up with a prediction (also called a hypothesis) about the answer to your question. Third, develop an experiment that can test the accuracy of your hypothesis.

Which choice completes the text with the most logical transition?

A) Therefore,

B) Instead,

C) For example,

D) Second,

23

In 1933, the Twentieth Amendment to the US Constitution was ratified. The amendment mandates that presidential inaugurations be held on January 20, approximately ten weeks after the November election. _____ this amendment requires newly elected US senators and representatives to be sworn into their respective offices on January 3.

Which choice completes the text with the most logical transition?

A) Instead,

B) For instance,

C) Specifically,

D) In addition,

24

At two weeks old, the time their critical socialization period begins, wolves can smell but cannot yet see or hear. Domesticated dogs, _____ can see, hear, and smell by the end of two weeks. This relative lack of sensory input may help explain why wolves behave so differently around humans than dogs do: from a very young age, wolves are more wary and less exploratory.

Which choice completes the text with the most logical transition?

A) in other words,

B) for instance,

C) by contrast,

D) accordingly,

Unauthorized copying or reuse of any part of this page is illegal.

CONTINUE

815

25

Some members of the US Supreme Court have resisted calls to televise the court's oral arguments, concerned that the participants would be tempted to perform for the cameras (and thus lower the quality of the discourse). _____ the justices worry that most viewers would not even watch the full deliberations, only short clips that could be misinterpreted and mischaracterized.

Which choice completes the text with the most logical transition?

A) However,

B) Additionally,

C) In comparison,

D) For example,

26

Roughly once an hour, a torrent of boiling water shoots up 100 feet or more from Yellowstone's Old Faithful geyser before plunging back to the surface—a cycle seemingly inhospitable to life. _____ as microbiologist Eric Boyd attests, "the geyser is…almost like a cradle for biodiversity," home to numerous bacteria species that thrive in its sulfurous waters.

Which choice completes the text with the most logical transition?

A) Thus,

B) Specifically,

C) Still,

D) In other words,

27

While researching a topic, a student has taken the following notes:

- Some sandstone arches in Utah's Arches National Park have been defaced by tourists' carvings.

- Park rangers can smooth away some carvings using power grinders.

- For deep carvings, power grinding is not always feasible because it can greatly alter or damage the rock.

- Park rangers can use an infilling technique, which involves filling in carvings with ground sandstone and a bonding agent.

- This technique is minimally invasive.

The student wants to explain an advantage of the infilling technique. Which choice most effectively uses relevant information from the notes to accomplish this goal?

A) To remove carvings from sandstone arches in Utah's Arches National Park, power grinding is not always feasible.

B) Filling in carvings with ground sandstone and a bonding agent is less invasive than smoothing them away with a power grinder, which can greatly alter or damage the sandstone arches.

C) Park rangers can use a power grinding technique to smooth away carvings or fill them in with ground sandstone and a bonding agent.

D) As methods for removing carvings from sandstone, power grinding and infilling differ in their level of invasiveness.

STOP

**If you finish before time is called, you may check your work on this module only.
Do not turn to any other module in the test.**

Test begins on the next page.

Reading and Writing

27 QUESTIONS

The questions in this section address a number of important reading and writing skills. Each question includes one or more passages, which may include a table or graph. Read each passage and question carefully, and then choose the best answer to the question based on the passage(s).

All questions in this section are multiple-choice with four answer choices. Each question has a single best answer.

1

In the Indigenous intercropping system known as the Three Sisters, maize, squash, and beans form an _____ web of relations: maize provides the structure on which the bean vines grow; the squash vines cover the soil, discouraging competition from weeds; and the beans aid their two "sisters" by enriching the soil with essential nitrogen.

Which choice completes the text with the most logical and precise word or phrase?

A) indecipherable

B) ornamental

C) obscure

D) intricate

2

For her 2021 art installation *Anthem*, Wu Tsang joined forces with singer and composer Beverly Glenn-Copeland to produce a piece that critics found truly _____: they praised Tsang for creatively transforming a museum rotunda into a dynamic exhibit by projecting filmed images of Glenn-Copeland onto a massive 84-foot curtain and filling the space with the sounds of his and other voices singing.

Which choice completes the text with the most logical and precise word or phrase?

A) restrained

B) inventive

C) inexplicable

D) mystifying

3

The author's claim about the relationship between Neanderthals and *Homo sapiens* is _____, as it fails to account for several recent archaeological discoveries. To be convincing, his argument would need to address recent finds of additional hominid fossils, such as the latest Denisovan specimens and *Homo longi*.

Which choice completes the text with the most logical and precise word or phrase?

A) disorienting

B) tenuous

C) nuanced

D) unoriginal

CONTINUE

4

Seminole/Muscogee director Sterlin Harjo _____ television's tendency to situate Native characters in the distant past: this rejection is evident in his series *Reservation Dogs*, which revolves around teenagers who dress in contemporary styles and whose dialogue is laced with current slang.

Which choice completes the text with the most logical and precise word or phrase?

A) repudiates

B) proclaims

C) foretells

D) recants

5

The following text is adapted from Zora Neale Hurston's 1921 short story "John Redding Goes to Sea." John is a child who lives in a town in the woods.

Perhaps ten-year-old John was puzzling to the folk there in the Florida woods for he was an imaginative child and fond of day-dreams. The St. John River flowed a scarce three hundred feet from his back door. On its banks at this point grow numerous palms, luxuriant magnolias and bay trees. On the bosom of the stream float millions of delicately colored hyacinths. [John Redding] loved to wander down to the water's edge, and, casting in dry twigs, watch them sail away down stream to Jacksonville, the sea, the wide world and [he] wanted to follow them.

Which choice best describes the function of the underlined sentence in the text as a whole?

A) It provides an extended description of a location that John likes to visit.

B) It reveals that some residents of John's town are confused by his behavior.

C) It illustrates the uniqueness of John's imagination compared to the imaginations of other children.

D) It suggests that John longs to experience a larger life outside the Florida woods.

6

Text 1
When companies in the same industry propose merging with one another, they often claim that the merger will benefit consumers by increasing efficiency and therefore lowering prices. Economist Ying Fan investigated this notion in the context of the United States newspaper market. She modeled a hypothetical merger of Minneapolis-area newspapers and found that subscription prices would rise following a merger.

Text 2
Economists Dario Focarelli and Fabio Panetta have argued that research on the effect of mergers on prices has focused excessively on short-term effects, which tend to be adverse for consumers. Using the case of consumer banking in Italy, they show that over the long term (several years, in their study), the efficiency gains realized by merged companies do result in economic benefits for consumers.

Based on the texts, how would Focarelli and Panetta (Text 2) most likely respond to Fan's findings (Text 1)?

A) They would recommend that Fan compare the near-term effect of a merger on subscription prices in the Minneapolis area with the effect of a merger in another newspaper market.

B) They would argue that over the long term the expenses incurred by the merged newspaper company will also increase.

C) They would encourage Fan to investigate whether the projected effect on subscription prices persists over an extended period.

D) They would claim that mergers have a different effect on consumer prices in the newspaper industry than in most other industries.

Unauthorized copying or reuse of any part of this page is illegal.

CONTINUE ▶

819

7

The following text is adapted from Lewis Carroll's 1889 satirical novel *Sylvie and Bruno*. A crowd has gathered outside a room belonging to the Warden, an official who reports to the Lord Chancellor.

One man, who was more excited than the rest, flung his hat high into the air, and shouted (as well as I could make out) "Who roar for the Sub-Warden?" Everybody roared, but whether it was for the Sub-Warden, or not, did not clearly appear: some were shouting "Bread!" and some "Taxes!", but no one seemed to know what it was they really wanted.

All this I saw from the open window of the Warden's breakfast-saloon, looking across the shoulder of the Lord Chancellor.

"What can it all mean?" he kept repeating to himself. "I never heard such shouting before—and at this time of the morning, too! And with such unanimity!"

Based on the text, how does the Lord Chancellor respond to the crowd?

A) He asks about the meaning of the crowd's shouting, even though he claims to know what the crowd wants.

B) He indicates a desire to speak to the crowd, even though the crowd has asked to speak to the Sub-Warden.

C) He expresses sympathy for the crowd's demands, even though the crowd's shouting annoys him.

D) He describes the crowd as being united, even though the crowd clearly appears otherwise.

8

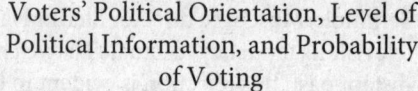

Voters' Political Orientation, Level of Political Information, and Probability of Voting

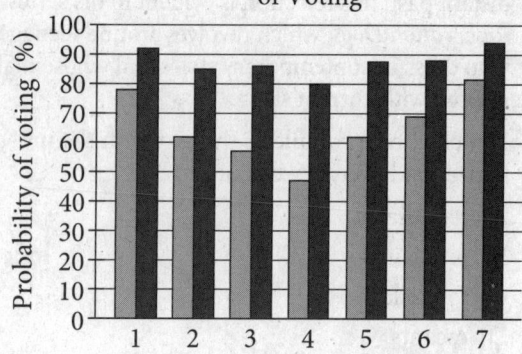

Voters' political orientation
(1 = strong Democrat/liberal;
4 = independent;
7 = strong Republican/conservative)

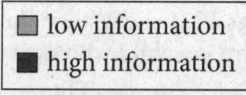

Economists Kerwin Kofi Charles and Melvin Stephens Jr. investigated a variety of factors that influence voter turnout in the United States. Using survey data that revealed whether respondents voted in national elections and how knowledgeable respondents are about politics, Charles and Stephens claim that the likelihood of voting is driven in part by potential voters' confidence in their assessments of candidates—essentially, the more informed voters are about politics, the more confident they are at evaluating whether candidates share their views, and thus the more likely they are to vote.

Which choice best describes data in the graph that support Charles and Stephens's claim?

A) At each point on the political orientation scale, high-information voters were more likely than low-information voters to vote.

B) Only low-information voters who identify as independents had a voting probability below 50%.

C) The closer that low-information voters are to the ends of the political orientation scale, the more likely they were to vote.

D) High-information voters were more likely to identify as strong Democrats or strong Republicans than low-information voters were.

CONTINUE ▶

9

Estimates of Tyrannosaurid Bite Force

Study	Year	Estimation method	Approximate bite force (newtons)
Cost et al.	2019	muscular and skeletal modeling	35,000–63,000
Gignac and Erickson	2017	tooth-bone interaction analysis	8,000–34,000
Meers	2002	body-mass scaling	183,000–235,000
Bates and Falkingham	2012	muscular and skeletal modeling	35,000–57,000

The largest tyrannosaurids—the family of carnivorous dinosaurs that includes *Tarbosaurus, Albertosaurus*, and, most famously, *Tyrannosaurus rex*—are thought to have had the strongest bites of any land animals in Earth's history. Determining the bite force of extinct animals can be difficult, however, and paleontologists Paul Barrett and Emily Rayfield have suggested that an estimate of dinosaur bite force may be significantly influenced by the methodology used in generating that estimate.

Which choice best describes data from the table that support Barrett and Rayfield's suggestion?

A) The study by Meers used body-mass scaling and produced the lowest estimated maximum bite force, while the study by Cost et al. used muscular and skeletal modeling and produced the highest estimated maximum.

B) In their study, Gignac and Erickson used tooth-bone interaction analysis to produce an estimated bite force range with a minimum of 8,000 newtons and a maximum of 34,000 newtons.

C) The bite force estimates produced by Bates and Falkingham and by Cost et al. were similar to each other, while the estimates produced by Meers and by Gignac and Erickson each differed substantially from any other estimate.

D) The estimated maximum bite force produced by Cost et al. exceeded the estimated maximum produced by Bates and Falkingham, even though both groups of researchers used the same method to generate their estimates.

CONTINUE

10

When digging for clams, their primary food, sea otters damage the roots of eelgrass plants growing on the seafloor. Near Vancouver Island in Canada, the otter population is large and well established, yet the eelgrass meadows are healthier than those found elsewhere off Canada's coast. To explain this, conservation scientist Erin Foster and colleagues compared the Vancouver Island meadows to meadows where otters are absent or were reintroduced only recently. Finding that the Vancouver Island meadows have a more diverse gene pool than the others do, Foster hypothesized that damage to eelgrass roots increases the plant's rate of sexual reproduction; this, in turn, boosts genetic diversity, which benefits the meadows' health overall.

Which finding, if true, would most directly undermine Foster's hypothesis?

A) At some sites in the study, eelgrass meadows are found near otter populations that are small and have only recently been reintroduced.

B) At several sites not included in the study, there are large, well-established sea otter populations but no eelgrass meadows.

C) At several sites not included in the study, eelgrass meadows' health correlates negatively with the length of residence and size of otter populations.

D) At some sites in the study, the health of plants unrelated to eelgrass correlates negatively with the length of residence and size of otter populations.

11

In the twentieth century, ethnographers made a concerted effort to collect Mexican American folklore, but they did not always agree about that folklore's origins. Scholars such as Aurelio Espinosa claimed that Mexican American folklore derived largely from the folklore of Spain, which ruled Mexico and what is now the southwestern United States from the sixteenth to early nineteenth centuries. Scholars such as Américo Paredes, by contrast, argued that while some Spanish influence is undeniable, Mexican American folklore is mainly the product of the ongoing interactions of various cultures in Mexico and the United States.

Which finding, if true, would most directly support Paredes's argument?

A) The folklore that the ethnographers collected included several songs written in the form of a *décima*, a type of poem originating in late sixteenth-century Spain.

B) Much of the folklore that the ethnographers collected had similar elements from region to region.

C) Most of the folklore that the ethnographers collected was previously unknown to scholars.

D) Most of the folklore that the ethnographers collected consisted of *corridos*—ballads about history and social life—of a clearly recent origin.

CONTINUE

12

Average Survival of Fruit Flies following Infection

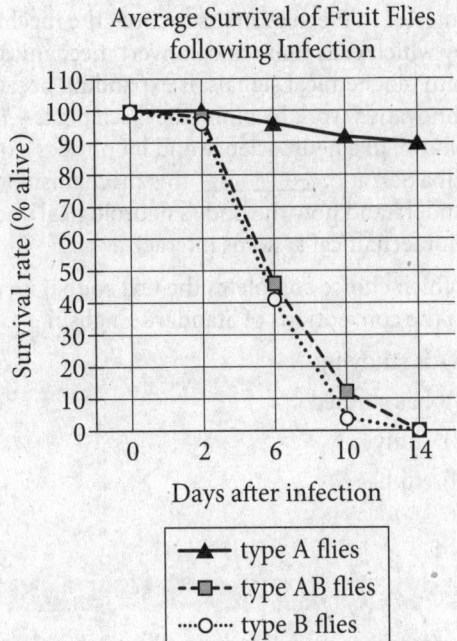

Days after infection

— type A flies
-■- type AB flies
···○··· type B flies

In a study of the evolution of *DptA* and *DptB*— *Diptericin* genes encoding antimicrobial peptides that combat pathogens and foster beneficial microbes in fruit flies (*Drosophila*)—researchers assessed *Drosophila melanogaster* resistance to pathogenic infections by *Providencia rettgeri* and *Acetobacter sicerae*, bacteria common in the flies' environments. Subjects included flies identified by mutations silencing *DptA*, *DptB*, or both *DptA* and *DptB* (termed types A, B, and AB, respectively). In conjunction with the observation that resistance to *P. rettgeri* correlates with *DptA* activity but is not significantly affected by *DptB* activity, data in the graph of survival rates post–*A. sicerae* infection suggest that _____

Which completion of the text is best supported by data in the graph?

A) *DptA* confers defense against *A. sicerae* regardless of the presence of *DptB*.

B) *DptB* protects against only one bacteria species, whereas *DptA* protects against multiple species.

C) *DptB* may have developed as a specific defense against *A. sicerae*.

D) defense against *A. sicerae* is strongest when both *DptA* and *DptB* are present.

13

Some economists have attributed the increasing adoption of automation technology by firms in the United States in part to the productivity gains firms can achieve by automating tasks previously requiring paid labor. Daron Acemoglu et al. recently complicated this account by showing not only that automation's productivity gains are often unremarkable, but that there is a disparity in the US tax code between automation technology and the labor it is nominally equivalent to: the tax code classifies automation-related technology as a depreciating asset, meaning that capital expenditures on that technology can reduce a firm's tax burden relative to its tax burden if equivalent expenditures were labor costs. Together, these findings suggest that _____

Which choice most logically completes the text?

A) the explanation that some economists have offered for US firms' increasing adoption of automation technology may be based on an overestimation of the tax benefits and productivity gains associated with that technology.

B) US firms' increasing adoption of automation technology may be driven more by the fact that the government indirectly incentivizes firms to adopt that technology than by the ongoing benefits that the technology has for firms' outputs.

C) changes to the US tax code that result in capital expenditures on automation technology being treated the same as expenditures on labor costs would likely have little effect on firms' productivity but may encourage further adoption of that technology.

D) US firms have actually tended to experience a decrease in productivity as a result of adopting automation technology, but that decrease is overlooked due to the tax advantages associated with the technology.

CONTINUE ▶

14

The morphological novelty of echinoderms—marine invertebrates with radial symmetry, usually starlike, around a central point—impedes comparisons with most other animals, in which bilateral symmetry on an anterior-posterior (head to tail) axis through a trunk is typical. Particularly puzzling are sea stars, thought to have evolved a headless layout from a known bilateral origin. Applying genomic knowledge of *Saccoglossus kowalevskii* acorn worms (close relatives of sea stars, and thus expected to have similar markers for corresponding anatomical regions) to the body patterning genes of *Patiria miniata* sea stars, Laurent Formery et al. observed activity only in anterior genes across *P. miniata*'s entire body and some posterior genes limited to the edges, suggesting that _____

Which choice most logically completes the text?

A) despite the greater prevalence of anterior genes in sea stars' genetic makeup, posterior genes active at the body's perimeter are primarily responsible for the starlike layout that distinguishes sea stars' radial symmetry from that of other echinoderms.

B) contrary to the belief that they evolved from early ancestors with the bilateral form typical of many other animals, sea stars instead originated with an atypical body layout that was neither bilaterally nor radially symmetrical.

C) although the two species are closely related, there is only minimal correspondence in the genetic markers for head, tail, and trunk region development in *P. miniata* sea stars and *S. kowalevskii* acorn worms.

D) rather than undergoing changes resulting in the eventual elimination of a head region in their radial body plan, as previously assumed, sea stars' morphology evolved to completely lack a trunk and consist primarily of a head region.

15

Interest in mechanotransduction, the mechanism by which cells sense and convert mechanical stimuli into biochemical signals, is expanding because of innovative work by biomedical scientists—many of whom, like neuroscience and biophysics expert Elba Serrano, _____ this mechanism to better understand how the body's neurological and biomechanical systems interact.

Which choice completes the text so that it conforms to the conventions of Standard English?

A) is studying

B) has studied

C) study

D) studies

16

Researchers studying magnetosensation have determined why some soil-dwelling roundworms in the Southern Hemisphere move in the opposite direction of Earth's magnetic field when searching for _____ in the Northern Hemisphere, the magnetic field points down, into the ground, but in the Southern Hemisphere, it points up, toward the surface and away from worms' food sources.

Which choice completes the text so that it conforms to the conventions of Standard English?

A) food:

B) food,

C) food while

D) food

CONTINUE

17

As cheesemaking practices spread throughout Europe and Asia during and after the Neolithic, divergent strategies for preserving milk _____ whereas rennet-coagulated cheesemaking became key to milk preservation in Europe and Southwest Asia, acid-heat coagulation methods became common among nomadic herding populations of the northeastern Eurasian steppe.

Which choice completes the text so that it conforms to the conventions of Standard English?

A) emerged

B) emerged and

C) emerged:

D) emerged,

18

Walt Whitman's *Leaves of Grass* first appeared in 1855 as a slim collection of twelve poems, but Whitman would revise and expand it substantially over the next four decades. These extensive _____ the addition of hundreds of new poems, the removal of some existing ones, and the insertion of prefatory material, reflected the poet's evolving literary perspective and experience of the US Civil War.

Which choice completes the text so that it conforms to the conventions of Standard English?

A) changes, including

B) changes would include

C) changes included

D) changes, include

19

English poet and Shakespeare contemporary John Donne's _____ much admired during his lifetime (1572–1631) and in the decades that followed, had, at the time of their enthusiastic rediscovery by the early twentieth-century modernists, been essentially gathering dust for the intervening 250 years.

Which choice completes the text so that it conforms to the conventions of Standard English?

A) works were

B) works, were

C) works,

D) works had been

20

Researchers studying the "terra-cotta army," the thousands of life-size statues of warriors found interred near the tomb of Emperor Qin Shi Huang of China, were shocked to realize that the shape of each statue's ears, like the shape of each person's ears, _____ unique.

Which choice completes the text so that it conforms to the conventions of Standard English?

A) are

B) is

C) were

D) have been

CONTINUE

21

A firefly uses specialized muscles to draw oxygen into its lower abdomen through narrow tubes, triggering a chemical reaction whereby the oxygen combines with chemicals in the firefly's abdomen to produce a glow. _____ when the firefly stops drawing in oxygen, the reaction—and the glow—cease.

Which choice completes the text with the most logical transition?

A) For instance,

B) By contrast,

C) Specifically,

D) In conclusion,

22

Upon first approaching artist Kurt Wenner's *Dies Irae*, a colorful scene painted on the surface of a cobblestone street in Mantua, Italy, one might assume a deep hole filled with life-sized, classically styled sculptures had opened up in the street. _____ by expertly applying the principles of perspective, Wenner created merely the illusion of depth.

Which choice completes the text with the most logical transition?

A) Additionally,

B) On the contrary,

C) As a result,

D) Next,

23

While researching a topic, a student has taken the following notes:

- The Philadelphia and Lancaster Turnpike was a road built between 1792 and 1794.
- It was the first private turnpike in the United States.
- It connected the cities of Philadelphia and Lancaster in the state of Pennsylvania.
- It was sixty-two miles long.

The student wants to emphasize the distance covered by the Philadelphia and Lancaster Turnpike. Which choice most effectively uses relevant information from the notes to accomplish this goal?

A) The sixty-two-mile-long Philadelphia and Lancaster Turnpike connected the Pennsylvania cities of Philadelphia and Lancaster.

B) The Philadelphia and Lancaster Turnpike was the first private turnpike in the United States.

C) The Philadelphia and Lancaster Turnpike, which connected two Pennsylvania cities, was built between 1792 and 1794.

D) A historic Pennsylvania road, the Philadelphia and Lancaster Turnpike was completed in 1794.

Unauthorized copying or reuse of any part of this page is illegal.

CONTINUE ▶

826

24

While researching a topic, a student has taken the following notes:

- In 2020, theater students at Radford and Virginia Tech chose an interactive, online format to present a play about woman suffrage activists.

- Their "Women and the Vote" website featured an interactive digital drawing of a Victorian-style house.

- Audiences were asked to focus on a room of their choice and select from that room an artifact related to the suffrage movement.

- One click took them to video clips, songs, artwork, and texts associated with the artifact.

- The play was popular with audiences because the format allowed them to control the experience.

The student wants to explain an advantage of the "Women and the Vote" format. Which choice most effectively uses relevant information from the notes to accomplish this goal?

A) "Women and the Vote" featured a drawing of a Victorian-style house with several rooms, each containing suffrage artifacts.

B) To access video clips, songs, artwork, and texts, audiences had to first click on an artifact.

C) The "Women and the Vote" format appealed to audiences because it allowed them to control the experience.

D) Using an interactive format, theater students at Radford and Virginia Tech created "Women and the Vote," a play about woman suffrage activists.

25

While researching a topic, a student has taken the following notes:

- Malapportionment is the over- or underrepresentation (relative to population size) of electoral districts in a governing body.

- It is a common feature of representative governments.

- There are 169 seats in Norway's supreme legislature (the Storting).

- Seats are distributed by a formula that awards 1 point per resident and 1.8 points per unit of land.

- Less populated rural districts with large tracts of land receive a disproportionate number of seats compared to smaller but more populated urban districts.

The student wants to refute a claim that malapportionment in the Storting favors small urban districts. Which choice most effectively uses relevant information from the notes to accomplish this goal?

A) Less populated rural districts are disproportionally underrepresented in the Storting, creating an unfair advantage for smaller but more populated urban districts.

B) It's untrue that malapportionment in the 169-seat Storting favors small urban districts; rather, the formula for distributing seats overrepresents more populated districts.

C) A common feature of representative governments, malapportionment occurs when electoral districts are over- or underrepresented.

D) Awarding more points per unit of land than points per resident, the formula for distributing Storting seats overrepresents less populated rural districts with large tracts of land.

CONTINUE

26

While researching a topic, a student has taken the following notes:

- Ducklings expend up to 62.8% less energy when swimming in a line behind their mother than when swimming alone.
- The physics behind this energy savings hasn't always been well understood.
- Naval architect Zhiming Yuan used computer simulations to study the effect of the mother duck's wake.
- The study revealed that ducklings are pushed in a forward direction by the wake's waves.
- Yuan determined this push reduces the effect of wave drag on the ducklings by 158%.

The student wants to present the study and its methodology. Which choice most effectively uses relevant information from the notes to accomplish this goal?

A) A study revealed that ducklings, which expend up to 62.8% less energy when swimming in a line behind their mother, also experience 158% less drag.

B) Seeking to understand how ducklings swimming in a line behind their mother save energy, Zhiming Yuan used computer simulations to study the effect of the mother duck's wake.

C) Zhiming Yuan studied the physics behind the fact that by being pushed in a forward direction by waves, ducklings save energy.

D) Naval architect Zhiming Yuan discovered that ducklings are pushed in a forward direction by the waves of their mother's wake, reducing the effect of drag by 158%.

27

While researching a topic, a student has taken the following notes:

- In North America, woodlands have expanded into areas that were once grasslands.
- Thomas Rogers and F. Leland Russell of Wichita State University investigated whether woodland expansion is related to changes in climate.
- Rogers and Russell analyzed core samples from oak trees on a site that was not wooded in the past and indexed the age of the trees with historical climate data to see if tree populations and climate were correlated.
- Tree population growth was associated with dry intervals.
- Droughts may have played a role in woodland expansion.

The student wants to emphasize the aim of the research study. Which choice most effectively uses relevant information from the notes to accomplish this goal?

A) Thomas Rogers and F. Leland Russell, researchers at Wichita State University, wanted to know if woodland expansion is related to changes in climate.

B) Thanks to the work done by Thomas Rogers and F. Leland Russell, we now know that droughts may have played a role in woodland expansion.

C) Wichita State University researchers have determined that tree population growth was associated with dry intervals.

D) Thomas Rogers and F. Leland Russell analyzed core samples from oak trees on a site that was not wooded in the past, indexing the age of the trees with historical climate data.

STOP

**If you finish before time is called, you may check your work on this module only.
Do not turn to any other module in the test.**

Test begins on the next page.

Math

22 QUESTIONS

DIRECTIONS

The questions in this section address a number of important math skills.
Use of a calculator is permitted for all questions.

NOTES

Unless otherwise indicated:

- All variables and expressions represent real numbers.
- Figures provided are drawn to scale.
- All figures lie in a plane.
- The domain of a given function f is the set of all real numbers x for which $f(x)$ is a real number.

REFERENCE

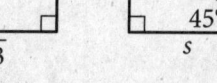

$A = \pi r^2$
$C = 2\pi r$

$A = \ell w$

$A = \frac{1}{2}bh$

$c^2 = a^2 + b^2$

Special Right Triangles

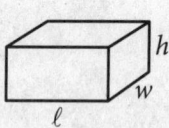

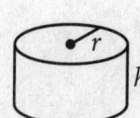

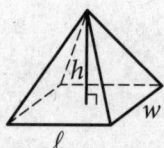

$V = \ell wh$

$V = \pi r^2 h$

$V = \frac{4}{3}\pi r^3$

$V = \frac{1}{3}\pi r^2 h$

$V = \frac{1}{3}\ell wh$

The number of degrees of arc in a circle is 360.

The number of radians of arc in a circle is 2π.

The sum of the measures in degrees of the angles of a triangle is 180.

CONTINUE

For multiple-choice questions, solve each problem, choose the correct answer from the choices provided, and then circle your answer in this book. Circle only one answer for each question. If you change your mind, completely erase the circle. You will not get credit for questions with more than one answer circled, or for questions with no answers circled.

For student-produced response questions, solve each problem and write your answer next to or under the question in the test book as described below.

- Once you've written your answer, circle it clearly. You will not receive credit for anything written outside the circle, or for any questions with more than one circled answer.

- If you find **more than one correct answer**, write and circle only one answer.

- Your answer can be up to 5 characters for a **positive** answer and up to 6 characters (including the negative sign) for a **negative** answer, but no more.

- If your answer is a **fraction** that is too long (over 5 characters for positive, 6 characters for negative), write the decimal equivalent.

- If your answer is a **decimal** that is too long (over 5 characters for positive, 6 characters for negative), truncate it or round at the fourth digit.

- If your answer is a **mixed number** (such as $3\frac{1}{2}$), write it as an improper fraction (7/2) or its decimal equivalent (3.5).

- Don't include **symbols** such as a percent sign, comma, or dollar sign in your circled answer.

CONTINUE

1

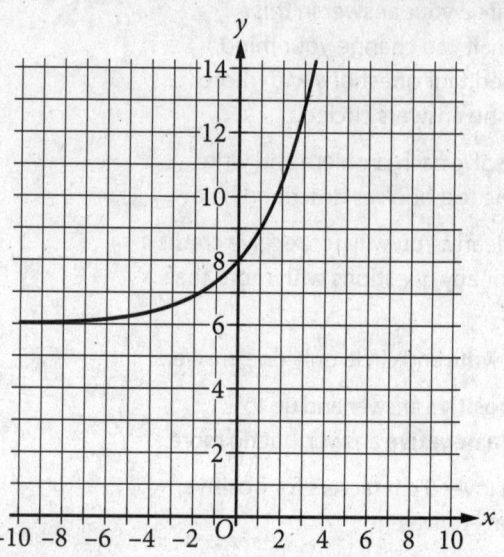

What is the *y*-intercept of the graph shown?

A) $(-8, 0)$

B) $(-6, 0)$

C) $(0, 6)$

D) $(0, 8)$

2

The function *f* is defined by $f(x) = -3x + 60$. What is the value of $f(x)$ when $x = -8$?

A) 49

B) 52

C) 57

D) 84

3

A producer is creating a video with a length of 70 minutes. The video will consist of segments that are 1 minute long and segments that are 3 minutes long. Which equation represents this situation, where *x* represents the number of 1-minute segments and *y* represents the number of 3-minute segments?

A) $4xy = 70$

B) $4(x + y) = 70$

C) $3x + y = 70$

D) $x + 3y = 70$

4

A bowl contains 20 ounces of water. When the bowl is uncovered, the amount of water in the bowl decreases by 1 ounce every 4 days. If 9 ounces of water remain in this bowl, for how many days has it been uncovered?

A) 3

B) 7

C) 36

D) 44

Unauthorized copying or reuse of any part of this page is illegal.

CONTINUE

832

5 ▬▬▬▬▬▬▬▬▬▬▬▬▬

Class A   Class B

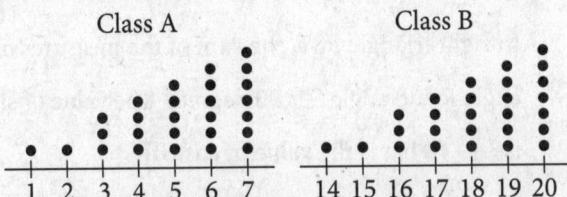

Each of the dot plots shown represents the number of glue sticks brought in by each student for two classes, class A and class B. Which statement best compares the standard deviations of the numbers of glue sticks brought in by each student for these two classes?

A) The standard deviation of the number of glue sticks brought in by each student for class A is less than the standard deviation of the number of glue sticks brought in by each student for class B.

B) The standard deviation of the number of glue sticks brought in by each student for class A is equal to the standard deviation of the number of glue sticks brought in by each student for class B.

C) The standard deviation of the number of glue sticks brought in by each student for class A is greater than the standard deviation of the number of glue sticks brought in by each student for class B.

D) There is not enough information to compare these standard deviations.

6 ▬▬▬▬▬▬▬▬▬▬▬▬▬

Which expression is equivalent to $(7x^3 + 7x) - (6x^3 - 3x)$?

A) $x^3 + 10x$

B) $-13x^3 + 10x$

C) $-13x^3 + 4x$

D) $x^3 + 4x$

7 ▬▬▬▬▬▬▬▬▬▬▬▬▬

In triangle ABC, the measure of angle A is 54°, the measure of angle B is 90°, and the measure of angle C is $\left(\frac{k}{2}\right)°$. What is the value of k?

A) 36

B) 45

C) 72

D) 108

8 ▬▬▬▬▬▬▬▬▬▬▬▬▬

$$3x(x - 4)(x + 5) = 0$$

What is one of the solutions to the given equation?

A) −4

B) 0

C) 3

D) 5

9 ▬▬▬▬▬▬▬▬▬▬▬▬▬

A chemist combines water and acetic acid to make a mixture with a volume of 56 milliliters (mL). The volume of acetic acid in the mixture is 10 mL. What is the volume of water, in mL, in the mixture? (Assume that the volume of the mixture is the sum of the volumes of water and acetic acid before they were mixed.)

10 ▬▬▬▬▬▬▬▬▬▬▬▬▬

A distance of 354 furlongs is equivalent to how many feet? (1 furlong = 220 yards and 1 yard = 3 feet)

A) 306

B) 402

C) 25,960

D) 233,640

CONTINUE ▶

11

$$y = 2x + 10$$
$$y = 2x - 1$$

At how many points do the graphs of the given equations intersect in the xy-plane?

A) Zero

B) Exactly one

C) Exactly two

D) Infinitely many

12

13 is p% of 25. What is the value of p?

13

The function $f(t) = 60,000(2)^{\frac{t}{410}}$ gives the number of bacteria in a population t minutes after an initial observation. How much time, in minutes, does it take for the number of bacteria in the population to double?

14

Each year, the value of an investment increases by 0.49% of its value the previous year. Which of the following functions best models how the value of the investment changes over time?

A) Decreasing exponential

B) Decreasing linear

C) Increasing exponential

D) Increasing linear

15

A circle in the xy-plane has a diameter with endpoints (2, 4) and (2, 14). An equation of this circle is $(x - 2)^2 + (y - 9)^2 = r^2$, where r is a positive constant. What is the value of r?

16

In right triangle RST, the sum of the measures of angle R and angle S is 90 degrees. The value of $\sin(R)$ is $\frac{\sqrt{15}}{4}$. What is the value of $\cos(S)$?

A) $\frac{\sqrt{15}}{15}$

B) $\frac{\sqrt{15}}{4}$

C) $\frac{4\sqrt{15}}{15}$

D) $\sqrt{15}$

17

$$p = \frac{k}{4j + 9}$$

The given equation relates the distinct positive numbers p, k, and j. Which equation correctly expresses $4j + 9$ in terms of p and k?

A) $4j + 9 = \frac{k}{p}$

B) $4j + 9 = kp$

C) $4j + 9 = k - p$

D) $4j + 9 = \frac{p}{k}$

CONTINUE

18

$$y > 13x - 18$$

For which of the following tables are all the values of x and their corresponding values of y solutions to the given inequality?

A)

x	y
3	21
5	47
8	86

B)

x	y
3	26
5	42
8	86

C)

x	y
3	16
5	42
8	81

D)

x	y
3	26
5	52
8	91

19

Line ℓ is defined by $3y + 12x = 5$. Line n is perpendicular to line ℓ in the xy-plane. What is the slope of line n?

20

$$y = 2(x - d)(x + d)(x + g)(x - d)$$

In the given equation, d and g are unique positive constants. When the equation is graphed in the xy-plane, how many distinct x-intercepts does the graph have?

A) 4

B) 3

C) 2

D) 1

21

For the exponential function f, the value of $f(1)$ is k, where k is a constant. Which of the following equivalent forms of the function f shows the value of k as the coefficient or the base?

A) $f(x) = 50(1.6)^{x+1}$

B) $f(x) = 80(1.6)^{x}$

C) $f(x) = 128(1.6)^{x-1}$

D) $f(x) = 204.8(1.6)^{x-2}$

22

$$f(x) = 4x^2 + 64x + 262$$

The function g is defined by $g(x) = f(x + 5)$. For what value of x does $g(x)$ reach its minimum?

A) -13

B) -8

C) -5

D) -3

STOP

**If you finish before time is called, you may check your work on this module only.
Do not turn to any other module in the test.**

Math

22 QUESTIONS

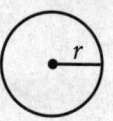 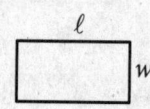 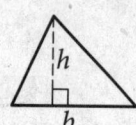 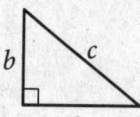 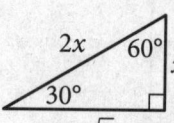 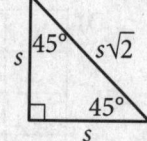

$A = \pi r^2$ $A = \ell w$ $A = \frac{1}{2}bh$ $c^2 = a^2 + b^2$ Special Right Triangles

$C = 2\pi r$

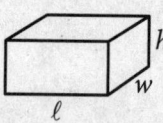    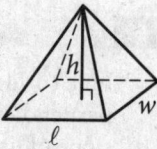

$V = \ell wh$ $V = \pi r^2 h$ $V = \frac{4}{3}\pi r^3$ $V = \frac{1}{3}\pi r^2 h$ $V = \frac{1}{3}\ell wh$

The number of degrees of arc in a circle is 360.

The number of radians of arc in a circle is 2π.

The sum of the measures in degrees of the angles of a triangle is 180.

Unauthorized copying or reuse of any part of this page is illegal.

CONTINUE ▶

836

For multiple-choice questions, solve each problem, choose the correct answer from the choices provided, and then circle your answer in this book. Circle only one answer for each question. If you change your mind, completely erase the circle. You will not get credit for questions with more than one answer circled, or for questions with no answers circled.

For student-produced response questions, solve each problem and write your answer next to or under the question in the test book as described below.

- Once you've written your answer, circle it clearly. You will not receive credit for anything written outside the circle, or for any questions with more than one circled answer.

- If you find **more than one correct answer**, write and circle only one answer.

- Your answer can be up to 5 characters for a **positive** answer and up to 6 characters (including the negative sign) for a **negative** answer, but no more.

- If your answer is a **fraction** that is too long (over 5 characters for positive, 6 characters for negative), write the decimal equivalent.

- If your answer is a **decimal** that is too long (over 5 characters for positive, 6 characters for negative), truncate it or round at the fourth digit.

- If your answer is a **mixed number** (such as $3\frac{1}{2}$), write it as an improper fraction (7/2) or its decimal equivalent (3.5).

- Don't include **symbols** such as a percent sign, comma, or dollar sign in your circled answer.

CONTINUE →

1

The line graph shows the percent of cars for sale at a used car lot on a given day by model year.

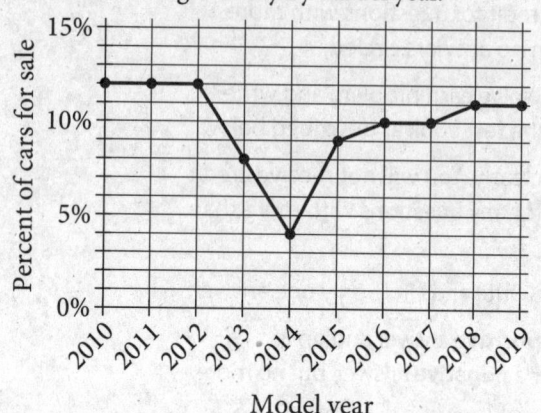

For what model year is the percent of cars for sale the smallest?

A) 2012

B) 2013

C) 2014

D) 2015

2

An object's speed is 64 yards per second. What is the object's speed, in <u>feet</u> per second? (1 yard = 3 feet)

A) 61

B) 67

C) 94

D) 192

3

The lengths of two sides of a triangle are 4 centimeters and 6 centimeters. If the perimeter of the triangle is 18 centimeters, what is the length, in centimeters, of the third side of this triangle?

A) 2

B) 8

C) 10

D) 24

4

A bus is traveling at a constant speed along a straight portion of road. The equation $d = 30t$ gives the distance d, in feet from a road marker, that the bus will be t seconds after passing the marker. How many feet from the marker will the bus be 2 seconds after passing the marker?

A) 30

B) 32

C) 60

D) 90

5

The total cost, in dollars, to rent a surfboard consists of a $25 service fee and a $10 per hour rental fee. A person rents a surfboard for t hours and intends to spend a maximum of $75 to rent the surfboard. Which inequality represents this situation?

A) $10t \leq 75$

B) $10 + 25t \leq 75$

C) $25t \leq 75$

D) $25 + 10t \leq 75$

CONTINUE ▶

6

	Live east of the river	Live west of the river	Total
Less than 40 years old	17	11	28
At least 40 years old	18	89	107
Total	35	100	135

The table summarizes members of a local organization by age and whether they live east or west of the river. If a member of the organization is selected at random, what is the probability that the selected member is at least 40 years old?

A) $\frac{28}{135}$

B) $\frac{35}{135}$

C) $\frac{100}{135}$

D) $\frac{107}{135}$

7

The function f is defined by $f(x) = \frac{1}{10}x - 2$. What is the y-intercept of the graph of $y = f(x)$ in the xy-plane?

A) $(-2, 0)$

B) $(0, -2)$

C) $\left(0, \frac{1}{10}\right)$

D) $\left(\frac{1}{10}, 0\right)$

8

The function g is defined by $g(x) = x^2 + 9$. For which value of x is $g(x) = 25$?

A) 4

B) 5

C) 9

D) 13

9

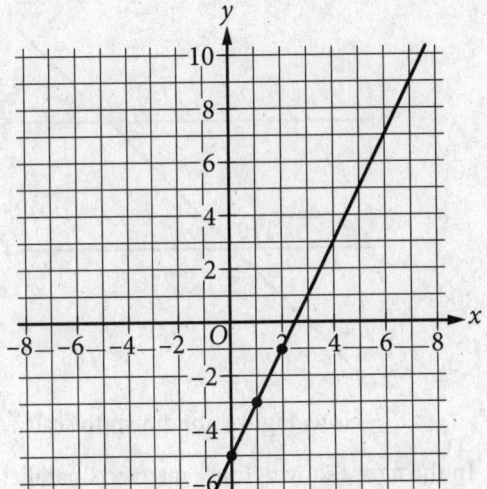

The graph shows the linear relationship between x and y. Which table gives three values of x and their corresponding values of y for this relationship?

A)

x	y
0	0
1	−7
2	−9

B)

x	y
0	0
1	−3
2	−1

C)

x	y
0	−5
1	−7
2	−9

D)

x	y
0	−5
1	−3
2	−1

CONTINUE

10

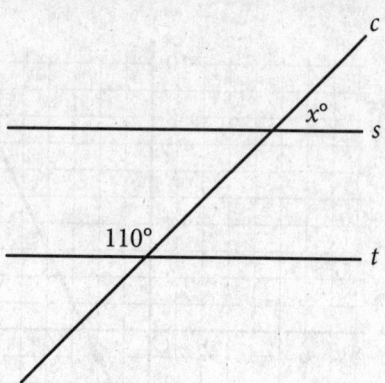

Note: Figure not drawn to scale.

In the figure shown, line c intersects parallel lines s and t. What is the value of x?

11

Each value in the data set shown represents the height, in centimeters, of a plant.

6, 10, 13, 2, 15, 22, 10, 4, 4, 4

What is the mean height, in centimeters, of these plants?

12

$$f(x) = 4x + b$$

For the linear function f, b is a constant and $f(7) = 28$. What is the value of b?

A) 0

B) 1

C) 4

D) 7

13

If $4x + 2 = 12$, what is the value of $16x + 8$?

A) 40

B) 48

C) 56

D) 60

14

$$y = 76$$
$$y = x^2 - 5$$

The graphs of the given equations in the xy-plane intersect at the point (x, y). What is a possible value of x?

A) $-\dfrac{76}{5}$

B) -9

C) 5

D) 76

15

$$y = -3x$$
$$4x + y = 15$$

The solution to the given system of equations is (x, y). What is the value of x?

A) 1

B) 5

C) 15

D) 45

CONTINUE ▶

16

An event planner is planning a party. It costs the event planner a onetime fee of $35 to rent the venue and $10.25 per attendee. The event planner has a budget of $300. What is the greatest number of attendees possible without exceeding the budget?

17

$$z^2 + 10z - 24 = 0$$

What is one of the solutions to the given equation?

18

A company opens an account with an initial balance of $36,100.00. The account earns interest, and no additional deposits or withdrawals are made. The account balance is given by an exponential function A, where $A(t)$ is the account balance, in dollars, t years after the account is opened. The account balance after 13 years is $68,071.93. Which equation could define A?

A) $A(t) = 36,100.00(1.05)^t$

B) $A(t) = 31,971.93(1.05)^t$

C) $A(t) = 31,971.93(0.05)^t$

D) $A(t) = 36,100.00(0.05)^t$

19

The perimeter of an equilateral triangle is 624 centimeters. The height of this triangle is $k\sqrt{3}$ centimeters, where k is a constant. What is the value of k?

20

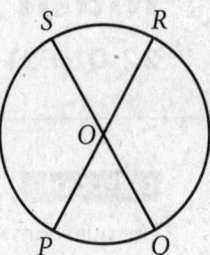

Note: Figure not drawn to scale.

The circle shown has center O, circumference 144π, and diameters $\overline{PR}$ and $\overline{QS}$. The length of arc PS is twice the length of arc PQ. What is the length of arc QR?

A) 24π

B) 48π

C) 72π

D) 96π

21

The expression $90y^5 - 54y^4$ is equivalent to $ry^4(15y - 9)$, where r is a constant. What is the value of r?

22

One leg of a right triangle has a length of 43.2 millimeters. The hypotenuse of the triangle has a length of 196.8 millimeters. What is the length of the other leg of the triangle, in millimeters?

A) 43.2

B) 120

C) 192

D) 201.5

STOP

**If you finish before time is called, you may check your work on this module only.
Do not turn to any other module in the test.**

Math

22 QUESTIONS

DIRECTIONS

The questions in this section address a number of important math skills.
Use of a calculator is permitted for all questions.

NOTES

Unless otherwise indicated:

- All variables and expressions represent real numbers.
- Figures provided are drawn to scale.
- All figures lie in a plane.
- The domain of a given function f is the set of all real numbers x for which $f(x)$ is a real number.

REFERENCE

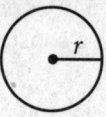 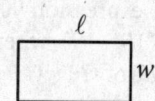 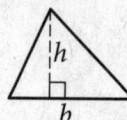 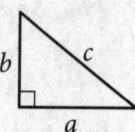 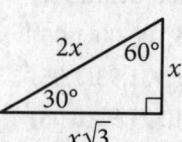

$A = \pi r^2$ $A = \ell w$ $A = \frac{1}{2}bh$ $c^2 = a^2 + b^2$ Special Right Triangles
$C = 2\pi r$

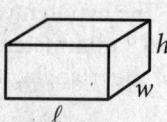 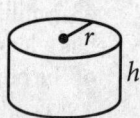  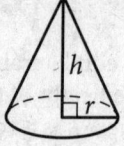 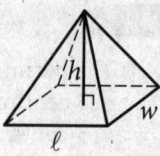

$V = \ell wh$ $V = \pi r^2 h$ $V = \frac{4}{3}\pi r^3$ $V = \frac{1}{3}\pi r^2 h$ $V = \frac{1}{3}\ell wh$

The number of degrees of arc in a circle is 360.

The number of radians of arc in a circle is 2π.

The sum of the measures in degrees of the angles of a triangle is 180.

CONTINUE ➡

For multiple-choice questions, solve each problem, choose the correct answer from the choices provided, and then circle your answer in this book. Circle only one answer for each question. If you change your mind, completely erase the circle. You will not get credit for questions with more than one answer circled, or for questions with no answers circled.

For student-produced response questions, solve each problem and write your answer next to or under the question in the test book as described below.

- Once you've written your answer, circle it clearly. You will not receive credit for anything written outside the circle, or for any questions with more than one circled answer.

- If you find **more than one correct answer**, write and circle only one answer.

- Your answer can be up to 5 characters for a **positive** answer and up to 6 characters (including the negative sign) for a **negative** answer, but no more.

- If your answer is a **fraction** that is too long (over 5 characters for positive, 6 characters for negative), write the decimal equivalent.

- If your answer is a **decimal** that is too long (over 5 characters for positive, 6 characters for negative), truncate it or round at the fourth digit.

- If your answer is a **mixed number** (such as $3\frac{1}{2}$), write it as an improper fraction (7/2) or its decimal equivalent (3.5).

- Don't include **symbols** such as a percent sign, comma, or dollar sign in your circled answer.

CONTINUE

1

$$4x + 6 = 18$$

Which equation has the same solution as the given equation?

A) $4x = 108$

B) $4x = 24$

C) $4x = 12$

D) $4x = 3$

2

The total cost $f(x)$, in dollars, to lease a car for 36 months from a particular car dealership is given by $f(x) = 36x + 1,000$, where x is the monthly payment, in dollars. What is the total cost to lease a car when the monthly payment is $400?

A) $13,400

B) $13,000

C) $15,400

D) $37,400

3

If the graph of $27x + 33y = 297$ is shifted down 5 units in the xy-plane, what is the y-intercept of the resulting graph?

A) $(0, 4)$

B) $(0, 6)$

C) $(0, 14)$

D) $(0, 28)$

4

The function f is defined by $f(x) = \frac{1}{10}x - 2$. What is the y-intercept of the graph of $y = f(x)$ in the xy-plane?

A) $(-2, 0)$

B) $(0, -2)$

C) $\left(0, \frac{1}{10}\right)$

D) $\left(\frac{1}{10}, 0\right)$

5

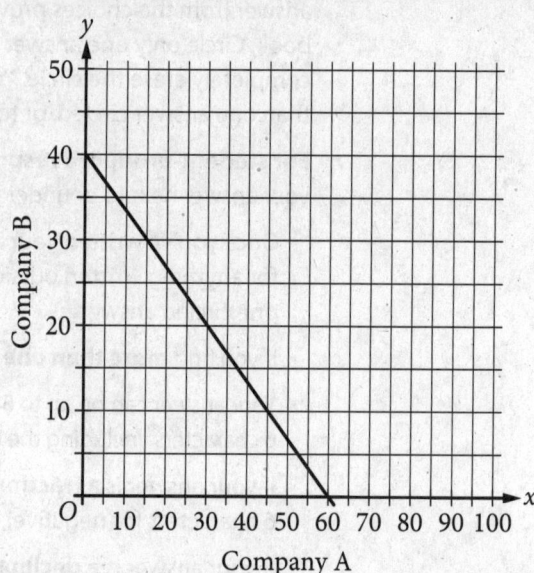

The graph shows the relationship between the number of shares of stock from Company A, x, and the number of shares of stock from Company B, y, that Simone can purchase. Which equation could represent this relationship?

A) $y = 8x + 12$

B) $8x + 12y = 480$

C) $y = 12x + 8$

D) $12x + 8y = 480$

6

$$\frac{7}{2}x + 6y = 25$$

$$\frac{5}{2}x + 6y = 23$$

The solution to the given system of equations is (x, y).

What is the value of $\frac{17}{2}x + 18y$?

A) 2

B) 3

C) 48

D) 71

CONTINUE ➤

7

$$f(x) = (x + 6)(x + 5)(x - 4)$$

The function f is given. Which table of values represents $y = f(x) - 3$?

A)

x	y
-6	-9
-5	-8
4	1

B)

x	y
-6	-3
-5	-3
4	-3

C)

x	y
-6	-3
-5	-2
4	7

D)

x	y
-6	3
-5	3
4	3

8

For the function q, the value of $q(x)$ decreases by 45% for every increase in the value of x by 1. If $q(0) = 14$, which equation defines q?

A) $q(x) = 0.55(14)^x$

B) $q(x) = 1.45(14)^x$

C) $q(x) = 14(0.55)^x$

D) $q(x) = 14(1.45)^x$

9

A submersible device is used for ocean research. The function $g(x) = -\frac{1}{55}(x + 19)(x - 35)$ gives the depth below the surface of the ocean, in meters, of the submersible device x minutes after collecting a sample, where $x > 0$. How many minutes after collecting the sample did it take for the submersible device to reach the surface of the ocean?

10

A cube has an edge length of 68 inches. A solid sphere with a radius of 34 inches is inside the cube, such that the sphere touches the center of each face of the cube. To the nearest cubic inch, what is the volume of the space in the cube not taken up by the sphere?

A) 149,796

B) 164,500

C) 190,955

D) 310,800

11

$$x(x + 1) - 56 = 4x(x - 7)$$

What is the sum of the solutions to the given equation?

CONTINUE

12

$$y < 6x + 2$$

For which of the following tables are all the values of x and their corresponding values of y solutions to the given inequality?

A)

x	y
3	20
5	32
7	44

B)

x	y
3	16
5	36
7	40

C)

x	y
3	16
5	28
7	40

D)

x	y
3	24
5	36
7	48

13

What is the diameter of the circle in the xy-plane with equation $(x - 5)^2 + (y - 3)^2 = 16$?

A) 4

B) 8

C) 16

D) 32

14

$$-9x^2 + 30x + c = 0$$

In the given equation, c is a constant. The equation has exactly one solution. What is the value of c?

A) 3

B) 0

C) −25

D) −53

15

In triangle XYZ, angle Y is a right angle, the measure of angle Z is 33°, and the length of $\overline{YZ}$ is 26 units. If the area, in square units, of triangle XYZ can be represented by the expression $k \tan 33°$, where k is a constant, what is the value of k?

16

The regular price of a shirt at a store is \$11.70. The sale price of the shirt is 80% less than the regular price, and the sale price is 30% greater than the store's cost for the shirt. What was the store's cost, in dollars, for the shirt? (Disregard the \$ sign when entering your answer. For example, if your answer is \$4.97, enter 4.97)

17

In triangles ABC and DEF, angles B and E each have measure 27° and angles C and F each have measure 41°. Which additional piece of information is sufficient to determine whether triangle ABC is congruent to triangle DEF?

A) The measure of angle A

B) The length of side AB

C) The lengths of sides BC and EF

D) No additional information is necessary.

CONTINUE ▶

18

$$48x - 72y = 30y + 24$$

$$ry = \frac{1}{6} - 16x$$

In the given system of equations, r is a constant. If the system has no solution, what is the value of r?

19

Which of the following expressions has a factor of $x + 2b$, where b is a positive integer constant?

A) $3x^2 + 7x + 14b$

B) $3x^2 + 28x + 14b$

C) $3x^2 + 42x + 14b$

D) $3x^2 + 49x + 14b$

20

The perimeter of an equilateral triangle is 624 centimeters. The height of this triangle is $k\sqrt{3}$ centimeters, where k is a constant. What is the value of k?

21

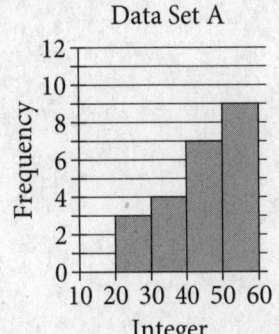 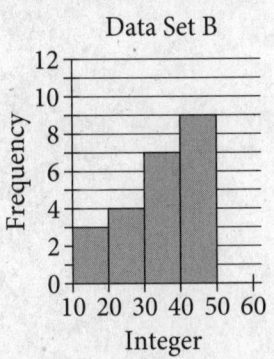

Two data sets of 23 integers each are summarized in the histograms shown. For each of the histograms, the first interval represents the frequency of integers greater than or equal to 10, but less than 20. The second interval represents the frequency of integers greater than or equal to 20, but less than 30, and so on. What is the smallest possible difference between the mean of data set A and the mean of data set B?

A) 0

B) 1

C) 10

D) 23

22

Poll Results	
Angel Cruz	483
Terry Smith	320

The table shows the results of a poll. A total of 803 voters selected at random were asked which candidate they would vote for in the upcoming election. According to the poll, if 6,424 people vote in the election, by how many votes would Angel Cruz be expected to win?

A) 163

B) 1,304

C) 3,864

D) 5,621

STOP

If you finish before time is called, you may check your work on this module only.
Do not turn to any other module in the test.

The SAT®

Practice Test #8

ANSWER EXPLANATIONS

These answer explanations are for students using
The Official SAT Study Guide.

Reading and Writing

Module 1
(27 questions)

QUESTION 1

Choice B is the best answer because it most logically completes the text's discussion of Juarez. In this context, "important" means marked by significant work or consequence. The text indicates that Juarez, who was the first president of Mexico from an Indigenous community, became a certain kind of figure in Mexico's history. It then supports that claim by describing some of the "many significant accomplishments" from Juarez's long tenure in office. This context conveys that Juarez is a significant and consequential figure in Mexico's history.

Choice A is incorrect because the text focuses on Juarez's role as the first president of Mexico from an Indigenous community and on his many major accomplishments during his lengthy time in office; nothing in the text suggests that Juarez was "unpredictable," or tended to behave in ways that couldn't be predicted. *Choice C* is incorrect because nothing in the text suggests that Juarez was a particularly "secretive" figure, or that he tended to keep things private or hidden from others. Instead, the text focuses on things that are known about Juarez: that he was the first president of Mexico from an Indigenous community, that he had a lengthy tenure, and that his many major accomplishments included consolidating the national government's authority and advancing Indigenous rights. *Choice D* is incorrect because the text focuses on the idea that Juarez, who was the first president of Mexico from an Indigenous community, had many major accomplishments during his lengthy time in office. Rather than suggesting that Juarez was an "ordinary," or common and typical, figure in Mexico's history, this context conveys that Juarez was instead a notable figure.

QUESTION 2

Choice B is the best answer because it most logically completes the text's discussion of Marilyn Dingle's baskets. In this context, to say that Dingle's baskets are "handmade from" particular plants means that Dingle creates baskets herself using those plants but without using machines. The text says that Dingle "skillfully winds" parts of palmetto palm plants around sweetgrass plants to make baskets with an appearance that "no factory can reproduce." This context suggests that Dingle's baskets are handmade from sweetgrass and palmetto palm.

Choice A is incorrect because the text describes how Dingle uses sweetgrass and palmetto palm to create her baskets, not how her baskets are "indicated by," or signified by, sweetgrass and palmetto palm. *Choice C* is incorrect. Although Dingle's baskets are described as being made using sweetgrass and palm, there's nothing in the text to suggest that the baskets are "represented by," or exemplified or portrayed by, sweetgrass and palmetto palm. Instead, the focus of the text is on Dingle's use of sweetgrass and palmetto palm and the impossibility of replicating the appearance of her baskets using machines. *Choice D* is incorrect because there's nothing in the text to suggest that Dingle's baskets are "collected with," or brought together in a group with, sweetgrass and palmetto palm. Instead, the text describes how Dingle uses those plants to make her baskets.

QUESTION 3

Choice C is the best answer because it logically and precisely completes the text's discussion of *The Mule Bone*, a play that Zora Neale Hurston and Langston Hughes wrote together. In this context, "collaboration" means working together with someone to write a literary work. The text indicates that most writers prefer to work alone and that working together destroyed the friendship between Hurston and Hughes. This establishes that *The Mule Bone* is a relatively rare example of collaboration in literature.

Choice A is incorrect because in this context, "characterization" would mean a literary work's portrayal of characters' psychological experiences and motivations, but the text doesn't discuss characterization in *The Mule Bone* specifically or in collaborative works more generally. *Choice B* is incorrect because in this context, "interpretation" would mean the explanation of a literary work's meaning or significance, but the text doesn't discuss how readers or critics have interpreted *The Mule Bone*; instead, the text discusses how the play was written collaboratively and how the writing process affected the two authors. *Choice D* is incorrect because in this context, "commercialization" would mean writing a literary work in such a way as to ensure its commercial appeal, but the text never discusses commercial appeal as a factor in the writing of *The Mule Bone* specifically or the writing of collaborative works more generally.

QUESTION 4

Choice C is the best answer because it most logically completes the discussion of the artist Diego Velázquez's influence outside Spain. As used in this context, "confined to" means restricted to. The text says that Velázquez was the leading artist in the Spanish court during the seventeenth century, but it also notes that other painters around the world were influenced by his techniques and style. Thus, Velázquez's influence was hardly (or almost not) confined to, or restricted to, Spain.

Choice A is incorrect because if Velázquez was a leading artist in Spain, it doesn't make logical sense to claim that his influence was hardly (or almost not) derived from, or obtained from, Spain. Moreover, the other painters around the world who employed Velázquez's techniques would by definition be influenced by Spanish style. *Choice B* is incorrect because if Velázquez was a leading artist in the court of King Philip IV of Spain, then his influence must have been widely recognized, or acknowledged, rather than being hardly (or almost not) recognized. *Choice D* is incorrect because the text gives no indication that deliberately limiting Velázquez's influence outside Spain was ever considered by anyone. Thus, even if it is true that his influence was not repressed, or restrained, it doesn't make logical sense to say so in this context.

QUESTION 5

Choice A is the best answer because it most logically completes the text's discussion of how biodiversity loss due to invasive species can be avoided. As used in this context, "preventable" means able to be stopped or kept from happening. The text indicates that "people can take simple steps" to avoid bringing possible invasive species into new environments. It presents these steps as an example of how biodiversity loss due to invasive species is preventable.

Choice B is incorrect because it wouldn't make sense to say that a simple step like washing your shoes after traveling is an example of biodiversity loss due to invasive species being "undeniable," or something that can't be proved to be wrong. Although the text may suggest that biodiversity loss due to invasive species is something that really happens, the word that completes the text must make the first sentence into an assertion that is illustrated by the second sentence, and the second sentence illustrates the idea that biodiversity loss due to invasive species is preventable, not undeniable. *Choice C* is incorrect because it wouldn't make sense to say that a simple step like washing your shoes after traveling is an example of biodiversity loss due to invasive species being "common," or something that happens regularly. Additionally, the text doesn't provide any information about how frequently invasive species cause biodiversity loss. *Choice D* is incorrect because it wouldn't make sense to say that a simple step like washing your shoes after traveling is an example of biodiversity loss due to invasive species being "concerning," or something that is troubling or causes worry. Although the text implies that the phenomenon of biodiversity loss due to invasive species is itself a concerning phenomenon, the word that completes the text must make the first sentence into an assertion that is illustrated by the second sentence, and the second sentence illustrates the idea that biodiversity loss due to invasive species is preventable, not concerning.

QUESTION 6

Choice C is the best answer because it presents the best description of the overall structure of the text. The text begins by stating that companies are increasingly giving consumers opportunities to customize products, allowing them to make design choices when buying certain sneakers, jewelry, and clothing. The text then indicates that although this trend benefits companies because they can successfully charge buyers more for customized products and don't have to rush production, it also poses a challenge because producing unique items may require different and more expensive methods than the ones typically used for mass production, raising the companies' costs. Thus, the text first introduces a trend in consumer products and then explains how the trend both benefits and poses a challenge to companies.

Choice A is incorrect because the text doesn't present the customization of various products as a recent innovation—the fact that there are "more opportunities" now indicates that there were opportunities before—and no other innovations, in product manufacturing or otherwise, are discussed. *Choice B* is incorrect because the text doesn't discuss any particular company or example and instead speaks broadly about the trend of companies providing customizable products. *Choice D* is incorrect. Although the text discusses companies offering something that consumers like and are willing to pay more for—the ability to customize products—it doesn't characterize this as a product-marketing technique and doesn't compare it to any other kind of offering or technique.

QUESTION 7

Choice A is the best answer because it accurately states the main purpose of the text. The text begins by discussing the promise of the future, with positive references to renewal such as "new roads," "new beating of the drum," and "fresh seeing." But with the "new sun," the text continues, there will still be "the same backs bending" and "the same sad feet" drumming, indicating that these difficulties will follow people into this new day. The poem thus considers both the rewards and challenges associated with the repetitiveness of human life.

Choice B is incorrect because the text doesn't say anything about how memorable activities are, let alone compare the memorability of activities completed at different times of the day. *Choice C* is incorrect. Although the text contrasts hope with difficulty, it does not compare the relative frequency of joyful feelings with that of sad feelings. *Choice D* is incorrect because the text makes no distinction between the experiences of individuals and the experiences of their communities.

QUESTION 8

Choice D is the best answer because it accurately describes the overall structure of the text. The text begins by pointing out an obstacle to observing the astronomical phenomenon of the NCP: the NCP is visible only at night. The text then indicates that, inspired by the ability of some insects and birds to navigate using visualizations of polarized sunlight, researchers devised a way to locate the NCP during daylight. The text then indicates that the researchers mimicked the insects' and birds' polarized-light visualization capabilities using a polarimetric camera. Thus, the text notes an obstacle to observing an astronomical phenomenon, mentions a navigational ability of certain animals that inspired a solution to that obstacle, and then explains how researchers used an optical device to mimic that ability.

Choice A is incorrect. Although it's reasonable to conjecture that humans have used the NCP for navigation, the text doesn't indicate this is the case, let alone that the NCP is relevant to a majority of navigational tools. Furthermore, the text doesn't state that researchers discovered that insects and birds navigate without the NCP; rather, it indicates that it's known that some animals navigate by using skylight polarization to locate the NCP during the day and that this knowledge inspired the method the researchers devised. *Choice B* is incorrect. Although it's reasonable to conjecture that humans have used the NCP for navigation, the text doesn't state that this is the case. Furthermore, the text discusses how some animals' use of navigational strategies based on the same celestial occurrence served as the inspiration for the researchers' polarized-light approach, not as the basis for a comparison of the relative effectiveness of animal and human methods of navigation. *Choice C* is incorrect. Although the text implies that humans have typically been able to locate the NCP visually at night and indicates that some animals use the NCP to navigate, the text doesn't state that humans use the NCP for navigation. The text therefore doesn't emphasize a difference between how humans and animals use the NCP for this purpose. Furthermore, the text doesn't suggest that existing navigational instruments will be augmented with polarimetric technologies.

QUESTION 9

Choice A is the best answer because it most accurately states the main idea of the text. The text describes the book *Vibration Cooking: or, the Travel Notes of a Geechee Girl* as Smart-Grosvenor's "most influential project" and as "unusual for its time." The text also notes that the book and author have influenced contemporary approaches to writing about food and cooking. Therefore, the text mainly conveys that *Vibration Cooking: or, the Travel Notes of a Geechee Girl* is an unconventional and important contribution to food writing.

Choice B is incorrect. Although the text mentions that Smart-Grosvenor worked in national public television and radio and was a food writer, these details aren't the main focus. Rather than focusing on Smart-Grosvenor's various jobs, the text focuses specifically on one specific book she wrote. *Choice C* is incorrect. Although the text suggests that *Vibration Cooking: or, the Travel Notes of a Geechee Girl* was groundbreaking, it doesn't suggest that the book didn't receive praise when it was published. In fact, the text states that the book is "long admired." *Choice D* is incorrect because the text states that Smart-Grosvenor was a culinary anthropologist and that her book influenced later approaches to food writing but doesn't indicate that Smart-Grosvenor or her book influenced people to begin cooking for themselves.

QUESTION 10

Choice C is the best answer because it presents a point that Prospero makes about Miranda. The text begins with Miranda responding to Prospero's claim that she probably doesn't remember her life before the island. She describes a distant memory, asking if she had "four or five women" caring for her. Prospero confirms this ("thou hadst") and then asks what else she can recall, stating that because she remembers one thing from the time before she lived on the island ("ought ere thou camest here"), she might also remember arriving on the island ("how thou camest here"). That is, Prospero indicates that Miranda's ability to summon details of an experience from before her arrival on the island suggests that she may also be able to summon details of her arrival.

Choice A is incorrect because Prospero doesn't say anything about how Miranda presents her early childhood memory of having several people care for her—he indicates only his surprise that she remembers something from so long ago ("the dark backward and abysm of time") and his thought that she may also be able to recall another childhood event: her arrival on the island. Further, Prospero doesn't suggest that he believes Miranda is discontent in her current circumstances. *Choice B* is incorrect. Although Miranda suggests some doubt about her recollection of a place other than the island, in that she describes it as "like a dream" she can't be certain of, Prospero doesn't mention her uncertainty—though he himself wonders how it is possible that she correctly recalls something from so long ago ("abysm of time"). Rather than indicating that doubt is making Miranda reluctant, Prospero simply states that Miranda may have the ability to remember traveling to the island. *Choice D* is incorrect. Although Miranda describes a vague impression of several people who cared for her as a young child and states that it is "rather like a dream" instead of something she is certain is real, Prospero doesn't indicate that Miranda is remembering a childhood daydream. Instead, he confirms that what Miranda remembers actually happened, answering her question about having had caregivers with "thou hadst," and asks her what else she can remember from long ago.

QUESTION 11

Choice C is the best answer because it illustrates the student's claim about some historians viewing Lumumba primarily as a symbol. This quotation argues that Lumumba "warrants" (or deserves) "scholarly attention" as a symbol and not for his "practical accomplishments"—that is, his actions as prime minister—which "can be passed over quickly," or dismissed as being of comparatively little importance. Thus, the quotation expresses the view that the student criticizes some historians for holding.

Choice A is incorrect. Although this quotation touches on the difficulty of evaluating Lumumba's legacy, it doesn't address how historians of modern African politics view him as a symbol. *Choice B* is incorrect. While this quotation mentions Lumumba's political beliefs, it doesn't discuss historians viewing him as a symbol. *Choice D* is incorrect. This quotation touches on Lumumba's vision for his country, but it doesn't discuss historians viewing him as a symbol.

QUESTION 12

Choice D is the best answer because it presents a finding that, if true, would most directly support the researchers' hypothesis about the connection between the dusky shark population decline and the eastern oyster population decline. The text indicates that although dusky sharks don't usually eat eastern oysters, they do consume cownose rays, which are the main predators of eastern oysters. An increase in the abundance of cownose rays in the region in response to a decline in the abundance of dusky sharks would directly support the researchers' hypothesis: a higher number of cownose rays would consume more eastern oysters, driving down the oyster population.

Choice A is incorrect because a finding that there's an association between a decline in the regional abundance of some of dusky sharks' prey and the regional abundance of dusky sharks wouldn't directly support the researchers' hypothesis that a decline in dusky sharks has led to a decline in eastern oysters in the region. Although such a finding might help explain why shark abundance has declined, it would reveal nothing about whether the shark decline is related to the oyster decline. *Choice B* is incorrect because a finding that eastern oyster abundance tends to be greater when dusky sharks and cownose rays are present than when only dusky sharks are present wouldn't support the researchers' hypothesis that a decline in dusky sharks has led to a decline in eastern oysters in the region. The text indicates that the sharks prey on the rays, which are the main predators of the oysters; if oyster abundance is found to be greater when rays are present than when rays are absent, that would suggest that rays aren't keeping oyster abundance down, and thus that a decline in rays' predators, which would be expected to lead to an increase in the abundance of rays, wouldn't bring about a decline in oyster abundance as the researchers hypothesize. *Choice C* is incorrect because a finding that consumption of eastern oysters by cownose rays increased substantially before dusky sharks declined in regional abundance wouldn't support the researchers' hypothesis that the decline in dusky sharks has led to a decline in eastern oysters in the region. Such a finding would suggest that some factor other than shark abundance led to an increase in rays' consumption of oysters and thus to a decrease in oyster abundance, thereby weakening the researchers' hypothesis.

QUESTION 13

Choice D is the best answer because it most logically completes the text's discussion of critic Jesse Green's review of the 2016 and 2019 productions of *Hadestown*. The text states that Green found the storytelling in the 2016 off-Broadway version to be "very confusing" but that he "enthusiastically praised" the storytelling in the revised 2019 Broadway version. This stark contrast in Green's opinions suggests that he believed the musical had significantly improved between 2016 and its 2019 Broadway premiere.

Choice A is incorrect because it contradicts the information in the text. The text indicates that Green found the storytelling in the 2016 version to be "very confusing," while he "enthusiastically praised" the storytelling in the 2019 version. This suggests that the 2019 version had fewer, not more, storytelling problems. *Choice B* is incorrect because the text doesn't provide any information about Green's opinion on the size of the 2019 Broadway production. While it mentions that the 2019 production was larger than the 2016 production, there's no indication in the text that Green thought the 2019 production should have been even larger than it was. *Choice C* is incorrect because it contradicts the information in the text. The text's description of Green's enthusiastic praise for the 2019 production suggests that he found this version more enjoyable, not less enjoyable, than the 2016 version, which he described as "very confusing."

QUESTION 14

Choice B is the best answer because it most logically completes the text's discussion of artifacts and Kuulo Kataa's founding date. If it were true both that Kuulo Kataa was founded in the fourteenth century CE and that artifacts found in excavations of the settlement are from the thirteenth century CE, it would be reasonable to conclude that the artifacts weren't created in the Kuulo Kataa settlement. That would suggest, then, that the artifacts originated somewhere else and eventually reached the settlement through trading or as people migrated.

Choice A is incorrect because the existence of thirteenth-century CE artifacts recovered during excavations of a settlement founded in the fourteenth century CE isn't logically connected to artifacts from one century being more commonly recovered than artifacts from another century. Rather than suggesting anything about how frequently artifacts from different times are found, the existence of artifacts confirmed as predating the settlement's founding suggests that those items arrived in Kuulo Kataa during or after its establishment. *Choice C* is incorrect because the text focuses on time periods and says nothing about which region the founders of Kuulo Kataa have been thought to come from; similarly, the text doesn't suggest anything about where the thirteenth-century CE artifacts originated other than not from Kuulo Kataa. Therefore, it isn't logical to conclude that the mere existence of artifacts confirmed as predating the Kuulo Kataa settlement suggests that the founders of the settlement came from a particular region other than one previously assumed. *Choice D* is incorrect because the existence of artifacts from the thirteenth century CE at a site dated to the fourteenth century CE doesn't imply that fourteenth-century objects were damaged during excavations. There's nothing in the text to suggest that any objects were damaged; rather, the existence of artifacts confirmed as predating the settlement's founding suggests that those items were brought to Kuulo Kataa during or after its establishment.

QUESTION 15

Choice D is the best answer because it most logically completes the text's discussion of Shultz's finding about male tanagers. The text explains that because carotenoids both contribute to deeply saturated feathers and offer health benefits, having deeply saturated feathers is usually "an honest signal" (a true indication) that a bird is generally fit. However, Shultz and others have found that certain male tanagers can appear to have deeply saturated feathers even if they haven't consumed a diet rich in carotenoids, thanks to microstructures in their feathers that manipulate light. If those birds aren't necessarily eating carotenoid-rich diets, they may actually be less fit than other birds that appear to have similarly saturated feathers; this suggests that a male tanager's appearance may function as a dishonest signal, or a false indication, of the bird's overall fitness.

Choice A is incorrect because Shultz's finding suggests that some tanagers can signal fitness without consuming the carotenoids that contribute to fitness, thereby making those signals dishonest, not that tanagers can give honest signals of their fitness without consuming carotenoids. *Choice B* is incorrect because Shultz's finding suggests that the microstructures in certain tanagers' feathers can give a dishonest signal of fitness, not that the microstructures are less effective than actual pigmentation for signaling fitness. Whether the signal of fitness is honest or dishonest has no bearing on how effective the signal is: a signal is effective if potential mates behave as though it's true, regardless of whether it's actually true. Since there's no information in the text about how potential mates respond to the dishonest signals of some tanagers, there's no support for the idea that the dishonest signals are less effective than the honest signals. *Choice C* is incorrect because Shultz's finding suggests that certain male tanagers may appear to be fitter than they actually are, not that scientists haven't determined why tanagers prefer mates with colorful appearances.

QUESTION 16

Choice B is the best answer. The convention being tested is the use of verbs to express tense. In this choice, the past perfect verb "had doubled" properly indicates that the doubling of the organization's initial membership occurred during a specific period before the present (between the organization's founding in 1967 and the end of the 1990s).

Choice A is incorrect because the present perfect verb "has doubled" doesn't indicate that the organization's doubling of its initial membership occurred during a specific period in the past. *Choice C* is incorrect because the present tense verb "doubles" doesn't indicate that the organization's doubling of its initial membership occurred during a specific period in the past. *Choice D* is incorrect because the future tense verb "will double" doesn't indicate that the organization's doubling of its initial membership occurred during a specific period in the past.

QUESTION 17

Choice B is the best answer. The convention being tested is pronoun-antecedent agreement. The plural pronoun "they" agrees in number with the plural antecedent "woodcuts" and clearly identifies what was exhibited at the Smithsonian American Art Museum.

Choice A is incorrect because the singular pronoun "it" doesn't agree in number with the plural antecedent "woodcuts." *Choice C* is incorrect because the singular pronoun "this" doesn't agree in number with the plural antecedent "woodcuts." *Choice D* is incorrect because the plural pronoun "some" is illogical in this context (referring to "some" of two woodcuts).

QUESTION 18

Choice C is the best answer. The convention being tested is the punctuation of a restrictive coordinated noun phrase. No punctuation is needed within or around the coordinated noun phrase "researchers Roberto Scandone and Christopher Kilburn" because it would create an illogical separation between the noun "researchers" and the coordinated noun phrase "Roberto Scandone and Christopher Kilburn."

Choice A is incorrect because no punctuation is needed. Placing a pair of commas around the coordinated noun phrase "Roberto Scandone and Christopher Kilburn" creates an illogical separation between the noun "researchers" and the aforementioned coordinated noun phrase. In this case, it illogically suggests that researchers in general bear the specific names Roberto Scandone and Christopher Kilburn. *Choice B* is incorrect because no punctuation is needed between the noun "researchers" and the coordinated noun phrase "Roberto Scandone and Christopher Kilburn." *Choice D* is incorrect because no punctuation is needed within the coordinated noun phrase "Roberto Scandone and Christopher Kilburn."

QUESTION 19

Choice C is the best answer. The convention being tested is punctuation use between a main clause and two supplementary elements. In this choice, the commas after "nickname" and "however" are correctly used to separate the supplementary adverb "however" from the main clause ("Scott-Heron… nickname") on one side and the supplementary participial phrase ("feeling… bluesologist") on the other.

Choice A is incorrect because it fails to mark the boundary between the supplementary adverb "however" and the supplementary phrase ("feeling… bluesologist"). *Choice B* is incorrect because a semicolon can't be used in this way to join the supplementary adverb "however" and the supplementary phrase ("feeling…bluesologist"). *Choice D* is incorrect because a semicolon can't be used in this way to join the main clause ("Scott-Heron…nickname") and the supplementary word and phrase ("however" and "feeling…bluesologist"). Moreover, placing the semicolon after "nickname" illogically signals that the following information (Scott-Heron's feeling that the nickname didn't encapsulate his devotion to the blues tradition) is contrary to the information in the previous clause (Scott-Heron's resistance to the nickname).

QUESTION 20

Choice A is the best answer. The convention being tested is the use of a colon within a sentence. In this choice, the colon is used in a conventional way to introduce the following description of how the number of jams available varied.

Choice B is incorrect because it creates a comma splice. A comma can't be used in this way to join two main clauses ("the number…varied" and "some…six"). *Choice C* is incorrect because it results in an illogical and confusing sentence. Using the conjunction "while" to join the main clause ("the number…varied") with the following clause's description of the number of jams available suggests that the variation in the number of jams is in contrast to some shoppers having twenty-four options. *Choice D* is incorrect because it results in an illogical and confusing sentence. Using "while" in this way suggests that the number of jams available varied during the time in which some shoppers had twenty-four options and others had six. The sentence makes clear, however, that what follows "varied" is a description of the variation, not a separate, simultaneous occurrence.

QUESTION 21

Choice B is the best answer. The convention being tested is the use of punctuation within a sentence. This choice uses a semicolon in a conventional way to join the first main clause ("Gitlin's…content") and the second main clause beginning with a supplementary phrase ("in…audiences"). Further, placing a comma after "era" separates the supplementary phrase "in that era" from the rest of the main clause that follows ("even…audiences").

Choice A is incorrect because it results in a comma splice. Without a conjunction following it, a comma can't be used in this way to join two main clauses. Further, this choice fails to mark the boundary between the supplementary phrase "in that era" and the rest of the main clause that follows ("even...audiences"). *Choice C* is incorrect because it results in a run-on sentence. The two main clauses ("Gitlin's...content" and "in...audiences") are fused without punctuation and/or a conjunction. *Choice D* is incorrect because it results in a comma splice. Without a conjunction following it, a comma can't be used in this way to join two main clauses.

QUESTION 22

Choice C is the best answer. "Consequently" logically signals that the information in this sentence—that many individual gold prospectors gave up their fortune-hunting dreams and became employees of mining companies—is a result or consequence of the previous information about the inaccessibility of the state's gold deposits.

Choice A is incorrect because "furthermore" illogically signals that the information in this sentence merely adds to the previous information about the inaccessibility of the state's gold deposits. Instead, it's a result or consequence of that information. *Choice B* is incorrect because "still" illogically signals that the information in this sentence offers a contrast or exception to the previous information about the inaccessibility of the state's gold deposits. Instead, it's a result or consequence of that information. *Choice D* is incorrect because "next" illogically signals that the information in this sentence is the next step in a process. Instead, it's a result or consequence of the previous information about the inaccessibility of the state's gold deposits.

QUESTION 23

Choice B is the best answer. "Specifically" logically signals that the information in this sentence—that Molina and Rowland's research laid the foundation for a later treaty—provides specific, precise details elaborating on the previous sentence's more general claim about the influence of the research.

Choice A is incorrect because "regardless" illogically signals that the information in this sentence is true despite the previous sentence's claim about the influence of Molina and Rowland's research. Instead, this information—that the research laid the foundation for a later treaty—provides specific details elaborating on the previous claim. *Choice C* is incorrect because "however" illogically signals that the information in this sentence contrasts with the previous sentence's claim about the influence of Molina and Rowland's research. Instead, this information—that the research laid the foundation for a later treaty—provides specific details elaborating on the previous claim. *Choice D* is incorrect because "earlier" illogically signals that the information in this sentence occurred at a time before Molina and Rowland's research influenced the fight against CFCs. Instead, this information—that the research laid the foundation for a later treaty—provides specific details elaborating on the previous claim about the research's influence.

QUESTION 24

Choice A is the best answer. The sentence emphasizes the order in which Alaska and Hawaii became US states, noting that Alaska became a US state several months before Hawaii did.

Choice B is incorrect. The sentence specifies when the 50-star US flag was unveiled; it doesn't emphasize the order in which Alaska and Hawaii became US states. *Choice C* is incorrect. While the sentence indicates that the 49th and 50th states became US states in the same year, it doesn't identify which state was the 49th and which was the 50th; as a result, it doesn't emphasize the order in which Alaska and Hawaii became states. *Choice D* is incorrect. The sentence indicates that a new US flag was unveiled when Hawaii became a US state; it doesn't emphasize the order in which Alaska and Hawaii became states.

QUESTION 25

Choice D is the best answer. The sentence uses "whereas" to contrast the emissivities of the two fibers, noting that the emissivity of the reflective metal fibers was just 0.02, far lower than that of the silicon carbide fibers (0.74).

Choice A is incorrect. The sentence emphasizes the ability of reflective metal fibers and silicon carbide fibers to emit heat; it doesn't contrast the emissivities of the two fibers. *Choice B* is incorrect. The sentence states a law of thermodynamics: the amount of heat a material absorbs is equal to the amount it emits. The sentence doesn't contrast the emissivity of reflective metal fibers with that of silicon carbide fibers. *Choice C* is incorrect. While the sentence includes a generalization about the emissivities of reflective metal fibers and silicon carbide fibers, it emphasizes Abebe's plans for their use in a garment; it doesn't contrast the emissivities of the two fibers.

QUESTION 26

Choice D is the best answer. The sentence emphasizes the role a misconception played in the naming of a place, explaining that Spanish explorers mistook a peninsula for an island and, as a result, named the peninsula after a fictional island, California.

Choice A is incorrect. The sentence mentions a novel that featured a fictional island, California; it doesn't emphasize the role a misconception played in the naming of a place. *Choice B* is incorrect. The sentence notes that Baja California was originally named after a fictional place; it doesn't emphasize the role a misconception—specifically, the Spanish explorers' mistaken belief that the peninsula was an island—played in the naming of a place. *Choice C* is incorrect. The sentence indicates when Spanish explorers learned of the peninsula they called California; it doesn't emphasize the role a misconception played in the naming of a place.

QUESTION 27

Choice C is the best answer. The sentence emphasizes the aim, or goal, of the research study, noting what Terada set out to do: determine whether some of the Moon's oxygen was coming from Earth.

Choice A is incorrect. The sentence focuses on how the Kaguya satellite collected data; it doesn't emphasize the aim of the research study. *Choice B* is incorrect. While the sentence mentions what Terada was curious about before conducting the research study, it doesn't emphasize his study's aim. *Choice D* is incorrect. The sentence presents the research study's conclusion; it doesn't emphasize the study's aim.

Reading and Writing

Module 2 — Lower Difficulty
(27 questions)

QUESTION 1

Choice C is the best answer because it most logically completes the text's discussion of how predators feed their young. As used in this context, "provide" means supply or make something that's needed available. The text indicates that some predators supply prey for their young by either leaving dead prey nearby or by bringing live prey to them. Other predators, the text states, feed their young directly from their own mouths. This context supports the idea that predatory animals have various ways to provide food for their young.

Choice A is incorrect because in this context, "avoid" would mean keep away from or refrain from, neither of which would make sense in context. Nothing in the text suggests that predators refrain from food for their young. *Choice B* is incorrect because in this context, "guess" would mean speculate or suppose, and it's unclear what it would mean for predators to speculate food for their young. *Choice D* is incorrect because in this context, "describe" would mean explain, and it's unclear what it would mean for predators to explain food for their young.

QUESTION 2

Choice D is the best answer because it most logically completes the text's discussion of the challenge of generating electricity from ocean waves. In this context, "consistent" means steady or unchanging over time. The text introduces a challenge and then explains that wave power varies, or changes, unpredictably in ways that cause problems for electricity generation. This context conveys that the challenge being described is a lack of consistency.

Choice A is incorrect because the text introduces a challenge and then elaborates on it by emphasizing that the unpredictable nature of variations in ocean waves causes problems, which doesn't indicate that wave power isn't "accidental," or isn't happening unintentionally. It wouldn't make sense to describe waves—a natural occurrence—as happening intentionally. *Choice B* is incorrect because "confident" means having a feeling of self-assurance, and it wouldn't make sense to describe wave power itself in terms of either having or lacking a sense of confidence. *Choice C* is incorrect because the text introduces a challenge and then elaborates on it by emphasizing that the unpredictable nature of variations in ocean waves causes problems, which doesn't indicate that wave power isn't "expensive," or isn't costly. If anything, technological and planning problems might actually increase the expense of generating electricity from waves.

QUESTION 3

Choice B is the best answer because it most logically completes the text's discussion of Jacob Lawrence's artistic process. In this context, "observant" means watchful and perceptive. The text emphasizes that the "close attention" Lawrence paid to "all the details" of his neighborhood allowed him to reflect subtle elements of "the beauty and vitality of the Black experience" in his artwork. This context indicates that being observant of his surroundings was an important part of Lawrence's work as an artist.

Choice A is incorrect because the text gives no indication that Lawrence was "skeptical," or had an attitude of doubt in general or about particular things, let alone that skepticism was important to him as an artist. Rather than indicating that he was skeptical, the text focuses on how Lawrence paid careful attention to everything around him and reflected his observations in his artwork. *Choice C* is incorrect because the text gives no indication that Lawrence was "critical," which in this context would mean inclined to criticize harshly or unfairly. Rather than indicating that Lawrence found fault in things, the text suggests that he paid careful attention to everything around him and that his artwork reflects this careful attention. *Choice D* is incorrect because the text doesn't suggest that Lawrence was "confident," or self-assured. Rather than addressing how Lawrence felt about himself and how that feeling affected his artistic process, the text emphasizes the careful attention Lawrence paid to everything around him—attention that allowed him to capture subtle elements of a particular place and time in his artwork.

QUESTION 4

Choice A is the best answer because it most logically completes the text's discussion of letters allegedly exchanged between President Lincoln and Rutledge. In this context, "validate" means to confirm that something is real or correct. According to the text, it was alleged, or claimed, that the newly discovered letters had been written by Lincoln and Rutledge. The text also indicates that historians ultimately decided the letters were a hoax, or fraudulent. This context suggests that the historians couldn't confirm that the letters were authentic.

Choice B is incorrect. The text focuses on the authenticity of the letters, which were claimed to have been written by Lincoln and Rutledge and were then quickly dismissed as fraudulent by historians. Rather than conveying that the historians simply weren't able to "interpret," or explain in an understandable way, the letters' authenticity, the text suggests that the historians decided the letters lacked authenticity altogether. *Choice C* is incorrect. The text states that the historians quickly dismissed the letters claimed to have been written by Lincoln and Rutledge as fraudulent; this suggests that rather than being unable to "relate," or tell others about, the letters' authenticity, the historians were able to share what they'd decided about the letters. *Choice D* is incorrect because it wouldn't make sense to suggest that the historians couldn't "accommodate," or give consideration to, the authenticity of the letters claimed to have been written by Lincoln and Rutledge; the text states that the historians decided that the letters were fraudulent, which indicates that they did consider whether the letters were authentic.

QUESTION 5

Choice A is the best answer because it most accurately states the main purpose of the text. After providing a brief introduction to computer scientist Luis von Ahn, the text focuses on discussing how von Ahn's digitization work led to the invention of a digital security test known as reCAPTCHA.

Choice B is incorrect because the text doesn't address how digital scanners work. *Choice C* is incorrect. Although the text mentions von Ahn's book-digitizing project, that information is provided as a detail, not as the main purpose of the text. *Choice D* is incorrect because the text doesn't provide any indication of reCAPTCHA's popularity; instead, it describes reCAPTCHA's origin.

QUESTION 6

Choice C is the best answer because it most accurately describes how the underlined sentence functions in the text as a whole. The underlined sentence establishes a difference between Uncle Katsuhisa and the narrator's father by describing Uncle Katsuhisa as "loud" and the narrator's father as "quiet." The text then elaborates on that contrast, describing some ways Uncle Katsuhisa is very noisy even when he isn't speaking.

Choice A is incorrect because the text doesn't indicate what kinds of topics Uncle Katsuhisa enjoys discussing, only that he is loud even when he isn't speaking. *Choice B* is incorrect because the text never indicates how Uncle Katsuhisa feels about meeting new people, only how loud he is. *Choice D* is incorrect because the text never describes a conversation occurring between any people; it refers to talking only when stating that Uncle Katsuhisa is loud even when he isn't speaking.

QUESTION 7

Choice A is the best answer because it reflects what the paleontologists in Text 2 would most likely say about what the researchers in Text 1 initially thought. Text 1 focuses on the discovery of a strange fossil consisting of the skull of the extinct species *Oculudentavis khaungraae*. According to Text 1, the fossil has features that appear to be avian, or related to birds, which led researchers to initially think that the fossil might be a very small avian dinosaur. Text 2 begins by noting the discovery of a second fossil similar to the one discussed in Text 1, then explains that based on detailed studies of both fossils, paleontologists think that the two creatures were probably unusual lizards, even though the skulls appeared avian at first. This suggests that the paleontologists in Text 2 recognize that the fossils do indeed look like they could be related to birds. For this reason, the paleontologists in Text 2 would most likely say that the initial thought of the researchers in Text 1—that the fossil was avian—is understandable, even if the fossil is probably not avian but rather is from a lizard.

Choice B is incorrect because Text 2 indicates that the fossils initially looked avian, so the paleontologists described in Text 2 wouldn't be confused by the researchers in Text 1 initially thinking that *O. khaungraae* might be related to birds. The paleontologists would find that initial thought understandable, not confusing. *Choice C* is incorrect because Text 1 never mentions lizards, so it wouldn't make sense for the paleontologists in Text 2 to say that the researchers in Text 1 mistakenly assumed that *O. khaungraae* must be a lizard. *Choice D* is incorrect. Although the paleontologists in Text 2 might agree that the initial thought of the researchers in Text 1 was reasonable, nothing in Text 2 suggests that the two skulls were shaped differently.

QUESTION 8

Choice B is the best answer because it presents a statement about Dorian that is directly supported by the text. The narrator of the text says that when Dorian sees his portrait, "his cheeks flushed for a moment with pleasure" and "a look of joy came into his eyes." The narrator goes on to say that Dorian looked at the portrait "in wonder" and presents him as being so entranced by the portrait that he doesn't notice what Hallward is saying to him. All these details support the description of Dorian as being delighted by what he sees in the portrait.

Choice A is incorrect because Dorian isn't depicted as interested in Hallward's opinion of the portrait but rather as so enraptured by the painting that he's hardly even aware of Hallward. *Choice C* is incorrect because the portrait of Dorian is the only painting that is mentioned in the text, so there's no evidence that Dorian prefers portraits to other types of paintings. Although Dorian is depicted as delighted with this particular portrait, there's no way of knowing from the text whether he likes portraits better than other kinds of paintings. *Choice D* is incorrect because nothing in the text suggests that Dorian is uncertain about Hallward's talent. Instead, the text is focused on Dorian's delight with the portrait.

QUESTION 9

Choice D is the best answer because it provides a detail about Elinor that is established in the text. The text indicates that although Elinor is "only nineteen," she gives good advice and exhibits such a high level of understanding and judgment that she serves as "the counsellor of her mother." Thus, Elinor is mature beyond her years.

Choice A is incorrect because it isn't supported by the text: although the text says that Elinor advises her mother and often counteracts her mother's impulses, there's no mention of Elinor arguing with her mother or failing to change her mother's mind. *Choice B* is incorrect because it isn't supported by the text: although the text mentions that Elinor has strong feelings, it doesn't indicate that she's excessively sensitive when it comes to family issues. *Choice C* is incorrect because it isn't supported by the text: there's no mention of what Elinor thinks about her mother and no suggestion that she thinks her mother is a bad role model. Because she's described as having "an excellent heart," Elinor likely doesn't think ill of her mother.

QUESTION 10

Choice A is the best answer because it presents an explanation that is directly stated in the text for why ecologists are worried about Pando. The text states that Pando is a colony of about 47,000 quaking aspen trees that represents one of the largest organisms on Earth. According to the text, ecologists are worried that Pando's growth is declining, partly because animals are feeding on the trees. In other words, the ecologists are worried that Pando isn't growing at the same rate it used to.

Choice B is incorrect. Rather than indicating that Pando isn't producing young trees anymore, the text reveals that Pando is indeed producing young trees, stating that those trees can be protected from grazing deer by strong fences. *Choice C* is incorrect because the text states that fences can be used to prevent deer from eating Pando's young trees, not that Pando itself can't grow in new areas because it's blocked by fences. *Choice D* is incorrect because the text offers no evidence that Pando's root system is incapable of supporting new trees or is otherwise a cause of worry for ecologists.

QUESTION 11

Choice B is the best answer because it most effectively uses data from the table to complete the statement about video game availability. The text states that just a few games released in the past are available today and then indicates that there is a period of years from which only 14.22 percent of the games released are available. The table shows that 14.22 percent of games are still available from the years 1995–1999.

Choice A is incorrect because the years 2000–2004 are not represented in the table. *Choice C* is incorrect because the years 1970–1974 are not represented in the table. *Choice D* is incorrect because the years 1985–1989 correspond to a percentage of games still available of 15.38 percent, not 14.22 percent.

QUESTION 12

Choice C is the best answer. The table shows the depths below the ocean surface at which four species of deep-sea fish live. According to the table, the range of depths at which the southern stoplight loosejaw lives is 500–2,000 meters below the surface.

Choice A is incorrect because the table indicates that the southern stoplight loosejaw lives 500–2,000 meters below the ocean surface, not at depths more than 2,000 meters below the surface. *Choice B* is incorrect because the table indicates that the southern stoplight loosejaw lives 500–2,000 meters below the ocean surface, not 150–400 meters below the surface. *Choice D* is incorrect because the table indicates that the southern stoplight loosejaw lives 500–2,000 meters below the ocean surface, not 250–500 meters below the surface.

QUESTION 13

Choice A is the best answer because it presents the quotation that most directly illustrates the claim that Cather portrays Alexandra as having a deep emotional connection to her natural surroundings. This quotation states that the country meant a great deal to Alexandra and then goes on to detail several ways in which her natural surroundings affect her emotionally: the insects sound like "the sweetest music," she feels as though "her heart were hiding" in the grass "with the quail and the plover," and near the ridges she feels "the future stirring."

Choice B is incorrect because the quotation doesn't suggest that Alexandra had a deep emotional connection to her natural surroundings but instead describes how she interacts with the people around her to learn more about crops, poultry, and experiments with clover hay. *Choice C* is incorrect because the quotation doesn't suggest that Alexandra has a deep emotional connection to her natural surroundings but instead describes her nighttime departure in a wagon. The quotation says nothing about Alexandra's emotional state. *Choice D* is incorrect because the quotation doesn't convey Alexandra's deep emotional connection to her natural surroundings; instead, this quotation describes how well she understands the markets and livestock.

QUESTION 14

Choice C is the best answer because it most effectively uses data from the table to complete the statement about the forestry student's project. The table shows five types of maple trees, each tree's maximum height, and whether each tree is native to North America. The text indicates that the student needs to recommend a maple tree that's native to North America and won't reach a height greater than 60 feet. The red maple is the only tree listed in the table that meets these criteria: its maximum height is 60 feet—meaning that it won't grow higher than 60 feet—and it's native to North America.

Choice A is incorrect because the text states that the student needs to recommend a tree that's native to North America and won't grow higher than 60 feet, but the table shows that the maximum height of the silver maple is 70 feet. *Choice B* is incorrect because the text states that the student needs to recommend a tree that's native to North America and won't grow higher than 60 feet, but the table shows that the maximum height of the sugar maple is 75 feet. *Choice D* is incorrect because the text states that the student needs to recommend a tree that's native to North America and won't grow higher than 60 feet, but the table shows that the Norway maple isn't native to North America.

QUESTION 15

Choice D is the best answer. The convention being tested is the use of verbs to express tense. In this choice, the present tense verb "is," used in conjunction with the word "today," correctly indicates that Paik is currently considered the first video artist.

Choice A is incorrect because the future-indicating verb "will be" doesn't indicate that Paik is currently considered the first video artist. *Choice B* is incorrect because the past perfect tense verb "had been" doesn't indicate that Paik is currently considered the first video artist. *Choice C* is incorrect because the past tense verb "was" doesn't indicate that Paik is currently considered the first video artist.

QUESTION 16

Choice D is the best answer. The convention being tested is the use of finite and nonfinite verb forms within a sentence. The nonfinite to-infinitive "to tell" is correctly used to form a nonfinite (infinitive) clause that explains the reason Engle uses poetry in her novel.

Choice A is incorrect because the finite present tense verb "tells" can't be used in this way to explain the reason that Engle uses poetry in her novel. *Choice B* is incorrect because the finite past tense verb "told" can't be used in this way to explain the reason that Engle uses poetry in her novel. *Choice C* is incorrect because the finite present progressive tense verb "is telling" can't be used in this way to explain the reason that Engle uses poetry in her novel.

QUESTION 17

Choice A is the best answer. The convention being tested is subject-verb agreement. The singular verb "allows" agrees in number with the singular subject "landing."

Choice B is incorrect because the plural verb "are allowing" doesn't agree in number with the singular subject "landing." *Choice C* is incorrect because the plural verb "have allowed" doesn't agree in number with the singular subject "landing." *Choice D* is incorrect because the plural verb "allow" doesn't agree in number with the singular subject "landing."

QUESTION 18

Choice C is the best answer. The convention being tested is the use of finite and nonfinite verb forms within a sentence. The nonfinite present participle "forcing" is correctly used to form a participial phrase that supplements the main clause "those...cover," describing the effects on monkeys of the lack of food sources.

Choice A is incorrect because the finite present tense verb "forces" can't be used in this way to supplement the main clause ("those...cover"). *Choice B* is incorrect. While the nonfinite to-infinitive "to force" could be used to form a subordinate clause that supplements the main clause ("those...cover"), to-infinitives conventionally express purpose, and nothing in the sentence suggests that the food sources become unavailable for the purpose of forcing monkeys to hunt marine animals. *Choice D* is incorrect because the finite past tense verb "forced" can't be used in this way to supplement the main clause ("those...cover").

QUESTION 19

Choice B is the best answer. The convention being tested is the coordination of main clauses within a sentence. This choice correctly uses a comma and the coordinating conjunction "but" to join the first main clause ("the Alvarez...out") and the second main clause ("it left...extinctions").

Choice A is incorrect because when coordinating two longer main clauses such as these, it's conventional to use a comma before the coordinating conjunction. *Choice C* is incorrect because it results in a run-on sentence. The two main clauses are fused without punctuation and/or a conjunction. *Choice D* is incorrect because it results in a comma splice. Without a conjunction following it, a comma can't be used in this way to join two main clauses.

QUESTION 20

Choice A is the best answer. The convention being tested is the use of verbs to express tense. In this choice, the simple past tense verb "suggested" properly indicates that Zufall offered her suggestion for the product's name in the past. This verb tense is consistent with the previous sentence's use of a simple past tense verb ("advised") to describe Zufall's advice to McVicker in the 1950s.

Choice B is incorrect because the present tense verb "suggests" doesn't indicate that Zufall offered her suggestion in the past. *Choice C* is incorrect because the past perfect verb "had suggested" isn't consistent with the previous sentence's use of the simple past tense verb "advised" to describe Zufall's advice to McVicker. *Choice D* is incorrect because the past progressive verb "was suggesting" isn't consistent with the previous sentence's use of the simple past tense verb "advised" to describe Zufall's advice to McVicker.

QUESTION 21

Choice D is the best answer. The convention being tested is the use of punctuation within a sentence. This choice uses a semicolon in a conventional way to join the first main clause ("In many...rare") and the second main clause ("in some...common") in this sentence.

Choice A is incorrect. Joining the first main clause ("In many...rare") and the second main clause ("in some...common") with the conjunction "and" conflicts with the use of "however" later in the sentence, resulting in a confusing and illogical sentence. *Choice B* is incorrect because it results in a comma splice. Without a conjunction following it, a comma can't be used in this way to join two main clauses. *Choice C* is incorrect because it results in a run-on sentence. The two main clauses are fused without punctuation and/or a conjunction.

QUESTION 22

Choice D is the best answer. "Second" logically signals that the activity described in this sentence—coming up with a prediction—is the next step in the three-part sequence of steps described in the text.

Choice A is incorrect because "therefore" illogically signals that coming up with a prediction is a result or consequence of the activity described in the previous sentence: researching a question. While a prediction may be influenced by prior research, these activities are distinct steps in planning a scientific inquiry. Coming up with a prediction is the next step in the three-part sequence of steps described in the text. *Choice B* is incorrect because "instead" illogically signals that coming up with a prediction is an alternative to the activity described in the previous sentence: researching a question. Rather, coming up with a prediction is the next step in the three-part sequence of steps described in the text. *Choice C* is incorrect because "for example" illogically signals that coming up with a prediction is an example of the activity described in the previous sentence: researching a question. Instead, coming up with a prediction is the next step in the three-part sequence of steps described in the text.

QUESTION 23

Choice D is the best answer. "In addition" logically signals that the information in this sentence—that the Twentieth Amendment requires newly elected US senators and representatives to be sworn in on January 3—is separate from and additional to the amendment's mandate concerning presidential inaugurations.

Choice A is incorrect because "instead" illogically signals that the information in the sentence presents an alternative to or substitute for the Twentieth Amendment's mandate concerning presidential inaugurations. Rather, the sentence presents a separate requirement in addition to that one. *Choice B* is incorrect because "for instance" illogically signals that the information in the sentence exemplifies the Twentieth Amendment's mandate concerning presidential inaugurations. Instead, the sentence presents a separate requirement in addition to that one. *Choice C* is incorrect because "specifically" illogically signals that the sentence provides specific, precise details elaborating on the Twentieth Amendment's mandate concerning presidential inaugurations. Instead, the sentence presents a separate requirement in addition to that one.

QUESTION 24

Choice C is the best answer. "By contrast" logically signals that the information in this sentence—that dogs can see, hear, and smell by the end of two weeks—contrasts with the preceding information (that wolves can smell but not see or hear at the same age).

Choice A is incorrect because "in other words" illogically signals that the information about domesticated dogs in this sentence paraphrases the information about wolves in the previous sentence. Instead, the information about dogs contrasts with what came before. *Choice B* is incorrect because "for instance" illogically signals that the information about domesticated dogs in this sentence exemplifies the information about wolves in the previous sentence. Instead, the information about dogs contrasts with what came before. *Choice D* is incorrect because "accordingly" illogically signals that the information about domesticated dogs in this sentence is in accordance with, or results from, the information about wolves in the previous sentence. Instead, the information about dogs contrasts with what came before.

QUESTION 25

Choice B is the best answer. "Additionally" logically signals that the claim in this sentence—that some Supreme Court justices worry that viewers (of televised court arguments) would watch only short, misleading clips—adds to the information in the previous sentence. Specifically, the previous sentence indicates one concern raised by those opposed to televising the court's oral arguments, and the claim that follows indicates a second, additional concern.

Choice A is incorrect because "however" illogically signals that the claim in this sentence contrasts with the information in the previous sentence. Instead, the claim adds to the information, indicating a second, additional concern that some Supreme Court justices have about televising the court's arguments. *Choice C* is incorrect because "in comparison" illogically signals that the claim in this sentence is being compared to the information in the previous sentence. Instead, the claim adds to the information, indicating a second, additional concern that some Supreme Court justices have about televising the court's arguments. *Choice D* is incorrect because "for example" illogically signals that the claim in this sentence exemplifies the information in the previous sentence. Instead, the claim adds to the information, indicating a second, additional concern that some Supreme Court justices have about televising the court's arguments.

QUESTION 26

Choice C is the best answer. "Still" logically signals that the information in this sentence about Old Faithful's thriving bacteria species is true despite the previous claim that conditions at the geyser seem as if they would be inhospitable to life.

Choice A is incorrect because "thus" illogically signals that the information in this sentence is a result or consequence of the previous claim about Old Faithful's seemingly inhospitable conditions. Instead, this information about the geyser's many thriving bacteria species is true despite the previous claim. *Choice B* is incorrect because "specifically" illogically signals that the information in this sentence provides specific, precise details elaborating on the previous claim about Old Faithful's seemingly inhospitable conditions. Instead, this information about the geyser's many thriving bacteria species is true despite the previous claim. *Choice D* is incorrect because "in other words" illogically signals that the information in this sentence serves as a paraphrase or restatement of the previous claim about Old Faithful's seemingly inhospitable conditions. Instead, this information about the geyser's many thriving bacteria species is true despite the previous claim.

QUESTION 27

Choice B is the best answer. The sentence effectively explains an advantage of infilling: it's less invasive than using a power grinder.

Choice A is incorrect. The sentence identifies a disadvantage of power grinding; it doesn't explain an advantage of infilling. *Choice C* is incorrect. The sentence identifies the two techniques park rangers use; it doesn't explain an advantage of infilling. *Choice D* is incorrect. The sentence indicates that power grinding and infilling are different in one aspect; it fails to explain an advantage of infilling.

Reading and Writing

Module 2 — Higher Difficulty
(27 questions)

QUESTION 1

Choice D is the best answer because it most logically completes the text's discussion of the Three Sisters intercropping system. As used in this context, "intricate" would mean made up of complexly related elements. The text indicates that in the Three Sisters system, maize, squash, and beans form a "web of relations" in which the crops interact in various ways. The text's description of these interactions—the bean vines growing on the maize stalks, the squash vines keeping weeds away, and the beans adding nutrients that the maize and squash use—provides context suggesting that this "web of relations" is intricate.

Choice A is incorrect because describing the relationship among the crops in the Three Sisters system as "indecipherable," or impossible to comprehend, would not make sense in context. Although the text presents the relationship as complex, the text's description of the role that each crop plays makes it clear that the relationship is well understood, not indecipherable. *Choice B* is incorrect because the text discusses the practical benefits that each plant in the Three Sisters system provides to other members of the system, showing that the relationship among the crops that make up the system is not "ornamental," or mainly serving a decorative purpose. *Choice C* is incorrect because describing the relationship among the crops in the Three Sisters system as "obscure," or unknown or poorly understood, would not make sense in context. Although the text presents the relationship as complex, the text's description of the role that each crop plays makes it clear that the relationship is well understood, not obscure.

QUESTION 2

Choice B is the best answer because it most logically completes the text's discussion of the art installation *Anthem*. In this context, "inventive" means characterized by invention and creativity. The text explains that critics' responses to the installation involved praise for Tsang's creative transformation of a space into a dynamic exhibit with huge images and lots of sound. This context conveys that the critics found the piece particularly creative.

Choice A is incorrect because the text indicates that critics praised the installation for being dynamic and including huge images and lots of sound, and it wouldn't make sense to describe such an exhibit as "restrained," or limited and not extravagant or showy. *Choice C* is incorrect because it wouldn't make sense to say that critics found the installation "inexplicable," or incapable of being explained or interpreted, since the critics were able to explain their praise for the installation's transformation of a space with huge images and lots of sound. *Choice D* is incorrect because the text focuses on the idea that critics praised Tsang for creatively transforming a space into a dynamic exhibit, not that they found the installation "mystifying," or bewildering and hard to understand. Nothing in the text suggests that the critics couldn't understand the piece.

QUESTION 3

Choice B is the best answer because it most logically completes the text's discussion of the author's claim about the relationship between Neanderthals and *Homo sapiens*. As used in this context, "tenuous" means lacking substance. The end of the first sentence states that the author's claim didn't consider certain key pieces of evidence—"recent archaeological discoveries"—and is therefore weak.

Choice A is incorrect because it wouldn't make sense in context to refer to the author's claim as "disorienting," or confusing. The text suggests that the author's claim is insubstantial, not that it's difficult to grasp. *Choice C* is incorrect because referring to the claim as "nuanced," or subtle, wouldn't make sense in context. According to the text, the claim is incomplete because it didn't consider certain key information about recent archaeological finds; it doesn't suggest that what's in the claim lacks precision. *Choice D* is incorrect because saying that the claim is "unoriginal," or imitative, wouldn't make sense in context. The text faults the claim because it doesn't consider certain key information about recent archaeological finds; it doesn't suggest that the author's claim lacks originality.

QUESTION 4

Choice A is the best answer because it most logically completes the text's discussion of Sterlin Harjo's approach to representing Native characters on television. As used in this context, "repudiates" means rejects or refuses to have anything to do with. The text indicates that television shows tend to depict Native characters as living long ago, but that Harjo's series *Reservation Dogs* focuses on Native teenagers in the present day, representing a "rejection" of the typical approach to depicting Native characters. This context thus indicates that Harjo repudiates television's general tendency regarding Native characters.

Choice B is incorrect because the text describes Harjo's "rejection" of the typical approach to representing Native characters on television, so it wouldn't make sense to say that Harjo "proclaims," or declares or affirms, television's general tendency regarding Native characters. Harjo is described as refusing to follow the pattern of depicting Native characters in the distant past, not as proclaiming that pattern. *Choice C* is incorrect because the text describes television's tendency to represent Native characters in the distant past as something that is already occurring, not as something that Harjo "foretells," or predicts will happen in the future. The text is focused on Harjo's "rejection" of this pattern, not on any predictions he may have about it. *Choice D* is incorrect because saying that Harjo "recants" something would mean that he withdraws a previously held belief, and it wouldn't make sense to say that Harjo recants television's tendency to represent Native characters as living in the past. No beliefs previously held by Harjo are mentioned. Additionally, a tendency isn't a belief and thus isn't something that can be recanted.

QUESTION 5

Choice D is the best answer because it accurately describes how the underlined sentence functions in the text as a whole. The text establishes that John has a strong imagination and then goes on to describe the St. John River near John's home in the Florida woods. The underlined sentence depicts John sending twigs sailing down the river while he imagines them reaching "Jacksonville, the sea, the wide world," where he wishes he could follow. This suggests that John longs to expand his life experiences beyond the Florida woods.

Choice A is incorrect because the second and third sentences of the text provide an extended description of the riverbank where John likes to go, whereas the underlined sentence describes what John does at that location. *Choice B* is incorrect because the first sentence of the text suggests that John's behavior "was puzzling" to others around him, whereas the underlined sentence concerns the content of John's imaginings. *Choice C* is incorrect because the underlined sentence elaborates on John's imagination but doesn't mention any other children to whom John could be compared.

QUESTION 6

Choice C is the best answer because, based on the information presented in the texts, it represents how Focarelli and Panetta would most likely respond to Fan's findings. Text 1 indicates that Fan found that a newspaper merger would result in a rise in subscription prices. This rise wouldn't benefit customers, who would have to pay more for news after a merger. Text 2 presents Focarelli and Panetta's argument that merger research tends to focus too much on what happens immediately after the merger. Text 2 goes on to describe their finding that mergers can be economically beneficial for consumers over the long term. This suggests that Focarelli and Panetta would encourage Fan to investigate the long-term effect of the hypothetical newspaper merger on subscription prices.

Choice A is incorrect because Text 2 doesn't indicate that Focarelli and Panetta connect the effects of mergers to specific locations. Instead, Focarelli and Panetta focus on the length of time over which the effects of mergers should be evaluated. *Choice B* is incorrect because Text 2 indicates that Focarelli and Panetta found that merged companies experience "efficiency gains" over the long term, meaning that their expenses go down relative to their output, not that their expenses increase. *Choice D* is incorrect because there's no indication in Text 2 that Focarelli and Panetta believe that the newspaper industry is different from any other industry when it comes to the effects of mergers. Although their own research was about consumer banking, Text 2 suggests that they view their conclusions as applicable to mergers in general.

QUESTION 7

Choice D is the best answer because it presents a statement about how the Lord Chancellor responds to the crowd that is supported by the text. The text indicates that the people in the crowd are roaring and shouting "Bread!" or "Taxes!" and presents them as not knowing what they really want. The Lord Chancellor's response is to ask what their shouting means but also to observe that they're shouting with "unanimity," or total agreement. Clearly, this isn't the case, which supports the statement that the Lord Chancellor describes the crowd as being united even though it's not.

Choice A is incorrect because it isn't supported by the text. Although the text indicates that the Lord Chancellor asks about the meaning of the crowd's shouting, it doesn't suggest that he knows what the crowd really wants. *Choice B* is incorrect because the text doesn't suggest that the Lord Chancellor wants to speak to the crowd. Furthermore, the text doesn't indicate that the crowd wants to hear from the Sub-Warden. Although the crowd roars when asked "Who roar for the Sub-Warden?" it's unclear what the roaring means. *Choice C* is incorrect because the text doesn't suggest that the Lord Chancellor knows of or sympathizes with the crowd's demands. In addition, the text doesn't indicate that the crowd's shouting annoys the Lord Chancellor, just that it causes him to keep repeating "What can it all mean?"

QUESTION 8

Choice A is the best answer because it uses data from the graph to effectively support Charles and Stephens's claim about how level of information affects voters. The graph shows the probability of voting for both high- and low-information voters in seven categories of political orientation. Charles and Stephens claim that "the more informed voters are about politics...the more likely they are to vote." This statement correctly asserts that the graph shows a higher probability of voting for high-information voters than for low-information voters at each of the seven political orientations. Thus, this statement accurately cites data from the graph that support Charles and Stephens's claim about how level of information affects voters.

Choice B is incorrect. Although this statement is correct that the only probability in the graph below 50% is for low-information voters categorized as independent (orientation 4), the claim in question is about the relative likelihood that low- and high-information voters will vote, and without some reference to high-information voters, this statement cannot help support such a comparison. *Choice C* is incorrect. Although this statement is correct that the highest probabilities of voting for low-information voters are at the ends of the orientation scale (1 and 7), the claim in question is about the relative likelihood that low- and high-information voters will vote, and without some reference to high-information voters, this statement cannot help support such a comparison. *Choice D* is incorrect because the graph does not give any information about how many people are represented in any of the categories, so this statement is not based on data from the graph. Furthermore, even if we did have this information, the claim is about how level of information affects voters' probability of voting, not whether they're likely to strongly identify with a particular political party.

QUESTION 9

Choice C is the best answer because it accurately describes data from the table that support Barrett and Rayfield's suggestion about bite force estimates. According to the text, Barrett and Rayfield believe that estimates of dinosaur bite force may be strongly influenced by the methods used to produce them— that is, that different methods may produce significantly different results. The table shows that the studies by Bates and Falkingham and by Cost et al. used the same estimation method (muscular and skeletal modeling) and produced similar bite force estimates (approximately 35,000–57,000 newtons and 35,000–63,000 newtons, respectively). The study by Meers, however, used body-mass scaling and produced a much higher bite force estimate (183,000–235,000 newtons), while the study by Gignac and Erickson used tooth-bone interaction analysis and produced a much lower bite force estimate (8,000–34,000 newtons). The fact that one method produced similar estimates in two different studies and that two different methods used in other studies produced substantially different estimates supports the idea that dinosaur bite force estimates are significantly influenced by the methodology used to produce them.

Choice A is incorrect because it inaccurately describes data from the table. The table does show that the studies by Meers and by Cost et al. used different estimation methods and produced very different ranges of estimated dinosaur bite force, which would support Barrett and Rayfield's suggestion that different methodologies may produce significantly different estimates. However, the table doesn't show that the study by Meers produced the lowest estimated maximum bite force while the study by Cost et al. produced the highest. In fact, the study by Meers estimated a maximum bite force of approximately 235,000 newtons, which is the highest of all the estimated maximums. *Choice B* is incorrect. Although the data from Gignac and Ericson's study are accurately described, a single set of findings from one study using only one methodology can't show that different methodologies may produce significantly different dinosaur bite force estimates, as Barrett and Rayfield suggest. *Choice D* is incorrect. Although the table shows that the maximum bite force estimated by Cost et al. was higher than that estimated by Bates and Falkingham, the difference is relatively small; in fact, both teams estimated a minimum bite force of approximately 35,000 newtons and a maximum bite force close to approximately 60,000 newtons. Because these findings demonstrate that a single methodology (muscular and skeletal modeling) produced similar overall results in two studies, the findings don't support Barrett and Rayfield's suggestion that different methodologies may produce significantly different dinosaur bite force estimates.

QUESTION 10

Choice C is the best answer because it presents a finding that, if true, would weaken Foster's hypothesis that damage to eelgrass roots improves the health of eelgrass meadows by boosting genetic diversity. The text indicates that sea otters damage eelgrass roots but that eelgrass meadows near Vancouver Island, where there's a large otter population, are comparatively healthy. When Foster and her colleagues compared the Vancouver Island eelgrass meadows to those that don't have established otter populations, the researchers found that the Vancouver Island meadows are more genetically diverse than the other meadows are. This finding led Foster to hypothesize that damage to the eelgrass roots encourages eelgrass reproduction, thereby improving genetic diversity and the health of the meadows. If, however, other meadows not included in the study are less healthy the larger the local otter population is and the longer the otters have been in residence, that would suggest that damage to the eelgrass roots, which would be expected to increase with the size and residential duration of the otter population, isn't leading meadows to be healthier. Such a finding would therefore weaken Foster's hypothesis.

Choice A is incorrect because finding that small, recently introduced otter populations are near other eelgrass meadows in the study wouldn't weaken Foster's hypothesis. If otter populations were small and only recently established, they wouldn't be expected to have caused much damage to eelgrass roots, so even if those eelgrass meadows were less healthy than the Vancouver Island meadows, that wouldn't undermine Foster's hypothesis. In fact, it would be consistent with Foster's hypothesis since it would suggest that the greater damage caused by larger, more established otter populations is associated with healthier meadows. *Choice B* is incorrect because the existence of areas with otters but without eelgrass meadows wouldn't reveal anything about whether the damage that otters cause to eelgrass roots ultimately benefits eelgrass meadows. *Choice D* is incorrect because the health of plants other than eelgrass would have no bearing on Foster's hypothesis that damage to eelgrass roots leads to greater genetic diversity and meadow health. It would be possible for otters to have a negative effect on other plants while nevertheless improving the health of eelgrass meadows by damaging eelgrass roots.

QUESTION 11

Choice D is the best answer because it presents a finding that, if true, would support Paredes's argument about the origin of Mexican American folklore. The text describes a disagreement among scholars about whether Mexican American folklore mostly derived from the folklore of Spain (the view held by Espinosa and others) or originated in Mexico and the United States through ongoing cultural interactions there (the view held by Paredes and others). If Mexican American folklore collected in the twentieth century mostly consists of ballads about history and social life that originated recently, then that would support Paredes's argument by suggesting that the folklore mostly arose after Spanish rule ended in the early nineteenth century and that the folklore reflects cultural interactions in Mexico and the United States rather than traditions from Spain.

Choice A is incorrect because the inclusion of songs influenced by sixteenth-century Spanish poetry among Mexican American folklore collected in the twentieth century would not support Paredes's view that the folklore was the result of cultural interactions in Mexico and the United States rather than an offshoot of Spanish folklore. If anything, the presence of such songs among the folklore collected in the twentieth century would weaken Paredes's argument, since it would reflect the influence of Spanish culture on the folklore. *Choice B* is incorrect because the mere presence of similarities in Mexican American folklore across regions would not be sufficient to draw a conclusion about where the folklore originated, let alone to support Paredes's argument that the folklore reflects various cultural interactions in Mexico and the United States. In fact, Paredes would likely expect there to be regional variations in folklore as different cultures have interacted in different places. *Choice C* is incorrect because scholars' previous ignorance of the folklore would have no bearing on Paredes's argument that Mexican American folklore mostly reflects cultural interactions in Mexico and the United States; the folklore's actual origins exist regardless of the scholars' awareness.

QUESTION 12

Choice C is the best answer because it most logically completes the text based on supporting data in the graph. The text indicates that in the fly *D. melanogaster*, *DptA* and *DptB* are genes that encode peptides that both fight pathogens and promote beneficial microbes. Researchers tested *D. melanogaster*'s resistance to *P. rettgeri* and *A. sicerae* bacteria based on which variation of the peptide-encoding gene the flies exhibit: *DptA* silenced (referred to as type A), *DptB* silenced (type B), or both silenced (type AB). The text also indicates that resistance to *P. rettgeri* correlates with *DptA* activity but not with *DptB* activity (which would manifest as type B flies surviving at a higher rate than other fly types when exposed to *P. rettgeri*). The graph shows the post–*A. sicerae* infection results, which indicate that *DptB* activity was most strongly associated with survival, whereas *DptA* activity was not (manifesting in the graph as the type A flies having greater survival rates than the other fly types). In other words, when *DptA* activity was silenced, the flies showed relatively high survival rates, but when *DptB* activity was silenced, whether on its own or in conjunction with *DptA* activity being silenced, survival rates were low, suggesting that *DptB* may have developed as a specific defense against *A. sicerae*.

Choice A is incorrect. The graph suggests that *DptA* activity is associated with a low rate of survival, not a high one. Furthermore, the graph shows results for flies where *DptA* alone was silenced, *DptB* alone was silenced, and both were silenced and thus does not show any flies with activity in both *DptA* and *DptB*, which would be necessary to determine whether *DptA* conferred defense against *A. sicerae* in the presence of *DptB*. *Choice B* is incorrect. Only two bacteria species were considered in the text: *P. rettgeri* and *A. sicerae*.

The text and graph taken together suggest that activity in *DptA* is associated with resistance to *P. rettgeri* while *DptB* activity is not, and that *DptB* activity is associated with resistance to *A. sicerae* while *DptA* is not. There is no further information to suggest one genetic type confers resistance to a greater number of pathogens than the other. *Choice D* is incorrect. The graph does not address flies with activity in both *DptA* and *DptB*. All flies represented in the graph had one or both of *DptA* and *DptB* silenced, or inactive.

QUESTION 13

Choice B is the best answer because it most logically completes the text's discussion of the research by Acemoglu et al. on the increasing adoption of automation technology by US firms. The text states that some economists have asserted that firms are increasingly using automation in part because doing so improves productivity. The text goes on to point out, however, that Acemoglu et al. have shown that automation does not necessarily lead to remarkable productivity gains. In addition, Acemoglu et al. have shown that the US tax code makes it more advantageous for firms to invest money in automation technology than to spend the same amount of money on labor—that is, on workers—to perform the same tasks. A firm that spends a certain amount of money on labor could instead spend that money on automation technology and reduce the amount of taxes it must pay, thereby benefiting the firm even if the firm saw no increase in productivity. These findings therefore suggest that the increasing adoption of automation technology by US firms may be more attributable to the US government indirectly incentivizing—through the tax code—the adoption of that technology than to automation being directly beneficial for firms' outputs.

Choice A is incorrect. Although the text does suggest that some economists may have overestimated the productivity gains associated with automation technology, nothing in the text supports the idea that those economists may have also overestimated the tax benefits of automation technology. Instead, the text presents the work of Acemoglu et al. as showing that the tax benefits of automation technology may be an important factor in explaining why firms have been increasingly adopting that technology. *Choice C* is incorrect. The text indicates that the current structure of the US tax code, which treats expenditures on automation technology differently than expenditures on labor, encourages firms to adopt that technology. If the tax code changed to treat expenditures on automation technology the same as it treats expenditures on labor, then automation technology would likely become less appealing to firms rather than more appealing, since that change would remove the relative tax benefit that firms currently receive from adopting the technology and since Acemoglu et al. suggest that the technology is not associated with remarkable productivity gains. *Choice D* is incorrect because nothing in the text suggests that automation leads to a decrease in productivity. Instead, the text states that Acemoglu et al. showed that productivity gains associated with automation technology "are often unremarkable," meaning that the gains associated with the technology are not particularly noteworthy.

QUESTION 14

Choice D is the best answer because it most logically completes the text's discussion of the morphology (form and structure) of sea stars, a type of echinoderm. The text indicates that echinoderms have radially symmetrical body plans (symmetrical around a central point, usually in the form of a star), whereas most animals have bilaterally symmetrical body plans (symmetrical along an axis running from head to tail through a trunk). According to the text, sea stars are unusual echinoderms because, despite their radial body plan, they descended from known bilateral ancestors. This shift in body plan was thought to be a process of losing the genetic markers associated with the head region. The text explains that by comparing the genes of one sea star species (*P. miniata*) to those of a close relative, the acorn worm, researchers determined that instead, anterior (head) genes are active across the sea star's entire body, posterior (tail) genes are active in limited, peripheral locations of the body, and no trunk-related genes are active. This finding strongly suggests that, rather than becoming "headless" as they evolved from a bilateral ancestor, sea stars developed a body plan consisting almost entirely of a head region with a minimal tail region and no trunk region present.

Choice A is incorrect because the text doesn't identify how any particular region of sea stars' bodies influences the layout of sea stars' radial symmetry. Moreover, the text indicates that the radial symmetry of echinoderms is "usually starlike," not that a starlike layout distinguishes sea stars from other echinoderms. *Choice B* is incorrect because the text doesn't suggest that the idea that sea stars evolved from an ancestor with bilateral symmetry is incorrect (describing the bilateral origin as "known") and doesn't address any body plans other than those with radial or bilateral symmetry. The text strongly suggests that rather than revealing something about sea stars' origin, Formery et al.'s findings contradict the assumption that the current body plan of sea stars is "headless." *Choice C* is incorrect because the text suggests that Formery et al. were able to make determinations about *P. miniata* sea stars' body plan based on the comparability of genetic markers between *P. miniata* and *S. kowalevskii* acorn worms. The text indicates only that little or no activity was observed in certain types of genes associated with body development in *P. miniata*, not that those genes turned out to largely differ from body-development genes in *S. kowalevskii*.

QUESTION 15

Choice C is the best answer. The convention being tested is the use of verb forms within a sentence. The plural verb "study" agrees in number with the plural subject "many."

Choice A is incorrect because the singular verb "is studying" doesn't agree in number with the plural subject "many." *Choice B* is incorrect because the singular verb "has studied" doesn't agree in number with the plural subject "many." *Choice D* is incorrect because the singular verb "studies" doesn't agree in number with the plural subject "many."

QUESTION 16

Choice A is the best answer. The convention being tested is colon use within a sentence. A colon used in this way introduces information that illustrates or explains information that has come before it. In this case, the colon introduces the following explanation of why some roundworms in the Southern Hemisphere move in the opposite direction of Earth's magnetic field.

Choice B is incorrect because it results in a comma splice. A comma can't be used in this way to join two long independent clauses ("Researchers...food" and "in...sources") such as these. *Choice C* is incorrect because it results in a run-on sentence. The two clauses ("Researchers...food" and "in...sources") are fused without punctuation. Furthermore, the conjunction "while" fails to indicate that what follows is an explanation of why some roundworms in the Southern Hemisphere move in the opposite direction of Earth's magnetic field. *Choice D* is incorrect because it results in a run-on sentence. The two clauses ("Researchers...food" and "in...sources") are fused without punctuation and/or a conjunction.

QUESTION 17

Choice C is the best answer. The convention being tested is punctuation use within a sentence. A colon can be used between two main clauses to signal that what follows is an elaboration of what came before. In this choice, the colon correctly introduces the following explanation of the divergent milk preservation strategies that emerged.

Choice A is incorrect because it results in a run-on sentence. The main clause ("As...emerged") and the subordinate clause followed by another main clause ("whereas...steppe") are fused without punctuation and/or a conjunction. *Choice B* is incorrect. Without a comma preceding it, the conjunction "and" can't be used in this way to join a main clause ("As...emerged") and a subordinate clause followed by another main clause ("whereas...steppe"). *Choice D* is incorrect because it results in a comma splice. A comma can't be used in this way to join a main clause ("As...emerged") and a subordinate clause followed by another main clause ("whereas...steppe").

QUESTION 18

Choice A is the best answer. The convention being tested is the use of verb forms within a sentence. The nonfinite present participle "including" is correctly used to form a supplementary element that interrupts the main clause "These extensive changes...reflected the poet's evolving literary perspective and experience of the US Civil War." This supplementary element, offset by commas after "changes" and "material," provides examples of the changes Whitman made to *Leaves of Grass*.

Choice B is incorrect because it results in an ungrammatical sentence. The finite modal verb "would include" can't be used in this way to form a supplementary element within the main clause. *Choice C* is incorrect because it results in an ungrammatical sentence. The finite past tense verb "included" can't be used in this way to form a supplementary element within the main clause. *Choice D* is incorrect because it results in an ungrammatical sentence. The finite present tense verb "include" can't be used in this way to form a supplementary element within the main clause.

QUESTION 19

Choice C is the best answer. The convention being tested is the use of punctuation and verb forms within a sentence. This choice leaves the verb "admired" in its nonfinite past participle form to function within a supplementary element ("much...followed"). Offset by commas after "works" and "followed," this supplementary element interrupts the main clause ("English poet and Shakespeare contemporary John Donne's works...had... been essentially gathering dust...") with additional information about the works' reception during Donne's lifetime.

Choice A is incorrect because it fails to offset the supplementary element ("much...followed") with appropriate punctuation, and using the finite verb "were much admired" results in an ungrammatical sentence. *Choice B* is incorrect because using the finite verb "were much admired" results in an ungrammatical sentence. *Choice D* is incorrect because it fails to offset the supplementary element ("much...followed") with appropriate punctuation, and using the finite verb "had been much admired" results in an ungrammatical sentence.

QUESTION 20

Choice B is the best answer. The convention being tested is subject–verb agreement. The singular verb "is" agrees in number with the singular subject "the shape."

Choice A is incorrect because the plural verb "are" doesn't agree in number with the singular subject "the shape." *Choice C* is incorrect because the plural verb "were" doesn't agree in number with the singular subject "the shape." *Choice D* is incorrect because the plural verb "have been" doesn't agree in number with the singular subject "the shape."

QUESTION 21

Choice B is the best answer. "By contrast" logically signals that the information in this sentence—that a firefly's glow ceases when it stops drawing in oxygen—contrasts with the previous sentence's discussion of the processes that cause a firefly to begin to glow.

Choice A is incorrect because "for instance" illogically signals that the information in the sentence exemplifies the previous sentence's discussion of how a firefly begins to glow. Instead, it contrasts with the previous sentence's discussion. *Choice C* is incorrect because "specifically" illogically signals that the information in the sentence provides specific details elaborating on the previous sentence's discussion of how a firefly begins to glow. Instead, it contrasts with the previous sentence's discussion. *Choice D* is incorrect because "in conclusion" illogically signals that the information in the sentence sums up the previous sentence's discussion of how a firefly begins to glow. Instead, it contrasts with the previous sentence's discussion.

QUESTION 22

Choice B is the best answer. "On the contrary" logically signals that the information in this sentence—that *Dies Irae*'s appearance of depth is merely an illusion—contrasts with the previous statement about a viewer's possible assumption regarding the street painting.

Choice A is incorrect because "additionally" illogically signals that this sentence is simply additional information about a viewer's possible assumption regarding the street painting. Instead, the information about how Wenner achieved the illusion of depth contrasts with the previous sentence's description of the illusion. *Choice C* is incorrect because "as a result" illogically signals that the information in this sentence is a result of, or caused by, a viewer's possible assumption regarding the street painting. Instead, the information about how Wenner achieved the illusion of depth contrasts with the previous sentence's description of the illusion. *Choice D* is incorrect because "next" illogically signals that the information in this sentence is the next step in a process. Instead, the information about how Wenner achieved the illusion of depth contrasts with the previous sentence's description of the illusion.

QUESTION 23

Choice A is the best answer. The sentence emphasizes the distance covered by the Philadelphia and Lancaster Turnpike, noting that the turnpike, which connected the two Pennsylvania cities in its name, was sixty-two miles long.

Choice B is incorrect. The sentence emphasizes the significance of the turnpike; it doesn't emphasize the distance that the turnpike covered. *Choice C* is incorrect. While the sentence mentions that the turnpike connected two Pennsylvania cities, it doesn't emphasize the specific distance covered by the turnpike. *Choice D* is incorrect. The sentence emphasizes when the turnpike was built; it doesn't emphasize the distance that the turnpike covered.

QUESTION 24

Choice C is the best answer. The sentence explains an advantage of the "Women and the Vote" format, noting that the format appealed to audiences because it allowed them to control the experience.

Choice A is incorrect. The sentence describes a digital drawing on the "Women and the Vote" website; it doesn't explain an advantage of the play's format. *Choice B* is incorrect. The sentence explains how audiences interacted with the "Women and the Vote" website; it doesn't explain an advantage of the play's format. *Choice D* is incorrect. While the sentence mentions that "Women and the Vote" had an interactive format, it doesn't explain what advantage this format might have.

QUESTION 25

Choice D is the best answer. By noting that the formula for distributing Storting seats overrepresents less populated rural districts, the sentence effectively refutes a claim that malapportionment in the Storting favors small urban districts.

Choice A is incorrect because the sentence claims that malapportionment in the Storting favors small urban districts; it doesn't refute such a claim. Moreover, it misrepresents information in the notes. According to the notes, the formula for distributing seats overrepresents less populated, not more populated, districts. *Choice B* is incorrect. While the sentence appears to refute a claim that malapportionment in the Storting favors small urban districts, it misrepresents information in the notes. According to the notes, the formula for distributing seats overrepresents less populated, not more populated, districts. *Choice C* is incorrect. The sentence explains what malapportionment is but doesn't address malapportionment in the Storting specifically.

QUESTION 26

Choice B is the best answer. The sentence presents both the study and its methodology (that is, the researcher's approach to the problem), explaining that Yuan used computer simulations to study the effect of the mother duck's wake on the ducklings' energy expenditure.

Choice A is incorrect. The sentence describes the findings of Yuan's study; it doesn't present the study and its methodology. *Choice C* is incorrect. While the sentence provides general information about Yuan's study, it doesn't present the study's methodology. *Choice D* is incorrect. The sentence describes the findings of Yuan's study; it doesn't present the study and its methodology.

QUESTION 27

Choice A is the best answer. The sentence effectively emphasizes the aim, or goal, of the research study (in other words, what the researchers hoped to learn from the study): Rogers and Russell wanted to know if woodland expansion is related to changes in climate.

Choice B is incorrect. The sentence emphasizes the researchers' findings; it doesn't emphasize the aim of the study. *Choice C* is incorrect. The sentence emphasizes the results of the study; it doesn't emphasize the aim. *Choice D* is incorrect. The sentence emphasizes the methodology of the study; it doesn't emphasize the aim.

Math

Module 1
(22 questions)

QUESTION 1

Choice D is correct. The y-intercept of a graph in the xy-plane is the point at which the graph crosses the y-axis. The graph shown crosses the y-axis at the point (0, 8). Therefore, the y-intercept of the graph shown is (0, 8).

Choice A is incorrect and may result from conceptual or calculation errors.
Choice B is incorrect and may result from conceptual or calculation errors.
Choice C is incorrect and may result from conceptual or calculation errors.

QUESTION 2

Choice D is correct. The value of $f(x)$ when $x = -8$ can be found by substituting -8 for x in the given function. This yields $f(-8) = -3(-8) + 60$, or $f(-8) = 84$. Therefore, when $x = -8$, the value of $f(x)$ is 84.

Choice A is incorrect. This is the value of $(-3 + (-8)) + 60$, not $-3(-8) + 60$.
Choice B is incorrect. This is the value of $-8 + 60$, not $-3(-8) + 60$. *Choice C* is incorrect. This is the value of $-3 + 60$, not $-3(-8) + 60$.

QUESTION 3

Choice D is correct. Since x represents the number of 1-minute segments and y represents the number of 3-minute segments, the total length of the video is $1 \cdot x + 3 \cdot y$, or $x + 3y$, minutes. Since the video is 70 minutes long, the equation $x + 3y = 70$ represents this situation.

Choice A is incorrect and may result from conceptual errors. *Choice B* is incorrect and may result from conceptual errors. *Choice C* is incorrect and may result from conceptual errors.

QUESTION 4

Choice D is correct. It's given that the bowl starts with 20 ounces of water and has 9 ounces of water remaining after a period of time has passed. The amount of water the bowl has lost during the time period can be found by subtracting the remaining amount of water from the amount of water the bowl starts with, which yields 20 − 9 ounces, or 11 ounces. This means the bowl loses 11 ounces of water during that period of time. It's given that the amount of water decreases by 1 ounce every 4 days. Letting t represent the number of days the bowl has been uncovered, it follows that $\frac{1}{4} = \frac{11}{t}$. Multiplying both sides of this equation by $4t$ yields $t = 44$. Therefore, the bowl has been uncovered for 44 days.

Choice A is incorrect and may result from conceptual or calculation errors. *Choice B* is incorrect and may result from conceptual or calculation errors.

Choice C is incorrect. This is the value of t for the equation $\frac{1}{4} = \frac{9}{t}$, not $\frac{1}{4} = \frac{11}{t}$.

QUESTION 5

Choice B is correct. Standard deviation is a measure of the spread of a data set from its mean. The dot plot for class A and the dot plot for class B have the same shape. Thus, the frequency distributions for both class A and class B are the same. Since both class A and class B have the same frequency distribution of glue sticks brought in by each student, it follows that both class A and class B have the same spread of the number of glue sticks brought in by each student from their respective means. Therefore, the standard deviation of the number of glue sticks brought in by each student for class A is equal to the standard deviation of the number of glue sticks brought in by each student for class B.

Choice A is incorrect and may result from conceptual or calculation errors. *Choice C* is incorrect and may result from conceptual or calculation errors. *Choice D* is incorrect and may result from conceptual or calculation errors.

QUESTION 6

Choice A is correct. Applying the distributive property, the given expression can be written as $7x^3 + 7x - 6x^3 + 3x$. Grouping like terms in this expression yields $(7x^3 - 6x^3) + (7x + 3x)$. Combining like terms in this expression yields $x^3 + 10x$.

Choice B is incorrect and may result from conceptual or calculation errors. *Choice C* is incorrect and may result from conceptual or calculation errors. *Choice D* is incorrect and may result from conceptual or calculation errors.

QUESTION 7

Choice C is correct. The sum of the interior angles of a triangle is 180°. It's given that the interior angles of triangle ABC are 54°, 90°, and $\left(\frac{k}{2}\right)°$. It follows that $54 + 90 + \frac{k}{2} = 180$, or $144 + \frac{k}{2} = 180$. Subtracting 144 from each side of this equation yields $\frac{k}{2} = 36$. Multiplying each side of this equation by 2 yields $k = 72$. Therefore, the value of k is 72.

Choice A is incorrect. This is the value of $\frac{k}{2}$, not k. *Choice B* is incorrect and may result from conceptual or calculation errors. *Choice D* is incorrect and may result from conceptual or calculation errors.

QUESTION 8

Choice B is correct. Applying the zero product property to the given equation yields $3x = 0$, $x - 4 = 0$, and $x + 5 = 0$. Dividing each side of the equation $3x = 0$ by 3 yields $x = 0$. Adding 4 to each side of the equation $x - 4 = 0$ yields $x = 4$. Subtracting 5 from each side of the equation $x + 5 = 0$ yields $x = -5$. Therefore, the solutions to the given equation are 0, 4, and -5. Thus, one of the solutions to the given equation is 0.

Choice A is incorrect and may result from conceptual or calculation errors.
Choice C is incorrect and may result from conceptual or calculation errors.
Choice D is incorrect and may result from conceptual or calculation errors.

QUESTION 9

The correct answer is 46. It's given that a chemist combines water and acetic acid to make a mixture with a volume of 56 milliliters (mL) and that the volume of acetic acid in the mixture is 10 mL. Let x represent the volume of water, in mL, in the mixture. The equation $x + 10 = 56$ represents this situation. Subtracting 10 from both sides of this equation yields $x = 46$. Therefore, the volume of water, in mL, in the mixture is 46.

QUESTION 10

Choice D is correct. It's given that 1 furlong = 220 yards and 1 yard = 3 feet. It follows that a distance of 354 furlongs is equivalent to

$(354 \text{ furlongs})\left(\dfrac{220 \text{ yards}}{1 \text{ furlong}}\right)\left(\dfrac{3 \text{ feet}}{1 \text{ yard}}\right)$, or 233,640 feet.

Choice A is incorrect and may result from conceptual or calculation errors.
Choice B is incorrect and may result from conceptual or calculation errors.
Choice C is incorrect and may result from conceptual or calculation errors.

QUESTION 11

Choice A is correct. A system of two linear equations in two variables, x and y, has zero points of intersection if the lines represented by the equations in the xy-plane are distinct and parallel. The graphs of two lines in the xy-plane represented by equations in slope-intercept form, $y = mx + b$, are distinct if the y-coordinates of their y-intercepts, b, are different and are parallel if their slopes, m, are the same. For the two equations in the given system, $y = 2x + 10$ and $y = 2x - 1$, the values of b are 10 and -1, respectively, and the values of m are both 2. Since the values of b are different, the graphs of these lines have different y-coordinates of the y-intercept and are distinct. Since the values of m are the same, the graphs of these lines have the same slope and are parallel. Therefore, the graphs of the given equations are lines that intersect at zero points in the xy-plane.

Choice B is incorrect. The graphs of a system of two linear equations have exactly one point of intersection if the lines represented by the equations have different slopes. Since the given equations represent lines with the same slope, there is not exactly one intersection point. *Choice C* is incorrect. The graphs of a system of two linear equations can never have exactly two intersection points. *Choice D* is incorrect. The graphs of a system of two linear equations have infinitely many intersection points when the lines represented by the equations have the same slope and the same y-coordinate of the y-intercept. Since the given equations represent lines with different y-coordinates of their y-intercepts, there are not infinitely many intersection points.

QUESTION 12

The correct answer is 52. It's given that 13 is p% of 25. It follows that $\dfrac{13}{25} = \dfrac{p}{100}$.

Multiplying both sides of this equation by 100 gives $52 = p$. Therefore, the value of p is 52.

QUESTION 13

The correct answer is 410. It's given that t minutes after an initial observation, the number of bacteria in a population is $60{,}000(2)^{\frac{t}{410}}$. This expression consists of the initial number of bacteria, 60,000, multiplied by the expression $2^{\frac{t}{410}}$.

The time it takes for the number of bacteria to double is the increase in the value of t that causes the expression $2^{\frac{t}{410}}$ to double. Since the base of the expression $2^{\frac{t}{410}}$ is 2, the expression $2^{\frac{t}{410}}$ will double when the exponent increases by 1. Since the exponent of the expression $2^{\frac{t}{410}}$ is $\frac{t}{410}$, the exponent will increase by 1 when t increases by 410. Therefore the time, in minutes, it takes for the number of bacteria in the population to double is 410.

QUESTION 14

Choice C is correct. Because the value of the investment increases each year, the function that best models how the value of the investment changes over time is an increasing function. It's given that each year, the value of the investment increases by 0.49% of its value the previous year. Since the value of the investment changes by a fixed percentage each year, the function that best models how the value of the investment changes over time is an exponential function. Therefore, the function that best models how the value of the investment changes over time is an increasing exponential function.

Choice A is incorrect and may result from conceptual errors. *Choice B* is incorrect and may result from conceptual errors. *Choice D* is incorrect and may result from conceptual errors.

QUESTION 15

The correct answer is 5. The standard form of an equation of a circle in the xy-plane is $(x - h)^2 + (y - k)^2 = r^2$, where h, k, and r are constants, the coordinates of the center of the circle are (h, k), and the length of the radius of the circle is r. It's given that an equation of the circle is $(x - 2)^2 + (y - 9)^2 = r^2$. Therefore, the center of this circle is $(2, 9)$. It's given that the endpoints of a diameter of the circle are $(2, 4)$ and $(2, 14)$. The length of the radius is the distance from the center of the circle to an endpoint of a diameter of the circle, which can be found using the distance formula, $\sqrt{(x_1 - x_2)^2 + (y_1 - y_2)^2}$.

Substituting the center of the circle $(2, 9)$ and one endpoint of the diameter $(2, 4)$ in this formula gives a distance of $\sqrt{(2 - 2)^2 + (9 - 4)^2}$, or $\sqrt{0^2 + 5^2}$, which is equivalent to 5. Since the distance from the center of the circle to an endpoint of a diameter is 5, the value of r is 5.

QUESTION 16

Choice B is correct. The sine of any acute angle is equal to the cosine of its complement. It's given that in right triangle RST, the sum of the measures of angle R and angle S is 90 degrees. Therefore, angle R and angle S are complementary, and the value of $\sin R$ is equal to the value of $\cos S$. It's given that the value of $\sin R$ is $\frac{\sqrt{15}}{4}$, so the value of $\cos S$ is also $\frac{\sqrt{15}}{4}$.

Choice A is incorrect. This is the value of tan *S*. *Choice C* is incorrect. This is the value of $\frac{1}{\cos S}$. *Choice D* is incorrect. This is the value of $\frac{1}{\tan S}$.

QUESTION 17

Choice A is correct. To express 4*j* + 9 in terms of *p* and *k*, the given equation must be solved for 4*j* + 9. Since it's given that *j* is a positive number, 4*j* + 9 is not equal to zero. Therefore, multiplying both sides of the given equation by 4*j* + 9 yields the equivalent equation *p*(4*j* + 9) = *k*. Since it's given that *p* is a positive number, *p* is not equal to zero. Therefore, dividing each side of the equation

p(4*j* + 9) = *k* by *p* yields the equivalent equation $4j + 9 = \frac{k}{p}$.

Choice B is incorrect. This equation is equivalent to $p = \frac{4j + 9}{k}$. *Choice C* is incorrect. This equation is equivalent to *p* = *k* − 4*j* − 9. *Choice D* is incorrect. This equation is equivalent to *p* = *k*(4*j* + 9).

QUESTION 18

Choice D is correct. All the tables in the choices have the same three values of *x*, so each of the three values of *x* can be substituted in the given inequality to compare the corresponding values of *y* in each of the tables. Substituting 3 for *x* in the given inequality yields *y* > 13(3) − 18, or *y* > 21. Therefore, when *x* = 3, the corresponding value of *y* is greater than 21. Substituting 5 for *x* in the given inequality yields *y* > 13(5) − 18, or *y* > 47. Therefore, when *x* = 5, the corresponding value of *y* is greater than 47. Substituting 8 for *x* in the given inequality yields *y* > 13(8) − 18, or *y* > 86. Therefore, when *x* = 8, the corresponding value of *y* is greater than 86. For the table in choice D, when *x* = 3, the corresponding value of *y* is 26, which is greater than 21; when *x* = 5, the corresponding value of *y* is 52, which is greater than 47; when *x* = 8, the corresponding value of *y* is 91, which is greater than 86. Therefore, the table in choice D gives values of *x* and their corresponding values of *y* that are all solutions to the given inequality.

Choice A is incorrect. In the table for choice A, when *x* = 3, the corresponding value of *y* is 21, which is not greater than 21; when *x* = 5, the corresponding value of *y* is 47, which is not greater than 47; when *x* = 8, the corresponding value of *y* is 86, which is not greater than 86. *Choice B* is incorrect. In the table for choice B, when *x* = 5, the corresponding value of *y* is 42, which is not greater than 47; when *x* = 8, the corresponding value of *y* is 86, which is not greater than 86. *Choice C* is incorrect. In the table for choice C, when *x* = 3, the corresponding value of *y* is 16, which is not greater than 21; when *x* = 5, the corresponding value of *y* is 42, which is not greater than 47; when *x* = 8, the corresponding value of *y* is 81, which is not greater than 86.

QUESTION 19

The correct answer is $\frac{1}{4}$. For an equation in slope-intercept form *y* = *mx* + *b*, *m* represents the slope of the line in the *xy*-plane defined by this equation. It's given that line ℓ is defined by 3*y* + 12*x* = 5. Subtracting 12*x* from both sides of this equation yields 3*y* = −12*x* + 5. Dividing both sides of this equation by 3 yields $y = -\frac{12}{3}x + \frac{5}{3}$, or $y = -4x + \frac{5}{3}$. Thus, the slope of line ℓ in the *xy*-plane is −4.

Since line n is perpendicular to line ℓ in the xy-plane, the slope of line n is the negative reciprocal of the slope of line ℓ. The negative reciprocal of -4 is $-\dfrac{1}{(-4)} = \dfrac{1}{4}$. Note that 1/4 and .25 are examples of ways to enter a correct answer.

QUESTION 20

Choice B is correct. An x-intercept of a graph in the xy-plane is a point on the graph where the value of y is 0. Substituting 0 for y in the given equation yields $0 = 2(x - d)(x + d)(x + g)(x - d)$. By the zero product property, the solutions to this equation are $x = d$, $x = -d$, $x = -g$, and $x = d$. However, $x = d$ and $x = d$ are identical. It's given that d and g are unique positive constants. It follows that the equation $0 = 2(x - d)(x + d)(x + g)(x - d)$ has 3 unique solutions: $x = d$, $x = -d$, and $x = -g$. Thus, the graph of the given equation has 3 distinct x-intercepts.

Alternate approach: The given equation is a polynomial equation in factored form. Therefore, when the given equation is graphed in the xy-plane, the number of distinct x-intercepts of the graph is the number of unique linear factors on the right-hand side of the equation. In the given equation, two of the factors are identical: $(x - d)$ and $(x - d)$; therefore, one of these factors isn't unique. It's given that d and g are unique positive constants. Thus, the right-hand side of the given equation has 3 unique linear factors: $(x - d)$, $(x + d)$, and $(x + g)$. It follows that the graph of the given equation in the xy-plane has 3 distinct x-intercepts.

Choice A is incorrect and may result from conceptual errors. *Choice C* is incorrect and may result from conceptual errors. *Choice D* is incorrect and may result from conceptual errors.

QUESTION 21

Choice C is correct. For the form of the function in choice C, $f(x) = 128(1.6)^{x-1}$, the value of $f(1)$ can be found as $128(1.6)^{1-1}$, which is equivalent to $128(1.6)^0$, or 128. Therefore, $k = 128$, which is shown in $f(x) = 128(1.6)^{x-1}$ as the coefficient.

Choice A is incorrect and may result from conceptual or calculation errors. *Choice B* is incorrect and may result from conceptual or calculation errors. *Choice D* is incorrect and may result from conceptual or calculation errors.

QUESTION 22

Choice A is correct. It's given that $g(x) = f(x + 5)$. Since $f(x) = 4x^2 + 64x + 262$, it follows that $f(x + 5) = 4(x + 5)^2 + 64(x + 5) + 262$. Expanding the quantity $(x + 5)^2$ in this equation yields $f(x + 5) = 4(x^2 + 10x + 25) + 64(x + 5) + 262$. Distributing the 4 and the 64 yields $f(x + 5) = 4x^2 + 40x + 100 + 64x + 320 + 262$. Combining like terms yields $f(x + 5) = 4x^2 + 104x + 682$. Therefore, $g(x) = 4x^2 + 104x + 682$. For a quadratic function defined by an equation of the form $g(x) = a(x - h)^2 + k$, where a, h, and k are constants and a is positive, $g(x)$ reaches its minimum, k, when the value of x is h. The equation $g(x) = 4x^2 + 104x + 682$ can be rewritten in this form by completing the square. This equation is equivalent to $g(x) = 4(x^2 + 26x) + 682$, or $g(x) = 4(x^2 + 26x + 169 - 169) + 682$. This equation can be rewritten as $g(x) = 4((x + 13)^2 - 169) + 682$, or $g(x) = 4(x + 13)^2 - 4(169) + 682$, which is equivalent to $g(x) = 4(x + 13)^2 + 6$. This equation is in the form $g(x) = a(x - h)^2 + k$, where $a = 4$, $h = -13$, and $k = 6$. Therefore, $g(x)$ reaches its minimum when the value of x is -13.

Choice B is incorrect. This is the value of x for which $f(x)$, rather than $g(x)$, reaches its minimum. *Choice C* is incorrect and may result from conceptual or calculation errors. *Choice D* is incorrect. This is the value of x for which $f(x - 5)$, rather than $f(x + 5)$, reaches its minimum.

Math

Module 2 — Lower Difficulty
(22 questions)

QUESTION 1

Choice C is correct. For the given line graph, the percent of cars for sale at a used car lot on a given day is represented on the vertical axis. The percent of cars for sale is the smallest when the height of the line graph is the lowest. The lowest height of the line graph occurs for cars with a model year of 2014.

Choice A is incorrect and may result from conceptual errors. *Choice B* is incorrect and may result from conceptual errors. *Choice D* is incorrect and may result from conceptual errors.

QUESTION 2

Choice D is correct. Since 1 yard is equal to 3 feet, 64 yards is equal to 64 yards $\left(\frac{3 \text{ feet}}{1 \text{ yard}}\right)$, or 192 feet. It follows that 64 yards per second is equivalent to 192 feet per second. Therefore, the object's speed is 192 feet per second.

Choice A is incorrect. A speed of 61 feet per second is equivalent to $\frac{61}{3}$, not 64, yards per second. *Choice B* is incorrect. A speed of 67 feet per second is equivalent to $\frac{67}{3}$, not 64, yards per second. *Choice C* is incorrect. A speed of 94 feet per second is equivalent to $\frac{94}{3}$, not 64, yards per second.

QUESTION 3

Choice B is correct. The perimeter of a triangle is the sum of the lengths of all three of its sides. It's given that the lengths of two sides of a triangle are 4 centimeters and 6 centimeters. Let x represent the length, in centimeters, of the third side of this triangle. The sum of the lengths, in centimeters, of all three sides of the triangle can be represented by the expression $4 + 6 + x$. Since it's given that the perimeter of the triangle is 18 centimeters, it follows that $4 + 6 + x = 18$, or $10 + x = 18$. Subtracting 10 from both sides of this equation yields $x = 8$. Therefore, the length, in centimeters, of the third side of this triangle is 8.

Choice A is incorrect. If the length of the third side of this triangle were 2 centimeters, the perimeter, in centimeters, of the triangle would be 4 + 6 + 2, or 12, not 18. *Choice C* is incorrect. If the length of the third side of this triangle were 10 centimeters, the perimeter, in centimeters, of the triangle would be 4 + 6 + 10, or 20, not 18. *Choice D* is incorrect. If the length of the third side of this triangle were 24 centimeters, the perimeter, in centimeters, of the triangle would be 4 + 6 + 24, or 34, not 18.

QUESTION 4

Choice C is correct. It's given that t represents the number of seconds after the bus passes the marker. Substituting 2 for t in the given equation $d = 30t$ yields $d = 30(2)$, or $d = 60$. Therefore, the bus will be 60 feet from the marker 2 seconds after passing it.

Choice A is incorrect. This is the distance, in feet, the bus will be from the marker 1 second, not 2 seconds, after passing it. *Choice B* is incorrect and may result from conceptual or calculation errors. *Choice D* is incorrect. This is the distance, in feet, the bus will be from the marker 3 seconds, not 2 seconds, after passing it.

QUESTION 5

Choice D is correct. The cost of the rental fee depends on the number of hours the surfboard is rented. Multiplying t hours by 10 dollars per hour yields a rental fee of $10t$ dollars. The total cost of the rental consists of the rental fee plus the 25 dollar service fee, which yields a total cost of $25 + 10t$ dollars. Since the person intends to spend a maximum of 75 dollars to rent the surfboard, the total cost must be at most 75 dollars. Therefore, the inequality $25 + 10t \leq 75$ represents this situation.

Choice A is incorrect. This represents a situation where the rental fee, not the total cost, is at most 75 dollars. *Choice B* is incorrect and may result from conceptual or calculation errors. *Choice C* is incorrect and may result from conceptual or calculation errors.

QUESTION 6

Choice D is correct. If a member of the organization is selected at random, the probability that the selected member is at least 40 years old is equal to the number of members who are at least 40 years old divided by the total number of members. According to the table, there are a total of 135 members of the organization, and 107 of these members are at least 40 years old. Therefore, the probability that the selected member is at least 40 years old is $\frac{107}{135}$.

Choice A is incorrect. This is the probability that the selected member is less than 40 years old. *Choice B* is incorrect. This is the probability that the selected member lives east of the river. *Choice C* is incorrect. This is the probability that the selected member lives west of the river.

QUESTION 7

Choice B is correct. The y-intercept of the graph of a function in the xy-plane is the point on the graph where $x = 0$. It's given that $f(x) = \frac{1}{10}x - 2$. Substituting 0 for x in this equation yields $f(0) = \frac{1}{10}(0) - 2$, or $f(0) = -2$. Since it's given that $y = f(x)$, it follows that $y = -2$ when $x = 0$. Therefore, the y-intercept of the graph of $y = f(x)$ in the xy-plane is $(0, -2)$.

Choice A is incorrect and may result from conceptual or calculation errors.
Choice C is incorrect and may result from conceptual or calculation errors.
Choice D is incorrect and may result from conceptual or calculation errors.

QUESTION 8

Choice A is correct. It's given that $g(x) = x^2 + 9$. Substituting 25 for $g(x)$ in this equation yields $25 = x^2 + 9$. Subtracting 9 from both sides of this equation yields $16 = x^2$. Taking the square root of each side of this equation yields $x = \pm 4$. It follows that $g(x) = 25$ when the value of x is 4 or −4. Only 4 is listed among the choices.

Choice B is incorrect and may result from conceptual or calculation errors.
Choice C is incorrect and may result from conceptual or calculation errors.
Choice D is incorrect and may result from conceptual or calculation errors.

QUESTION 9

Choice D is correct. It's given that the graph shows the linear relationship between x and y. The given graph passes through the points (0, −5), (1, −3), and (2, −1). It follows that when $x = 0$, the corresponding value of y is −5, when $x = 1$, the corresponding value of y is −3, and when $x = 2$, the corresponding value of y is −1. Of the given choices, only the table in choice D gives these three values of x and their corresponding values of y for the relationship shown in the graph.

Choice A is incorrect. This table represents a relationship between x and y such that the graph passes through the points (0, 0), (1, −7), and (2, −9). *Choice B* is incorrect. This table represents a relationship between x and y such that the graph passes through the points (0, 0), (1, −3), and (2, −1). *Choice C* is incorrect. This table represents a linear relationship between x and y such that the graph passes through the points (0, −5), (1, −7), and (2, −9).

QUESTION 10

The correct answer is 70. Based on the figure, the angle with measure 110° and the angle vertical to the angle with measure $x°$ are same side interior angles. Since vertical angles are congruent, the angle vertical to the angle with measure $x°$ also has measure $x°$. It's given that lines s and t are parallel. Therefore, same side interior angles between lines s and t are supplementary. It follows that $x + 110 = 180$. Subtracting 110 from both sides of this equation yields $x = 70$.

QUESTION 11

The correct answer is 9. The mean of a data set is the sum of the values in the data set divided by the number of values in the data set. It follows that the mean height, in centimeters, of these plants is the sum of the heights, in centimeters, of each plant, 6 + 10 + 13 + 2 + 15 + 22 + 10 + 4 + 4 + 4, or 90, divided by the number of plants in the data set, 10. Therefore, the mean height, in centimeters, of these plants is $\frac{90}{10}$, or 9.

QUESTION 12

Choice A is correct. For the linear function f, it's given that $f(7) = 28$. Substituting 7 for x and 28 for $f(x)$ in the given function yields $28 = 4(7) + b$, or $28 = 28 + b$. Subtracting 28 from each side of this equation yields $0 = b$. Therefore, the value of b is 0.

Choice B is incorrect. Substituting 1 for b in the given function yields $f(x) = 4x + 1$. For this function, when the value of x is 7, the value of $f(x)$ is 29, not 28. *Choice C* is incorrect. Substituting 4 for b in the given function yields $f(x) = 4x + 4$. For this function, when the value of x is 7, the value of $f(x)$ is 32, not 28. *Choice D* is incorrect. Substituting 7 for b in the given function yields $f(x) = 4x + 7$. For this function, when the value of x is 7, the value of $f(x)$ is 35, not 28.

QUESTION 13

Choice B is correct. Multiplying both sides of the given equation by 4 yields $(4)(4x + 2) = (4)(12)$, or $16x + 8 = 48$. Therefore, the value of $16x + 8$ is 48.

Choice A is incorrect and may result from conceptual or calculation errors. *Choice C* is incorrect and may result from conceptual or calculation errors. *Choice D* is incorrect and may result from conceptual or calculation errors.

QUESTION 14

Choice B is correct. Since the point (x, y) is an intersection point of the graphs of the given equations in the xy-plane, the pair (x, y) should satisfy both equations, and thus is a solution of the given system. According to the first equation, $y = 76$. Substituting 76 in place of y in the second equation yields $x^2 - 5 = 76$. Adding 5 to both sides of this equation yields $x^2 = 81$. Taking the square root of both sides of this equation yields two solutions: $x = 9$ and $x = -9$. Of these two solutions, only -9 is given as a choice.

Choice A is incorrect and may result from conceptual or calculation errors. *Choice C* is incorrect and may result from conceptual or calculation errors. *Choice D* is incorrect. This is the value of coordinate y, rather than x, of the intersection point (x, y).

QUESTION 15

Choice C is correct. The given system of linear equations can be solved by the substitution method. Substituting $-3x$ for y from the first equation in the given system into the second equation yields $4x + (-3x) = 15$, or $x = 15$.

Choice A is incorrect and may result from conceptual or calculation errors. *Choice B* is incorrect and may result from conceptual or calculation errors. *Choice D* is incorrect. This is the absolute value of y, not the value of x.

QUESTION 16

The correct answer is 25. The total cost of the party is found by adding the onetime fee of the venue to the cost per attendee times the number of attendees. Let x be the number of attendees. The expression $35 + 10.25x$ thus represents the total cost of the party. It's given that the budget is $300, so this situation can be represented by the inequality $35 + 10.25x \leq 300$. Subtracting 35 from both sides of this inequality gives $10.25x \leq 265$. Dividing both sides of this inequality by 10.25 results in approximately $x \leq 25.854$. Since the question is stated in terms of attendees, rounding 25.854 down to the greatest whole number gives the greatest number of attendees possible, which is 25.

QUESTION 17

The correct answer is either 2 or -12. The left-hand side of the given equation can be rewritten by factoring. The two values that multiply to -24 and add to 10 are 12 and -2. It follows that the given equation can be rewritten as $(z + 12)(z - 2) = 0$. Setting each factor equal to 0 yields two equations: $z + 12 = 0$ and $z - 2 = 0$.

Subtracting 12 from both sides of the equation $z + 12 = 0$ results in $z = -12$. Adding 2 to both sides of the equation $z - 2 = 0$ results in $z = 2$. Note that 2 and -12 are examples of ways to enter a correct answer.

QUESTION 18

Choice A is correct. Since it's given that the account balance, $A(t)$, in dollars, after t years can be modeled by an exponential function, it follows that function A can be written in the form $A(t) = Nr^t$, where N is the initial value of the function and r is a constant related to the growth of the function. It's given that the initial balance of the account is \$36,100.00, so it follows that the initial value of the function, or N, must be 36,100.00. Substituting 36,100.00 for N in the equation $A(t) = Nr^t$ yields $A(t) = 36,100.00r^t$. It's given that the account balance after 13 years, or when $t = 13$, is \$68,071.93. It follows that $A(13) = 68,071.93$, or $36,100.00r^{13} = 68,071.93$. Dividing each side of the

equation $36,100.00r^{13} = 68,071.93$ by 36,100.00 yields $r^{13} = \dfrac{68,071.93}{36,100.00}$.

Taking the 13th root of both sides of this equation yields $r = \sqrt[13]{\dfrac{68,071.93}{36,100.00}}$, or

r is approximately equal to 1.05. Substituting 1.05 for r in the equation $A(t) = 36,100.00r^t$ yields $A(t) = 36,100.00(1.05)^t$, so the equation $A(t) = 36,100.00(1.05)^t$ could define A.

Choice B is incorrect. Substituting 0 for t in this function indicates an initial balance of \$31,971.93, rather than \$36,100.00. *Choice C* is incorrect. Substituting 0 for t in this function indicates an initial balance of \$31,971.93, rather than \$36,100.00. Additionally, this function indicates the account balance is decreasing, rather than increasing, over time. *Choice D* is incorrect. This function indicates the account balance is decreasing, rather than increasing, over time.

QUESTION 19

The correct answer is 104. An equilateral triangle is a triangle in which all three sides have the same length and all three angles have a measure of 60°. The height of the triangle, $k\sqrt{3}$, is the length of the altitude from one vertex. The altitude divides the equilateral triangle into two congruent 30-60-90 right triangles, where the altitude is the side across from the 60° angle in each 30-60-90 right triangle. Since the altitude has a length of $k\sqrt{3}$, it follows from the properties of 30-60-90 right triangles that the side across from each 30° angle has a length of k and each hypotenuse has a length of $2k$. In this case, the hypotenuse of each 30-60-90 right triangle is a side of the equilateral triangle; therefore, each side length of the equilateral triangle is $2k$. The perimeter of a triangle is the sum of the lengths of each side. It's given that the perimeter of the equilateral triangle is 624; therefore, $2k + 2k + 2k = 624$, or $6k = 624$. Dividing both sides of this equation by 6 yields $k = 104$.

QUESTION 20

Choice B is correct. Since $\overline{PR}$ and $\overline{QS}$ are diameters of the circle shown, $\overline{OS}$, $\overline{OR}$, $\overline{OP}$, and $\overline{OQ}$ are radii of the circle and are therefore congruent. Since $\angle SOP$ and $\angle ROQ$ are vertical angles, they are congruent. Therefore, arc PS and arc QR are formed by congruent radii and have the same angle measure, so they are congruent arcs. Similarly, $\angle SOR$ and $\angle POQ$ are vertical angles, so they are congruent. Therefore, arc SR and arc PQ are formed by congruent radii and have the same angle measure, so they are congruent arcs. Let x represent the length of arc SR. Since arc SR and arc PQ are congruent arcs, the length of arc *PQ* can also be represented by *x*. It's given that the length of arc *PS* is twice the length of arc *PQ*. Therefore, the length of arc *PS* can be represented by the expression 2*x*. Since arc *PS* and arc *QR* are congruent arcs, the length of arc *QR* can also be represented by 2*x*. This gives the expression *x* + *x* + 2*x* + 2*x*. Since it's given that the circumference is 144π, the expression *x* + *x* + 2*x* + 2*x* is equal to 144π. Thus *x* + *x* + 2*x* + 2*x* = 144π, or 6*x* = 144π. Dividing both sides of this equation by 6 yields *x* = 24π. Therefore, the length of arc *QR* is 2(24π), or 48π.

Choice A is incorrect. This is the length of arc *PQ*, not arc *QR*. *Choice C* is incorrect and may result from conceptual or calculation errors. *Choice D* is incorrect and may result from conceptual or calculation errors.

QUESTION 21

The correct answer is 6. Applying the distributive property to the expression $ry^4(15y - 9)$ yields $15ry^5 - 9ry^4$. Since $90y^5 - 54y^4$ is equivalent to $ry^4(15y - 9)$, it follows that $90y^5 - 54y^4$ is also equivalent to $15ry^5 - 9ry^4$. Since these expressions are equivalent, it follows that corresponding coefficients are equivalent. Therefore, $90 = 15r$ and $-54 = -9r$. Solving either of these equations for *r* will yield the value of *r*. Dividing both sides of $90 = 15r$ by 15 yields $6 = r$. Therefore, the value of *r* is 6.

QUESTION 22

Choice C is correct. The Pythagorean theorem states that for a right triangle, the sum of the squares of the lengths of the two legs is equal to the square of the length of the hypotenuse. It's given that one leg of a right triangle has a length of 43.2 millimeters. It's also given that the hypotenuse of the triangle has a length of 196.8 millimeters. Let *b* represent the length of the other leg of the triangle, in millimeters. Therefore, by the Pythagorean theorem, $43.2^2 + b^2 = 196.8^2$, or $1{,}866.24 + b^2 = 38{,}730.24$. Subtracting 1,866.24 from both sides of this equation yields $b^2 = 36{,}864$. Taking the positive square root of both sides of this equation yields $b = 192$. Therefore, the length of the other leg of the triangle, in millimeters, is 192.

Choice A is incorrect and may result from conceptual or calculation errors. *Choice B* is incorrect and may result from conceptual or calculation errors. *Choice D* is incorrect and may result from conceptual or calculation errors.

Math

Module 2 — Higher Difficulty
(22 questions)

QUESTION 1

Choice C is correct. Subtracting 6 from both sides of the given equation yields $4x = 12$, which is the equation given in choice C. Since this equation is equivalent to the given equation, it has the same solution as the given equation.

Choice A is incorrect and may result from conceptual or calculation errors.
Choice B is incorrect and may result from conceptual or calculation errors.
Choice D is incorrect and may result from conceptual or calculation errors.

QUESTION 2

Choice C is correct. It's given that $f(x)$ is the total cost, in dollars, to lease a car from this dealership with a monthly payment of x dollars. Therefore, the total cost, in dollars, to lease the car when the monthly payment is $400 is represented by the value of $f(x)$ when $x = 400$. Substituting 400 for x in the equation $f(x) = 36x + 1,000$ yields $f(400) = 36(400) + 1,000$, or $f(400) = 15,400$. Thus, when the monthly payment is $400, the total cost to lease a car is $15,400.

Choice A is incorrect and may result from conceptual or calculation errors.
Choice B is incorrect and may result from conceptual or calculation errors.
Choice D is incorrect and may result from conceptual or calculation errors.

QUESTION 3

Choice A is correct. When the graph of an equation in the form $Ax + By = C$, where A, B, and C are constants, is shifted down k units in the xy-plane, the resulting graph can be represented by the equation $Ax + B(y + k) = C$. It's given that the graph of $27x + 33y = 297$ is shifted down 5 units in the xy-plane. Therefore, the resulting graph can be represented by the equation $27x + 33(y + 5) = 297$, or $27x + 33y + 165 = 297$. Subtracting 165 from both sides of this equation yields $27x + 33y = 132$. The y-intercept of the graph of an equation in the xy-plane is the point where the line intersects the y-axis, represented by the point $(0, y)$. Substituting 0 for x in the equation $27x + 33y = 132$ yields $27(0) + 33y = 132$, or $33y = 132$. Dividing both sides of this equation by 33 yields $y = 4$. Therefore, if the graph of $27x + 33y = 297$ is shifted down 5 units, the y-intercept of the resulting graph is $(0, 4)$.

Choice B is incorrect and may result from conceptual or calculation errors. *Choice C* is incorrect. This is the y-intercept of the graph of $27x + 33y = 297$ shifted up, not down, 5 units. *Choice D* is incorrect and may result from conceptual or calculation errors.

QUESTION 4

Choice B is correct. The y-intercept of the graph of a function in the xy-plane is the point on the graph where $x = 0$. It's given that $f(x) = \frac{1}{10}x - 2$. Substituting 0 for x in this equation yields $f(0) = \frac{1}{10}(0) - 2$, or $f(0) = -2$. Since it's given that $y = f(x)$, it follows that $y = -2$ when $x = 0$. Therefore, the y-intercept of the graph of $y = f(x)$ in the xy-plane is $(0, -2)$.

Choice A is incorrect and may result from conceptual or calculation errors. *Choice C* is incorrect and may result from conceptual or calculation errors. *Choice D* is incorrect and may result from conceptual or calculation errors.

QUESTION 5

Choice B is correct. The graph shown is a line passing through the points $(0, 40)$ and $(60, 0)$. Since the relationship between x and y is linear, if two points on the graph make a linear equation true, then the equation represents the relationship. Substituting 0 for x and 40 for y in the equation in choice B, $8x + 12y = 480$, yields $8(0) + 12(40) = 480$, or $480 = 480$, which is true. Substituting 60 for x and 0 for y in the equation $8x + 12y = 480$ yields $8(60) + 12(0) = 480$, or $480 = 480$, which is true. Therefore, the equation $8x + 12y = 480$ represents the relationship between x and y.

Choice A is incorrect. The point $(0, 40)$ is not on the graph of this equation, since $40 = 8(0) + 12$, or $40 = 12$, is not true. *Choice C* is incorrect. The point $(0, 40)$ is not on the graph of this equation, since $40 = 12(0) + 8$, or $40 = 8$, is not true. *Choice D* is incorrect. The point $(0, 40)$ is not on the graph of this equation, since $12(0) + 8(40) = 480$, or $320 = 480$, is not true.

QUESTION 6

Choice D is correct. Multiplying the second equation in the given system by 2 yields $\frac{10}{2}x + 12y = 46$. Adding this equation to the first equation in the system yields $\left(\frac{7}{2}x + 6y\right) + \left(\frac{10}{2}x + 12y\right) = 25 + 46$, which is equivalent to $\left(\frac{7}{2}x + \frac{10}{2}x\right) + (6y + 12y) = 25 + 46$, or $\frac{17}{2}x + 18y = 71$. Therefore, the value of $\frac{17}{2}x + 18y$ is 71.

Choice A is incorrect. This is the value of x, not the value of $\frac{17}{2}x + 18y$.

Choice B is incorrect. This is the value of y, not the value of $\frac{17}{2}x + 18y$.

Choice C is incorrect. This the value of $\left(\frac{7}{2}x + 6y\right) + \left(\frac{5}{2}x + 6y\right)$, or $6x + 12y$, not the value of $\frac{17}{2}x + 18y$.

QUESTION 7

Choice B is correct. It's given that $f(x) = (x + 6)(x + 5)(x - 4)$ and $y = f(x) - 3$. Substituting $(x + 6)(x + 5)(x - 4)$ for $f(x)$ in the equation $y = f(x) - 3$ yields $y = (x + 6)(x + 5)(x - 4) - 3$. Substituting -6 for x in this equation yields $y = (-6 + 6)(-6 + 5)(-6 - 4) - 3$, or $y = -3$. Substituting -5 for x in the equation $y = (x + 6)(x + 5)(x - 4) - 3$ yields $y = (-5 + 6)(-5 + 5)(-5 - 4) - 3$, or $y = -3$. Substituting 4 for x in the equation $y = (x + 6)(x + 5)(x - 4) - 3$ yields $y = (4 + 6)(4 + 5)(4 - 4) - 3$, or $y = -3$. Therefore, when $x = -6$ then $y = -3$, when $x = -5$ then $y = -3$, and when $x = 4$ then $y = -3$. Thus, the table of values in choice B represents $y = f(x) - 3$.

Choice A is incorrect. This table represents $y = x - 3$ rather than $y = f(x) - 3$.
Choice C is incorrect. This table represents $y = x + 3$ rather than $y = f(x) - 3$.
Choice D is incorrect. This table represents $y = f(x) + 3$ rather than $y = f(x) - 3$.

QUESTION 8

Choice C is correct. Since the value of $q(x)$ decreases by a fixed percentage, 45%, for every increase in the value of x by 1, the function q is a decreasing exponential function. A decreasing exponential function can be written in the form $q(x) = a\left(1 - \frac{p}{100}\right)^x$, where a is the value of $q(0)$ and the value of $q(x)$ decreases by p% for every increase in the value of x by 1. If $q(0) = 14$, then $a = 14$. Since the value of $q(x)$ decreases by 45% for every increase in the value of x by 1, $p = 45$. Substituting 14 for a and 45 for p in the equation $q(x) = a\left(1 - \frac{p}{100}\right)^x$ yields $q(x) = 14\left(1 - \frac{45}{100}\right)^x$, which is equivalent to $q(x) = 14(1 - 0.45)^x$, or $q(x) = 14(0.55)^x$.

Choice A is incorrect and may result from conceptual or calculation errors.
Choice B is incorrect and may result from conceptual or calculation errors.
Choice D is incorrect. For this function, the value of $q(x)$ increases, rather than decreases, by 45% for every increase in the value of x by 1.

QUESTION 9

The correct answer is 35. It's given that the function $g(x) = -\frac{1}{55}(x + 19)(x - 35)$ gives the depth below the surface of the ocean, in meters, of the submersible device x minutes after collecting a sample, where $x > 0$. It follows that when the submersible device is at the surface of the ocean, the value of $g(x)$ is 0.

Substituting 0 for $g(x)$ in the equation $g(x) = -\frac{1}{55}(x + 19)(x - 35)$ yields $0 = -\frac{1}{55}(x + 19)(x - 35)$. Multiplying both sides of this equation by -55 yields $0 = (x + 19)(x - 35)$. Since a product of two factors is equal to 0 if and only if at least one of the factors is 0, either $x + 19 = 0$ or $x - 35 = 0$. Subtracting 19 from both sides of the equation $x + 19 = 0$ yields $x = -19$. Adding 35 to both sides of the equation $x - 35 = 0$ yields $x = 35$. Since $x > 0$, 35 minutes after collecting the sample the submersible device reached the surface of the ocean.

QUESTION 10

Choice A is correct. The volume of a cube can be found by using the formula $V = s^3$, where V is the volume and s is the edge length of the cube. Therefore, the volume of the given cube is $V = 68^3$, or 314,432 cubic inches. The volume of a sphere can be found by using the formula $V = \frac{4}{3}\pi r^3$, where V is the volume and r is the radius of the sphere. Therefore, the volume of the given sphere is $V = \frac{4}{3}\pi(34)^3$, or approximately 164,636 cubic inches. The volume of the space in the cube not taken up by the sphere is the difference between the volume of the cube and volume of the sphere. Subtracting the approximate volume of the sphere from the volume of the cube gives 314,432 − 164,636 = 149,796 cubic inches.

Choice B is incorrect and may result from conceptual or calculation errors. *Choice C* is incorrect and may result from conceptual or calculation errors. *Choice D* is incorrect and may result from conceptual or calculation errors.

QUESTION 11

The correct answer is $\frac{29}{3}$. Applying the distributive property to the left-hand side of the given equation, $x(x + 1) - 56$, yields $x^2 + x - 56$. Applying the distributive property to the right-hand side of the given equation, $4x(x - 7)$, yields $4x^2 - 28x$. Thus, the equation becomes $x^2 + x - 56 = 4x^2 - 28x$. Combining like terms on the left- and right-hand sides of this equation yields $0 = (4x^2 - x^2) + (-28x - x) + 56$, or $3x^2 - 29x + 56 = 0$. For a quadratic equation in the form $ax^2 + bx + c = 0$, where a, b, and c are constants, the quadratic formula gives the solutions to the equation in the form $x = \frac{\left(-b \pm \sqrt{b^2 - 4ac}\right)}{2a}$.

Substituting 3 for a, −29 for b, and 56 for c from the equation $3x^2 - 29x + 56 = 0$ into the quadratic formula yields $x = \frac{\left(29 \pm \sqrt{(-29)^2 - 4(3)(56)}\right)}{2(3)}$, or $x = \frac{29}{6} \pm \frac{13}{6}$.

It follows that the solutions to the given equation are $\frac{29}{6} + \frac{13}{6}$ and $\frac{29}{6} - \frac{13}{6}$.

Adding these two solutions gives the sum of the solutions: $\frac{29}{6} + \frac{13}{6} + \frac{29}{6} - \frac{13}{6}$, which is equivalent to $\frac{29}{6} + \frac{29}{6}$, or $\frac{29}{3}$. Note that 29/3, 9.666, and 9.667 are examples of ways to enter a correct answer.

QUESTION 12

Choice C is correct. All the tables in the choices have the same three values of x, so each of the three values of x can be substituted in the given inequality to compare the corresponding values of y in each of the tables. Substituting 3 for x in the given inequality yields $y < 6(3) + 2$, or $y < 20$. Therefore, when $x = 3$, the corresponding value of y is less than 20. Substituting 5 for x in the given inequality yields $y < 6(5) + 2$, or $y < 32$. Therefore, when $x = 5$, the corresponding value of y is less than 32. Substituting 7 for x in the given inequality yields $y < 6(7) + 2$, or $y < 44$. Therefore, when $x = 7$, the corresponding value of y is less than 44. For the table in choice C, when $x = 3$, the corresponding value of y is 16, which is less than 20; when $x = 5$, the corresponding value of y is 28, which is less than 32; when $x = 7$, the corresponding value of y is 40, which is less than 44. Therefore, the table in choice C gives values of x and their corresponding values of y that are all solutions to the given inequality.

Choice A is incorrect. In the table for choice A, when $x = 3$, the corresponding value of y is 20, which is not less than 20; when $x = 5$, the corresponding value of y is 32, which is not less than 32; when $x = 7$, the corresponding value of y is 44, which is not less than 44. *Choice B* is incorrect. In the table for choice B, when $x = 5$, the corresponding value of y is 36, which is not less than 32.

Choice D is incorrect. In the table for choice D, when $x = 3$, the corresponding value of y is 24, which is not less than 20; when $x = 5$, the corresponding value of y is 36, which is not less than 32; when $x = 7$, the corresponding value of y is 48, which is not less than 44.

QUESTION 13

Choice B is correct. The standard form of an equation of a circle in the xy-plane is $(x - h)^2 + (y - k)^2 = r^2$, where the coordinates of the center of the circle are (h, k) and the length of the radius of the circle is r. For the circle in the xy-plane with equation $(x - 5)^2 + (y - 3)^2 = 16$, it follows that $r^2 = 16$. Taking the square root of both sides of this equation yields $r = 4$ or $r = -4$. Because r represents the length of the radius of the circle and this length must be positive, $r = 4$. Therefore, the radius of the circle is 4. The diameter of a circle is twice the length of the radius of the circle. Thus, 2(4) yields 8. Therefore, the diameter of the circle is 8.

Choice A is incorrect. This is the radius of the circle. *Choice C* is incorrect. This is the square of the radius of the circle. *Choice D* is incorrect and may result from conceptual or calculation errors.

QUESTION 14

Choice C is correct. It's given that the equation $-9x^2 + 30x + c = 0$ has exactly one solution. A quadratic equation of the form $ax^2 + bx + c = 0$ has exactly one solution if and only if its discriminant, $-4ac + b^2$, is equal to zero. It follows that for the given equation, $a = -9$ and $b = 30$. Substituting -9 for a and 30 for b into $b^2 - 4ac$ yields $30^2 - 4(-9)(c)$, or $900 + 36c$. Since the discriminant must equal zero, $900 + 36c = 0$. Subtracting $36c$ from both sides of this equation yields $900 = -36c$. Dividing each side of this equation by -36 yields $-25 = c$. Therefore, the value of c is -25.

Choice A is incorrect. If the value of c is 3, this would yield a discriminant that is greater than zero. Therefore, the given equation would have two solutions, rather than exactly one solution. *Choice B* is incorrect. If the value of c is 0, this would yield a discriminant that is greater than zero. Therefore, the given equation would have two solutions, rather than exactly one solution. *Choice D* is incorrect. If the value of c is -53, this would yield a discriminant that is less than zero. Therefore, the given equation would have no real solutions, rather than exactly one solution.

QUESTION 15

The correct answer is 338. The tangent of an acute angle in a right triangle is the ratio of the length of the leg opposite the angle to the length of the leg adjacent to the angle. In triangle XYZ, it's given that angle Y is a right angle. Thus, $\overline{XY}$ is the leg opposite of angle Z and $\overline{YZ}$ is the leg adjacent to angle Z.

It follows that $\tan Z = \frac{XY}{YZ}$. It's also given that the measure of angle Z is 33° and the length of $\overline{YZ}$ is 26 units. Substituting 33° for Z and 26 for YZ in the equation $\tan Z = \frac{XY}{YZ}$ yields $\tan 33° = \frac{XY}{26}$. Multiplying each side of this equation by 26 yields $26 \tan 33° = XY$. Therefore, the length of $\overline{XY}$ is $26 \tan 33°$. The area of a triangle is half the product of the lengths of its legs. Since the length of $\overline{YZ}$ is 26 and the length of $\overline{XY}$ is $26 \tan 33°$, it follows that the area of triangle XYZ is

$\frac{1}{2}(26)(26 \tan 33°)$ square units, or 338 tan 33° square units. It's given that the area, in square units, of triangle XYZ can be represented by the expression $k \tan 33°$, where k is a constant. Therefore, 338 is the value of k.

QUESTION 16

The correct answer is 1.8. It's given that the regular price of a shirt at a store is $11.70, and the sale price of the shirt is 80% less than the regular price.

It follows that the sale price of the shirt is 11.70\left(1 - \frac{80}{100}\right)$, or $11.70(1 − 0.8),

which is equivalent to $2.34. It's also given that the sale price of the shirt is 30% greater than the store's cost for the shirt. Let x represent the store's cost for

the shirt. It follows that 2.34 = $\left(1 + \frac{30}{100}\right)x$, or 2.34 = 1.3$x$. Dividing both sides of

this equation by 1.3 yields x = 1.80. Therefore, the store's cost, in dollars, for the shirt is 1.80. Note that 1.8 and 9/5 are examples of ways to enter a correct answer.

QUESTION 17

Choice C is correct. Since angles *B* and *E* each have the same measure and angles *C* and *F* each have the same measure, triangles *ABC* and *DEF* are similar, where side *BC* corresponds to side *EF*. To determine whether two similar triangles are congruent, it is sufficient to determine whether one pair of corresponding sides are congruent. Therefore, to determine whether triangles *ABC* and *DEF* are congruent, it is sufficient to determine whether sides *BC* and *EF* have equal length. Thus, the lengths of *BC* and *EF* are sufficient to determine whether triangle *ABC* is congruent to triangle *DEF*.

Choice A is incorrect and may result from conceptual errors. *Choice B* is incorrect and may result from conceptual errors. *Choice D* is incorrect. The given information is sufficient to determine that triangles *ABC* and *DEF* are similar, but not whether they are congruent.

QUESTION 18

The correct answer is −34. A system of two linear equations in two variables, *x* and *y*, has no solution if the lines represented by the equations in the *xy*-plane are distinct and parallel. Two lines represented by equations in standard form *Ax* + *By* = *C*, where *A*, *B*, and *C* are constants, are parallel if the coefficients for *x* and *y* in one equation are proportional to the corresponding coefficients in the other equation. The first equation in the given system can be written in standard form by subtracting 30*y* from both sides of the equation to yield 48*x* − 102*y* = 24. The second equation in the given system can be written in

standard form by adding 16*x* to both sides of the equation to yield 16*x* + *ry* = $\frac{1}{6}$.

The coefficient of *x* in this second equation, 16, is $\frac{1}{3}$ times the coefficient of

x in the first equation, 48. For the lines to be parallel the coefficient of *y* in

the second equation, *r*, must also be $\frac{1}{3}$ times the coefficient of *y* in the first

equation, −102. Thus, *r* = $\frac{1}{3}$(−102), or *r* = −34. Therefore, if the given system has

no solution, the value of *r* is −34.

QUESTION 19

Choice D is correct. Since each choice has a term of 3x^2, which can be written as (3*x*)(*x*), and each choice has a term of 14*b*, which can be written as (7)(2*b*), the expression that has a factor of *x* + 2*b*, where *b* is a positive integer constant, can be represented as (3*x* + 7)(*x* + 2*b*). Using the distributive property of multiplication, this expression is equivalent to 3*x*(*x* + 2*b*) + 7(*x* + 2*b*), or 3x^2 + 6*xb* + 7*x* + 14*b*.

Combining the *x*-terms in this expression yields $3x^2 + (7 + 6b)x + 14b$. It follows that the coefficient of the *x*-term is equal to $7 + 6b$. Thus, from the given choices, $7 + 6b$ must be equal to 7, 28, 42, or 49. Therefore, $6b$ must be equal to 0, 21, 35, or 42, respectively, and *b* must be equal to $\frac{0}{6}$, $\frac{21}{6}$, $\frac{35}{6}$, or $\frac{42}{6}$, respectively.

Of these four values of *b*, only $\frac{42}{6}$, or 7, is a positive integer. It follows that $7 + 6b$ must be equal to 49 because this is the only choice for which the value of *b* is a positive integer constant. Therefore, the expression that has a factor of $x + 2b$ is $3x^2 + 49x + 14b$.

Choice A is incorrect. If this expression has a factor of $x + 2b$, then the value of *b* is 0, which isn't positive. *Choice B is incorrect.* If this expression has a factor of $x + 2b$, then the value of *b* is $\frac{21}{6}$, which isn't an integer. *Choice C is incorrect.* If this expression has a factor of $x + 2b$, then the value of *b* is $\frac{35}{6}$, which isn't an integer.

QUESTION 20

The correct answer is 104. An equilateral triangle is a triangle in which all three sides have the same length and all three angles have a measure of 60°. The height of the triangle, $k\sqrt{3}$, is the length of the altitude from one vertex. The altitude divides the equilateral triangle into two congruent 30-60-90 right triangles, where the altitude is the side across from the 60° angle in each 30-60-90 right triangle. Since the altitude has a length of $k\sqrt{3}$, it follows from the properties of 30-60-90 right triangles that the side across from each 30° angle has a length of *k* and each hypotenuse has a length of $2k$. In this case, the hypotenuse of each 30-60-90 right triangle is a side of the equilateral triangle; therefore, each side length of the equilateral triangle is $2k$. The perimeter of a triangle is the sum of the lengths of each side. It's given that the perimeter of the equilateral triangle is 624; therefore, $2k + 2k + 2k = 624$, or $6k = 624$. Dividing both sides of this equation by 6 yields $k = 104$.

QUESTION 21

Choice B is correct. The histograms shown have the same shape, but data set A contains values between 20 and 60 and data set B contains values between 10 and 50. Thus, the mean of data set A is greater than the mean of data set B. Therefore, the smallest possible difference between the mean of data set A and the mean of data set B is the difference between the smallest possible mean of data set A and the greatest possible mean of data set B. In data set A, since there are 3 integers in the interval greater than or equal to 20 but less than 30, 4 integers greater than or equal to 30 but less than 40, 7 integers greater than or equal to 40 but less than 50, and 9 integers greater than or equal to 50 but less than 60, the smallest possible mean for data set A is $\frac{(3 \cdot 20) + (4 \cdot 30) + (7 \cdot 40) + (9 \cdot 50)}{23}$. In data set B, since there are 3 integers greater than or equal to 10 but less than 20, 4 integers greater than or equal to 20 but less than 30, 7 integers greater than or equal to 30 but less than 40, and 9 integers greater than or equal to 40 but less than 50, the largest possible mean for data set B is $\frac{(3 \cdot 19) + (4 \cdot 29) + (7 \cdot 39) + (9 \cdot 49)}{23}$. Therefore, the smallest possible difference between the mean of data set A and the mean of data set B is

$$\frac{(3 \cdot 20) + (4 \cdot 30) + (7 \cdot 40) + (9 \cdot 50)}{23} - \frac{(3 \cdot 19) + (4 \cdot 29) + (7 \cdot 39) + (9 \cdot 49)}{23},$$

which is equivalent to

$$\frac{(3 \cdot 20) - (3 \cdot 19) + (4 \cdot 30) - (4 \cdot 29) + (7 \cdot 40) - (7 \cdot 39) + (9 \cdot 50) - (9 \cdot 49)}{23}$$. This

expression can be rewritten as $\frac{3(20 - 19) + 4(30 - 29) + 7(40 - 39) + 9(50 - 49)}{23}$,

or $\frac{23}{23}$, which is equal to 1. Therefore, the smallest possible difference between

the mean of data set A and the mean of data set B is 1.

Choice A is incorrect. This is the smallest possible difference between the ranges, not the means, of the data sets. *Choice C* is incorrect. This is the difference between the greatest possible mean, not the smallest possible mean, of data set A and the greatest possible mean of data set B. *Choice D* is incorrect. This is the smallest possible difference between the sum of the values in data set A and the sum of the values in data set B, not the smallest possible difference between the means.

QUESTION 22

Choice B is correct. It's given that 483 out of 803 voters responded that they would vote for Angel Cruz. Therefore, the proportion of voters from the poll who

responded they would vote for Angel Cruz is $\frac{483}{803}$. It's also given that there are a

total of 6,424 voters in the election. Therefore, the total number of people who

would be expected to vote for Angel Cruz is $6,424\left(\frac{483}{803}\right)$, or 3,864. Since, 3,864

of the 6,424 total voters would be expected to vote for Angel Cruz, it follows that 6,424 − 3,864, or 2,560 voters would be expected not to vote for Angel Cruz. The difference in the number of votes for and against Angel Cruz is 3,864 − 2,560, or 1,304 votes. Therefore, if 6,424 people vote in the election, Angel Cruz would be expected to win by 1,304 votes.

Choice A is incorrect. This is the difference in the number of voters from the poll who responded that they would vote for and against Angel Cruz. *Choice C* is incorrect. This is the total number of people who would be expected to vote for Angel Cruz. *Choice D* is incorrect. This is the difference between the total number of people who vote in the election and the number of voters from the poll.

Scoring Your Paper SAT Practice Test #8

Congratulations on completing an SAT® practice test. To score your test, follow the instructions in this scoring guide.

IMPORTANT: *This scoring guide is for students who completed SAT Practice Test #8 in The Official SAT Study Guide™. We recommend reading through these instructions and explanations before scoring so that you understand the specifics and limitations of scoring this practice test.*

The total score on your practice test reflects the sum of the (1) Reading and Writing and (2) Math section scores, as indicated below. If you decided to take both the lower- and higher-difficulty modules, choose which one you will use to score.

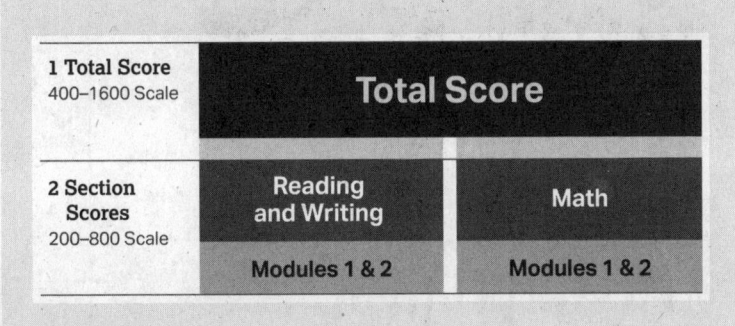

Scores Overview

Each assessment in the SAT Suite (SAT, PSAT/NMSQT®, PSAT™ 10, and PSAT™ 8/9) reports test scores on a common scale.

For more details about scores, visit **sat.org/scores**.

How to Calculate Your Practice Test Scores

The worksheets on the pages that follow help you calculate your test scores.

GET SET UP

1 In addition to your practice test, you'll need the answer keys and conversion tables at the end of this scoring guide.

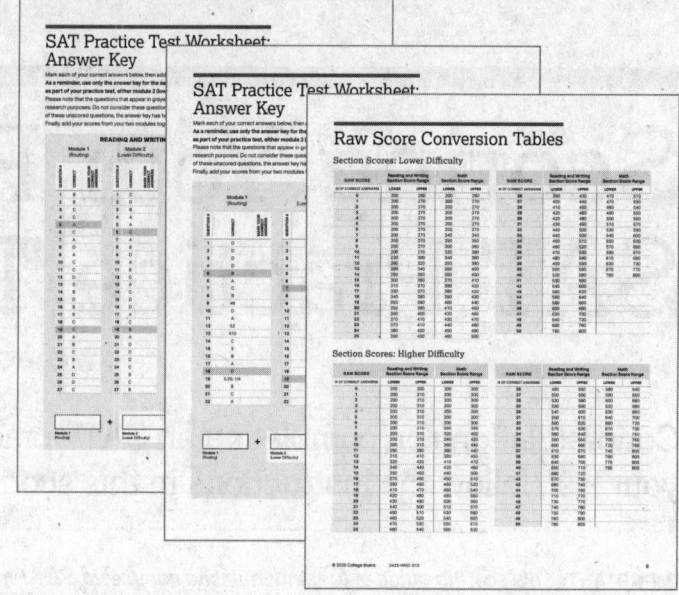

SCORE YOUR PRACTICE TEST

2 Compare your answers to the answer keys later in this scoring guide and count up the total number of correct answers for each section. Write the number of correct answers for each section in the boxes at the bottom of the pages.

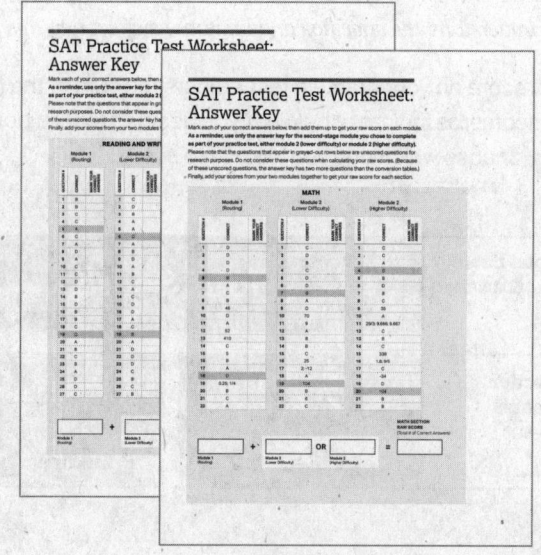

CALCULATE YOUR SCORES

3 Using your marked-up answer keys and the conversion tables, follow the directions on the SAT Practice Test Worksheet: Section and Total Scores page to get your section and total scores.

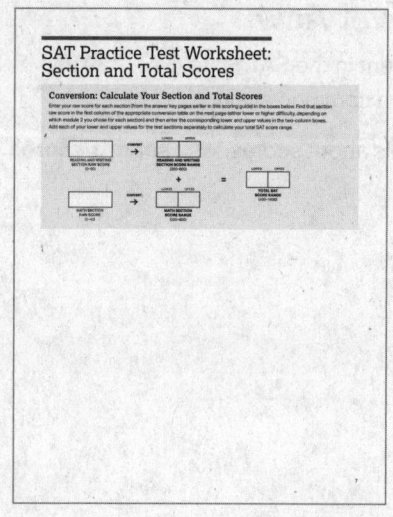

Get Section and Total Scores

Section and total scores for this paper version of SAT Practice Test #8 are expressed as ranges. That's because the scoring method described in this guide is a different (and therefore less precise) version of the one used in the actual adaptive test.

This practice test contains three modules for each test section: (1) a single first-stage (routing) module and (2) two second-stage modules. The two second-stage modules differ by average question difficulty and are marked as either "module 2 (lower difficulty)" or "module 2 (higher difficulty)." You get to choose which module 2 you would like to take for this practice test. **An actual testing experience consists of one routing and one second-stage module per test section.** To obtain your Reading and Writing and Math section scores, you will refer to the answer key and conversion table for the second-stage module you chose (either lower or higher difficulty).

GET YOUR READING AND WRITING SECTION SCORE

Calculate your SAT Reading and Writing section score (it's on a scale of 200–800).

1. Use the answer key for Reading and Writing to find the number of questions in module 1 and the module 2 you chose (either lower or higher difficulty) that you answered correctly.

2. To determine your Reading and Writing raw score, add the number of correct answers you got in module 1 and the module 2 you chose (either lower or higher difficulty). **Exclude the questions in grayed-out rows in your calculation.**

3. Use the appropriate Raw Score Conversion Table to turn your raw score into your Reading and Writing section score.

4. The lower and upper values associated with your raw score establish the range of scores you might expect to receive had this been an actual adaptive test.

GET YOUR MATH SECTION SCORE

Calculate your SAT Math section score (it's on a scale of 200–800).

1. Use the answer key for Math to find the number of questions in module 1 and the module 2 you chose (either lower or higher difficulty) that you answered correctly.

2. To determine your Math raw score, add the number of correct answers you got in module 1 and the module 2 you chose (either lower or higher difficulty). **Exclude the questions in grayed-out rows in your calculation.**

3. Use the appropriate Raw Score Conversion Table to turn your raw score into your Math section score.

4. The lower and upper values associated with your raw score establish the range of scores you might expect to receive had this been an actual adaptive test.

GET YOUR TOTAL SCORE

Add together the lower values for the Reading and Writing and Math sections, and then add together the upper values for the two sections. The result is your total score, expressed as a range, for this SAT practice test. The total score is on a scale of 400–1600.

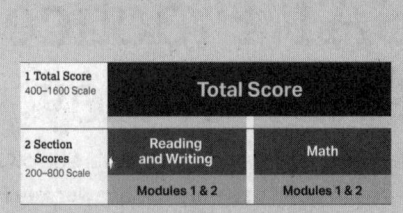

1 Total Score 400–1600 Scale	Total Score	
2 Section Scores 200–800 Scale	Reading and Writing	Math
	Modules 1 & 2	Modules 1 & 2

Your total score on this SAT practice test is the sum of your Reading and Writing section score and your Math section score. For this practice test, you'll receive a lower and upper score for each test section and the total score. This is the range of scores that you might expect to receive.

Use the worksheets on the pages that follow to calculate your section and total scores.

SAT Practice Test Worksheet: Answer Key

Mark each of your correct answers below, then add them up to get your raw score on each module. **As a reminder, use only the answer key for the second-stage module you chose to complete as part of your practice test, either module 2 (lower difficulty) or module 2 (higher difficulty).** Please note that the questions that appear in grayed-out rows below are unscored questions for research purposes. Do not consider these questions when calculating your raw scores. (Because of these unscored questions, the answer key has two more questions than the conversion tables.) Finally, add your scores from your two modules together to get your raw score for each section.

READING AND WRITING

Module 1 (Routing)			Module 2 (Lower Difficulty)			Module 2 (Higher Difficulty)		
QUESTION #	CORRECT	MARK YOUR CORRECT ANSWERS	QUESTION #	CORRECT	MARK YOUR CORRECT ANSWERS	QUESTION #	CORRECT	MARK YOUR CORRECT ANSWERS
1	B		1	C		1	D	
2	B		2	D		2	B	
3	C		3	B		3	B	
4	C		4	A		4	A	
5	A		5	A		5	D	
6	C		6	C		6	C	
7	A		7	A		7	D	
8	D		8	B		8	A	
9	A		9	D		9	C	
10	C		10	A		10	C	
11	C		11	B		11	D	
12	D		12	C		12	C	
13	D		13	A		13	B	
14	B		14	C		14	D	
15	D		15	D		15	C	
16	B		16	D		16	A	
17	B		17	A		17	C	
18	C		18	C		18	A	
19	C		19	B		19	C	
20	A		20	A		20	B	
21	B		21	D		21	B	
22	C		22	D		22	B	
23	B		23	D		23	A	
24	A		24	C		24	C	
25	D		25	B		25	D	
26	D		26	C		26	B	
27	C		27	B		27	A	

READING AND WRITING SECTION RAW SCORE
(Total # of Correct Answers)

[___] **+** [___] **OR** [___] **=** [___]

Module 1 (Routing)   Module 2 (Lower Difficulty)   Module 2 (Higher Difficulty)

SAT Practice Test Worksheet: Answer Key

Mark each of your correct answers below, then add them up to get your raw score on each module.

As a reminder, use only the answer key for the second-stage module you chose to complete as part of your practice test, either module 2 (lower difficulty) or module 2 (higher difficulty).

Please note that the questions that appear in grayed-out rows below are unscored questions for research purposes. Do not consider these questions when calculating your raw scores. (Because of these unscored questions, the answer key has two more questions than the conversion tables.)

Finally, add your scores from your two modules together to get your raw score for each section.

MATH

QUESTION #	Module 1 (Routing) CORRECT	MARK YOUR CORRECT ANSWERS	QUESTION #	Module 2 (Lower Difficulty) CORRECT	MARK YOUR CORRECT ANSWERS	QUESTION #	Module 2 (Higher Difficulty) CORRECT	MARK YOUR CORRECT ANSWERS
1	D		1	C		1	C	
2	D		2	D		2	C	
3	D		3	B		3	A	
4	D		4	C		4	B	
5	B		5	D		5	B	
6	A		6	D		6	D	
7	C		7	B		7	B	
8	B		8	A		8	C	
9	46		9	D		9	35	
10	D		10	70		10	A	
11	A		11	9		11	29/3; 9.666; 9.667	
12	52		12	A		12	C	
13	410		13	B		13	B	
14	C		14	B		14	C	
15	5		15	C		15	338	
16	B		16	25		16	1.8; 9/5	
17	A		17	2; -12		17	C	
18	D		18	A		18	-34	
19	0.25; 1/4		19	104		19	D	
20	B		20	B		20	104	
21	C		21	6		21	B	
22	A		22	C		22	B	

MATH SECTION RAW SCORE
(Total # of Correct Answers)

[ ]	+	[ ]	OR	[ ]	=	[ ]	
Module 1 (Routing)		Module 2 (Lower Difficulty)		Module 2 (Higher Difficulty)			

Understanding the SAT Practice Test Conversion Tables and Total Score Ranges

As mentioned earlier in this scoring guide, the scoring method for the practice tests that appear in *The Official SAT Study Guide* is different (and therefore less precise) than the method used in the actual adaptive test. Your practice test may result in a larger score range than what you hoped to see, but it's not feasible to estimate your performance on the practice tests in the study guide as precisely as we could for an actual test. As the test developers, College Board is committed to providing the most accurate conversion possible to help you understand your scores and guide your practice most effectively.

There are two conversion tables in this scoring guide. Use the conversion table labelled lower difficulty if you took module 2 (lower difficulty). Use the conversion table labelled higher difficulty if you took module 2 (higher difficulty). You might need both conversion tables if you took the lower-difficulty option for one section (e.g., Reading and Writing) and the higher-difficulty option for the other section (e.g., Math).

Because the lower- and higher-difficulty conversion tables share the same questions for module 1 (routing), you may encounter different score ranges based on the conversion table you use. For example, if you got all the module 1 (routing) questions correct, the lower-difficulty conversion table and the higher-difficulty conversion table will give you different score ranges. This is to be expected because the conversion tables account for all items within the two modules that make up the test. Answering only items on the first half of the test assumes you answered the other questions (module 2) incorrectly. Recall that when taking the actual SAT on test day, the test will adapt to your ability based on how you perform on the first half. Because of the differences between the actual test and providing a paper approximation of that (the practice test you're currently scoring), you should select the second-stage module that feels most appropriate for you. For example, if you were to answer all items on the first module correctly on the actual test, you would not be routed to the easier second-stage module. The converse would also be true. For many users of moderate ability either second-stage would be acceptable, but very high or low performers should be cautioned about taking the second-stage module that doesn't align well with their ability.

SAT Practice Test Worksheet: Section and Total Scores

Conversion: Calculate Your Section and Total Scores

Enter your raw score for each section (from the answer key pages earlier in this scoring guide) in the boxes below. Find that section raw score in the first column of the appropriate conversion table on the next page (either lower or higher difficulty, depending on which module 2 you chose for each section) and then enter the corresponding lower and upper values in the two-column boxes. Add each of your lower and upper values for the test sections separately to calculate your total SAT score range.

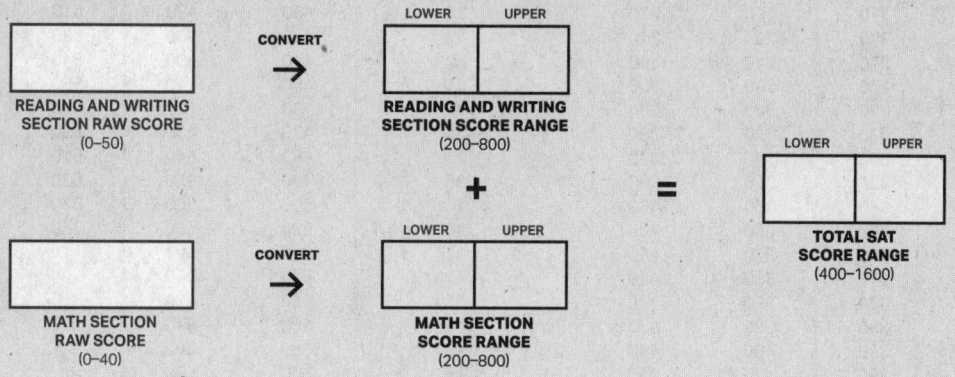

READING AND WRITING
SECTION RAW SCORE
(0–50)

CONVERT →

LOWER   UPPER

READING AND WRITING
SECTION SCORE RANGE
(200–800)

+

MATH SECTION
RAW SCORE
(0–40)

CONVERT →

LOWER   UPPER

MATH SECTION
SCORE RANGE
(200–800)

=

LOWER   UPPER

TOTAL SAT
SCORE RANGE
(400–1600)

Raw Score Conversion Tables

Section Scores: Lower Difficulty

RAW SCORE	Reading and Writing Section Score Range		Math Section Score Range	
(# OF CORRECT ANSWERS)	LOWER	UPPER	LOWER	UPPER
0	200	260	200	260
1	200	270	200	270
2	200	270	200	270
3	200	270	200	270
4	200	270	200	270
5	200	270	200	270
6	200	270	200	270
7	200	270	240	340
8	200	270	290	350
9	200	270	300	360
10	200	270	320	380
11	220	300	340	380
12	260	320	350	390
13	280	340	360	400
14	290	350	360	400
15	300	360	370	410
16	310	370	380	420
17	330	370	380	420
18	340	380	390	430
19	350	390	400	440
20	350	390	410	450
21	360	400	420	460
22	370	410	430	470
23	370	410	440	480
24	380	420	450	490
25	390	430	460	500

RAW SCORE	Reading and Writing Section Score Range		Math Section Score Range	
(# OF CORRECT ANSWERS)	LOWER	UPPER	LOWER	UPPER
26	390	430	470	510
27	400	440	470	530
28	410	450	480	540
29	420	460	490	550
30	420	480	500	560
31	430	490	510	570
32	440	500	530	590
33	440	500	540	600
34	450	510	550	630
35	460	520	570	650
36	470	530	590	670
37	480	540	610	690
38	490	550	630	730
39	500	560	670	770
40	520	580	760	800
41	530	590		
42	540	600		
43	560	620		
44	560	640		
45	580	660		
46	600	680		
47	620	700		
48	640	720		
49	680	760		
50	760	800		

Section Scores: Higher Difficulty

RAW SCORE	Reading and Writing Section Score Range		Math Section Score Range	
(# OF CORRECT ANSWERS)	LOWER	UPPER	LOWER	UPPER
0	200	300	200	300
1	200	310	200	300
2	200	310	200	300
3	200	310	200	300
4	200	310	200	300
5	200	310	200	300
6	200	310	200	300
7	200	310	260	360
8	200	310	320	400
9	200	310	340	420
10	200	310	360	440
11	290	390	380	440
12	310	410	390	450
13	320	420	410	470
14	340	440	420	480
15	350	450	440	500
16	370	450	450	510
17	390	450	460	520
18	410	470	480	540
19	420	480	490	550
20	430	490	500	560
21	440	500	510	570
22	450	510	530	590
23	460	520	540	600
24	470	530	550	610
25	480	540	560	620

RAW SCORE	Reading and Writing Section Score Range		Math Section Score Range	
(# OF CORRECT ANSWERS)	LOWER	UPPER	LOWER	UPPER
26	490	550	580	640
27	500	560	590	650
28	520	580	600	660
29	530	590	620	680
30	540	600	630	690
31	550	610	640	700
32	560	620	660	720
33	570	630	670	730
34	580	640	690	750
35	590	650	700	760
36	600	660	720	780
37	610	670	740	800
38	630	690	760	800
39	640	700	770	800
40	650	710	780	800
41	660	720		
42	670	730		
43	680	740		
44	700	760		
45	710	770		
46	730	770		
47	740	780		
48	750	790		
49	760	800		
50	780	800		

The SAT®
Practice Test #9

Make time to take the practice test. It is one of the best ways to get ready for the SAT.

Note: The practice tests in this guide include two second modules so that you can experience both the lower- and higher-difficulty modules. On the actual test, you will be presented with only one second module.

After you have taken the practice test, score it right away using materials provided in *The Official SAT Study Guide*.

This version of the SAT Practice Test is for students using this Study Guide. As a reminder, most students taking the SAT will do so using Bluebook™, the digital testing application. To best prepare for test day, download Bluebook at **bluebook.app.collegeboard.org** to take the practice test in the digital format.

Test begins on the next page.

Reading and Writing

27 QUESTIONS

1

Researchers have struggled to pinpoint specific causes for hiccups, which happen when a person's diaphragm contracts _____. However, neuroscientist Kimberley Whitehead has found that these uncontrollable contractions may play an important role in helping infants regulate their breathing.

Which choice completes the text with the most logical and precise word or phrase?

A) involuntarily

B) beneficially

C) strenuously

D) smoothly

2

Ofelia Zepeda's contributions to the field of linguistics are _____: her many accomplishments include working as a linguistics professor and bilingual poet, authoring the first Tohono O'odham grammar book, and co-founding the American Indian Language Development Institute.

Which choice completes the text with the most logical and precise word or phrase?

A) pragmatic

B) controversial

C) extensive

D) universal

3

Some researchers believe that the genes that enable groundhogs and certain other mammals to hibernate through the winter by slowing their breathing and heart rates and lowering their body temperature may be _____ in humans: present yet having essentially no effect on our bodily processes.

Which choice completes the text with the most logical and precise word or phrase?

A) decisive

B) lacking

C) variable

D) dormant

4

Although science fiction was dominated mostly by white male authors when Octavia Butler, a Black woman, began writing, she did not view the genre as _____: Butler broke into the field with the publication of several short stories and her 1976 novel *Patternmaster*, and she later became the first science fiction writer to win a prestigious MacArthur Fellowship.

Which choice completes the text with the most logical and precise word or phrase?

A) legitimate

B) impenetrable

C) compelling

D) indecipherable

5

Oral histories—whether they consist of interviews or recordings of songs and stories—can offer researchers a rich view of people's everyday experiences. For her book about coal mining communities in Kentucky during the twentieth century, Karida Brown therefore relied in part on interviews with coal miners and their families. <u>By doing so, she gained valuable insights into her subjects' day-to-day lives.</u>

Which choice best describes the function of the underlined sentence in the text as a whole?

A) It provides a little-known geographical fact about Kentucky.

B) It argues that Karida Brown is an expert on United States politics.

C) It presents a major historical event that took place in the twentieth century.

D) It describes how Karida Brown benefited from incorporating oral history in her book.

6

The following text is from Sarah Orne Jewett's 1899 short story "Martha's Lady." Martha is employed by Miss Pyne as a maid.

> Miss Pyne sat by the window watching, in her best dress, looking stately and calm; she seldom went out now, and it was almost time for the carriage. Martha was just coming in from the garden with the strawberries, and with more flowers in her apron. It was a bright cool evening in June, the golden robins sang in the elms, and the sun was going down behind the apple-trees at the foot of the garden. The beautiful old house stood wide open to the long-expected guest.

Which choice best states the main purpose of the text?

A) To convey the worries brought about by a new guest

B) To describe how the characters have changed over time

C) To contrast the activity indoors with the stillness outside

D) To depict the setting as the characters await a visitor's arrival

CONTINUE

7

The following text is adapted from George Bernard Shaw's 1912 play *Pygmalion*. Henry Higgins has just arrived at the house of his mother (Mrs. Higgins). She is expecting her friends to visit soon.

MRS. HIGGINS: I'm serious, Henry. You offend all my friends: they stop coming whenever they meet you.

HIGGINS: Nonsense! I know I have no small talk; but people don't mind.

MRS. HIGGINS: Oh! don't they? Small talk indeed! What about your large talk? Really, dear, you mustn't stay.

Which choice best states the main purpose of the text?

A) To describe what Henry's mother does when she goes out with her friends

B) To show that Henry's mother wants him to leave

C) To present a detailed account of what Henry's home looks like

D) To explain why Henry often visits his mother

8

In response to concerns that some recent financial crises were exacerbated by consumers misunderstanding risks associated with credit cards, loans, and other financial products, policymakers in many countries have instituted risk-disclosure requirements on sellers of those products. Enrique Seira et al. investigated a variety of risk-disclosure messages sent to thousands of credit card customers and found that the messages had only small and short-lived effects on behavior. Seira et al. asserted that such effects may nevertheless be worth pursuing, given the negligible cost of messaging.

Which choice best describes the function of the underlined portion in the text as a whole?

A) It notes a factor that led Seira et al. to not dismiss risk-disclosure messaging altogether despite their evidence of its limited utility.

B) It acknowledges a type of risk-disclosure messaging that Seira et al. may not have fully accounted for in their study.

C) It describes a consideration that explains why Seira et al. recommended risk-disclosure messaging even though its effects may be small relative to its costs.

D) It points out a circumstance that Seira et al. conceded may make risk-disclosure messaging more effective than their study suggests.

CONTINUE

9

The following text is adapted from Charles W. Chesnutt's 1901 novel *The Marrow of Tradition*.

Mrs. Ochiltree was a woman of strong individuality, whose comments upon her acquaintance[s], present or absent, were marked by a frankness at times no less than startling. This characteristic caused her to be more or less avoided. Mrs. Ochiltree was aware of this sentiment on the part of her acquaintance[s], and rather exulted in it.

Based on the text, what is true about Mrs. Ochiltree's acquaintances?

A) They try to refrain from discussing topics that would upset Mrs. Ochiltree.

B) They are unable to spend as much time with Mrs. Ochiltree as she would like.

C) They are too preoccupied with their own concerns to speak with Mrs. Ochiltree.

D) They are likely offended by what Mrs. Ochiltree has said about them.

10

"Mrs. Spring Fragrance" is a 1912 short story by Sui Sin Far. In the story, Mrs. Spring Fragrance, a Chinese immigrant living in Seattle, is traveling in California. In letters to her husband and friend, she demonstrates her concern for what's happening at her home in Seattle while she is away: _____

Which quotation from Mrs. Spring Fragrance's letters most effectively illustrates the claim?

A) "My honorable cousin is preparing for the Fifth Moon Festival, and wishes me to compound for the occasion some American 'fudge,' for which delectable sweet, made by my clumsy hands, you have sometimes shown a slight prejudice."

B) "Next week I accompany Ah Oi to the beauteous town of San José. There will we be met by the son of the Illustrious Teacher."

C) "Forget not to care for the cat, the birds, and the flowers. Do not eat too quickly nor fan too vigorously now that the weather is warming."

D) "I am enjoying a most agreeable visit, and American friends, as also our own, strive benevolently for the accomplishment of my pleasure."

CONTINUE

11

A student is examining a long, challenging poem that was initially published in a quarterly journal without explanatory notes, then later republished in a stand-alone volume containing only that poem and accompanying explanatory notes written by the poet. The student asserts that the explanatory notes were included in the republication primarily as a marketing device to help sell the stand-alone volume.

Which statement, if true, would most directly support the student's claim?

A) The text of the poem as published in the quarterly journal is not identical to the text of the poem published in the stand-alone volume.

B) Many critics believe that the poet's explanatory notes remove certain ambiguities of the poem and make it less interesting as a result.

C) The publishers of the stand-alone volume requested the explanatory notes from the poet in order to make the book attractive to readers who already had a copy of the poem in a journal issue.

D) Correspondence between the poet and the publisher reveals that the poet's explanatory notes went through several drafts.

12

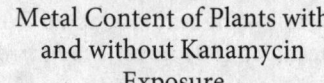

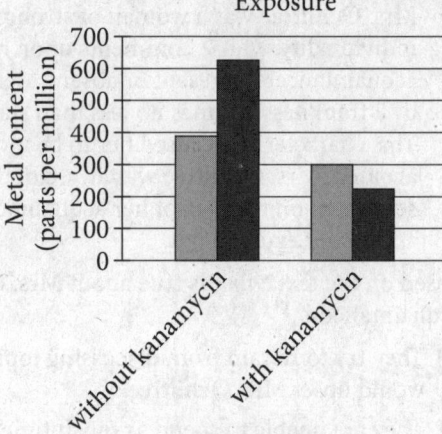

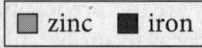

Metal Content of Plants with and without Kanamycin Exposure

Experimental condition

zinc   iron

Many plants lose their leaf color when exposed to kanamycin, an antibiotic produced by some soil microorganisms. Spelman College biologist Mentewab Ayalew and her colleagues hypothesized that plants' response to kanamycin exposure involves altering their uptake of metals, such as iron and zinc. The researchers grew two groups of seedlings of the plant *Arabidopsis thaliana*, half of which were exposed to kanamycin and half of which were a control group without exposure to kanamycin, and measured the plants' metal content five days after germination.

Which choice best describes data in the graph that support Ayalew and her colleagues' hypothesis?

A) The control plants contained higher levels of zinc than iron, but plants exposed to kanamycin contained higher levels of iron than zinc.

B) Both groups of plants contained more than 200 parts per million of both iron and zinc.

C) Zinc levels were around 300 parts per million in the control plants but nearly 400 parts per million in the plants exposed to kanamycin.

D) The plants exposed to kanamycin showed lower levels of iron and zinc than the control plants did.

CONTINUE

13

Characteristics of Five Recently Discovered Gas Exoplanets

Exoplanet designation	Mass (Jupiters)	Radius (Jupiters)	Orbital period (days)	Distance from the Sun (parsecs)
TOI-640 b	0.88	1.771	5.003	340
TOI-1601 b	0.99	1.239	5.331	336
TOI-628 b	6.33	1.060	3.409	178
TOI-1478 b	0.85	1.060	10.180	153
TOI-1333 b	2.37	1.396	4.720	200

"Hot Jupiters" are gas planets that have a mass of at least 0.25 Jupiters (meaning that their mass is at least 25% of that of Jupiter) and an orbital period of less than 10 days (meaning that they complete one orbit around their star in less than 10 days), while "warm Jupiters" are gas planets that meet the same mass criterion but have orbital periods of more than 10 days. In 2021, Michigan State University astronomer Joseph Rodriguez and colleagues announced the discovery of five new gas exoplanets and asserted that four are hot Jupiters and one is a warm Jupiter.

Which choice best describes data from the table that support Rodriguez and colleagues' assertion?

A) None of the planets have an orbital period of more than 10 days, and TOI-628 b has a mass of 6.33 Jupiters.

B) TOI-1478 b has an orbital period of 153 days, and the masses of all the planets range from 0.85 to 6.33 Jupiters.

C) All the planets have a radius between 1.060 and 1.771 Jupiters, and only TOI-1333 b has an orbital period of more than 10 days.

D) Each of the planets has a mass greater than 0.25 Jupiters, and all except for TOI-1478 b have an orbital period of less than 10 days.

CONTINUE

14

Archaeologist Christiana Kohler and her team excavated the Egyptian tomb of Queen Merneith, the wife of a First Dynasty pharaoh. Some scholars claim that she also ruled Egypt on her own and was actually the first female pharaoh. The team found a tablet in Merneith's tomb with writing suggesting that she was in charge of the country's treasury and other central offices. Whether Merneith was a pharaoh or not, this discovery supports the idea that Merneith likely _____

Which choice most logically completes the text?

A) had an important role in Egypt's government.

B) lived after rather than before the First Dynasty of Egypt.

C) traveled beyond Egypt's borders often.

D) created a new form of writing in Egypt.

15

The widespread use of social media enables linguists to study changes in language usage in real time. A notable recent example is the proliferation of the affix *meng-* among speakers of Bahasa Indonesia, the official language of Indonesia. Linguists observed *meng-* originate as an onomatopoetic tag that social-media users applied to images of cats they posted; over time, users increasingly applied it as a prefix to existing words (e.g., *mengsedih* affixes *meng-* to the word for *sad*) in text that they posted. From there, it has begun to move into spoken Bahasa Indonesia. Linguists have noted many similar examples of this phenomenon occurring in other languages, suggesting that social media _____

Which choice most logically completes the text?

A) is more useful for studying informal language than for studying formal or official language.

B) appears to be exerting an exceptionally strong influence on the evolution of Bahasa Indonesia.

C) may give linguists a somewhat misleading sense of how languages are changing.

D) does not merely register changes in language usage but can facilitate such changes.

CONTINUE

16

For thousands of years, people in the Americas _____ the bottle gourd, a large bitter fruit with a thick rind, to make bottles, other types of containers, and even musical instruments. Oddly, there is no evidence that any type of bottle gourd is native to the Western Hemisphere; either the fruit or its seeds must have somehow been carried from Asia or Africa.

Which choice completes the text so that it conforms to the conventions of Standard English?

A) to use

B) have used

C) having used

D) using

17

Lucía Michel of the University of Chile observed that alkaline soils contain an insoluble form of iron that blueberry plants cannot absorb, thus inhibiting blueberry growth. If these plants were grown in alkaline soil alongside grasses that aid in iron solubilization, _____ Michel was determined to find out.

Which choice completes the text so that it conforms to the conventions of Standard English?

A) could the blueberries thrive.

B) the blueberries could thrive.

C) the blueberries could thrive?

D) could the blueberries thrive?

18

The intense pressure found in the deep ocean can affect the structure of proteins in fish's cells, distorting the proteins' shape. The chemical trimethylamine N-oxide (TMAO) counters this effect, ensuring that proteins retain their original _____ is found in high concentrations in the cells of the deepest-dwelling fish.

Which choice completes the text so that it conforms to the conventions of Standard English?

A) configurations. TMAO

B) configurations TMAO

C) configurations, TMAO

D) configurations and TMAO

19

Mathematician Grigori Perelman, sometimes in conjunction with mathematicians Richard S. Hamilton and Shing-Tung Yau, _____ credited with proving the Poincaré conjecture. Having built on Hamilton's previous work to solve the proof, Perelman has insisted that Hamilton receive credit. Yau later found and closed gaps in Perelman's proof, persuading some mathematicians that he deserves credit as well.

Which choice completes the text so that it conforms to the conventions of Standard English?

A) are

B) have been

C) are being

D) is

Unauthorized copying or reuse of any part of this page is illegal.

CONTINUE

919

20

Jetties—long, narrow structures that extend from a landmass into the water—are often constructed to protect coastlines from erosion. Jetties can sometimes have the opposite _____ obstructing the natural flow of sand along the shore can lead to increased erosion in some areas.

Which choice completes the text so that it conforms to the conventions of Standard English?

A) effect, though;

B) effect, though

C) effect; though

D) effect, though,

21

Archaeologist Sue Brunning explains why the seventh-century ship burial site at Sutton Hoo in England was likely the tomb of a king. First, the gold artifacts inside the ship suggest that the person buried with them was a wealthy and respected leader. _____ the massive effort required to bury the ship would likely only have been undertaken for a king.

Which choice completes the text with the most logical transition?

A) Instead,

B) Still,

C) Specifically,

D) Second,

22

Earth's auroras—colorful displays of light seen above the northern and southern poles—result, broadly speaking, from the Sun's activity. _____ the Sun releases charged particles that are captured by Earth's magnetic field and channeled toward the poles. These particles then collide with atoms in the atmosphere, causing the atoms to emit auroral light.

Which choice completes the text with the most logical transition?

A) Specifically,

B) Similarly,

C) Nevertheless,

D) Hence,

23

The Coastal Virginia Offshore Wind project is anticipated to generate 2.6 gigawatts of energy, enough to power almost one million homes. As its name indicates, the project—currently in development—consists of wind turbines located off the Virginia coast. _____ the project plan calls for 176 large turbines to be placed at a site 27 miles east of Virginia Beach.

Which choice completes the text with the most logical transition?

A) To be exact,

B) In conclusion,

C) As a result,

D) In contrast,

CONTINUE

24

While researching a topic, a student has taken the following notes:

- If a moon orbiting a planet comes close enough to that planet, tidal forces can cause the moon to break apart.

- In a 2022 study, researchers proposed that Saturn was once orbited by a large moon they named Chrysalis.

- Their simulations indicated that Chrysalis would likely have come very close to Saturn around 160 million years ago.

- At that distance, Chrysalis would have been broken apart by tidal forces.

- The researchers hypothesized that the resulting debris formed Saturn's rings.

The student wants to recount the sequence of events proposed by the researchers. Which choice most effectively uses relevant information from the notes to accomplish this goal?

A) According to researchers' simulations, two events likely occurred around 160 million years ago: first, Chrysalis came very close to Saturn, and second, debris from Saturn's rings caused the moon to break apart.

B) If a moon orbiting a planet (like Saturn) comes close enough to that planet, tidal forces can cause the moon to break apart.

C) Around 160 million years ago, a large moon (Chrysalis) came close enough to Saturn that tidal forces broke the moon apart; its debris then formed the planet's rings.

D) First, researchers proposed that Saturn was orbited by a large moon (Chrysalis); next, they conducted simulations; and, finally, they formed a hypothesis.

25

While researching a topic, a student has taken the following notes:

- Pinnipeds, which include seals, sea lions, and walruses, live in and around water.

- Pinnipeds are descended not from sea animals but from four-legged, land-dwelling carnivores.

- Canadian paleobiologist Natalia Rybczynski recently found a fossil with four legs, webbed toes, and the skull and teeth of a seal.

- Rybczynski refers to her rare find as a "transitional fossil."

- The fossil illustrates an early stage in the evolution of pinnipeds from their land-dwelling ancestors.

The student wants to emphasize the fossil's significance. Which choice most effectively uses relevant information from the notes to accomplish this goal?

A) Canadian paleobiologist Natalia Rybczynski's fossil has the skull and teeth of a seal, which, like sea lions and walruses, is a pinniped.

B) Pinnipeds are descended from four-legged, land-dwelling carnivores; a fossil that resembles both was recently found.

C) Having four legs but the skull and teeth of a seal, the rare fossil illustrates an early stage in the evolution of pinnipeds from their land-dwelling ancestors.

D) A "transitional fossil" was recently found by paleobiologist Natalia Rybczynski.

CONTINUE

26

While researching a topic, a student has taken the following notes:

- Started in 1925, the Scripps National Spelling Bee is a US-based spelling competition.
- The words used in the competition have diverse linguistic origins.
- In 2008, Sameer Mishra won by correctly spelling the word "guerdon."
- "Guerdon" derives from the Anglo-French word "guerdun."
- In 2009, Kavya Shivashankar won by correctly spelling the word "Laodicean."
- "Laodicean" derives from the ancient Greek word "Laodíkeia."

The student wants to emphasize a difference in the origins of the two words. Which choice most effectively uses relevant information from the notes to accomplish this goal?

A) "Guerdon," the final word of the 2008 Scripps National Spelling Bee, is of Anglo-French origin, while the following year's final word, "Laodicean," derives from ancient Greek.

B) In 2008, Sameer Mishra won the Scripps National Spelling Bee by correctly spelling the word "guerdon"; however, the following year, Kavya Shivashankar won based on spelling the word "Laodicean."

C) Kavya Shivashankar won the 2009 Scripps National Spelling Bee by correctly spelling "Laodicean," which derives from the ancient Greek word "Laodíkeia."

D) The Scripps National Spelling Bee uses words from diverse linguistic origins, such as "guerdon" and "Laodicean."

27

While researching a topic, a student has taken the following notes:

- In 1851, German American artist Emanuel Leutze painted *Washington Crossing the Delaware.*
- His huge painting (149 × 255 inches) depicts the first US president crossing a river with soldiers in the Revolutionary War.
- In 2019, Cree artist Kent Monkman painted *mistikôsiwak (Wooden Boat People): Resurgence of the People.*
- Monkman's huge painting (132 × 264 inches) was inspired by Leutze's.
- It portrays Indigenous people in a boat rescuing refugees.

The student wants to emphasize a similarity between the two paintings. Which choice most effectively uses relevant information from the notes to accomplish this goal?

A) Monkman, a Cree artist, finished his painting in 2019; Leutze, a German American artist, completed his in 1851.

B) Although Monkman's painting was inspired by Leutze's, the people and actions the two paintings portray are very different.

C) Leutze's and Monkman's paintings are both huge, measuring 149 × 255 inches and 132 × 264 inches, respectively.

D) Leutze's painting depicts Revolutionary War soldiers, while Monkman's depicts Indigenous people and refugees.

STOP

If you finish before time is called, you may check your work on this module only. Do not turn to any other module in the test.

Test begins on the next page.

Reading and Writing

27 QUESTIONS

The questions in this section address a number of important reading and writing skills. Each question includes one or more passages, which may include a table or graph. Read each passage and question carefully, and then choose the best answer to the question based on the passage(s).

All questions in this section are multiple-choice with four answer choices. Each question has a single best answer.

1

Nigerian American author Teju Cole's _____ his two passions—photography and the written word—culminates in his 2017 book, *Blind Spot*, which evocatively combines his original photographs from his travels with his poetic prose.

Which choice completes the text with the most logical and precise word or phrase?

A) indifference to

B) enthusiasm for

C) concern about

D) surprise at

2

Mônica Lopes-Ferreira and others at Brazil's Butantan Institute are studying the freshwater stingray species *Potamotrygon rex* to determine whether biological characteristics such as the rays' age and sex have _____ effect on the toxicity of their venom—that is, to see if differences in these traits are associated with considerable variations in venom potency.

Which choice completes the text with the most logical and precise word or phrase?

A) a disconcerting

B) an acceptable

C) an imperceptible

D) a substantial

Unauthorized copying or reuse of any part of this page is illegal.

924

CONTINUE ▶

3

Former astronaut Ellen Ochoa says that although she doesn't have a definite idea of when it might happen, she _____ that humans will someday need to be able to live in other environments than those found on Earth. This conjecture informs her interest in future research missions to the moon.

Which choice completes the text with the most logical and precise word or phrase?

A) demands

B) speculates

C) doubts

D) establishes

4

In habitats with limited nutrients, certain fungus species grow on the roots of trees, engaging in mutually beneficial relationships known as ectomycorrhizae: in this symbiotic exchange, the tree provides the fungus with carbon, a nutrient necessary for both species, and the fungus _____ by enhancing the tree's ability to absorb nitrogen, another key nutrient, from the soil.

Which choice completes the text with the most logical and precise word or phrase?

A) overreacts

B) reciprocates

C) retaliates

D) deviates

5

The following text is from Georgia Douglas Johnson's 1922 poem "Benediction."

> Go forth, my son,
> Winged by my heart's desire!
> Great reaches, yet unknown,
> Await
> For your possession.
> I may not, if I would,
> Retrace the way with you,
> My pilgrimage is through,
> But life is calling you!

Which choice best states the main purpose of the text?

A) To express hope that a child will have the same accomplishments as his parent did

B) To suggest that raising a child involves many struggles

C) To warn a child that he will face many challenges throughout his life

D) To encourage a child to embrace the experiences life will offer

CONTINUE →

6

According to historian Vicki L. Ruiz, Mexican American women made crucial contributions to the labor movement during World War II. At the time, food processing companies entered into contracts to supply United States armed forces with canned goods. Increased production quotas conferred greater bargaining power on the companies' employees, many of whom were Mexican American women: <u>employees insisted on more favorable benefits, and employers, who were anxious to fulfill the contracts, complied.</u> Thus, labor activism became a platform for Mexican American women to assert their agency.

Which choice best describes the function of the underlined portion in the text as a whole?

A) It elaborates on a claim about labor relations in a particular industry made earlier in the text.

B) It offers an example of a trend in the World War II–era economy discussed earlier in the text.

C) It notes a possible exception to the historical narrative of labor activism sketched earlier in the text.

D) It provides further details about the identities of the workers discussed earlier in the text.

7

Text 1
Astronomer Mark Holland and colleagues examined four white dwarfs—small, dense remnants of past stars—in order to determine the composition of exoplanets that used to orbit those stars. Studying wavelengths of light in the white dwarf atmospheres, the team reported that traces of elements such as lithium and sodium support the presence of exoplanets with continental crusts similar to Earth's.

Text 2
Past studies of white dwarf atmospheres have concluded that certain exoplanets had continental crusts. Geologist Keith Putirka and astronomer Siyi Xu argue that those studies unduly emphasize atmospheric traces of lithium and other individual elements as signifiers of the types of rock found on Earth. The studies don't adequately account for different minerals made up of various ratios of those elements, and the possibility of rock types not found on Earth that contain those minerals.

Based on the texts, how would Putirka and Xu (Text 2) most likely characterize the conclusion presented in Text 1?

A) As unexpected, because it was widely believed at the time that white dwarf exoplanets lack continental crusts

B) As premature, because researchers have only just begun trying to determine what kinds of crusts white dwarf exoplanets had

C) As questionable, because it rests on an incomplete consideration of potential sources of the elements detected in white dwarf atmospheres

D) As puzzling, because it's unusual to successfully detect lithium and sodium when analyzing wavelengths of light in white dwarf atmospheres

CONTINUE ▶

8

The following text is from David Barclay Moore's 2022 novel *Holler of the Fireflies*. The narrator has just arrived at summer camp, which is far away from his home.

> This place was different than I thought it would be. I'd never been somewhere like this before. I did feel scared, but also excited.

©2022 by David Barclay Moore

According to the text, how does the narrator feel about being at summer camp?

A) He feels overjoyed.

B) He feels peaceful.

C) He feels both scared and excited.

D) He feels both angry and jealous.

9

In the 1700s and 1800s, European composers experimented with volume in their musical works. They did so by increasing the number of musicians playing in the orchestra. For example, in some of his operas, German composer Richard Wagner added more horns, trombones, and tubas to the orchestra. With more instruments playing at the same time, the orchestra could play extremely loudly at key moments in his operas.

According to the text, how did Richard Wagner achieve moments of extremely high volume in his operas?

A) By moving the performances of his operas from outdoor stages to indoor ones

B) By increasing the number of musicians playing horns, trombones, and tubas in the orchestra

C) By building a concert hall whose shape would cause sounds to echo

D) By insisting that the singers undergo special training to sing for extended periods of time

10

At over a thousand pages across two volumes, *The Fifty-Year Mission*, compiled by Edward Gross and Mark A. Altman, is presented as the "complete, uncensored, unauthorized oral history" as told by the people behind the media franchise *Star Trek*. The work aspires to be comprehensive by, for example, including accounts from cast and crew members of every *Star Trek* television series and film to date. But while *The Fifty-Year Mission* is clearly a unique and valuable resource, it has a shortcoming common among oral histories: it lacks a clear authorial point of view that could otherwise unite the various accounts into a cohesive whole.

Which choice best states the main idea of the text?

A) The compilers of *The Fifty-Year Mission* had lofty goals for their oral history of the *Star Trek* franchise, but the published work lacks information about many key events in the franchise's history.

B) *The Fifty-Year Mission* includes more accounts from people involved with *Star Trek* television shows than it does from people involved with *Star Trek* films.

C) The large amount of material compiled into *The Fifty-Year Mission* is surprising given that many of the people involved in the *Star Trek* franchise did not participate in the oral history project.

D) *The Fifty-Year Mission* represents a worthwhile attempt to thoroughly recount the history of the *Star Trek* franchise, but its approach has an important limitation.

CONTINUE

11

Recordings of
Female Bottlenose Dolphins
with Their Calves

Dolphin ID	Recording year
FB07	2012
FB25	1989
FB43	1992
FB79	2018

In a study of bottlenose dolphins, biologist Laela S. Sayigh and a team of researchers analyzed recordings of female bottlenose dolphins interacting with their calves.

According to the table, in which year was the dolphin with the ID FB43 recorded with her calf?

A) 1999

B) 2012

C) 2020

D) 1992

12

The novelist Toni Morrison was the first Black woman to work as an editor at the publishing company Random House, from 1967 to 1983. A scholar asserts that one of Morrison's likely aims during her time as an editor was to strengthen the presence of Black writers on the list of Random House's published authors.

Which finding, if true, would most strongly support the scholar's claim?

A) The percentage of authors published by Random House who were Black rose in the early 1970s and stabilized throughout the decade.

B) Black authors who were interviewed in the 1980s and 1990s were highly likely to cite Toni Morrison's novels as a principal influence on their work.

C) The novels written by Toni Morrison that were published after 1983 sold significantly more copies and received wider critical acclaim than the novels she wrote that were published before 1983.

D) Works that were edited by Toni Morrison during her time at Random House displayed stylistic characteristics that distinguished them from works that were not edited by Morrison.

CONTINUE

13

Number and Origin of Clamshell Tools Found at Different Levels Below the Surface in Neanderthal Cave

Depth of tools found below surface in cave (meters)	Clamshells that Neanderthals collected from the beach	Clamshells that Neanderthals harvested from the seafloor
3–4	99	33
6–7	1	0
4–5	2	0
2–3	7	0
5–6	18	7

Studying tools unearthed at a cave site on the western coast of Italy, archaeologist Paola Villa and colleagues have determined that prehistoric Neanderthal groups fashioned them from shells of clams that they harvested from the seafloor while wading or diving or that washed up on the beach. Clamshells become thin and eroded as they wash up on the beach, while those on the seafloor are smooth and sturdy, so the research team suspects that Neanderthals prized the tools made with seafloor shells. However, the team also concluded that those tools were likely more challenging to obtain, noting that _____

Which choice most effectively uses data from the table to support the research team's conclusion?

A) at each depth below the surface in the cave, the difference in the numbers of tools of each type suggests that shells were easier to collect from the beach than to harvest from the seafloor.

B) the highest number of tools were at a depth of 3–4 meters below the surface, which suggests that the Neanderthal population at the site was highest during the related period of time.

C) at each depth below the surface in the cave, the difference in the numbers of tools of each type suggests that Neanderthals preferred to use clamshells from the beach because of their durability.

D) the higher number of tools at depths of 5–6 meters below the surface in the cave than at depths of 4–5 meters below the surface suggests that the size of clam populations changed over time.

14

In documents called judicial opinions, judges explain the reasoning behind their legal rulings, and in those explanations they sometimes cite and discuss historical and contemporary philosophers. Legal scholar and philosopher Anita L. Allen argues that while judges are naturally inclined to mention philosophers whose views align with their own positions, the strongest judicial opinions consider and rebut potential objections; discussing philosophers whose views conflict with judges' views could therefore _____

Which choice most logically completes the text?

A) allow judges to craft judicial opinions without needing to consult philosophical works.

B) help judges improve the arguments they put forward in their judicial opinions.

C) make judicial opinions more comprehensible to readers without legal or philosophical training.

D) bring judicial opinions in line with views that are broadly held among philosophers.

15

Public-awareness campaigns about the need to reduce single-use plastics can be successful, says researcher Kim Borg of Monash University in Australia, when these campaigns give consumers a choice: for example, Japan achieved a 40 percent reduction in plastic-bag use after cashiers were instructed to ask customers whether _____ wanted a bag.

Which choice completes the text so that it conforms to the conventions of Standard English?

A) they

B) one

C) you

D) it

CONTINUE

16

When writing *The Other Black Girl* (2021), novelist Zakiya Dalila Harris drew on her own experiences working at a publishing office. The award-winning book is Harris's first novel, but her writing _____ honored before. At the age of twelve, she entered a contest to have a story published in *American Girl* magazine—and won.

Which choice completes the text so that it conforms to the conventions of Standard English?

A) were

B) have been

C) has been

D) are

17

To survive when water is scarce, embryos inside African turquoise killifish eggs _____ a dormant state known as diapause. In this state, embryonic development is paused for as long as two years—longer than the life span of an adult killifish.

Which choice completes the text so that it conforms to the conventions of Standard English?

A) enter

B) to enter

C) having entered

D) entering

18

Typically, underlines, scribbles, and notes left in the margins by a former owner lower a book's _____ when the former owner is a famous poet like Walt Whitman, such markings, known as marginalia, can be a gold mine to literary scholars.

Which choice completes the text so that it conforms to the conventions of Standard English?

A) value, but

B) value

C) value,

D) value but

19

Former First Lady of the United States Eleanor Roosevelt and Indian activist and educator Hansa Mehta were instrumental in drafting the United Nations' Universal Declaration of Human Rights, a document that _____ the basic freedoms to which all people are entitled.

Which choice completes the text so that it conforms to the conventions of Standard English?

A) have outlined

B) were outlining

C) outlines

D) outline

20

Atoms in a synchrotron, a type of circular particle accelerator, travel faster and faster until they _____ a desired energy level, at which point they are diverted to collide with a target, smashing the atoms.

Which choice completes the text so that it conforms to the conventions of Standard English?

A) will reach

B) reach

C) had reached

D) are reaching

21

The forty-seven geothermal springs of Arkansas' Hot Springs National Park are sourced via a process known as natural groundwater recharge, in which rainwater percolates downward through the earth—in this case, the porous rocks of the hills around Hot _____ collect in a subterranean basin.

Which choice completes the text so that it conforms to the conventions of Standard English?

A) Springs to

B) Springs: to

C) Springs—to

D) Springs, to

CONTINUE →

22

The Alaska Native Language Archive (ANLA) is known for its impressive audio collection. _____ the ANLA has more than 5,000 audio recordings of Native Alaskan languages dating as far back as 1943.

Which choice completes the text with the most logical transition?

A) In fact,

B) After,

C) Regardless,

D) Instead,

23

When Chinese director Chloé Zhao accepted the Oscar in 2021 for her film *Nomadland*, she made Academy Award history. _____ only one other woman, Kathryn Bigelow of the United States, had been named best director at the Oscars, making Zhao the second woman and the first Asian woman to win the award.

Which choice completes the text with the most logical transition?

A) As a result,

B) Previously,

C) However,

D) Likewise,

24

Neuroscientist Karen Konkoly wanted to determine whether individuals can understand and respond to questions during REM sleep. She first taught volunteers eye movements they would use to respond to basic math problems while asleep (a single left-right eye movement indicated the number one). _____ she attached electrodes to the volunteers' faces to record their eye movements during sleep.

Which choice completes the text with the most logical transition?

A) Specifically,

B) Next,

C) For instance,

D) In sum,

25

While researching a topic, a student has taken the following notes:

• The green iguana is a species of reptile.

• It can be found in Central America and Brazil.

• The green iguana primarily eats leaves and fruit.

• It has an average length of 4.8 feet.

The student wants to specify the average length of the green iguana. Which choice most effectively uses relevant information from the notes to accomplish this goal?

A) The green iguana can be found in Central America.

B) The green iguana has an average length of 4.8 feet.

C) One species of reptile found in Brazil primarily eats leaves and fruit.

D) The green iguana is a reptile that primarily eats leaves and fruit.

Unauthorized copying or reuse of any part of this page is illegal.

CONTINUE ▶

931

26

While researching a topic, a student has taken the following notes:

- Ibn Sina was a Persian philosopher and physician.
- His book *The Canon of Medicine* recorded the most advanced medical knowledge of his time.
- It was published in the year 1025 CE.
- It was used as a medical textbook in Middle Eastern and European universities for centuries.

The student wants to identify the year that *The Canon of Medicine* was published. Which choice most effectively uses relevant information from the notes to accomplish this goal?

A) Ibn Sina's book *The Canon of Medicine* was published in the year 1025 CE.

B) A Persian philosopher and physician wrote a medical textbook called *The Canon of Medicine*.

C) *The Canon of Medicine* was a medical textbook used by Middle Eastern and European universities for centuries.

D) Ibn Sina recorded the most advanced medical knowledge of his time in his book *The Canon of Medicine*.

27

While researching a topic, a student has taken the following notes:

- Gaspar Enriquez is an artist.
- He specializes in portraits of Mexican Americans.
- A portrait is an artistic representation of a person.
- Enriquez completed a painting of the sculptor Luis Jimenez in 2003.
- He completed a drawing of the writer Rudolfo Anaya in 2016.

The student wants to emphasize a difference between the two portraits. Which choice most effectively uses relevant information from the notes to accomplish this goal?

A) The portraits, or artistic representations, of Luis Jimenez and Rudolfo Anaya were both completed by Enriquez in the early 2000s.

B) Enriquez has completed portraits of numerous Mexican Americans, including sculptor Luis Jimenez and writer Rudolfo Anaya.

C) While both are by Enriquez, the 2003 portrait of Luis Jimenez is a painting, and the 2016 portrait of Rudolfo Anaya is a drawing.

D) Luis Jimenez was a Mexican American sculptor, and Rudolfo Anaya was a Mexican American writer.

STOP

If you finish before time is called, you may check your work on this module only. Do not turn to any other module in the test.

Test begins on the next page.

Reading and Writing

27 QUESTIONS

The questions in this section address a number of important reading and writing skills. Each question includes one or more passages, which may include a table or graph. Read each passage and question carefully, and then choose the best answer to the question based on the passage(s).

All questions in this section are multiple-choice with four answer choices. Each question has a single best answer.

1

Within baleen whale species, some individuals develop an accessory spleen—a seemingly functionless formation of splenetic tissue outside the normal spleen. Given the formation's greater prevalence among whales known to make deeper dives, some researchers hypothesize that its role isn't _____; rather, the accessory spleen may actively support diving mechanisms.

Which choice completes the text with the most logical and precise word or phrase?

A) replicable

B) predetermined

C) operative

D) latent

2

The province of Xoconochco was situated on the Pacific coast, hundreds of kilometers southeast of Tenochtitlan, the capital of the Aztec Empire. Because Xoconochco's location within the empire was so _____, cacao and other trade goods produced there could reach the capital only after a long overland journey.

Which choice completes the text with the most logical and precise word or phrase?

A) unobtrusive

B) concealed

C) approximate

D) peripheral

Unauthorized copying or reuse of any part of this page is illegal.

CONTINUE

934

3

In 2016, Gabriela González and team announced that a chirping sound captured by Laser Interferometer Gravitational-Wave Observatory antennas was direct evidence of gravitational waves, which skeptics had argued would be too faint for detection. Detailed statistical analysis helped preclude claims of the event's _____, confirming the signal at a confidence level of over 99%.

Which choice completes the text with the most logical and precise word or phrase?

A) inconspicuousness

B) discretion

C) ambiguity

D) probability

4

Political blogs with conspicuous ideological alignments became an integral component of US media in the early 2000s. While some commentators lauded this development, asserting that such blogs had a welcome transparency missing from traditional news, less _____ observers countered that such blogs tended to ideological extremes that exacerbated political polarization to problematic levels.

Which choice completes the text with the most logical and precise word or phrase?

A) sanguine

B) recalcitrant

C) misanthropic

D) earnest

CONTINUE ▶

5

The following text is from Charlotte Forten Grimké's 1888 poem "At Newport."

> Oh, deep delight to watch the gladsome waves
> Exultant leap upon the rugged rocks;
> <u>Ever repulsed, yet ever rushing on—</u>
> <u>Filled with a life that will not know defeat;</u>
> To see the glorious hues of sky and sea.
> The distant snowy sails, glide spirit like,
> Into an unknown world, to feel the sweet
> Enchantment of the sea thrill all the soul,
> Clearing the clouded brain, making the heart
> Leap joyous as it own bright, singing waves!

Which choice best describes the function of the underlined portion in the text as a whole?

A) It portrays the surroundings as an imposing and intimidating scene.

B) It characterizes the sea's waves as a relentless and enduring force.

C) It conveys the speaker's ambivalence about the natural world.

D) It draws a contrast between the sea's waves and the speaker's thoughts.

6

Text 1
Ecologists have long wondered how thousands of microscopic phytoplankton species can live together near ocean surfaces competing for the same resources. According to <u>conventional wisdom</u>, one species should emerge after outcompeting the rest. So why do so many species remain? Ecologists' many efforts to explain this phenomenon still haven't uncovered a satisfactory explanation.

Text 2
Ecologist Michael Behrenfeld and colleagues have connected phytoplankton's diversity to their microscopic size. Because these organisms are so tiny, they are spaced relatively far apart from each other in ocean water and, moreover, experience that water as a relatively dense substance. This in turn makes it hard for them to move around and interact with one another. Therefore, says Behrenfeld's team, direct competition among phytoplankton probably happens much less than previously thought.

Based on the texts, how would Behrenfeld and colleagues (Text 2) most likely respond to the "conventional wisdom" discussed in Text 1?

A) By arguing that it is based on a misconception about phytoplankton species competing with one another

B) By asserting that it fails to recognize that routine replenishment of ocean nutrients prevents competition between phytoplankton species

C) By suggesting that their own findings help clarify how phytoplankton species are able to compete with larger organisms

D) By recommending that more ecologists focus their research on how competition among phytoplankton species is increased with water density

CONTINUE ➤

7

For many years, the only existing fossil evidence of mixopterid eurypterids—an extinct family of large aquatic arthropods known as sea scorpions and related to modern arachnids and horseshoe crabs—came from four species living on the paleocontinent of Laurussia. In a discovery that expands our understanding of the geographical distribution of mixopterids, paleontologist Bo Wang and others have identified fossilized remains of a new mixopterid species, *Terropterus xiushanensis*, that lived over 400 million years ago on the paleocontinent of Gondwana.

According to the text, why was Wang and his team's discovery of the *Terropterus xiushanensis* fossil significant?

A) The fossil constitutes the first evidence found by scientists that mixopterids lived more than 400 million years ago.

B) The fossil helps establish that mixopterids are more closely related to modern arachnids and horseshoe crabs than previously thought.

C) The fossil helps establish a more accurate timeline of the evolution of mixopterids on the paleocontinents of Laurussia and Gondwana.

D) The fossil constitutes the first evidence found by scientists that mixopterids existed outside the paleocontinent of Laurussia.

8

Poetry in Classical Nahuatl, the language of the Aztec Empire, relies on *difrasismo*, or a parallel noun construction that conventionally operates as a single metaphor. For example, the common difrasismo *in cuauhtli in ocelotl* (literally, "the eagle, the jaguar") signifies "warrior." The device's function is both formal—providing structure to lines of verse—and ritual: semantic relations among the two nouns and the concept they signify can be tenuous, as in the previous example, such that difrasismos are often only intelligible according to the conceptual associations observed in Aztec ceremonial culture.

Which statement about the difrasismo *in cuauhtli in ocelotl* is most strongly supported by the text?

A) Its metaphorical significance derives from the semantic equivalence of the two nouns constituting the difrasismo.

B) Its unintelligibility may cause its formal function within a line of verse to go unnoticed by present-day readers.

C) Its apparent obscurity can be resolved when considered in the proper cultural context.

D) Its frequency in Classical Nahuatl poetry confirms its intelligibility to the Aztec audience.

Unauthorized copying or reuse of any part of this page is illegal.

CONTINUE

937

9

Ratio of Manganese to Calcium in Samples from Alboran Sea and Mauritanian Coast

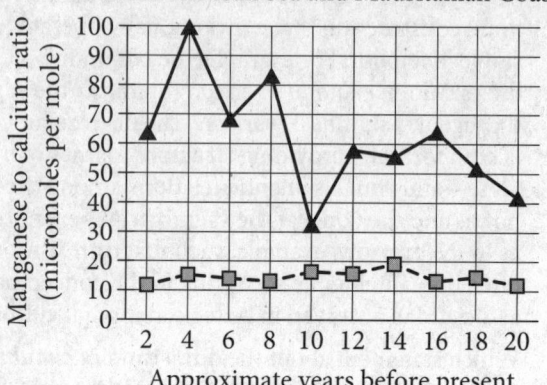

Alboran Sea
Mauritanian coast

The population of the coral *Lophelia pertusa* declined significantly around 9,000 years ago in the Alboran Sea and around 11,000 years ago near the Mauritanian coast. Using the ratio of manganese to calcium, which inversely correlates with ocean oxygenation levels, marine scientist Rodrigo da Costa Portilho-Ramos and colleagues evaluated whether oxygenation played a role in the declines of *L. pertusa*. The researchers concluded that oxygenation may have been important in the Alboran Sea but not near the Mauritanian coast, since _____.

Which choice most effectively uses data from the graph to complete the statement?

A) a substantial increase in oxygenation in the Alboran Sea corresponded with the local decline in *L. pertusa*, but the opposite relationship between oxygenation and *L. pertusa* was found near the Mauritanian coast.

B) *L. pertusa* declined in the Alboran Sea during a period of substantial local decline in oxygenation, but *L. pertusa* declined near the Mauritanian coast during a period of little local change in oxygenation.

C) oxygenation in the Alboran Sea was higher before the decline in *L. pertusa* than after the decline, whereas oxygenation near the Mauritanian coast was relatively low both before and after the decline in *L. pertusa*.

D) oxygenation in the Alboran Sea tended to be substantially higher than oxygenation near the Mauritanian coast during the period studied.

10

Psychologists Dacher Keltner and Jonathan Haidt have argued that experiencing awe—a sensation of reverence and wonder typically brought on by perceiving something grand or powerful—can enable us to feel more connected to others and thereby inspire us to act more altruistically. Keltner, along with Paul K. Piff, Pia Dietze, and colleagues, claims to have found evidence for this effect in a recent study where participants were asked to either gaze up at exceptionally tall trees in a nearby grove (reported to be a universally awe-inspiring experience) or stare at the exterior of a nearby, nondescript building. After one minute, an experimenter deliberately spilled a box of pens nearby.

Which finding from the researchers' study, if true, would most strongly support their claim?

A) Participants who had been looking at the trees helped the experimenter pick up significantly more pens than did participants who had been looking at the building.

B) Participants who helped the experimenter pick up the pens used a greater number of positive words to describe the trees and the building in a postexperiment survey than did participants who did not help the experimenter.

C) Participants who did not help the experimenter pick up the pens were significantly more likely to report having experienced a feeling of awe, regardless of whether they looked at the building or the trees.

D) Participants who had been looking at the building were significantly more likely to notice that the experimenter had dropped the pens than were participants who had been looking at the trees.

CONTINUE

11

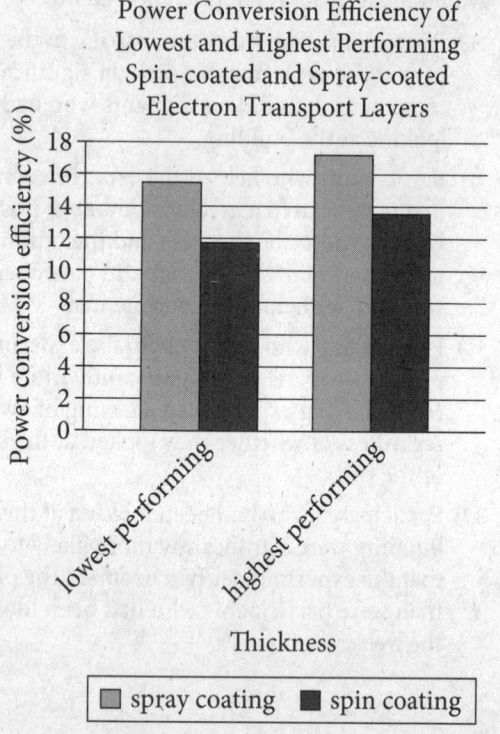

Power Conversion Efficiency of
Lowest and Highest Performing
Spin-coated and Spray-coated
Electron Transport Layers

Thickness

☐ spray coating   ■ spin coating

Perovskite solar cells convert light into electricity more efficiently than earlier kinds of solar cells, and manufacturing advances have recently made them commercially attractive. One limitation of the cells, however, has to do with their electron transport layer (ETL), through which absorbed electrons must pass. Often the ETL is applied through a process called spin coating, but such ETLs are fairly inefficient at converting input power to output power. André Taylor and colleagues tested a novel spray coating method for applying the ETL.
The team produced ETLs of various thicknesses and concluded that spray coating holds promise for improving the power conversion efficiency of ETLs in perovskite solar cells.

Which choice best describes data from the graph that support Taylor and colleagues' conclusion?

A) Both the ETL applied through spin coating and the ETL applied through spray coating showed a power conversion efficiency greater than 10% at their lowest performing thickness.

B) The lowest performing ETL applied through spray coating had a higher power conversion efficiency than the highest performing ETL applied through spin coating.

C) The highest performing ETL applied through spray coating showed a power conversion efficiency of approximately 13%, while the highest performing ETL applied through spin coating showed a power conversion efficiency of approximately 11%.

D) There was a substantial difference in power conversion efficiency between the lowest and highest performing ETLs applied through spray coating.

CONTINUE ➤

12

Political scientists who favor the traditional view of voter behavior claim that voting in an election does not change a voter's attitude toward the candidates in that election. Focusing on each US presidential election from 1976 to 1996, Ebonya Washington and Sendhil Mullainathan tested this claim by distinguishing between subjects who had just become old enough to vote (around half of whom actually voted) and otherwise similar subjects who were slightly too young to vote (and thus none of whom voted). Washington and Mullainathan compared the attitudes of the groups of subjects toward the winning candidate two years after each election.

Which finding from Washington and Mullainathan's study, if true, would most directly weaken the claim made by people who favor the traditional view of voter behavior?

A) Subjects' attitudes toward the winning candidate two years after a given election were strongly predicted by subjects' general political orientation, regardless of whether subjects were old enough to vote at the time of the election.

B) Subjects who were not old enough to vote in a given election held significantly more positive attitudes towards the winning candidate two years later than they held at the time of the election.

C) Subjects who voted in a given election held significantly more polarized attitudes toward the winning candidate two years later than did subjects who were not old enough to vote in that election.

D) Two years after a given election, subjects who voted and subjects who were not old enough to vote were significantly more likely to express negative attitudes than positive attitudes toward the winning candidate in that election.

13

Among social animals that care for their young, such as chickens, macaque monkeys, and humans, newborns appear to show an innate attraction to faces and face-like stimuli. Elisabetta Versace and her colleagues used an image of three black dots arranged in the shape of eyes and a nose or mouth to test whether this trait also occurs in *Testudo* tortoises, which live alone and do not engage in parental care. They found that tortoise hatchlings showed a significant preference for the image, suggesting that _____

Which choice most logically completes the text?

A) face-like stimuli are likely perceived as harmless by newborns of social species that practice parental care but as threatening by newborns of solitary species without parental care.

B) researchers should not assume that an innate attraction to face-like stimuli is necessarily an adaptation related to social interaction or parental care.

C) researchers can assume that the attraction to face-like stimuli that is seen in social species that practice parental care is learned rather than innate.

D) newly hatched *Testudo* tortoises show a stronger preference for face-like stimuli than adult *Testudo* tortoises do.

CONTINUE ➡

14

In a study of the cognitive abilities of white-faced capuchin monkeys (*Cebus imitator*), researchers neglected to control for the physical difficulty of the tasks they used to evaluate the monkeys. The cognitive abilities of monkeys given problems requiring little dexterity, such as sliding a panel to retrieve food, were judged by the same criteria as were those of monkeys given physically demanding problems, such as unscrewing a bottle and inserting a straw. The results of the study, therefore, _____

Which choice most logically completes the text?

A) could suggest that there are differences in cognitive ability among the monkeys even though such differences may not actually exist.

B) are useful for identifying tasks that the monkeys lack the cognitive capacity to perform but not for identifying tasks that the monkeys can perform.

C) should not be taken as indicative of the cognitive abilities of any monkey species other than *C. imitator*.

D) reveal more about the monkeys' cognitive abilities when solving artificial problems than when solving problems encountered in the wild.

15

In crafting her fantasy fiction, Nigerian-born British author Helen Oyeyemi has drawn inspiration from the classic nineteenth-century fairy tales of the Brothers Grimm. Her 2014 novel *Boy, Snow, Bird*, for instance, is a complex retelling of the story of Snow White, while her 2019 novel _____ offers a delicious twist on the classic tale of Hansel and Gretel.

Which choice completes the text so that it conforms to the conventions of Standard English?

A) *Gingerbread*—

B) *Gingerbread*,

C) *Gingerbread*

D) *Gingerbread*:

16

When external forces are applied to common glass made from silicates, energy builds up around minuscule defects in the material, resulting in fractures. Recently, engineer Erkka Frankberg of Tampere University in Finland used the chemical _____ to make a glassy solid that can withstand higher strain than silicate glass can before fracturing.

Which choice completes the text so that it conforms to the conventions of Standard English?

A) compound, aluminum oxide

B) compound aluminum oxide,

C) compound, aluminum oxide,

D) compound aluminum oxide

Unauthorized copying or reuse of any part of this page is illegal.

942

CONTINUE ▶

17

In 1943, in the midst of World War II, mathematics professor Grace Hopper was recruited by the US military to help the war effort by solving complex equations. Hopper's subsequent career would involve more than just _____ as a pioneering computer programmer, Hopper would help usher in the digital age.

Which choice completes the text so that it conforms to the conventions of Standard English?

A) equations, though:

B) equations, though,

C) equations. Though,

D) equations though

18

Increased gender diversity is revitalizing the field of economics, according to Harvard's Claudia Goldin. The trailblazing accomplishments of Goldin, winner of the 2023 Nobel Prize in Economics for her work on women in the labor force, _____ to the value of scholars of diverse backgrounds in spurring research into previously unexplored, but vitally important, topics.

Which choice completes the text so that it conforms to the conventions of Standard English?

A) attests

B) has attested

C) is attesting

D) attest

19

Recent pollen analyses of the Aran Islands have led some researchers to propose that the now treeless islands were once wooded. This hypothesis _____ that certain trees, such as *P. sylvestris*, survived without interruption or human intervention throughout the Holocene cannot stand, researchers Michael O'Connell and Karen Molloy counter, unless other explanations can first be ruled out.

Which choice completes the text so that it conforms to the conventions of Standard English?

A) suggesting

B) suggested

C) suggests

D) has suggested

20

Atoms in a synchrotron, a type of circular particle accelerator, travel faster and faster until they _____ a desired energy level, at which point they are diverted to collide with a target, smashing the atoms.

Which choice completes the text so that it conforms to the conventions of Standard English?

A) will reach

B) reach

C) had reached

D) are reaching

Unauthorized copying or reuse of any part of this page is illegal.

CONTINUE

943

21

Compared to that of alumina glass, _____ silica glass atoms are so far apart that they are unable to reform bonds after being separated.

Which choice completes the text so that it conforms to the conventions of Standard English?

A) silica glass is at a significant disadvantage due to its more dispersed atomic arrangement:

B) silica glass has a more dispersed atomic arrangement, resulting in a significant disadvantage:

C) a significant disadvantage of silica glass is that its atomic arrangement is more dispersed:

D) silica glass's atomic arrangement is more dispersed, resulting in a significant disadvantage:

22

With his room-sized installation *Unicorn/My Private Sky*, Norwegian artist Børre Sæthre succeeds in creating a whimsical yet perplexing experience. _____ when visitors set foot inside the fantastically blue room and encounter the life-sized stuffed unicorn preening at the far end of it, they are both dazzled and confused—as if stepping into a strange and enchanting new world.

Which choice completes the text with the most logical transition?

A) Second,

B) Instead,

C) Indeed,

D) Nevertheless,

23

Economist Elinor Ostrom's studies of communities around the world have empirically demonstrated that common pool resources, such as grazing lands, can be sustainably managed by the people who use them (rather than through private entities or centralized governments). _____ Ostrom's work is a repudiation of the "tragedy of the commons," the view that individuals will inevitably overexploit a finite shared resource if given unfettered access to it.

Which choice completes the text with the most logical transition?

A) By contrast,

B) For example,

C) That said,

D) As such,

CONTINUE

24

While researching a topic, a student has taken the following notes:

- Shaun Tan is an Australian author.
- In 2008, he published *Tales from Outer Suburbia*, a book of fifteen short stories.
- The stories describe surreal events occurring in otherwise ordinary suburban neighborhoods.
- In 2018, he published *Tales from the Inner City*, a book of twenty-five short stories.
- The stories describe surreal events occurring in otherwise ordinary urban settings.

The student wants to emphasize a similarity between the two books by Shaun Tan. Which choice most effectively uses relevant information from the notes to accomplish this goal?

A) Shaun Tan's book *Tales from Outer Suburbia*, which describes surreal events occurring in otherwise ordinary places, contains fewer short stories than *Tales from the Inner City* does.

B) *Tales from Outer Suburbia* was published in 2008, and *Tales from the Inner City* was published in 2018.

C) Unlike *Tales from the Inner City*, Shaun Tan's book *Tales from Outer Suburbia* is set in suburban neighborhoods.

D) Shaun Tan's books *Tales from Outer Suburbia* and *Tales from the Inner City* both describe surreal events occurring in otherwise ordinary places.

25

While researching a topic, a student has taken the following notes:

- In 2013, archaeologists studied cat bone fragments they had found in the ruins of Quanhucun, a Chinese farming village.
- The fragments were estimated to be 5,300 years old.
- A chemical analysis of the fragments revealed that the cats had consumed large amounts of grain.
- The grain consumption is evidence that the Quanhucun cats may have been domesticated.

The student wants to present the Quanhucun study and its conclusions. Which choice most effectively uses relevant information from the notes to accomplish this goal?

A) As part of a 2013 study of cat domestication, a chemical analysis was conducted on cat bone fragments found in Quanhucun, China.

B) A 2013 analysis of cat bone fragments found in Quanhucun, China, suggests that cats there may have been domesticated 5,300 years ago.

C) In 2013, archaeologists studied what cats in Quanhucun, China, had eaten more than 5,000 years ago.

D) Cat bone fragments estimated to be 5,300 years old were found in Quanhucun, China, in 2013.

Unauthorized copying or reuse of any part of this page is illegal.

CONTINUE

945

26

While researching a topic, a student has taken the following notes:

- Cecilia Vicuña is a multidisciplinary artist.
- In 1971, her first solo art exhibition, *Pinturas, poemas y explicaciones*, was shown at the Museo Nacional de Bellas Artes in Santiago, Chile.
- Her poetry collection *Precario/Precarious* was published in 1983 by Tanam Press.
- Her poetry collection *Instan* was published in 2002 by Kelsey St. Press.
- She lives part time in Chile, where she was born, and part time in New York.

The student wants to introduce the artist's 1983 poetry collection. Which choice most effectively uses relevant information from the notes to accomplish this goal?

A) Before she published the books *Precario/Precarious* (1983) and *Instan* (2002), Cecilia Vicuña exhibited visual art at the Museo Nacional de Bellas Artes in Santiago, Chile.

B) Cecilia Vicuña is a true multidisciplinary artist whose works include numerous poetry collections and visual art exhibitions.

C) Published in 1983 by Tanam Press, *Precario/Precarious* is a collection of poetry by the multidisciplinary artist Cecilia Vicuña.

D) In 1971, Cecilia Vicuña exhibited her first solo art exhibition, *Pinturas, poemas y explicaciones*, in Chile, her country of birth.

27

While researching a topic, a student has taken the following notes:

- The factors that affect clutch size (the number of eggs laid at one time) have been well studied in birds but not in lizards.
- A team led by Shai Meiri of Tel Aviv University investigated which factors influence lizard clutch size.
- Meiri's team obtained clutch-size and habitat data for over 3,900 lizard species and analyzed the data with statistical models.
- Larger clutch size was associated with environments in higher latitudes that have more seasonal change.
- Lizards in higher-latitude environments may lay larger clutches to take advantage of shorter windows of favorable conditions.

The student wants to emphasize the aim of the research study. Which choice most effectively uses relevant information from the notes to accomplish this goal?

A) Researchers wanted to know which factors influence lizard egg clutch size because such factors have been well studied in birds but not in lizards.

B) After they obtained data for over 3,900 lizard species, researchers determined that larger clutch size was associated with environments in higher latitudes that have more seasonal change.

C) We now know that lizards in higher-latitude environments may lay larger clutches to take advantage of shorter windows of favorable conditions.

D) Researchers obtained clutch-size and habitat data for over 3,900 lizard species and analyzed the data with statistical models.

STOP

If you finish before time is called, you may check your work on this module only.
Do not turn to any other module in the test.

Test begins on the next page.

Math

22 QUESTIONS

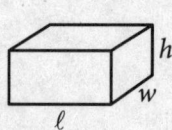

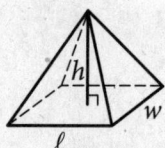

$$A = \pi r^2$$
$$C = 2\pi r$$

$$A = \ell w$$

$$A = \frac{1}{2} bh$$

$$c^2 = a^2 + b^2$$

Special Right Triangles

$$V = \ell w h$$

$$V = \pi r^2 h$$

$$V = \frac{4}{3}\pi r^3$$

$$V = \frac{1}{3}\pi r^2 h$$

$$V = \frac{1}{3}\ell w h$$

The number of degrees of arc in a circle is 360.

The number of radians of arc in a circle is 2π.

The sum of the measures in degrees of the angles of a triangle is 180.

CONTINUE

For multiple-choice questions, solve each problem, choose the correct answer from the choices provided, and then circle your answer in this book. Circle only one answer for each question. If you change your mind, completely erase the circle. You will not get credit for questions with more than one answer circled, or for questions with no answers circled.

For student-produced response questions, solve each problem and write your answer next to or under the question in the test book as described below.

- Once you've written your answer, circle it clearly. You will not receive credit for anything written outside the circle, or for any questions with more than one circled answer.

- If you find **more than one correct answer**, write and circle only one answer.

- Your answer can be up to 5 characters for a **positive** answer and up to 6 characters (including the negative sign) for a **negative** answer, but no more.

- If your answer is a **fraction** that is too long (over 5 characters for positive, 6 characters for negative), write the decimal equivalent.

- If your answer is a **decimal** that is too long (over 5 characters for positive, 6 characters for negative), truncate it or round at the fourth digit.

- If your answer is a **mixed number** (such as $3\frac{1}{2}$), write it as an improper fraction (7/2) or its decimal equivalent (3.5).

- Don't include **symbols** such as a percent sign, comma, or dollar sign in your circled answer.

CONTINUE

1

Which expression is equivalent to
$(2x^2 + x - 9) + (x^2 + 6x + 1)$?

A) $2x^2 + 7x + 10$

B) $2x^2 + 6x - 8$

C) $3x^2 + 7x - 10$

D) $3x^2 + 7x - 8$

2

John paid a total of $165 for a microscope by making a down payment of $37 plus p monthly payments of $16 each. Which of the following equations represents this situation?

A) $16p - 37 = 165$

B) $37p - 16 = 165$

C) $16p + 37 = 165$

D) $37p + 16 = 165$

3

$$7m = 2(n + p)$$

The given equation relates the positive numbers m, n, and p. Which equation correctly gives m in terms of n and p?

A) $m = \dfrac{2(n + p)}{7}$

B) $m = 2(n + p)$

C) $m = 2(n + p) - 7$

D) $m = 2 - n - p - 7$

4

The function g is defined by $g(x) = \sqrt{8x + 1}$. What is the value of $g(3)$?

A) $\dfrac{5}{8}$

B) $\dfrac{25}{8}$

C) 5

D) 25

5

The table gives the distribution of votes for a new school mascot and grade level for 80 students.

Mascot	Grade level			
	Sixth	Seventh	Eighth	Total
Badger	4	9	9	22
Lion	9	2	9	20
Longhorn	4	6	4	14
Tiger	6	9	9	24
Total	23	26	31	80

If one of these students is selected at random, what is the probability of selecting a student whose vote for new mascot was for a lion?

A) $\dfrac{1}{9}$

B) $\dfrac{1}{5}$

C) $\dfrac{1}{4}$

D) $\dfrac{2}{3}$

6

A student council group is selling school posters for a fundraiser. They use the function $p(x) = 5x - 220$ to determine their profit $p(x)$, in dollars, for selling x school posters. In order to earn a profit of $900, how many school posters must they sell?

CONTINUE

7

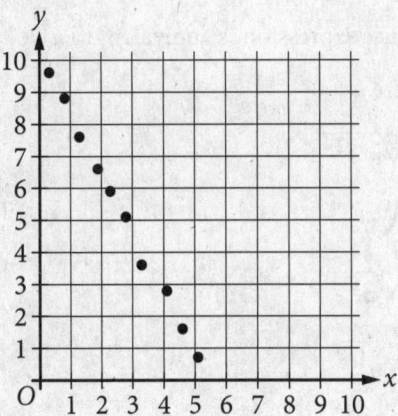

Which of the following equations is the most appropriate linear model for the data shown in the scatterplot?

A) $y = -1.9x - 10.1$

B) $y = -1.9x + 10.1$

C) $y = 1.9x - 10.1$

D) $y = 1.9x + 10.1$

8

$$3x + 6 = 4y$$
$$3x + 4 = 2y$$

The solution to the given system of equations is (x, y). What is the value of y?

9

Data value	Frequency
6	3
7	3
8	8
9	8
10	9
11	11
12	9
13	0
14	6

The frequency table summarizes the 57 data values in a data set. What is the maximum data value in the data set?

10

Circle K has a radius of 4 millimeters (mm). Circle L has an area of 100π mm^2. What is the total area, in mm^2, of circles K and L?

A) 14π

B) 28π

C) 56π

D) 116π

11

If $9(4 - 3x) + 2 = 8(4 - 3x) + 18$, what is the value of $4 - 3x$?

A) -16

B) -4

C) 4

D) 16

CONTINUE

12

Triangle FGH is similar to triangle JKL, where angle F corresponds to angle J and angles G and K are right angles. If $\sin(F) = \frac{308}{317}$, what is the value of $\sin(J)$?

A) $\frac{75}{317}$

B) $\frac{308}{317}$

C) $\frac{317}{308}$

D) $\frac{317}{75}$

13

A wire with a length of 106 inches is cut into two parts. One part has a length of x inches, and the other part has a length of y inches. The value of x is 6 more than 4 times the value of y. What is the value of x?

A) 25

B) 28

C) 56

D) 86

14

A certain township consists of a 5-hectare industrial park and a 24-hectare neighborhood. The total number of trees in the township is 4,529. The equation $5x + 24y = 4,529$ represents this situation. Which of the following is the best interpretation of x in this context?

A) The average number of trees per hectare in the industrial park

B) The average number of trees per hectare in the neighborhood

C) The total number of trees in the industrial park

D) The total number of trees in the neighborhood

15

Which expression is equivalent to $a^{\frac{11}{12}}$, where $a > 0$?

A) $\sqrt[12]{a^{132}}$

B) $\sqrt[144]{a^{132}}$

C) $\sqrt[121]{a^{132}}$

D) $\sqrt[11]{a^{132}}$

16

The function f is defined by $f(x) = (x - 6)(x - 2)(x + 6)$. In the xy-plane, the graph of $y = g(x)$ is the result of translating the graph of $y = f(x)$ up 4 units. What is the value of $g(0)$?

17

$$y = 4x + 1$$
$$4y = 15x - 8$$

The solution to the given system of equations is (x, y). What is the value of $x - y$?

CONTINUE

18

$$f(t) = 8,000(0.65)^t$$

The given function f models the number of coupons a company sent to their customers at the end of each year, where t represents the number of years since the end of 1998, and $0 \le t \le 5$. If $y = f(t)$ is graphed in the ty-plane, which of the following is the best interpretation of the y-intercept of the graph in this context?

A) The minimum estimated number of coupons the company sent to their customers during the 5 years was 1,428.

B) The minimum estimated number of coupons the company sent to their customers during the 5 years was 8,000.

C) The estimated number of coupons the company sent to their customers at the end of 1998 was 1,428.

D) The estimated number of coupons the company sent to their customers at the end of 1998 was 8,000.

19

A landscaper uses a hose that puts $88x$ ounces of water in a bucket in $5y$ minutes. Which expression represents the number of ounces of water the hose puts in the bucket in $9y$ minutes at this rate?

A) $\dfrac{9x}{440}$

B) $\dfrac{440x}{9}$

C) $\dfrac{5x}{792}$

D) $\dfrac{792x}{5}$

20

$$\sqrt{(x-2)^2} = \sqrt{3x + 34}$$

What is the smallest solution to the given equation?

21

Triangle XYZ is similar to triangle RST such that X, Y, and Z correspond to R, S, and T, respectively. The measure of $\angle Z$ is 20° and $2XY = RS$. What is the measure of $\angle T$?

A) 2°

B) 10°

C) 20°

D) 40°

22

$$f(x) = 9(4)^x$$

The function f is defined by the given equation. If $g(x) = f(x + 2)$, which of the following equations defines the function g?

A) $g(x) = 18(4)^x$

B) $g(x) = 144(4)^x$

C) $g(x) = 18(8)^x$

D) $g(x) = 81(16)^x$

STOP

If you finish before time is called, you may check your work on this module only.
Do not turn to any other module in the test.

Math
22 QUESTIONS

The questions in this section address a number of important math skills.
Use of a calculator is permitted for all questions.

NOTES

Unless otherwise indicated:

- All variables and expressions represent real numbers.
- Figures provided are drawn to scale.
- All figures lie in a plane.
- The domain of a given function f is the set of all real numbers x for which $f(x)$ is a real number.

REFERENCE

 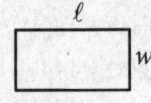 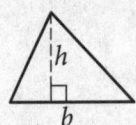 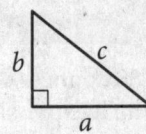 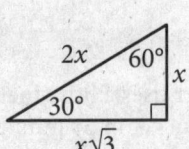

$A = \pi r^2$ $\quad$ $A = \ell w$ $\quad$ $A = \frac{1}{2}bh$ $\quad$ $c^2 = a^2 + b^2$ $\quad$ Special Right Triangles
$C = 2\pi r$

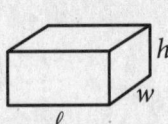    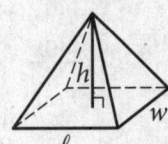

$V = \ell wh$ $\quad$ $V = \pi r^2 h$ $\quad$ $V = \frac{4}{3}\pi r^3$ $\quad$ $V = \frac{1}{3}\pi r^2 h$ $\quad$ $V = \frac{1}{3}\ell wh$

The number of degrees of arc in a circle is 360.

The number of radians of arc in a circle is 2π.

The sum of the measures in degrees of the angles of a triangle is 180.

CONTINUE

For multiple-choice questions, solve each problem, choose the correct answer from the choices provided, and then circle your answer in this book. Circle only one answer for each question. If you change your mind, completely erase the circle. You will not get credit for questions with more than one answer circled, or for questions with no answers circled.

For student-produced response questions, solve each problem and write your answer next to or under the question in the test book as described below.

- Once you've written your answer, circle it clearly. You will not receive credit for anything written outside the circle, or for any questions with more than one circled answer.

- If you find **more than one correct answer**, write and circle only one answer.

- Your answer can be up to 5 characters for a **positive** answer and up to 6 characters (including the negative sign) for a **negative** answer, but no more.

- If your answer is a **fraction** that is too long (over 5 characters for positive, 6 characters for negative), write the decimal equivalent.

- If your answer is a **decimal** that is too long (over 5 characters for positive, 6 characters for negative), truncate it or round at the fourth digit.

- If your answer is a **mixed number** (such as $3\frac{1}{2}$), write it as an improper fraction (7/2) or its decimal equivalent (3.5).

- Don't include **symbols** such as a percent sign, comma, or dollar sign in your circled answer.

CONTINUE ▶

1

$$k + 12 = 336$$

What is the solution to the given equation?

A) 28

B) 324

C) 348

D) 4,032

2

What length, in <u>centimeters</u>, is equivalent to a length of 51 meters? (1 meter = 100 centimeters)

A) 0.051

B) 0.51

C) 5,100

D) 51,000

3

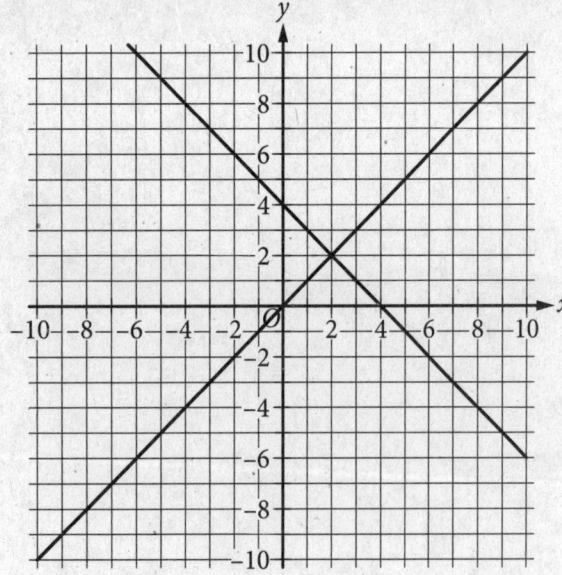

The graph of a system of two linear equations is shown. What is the solution (x, y) to the system?

A) (0, 4)

B) (2, 2)

C) (4, 0)

D) (4, 4)

4

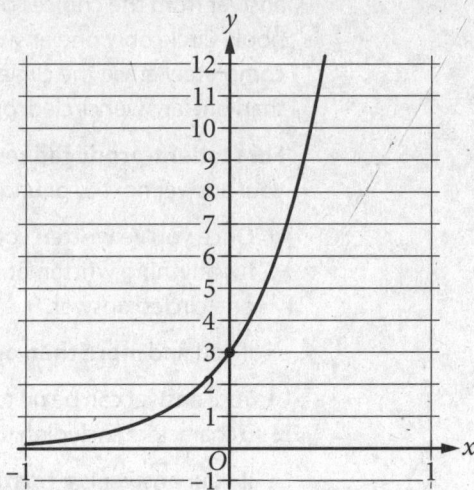

The graph of the exponential function f is shown, where $y = f(x)$. The y-intercept of the graph is $(0, y)$. What is the value of y?

5

The bar graph shows the distribution of the number of students in each of four extracurricular activities at a high school.

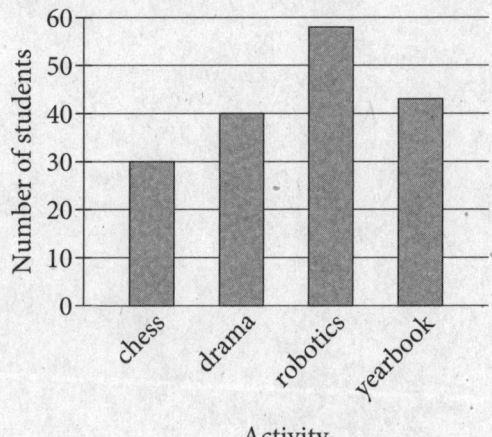

How many more students are in drama than in chess?

A) 10

B) 30

C) 40

D) 70

CONTINUE

6

Which expression is equivalent to
$\dfrac{8x(x-7) - 3(x-7)}{2x - 14}$, where $x > 7$?

A) $\dfrac{x-7}{5}$

B) $\dfrac{8x-3}{2}$

C) $\dfrac{8x^2 - 3x - 14}{2x - 14}$

D) $\dfrac{8x^2 - 3x - 77}{2x - 14}$

7

Out of 300 seeds that were planted, 80% sprouted. How many of these seeds sprouted?

8

Ty set a goal to walk at least 24 kilometers every day to prepare for a multiday hike. On a certain day, Ty plans to walk at an average speed of 4 kilometers per hour. What is the minimum number of hours Ty must walk on that day to fulfill the daily goal?

A) 4

B) 6

C) 20

D) 24

9

$$y = x + 4$$

Which table gives three values of x and their corresponding values of y for the given equation?

A)

x	y
0	4
1	5
2	6

B)

x	y
0	6
1	5
2	4

C)

x	y
0	2
1	1
2	0

D)

x	y
0	0
1	1
2	2

CONTINUE

10

The function g is defined by $g(x) = 6x$. For what value of x is $g(x) = 54$?

11

Sean rents a tent at a cost of $11 per day plus a onetime insurance fee of $10. Which equation represents the total cost c, in dollars, to rent the tent with insurance for d days?

A) $c = 11(d + 10)$

B) $c = 10(d + 11)$

C) $c = 11d + 10$

D) $c = 10d + 11$

12

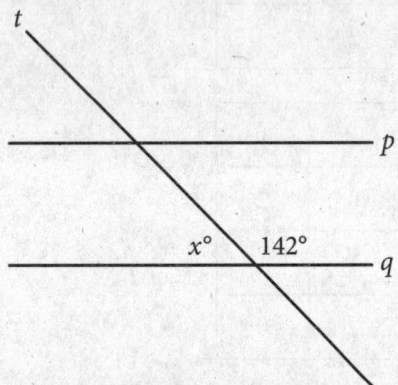

Note: Figure not drawn to scale.

In the figure, line p is parallel to line q, and line t intersects both lines. What is the value of $x + 142$?

A) 52

B) 90

C) 142

D) 180

13

What is the area, in square centimeters, of a rectangle with a length of 34 centimeters (cm) and a width of 29 cm?

14

$$h(x) = x + b$$

For the linear function h, b is a constant and $h(0) = 45$. What is the value of b?

15

What is the equation of the line that passes through the point $(0, 5)$ and is parallel to the graph of $y = 7x + 4$ in the xy-plane?

A) $y = 5x$

B) $y = 7x + 5$

C) $y = 7x$

D) $y = 5x + 7$

16

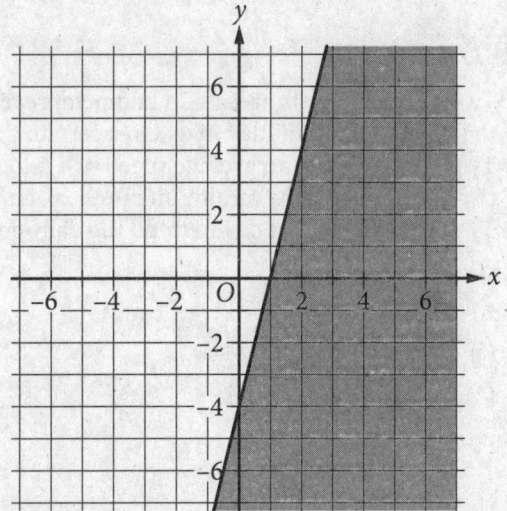

The shaded region shown represents the solutions to an inequality. Which ordered pair (x, y) is a solution to this inequality?

A) $(-5, -6)$

B) $(-2, 5)$

C) $(1, 4)$

D) $(6, -2)$

CONTINUE

17

The number of bacteria in a liquid medium doubles every day. There are 44,000 bacteria in the liquid medium at the start of an observation. Which of the following represents the number of bacteria, y, in the liquid medium t days after the start of the observation?

A) $y = \frac{1}{2}(44,000)^t$

B) $y = 2(44,000)^t$

C) $y = 44,000\left(\frac{1}{2}\right)^t$

D) $y = 44,000(2)^t$

18

The product of a positive number x and the number that is 8 more than x is 180. What is the value of x?

A) 5

B) 10

C) 18

D) 36

19

$$(5x + 4)(2x - 5) = 0$$

Which of the following is a solution to the given equation?

A) $-\frac{5}{2}$

B) $-\frac{5}{4}$

C) $-\frac{4}{5}$

D) $-\frac{2}{5}$

20

Keenan made 32 cups of vegetable broth. Keenan then filled x small jars and y large jars with all the vegetable broth he made. The equation $3x + 5y = 32$ represents this situation. Which is the best interpretation of $5y$ in this context?

A) The number of large jars Keenan filled

B) The number of small jars Keenan filled

C) The total number of cups of vegetable broth in the large jars

D) The total number of cups of vegetable broth in the small jars

21

The area A, in square centimeters, of a rectangular cutting board can be represented by the expression $w(w + 9)$, where w is the width, in centimeters, of the cutting board. Which expression represents the length, in centimeters, of the cutting board?

A) $w(w + 9)$

B) w

C) 9

D) $(w + 9)$

22

The measure of angle R is $\frac{2\pi}{3}$ radians. The measure of angle T is $\frac{5\pi}{12}$ radians greater than the measure of angle R. What is the measure of angle T, in <u>degrees</u>?

A) 75

B) 120

C) 195

D) 390

STOP

**If you finish before time is called, you may check your work on this module only.
Do not turn to any other module in the test.**

Math

22 QUESTIONS

DIRECTIONS

The questions in this section address a number of important math skills.

Use of a calculator is permitted for all questions.

NOTES

Unless otherwise indicated:

- All variables and expressions represent real numbers.
- Figures provided are drawn to scale.
- All figures lie in a plane.
- The domain of a given function f is the set of all real numbers x for which $f(x)$ is a real number.

REFERENCE

 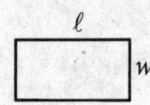 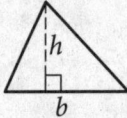 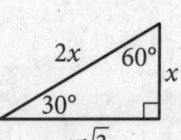

$A = \pi r^2$
$C = 2\pi r$ $A = \ell w$ $A = \frac{1}{2}bh$ $c^2 = a^2 + b^2$ Special Right Triangles

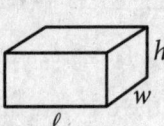   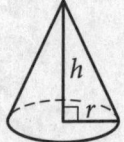 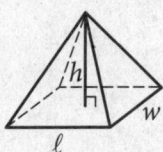

$V = \ell w h$ $V = \pi r^2 h$ $V = \frac{4}{3}\pi r^3$ $V = \frac{1}{3}\pi r^2 h$ $V = \frac{1}{3}\ell w h$

The number of degrees of arc in a circle is 360.

The number of radians of arc in a circle is 2π.

The sum of the measures in degrees of the angles of a triangle is 180.

CONTINUE ➤

For multiple-choice questions, solve each problem, choose the correct answer from the choices provided, and then circle your answer in this book. Circle only one answer for each question. If you change your mind, completely erase the circle. You will not get credit for questions with more than one answer circled, or for questions with no answers circled.

For student-produced response questions, solve each problem and write your answer next to or under the question in the test book as described below.

- Once you've written your answer, circle it clearly. You will not receive credit for anything written outside the circle, or for any questions with more than one circled answer.

- If you find **more than one correct answer**, write and circle only one answer.

- Your answer can be up to 5 characters for a **positive** answer and up to 6 characters (including the negative sign) for a **negative** answer, but no more.

- If your answer is a **fraction** that is too long (over 5 characters for positive, 6 characters for negative), write the decimal equivalent.

- If your answer is a **decimal** that is too long (over 5 characters for positive, 6 characters for negative), truncate it or round at the fourth digit.

- If your answer is a **mixed number** (such as $3\frac{1}{2}$), write it as an improper fraction (7/2) or its decimal equivalent (3.5).

- Don't include **symbols** such as a percent sign, comma, or dollar sign in your circled answer.

CONTINUE ➡

1

$$73, 74, 75, 77, 79, 82, 84, 85, 91$$

What is the median of the data shown?

2

Right triangles LMN and PQR are similar, where L and M correspond to P and Q, respectively. Angle M has a measure of 53°. What is the measure of angle Q?

A) 37°

B) 53°

C) 127°

D) 143°

3

x	y
1	11
2	19
3	a

The table shows three values of x and their corresponding values of y for the equation $y = 4(2)^x + 3$. In the table, a is a constant. What is the value of a?

A) 67

B) 35

C) 32

D) 27

4

$$66x = 66x$$

How many solutions does the given equation have?

A) Exactly one

B) Exactly two

C) Infinitely many

D) Zero

5

A model predicts that the population of Bergen was 15,000 in 2005. The model also predicts that each year for the next 5 years, the population p increased by 4% of the previous year's population. Which equation best represents this model, where x is the number of years after 2005, for $x \le 5$?

A) $p = 0.96(15{,}000)^x$

B) $p = 1.04(15{,}000)^x$

C) $p = 15{,}000(0.96)^x$

D) $p = 15{,}000(1.04)^x$

6

The function h is defined by $h(x) = 4x + 28$. The graph of $y = h(x)$ in the xy-plane has an x-intercept at $(a, 0)$ and a y-intercept at $(0, b)$, where a and b are constants. What is the value of $a + b$?

A) 21

B) 28

C) 32

D) 35

7

Which expression is equivalent to $\dfrac{8x(x-7) - 3(x-7)}{2x - 14}$, where $x > 7$?

A) $\dfrac{x-7}{5}$

B) $\dfrac{8x-3}{2}$

C) $\dfrac{8x^2 - 3x - 14}{2x - 14}$

D) $\dfrac{8x^2 - 3x - 77}{2x - 14}$

CONTINUE ▶

8

Circle A has a radius of $3n$ and circle B has a radius of $129n$, where n is a positive constant. The area of circle B is how many times the area of circle A?

A) 43

B) 86

C) 129

D) 1,849

9

A circle has center O, and points R and S lie on the circle. In triangle ORS, the measure of $\angle ROS$ is 88°. What is the measure of $\angle RSO$, in degrees? (Disregard the degree symbol when entering your answer.)

10

A business owner plans to purchase the same model of chair for each of the 81 employees. The total budget to spend on these chairs is $14,000, which includes a 7% sales tax. Which of the following is closest to the maximum possible price per chair, before sales tax, the business owner could pay based on this budget?

A) $148.15

B) $161.53

C) $172.84

D) $184.94

11

A right triangle has legs with lengths of 24 centimeters and 21 centimeters. If the length of this triangle's hypotenuse, in centimeters, can be written in the form $3\sqrt{d}$, where d is an integer, what is the value of d?

12

The positive number a is 230% of the number b, and a is 60% of the number c. If c is p% of b, which of the following is closest to the value of p?

A) 138

B) 217

C) 283

D) 383

13

For $x > 0$, the function f is defined as follows:

$$f(x) \text{ equals 201\% of } x$$

Which of the following could describe this function?

A) Decreasing exponential

B) Decreasing linear

C) Increasing exponential

D) Increasing linear

14

x	y
k	13
$k+7$	-15

The table gives the coordinates of two points on a line in the xy-plane. The y-intercept of the line is $(k-5, b)$, where k and b are constants. What is the value of b?

CONTINUE

15

Keenan made 32 cups of vegetable broth. Keenan then filled x small jars and y large jars with all the vegetable broth he made. The equation $3x + 5y = 32$ represents this situation. Which is the best interpretation of $5y$ in this context?

A) The number of large jars Keenan filled

B) The number of small jars Keenan filled

C) The total number of cups of vegetable broth in the large jars

D) The total number of cups of vegetable broth in the small jars

16

$$3x = 36y - 45$$

One of the two equations in a system of linear equations is given. The system has no solution. Which equation could be the second equation in this system?

A) $x = 4y$

B) $\frac{1}{3}x = 4y$

C) $x = 12y - 15$

D) $\frac{1}{3}x = 12y - 15$

17

$$x - 29 = (x - a)(x - 29)$$

Which of the following are solutions to the given equation, where a is a constant and $a > 30$?

  I. a

  II. $a + 1$

  III. 29

A) I and II only

B) I and III only

C) II and III only

D) I, II, and III

18

One gallon of stain will cover 170 square feet of a surface. A yard has a total fence area of w square feet. Which equation represents the total amount of stain S, in gallons, needed to stain the fence in this yard twice?

A) $S = \frac{w}{170}$

B) $S = 170w$

C) $S = 340w$

D) $S = \frac{w}{85}$

19

In the xy-plane, the graph of the equation $y = -x^2 + 9x - 100$ intersects the line $y = c$ at exactly one point. What is the value of c?

A) $-\frac{481}{4}$

B) -100

C) $-\frac{319}{4}$

D) $-\frac{9}{2}$

20

The quadratic function g models the depth, in meters, below the surface of the water of a seal t minutes after the seal entered the water during a dive. The function estimates that the seal reached its maximum depth of 302.4 meters 6 minutes after it entered the water and then reached the surface of the water 12 minutes after it entered the water. Based on the function, what was the estimated depth, to the nearest meter, of the seal 10 minutes after it entered the water?

CONTINUE

21

The area of a rectangular region is increasing at a rate of 250 square feet per hour. Which of the following is closest to this rate in <u>square meters per minute</u>? (Use 1 meter = 3.28 feet.)

A) 0.39

B) 1.27

C) 13.67

D) 23.24

22

$$5x + 7y = 1$$
$$ax + by = 1$$

In the given pair of equations, a and b are constants. The graph of this pair of equations in the xy-plane is a pair of perpendicular lines. Which of the following pairs of equations also represents a pair of perpendicular lines?

A) $10x + 7y = 1$
$ax - 2by = 1$

B) $10x + 7y = 1$
$ax + 2by = 1$

C) $10x + 7y = 1$
$2ax + by = 1$

D) $5x - 7y = 1$
$ax + by = 1$

STOP

**If you finish before time is called, you may check your work on this module only.
Do not turn to any other module in the test.**

The SAT

Practice Test #9

ANSWER EXPLANATIONS

These answer explanations are for students using
The Official SAT Study Guide.

Reading and Writing

Module 1
(27 questions)

QUESTION 1

Choice A is the best answer because it most logically completes the text's discussion of diaphragm contractions and hiccups. In this context, "involuntarily" means done without any control, or by reflex. The text explains that when a person's diaphragm repeatedly contracts and results in hiccups (which may be important for infants), those muscle contractions are "uncontrollable." This context indicates that the diaphragm contractions occur without the person's control.

Choice B is incorrect because the text indicates that researchers haven't determined exactly why people hiccup, suggesting that it isn't known that the uncontrollable muscle contractions generally occur "beneficially," or with a good or helpful effect—even if one neuroscientist has now found that it's possible hiccups play an important positive role for a specific group of people (infants). *Choice C* is incorrect because the text indicates that the diaphragm contractions that result in hiccups are "uncontrollable." Because those muscle contractions are described as happening without the person's control, it wouldn't make sense to describe them as occurring "strenuously," or in a way that requires great effort or energy. *Choice D* is incorrect because the text doesn't describe the quality of the diaphragm contractions that result in hiccups beyond stating that they are "uncontrollable." Nothing in the text indicates that those muscle contractions occur "smoothly," or evenly and continuously.

QUESTION 2

Choice C is the best answer because it most logically completes the text's discussion of how Ofelia Zepeda has contributed to the field of linguistics. As used in this context, "extensive" means having a wide or considerable extent. The text indicates that Zepeda's many accomplishments in linguistics are varied, including teaching linguistics, writing poetry in more than one language, creating a grammar book, and co-founding a language institute. This context supports the idea that Zepeda's contributions to the field are extensive.

Choice A is incorrect because the sentence presents Zepeda's accomplishments as examples to support the claim made in the first part of the sentence. It wouldn't make sense to say that achievements as a professor, poet and author, and co-founder of a language institute demonstrate that Zepeda's contributions in her field are "pragmatic," or related to practical matters and not involving intellectual or artistic matters. *Choice B* is incorrect because the sentence presents Zepeda's accomplishments as a professor, poet and author, and co-founder of a language institute as examples to support the claim made in the first part of the sentence. There's no reason to believe that the positive achievements listed demonstrate that Zepeda's contributions in her field are "controversial," or have caused disputes and opposing viewpoints. *Choice D* is incorrect because in this context, "universal" would mean including or covering everything in a group. The sentence presents Zepeda's accomplishments as examples to support the claim made in the first part of the sentence, and it wouldn't make sense to say that these specific achievements—particularly as the author of a grammar book specific to the Tohono O'odham language—demonstrate that Zepeda's contributions relate to everything in the field of linguistics.

QUESTION 3

Choice D is the best answer because it logically completes the text's discussion about genes related to hibernation. In this context, "dormant" means inactive. The text explains that the same genes that enable certain nonhuman mammal species to hibernate during the winter by altering their bodily processes are also found in our species but have "essentially no effect" on humans' bodily processes. In other words, these genes don't function in humans.

Choice A is incorrect because in this context, "decisive" means has the power to affect the outcome of something, but the text states that genes related to hibernation are instead inactive in humans—that is, the genes don't affect humans' bodily processes, although they are present in their bodies. *Choice B* is incorrect because in this context, "lacking" means missing, but the text states that the genes are present in humans, though inactive. *Choice C* is incorrect because "variable" means characterized by the potential to change, but the text indicates that these genes don't change in their effect on humans' bodily processes; instead, the genes are consistently inactive in humans.

QUESTION 4

Choice B is the best answer because it most logically completes the discussion of Octavia Butler's career. In this context, "impenetrable" means impossible to enter. The text indicates that the field of science fiction was dominated by white males when Butler, a Black woman, started writing, but she published several science fiction short stories and a novel and later won a prestigious award; that is, Butler pursued science fiction writing and had success. This context suggests that Butler didn't view the genre as impossible to enter.

Choice A is incorrect. In this context, "legitimate" would mean genuinely good or valid. Nothing in the text suggests that Butler didn't think the science fiction genre was good or valid; in fact, it indicates that she pursued and made a successful career of publishing work in that field. *Choice C* is incorrect. In this context, "compelling" would mean attracting or demanding attention. The text indicates that Butler chose to write science fiction, so it wouldn't make sense to say that she didn't see the field as drawing her attention. *Choice D* is incorrect. To say that Butler didn't consider science fiction "indecipherable," or impossible to understand, would suggest that Butler did understand it. However, the text doesn't address Butler's ability to interpret works in the genre; rather, it focuses on Butler's successful pursuit of writing science fiction.

QUESTION 5

Choice D is the best answer because it most accurately describes how the underlined sentence functions in the text as a whole. The text begins by pointing out one of the advantages of oral histories: that they allow researchers to document the daily experiences of people. The text then goes on to describe how Karida Brown utilized interviews with coal miners and their families for her book about twentieth-century coal mining in Kentucky. The underlined sentence affirms that the general advantages of oral histories mentioned earlier in the text were also benefits in Brown's particular case. Thus, the underlined sentence describes how Karida Brown benefited from incorporating oral history in her book.

Choice A is incorrect because though the text mentions coal miners who live in Kentucky, the underlined sentence does not offer a geographical fact about Kentucky. *Choice B* is incorrect because the underlined sentence does not mention United States politics or that Brown is an expert in this particular area. *Choice C* is incorrect. Although the text mentions that Brown's book revolved around coal miners during the twentieth century, the underlined sentence does not focus on a major historical event during this time.

QUESTION 6

Choice D is the best answer because it most accurately reflects the main purpose of the text. The text portrays Miss Pyne as awaiting the arrival of a carriage while Martha brings strawberries and flowers from the garden into the house. The text also describes the surroundings of the scene, stating that Miss Pyne looks "stately and calm," the evening is bright and cool, and birds are singing in the garden as the sun sets. Then the last sentence states that the house was "wide open to the long-expected guest," which strongly suggests that Miss Pyne's anticipation and Martha's activities were in preparation for the guest who is expected to arrive in the carriage. Thus, the text depicts the setting and conveys what these characters are doing as they await the arrival of their visitor.

Choice A is incorrect because there is nothing in the text to indicate that the characters feel any worry about the guest's arrival. The text indicates that the guest was "long-expected," but characterizing Miss Pyne as "stately and calm" conflicts with the idea that the characters are worried about the guest. *Choice B* is incorrect because the text describes a moment in time when two characters are awaiting the arrival of a visitor rather than an extended period over which characters could be seen changing. *Choice C* is incorrect. Although the text describes the activity indoors (Miss Pyne sitting calmly), it describes a higher level of activity, not stillness, outside (Martha bringing fruit and flowers and birds singing).

QUESTION 7

Choice B is the best answer because it most accurately states the main purpose of the text, which is to show that Henry's mother, Mrs. Higgins, wants Henry to leave her house. In the text, Mrs. Higgins complains that Henry offends all her friends and that they stop coming when he's also visiting. She then tells him directly, "you mustn't stay." The overall exchange conveys Mrs. Higgins's intention for Henry to leave so as not to drive away her friends with his behavior.

Choice A is incorrect because the text doesn't indicate what Henry's mother does when she's out with her friends. Instead, it focuses on what goes on when Henry and her friends visit her at the same time, indicating that since her friends find Henry's company disagreeable, she wishes him to leave before they arrive. *Choice C* is incorrect because the text doesn't contain an account of what Henry's home looks like. The setting is established as the house of Henry's mother, and the dialogue focuses solely on her wish that Henry should depart before her friends arrive. *Choice D* is incorrect because the text doesn't mention how often Henry visits his mother nor does it provide any explanation for why he visits his mother. Instead, it indicates that she thinks her friends dislike Henry and that she therefore wants him to depart before they arrive.

QUESTION 8

Choice A is the best answer because it most accurately describes the function of the underlined portion in the text as a whole. The text establishes that many countries have adopted risk-disclosure requirements for financial products due to concerns that consumers don't understand the risks associated with the products. According to the text, Seira et al. found that the effects of such messaging on consumer behavior were small and temporary. The text then adds that the researchers assert that because the cost of the messaging is negligible, the approach may be worth doing even if the effects are limited. Thus, the underlined portion notes a factor—very low cost—that led the researchers to not completely dismiss risk-disclosure messaging despite their evidence of its limited utility.

Choice B is incorrect because the underlined portion doesn't refer to a particular type of risk-disclosure messaging, whether Seira et al. considered it or not; the underlined portion simply indicates that the cost of the messaging (broadly) is very low, which makes the approach worth pursuing even if its effects are limited. *Choice C* is incorrect. Although the underlined portion does describe a consideration that led the researchers to recommend risk-disclosure messaging despite the messaging's small effects on consumer behavior, it directly states that the cost of such messaging is negligible, or very low—meaning that both the effects and the costs are small, not that the effects are small only relative to the costs. *Choice D* is incorrect because there's no indication that Seira et al. suggest that risk-disclosure messaging could be more effective if it had lower costs; rather, the underlined portion indicates that Seira et al. believe the already negligible cost of messaging makes the approach worth pursuing even if its effects are limited.

QUESTION 9

Choice D is the best answer because it presents a statement about Mrs. Ochiltree's acquaintances that is supported by the text. The text indicates that Mrs. Ochiltree makes comments about her acquaintances that are frank, or direct and blunt, and sometimes startling. It also states that because of this behavior, the acquaintances tend to avoid Mrs. Ochiltree. Together, these details suggest that the acquaintances choose not to be around Mrs. Ochiltree because they are offended by the things she has said about them.

Choice A is incorrect because the text doesn't suggest that Mrs. Ochiltree's acquaintances avoid discussing topics that would upset Mrs. Ochiltree; instead, it states that they avoid being around Mrs. Ochiltree at all. *Choice B* is incorrect because the text makes it clear that Mrs. Ochiltree knows her acquaintances often avoid her and is pleased about it (she "rather exulted in it"), not that she wants to spend more time with them. *Choice C* is incorrect because the text doesn't suggest that Mrs. Ochiltree's acquaintances don't speak with Mrs. Ochiltree because they are too focused on their own concerns, but rather because they don't like the frank comments she makes.

QUESTION 10

Choice C is the best answer because it presents a quotation that illustrates the claim that Mrs. Spring Fragrance demonstrates concern for what's happening at home while she's in California. By giving reminders to "care for the cat, the birds, and the flowers," "not eat too quickly," and avoid engaging in strenuous activity in the heat, Mrs. Spring Fragrance shows that she's thinking about what's happening at home and wants to ensure everything is taken care of.

Choice A is incorrect because the quotation, while it does suggest that Mrs. Spring Fragrance has made fudge at home before, is focused on preparations for an upcoming festival, not on concerns for anything happening at home while Mrs. Spring Fragrance is away. *Choice B* is incorrect because the quotation has to do with an upcoming event during Mrs. Spring Fragrance's trip—visiting San José and meeting someone new—rather than her concern for what's happening at home. *Choice D* is incorrect because the quotation is focused on how Mrs. Spring Fragrance feels about her trip and the friends she's seeing, not on her concern for what's happening at home.

QUESTION 11

Choice C is the best answer because it would most directly support the student's claim about the motivation for including explanatory notes with the stand-alone volume of the poem. The text explains that the poem had previously been published without the notes in a quarterly journal. It stands to reason that readers who had purchased the journal issue containing the poem would be unlikely to purchase an unchanged version of the poem in a stand-alone volume. However, the inclusion of notes in that volume would encourage the purchase of a stand-alone volume, since the later text would differ from the original by including the author's own explanation of the poem. Therefore, if it were true that the publishers of the stand-alone volume had requested the notes to make the book attractive to readers who already had a copy of the journal issue, this fact would support the student's claim that the notes were included primarily as a marketing device.

Choice A is incorrect because the student's claim is about the motivation for including the explanatory notes in the stand-alone volume, not about changes that might have been made to the poem itself for publication in that volume; moreover, the text never suggests that such changes were made. *Choice B* is incorrect because the student's claim is about why the explanatory notes were included in the stand-alone volume, not about how the notes affected readers' and critics' subsequent experience of the poem. *Choice D* is incorrect because the fact that the poet drafted multiple versions of the explanatory notes doesn't directly address the issue of whether the notes were intended as a marketing device, as the student claims; the correspondence would support this claim only if it showed that the poet had revised the notes specifically to make them useful to the marketing of the stand-alone volume.

QUESTION 12

Choice D is the best answer because it best describes data in the graph supporting Ayalew and her colleagues' hypothesis that plants' response to kanamycin exposure involves altering their uptake of metals. The graph compares the metal content of two groups of plants, one with kanamycin exposure and a control group without such exposure. The amount of zinc in plants without kanamycin exposure is around 400 parts per million, while the amount of zinc in plants with kanamycin exposure is lower, at around 300 parts per million. Similarly, the amount of iron in plants without kanamycin exposure is a little over 600 parts per million, while the amount of iron in plants with kanamycin exposure is lower, at a little over 200 parts per million. Thus, the graph shows that plants with kanamycin exposure have significantly lower levels of both iron and zinc than the plants without kanamycin exposure. This is evidence supporting the hypothesis that kanamycin exposure results in plants altering their uptake of metals.

Choice A is incorrect because the graph shows that control plants contained higher levels of iron than zinc, not higher levels of zinc than iron; similarly, the plants exposed to kanamycin contained higher levels of zinc than iron, not higher levels of iron than zinc. *Choice B* is incorrect. Though the claim that both groups of plants contained more than 200 parts per million of both iron and zinc is supported by the graph, this alone does not state whether plants with kanamycin exposure have a different metal content than plants without kanamycin exposure. *Choice C* is incorrect. The graph shows that the zinc levels for the control plants (those without kanamycin exposure) were around 400 parts per million, not 300 parts per million, and that the zinc levels for plants with kanamycin exposure were around 300 parts per million, not 400 parts per million.

QUESTION 13

Choice D is the best answer because it accurately describes data from the table that support Rodriguez and colleagues' assertion about the classifications of the five new gas exoplanets. The text describes two categories of gas planets: hot Jupiters, which have a mass of at least 0.25 Jupiters and an orbital period of less than 10 days, and warm Jupiters, which have the same mass characteristic but have orbital periods of more than 10 days. According to the table, four of the gas exoplanets discovered by Rodriguez and colleagues have a mass of at least 0.25 Jupiters and an orbital period of less than 10 days, while one of the planets has a mass of at least 0.25 Jupiters and an orbital period of more than 10 days. These data therefore support Rodriguez and colleagues' assertion that four of the new exoplanets are hot Jupiters and one is a warm Jupiter.

Choice A is incorrect because it doesn't accurately describe the data from the table. Although the table shows that TOI-628 b has a mass equivalent to 6.33 Jupiters, the table also shows that one of the planets—TOI-1478 b— does indeed have an orbital period of more than 10 days. *Choice B* is incorrect because it doesn't accurately describe the data from the table. Although the table does show that the masses of the five planets range from 0.85 to 6.33 Jupiters, the table also shows that TOI-1478 b has an orbital period of 10.180 days, not 153 days. *Choice C* is incorrect. According to the table, TOI-1333 b has an orbital period of only 4.720 days, not more than 10 days. Additionally, although the table does show that all the planets have a radius between 1.060 and 1.771 Jupiters, the text indicates that a planet may be classified as a hot Jupiter or a warm Jupiter based on its mass and orbital period, not on its radius, making the information about the range of the five planets' radius values irrelevant.

QUESTION 14

Choice A is the best answer because it most logically completes the text's discussion of the evidence found in Queen Merneith's tomb. The text begins by mentioning archaeologists' efforts to excavate the tomb of Queen Merneith, the wife of a pharaoh who some scholars think was actually the first female pharaoh. The text states that a tablet discovered in her tomb suggests she "was in charge of the country's treasury and other central offices," which supports the idea that she had an important role in Egypt's government.

Choice B is incorrect because since the text explicitly states that Merneith's husband was a First Dynasty pharaoh, it can be inferred that she lived during the First Dynasty, not after it. *Choice C* is incorrect because the text does not provide any evidence that Merneith traveled beyond Egypt's borders often. The text is focused on the archaeological discovery in her tomb and the implications about her potential role as a ruler in Egypt but does not mention anything about her traveling habits. *Choice D* is incorrect because the text does not mention anything about Merneith creating a new form of writing in Egypt. The text discusses the discovery of a tablet with writing suggesting her governmental role but does not imply that this writing represented a new form created by Merneith.

QUESTION 15

Choice D is the best answer because it most logically completes the text's discussion of linguists using social media to study changes in language usage in real time, providing the specific example of the affix *meng-* in Bahasa Indonesia. The text states that linguists first observed *meng-* being used as an onomatopoeic tag on social media, which then spread to being affixed to existing words in text posted on social media; from there, it has begun to move into spoken Bahasa Indonesia. As presented in the text, this progression from online usage to spoken language suggests that social media does more than just register or reflect changes in language—it can actively drive such changes. In the case of *meng-*, the text suggests, social media facilitated the movement of the affix from an online tag to part of spoken Bahasa Indonesia.

Choice A is incorrect because the text doesn't differentiate between social media's usefulness for studying informal versus formal or official language; it merely notes that Bahasa Indonesia is an official language. *Choice B* is incorrect because while the example given in the text focuses on changes in Bahasa Indonesia, the text doesn't provide any evidence that social media is exerting an exceptionally strong influence on the evolution of this particular language compared to others. In fact, the text states that "linguists have noted many similar examples of this phenomenon occurring in other languages," suggesting that social media's influence is evident across multiple languages and not unique to Bahasa Indonesia. *Choice C* is incorrect because the text never suggests that social media provides a somewhat misleading sense of how languages are changing. Rather, the text suggests that by allowing linguists to directly observe linguistic changes, social media offers a clear window into language evolution.

QUESTION 16

Choice B is the best answer. The convention being tested is finite and nonfinite verb forms within a sentence. A main clause requires a finite verb to perform the action of the subject (in this case, "people in the Americas"), and this choice supplies the finite past perfect tense verb "have used" to indicate what people in the Americas used the gourd for.

Choice A is incorrect because the nonfinite to-infinitive "to use" doesn't supply the main clause with a finite verb. *Choice C* is incorrect because the nonfinite participle "having used" doesn't supply the main clause with a finite verb. *Choice D* is incorrect because the nonfinite participle "using" doesn't supply the main clause with a finite verb.

QUESTION 17

Choice D is the best answer. The convention being tested is end-of-sentence punctuation. This choice correctly uses a question mark to punctuate the interrogative clause "could the blueberries thrive," which asks a direct question at the end of the sentence.

Choice A is incorrect because a period can't be used in this way to punctuate an interrogative clause, such as "could the blueberries thrive," at the end of a sentence. *Choice B* is incorrect because the context requires an interrogative clause. The declarative clause "the blueberries could thrive" incorrectly indicates that it was known that the blueberries could thrive in alkaline soil, whereas Michel had yet to find this out. *Choice C* is incorrect because a question mark can't be used in this way to punctuate a declarative clause, such as "the blueberries could thrive," at the end of a sentence.

QUESTION 18

Choice A is the best answer. The convention being tested is punctuation use between sentences. In this choice, the period after "configurations" is used correctly to mark the boundary between one sentence ("The intense… configurations") and another ("TMAO…fish"). The supplementary phrase ("ensuring…configurations") modifies the main clause of the first sentence ("The chemical…effect"), and "TMAO" is the subject of the second sentence.

Choice B is incorrect because it results in a run-on sentence. The sentences ("The intense…configurations" and "TMAO…fish") are fused without punctuation and/or a conjunction. *Choice C* is incorrect because it results in a comma splice. A comma can't be used in this way to mark the boundary between sentences. *Choice D* is incorrect. Without a comma preceding it, the conjunction "and" can't be used in this way to join sentences.

QUESTION 19

Choice D is the best answer. The convention being tested is subject-verb agreement. The singular verb "is credited" agrees in number with the singular subject "mathematician Grigori Perelman."

Choice A is incorrect because the plural verb "are credited" doesn't agree in number with the singular subject "mathematician Grigori Perelman." *Choice B* is incorrect because the plural verb "have been credited" doesn't agree in number with the singular subject "mathematician Grigori Perelman." *Choice C* is incorrect because the plural verb "are being credited" doesn't agree in number with the singular subject "mathematician Grigori Perelman."

QUESTION 20

Choice A is the best answer. The convention being tested is the use of punctuation within a sentence. This choice correctly uses a comma to separate the supplementary adverb "though" from the preceding main clause ("Jetties can sometimes have the opposite effect") and uses a semicolon to join the next main clause ("obstructing…areas") to the rest of the sentence. Further, placing the semicolon after "though" logically indicates that the information earlier in this sentence (that jetties can sometimes cause erosion) is contrary to what might be assumed from the information in the previous sentence (that jetties are often constructed for the purpose of protecting coastlines from erosion).

Choice B is incorrect because it fails to mark the boundary between the two main clauses with appropriate punctuation. With "though…areas" functioning as a subordinate clause following the comma, this choice illogically indicates that the following information (that obstructing the natural flow of sand along the shore can sometimes lead to erosion) is contrary to the information earlier in the sentence (that jetties can sometimes cause erosion). Instead, the information following "though" supports the previous claim about the erosive effects of jetties. *Choice C* is incorrect because it's not conventional to use a semicolon in this way to separate a main clause from a dependent clause. Further, it illogically indicates that the following information (that obstructing the natural flow of sand along the shore can sometimes lead to erosion) is contrary to the information earlier in the sentence (that jetties can sometimes cause erosion). Instead, the information following "though" supports the previous claim about the erosive effects of jetties. *Choice D* is incorrect because it results in a comma splice. Commas can't be used in this way to set off a supplementary word or phrase between two main clauses.

QUESTION 21

Choice D is the best answer. "Second" logically signals that the information in this sentence—that the effort to bury the ship would likely only have been made for a king—joins the information in the previous sentence ("first...") in supporting Brunning's claim that the burial site was likely the tomb of a king.

Choice A is incorrect because "instead" illogically signals that the information in this sentence presents an alternative or substitute to the previous information about the gold artifacts inside the ship. Rather, this sentence presents a second piece of information that supports Brunning's claim. *Choice B* is incorrect because "still" illogically signals that the information in this sentence exists in contrast to or despite the previous information about the gold artifacts inside the ship. Instead, this sentence presents a second piece of information that supports Brunning's claim. *Choice C* is incorrect because "specifically" illogically signals that the information in this sentence specifies or elaborates on the previous information about the gold artifacts inside the ship. Instead, this sentence presents a second piece of information that supports Brunning's claim.

QUESTION 22

Choice A is the best answer. "Specifically" logically signals that the information in this sentence—that the Sun releases charged particles that later collide with atoms, resulting in auroral light—provides specific, precise details about how auroras result from the Sun's activity.

Choice B is incorrect because "similarly" illogically signals that the information in this sentence is similar to the general information about auroras in the previous sentence. Instead, this sentence provides specific, precise details about how auroras form. *Choice C* is incorrect because "nevertheless" illogically signals that the information in this sentence is despite the general information about auroras in the previous sentence. Instead, this sentence provides specific, precise details about how auroras form. *Choice D* is incorrect because "hence" illogically signals that the information in this sentence is a result of the general information about auroras in the previous sentence. Instead, this sentence provides specific, precise details about how auroras form.

QUESTION 23

Choice A is the best answer. "To be exact" logically signals that this sentence about the Coastal Virginia Offshore Wind project plan provides specific, precise details—number of turbines, location of site—elaborating on the more general information about the project in the previous sentence.

Choice B is incorrect because "in conclusion" illogically signals that the information in this sentence about the Coastal Virginia Offshore Wind project plan concludes or summarizes the discussion of the project in the previous sentences. Instead, the sentence provides specific, precise details elaborating on the previous information. *Choice C* is incorrect because "as a result" illogically signals that the information in this sentence about the Coastal Virginia Offshore Wind project plan is caused by, or occurs as a result of, the information about the project in the previous sentence. Instead, the sentence provides specific, precise details elaborating on the previous information. *Choice D* is incorrect because "in contrast" illogically signals that the information in this sentence about the Coastal Virginia Offshore Wind project plan contrasts with information about the project in the previous sentence. Instead, the sentence provides specific, precise details elaborating on the previous information.

QUESTION 24

Choice C is the best answer. The sentence recounts the sequence of events proposed by the researchers: a large moon orbiting Saturn came close enough to the planet that it was broken apart by tidal forces, and the resulting debris formed Saturn's rings.

Choice A is incorrect because the sentence misrepresents information from the notes; according to the notes, tidal forces, not debris, caused the moon to break apart. *Choice B* is incorrect. The sentence offers information relevant to the 2022 study but doesn't recount the sequence of events proposed by the researchers. *Choice D* is incorrect. The sentence recounts a sequence, but it's a sequence of the researchers' activities, not the sequence of events proposed by the researchers.

QUESTION 25

Choice C is the best answer. The sentence effectively emphasizes the fossil's significance, explaining that the fossil is rare and illustrates an early stage in the evolution of pinnipeds from their land-dwelling ancestors.

Choice A is incorrect. The sentence describes the fossil Rybczynski found; it doesn't emphasize the fossil's significance. *Choice B* is incorrect. The sentence mentions that a fossil resembling both pinnipeds and their ancestors was found; it doesn't emphasize the fossil's significance. *Choice D* is incorrect. The sentence notes a term used to describe the fossil Rybczynski found; it doesn't emphasize the fossil's significance.

QUESTION 26

Choice A is the best answer. Noting that "guerdon" is of Anglo-French origin and "Laodicean" is of ancient Greek origin, the sentence uses "while" to emphasize a difference in the origins of the two words.

Choice B is incorrect. While the sentence emphasizes two words used in the Scripps National Spelling Bee, it doesn't emphasize (or mention) the words' linguistic origins. *Choice C* is incorrect. While the sentence specifies the linguistic origin of one word used in the Scripps National Spelling Bee, it doesn't mention the other word or emphasize a difference in the two words' origins. *Choice D* is incorrect. While the sentence makes a generalization about words used in the Scripps National Spelling Bee, it doesn't emphasize a difference in the words' origins.

QUESTION 27

Choice C is the best answer. The sentence emphasizes a similarity between the two paintings, noting that Leutze's painting (which measures 149 × 255 inches) and Monkman's painting (which measures 132 × 264 inches) are both very large.

Choice A is incorrect. The sentence mentions that Monkman's painting was completed in 2019 and Leutze's was completed in 1851; it doesn't emphasize a similarity between the two paintings. *Choice B* is incorrect. While the sentence acknowledges that one painting was inspired by the other, it emphasizes differences between the two paintings; it doesn't emphasize a similarity between them. *Choice D* is incorrect. The sentence mentions a difference between the two paintings; it doesn't emphasize a similarity between them.

Reading and Writing

Module 2 — Lower Difficulty
(27 questions)

QUESTION 1

Choice B is the best answer because it most logically completes the text's discussion of Cole's book *Blind Spot*. In this context, "enthusiasm for" means excitement about. The text explains that *Blind Spot* consists of original photographs as well as poetic prose—two elements that correspond to Cole's passions, identified in the text, for photography and the written word. This context suggests that Cole's excitement about photography and writing led him to create a book that successfully combines the two mediums.

Choice A is incorrect because describing Cole as feeling "indifference to" his two passions wouldn't make sense in context. If Cole is indifferent to his passions, that would mean he doesn't care about photography or writing— in which case they wouldn't be his passions at all. *Choice C* is incorrect because there's nothing in the text to suggest that Cole feels "concern about," or uneasiness about, his passions. The text's use of the word "culminates" indicates that *Blind Spot* represents a triumphant climax of Cole's passions, not a work that results from his sense of discomfort with photography and writing. *Choice D* is incorrect because there's nothing in the text to suggest that Cole feels "surprise at," or astonished by, his passions. The text indicates that Cole's feeling about his passions "culminates" in a book that "evocatively" combines photographs and writing, suggesting that Cole has a long-standing and skillful relationship to his passions, not that he is startled by them.

QUESTION 2

Choice D is the best answer because it most logically completes the text's discussion of the research that Lopes-Ferreira and her colleagues are conducting on the stingray species *Potamotrygon rex.* As used in this context, "a substantial" effect means an effect that is sizable or noteworthy. The text indicates that the researchers are seeking to determine whether there are "considerable variations" in the potency of stingray venom that are associated with variation in the stingrays' age and sex. This context suggests that the researchers want to find out whether stingray age and sex have a substantial effect on venom toxicity.

Choice A is incorrect because there's nothing in the text that suggests that the researchers have been studying whether the stingrays' age and sex have "a disconcerting," or an unsettling and disturbing, effect on the stingrays' venom. The text indicates that the researchers wish to determine if stingray age and sex cause large variations in the toxicity of stingray venom, not if the effect of age and sex is disconcerting. *Choice B* is incorrect because the text indicates that researchers want to find out whether differences in stingray age and sex produce differences in stingray venom, not that the researchers want to find out whether age and sex have "an acceptable," or a satisfactory, effect on venom. The text makes no mention of what would make an effect on venom toxicity acceptable and gives no indication that the researchers are interested in that question. *Choice C* is incorrect because it wouldn't make sense in context for the researchers to be looking for "an imperceptible," or an unnoticeable, effect of age and sex on stingray venom. The text says that the researchers are trying to determine if there are "considerable variations" in venom toxicity linked to age and sex, not that the researchers are trying to find effects that they can't perceive.

QUESTION 3

Choice B is the best answer because it most logically completes the text's discussion of Ochoa's prediction that humans will one day need to live in places other than Earth. As used in this context, "speculates" would mean puts forward an idea without firm evidence. The text states that Ochoa "doesn't have a definite idea" about when humans might need to live in other environments and characterizes Ochoa's prediction as a "conjecture," or a conclusion presented without convincing evidence. This context indicates that Ochoa speculates when she makes this prediction.

Choice A is incorrect because saying that Ochoa "demands," or insists or requires, that humans will one day need to live in other environments than Earth's would not make sense in context. The text indicates that she's unsure about the timing but hypothesizes that it will someday happen. *Choice C* is incorrect because saying that Ochoa "doubts," or questions or disbelieves, that humans will one day need to live in other environments than Earth's would not make sense in context. The text indicates that although Ochoa is unsure about the timing, she hypothesizes that humans will need to live in places other than Earth and encourages research into future travel to the moon. *Choice D* is incorrect because saying that Ochoa "establishes," or proves, that humans will one day need to live in other environments than Earth's would not make sense in context. Rather than stating that Ochoa discusses her idea with certainty and supports it with evidence, the text indicates that Ochoa is unsure about when humans might need to live in other environments.

QUESTION 4

Choice B is the best answer because it most logically completes the text's discussion of ectomycorrhizae relationships. In this context, "reciprocates" means responds in kind or degree. The text indicates that the relationship between certain fungi and trees in some habitats is "mutually beneficial" and involves a "symbiotic exchange" in which each organism helps the other access an important nutrient. In other words, each organism provides the same kind of benefit it receives: the tree provides a nutrient (carbon) for the fungus and the fungus reciprocates by helping the tree to absorb more of another nutrient (nitrogen).

Choice A is incorrect because the text emphasizes that the relationship between certain fungi and trees in some habitats involves a "symbiotic exchange" in which each organism helps the other access an important nutrient. Nothing in the text suggests that the fungus "overreacts," or responds too strongly, by allowing the tree to be better able to absorb a beneficial nutrient. *Choice C* is incorrect because "retaliates" means responds to a harmful action with a similarly harmful action. The text indicates that the relationship between certain fungi and trees in some habitats is "mutually beneficial" and involves a "symbiotic exchange" in which each organism helps the other, not that the relationship is one in which the organisms harm one another. *Choice D is incorrect.* In this context, "deviates" would mean departs from an established course or norm. The text explains that the relationship between certain fungi and trees in some habitats involves a "symbiotic exchange" in which each organism helps the other access an important nutrient. Because the relationship involves benefits for both the fungus and the tree, it wouldn't make sense to say that the fungus deviates by helping the tree be better able to absorb a beneficial nutrient.

QUESTION 5

Choice D is the best answer because it accurately states the text's main purpose. The poem begins with the speaker urging a child to "go forth" with her encouragement ("my heart's desire"). The speaker goes on to suggest that new experiences ("Great reaches, yet unknown") lie ahead for the son that "life is calling" him to seek out. Thus, the main purpose is to encourage a child to embrace the experiences available to him in his life.

Choice A is incorrect because the speaker encourages the child to pursue new experiences ("Great reaches") without knowing exactly what those experiences will be ("yet unknown") or suggesting that they should match the speaker's own accomplishments. *Choice B* is incorrect because the speaker focuses on positive possibilities for her son ("Great reaches, yet unknown") and her enthusiastic encouragement to embrace those possibilities ("life is calling you!"), while there is no mention of raising a child or associated struggles. *Choice C* is incorrect because the speaker frames the possibilities for her son in a positive light when she says that "great reaches, yet unknown" are waiting for him, and this positive outlook for the son is consistent throughout the text.

QUESTION 6

Choice A is the best answer because it best describes how the underlined portion functions in the text as a whole. The text says that the increased production quotas of food processing companies during World War II enabled employees to make better bargains in exchange for their labor. The underlined portion presents an example of this increased bargaining power: employees requested more favorable benefits, and employers complied because they were under pressure to fulfill the demanding terms of their contracts. Thus, the underlined portion of the text elaborates on a claim about labor relations in a particular industry (food processing) made earlier in the text.

Choice B is incorrect because there is no indication in the text that the economic factors that influenced food processing also influenced other parts of the economy; thus, the bargaining described in the underlined portion of the text cannot be called an example of a trend. *Choice C* is incorrect because the underlined portion supports the historical narrative of labor activism in food processing that is sketched in the text, instead of noting an exception to that narrative. *Choice D* is incorrect because while the underlined portion does discuss the demands that workers made in exchange for their labor, it does not discuss the identities of the workers.

QUESTION 7

Choice C is the best answer because it reflects how Putirka and Xu (Text 2) would likely characterize the conclusion presented in Text 1. Text 1 discusses a study by Mark Holland and colleagues in which they detected traces of lithium and sodium in the atmospheres of four white dwarf stars. The team claims that this supports the idea that exoplanets with continental crusts like Earth's once orbited these stars. Text 2 introduces Putirka and Xu, who indicate that sodium and lithium are present in several different minerals and that some of those minerals might exist in types of rock that are not found on Earth. Therefore, Putirka and Xu would likely describe the conclusion in Text 1 as questionable because it does not consider that lithium and sodium are also found in rocks that are not like Earth's continental crust.

Choice A is incorrect because the texts do not indicate how widely held any of the viewpoints described are. *Choice B* is incorrect because neither text discusses how new this area of study is. *Choice D* is incorrect because neither text discusses how likely lithium and sodium are to be detected by analyzing wavelengths of light.

QUESTION 8

Choice C is the best answer because it most accurately states how the narrator feels about being at summer camp. In the text, the narrator states that after arriving at the camp, he found it to be different than he'd expected and that as a result, he felt "scared, but also excited."

Choice A is incorrect. In the text, the narrator describes himself as "excited." Although excitement is a positive emotion, it isn't as intensely positive as feeling overjoyed is. Moreover, the narrator also notes that he felt "scared." In other words, his excitement (a positive emotion) is balanced with fear (a negative emotion). Given this mixture of positive and negative emotions, it would be inaccurate to characterize the narrator as overjoyed. *Choice B* is incorrect because in the text, the narrator describes himself as having felt both fear and excitement. Neither of these emotions can be thought of as peaceful and, in fact, are almost the opposite of a sense of peace. *Choice D* is incorrect because in the text, the narrator describes himself as both "scared" and "excited," not angry and jealous.

QUESTION 9

Choice B is the best answer because it presents a statement about how Richard Wagner achieved moments of extremely high volume in his operas that is supported by the text. The text states that European composers experimented with volume in their works by increasing the number of musicians in the orchestra and provides the example of Wagner, who "added more horns, trombones, and tubas to the orchestra." The text explains that by having more of these instruments playing at the same time, the overall volume of the orchestra could be dramatically increased at key moments in Wagner's operas.

Choice A is incorrect because the text never indicates that Wagner moved his operas indoors to achieve moments of extremely high volume, nor does it indicate that his operas were previously performed outdoors. The only technique discussed in the text for achieving extremely high volume is Wagner's addition of more instruments to create a bigger, louder orchestra. *Choice C* is incorrect because the text never says that Wagner built or used a specially designed concert hall to increase volume through echoes. The only technique discussed in the text is Wagner's addition of more instruments to create a bigger, louder orchestra. *Choice D* is incorrect because the text never mentions any special training for singers related to volume or singing for extended periods. The text's focus is entirely on the orchestra and how Wagner and other European composers used instruments to experiment with volume in their musical works.

QUESTION 10

Choice D is the best answer because it most accurately states the main idea of the text. According to the text, Gross and Altman's book is a "valuable resource" because it's a "complete, uncensored, unauthorized oral history" that features accounts from people involved with "every *Star Trek* television series and film" made. However, the text also points out an inherent shortcoming of the oral history approach used by the book's creators: the lack of an authorial voice that could unify the many accounts into a coherent narrative. Thus, the text's main idea is that while the book's attempt at presenting a comprehensive oral history of the *Star Trek* franchise is a worthwhile one, the approach the creators selected has an important limitation.

Choice A is incorrect. While the goal of the book's creators (providing a comprehensive history of the *Star Trek* franchise) could be described as lofty, the text's criticism of the book is focused on the shortcomings of the oral history form, not on events in the *Star Trek* franchise that were not reflected in the book. *Choice B* is incorrect because the text doesn't suggest that the book includes more accounts from people involved with television shows than with films. In fact, the text explicitly states that the book includes accounts from people involved with "every *Star Trek* television series and film" ever made. *Choice C* is incorrect because the text doesn't indicate that many people involved with the *Star Trek* franchise failed to participate in the book's oral history project. The only mention of the scope of participation states that the book includes accounts "from cast and crew members of every *Star Trek* television series and film to date." This information implies a high level of participation from relevant individuals, not a lack of participation.

QUESTION 11

Choice D is the best answer because it accurately reflects the data in the table. According to the table, the dolphin with ID FB43 has a recording year of 1992.

Choice A is incorrect. None of the dolphins in the table have a recording year of 1999. *Choice B* is incorrect. The table shows 2012 as the recording year for the dolphin with ID FB07, not ID FB43. *Choice C* is incorrect. None of the dolphins in the table have a recording year of 2020.

QUESTION 12

Choice A is the best answer because it presents a finding that, if true, would support the scholar's claim about Toni Morrison's likely goal of strengthening the presence of Black writers on Random House's list of published authors. The text explains that Morrison was the first Black woman to be an editor for Random House and that she was an editor there from 1967 to 1983. If it were true that Random House published a higher percentage of works by Black authors throughout the 1970s—during most of Morrison's time working there—than it had previously published, that would suggest that Morrison may have made a deliberate effort to strengthen the presence of Black authors on the list of Random House's published authors, thus supporting the scholar's claim.

Choice B is incorrect because the scholar's claim is about Morrison's work as an editor at a publishing company and her likely effort to strengthen the presence of Black writers on that company's list of published authors. It might be true that Black authors interviewed in the 1980s and 1990s often cited Morrison's novels as an influence on their work, but that finding would simply suggest something about how those authors approached their work; it wouldn't show that Morrison intended to increase the number of Black writers among the published authors specifically at Random House. *Choice C* is incorrect because the scholar's claim is about Morrison's work as an editor at a publishing company, not about her work as a novelist. Therefore, a finding that Morrison's novels published after 1983 sold more copies and were more widely acclaimed than her earlier novels would have no bearing on the claim that as an editor Morrison made an effort to ensure that more Black writers were present on Random House's list of published authors. *Choice D* is incorrect. Although the text discusses Morrison's work as an editor at Random House, the scholar's claim focuses on Morrison's likely effort in that role to increase the number of Black writers present on Random House's list of published authors, not on the influence she may have had on the content of the works she edited. Without knowing whether Morrison's stylistic influence led to more publications or if Morrison applied her influence specifically to works by Black writers, the finding that works edited by Morrison could be identified by stylistic characteristics would have no bearing on the claim that Morrison intended to strengthen the presence of Black writers among the published authors at Random House.

QUESTION 13

Choice A is the best answer because it most effectively uses data from the table to support the researchers' conclusion about the harvesting of clamshells by Neanderthals for use as tools. The text explains that Neanderthals used clamshells to make tools and that the sturdiest, and therefore the most desirable, shells for this purpose are found on the seafloor, not on the beach. However, the researchers also concluded that the clamshell tools made from shells from the seafloor are rarer than those made from shells from the beach. Meanwhile the table shows that at each depth, the number of tools made from shells from the beach exceeds the number made from the more desirable shells from the seafloor. The fact that the more desirable shells are less common suggests that it was significantly more difficult to harvest shells from the seafloor than from the beach.

Choice B is incorrect because knowing which depth represents the period of time with the highest Neanderthal population does not help answer the question of why the Neanderthals consistently made more tools from the less desirable shells from the beach than they made from the more desirable shells from the seafloor. *Choice C* is incorrect because it claims that the beach shells are more durable than the seafloor shells, which contradicts the text's description of shells from the seafloor as smoother and sturdier than shells from the beach. *Choice D* is incorrect because knowing which depth has the most artifacts or whether the clam population fluctuated does not help explain why tools made from the less desirable shells from the beach outnumber tools made from the more desirable shells from the seafloor.

QUESTION 14

Choice B is the best answer because it most logically completes the text's discussion of Anita Allen's argument about judges citing philosophers in their judicial opinions. The text indicates that judges sometimes cite philosophers when writing their judicial opinions and that, according to Allen, judges tend to cite philosophers whose views are in agreement with those of the judges themselves. Allen claims, however, that the best judicial opinions consider potential objections and rebut them, which suggests that judges may be able to strengthen their opinions by including discussions of philosophers with views contrary to their own.

Choice A is incorrect because Allen's claim is that judges could improve their judicial opinions by citing philosophers who disagree with the views expressed in the opinions, which would necessarily require judges to consult philosophical works. *Choice C* is incorrect because there's no discussion in the text about making judicial opinions more easily understood by any particular group of readers. The focus of the text is on Allen's claim that judicial opinions could be strengthened by the inclusion of discussions of philosophers whose views disagree with those of the judges authoring the opinions. *Choice D* is incorrect because the text presents Allen's argument that discussing philosophers whose views judges disagree with could strengthen judicial opinions, not that doing so could bring those opinions into line with views that are popular among philosophers.

QUESTION 15

Choice A is the best answer. The convention being tested is pronoun-antecedent agreement. The plural pronoun "they" agrees in number with the plural antecedent "customers."

Choice B is incorrect because the singular pronoun "one" doesn't agree in number with the plural antecedent "customers." *Choice C* is incorrect because the second person pronoun "you" isn't conventional as a substitute for "customers." It suggests that the audience ("you") is the customer. *Choice D* is incorrect because the singular pronoun "it" doesn't agree in number with the plural antecedent "customers."

QUESTION 16

Choice C is the best answer. The convention being tested is subject-verb agreement. The singular verb "has been" agrees in number with the singular subject "writing."

Choice A is incorrect because the plural verb "were" doesn't agree in number with the singular subject "writing." *Choice B* is incorrect because the plural verb "have been" doesn't agree in number with the singular subject "writing." *Choice D* is incorrect because the plural verb "are" doesn't agree in number with the singular subject "writing."

QUESTION 17

Choice A is the best answer. The convention being tested is finite and nonfinite verb forms within a sentence. A main clause requires a finite verb to perform the action of the subject (in this case, "embryos"), and this choice supplies the clause with the finite present tense verb "enter" to indicate how the embryos achieve diapause.

Choice B is incorrect because the nonfinite to-infinitive "to enter" doesn't supply the main clause with a finite verb. *Choice C* is incorrect because the nonfinite participle "having entered" doesn't supply the main clause with a finite verb. *Choice D* is incorrect because the nonfinite participle "entering" doesn't supply the main clause with a finite verb.

QUESTION 18

Choice A is the best answer. The convention being tested is the coordination of independent clauses within a sentence. An independent clause is a phrase containing a subject and a verb that can stand on its own as a sentence. This choice uses a comma and the coordinating conjunction "but" to join the first independent clause ("underlines...lower a book's value") and the second independent clause ("such markings...can be a gold mine to scholars") to create a compound sentence.

Choice B is incorrect because it results in a run-on sentence. The two independent clauses are fused without punctuation and/or a conjunction. *Choice C* is incorrect because it results in a comma splice. A comma can't be used in this way to mark the boundary between two independent clauses. *Choice D* is incorrect because a comma is needed to mark the boundary between two coordinated independent clauses.

QUESTION 19

Choice C is the best answer. The convention being tested is subject-verb agreement. The singular verb "outlines" agrees in number with the singular subject "document."

Choice A is incorrect because the plural verb "have outlined" doesn't agree in number with the singular subject "document." *Choice B* is incorrect because the plural verb "were outlining" doesn't agree in number with the singular subject "document." *Choice D* is incorrect because the plural verb "outline" doesn't agree in number with the singular subject "document."

QUESTION 20

Choice B is the best answer. The convention being tested is the use of verbs to express tense in a sentence. In this choice, the present tense verb "reach" is consistent with the present tense verbs "travel" and "are diverted" used to describe how atoms move through the synchrotron.

Choice A is incorrect because the future tense verb "will reach" is inconsistent with the present tense verbs used to describe how atoms move through the synchrotron. Though the atoms' movement is a recurring action and "will reach" can also be used to indicate a habitual or recurring action, it creates a logical inconsistency in this sentence when paired with the present tense verbs "travel" and "are diverted." *Choice C* is incorrect because the past perfect tense verb "had reached" is inconsistent with the present tense verbs used to describe how atoms move through the synchrotron. *Choice D* is incorrect because the present progressive tense verb "are reaching" is inconsistent with the present tense verbs used to describe how atoms move through the synchrotron. While both verbs occur in the present, the present progressive tense suggests that the action is currently in progress. This creates a logical inconsistency when paired with the present tense verbs "travel" and "are diverted," which offer a general description of the tendencies of the atoms' movement, rather than a description of an action that is currently in progress.

QUESTION 21

Choice C is the best answer. The convention being tested is the punctuation of a supplementary element within a sentence. The dash after "Springs" pairs with the dash after "earth" to separate the supplementary element "in this case, the porous rocks of the hills around Hot Springs" from the rest of the sentence.

Choice A is incorrect because it fails to use appropriate punctuation to separate the supplementary element from the rest of the sentence. *Choice B* is incorrect because a colon can't be paired with a dash in this way to separate the supplementary element from the rest of the sentence. *Choice D* is incorrect because a comma can't be paired with a dash in this way to separate the supplementary element from the rest of the sentence.

QUESTION 22

Choice A is the best answer. "In fact" logically signals that the information in this sentence about the large number of recordings in ANLA's collection emphasizes and supports the previous claim that ANLA is known for its impressive audio collection.

Choice B is incorrect because "after" illogically signals that the information in this sentence occurs later in a sequence of events than the previous claim about ANLA's impressive audio collection. Instead, the information about the large number of recordings emphasizes and supports that claim. *Choice C* is incorrect because "regardless" illogically signals that the information in this sentence is true despite the previous claim about ANLA's impressive audio collection. Instead, the information about the large number of recordings emphasizes and supports that claim. *Choice D* is incorrect because "instead" illogically signals that the information in this sentence presents an alternative to the previous claim about ANLA's impressive audio collection. Rather, the information about the large number of recordings emphasizes and supports that claim.

QUESTION 23

Choice B is the best answer. "Previously" logically signals that the event described in this sentence—Bigelow being named best director—occurred before Zhao's win. The fact that only one other woman had won the award before puts Zhao's win in perspective.

Choice A is incorrect because "as a result" illogically signals that the event described in this sentence occurred as a result or consequence of Zhao's win. Instead, it occurred before Zhao was named best director and puts Zhao's win in perspective. *Choice C* is incorrect because "however" illogically signals that the event described in this sentence occurred in spite of or in contrast to Zhao's win. Instead, it occurred before Zhao was named best director and puts Zhao's win in perspective. *Choice D* is incorrect because "likewise" illogically signals that this sentence merely adds a second, similar piece of information to the information about Zhao's win. Instead, the fact that only one other woman had won the award before puts Zhao's win in perspective.

QUESTION 24

Choice B is the best answer. "Next" logically signals that the action described in this sentence—Konkoly recording participants' eye movements—is the next step in Konkoly's experiment.

Choice A is incorrect because "specifically" illogically signals that this sentence specifies or elaborates on an aspect of the action described in the previous sentence. Instead, it describes the next step in Konkoly's experiment. *Choice C* is incorrect because "for instance" illogically signals that the action described in this sentence is an example of the action described in the previous sentence. Instead, it is the next step in Konkoly's experiment. *Choice D* is incorrect because "in sum" illogically signals that this sentence summarizes or concludes the action described in the previous sentence. Instead, it describes the next step in Konkoly's experiment.

QUESTION 25

Choice B is the best answer. The sentence specifies the average length of the green iguana: 4.8 feet.

Choice A is incorrect. While the sentence provides information about the green iguana, it doesn't specify the green iguana's average length. *Choice C* is incorrect. The sentence describes the diet of a species of reptile in Brazil; it doesn't specify the green iguana's average length. *Choice D* is incorrect. While the sentence provides information about the green iguana, it doesn't specify the green iguana's average length.

QUESTION 26

Choice A is the best answer. The sentence identifies the year in which the book was published.

Choice B is incorrect. While the sentence provides information about the book's author, it doesn't identify the year in which the book was published. *Choice C* is incorrect. While the sentence provides information about the book's historical use, it doesn't identify the year in which the book was published. *Choice D* is incorrect. While the sentence provides information about the book's contents, it doesn't identify the year in which the book was published.

QUESTION 27

Choice C is the best answer. The sentence emphasizes a difference between the portraits, noting that one is a painting and the other is a drawing.

Choice A is incorrect. The sentence emphasizes a similarity between the two portraits rather than a difference. *Choice B* is incorrect. The sentence makes a generalization about Enriquez's portraits; it doesn't emphasize a difference between the portraits of Jimenez and Anaya. *Choice D* is incorrect. While the sentence notes a difference between Jimenez and Anaya, it doesn't emphasize a difference between, or even mention, their portraits.

Reading and Writing

Module 2 — Higher Difficulty
(27 questions)

QUESTION 1

Choice D is the best answer because it most logically completes the text's discussion of baleen whale accessory spleens. In this context, "latent" means dormant or functionless. The text sets up a contrast between the idea that baleen whale accessory spleens appear not to have a function and the research indicating that the accessory spleen may actually have a role in supporting the whales' diving mechanisms. This context therefore conveys the idea that the assumption that baleen whale accessory spleens are latent may be incorrect.

Choice A is incorrect because it wouldn't make sense to say that the role of the accessory spleen is "replicable," or capable of being reproduced. The text indicates that the role of the accessory spleen seems to have no function, but some researchers think it does have a role; the text doesn't address whether the role of the accessory spleen could or couldn't be reproduced. *Choice B* is incorrect because suggesting that the role of the accessory spleen is "predetermined," or decided in advance, wouldn't make sense in context. Although the researchers may agree that the role of the accessory spleen or any other organ hasn't been determined in advance, the text focuses on the idea that the accessory spleen was thought to have been functionless but may in fact serve an active role for baleen whales. *Choice C* is incorrect because it's the opposite of what the context of the text is conveying. The second sentence of the text indicates that baleen whale accessory spleens may not be useless, not that they aren't "operative," or functional.

QUESTION 2

Choice D is the best answer because it most logically completes the text's discussion of the location of the province of Xoconochco within the Aztec Empire. As used in this context, "peripheral" means situated toward the outer bounds rather than the center. The text indicates that Xoconochco was located on a coast, hundreds of kilometers away from the capital of the Aztec Empire. The text also states that trade between the province and the capital required "a long overland journey." This context suggests that Xoconochco was situated toward an edge of the empire's territory rather than near its center.

Choice A is incorrect because it wouldn't make sense in context to refer to Xoconochco's location within the Aztec Empire as "unobtrusive," or not blatant or undesirably prominent; it's not clear how a province's physical location would or wouldn't be blatant. Instead of focusing on how noticeable

Xoconochco's location was, the text emphasizes the province's distance from the capital of the empire, pointing out that because of this distance trade between the two required "a long overland journey." *Choice B* is incorrect because the text indicates that the province of Xoconochco was located on a coast far from the capital of the Aztec Empire, not that it was "concealed," or kept out of sight or hidden from view. Nothing in the text suggests that Xoconochco was actually hidden such that people couldn't see it, and being hidden wouldn't necessarily result in trade between the province and the capital requiring "a long overland journey." *Choice C* is incorrect because to say that Xoconochco's location within the Aztec Empire was "approximate" would mean that the location either wasn't precisely correct or was close to some other location. Neither of these meanings would make sense in context because the text indicates that Xoconochco's location is known and that it was far from the empire's capital, so there's no reason to characterize the location as either not precisely correct or close to another location.

QUESTION 3

Choice C is the best answer because it most logically completes the text's discussion of Gabriela González and team's detection of gravitational waves. In this context, "ambiguity" means uncertainty or doubtfulness. The text explains that although skeptics had thought that direct evidence of gravitational waves would be too faint to be detected, researchers led by González claimed that a chirping sound captured by Laser Interferometer Gravitational-Wave Observatory antennas nevertheless provided such evidence. The text goes on to say that detailed statistical analysis confirmed the observation of gravitational waves with a high degree of confidence— that is, with near certainty—a finding that helped to preclude, or rule out, any claims that the signal's attribution to gravitational waves might be ambiguous or doubtful.

Choice A is incorrect. In this context, "inconspicuousness" would mean the quality of being unnoticeable or difficult to detect. Although the text indicates that skeptics had doubted whether gravitational waves could be observed directly because of their presumed faintness (which suggests that gravitational waves were expected to be difficult to detect), the blank portion of the text isn't referring to the possibility that gravitational waves are unnoticeable or undetectable. Instead, the focus of the last sentence is González's team's observation of a chirping sound that they attributed to gravitational waves, and it wouldn't make sense to say that through statistical analysis, they ruled out the possibility that the sound they observed was undetectable. Rather, the skeptical view presented in the text suggests that there could be some ambiguity about the source of the chirping, but statistical analysis virtually eliminated this uncertainty. *Choice B* is incorrect because in this context, "discretion" would mean good judgment, and it wouldn't make sense to say that an event, such as the detection of gravitational waves, would show judgment, much less that the event's capacity to exercise good judgment would be precluded by statistical analysis confirming its attribution. *Choice D* is incorrect because in this context, "probability" would mean likelihood, and the text states that statistical analysis, which confirmed the signal with a high degree of confidence, suggests the likelihood that the chirping sound was produced by gravitational waves, not that the analysis helped to preclude this likelihood.

QUESTION 4

Choice A is the best answer because it most logically completes the text's discussion of political blogs. In this context, "sanguine" means optimistic. The text begins by noting the rise of political blogs with readily identifiable ideological alignments in the early 2000s. The text then indicates that some commentators saw this as a positive development, citing a reason why (their difference from traditional news). Finally, the text goes on to contrast those commentators with others who have a negative opinion of the rise of political blogs (because they increase political polarization among their readers). This context supports the idea that the second group of commentators is less positive than the first: thus, the second group of commentators is less optimistic, or sanguine.

Choice B is incorrect because it would not make sense in this context to describe those commentators who have a negative opinion of political blogs as less "recalcitrant," or obstinately uncooperative, than those commentators who supported political blogs. *Choice C* is incorrect because the text gives no indication that those commentators who have a negative opinion of political blogs are less "misanthropic," or less contemptuous of humankind, than those commentators who have a positive opinion of political blogs—there is no indication in the text that those commentators who like political blogs would be contemptuous of humankind at all. *Choice D* is incorrect because there is no evidence that those commentators who have a negative opinion of political blogs are less "earnest," or sincere, than those who have a positive opinion of such blogs—presumably, both groups of commentators hold their beliefs with equal conviction.

QUESTION 5

Choice B is the best answer because it most accurately describes how the underlined portion functions in the text as a whole. The text presents the speaker's experience of viewing the sea. In the underlined portion, the speaker focuses on the idea that the waves hitting rocks on the shore are a relentless and enduring force: they are constantly pushed back ("ever repulsed") but always return ("ever rushing on"), as though they have an energy that can't be overcome ("a life that will not know defeat").

Choice A is incorrect. Although the underlined portion characterizes the waves as a relentless force (always "repulsed" but still "rushing on" and never being defeated), the speaker doesn't suggest that the surroundings are intimidating. Instead, the speaker presents the scene in a positive way, describing the "deep delight" of the "gladsome," or cheerful, waves and feeling "the heart / Leap joyous" while viewing the sea. *Choice C* is incorrect because the underlined portion doesn't suggest that the speaker is ambivalent, or has mixed feelings about, the natural world. Instead, it presents a single view of one part of the immediate surroundings: the speaker characterizes the sea's waves as an unstoppable force, since they are constantly pushed back but always return ("ever repulsed, yet ever rushing on"). *Choice D* is incorrect. Although the text later suggests the speaker's view of her own thoughts by referring to a "clouded brain" and a heart that leaps joyously, this reference neither occurs within the underlined portion nor establishes a clear contrast with the relentless determination of the waves. The underlined portion addresses only the speaker's view of the waves and doesn't suggest what her own thoughts might be.

QUESTION 6

Choice A is the best answer because based on Text 2, it represents how Behrenfeld and colleagues would most likely respond to the "conventional wisdom" discussed in Text 1. The conventional wisdom cited holds the opinion that when there is species diversity within a phytoplankton population, "one species should emerge after outcompeting the rest"—that is, after being so successful in competing for resources that the other species vanish from the population. However, Text 2 explains that according to Behrenfeld and colleagues, phytoplankton are so small and spaced so far apart in the water that there is "much less" direct competition for resources within phytoplankton populations than scientists had previously thought.

Choice B is incorrect because Text 2 never discusses whether routine replenishment of ocean nutrients affects competition between phytoplankton species. *Choice C* is incorrect because the interspecies competition discussed in both texts is specifically between phytoplankton species, and neither text considers whether phytoplankton compete for resources with larger nonphytoplankton species. *Choice D* is incorrect because according to Text 2, Behrenfeld and colleagues argue that water density decreases, not increases, competition between phytoplankton species.

QUESTION 7

Choice D is the best answer because it states why Wang and his team's discovery of the *Terropterus xiushanensis* fossil was significant. The text explains that up until Wang and his team's discovery, the only fossil evidence of mixopterids came from the paleocontinent of Laurussia. Wang and his team, however, identified fossil remains of a mixopterid species from the paleocontinent Gondwana. Therefore, the team's discovery was significant because the fossil remains of a mixopterid species were outside of the paleocontinent Laurussia.

Choice A is incorrect. Although the text states that Wang and his team identified fossilized remains of a mixopterid species that lived more than 400 million years ago, it doesn't indicate that mixopterid fossils previously found by scientists dated to a more recent period than that. *Choice B* is incorrect. Although the text states that mixopterids are related to modern arachnids and horseshoe crabs, it doesn't suggest that the fossil discovered by Wang and his team confirmed that this relationship is closer than scientists had previously thought. *Choice C* is incorrect because the team's fossil established the presence of mixopterids on Gondwana, not on Laurussia. Moreover, the text only discusses the fossil in relation to the geographical distribution of mixopterids, not in relation to their evolution.

QUESTION 8

Choice C is the best answer because it presents a statement about the difrasismo *in cuauhtli in ocelotl* that is directly supported by the text. The text begins by describing difrasismo, a device used in Classical Nahuatl poetry. The text then mentions the device's two functions: a formal one (giving structure to lines of verse) and a ritualistic one. The text indicates that the relation between the words in a difrasismo may appear tenuous without the additional information supplied by Aztec ceremonial culture but that the meaning becomes intelligible in the context of that information. Therefore, the difrasismo's apparent obscurity can be resolved when considered in the proper cultural context.

Choice A is incorrect because the text doesn't indicate that the two nouns used in a difrasismo are semantically equivalent; instead, the text indicates that the two nouns used in a difrasismo make up a single metaphor whose meaning is often intelligible only in the context of information supplied by Aztec ceremonial culture. *Choice B* is incorrect because the text doesn't indicate that there's a relationship between the formal function of the difrasismo and the difrasismo's intelligibility. Additionally, the text suggests that present-day readers who are familiar with Aztec ceremonial culture wouldn't find the difrasismo to be unintelligible.

Choice D is incorrect because the text doesn't indicate that the frequency of difrasismo's use in Classical Nahuatl is a necessary feature of intelligibility: the text indicates that an infrequently used difrasismo would presumably also be intelligible to members of an Aztec audience who are sufficiently familiar with Aztec ceremonial culture.

QUESTION 9

Choice B is the best answer because it effectively uses data from the graph to complete the statement about Rodrigo da Costa Portilho-Ramos and colleagues' conclusion. The graph shows the ratio of manganese to calcium in *L. pertusa* coral samples from the Alboran Sea and the Mauritanian coast. The graph reflects time in approximate years before present: in other words, the greater the number in years noted on the graph's horizontal axis, the farther that moment is in the past. The text indicates that the researchers tested the samples to determine whether oxygenation played a role in the decline of *L. pertusa*. The text goes on to note that a change in the ratio of manganese to calcium would signal an inverse, or opposite, change in oxygenation. According to the graph, the ratio of manganese to calcium in samples from the Alboran Sea increased from about 30 micromoles per mole 10,000 years ago to about 80 micromoles per mole 8,000 years ago, which means that oxygenation decreased between 10,000 and 8,000 years ago. Meanwhile, there was almost no discernible change in the ratio of manganese to calcium in samples from the Mauritanian coast between 12,000 and 10,000 years ago. According to the text, the population of *L. pertusa* declined significantly around 9,000 years ago in the Alboran Sea and around 11,000 years ago near the Mauritanian coast. Thus, the increase in the ratio of manganese to calcium around 9,000 years ago in the Alboran Sea coincides with the decline in the *L. pertusa* population, suggesting an association between the decrease in oxygenation and the decline in population of the coral. No such relationship is suggested around 11,000 years ago near the Mauritanian coast. So, oxygenation likely played a role in the *L. pertusa* decline in the Alboran Sea but not in the coral's decline near the Mauritanian coast.

Choice A is incorrect because it asserts the opposite of what the graph indicates regarding oxygenation in the Alboran Sea, and it misrepresents what the graph indicates about oxygenation near the Mauritanian coast. The graph indicates that at the time of the decline in *L. pertusa* (approximately 9,000 years ago), the samples from the Alboran Sea contained a ratio of manganese to calcium that was increasing. According to the text, this ratio inversely correlates with ocean oxygenation levels, so if the ratio was increasing, oxygenation was decreasing, not substantially increasing. Furthermore, the graph shows that the ratio of manganese to calcium remained relatively stable in coral samples from the Mauritanian coast during the period studied, which suggests that there was no discernible relationship between oxygenation and the coral's population decline in that location, not that there was a substantial decrease in oxygenation corresponding to the coral's decline. *Choice C* is incorrect. Although the graph suggests that the level of oxygenation in the Alboran Sea was higher before the decline in *L. pertusa* than after—because the ratio of manganese to calcium inversely correlates with ocean oxygenation levels and this ratio was lower before the decline than after—the graph doesn't support the claim that oxygenation near the Mauritanian coast was consistently low before and after the coral's decline there. Rather, the graph indicates that relative to coral samples from the Alboran Sea, the ratio of manganese to calcium in samples from near the Mauritanian coast was consistently low, which suggests that oxygenation levels were relatively high both before and after the decline of *L. pertusa*. *Choice D* is incorrect because it states the opposite of what the graph indicates: the graph shows that throughout the period studied, the ratio of manganese to calcium was higher in coral samples from the Alboran Sea than it was in samples from near the Mauritanian coast. Since the text indicates that the ratio of manganese to calcium inversely correlates with ocean oxygenation levels, oxygenation in the Alboran Sea was therefore lower than, not higher than, oxygenation near the Mauritanian coast during the period studied. Moreover, even if choice D did accurately represent the graph, it wouldn't effectively complete the statement since a comparison of the ocean oxygenation levels at the two locations is not relevant to the claim that a decline in oxygenation levels was associated with the decline of *L. pertusa* in the Alboran Sea but not near the Mauritanian coast.

QUESTION 10

Choice A is the best answer because it presents a finding that, if true, would most strongly support the researchers' claim that they found evidence that experiencing awe can make people feel more connected to others and thus more likely to behave altruistically (with beneficial and unselfish concern for others). According to the text, the researchers tested for this effect by first having participants look at either something known to be awe-inspiring (very tall trees) or something ordinary (a plain building) and then purposely spilling pens near the participants. The finding that participants who had looked at the trees helped pick up significantly more pens than did participants who had looked at the building would support the researchers' claim by demonstrating that the people who had experienced awe behaved more altruistically when the experimenter needed help than the other participants did.

Choice B is incorrect because a finding about helpful participants using positive words to describe the trees and the building after the experiment was over wouldn't have any bearing on the researchers' claim that experiencing awe increases altruistic behavior. The text doesn't address the use of positive words to describe things or suggest any connection between using such words and having experienced awe, so that behavior wouldn't serve as evidence that experiencing awe played a role in promoting helpful behavior. *Choice C* is incorrect because a finding that participants who didn't help the experimenter were significantly more likely than others to report having experienced awe whether they had looked at the building or the trees would weaken the researchers' claim that experiencing awe increases altruistic behavior by suggesting that the opposite might be true—that experiencing awe is in fact linked to choosing not to act in a way that benefits someone else. *Choice D* is incorrect because a finding about participants noticing that the experimenter had dropped the pens wouldn't have any bearing on the researchers' claim about people behaving altruistically. Being aware of a challenge or problem isn't necessarily beneficial on its own and isn't the same as offering help, so the finding wouldn't support the idea that experiencing awe increases altruistic behavior.

QUESTION 11

Choice B is the best answer because it describes data from the graph that support Taylor and colleagues' conclusion that spray coating holds promise for improving the power conversion efficiency of ETLs in perovskite solar cells. The text explains that perovskite solar cells' efficiency at converting light into electricity is diminished by their electron transport layer (ETL), which is applied through spin coating, but that Taylor's team devised a new spray coating method for applying the ETL that improves its power conversion efficiency. The graph displays data on the power conversion efficiency of solar cells in tests conducted by Taylor's team, with bars for both the highest- and lowest-performing ETLs in two data categories: spray coating and spin coating. According to the graph, the lowest-performing ETL applied through spray coating had a power conversion efficiency of between 14% and 16%, while the highest-performing ETL applied through spin coating had a power conversion efficiency of less than 14%. These data confirm that ETLs applied through novel spray coating are more efficient than those applied though traditional spin coating. Thus, the data support Taylor and colleagues' conclusion about spray coating's potential value.

Choice A is incorrect. Although this claim correctly describes the data in the graph by stating that both the lowest-performing ETL applied through spin coating and the lowest-performing ETL applied through spray coating had a power conversion efficiency greater than 10%, this relationship in the data doesn't support or relate to Taylor and colleagues' conclusion that spray coating promises greater efficiency for solar cells than traditional spin coating does. *Choice C* is incorrect. This claim does address the greater power conversion efficiency of the highest-performing ETL applied through spray coating, compared with the highest-performing ETL applied through spin coating. However, it also incorrectly cites the value for the efficiency of the highest-performing ETL applied through spray coating as approximately 13%, instead of a value between 14% and 16%, and the value for the efficiency of the highest-performing ETL applied through spin coating as approximately 11%, instead of a value between 12% and 14%, as shown in the graph. *Choice D* is incorrect because Taylor and colleagues' conclusion is based on the difference in the power conversion efficiency of ETLs applied through spray coating and that of ETLs applied through spin coating, not on the difference between the highest- and lowest-performing ETLs applied through just spray coating.

QUESTION 12

Choice C is the best answer because it presents a finding that, if true, would weaken the claim made by people who favor the traditional view of voter behavior. According to the text, people who favor that view believe that voting in an election doesn't change a voter's attitude toward the candidates in that election. If Washington and Mullainathan found that two years after an election, attitudes toward the winning candidate were significantly more polarized among subjects who had voted than among subjects who had been too young to vote, that would suggest that the act of voting did have an effect on the voters' attitudes toward the candidates, which would undermine the claim that voting doesn't change voters' attitudes.

Choice A is incorrect because a finding about links between subjects' attitudes and general political orientation, regardless of age and ability to vote, wouldn't address the presence or absence of changes in attitudes among those subjects who did actually vote. Therefore, the finding wouldn't have any bearing on the claim that voting in an election doesn't change a voter's attitude toward the candidates in that election. *Choice B* is incorrect because a finding that positive attitudes toward a winning candidate significantly increased in the two years after the election among subjects who had been too young to vote would involve only people who didn't vote; therefore, the finding wouldn't have any bearing on the claim that when people do vote, the act of voting doesn't change their attitudes toward the candidates. *Choice D* is incorrect because the finding that subjects in both groups were more likely to have negative attitudes than positive attitudes toward the winning candidate two years after an election would reflect all subjects' attitudes at one particular time whether they voted or not, rather than the presence or absence of a change in voters' attitudes after voting. Therefore, the finding would neither weaken nor strengthen the claim that voting in an election doesn't change a voter's attitude toward the candidates.

QUESTION 13

Choice B is the best answer because it presents the conclusion that most logically follows from the text's discussion of the study by Versace and colleagues. The text indicates that newborn animals of some species are attracted to faces and to stimuli that resemble faces. These species, the text says, share two characteristics: they're social and they practice parental care, meaning that parents care for their young. The text goes on to describe Versace and colleagues' experiment, which showed that *Testudo* tortoises, which aren't social and don't practice parental care, were attracted to a stimulus that resembles a face. Since Versace and colleagues have shown that a species that isn't social and doesn't practice parental care nevertheless has the innate characteristic of being attracted to face-like stimuli, it follows that this characteristic shouldn't be assumed to be an adaptation related to social interaction or parental care.

Choice A is incorrect because the text indicates that the tortoise hatchlings, which are solitary and don't practice parental care, were attracted to the face-like stimuli, not that they perceived the stimuli as threatening. *Choice C* is incorrect because the phenomenon discussed in the text is an attraction to faces and face-like stimuli on the part of newborn animals, which can't show any learned characteristics since they were just born. Additionally, the text tells us that the tortoises Versace and colleagues studied aren't social and don't practice parental care, so any findings about those tortoises wouldn't be relevant to the question of whether an attraction to faces in social species that practice parental care is innate or learned. *Choice D* is incorrect because the text gives no indication that adult tortoises were tested on face-like stimuli and, if adults were in fact tested, no information about how they responded is provided. Since no information about adult tortoises' responses is provided, no conclusion comparing those responses to the responses of newly hatched tortoises can be supported.

QUESTION 14

Choice A is the best answer because it presents the conclusion that most logically follows from the text's discussion of the study of capuchin monkeys' cognitive abilities. The text explains that the study failed to distinguish between outcomes for the tasks performed by the capuchin monkeys, such that simpler tasks requiring less dexterity, or skill, were judged by the same criteria as tasks that demanded more dexterity. Because the study didn't account for this discrepancy, the researchers might have assumed that observed differences in performance were due to the abilities of the monkeys rather than the complexity of the tasks. In other words, the results may suggest cognitive differences among the monkeys even though such differences may not really exist.

Choice B is incorrect because the text focuses on the fact that the tasks assigned to the capuchin monkeys in the study varied in difficulty and that the variety wasn't taken into consideration. The text doesn't suggest that the capuchin monkeys couldn't perform certain tasks, just that some tasks were more difficult to do. *Choice C* is incorrect because the text doesn't suggest that the study's results are indicative of the abilities of capuchin monkeys but not of other monkey species; in fact, the text suggests that the results may not even be an accurate reflection of capuchin monkeys' abilities. *Choice D* is incorrect because the text doesn't indicate that the researchers compared results for artificial tasks with those for tasks encountered in the wild, although the tasks described in the text—sliding a panel and putting a straw in a bottle—are presumably artificial.

QUESTION 15

Choice C is the best answer. The convention being tested is punctuation between a subject and a verb. When, as in this case, a subject ("her 2019 novel *Gingerbread*") is immediately followed by a verb ("offers"), no punctuation is needed.

Choice A is incorrect because no punctuation is needed between the subject and the verb. *Choice B* is incorrect because no punctuation is needed between the subject and the verb. *Choice D* is incorrect because no punctuation is needed between the subject and the verb.

QUESTION 16

Choice D is the best answer. The convention being tested is the use of punctuation around noun phrases. No punctuation is needed because the noun phrase "aluminum oxide" is a restrictive appositive, meaning that it provides essential identifying information about the noun phrase before it, "the chemical compound," and thus doesn't require punctuation around it.

Choice A is incorrect because no punctuation is needed. *Choice B* is incorrect because no punctuation is needed. *Choice C* is incorrect because the noun phrase "aluminum oxide" is a restrictive appositive. Setting the phrase off with punctuation suggests that it could be removed without affecting the coherence of the sentence, which isn't the case.

QUESTION 17

Choice A is the best answer. The convention being tested is the use of punctuation to mark boundaries between supplements and clauses. The comma after "equations" is used to separate the independent clause ("Hopper's...equation") from the supplementary adverb phrase "though." The colon after "though" is used to mark the boundary between the clause ending with "though" and the following clause ("as...age"). A colon used in this way introduces information that illustrates or explains information that has come before it. In this case, the colon after "though" introduces the following explanation of how Hopper's subsequent career would involve more than just solving equations: she would become a pioneering computer programmer.

Choice B is incorrect because it results in a comma splice. A comma can't be used in this way to join two independent clauses ("Hopper's...though" and "as...age") such as these. *Choice C* is incorrect because it results in an illogical sequence of sentences. Placing the period after "equations" and beginning the next sentence with "Though" illogically suggests that the following information (that Hopper would help usher in the digital age) is contrary to the information in the previous sentence (Hopper's subsequent career would involve more than just solving equations). Instead, the information that follows supports the information from the previous sentence by explaining how her work and influence extended beyond solely solving equations. *Choice D* is incorrect because it results in a run-on sentence. The two independent clauses ("Hopper's...though" and "as...age") are fused without punctuation.

QUESTION 18

Choice D is the best answer. The convention being tested is subject-verb agreement. The plural verb "attest" agrees in number with the plural subject "trailblazing accomplishments."

Choice A is incorrect because the singular verb "attests" doesn't agree in number with the plural subject "trailblazing accomplishments." *Choice B* is incorrect because the singular verb "has attested" doesn't agree in number with the plural subject "trailblazing accomplishments." *Choice C* is incorrect because the singular verb "is attesting" doesn't agree in number with the plural subject "trailblazing accomplishments."

QUESTION 19

Choice A is the best answer. The convention being tested is the use of verb forms within a sentence. The nonfinite present participle "suggesting" is correctly used to form a restrictive participial phrase ("suggesting...Holocene") within the main clause ("This hypothesis...cannot stand..."). This participial phrase functions as part of the sentence's subject ("This...Holocene"), providing essential identifying information about what the hypothesis states— namely, that certain trees survived without interruption or human intervention throughout the Holocene.

Choice B is incorrect because it results in an ungrammatical sentence. The finite verb "suggested" can't be used in this way within the subject of the sentence. *Choice C* is incorrect because it results in an ungrammatical sentence. The finite verb "suggests" can't be used in this way within the subject of the sentence. *Choice D* is incorrect because it results in an ungrammatical sentence. The finite verb "has suggested" can't be used in this way within the subject of the sentence.

QUESTION 20

Choice B is the best answer. The convention being tested is the use of verbs to express tense in a sentence. In this choice, the present tense verb "reach" is consistent with the present tense verbs "travel" and "are diverted" used to describe how atoms move through the synchrotron.

Choice A is incorrect because the future tense verb "will reach" is inconsistent with the present tense verbs used to describe how atoms move through the synchrotron. Though the atoms' movement is a recurring action and "will reach" can also be used to indicate a habitual or recurring action, it creates a logical inconsistency in this sentence when paired with the present tense verbs "travel" and "are diverted." *Choice C* is incorrect because the past perfect tense verb "had reached" is inconsistent with the present tense verbs used to describe how atoms move through the synchrotron. *Choice D* is incorrect because the present progressive tense verb "are reaching" is inconsistent with the present tense verbs used to describe how atoms move through the synchrotron. While both verbs occur in the present, the present progressive tense suggests that the action is currently in progress. This creates a logical inconsistency when paired with the present tense verbs "travel" and "are diverted," which offer a general description of the tendencies of the atoms' movement, rather than a description of an action that is currently in progress.

QUESTION 21

Choice D is the best answer. The convention being tested is subject-modifier placement. This choice makes "silica glass's atomic arrangement" the subject of the sentence and places it immediately after the modifying phrase "compared to that of alumina glass." In doing so, this choice clearly establishes that silica glass's atomic arrangement—and not another noun in the sentence— is being compared to the atomic arrangement ("that") of alumina glass.

Choice A is incorrect because it results in a dangling modifier. The placement of the noun phrase "silica glass" immediately after the modifying phrase illogically suggests that silica glass itself (rather than its atomic arrangement) is being compared to alumina glass's atomic arrangement. *Choice B* is incorrect because it results in a dangling modifier. The placement of the noun phrase "silica glass" immediately after the modifying phrase illogically suggests that silica glass itself (rather than its atomic arrangement) is being compared to alumina glass's atomic arrangement. *Choice C* is incorrect because it results in a dangling modifier. The placement of the noun phrase "a significant disadvantage" immediately after the modifying phrase illogically suggests that "a significant disadvantage" is being compared to alumina glass's atomic arrangement.

QUESTION 22

Choice C is the best answer. "Indeed" logically signals that the description of the art installation in this sentence—its blue room and preening unicorn that leave visitors "dazzled and confused"—offers additional emphasis in support of the previous sentence's claim about the installation's "whimsical yet perplexing experience."

Choice A is incorrect because "second" illogically signals that the description in this sentence is a second, separate claim from the previous sentence's claim about the installation's "whimsical yet perplexing experience." Instead, the specific details describing the installation emphasize and support the previous claim. *Choice B* is incorrect because "instead" illogically signals that the description in this sentence is an alternative to the previous sentence's claim about the installation's "whimsical yet perplexing experience." Rather, the specific details describing the installation emphasize and support that claim. *Choice D* is incorrect because "nevertheless" illogically signals that the description in this sentence is true despite the previous sentence's claim about the installation's "whimsical yet perplexing experience." Instead, the specific details describing the installation emphasize and support that claim.

QUESTION 23

Choice D is the best answer. "As such" correctly signals that the claim in this sentence—that Ostrom's work is a repudiation of the "tragedy of the commons" view—follows logically from the information about Ostrom's studies in the previous sentence. According to that sentence, Ostrom's studies demonstrate that common pool resources can in fact be sustainably managed by the people who use them.

Choice A is incorrect because "by contrast" illogically signals that the information in this sentence contrasts with the information about Ostrom's studies in the previous sentence. Instead, the claim that Ostrom's work repudiates the "tragedy of the commons" view follows logically from that information. *Choice B* is incorrect because "for example" illogically signals that the claim in this sentence exemplifies the information about Ostrom's studies in the previous sentence. Instead, the claim that Ostrom's work repudiates the "tragedy of the commons" view follows logically from that information. *Choice C* is incorrect because "that said" illogically signals that the information in this sentence is an exception or caveat to the information about Ostrom's studies in the previous sentence. Instead, the claim that Ostrom's work repudiates the "tragedy of the commons" view follows logically from that information.

QUESTION 24

Choice D is the best answer. The sentence uses "both" to emphasize a thematic similarity between Tan's two books, noting that both *Tales from Outer Suburbia* and *Tales from the Inner City* describe surreal events occurring in otherwise ordinary places.

Choice A is incorrect. The sentence emphasizes a difference (one contains fewer stories than the other), not a similarity, between the two books. *Choice B* is incorrect. The sentence indicates that Tan's books were published ten years apart; it doesn't emphasize a similarity between the two books. *Choice C* is incorrect. The sentence uses "unlike" to emphasize a difference between *Tales from Outer Suburbia* and *Tales from the Inner City*; it doesn't emphasize a similarity between the two books.

QUESTION 25

Choice B is the best answer. The sentence presents the study, describing it as a 2013 analysis of Quanhucun cat bone fragments, and its conclusions, indicating what the analysis suggests about cat domestication in Quanhucun.

Choice A is incorrect because the sentence focuses on the study's methodology; it doesn't present conclusions from the study. *Choice C* is incorrect. While the sentence provides a general overview of the study, it doesn't present conclusions from the study. *Choice D* is incorrect. The sentence describes a finding from the study; it doesn't present conclusions from the study.

QUESTION 26

Choice C is the best answer. The sentence effectively introduces the poetry collection *Precario/Precarious*, noting that it is a collection by Vicuña that was published in 1983 by Tanam Press.

Choice A is incorrect. While the sentence mentions the 1983 poetry collection *Precario/Precarious*, it focuses mainly on Vicuña's visual art. *Choice B* is incorrect. The sentence doesn't introduce the 1983 poetry collection *Precario/Precarious*; instead, it introduces Vicuña. *Choice D* is incorrect. The sentence emphasizes the location of Vicuña's 1971 exhibition *Pinturas, poemas y explicaciones*; it doesn't introduce the 1983 poetry collection *Precario/Precarious*.

QUESTION 27

Choice A is the best answer. The sentence emphasizes the aim of the research study by highlighting what the researchers conducting the study wanted to know—specifically, which factors influence clutch size among lizards.

Choice B is incorrect because the sentence emphasizes what researchers determined at the end of the study, not what the study's aim was. *Choice C* is incorrect because the sentence emphasizes a finding from the research study, not the aim of the study. *Choice D* is incorrect because the sentence emphasizes the research study's methodology, not its aim.

Math

Module 1
(22 questions)

QUESTION 1

Choice D is correct. The given expression is equivalent to $(2x^2 + x + (-9)) + (x^2 + 6x + 1)$, which can be rewritten as $(2x^2 + x^2) + (x + 6x) + (-9 + 1)$. Adding like terms in this expression yields $3x^2 + 7x + (-8)$, or $3x^2 + 7x - 8$.

Choice A is incorrect and may result from conceptual or calculation errors.
Choice B is incorrect and may result from conceptual or calculation errors.
Choice C is incorrect and may result from conceptual or calculation errors.

QUESTION 2

Choice C is correct. It's given that John made a $16 payment each month for p months. The total amount of these payments can be represented by the expression $16p$. The down payment can be added to that amount to find the total amount John paid, yielding the expression $16p + 37$. It's given that John paid a total of $165. Therefore, the expression for the total amount John paid can be set equal to that amount, yielding the equation $16p + 37 = 165$.

Choice A is incorrect and may result from conceptual or calculation errors.
Choice B is incorrect and may result from conceptual or calculation errors.
Choice D is incorrect and may result from conceptual or calculation errors.

QUESTION 3

Choice A is correct. Dividing each side of the given equation by 7 yields $m = \dfrac{2(n + p)}{7}$.

Choice B is incorrect and may result from conceptual or calculation errors.
Choice C is incorrect. This equation is equivalent to $7 + m = 2(n + p)$, not $7m = 2(n + p)$. *Choice D is incorrect and may result from conceptual or calculation errors.*

QUESTION 4

Choice C is correct. It's given that the function g is defined by $g(x) = \sqrt{8x + 1}$. Substituting 3 for x in the given function yields $g(3) = \sqrt{8(3) + 1}$, which is equivalent to $g(3) = \sqrt{25}$, or $g(3) = 5$. Therefore, the value of $g(3)$ is 5.

Choice A is incorrect and may result from conceptual or calculation errors. *Choice B* is incorrect and may result from conceptual or calculation errors. *Choice D* is incorrect. This is the value of 8(3) + 1, not $\sqrt{8(3) + 1}$.

QUESTION 5

Choice C is correct. If one of these students is selected at random, the probability of selecting a student whose vote for the new mascot was for a lion is given by the number of votes for a lion divided by the total number of votes. The given table indicates that the number of votes for a lion is 20 votes, and the total number of votes is 80 votes. The table gives the distribution of votes for 80 students, and the table shows a total of 80 votes were counted. It follows that each of the 80 students voted exactly once. Thus, the probability of

selecting a student whose vote for the new mascot was for a lion is $\frac{20}{80}$, or $\frac{1}{4}$.

Choice A is incorrect and may result from conceptual or calculation errors. *Choice B* is incorrect and may result from conceptual or calculation errors. *Choice D* is incorrect and may result from conceptual or calculation errors.

QUESTION 6

The correct answer is 224. It's given that a student council group uses the function $p(x) = 5x - 220$ to determine their profit $p(x)$, in dollars, for selling x school posters. Substituting 900 for $p(x)$ in the given function yields $900 = 5x - 220$. Adding 220 to each side of this equation yields $1,120 = 5x$. Dividing each side of this equation by 5 yields $224 = x$. Therefore, in order to earn a profit of $900, they must sell 224 school posters.

QUESTION 7

Choice B is correct. The equation representing a linear model can be written in the form $y = a + bx$, or $y = bx + a$, where b is the slope of the graph of the model and $(0, a)$ is the y-intercept of the graph of the model. The scatterplot shows that as the x-values of the data points increase, the y-values of the data points decrease, which means the graph of an appropriate linear model has a negative slope. Therefore, $b < 0$. The scatterplot also shows that the data points are close to the y-axis at a positive value of y. Therefore, the y-intercept of the graph of an appropriate linear model has a positive y-coordinate, which means $a > 0$. Of the given choices, only choice B, $y = -1.9x + 10.1$, has a negative value for b, the slope, and a positive value for a, the y-coordinate of the y-intercept.

Choice A is incorrect. The graph of this model has a y-intercept with a negative y-coordinate, not a positive y-coordinate. *Choice C* is incorrect. The graph of this model has a positive slope, not a negative slope, and a y-intercept with a negative y-coordinate, not a positive y-coordinate. *Choice D* is incorrect. The graph of this model has a positive slope, not a negative slope.

QUESTION 8

The correct answer is 1. Subtracting the second equation from the first equation in the given system of equations yields $(3x - 3x) + (6 - 4) = 4y - 2y$, which is equivalent to $0 + 2 = 2y$, or $2 = 2y$. Dividing each side of this equation by 2 yields $1 = y$.

QUESTION 9

The correct answer is 14. The maximum value is the largest value in the data set. The frequency refers to the number of times a data value occurs. The given frequency table shows that for this data set, the data value 6 occurs three times, the data value 7 occurs three times, the data value 8 occurs eight times, the data value 9 occurs eight times, the data value 10 occurs nine times, the data value 11 occurs eleven times, the data value 12 occurs nine times, the data value 13 occurs zero times, and the data value 14 occurs six times. Therefore, the maximum data value in the data set is 14.

QUESTION 10

Choice D is correct. The area, A, of a circle is given by the formula $A = \pi r^2$, where r represents the radius of the circle. It's given that circle K has a radius of 4 millimeters (mm). Substituting 4 for r in the formula $A = \pi r^2$ yields $A = \pi(4)^2$, or $A = 16\pi$. Therefore, the area of circle K is 16π mm^2. It's given that circle L has an area of 100π mm^2. Therefore, the total area, in mm^2, of circles K and L is $16\pi + 100\pi$, or 116π.

Choice A is incorrect. This is the sum of the radii, in mm, of circles K and L multiplied by π, not the total area, in mm^2, of the circles. *Choice B* is incorrect. This is the sum of the diameters, in mm, of circles K and L multiplied by π, not the total area, in mm^2, of the circles. *Choice C* is incorrect and may result from conceptual or calculation errors.

QUESTION 11

Choice D is correct. The value of $4 - 3x$ can be found by isolating this expression in the given equation. Subtracting 2 from both sides of the given equation yields $9(4 - 3x) = 8(4 - 3x) + 16$. Subtracting $8(4 - 3x)$ from both sides of this equation yields $9(4 - 3x) - 8(4 - 3x) = 16$, which gives $1(4 - 3x) = 16$, or $4 - 3x = 16$. Therefore, the value of $4 - 3x$ is 16.

Choice A is incorrect and may result from conceptual or calculation errors. *Choice B* is incorrect. This is the value of x, not $4 - 3x$. *Choice C* is incorrect and may result from conceptual or calculation errors.

QUESTION 12

Choice B is correct. If two triangles are similar, then their corresponding angles are congruent. It's given that right triangle FGH is similar to right triangle JKL and angle F corresponds to angle J. It follows that angle F is congruent to angle J and, therefore, the measure of angle F is equal to the measure of angle J. The sine ratios of angles of equal measure are equal. Since the measure of angle F is equal to the measure of angle J, $\sin(F) = \sin(J)$. It's given that $\sin(F) = \frac{308}{317}$. Therefore, $\sin(J)$ is $\frac{308}{317}$.

Choice A is incorrect. This is the value of $\cos(J)$, not the value of $\sin(J)$. *Choice C* is incorrect. This is the reciprocal of the value of $\sin(J)$, not the value of $\sin(J)$. *Choice D* is incorrect. This is the reciprocal of the value of $\cos(J)$, not the value of $\sin(J)$.

QUESTION 13

Choice D is correct. It's given that a wire with a length of 106 inches is cut into two parts. It's also given that one part has a length of x inches and the other part has a length of y inches. This can be represented by the equation $x + y = 106$.

It's also given that the value of x is 6 more than 4 times the value of y. This can be represented by the equation $x = 4y + 6$. Substituting $4y + 6$ for x in the equation $x + y = 106$ yields $4y + 6 + y = 106$, or $5y + 6 = 106$. Subtracting 6 from each side of this equation yields $5y = 100$. Dividing each side of this equation by 5 yields $y = 20$. Substituting 20 for y in the equation $x = 4y + 6$ yields $x = 4(20) + 6$, or $x = 86$.

Choice A is incorrect. This value represents less than half of the total length of 106 inches; however, x represents the length of the longer part of the wire, since it's given that the value of x is 6 more than 4 times the value of y. *Choice B* is incorrect. This value represents less than half of the total length of 106 inches; however, x represents the length of the longer part of the wire, since it's given that the value of x is 6 more than 4 times the value of y. *Choice C* is incorrect. This represents a part that is 6 more than the length of the other part, rather than 6 more than 4 times the length of the other part.

QUESTION 14

Choice A is correct. It's given that a certain township consists of a 5-hectare industrial park and a 24-hectare neighborhood and that the total number of trees in the township is 4,529. It's also given that the equation $5x + 24y = 4{,}529$ represents this situation. Since the total number of trees for a given area can be determined by taking the size of the area, in hectares, times the average number of trees per hectare, the best interpretation of $5x$ is the number of trees in the industrial park and the best interpretation of $24y$ is the number of trees in the neighborhood. Since 5 is the size of the industrial park, in hectares, the best interpretation of x is the average number of trees per hectare in the industrial park.

Choice B is incorrect and may result from conceptual errors. *Choice C* is incorrect and may result from conceptual errors. *Choice D* is incorrect and may result from conceptual errors.

QUESTION 15

Choice B is correct. Since $\frac{12}{12} = 1$, multiplying the exponent of the given expression by $\frac{12}{12}$ yields an equivalent expression: $a^{\left(\frac{11}{12}\right)\left(\frac{12}{12}\right)} = a^{\left(\frac{132}{144}\right)}$.

Since $\frac{132}{144} = 132\left(\frac{1}{144}\right)$, the expression $a^{\frac{132}{144}}$ can be rewritten as $a^{(132)\left(\frac{1}{144}\right)}$.

Applying properties of exponents, this expression can be rewritten as $(a^{132})^{\frac{1}{144}}$.

An expression of the form $(m)^{\frac{1}{k}}$, where $m > 0$ and $k > 0$, is equivalent to $\sqrt[k]{m}$.

Therefore, $(a^{132})^{\frac{1}{144}}$ is equivalent to $\sqrt[144]{a^{132}}$.

Choice A is incorrect and may result from conceptual or calculation errors. *Choice C* is incorrect and may result from conceptual or calculation errors. *Choice D* is incorrect and may result from conceptual or calculation errors.

QUESTION 16

The correct answer is 76. It's given that the graph of $y = g(x)$ is the result of translating the graph of $y = f(x)$ up 4 units in the xy-plane. It follows that the graph of $y = g(x)$ is the same as the graph of $y = f(x) + 4$. Substituting $g(x)$ for y in the equation $y = f(x) + 4$ yields $g(x) = f(x) + 4$. It's given that $f(x) = (x - 6)(x - 2)(x + 6)$. Substituting $(x - 6)(x - 2)(x + 6)$ for $f(x)$ in the equation $g(x) = f(x) + 4$ yields $g(x) = (x - 6)(x - 2)(x + 6) + 4$. Substituting 0 for x in this equation yields $g(0) = (0 - 6)(0 - 2)(0 + 6) + 4$, or $g(0) = 76$. Thus, the value of $g(0)$ is 76.

QUESTION 17

The correct answer is 35. The first equation in the given system of equations defines y as $4x + 1$. Substituting $4x + 1$ for y in the second equation in the given system of equations yields $4(4x + 1) = 15x - 8$. Applying the distributive property on the left-hand side of this equation yields $16x + 4 = 15x - 8$. Subtracting $15x$ from each side of this equation yields $x + 4 = -8$. Subtracting 4 from each side of this equation yields $x = -12$. Substituting -12 for x in the first equation of the given system of equations yields $y = 4(-12) + 1$, or $y = -47$. Substituting -12 for x and -47 for y into the expression $x - y$ yields $-12 - (-47)$, or 35.

QUESTION 18

Choice D is correct. The y-intercept of a graph in the ty-plane is the point where $t = 0$. For the given function f, the y-intercept of the graph of $y = f(t)$ in the ty-plane can be found by substituting 0 for t in the equation $y = 8,000(0.65)^t$, which gives $y = 8,000(0.65)^0$. This is equivalent to $y = 8,000(1)$, or $y = 8,000$. Therefore, the y-intercept of the graph of $y = f(t)$ is $(0, 8,000)$. It's given that the function f models the number of coupons a company sent to their customers at the end of each year. Therefore, $f(t)$ represents the estimated number of coupons the company sent to their customers at the end of each year. It's also given that t represents the number of years since the end of 1998. Therefore, $t = 0$ represents 0 years since the end of 1998, or the end of 1998. Thus, the best interpretation of the y-intercept of the graph of $y = f(t)$ is that the estimated number of coupons the company sent to their customers at the end of 1998 was 8,000.

Choice A is incorrect and may result from conceptual or calculation errors.
Choice B is incorrect and may result from conceptual or calculation errors.
Choice C is incorrect and may result from conceptual or calculation errors.

QUESTION 19

Choice D is correct. It's given that a hose puts $88x$ ounces of water in a bucket in $5y$ minutes. Therefore, the rate at which the hose puts water in the bucket, in ounces per minute, can be represented by the expression $\frac{88x}{5y}$.

Let w represent the number of ounces of water the hose puts in the bucket in $9y$ minutes at this rate. It follows that the rate at which the hose puts water in the bucket, in ounces per minute, can be represented by the expression $\frac{w}{9y}$.

The expressions $\frac{88x}{5y}$ and $\frac{w}{9y}$ represent the same rate, so it follows that $\frac{88x}{5y} = \frac{w}{9y}$. Multiplying both sides of this equation by $9y$ yields $\frac{792xy}{5y} = w$, or $\frac{792x}{5} = w$.

Therefore, the number of ounces of water the hose puts in the bucket in $9y$ minutes can be represented by the expression $\frac{792x}{5}$.

Choice A is incorrect and may result from conceptual or calculation errors.
Choice B is incorrect and may result from conceptual or calculation errors.
Choice C is incorrect and may result from conceptual or calculation errors.

QUESTION 20

The correct answer is -3. Squaring both sides of the given equation yields $(x - 2)^2 = 3x + 34$, which can be rewritten as $x^2 - 4x + 4 = 3x + 34$. Subtracting $3x$ and 34 from both sides of this equation yields $x^2 - 7x - 30 = 0$. This quadratic equation can be rewritten as $(x - 10)(x + 3) = 0$. According to the zero product property, $(x - 10)(x + 3)$ equals zero when either $x - 10 = 0$ or $x + 3 = 0$. Solving each of these equations for x yields $x = 10$ or $x = -3$. Therefore, the given equation has two solutions, 10 and −3. Of these two solutions, −3 is the smallest solution to the given equation.

QUESTION 21

Choice C is correct. It's given that triangle *XYZ* is similar to triangle *RST*, such that *X*, *Y*, and *Z* correspond to *R*, *S*, and *T*, respectively. Since corresponding angles of similar triangles are congruent, it follows that the measure of $\angle Z$ is congruent to the measure of $\angle T$. It's given that the measure of $\angle Z$ is 20°. Therefore, the measure of $\angle T$ is 20°.

Choice A is incorrect and may result from a conceptual error. *Choice B* is incorrect. This is half the measure of $\angle Z$. *Choice D* is incorrect. This is twice the measure of $\angle Z$.

QUESTION 22

Choice B is correct. It's given that $f(x) = 9(4)^x$ and $g(x) = f(x + 2)$. Substituting $x + 2$ for x in $f(x) = 9(4)^x$ gives $f(x + 2) = 9(4)^{x+2}$. Rewriting this equation using properties of exponents gives $f(x + 2) = 9(4)^x(4)^2$, which is equivalent to $f(x + 2) = 9(4)^x(16)$. Multiplying 9 and 16 in this equation gives $f(x + 2) = 144(4)^x$. Since $g(x) = f(x + 2)$, $g(x) = 144(4)^x$.

Choice A is incorrect and may result from conceptual or calculation errors. *Choice C* is incorrect and may result from conceptual or calculation errors. *Choice D* is incorrect and may result from conceptual or calculation errors.

Math

Module 2 — Lower Difficulty
(22 questions)

QUESTION 1

Choice B is correct. Subtracting 12 from both sides of the given equation yields $k = 324$. Therefore, the solution to the given equation is 324.

Choice A is incorrect and may result from conceptual or calculation errors.
Choice C is incorrect and may result from conceptual or calculation errors.
Choice D is incorrect and may result from conceptual or calculation errors.

QUESTION 2

Choice C is correct. Since 1 meter is equal to 100 centimeters, 51 meters is equal to 51 meters $\left(\dfrac{100 \text{ centimeters}}{1 \text{ meter}}\right)$, or 5,100 centimeters.

Choice A is incorrect and may result from conceptual or calculation errors. *Choice B* is incorrect and may result from dividing, rather than multiplying, 51 by 100. *Choice D* is incorrect. This is the length, in millimeters rather than centimeters, that is equivalent to a length of 51 meters.

QUESTION 3

Choice B is correct. The solution to this system of linear equations is represented by the point that lies on both lines shown, or the point of intersection of the two lines. According to the graph, the point of intersection occurs when $x = 2$ and $y = 2$, or at the point (2, 2). Therefore, the solution (x, y) to the system is (2, 2).

Choice A is incorrect and may result from conceptual or calculation errors.
Choice C is incorrect and may result from conceptual or calculation errors.
Choice D is incorrect and may result from conceptual or calculation errors.

QUESTION 4

The correct answer is 3. For the graph of the exponential function f shown, where $y = f(x)$, it's given that the y-intercept of the graph is $(0, y)$. The graph intersects the y-axis at the point (0, 3). Therefore, the value of y is 3.

QUESTION 5

Choice A is correct. It's given that the bar graph shows the distribution of the number of students in each of four extracurricular activities at a high school. The bar representing drama has a height of 40; therefore, there are 40 students in drama. The bar representing chess has a height of 30; therefore, there are 30 students in chess. Thus, there are 40 – 30, or 10 more students in drama than in chess.

Choice B is incorrect. This is the number of students in chess. *Choice C* is incorrect. This is the number of students in drama. *Choice D* is incorrect. This is the sum of the number of students in drama and in chess.

QUESTION 6

Choice B is correct. The given expression has a common factor of 2 in the denominator, so the expression can be rewritten as $\frac{8x(x-7)-3(x-7)}{2(x-7)}$.

The three terms in this expression have a common factor of $(x-7)$. Since it's given that $x > 7$, x can't be equal to 7, which means $(x-7)$ can't be equal to 0. Therefore, each term in the expression, $\frac{8x(x-7)-3(x-7)}{2(x-7)}$, can be divided by $(x-7)$, which gives $\frac{8x-3}{2}$.

Choice A is incorrect and may result from conceptual or calculation errors. *Choice C* is incorrect and may result from conceptual or calculation errors. *Choice D* is incorrect and may result from conceptual or calculation errors.

QUESTION 7

The correct answer is 240. It's given that 80% of the 300 seeds sprouted. Therefore, the number of seeds that sprouted can be calculated by multiplying the number of seeds that were planted by $\frac{80}{100}$, which gives $300\left(\frac{80}{100}\right)$, or 240.

QUESTION 8

Choice B is correct. It's given that Ty plans to walk at an average speed of 4 kilometers per hour. The number of kilometers Ty will walk is determined by the expression $4s$, where s is the number of hours Ty walks. The given goal of at least 24 kilometers means that the inequality $4s \geq 24$ represents the situation. Dividing both sides of this inequality by 4 gives $s \geq 6$, which corresponds to a minimum of 6 hours Ty must walk.

Choice A is incorrect and may result from conceptual or calculation errors. *Choice C* is incorrect and may result from conceptual or calculation errors. *Choice D* is incorrect and may result from conceptual or calculation errors.

QUESTION 9

Choice A is correct. Substituting 0 for x into the given equation yields $y = 0 + 4$, or $y = 4$. Therefore, when $x = 0$, the corresponding value of y for the given equation is 4. Substituting 1 for x into the given equation yields $y = 1 + 4$, or $y = 5$. Therefore, when $x = 1$, the corresponding value of y for the given equation is 5. Substituting 2 for x into the given equation yields $y = 2 + 4$, or $y = 6$. Therefore, when $x = 2$, the corresponding value of y for the given equation is 6. Of the choices given, only the table in choice A gives these three values of x and their corresponding values of y for the given equation.

Choice B is incorrect. This table gives three values of *x* and their corresponding values of *y* for the equation $y = -x + 6$. *Choice C* is incorrect. This table gives three values of *x* and their corresponding values of *y* for the equation $y = -x + 2$. *Choice D* is incorrect. This table gives three values of *x* and their corresponding values of *y* for the equation $y = x$.

QUESTION 10

The correct answer is 9. It's given that $g(x) = 6x$. Substituting 54 for $g(x)$ in the given function yields $54 = 6x$. Dividing both sides of this equation by 6 yields $x = 9$. Therefore, the value of *x* when $g(x) = 54$ is 9.

QUESTION 11

Choice C is correct. It's given that the cost of renting a tent is $11 per day for *d* days. Multiplying the rental cost by the number of days yields $11*d*, which represents the cost of renting the tent for *d* days before the insurance is added. Adding the onetime insurance fee of $10 to the rental cost of $11*d* gives the total cost *c*, in dollars, which can be represented by the equation $c = 11d + 10$.

Choice A is incorrect. This equation represents the total cost to rent the tent if the insurance fee was charged every day. *Choice B* is incorrect. This equation represents the total cost to rent the tent if the daily fee was $(*d* + 11) for 10 days. *Choice D* is incorrect. This equation represents the total cost to rent the tent if the daily fee was $10 and the onetime fee was $11.

QUESTION 12

Choice D is correct. In the figure shown, the angle marked *x*° and the angle marked 142° form a linear pair of angles. If two angles form a linear pair of angles, the sum of the measures of the angles is 180°. Therefore, the value of $x + 142$ is 180.

Choice A is incorrect. This is 90 less than 142, not the sum of *x* and 142. *Choice B* is incorrect and may result from conceptual or calculation errors. *Choice C* is incorrect. This is the measure, in degrees, of one of the angles shown.

QUESTION 13

The correct answer is 986. The area, *A*, of a rectangle is given by $A = \ell w$, where ℓ is the length of the rectangle and *w* is its width. It's given that the length of the rectangle is 34 centimeters (cm) and the width is 29 cm. Substituting 34 for ℓ and 29 for *w* in the equation $A = \ell w$ yields $A = (34)(29)$, or $A = 986$. Therefore, the area, in square centimeters, of this rectangle is 986.

QUESTION 14

The correct answer is 45. It's given that $h(0) = 45$. Therefore, for the given function *h*, when $x = 0$, $h(x) = 45$. Substituting 0 for *x* and 45 for $h(x)$ in the given function, $h(x) = x + b$, yields $45 = 0 + b$, or $45 = b$. Therefore, the value of *b* is 45.

QUESTION 15

Choice B is correct. The equation of a line in the *xy*-plane can be written in slope-intercept form $y = mx + b$, where *m* is the slope of the line and (0, *b*) is its *y*-intercept. It's given that the line passes through the point (0, 5). Therefore, $b = 5$. It's also given that the line is parallel to the graph of $y = 7x + 4$, which means the line has the same slope as the graph of $y = 7x + 4$. The slope of the graph of $y = 7x + 4$ is 7. Therefore, $m = 7$. Substituting 7 for *m* and 5 for *b* in the equation $y = mx + b$ yields $y = 7x + 5$.

Choice A is incorrect. The graph of this equation passes through the point (0, 0), not (0, 5), and has a slope of 5, not 7. *Choice C* is incorrect. The graph of this equation passes through the point (0, 0), not (0, 5). *Choice D* is incorrect. The graph of this equation passes through the point (0, 7), not (0, 5), and has a slope of 5, not 7.

QUESTION 16

Choice D is correct. Since the shaded region shown represents the solutions to an inequality, an ordered pair (x, y) is a solution to the inequality if it's represented by a point in the shaded region. Of the given choices, only (6, −2) is represented by a point in the shaded region. Therefore, the ordered pair (6, −2) is a solution to this inequality.

Choice A is incorrect and may result from conceptual errors. *Choice B* is incorrect and may result from conceptual errors. *Choice C* is incorrect and may result from conceptual errors.

QUESTION 17

Choice D is correct. Since the number of bacteria doubles every day, the relationship between t and y can be represented by an exponential equation of the form $y = a(b)^t$, where a is the number of bacteria at the start of the observation and the number of bacteria increases by a factor of b every day. It's given that there are 44,000 bacteria at the start of the observation. Therefore, $a = 44,000$. It's also given that the number of bacteria doubles, or increases by a factor of 2, every day. Therefore, $b = 2$. Substituting 44,000 for a and 2 for b in the equation $y = a(b)^t$ yields $y = 44,000(2)^t$.

Choice A is incorrect and may result from conceptual or calculation errors. *Choice B* is incorrect and may result from conceptual or calculation errors. *Choice C* is incorrect. This equation represents a situation where the number of bacteria is decreasing by half, not doubling, every day.

QUESTION 18

Choice B is correct. The number that's 8 more than x can be represented by the expression $x + 8$. It's given that the product of x and $x + 8$ is 180, so it follows that $(x)(x + 8) = 180$, or $x^2 + 8x = 180$. Subtracting 180 from each side of this equation yields $x^2 + 8x - 180 = 0$. Factoring the left-hand side of this equation yields $(x - 10)(x + 18) = 0$. Applying the zero product property to this equation yields two solutions: $x = 10$ and $x = -18$. Since x is a positive number, the value of x is 10.

Choice A is incorrect. If $x = 5$, the product of x and the number that's 8 more than x would be (5)(13), or 65, not 180. *Choice C* is incorrect. This is the value of the number that's 8 more than x, not the value of x. *Choice D* is incorrect. If $x = 36$, the product of x and the number that's 8 more than x would be (36)(44), or 1,584, not 180.

QUESTION 19

Choice C is correct. Since a product of two factors is equal to 0 if and only if at least one of the factors is 0, either $5x + 4 = 0$ or $2x - 5 = 0$. Subtracting 4 from each side of the equation $5x + 4 = 0$ yields $5x = -4$. Dividing each side of this equation by 5 yields $x = -\frac{4}{5}$. Adding 5 to each side of the equation $2x - 5 = 0$ yields $2x = 5$. Dividing each side of this equation by 2 yields $x = \frac{5}{2}$.

It follows that the solutions to the given equation are $-\frac{4}{5}$ and $\frac{5}{2}$. Therefore, $-\frac{4}{5}$ is a solution to the given equation.

Choice A is incorrect and may result from conceptual or calculation errors.
Choice B is incorrect and may result from conceptual or calculation errors.
Choice D is incorrect and may result from conceptual or calculation errors.

QUESTION 20

Choice C is correct. It's given that the equation $3x + 5y = 32$ represents the situation where Keenan filled x small jars and y large jars with all the vegetable broth he made, which was 32 cups. Therefore, $3x$ represents the total number of cups of vegetable broth in the small jars and $5y$ represents the total number of cups of vegetable broth in the large jars.

Choice A is incorrect. The number of large jars Keenan filled is represented by y, not $5y$. *Choice B* is incorrect. The number of small jars Keenan filled is represented by x, not $5y$. *Choice D* is incorrect. The total number of cups of vegetable broth in the small jars is represented by $3x$, not $5y$.

QUESTION 21

Choice D is correct. It's given that the expression $w(w + 9)$ represents the area, in square centimeters, of a rectangular cutting board, where w is the width, in centimeters, of the cutting board. The area of a rectangle can be calculated by multiplying its length by its width. It follows that the length, in centimeters, of the cutting board is represented by the expression $(w + 9)$.

Choice A is incorrect. This expression represents the area, in square centimeters, of the cutting board, not its length, in centimeters. *Choice B* is incorrect. This expression represents the width, in centimeters, of the cutting board, not its length. *Choice C* is incorrect. This is the difference between the length, in centimeters, and the width, in centimeters, of the cutting board, not its length, in centimeters.

QUESTION 22

Choice C is correct. It's given that the measure of angle R is $\frac{2\pi}{3}$ radians, and the measure of angle T is $\frac{5\pi}{12}$ radians greater than the measure of angle R. Therefore, the measure of angle T is equal to $\frac{2\pi}{3} + \frac{5\pi}{12}$ radians. Multiplying $\frac{2\pi}{3}$ by $\frac{4}{4}$ to get a common denominator with $\frac{5\pi}{12}$ yields $\frac{8\pi}{12}$. Therefore, $\frac{2\pi}{3} + \frac{5\pi}{12}$ is equivalent to $\frac{8\pi}{12} + \frac{5\pi}{12}$, or $\frac{13\pi}{12}$. Therefore, the measure of angle T is $\frac{13\pi}{12}$ radians. The measure of angle T, in degrees, can be found by multiplying its measure, in radians, by $\frac{180}{\pi}$. This yields $\frac{13\pi}{12} \times \frac{180}{\pi}$, which is equivalent to 195 degrees. Therefore, the measure of angle T is 195 degrees.

Choice A is incorrect. This is the number of degrees that the measure of angle T is greater than the measure of angle R. *Choice B* is incorrect. This is the measure of angle R, in degrees. *Choice D* is incorrect and may result from conceptual or calculation errors.

Math

Module 2 — Higher Difficulty
(22 questions)

QUESTION 1

The correct answer is 79. The median of a data set with an odd number of values is the middle value of the set when the values are ordered from least to greatest. Because the given data set consists of nine values that are ordered from least to greatest, the median is the fifth value in the data set. Therefore, the median of the data shown is 79.

QUESTION 2

Choice B is correct. It's given that triangle *LMN* is similar to triangle *PQR*. Corresponding angles of similar triangles are congruent. Since angle *M* and angle *Q* correspond to each other, they must be congruent. Therefore, if the measure of angle *M* is 53°, then the measure of angle *Q* is also 53°.

Choice A is incorrect and may result from concluding that angle *M* and angle *Q* are complementary rather than congruent. *Choice C* is incorrect and may result from concluding that angle *M* and angle *Q* are supplementary rather than congruent. *Choice D* is incorrect and may result from conceptual or calculation errors.

QUESTION 3

Choice B is correct. It's given that the table shows three values of *x* and their corresponding values of *y* for the equation $y = 4(2)^x + 3$. It's also given that when $x = 3$ the corresponding value of *y* is *a*, and *a* is a constant. Substituting 3 for *x* and *a* for *y* in the given equation yields $a = 4(2)^3 + 3$, or $a = 35$. Therefore, the value of *a* is 35.

Choice A is incorrect and may result from conceptual or calculation errors.
Choice C is incorrect and may result from conceptual or calculation errors.
Choice D is incorrect and may result from conceptual or calculation errors.

QUESTION 4

Choice C is correct. If the two sides of a linear equation are equivalent, then the equation is true for any value. If an equation is true for any value, it has infinitely many solutions. Since the two sides of the given linear equation $66x = 66x$ are equivalent, the given equation has infinitely many solutions.

Choice A is incorrect and may result from conceptual or calculation errors.
Choice B is incorrect and may result from conceptual or calculation errors.
Choice D is incorrect and may result from conceptual or calculation errors.

QUESTION 5

Choice D is correct. It's given that a model predicts the population of Bergen in 2005 was 15,000. The model also predicts that each year for the next 5 years, the population increased by 4% of the previous year's population. The predicted population in one of these years can be found by multiplying the predicted population from the previous year by 1.04. Since the predicted population in 2005 was 15,000, the predicted population 1 year later is 15,000(1.04). The predicted population 2 years later is this value times 1.04, which is 15,000(1.04)(1.04), or $15,000(1.04)^2$. The predicted population 3 years later is this value times 1.04, or $15,000(1.04)^3$. More generally, the predicted population, p, x years after 2005 is represented by the equation $p = 15,000(1.04)^x$.

Choice A is incorrect. Substituting 0 for x in this equation indicates the predicted population in 2005 was 0.96 rather than 15,000. *Choice B* is incorrect. Substituting 0 for x in this equation indicates the predicted population in 2005 was 1.04 rather than 15,000. *Choice C* is incorrect. This equation indicates the predicted population is decreasing, rather than increasing, by 4% each year.

QUESTION 6

Choice A is correct. The x-intercept of a graph in the xy-plane is the point on the graph where $y = 0$. It's given that function h is defined by $h(x) = 4x + 28$. Therefore, the equation representing the graph of $y = h(x)$ is $y = 4x + 28$. Substituting 0 for y in the equation $y = 4x + 28$ yields $0 = 4x + 28$. Subtracting 28 from both sides of this equation yields $-28 = 4x$. Dividing both sides of this equation by 4 yields $-7 = x$. Therefore, the x-intercept of the graph of $y = h(x)$ in the xy-plane is $(-7, 0)$. It's given that the x-intercept of the graph of $y = h(x)$ is $(a, 0)$. Therefore, $a = -7$. The y-intercept of a graph in the xy-plane is the point on the graph where $x = 0$. Substituting 0 for x in the equation $y = 4x + 28$ yields $y = 4(0) + 28$, or $y = 28$. Therefore, the y-intercept of the graph of $y = h(x)$ in the xy-plane is $(0, 28)$. It's given that the y-intercept of the graph of $y = h(x)$ is $(0, b)$. Therefore, $b = 28$. If $a = -7$ and $b = 28$, then the value of $a + b$ is $-7 + 28$, or 21.

Choice B is incorrect. This is the value of b, not $a + b$. *Choice C* is incorrect and may result from conceptual or calculation errors. *Choice D* is incorrect. This is the value of $-a + b$, not $a + b$.

QUESTION 7

Choice B is correct. The given expression has a common factor of 2 in the denominator, so the expression can be rewritten as $\dfrac{8x(x - 7) - 3(x - 7)}{2(x - 7)}$.

The three terms in this expression have a common factor of $(x - 7)$. Since it's given that $x > 7$, x can't be equal to 7, which means $(x - 7)$ can't be equal to 0. Therefore, each term in the expression, $\dfrac{8x(x - 7) - 3(x - 7)}{2(x - 7)}$, can be divided by $(x - 7)$, which gives $\dfrac{8x - 3}{2}$.

Choice A is incorrect and may result from conceptual or calculation errors. *Choice C* is incorrect and may result from conceptual or calculation errors. *Choice D* is incorrect and may result from conceptual or calculation errors.

QUESTION 8

Choice D is correct. The area of a circle can be found by using the formula $A = \pi r^2$, where A is the area and r is the radius of the circle. It's given that the radius of circle A is $3n$. Substituting this value for r into the formula $A = \pi r^2$

gives $A = \pi(3n)^2$, or $9\pi n^2$. It's also given that the radius of circle B is $129n$. Substituting this value for r into the formula $A = \pi r^2$ gives $A = \pi(129n)^2$, or

$16,641\pi n^2$. Dividing the area of circle B by the area of circle A gives $\frac{16,641\pi n^2}{9\pi n^2}$, which simplifies to $1,849$. Therefore, the area of circle B is $1,849$ times the area of circle A.

Choice A is incorrect. This is how many times greater the radius of circle B is than the radius of circle A. *Choice B is incorrect* and may result from conceptual or calculation errors. *Choice C is incorrect.* This is the coefficient on the term that describes the radius of circle B.

QUESTION 9

The correct answer is 46. It's given that O is the center of a circle and that points R and S lie on the circle. Therefore, $\overline{OR}$ and $\overline{OS}$ are radii of the circle. It follows that $OR = OS$. If two sides of a triangle are congruent, then the angles opposite them are congruent. It follows that the angles $\angle RSO$ and $\angle ORS$, which are across from the sides of equal length, are congruent. Let $x°$ represent the measure of $\angle RSO$. It follows that the measure of $\angle ORS$ is also $x°$. It's given that the measure of $\angle ROS$ is $88°$. Because the sum of the measures of the interior angles of a triangle is $180°$, the equation $x° + x° + 88° = 180°$, or $2x + 88 = 180$, can be used to find the measure of $\angle RSO$. Subtracting 88 from both sides of this equation yields $2x = 92$. Dividing both sides of this equation by 2 yields $x = 46$. Therefore, the measure of $\angle RSO$, in degrees, is 46.

QUESTION 10

Choice B is correct. It's given that a business owner plans to purchase 81 chairs. If p is the price per chair, the total price of purchasing 81 chairs is $81p$. It's also given that 7% sales tax is included, which is equivalent to $81p$ multiplied by 1.07, or $81(1.07)p$. Since the total budget is $14,000, the inequality representing the situation is given by $81(1.07)p \le 14,000$. Dividing both sides of this inequality by $81(1.07)$ and rounding the result to two decimal places gives $p \le 161.53$. To not exceed the budget, the maximum possible price per chair is $161.53.

Choice A is incorrect and may result from conceptual or calculation errors. *Choice C is incorrect.* This is the maximum possible price per chair including sales tax, not the maximum possible price per chair before sales tax. *Choice D is incorrect.* This is the maximum possible price if the sales tax is added to the total budget, not the maximum possible price per chair before sales tax.

QUESTION 11

The correct answer is 113. It's given that the legs of a right triangle have lengths 24 centimeters and 21 centimeters. In a right triangle, the square of the length of the hypotenuse is equal to the sum of the squares of the lengths of the two legs. It follows that if h represents the length, in centimeters, of the hypotenuse of the right triangle, $h^2 = 24^2 + 21^2$. This equation is equivalent to $h^2 = 1,017$. Taking the square root of each side of this equation yields $h = \sqrt{1,017}$. This equation can be rewritten as $h = \sqrt{9 \cdot 113}$, or $h = \sqrt{9} \cdot \sqrt{113}$. This equation is equivalent to $h = 3\sqrt{113}$. It's given that the length of the triangle's hypotenuse, in centimeters, can be written in the form $3\sqrt{d}$. It follows that the value of d is 113.

QUESTION 12

Choice D is correct. It's given that a is 230% of b. It follows that $a = \frac{230}{100}b$.

It's also given that a is 60% of c. It follows that $a = \frac{60}{100}c$. Since $a = \frac{230}{100}b$ and

$a = \frac{60}{100}c$, it follows that $\frac{230}{100}b = \frac{60}{100}c$. Multiplying each side of this equation

by $\frac{100}{60}$ yields $\frac{23}{6}b = c$. If c is $p\%$ of b, then $c = \frac{p}{100}b$. It follows that $\frac{23}{6} = \frac{p}{100}$.

Multiplying each side of this equation by 100 yields $\frac{2,300}{6} = p$. It follows that

the value of p is approximately 383.33. Therefore, of the given choices, 383 is closest to the value of p.

Choice A is incorrect. This is closest to the value of p if b is 230% of a, rather than if a is 230% of b, and if b is $p\%$ of c, rather than if c is $p\%$ of b. *Choice B is incorrect.* This is closest to the value of p if a is 230% greater than b, rather than 230% of b. *Choice C is incorrect.* This is closest to the value of p if c is $p\%$ greater than b, rather than $p\%$ of b.

QUESTION 13

Choice D is correct. It's given that for $x > 0$, $f(x)$ is equal to 201% of x. This is

equivalent to $f(x) = \frac{201}{100}x$, or $f(x) = 2.01x$, for $x > 0$. This function indicates that

as x increases, $f(x)$ also increases, which means f is an increasing function. Furthermore, $f(x)$ increases at a constant rate of 2.01 for each increase of x by 1. A function with a constant rate of change is linear. Thus, the function f can be described as an increasing linear function.

Choice A is incorrect and may result from conceptual errors. Choice B is incorrect and may result from conceptual errors. Choice C is incorrect. This could describe the function $f(x) = (2.01)^x$, where $f(x)$ is equal to 201% of $f(x - 1)$, not x, for $x > 0$.

QUESTION 14

The correct answer is 33. It's given in the table that the coordinates of two points on a line in the xy-plane are $(k, 13)$ and $(k + 7, -15)$. The y-intercept is another point on the line. The slope computed using any pair of points from the line will be the same. The slope of a line, m, between any two points, (x_1, y_1) and (x_2, y_2),

on the line can be calculated using the slope formula, $m = \frac{(y_2 - y_1)}{(x_2 - x_1)}$. It follows

that the slope of the line with the given points from the table, $(k, 13)$ and $(k + 7, -15)$,

is $m = \frac{-15 - 13}{k + 7 - k}$, which is equivalent to $m = \frac{-28}{7}$, or $m = -4$. It's given that the

y-intercept of the line is $(k - 5, b)$. Substituting -4 for m and the coordinates of

the points $(k - 5, b)$ and $(k, 13)$ into the slope formula yields $-4 = \frac{13 - b}{k - (k - 5)}$,

which is equivalent to $-4 = \frac{13 - b}{k - k + 5}$, or $-4 = \frac{13 - b}{5}$. Multiplying both sides of

this equation by 5 yields $-20 = 13 - b$. Subtracting 13 from both sides of this equation yields $-33 = -b$. Dividing both sides of this equation by -1 yields $b = 33$. Therefore, the value of b is 33.

QUESTION 15

Choice C is correct. It's given that the equation $3x + 5y = 32$ represents the situation where Keenan filled x small jars and y large jars with all the vegetable broth he made, which was 32 cups. Therefore, $3x$ represents the total number of cups of vegetable broth in the small jars and $5y$ represents the total number of cups of vegetable broth in the large jars.

Choice A is incorrect. The number of large jars Keenan filled is represented by y, not $5y$. Choice B is incorrect. The number of small jars Keenan filled is represented by x, not $5y$. Choice D is incorrect. The total number of cups of vegetable broth in the small jars is represented by $3x$, not $5y$.

QUESTION 16

Choice B is correct. A system of two linear equations in two variables, x and y, has no solution when the lines in the xy-plane representing the equations are parallel and distinct. Two lines are parallel and distinct if their slopes are the same and their y-intercepts are different. The slope of the graph of the given equation, $3x = 36y - 45$, in the xy-plane can be found by rewriting the equation in the form $y = mx + b$, where m is the slope of the graph and $(0, b)$ is the y-intercept. Adding 45 to each side of the given equation yields $3x + 45 = 36y$.

Dividing each side of this equation by 36 yields $\frac{1}{12}x + \frac{5}{4} = y$, or $y = \frac{1}{12}x + \frac{5}{4}$.

It follows that the slope of the graph of the given equation is $\frac{1}{12}$ and the

y-intercept is $\left(0, \frac{5}{4}\right)$. Therefore, the graph of the second equation in the system

must also have a slope of $\frac{1}{12}$, but must not have a y-intercept of $\left(0, \frac{5}{4}\right)$.

Multiplying each side of the equation given in choice B by $\frac{1}{4}$ yields $\frac{1}{12}x = y$,

or $y = \frac{1}{12}x$. It follows that the graph representing the equation in choice B has

a slope of $\frac{1}{12}$ and a y-intercept of $(0, 0)$. Since the slopes of the graphs of the

two equations are equal and the y-intercepts of the graphs of the two equations are different, the equation in choice B could be the second equation in the system.

Choice A is incorrect. This equation can be rewritten as $y = \frac{1}{4}x$. It follows that

the graph of this equation has a slope of $\frac{1}{4}$, so the system consisting of this

equation and the given equation has exactly one solution, rather than no

solution. Choice C is incorrect. This equation can be rewritten as $y = \frac{1}{12}x + \frac{5}{4}$.

It follows that the graph of this equation has a slope of $\frac{1}{12}$ and a y-intercept

of $\left(0, \frac{5}{4}\right)$, so the system consisting of this equation and the given equation

has infinitely many solutions, rather than no solution. Choice D is incorrect.

This equation can be rewritten as $y = \frac{1}{36}x + \frac{5}{4}$. It follows that the graph of this

equation has a slope of $\frac{1}{36}$, so the system consisting of this equation and the

given equation has exactly one solution, rather than no solution.

QUESTION 17

Choice C is correct. Subtracting the expression $(x - 29)$ from both sides of the given equation yields $0 = (x - a)(x - 29) - (x - 29)$, which can be rewritten as $0 = (x - a)(x - 29) + (-1)(x - 29)$. Since the two terms on the right-hand side of this equation have a common factor of $(x - 29)$, it can be rewritten as $0 = (x - 29)(x - a + (-1))$, or $0 = (x - 29)(x - a - 1)$. Since $x - a - 1$ is equivalent to $x - (a + 1)$, the equation $0 = (x - 29)(x - a - 1)$ can be rewritten as $0 = (x - 29)(x - (a + 1))$. By the zero product property, it follows that $x - 29 = 0$ or $x - (a + 1) = 0$. Adding 29 to both sides of the equation $x - 29 = 0$ yields

$x = 29$. Adding $a + 1$ to both sides of the equation $x - (a + 1) = 0$ yields $x = a + 1$. Therefore, the two solutions to the given equation are 29 and $a + 1$. Thus, only $a + 1$ and 29, not a, are solutions to the given equation.

Choice A is incorrect and may result from conceptual or calculation errors.
Choice B is incorrect and may result from conceptual or calculation errors.
Choice D is incorrect and may result from conceptual or calculation errors.

QUESTION 18

Choice D is correct. It's given that w represents the total fence area, in square feet. Since the fence will be stained twice, the amount of stain, in gallons, will need to cover $2w$ square feet. It's also given that one gallon of stain will cover 170 square feet. Dividing the total area, in square feet, of the surface to be stained by the number of square feet covered by one gallon of stain gives the number of gallons of stain that will be needed. Dividing $2w$ by 170 yields $\frac{2w}{170}$, or $\frac{w}{85}$. Therefore, the equation that represents the total amount of stain S, in gallons, needed to stain the fence of the yard twice is $S = \frac{w}{85}$.

Choice A is incorrect. This equation represents the total amount of stain, in gallons, needed to stain the fence once, not twice. Choice B is incorrect and may result from conceptual or calculation errors. Choice C is incorrect and may result from conceptual or calculation errors.

QUESTION 19

Choice C is correct. In the xy-plane, the graph of the line $y = c$ is a horizontal line that crosses the y-axis at $y = c$ and the graph of the quadratic equation $y = -x^2 + 9x - 100$ is a parabola. A parabola can intersect a horizontal line at exactly one point only at its vertex. Therefore, the value of c should be equal to the y-coordinate of the vertex of the graph of the given equation. For a quadratic equation in vertex form, $y = a(x - h)^2 + k$, the vertex of its graph in the xy-plane is (h, k). The given quadratic equation, $y = -x^2 + 9x - 100$, can be rewritten as $y = -\left(x^2 - 2\left(\frac{9}{2}\right)x + \left(\frac{9}{2}\right)^2\right) + \left(\frac{9}{2}\right)^2 - 100$, or $y = -\left(x - \frac{9}{2}\right)^2 + \left(-\frac{319}{4}\right)$. Thus, the value of c is equal to $-\frac{319}{4}$.

Choice A is incorrect and may result from conceptual or calculation errors.
Choice B is incorrect and may result from conceptual or calculation errors.
Choice D is incorrect and may result from conceptual or calculation errors.

QUESTION 20

The correct answer is 168. The quadratic function g gives the estimated depth of the seal, $g(t)$, in meters, t minutes after the seal enters the water. It's given that function g estimates that the seal reached its maximum depth of 302.4 meters 6 minutes after it entered the water. Therefore, function g can be expressed in vertex form as $g(t) = a(t - 6)^2 + 302.4$, where a is a constant. Since it's also given that the seal reached the surface of the water after 12 minutes, $g(12) = 0$. Substituting 12 for t and 0 for $g(t)$ in $g(t) = a(t - 6)^2 + 302.4$ yields $0 = a(12 - 6)^2 + 302.4$, or $36a = -302.4$. Dividing both sides of this equation by 36 gives $a = -8.4$. Substituting -8.4 for a in $g(t) = a(t - 6)^2 + 302.4$ gives $g(t) = -8.4(t - 6)^2 + 302.4$. Substituting 10 for t in $g(t)$ gives $g(10) = -8.4(10 - 6)^2 + 302.4$, which is equivalent to $g(10) = -8.4(4)^2 + 302.4$, or $g(10) = 168$. Therefore, the estimated depth, to the nearest meter, of the seal 10 minutes after it entered the water was 168 meters.

QUESTION 21

Choice A is correct. It's given that 1 meter = 3.28 feet. It follows that 1^2 square meter = 3.28^2 square feet, or 1 square meter = 10.7584 square feet. Since 1 hour = 60 minutes, it follows that 250 square feet per hour is equivalent to

$$\left(\frac{250 \text{ square feet}}{1 \text{ hour}}\right)\left(\frac{1 \text{ square meter}}{10.7584 \text{ square feet}}\right)\left(\frac{1 \text{ hour}}{60 \text{ minutes}}\right), \text{ or } \frac{250 \text{ square meters}}{645.504 \text{ minutes}},$$

which is approximately 0.3873 square meters per minute. Of the given choices, 0.39 is closest to 0.3873.

Choice B is incorrect and may result from conceptual or calculation errors.
Choice C is incorrect and may result from conceptual or calculation errors.
Choice D is incorrect and may result from conceptual or calculation errors.

QUESTION 22

Choice B is correct. Two lines are perpendicular if their slopes are negative reciprocals, meaning that the slope of the first line is equal to −1 divided by the slope of the second line. Each equation in the given pair of equations can be written in slope-intercept form, $y = mx + b$, where m is the slope of the graph of the equation in the xy-plane and $(0, b)$ is the y-intercept. For the first equation, $5x + 7y = 1$, subtracting $5x$ from both sides gives $7y = -5x + 1$, and dividing both sides of this equation by 7 gives $y = -\frac{5}{7}x + \frac{1}{7}$. Therefore, the slope of the graph of this equation is $-\frac{5}{7}$. For the second equation, $ax + by = 1$, subtracting ax from both sides gives $by = -ax + 1$, and dividing both sides of this equation by b gives $y = -\frac{a}{b}x + \frac{1}{b}$. Therefore, the slope of the graph of this equation is $-\frac{a}{b}$. Since the graph of the given pair of equations is a pair of perpendicular lines, the slope of the graph of the second equation, $-\frac{a}{b}$, must be the negative reciprocal of the slope of the graph of the first equation, $-\frac{5}{7}$. The negative reciprocal of $-\frac{5}{7}$ is $\frac{-1}{\left(-\frac{5}{7}\right)}$, or $\frac{7}{5}$. Therefore, $-\frac{a}{b} = \frac{7}{5}$, or $\frac{a}{b} = -\frac{7}{5}$. Similarly, rewriting the equations in choice B in slope-intercept form yields $y = -\frac{10}{7}x + \frac{1}{7}$ and $y = -\frac{a}{2b}x + \frac{1}{2b}$. It follows that the slope of the graph of the first equation in choice B is $-\frac{10}{7}$ and the slope of the graph of the second equation in choice B is $-\frac{a}{2b}$. Since $\frac{a}{b} = -\frac{7}{5}$, $-\frac{a}{2b}$ is equal to $-\left(\frac{1}{2}\right)\left(-\frac{7}{5}\right)$, or $\frac{7}{10}$. Since $\frac{7}{10}$ is the negative reciprocal of $-\frac{10}{7}$, the pair of equations in choice B represents a pair of perpendicular lines.

Choice A is incorrect and may result from conceptual or calculation errors.
Choice C is incorrect and may result from conceptual or calculation errors.
Choice D is incorrect and may result from conceptual or calculation errors.

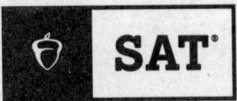

Scoring Your Paper SAT Practice Test #9

Congratulations on completing an SAT® practice test. To score your test, follow the instructions in this scoring guide.

IMPORTANT: *This scoring guide is for students who completed SAT Practice Test #9 in The Official SAT Study Guide™. We recommend reading through these instructions and explanations before scoring so that you understand the specifics and limitations of scoring this practice test.*

The total score on your practice test reflects the sum of the (1) Reading and Writing and (2) Math section scores, as indicated below. If you decided to take both the lower- and higher-difficulty modules, choose which one you will use to score.

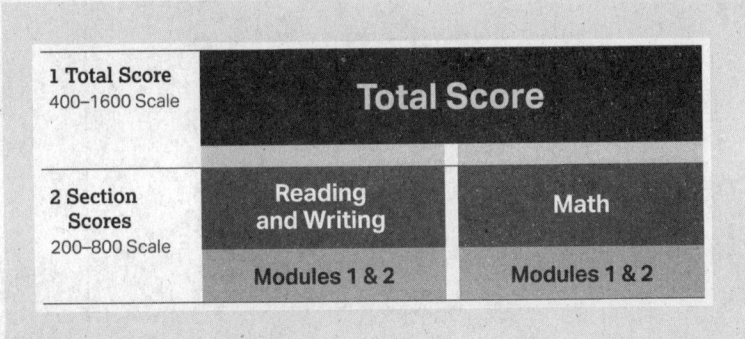

1 Total Score 400–1600 Scale	Total Score	
2 Section Scores 200–800 Scale	Reading and Writing Modules 1 & 2	Math Modules 1 & 2

Scores Overview

Each assessment in the SAT Suite (SAT, PSAT/NMSQT®, PSAT™ 10, and PSAT™ 8/9) reports test scores on a common scale.

For more details about scores, visit **sat.org/scores**.

How to Calculate Your Practice Test Scores

The worksheets on the pages that follow help you calculate your test scores.

GET SET UP

1 In addition to your practice test, you'll need the answer keys and conversion tables at the end of this scoring guide.

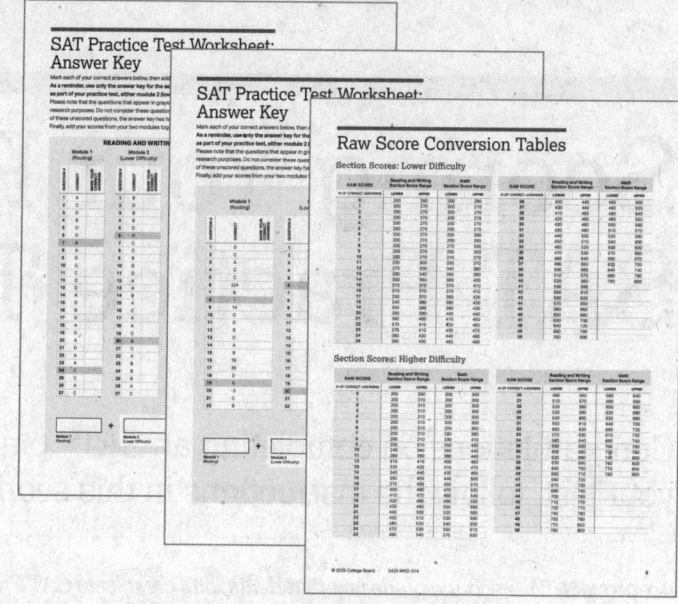

SCORE YOUR PRACTICE TEST

2 Compare your answers to the answer keys later in this scoring guide and count up the total number of correct answers for each section. Write the number of correct answers for each section in the boxes at the bottom of the pages.

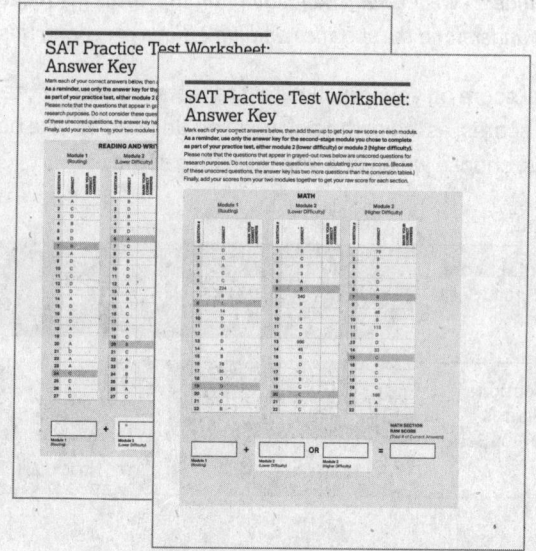

CALCULATE YOUR SCORES

3 Using your marked-up answer keys and the conversion tables, follow the directions on the SAT Practice Test Worksheet: Section and Total Scores page to get your section and total scores.

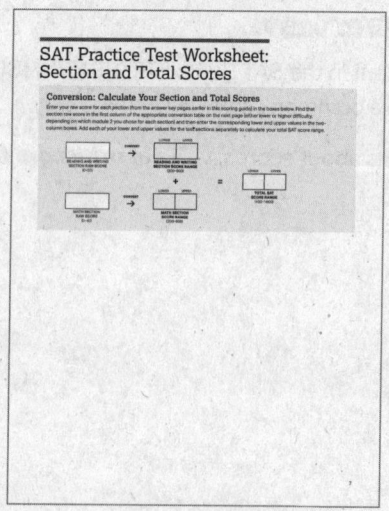

Get Section and Total Scores

Section and total scores for this paper version of SAT Practice Test #9 are expressed as ranges. That's because the scoring method described in this guide is a different (and therefore less precise) version of the one used in the actual adaptive test.

This practice test contains three modules for each test section: (1) a single first-stage (routing) module and (2) two second-stage modules. The two second-stage modules differ by average question difficulty and are marked as either "module 2 (lower difficulty)" or "module 2 (higher difficulty)." You get to choose which module 2 you would like to take for this practice test. **An actual testing experience consists of one routing and one second-stage module per test section.** To obtain your Reading and Writing and Math section scores, you will refer to the answer key and conversion table for the second-stage module you chose (either lower or higher difficulty).

GET YOUR READING AND WRITING SECTION SCORE

Calculate your SAT Reading and Writing section score (it's on a scale of 200–800).

1. Use the answer key for Reading and Writing to find the number of questions in module 1 and the module 2 you chose (either lower or higher difficulty) that you answered correctly.

2. To determine your Reading and Writing raw score, add the number of correct answers you got in module 1 and the module 2 you chose (either lower or higher difficulty). **Exclude the questions in grayed-out rows in your calculation.**

3. Use the appropriate Raw Score Conversion Table to turn your raw score into your Reading and Writing section score.

4. The lower and upper values associated with your raw score establish the range of scores you might expect to receive had this been an actual adaptive test.

GET YOUR MATH SECTION SCORE

Calculate your SAT Math section score (it's on a scale of 200–800).

1. Use the answer key for Math to find the number of questions in module 1 and the module 2 you chose (either lower or higher difficulty) that you answered correctly.

2. To determine your Math raw score, add the number of correct answers you got in module 1 and the module 2 you chose (either lower or higher difficulty). **Exclude the questions in grayed-out rows in your calculation.**

3. Use the appropriate Raw Score Conversion Table to turn your raw score into your Math section score.

4. The lower and upper values associated with your raw score establish the range of scores you might expect to receive had this been an actual adaptive test.

GET YOUR TOTAL SCORE

Add together the lower values for the Reading and Writing and Math sections, and then add together the upper values for the two sections. The result is your total score, expressed as a range, for this SAT practice test. The total score is on a scale of 400–1600.

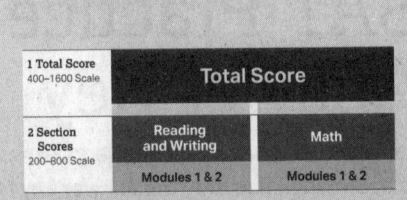

1 Total Score 400–1600 Scale	Total Score	
2 Section Scores 200–800 Scale	Reading and Writing	Math
	Modules 1 & 2	Modules 1 & 2

Your total score on this SAT practice test is the sum of your Reading and Writing section score and your Math section score. For this practice test, you'll receive a lower and upper score for each test section and the total score. This is the range of scores that you might expect to receive.

Use the worksheets on the pages that follow to calculate your section and total scores.

SAT Practice Test Worksheet: Answer Key

Mark each of your correct answers below, then add them up to get your raw score on each module.
As a reminder, use only the answer key for the second-stage module you chose to complete as part of your practice test, either module 2 (lower difficulty) or module 2 (higher difficulty).
Please note that the questions that appear in grayed-out rows below are unscored questions for research purposes. Do not consider these questions when calculating your raw scores. (Because of these unscored questions, the answer key has two more questions than the conversion tables.)
Finally, add your scores from your two modules together to get your raw score for each section.

READING AND WRITING

Module 1 (Routing)			Module 2 (Lower Difficulty)			Module 2 (Higher Difficulty)		
QUESTION #	CORRECT	MARK YOUR CORRECT ANSWERS	QUESTION #	CORRECT	MARK YOUR CORRECT ANSWERS	QUESTION #	CORRECT	MARK YOUR CORRECT ANSWERS
1	A		1	B		1	D	
2	C		2	D		2	D	
3	D		3	B		3	C	
4	B		4	B		4	A	
5	D		5	D		5	B	
6	D		6	A		6	A	
7	B		7	C		7	D	
8	A		8	C		8	C	
9	D		9	B		9	B	
10	C		10	D		10	A	
11	C		11	D		11	B	
12	D		12	A		12	C	
13	D		13	A		13	B	
14	A		14	B		14	A	
15	D		15	A		15	C	
16	B		16	C		16	D	
17	D		17	A		17	A	
18	A		18	A		18	D	
19	D		19	C		19	A	
20	A		20	B		20	B	
21	D		21	C		21	D	
22	A		22	A		22	C	
23	A		23	B		23	D	
24	C		24	B		24	D	
25	C		25	B		25	B	
26	A		26	A		26	C	
27	C		27	C		27	A	

READING AND WRITING SECTION RAW SCORE
(Total # of Correct Answers)

☐ Module 1 (Routing)	**+**	☐ Module 2 (Lower Difficulty)	**OR** ☐ Module 2 (Higher Difficulty)	**=**	☐

SAT Practice Test Worksheet: Answer Key

Mark each of your correct answers below, then add them up to get your raw score on each module. **As a reminder, use only the answer key for the second-stage module you chose to complete as part of your practice test, either module 2 (lower difficulty) or module 2 (higher difficulty).** Please note that the questions that appear in grayed-out rows below are unscored questions for research purposes. Do not consider these questions when calculating your raw scores. (Because of these unscored questions, the answer key has two more questions than the conversion tables.) Finally, add your scores from your two modules together to get your raw score for each section.

MATH

Module 1 (Routing)			Module 2 (Lower Difficulty)			Module 2 (Higher Difficulty)		
QUESTION #	CORRECT	MARK YOUR CORRECT ANSWERS	QUESTION #	CORRECT	MARK YOUR CORRECT ANSWERS	QUESTION #	CORRECT	MARK YOUR CORRECT ANSWERS
1	D		1	B		1	79	
2	C		2	C		2	B	
3	A		3	B		3	B	
4	C		4	3		4	C	
5	C		5	A		5	D	
6	224		6	B		6	A	
7	B		7	240		7	B	
8	1		8	B		8	D	
9	14		9	A		9	46	
10	D		10	9		10	B	
11	D		11	C		11	113	
12	B		12	D		12	D	
13	D		13	986		13	D	
14	A		14	45		14	33	
15	B		15	B		15	C	
16	76		16	B		16	B	
17	35		17	D		17	C	
18	D		18	B		18	D	
19	D		19	C		19	C	
20	-3		20	C		20	168	
21	C		21	D		21	A	
22	B		22	C		22	B	

MATH SECTION RAW SCORE
(Total # of Correct Answers)

____	+	____	OR	____	=	____

Module 1 (Routing)   Module 2 (Lower Difficulty)   Module 2 (Higher Difficulty)

Understanding the SAT Practice Test Conversion Tables and Total Score Ranges

As mentioned earlier in this scoring guide, the scoring method for the practice tests that appear in *The Official SAT Study Guide* is different (and therefore less precise) than the method used in the actual adaptive test. Your practice test may result in a larger score range than what you hoped to see, but it's not feasible to estimate your performance on the practice tests in the study guide as precisely as we could for an actual test. As the test developers, College Board is committed to providing the most accurate conversion possible to help you understand your scores and guide your practice most effectively.

There are two conversion tables in this scoring guide. Use the conversion table labelled lower difficulty if you took module 2 (lower difficulty). Use the conversion table labelled higher difficulty if you took module 2 (higher difficulty). You might need both conversion tables if you took the lower-difficulty option for one section (e.g., Reading and Writing) and the higher-difficulty option for the other section (e.g., Math).

Because the lower- and higher-difficulty conversion tables share the same questions for module 1 (routing), you may encounter different score ranges based on the conversion table you use. For example, if you got all the module 1 (routing) questions correct, the lower-difficulty conversion table and the higher-difficulty conversion table will give you different score ranges. This is to be expected because the conversion tables account for all items within the two modules that make up the test. Answering only items on the first half of the test assumes you answered the other questions (module 2) incorrectly. Recall that when taking the actual SAT on test day, the test will adapt to your ability based on how you perform on the first half. Because of the differences between the actual test and providing a paper approximation of that (the practice test you're currently scoring), you should select the second-stage module that feels most appropriate for you. For example, if you were to answer all items on the first module correctly on the actual test, you would not be routed to the easier second-stage module. The converse would also be true. For many users of moderate ability either second-stage would be acceptable, but very high or low performers should be cautioned about taking the second-stage module that doesn't align well with their ability.

SAT Practice Test Worksheet: Section and Total Scores

Conversion: Calculate Your Section and Total Scores

Enter your raw score for each section (from the answer key pages earlier in this scoring guide) in the boxes below. Find that section raw score in the first column of the appropriate conversion table on the next page (either lower or higher difficulty, depending on which module 2 you chose for each section) and then enter the corresponding lower and upper values in the two-column boxes. Add each of your lower and upper values for the test sections separately to calculate your total SAT score range.

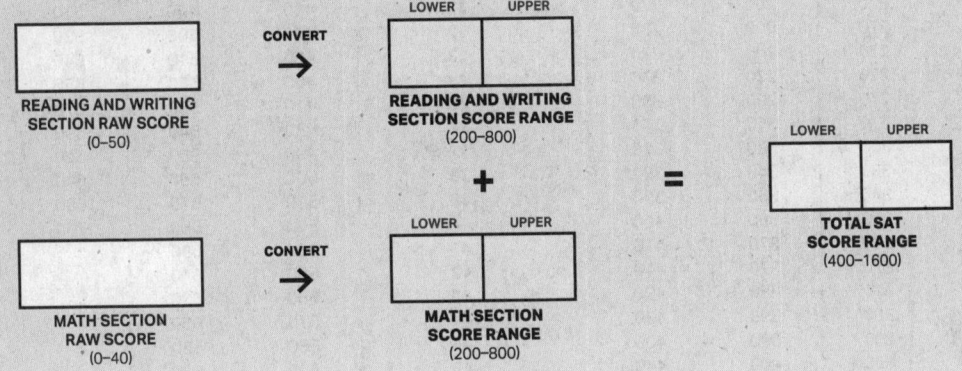

READING AND WRITING
SECTION RAW SCORE
(0–50)

CONVERT →

LOWER   UPPER

READING AND WRITING
SECTION SCORE RANGE
(200–800)

+

MATH SECTION
RAW SCORE
(0–40)

CONVERT →

LOWER   UPPER

MATH SECTION
SCORE RANGE
(200–800)

=

LOWER   UPPER

TOTAL SAT
SCORE RANGE
(400–1600)

Raw Score Conversion Tables

Section Scores: Lower Difficulty

RAW SCORE	Reading and Writing Section Score Range		Math Section Score Range	
(# OF CORRECT ANSWERS)	LOWER	UPPER	LOWER	UPPER
0	200	260	200	260
1	200	270	200	270
2	200	270	200	270
3	200	270	200	270
4	200	270	200	270
5	200	270	200	270
6	200	270	200	280
7	200	270	200	290
8	200	270	270	330
9	200	270	290	350
10	200	270	310	370
11	220	300	330	370
12	270	330	340	380
13	280	340	350	390
14	300	360	360	400
15	310	370	370	410
16	310	370	370	410
17	330	370	380	420
18	340	380	390	430
19	350	390	390	430
20	350	390	400	440
21	360	400	410	450
22	370	410	420	460
23	370	410	430	470
24	380	420	440	480
25	390	430	450	490

RAW SCORE	Reading and Writing Section Score Range		Math Section Score Range	
(# OF CORRECT ANSWERS)	LOWER	UPPER	LOWER	UPPER
26	400	440	460	500
27	400	440	460	520
28	410	450	480	540
29	420	460	490	550
30	420	480	500	560
31	430	490	510	570
32	440	500	530	590
33	450	510	540	600
34	460	520	550	630
35	470	530	570	650
36	480	540	590	670
37	490	550	620	700
38	500	560	640	740
39	510	570	680	780
40	520	580	760	800
41	530	590		
42	550	610		
43	560	620		
44	570	650		
45	580	660		
46	600	680		
47	620	700		
48	640	720		
49	680	760		
50	760	800		

Section Scores: Higher Difficulty

RAW SCORE	Reading and Writing Section Score Range		Math Section Score Range	
(# OF CORRECT ANSWERS)	LOWER	UPPER	LOWER	UPPER
0	200	300	200	300
1	200	310	200	300
2	200	310	200	300
3	200	310	200	300
4	200	310	200	300
5	200	310	200	300
6	200	310	200	300
7	200	310	280	380
8	200	310	330	410
9	200	310	350	430
10	240	360	360	440
11	290	390	380	440
12	310	410	400	460
13	320	420	410	470
14	340	440	430	490
15	350	450	440	500
16	370	450	450	510
17	400	460	470	530
18	410	470	480	540
19	420	480	490	550
20	430	490	500	560
21	440	500	520	580
22	450	510	530	590
23	460	520	540	600
24	470	530	550	610
25	480	540	570	630

RAW SCORE	Reading and Writing Section Score Range		Math Section Score Range	
(# OF CORRECT ANSWERS)	LOWER	UPPER	LOWER	UPPER
26	490	550	580	640
27	510	570	590	650
28	520	580	600	660
29	530	590	620	680
30	540	600	630	690
31	550	610	640	700
32	560	620	660	720
33	570	630	670	730
34	580	640	690	750
35	590	650	700	760
36	600	660	720	780
37	620	680	740	800
38	630	690	760	800
39	640	700	770	800
40	650	710	780	800
41	660	720		
42	670	730		
43	680	740		
44	700	760		
45	710	770		
46	730	770		
47	740	780		
48	750	790		
49	770	800		
50	780	800		

The SAT®
Practice Test #10

Make time to take the practice test.
It is one of the best ways to get ready for the SAT.

Note: The practice tests in this guide include two second modules so that you can experience both the lower- and higher-difficulty modules. On the actual test, you will be presented with only one second module.

After you have taken the practice test, score it right away using materials provided in *The Official SAT Study Guide*.

This version of the SAT Practice Test is for students using this Study Guide. As a reminder, most students taking the SAT will do so using Bluebook™, the digital testing application. To best prepare for test day, download Bluebook at **bluebook.app.collegeboard.org** to take the practice test in the digital format.

Test begins on the next page.

Reading and Writing

27 QUESTIONS

DIRECTIONS

The questions in this section address a number of important reading and writing skills. Each question includes one or more passages, which may include a table or graph. Read each passage and question carefully, and then choose the best answer to the question based on the passage(s).

All questions in this section are multiple-choice with four answer choices. Each question has a single best answer.

1

In the early 1800s, the Cherokee scholar Sequoyah created the first script, or writing system, for an Indigenous language in the United States. Because it represented the sounds of spoken Cherokee so accurately, his script was easy to learn and thus quickly achieved _____ use: by 1830, over 90 percent of the Cherokee people could read and write it.

Which choice completes the text with the most logical and precise word or phrase?

A) widespread

B) careful

C) unintended

D) infrequent

2

Due to their often strange images, highly experimental syntax, and opaque subject matter, many of John Ashbery's poems can be quite difficult to _____ and thus are the object of heated debate among scholars.

Which choice completes the text with the most logical and precise word or phrase?

A) delegate

B) compose

C) interpret

D) renounce

3

Beginning in the 1950s, Navajo Nation legislator Annie Dodge Wauneka continuously worked to promote public health; this _____ effort involved traveling throughout the vast Navajo homeland and writing a medical dictionary for speakers of *Diné bizaad*, the Navajo language.

Which choice completes the text with the most logical and precise word or phrase?

A) impartial

B) offhand

C) persistent

D) mandatory

4

Kelp forests grow underwater along the eastern Pacific Coast. These underwater forests are important to fish and other marine animals. Ocean currents can be powerful and rough, making it difficult for animals to find safe places to hide from predators. The underwater forests slow down the currents. This creates a more _____ environment with calmer waters where animals can take shelter.

Which choice completes the text with the most logical and precise word or phrase?

A) tranquil

B) dangerous

C) imaginative

D) surprising

CONTINUE →

5

People sometimes dismiss a claim if it comes from a source they regard as self-interested, but from a strictly logical perspective, the source of a claim is _____: it has no direct bearing on whether the claim is true.

Which choice completes the text with the most logical and precise word or phrase?

A) indistinct

B) irrelevant

C) indisputable

D) implicit

6

Jazz tap is a dance form that was first developed in African American communities. Jazz tap was heavily influenced by jazz music, which became widely popular in the United States in the 1920s. Tap dancers were inspired by jazz music's quick rhythms and by the way jazz musicians would make up melodies as they played. As jazz music continued to develop in the 1930s and 1940s, jazz tap evolved with it. Because of jazz music's influence, jazz tap quickly developed into a dance form that was very different from earlier kinds of tap dance.

Which choice best states the main purpose of the text?

A) It explains why audiences prefer some kinds of music over others.

B) It discusses the development of a dance form.

C) It describes how to play a musical instrument.

D) It emphasizes the popularity of a famous dancer.

7

The following text is adapted from Jane Austen's 1814 novel *Mansfield Park*. The speaker, Tom, is considering staging a play at home with a group of his friends and family.

We mean nothing but a little amusement among ourselves, just to vary the scene, and exercise our powers in something new. We want no audience, no publicity. We may be trusted, I think, in choosing some play most perfectly unexceptionable; and I can conceive no greater harm or danger to any of us in conversing in the elegant written language of some respectable author than in chattering in words of our own.

Which choice best states the main purpose of the text?

A) To offer Tom's assurance that the play will be inoffensive and involve only a small number of people

B) To clarify that the play will not be performed in the manner Tom had originally intended

C) To elaborate on the idea that the people around Tom lack the skills to successfully stage a play

D) To assert that Tom believes the group performing the play will be able to successfully promote it

Unauthorized copying or reuse of any part of this page is illegal.

CONTINUE ▶

1031

Text 1

French Impressionist artist Edgar Degas insisted that his paintings be kept in their original frames after they were sold. Like many Impressionist painters, Degas used painted frames that stood in contrast to the gold frames frequently seen at the Paris Salon, a prestigious art exhibition that was sponsored by the French government and promoted traditional painting styles. Impressionist painters likely chose these colorful frames to distinguish themselves from what was considered conventional at the time.

Text 2

Impressionist painters often focused on the interplay of color and light in their works. As such, those Impressionists who placed their works in painted frames instead of the more traditional gold ones did so for aesthetic reasons: a frame's color was likely chosen because it would harmonize with the colors or subjects in a painting. Gold, conversely, could distract from the subtleties in a painted scene.

Based on the texts, both authors would most likely agree with which statement?

A) Gold frames were considered especially desirable by those who purchased works from Impressionist painters.

B) The colors in an Impressionist painting were often chosen to complement the colors of the frame it would be placed in.

C) Many Impressionist painters were intentional about the frames they selected for their works.

D) Degas's preferred framing style was different from that of most Impressionist painters.

Choctaw/Cherokee artist Jeffrey Gibson turns punching bags used by boxers into art by decorating them with beadwork and elements of Native dressmaking. These elements include leather fringe and jingles, the metal cones that cover the dresses worn in the jingle dance, a women's dance of the Ojibwe people. Thus, Gibson combines an object commonly associated with masculinity (a punching bag) with art forms traditionally practiced by women in most Native communities (beadwork and dressmaking). In this way, he rejects the division of male and female gender roles.

Which choice best describes Gibson's approach to art, as presented in the text?

A) He draws from traditional Native art forms to create his original works.

B) He has been influenced by Native and non-Native artists equally.

C) He finds inspiration from boxing in designing the dresses he makes.

D) He rejects expectations about color and pattern when incorporating beadwork.

Unauthorized copying or reuse of any part of this page is illegal.

1032

CONTINUE ➤

Believing that living in an impractical space can heighten awareness and even improve health, conceptual artists Madeline Gins and Shusaku Arakawa designed an apartment building in Japan to be more fanciful than functional. A kitchen counter is chest-high on one side and knee-high on the other; a ceiling has a door to nowhere. The effect is disorienting but invigorating: after four years there, filmmaker Nobu Yamaoka reported significant health benefits.

Which choice best states the main idea of the text?

A) Although inhabiting a home surrounded by fanciful features such as those designed by Gins and Arakawa can be rejuvenating, it is unsustainable.

B) Designing disorienting spaces like those in the Gins and Arakawa building is the most effective way to create a physically stimulating environment.

C) As a filmmaker, Yamaoka has long supported the designs of conceptual artists such as Gins and Arakawa.

D) Although impractical, the design of the apartment building by Gins and Arakawa may improve the well-being of the building's residents.

Many insects are iridescent, or have colors that appear to shimmer and change when seen from different angles. Scientists have assumed that this feature helps to attract mates but could also attract predators. But biologist Karin Kjernsmo and a team had the idea that the shifting appearance of colors might actually make it harder for other animals to see iridescent insects. To test this idea, the team put beetle forewings on leaves along a forest path and then asked human participants to look for them. Some of the wings were naturally iridescent. Others were painted with a nonchanging color from the iridescent spectrum, such as purple or blue.

Which finding, if true, would most directly support the team's idea?

A) On average, participants found most of the purple wings and blue wings and far fewer of the iridescent wings.

B) On average, participants found the iridescent wings faster than they found the purple wings or blue wings.

C) Some participants reported that the purple wings were easier to see than the blue wings.

D) Some participants successfully found all of the wings on the leaves.

Unauthorized copying or reuse of any part of this page is illegal.

CONTINUE

1033

12

The Post Office is a 1912 play by Rabindranath Tagore, originally written in Bengali. The character Amal is a young boy who imagines that the people he sees passing the window of his home are carefree even when engaged in work or chores, as is evident when he says to the daughter of a flower seller, _____

Which quotation from *The Post Office* most effectively illustrates the claim?

A) "I see, you don't wish to stop; I don't care to stay on here either."

B) "Oh, flower gathering? That is why your feet seem so glad and your anklets jingle so merrily as you walk."

C) "I'll pay when I grow up—before I leave to look for work out on the other side of that stream there."

D) "Wish I could be out too. Then I would pick some flowers for you from the very topmost branches right out of sight."

13

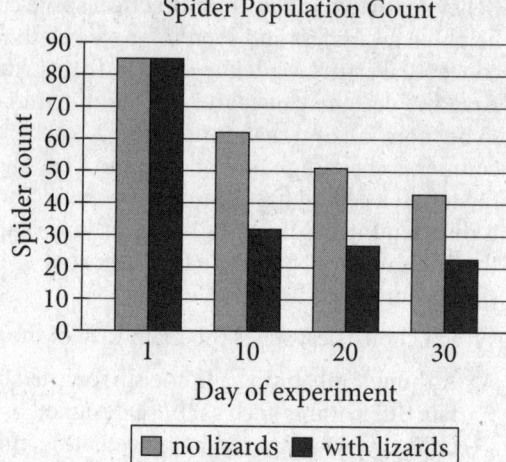

Spider Population Count

To investigate the effect of lizard predation on spider populations, a student in a biology class placed spiders in two enclosures, one with lizards and one without, and tracked the number of spiders in the enclosures for 30 days. The student concluded that the reduction in the spider population count in the enclosure with lizards by day 30 was entirely attributable to the presence of the lizards.

Which choice best describes data from the graph that weaken the student's conclusion?

A) The spider population count was the same in both enclosures on day 1.

B) The spider population count also substantially declined by day 30 in the enclosure without lizards.

C) The largest decline in spider population count in the enclosure with lizards occurred from day 1 to day 10.

D) The spider population count on day 30 was lower in the enclosure with lizards than in the enclosure without lizards.

CONTINUE ▶

14

Many mosquito repellents contain natural components that work by activating multiple odor receptors on mosquitoes' antennae. As the insects develop resistance, new repellents are needed. Ke Dong and her team found that EBF, a molecular component of a chrysanthemum-flower extract, can repel mosquitoes by activating just one odor receptor—and this receptor, Or31, is present in all mosquito species known to carry diseases. Therefore, the researchers suggest that in developing new repellents, it would be most useful to _____

Which choice most logically completes the text?

A) identify molecular components similar to EBF that target the activation of Or31 receptors.

B) investigate alternative methods for extracting EBF molecules from chrysanthemums.

C) verify the precise locations of Or31 and other odor receptors on mosquitoes' antennae.

D) determine the maximum number of different odor receptors that can be activated by a single molecule.

15

Euphorbia esula (leafy spurge) is a Eurasian plant that has become invasive in North America, where it displaces native vegetation and sickens cattle. *E. esula* can be controlled with chemical herbicides, but that approach can also kill harmless plants nearby. Recent research on introducing engineered DNA into plant species to inhibit their reproduction may offer a path toward exclusively targeting *E. esula*, consequently _____

Which choice most logically completes the text?

A) making individual *E. esula* plants more susceptible to existing chemical herbicides.

B) enhancing the ecological benefits of *E. esula* in North America.

C) enabling cattle to consume *E. esula* without becoming sick.

D) reducing invasive *E. esula* numbers without harming other organisms.

16

While many video game creators strive to make their graphics ever more _____ others look to the past, developing titles with visuals inspired by the "8-bit" games of the 1980s and 1990s. (The term "8-bit" refers to a console whose processor could only handle eight bits of data at once.)

Which choice completes the text so that it conforms to the conventions of Standard English?

A) lifelike but

B) lifelike

C) lifelike,

D) lifelike, but

17

As British scientist Peter Whibberley has observed, "the Earth is not a very good timekeeper." Earth's slightly irregular rotation rate means that measurements of time must be periodically adjusted. Specifically, an extra "leap second" (the 86,401st second of the day) is _____ time based on the planet's rotation lags a full nine-tenths of a second behind time kept by precise atomic clocks.

Which choice completes the text so that it conforms to the conventions of Standard English?

A) added, whenever

B) added; whenever

C) added. Whenever

D) added whenever

CONTINUE

18

In Death Valley National Park's Racetrack Playa, a flat, dry lakebed, are 162 rocks—some weighing less than a pound but others almost 700 pounds—that move periodically from place to place, seemingly of their own volition. Racetrack-like trails in the _____ mysterious migration.

Which choice completes the text so that it conforms to the conventions of Standard English?

A) playas sediment mark the rock's

B) playa's sediment mark the rocks

C) playa's sediment mark the rocks'

D) playas' sediment mark the rocks'

19

Along with carbon dioxide concentration and temperature, light intensity affects the chemical reaction rate of _____ as light intensity increases, so does the rate at which the reactants (water and carbon dioxide) are converted into their products (glucose and oxygen).

Which choice completes the text so that it conforms to the conventions of Standard English?

A) photosynthesis and

B) photosynthesis,

C) photosynthesis:

D) photosynthesis

20

Paintings by the renowned twentieth-century US _____ were featured in _Artist to Artist_, an exhibition at the Smithsonian Art Museum that paired the works of artists whose career trajectories intersected in meaningful ways.

Which choice completes the text so that it conforms to the conventions of Standard English?

A) artists: Thomas Hart Benton and Jackson Pollock,

B) artists Thomas Hart Benton and Jackson Pollock

C) artists Thomas Hart Benton, and Jackson Pollock,

D) artists, Thomas Hart Benton and Jackson Pollock

21

In her 2012 analysis of tree rings from Japan's Yaku Island, cosmic ray physicist Fusa Miyake noted an anomalous carbon-14 spike dating to 774–775 CE, indicating that a massive burst of radiation reached Earth during that time. _____ this unprecedented radiocarbon surge was dubbed a "Miyake event" in honor of its discoverer.

Which choice completes the text with the most logical transition?

A) Fittingly,

B) Similarly,

C) However,

D) In other words,

22

One poll taken after the first 1960 presidential debate suggested that John Kennedy lost badly: only 21 percent of those who listened on the radio rated him the winner. _____ the debate was ultimately considered a victory for the telegenic young senator, who rated higher than his opponent, Vice President Richard Nixon, among those watching on the new medium of television.

Which choice completes the text with the most logical transition?

A) In other words,

B) Therefore,

C) Likewise,

D) Nevertheless,

Unauthorized copying or reuse of any part of this page is illegal.

1036

CONTINUE

23

In his 1925 book *The Morphology of Landscape*, US geographer Carl Sauer challenged prevailing views about how natural landscapes influence human cultures. _____ Sauer argued that instead of being shaped entirely by their natural surroundings, cultures play an active role in their own development by virtue of their interactions with the environment.

Which choice completes the text with the most logical transition?

A) Similarly,

B) Finally,

C) Therefore,

D) Specifically,

24

While researching a topic, a student has taken the following notes:

- Dr. Sunil Bajpai studies dinosaurs at the Indian Institute of Technology.

- Bajpai's research team recently found a 167-million-year-old dicraeosaurid fossil.

- It is the oldest fossil from the dicraeosaurid dinosaur group ever recovered.

- It was found in the Thar Desert in western India.

The student wants to indicate where the dicraeosaurid fossil was found. Which choice most effectively uses relevant information from the notes to accomplish this goal?

A) The dicraeosaurid fossil was found in western India's Thar Desert.

B) Bajpai's team recently found the oldest dicraeosaurid fossil ever recovered.

C) Dr. Sunil Bajpai, of the Indian Institute of Technology, is part of a research team.

D) The fossil, which is from the dicraeosaurid dinosaur group, is 167 million years old.

25

While researching a topic, a student has taken the following notes:

- Ancient Native American and Australian Aboriginal cultures described the Pleiades star cluster as having seven stars.

- It was referred to as the Seven Sisters in the mythology of ancient Greece.

- Today, the cluster appears to have only six stars.

- Two of the stars have moved so close together that they now appear as one.

The student wants to specify the reason the Pleiades' appearance changed. Which choice most effectively uses relevant information from the notes to accomplish this goal?

A) Ancient Native American and Australian Aboriginal cultures described the Pleiades, which was referred to in Greek mythology as the Seven Sisters, as having seven stars.

B) Although once referred to as the Seven Sisters, the Pleiades appears to have only six stars today.

C) In the time since ancient cultures described the Pleiades as having seven stars, two of the cluster's stars have moved so close together that they now appear as one.

D) The Pleiades has seven stars, but two are so close together that they appear to be a single star.

Unauthorized copying or reuse of any part of this page is illegal.

CONTINUE

1037

While researching a topic, a student has taken the following notes:

- Severo Ochoa discovered the enzyme PNPase in 1955.

- PNPase is involved in both the creation and degradation of mRNA.

- Ochoa incorrectly hypothesized that PNPase provides the genetic blueprints for mRNA.

- The discovery of PNPase proved critical to deciphering the human genetic code.

- Deciphering the genetic code has led to a better understanding of how genetic variations affect human health.

The student wants to emphasize the significance of Ochoa's discovery. Which choice most effectively uses relevant information from the notes to accomplish this goal?

A) Ochoa's 1955 discovery of PNPase proved critical to deciphering the human genetic code, leading to a better understanding of how genetic variations affect human health.

B) Ochoa first discovered PNPase, an enzyme that he hypothesized contained the genetic blueprints for mRNA, in 1955.

C) In 1955, Ochoa discovered the PNPase enzyme, which is involved in both the creation and degradation of mRNA.

D) Though his discovery of PNPase was critical to deciphering the human genetic code, Ochoa incorrectly hypothesized that the enzyme was the source of mRNA's genetic blueprints.

While researching a topic, a student has taken the following notes:

- In the late 1890s, over 14,000 unique varieties of apples were grown in the US.

- The rise of industrial agriculture in the mid-1900s narrowed the range of commercially grown crops.

- Thousands of apple varieties considered less suitable for commercial growth were lost.

- Today, only 15 apple varieties dominate the market, making up 90% of apples purchased in the US.

- The Lost Apple Project, based in Washington State, attempts to find and grow lost apple varieties.

The student wants to emphasize the decline in unique apple varieties in the US and specify why this decline occurred. Which choice most effectively uses relevant information from the notes to accomplish these goals?

A) The Lost Apple Project is dedicated to finding some of the apple varieties lost following a shift in agricultural practices in the mid-1900s.

B) While over 14,000 apple varieties were grown in the US in the late 1890s, only 15 unique varieties make up most of the apples sold today.

C) Since the rise of industrial agriculture, US farmers have mainly grown the same few unique apple varieties, resulting in the loss of thousands of varieties less suitable for commercial growth.

D) As industrial agriculture rose to prominence in the mid-1900s, the number of crops selected for cultivation decreased dramatically.

STOP

If you finish before time is called, you may check your work on this module only.
Do not turn to any other module in the test.

Test begins on the next page.

Reading and Writing

27 QUESTIONS

1

The general store was essential to daily life in the rural United States during the 1800s because it provided the supplies that the people living in nearby communities needed. Also, the store was a _____ of information. People socializing at the general store would share news and help spread it throughout their communities.

Which choice completes the text with the most logical and precise word or phrase?

A) source

B) rival

C) condition

D) waste

2

According to Potawatomi ecologist Robin Wall Kimmerer, the Indigenous method of harvesting *Hierochloe odorata*, or sweetgrass, by snapping the plant off at the root actually _____ wild populations: it may seem counterintuitive, she says, but this method of removal allows new sweetgrass plants to repopulate the space, with an overall increase in number and vigor.

Which choice completes the text with the most logical and precise word or phrase?

A) selects

B) originates

C) conditions

D) replenishes

Unauthorized copying or reuse of any part of this page is illegal.

1040

CONTINUE →

3

The process of mechanically recycling plastics is often considered _____ because of the environmental impact and the loss of material quality that often occurs. But chemist Takunda Chazovachii has helped develop a cleaner process of chemical recycling that converts superabsorbent polymers from diapers into a desirable reusable adhesive.

Which choice completes the text with the most logical and precise word or phrase?

A) resilient

B) inadequate

C) dynamic

D) satisfactory

4

The parasitic dodder plant increases its reproductive success by flowering at the same time as the host plant it has latched onto. In 2020, Jianqiang Wu and his colleagues determined that the tiny dodder achieves this _____ with its host by absorbing and utilizing a protein the host produces when it is about to flower.

Which choice completes the text with the most logical and precise word or phrase?

A) synchronization

B) hibernation

C) prediction

D) moderation

5

The following text is adapted from Pam Muñoz Ryan's 2020 novel *Mañanaland*. In the village where Max lives, there is an old fortress called La Reina. Children in the village say that the fortress is haunted.

> For as long as he could remember, Max had begged Papá [his father] to take him to see La Reina and the ruins up close. He'd be a hero among his friends if he was the first boy to cross the haunted gates! Just because Papá didn't believe in ghosts didn't mean they weren't there. Maybe this summer Papá would finally take him. He *was* almost twelve.

©2020 by Pam Muñoz Ryan

Which choice best describes the overall purpose of the text?

A) To portray how proud Max's father is of Max

B) To explain why Max doesn't want to grow up yet

C) To criticize Max for disliking summer

D) To show how much Max wants to visit La Reina

6

The following text is adapted from Gwendolyn Bennett's 1926 poem "Street Lamps in Early Spring."

> Night wears a garment
> All velvet soft, all violet blue…
> And over her face she draws a veil
> As shimmering fine as floating dew…
> And here and there
> In the black of her hair
> The subtle hands of Night
> Move slowly with their gem-starred light.

Which choice best describes the overall structure of the text?

A) It presents alternating descriptions of night in a rural area and in a city.

B) It sketches an image of nightfall, then an image of sunrise.

C) It makes an extended comparison of night to a human being.

D) It portrays how night changes from one season of the year to the next.

Unauthorized copying or reuse of any part of this page is illegal.

CONTINUE

1041

7

The following text is adapted from Sylvia Acevedo's 2018 memoir *Path to the Stars: My Journey from Girl Scout to Rocket Scientist*. The narrator is traveling by car with her family to Mexico City. Mario and Laura are her brother and sister.

Mario and I played games to see how many different license plates we could spot, and Laura liked to look for children in the back seats of the cars we passed. We were used to the forty-five-minute drive to El Paso and familiar with the six-hour ride to Chihuahua, but I wondered what the long journey to Mexico City would be like.

©2018 by Sylvia Acevedo

According to the text, what did the narrator and Mario do while riding in the car?

A) They read books.

B) They sang songs.

C) They went to sleep.

D) They played games.

8

In the 1960s, Gloria Richardson led a movement to promote racial equality. Her involvement in this effort was inspired by her daughter, Donna Richardson. In 1961, Donna joined protests organized by the Student Nonviolent Coordinating Committee in Cambridge, Maryland. Following her daughter, Gloria joined these protests too. Gloria soon became the cochair of the Cambridge Nonviolent Action Committee. She was also the leader of what became known as the Cambridge movement.

According to the text, what did Gloria Richardson lead?

A) The Cambridge movement

B) Her daughter Donna's high school

C) Protests to support environmental protections

D) A new business in Cambridge, Maryland

9

Archaeologist Petra Vaiglova, anthropologist Xinyi Liu, and their colleagues investigated the domestication of farm animals in China during the Bronze Age (approximately 2000 to 1000 BCE). By analyzing the chemical composition of the bones of sheep, goats, and cattle from this era, the team determined that wild plants made up the bulk of sheep's and goats' diets, while the cattle's diet consisted largely of millet, a crop cultivated by humans. The team concluded that cattle were likely raised closer to human settlements, whereas sheep and goats were allowed to roam farther away.

Which finding, if true, would most strongly support the team's conclusion?

A) Analysis of the animal bones showed that the cattle's diet also consisted of wheat, which humans widely cultivated in China during the Bronze Age.

B) Further investigation of sheep and goat bones revealed that their diets consisted of small portions of millet as well.

C) Cattle's diets generally require larger amounts of food and a greater variety of nutrients than do sheep's and goats' diets.

D) The diets of sheep, goats, and cattle were found to vary based on what the farmers in each Bronze Age settlement could grow.

CONTINUE →

10

Top Four Species of Wild Land Mammals by Global Biomass

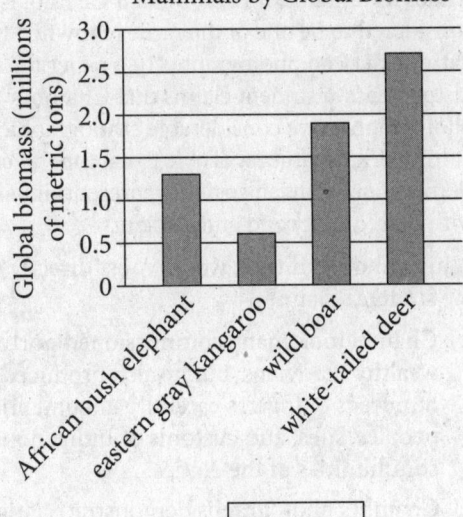

species

Global biomass is the total mass of living material, such as animals and plants, on Earth. A team of scientists estimated the global biomass, by species, of various wild land mammals. The team found that the species with the highest global biomass is the _____

Which choice most effectively uses data from the graph to complete the sentence?

A) wild boar.

B) eastern gray kangaroo.

C) African bush elephant.

D) white-tailed deer.

11

Housing Starts in the US, January–April 2022 (in thousands)

Month	Housing starts
January	1,669
February	1,771
March	1,713
April	1,803

When construction of a single-family house begins, it is called a housing start. In the first four months of 2022, the highest number of housing starts in the United States was in _____

Which choice most effectively uses data from the table to complete the statement?

A) April.

B) March.

C) January.

D) February.

CONTINUE ▶

12

Approximate Rates of Speech and Information
Conveyed for Five Languages

Language	Rate of speech (syllables per second)	Rate of information conveyed (bits per second)
Serbian	7.2	39.1
Spanish	7.7	42.0
Vietnamese	5.3	42.5
Thai	4.7	33.8
Hungarian	5.9	34.6

A group of researchers working in Europe, Asia, and Oceania conducted a study to determine how quickly different Eurasian languages are typically spoken (in syllables per second) and how much information they can effectively convey (in bits per second). They found that, although languages vary widely in the speed at which they are spoken, the amount of information languages can effectively convey tends to vary much less. Thus, they claim that two languages with very different spoken rates can nonetheless convey the same amount of information in a given amount of time.

Which choice best describes data from the table that support the researchers' claim?

A) Among the five languages in the table, Thai and Hungarian have the lowest rates of speech and the lowest rates of information conveyed.

B) Vietnamese conveys information at approximately the same rate as Spanish despite being spoken at a slower rate.

C) Among the five languages in the table, the language that is spoken the fastest is also the language that conveys information the fastest.

D) Serbian and Spanish are spoken at approximately the same rate, but Serbian conveys information faster than Spanish does.

13

Born in 1891 to a Quechua-speaking family in the Andes Mountains of Peru, Martín Chambi is today considered to be one of the most renowned figures of Latin American photography. In a paper for an art history class, a student claims that Chambi's photographs have considerable ethnographic value—in his work, Chambi was able to capture diverse elements of Peruvian society, representing his subjects with both dignity and authenticity.

Which finding, if true, would most directly support the student's claim?

A) Chambi took many commissioned portraits of wealthy Peruvians, but he also produced hundreds of images carefully documenting the peoples, sites, and customs of Indigenous communities of the Andes.

B) Chambi's photographs demonstrate a high level of technical skill, as seen in his strategic use of illumination to create dramatic light and shadow contrasts.

C) During his lifetime, Chambi was known and celebrated both within and outside his native Peru, as his work was published in places like Argentina, Spain, and Mexico.

D) Some of the peoples and places Chambi photographed had long been popular subjects for Peruvian photographers.

Unauthorized copying or reuse of any part of this page is illegal.

CONTINUE

1044

14

Although military veterans make up a small proportion of the total population of the United States, they occupy a significantly higher proportion of the jobs in the civilian government. One possible explanation for this disproportionate representation is that military service familiarizes people with certain organizational structures that are also reflected in the civilian government bureaucracy, and this familiarity thus _____

Which choice most logically completes the text?

A) makes civilian government jobs especially appealing to military veterans.

B) alters the typical relationship between military service and subsequent career preferences.

C) encourages nonveterans applying for civilian government jobs to consider military service instead.

D) increases the number of civilian government jobs that require some amount of military experience to perform.

15

British scientists James Watson and Francis Crick won the Nobel Prize in part for their 1953 paper announcing the double helix structure of DNA, but it is misleading to say that Watson and Crick discovered the double helix. _____ findings were based on a famous X-ray image of DNA fibers, "Photo 51," developed by X-ray crystallographer Rosalind Franklin and her graduate student Raymond Gosling.

Which choice completes the text so that it conforms to the conventions of Standard English?

A) They're

B) It's

C) Their

D) Its

16

A member of the Cherokee Nation, Mary Golda Ross is renowned for her contributions to NASA's Planetary Flight Handbook, which _____ detailed mathematical guidance for missions to Mars and Venus.

Which choice completes the text so that it conforms to the conventions of Standard English?

A) provided

B) having provided

C) to provide

D) providing

17

In order to prevent nonnative fish species from moving freely between the Mediterranean and Red Seas, marine biologist Bella Galil has proposed that a saline lock system be installed along the Suez Canal in Egypt's Great Bitter Lakes. The lock would increase the salinity of the lakes and _____ a natural barrier of water most marine creatures would be unable to cross.

Which choice completes the text so that it conforms to the conventions of Standard English?

A) creates

B) create

C) creating

D) created

18

After the United Kingdom began rolling out taxes equivalent to a few cents on single-use plastic grocery bags in 2011, plastic-bag consumption decreased by up to ninety _____ taxes are subject to what economists call the "rebound effect": as the change became normalized, plastic-bag use started to creep back up.

Which choice completes the text so that it conforms to the conventions of Standard English?

A) percent, such

B) percent and such

C) percent. Such

D) percent such

Unauthorized copying or reuse of any part of this page is illegal.

CONTINUE ▶

1045

19

Food and the sensation of taste are central to Monique Truong's novels. In *The Book of Salt*, for example, the exiled character of Binh connects to his native Saigon through the food he prepares, while in *Bitter in the Mouth*, the character of Linda _____ a form of synesthesia whereby the words she hears evoke tastes.

Which choice completes the text so that it conforms to the conventions of Standard English?

A) experienced

B) had experienced

C) experiences

D) will be experiencing

20

In February 1919, following the end of the First World War, women from ten countries around the world convened the Inter-Allied Women's Conference in Paris. The conference's goals were _____ ensure women's participation in the proceedings of the Paris Peace Conference, to secure the right of women to serve in the League of Nations, and to advocate for human rights.

Which choice completes the text so that it conforms to the conventions of Standard English?

A) threefold: to

B) threefold. To

C) threefold to

D) threefold; to

21

Most conifers (trees belonging to the phylum Coniferophyta) are evergreen. That is, they keep their green leaves or needles year-round. However, not all conifer species are evergreen. Larch trees, _____ lose their needles every fall.

Which choice completes the text with the most logical transition?

A) for instance,

B) nevertheless,

C) meanwhile,

D) in addition,

22

Etched into Peru's Nazca Desert are line drawings so large that they can only be fully seen from high above. Archaeologists have known of the lines since the 1920s, when a researcher spotted some from a nearby foothill, and they have been studying the markings ever since. _____ archaeologists' efforts are aided by drones that capture high-resolution aerial photographs of the lines.

Which choice completes the text with the most logical transition?

A) Currently,

B) In comparison,

C) Still,

D) However,

CONTINUE ➡

23

Organisms have evolved a number of surprising adaptations to ensure their survival in adverse conditions. Tadpole shrimp (*Triops longicaudatus*) embryos, _____ can pause development for over ten years during extended periods of drought.

Which choice completes the text with the most logical transition?

A) in contrast,

B) for example,

C) meanwhile,

D) consequently,

24

Chimamanda Ngozi Adichie's 2013 novel *Americanah* chronicles the divergent experiences of Ifemelu and Obinze, a young Nigerian couple, after high school. Ifemelu moves to the United States to attend a prestigious university. _____ Obinze travels to London, hoping to start a career there. However, frustrated with the lack of opportunities, he soon returns to Nigeria.

Which choice completes the text with the most logical transition?

A) Meanwhile,

B) Nevertheless,

C) Secondly,

D) In fact,

25

While researching a topic, a student has taken the following notes:

- Little is known about the life of Wong Fei-hung (1847–1925).

- He was born near Foshan, China, and gained local recognition as a physician and Hung Ga (also known as Hung Gar) Kung Fu master.

- He achieved many incredible martial arts feats— some confirmed and some rumored.

- He has become an internationally known folk hero thanks to his depiction in over a hundred films, television shows, and other media.

- In the 1991 film *Once Upon a Time in China*, actor Jet Li portrays Wong Fei-hung using superhuman kung fu abilities to save his community.

The student wants to emphasize the effect media had on building Wong Fei-hung's legacy. Which choice most effectively uses relevant information from the notes to accomplish this goal?

A) Thanks to his depiction in over a hundred pieces of media, Wong Fei-hung was locally known as a successful physician and Hung Ga Kung Fu master.

B) Though he was known locally during his lifetime, Wong Fei-hung's later depiction in television, film, and other media has turned him into an internationally known folk hero.

C) Various media have depicted Wong Fei-hung, the successful physician and kung fu master who became an internationally known folk hero.

D) Wong Fei-hung's abilities as a kung fu master are depicted in many media, including the 1991 film *Once Upon a Time in China*.

CONTINUE ▶

26

While researching a topic, a student has taken the following notes:

- The Seikan Tunnel is a rail tunnel in Japan.
- It connects the island of Honshu to the island of Hokkaido.
- It is roughly 33 miles long.
- The Channel Tunnel is a rail tunnel in Europe.
- It connects Folkestone, England, to Coquelles, France.
- It is about 31 miles long.

The student wants to compare the lengths of the two rail tunnels. Which choice most effectively uses relevant information from the notes to accomplish this goal?

A) Some of the world's rail tunnels, including one tunnel that extends from Folkestone, England, to Coquelles, France, are longer than 30 miles.

B) The Seikan Tunnel is roughly 33 miles long, while the slightly shorter Channel Tunnel is about 31 miles long.

C) The Seikan Tunnel, which is roughly 33 miles long, connects the Japanese islands of Honshu and Hokkaido.

D) Both the Seikan Tunnel, which is located in Japan, and the Channel Tunnel, which is located in Europe, are examples of rail tunnels.

27

While researching a topic, a student has taken the following notes:

- The Gullah are a group of African Americans who have lived in parts of the southeastern United States since the 18th century.
- Gullah culture is influenced by West African and Central African traditions.
- Louise Miller Cohen is a Gullah historian, storyteller, and preservationist.
- She founded the Gullah Museum of Hilton Head Island, South Carolina, in 2003.
- Vermelle Rodrigues is a Gullah historian, artist, and preservationist.
- She founded the Gullah Museum of Georgetown, South Carolina, in 2003.

The student wants to emphasize the duration and purpose of Cohen's and Rodrigues's work. Which choice most effectively uses relevant information from the notes to accomplish this goal?

A) At the Gullah Museums in Hilton Head Island and Georgetown, South Carolina, visitors can learn more about the Gullah people who have lived in the region for centuries.

B) Louise Miller Cohen and Vermelle Rodrigues have worked to preserve the culture of the Gullah people, who have lived in the United States since the 18th century.

C) Since 2003, Louise Miller Cohen and Vermelle Rodrigues have worked to preserve Gullah culture through their museums.

D) Influenced by the traditions of West and Central Africa, Gullah culture developed in parts of the southeastern United States in the 18th century.

STOP

**If you finish before time is called, you may check your work on this module only.
Do not turn to any other module in the test.**

Test begins on the next page.

Reading and Writing

27 QUESTIONS

The questions in this section address a number of important reading and writing skills. Each question includes one or more passages, which may include a table or graph. Read each passage and question carefully, and then choose the best answer to the question based on the passage(s).

All questions in this section are multiple-choice with four answer choices. Each question has a single best answer.

1

Critics have asserted that fine art and fashion rarely _____ in a world where artists create timeless works for exhibition and designers periodically produce new styles for the public to buy. Luiseño/Shoshone-Bannock beadwork artist and designer Jamie Okuma challenges this view: her work can be seen in the Metropolitan Museum of Art and purchased through her online boutique.

Which choice completes the text with the most logical and precise word or phrase?

A) prevail

B) succumb

C) diverge

D) intersect

2

Barring major archaeological discoveries, we are unlikely to ever have _____ account of ancient Egypt under the female pharaoh Hatshepsut, as much of the evidence of her reign was deliberately destroyed by her successors.

Which choice completes the text with the most logical and precise word or phrase?

A) an imaginative

B) a superficial

C) an exhaustive

D) a questionable

3

The work of Kiowa painter T.C. Cannon derives its power in part from the tension among his _____ influences: classic European portraiture, with its realistic treatment of faces; the American pop art movement, with its vivid colors; and flatstyle, the intertribal painting style that rejects the effect of depth typically achieved through shading and perspective.

Which choice completes the text with the most logical and precise word or phrase?

A) complementary

B) unknown

C) disparate

D) interchangeable

CONTINUE

Proposals to raise the age at which retirees begin receiving government transfers of funds are generally discussed in terms of the effects on transfer recipients, but Andria Smythe has argued that delaying such transfers could _____ wealth creation among working adults by lengthening the period in which they are providing financial support to their nonworking parents.

Which choice completes the text with the most logical and precise word or phrase?

A) stymie

B) compound

C) disparage

D) outstrip

The following text is adapted from Aphra Behn's 1689 novel *The Lucky Mistake*. Atlante and Rinaldo are neighbors who have been secretly exchanging letters through Charlot, Atlante's sister.

[Atlante] gave this letter to Charlot; who immediately ran into the balcony with it, where she still found Rinaldo in a melancholy posture, leaning his head on his hand: She showed him the letter, but was afraid to toss it to him, for fear it might fall to the ground; so he ran and fetched a long cane, which he cleft at one end, and held it while she put the letter into the cleft, and stayed not to hear what he said to it. But never was man so transported with joy, as he was at the reading of this letter; it gives him new wounds; for to the generous, nothing obliges love so much as love.

Which choice best describes the overall structure of the text?

A) It describes the delivery of a letter, and then portrays a character's happiness at reading that letter.

B) It establishes that a character is desperate to receive a letter, and then explains why another character has not yet written that letter.

C) It presents a character's concerns about delivering a letter, and then details the contents of that letter.

D) It reveals the inspiration behind a character's letter, and then emphasizes the excitement that another character feels upon receiving that letter.

CONTINUE

6

The following text is from Edith Wharton's 1905 novel *The House of Mirth*. Lily Bart and a companion are walking through a park.

Lily had no real intimacy with nature, but she had a passion for the appropriate and could be keenly sensitive to a scene which was the fitting background of her own sensations. The landscape outspread below her seemed an enlargement of her present mood, and she found something of herself in its calmness, its breadth, its long free reaches. On the nearer slopes the sugar-maples wavered like pyres of light; lower down was a massing of grey orchards, and here and there the lingering green of an oak-grove.

Which choice best describes the function of the underlined sentence in the text as a whole?

A) It creates a detailed image of the physical setting of the scene.

B) It establishes that a character is experiencing an internal conflict.

C) It makes an assertion that the next sentence then expands on.

D) It illustrates an idea that is introduced in the previous sentence.

7

Several studies have found negligible electoral consequences for governments that impose fiscal austerity measures, yet some European governments recently suffered electorally due to their austerity programs. Evelyne Huebscher and colleagues attribute this incongruity to governments' tendency—not followed in the recent European cases—to implement austerity programs strategically to avoid electoral costs (e.g., setting spending cuts to take effect only after the next election), which has obscured the inherent political risks of austerity measures in the election data scholars have examined.

Which choice best describes the function of the underlined sentence in the text as a whole?

A) It explains a discrepancy between what has been observed in study settings and what has been observed in real-world settings that the text goes on to assert is attributable to the studies not using real-world data.

B) It identifies a conflict between research findings and recent events that the text goes on to suggest is a consequence of a complicating factor in the data used to generate those findings.

C) It presents a long-standing divergence in research findings that the text goes on to say is due to different groups of researchers using data that derive from different electoral circumstances.

D) It describes a recent exception to a general pattern in research findings that the text goes on to explain is a result of researchers underestimating the significance of inconsistencies in the data they've analyzed.

CONTINUE →

8

Eighteenth-century economist Adam Smith is famed for his metaphor of the invisible hand, which he putatively used to illustrate a robust model of how individuals produce aggregate benefits by pursuing their own economic interests. Note "putatively": as Gavin Kennedy has shown, Smith deploys this metaphor only once in his economic writings—to make a narrow point about the then-dominant economic theory of mercantilism—and it was largely ignored until some twentieth-century economists eager to secure an intellectual pedigree for their views elevated it to a fully-fledged paradigm.

Which choice best states the main idea of the text?

A) Although Smith is famed for his metaphor of the invisible hand, the metaphor was largely ignored until economists in the twentieth century came to realize that the metaphor was a robust model that anticipated their own views.

B) Some twentieth-century economists gave Smith's metaphor of the invisible hand a significance it does not have in Smith's work, but it is nevertheless a useful model of how individuals produce aggregate benefits by pursuing their own economic interests.

C) Smith's metaphor of the invisible hand has been interpreted as a model of how individuals acting in their own interest produce aggregate benefits, but it was intended as a subtle critique of the economic theory of mercantilism.

D) The reputation of Smith's metaphor of the invisible hand is not due to the importance of the metaphor in Smith's work but rather to the promotion of the metaphor by some later economists for their own ends.

9

"To You" is an 1856 poem by Walt Whitman. In the poem, Whitman suggests that he deeply understands the reader, whom he addresses directly, writing, _____

Which quotation from "To You" most effectively illustrates the claim?

A) "Your true soul and body appear before me."

B) "Whoever you are, now I place my hand upon you, that you be my poem."

C) "I should have made my way straight to you long ago."

D) "Whoever you are, I fear you are walking the walks of dreams."

CONTINUE ➤

10

Average Number and Duration of Torpor Bouts and Arousal Episodes for Alaska Marmots and Arctic Ground Squirrels, 2008–2011

Feature	Alaska marmots	Arctic ground squirrels
torpor bouts	12	10.5
duration per bout	13.81 days	16.77 days
arousal episodes	11	9.5
duration per episode	21.2 hours	14.2 hours

When hibernating, Alaska marmots and Arctic ground squirrels enter a state called torpor, which minimizes the energy their bodies need to function. Often a hibernating animal will temporarily come out of torpor (called an arousal episode) and its metabolic rate will rise, burning more of the precious energy the animal needs to survive the winter. Alaska marmots hibernate in groups and therefore burn less energy keeping warm during these episodes than they would if they were alone. A researcher hypothesized that because Arctic ground squirrels hibernate alone, they would likely exhibit longer bouts of torpor and shorter arousal episodes than Alaska marmots.

Which choice best describes data from the table that support the researcher's hypothesis?

A) The Alaska marmots' arousal episodes lasted for days, while the Arctic ground squirrels' arousal episodes lasted less than a day.

B) The Alaska marmots and the Arctic ground squirrels both maintained torpor for several consecutive days per bout, on average.

C) The Alaska marmots had shorter torpor bouts and longer arousal episodes than the Arctic ground squirrels did.

D) The Alaska marmots had more torpor bouts than arousal episodes, but their arousal episodes were much shorter than their torpor bouts.

11

In the mountains of Brazil, *Barbacenia tomentosa* and *Barbacenia macrantha*—two plants in the Velloziaceae family—establish themselves on soilless, nutrient-poor patches of quartzite rock. Plant ecologists Anna Abrahão and Patricia de Britto Costa used microscopic analysis to determine that the roots of *B. tomentosa* and *B. macrantha*, which grow directly into the quartzite, have clusters of fine hairs near the root tip; further analysis indicated that these hairs secrete both malic and citric acids. The researchers hypothesize that the plants depend on dissolving underlying rock with these acids, as the process not only creates channels for continued growth but also releases phosphates that provide the vital nutrient phosphorus.

Which finding, if true, would most directly support the researchers' hypothesis?

A) Other species in the Velloziaceae family are found in terrains with more soil but have root structures similar to those of *B. tomentosa* and *B. macrantha*.

B) Though *B. tomentosa* and *B. macrantha* both secrete citric and malic acids, each species produces the acids in different proportions.

C) The roots of *B. tomentosa* and *B. macrantha* carve new entry points into rocks even when cracks in the surface are readily available.

D) *B. tomentosa* and *B. macrantha* thrive even when transferred to the surfaces of rocks that do not contain phosphates.

CONTINUE

12

Employment by Sector in France and the United States, 1800–2012
(% of total employment)

Year	Agriculture in France	Manufacturing in France	Services in France	Agriculture in US	Manufacturing in US	Services in US
1800	64	22	14	68	18	13
1900	43	29	28	41	28	31
1950	32	33	35	14	33	53
2012	3	21	76	2	18	80

Rows in table may not add up to 100 due to rounding.

Over the past two hundred years, the percentage of the population employed in the agricultural sector has declined in both France and the United States, while employment in the service sector (which includes jobs in retail, consulting, real estate, etc.) has risen. However, this transition happened at very different rates in the two countries. This can be seen most clearly by comparing the employment by sector in both countries in _____

Which choice most effectively uses data from the table to complete the statement?

A) 1900 with the employment by sector in 1950.

B) 1800 with the employment by sector in 2012.

C) 1900 with the employment by sector in 2012.

D) 1800 with the employment by sector in 1900.

Unauthorized copying or reuse of any part of this page is illegal.

CONTINUE ▶

1055

13

A team of biologists led by Jae-Hoon Jung, Antonio D. Barbosa, and Stephanie Hutin investigated the mechanism that allows *Arabidopsis thaliana* (thale cress) plants to accelerate flowering at high temperatures. They replaced the protein ELF3 in the plants with a similar protein found in another species (stiff brome) that, unlike *A. thaliana*, displays no acceleration in flowering with increased temperature. A comparison of unmodified *A. thaliana* plants with the altered plants showed no difference in flowering at 22° Celsius, but at 27° Celsius, the unmodified plants exhibited accelerated flowering while the altered ones did not, which suggests that _____

Which choice most logically completes the text?

A) temperature-sensitive accelerated flowering is unique to *A. thaliana*.

B) *A. thaliana* increases ELF3 production as temperatures rise.

C) ELF3 enables *A. thaliana* to respond to increased temperatures.

D) temperatures of at least 22° Celsius are required for *A. thaliana* to flower.

14

The domestic sweet potato (*Ipomoea batatas*) descends from a wild plant native to South America. It also populates the Polynesian Islands, where evidence confirms that Native Hawaiians and other Indigenous peoples were cultivating the plant centuries before seafaring first occurred over the thousands of miles of ocean separating them from South America. To explain how the sweet potato was first introduced in Polynesia, botanist Pablo Muñoz-Rodríguez and colleagues analyzed the DNA of numerous varieties of the plant, concluding that Polynesian varieties diverged from South American ones over 100,000 years ago. Given that Polynesia was peopled only in the last three thousand years, the team concluded that _____

Which choice most logically completes the text?

A) the cultivation of the sweet potato in Polynesia likely predates its cultivation in South America.

B) Polynesian peoples likely acquired the sweet potato from South American peoples only within the last three thousand years.

C) human activity likely played no role in the introduction of the sweet potato in Polynesia.

D) Polynesian sweet potato varieties likely descend from a single South American variety that was domesticated, not wild.

15

In 1966, Emmett Ashford became the first African American to umpire a Major League Baseball game. His energetic gestures announcing when a player had struck out and his habit of barreling after a hit ball to see if it would land out of _____ transform the traditionally solemn umpire role into a dynamic one.

Which choice completes the text so that it conforms to the conventions of Standard English?

A) bounds helped

B) bounds, helping

C) bounds that helped

D) bounds to help

CONTINUE

16

Stomata, tiny pore structures in a leaf that absorb gases needed for plant growth, open when guard cells surrounding each pore swell with water. In a pivotal 2007 article, plant cell _____ showed that lipid molecules called phosphatidylinositol phosphates are responsible for signaling guard cells to open stomata.

Which choice completes the text so that it conforms to the conventions of Standard English?

A) biologist, Yuree Lee

B) biologist Yuree Lee,

C) biologist Yuree Lee

D) biologist, Yuree Lee,

17

In the late nineteenth and early twentieth centuries, automobiles were commonly referred to as horseless carriages after the older technology they still resembled. Known as the Brass Era, this period in automotive design is remembered for its grandeur and artistry, its vehicles _____ by collectors for their ornate detailing and gleaming brass fittings.

Which choice completes the text so that it conforms to the conventions of Standard English?

A) are highly prized

B) had been highly prized

C) highly prized

D) were highly prized

18

During the English neoclassical period (1660–1789), many writers imitated the epic poetry and satires of ancient Greece and Rome. They were not the first in England to adopt the literary modes of classical _____ some of the most prominent figures of the earlier Renaissance period were also influenced by ancient Greek and Roman literature.

Which choice completes the text so that it conforms to the conventions of Standard English?

A) antiquity, however

B) antiquity, however,

C) antiquity, however;

D) antiquity; however,

19

With the development of new technologies that use natural resources more efficiently, the overall consumption of those resources might be expected to decrease. Economists have observed that improvements in efficiency often correlate negatively with resource _____ efficiency gains, lowering the cost of use, may increase demand to the extent that resource consumption ultimately rises.

Which choice completes the text so that it conforms to the conventions of Standard English?

A) conservation, though,

B) conservation; though

C) conservation, though;

D) conservation, though

CONTINUE

20

The ghazal, a poetic form originating in seventh-century Arabic poetry, has an intricate structure. The twentieth-century Kashmiri American poet Agha Shahid Ali explains that each one of a ghazal's couplets, while adhering to the patterns of rhyme (*qafia*) and refrain (*radif*) established in the poem's opening lines (*matla*), _____ thematically and logically autonomous, resulting in a poem with "a stringently formal disunity."

Which choice completes the text so that it conforms to the conventions of Standard English?

A) is

B) were

C) have been

D) are

21

In November 1934, Amrita Sher-Gil was living in what must have seemed like the ideal city for a young artist: Paris. She was studying firsthand the color-saturated style of France's modernist masters and beginning to make a name for herself as a painter. _____ Sher-Gil longed to return to her childhood home of India; only there, she believed, could her art truly flourish.

Which choice completes the text with the most logical transition?

A) Still,

B) Therefore,

C) Indeed,

D) Furthermore,

22

Researchers Helena Mihaljević-Brandt, Lucía Santamaría, and Marco Tullney report that while mathematicians may have traditionally worked alone, evidence points to a shift in the opposite direction. _____ mathematicians are choosing to collaborate with their peers—a trend illustrated by a rise in the number of mathematics publications credited to multiple authors.

Which choice completes the text with the most logical transition?

A) Similarly,

B) For this reason,

C) Furthermore,

D) Increasingly,

23

The prime meridian, the global indicator of zero degrees longitude established in 1884, was originally determined using astronomically derived coordinates. _____ as decades passed, new calculations would reveal increasingly precise coordinates, yet the prime meridian remained unchanged; it wasn't until the 1980s that, spurred by improved geodetic data, the prime meridian was officially moved—roughly one hundred meters east.

Which choice completes the text with the most logical transition?

A) Specifically,

B) To that end,

C) Again and again,

D) Granted,

CONTINUE ▶

24

While researching a topic, a student has taken the following notes:

- *Puntius javanicus* is a species of commercially raised fish.
- Researchers in Indonesia recently found that adding pineapple extract to fish food increased both the feed utilization efficiency and the growth rate of *P. javanicus*.
- Adding the pineapple extract did not affect total food consumption.
- The researchers thus determined that the increased growth rate resulted from the increased feed utilization efficiency.
- The enzyme bromelain in pineapple extract enhances the hydrolysis of ingested proteins.
- This allows the fish to more readily absorb them.

The student wants to explain how pineapple extract increased the growth rate of *P. javanicus*. Which choice most effectively uses relevant information from the notes to accomplish this goal?

A) Researchers in Indonesia recently found that adding pineapple extract to fish food increased the growth rate of *P. javanicus*.

B) An enzyme in pineapple extract, bromelain increased the growth rate of *P. javanicus* by enhancing the hydrolysis of ingested proteins, in turn affecting the fish's total food consumption.

C) According to the researchers, the growth rate of *P. javanicus* was affected not by food consumption but by feed utilization efficiency.

D) The enzyme bromelain enhanced *P. javanicus*'s absorption of ingested proteins, increasing the growth rate of fish fed pineapple extract.

25

While researching a topic, a student has taken the following notes:

- NASA uses rovers, large remote vehicles with wheels, to explore the surface of Mars.
- NASA's rovers can't explore regions inaccessible to wheeled vehicles.
- Rovers are also heavy, making them difficult to land on the planet's surface.
- Microprobes, robotic probes that weigh as little as 50 milligrams, could be deployed virtually anywhere on the surface of Mars.
- Microprobes have been proposed as an alternative to rovers.

The student wants to explain an advantage of microprobes. Which choice most effectively uses relevant information from the notes to accomplish this goal?

A) Despite being heavy, NASA's rovers can land successfully on the surface of Mars.

B) Microprobes, which weigh as little as 50 milligrams, could explore areas of Mars that are inaccessible to NASA's heavy, wheeled rovers.

C) NASA currently uses its rovers on Mars, but microprobes have been proposed as an alternative.

D) Though they are different sizes, both microprobes and rovers can be used to explore the surface of Mars.

CONTINUE

26

While researching a topic, a student has taken the following notes:

- When medical students mention their patients on social media, they may violate patient confidentiality.

- Terry Kind led a study to determine how many medical schools have student policies that mention social media use.

- Kind and her team reviewed 132 medical school websites, examining publicly available student policies.

- Only thirteen medical schools had guidelines that explicitly mention social media, and only five defined what constitutes acceptable social media use.

The student wants to emphasize the study's methodology. Which choice most effectively uses relevant information from the notes to accomplish this goal?

A) The student policies of 132 medical schools can be found online, according to research by Terry Kind.

B) To find out how many medical schools have guidelines about student social media use, Terry Kind and her team examined the student policies of 132 medical schools.

C) Out of 132 medical schools, only thirteen had student policies that mentioned social media, and only five specified what use was acceptable.

D) Terry Kind and her team wanted to know how many medical schools have student social media policies in place about protecting patient confidentiality.

27

While researching a topic, a student has taken the following notes:

- British musicians John Lennon and Paul McCartney shared writing credit for numerous Beatles songs.

- Many Lennon-McCartney songs were actually written by either Lennon or McCartney, not by both.

- The exact authorship of specific parts of many Beatles songs, such as the verse for "In My Life," is disputed.

- Mark Glickman, Jason Brown, and Ryan Song used statistical methods to analyze the musical content of Beatles songs.

- They concluded that there is 18.9% probability that McCartney wrote the verse for "In My Life," stating that the verse is "consistent with Lennon's songwriting style."

The student wants to make a generalization about the kind of study conducted by Glickman, Brown, and Song. Which choice most effectively uses relevant information from the notes to accomplish this goal?

A) Based on statistical analysis, Glickman, Brown, and Song claim that John Lennon wrote the verse of "In My Life."

B) There is only an 18.9% probability that Paul McCartney wrote the verse for "In My Life"; John Lennon is the more likely author.

C) It is likely that John Lennon, not Paul McCartney, wrote the verse for "In My Life."

D) Researchers have used statistical methods to address questions of authorship within the field of music.

STOP

If you finish before time is called, you may check your work on this module only.
Do not turn to any other module in the test.

Test begins on the next page.

Math

22 QUESTIONS

DIRECTIONS

The questions in this section address a number of important math skills.
Use of a calculator is permitted for all questions.

NOTES

Unless otherwise indicated:

- All variables and expressions represent real numbers.
- Figures provided are drawn to scale.
- All figures lie in a plane.
- The domain of a given function f is the set of all real numbers x for which $f(x)$ is a real number.

REFERENCE

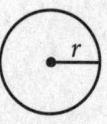
$A = \pi r^2$
$C = 2\pi r$

$A = \ell w$

$A = \frac{1}{2} bh$

$c^2 = a^2 + b^2$

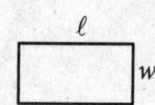

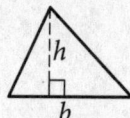
Special Right Triangles

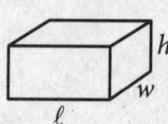
$V = \ell wh$

$V = \pi r^2 h$

$V = \frac{4}{3} \pi r^3$

$V = \frac{1}{3} \pi r^2 h$

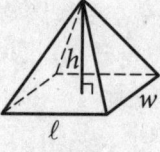
$V = \frac{1}{3} \ell wh$

The number of degrees of arc in a circle is 360.

The number of radians of arc in a circle is 2π.

The sum of the measures in degrees of the angles of a triangle is 180.

CONTINUE ➡

For multiple-choice questions, solve each problem, choose the correct answer from the choices provided, and then circle your answer in this book. Circle only one answer for each question. If you change your mind, completely erase the circle. You will not get credit for questions with more than one answer circled, or for questions with no answers circled.

For student-produced response questions, solve each problem and write your answer next to or under the question in the test book as described below.

- Once you've written your answer, circle it clearly. You will not receive credit for anything written outside the circle, or for any questions with more than one circled answer.

- If you find **more than one correct answer**, write and circle only one answer.

- Your answer can be up to 5 characters for a **positive** answer and up to 6 characters (including the negative sign) for a **negative** answer, but no more.

- If your answer is a **fraction** that is too long (over 5 characters for positive, 6 characters for negative), write the decimal equivalent.

- If your answer is a **decimal** that is too long (over 5 characters for positive, 6 characters for negative), truncate it or round at the fourth digit.

- If your answer is a **mixed number** (such as $3\frac{1}{2}$), write it as an improper fraction (7/2) or its decimal equivalent (3.5).

- Don't include **symbols** such as a percent sign, comma, or dollar sign in your circled answer.

CONTINUE →

1

For a particular machine that produces beads, 29 out of every 100 beads it produces have a defect. A bead produced by the machine will be selected at random. What is the probability of selecting a bead that has a defect?

A) $\dfrac{1}{2,900}$

B) $\dfrac{1}{29}$

C) $\dfrac{29}{100}$

D) $\dfrac{29}{10}$

2

$$s = 40 + 3t$$

The equation gives the speed s, in miles per hour, of a certain car t seconds after it began to accelerate. What is the speed, in miles per hour, of the car 5 seconds after it began to accelerate?

A) 40

B) 43

C) 45

D) 55

3

If $4x = 3$, what is the value of $24x$?

A) $\dfrac{9}{2}$

B) 6

C) 18

D) 72

4

The scatterplot shows the relationship between two variables, x and y. A line of best fit is also shown.

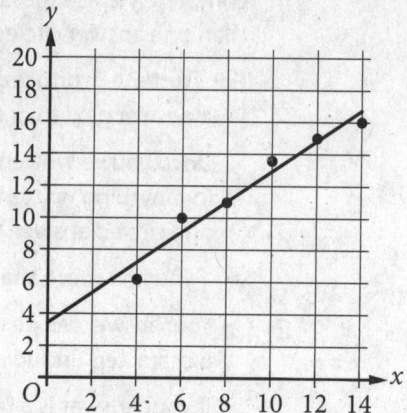

Which of the following equations best represents the line of best fit shown?

A) $y = x + 3.4$

B) $y = x - 3.4$

C) $y = -x + 3.4$

D) $y = -x - 3.4$

5

Of 300,000 paper clips, 234,000 are size large. What percentage of the paper clips are size large?

A) 22%

B) 33%

C) 66%

D) 78%

CONTINUE

6

x	y
0	18
1	13
2	8

The table shows three values of x and their corresponding values of y. There is a linear relationship between x and y. Which of the following equations represents this relationship?

A) $y = 18x + 13$

B) $y = 18x + 18$

C) $y = -5x + 13$

D) $y = -5x + 18$

7

The function f is defined by $f(x) = x^2 + x + 71$. What is the value of $f(2)$?

8

Which expression is equivalent to $(m^4 q^4 z^{-1})(mq^5 z^3)$, where m, q, and z are positive?

A) $m^4 q^{20} z^{-3}$

B) $m^5 q^9 z^2$

C) $m^6 q^8 z^{-1}$

D) $m^{20} q^{12} z^{-2}$

9

Triangle ABC is similar to triangle XYZ, where A, B, and C correspond to X, Y, and Z, respectively. In triangle ABC, the length of $\overline{AB}$ is 170 and the length of $\overline{BC}$ is 850. In triangle XYZ, the length of $\overline{YZ}$ is 60. What is the length of $\overline{XY}$?

A) 204

B) 182

C) 60

D) 12

10

If $\frac{x}{y} = 4$ and $\frac{24x}{ny} = 4$, what is the value of n?

11

$$w(t) = 300 - 4t$$

The function w models the volume of liquid, in milliliters, in a container t seconds after it begins draining from a hole at the bottom. According to the model, what is the predicted volume, in milliliters, draining from the container each second?

A) 300

B) 296

C) 75

D) 4

12

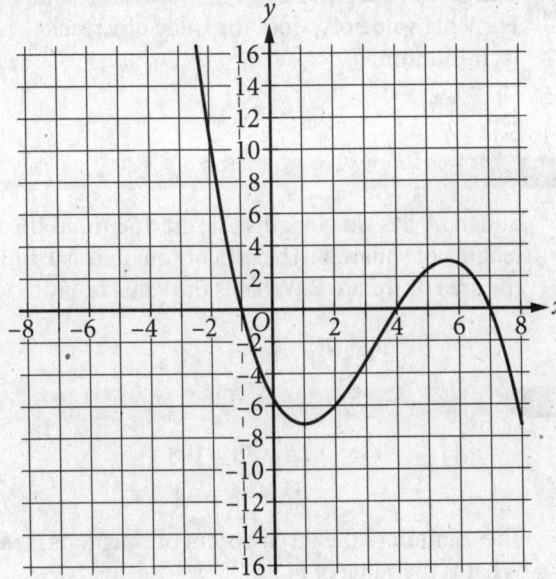

The graph of $y = f(x)$ is shown, where the function f is defined by $f(x) = ax^3 + bx^2 + cx + d$ and a, b, c, and d are constants. For how many values of x does $f(x) = 0$?

A) One

B) Two

C) Three

D) Four

CONTINUE

13

$$f(x) = 3{,}000(0.75)^x$$

A conservation scientist implemented a program to reduce the population of a certain species in an area. The given function estimates this species' population x years after 2008, where $x \le 8$. Which of the following is the best interpretation of 3,000 in this context?

A) The estimated percent decrease in the population for this species and area every 8 years after 2008

B) The estimated percent decrease in the population for this species and area each year after 2008

C) The estimated population for this species and area 8 years after 2008

D) The estimated initial population for this species and area in 2008

14

$$y = x^2 - 14x + 22$$

The given equation relates the variables x and y. For what value of x does the value of y reach its minimum?

15

Square A has side lengths that are 166 times the side lengths of square B. The area of square A is k times the area of square B. What is the value of k?

16

$$2a + 8b = 198$$
$$2a + 4b = 98$$

The solution to the given system of equations is (a, b). What is the value of b?

17

The function f is defined by $f(x) = (-8)(2)^x + 22$. What is the y-intercept of the graph of $y = f(x)$ in the xy-plane?

A) (0, 14)

B) (0, 2)

C) (0, 22)

D) (0, −8)

18

Two variables, x and y, are related such that for each increase of 1 in the value of x, the value of y increases by a factor of 4. When $x = 0$, $y = 200$. Which equation represents this relationship?

A) $y = 4(x)^{200}$

B) $y = 4(200)^x$

C) $y = 200(x)^4$

D) $y = 200(4)^x$

19

What is the value of $\sin 42\pi$?

A) 0

B) $\frac{1}{2}$

C) $\frac{\sqrt{2}}{2}$

D) 1

20

$$4x - 9y = 9y + 5$$
$$hy = 2 + 4x$$

In the given system of equations, h is a constant. If the system has no solution, what is the value of h?

A) −9

B) 0

C) 9

D) 18

CONTINUE

21

$$x^2 - 2x - 9 = 0$$

One solution to the given equation can be written as $1 + \sqrt{k}$, where k is a constant. What is the value of k?

A) 8

B) 10

C) 20

D) 40

22

$$\frac{x^2}{\sqrt{x^2 - c^2}} = \frac{c^2}{\sqrt{x^2 - c^2}} + 39$$

In the given equation, c is a positive constant. Which of the following is one of the solutions to the given equation?

A) $-c$

B) $-c^2 - 39^2$

C) $-\sqrt{39^2 - c^2}$

D) $-\sqrt{c^2 + 39^2}$

STOP

If you finish before time is called, you may check your work on this module only.
Do not turn to any other module in the test.

Math

22 QUESTIONS

The questions in this section address a number of important math skills.
Use of a calculator is permitted for all questions.

NOTES

Unless otherwise indicated:

- All variables and expressions represent real numbers.
- Figures provided are drawn to scale.
- All figures lie in a plane.
- The domain of a given function f is the set of all real numbers x for which $f(x)$ is a real number.

REFERENCE

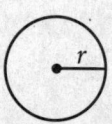 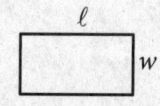 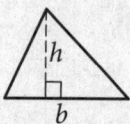 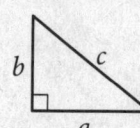 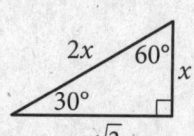

$A = \pi r^2$
$C = 2\pi r$ $A = \ell w$ $A = \frac{1}{2}bh$ $c^2 = a^2 + b^2$ Special Right Triangles

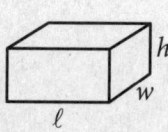    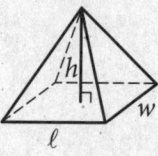

$V = \ell wh$ $V = \pi r^2 h$ $V = \frac{4}{3}\pi r^3$ $V = \frac{1}{3}\pi r^2 h$ $V = \frac{1}{3}\ell wh$

The number of degrees of arc in a circle is 360.

The number of radians of arc in a circle is 2π.

The sum of the measures in degrees of the angles of a triangle is 180.

CONTINUE ➡

For multiple-choice questions, solve each problem, choose the correct answer from the choices provided, and then circle your answer in this book. Circle only one answer for each question. If you change your mind, completely erase the circle. You will not get credit for questions with more than one answer circled, or for questions with no answers circled.

For student-produced response questions, solve each problem and write your answer next to or under the question in the test book as described below.

- Once you've written your answer, circle it clearly. You will not receive credit for anything written outside the circle, or for any questions with more than one circled answer.

- If you find **more than one correct answer**, write and circle only one answer.

- Your answer can be up to 5 characters for a **positive** answer and up to 6 characters (including the negative sign) for a **negative** answer, but no more.

- If your answer is a **fraction** that is too long (over 5 characters for positive, 6 characters for negative), write the decimal equivalent.

- If your answer is a **decimal** that is too long (over 5 characters for positive, 6 characters for negative), truncate it or round at the fourth digit.

- If your answer is a **mixed number** (such as $3\frac{1}{2}$), write it as an improper fraction (7/2) or its decimal equivalent (3.5).

- Don't include **symbols** such as a percent sign, comma, or dollar sign in your circled answer.

CONTINUE

1

$$4x + 5 = 165$$

What is the solution to the given equation?

2

Type of store	Average number of employees
Warehouse store	365
Department store	213
Supermarket	130

For a certain region, the table shows the average number of store employees in 2016 by type of store. Based on the table, how much greater was the average number of store employees in warehouse stores than in supermarkets?

A) 83

B) 152

C) 235

D) 495

3

Julissa needs at least 100 hours of flight time to get her private pilot certification. If Julissa already has 86 hours of flight time, what is the minimum number of additional hours of flight time Julissa needs to get her private pilot certification?

A) 14

B) 76

C) 86

D) 186

4

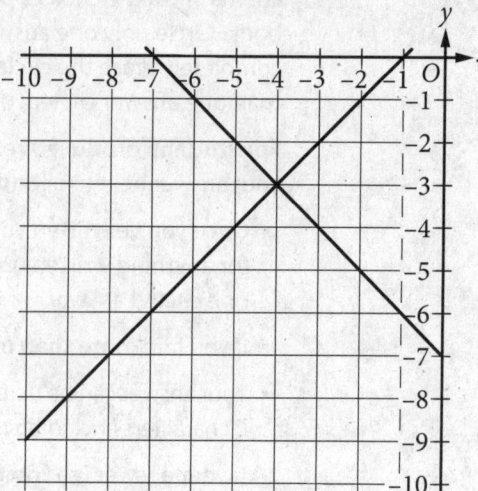

The graph of a system of linear equations is shown. What is the solution (x, y) to the system?

A) $(0, -7)$

B) $(0, -3)$

C) $(-4, -3)$

D) $(-4, 0)$

5

A giant armadillo has a mass of 39 kilograms. What is the giant armadillo's mass in **grams**? (1 kilogram = 1,000 grams)

6

The function f is defined by $f(x) = 4x$. For what value of x does $f(x) = 8$?

7

Triangles ABC and DEF are congruent, where A corresponds to D, and B and E are right angles. The measure of angle A is 18°. What is the measure of angle F?

A) 18°

B) 72°

C) 90°

D) 162°

CONTINUE ▶

8

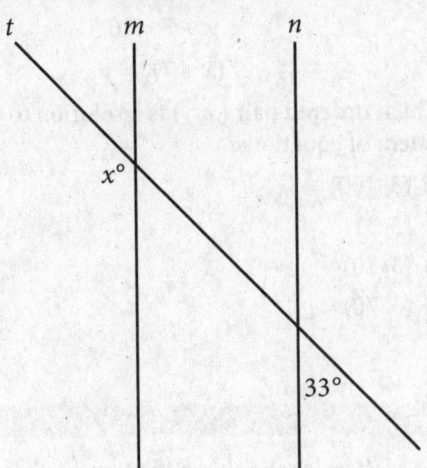

Note: Figure not drawn to scale.

In the figure, line *m* is parallel to line *n*, and line *t* intersects both lines. What is the value of *x*?

A) 33

B) 57

C) 123

D) 147

9

$$3x = 12$$
$$-3x + y = -6$$

The solution to the given system of equations is (x, y). What is the value of *y*?

A) −3

B) 6

C) 18

D) 30

10

Which expression is equivalent to $9x^2 + 5x$?

A) $x(9x + 5)$

B) $5x(9x + 1)$

C) $9x(x + 5)$

D) $x^2(9x + 5)$

11

Jay walks at a speed of 3 miles per hour and runs at a speed of 5 miles per hour. He walks for *w* hours and runs for *r* hours for a combined total of 14 miles. Which equation represents this situation?

A) $3w + 5r = 14$

B) $\frac{1}{3}w + \frac{1}{5}r = 14$

C) $\frac{1}{3}w + \frac{1}{5}r = 112$

D) $3w + 5r = 112$

12

What is the perimeter, in inches, of a rectangle with a length of 4 inches and a width of 9 inches?

A) 13

B) 17

C) 22

D) 26

13

A line in the *xy*-plane has a slope of $\frac{1}{9}$ and passes through the point $(0, 14)$. Which equation represents this line?

A) $y = -\frac{1}{9}x - 14$

B) $y = -\frac{1}{9}x + 14$

C) $y = \frac{1}{9}x - 14$

D) $y = \frac{1}{9}x + 14$

Unauthorized copying or reuse of any part of this page is illegal.

CONTINUE

1071

14

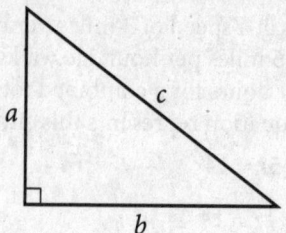

Note: Figure not drawn to scale.

For the right triangle shown, $a = 4$ and $b = 5$. Which expression represents the value of c?

A) $4 + 5$

B) $\sqrt{(4)(5)}$

C) $\sqrt{4 + 5}$

D) $\sqrt{4^2 + 5^2}$

15

Vivian bought party hats and cupcakes for $71. Each package of party hats cost $3, and each cupcake cost $1. If Vivian bought 10 packages of party hats, how many cupcakes did she buy?

16

The function f is defined by $f(x) = 7x^3$. In the xy-plane, the graph of $y = g(x)$ is the result of shifting the graph of $y = f(x)$ down 2 units. Which equation defines function g?

A) $g(x) = \frac{7}{2}x^3$

B) $g(x) = 7x^{\frac{3}{2}}$

C) $g(x) = 7x^3 + 2$

D) $g(x) = 7x^3 - 2$

17

$$x + 7 = 10$$
$$(x + 7)^2 = y$$

Which ordered pair (x, y) is a solution to the given system of equations?

A) $(3, 100)$

B) $(3, 3)$

C) $(3, 10)$

D) $(3, 70)$

18

The scatterplot shows the relationship between two variables, x and y. A line of best fit is also shown.

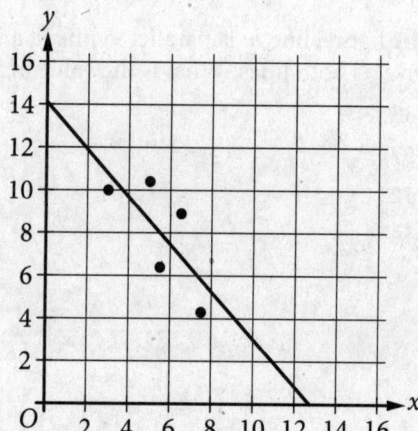

Which of the following is closest to the slope of this line of best fit?

A) -3.3

B) -1.1

C) 1.1

D) 3.3

CONTINUE

19

$$y = 6x + 18$$

One of the equations in a system of two linear equations is given. The system has no solution. Which equation could be the second equation in the system?

A) $-6x + y = 18$

B) $-6x + y = 22$

C) $-12x + y = 36$

D) $-12x + y = 18$

20

The function f is defined by $f(x) = 7x - 84$. What is the x-intercept of the graph of $y = f(x)$ in the xy-plane?

A) $(-12, 0)$

B) $(-7, 0)$

C) $(7, 0)$

D) $(12, 0)$

21

The exponential function g is defined by $g(x) = 19 \cdot a^x$, where a is a positive constant. If $g(3) = 2{,}375$, what is the value of $g(4)$?

22

The population of Greenville increased by 7% from 2015 to 2016. If the 2016 population is k times the 2015 population, what is the value of k?

A) 0.07

B) 0.7

C) 1.07

D) 1.7

STOP

If you finish before time is called, you may check your work on this module only. Do not turn to any other module in the test.

Math

22 QUESTIONS

DIRECTIONS

The questions in this section address a number of important math skills.

Use of a calculator is permitted for all questions.

NOTES

Unless otherwise indicated:

- All variables and expressions represent real numbers.
- Figures provided are drawn to scale.
- All figures lie in a plane.
- The domain of a given function f is the set of all real numbers x for which $f(x)$ is a real number.

REFERENCE

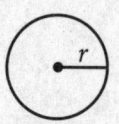

$A = \pi r^2$
$C = 2\pi r$

$A = \ell w$

$A = \frac{1}{2}bh$

$c^2 = a^2 + b^2$

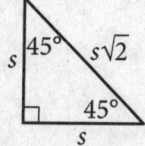

Special Right Triangles

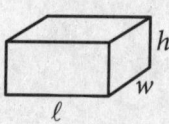

$V = \ell wh$

$V = \pi r^2 h$

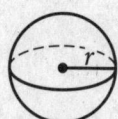

$V = \frac{4}{3}\pi r^3$

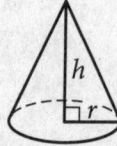

$V = \frac{1}{3}\pi r^2 h$

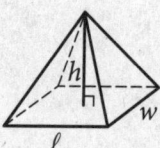

$V = \frac{1}{3}\ell wh$

The number of degrees of arc in a circle is 360.

The number of radians of arc in a circle is 2π.

The sum of the measures in degrees of the angles of a triangle is 180.

CONTINUE ➔

For multiple-choice questions, solve each problem, choose the correct answer from the choices provided, and then circle your answer in this book. Circle only one answer for each question. If you change your mind, completely erase the circle. You will not get credit for questions with more than one answer circled, or for questions with no answers circled.

For student-produced response questions, solve each problem and write your answer next to or under the question in the test book as described below.

- Once you've written your answer, circle it clearly. You will not receive credit for anything written outside the circle, or for any questions with more than one circled answer.

- If you find **more than one correct answer**, write and circle only one answer.

- Your answer can be up to 5 characters for a **positive** answer and up to 6 characters (including the negative sign) for a **negative** answer, but no more.

- If your answer is a **fraction** that is too long (over 5 characters for positive, 6 characters for negative), write the decimal equivalent.

- If your answer is a **decimal** that is too long (over 5 characters for positive, 6 characters for negative), truncate it or round at the fourth digit.

- If your answer is a **mixed number** (such as $3\frac{1}{2}$), write it as an improper fraction (7/2) or its decimal equivalent (3.5).

- Don't include **symbols** such as a percent sign, comma, or dollar sign in your circled answer.

Unauthorized copying or reuse of any part of this page is illegal.

CONTINUE

1075

1

An airplane descends from an altitude of 9,500 feet to 5,000 feet at a constant rate of 400 feet per minute. What type of function best models the relationship between the descending airplane's altitude and time?

A) Decreasing exponential

B) Decreasing linear

C) Increasing exponential

D) Increasing linear

2

Line k is defined by $y = \frac{17}{7}x + 4$. Line j is parallel to line k in the xy-plane. What is the slope of line j?

A) $\frac{7}{17}$

B) $\frac{17}{7}$

C) 4

D) 17

3

Caleb used juice to make popsicles. The function $f(x) = -5x + 30$ approximates the volume, in fluid ounces, of juice Caleb had remaining after making x popsicles. Which statement is the best interpretation of the y-intercept of the graph of $y = f(x)$ in the xy-plane in this context?

A) Caleb used approximately 5 fluid ounces of juice for each popsicle.

B) Caleb had approximately 5 fluid ounces of juice when he began to make the popsicles.

C) Caleb had approximately 30 fluid ounces of juice when he began to make the popsicles.

D) Caleb used approximately 30 fluid ounces of juice for each popsicle.

4

A physics class is planning an experiment about a toy rocket. The equation $y = -16(x - 5.6)^2 + 502$ gives the estimated height y, in feet, of the toy rocket x seconds after it is launched into the air. Which of the following is the best interpretation of the vertex of the graph of the equation in the xy-plane?

A) This toy rocket reaches an estimated maximum height of 502 feet 16 seconds after it is launched into the air.

B) This toy rocket reaches an estimated maximum height of 502 feet 5.6 seconds after it is launched into the air.

C) This toy rocket reaches an estimated maximum height of 16 feet 502 seconds after it is launched into the air.

D) This toy rocket reaches an estimated maximum height of 5.6 feet 502 seconds after it is launched into the air.

5

The function f is defined by $f(x) = 4x + k(x - 1)$, where k is a constant, and $f(5) = 32$. What is the value of $f(10)$?

6

Triangles ABC and DEF are congruent, where A corresponds to D, and B and E are right angles. The measure of angle A is 18°. What is the measure of angle F?

A) 18°

B) 72°

C) 90°

D) 162°

Unauthorized copying or reuse of any part of this page is illegal.

1076

CONTINUE →

7

$$y \leq x + 7$$
$$y \geq -2x - 1$$

Which point (x, y) is a solution to the given system of inequalities in the xy-plane?

A) $(-14, 0)$

B) $(0, -14)$

C) $(0, 14)$

D) $(14, 0)$

8

The dot plots represent the distributions of values in data sets A and B.

Data Set A   Data Set B

Value   Value

Which of the following statements must be true?

I. The median of data set A is equal to the median of data set B.

II. The standard deviation of data set A is equal to the standard deviation of data set B.

A) I only

B) II only

C) I and II

D) Neither I nor II

9

A scientist initially measures 12,000 bacteria in a growth medium. 4 hours later, the scientist measures 24,000 bacteria. Assuming exponential growth, the formula $P = C(2)^{rt}$ gives the number of bacteria in the growth medium, where r and C are constants and P is the number of bacteria t hours after the initial measurement. What is the value of r?

A) $\dfrac{1}{12,000}$

B) $\dfrac{1}{4}$

C) 4

D) $12,000$

10

A cube has a volume of 474,552 cubic units. What is the surface area, in square units, of the cube?

11

$$2(8x) + 4(7y) = 12$$
$$-2(8x) + 4(7y) = 12$$

The solution to the given system of equations is (x, y). What is the value of $8x + 7y$?

12

A certain town has an area of 4.36 square miles. What is the area, in square yards, of this town? (1 mile = 1,760 yards)

A) 404

B) 7,674

C) 710,459

D) 13,505,536

CONTINUE ➤

13

Triangles PQR and LMN are graphed in the xy-plane. Triangle PQR has vertices P, Q, and R at $(4, 5)$, $(4, 7)$, and $(6, 5)$, respectively. Triangle LMN has vertices L, M, and N at $(4, 5)$, $(4, 7 + k)$, and $(6 + k, 5)$, respectively, where k is a positive constant. If the measure of $\angle Q$ is $t°$, what is the measure of $\angle N$?

A) $(90 - (t - k))°$

B) $(90 - (t + k))°$

C) $(90 - t)°$

D) $(90 + k)°$

14

A small business owner budgets \$2,200 to purchase candles. The owner must purchase a minimum of 200 candles to maintain the discounted pricing. If the owner pays \$4.90 per candle to purchase small candles and \$11.60 per candle to purchase large candles, what is the maximum number of large candles the owner can purchase to stay within the budget and maintain the discounted pricing?

15

A square is inscribed in a circle. The radius of the circle is $\frac{20\sqrt{2}}{2}$ inches. What is the side length, in inches, of the square?

A) 20

B) $\frac{20\sqrt{2}}{2}$

C) $20\sqrt{2}$

D) 40

16

Which of the following equations represents a circle in the xy-plane that intersects the y-axis at exactly one point?

A) $(x - 8)^2 + (y - 8)^2 = 16$

B) $(x - 8)^2 + (y - 4)^2 = 16$

C) $(x - 4)^2 + (y - 9)^2 = 16$

D) $x^2 + (y - 9)^2 = 16$

17

$$y = 6x + 18$$

One of the equations in a system of two linear equations is given. The system has no solution. Which equation could be the second equation in the system?

A) $-6x + y = 18$

B) $-6x + y = 22$

C) $-12x + y = 36$

D) $-12x + y = 18$

18

Which expression is equivalent to $\dfrac{y + 12}{x - 8} + \dfrac{y(x - 8)}{x^2 y - 8xy}$?

A) $\dfrac{xy + y + 4}{x^3 y - 16x^2 y + 64xy}$

B) $\dfrac{xy + 9y + 12}{x^2 y - 8xy + x - 8}$

C) $\dfrac{xy^2 + 13xy - 8y}{x^2 y - 8xy}$

D) $\dfrac{xy^2 + 13xy - 8y}{x^3 y - 16x^2 y + 64xy}$

CONTINUE ▶

19

$$\frac{20}{p} = \frac{20}{q} - \frac{20}{r} - \frac{20}{s}$$

The given equation relates the positive variables p, q, r, and s. Which of the following is equivalent to q?

A) $p + r + s$

B) $20(p + r + s)$

C) $\dfrac{prs}{pr + ps + rs}$

D) $\dfrac{prs}{20p + 20r + 20s}$

20

$$x(kx - 56) = -16$$

In the given equation, k is an integer constant. If the equation has no real solution, what is the least possible value of k?

21

$$2x + 3y = 7$$
$$10x + 15y = 35$$

For each real number r, which of the following points lies on the graph of each equation in the xy-plane for the given system?

A) $\left(\dfrac{r}{5} + 7, -\dfrac{r}{5} + 35\right)$

B) $\left(-\dfrac{3r}{2} + \dfrac{7}{2}, r\right)$

C) $\left(r, \dfrac{2r}{3} + \dfrac{7}{3}\right)$

D) $\left(r, -\dfrac{3r}{2} + \dfrac{7}{2}\right)$

22

A window repair specialist charges $220 for the first two hours of repair plus an hourly fee for each additional hour. The total cost for 5 hours of repair is $400. Which function f gives the total cost, in dollars, for x hours of repair, where $x \geq 2$?

A) $f(x) = 60x + 100$

B) $f(x) = 60x + 220$

C) $f(x) = 80x$

D) $f(x) = 80x + 220$

STOP

If you finish before time is called, you may check your work on this module only. Do not turn to any other module in the test.

The SAT®

Practice Test #10

ANSWER EXPLANATIONS

These answer explanations are for students using
The Official SAT Study Guide.

Reading and Writing

Module 1
(27 questions)

QUESTION 1

Choice A is the best answer because it most logically completes the text's discussion of the writing system created by Sequoyah. In this context, "widespread" means widely accepted or practiced. The text indicates that because Sequoyah's script accurately represented the spoken sounds of the Cherokee language and was easy to learn, nearly all Cherokee people were able to read and write it soon after it was created. This context demonstrates that the script was widely used by the Cherokee people.

Choice B is incorrect. In this context, "careful" would mean exercised with care and attentive concern. Although the work of creating a writing system likely involved great care, the text indicates that the system was "easy to learn," which conflicts with the idea that using this system requires a noteworthy amount of care. *Choice C* is incorrect because in this context "unintended" means not deliberate. The idea that using Sequoyah's script was unintentional conflicts directly with the claim that it was easy to learn and used by "over 90% of the Cherokee people" by 1830. In fact, because one had to learn this system, it's not clear how one could use it unintentionally. *Choice D* is incorrect because in this context "infrequent" means rare or not occurring often, which conflicts directly with the claim that "over 90% of the Cherokee people" were using Sequoyah's script by 1830.

QUESTION 2

Choice C is the best answer because it most logically completes the text's discussion of John Ashbery's poems. As used in this context, "interpret" would mean decipher the meaning of. The text indicates that Ashbery's poems have many unusual features, that it's difficult to tell what exactly the poems' subject matter is, and that scholars strongly disagree about the poems. This context conveys the idea that it's difficult to interpret Ashbery's poems.

Choice A is incorrect because "delegate" means to assign someone as a representative of another person or to entrust something to someone else, neither of which would make sense in context. The text is focused only on the difficulty that readers have interpreting Ashbery's poems due to their many unusual features; it doesn't suggest anything about the poems being difficult to delegate. *Choice B* is incorrect because describing Ashbery's poems as difficult to "compose," or put together or produce, would make sense only if the text were about Ashbery's experience of writing the poems. It could be true that

ANSWER EXPLANATIONS | *SAT Practice Test #10*

it was difficult for Ashbery to compose his poems, but the text doesn't address this; it instead discusses how readers interpret and engage with the poems. *Choice D* is incorrect because describing Ashbery's poems as being difficult to "renounce," or give up or refuse, wouldn't make sense in context. The text focuses on the idea that features of Ashbery's poems are odd or unclear and have caused heated scholarly debate. This context suggests that the poems are difficult to interpret, not that the poems are difficult to renounce.

QUESTION 3

Choice C is the best answer because it most logically completes the text's discussion of Annie Dodge Wauneka's work as a Navajo Nation legislator. As used in this context, "persistent" means existing continuously. The text states that Wauneka "continuously worked to promote public health," traveling extensively and authoring a medical dictionary; this indicates that Wauneka's effort was persistent.

Choice A is incorrect because describing Wauneka's effort related to public health as "impartial," or not partial or biased and treating all things equally, wouldn't make sense in context. The text suggests that Wauneka's continuous work was partial in one way, as she focused specifically on promoting public health throughout the Navajo homeland and to speakers of the Navajo language. *Choice B* is incorrect because the text emphasizes that Wauneka's effort to promote public health as a Navajo Nation legislator was continuous and extensive, involving wide travels and the authoring of a medical dictionary. Because this work clearly involved care and dedication, it wouldn't make sense to describe it as "offhand," or casual and informal. *Choice D* is incorrect because nothing in the text suggests that Wauneka's effort to promote public health was "mandatory," or required by law or rule, even though Wauneka was a Navajo Nation legislator. Rather than suggesting that Wauneka's effort was required for any reason, the text emphasizes the continuous and extensive nature of her work.

QUESTION 4

Choice A is the best answer because it most logically completes the text's discussion of how kelp forests help marine animals. In this context, "tranquil" means free from disturbance, or calm. The text indicates that ocean currents are powerful and make it difficult for marine animals to hide from predators and that kelp forests slow currents down to create calmer areas. In other words, kelp forests create a more tranquil environment.

Choice B is incorrect because the text indicates that kelp forests provide shelter for marine animals, meaning they create environments that are safer, not more "dangerous." *Choice C* is incorrect because the text discusses how kelp forests affect currents in the ocean, and it isn't clear how an ocean environment could be "imaginative," or full of imagination. *Choice D* is incorrect because the text indicates that kelp forests create a calm and safe environment, and an environment that is "surprising" would be characterized by unexpected occurrences, not calmness.

QUESTION 5

Choice B is the best answer because it most logically completes the text's discussion about people's tendency to dismiss claims from sources perceived as self-interested, or acting for their own advantage. In this context, "irrelevant" means not applicable to the matter at hand. The text explains that as a matter of logical reasoning, the source of a claim has nothing to do with the claim's truthfulness—a claim is either true or false in actuality, regardless of where it originates. This context suggests that even though people may distrust a claim based on its source, the source of the claim is actually irrelevant.

Choice A is incorrect because in this context, "indistinct" would mean uncertain or not clearly recognizable. Instead of suggesting that the source of a claim can't be determined with certainty, the text suggests that recognizing a source and having an opinion of it simply doesn't matter because as a matter of logic, a claim is true or false in actuality, regardless of where it originates. *Choice C* is incorrect because in this context, "indisputable" would mean impossible to question or deny. Although the text suggests that it isn't logical to assume a claim is false just because its source appears to be self-interested, it doesn't go so far as to suggest that the source of a claim can't be questioned—the text instead makes the point that from a logical standpoint, the source of a claim doesn't matter because the claim is either true or false in and of itself. *Choice D* is incorrect because in this context, "implicit" would mean suggested or understood without being directly expressed. Nothing in the text suggests that logically, the source of a claim is only suggested; instead of addressing whether sources can be directly identified, the text focuses on the idea that sources don't matter because a claim is true or false in actuality, regardless of where it originates.

QUESTION 6

Choice B is the best answer because it best describes the main purpose of the text. The text indicates where and when jazz tap first developed (in African American communities in the 1920s) and what influenced it (the quick rhythms and improvisations in jazz music) and then explains that it evolved alongside jazz music in the 1930s and 1940s, resulting in a very different form of tap dance than had existed before. Therefore, the main purpose of the text is to discuss jazz tap's development.

Choice A is incorrect. Although the text indicates that jazz music became widely popular in the US in the 1920s and describes some of jazz music's qualities, the text never explains why audiences prefer some kinds of music— jazz or otherwise—over others. *Choice C* is incorrect because the text never mentions any musical instruments and doesn't describe how to play one. *Choice D* is incorrect because the text discusses jazz tap generally and never identifies a particular dancer, famous or otherwise.

QUESTION 7

Choice A is the best answer because it most accurately portrays the main purpose of the text. At the beginning of the text, Tom asserts that he and the other people staging the play are doing so only for "a little amusement among ourselves" and aren't interested in attracting an audience or any attention with the production. Then, Tom promises that the play they chose is modest and appropriate, and he further reasons that using the well-written prose of "some respectable author" is better than using their own words. Overall, the main purpose of the text is to convey Tom's promise that the play will be inoffensive and involve only a few people.

Choice B is incorrect because the text doesn't indicate that Tom had earlier intentions for the play's performance or that anything has changed since the group first decided to stage a play. Instead, the text focuses on how harmless the entire endeavor will be. *Choice C* is incorrect. Although Tom mentions that using the words of a "respectable author" will be better than using their own words, he never addresses the idea that the people around him generally aren't skilled enough to stage a play. *Choice D* is incorrect because in the text Tom specifically says that they "want no audience, no publicity," which indicates that they don't plan on promoting the play at all.

QUESTION 8

Choice C is the best answer because it presents the statement about the use of painted frames in Impressionist painting that both authors would be most likely to agree with. Text 1 discusses painter Edgar Degas's insistence that his works remain in their original painted frames, which contrasted with the gold frames that were typical of the Paris art scene at the time. The text then argues that the preference of Degas and other French Impressionist painters for colorful frames can likely be attributed to their desire "to distinguish themselves from what was considered conventional at the time." Text 2 also notes that Impressionist painters "placed their works in painted frames" but argues that they probably did so for a purely aesthetic reason: to ensure that "the frame's color...would harmonize with the colors or subjects in a painting." Though differing on Impressionist painters' rationale for using painted frames, the authors of both texts would agree that many Impressionist painters were intentional about the frames they selected for their works.

Choice A is incorrect because neither text suggests that gold frames were considered desirable by those purchasing Impressionist works. Indeed, it can be inferred from the fact that Impressionist painters used painted frames that those who purchased those works wouldn't have had a strong preference for gold frames. *Choice B* is incorrect because neither text suggests that Impressionist painters chose colors for their paintings based on planned frame colors. Indeed, Text 2 states that frame colors were chosen to "harmonize with the colors or subjects in a painting," implying that the color scheme of paintings predated and took precedence over the choice of the colors of frames. *Choice D* is incorrect because Text 1 presents Degas's preference for painted frames as being typical of Impressionist painters' attitudes toward the framing of their works. Moreover, although Text 2 doesn't specifically discuss Degas, it concurs with Text 1's assertion that these painters preferred painted frames. Thus, both texts position painted frames as a hallmark of French Impressionist painting, not as a deviation from it.

QUESTION 9

Choice A is the best answer because it most accurately describes Gibson's approach to art. As the text explains, Gibson, who is Cherokee and Choctaw, transforms punching bags into art pieces by applying (or attaching) to them beadwork and elements of Native dressmaking, including leather fringe and the jingles of the jingle dress. The text goes on to say that in most Native communities, the art forms of beadwork and dressmaking are traditionally practiced by women. Therefore, Gibson's approach to art consists of creating original works by drawing from traditional Native art forms.

Choice B is incorrect. Because Gibson incorporates Native art forms into his own original artwork, it can be inferred that he has been influenced by other Native artists, but the text never suggests that non-Native artists have influenced him. *Choice C* is incorrect because the text doesn't indicate that Gibson designs dresses influenced by boxing but instead that he turns punching bags, which are used in boxing, into works of art by applying elements of Native dressmaking to them. *Choice D* is incorrect. Although Gibson does incorporate beadwork into his art, the text never mentions the colors or patterns that he uses or suggests that his art defies the expectations that people might have about color and pattern in beadwork.

QUESTION 10

Choice D is the best answer because it most accurately states the main idea of the text. According to the text, conceptual artists Gins and Arakawa have designed an apartment building that is disorienting because of several unconventional elements, such as uneven kitchen counters and "a door to nowhere." The text goes on to suggest that there may be benefits to this kind of design because filmmaker Yamaoka lived in the apartment building for four years and reported health benefits. Thus, although the design is impractical, it may improve the well-being of the apartment building's residents.

Choice A is incorrect. Although the text mentions that Yamaoka lived in the apartment for four years, it doesn't address how long someone can beneficially live in a home surrounded by fanciful features or whether doing so can be sustained. *Choice B* is incorrect. Although the text mentions the potential benefits of living in a home with disorienting design features, it doesn't suggest that this is the most effective method to create a physically stimulating environment. *Choice C* is incorrect because the text refers to Yamaoka to support the claim that Gins and Arakawa's apartment building design may be beneficial, but the text doesn't indicate that Yamaoka supports the designs of other conceptual artists.

QUESTION 11

Choice A is the best answer because it presents the finding that, if true, would most strongly support the research team's idea about the effect of iridescence, or colors that appear to shimmer and change. The text indicates that although some scientists have assumed that iridescence could attract predators, Kjernsmo's team wondered if iridescent insects might be harder for other animals to see. The team tested this idea by asking human participants to look for both iridescent beetle wings and beetle wings that weren't iridescent but that had been painted colors such as purple or blue. If participants located most of the purple or blue wings but far fewer of the iridescent wings, that finding would support the team's idea since it would suggest that noniridescent wings are easier to see than iridescent wings.

Choice B is incorrect because if participants located the iridescent wings more quickly than the purple or blue wings, that finding would weaken the team's idea, not support the team's idea, since it would suggest that the iridescent wings were easier to see than the iridescent wings. *Choice C* is incorrect because finding that some participants believed that the purple wings were easier to see than the blue wings would be irrelevant to the team's idea. The purple and blue wings were both noniridescent, so any difference in how easy those two colors were to see would have nothing to do with the idea that iridescent insects are harder to see than noniridescent insects. *Choice D* is incorrect because if some participants found all the wings, that wouldn't support the team's idea that iridescent insects may be harder to see than noniridescent insects. If anything, this finding might weaken the team's idea since it could suggest that iridescence had no effect on how difficult the wings were to see.

QUESTION 12

Choice B is the best answer because it most effectively illustrates the claim that Amal imagines the people he sees are carefree even when engaged in work. In the quotation, Amal observes that the flower seller's daughter is "flower gathering," or working, as the text indicates. Moreover, Amal notes that the daughter's feet "seem so glad" and her "anklets jingle so merrily," suggesting that Amal believes that the flower seller's daughter is cheerful.

Choice A is incorrect because the quotation makes no observation about the cheerful mood of the flower seller's daughter. *Choice C* is incorrect because the quotation discusses how Amal envisions his future, not the feelings of the flower seller's daughter. *Choice D* is incorrect because the quotation discusses Amal's wishes, not the feelings of the flower seller's daughter.

QUESTION 13

Choice B is the best answer because it describes data from the graph that weaken the student's conclusion about the reduction in the spider population in the enclosure with lizards. The graph shows that the enclosure with lizards and the enclosure without lizards each began with about 85 spiders, and that the number of spiders in each enclosure fell over the 30 days of the study. The student's claim is that the reduction in spiders in the enclosure with lizards is "entirely attributable to the presence of the lizards," meaning that the spider population wouldn't have declined except for the presence of the lizards. This claim is weakened, however, by the fact that the enclosure without lizards also saw a substantial reduction in the number of spiders. Since the number of spiders fell in the enclosure without lizards as well as in the enclosure with lizards, there must be some other factor than just the presence of the lizards that contributed to the reduction in the spider population.

Choice A is incorrect because the fact that the two enclosures started with the same number of spiders is irrelevant to the claim that the reduction in spider population by day 30 in the enclosure with lizards can be entirely attributed to the lizards. *Choice C* is incorrect because the fact that the spider population in the enclosure with lizards fell more between days 1 and 10 than in other periods has nothing to do with the student's claim that the reduction in spiders in that enclosure by day 30 can be entirely attributed to the lizards. *Choice D* is incorrect. Although it's true that on day 30 the spider population was lower in the enclosure with lizards than in the enclosure without lizards, this fact doesn't weaken the student's claim that the reduction in the spider population in the enclosure with lizards can be entirely attributed to the lizards. Indeed, the lower spider population in the enclosure with lizards suggests that the lizards are contributing to the reduction in the spider population, though the fact that the spider population also fell substantially in the other enclosure means that the lizards aren't the only cause of the reduction.

QUESTION 14

Choice A is the best answer because it most logically completes the text's discussion of mosquito repellents. The text begins by explaining that many repellents work by using natural components to activate multiple odor receptors on mosquitoes' antennae, and that new repellents must be created whenever mosquitoes become resistant to older ones. The text then highlights a research team's discovery that EBF, a molecular component of a chrysanthemum-flower extract, can repel mosquitoes by activating a single odor receptor, Or31, that is shared by all species of mosquitoes known to carry diseases. The text suggests that compared to the repellents mentioned earlier, a repellent that acts on the Or31 receptor would be more effective: by noting that all mosquito species known to carry diseases share the Or31 receptor, the text suggests that the Or31 receptor may be unique in this respect, meaning that a repellent such as EBF that acts on it would be more effective since it works on a single receptor shared by all mosquito species that carry diseases, rather than a combination of receptors that is not shared by all species. Once mosquitoes become resistant to EBF, it would therefore make sense for researchers to look for other molecular components similar to EBF that target the activation of Or31 receptors, since a single such component could also repel all disease-carrying mosquitoes.

Choice B is incorrect because nothing in the text suggests that EBF molecules are difficult to extract from chrysanthemums and that investigating alternative extraction methods would therefore be useful for developing efficient and effective mosquito repellents. Rather, the text suggests that researchers developing new mosquito repellents should aim to identify molecular components similar to EBF, since that component targets the Or31 odor receptor shared by all species of mosquitoes known to carry diseases. *Choice C* is incorrect because nothing in the text suggests that researchers are unaware of the precise location of Or31 and other odor receptors in mosquitoes' antennae or that knowing this information would be useful for developing efficient and effective mosquito repellents. Rather, the text suggests that researchers developing new mosquito repellents should aim to identify molecular components similar to EBF, which targets the Or31 odor receptor. *Choice D* is incorrect because it doesn't logically follow that the discovery of one odor receptor shared by all disease-bearing mosquitoes should lead to further research into which repellents might activate the greatest number of odor receptors. Rather, the text suggests that researchers developing new mosquito repellents should instead search for additional molecular components that, like EBF, activate the one odor receptor that is known to be shared by all disease-bearing mosquitoes.

QUESTION 15

Choice D is the best answer because it presents the conclusion that most logically follows from the text's discussion of leafy spurge and engineered DNA. The text establishes that using chemical herbicides to control leafy spurge in North America can also harm other plants nearby. The text then indicates that it might be possible to use engineered DNA to prevent plants from reproducing, which would be useful for "exclusively targeting" leafy spurge. If it's possible to exclusively target leafy spurge with engineered DNA—meaning that only leafy spurge is affected by the engineered DNA—and prevent the plant from reproducing, then leafy spurge numbers could be reduced "without harming other organisms."

Choice A is incorrect because the text raises the possibility of using engineered DNA to prevent leafy spurge from reproducing, not to make individual leafy spurge plants more vulnerable to chemical herbicides that already exist. *Choice B* is incorrect because the text doesn't describe any ecological benefits of leafy spurge in North America; instead, the text is focused on using engineered DNA to prevent leafy spurge from reproducing and thereby reduce its numbers. The only ecological effects of leafy spurge in North America that are described in the text are harmful. *Choice C* is incorrect because the text describes the possibility of using engineered DNA to prevent leafy spurge from reproducing; it doesn't offer a way to enable cattle to eat leafy spurge without becoming sick.

QUESTION 16

Choice C is the best answer. The convention being tested is punctuation between a subordinate clause and a main clause. This choice correctly uses a comma to mark the boundary between the subordinate clause ("While...lifelike") and the main clause ("others look to the past").

Choice A is incorrect because it results in an incomplete sentence with no main clause. *Choice B* is incorrect because it fails to mark the boundary between the subordinate clause ("While...lifelike") and the main clause ("others...past"). *Choice D* is incorrect because it results in an incomplete sentence with no main clause.

QUESTION 17

Choice D is the best answer. The convention being tested is punctuation between a verb and a preposition. When, as in this case, a verb ("is added") is immediately followed by a preposition ("whenever"), no punctuation is needed.

Choice A is incorrect because no punctuation is needed between the verb and the preposition. *Choice B* is incorrect because no punctuation is needed between the verb and the preposition. *Choice C* is incorrect because no punctuation is needed between the verb and the preposition.

QUESTION 18

Choice C is the best answer. The convention being tested is the use of plural and possessive nouns. The singular possessive noun "playa's" and the plural possessive noun "rocks'" correctly indicate that the sediment is that of one playa (the Racetrack Playa) and that there are multiple rocks that have mysteriously migrated across the sediment.

Choice A is incorrect because the context requires the singular possessive noun "playa's" and the plural possessive noun "rocks'," not the plural noun "playas" and the singular possessive noun "rock's." *Choice B* is incorrect because the context requires the plural possessive noun "rocks'," not the plural noun "rocks." *Choice D* is incorrect because the context requires the singular possessive noun "playa's," not the plural possessive noun "playas'."

QUESTION 19

Choice C is the best answer. The convention being tested is the use of punctuation in a sentence. In this choice, a colon is correctly used to mark the boundary between one main clause ("Along with...photosynthesis") and another main clause ("as light...oxygen") and to introduce the following explanation of how light intensity affects photosynthesis.

Choice A is incorrect because when coordinating two longer main clauses such as these, it's conventional to use a comma before the coordinating conjunction ("and"). *Choice B* is incorrect because it results in a comma splice. Without a coordinating conjunction following it, a comma can't be used in this way to join two main clauses ("Along with...photosynthesis" and "as light...oxygen"). *Choice D* is incorrect because it results in a run-on sentence. The two main clauses ("Along with...photosynthesis" and "as light...oxygen") are fused without punctuation and/or a conjunction.

QUESTION 20

Choice B is the best answer. The convention being tested is the use of punctuation around noun phrases. No punctuation is needed because the coordinated noun phrase "Thomas Hart Benton and Jackson Pollock" is a restrictive appositive, meaning that it provides essential identifying information about the noun phrase before it, "the renowned twentieth-century US artists."

Choice A is incorrect because no punctuation is needed between the noun phrase "the renowned twentieth-century US artists" and the restrictive appositive "Thomas Hart Benton and Jackson Pollock." Additionally, no punctuation is needed between the sentence's subject ("paintings by the renowned twentieth-century US artists Thomas Hart Benton and Jackson Pollock") and the main verb ("were featured"). *Choice C* is incorrect because no punctuation is needed between the coordinated elements "Thomas Hart Benton" and "Jackson Pollock." Additionally, no punctuation is needed between the sentence's subject ("paintings by the renowned twentieth-century US artists Thomas Hart Benton and Jackson Pollock") and the main verb ("were featured"). *Choice D* is incorrect because no punctuation is needed between the noun phrase "the renowned twentieth-century US artists" and the restrictive appositive "Thomas Hart Benton and Jackson Pollock."

QUESTION 21

Choice A is the best answer. "Fittingly" logically signals that the naming of an unprecedented radiocarbon surge for Fusa Miyake is appropriate to the situation, since Miyake is the person who identified the surge (through her Yaku Island tree-ring analysis).

Choice B is incorrect because "similarly" illogically signals that the information in this sentence is similar to the previous information about Miyake's identification of a massive radiation burst through tree-ring analysis. Instead, the naming of the event for its discoverer is a fitting and appropriate outcome. *Choice C* is incorrect because "however" illogically signals that the information in this sentence contrasts with the previous information about Miyake's identification of a massive radiation burst through tree-ring analysis. Instead, the naming of the event for its discoverer is a fitting and appropriate outcome. *Choice D* is incorrect because "in other words" illogically signals that the information in this sentence is a paraphrase or restatement of the previous information about Miyake's identification of a massive radiation burst through tree-ring analysis. Instead, the naming of the event for its discoverer is a fitting and appropriate outcome.

QUESTION 22

Choice D is the best answer. "Nevertheless" logically signals that the claim in this sentence—that the telegenic Kennedy was ultimately considered the winner of the debate—is true despite the previous information about the poll of radio listeners.

Choice A is incorrect because "in other words" illogically signals that the claim in this sentence is a paraphrase of the previous information about the poll of radio listeners. Instead, Kennedy was ultimately considered the winner despite what that poll suggested about his performance. *Choice B* is incorrect because "therefore" illogically signals that the claim in this sentence is a result of the previous information about the poll of radio listeners. Instead, Kennedy was ultimately considered the winner despite what that poll suggested about his performance. *Choice C* is incorrect because "likewise" illogically signals that the claim in this sentence is similar to the previous information about the poll of radio listeners. Instead, Kennedy was ultimately considered the winner despite what that poll suggested about his performance.

QUESTION 23

Choice D is the best answer. "Specifically" logically signals that the information in this sentence about Sauer's argument—that, according to Sauer, cultures play a role in their own development, as opposed to being shaped solely by natural surroundings—provides specific, precise details elaborating on the more general information in the previous sentence about how Sauer challenged prevailing views about how natural landscapes influence human cultures.

Choice A is incorrect because "similarly" illogically signals that the information in this sentence about Sauer's argument is similar to, but separate from, the more general information in the previous sentence. Instead, it provides specific, precise details elaborating on that information. *Choice B* is incorrect because "finally" illogically signals that the information in this sentence about Sauer's argument indicates a last step in a process or a concluding summary. Instead, it provides specific, precise details elaborating on the general information in the previous sentence. *Choice C* is incorrect because "therefore" illogically signals that the information in this sentence about Sauer's argument is a result of the more general information in the previous sentence. Instead, it provides specific, precise details elaborating on that information.

QUESTION 24

Choice A is the best answer. The sentence indicates where the dicraeosaurid fossil was found: western India's Thar Desert.

Choice B is incorrect. The sentence states that Bajpai's team discovered the dicraeosaurid fossil; it doesn't specify where they found it. *Choice C* is incorrect. The sentence provides information about Dr. Sunil Bajpai; it doesn't indicate where the fossil was found. *Choice D* is incorrect. While the sentence provides information about the fossil, it doesn't indicate where the fossil was found.

QUESTION 25

Choice C is the best answer. The sentence specifies the reason the Pleiades' appearance changed, noting that two of the cluster's stars have moved so close together that they now appear as one star.

Choice A is incorrect. The sentence specifies how ancient Native American and Australian Aboriginal cultures described the Pleiades; it doesn't specify the reason the Pleiades' appearance changed. *Choice B* is incorrect. The sentence describes the appearance of the Pleiades today; it doesn't specify the reason the Pleiades' appearance changed. *Choice D* is incorrect. The sentence explains why two of the Pleiades' stars appear to be a single star; it doesn't specify the reason the Pleiades' appearance changed.

QUESTION 26

Choice A is the best answer. The sentence emphasizes the significance of Ochoa's discovery, noting that it proved critical to deciphering the human genetic code, which resulted in a better understanding of how genetic variations affect human health.

Choice B is incorrect. While the sentence explains what Ochoa discovered, it doesn't emphasize the significance of the discovery. *Choice C* is incorrect. While the sentence explains what Ochoa discovered, it doesn't emphasize the significance of the discovery. *Choice D* is incorrect. While the sentence mentions that Ochoa's discovery was crucial, it emphasizes Ochoa's incorrect hypothesis, not the significance of the discovery.

QUESTION 27

Choice C is the best answer. The sentence emphasizes the decline in unique apple varieties in the US and specifies why this decline occurred, noting that thousands of apple varieties were lost because US farmers started mainly growing the same few unique varieties.

Choice A is incorrect. The sentence introduces the Lost Apple Project; it doesn't emphasize the decline in unique apple varieties in the US and specify why this decline occurred. *Choice B* is incorrect. While the sentence emphasizes the decline in unique apple varieties in the US, it doesn't explain why this decline occurred. *Choice D* is incorrect. The sentence emphasizes the general decline of crop varieties in the mid-1900s; it doesn't emphasize the specific decline in unique apple varieties in the US.

Reading and Writing

Module 2 — Lower Difficulty
(27 questions)

QUESTION 1

Choice A is the best answer because it most logically completes the text's discussion of the role of the general store in US rural communities during the 1800s. In this context, "source" means a place where something originates or is obtained. The text states that people would share news while socializing at the general store. This context supports the idea that the store served as a source of information in rural communities.

Choice B is incorrect because "rival" would mean competitor or opponent. The text doesn't indicate that the general store was a rival of anything. Instead, the text describes the general store as a place that enabled the sharing of information within rural communities. *Choice C* is incorrect because in this context, "condition" would mean state, circumstance, or requirement. Although the text implies that visiting the store was helpful for acquiring information since people shared news there, it wouldn't make sense to say that the general store was a condition of information. *Choice D* is incorrect because "waste" would mean something that is unused, discarded, or spent unnecessarily, which would not make sense in context. The text describes the general store as an essential part of daily life and a place for socializing and information sharing. The store was therefore a source, not a waste, of information.

QUESTION 2

Choice D is the best answer because it most logically completes the text's discussion of the Indigenous method of harvesting *Hierochloe odorata*. As used in this context, "replenishes" means helps increase the population or helps it recover. The text explains that although snapping off a wild plant at the root might seem detrimental to the wild population, it actually helps *Hierochloe odorata*, increasing both their "number and vigor." This context conveys the idea that even though it seems counterintuitive, the Indigenous method of harvesting *Hierochloe odorata* actually replenishes the wild population.

Choice A is incorrect. Although a harvesting method could be used to select for certain traits in plants, it's not clear what it would mean for a harvesting method to select "wild populations" of plants. *Choice B* is incorrect because as used in this context, "originates" means creates. The text doesn't address the origin of *Hierochloe odorata*, but rather how the Indigenous harvesting method affects it. *Choice C* is incorrect because in this context, "conditions" means to influence someone or something to behave in a certain way, and the text doesn't suggest the new plants that replace the harvested ones differ in any meaningful way, or in any way that could be the result of conditioning.

QUESTION 3

Choice B is the best answer because it most logically completes the text's discussion about recycling plastics. In this context, "inadequate" means not satisfactory. The text indicates that the mechanical plastic-recycling process affects the environment and causes "the loss of material quality." The text contrasts that with Chazovachii's chemical plastic-recycling process, which is cleaner and produces a desirable product. The text's emphasis on the negative aspects of mechanical recycling suggests that it is inadequate in terms of environmental impact and the quality of the material the process yields.

Choice A is incorrect because in this context "resilient" would mean able to withstand difficulty and the text does not characterize the plastic-recycling process as having this quality or describe any difficulties that these processes might need to overcome. *Choice C* is incorrect because in this context "dynamic" would mean constantly changing. Although the text suggests that there have been changes in the field of recycling, as is the case with the advent of Chazovachii's chemical recycling process, there is nothing to suggest that the mechanical process itself has changed or is prone to change. *Choice D* is incorrect because in this context "satisfactory" would mean acceptable but not perfect. The text mentions only shortcomings of the mechanical process (environmental effects and lower material quality), so the text more strongly supports a negative view of this process and provides no evidence that it would be considered satisfactory.

QUESTION 4

Choice A is the best answer because it most logically completes the text's discussion of a relationship between the dodder plant and its host plant. As used in this context, "synchronization" means the act of things happening at the same time. The text indicates that the dodder and its host plant flower in unison and that this synchronization occurs because the dodder makes use of a protein produced by the host shortly before flowering.

Choice B is incorrect because referring to "hibernation," or the state of being dormant or inactive, wouldn't make sense in context. The text focuses on something the dodder plant actively engages in—making use of a protein and producing flowers. *Choice C* is incorrect because stating that the dodder plant and its host engage together in "prediction," or the act of declaring or indicating something in advance, wouldn't make sense in context. Rather than indicating that the dodder plant and its host plant make a prediction about flowering activity, the text suggests that the host produces a protein as part of its regular flowering process and that the dodder then absorbs and uses that protein to flower at the same time. *Choice D* is incorrect because referring to "moderation," or the act of causing something to become less intense or extreme, wouldn't make sense in context. Although the text states that the dodder plant absorbs and uses a protein made by its host plant, it doesn't suggest that the dodder lessens the host plant's flowering activity; the two plants simply flower in unison.

QUESTION 5

Choice D is the best answer because it most accurately describes the overall purpose of the text. The text indicates that "for as long as he could remember," Max had "begged" his father to take him to La Reina. This point is later emphasized in the text by indicating that "this summer" his father might "finally take" Max to visit La Reina. Thus, the purpose of the text as a whole is to show how much Max wants to visit La Reina.

Choice A is incorrect. The text does not discuss Papa's feelings toward Max. Rather, it mentions that Max has long wanted Papa to take him to La Reina and that, unlike Max and some other children, Papa does not believe that La Reina is haunted. *Choice B* is incorrect. The text mentions that Max is "almost twelve" at the time, which suggests anticipation of growing up rather than refusal to. *Choice C* is incorrect. The text indicates that Max hopes to visit La Reina during the current summer, but nothing suggests that Max dislikes summer.

QUESTION 6

Choice C is the best answer because it most accurately describes the overall structure of the text. Throughout the text, the speaker characterizes nighttime as if it were a person who wears clothing ("a garment" that is "velvet soft" and "violet blue") and a veil "over her face" and who moves her hands "slowly with their gem-starred light" through her dark hair. Thus, the text is structured as an extended comparison of night to a human being.

Choice A is incorrect because the text never mentions any particular location; instead, it focuses on presenting a single description of night as a person with certain clothing and features. *Choice B* is incorrect because the text doesn't make any reference to the sun or sunrise; instead, it focuses on presenting a single image of night as a person with certain clothing and features. *Choice D* is incorrect. Rather than describing how nighttime changes seasonally (or in any other way), the text presents a single image of night as a person with certain clothing and features.

QUESTION 7

Choice D is the best answer because it most accurately describes what the narrator and Mario did while riding in the car. The text describes a car trip that the narrator is taking with her family. The text states that during the car ride, the narrator and Mario "played games" to see how many different license plates they could spot.

Choice A is incorrect because the text doesn't mention the narrator and Mario reading during the car ride and instead describes them playing games. *Choice B* is incorrect because the text doesn't mention the narrator and Mario singing songs during the car ride and instead describes them playing games. *Choice C* is incorrect because the text doesn't mention the narrator and Mario sleeping during the car ride and instead describes them playing games.

QUESTION 8

Choice A is the best answer because it presents information about Gloria Richardson that is supported by the text. The text provides a number of details about Gloria's involvement in efforts to promote racial equality, including that she was the leader of what became known as the Cambridge movement.

Choice B is incorrect because the text never indicates that Gloria Richardson led her daughter Donna's high school. The text says only that Gloria was inspired by her daughter to become involved in efforts to promote racial equality.

Choice C is incorrect because the text doesn't mention protests related to environmental protections. Rather, the text discusses Gloria Richardson's involvement in efforts to promote racial equality. *Choice D* is incorrect because the text doesn't indicate that Gloria Richardson led a new business in Cambridge, Maryland. Rather, the text states that she led what became known as the Cambridge movement.

QUESTION 9

Choice A is the best answer because it presents a finding that, if true, would most strongly support the team's conclusion that cattle were likely raised closer to human settlements than sheep and goats were. The text explains that Vaiglova, Liu, and their colleagues analyzed the chemical composition of sheep, goat, and cattle bones from the Bronze Age in China in order to investigate the animals' domestication, or their adaptation from a wild state to a state in which they existed in close connection with humans. According to the text, the team's analysis showed that sheep and goats of the era fed largely on wild plants, whereas cattle fed on millet—importantly, a crop cultivated by humans. If analysis of the animal bones shows that the cattle's diet also consisted of wheat, another crop cultivated by humans in China during the Bronze Age, the finding would support the team's conclusion by offering additional evidence that cattle during this era fed on human-grown crops—and, by extension, that humans raised cattle relatively close to the settlements where they grew these crops, leaving goats and sheep to roam farther away in areas with wild vegetation, uncultivated by humans.

Choice B is incorrect because if it were true that sheep's and goats' diets consisted of small portions of millet, which the text states was a crop cultivated by humans, the finding would suggest that sheep and goats were raised relatively close to human settlements, weakening the team's conclusion that cattle were likely raised closer to those settlements than sheep and goats were. *Choice C* is incorrect because the finding that cattle generally require more food and nutrients than do sheep and goats wouldn't support the team's conclusion that cattle were likely raised closer to human settlements than sheep and goats were. Nothing in the text suggests that cattle were incapable of obtaining sufficient food and nutrients without access to human-grown crops. Hence, even if cattle's diets are found to have different requirements than the diets of sheep and goats, the cattle could have met those requirements from food located far from human settlements. *Choice D* is incorrect because if it were true that the diets of sheep, goats, and cattle varied based on what the farmers in each Bronze Age settlement could grow, the finding would weaken the team's conclusion that cattle were likely raised closer to human settlements than sheep and goats were, suggesting instead that all three types of animals were raised close enough to human settlements to feed on those settlements' crops.

QUESTION 10

Choice D is the best answer because it accurately identifies the species with the highest global biomass, the white-tailed deer at approximately 2.7 million metric tons. The graph shows the global biomass for four wild land mammal species with the highest global biomass. The graph indicates that the African bush elephant's global biomass is about 1.3 million metric tons, the eastern gray kangaroo's is about 0.6 million metric tons, and the wild boar's is about 1.9 million metric tons. These values are all lower than the global biomass for the white-tailed deer's approximately 2.7 million metric tons. Thus, the white-tailed deer is the species with the highest global biomass.

Choice A is incorrect because although the graph indicates that the wild boar has a relatively high global biomass of about 1.9 million metric tons, it is not the species with the highest value. The white-tailed deer is the species with the highest global biomass at about 2.7 million metric tons. *Choice B* is incorrect because the eastern gray kangaroo has the lowest global biomass value shown on the graph at about 0.6 million metric tons, not the highest global biomass. The white-tailed deer has the highest at about 2.7 million metric tons. *Choice C* is incorrect because although the African bush elephant has a substantial global biomass of about 1.3 million metric tons, it is not the species with the highest value according to the graph. The white-tailed deer has the highest global biomass at about 2.7 million metric tons.

QUESTION 11

Choice A is the best answer because it effectively uses data from the table to complete the statement, identifying the month in which the United States had the highest number of housing starts in 2022. According to the table, which shows the number of US housing starts from January to April 2022, the highest number of housing starts was 1,803 thousand, which occurred in April.

Choice B is incorrect because March had 1,713 thousand housing starts, which is lower than the number of starts in April and in February. *Choice C* is incorrect because January had 1,669 thousand housing starts, which is the lowest of all the months listed in the table. *Choice D* is incorrect because February had 1,771 thousand housing starts, which is lower than the number of starts in April.

QUESTION 12

Choice B is the best answer because it provides the most direct support from the table for the claim that two languages can convey similar amounts of information even if they're spoken at different rates. The table shows the approximate rates at which five languages are spoken and the rates at which those five languages convey information. Vietnamese is spoken at around 5.3 syllables per second, whereas Spanish is spoken at around 7.7 syllables per second, but the two languages convey information at very similar rates: Vietnamese at a rate of around 42.5 bits per second and Spanish at a rate of around 42.0 bits per second. Thus, the description of Vietnamese conveying information at around the same rate that Spanish does despite being spoken more slowly supports the claim in the text that languages can convey the same amount of information even if spoken at different rates.

Choice A is incorrect because it isn't true that Thai and Hungarian have the lowest rates of speech of the five languages shown. According to the table, Hungarian is spoken at around 5.9 syllables per second, which is faster than Vietnamese (5.3 syllables per second). Additionally, even if this statement were true, the assertion that two languages are spoken the slowest and convey information the slowest wouldn't support the claim that languages can convey the same amount of information even if they're spoken at different rates. *Choice C* is incorrect because it isn't true that the fastest-spoken language (Spanish, at 7.7 syllables per second) also conveys information the fastest: Spanish conveys information at 42.0 bits per second, which is slower than the 42.5 bits-per-second rate at which Vietnamese conveys information. Additionally, even if this statement were true, the assertion that the language spoken the fastest also conveys information the fastest has no bearing on the claim that languages can convey the same amount of information even if they're spoken at different rates. *Choice D* is incorrect because it isn't true that Serbian conveys information faster than Spanish does. According to the table, Serbian conveys information at a rate of around 39.1 bits per second, which is slower than the 42.0 bits-per-second rate at which Spanish conveys information.

QUESTION 13

Choice A is the best answer because it presents a finding that, if true, would support the claim about Chambi's photographs. The text describes a student advancing the claim that Chambi's photographs "have considerable ethnographic value"—meaning that they are valuable as records of cultures—and that they "capture diverse elements of Peruvian society" in a respectul way. If it's true that Chambi carefully photographed people from a range of different communities in Peru as well as photographed the customs and sites of different communities, that would lend support to the claim that the photographs have ethnographic value as depictions of diverse elements of society in Peru.

Choice B is incorrect because the student's claim is that Chambi's photographs have considerable ethnographic value because they depict diverse elements of Peruvian society; the student doesn't claim anything about the technical skill demonstrated in the photographs. *Choice C* is incorrect because neither Chambi's reputation nor the locations where his photographs may have been published would be relevant to the student's claim that his photographs are valuable as an ethnographic record of Peru's diverse society. *Choice D* is incorrect because the popularity among other photographers of the people and places that Chambi photographed would be irrelevant to the student's claim that Chambi's photographs are valuable as an ethnographic record of Peru's diverse society.

QUESTION 14

Choice A is the best answer because it presents the conclusion that most logically follows from the text's discussion of military veterans working in civilian government jobs in the United States. The text indicates that the proportion of military veterans working in civilian government jobs is considerably higher than the proportion of military veterans in the population as a whole. The text also notes that the unusually high representation of military veterans in these jobs may be a result of the organizational structures shared by civilian government entities and the military. Hence, it's reasonable to infer that it's the familiarity of the structures of civilian government that makes jobs there particularly attractive to military veterans.

Choice B is incorrect because the text doesn't address what a typical relationship between military service and later career preferences would be, and there's no indication that it's atypical for veterans to work in civilian government jobs after they've left the military. On the contrary, the text suggests that many military veterans are drawn to such jobs. *Choice C* is incorrect because the text is focused on the high representation of military veterans in civilian government jobs and doesn't address nonveterans or their possible interest in military service. *Choice D* is incorrect because the text conveys that military veterans may be particularly interested in civilian government jobs due to the familiarity of organizational structures that are already in place, but there's no reason to think that this interest would mean that more civilian government jobs will start to require military experience.

QUESTION 15

Choice C is the best answer. The convention being tested is the use of possessive determiners. The plural possessive determiner "their" agrees in number with the plural conjoined noun phrase "Watson and Crick" and thus indicates that the findings were those of Watson and Crick.

Choice A is incorrect because "they're" is the contraction for "they are," not a possessive determiner. *Choice B* is incorrect because "it's" is the contraction for "it is" or "it has," not a possessive determiner. *Choice D* is incorrect because the singular possessive determiner "its" doesn't agree in number with the plural conjoined noun phrase "Watson and Crick."

QUESTION 16

Choice A is the best answer. The convention being tested is the use of finite verbs in a relative clause. Relative clauses, such as the one beginning with "which," require a finite verb, a verb that can function as the main verb of a clause. This choice correctly supplies the clause with the finite past tense verb "provided."

Choice B is incorrect because the non-finite participle "having provided" doesn't supply the clause with a finite verb. *Choice C* is incorrect because the non-finite to-infinitive "to provide" doesn't supply the clause with a finite verb. *Choice D* is incorrect because the non-finite participle "providing" doesn't supply the clause with a finite verb.

QUESTION 17

Choice B is the best answer. The convention being tested is the use of non-finite (untensed) verb forms in a sentence. The modal "would," which indicates the future from a perspective in the past, should be accompanied by a non-finite plain form verb. In this choice, the non-finite plain form verb "create" is used correctly in conjunction with the non-finite plain form verb "increase" to describe what the lock would do.

Choice A is incorrect because the finite present tense verb "creates" can't be used in this way with the modal "would" to describe what the lock would do. *Choice C* is incorrect because the present participle "creating" can't be used in this way with the modal "would" to describe what the lock would do. *Choice D* is incorrect because the finite past tense verb "created" can't be used in this way with the modal "would" to describe what the lock would do.

QUESTION 18

Choice C is the best answer. The convention being tested is punctuation use between sentences. In this choice, the period after "percent" is used correctly to mark the boundary between one sentence ("After...percent") and another ("Such...up").

Choice A is incorrect because it results in a comma splice. A comma can't be used in this way to mark the boundary between sentences. *Choice B* is incorrect. Without a comma preceding it, the conjunction "and" can't be used in this way to join sentences. *Choice D* is incorrect because it results in a run-on sentence. The sentences ("After...percent" and "Such...up") are fused without punctuation and/or a conjunction.

QUESTION 19

Choice C is the best answer. The convention being tested is the use of verbs to express tense. In this choice, the present tense verb "experiences" is consistent with the other present tense verbs (e.g., "connects" and "prepares") used to describe the events in Truong's novels. Furthermore, it's conventional to use the present tense when discussing a literary work.

Choice A is incorrect because the past tense verb "experienced" isn't consistent with the other present tense verbs used to describe the events in Truong's novels. *Choice B* is incorrect because the past perfect tense verb "had experienced" isn't consistent with the other present tense verbs used to describe the events in Truong's novels. *Choice D* is incorrect because the future progressive tense verb "will be experiencing" isn't consistent with the other present tense verbs used to describe the events in Truong's novels.

QUESTION 20

Choice A is the best answer. The convention being tested is the use of punctuation within a sentence. In this choice, the colon correctly introduces the series of goals held by the 1919 Inter-Allied Women's Conference.

Choice B is incorrect because placing a period after "threefold" results in a rhetorically unacceptable sentence fragment beginning with "To." *Choice C* is incorrect because it results in a run-on sentence. The main clause ("The conference's goals were threefold") and the series supplement ("to...rights") are fused without punctuation. *Choice D* is incorrect because a semicolon can't be used in this way to introduce a series. A semicolon is conventionally used to join two main clauses, whereas a colon is conventionally used to introduce a series, making the colon the better choice in this context.

QUESTION 21

Choice A is the best answer. "For instance" logically signals that the information in this sentence—that larch trees lose their needles every fall—is an example supporting the claim in the previous sentence (that not all conifer species keep their leaves or needles year-round).

Choice B is incorrect because "nevertheless" illogically signals that the information in this sentence is true in spite of the claim about conifer species in the previous sentence. Instead, it's an example supporting that claim. *Choice C* is incorrect because "meanwhile" illogically signals that the information in this sentence is separate from (while occurring simultaneously with) the claim about conifer species in the previous sentence. Instead, it's an example supporting that claim. *Choice D* is incorrect because "in addition" illogically signals that the information in this sentence is merely an additional fact related to the claim about conifer species in the previous sentence. Instead, it's an example supporting that claim.

QUESTION 22

Choice A is the best answer. "Currently" logically signals that the archaeologists' use of drones (a current technology) to photograph the lines is the present-day continuation of the ongoing archaeological research described in the previous sentence.

Choice B is incorrect because "in comparison" illogically signals that the action described in this sentence offers a comparison to the ongoing archaeological research described in the previous sentence. Instead, the use of drones is the present-day continuation of that research. *Choice C* is incorrect because "still" illogically signals that the action described in this sentence occurs despite the ongoing archaeological research described in the previous sentence. Instead, the use of drones is the present-day continuation of that research. *Choice D* is incorrect because "however" illogically signals that the action described in this sentence occurs either despite or in contrast to the ongoing archaeological research described in the previous sentence. Instead, the use of drones is the present-day continuation of that research.

QUESTION 23

Choice B is the best answer. "For example" logically signals that the information in this sentence—that tadpole shrimp embryos can pause development during extended periods of drought—exemplifies the previous sentence's claim that organisms have evolved surprising adaptations to survive in adverse conditions.

Choice A is incorrect because "in contrast" illogically signals that the information in this sentence contrasts with the claim about organisms in the previous sentence. Instead, it exemplifies this claim. *Choice C* is incorrect because "meanwhile" illogically signals that the information in this sentence is separate from (while occurring simultaneously with) the claim about organisms in the previous sentence. Instead, it exemplifies this claim. *Choice D* is incorrect because "consequently" illogically signals that the information in this sentence is a consequence, or result, of the claim about organisms in the previous sentence. Instead, it exemplifies this claim.

QUESTION 24

Choice A is the best answer. "Meanwhile" logically signals that the action described in this sentence (Obinze's move to London to pursue a career) is simultaneous with the action described in the previous sentence (Ifemelu's move to the United States). The first sentence establishes that the actions take place around the same time, referring to the characters' "divergent experiences" following high school.

Choice B is incorrect because "nevertheless" illogically signals that the information in this sentence about Obinze's move to London is true despite the previous information about Ifemelu's move to the United States. Instead, as the first sentence establishes, Obinze's move and Ifemelu's move are related, parallel experiences that occur around the same time. *Choice C* is incorrect because "secondly" illogically signals that the information in this sentence is a second point or reason separate from the previous information about Ifemelu's move to the United States. Instead, as the first sentence establishes, Obinze's move and Ifemelu's move are related, parallel experiences that occur around the same time. *Choice D* is incorrect because "in fact" illogically signals that the information in this sentence emphasizes, modifies, or contradicts the previous information about Ifemelu's move to the United States. Instead, as the first sentence establishes, Obinze's move and Ifemelu's move are related, parallel experiences that occur around the same time.

QUESTION 25

Choice B is the best answer. The sentence emphasizes the effect media had on building Wong Fei-hung's legacy, noting that media depictions after his lifetime turned Wong Fei-hung into an internationally known folk hero.

Choice A is incorrect. While it appears to emphasize the effect of media depictions of Wong Fei-hung, the sentence misrepresents information from the notes. According to the notes, media depictions resulted in Wong Fei-hung becoming an internationally known folk hero, not a locally known physician and kung fu master. *Choice C* is incorrect. The sentence discusses Wong Fei-hung's legacy, noting that he became an internationally known folk hero, but it doesn't emphasize the effect media had on building that legacy. *Choice D* is incorrect. The sentence indicates that Wong Fei-hung has been depicted in many media but doesn't emphasize the effect of these media depictions on building his legacy.

QUESTION 26

Choice B is the best answer. The sentence compares the lengths of the two rail tunnels, noting that the Channel Tunnel (about 31 miles long) is slightly shorter than the Seikan Tunnel (roughly 33 miles long).

Choice A is incorrect. The sentence makes a generalization about the length of some rail tunnels; it doesn't compare the lengths of the two rail tunnels. *Choice C* is incorrect. The sentence describes a single rail tunnel; it doesn't compare the lengths of the two rail tunnels. *Choice D* is incorrect. While the sentence mentions the two rail tunnels, it doesn't compare their lengths.

QUESTION 27

Choice C is the best answer. The sentence emphasizes both the duration (the length of time) and the purpose of Cohen's and Rodrigues's work by noting that the women have been working since 2003 to preserve Gullah culture.

Choice A is incorrect. While the sentence emphasizes what visitors to Cohen's and Rodrigues's museums can learn, it doesn't mention the duration or purpose of the women's work. *Choice B* is incorrect. While the sentence emphasizes the purpose of Cohen's and Rodrigues's work, it doesn't mention the duration of that work (the length of time the women have been working to preserve Gullah culture). *Choice D* is incorrect. While the sentence emphasizes where and when Gullah culture developed, it doesn't mention the duration or purpose of Cohen's and Rodrigues's work.

Reading and Writing

Module 2 — Higher Difficulty
(27 questions)

QUESTION 1

Choice D is the best answer because it most logically completes the text's discussion about the relationship between fine art and fashion. As used in this context, "intersect" means to connect or overlap. The text indicates that Jamie Okuma challenges the position held by critics because her work can be seen at an art museum and can be bought by the public from her online boutique. The text also presents the critics' view as being influenced by a perception that fine artists create works that are "timeless" and meant for exhibition, whereas fashion designers periodically produce new styles that are meant for purchase. This context suggests that the critics believe that fine art and fashion tend not to overlap—in other words, that they rarely intersect.

Choice A is incorrect because it wouldn't make sense in context to say that critics contend that fine art and fashion rarely "prevail," or prove to be triumphant or widespread. The text indicates that Okuma is an example of an artist who demonstrates that it's possible to make fine art that is also available to the public as fashion. *Choice B* is incorrect because it wouldn't make sense in context to say that fine art and fashion rarely "succumb," or surrender. The text establishes that unlike what critics believe, Okuma creates works that are in art museums and available for the public to purchase, suggesting that critics believe fine art and fashion rarely overlap, not that they rarely succumb. *Choice C* is incorrect because saying that critics believe that fine art and fashion rarely "diverge," or disagree or move in different directions, wouldn't make sense in context. The text presents Okuma's work as both fine art and fashion, thereby undermining what the critics assert. This suggests that the critics believe that fine art and fashion rarely intersect rather than that the two rarely diverge.

QUESTION 2

Choice C is the best answer because it most logically completes the text's discussion of historical evidence about ancient Egypt under the reign of the pharaoh Hatshepsut. In this context, "an exhaustive" account would be a thorough one. The text states that much of the evidence from her reign was purposely destroyed—in other words, there is a lack of surviving records. This context conveys that unless there are major new archaeological discoveries, an exhaustive account of Hatshepsut's reign is unlikely.

Choice A is incorrect because in this context, "an imaginative" account would be an account based on imagination, or ideas and speculation, rather than facts. The text indicates that much of the evidence of Hatshepsut's reign was deliberately destroyed, and a lack of evidence actually makes it more likely that accounts will be imaginative to some degree and not strictly factual. *Choice B* is incorrect because in this context, "a superficial" account would be one that is lacking in depth or concerned only with what is obvious. The text indicates that most evidence of Hatshepsut's reign was purposely destroyed, which suggests that accounts of that time are likely already somewhat superficial, since there is little information available to support deeper knowledge. Further, it would be illogical to suggest that discovering major new evidence would make it more likely that accounts would be superficial. *Choice D* is incorrect because "a questionable" account would be one likely to be challenged or doubted, and since the text suggests that little evidence of Hatshepsut's reign has survived, accounts of that time probably involve some speculation and thus may already be open to doubt. Further, it would be illogical to suggest that discovering major new evidence would make it more likely that accounts would be questionable.

QUESTION 3

Choice C is the best answer because it most logically completes the text's discussion of the artistic styles that have influenced Cannon's work. As used in this context, "disparate" means distinct or dissimilar. The text indicates that a tension exists among the styles that have influenced Cannon's work and goes on to describe how those styles differ: classic European portraiture favors realism, American pop art uses vivid colors, and intertribal flatstyle rejects the use of shading and perspective to achieve depth. This context suggests that the styles that have influenced Cannon's work are disparate.

Choice A is incorrect because the text indicates that there is a tension among the influences on Cannon's artwork, so it wouldn't make sense to say that the influences are "complementary," or that they complete one another or make up for one another's deficiencies. *Choice B* is incorrect because it wouldn't make sense to characterize Cannon's influences as "unknown," or not familiar; it's clear that the influences are known because the text goes on to list them. *Choice D* is incorrect because the text indicates that there is a tension among the influences on Cannon's work, not that they are "interchangeable," or capable of being used in one another's place.

QUESTION 4

Choice A is the best answer because it most logically completes the text's discussion of the consequences of raising the age at which retirees begin receiving government funds. The text indicates that raising the age for these funds is usually discussed in terms of effects on fund recipients but that Andria Smythe is instead considering the effects on working family members who care for retirees. Smythe notes that raising the age for the funds would increase the length of time retirees are dependent on financial assistance from working family members. This is suggested to have an effect on wealth creation for those workers, and most logically, that effect would be disadvantageous. Thus, "stymie," which means to prevent or greatly hinder, is the most logical choice in context.

Choice B is incorrect because in this context, "compound" would most nearly mean multiply or greatly enhance. The text indicates that raising the age at which retirees are eligible for government funds will increase the amount of time retirees are dependent on working family members for financial support. This would likely have a negative rather than a positive effect on wealth creation. *Choice C* is incorrect because in this context, "disparage" would most nearly mean criticize or defame. Nothing in the text suggests that raising the age at which retirees are eligible for government funds would defame wealth creation among working adults. *Choice D* is incorrect because in this context, "outstrip" would most nearly mean to exceed, and nothing in the text indicates that the financial support provided to retirees would exceed the amount of wealth these workers can create. The text does suggest that workers providing funds to retirees works against those workers' wealth accumulation, but not that the support to retirees exceeds the workers' accumulated wealth.

QUESTION 5

Choice A is the best answer because it most accurately describes the overall structure of the text. The narrator begins by explaining how Charlot carefully delivers Atlante's letter to Rinaldo, and then relates that Rinaldo feels "transported with joy" after reading the letter. Therefore, the overall structure of the text is best described as a description of the delivery of a letter followed by the portrayal of a character's happiness after reading the letter.

Choice B is incorrect because the text indicates that the letter has been written; there's no explanation why another character hasn't written one. In addition, the text's description of Rinaldo "in a melancholy posture" suggests that he's sad and thoughtful, not that he's desperate to receive the letter. *Choice C* is incorrect. Although the text states that Charlot won't toss the letter to Rinaldo because she doesn't want it to fall, the text doesn't refer to the contents of the letter. Instead, the text describes how happy Rinaldo feels after reading it. *Choice D* is incorrect. Although the text does describe Rinaldo's reaction to the letter, the text doesn't begin by discussing Atlante's inspiration for writing the letter. Instead, the text begins by discussing the delivery of the letter.

QUESTION 6

Choice D is the best answer because it best describes how the underlined sentence functions in the text as a whole. The first sentence of the text establishes that Lily can be "keenly sensitive to" scenes that serve as a "fitting background" for her feelings—that is, she's very aware of when a setting seems to reflect her mood. The next sentence, which is underlined, then demonstrates this awareness: Lily views the landscape she's in as a large-scale reflection of her current mood, identifying with elements such as its calmness. Thus, the function of the underlined sentence is to illustrate an idea introduced in the previous sentence.

Choice A is incorrect because the underlined sentence describes the scene only in very general terms, referring to its calmness, breadth, and long stretches of land. It's the next sentence that adds specific details about colors, light, and various trees nearby. *Choice B* is incorrect because nothing in the underlined sentence suggests that Lily is experiencing an internal conflict. In fact, the sentence indicates that Lily thinks the landscape reflects her own feeling of calmness. *Choice C* is incorrect because the only assertion in the underlined sentence is that Lily feels that broad aspects of the landscape, such as its calmness, reflect her current mood, and that assertion isn't expanded on in the next sentence. Instead, the next sentence describes specific details of the scene without connecting them to Lily's feelings.

QUESTION 7

Choice B is the best answer because it best describes how the underlined sentence functions in the text as a whole. The underlined sentence explains that contrary to what several studies would suggest, recent European governments suffered electorally after the launch of fiscal austerity programs. The text goes on to indicate that the researchers generated their findings from data that didn't reveal the true political risk of austerity measures because the data were based on cases in which governments had set austerity programs to take effect after the next election, a practice the European governments that recently suffered electorally didn't adhere to, thus introducing a complicating factor resulting in a conflict between the research findings and recent events.

Choice A is incorrect because the underlined sentence doesn't indicate that the discrepancy described in the text is between observations made in study settings and observations made in real-world settings. Rather, the underlined sentence indicates that the outcome of recent events is contrary to what would be expected based on the findings of several studies. Additionally, there is nothing in the text to suggest that the studies mentioned did not use real-world data; instead, the text indicates that the data used was generated under potentially different circumstances than the recent events. *Choice C* is incorrect because the underlined sentence doesn't present a long-standing divergence in research findings but rather a discrepancy between past research findings and recent events that the text goes on to attribute to researchers' use of data that didn't reveal the true political risk of austerity measures. *Choice D* is incorrect because while the underlined sentence notes that there have been some recent exceptions to a general pattern observed in several research studies, it does not go on to attribute this exception to the researchers underestimating inconsistencies in the data. Rather, the text goes on to attribute this to a circumstance (fiscal austerity measures being implemented before an election rather than after) which adds a complicating factor into the data not accounted for in past studies.

QUESTION 8

Choice D is the best answer because it most accurately states the main idea of the text. The text explains that economist Adam Smith's famous metaphor of the invisible hand was putatively (that is, widely assumed but not proven) intended to illustrate a robust model (a consistently accurate generalization) of how individuals pursuing their own economic interests can create broader benefits for the population. The text then emphasizes the lack of affirmative evidence for this idea by calling out the term "putatively," and explaining that, according to Gavin Kennedy, Smith used the metaphor only once in his works, in reference to specific circumstances related to the now-outdated economic view known as mercantilism, and that the metaphor didn't garner much attention until economists in the twentieth century held it up as a paradigm (a theoretical framework in the field) and thereby implied that Smith shared some of their views on economics. By emphasizing "putatively," the text implies that there is no independent reason to believe that Smith would agree with the metaphor's use outside of the specific context for which he wrote it and that, therefore, the twentieth-century economists who used it did so to support their own views without regard for the metaphor's importance to Smith's work.

Choice A is incorrect. Although the text indicates that Smith's metaphor was largely ignored until some twentieth-century economists revived it and bolstered its status, the text suggests that the later economists used Smith's metaphor to self-servingly boost their own work while ignoring the original context in which Smith wrote it. Moreover, the statement in this choice fails to reflect the text's emphasis on Smith's limited use of the metaphor in his work. *Choice B* is incorrect. Although the text indicates that some twentieth-century economists altered the significance of Smith's metaphor, the text doesn't suggest that the metaphor is a "useful model" of how aggregate benefits arise from individuals' selfish actions, let alone that this usefulness is unaffected by taking the metaphor out of its original context. *Choice C* is incorrect. Although the text indicates that Smith's metaphor was intended as a model of how individuals acting in their own interest produce aggregate benefits and it was written within the context of the now-outdated economic theory of mercantilism, these points are subordinate to the primary idea in the text, which is that Smith's use of the metaphor was tightly constrained but twentieth-century economists ignored the original context so that they could use the metaphor to suggest, without support, that Smith would agree with their economic views.

QUESTION 9

Choice A is the best answer because it most directly illustrates the text's claim about Whitman's poem, "To You." The text says that in this poem, Whitman suggests that he deeply understands the poem's reader. This quotation says that the reader's "true soul and body appear before" Whitman, thereby asserting that he can see the reader as the reader truly is, suggesting that he deeply understands the reader.

Choice B is incorrect because this quotation describes Whitman making the reader the subject of the poem ("you be my poem"), not Whitman deeply understanding the reader. *Choice C* is incorrect because instead of suggesting that Whitman deeply understands the reader, it emphasizes Whitman's regret at not having addressed the reader sooner. *Choice D* is incorrect. Although this quotation shows Whitman directly addressing the reader and expressing concern about the reader, it doesn't illustrate the idea that Whitman suggests that he deeply understands the reader. The quotation is simply expressing concern about the reader, which doesn't necessarily imply deep understanding of the reader.

QUESTION 10

Choice C is the best answer because it describes data from the table that support the researcher's hypothesis. According to the text, the researcher hypothesized that Arctic ground squirrels would exhibit longer torpor bouts and shorter arousal episodes than Alaska marmots do—or, put the other way, that the marmots would show shorter torpor bouts and longer arousal episodes than the ground squirrels do. The table shows data about torpor bouts and arousal episodes for the two species from 2008 to 2011. According to the table, the average duration of torpor bouts was 13.81 days for Alaska marmots, shorter than the average of 16.77 days for Arctic ground squirrels, and the average duration of arousal episodes was 21.2 hours for Alaska marmots, longer than the average of 14.2 hours for Arctic ground squirrels. Thus, the table supports the researcher's hypothesis by showing that Alaska marmots had shorter bouts of torpor and longer arousal episodes than Arctic ground squirrels did.

Choice A is incorrect because it inaccurately describes data from the table and doesn't support the researcher's hypothesis. The table shows that the average duration of arousal episodes was less than a day for both Alaska marmots (21.2 hours) and Arctic ground squirrels (14.2 hours). Additionally, information about arousal episodes for Alaska marmots and Arctic ground squirrels isn't sufficient to support a hypothesis involving comparisons of both arousal episodes and torpor bouts for those animals. *Choice B* is incorrect because it doesn't support the researcher's hypothesis, which involves comparisons of arousal episodes as well as torpor bouts for Alaska marmots and Arctic ground squirrels. Noting that both animals had torpor bouts lasting several days, on average, doesn't address arousal episodes at all, nor does it reveal how the animals' torpor bouts compared. *Choice D* is incorrect because it doesn't support the researcher's hypothesis. Although the table does show that Alaska marmots had more torpor bouts (12) than arousal episodes (11) and that their arousal episodes were much shorter than their torpor bouts

(21.2 hours and 13.81 days, respectively), comparing data across only Alaska marmot behaviors isn't sufficient to support a hypothesis about torpor and arousal behaviors of both Alaska marmots and Arctic ground squirrels.

QUESTION 11

Choice C is the best answer because it presents a finding that, if true, would support the researchers' hypothesis about the plants' dependence on dissolving rock. The text indicates that the roots of the two plant species grow directly into quartzite rock, where hairs on the roots secrete acids that dissolve the rock. The researchers hypothesize that the plants depend on this process because dissolving rock opens spaces for the roots to grow and releases phosphates that provide the plants with phosphorus, a vital nutrient. If the plants carry out this process of dissolving rock even when the rock already has spaces into which the roots could grow, that would support the researchers' hypothesis because it suggests that the plants are getting some advantage— such as access to phosphorus—from the action of dissolving rock. If the plants don't benefit from dissolving rock, they would be expected to grow in the cracks that already exist, as doing so would mean that the plants don't have to spend energy creating and secreting acids; if, however, the plants create new entry points by dissolving rock even when cracks already exist, that would support the hypothesis that they depend on dissolving rock for some benefit.

Choice A is incorrect because the existence of soil-inhabiting members of the Velloziaceae family with similar root structures to those of the two species discussed in the text wouldn't support the researchers' hypothesis that the species discussed in the text depend on dissolving rock. If other such members exist, that might suggest that the root structures can serve more functions than secreting acids to dissolve rock (since dissolving rock may not be necessary for plants living in soil), but that wouldn't suggest anything about whether the species discussed in the text benefit from dissolving rock. *Choice B* is incorrect because differences in the proportions of citric and malic acid secreted by the two species would be irrelevant to the hypothesis that the plants depend on dissolving rock. There's no information in the text to suggest that the proportion of each acid has any bearing on the process of dissolving rock or on any benefits the plants might receive from that process. *Choice D* is incorrect because if the two species thrive on rocks without phosphates, that would weaken the researchers' hypothesis that the plants depend on dissolving rock partly because dissolving rock gives them access to phosphates. If the plants can survive on rocks without getting a vital nutrient by dissolving those rocks, then either the nutrient isn't actually vital for those plants or they can get the nutrient in some way other than by dissolving rocks.

QUESTION 12

Choice A is the best answer because it presents data from the table that most effectively complete the statement about the rates at which employment shifted in France and the United States. The text states that over the last two hundred years employment in the agricultural sector has declined while employment in the service sector has risen in both France and the US, and the data from the table reflect these trends. The text asserts, however, that the transition from agriculture to services "happened at very different rates in the two countries." This assertion is best supported by a comparison of data from 1900 and 1950: the table shows that in those years, employment in agriculture went from 43% to 32% in France (a decline of 11 percentage points) and from 41% to 14% in the US (a decline of 27 percentage points), and that employment in services went from 28% to 35% in France (an increase of 7 percentage points) and from 31% to 53% in the US (an increase of 22 percentage points). In other words, the rate of change was greater in the US than in France for both sectors.

Choice B is incorrect because comparing the data for 1800 and 2012 would suggest a similar rate of change in the two countries, not very different rates: employment in agriculture went from 64% in 1800 to 3% in 2012 in France, which is close to the change from 68% in 1800 to 2% in 2012 in the US, while employment in services went from 14% in 1800 to 76% in 2012 in France, which is close to the change from 13% in 1800 to 80% in 2012 in the US. *Choice C* is incorrect because comparing the data for 1900 and 2012 would suggest a similar rate of change in the two countries rather than very different rates: employment in agriculture went from 43% in 1900 to 3% in 2012 in France, which is close to the change from 41% in 1900 to 2% in 2012 in the US, while employment in services went from 28% in 1900 to 76% in 2012 in France, which is close to the change from 31% in 1900 to 80% in 2012 in the US. *Choice D* is incorrect because comparing the data for 1800 and 1900 would suggest a similar rate of change in the two countries, not very different rates: employment in agriculture went from 64% in 1800 to 43% in 1900 in France, which is fairly close to the change from 68% in 1800 to 41% in 1900 in the US, while employment in services went from 14% in 1800 to 28% in 1900 in France, which is close to the change from 13% in 1800 to 31% in 1900 in the US.

QUESTION 13

Choice C is the best answer because it most logically completes the text's discussion of accelerated flowering in *A. thaliana* plants. The text indicates that *A. thaliana* plants show accelerated flowering at high temperatures. To investigate the mechanism for this accelerated flowering, biologists replaced the ELF3 protein in one group of *A. thaliana* plants with a similar protein found in another plant species that doesn't show accelerated flowering. The team then compared these modified plants to *A. thaliana* plants that retained their original ELF3 protein. The text states that the two samples of plants showed no difference in flowering at 22° Celsius, but at 27° Celsius the unaltered plants with ELF3 showed accelerated flowering while the plants without ELF3 didn't. If accelerated flowering at the higher temperature occurred in the *A. thaliana* plants with ELF3 but not in the plants without the protein, then ELF3 likely enables *A. thaliana* to respond to increased temperatures.

Choice A is incorrect because the text doesn't mention whether any plants other than *A. thaliana* and stiff brome show temperature-sensitive flowering, so there is no support for the idea that this type of flowering is unique to *A. thaliana*. *Choice B* is incorrect because the text discusses the effects of ELF3 and not the production of it. There's nothing in the text to suggest that the amount of ELF3 in *A. thaliana* varies with temperature. *Choice D* is incorrect. While the text states that there was no difference in the flowering of modified and unmodified *A. thaliana* plants at 22° Celsius, there's no suggestion that *A. thaliana* only begins to flower at 22° Celsius; the text doesn't mention a specific temperature threshold required for *A. thaliana* flowering.

QUESTION 14

Choice C is the best answer because it most logically completes the text's discussion of the sweet potato in Polynesia. The text indicates that the sweet potato is found in Polynesia but originated in South America, and that the sweet potato was being cultivated by Native Hawaiians and other Indigenous peoples in Polynesia long before sea voyages between South America and Polynesia began. The text goes on to note that research by Muñoz-Rodríguez and colleagues has established that the Polynesian varieties of sweet potato split from South American varieties more than 100,000 years ago, which is thousands of years before humans settled in Polynesia. If Polynesian peoples were cultivating the sweet potato before sea voyages between Polynesia and South America began, and if Polynesian varieties of sweet potato diverged from South American varieties well before people were in Polynesia, it can reasonably be concluded that humans didn't play a role in bringing the sweet potato to Polynesia.

Choice A is incorrect. The text doesn't provide any information about when the sweet potato began to be cultivated in South America, so there's no support for the conclusion that cultivation began in Polynesia before it began in South America. *Choice B* is incorrect because the text indicates that the sweet potato was being cultivated in Polynesia long before sea journeys between Polynesia and South America began. Therefore, it wouldn't be reasonable to conclude that Polynesian peoples acquired the sweet potato from South American peoples. Additionally, the text indicates that the Polynesian varieties of sweet potato diverged from the South American varieties thousands of years before people settled in Polynesia, which suggests that the sweet potato was already present in Polynesia when people arrived. *Choice D* is incorrect because the text states that the domestic sweet potato, which is found in Polynesia, descends from a wild South American plant, not from a domesticated South American plant. The only people that the text describes as cultivating the sweet potato are Native Hawaiians and other Indigenous peoples of Polynesia.

QUESTION 15

Choice A is the best answer. The convention being tested is finite verb use in a main clause. A main clause requires a finite verb to perform the action of the subject (in this case, Ashford's "gestures" and "habit"), and this choice supplies the finite past tense verb "helped" to indicate what Ashford's gestures and habit helped accomplish.

Choice B is incorrect because the non-finite participle "helping" doesn't supply the main clause with a finite verb. *Choice C* is incorrect because the relative clause "that helped" doesn't supply the main clause with a finite verb. *Choice D* is incorrect because the non-finite to-infinitive "to help" doesn't supply the main clause with a finite verb.

QUESTION 16

Choice C is the best answer. The convention being tested is the use of punctuation between titles and proper nouns. No punctuation is needed to offset the proper noun "Yuree Lee" from the title "plant cell biologist" that describes Lee.

Choice A is incorrect because no punctuation is needed. *Choice B* is incorrect because no punctuation is needed. *Choice D* is incorrect because no punctuation is needed around the proper noun "Yuree Lee." Setting the phrase off with punctuation suggests that it could be removed without affecting the coherence of the sentence, which isn't the case.

QUESTION 17

Choice C is the best answer. The convention being tested is the use of verb forms in a sentence. The nonfinite past participle phrase "highly prized" is correctly used to form a supplementary element that modifies the main clause "this...artistry," describing memorable features of Brass Era automotive design.

Choice A is incorrect because it results in a comma splice. Using the finite present tense verb phrase "are highly prized" creates a second main clause in the sentence, and two main clauses can't be joined in this way with only a comma after "artistry." *Choice B* is incorrect because it results in a comma splice. Using the finite past perfect tense verb phrase "had been highly prized" creates a second main clause in the sentence, and two main clauses can't be joined in this way with only a comma after "artistry." *Choice D* is incorrect because it results in a comma splice. Using the finite past tense verb phrase "were highly prized" creates a second main clause in the sentence, and two main clauses can't be joined in this way with only a comma after "artistry."

QUESTION 18

Choice C is the best answer. The convention being tested is the punctuation of a supplementary phrase following a clause. This choice uses a comma to separate the supplementary adverb phrase "however" from the independent clause it modifies ("They...antiquity") and uses a semicolon to join the first independent clause ("They...antiquity") and the second independent clause ("some...literature"). Further, placing the semicolon after "however" indicates that the information in the clause that this is part of (that neoclassical writers were not the first to adopt classical literary modes) is contrary to what might be assumed from the information in the previous sentence (that the neoclassical writers were unique in imitating classical epic poetry and satires).

Choice A is incorrect because it fails to mark the boundary after "however" between the two independent clauses with appropriate punctuation. *Choice B* is incorrect because the comma after "however" can't be used in this way to mark the boundary between the two independent clauses. *Choice D* is incorrect because placing the semicolon after "antiquity" illogically indicates that the information in the clause that this is part of (that prominent Renaissance figures were also influenced by classical literature) is contrary to the information in the previous clause (that neoclassical writers were not the first to adopt classical literary modes).

QUESTION 19

Choice C is the best answer. The convention being tested is the use of punctuation within a sentence. This choice correctly uses a comma to separate the supplementary adverb "though" from the preceding main clause ("Economists...conservation") and uses a semicolon to join the next main clause ("efficiency gains...rises") to the rest of the sentence. Further, placing the semicolon after "though" indicates that the information in the preceding main clause ("improvements in efficiency often correlate negatively with resource conservation") is contrary to what might be assumed from the information in the previous sentence (resource consumption would be expected to decrease with the development of new, more efficient technologies).

Choice A is incorrect because it results in a comma splice. Commas can't be used in this way to punctuate a supplementary word or phrase between two main clauses. *Choice B* is incorrect because it fails to mark the boundary between the two main clauses ("Economists...though" and "efficiency gains....rises") with appropriate punctuation. Moreover, placing the semicolon after "conservation" illogically indicates that the information in the next clause (gains in efficiency may lead to an increase in resource consumption) is contrary to the information in the previous clause ("improvements in efficiency often correlate negatively with resource conservation"). *Choice D* is incorrect because placing a comma after "conservation" illogically indicates that the information in the next clause (gains in efficiency may lead to an increase in resource consumption) is contrary to the information in the previous clause ("improvements in efficiency often correlate negatively with resource conservation").

QUESTION 20

Choice A is the best answer. The convention being tested is the use of verb forms within a sentence. The singular verb "is" agrees in number with the singular subject "each one of a ghazal's couplets." While the prepositional phrase "of a ghazal's couplets" within the subject contains a plural noun, the head of the subject ("each one") is singular, indicating that each individual couplet (not the couplets as a group) is "thematically and logically autonomous," or self-standing.

Choice B is incorrect because the plural verb "were" doesn't agree in number with the singular subject "each one of a ghazal's couplets." *Choice C* is incorrect because the plural verb "have been" doesn't agree in number with the singular subject "each one of a ghazal's couplets." *Choice D* is incorrect because the plural verb "are" doesn't agree in number with the singular subject "each one of a ghazal's couplets."

QUESTION 21

Choice A is the best answer. "Still" logically signals that the information about Sher-Gil in this sentence—that she longed to leave Paris and return to India—contrasts with what one would expect after reading about Sher-Gil's experiences in Paris in the previous sentences.

Choice B is incorrect because "therefore" illogically signals that the information about Sher-Gil in this sentence is a result or consequence of the descriptions in the previous sentences. Instead, this information contrasts with what one would expect after reading about Sher-Gil's experiences in Paris. *Choice C* is incorrect because "indeed" illogically signals that the information about Sher-Gil in this sentence offers additional emphasis in support of the descriptions in the previous sentences. Instead, this information contrasts with what one would expect after reading about Sher-Gil's experiences in Paris. *Choice D* is incorrect because "furthermore" illogically signals that the information about Sher-Gil in this sentence offers additional support for or confirmation of the descriptions in the previous sentences. Instead, this information contrasts with what one would expect after reading about Sher-Gil's experiences in Paris.

QUESTION 22

Choice D is the best answer. "Increasingly" logically signals that the claim in this sentence—that mathematicians are collaborating with their peers—marks a change relative to what was traditionally done. As the previous sentence explains, while mathematicians may have traditionally worked alone, evidence points to a shift in the opposite direction. The claim describes the shift: a rise in collaboration.

Choice A is incorrect because "similarly" illogically signals that the claim in this sentence is similar to, but separate from, the previous claim about the shift away from mathematicians working alone. Instead, the claim about the rise in collaboration elaborates on the previous claim, describing the shift. *Choice B* is incorrect because "for this reason" illogically signals that the claim in this sentence is caused by the previous claim about the shift away from mathematicians working alone. Instead, the claim about the rise in collaboration elaborates on the previous claim, describing the shift. *Choice C* is incorrect because "furthermore" illogically signals that the claim in this sentence is in addition to the previous claim about the shift away from mathematicians working alone. Instead, the claim about the rise in collaboration elaborates on the previous claim, describing the shift.

QUESTION 23

Choice C is the best answer. "Again and again" logically signals that the information in this sentence—that new calculations revealed increasingly precise coordinates for the location of the prime meridian—refers to events that occurred multiple times in the decades after the establishment of the prime meridian in 1884 (which is described in the preceding sentence).

Choice A is incorrect because "specifically" illogically signals that the information in this sentence provides specific, precise details elaborating on the description of the prime meridian's establishment in the previous sentence. Instead, the sentence indicates that increasingly precise coordinates were revealed on multiple occasions in the decades following the meridian's establishment. *Choice B* is incorrect because "to that end" illogically signals that the information in this sentence is a means of accomplishing a goal established in the previous sentence about the prime meridian's establishment. Instead, the sentence indicates that increasingly precise coordinates were revealed on multiple occasions in the decades following the meridian's establishment. *Choice D* is incorrect because "granted" illogically signals that the information in this sentence is in opposition to the information about the prime meridian's establishment in the previous sentence. Instead, the sentence indicates that increasingly precise coordinates were revealed on multiple occasions in the decades following the meridian's establishment.

QUESTION 24

Choice D is the best answer. The sentence effectively explains how pineapple extract increased the fish's growth rate, noting that the enzyme bromelain (which is in pineapple extract) enhanced the absorption of proteins ingested by fish fed pineapple extract.

Choice A is incorrect. The sentence indicates that adding pineapple extract to fish food increased the fish's growth rate; it does not explain how this was accomplished. *Choice B* is incorrect. While the sentence appears to explain how pineapple extract increased the fish's growth rate, it misrepresents the information provided about the effect on the fish's food consumption. As the notes indicate, adding the pineapple extract did not affect total food consumption. *Choice C* is incorrect. The sentence discusses the fish's growth rate but does not indicate how pineapple extract increased that rate.

QUESTION 25

Choice B is the best answer. The sentence explains an advantage of microprobes, noting that because microprobes weigh as little as 50 milligrams, they can explore areas inaccessible to rovers.

Choice A is incorrect. The sentence indicates that rovers can land successfully on Mars despite their weight; it doesn't explain an advantage of microprobes. *Choice C* is incorrect. While the sentence mentions that microprobes have been proposed as an alternative to rovers, it doesn't explain an advantage of microprobes. *Choice D* is incorrect. The sentence emphasizes a similarity between microprobes and rovers; it doesn't explain an advantage of microprobes.

QUESTION 26

Choice B is the best answer. The sentence effectively emphasizes Kind's methodology: examining the student policies of 132 medical schools for guidelines about student social media use.

Choice A is incorrect. The sentence specifies how many medical schools' student policies are available online; it doesn't emphasize the study's methodology. *Choice C* is incorrect. The sentence emphasizes the study's results, not the study's methodology. *Choice D* is incorrect. The sentence emphasizes the aim of the study, not the study's methodology.

QUESTION 27

Choice D is the best answer. The sentence uses information from the notes to make a generalization about the kind of study Glickman, Brown, and Song conducted. Specifically, the sentence indicates that the study was of a kind that used statistical methods to address questions of authorship within the field of music.

Choice A is incorrect because the sentence summarizes the methodology and findings of a particular analysis of a single song; it doesn't make a generalization about the kind of study conducted. *Choice B* is incorrect because the sentence mentions the data and conclusion of a particular analysis of a single song; it doesn't make a generalization about the kind of study conducted. *Choice C* is incorrect because the sentence focuses on a specific conclusion from a particular analysis of a single song; it doesn't make a generalization about the kind of study conducted.

Math

Module 1
(22 questions)

QUESTION 1

Choice C is correct. It's given that 29 out of every 100 beads that the machine produces have a defect. It follows that if the machine produces k beads,

then the number of beads that have a defect is $\frac{29}{100}k$, for some constant k.

If a bead produced by the machine will be selected at random, the probability of selecting a bead that has a defect is given by the number of beads with a

defect, $\frac{29}{100}k$, divided by the number of beads produced by the machine, k.

Therefore, the probability of selecting a bead that has a defect is $\frac{\frac{29}{100}k}{k}$, or $\frac{29}{100}$.

Choice A is incorrect and may result from conceptual or computational errors.
Choice B is incorrect and may result from conceptual or computational errors.
Choice D is incorrect and may result from conceptual or computational errors.

QUESTION 2

Choice D is correct. In the given equation, s is the speed, in miles per hour, of a certain car t seconds after it began to accelerate. Therefore, the speed of the car, in miles per hour, 5 seconds after it began to accelerate can be found by substituting 5 for t in the given equation, which yields $s = 40 + 3(5)$, or $s = 55$. Thus, the speed of the car 5 seconds after it began to accelerate is 55 miles per hour.

Choice A is incorrect and may result from conceptual or calculation errors.
Choice B is incorrect and may result from conceptual or calculation errors.
Choice C is incorrect and may result from conceptual or calculation errors.

QUESTION 3

Choice C is correct. It's given that $4x = 3$. Multiplying each side of this equation by 6 yields $24x = 18$. Therefore, the value of $24x$ is 18.

Choice A is incorrect. This is the value of $6x$, not $24x$. *Choice B* is incorrect. This is the value of $8x$, not $24x$. *Choice D* is incorrect. This is the value of $96x$, not $24x$.

QUESTION 4

Choice A is correct. The line of best fit shown has a positive slope and intersects the y-axis at a positive y-value. The graph of an equation of the form $y = mx + b$, where m and b are constants, has a slope of m and intersects the y-axis at a y-value of b. Of the given choices, only $y = x + 3.4$ represents a line that has a positive slope, 1, and intersects the y-axis at a positive y-value, 3.4.

Choice B is incorrect. This equation represents a line that intersects the y-axis at a negative y-value, not a positive y-value. *Choice C* is incorrect. This equation represents a line that has a negative slope, not a positive slope. *Choice D* is incorrect. This equation represents a line that has a negative slope, not a positive slope, and intersects the y-axis at a negative y-value, not a positive y-value.

QUESTION 5

Choice D is correct. The proportion of the paper clips that are size large can be written as $\frac{234,000}{300,000}$, or 0.78. Therefore, the percentage of the paper clips that are size large is 0.78(100), or 78%.

Choice A is incorrect. This is the percentage of the paper clips that are not size large. *Choice B* is incorrect and may result from conceptual or calculation errors. *Choice C* is incorrect and may result from conceptual or calculation errors.

QUESTION 6

Choice D is correct. A linear relationship can be represented by an equation of the form $y = mx + b$, where m and b are constants. It's given in the table that when $x = 0$, $y = 18$. Substituting 0 for x and 18 for y in $y = mx + b$ yields $18 = m(0) + b$, or $18 = b$. Substituting 18 for b in the equation $y = mx + b$ yields $y = mx + 18$. It's also given in the table that when $x = 1$, $y = 13$. Substituting 1 for x and 13 for y in the equation $y = mx + 18$ yields $13 = m(1) + 18$, or $13 = m + 18$. Subtracting 18 from both sides of this equation yields $-5 = m$. Therefore, the equation $y = -5x + 18$ represents the relationship between x and y.

Choice A is incorrect and may result from conceptual or calculation errors. *Choice B* is incorrect and may result from conceptual or calculation errors. *Choice C* is incorrect and may result from conceptual or calculation errors.

QUESTION 7

The correct answer is 77. It's given that the function f is defined by $f(x) = x^2 + x + 71$. Substituting 2 for x in function f yields $f(2) = (2)^2 + 2 + 71$, which is equivalent to $f(2) = 4 + 2 + 71$, or $f(2) = 77$. Therefore, the value of $f(2)$ is 77.

QUESTION 8

Choice B is correct. Applying the commutative property of multiplication, the expression $(m^4 q^4 z^{-1})(mq^5 z^3)$ can be rewritten as $(m^4 m)(q^4 q^5)(z^{-1} z^3)$. For positive values of x, $(x^a)(x^b) = x^{a+b}$. Therefore, the expression $(m^4 m)(q^4 q^5)(z^{-1} z^3)$ can be rewritten as $(m^{4+1})(q^{4+5})(z^{-1+3})$, or $m^5 q^9 z^2$.

Choice A is incorrect and may result from multiplying, not adding, the exponents. *Choice C* is incorrect and may result from conceptual or calculation errors. *Choice D* is incorrect and may result from conceptual or calculation errors.

QUESTION 9

Choice D is correct. It's given that triangle *ABC* is similar to triangle *XYZ*, where *A*, *B*, and *C* correspond to *X*, *Y*, and *Z*, respectively. It follows that side *AB* corresponds to side *XY* and side *BC* corresponds to side *YZ*. Since the lengths of corresponding sides in similar triangles are proportional, it follows that

$\frac{XY}{AB} = \frac{YZ}{BC}$. Substituting 170 for *AB*, 60 for *YZ*, and 850 for *BC* in this equation

yields $\frac{XY}{170} = \frac{60}{850}$. Multiplying each side of this equation by 170 yields *XY* = 12.

Therefore, the length of $\overline{XY}$ is 12.

Choice A is incorrect and may result from conceptual or calculation errors.
Choice B is incorrect and may result from conceptual or calculation errors.
Choice C is incorrect. This is the length of $\overline{YZ}$, not $\overline{XY}$.

QUESTION 10

The correct answer is 24. The equation $\frac{24x}{ny} = 4$ can be rewritten as $\left(\frac{24}{n}\right)\left(\frac{x}{y}\right) = 4$.

It's given that $\frac{x}{y} = 4$. Substituting 4 for $\frac{x}{y}$ in the equation $\left(\frac{24}{n}\right)\left(\frac{x}{y}\right) = 4$ yields

$\left(\frac{24}{n}\right)(4) = 4$. Multiplying both sides of this equation by *n* yields (24)(4) = 4*n*.

Dividing both sides of this equation by 4 yields 24 = *n*. Therefore, the value of *n* is 24.

QUESTION 11

Choice D is correct. It's given that the function *w* models the volume of liquid, in milliliters, in a container *t* seconds after it begins draining from a hole at the bottom. The given function *w*(*t*) = 300 − 4*t* can be rewritten as *w*(*t*) = −4*t* + 300. Thus, for each increase of *t* by 1, the value of *w*(*t*) decreases by 4(1), or 4. Therefore, the predicted volume, in milliliters, draining from the container each second is 4 milliliters.

Choice A is incorrect. This is the amount of liquid, in milliliters, in the container before the liquid begins draining. *Choice B* is incorrect and may result from conceptual errors. *Choice C* is incorrect and may result from conceptual errors.

QUESTION 12

Choice C is correct. If a value of *x* satisfies *f*(*x*) = 0, the graph of *y* = *f*(*x*) will contain a point (*x*, 0) and thus touch the *x*-axis. Since there are 3 points at which this graph touches the *x*-axis, there are 3 values of *x* for which *f*(*x*) = 0.

Choice A is incorrect and may result from conceptual or calculation errors.
Choice B is incorrect and may result from conceptual or calculation errors.
Choice D is incorrect and may result from conceptual or calculation errors.

QUESTION 13

Choice D is correct. Substituting 0 for *x* in the given equation yields *f*(0) = 3,000(0.75)^0, which is equivalent to *f*(0) = 3,000(1), or *f*(0) = 3,000. It's given that the function estimates the species' population *x* years after 2008, so it follows that the estimated population of the species is 3,000 in 2008. Therefore, the best interpretation of 3,000 in this context is the estimated initial population for this species and area in 2008.

Choice A is incorrect and may result from conceptual errors. *Choice B* is incorrect. The estimated percent decrease in the population for this species and area each year after 2008 is 25%, not 3,000. *Choice C* is incorrect. The estimated population for this species and area 8 years after 2008 is $3,000(0.75)^8$, or approximately 300, not 3,000.

QUESTION 14

The correct answer is 7. When an equation is of the form $y = ax^2 + bx + c$, where

a, b, and c are constants, the value of y reaches its minimum when $x = -\dfrac{b}{2a}$.

Since the given equation is of the form $y = ax^2 + bx + c$, it follows that $a = 1$, $b = -14$, and $c = 22$. Therefore, the value of y reaches its minimum when

$x = -\dfrac{(-14)}{2(1)}$, or $x = 7$.

QUESTION 15

The correct answer is 27,556. The area of a square is s^2, where s is the side length of the square. Let x represent the length of each side of square B. Substituting x for s in s^2 yields x^2. It follows that the area of square B is x^2. It's given that square A has side lengths that are 166 times the side lengths of square B. Since x represents the length of each side of square B, the length of each side of square A can be represented by the expression $166x$. It follows that the area of square A is $(166x)^2$, or $27,556x^2$. It's given that the area of square A is k times the area of square B. Since the area of square A is equal to $27,556x^2$, and the area of square B is equal to x^2, an equation representing the given statement is $27,556x^2 = kx^2$. Since x represents the length of each side of square B, the value of x must be positive. Therefore, the value of x^2 is also positive, so it does not equal 0. Dividing by x^2 on both sides of the equation $27,556x^2 = kx^2$ yields $27,556 = k$. Therefore, the value of k is 27,556.

QUESTION 16

The correct answer is 25. Subtracting the second equation from the first equation in the given system of equations yields $(2a - 2a) + (8b - 4b) = 198 - 98$, which is equivalent to $0 + 4b = 100$, or $4b = 100$. Dividing each side of this equation by 4 yields $b = 25$.

QUESTION 17

Choice A is correct. The y-intercept of the graph of $y = f(x)$ in the xy-plane occurs at the point on the graph where $x = 0$. In other words, when $x = 0$, the corresponding value of $f(x)$ is the y-coordinate of the y-intercept. Substituting 0 for x in the given equation yields $f(0) = (-8)(2)^0 + 22$, which is equivalent to $f(0) = (-8)(1) + 22$, or $f(0) = 14$. Thus, when $x = 0$, the corresponding value of $f(x)$ is 14. Therefore, the y-intercept of the graph of $y = f(x)$ in the xy-plane is (0, 14).

Choice B is incorrect and may result from conceptual or calculation errors. *Choice C* is incorrect and may result from conceptual or calculation errors. *Choice D* is incorrect. This could be the y-intercept for $f(x) = (-8)(2)^x$, not $f(x) = (-8)(2)^x + 22$.

QUESTION 18

Choice D is correct. Since the value of y increases by a constant factor, 4, for each increase of 1 in the value of x, the relationship between x and y is exponential. An exponential relationship between x and y can be represented by an equation of the form $y = a(b)^x$, where a is the value of x when $y = 0$ and y increases by a factor of b for each increase of 1 in the value of x. Since $y = 200$ when $x = 0$, $a = 200$. Since y increases by a factor of 4 for each increase of 1 in the value of x, $b = 4$. Substituting 200 for a and 4 for b in the equation $y = a(b)^x$ yields $y = 200(4)^x$. Thus, the equation $y = 200(4)^x$ represents the relationship between x and y.

Choice A is incorrect and may result from conceptual errors. *Choice B* is incorrect. This equation represents a relationship where for each increase of 1 in the value of x, the value of y increases by a factor of 200, not 4, and when $x = 0$, y is equal to 4, not 200. *Choice C* is incorrect and may result from conceptual errors.

QUESTION 19

Choice A is correct. The sine of a number t is the y-coordinate of the point arrived at by traveling a distance of t units counterclockwise around the unit circle from the starting point $(1, 0)$. Since the unit circle has a circumference of 2π units, it follows that one full rotation around the circle is equal to a distance of 2π units. Therefore, a distance of 42π units around the circle from the starting point $(1, 0)$ would result in exactly 21 full rotations, arriving back at the point $(1, 0)$. So, $\sin 42\pi$ is equal to the y-coordinate of the point $(1, 0)$, which is 0.

Alternate approach: The sine of an angle is equal to the sine of 2π radians more than the angle. Since 42π is equal to $21(2\pi)$, $\sin 42\pi$ can be rewritten as $\sin(0 + 21(2\pi))$, which is equal to $\sin 0$. Since $\sin 42\pi = \sin 0$ and $\sin 0 = 0$, it follows that $\sin 42\pi = 0$.

Choice B is incorrect and may result from conceptual or calculation errors. *Choice C* is incorrect and may result from conceptual or calculation errors. *Choice D* is incorrect. This is the value of $\cos 42\pi$, not $\sin 42\pi$.

QUESTION 20

Choice D is correct. A system of two linear equations in two variables, x and y, has no solution if the lines represented by the equations in the xy-plane are distinct and parallel. The graphs of two lines in the xy-plane represented by equations in the form $Ax + By = C$, where A, B, and C are constants, are parallel if the coefficients for x and y in one equation are proportional to the corresponding coefficients in the other equation. The first equation in the given system can be written in the form $Ax + By = C$ by subtracting $9y$ from both sides of the equation to yield $4x - 18y = 5$. The second equation in the given system can be written in the form $Ax + By = C$ by subtracting $4x$ from both sides of the equation to yield $-4x + hy = 2$. The coefficient of x in this second equation, -4, is -1 times the coefficient of x in the first equation, 4. For the lines to be parallel, the coefficient of y in the second equation, h, must also be -1 times the coefficient of y in the first equation, -18. Thus, $h = -1(-18)$, or $h = 18$. Therefore, if the given system has no solution, the value of h is 18.

Choice A is incorrect. If the value of h is -9, then the given system would have one solution, rather than no solution. *Choice B* is incorrect. If the value of h is 0, then the given system would have one solution, rather than no solution. *Choice C* is incorrect. If the value of h is 9, then the given system would have one solution, rather than no solution.

QUESTION 21

Choice B is correct. Adding 9 to each side of the given equation yields $x^2 - 2x = 9$. To complete the square, adding 1 to each side of this equation yields $x^2 - 2x + 1 = 9 + 1$, or $(x - 1)^2 = 10$. Taking the square root of each side of this equation yields $x - 1 = \pm\sqrt{10}$. Adding 1 to each side of this equation yields $x = 1 \pm \sqrt{10}$. Since it's given that one of the solutions to the equation can be written as $1 + \sqrt{k}$, the value of k must be 10.

Alternate approach: It's given that $1 + \sqrt{k}$ is a solution to the given equation. It follows that $x = 1 + \sqrt{k}$. Substituting $1 + \sqrt{k}$ for x in the given equation yields $(1 + \sqrt{k})^2 - 2(1 + \sqrt{k}) - 9 = 0$, or $(1 + \sqrt{k})(1 + \sqrt{k}) - 2(1 + \sqrt{k}) - 9 = 0$. Expanding the products on the left-hand side of this equation yields $1 + 2\sqrt{k} + k - 2 - 2\sqrt{k} - 9 = 0$, or $k - 10 = 0$. Adding 10 to each side of this equation yields $k = 10$.

Choice A is incorrect and may result from conceptual or calculation errors.
Choice C is incorrect and may result from conceptual or calculation errors.
Choice D is incorrect and may result from conceptual or calculation errors.

QUESTION 22

Choice D is correct. If $x^2 - c^2 \leq 0$, then neither side of the given equation is defined and there can be no solution. Therefore, $x^2 - c^2 > 0$. Subtracting $\dfrac{c^2}{\sqrt{x^2 - c^2}}$ from both sides of the given equation yields

$\dfrac{x^2}{\sqrt{x^2 - c^2}} - \dfrac{c^2}{\sqrt{x^2 - c^2}} = 39$, or $\dfrac{x^2 - c^2}{\sqrt{x^2 - c^2}} = 39$. Squaring both sides of this equation

yields $\left(\dfrac{x^2 - c^2}{\sqrt{x^2 - c^2}}\right)^2 = 39^2$, or $\dfrac{(x^2 - c^2)(x^2 - c^2)}{x^2 - c^2} = 39^2$. Since $x^2 - c^2$ is positive and,

therefore, nonzero, the expression $\dfrac{x^2 - c^2}{x^2 - c^2}$ is defined and equivalent to 1.

It follows that the equation $\dfrac{(x^2 - c^2)(x^2 - c^2)}{x^2 - c^2} = 39^2$ can be rewritten as

$\left(\dfrac{x^2 - c^2}{x^2 - c^2}\right)(x^2 - c^2) = 39^2$, or $(1)(x^2 - c^2) = 39^2$, which is equivalent to $x^2 - c^2 = 39^2$.

Adding c^2 to both sides of this equation yields $x^2 = c^2 + 39^2$. Taking the square

root of both sides of this equation yields two solutions: $x = \sqrt{c^2 + 39^2}$ and

$x = -\sqrt{c^2 + 39^2}$. Therefore, of the given choices, $-\sqrt{c^2 + 39^2}$ is one of the

solutions to the given equation.

Choice A is incorrect and may result from conceptual or calculation errors.
Choice B is incorrect and may result from conceptual or calculation errors.
Choice C is incorrect and may result from conceptual or calculation errors.

Math

Module 2 — Lower Difficulty
(22 questions)

QUESTION 1

The correct answer is 40. Subtracting 5 from both sides of the given equation yields $4x = 160$. Dividing both sides of this equation by 4 yields $x = 40$. Therefore, the solution to the given equation is 40.

QUESTION 2

Choice C is correct. The table shows that for a certain region in 2016, the average number of store employees in warehouse stores was 365 and the average number of store employees in supermarkets was 130. Subtracting 130 from 365 yields $365 - 130$, or 235. Therefore, the average number of store employees was 235 greater in warehouse stores than in supermarkets.

Choice A is incorrect. For this region in 2016, this is how much greater the average number of store employees was in department stores than in supermarkets.
Choice B is incorrect. For this region in 2016, this is how much greater the average number of store employees was in warehouse stores than in department stores.
Choice D is incorrect. For this region in 2016, this is the sum of the average number of store employees in warehouse stores and in supermarkets.

QUESTION 3

Choice A is correct. It's given that Julissa already has 86 hours of flight time. Let x represent the number of additional hours of flight time Julissa needs to get her private pilot certification. After completing x hours of flight time, Julissa will have completed a total of $86 + x$ hours of flight time. It's given that Julissa needs at least 100 hours of flight time to get her private pilot certification. Therefore, $86 + x \geq 100$. Subtracting 86 from both sides of this inequality yields $x \geq 14$. Thus, 14 is the minimum number of additional hours of flight time Julissa needs to get her private pilot certification.

Choice B is incorrect and may result from conceptual or calculation errors.
Choice C is incorrect. This is the number of hours of flight time Julissa already has, rather than the minimum number of additional hours of flight time Julissa needs.
Choice D is incorrect. This is the number of hours of flight time Julissa will have if she completes 100 more hours of flight time, rather than the minimum number of additional hours of flight time Julissa needs.

QUESTION 4

Choice C is correct. The solution to a system of linear equations is represented by the point that lies on the graph of each equation in the system, or the point where the lines intersect on a graph. On the graph shown, the two lines intersect at the point (−4, −3). Therefore, the solution to the system is (−4, −3).

Choice A is incorrect. This is the *y*-intercept of the graph of one of the lines shown, not the intersection point of the two lines. *Choice B* is incorrect and may result from conceptual or calculation errors. *Choice D* is incorrect and may result from conceptual or calculation errors.

QUESTION 5

The correct answer is 39,000. It's given that the giant armadillo has a mass of 39 kilograms. Since 1 kilogram is equal to 1,000 grams, 39 kilograms is equal to 39 kilograms $\left(\frac{1,000 \text{ grams}}{1 \text{ kilogram}}\right)$, or 39,000 grams. Therefore, the giant armadillo's mass, in grams, is 39,000.

QUESTION 6

The correct answer is 2. Substituting 8 for $f(x)$ in the given equation yields $8 = 4x$. Dividing the left- and right-hand sides of this equation by 4 yields $x = 2$. Therefore, the value of x is 2 when $f(x) = 8$.

QUESTION 7

Choice B is correct. It's given that triangle *ABC* is congruent to triangle *DEF*. Corresponding angles of congruent triangles are congruent and, therefore, have equal measure. It's given that angle *A* corresponds to angle *D*, and that the measure of angle *A* is 18°. It's also given that the measures of angles *B* and *E* are 90°. Since these angles have equal measure, they are corresponding angles. It follows that angle *C* corresponds to angle *F*. Let $x°$ represent the measure of angle *C*. Since the sum of the measures of the interior angles of a triangle is 180°, it follows that $18° + 90° + x° = 180°$, or $108° + x° = 180°$. Subtracting 108° from both sides of this equation yields $x° = 72°$. Therefore, the measure of angle *C* is 72°. Since angle *C* corresponds to angle *F*, it follows that the measure of angle *F* is also 72°.

Choice A is incorrect. This is the measure of angle *D*, not the measure of angle *F*. *Choice C* is incorrect. This is the measure of angle *E*, not the measure of angle *F*. *Choice D* is incorrect. This is the sum of the measures of angles *E* and *F*, not the measure of angle *F*.

QUESTION 8

Choice D is correct. It's given that line *m* is parallel to line *n*, and line *t* intersects both lines. It follows that line *t* is a transversal. When two lines are parallel and intersected by a transversal, exterior angles on the same side of the transversal are supplementary. Thus, $x + 33 = 180$. Subtracting 33 from both sides of this equation yields $x = 147$. Therefore, the value of *x* is 147.

Choice A is incorrect and may result from conceptual or calculation errors. *Choice B* is incorrect and may result from conceptual or calculation errors. *Choice C* is incorrect and may result from conceptual or calculation errors.

QUESTION 9

Choice B is correct. Adding the second equation in the given system to the first equation in the given system yields $3x + (-3x + y) = 12 + (-6)$, which is equivalent to $y = 6$.

Choice A is incorrect and may result from conceptual or calculation errors.
Choice C is incorrect and may result from conceptual or calculation errors.
Choice D is incorrect and may result from conceptual or calculation errors.

QUESTION 10

Choice A is correct. Since x is a factor of each term in the given expression, the expression is equivalent to $x(9x) + x(5)$, or $x(9x + 5)$.

Choice B is incorrect. This expression is equivalent to $45x^2 + 5x$, not $9x^2 + 5x$.
Choice C is incorrect. This expression is equivalent to $9x^2 + 45x$, not $9x^2 + 5x$.
Choice D is incorrect. This expression is equivalent to $9x^3 + 5x^2$, not $9x^2 + 5x$.

QUESTION 11

Choice A is correct. Since Jay walks at a speed of 3 miles per hour for w hours, Jay walks a total of $3w$ miles. Since Jay runs at a speed of 5 miles per hour for r hours, Jay runs a total of $5r$ miles. Therefore, the total number of miles Jay travels can be represented by $3w + 5r$. Since the combined total number of miles is 14, the equation $3w + 5r = 14$ represents this situation.

Choice B is incorrect and may result from conceptual errors. *Choice C* is incorrect and may result from conceptual errors. *Choice D* is incorrect and may result from conceptual errors.

QUESTION 12

Choice D is correct. The perimeter of a figure is equal to the sum of the measurements of the sides of the figure. It's given that the rectangle has a length of 4 inches and a width of 9 inches. Since a rectangle has 4 sides, of which opposite sides are parallel and equal, it follows that the rectangle has two sides with a length of 4 inches and two sides with a width of 9 inches. Therefore, the perimeter of this rectangle is $4 + 4 + 9 + 9$, or 26 inches.

Choice A is incorrect. This is the sum, in inches, of the length and the width of the rectangle. *Choice B* is incorrect. This is the sum, in inches, of the two lengths and the width of the rectangle. *Choice C* is incorrect. This is the sum, in inches, of the length and the two widths of the rectangle.

QUESTION 13

Choice D is correct. The equation of a line in the xy-plane can be written as $y = mx + b$, where m represents the slope of the line and $(0, b)$ represents the y-intercept of the line. It's given that the slope of the line is $\frac{1}{9}$. It follows that $m = \frac{1}{9}$. It's also given that the line passes through the point $(0, 14)$. It follows that $b = 14$. Substituting $\frac{1}{9}$ for m and 14 for b in $y = mx + b$ yields $y = \frac{1}{9}x + 14$. Thus, the equation $y = \frac{1}{9}x + 14$ represents this line.

Choice A is incorrect. This equation represents a line with a slope of $-\frac{1}{9}$ and a *y*-intercept of (0, −14). *Choice B* is incorrect. This equation represents a line with a slope of $-\frac{1}{9}$ and a *y*-intercept of (0, 14). *Choice C* is incorrect. This equation represents a line with a slope of $\frac{1}{9}$ and a *y*-intercept of (0, −14).

QUESTION 14

Choice D is correct. By the Pythagorean theorem, if a right triangle has a hypotenuse with length *c* and legs with lengths *a* and *b*, then $c^2 = a^2 + b^2$. In the right triangle shown, the hypotenuse has length *c* and the legs have lengths *a* and *b*. It's given that *a* = 4 and *b* = 5. Substituting 4 for *a* and 5 for *b* in the Pythagorean theorem yields $c^2 = 4^2 + 5^2$. Taking the square root of both sides of this equation yields $c = \pm\sqrt{4^2 + 5^2}$. Since the length of a side of a triangle must be positive, the value of *c* is $\sqrt{4^2 + 5^2}$.

Choice A is incorrect and may result from conceptual or calculation errors. *Choice B* is incorrect and may result from conceptual or calculation errors. *Choice C* is incorrect and may result from conceptual or calculation errors.

QUESTION 15

The correct answer is 41. The number of cupcakes Vivian bought can be found by first finding the amount Vivian spent on cupcakes. The amount Vivian spent on cupcakes can be found by subtracting the amount Vivian spent on party hats from the total amount Vivian spent. The amount Vivian spent on party hats can be found by multiplying the cost per package of party hats by the number of packages of party hats, which yields $3 · 10, or $30. Subtracting the amount Vivian spent on party hats, $30, from the total amount Vivian spent, $71, yields $71 − $30, or $41. Since the amount Vivian spent on cupcakes was $41 and each cupcake cost $1, it follows that Vivian bought 41 cupcakes.

QUESTION 16

Choice D is correct. If the graph of *y* = *g*(*x*) is the result of shifting the graph of *y* = *f*(*x*) down *k* units in the *xy*-plane, the function *g* can be defined by an equation of the form *g*(*x*) = *f*(*x*) − *k*. It's given that $f(x) = 7x^3$ and the graph of *y* = *g*(*x*) is the result of shifting the graph of *y* = *f*(*x*) down 2 units. Substituting $7x^3$ for *f*(*x*) and 2 for *k* in the equation *g*(*x*) = *f*(*x*) − *k* yields $g(x) = 7x^3 - 2$.

Choice A is incorrect and may result from conceptual errors. *Choice B* is incorrect and may result from conceptual errors. *Choice C* is incorrect. This equation defines a function *g* for which the graph of *y* = *g*(*x*) is the result of shifting the graph of *y* = *f*(*x*) up, not down, 2 units.

QUESTION 17

Choice A is correct. The solution to a system of equations is the ordered pair (*x*, *y*) that satisfies all equations in the system. It's given by the first equation in the system that *x* + 7 = 10. Substituting 10 for *x* + 7 into the second equation yields $10^2 = y$, or *y* = 100. The *x*-coordinate of the solution to the system of equations can be found by subtracting 7 from both sides of the equation *x* + 7 = 10, which yields *x* = 3. Therefore, the ordered pair (3, 100) is a solution to the given system of equations.

Choice B is incorrect and may result from conceptual or calculation errors. *Choice C* is incorrect and may result from conceptual or calculation errors. *Choice D* is incorrect and may result from conceptual or calculation errors.

QUESTION 18

Choice B is correct. A line in the *xy*-plane that passes through points (x_1, y_1) and (x_2, y_2) has a slope of $\frac{y_2 - y_1}{x_2 - x_1}$. The line of best fit shown passes approximately through the points (0, 14) and (13, 0). It follows that the slope of this line of best fit is approximately $\frac{0 - 14}{13 - 0}$, or $-\frac{14}{13}$. Of the given choices, −1.1 is closest to $-\frac{14}{13}$.

Choice A is incorrect and may result from conceptual or calculation errors. *Choice C* is incorrect and may result from conceptual or calculation errors. *Choice D* is incorrect and may result from conceptual or calculation errors.

QUESTION 19

Choice B is correct. A system of two linear equations in two variables, *x* and *y*, has no solution if the lines represented by the equations in the *xy*-plane are parallel and distinct. Lines represented by equations in standard form, $Ax + By = C$ and $Dx + Ey = F$, are parallel if the coefficients for *x* and *y* in one equation are proportional to the corresponding coefficients in the other equation, meaning $\frac{D}{A} = \frac{E}{B}$, and the lines are distinct if the constants are not proportional, meaning $\frac{F}{C}$ is not equal to $\frac{D}{A}$ or $\frac{E}{B}$. The given equation, $y = 6x + 18$, can be written in standard form by subtracting 6x from both sides of the equation to yield $-6x + y = 18$. Therefore, the given equation can be written in the form $Ax + By = C$, where $A = -6$, $B = 1$, and $C = 18$. The equation in choice B, $-6x + y = 22$, is written in the form $Dx + Ey = F$, where $D = -6$, $E = 1$, and $F = 22$. Therefore, $\frac{D}{A} = \frac{-6}{-6}$, which can be rewritten as $\frac{D}{A} = 1$; $\frac{E}{B} = \frac{1}{1}$, which can be rewritten as $\frac{E}{B} = 1$; and $\frac{F}{C} = \frac{22}{18}$, which can be rewritten as $\frac{F}{C} = \frac{11}{9}$. Since $\frac{D}{A} = 1$, $\frac{E}{B} = 1$, and $\frac{F}{C}$ is not equal to 1, it follows that the given equation and the equation $-6x + y = 22$ are parallel and distinct. Therefore, a system of two linear equations consisting of the given equation and the equation $-6x + y = 22$ has no solution. Thus, the equation in choice B could be the second equation in the system.

Choice A is incorrect. The equation $-6x + y = 18$ and the given equation represent the same line in the *xy*-plane. Therefore, a system of these linear equations would have infinitely many solutions, rather than no solution. *Choice C* is incorrect. The equation $-12x + y = 36$ and the given equation represent lines in the *xy*-plane that are distinct and not parallel. Therefore, a system of these linear equations would have exactly one solution, rather than no solution. *Choice D* is incorrect. The equation $-12x + y = 18$ and the given equation represent lines in the *xy*-plane that are distinct and not parallel. Therefore, a system of these linear equations would have exactly one solution, rather than no solution.

QUESTION 20

Choice D is correct. The given function *f* is a linear function. Therefore, the graph of $y = f(x)$ in the *xy*-plane has one *x*-intercept at the point $(k, 0)$, where *k* is a constant. Substituting 0 for $f(x)$ and *k* for *x* in the given function yields $0 = 7k - 84$. Adding 84 to both sides of this equation yields $84 = 7k$. Dividing both sides of this equation by 7 yields $12 = k$. Therefore, the *x*-intercept of the graph of $y = f(x)$ in the *xy*-plane is (12, 0).

Choice A is incorrect and may result from conceptual or calculation errors.
Choice B is incorrect and may result from conceptual or calculation errors.
Choice C is incorrect and may result from conceptual or calculation errors.

QUESTION 21

The correct answer is 11,875. It's given that the exponential function *g* is defined by $g(x) = 19 \cdot a^x$, where *a* is a positive constant, and $g(3) = 2,375$. It follows that when $x = 3$, $g(x) = 2,375$. Substituting 3 for *x* and 2,375 for $g(x)$ in the given equation yields $2,375 = 19 \cdot a^3$. Dividing each side of this equation by 19 yields $125 = a^3$. Taking the cube root of both sides of this equation gives $a = 5$. Substituting 4 for *x* and 5 for *a* in the equation $g(x) = 19 \cdot a^x$ yields $g(4) = 19 \cdot 5^4$, or $g(4) = 11,875$. Therefore, the value of $g(4)$ is 11,875.

QUESTION 22

Choice C is correct. Let *x* be the 2015 population of Greenville. It's given that the population increased by 7% from 2015 to 2016. The increase in population can be written as $(0.07)x$. The 2016 population of Greenville is given as the sum of the 2015 population of Greenville and the increase in population from 2015 to 2016. This can be rewritten as $x + (0.07)x$, or $1.07x$. Therefore, the value of *k* is 1.07.

Choice A is incorrect. This is the percent, represented as a decimal, that the population increased from 2015 to 2016, not the value of *k*. *Choice B* is incorrect and may result from conceptual or calculation errors. *Choice D* is incorrect. This is the value of *k* if the population increased by 70%, not 7%, from 2015 to 2016.

Math

Module 2 — Higher Difficulty
(22 questions)

QUESTION 1

Choice B is correct. It's given that the airplane descends at a constant rate of 400 feet per minute. Since the altitude decreases by a constant amount during each fixed time period, the relationship between the airplane's altitude and time is linear. Since the airplane descends from an altitude of 9,500 feet to 5,000 feet, the airplane's altitude is decreasing with time. Thus, the relationship is best modeled by a decreasing linear function.

Choice A is incorrect and may result from conceptual or calculation errors. *Choice C* is incorrect and may result from conceptual or calculation errors. *Choice D* is incorrect and may result from conceptual or calculation errors.

QUESTION 2

Choice B is correct. It's given that line *k* is defined by $y = \frac{17x}{7} + 4$. For an equation of a line written in the form $y = mx + b$, *m* is the slope of the line and *b* is the *y*-coordinate of the *y*-intercept of the line. It follows that the slope of line *k* is $\frac{17}{7}$. It's also given that line *j* is parallel to line *k* in the *xy*-plane. Since parallel lines have equal slopes, line *j* also has a slope of $\frac{17}{7}$.

Choice A is incorrect and may result from conceptual or calculation errors. *Choice C* is incorrect. This is the *y*-coordinate of the *y*-intercept of line *k*, not the slope of line *j*. *Choice D* is incorrect and may result from conceptual or calculation errors.

QUESTION 3

Choice C is correct. An equation that defines a linear function *f* can be written in the form $f(x) = mx + b$, where *m* represents the slope and *b* represents the *y*-intercept, (0, *b*), of the line of $y = f(x)$ in the *xy*-plane. The function $f(x) = -5x + 30$ is linear. Therefore, the graph of the given function $y = f(x)$ in the *xy*-plane has a *y*-intercept of (0, 30). It's given that $f(x)$ gives the approximate volume, in fluid ounces, of juice Caleb had remaining after making *x* popsicles. It follows that the *y*-intercept of (0, 30) means that Caleb had approximately 30 fluid ounces of juice remaining after making 0 popsicles. In other words, Caleb had approximately 30 fluid ounces of juice when he began to make the popsicles.

Choice A is incorrect. This is an interpretation of the slope, rather than the *y*-intercept, of the graph of *y* = *f*(*x*) in the *xy*-plane. *Choice B* is incorrect and may result from conceptual errors. *Choice D* is incorrect and may result from conceptual errors.

QUESTION 4

Choice B is correct. The vertex of the graph of a quadratic equation is where it reaches its minimum or maximum value. When a quadratic equation is written in the form $y = a(x - h)^2 + k$, the vertex of the parabola represented by the equation is (*x*, *y*) = (*h*, *k*). In the given equation $y = -16(x - 5.6)^2 + 502$, the value of *h* is 5.6 and the value of *k* is 502. It follows that the vertex of the graph of this equation in the *xy*-plane is (*x*, *y*) = (5.6, 502). Additionally, since *a* = −16 in the given equation, the graph of the quadratic equation opens down, and the vertex represents a maximum. It's given that the value of *y* represents the estimated height, in feet, of the toy rocket *x* seconds after it is launched into the air. Therefore, this toy rocket reaches an estimated maximum height of 502 feet 5.6 seconds after it is launched into the air.

Choice A is incorrect. The 16 in the equation is an indicator of how narrow the graph of the equation is rather than where it reaches its maximum. *Choice C* is incorrect. The 16 in the equation is an indicator of how narrow the graph of the equation is rather than where it reaches its maximum. *Choice D* is incorrect. This is an interpretation of the vertex of the graph of the equation $y = -16(x - 502)^2 + 5.6$, not of the equation $y = -16(x - 5.6)^2 + 502$.

QUESTION 5

The correct answer is 67. It's given that *f*(5) = 32. Therefore, for the given function *f*, when *x* = 5, *f*(*x*) = 32. Substituting 5 for *x* and 32 for *f*(*x*) in the given function $f(x) = 4x + k(x - 1)$ yields 32 = 4(5) + *k*(5 − 1), or 32 = 20 + 4*k*. Subtracting 20 from each side of this equation yields 12 = 4*k*. Dividing each side of this equation by 4 yields *k* = 3. Substituting 3 for *k* in the given function $f(x) = 4x + k(x - 1)$ yields *f*(*x*) = 4*x* + 3(*x* − 1), which is equivalent to *f*(*x*) = 4*x* + 3*x* − 3, or *f*(*x*) = 7*x* − 3. Substituting 10 for *x* into this equation yields *f*(10) = 7(10) − 3, or *f*(10) = 67. Therefore, the value of *f*(10) is 67.

QUESTION 6

Choice B is correct. It's given that triangle *ABC* is congruent to triangle *DEF*. Corresponding angles of congruent triangles are congruent and, therefore, have equal measure. It's given that angle *A* corresponds to angle *D*, and that the measure of angle *A* is 18°. It's also given that the measures of angles *B* and *E* are 90°. Since these angles have equal measure, they are corresponding angles. It follows that angle *C* corresponds to angle *F*. Let *x*° represent the measure of angle *C*. Since the sum of the measures of the interior angles of a triangle is 180°, it follows that 18° + 90° + *x*° = 180°, or 108° + *x*° = 180°. Subtracting 108° from both sides of this equation yields *x*° = 72°. Therefore, the measure of angle *C* is 72°. Since angle *C* corresponds to angle *F*, it follows that the measure of angle *F* is also 72°.

Choice A is incorrect. This is the measure of angle *D*, not the measure of angle *F*. *Choice C* is incorrect. This is the measure of angle *E*, not the measure of angle *F*. *Choice D* is incorrect. This is the sum of the measures of angles *E* and *F*, not the measure of angle *F*.

QUESTION 7

Choice D is correct. A point (x, y) is a solution to a system of inequalities in the xy-plane if substituting the x-coordinate and the y-coordinate of the point for x and y, respectively, in each inequality makes both of the inequalities true. Substituting the x-coordinate and the y-coordinate of choice D, 14 and 0, for x and y, respectively, in the first inequality in the given system, $y \leq x + 7$, yields $0 \leq 14 + 7$, or $0 \leq 21$, which is true. Substituting 14 for x and 0 for y in the second inequality in the given system, $y \geq -2x - 1$, yields $0 \geq -2(14) - 1$, or $0 \geq -29$, which is true. Therefore, the point (14, 0) is a solution to the given system of inequalities in the xy-plane.

Choice A is incorrect. Substituting −14 for x and 0 for y in the inequality $y \leq x + 7$ yields $0 \leq -14 + 7$, or $0 \leq -7$, which is not true. *Choice B* is incorrect. Substituting 0 for x and −14 for y in the inequality $y \geq -2x - 1$ yields $-14 \geq -2(0) - 1$, or $-14 \geq -1$, which is not true. *Choice C* is incorrect. Substituting 0 for x and 14 for y in the inequality $y \leq x + 7$ yields $14 \leq 0 + 7$, or $14 \leq 7$, which is not true.

QUESTION 8

Choice A is correct. The median of a data set with an odd number of values that are in ascending or descending order is the middle value of the data set. Since the distribution of the values of both data set A and data set B form symmetric dot plots, and each data set has an odd number of values, it follows that the median is given by the middle value in each of the dot plots. Thus, the median of data set A is 13, and the median of data set B is 13. Therefore, statement I is true. Data set A and data set B have the same frequency for each of the values 11, 12, 14, and 15. Data set A has a frequency of 1 for values 10 and 16, whereas data set B has a frequency of 2 for values 10 and 16. Standard deviation is a measure of the spread of a data set; it is larger when there are more values farther from the mean, and smaller when there are more values closer to the mean. Since both distributions are symmetric with an odd number of values, the mean of each data set is equal to its median. Thus, each data set has a mean of 13. Since more of the values in data set A are closer to 13 than in data set B, it follows that data set A has a smaller standard deviation than data set B. Thus, statement II is false. Therefore, only statement I must be true.

Choice B is incorrect and may result from conceptual or calculation errors. *Choice C* is incorrect and may result from conceptual or calculation errors. *Choice D* is incorrect and may result from conceptual or calculation errors.

QUESTION 9

Choice B is correct. It's given that the formula $P = C(2)^{rt}$ gives the number of bacteria in a growth medium, where r and C are constants and P is the number of bacteria t hours after the initial measurement. It's also given that a scientist initially measures 12,000 bacteria in the growth medium. Since the initial measurement is 0 hours after the initial measurement, it follows that when t = 0, P = 12,000. Substituting 0 for t and 12,000 for P in the given equation yields $12,000 = C(2)^{r(0)}$, or $12,000 = C(2)^0$, which is equivalent to 12,000 = C. It's given that 4 hours later, the scientist measures 24,000 bacteria, or when t = 4, P = 24,000. Substituting 4 for t, 24,000 for P, and 12,000 for C in the given equation yields $24,000 = 12,000(2)^{4r}$. Dividing each side of this equation by 12,000 yields $2 = 2^{4r}$, or $2^1 = 2^{4r}$, which is equivalent to 1 = 4r. Dividing both sides of this equation by 4 yields $\frac{1}{4} = r$. Therefore, the value of r is $\frac{1}{4}$.

Choice A is incorrect. This is the value of the reciprocal of C. *Choice C* is incorrect. This is the value of the reciprocal of r. *Choice D* is incorrect. This is the value of C.

QUESTION 10

The correct answer is 36,504. The volume of a cube can be found using the formula $V = s^3$, where s represents the edge length of a cube. It's given that this cube has a volume of 474,552 cubic units. Substituting 474,552 for V in $V = s^3$ yields $474{,}552 = s^3$. Taking the cube root of both sides of this equation yields $78 = s$. Thus, the edge length of the cube is 78 units. Since each face of a cube is a square, it follows that each face has an edge length of 78 units. The area of a square can be found using the formula $A = s^2$. Substituting 78 for s in this formula yields $A = 78^2$, or $A = 6{,}084$. Therefore, the area of one face of this cube is 6,084 square units. Since a cube has 6 faces, the surface area, in square units, of this cube is 6(6,084), or 36,504.

QUESTION 11

The correct answer is 3. Adding the second equation to the first equation in the given system of equations yields $(2(8x) - 2(8x)) + (4(7y) + 4(7y)) = 12 + 12$, or $8(7y) = 24$. Dividing both sides of this equation by 8 yields $7y = 3$. Substituting 3 for $7y$ in the first equation, $2(8x) + 4(7y) = 12$, yields $2(8x) + 4(3) = 12$, or $2(8x) + 12 = 12$. Subtracting 12 from both sides of this equation yields $2(8x) = 0$. Dividing both sides of this equation by 2 yields $8x = 0$. Substituting 0 for $8x$ and 3 for $7y$ in the expression $8x + 7y$ yields $0 + 3$, or 3. Therefore, the value of $8x + 7y$ is 3.

QUESTION 12

Choice D is correct. Since the number of yards in 1 mile is 1,760, the number of square yards in 1 square mile is (1,760)(1,760) = 3,097,600. Therefore, if the area of the town is 4.36 square miles, it is 4.36(3,097,600) = 13,505,536, in square yards.

Choice A is incorrect and may result from dividing the number of yards in a mile by the square mileage of the town. *Choice B* is incorrect and may result from multiplying the number of yards in a mile by the square mileage of the town. *Choice C* is incorrect and may result from dividing the number of square yards in a square mile by the square mileage of the town.

QUESTION 13

Choice C is correct. Since $P = (4, 5)$ and $Q = (4, 7)$, side PQ is parallel to the y-axis and has a length of 2. Since $P = (4, 5)$ and $R = (6, 5)$, side PR is parallel to the x-axis and has a length of 2. Therefore, triangle PQR is a right isosceles triangle, where $\angle P$ has measure 90° and $\angle Q$ and $\angle R$ each have measure 45°. It follows that if the measure of $\angle Q$ is $t°$, then $t = 45$. Since $L = (4, 5)$ and $M = (4, 7 + k)$, side LM is parallel to the y-axis and has a length of $k + 2$. Since $L = (4, 5)$ and $N = (6 + k, 5)$, side LN is parallel to the x-axis and has a length of $k + 2$. Therefore, triangle LMN is a right isosceles triangle, where $\angle L$ has measure 90° and $\angle M$ and $\angle N$ each have measure 45°. Of the given choices, only $(90 - t)°$ is equal to 45°, so the measure of $\angle N$ is $(90 - t)°$.

Choice A is incorrect and may result from conceptual or calculation errors. *Choice B* is incorrect and may result from conceptual or calculation errors. *Choice D* is incorrect and may result from conceptual or calculation errors.

QUESTION 14

The correct answer is 182. Let s represent the number of small candles the owner can purchase, and let ℓ represent the number of large candles the owner can purchase. It's given that the owner pays $4.90 per candle to purchase small candles and $11.60 per candle to purchase large candles. Therefore, the owner pays 4.90s dollars for s small candles and 11.60ℓ dollars for ℓ large candles, which means the owner pays a total of 4.90s + 11.60ℓ dollars to purchase candles. It's given that the owner budgets $2,200 to purchase candles. Therefore, 4.90s + 11.60ℓ ≤ 2,200. It's also given that the owner must purchase a minimum of 200 candles. Therefore, $s + \ell$ ≥ 200. The inequalities 4.90s + 11.60ℓ ≤ 2,200 and $s + \ell$ ≥ 200 can be combined into one compound inequality by rewriting the second inequality so that its left-hand side is equivalent to the left-hand side of the first inequality. Subtracting ℓ from both sides of the inequality $s + \ell$ ≥ 200 yields s ≥ 200 − ℓ. Multiplying both sides of this inequality by 4.90 yields 4.90s ≥ 4.90(200 − ℓ), or 4.90s ≥ 980 − 4.90ℓ. Adding 11.60ℓ to both sides of this inequality yields 4.90s + 11.60ℓ ≥ 980 − 4.90ℓ + 11.60ℓ, or 4.90s + 11.60ℓ ≥ 980 + 6.70ℓ. This inequality can be combined with the inequality 4.90s + 11.60ℓ ≤ 2,200, which yields the compound inequality 980 + 6.70ℓ ≤ 4.90s + 11.60ℓ ≤ 2,200. It follows that 980 + 6.70ℓ ≤ 2,200. Subtracting 980 from both sides of this inequality yields 6.70ℓ ≤ 1,220. Dividing both sides of this inequality by 6.70 yields approximately ℓ ≤ 182.09. Since the number of large candles the owner purchases must be a whole number, the maximum number of large candles the owner can purchase is the largest whole number less than 182.09, which is 182.

QUESTION 15

Choice A is correct. When a square is inscribed in a circle, a diagonal of the square is a diameter of the circle. It's given that a square is inscribed in a circle and the length of a radius of the circle is $\frac{20\sqrt{2}}{2}$ inches. Therefore, the length of a diameter of the circle is $2\left(\frac{20\sqrt{2}}{2}\right)$ inches, or $20\sqrt{2}$ inches. It follows that the length of a diagonal of the square is $20\sqrt{2}$ inches. A diagonal of a square separates the square into two right triangles in which the legs are the sides of the square and the hypotenuse is a diagonal. Since a square has 4 congruent sides, each of these two right triangles has congruent legs and a hypotenuse of length $20\sqrt{2}$ inches. Since each of these two right triangles has congruent legs, they are both 45-45-90 triangles. In a 45-45-90 triangle, the length of the hypotenuse is $\sqrt{2}$ times the length of a leg. Let s represent the length of a leg of one of these 45-45-90 triangles. It follows that $20\sqrt{2} = \sqrt{2}(s)$. Dividing both sides of this equation by $\sqrt{2}$ yields 20 = s. Therefore, the length of a leg of one of these 45-45-90 triangles is 20 inches. Since the legs of these two 45-45-90 triangles are the sides of the square, it follows that the side length of the square is 20 inches.

Choice B is incorrect. This is the length of a radius, in inches, of the circle.
Choice C is incorrect. This is the length of a diameter, in inches, of the circle.
Choice D is incorrect and may result from conceptual or calculation errors.

QUESTION 16

Choice C is correct. The graph of the equation $(x - h)^2 + (y - k)^2 = r^2$ in the xy-plane is a circle with center (h, k) and a radius of length r. The radius of a circle is the distance from the center of the circle to any point on the circle. If a circle in the xy-plane intersects the y-axis at exactly one point, then the perpendicular distance from the center of the circle to this point on the y-axis must be equal to the length of the circle's radius. It follows that the x-coordinate of the circle's center must be equivalent to the length of the circle's radius. In other words, if the graph of $(x - h)^2 + (y - k)^2 = r^2$ is a circle that intersects the y-axis at exactly one point, then $r = |h|$ must be true. The equation in choice C is $(x - 4)^2 + (y - 9)^2 = 16$, or $(x - 4)^2 + (y - 9)^2 = 4^2$. This equation is in the form

$(x - h)^2 + (y - k)^2 = r^2$, where $h = 4$, $k = 9$, and $r = 4$, and represents a circle in the xy-plane with center $(4, 9)$ and radius of length 4. Substituting 4 for r and 4 for h in the equation $r = |h|$ yields $4 = |4|$, or $4 = 4$, which is true. Therefore, the equation in choice C represents a circle in the xy-plane that intersects the y-axis at exactly one point.

Choice A is incorrect. This is the equation of a circle that does not intersect the y-axis at any point. *Choice B* is incorrect. This is an equation of a circle that intersects the x-axis, not the y-axis, at exactly one point. *Choice D* is incorrect. This is the equation of a circle with the center located on the y-axis and thus intersects the y-axis at exactly two points, not exactly one point.

QUESTION 17

Choice B is correct. A system of two linear equations in two variables, x and y, has no solution if the lines represented by the equations in the xy-plane are parallel and distinct. Lines represented by equations in standard form, $Ax + By = C$ and $Dx + Ey = F$, are parallel if the coefficients for x and y in one equation are proportional to the corresponding coefficients in the other equation, meaning $\frac{D}{A} = \frac{E}{B}$, and the lines are distinct if the constants are not proportional, meaning $\frac{F}{C}$ is not equal to $\frac{D}{A}$ or $\frac{E}{B}$. The given equation, $y = 6x + 18$, can be written in standard form by subtracting $6x$ from both sides of the equation to yield $-6x + y = 18$. Therefore, the given equation can be written in the form $Ax + By = C$, where $A = -6$, $B = 1$, and $C = 18$. The equation in choice B, $-6x + y = 22$, is written in the form $Dx + Ey = F$, where $D = -6$, $E = 1$, and $F = 22$. Therefore, $\frac{D}{A} = \frac{-6}{-6}$, which can be rewritten as $\frac{D}{A} = 1$; $\frac{E}{B} = \frac{1}{1}$, which can be rewritten as $\frac{E}{B} = 1$; and $\frac{F}{C} = \frac{22}{18}$, which can be rewritten as $\frac{F}{C} = \frac{11}{9}$. Since $\frac{D}{A} = 1$, $\frac{E}{B} = 1$, and $\frac{F}{C}$ is not equal to 1, it follows that the given equation and the equation $-6x + y = 22$ are parallel and distinct. Therefore, a system of two linear equations consisting of the given equation and the equation $-6x + y = 22$ has no solution. Thus, the equation in choice B could be the second equation in the system.

Choice A is incorrect. The equation $-6x + y = 18$ and the given equation represent the same line in the xy-plane. Therefore, a system of these linear equations would have infinitely many solutions, rather than no solution. *Choice C* is incorrect. The equation $-12x + y = 36$ and the given equation represent lines in the xy-plane that are distinct and not parallel. Therefore, a system of these linear equations would have exactly one solution, rather than no solution. *Choice D* is incorrect. The equation $-12x + y = 18$ and the given equation represent lines in the xy-plane that are distinct and not parallel. Therefore, a system of these linear equations would have exactly one solution, rather than no solution.

QUESTION 18

Choice C is correct. Factoring the denominator in the second term of the given expression gives $\frac{y + 12}{x - 8} + \frac{y(x - 8)}{xy(x - 8)}$. This expression can be rewritten with common denominators by multiplying the first term by $\frac{xy}{xy}$, giving $\frac{xy(y + 12)}{xy(x - 8)} + \frac{y(x - 8)}{xy(x - 8)}$. Adding these two terms yields $\frac{xy(y + 12) + y(x - 8)}{xy(x - 8)}$.

Using the distributive property to rewrite this expression gives

$\dfrac{xy^2 + 12xy + xy - 8y}{x^2y - 8xy}$. Combining the like terms in the numerator of this

expression gives $\dfrac{xy^2 + 13xy - 8y}{x^2y - 8xy}$.

Choice A is incorrect and may result from conceptual or calculation errors.
Choice B is incorrect and may result from conceptual or calculation errors.
Choice D is incorrect and may result from conceptual or calculation errors.

QUESTION 19

Choice C is correct. Multiplying each side of the given equation by $\dfrac{1}{20}$ yields

$\dfrac{1}{20}\left(\dfrac{20}{p}\right) = \dfrac{1}{20}\left(\dfrac{20}{q} - \dfrac{20}{r} - \dfrac{20}{s}\right)$. Distributing $\dfrac{1}{20}$ on each side of this equation

yields $\dfrac{20}{20p} = \dfrac{20}{20q} - \dfrac{20}{20r} - \dfrac{20}{20s}$, or $\dfrac{1}{p} = \dfrac{1}{q} - \dfrac{1}{r} - \dfrac{1}{s}$. Adding $\dfrac{1}{r} + \dfrac{1}{s}$ to each side of

this equation yields $\dfrac{1}{s} + \dfrac{1}{r} + \dfrac{1}{p} = \dfrac{1}{q}$. Multiplying $\dfrac{1}{s}$ by $\dfrac{pr}{pr}$, $\dfrac{1}{r}$ by $\dfrac{ps}{ps}$, and $\dfrac{1}{p}$ by $\dfrac{rs}{rs}$

yields $\dfrac{pr}{prs} + \dfrac{ps}{prs} + \dfrac{rs}{prs} = \dfrac{1}{q}$, which is equivalent to $\dfrac{pr + ps + rs}{prs} = \dfrac{1}{q}$. Since

$\dfrac{pr + ps + rs}{prs} = \dfrac{1}{q}$, and it's given that p, q, r, and s are positive, it follows that the

reciprocals of each side of this equation are also equal. Thus, $\dfrac{prs}{pr + ps + rs} = \dfrac{q}{1}$,

or $\dfrac{prs}{pr + ps + rs} = q$. Therefore, $\dfrac{prs}{pr + ps + rs}$ is equivalent to q.

Choice A is incorrect and may result from conceptual or calculation errors.
Choice B is incorrect and may result from conceptual or calculation errors.
Choice D is incorrect and may result from conceptual or calculation errors.

QUESTION 20

The correct answer is 50. An equation of the form $ax^2 + bx + c = 0$, where a, b, and c are constants, has no real solutions if and only if its discriminant, $b^2 - 4ac$, is negative. Applying the distributive property to the left-hand side of the equation $x(kx - 56) = -16$ yields $kx^2 - 56x = -16$. Adding 16 to each side of this equation yields $kx^2 - 56x + 16 = 0$. Substituting k for a, -56 for b, and 16 for c in $b^2 - 4ac$ yields a discriminant of $(-56)^2 - 4(k)(16)$, or $3{,}136 - 64k$. If the given equation has no real solution, it follows that the value of $3{,}136 - 64k$ must be negative. Therefore, $3{,}136 - 64k < 0$. Adding $64k$ to both sides of this inequality yields $3{,}136 < 64k$. Dividing both sides of this inequality by 64 yields $49 < k$, or $k > 49$. Since it's given that k is an integer, the least possible value of k is 50.

QUESTION 21

Choice B is correct. The two given equations are equivalent because the second equation can be obtained from the first equation by multiplying each side of the equation by 5. Thus, the graphs of the equations are coincident, so if a point lies on the graph of one of the equations, it also lies on the graph of the other equation. A point (x, y) lies on the graph of an equation in the xy-plane if and only if this point represents a solution to the equation. It is sufficient, therefore, to find the point that represents a solution to the first given equation.

Substituting the x- and y-coordinates of choice B, $-\dfrac{3r}{2} + \dfrac{7}{2}$ and r, for x and y,

respectively, in the first equation yields $2\left(-\dfrac{3r}{2} + \dfrac{7}{2}\right) + 3r = 7$, which is equivalent to $-3r + 7 + 3r = 7$, or $7 = 7$. Therefore, the point $\left(-\frac{3r}{2} + \frac{7}{2}, r\right)$ represents a

solution to the first equation and thus lies on the graph of each equation in the xy-plane for the given system.

Choice A is incorrect and may result from conceptual or calculation errors.
Choice C is incorrect and may result from conceptual or calculation errors.
Choice D is incorrect and may result from conceptual or calculation errors.

QUESTION 22

Choice A is correct. It's given that the window repair specialist charges $220 for the first two hours of repair plus an hourly fee for each additional hour. Let n represent the hourly fee for each additional hour after the first two hours. Since it's given that x is the number of hours of repair, it follows that the charge generated by the hourly fee after the first two hours can be represented by the expression $n(x - 2)$. Therefore, the total cost, in dollars, for x hours of repair is $f(x) = 220 + n(x - 2)$. It's given that the total cost for 5 hours of repair is $400. Substituting 5 for x and 400 for $f(x)$ into the equation $f(x) = 220 + n(x - 2)$ yields $400 = 220 + n(5 - 2)$, or $400 = 220 + 3n$. Subtracting 220 from both sides of this equation yields $180 = 3n$. Dividing both sides of this equation by 3 yields $n = 60$. Substituting 60 for n in the equation $f(x) = 220 + n(x - 2)$ yields $f(x) = 220 + 60(x - 2)$, which is equivalent to $f(x) = 220 + 60x - 120$, or $f(x) = 60x + 100$. Therefore, the total cost, in dollars, for x hours of repair is $f(x) = 60x + 100$.

Choice B is incorrect. This function represents the total cost, in dollars, for x hours of repair where the specialist charges $340, rather than $220, for the first two hours of repair. *Choice C* is incorrect. This function represents the total cost, in dollars, for x hours of repair where the specialist charges $160, rather than $220, for the first two hours of repair, and an hourly fee of $80, rather than $60, after the first two hours. *Choice D* is incorrect. This function represents the total cost, in dollars, for x hours of repair where the specialist charges $380, rather than $220, for the first two hours of repair, and an hourly fee of $80, rather than $60, after the first two hours.

Scoring Your Paper SAT Practice Test #10

Congratulations on completing an SAT® practice test. To score your test, follow the instructions in this scoring guide.

IMPORTANT: *This scoring guide is for students who completed SAT Practice Test #10 in The Official SAT Study Guide™. We recommend reading through these instructions and explanations before scoring so that you understand the specifics and limitations of scoring this practice test.*

The total score on your practice test reflects the sum of the (1) Reading and Writing and (2) Math section scores, as indicated below. If you decided to take both the lower- and higher-difficulty modules, choose which one you will use to score.

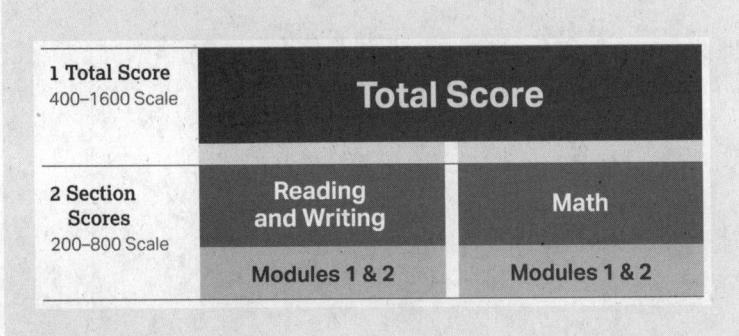

Scores Overview

Each assessment in the SAT Suite (SAT, PSAT/NMSQT®, PSAT™ 10, and PSAT™ 8/9) reports test scores on a common scale.

For more details about scores, visit **sat.org/scores**.

How to Calculate Your Practice Test Scores

The worksheets on the pages that follow help you calculate your test scores.

GET SET UP

1 In addition to your practice test, you'll need the answer keys and conversion tables at the end of this scoring guide.

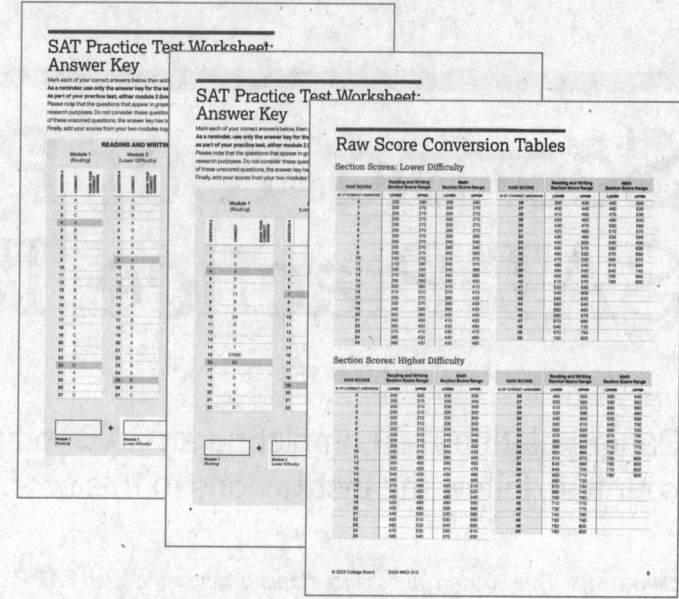

SCORE YOUR PRACTICE TEST

2 Compare your answers to the answer keys later in this scoring guide, and count up the total number of correct answers for each section. Write the number of correct answers for each section in the boxes at the bottom of the pages.

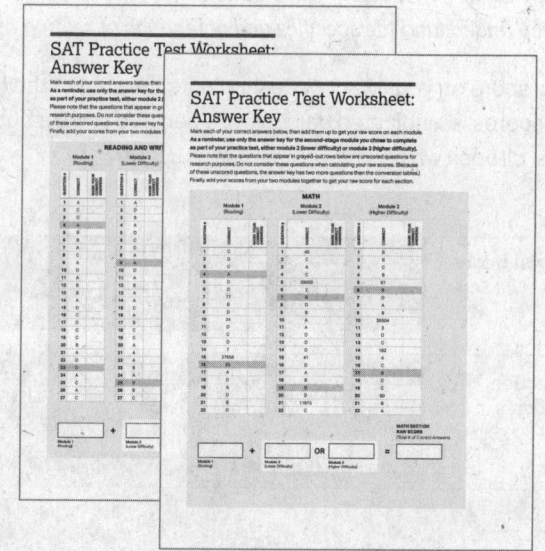

CALCULATE YOUR SCORES

3 Using your marked-up answer keys and the conversion tables, follow the directions on the SAT Practice Test Worksheet: Section and Total Scores page to get your section and total scores.

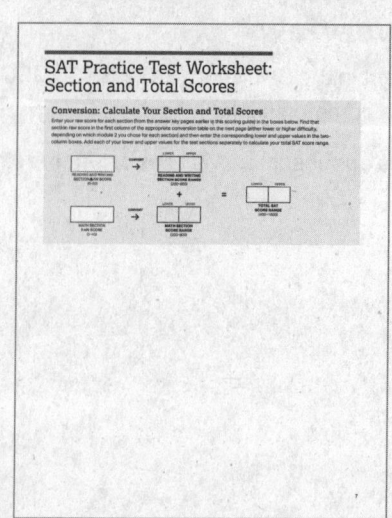

Get Section and Total Scores

Section and total scores for this paper version of SAT Practice Test #10 are expressed as ranges. That's because the scoring method described in this guide is a different (and therefore less precise) version of the one used in the actual adaptive test.

This practice test contains three modules for each test section: (1) a single first-stage (routing) module and (2) two second-stage modules. The two second-stage modules differ by average question difficulty and are marked as either "module 2 (lower difficulty)" or "module 2 (higher difficulty)." You get to choose which module 2 you would like to take for this practice test. **An actual testing experience consists of one routing and one second-stage module per test section.** To obtain your Reading and Writing and Math section scores, you will refer to the answer key and conversion table for the second-stage module you chose (either lower or higher difficulty).

GET YOUR READING AND WRITING SECTION SCORE

Calculate your SAT Reading and Writing section score (it's on a scale of 200–800).

1. Use the answer key for Reading and Writing to find the number of questions in module 1 and the module 2 you chose (either lower or higher difficulty) that you answered correctly.

2. To determine your Reading and Writing raw score, add the number of correct answers you got in module 1 and the module 2 you chose (either lower or higher difficulty). **Exclude the questions in grayed-out rows in your calculation.**

3. Use the appropriate Raw Score Conversion Table to turn your raw score into your Reading and Writing section score.

4. The lower and upper values associated with your raw score establish the range of scores you might expect to receive had this been an actual adaptive test.

GET YOUR MATH SECTION SCORE

Calculate your SAT Math section score (it's on a scale of 200–800).

1. Use the answer key for Math to find the number of questions in module 1 and the module 2 you chose (either lower or higher difficulty) that you answered correctly.

2. To determine your Math raw score, add the number of correct answers you got in module 1 and the module 2 you chose (either lower or higher difficulty). **Exclude the questions in grayed-out rows in your calculation.**

3. Use the appropriate Raw Score Conversion Table to turn your raw score into your Math section score.

4. The lower and upper values associated with your raw score establish the range of scores you might expect to receive had this been an actual adaptive test.

GET YOUR TOTAL SCORE

Add together the lower values for the Reading and Writing and Math sections, and then add together the upper values for the two sections. The result is your total score, expressed as a range, for this SAT practice test. The total score is on a scale of 400–1600.

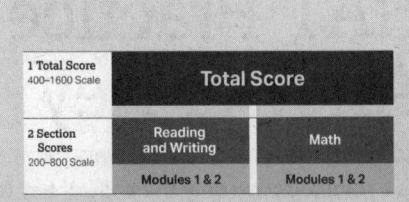

	Total Score	
1 Total Score 400–1600 Scale		
2 Section Scores 200–800 Scale	Reading and Writing	Math
	Modules 1 & 2	Modules 1 & 2

Your total score on this SAT practice test is the sum of your Reading and Writing section score and your Math section score. For this practice test, you'll receive a lower and upper score for each test section and the total score. This is the range of scores that you might expect to receive.

Use the worksheets on the pages that follow to calculate your section and total scores.

SAT Practice Test Worksheet: Answer Key

Mark each of your correct answers below, then add them up to get your raw score on each module. **As a reminder, use only the answer key for the second-stage module you chose to complete as part of your practice test, either module 2 (lower difficulty) or module 2 (higher difficulty).** Please note that the questions that appear in grayed-out rows below are unscored questions for research purposes. Do not consider these questions when calculating your raw scores. (Because of these unscored questions, the answer key has two more questions than the conversion tables.) Finally, add your scores from your two modules together to get your raw score for each section.

READING AND WRITING

Module 1 (Routing)			Module 2 (Lower Difficulty)			Module 2 (Higher Difficulty)		
QUESTION #	CORRECT	MARK YOUR CORRECT ANSWERS	QUESTION #	CORRECT	MARK YOUR CORRECT ANSWERS	QUESTION #	CORRECT	MARK YOUR CORRECT ANSWERS
1	A		1	A		1	D	
2	C		2	D		2	C	
3	C		3	B		3	C	
4	A		4	A		4	A	
5	B		5	D		5	A	
6	B		6	C		6	D	
7	A		7	D		7	B	
8	C		8	A		8	D	
9	A		9	A		9	A	
10	D		10	D		10	C	
11	A		11	A		11	C	
12	B		12	B		12	A	
13	B		13	A		13	C	
14	A		14	A		14	C	
15	D		15	C		15	A	
16	C		16	A		16	C	
17	D		17	B		17	C	
18	D		18	C		18	C	
19	C		19	C		19	C	
20	B		20	A		20	A	
21	A		21	A		21	A	
22	D		22	A		22	D	
23	D		23	B		23	C	
24	A		24	A		24	D	
25	C		25	B		25	B	
26	A		26	B		26	B	
27	C		27	C		27	D	

READING AND WRITING SECTION RAW SCORE
(Total # of Correct Answers)

[ ] **+** [ ] **OR** [ ] **=** [ ]

Module 1 (Routing)   Module 2 (Lower Difficulty)   Module 2 (Higher Difficulty)

SAT Practice Test Worksheet: Answer Key

Mark each of your correct answers below, then add them up to get your raw score on each module.
As a reminder, use only the answer key for the second-stage module you chose to complete as part of your practice test, either module 2 (lower difficulty) or module 2 (higher difficulty).
Please note that the questions that appear in grayed-out rows below are unscored questions for research purposes. Do not consider these questions when calculating your raw scores. (Because of these unscored questions, the answer key has two more questions than the conversion tables.)
Finally, add your scores from your two modules together to get your raw score for each section.

MATH

Module 1 (Routing)			Module 2 (Lower Difficulty)			Module 2 (Higher Difficulty)		
QUESTION #	CORRECT	MARK YOUR CORRECT ANSWERS	QUESTION #	CORRECT	MARK YOUR CORRECT ANSWERS	QUESTION #	CORRECT	MARK YOUR CORRECT ANSWERS
1	C		1	40		1	B	
2	D		2	C		2	B	
3	C		3	A		3	C	
4	A		4	C		4	B	
5	D		5	39000		5	67	
6	D		6	2		6	B	
7	77		7	B		7	D	
8	B		8	D		8	A	
9	D		9	B		9	B	
10	24		10	A		10	36504	
11	D		11	A		11	3	
12	C		12	D		12	D	
13	D		13	D		13	C	
14	7		14	D		14	182	
15	27556		15	41		15	A	
16	25		16	D		16	C	
17	A		17	A		17	B	
18	D		18	B		18	C	
19	A		19	B		19	C	
20	D		20	D		20	50	
21	B		21	11875		21	B	
22	D		22	C		22	A	

MATH SECTION RAW SCORE
(Total # of Correct Answers)

[___] **+** [___] **OR** [___] **=** [___]

Module 1 (Routing)   Module 2 (Lower Difficulty)   Module 2 (Higher Difficulty)

Understanding the SAT Practice Test Conversion Tables and Total Score Ranges

As mentioned earlier in this scoring guide, the scoring method for the practice tests that appear in *The Official SAT Study Guide* is different (and therefore less precise) than the method used in the actual adaptive test. Your practice test may result in a larger score range than what you hoped to see, but it's not feasible to estimate your performance on the practice tests in the study guide as precisely as we could for an actual test. As the test developers, College Board is committed to providing the most accurate conversion possible to help you understand your scores and guide your practice most effectively.

There are two conversion tables in this scoring guide. Use the conversion table labelled lower difficulty if you took module 2 (lower difficulty). Use the conversion table labelled higher difficulty if you took module 2 (higher difficulty). You might need both conversion tables if you took the lower-difficulty option for one section (e.g., Reading and Writing) and the higher-difficulty option for the other section (e.g., Math).

Because the lower- and higher-difficulty conversion tables share the same questions for module 1 (routing), you may encounter different score ranges based on the conversion table you use. For example, if you got all the module 1 (routing) questions correct, the lower-difficulty conversion table and the higher-difficulty conversion table will give you different score ranges. This is to be expected because the conversion tables account for all items within the two modules that make up the test. Answering only items on the first half of the test assumes you answered the other questions (module 2) incorrectly. Recall that when taking the actual SAT on test day, the test will adapt to your ability based on how you perform on the first half. Because of the differences between the actual test and providing a paper approximation of that (the practice test you're currently scoring), you should select the second-stage module that feels most appropriate for you. For example, if you were to answer all items on the first module correctly on the actual test, you would not be routed to the easier second-stage module. The converse would also be true. For many users of moderate ability either second-stage would be acceptable, but very high or low performers should be cautioned about taking the second-stage module that doesn't align well with their ability.

SAT Practice Test Worksheet: Section and Total Scores

Conversion: Calculate Your Section and Total Scores

Enter your raw score for each section (from the answer key pages earlier in this scoring guide) in the boxes below. Find that section raw score in the first column of the appropriate conversion table on the next page (either lower or higher difficulty, depending on which module 2 you chose for each section) and then enter the corresponding lower and upper values in the two-column boxes. Add each of your lower and upper values for the test sections separately to calculate your total SAT score range.

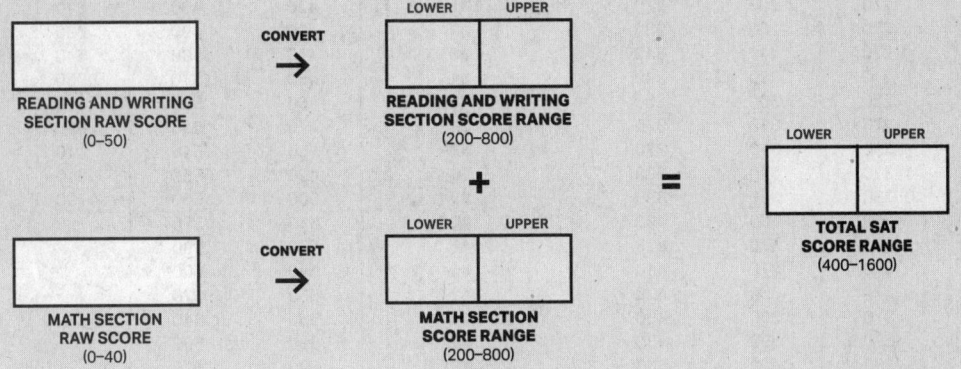

CONVERT →

LOWER   UPPER

READING AND WRITING
SECTION RAW SCORE
(0–50)

READING AND WRITING
SECTION SCORE RANGE
(200–800)

+

LOWER   UPPER

CONVERT →

MATH SECTION
RAW SCORE
(0–40)

MATH SECTION
SCORE RANGE
(200–800)

=

LOWER   UPPER

TOTAL SAT
SCORE RANGE
(400–1600)

Raw Score Conversion Tables

Section Scores: Lower Difficulty

RAW SCORE (# OF CORRECT ANSWERS)	Reading and Writing Section Score Range		Math Section Score Range		RAW SCORE (# OF CORRECT ANSWERS)	Reading and Writing Section Score Range		Math Section Score Range	
	LOWER	UPPER	LOWER	UPPER		LOWER	UPPER	LOWER	UPPER
0	200	260	200	260	26	390	430	460	500
1	200	270	200	270	27	400	440	460	520
2	200	270	200	270	28	410	450	470	530
3	200	270	200	270	29	420	460	480	540
4	200	270	200	270	30	420	470	500	560
5	200	270	200	270	31	420	480	510	570
6	200	270	200	280	32	430	490	530	590
7	200	270	240	340	33	440	500	540	600
8	200	270	280	340	34	450	510	550	630
9	200	270	300	360	35	460	520	570	650
10	200	270	310	370	36	470	530	590	670
11	210	290	330	370	37	480	540	610	690
12	260	320	340	380	38	490	550	640	740
13	270	330	350	390	39	500	560	700	800
14	290	350	360	400	40	510	570	760	800
15	300	360	370	410	41	530	590		
16	310	370	370	410	42	540	600		
17	330	370	380	420	43	560	620		
18	330	370	390	430	44	560	640		
19	340	380	390	430	45	580	660		
20	350	390	400	440	46	590	670		
21	360	400	410	450	47	610	690		
22	360	400	420	460	48	640	720		
23	370	410	430	470	49	670	750		
24	380	420	440	480	50	760	800		
25	380	420	450	490					

Section Scores: Higher Difficulty

RAW SCORE (# OF CORRECT ANSWERS)	Reading and Writing Section Score Range		Math Section Score Range		RAW SCORE (# OF CORRECT ANSWERS)	Reading and Writing Section Score Range		Math Section Score Range	
	LOWER	UPPER	LOWER	UPPER		LOWER	UPPER	LOWER	UPPER
0	200	300	200	300	26	490	550	580	640
1	200	310	200	300	27	500	560	590	650
2	200	310	200	300	28	510	570	600	660
3	200	310	200	300	29	520	580	620	680
4	200	310	200	300	30	540	600	630	690
5	200	310	200	300	31	550	610	640	700
6	200	310	200	300	32	560	620	660	720
7	200	310	240	340	33	570	630	670	730
8	200	310	310	390	34	580	640	690	750
9	200	310	340	420	35	590	650	710	770
10	200	310	350	430	36	600	660	730	790
11	280	380	380	440	37	610	670	750	800
12	300	400	390	450	38	620	680	760	800
13	320	420	410	470	39	640	700	770	800
14	340	420	420	480	40	650	710	780	800
15	360	440	440	500	41	660	720		
16	370	450	450	510	42	670	730		
17	390	450	460	520	43	680	740		
18	400	460	480	540	44	700	760		
19	420	480	490	550	45	710	770		
20	430	490	500	560	46	730	770		
21	440	500	520	580	47	740	780		
22	450	510	530	590	48	750	790		
23	460	520	540	600	49	760	800		
24	470	530	550	610	50	780	800		
25	480	540	570	630					